VOLUME ONE

The Great Republic

A History of the American People

FOURTH EDITION

Bernard Bailyn
Harvard University

Robert Dallek
*University of California,
Los Angeles*

David Brion Davis
Yale University

David Herbert Donald
Harvard University

John L. Thomas
Brown University

Gordon S. Wood
Brown University

D. C. HEATH AND COMPANY
LEXINGTON, MASSACHUSETTS TORONTO

Address editorial correspondence to:

D. C. Heath
125 Spring Street
Lexington, MA 02173

Cover: "America," London 1804, oil on Glass. Height 8⅞″, width 6¼″. Winterthur Museum.

For permission to use illustrations, grateful acknowledgment is made to the copyright holders listed on pages xxxiii–xxxiv, which are hereby considered an extension of this copyright page.

Published simultaneously in Canada.

Printed in the United States of America.

International Standard Book Number: 0-669-20986-4

Library of Congress Catalog Number: 91-71285

10 9 8 7

PUBLISHER'S FOREWORD

$\int$INCE it was first published in 1977 *The Great Republic* has held an honored place in the small company of truly distinguished and pathbreaking textbooks in American history. The work's authoritative scholarship, interpretive richness, and elegant style have been widely recognized and admired, not only among teachers of United States history courses but among historians in general. As Bernard Bailyn recently stated, "Every historian—however technical—has an obligation to reach out to a broad public because the purpose of the whole effort is to make a culture aware of its origins and development." D. C. Heath is proud to be the publisher of this work in which these distinguished historians have set out to reach that wider public.

Those familiar with earlier editions will find all the original qualities still here: a supple literary style; sufficient detail to provide supporting evidence and memorable examples; special attention to the colonial- and Revolutionary-era origins of the American experience; a dedication to tracing the subtle interconnections of social, economic, and cultural strands with the history of public events; and a consistent commitment to explaining the importance of ideas— whether formally articulated or unspoken—in the shaping of history. But over the years *The Great Republic* has been refined in response to classroom experience and the evolution of historical scholarship, and we believe that this fourth edition is the finest version yet. Throughout the book, of course, the authors have drawn upon recent research to keep the interpretation up-to-date. For example, contemporary historians' fruitful work on the history of native Americans has enriched this account of our history. In the antebellum chapters, previous limitations of space have been slightly relaxed, allowing for more contemporary quotations and anecdotes that render the analysis less abstract, and the role of the 1857 depression in shaping the decade's disastrous political crisis receives more attention. The treatment of Reconstruction has been reorganized for greater clarity and to eliminate overlapping coverage of post–Civil War economic and political issues at the end of Part Four and the beginning of Part Five. Chapters 22 and 23 have been thoroughly rewritten, not only to achieve a more concentrated focus on Gilded Age economic and political topics, but also for greater interpretive clarity. And Part Six, which traces American history since 1920, has been expanded and rewritten. Readers will now find its central thread—the reshaping of progressivism into modern liberalism in the New Deal era, the liberal triumph in the 1960s, and the subsequent crisis of liberal ideas and policies—much more clearly described.

An even more dramatic change in the fourth edition is the book's format. As a publisher, D. C. Heath is acutely aware of the rapidly rising cost of producing elaborate full-color textbooks. Clearly, such a format has pedagogical as well as aesthetic justifications. But many instructors object to the higher price that their students must inevitably pay for a full-color textbook. We believe that *The Great Republic* will have a particularly strong appeal to those history teachers for whom the sacrifice of color illustrations is worth a substantial reduction in the net cost of the book. With this edition we have striven for a clean, elegant appearance, well illustrated with crisply reproduced black-and-white photographs chosen for their quality as visual documents. At the same time we have retained color where it is most necessary—in the book's broad array of maps.

Instructors should also welcome another feature of the fourth edition: the extensive set of supplements that they can add to the textbook, mostly at little or no cost. Neal Stout of the University of Vermont has written a stimulating student's guide to the study of history, *Getting the Most Out of Your U.S. History Course,* that is available free of charge to every student who purchases a new copy of either volume. A challenging workbook in historical geography, *Surveying the Land* by Robert Grant of Framingham State University, is also available to student readers at their instructor's request. So are two documentary anthologies that focus on American regional history: *Document Sets for the South in U.S. History* by Richard Purday of North Georgia College and *Document Sets for Texas and the Southwest in U.S. History* by J'Nell L. Pate of Collin County Community College. The *Study Guide* that accompanies *The Great Republic,* revised for this edition by Patrick Reagan of Tennessee Technological University, offers students a wealth of practical aids. Instructors may also order for their students' use a menu-driven computerized version of the *Study Guide,* available for Macintosh, IBM, and IBM-compatible computers.

For instructors' use, Heath also makes available an *Instructor's Guide and Test Item File,* revised for this edition by Herbert Lasky of Eastern Illinois University, offering a great many classroom-tested suggestions for teaching the survey course with *The Great Republic,* as well as over a thousand questions for quizzes and examinations. These questions are also available on disk—for IBM computers in both 3½- and 5¼-inch formats, and for the Macintosh computer. All the book's maps are reproduced on acetate transparencies. Ivan Steen of the State University of New York, Albany, has created for Heath a cassette tape of recordings of speeches, songs, and other aural documents from American history, which many instructors will find an important and intriguing supplement to their lectures.

For further information about these supplements and to arrange to receive them, instructors should contact their D. C. Heath campus or telemarketing representative, or telephone D. C. Heath toll-free at 1-800-235-3565.

Publisher and authors alike owe a deep debt of gratitude to the historians who reviewed the book, in whole or in part, specifically: **Carl Abbott,** Portland State University; **Guy Alchon,** University of Delaware; **Charles Alexander,** Ohio University; **David Bernstein,** California State University, Long Beach; **Iver Bernstein,** Washington University; **W. Roger Biles,** Oklahoma State University; **Bernard Burke,** Portland State University; **David Burner,** State University of New York, Stony Brook; **Paul Bushnell,** Illinois Wesleyan University; **Dorothy Brown,** Georgetown University; **David Colburn,** University of Florida; **John Milton**

Cooper, University of Wisconsin, Madison; **David Danbom,** North Dakota State University; **Michael Ebner,** Lake Forest College; **Leon Fink,** University of North Carolina, Chapel Hill; **Larry Gerber,** Auburn University; **David Hammack,** Case Western University; **Michael W. Homel,** East Michigan University; **Bruce Kuklick,** University of Pennsylvania; **Allan Lichtman,** American University; **Norman Markowitz,** Rutgers University; **Alan Matusow,** Rice University; **George McJimsey,** Iowa State University; **Anne McLaurin,** Louisiana State University, Shreveport; **Samuel T. McSeveney,** Vanderbilt University; **Thomas Mega,** University of St. Thomas; **Keith Olson,** University of Maryland, College Park; **Richard Pohlenberg,** Cornell University; **Carroll Pursell,** Case Western Reserve University; **James Rawley,** University of Nebraska, Lincoln; **Patrick Reagan,** Tennessee Technological University; **Leo Ribuffo,** George Washington University; **Judith Riddle,** Jefferson College; **Donald Rogers,** University of Hartford; **Nick Salvatore,** Cornell University; **Robert D. Schulzinger,** University of Colorado, Boulder; **June Sochen,** Northeast Illinois University; **Robert Thomas,** University of Washington; **Charles Tull,** Indiana University, South Bend; **Jules Tygiel,** San Francisco State University; and **William Wagnon,** Washburn University.

Many members of D. C. Heath's staff assisted ably in producing this edition. Special thanks are due to Andrea Cava and Martha Wetherill for long hours of painstaking work as production editors, to Henry Rachlin for design, to Martha Friedman and Martha Shethar for photo research, to Charles Dutton for overseeing the manufacturing process, and to Irene Cinelli for expertly producing the supplements.

James Miller
Senior Editor, History

INTRODUCTION

*T*HIS book is a history of the American people, from the earliest European settlements in the New World to the present. We call our book "The Great Republic," adopting a phrase that Winston Churchill used to describe the United States. No one can doubt the greatness of the American Republic if it is measured by the size of our national domain, the vastness of our economic productivity, or the stability of our governmental institutions. Less certain has been its greatness in the realm of culture, in the uses of power, and in the distribution of social justice. Our purpose has been to present a balanced story of American development—a story of great achievement, of enormous material success, and of soaring idealism, but also one of conflict, of turbulent factionalism, and of injustice, rootlessness, and grinding disorder.

Three general themes unify the six sections of this book. The first is the development of free political institutions in America. Understanding the United States today requires knowledge of conditions in the colonial period that made popular self-government at first possible, then likely, and in the end necessary. In the American Revolution the longings of provincial Britons for a total reformation of political culture were implemented in American political institutions. During the first half of the nineteenth century, democratic institutions and practices expanded to the limits of the continent, and they received their crucial testing in the American Civil War. By the twentieth century, urbanization and industrialization profoundly changed American society, but our democracy survived all of these changes, as well as depressions, international crises, and world wars. To understand why today, in the last decade of the twentieth century, no significant groups of Americans question our free institutions requires an understanding of how these institutions evolved from eighteenth-century republicanism to modern mass democracy.

Our second theme is the tension that has always existed in America between the interests of groups with special goals and needs and those of the society as a whole. From the beginning the New World, with its abundant resources, stimulated ambitions among the shrewd, the enterprising, and the energetic that often conflicted with the shared needs of the entire populace. The enormous expanse of the country and the admixture of peoples from every quarter of the world encouraged social fragmentation and fostered cultural diversity. But from colonial times to the present, there have been countervailing forces working for social stability and cultural homogeneity.

The Founding Fathers of the Republic were aware that there would be no automatic harmonizing of regional, economic, and social interests, and they worried that minorities might become subject to the tyranny of majorities. At the same time, they feared a centralized government powerful enough to impose order on these conflicting and local interests and active enough to defend the weak against the powerful. In the national and state constitutions they devised a mechanism for the mediation of struggles and for the protection of human rights. In the years since, the balance between the general welfare and the welfare of regions, states, and economic and social groups has often been precarious, and our book shows how, from time to time, that balance has tipped, sometimes in the direction of social order and stability, sometimes in favor of minority interests and individual rights. Much of our story deals with successive attempts, never fully satisfactory, to reconcile the needs of the whole country with the interests of the parts.

Our third theme reflects our recognition that the history of the United States has always been part of a larger history. Except for the native Americans, who had developed a complex and diverse indigenous civilization, the early settlers in America were all immigrants who brought with them the beliefs, values, and cultural legacy of the European and African societies in which they had been born. Naturally, then, developments in America have been closely and inextricably related to those abroad. We believe that the American Revolution, for all of its distinctiveness, needs to be viewed as one in a series of great democratic revolutions that swept the Western world. We think the leveling of social distinctions and the democratization of political life in Jacksonian America are closely related to similar contemporary movements in Europe. And we have stressed that the urbanization, mechanization, and bureaucratization of the United States by the end of the nineteenth century paralleled, copied, and influenced like transformations in the other modernizing nations.

By the twentieth century the connections between developments in the United States and those in the world at large became even closer, and the final sections of our book trace the emergence of the United States as a world power. We have told the story of our involvement in two devastating world wars, in addition to other, smaller conflicts all over the globe, from Korea to Vietnam to the Persian Gulf. We have shown how, in recent decades, the president of the United States has become the most influential political leader in the world, how variations in the American economy have affected the well-being of all other nations, and how, for better or worse, American popular culture has reached a global audience. At the same time, we have emphasized that changes in other parts of the world have profoundly affected American political life, economic growth, and social organization. In short, we have written an American history that is part of world history.

In presenting these three themes, the authors have started from a shared view of the nature of history. We all believe that history is a mode of understanding, not merely a collection of information about the past. Our obligation is not simply to describe what happened, but to explain it, to make clear why things developed as they did. We share, too, an aversion to any deterministic interpretation of history. At certain times economic and demographic forces are dominant, but they are themselves shaped by cultural forces. Great political events are sometimes triggered by economic drives, but at other times they are responses to ideologies.

We do not believe, then, that the course of American history was predetermined. The present condition of our national life has to be explained historically, stage by stage. In the pages that follow, we present both a narrative and an analysis of how the United States has come to be what it is today—a great power, but still a Great Republic, where freedom and equality are dreams that can become realities.

B. B.   D. H. D.
R. D.   J. L. T.
D. B. D.   G. S. W.

CONTENTS

PART ONE

Shaping the Republic, to 1760   1
Bernard Bailyn
Introduction   2

Chapter 1   *The Background of English Colonization*   5
Points of Contrast: Spain in America   5
England's Overseas Expansion   16
Personnel and the Role of the State   23
Financial Limitations and the "Starving Times"   24
Chronology   29
Suggested Readings   30

Chapter 2   *Transplantation*   33
Virginia: Squalor, Struggle, and a New Way of Life   36
The Pilgrims' "Sweet Communion"   43
The Puritans: Power in the Service of God   47
A Catholic Refuge on the Chesapeake   54
The Failure of the Dutch   58
Royal Rewards: Carolina and the Jerseys   62
Pennsylvania: A Godly Experiment and a Worldly Success   69
Chronology   74
Suggested Readings   75

Chapter 3   *The Colonists' World: American Society in
the Seventeenth Century*   78
Growth and Structure of the Settling Population   79
Economic Instability   84
Social Instability   91
Religion   98
Suggested Readings   110

Chapter 4   *Elements of Change, 1660–1720*   112
Empire   112
Anglo-American Aristocracy   121

Rebellion: The Measure of Social Strain   132
Provincial Culture   138
Chronology   145
Suggested Readings   146

Chapter 5   *American Society in the Eighteenth Century*   149
The New Population: Sources and Impact   149
A Maturing Economy and a Society in Flux   157
Religion: The Sources of American Denominationalism   166
The Origins of American Politics   174
Suggested Readings   182

Chapter 6   *The Enlightenment's New World*   185
"Rule Britannia"   186
The Alienation of the State   193
The American and the Enlightenment   199
Chronology   206
Suggested Readings   207

PART TWO
Framing the Republic, 1760–1820   209
Gordon S. Wood
Introduction   210

Chapter 7   *Sources of the Revolution*   212
The Changing Empire   212
The Reorganization of the Empire   223
American Resistance   229
The Imperial Debate   240
Chronology   244
Suggested Readings   245

Chapter 8   *Independence and War*   248
The Coming of Independence   248
The Declaration of Independence   252
An Asylum for Liberty   256
The War for Independence   260
Chronology   270
Suggested Readings   271

Chapter 9   *Republicanism*   273
             Republican Idealism   273
             State Constitution Making   277
             The Articles of Confederation   280
             Republican Society   285
             The Betterment of Humanity   291
             Suggested Readings   295

Chapter 10   *The Federalist Age*   298
             The Critical Period   298
             The Federal Constitution   307
             The Hamiltonian Program   314
             The Republican Opposition   322
             Chronology   331
             Suggested Readings   332

Chapter 11   *The Jeffersonian Revolution*   335
             The Revolution of 1800   335
             An Empire of Liberty   343
             The Origins of Judicial Review   350
             Republican Religion   354
             Republican Diplomacy   359
             The War of 1812   364
             Chronology   368
             Suggested Readings   370

                         PART THREE
             Expanding the Republic, 1820–1860   373
                      David Brion Davis
                      Introduction   374

Chapter 12   *Population Growth and Economic Expansion*   377
             Population Growth, Immigration, and Urbanization   379
             Agriculture   383
             Industrialization and Railroads   390
             Population Distribution and Opportunity   396
             The Cost of Expansion: The Indians   401
             Suggested Readings   407

Chapter 13 *Shaping the American Character: Reform, Protest, Dissent, Artistic Creativity*   411
  "We Must Educate or Perish"   413
  The Evangelical Age   417
  The Cult of Self-Improvement   424
  Dissent: The Mormons as a Test Case   428
  The Benevolent Empire   435
  Feminism and Perfectionism   442
  The Tensions of Democratic Art   446
  Suggested Readings   449

Chapter 14 *The Peculiar Institution*   454
  Rise of the Cotton Kingdom   454
  The South as a "Slave Society"   468
  Radical Abolitionism   472
  Suggested Readings   483

Chapter 15 *Politics: Cohesion and Division, 1820–1840*   486
  "A Fire Bell in the Night": The Missouri Compromise   488
  The End of Republican Unity   492
  Jackson's Rise to Power   496
  The Threat of National Division: Tariffs, Nullification, and the Gag Rule   500
  The Bank War, the Panic of 1837, and Political Realignments   504
  Whigs and the Two-Party System   509
  Jacksonian Democracy   517
  Chronology   518
  Suggested Readings   519

Chapter 16 *Expansion and New Boundaries*   522
  Foreign Dangers, American Expansion, and the Monroe Doctrine   523
  The Mexican War and Manifest Destiny   535
  Chronology   544
  Suggested Readings   544

Chapter 17 *Compromise and Conflict*   547
  Free Soil and the Challenge of California   548
  The Crisis of 1850   552
  Destabilizing the Two-Party System   559

The Know-Nothing Upsurge   562
The Confrontation over Kansas   564
Dred Scott and the Lincoln-Douglas Debates   571
The Ultimate Failure of Compromise   578
Chronology   584
Suggested Readings   585

PART FOUR
Uniting the Republic, 1860–1877   587
David Herbert Donald
Introduction   588

Chapter 18   *Stalemate, 1861–1862*   589
The Rival Governments   589
Winning the Border States   593
Raising the Armies   599
Financing the War   604
Wartime Diplomacy   606
Battles and Leaders   610
Chronology   617
Suggested Readings   618

Chapter 19   *Experimentation, 1862–1865*   620
Evolution of a Command System   620
The Naval War   627
The Wartime Economy   629
Inflation and Its Consequences   631
Conscription and Conflict   634
Steps Toward Emancipation   636
Europe and the War   641
Wartime Politics in the Confederacy   643
Wartime Politics in the North   644
Northern Victory   647
Chronology   654
Suggested Readings   655

Chapter 20   *Reconstruction, 1865–1869*   657
Paths Not Taken   658
Constitutionalism as a Limit to Change   661

Laissez-Faire as a Limit to Change   668
Political Parties as a Limit to Change   673
Racism as a Limit to Change   681
Chronology   691
Suggested Readings   692

Chapter 21   *Compromises, 1869–1877*   694
Compromises Between Equal Forces   695
Where Compromise Did Not Work   708
The Restoration of "Home Rule" in the South   714
Chronology   721
Suggested Readings   722

Appendix   i
Declaration of Independence   i
The Articles of Confederation and Perpetual Union   iv
Constitution of the United States of America   x
Presidential Elections   xxvi
Presidents and Vice-Presidents   xxx
Growth of U.S. Population and Area   xxxii

Illustration Credits   xxxiii

Index   xxxv

MAPS AND CHARTS

The United States of America   xx–xxi
Spanish Conquests in America   7
Spanish and Portuguese Empires in the New World   10
Spain's Imperial Government in the New World, 1550   11
Raleigh's Virginia, 1584–1590   22
The Arc of Empire in the Seventeenth Century: Ireland and America   25
Jamestown, 1607–1612   37
Southern British Settlements, 1700   63
Northern British Settlements, 1700   73
English Origins of New England Settlers, 1620–1650   80
Hudson River Estates in Colonial New York   126
The French Wars, 1680–1713   128
German Settlements in 18th-Century America   152
Mount Vernon Plantation   160
18th-Century Atlantic Trade Routes   163
The French and Indian War, 1755–1760   189
North America in 1763   214
Frontier Expansion, 1760s   216
Concentration of Population in the Colonies, 1760   218
Trade Between the Colonies and Britain, 1763–76   238
Northern Campaigns, 1775–1776   261
Northern Campaigns, 1777   265
Yorktown and the Southern Campaigns, 1778–1781   268
State Claims to Western Lands and Cessions   283
Northwest Ordinance of 1785 Land Survey   284
The Treaty of Greenville, 1795   322
Density of Population, 1810   343
The United States, 1803–1807   345
American Foreign Trade, 1790–1812   361
The War of 1812—Major Campaigns   364
Population, 1820   378
Population, 1860   379

The United States, 1820–1860   383
Main Roads, Canals, River and Lake Transportation, 1840s   389
Principal Railroads, 1860   395
Indian Removal to Western Territories, 1820–1840   407
The Mormon Trail   432
Geographical Distribution of Slaves in 1820   456
Geographical Distribution of Slaves in 1860   457
The Two-Party System   488
The Missouri Compromise, 1820–1821   491
The Election of 1828   497
The Election of 1840   516
Continental Expansion, 1819–1854   526
The Election of 1844   534
Wagon Trails Westward, 1840   536
Major Campaigns of the Mexican War   538
The Compromise of 1850   556
The Kansas-Nebraska Act, 1854   566
The Election of 1860   582
Secession   596
Operations in the West, February–April 1862   613
Operations in the East, July 1861–November 1862   614
The Confederate Offensive in the West, August–October 1862   616
Operations in the East, December 1862–July 1863   623
Operations in the West, 1863, The Vicksburg Campaign   624
Operations in the East, May 1864–April 1865   648
Sherman's March to the Sea   649
The Same Georgia Plantation in 1860 and in 1880   671
Reconstruction   678
Black Population, 1880   685
Westward Expansion and Indian Wars, 1864–1876   713
Hayes-Tilden Disputed Election of 1876   717

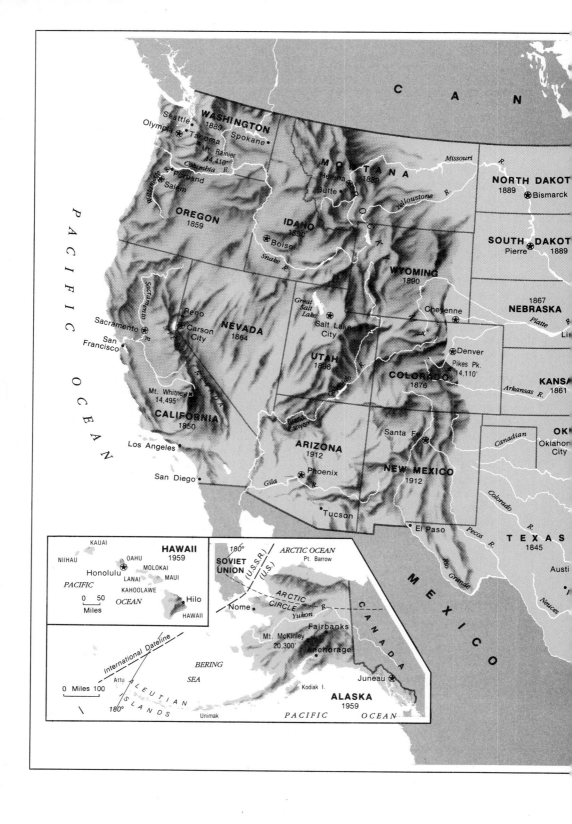

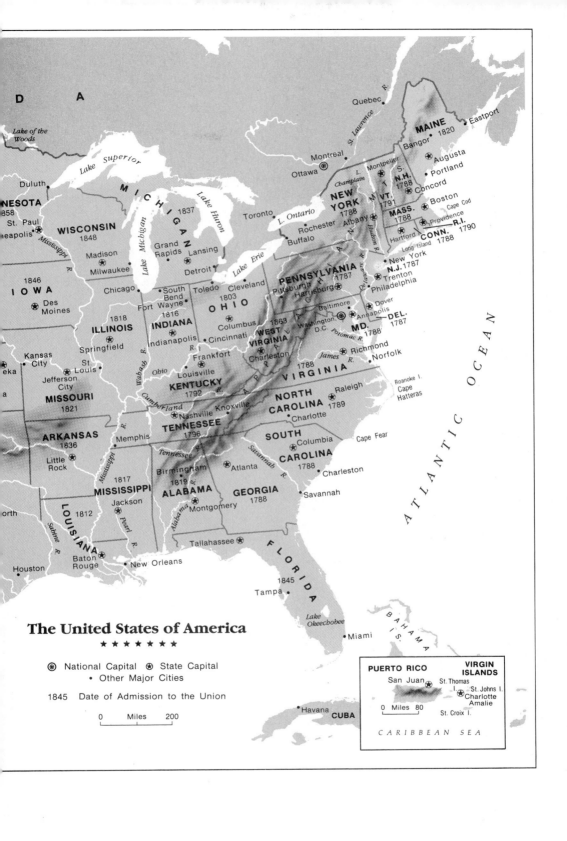

The United States of America

★ ★ ★ ★ ★ ★ ★

◉ National Capital ✪ State Capital
• Other Major Cities

1845 Date of Admission to the Union

0   Miles   200

PUERTO RICO	VIRGIN ISLANDS
San Juan ✪	St. Thomas
	St. Johns I.
	✪ Charlotte Amalie
0 Miles 80	St. Croix I.

CARIBBEAN SEA

PART ONE

Shaping the Republic

to 1760

Bernard Bailyn

$\mathcal{T}$HE American Republic was created only in a legal sense in 1776. In a deeper and more general sense it was the product of a century and a half of development that preceded the establishment of American independence. The ultimate origins of this "Great Republic," as Winston Churchill called the American nation, lie far back in time. America's historical roots lie in the fortunes and fortitude of a multitude of native peoples who struggled to maintain their integrity in the face of severe adversity, in desperate gambles of sixteenth- and seventeenth-century European merchants involved in overseas trade, and in Elizabethans' visions of a western passage to the vast wealth of the Far East. They lie in the courage and single-mindedness of religious refugees determined to carve out a new life in the wilderness rather than compromise their beliefs. They lie in the lifelong labors of a quarter of a million Africans transported in bondage to the New World. And they lie in the everyday struggles of five generations of transplanted Europeans and their descendants—primarily farmers and artisans—who vaguely sensed that theirs was a new and freer world, more supportive of human dignity and richer, for those whose risks succeeded, than any land known before.

Most of the people in colonial North America did not seek to transform the world. Although they were adventurous, they were conservative by instinct, or they became conservative as they sought to establish familiar forms of life in an unfamiliar environment. But traditions could not be maintained in wilderness communities whose basic conditions were so different from those of the Old World. A new pattern of life evolved in the course of the century and a half that spanned the first permanent English settlement in North America and the American Revolution. Gradually the character of community life was transformed—its demographic foundations, economy, social organization, religion, and politics. No theory or grand design guided this transformation; change did not come about because of anyone's desire or will, or in an effort to attain an ideal. Change simply took place as a matter of fact.

In the years before the American Revolution, some looked on change with suspicion. It was resisted in part, and its effects were limited as the colonists sought to copy the pattern of life in the more traditional societies of Europe. Many saw their provincial world not as a model for future societies, but as a regression to a more primitive way of life. Behavior had changed—had had to change—with the circumstances of everyday life. But habits of mind and the sense of the rightness of things changed more slowly. Many felt that the changes that had taken place in the years before the Revolution meant a movement away from, not toward, something; that these changes meant deviance; that they lacked, in a word, legitimacy.

For most Americans this divergence between ideals, habits of mind, and beliefs on the one hand, and experience and patterns of behavior on the other, ended at the Revolution. The American Revolution was an upheaval that destroyed the traditional sources of public authority and called forth the full range of advanced and enlightened ideas. Long-settled attitudes were jolted and loosened. People came to believe that the erosion in patterns of social life that had taken place in the colonial period had been good and proper. In the context of Revolutionary beliefs, these changes were viewed as steps toward a new ideal— the ideal of a simpler existence in which the individual would count for more, and the state for less. In this new way of life, the weight of burdensome social institutions would be permanently lifted. The blight of privilege and the misuse of power, it was expected, would be destroyed, and corruption would be exposed before it could sap the nation's strength. As a result of all these changes, the ordinary person's desire for personal fulfillment could at long last be satisfied.

These were the ideals of the Revolution, shaped by a generation of brilliant political thinkers who were convinced that it was their great historic role to set the world on a new course. And in the context of these ideals—which, however modified, remain the highest aspirations of the American people—the changes of the colonial years took on a new meaning. The settlement and development of the colonies, John Adams wrote, could now be seen as "the opening of a grand scene and design in providence for the illumination of the ignorant and the emancipation of the slavish part of mankind all over the earth." The glass was half full, not half empty; and to complete the work of fate and nature, further thought must be taken, and changes accelerated rather than restrained.

Social change and social conflict took place during the Revolutionary years, but the beliefs and aspirations of America's founders, unlike those of the leaders of the later French and Russian revolutions, did not require the destruction and remaking of society. The American Revolution did not create new social and political forces; it released forces and intensified changes that had been developing from the day Englishmen first permanently settled in America. Modern America's massively developed, affluent, and tumultuous technological society of more than 240 million people is worlds away from the seventeenth century's tiny farming communities and obscure port towns, huddled along the coast of an almost undeveloped continent. Yet there is a clear line of continuity in American history that links those primitive settlements to the sophisticated, dynamic world power of the late twentieth century. Modern America is not simply the product of modern forces—industrialism, political democracy, universal education, a consumer culture. It is the product too of the idealism of the eighteenth-century Enlightenment, reinforced and intensified by the openness and affluence of American life.

This powerful strain of idealism flowing from the very different world of the eighteenth century into all the complexities of modern America is the most distinctive feature of the American Republic as it enters its third century of existence. The central theme of the colonial period of American history is the story of how that strain first entered American life, of how it was nourished in the soil of a strangely altered society that grew from confused seventeenth-century origins, and of how the characteristic American mixture of idealism and materialism was first created—reaching so soon an apparently absolute and perfect form in the subtle figure of Benjamin Franklin.

Far from being a quaint introduction to the main story, therefore, the settlement of the American colonies and the early development of American society constitute a critically important phase of our history. Without an understanding of the pre-Revolutionary era, none of the rest of our history can be properly understood.

1

The Background of English Colonization

⁓

*T*HE United States evolved from British settlements on the North American mainland, first permanently established in 1607. But a century earlier a more powerful European state, Spain, had founded an empire in the Western Hemisphere that was highly developed when the British first entered the colonial world. The growth of the Spanish Empire in the Western Hemisphere and of Spanish-American society forms a remarkable—and revealing—contrast to the evolution of the British Empire and of Anglo-American society. In some ways, to be sure, Anglo-American society in British North America and Indo-Hispanic society in Central America and South America are so different that they can hardly be compared. But we can learn much by contrasting government and politics in the two empires.

By the early eighteenth century, political life in British North America had become distinctive. Anglo-American society was marked by free, open political competition, which was made possible by certain underlying institutional and cultural conditions. Nothing quite like this society's brawling political struggles—faction against faction, groups against the state—existed in any other colonial region of the world, and certainly not in Spanish America. Yet there had been a time when this kind of political life might have evolved in the Spanish colonies as well. It is therefore worthwhile at the outset to explore the basic reasons why Spanish America did not have a free competitive political system at the height of the colonial period. By studying this contrast, we can better understand the forces and circumstances that made for so dynamic a political society in the British-American colonies on the eve of the American Revolution.

Points of Contrast: Spain in America

There are important contrasts between Spanish and British America at every stage of development. Whereas it took England half a century after its first contact with the Western Hemisphere to establish even a temporary colony there,

5

One of a Large Number of Imaginary Portraits of Columbus
No likeness of Columbus was made in his lifetime, and this painting by Sebastiano del Piombo, like all others, says as much about the artist's imagination as it does about Columbus. In fact the great mariner, his biographer S. E. Morison has written, was "tall and well-built, red-haired with a ruddy and freckled complexion, hawk-nosed and long of visage, blue-eyed and with high cheekbones."

Spain proceeded swiftly to exploit the lands that had been claimed for it by Christopher Columbus in 1492. Led by its courageous, greedy, and often brutal *conquistadores*—adventurers for whom there are no British equivalents—Spain's exploration of the Western Hemisphere, its conquest of the native peoples, and its establishment of a new civilization swept forward in three main waves.

The Spanish Conquests

Columbus himself explored much of the Caribbean on his four voyages between 1492 and 1504. Within a generation of his death in 1506, Spanish adventurers had seized possession of most of the coastal lands of Central America and South America. The conquest of the Caribbean basin climaxed in 1513 with Vasco Núñez de Balboa's exploration of the Isthmus of Panama and his discovery of the Pacific Ocean, and with Juan Ponce de Leon's discovery of the Florida mainland.

The second wave of Spanish expansion in America was stimulated by rumors of vast treasures hidden in a highly civilized state deep in the interior. In the course of this second wave, the empire of the Aztec ruler Montezuma in Mexico was conquered between 1519 and 1521. This most dramatic and bloody conquest was led by the resourceful, ruthless, and incredibly energetic *conquistador* Hernando Cortés. There are no heroes in this tale of slaughter and conquest. On one side were the passionately determined Spanish adventurers, who overcame fearful hardships to plunder and ultimately to destroy an ancient civilization. On the other side were the equally courageous but bewildered and unsophisticated

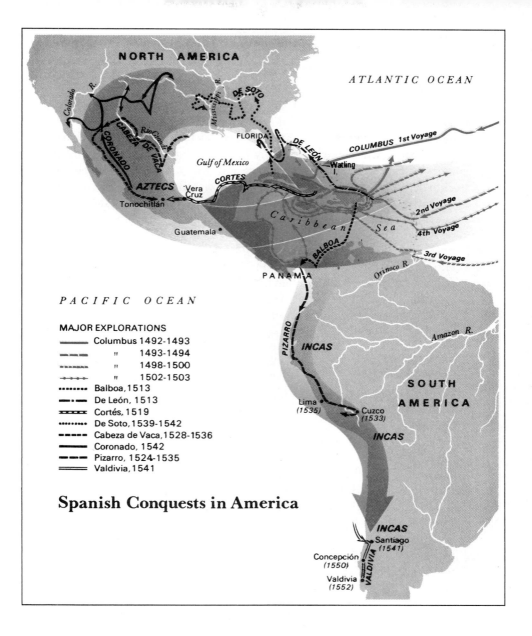

Spanish Conquests in America

MAJOR EXPLORATIONS
- Columbus 1492-1493
- " 1493-1494
- " 1498-1500
- " 1502-1503
- Balboa, 1513
- De León, 1513
- Cortés, 1519
- De Soto, 1539-1542
- Cabeza de Vaca, 1528-1536
- Coronado, 1542
- Pizarro, 1524-1535
- Valdivia, 1541

natives. Other *conquistadores* extended Cortés's conquest of the Mexican world into North America. Between 1528 and 1536 Alvar Núñez Cabeza de Vaca circled the northern edge of the Gulf of Mexico and reached the Gulf of California. Between 1539 and 1541 Hernando de Soto cut through the forests of northern Florida and what would later be the southeastern United States and discovered the Mississippi River. And in 1542 Francisco Coronado, seeking El Dorado, a mythical city of gold and jewels, explored the native villages of what is now

Arizona, New Mexico, Colorado, Oklahoma, and Kansas. While these conquerors were exploring and subduing what would become the northern borderlands of Spain's empire, other followers of Cortés swept through Central America and established Spanish rule in Honduras and Guatemala.

The third great wave of Spanish conquest was led by an illiterate adventurer, Francisco Pizarro, who launched a series of expeditions from Panama through the jungles of Ecuador and northern Peru into the heartland of the elaborate Incan empire, which was then weakened by civil war. By a trick Pizarro managed to capture the Incan emperor, whom he murdered after extracting a heavy ransom of gold and silver, and then destroyed much of the Incan army and nobility. Next he proceeded to strip city after city of their treasures, to embroil both natives and conquerors in devastating warfare, and to establish in 1535 the new central city of Lima. From the plundered Incan lands further expeditions were begun—first into Ecuador, then into Chile and northern Argentina (1535–37), and finally into Bolivia (1539). The full conquest of Chile was the work of another almost unbelievably determined and ruthless conquistador, Pedro de Valdivia. His small troop of Spanish adventurers and Indian followers survived journeys through the desert, near starvation, and attacks by native peoples to found Santiago, Concepción, and Valdivia before succumbing to a native rebellion in 1553.

Radiating out from these three main lines of conquest (first, the subjugation of the Caribbean islands and coastal areas; then the reduction of Mexico and the exploration of southern North America; and finally the invasion of Peru, Chile, and northern Argentina), Spain's empire in America expanded in all directions. By 1607, when England established Jamestown, its first permanent settlement in America, Spain's American empire extended nearly 8,000 miles, from California to the southern tip of South America. The empire was the largest the Western world had known since the fall of Rome. Its only competitor in the Western Hemisphere had been Portugal, which had controlled the coastal areas of Brazil until the union of the Spanish and Portuguese thrones (1580–1640) gave Spain legal jurisdiction even there.

Spain's fabulous empire had been acquired through greed, lust for adventure, and a passion to convert the native people to Christianity. But it was also the product of remarkable administrative skill.

The Spanish Empire Despite the difficulties of effectively managing so vast a territory, Spain's American empire was well organized. The structure of government that had evolved during the sixteenth century was elaborate, skillfully designed, and—except for periods when royal authority collapsed in Spain itself—successful. And it was utterly different from the imperial system that Britain would set up during the seventeenth and early eighteenth centuries. Spain's rule of its empire was highly bureaucratic: full-time salaried officials enforced decrees and laws governing the behavior of both the rulers and the ruled. These regulations reached down into the daily life of the poorest peasants in the most remote corners of the empire, half a world away from the central administrative agencies in Spain. And the system was hierarchical in structure, all authority ultimately centering in the patriarchal figure of the monarch of Castile,* whose rule in his American lands was conceived of as personal, an extension of his domestic authority.

The establishment of royal power in overseas territories by means of a complex bureaucracy began almost as soon as Spain learned of Columbus's discoveries. This quick response contrasts sharply with the plodding actions of the British government a century later. By 1503 the first major Spanish imperial institution had been created, the *Casa de Contratación* (board of trade). With its headquarters in Spain's leading port, Seville, the *Casa* licensed all trade with America, enforced commercial laws and regulations, collected customs duties and colonial crown revenues, and kept the commercial accounts of the entire empire. Because of its power over colonial commerce and over the flow of money that poured into Spain from America, the *Casa* became in effect a major branch of the royal treasury.

In all its work, the *Casa de Contratación* was controlled by the Council of the Indies, which was created in 1524. The council was composed of some of the Spanish king's highest advisers, and it acted in the king's name. It dominated both the making and the enforcing of laws—civil and religious alike—in the Spanish colonies, and it constituted a branch of the royal court of justice. The council appointed all the clerical and secular officials who enforced its laws. It had a special responsibility for the spiritual and physical welfare of the Indians; it was the court of highest appeal for the entire colonial judicial system; it censored all publications in America; and it audited the accounts of the colonial treasurers.

All government agencies and officials in America reported in some way to the Council of the Indies. The chief governmental unit in America was the viceroyalty. Two viceroyalties were created in the sixteenth century: New Spain (1535), which included all Spanish territory north of the Isthmus of Panama; and Peru (1542), which covered all to the south of the Isthmus except the coast of what is today Venezuela. The viceroys ruled these two huge jurisdictions with broad but somewhat ambiguous authority to act in the king's name, and their capitals were centers of glittering splendor.

The level of government below the viceroyalties was that of the *audiencias.* There were seven *audiencias* by 1550; five more were added by 1661. Originally they were royal courts with direct access to the Council of the Indies and were subject to the council's veto. Soon, however, the *audiencias* acquired administrative and political authority—power that they shared or contested with the viceroys. More clearly below the viceroyalties were lesser jurisdictions—*presiden-*

---

*Castile was the largest and most important of the kingdoms that had been united in the fifteenth century to form the Spanish monarchy. Isabella was queen of Castile; Ferdinand ruled the smaller kingdom of Aragon. Strictly speaking, America belonged to—and was governed by—Castile alone.

Spanish and Portuguese Empires in the New World

cias and captaincies-general—that were deliberately created as administrative subdivisions of the larger territorial governments.

These were the main jurisdictions. Below them lay many lower units, whose chief officers were usually appointed by the viceroys or *audiencias.* Normally the Council of the Indies had to approve these appointments; occasionally the king himself did. Below them was the lowest level of civil government, the municipal corporation (*cabildo*). Finally, there were various investigating and superintending officials who were appointed in Spain to strengthen the crown's authority throughout its American territories.

Thus Spain's imperial government, reaching lands in all parts of the globe and bound together by hundreds of rules enforced by thousands of officials, had taken shape within a single generation. It is true, however, that this imperial government was neither completely rational in its construction, nor altogether efficient in its operation, nor comprehensive in its reach. There were clumsy gaps

AUDIENCIA OF NUEVA GALICIA (1548)

AUDIENCIA OF MEXICO (1527) **VICEROYALTY OF NEW SPAIN 1535**

AUDIENCIA OF GUATEMALA (1543)

AUDIENCIA OF SANTO DOMINGO (1526)

AUDIENCIA OF PANAMA (1535)

AUDIENCIA OF NUEVA GRANADA (1549)

SOUTH AMERICA

VICEROYALTY OF PERU 1542

AUDIENCIA OF LIMA (1542)

Spain's Imperial Government in the New World, 1550

and overlaps in authority. Lower jurisdictions, especially those in remote areas, found many ways of ignoring the higher authorities; and corruption was widespread, especially in the lower offices. But despite these weaknesses, the Spanish Empire functioned as a reasonably coherent state system for more than three hundred years. And the system was largely unchallenged. Of course there was resistance to certain regulations and to some of the officials sent from Spain. But there was no openly organized political opposition to the state, only the passive refusal to comply with unacceptable or unenforceable crown orders (a foot dragging that was reflected in the well-known phrase "I obey but I do not execute"). Nor was there a body of ideas that would justify sustained opposition to the crown, nor political leaders who were experienced in challenging state authority and motivated to do so. When, more than three hundred years after its founding, Spain's empire in America finally succumbed to corruption, misgovernment, and rising democratic aspirations, there was no corps of native politicians experienced in managing free governments and in creating responsible, stable self-government.

Contrast with the British Empire   The contrast with British America could hardly be sharper or more significant. There was never an effective structure of imperial government in the Anglo-American empire, from which the United States evolved. The authority of the British crown and of Parliament was scattered through half a dozen uncoordinated agencies of government, and it was always superficial. It seldom penetrated much beyond the docks or the customhouses, and British control of the American political system was weak. Yet, surprisingly, there *was* organized resistance to this weak and scattered authority from the start. By the middle of the eighteenth century, resistance had grown into a sophisticated process of competitive politics and had bred politicians who were long experienced in local self-government. Consequently, the transition to independence and to responsible self-government was smooth and, once the War of Independence was concluded, entirely bloodless.

This stark contrast between the Spanish-American and the British-American patterns becomes even more vivid and surprising if one considers the fact that, in the early years of the Spanish-American empire, institutions had existed that could have developed into bases for just the kind of competitive politics that evolved in North America. But instead of maturing into centers of open competition with the state, these institutions withered and disappeared.

At the start, for example, the most powerful figures in Latin America were the *adelantados*—feudal lords to whom the crown had granted extraordinary powers to subjugate the American frontiers. These men exercised executive and judicial authority that from the beginning was understood to be competitive with the crown's own authority. Yet few of the *adelantados* managed to transmit their authority to a second generation. Another potential threat to the state's overall authority in the sixteenth century was the *encomienda,* a grant of the labor of a specific number of native Americans for agriculture or mining—along with the land they occupied. This was, in effect, a gift of slaves or serfs. The crown had intended to protect the Indians' spiritual and physical well-being, but the *encomiendas* quickly became agencies of vicious oppression. Determined to eliminate the institution, the crown gradually succeeded in reducing the powers of the roughly 4,000 *encomienda* holders by draining away their incomes and eliminating their right to pass the original grants on to their heirs. The dramatic decline of the Indian population also undermined the *encomiendas.* By the early eighteenth century the *encomienda* was no longer a political danger to the crown. In similar ways the threat of other, lesser competing political authorities—provincial assemblies and municipal corporations—was eliminated or reduced.

Why had all these semi-independent agencies and institutions been weakened or absorbed into the state apparatus? Why had organized competitive politics died almost at birth in Spanish America, whereas in British America it

Facade, Church of La Soledad, Oaxaca, Mexico
*This masterpiece of baroque architecture, built in 1695, reflects the great wealth of the
established Catholic church in Spanish America, so different from the many scattered
Protestant churches in British North America, none of them wealthy, clearly established, or
secure. Compare this magnificent facade with that of St. Luke's Church, Virginia, p. 100.*

grew so quickly and so strongly? There is no simple explanation, but there were
certain circumstances in Spanish America that provide part of an explanation,
and these contrast sharply with the conditions that shaped the development of
the British-American communities.

From the very start the Spanish crown had actively and directly asserted its
authority. Even before Columbus's discovery, the monarchy had proclaimed its
rule over the lands that had been conquered in its name, and it intended to use
this power not merely to regulate commerce, but also to impose far-reaching
governmental authority in newly acquired territories. The Spanish monarchs of
Columbus's time, Ferdinand and Isabella, declared America to be a separate
kingdom under the jurisdiction of Castile. The native American peoples thus
became direct subjects of the Spanish crown, and the governmental jurisdictions
in America were regarded as subordinate agencies of the crown.

The papacy—the highest moral authority in the Western world—supported
Ferdinand and Isabella's claims. The popes assigned to the monarch of Castile

the responsibility for the welfare of the native Americans, which meant primarily the task of converting them to Christianity. Building on that central Christian responsibility, legal and religious scholars in Spain developed an imposing body of writings that strongly reinforced and justified the Spanish monarch's claims to personal rule in America. Further, there were no competing intellectual centers from which contrary ideas could develop. The Catholic church, conservative in doctrine and royalist in politics, dominated the intellectual life of Spanish America. Whereas British America became a refuge for religious dissenters, Spanish America became a fortress of Catholic orthodoxy, even more tightly controlled than Spain itself. Dissenters and heretics of all kinds were generally barred by law from emigrating to Spanish America.

Yet declarations and theories do not in themselves create political realities. There was something in the conditions of Spanish-American life that guaranteed a welcome for the crown's supremacy and that helped stifle competitive institutions at their birth. The situation becomes clearer if one turns from institutions to population characteristics and considers what groups would have had both the capacity to oppose the crown and an interest in active, organized resistance. Here again the contrast with British America is striking.

The Spanish-American Population There were five principal categories in the Spanish-American population, of which the most numerous by far was that of the native Indians. The Aztecs, the Incas, and the other Americans whom the Spanish encountered were advanced people in certain ways. But to Europeans of the time they seemed primitive, particularly in technology and weaponry, and they were helpless before the Spanish conquerors. The native Americans were quickly transformed by conquest into a mass laboring population. And beyond the deprivation of their political rights and their severe exploitation under the *encomienda* system, the Indians were being decimated by diseases brought by the Spanish. Reliable studies estimate that the population of the Viceroyalty of New Spain declined from about 25 million at the time of the Spanish conquest to slightly over 1 million at the beginning of the seventeenth century. Losses in the Viceroyalty of Peru may have been equally severe. As the Indian population plummeted, the Indians' abandoned land claimed by Spanish landlords, and the surviving native Americans found themselves bound in a form of permanent debt servitude, called peonage. It is scarcely surprising that the Indians, struggling for basic survival, were incapable of organizing their own political institutions to resist the Spanish state.

At the other extreme from the Indians in the Spanish-American population were the major imperial officeholders—the viceroys, *audiencia* judges, high church officials, and governors—who might most readily have achieved some independent authority. But the crown's policies in recruiting and controlling these officers prevented them from developing political independence. Most of the high church and state officials who served in Spanish America in the three-hundred-year colonial period had been born in Spain. They had no vested interests in America, and they expected to return home to Spain after completing their tour of duty abroad. Further, their time in office was strictly limited, and they were frequently transferred to prevent them from acquiring too strong an identification with any particular locality. Moreover, they depended on the royal treasury for their salaries, and their conduct of office was carefully examined.

A third group was the Creoles, the American-born leaders of Spanish descent. Under favorable conditions they might well have organized and become an active political force. Unlike the Indians they were politically sophisticated, and unlike most high church and state officials they were Americans by birth, with American interests. And indeed, there were conflicts between the Creoles and the Spanish officials, particularly over officeholding and the enforcement of trade regulations. Further, by the eighteenth century the sale of public offices by the bankrupt Spanish state gave the Creoles increasing access to public authority. But in general the Creoles' small numbers and their social position forced them into a dependent political role. Of the total population of more than 9 million in Spanish America in the 1570s, only 118,000—or 1.25 percent—were Creoles. In the entire first century of Spain's colonial period, no more than 250,000 Spaniards emigrated to America. The contrast with British America is startling. In the equivalent period (that is, from 1607 to 1700), approximately 390,000 emigrants left the British Isles for the Western Hemisphere, a yearly average two-thirds greater than that of the Spanish. The Creoles' small numbers account for the kinds of occupations they pursued. As a thin overlay on a comparatively large population of Indians, the Creoles never became the mass base of the social structure. Instead they filled the upper strata of the American communities: they were landowners, clergymen, army officers, and merchants. Their identity as a ruling class, and consequently their well-being, derived not from their American birth but from their European descent, which distinguished them racially from the mass of the population. Thus, despite their local interests, the Creoles continued to identify themselves with Spain, the source of their status, wealth, and power.

Finally, there were two other groups in the Spanish-American population. Blacks were imported as slaves and never acquired an active political role. Politically more important was the increasingly large number of racially mixed persons. By the 1570s the racially mixed elements constituted approximately 2.5 percent of the entire populace. By the end of the colonial period in the early nineteenth century, that figure had risen to more than 30 percent. (This presents another striking contrast with British America, where the racially mixed population was quite small.) Many racial combinations existed, but the most important element by far was the *mestizos,* people of mixed European and Indian ancestry. Yet, although numerous, the *mestizos* were generally considered socially inferior to the dominant Spanish elements, and they constituted a lower-middle class of small farmers and shopkeepers. In a society where status, wealth, and power were controlled by those of pure Spanish heritage, *mestizos* avoided asserting their identity through politics and chose rather to fit themselves as inconspicuously as possible into existing situations. Only a profound cultural change would release their suppressed aspirations and free them to assume effective political roles. When that cultural change took place—and only then—the colonial era of Spanish-American history was over.

These population characteristics, so different from those of the British-American world, go far toward explaining the failure of a free competitive political system to develop in colonial Spanish America. Institutions that originally could have supported these politics were available. But the small elite of high state officials was bound to Spain in every way. The Creoles were a small, self-conscious ruling class in a great sea of Indians, blacks, and racially mixed persons. Their well-being depended on their continuing identification with the sources of authority in Europe. Only the racially mixed were disposed to move toward self-government, but through most of the colonial period they lacked the numbers, the self-esteem, and the experience to create effective political weapons against the overwhelming Spanish establishment.

England's Overseas Expansion

England's entry into the Western Hemisphere was the very opposite of Spain's. Where Spain had been swift, England was slow; where Spain had been deliberate and decisive, England was muddled in purpose. For Spain, America almost immediately yielded immense wealth. For England, America created more losses than profits, at least at the start. The differences were most extreme and of most consequence at the very beginning of exploration and settlement.

For no less than fifty years, while Spain was conquering and exploiting vast areas of Central America and South America, England did nothing to develop its claims to North America. These claims had been established in 1497–98, when John Cabot, who had been commissioned by Henry VII, had discovered and begun the exploration of Newfoundland, Labrador, and Nova Scotia. Cabot's son Sebastian had continued the exploration into the Hudson Bay region of Canada in 1508–09; but throughout the reign of Henry VIII (1509–47), neither the crown nor private enterprise showed any interest in developing these distant territories. The only English contact with America that remained throughout these years was the work of fishermen from England's West Country—the counties of Cornwall, Devonshire, and Dorsetshire—who, together with fishermen from France, Spain, and Portugal, had begun to exploit the excellent fishing waters of the Grand Banks (off Newfoundland) and the mouth of the St. Lawrence River. These fishermen had become familiar with the southern Canadian and northern New England coasts. They had built crude shacks for use during the fishing seasons, but they had made no attempt to establish permanent settlements or otherwise assert England's claims to the land.

Then suddenly, in the early 1550s, the situation changed. This abrupt reversal marked the beginnings of British colonization. The development was complex, and it is as important to understand what did *not* happen as it is to know what *did* happen. For there was no sudden emphasis on overseas settlement as such, and there was no immediate English determination to assert claims to America. Instead there were two basic shifts in orientation, both of which would eventually involve colonization, but neither of which was originally directed toward that goal. The first shift was in England's economy, the second in its international relations.

Economic and Diplomatic Changes England's prosperity in the first half of the sixteenth century had been based on the growing European demand for its raw wool and woolen cloth, which were marketed largely in Antwerp, in what is now Belgium. Throughout the reign of Henry VIII, more and more capital and labor had become involved in this dominant commercial enterprise, more and more farmland had been converted to pastureland for sheep, and England's financial stability had become increasingly dependent on Antwerp. Then in the late 1540s this elaborate commercial structure began to weaken. By 1550 the Antwerp wool market was saturated, and in 1551 it collapsed. English cloth exports fell off 35 percent within a year, and the financial world was thrown into turmoil. The merchants were forced to reconsider the whole of their activities. New markets and new trade routes would have to be found, and capital would have to be risked in ways that a previous generation would have thought wildly speculative.

Changes in England's international position helped channel the merchants' suddenly mobilized energies. Antagonism with France had dominated England's policies throughout Henry VIII's reign, and in this rivalry Spain had been England's natural ally. As a result England had been willing to support Spain's claim to the entire Western Hemisphere except Portuguese Brazil, a claim recognized by the Pope and confirmed by the Spanish-Portuguese Treaty of Tordesillas (1494). This alliance was confirmed by the marriage of England's Queen Mary (1553–58) to King Philip II of Spain.

But when Mary's half-sister Elizabeth became queen in 1558, a reversal in England's international relations began. In contrast to her predecessor, Elizabeth was inclined toward Protestantism, and Protestant political considerations gradually came to shape England's foreign policy. By the mid-1560s it was becoming clear that Catholic Spain threatened England's independence as a Protestant nation, and that England's long-range interests in Europe lay in the support of the rebellious Protestants in France and of their counterparts in the Netherlands who were struggling against Spanish rule. From an ally of Spain, England gradually became an enemy. Although England felt too weak until the 1580s to engage in open warfare with the great imperial power, the country had every reason to want to harass the Spanish people and to plunder Spanish territories in any way possible.

Thus, impelled by a sudden economic need to break out of the safe, conservative commerce of earlier years, and no longer hesitant to attack Spain's overseas territories, England entered a new phase in its history. It did not,

Elizabeth I
In the so-called Armada Portrait, painted in 1588, Elizabeth's hand, holding a globe of the world, covers most of North America.

however, plunge directly and immediately into colonization; it attempted over-seas settlement only eventually, and almost incidentally. In response to the new economic pressures, England expelled foreign merchants and favored English merchants in the conduct of trade. Land that had been converted to sheep grazing in order to supply wool for export was now forced back into crop raising. Textile production was deliberately limited, and new merchants were restrained from entering into trade. Above all, the commercial community poured capital into a search for new kinds of overseas trade and for new, distant markets that would be free of the influence of European middlemen. In 1555 enterprising merchants formed the Guinea Company for trade to Africa, and the Muscovy Company for trade with Russia. In 1579 the Eastland Company organized English trade to the Baltic region. In 1581 the Levant Company was created to control England's commerce with the Middle East. Finally, a series of contacts with India and Southeast Asia led to the formation of the East India Company in 1600.

These were legitimate and official enterprises, but during the same years less legitimate activities were also unfolding. Risk capital, some of it secretly supplied from royal sources, was being channeled into semipiratical raids on Spanish commerce and shipping. These enterprises began in 1562 when John Hawkins of the southwestern town of Plymouth broke into the Spanish trade monopoly in the West Indies and the South American mainland (the "Spanish Main") with the first in a series of illegal but highly lucrative peddling voyages. Hawkins's third voyage, in 1567, led to open conflict with the Spanish. Francis Drake took up the challenge at that point and began what proved to be twenty years of wildly adventurous raids on the Spanish colonial properties. The climax of Drake's career was his famous voyage around the world between 1577 and 1580, a joint-stock enterprise (see pp. 26–27) that yielded a 4,600 percent profit for the shareholders.

By then there was rising English interest in the Western Hemisphere—not primarily as a location for English colonies, but as a route to Asian markets. The Cabots' explorations at the turn of the sixteenth century were recalled, and new commercial and geographical information flowed in to help justify the enthusiasm of a group of adventurers from England's West Country. Led by Sir Humphrey Gilbert, this group was determined to find a northwestern passage through the Western Hemisphere to the Far East. In 1565 Queen Elizabeth's most important official advisers, the Privy Council, heard a formal debate on possible new routes. The merchants of the Muscovy Company urged endorsement of efforts to find an eastern passage, north of Siberia, and to exploit the trade of the Baltic region and Russia. The merchants and landowning gentry of the West Country, long familiar with the North American coastal waters, argued for expeditions to the west, through what is now Canada. Gilbert and the westerners were defeated in that debate, but with their support an enterprising mariner, Martin Frobisher, in 1576–78 led three expeditions into the region northeast of Hudson Bay. Frobisher and his London backers, under the direction of a merchant, Michael Lok, organized the short-lived Company of Cathay in response to the reports of gold—which later proved to be false—that were carried back. There were continuous frustrations in all these western ventures, but the search for the northwest passage went on. In the end, after vain and desperate efforts to get through the ice and snow of the Canadian wilderness, Englishmen at least gained a reasonably clear picture of that forbidding region of the globe.

First Attempts at Colonization

As these overseas enterprises progressed, the idea of colonization gradually developed. In his appearance before the Privy Council in 1565, Gilbert had suggested the value of establishing colonies as way stations along the proposed routes to the Far East. In 1578 he sought and received a crown charter for establishing a colony in America.

Gilbert's attempt in 1578 to establish a colony in New England or Nova Scotia—the first English attempt to colonize the Western Hemisphere—failed almost before it began. His small exploratory fleet was scattered by storms and diverted by the lure of privateering. Yet, in the process of launching this expedi-

Sir Walter Raleigh and His Son, 1602
A statesman, courtier, adventurer, and man of letters, once a favorite of Queen Elizabeth, Raleigh was executed by James I in 1618 on trumped-up charges of treason. Raleigh's sponsorship of the Roanoke voyages was part of his general interest in overseas discovery and settlement. He financed expeditions to the Orinoco River in South America and developed a large personal estate in Ireland.

tion, Gilbert acquired valuable experience in the financial aspects of colonization. He also won the enthusiasm of his gifted half-brother, Sir Walter Raleigh, and captured the interest of two cousins, both named Richard Hakluyt and both experts on overseas geography, who became important propagandists for colonization.

The younger Hakluyt's *Discourse Concerning Western Planting* (1584) shows the mixed motives of this advanced circle of enthusiasts. Hakluyt argued that it was England's duty to Christianize the American pagans, especially because an American colony would serve as a base for attacks on Spanish lands and Spanish treasure ships. More important, he continued, American colonies would provide long-term economic gains. They could supply England with exotic goods that otherwise would have to be bought from Spain, and they would create new markets for English consumer goods. The colonies would also absorb England's unemployed workers and turn their labor to advantage. New routes to Asia, new weapons against Spain, a new source of exotic supplies, a new market for English goods, and a new use for England's "surplus" population—all this would justify England's support of colonization.

"The Aged Man in His Wynter Garment"
One of the accurate and superbly colored scenes of native life and the natural environment of coastal North Carolina painted by John White on his voyages to Raleigh's "Virginia" in 1585 and 1587.

But Raleigh's and Hakluyt's ideas were not widely shared, and they did not become state policy. In 1584, after Gilbert had died on a voyage from Newfoundland, Queen Elizabeth transferred his charter to Raleigh; but she kept her government from directly supporting his plans for colonization. When Raleigh was planning the expedition that would lead to the establishment of his famous "lost" colony in America in 1585, the queen made a minor financial contribution to the venture and gave it her personal blessing. But her government did nothing to help launch or sustain the enterprise. This one English settlement in America in the sixteenth century was thus of necessity almost entirely the private undertaking of a group of merchants and gentlemen from the west of England.

The story of this first English colony in the Western Hemisphere, in the region that the English named Virginia in honor of Elizabeth, the "Virgin Queen," is quickly told. In three successive years separate groups of settlers were landed on Roanoke Island, a heavily wooded spot off the coast of present-day North Carolina. The first group, 108 men, arrived in 1585. The settlers clashed with the Indians and used up their food supply as they explored the North Carolina coast, and they returned hurriedly to England the next year with Francis Drake, who had unexpectedly appeared on his way home from a successful raid on the West Indies. Late in 1586 a party was sent from England to relieve the first group; of this party, 18 men were left behind on Roanoke Island, but this forlorn and helpless crew was soon killed by the Indians. The island was therefore deserted when in the summer of 1587 the third and largest contingent of set-

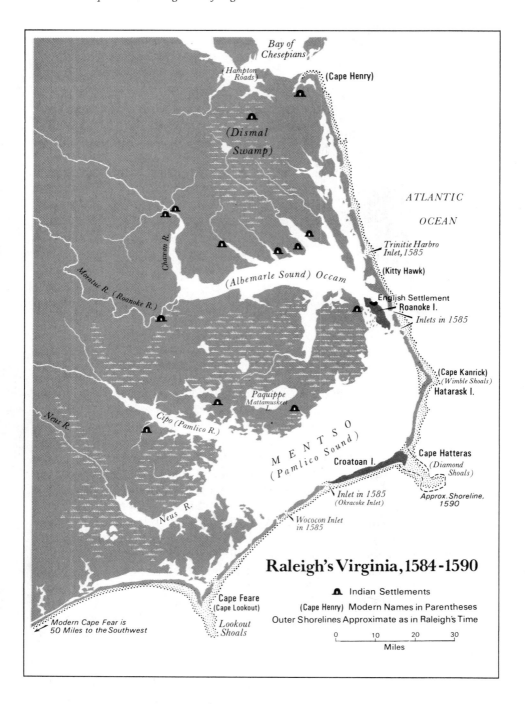

Bay of
Chesepians

*(Hampton
Roads)*

(Cape Henry)

*(Dismal

Swamp)*

ATLANTIC

OCEAN

*Trinitie Harbro
Inlet, 1585*

(Kitty Hawk)

Chavan R.

Moratu R. (Roanoke R.)

(Albemarle Sound) Occam

English Settlement
Roanoke I.

Inlets in 1585

(Cape Kanrick)
(Wimble Shoals)
Hatarask I.

*Paquippe
Mattamuskeet
L.*

Neus R.

Cipo (Pamlico R.)

M E N T S O
(Pamlico Sound)

Croatoan I.

Cape Hatteras
*(Diamond
Shoals)*

*Inlet in 1585
(Okracoke Inlet)*

*Approx. Shoreline,
1590*

Neus R.

*Wococon Inlet
in 1585*

Raleigh's Virginia, 1584-1590

🛖 Indian Settlements

(Cape Henry) Modern Names in Parentheses

Outer Shorelines Approximate as in Raleigh's Time

Cape Feare
(Cape Lookout)

*Lookout
Shoals*

*Modern Cape Fear is
50 Miles to the Southwest*

0	10	20	30

Miles

tlers—117 men, women, and children—arrived under Governor John White. The precise fate of these people, the best-equipped of Raleigh's settlers, has never been discovered. White had to return quickly to England to speed on more supplies, but the threat of open war with Spain* and the attractions of privateering kept relief vessels from reaching the colony. When White finally managed to return in 1590, he found all the settlers gone. Apparently they had moved south to Croatoan Island, and there they had vanished. Their disappearance marks the end of Raleigh's efforts at colonization.

In comparison with the bold and hugely successful first thrusts of the Spanish in America, this was a fumbling, failing, almost pathetic affair. Raleigh's Roanoke venture dramatically underscored the limitations that defeated English colonization in the reign of Elizabeth I. Yet it also revealed the basic conditions that would shape the successful English settlements in the early seventeenth century.

Personnel and the Role of the State

Several things of permanent importance had become clear during these earliest and least successful years of English colonization in America. First, there existed in England, available for colonization, a leadership group whose members were quite different from the Spanish conquerors, "drunk with a heroic and brutal dream," as a Spanish poet later described the *conquistadores.* The Spanish conquerors had been the sons of poor farmers and townsmen, many of them illiterate. But the leaders of English overseas enterprise—Gilbert, Raleigh, Hawkins, Drake—were the well-educated younger sons of the West Country gentry, bred in secure landed establishments and familiar with the sea from childhood. English law barred younger sons from inheriting family properties, and these men were eager to find a way of reestablishing themselves on the land in the same genteel condition they had known before.

Second, it was clear that there was in England a mass of laborers available for emigration to overseas colonies. London, whose population rose from 60,000 in 1500 to 200,000 in 1600, was swollen with unemployed workers. The countryside was swarming with migrant farmhands; and in the centers of the wool industry, the West Country and East Anglia (the eastern counties of Essex, Suffolk, and Norfolk), underemployment was generating the discontent that would express itself forcefully in the religious protest of Puritanism. Elizabethans spoke of the "multitude of increase in our people." Responsible officials were convinced that England was overpopulated and that its well-being was threatened by an idle labor force that consumed more than it contributed to the national wealth. For many, the most attractive remedy was colonization and emigration. We know now that there was no real "surplus" of people in seventeenth-century England, even though the population of the kingdom rose from just over 3 million in 1550 to just

---

*This war climaxed, but did not end, with the famous defeat of the Spanish Armada in 1588.

over 4 million in 1600, and then to 5.2 million in 1695, and to 6 million in 1720. The sense of overpopulation arose from the widespread displacement of a mass population and from the high geographical mobility that had resulted from rapid economic growth, inflation, and the commercialization of agriculture. But however these developments were viewed, they proved crucial to the early settlement of British North America by making a mass of ordinary farm and town workers available for recruitment.

Third, it became evident that there was plentiful capital available for investment in overseas ventures, as well as abundant business interest in mobilizing that capital and directing it to profitable uses in colonization. The costs of financing the Roanoke voyages and the first efforts at colonization had been borne almost entirely by landowning West Country gentlemen, but their resources were clearly inadequate to support further, larger-scale efforts. In 1589 Raleigh transferred control of the Virginia enterprise to a London business syndicate that was headed by Sir Thomas Smith, one of the most powerful merchants of the era. The capital available to these merchants was far greater than that of the West Country gentry, and it would be these businessmen who would launch the first new wave of colonization in the early seventeenth century.

It had become clear too, in the later years of Elizabeth's reign, that when colonization efforts would be resumed the crown would continue to play only a minor role. It would legalize exploration and settlement and would have some say in the plans that were made. But the crown would initiate nothing and organize nothing, nor would it sustain or reinforce any enterprise that was begun. More important, the English crown had no desire to extend its direct rule over distant territories conquered or settled by Englishmen. Some form of government would be provided, but it would not be direct crown government in depth. The burden of governing the colonies, like the burden of financing them, would have to be borne by the organizers of the settlement or by the settlers themselves. At the start at least, colonial government would have to be self-government of some sort, and the imperial government would be a superstructure, an overlay imposed on semi-independent units of local government.

Financial Limitations and the "Starving Times"

England's war with Spain, which had begun in the 1580s, finally ended in 1604. Peace released the powerful expansionist impulses that had been building up in England for half a century, and the resulting lunge into overseas enterprise in the reigns of James I (1603–25) and his son Charles I (1625–49) was spectacular. The famous settlements at Jamestown, at Plymouth, and around Massachusetts Bay were only fragments of a huge overall effort that reached into many areas of the globe, involved hundreds of thousands of Englishmen of all descriptions, and cost millions of pounds.

The chief target of this great expansion was not North America but Ireland, which in the sixteenth century had been the scene of England's first extensive and

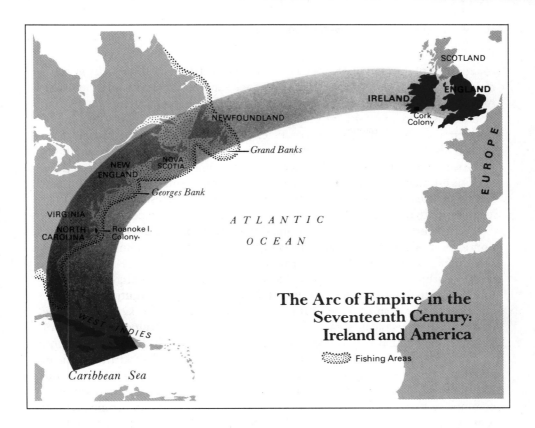

The Arc of Empire in the Seventeenth Century: Ireland and America

Fishing Areas

SCOTLAND

IRELAND ENGLAND

EUROPE

Cork Colony

NEWFOUNDLAND

Grand Banks

NEW ENGLAND

NOVA SCOTIA

Georges Bank

VIRGINIA

NORTH CAROLINA — Roanoke I. Colony

ATLANTIC OCEAN

WEST INDIES

Caribbean Sea

sustained efforts at overseas colonization. Henry VIII had tried to bind the native Irish chiefs to him by feudal ties and gradually to introduce the Church of England and elements of English law. But he had failed to win over the rebellious Irishmen, and in 1566 English armies moved in to conquer what they could by force. British settlements were then established in certain parts of southern Ireland, which formed a "pale of settlement" beyond which lived the native people whom Englishmen considered savage and ungovernable.

By 1604 the English saw Ireland and America as similar targets of overseas expansion and in their minds linked the two lands geographically. As they looked out at the world beyond England, they saw a single arc of overseas territories suitable for colonization sweeping out from their own island. This arc enclosed Ireland, Newfoundland, and the mainland coast of North America south to the Caribbean. It was natural for the English to consider nearby Ireland, which was described in a travel book of 1617 as "this famous island in the Virginia Sea," as the first and primary object of their colonization efforts in the early seventeenth century. When in 1607 two of the most powerful Irish earls resisted English authority and ultimately fled the British Isles, the English confiscated their vast properties. They largely cleared this immense territory—which covered six of the nine counties of the northern province of Ulster—of its native population and sold parcels of the land to prospective "planters" (settlers). London's city government and its major guild corporations took up large grants. After an Irish rebellion in 1641, 7 million more acres were cleared of their native inhabitants. Thousands of native Irish were severely punished for their part—proved or suspected—in the rebellion, and most were driven beyond the English pale. Into these Irish "plantations" came a steady stream of English and Scottish emigrants in the same years that the North American settlements were being established. By 1642 an estimated 120,000 English and Scottish men, women, and children had settled in Ireland. This migration was six times larger than the famous "Great Migration" that settled New England in the same period.

Yet Ulster was the scene of only one—if the most extensive—of the colonization efforts of the time. Besides Ireland, Virginia, and Massachusetts, English settlements were established in Bermuda, on several Caribbean islands (Providence, Barbados, St. Christopher, Nevis, Montserrat, and Antigua), in Newfoundland, in Nova Scotia, and on the mainland coast of South America. In addition the English developed fragile contacts with India, first in flourishing trading settlements (called factories) and then in the beginning of a network of political control that would eventually cover much of the Indian subcontinent.

In this global context the first English settlements on the North American mainland were relatively small undertakings, and their early histories become understandable only in terms of the greater whole. For while these American communities would in time have a unique historical importance, originally they shared characteristics common to the rest of the earliest seventeenth-century enterprises. And of these common characteristics, none was more important than the way in which they were financed.

The Financing of the Colonies

Whatever their founders' ultimate dreams, these earliest English colonies—whether in Newfoundland, Barbados, Ulster, Plymouth, or Virginia—had to be financed at the start by profit-seeking joint-stock companies. Eleven commercial companies bore the main financial burden of the settlements that were launched before 1640. They raised their capital (an estimated £3 million) by selling stock to a remarkably broad range of the English population. Thousands invested— landowners as well as merchants, people of ordinary means as well as those of wealth. The funds that were raised by these investments were, for the most part, managed by men who worked not only within the usual constraints of business operations, but also under two very special pressures. These pressures explain much of the hardship and tragedy of life in the earliest American settlements.

First, the joint stocks—the initial capital funds—of these ventures were not expected to endure. That is, shareholders did not expect to leave their funds in these companies over a long period and to draw a steady dividend income from them. Instead investors hoped to benefit from the quick liquidation of the whole enterprise at the end of a single voyage or after a set number of years. It was expected that at such a time the original capital plus accumulated profits would be distributed to investors. Whether there would be any further investments beyond the initial one would depend on the business prospects at the time of this complete division of the company's assets. Many of the settlers were in effect employees of the company that had organized the venture, for a stated term of years; thus they were under great pressure to produce an immediate profit. If they failed to ship back tangible proof of the financial value of the settlement, they would be cut off and would be forced to fend for themselves. As a consequence, instead of carefully exploring their surroundings and acclimatizing themselves to the strange American environment, the first settlers spent much of their time scrabbling for gold in every shallow stream, searching for routes to the Pacific Ocean around the bend of every broad river, and plunging almost suicidally into the backcountry to investigate confused Indian reports of great cities or of vast sources of furs or precious metals.

The pressures on the settlers were further intensified by the technical fact that the shareholders in these early joint-stock companies had unlimited legal liability. The backers of the settlements were personally liable, without limit, for all debts the settlement companies might incur. Investors were therefore extremely sensitive to any possibility of failure. They had no choice but to abandon doubtful enterprises as quickly as possible.

The "Starving Times" The result of these conditions was desperation, starvation, and at times chaos in England's first North American colonies, as well as bankruptcy in the companies that first colonized mainland North America. For there were only three possible sources of quick profits for colonists. First, they might have found valuable resources on the surface of the land, loaded them onto boats, and rushed them back to investors. Second, they might have encountered a docile native population and organized it quickly into labor gangs to dig out the less accessible resources. Third, settlers might have discovered new routes to rich, exotic markets. None of these possibilities proved realistic on the coasts of North America. Consequently, after the first shipments, investors withheld life-sustaining supplies from the settlements, and one company after another failed. Sheer accident provided most of the profits that were made at the start. In Bermuda, for example, ambergris (a substance, produced by whales, that was used in making perfume and medicine) was found in large quantities; a shipment of £10,000 worth of this substance saved the Bermuda Company. (Subsequently the company profited steadily from tobacco production.) Similarly, the Providence Island Company had the good fortune to capture a Spanish treasure ship worth £50,000.

Lucky accidents of this kind were rare, however. Sooner or later almost every one of the companies that had financed settlements in British North America failed, and as they did so the original investors sought desperately to find secondary sources of profit. Some of the stockholders, seeking to recover their losses, funded "magazines"—stores of goods to be sold at high prices to the needy settlers. Some stockholders set up secondary enterprises: glass manufac-

"Virginia," c. 1590

This interesting detail of a map-picture dating from 1590 shows the coast of "Virginia" (present-day North Carolina) and the perilous shoals off Cape Hatteras where many early sailing vessels foundered. The rendering shows Indian settlements on Roanoke Island.

turing and silk making were favored in Virginia. Others attempted to develop "private plantations," that is, personal estates and jurisdictions, in the new land given to them in place of the missing company profits. The Virginia Company alone created fifty of these private domains, but few of these secondary enterprises succeeded. Perhaps the most successful of the lesser ventures within the Virginia Company was the fund established to send over a hundred "maids" to Jamestown "to be made wives of." The investors in this venture realized a 47 percent profit on their shares when they sold the women's work contracts to the colonists.

As their financial prospects dimmed, many investors withdrew altogether from the ventures. In these cases colonists found themselves abruptly cut off from their backers, and for most of them the transition to self-sustained community life was desperately difficult. Even in the best of circumstances, the first inhabitants of Jamestown or Bermuda or Plymouth would have had a shock in adjusting to the wilderness environment. Forced to search for sources of immediate profit while neglecting the basics of survival, many found the struggle unendurable and succumbed—to despair, to disease, and to the harassment of hostile natives.

The narratives of the first settlements make painful reading. There was heroism, but there was also murderous selfishness; there was industry, but also laziness and at times suicidal inertia. Death and misery were everywhere. It is perhaps not surprising that the best-organized and most successful of the earliest communities were those in which strong religious beliefs prevailed. For only the otherworldly goals, the fierce determination, and the inner certainty of the Pilgrim and Puritan leaders could withstand the disintegrating effects of the "starving times."

CHRONOLOGY

1492–1504	Columbus's four voyages to New World.
1494	Treaty of Tordesillas divides non-Christian world between Spain and Portugal.
1497–1498	John Cabot explores Newfoundland, Labrador, and Nova Scotia, and establishes English claim to North America.
1503	Spain establishes board of trade, Casa de Contratacion.
1508–1509	Sebastian Cabot explores Hudson Bay region.
1509–1547	Reign of Henry VIII.
1513	Balboa discovers Pacific Ocean after crossing Isthmus of Panama.
1513	Ponce de Leon discovers mainland of Florida.
1519–1521	Cortes conquers Mexico.
1523	Verrazano explores coast of North America, establishing French claim.
1523–1530	Spaniards conquer Honduras and Guatemala.
1524	Spain creates Council of the Indies.
1528–1536	Cabeza de Vaca explores northern periphery of Gulf of Mexico, west to Gulf of California.
1532–1535	Pizarro conquers Peru.
1535	Viceroyalty of New Spain created.
1535–1539	Initial Spanish conquest of Ecuador, Chile, northern Argentina, and Bolivia.
1539–1541	De Soto explores southeastern United States and discovers the Mississippi.
1540–1542	Coronado seeks legendary cities of wealth in North American Southwest.
1540–1553	Valdivia extends Spanish conquest of Chile.
1542	Viceroyalty of Peru established.
1551	Antwerp market for English woolen goods fails.
1553–1558	Queen Mary reigns in England.
1558–1603	Elizabeth's reign in England
1562–1567	Hawkins trades and plunders in Spanish America.
1566	England begins conquest of Ireland.

1574	Gilbert leads expedition to Hudson Bay.
1577–1580	Drake circumnavigates globe.
1578	Gilbert fails to establish colony in North America.
1584	Richard Hakluyt (the younger) publishes *A Discourse Concerning Western Planting.*

1585–1587	Raleigh fails to establish Roanoke Colony.
1585–1598	England colonizes Ireland.
1603–1625	Reign of James I.
1606	Virginia Company chartered; includes two subcompanies.
1607	English colony established at Jamestown.

SUGGESTED READINGS

For an overview of European expansion and a geographer's interpretation of the settlement process: D. W. Meinig, *The Shaping of America* (I: *Atlantic America, 1492–1800,* 1986).

The discovery and conquest of Central and South America by Spain had been the subject of some of the greatest narrative histories written in the nineteenth century, notably William H. Prescott's *History of the Conquest of Mexico* (1843) and his *Conquest of Peru* (1847). This tradition of dramatic narratives continues in our own time in the writings of Samuel E. Morison, particularly in his biography of Columbus, *Admiral of the Ocean Sea* (2 vol. and 1 vol. eds., 1942, condensed as *Christopher Columbus, Mariner,* 1956), and his *The European Discovery of America: The Southern Voyages, A.D. 1492–1616* (1974), a volume crowded with maps and photographs that was written after the author retraced the routes of the Spanish discoverers by ship and plane. John H. Parry has sketched the general development of European expansion, geographical discovery, and initial overseas settlements in two very readable books, *Europe and a Wider World, 1415–1715* (1949) and *The Age of Reconnaissance* (1963). And David B. Quinn has summarized the first efforts of the Spanish, English, and French to explore and settle North America in his *North America from Earliest Discovery to First Settlements* (1977).

There are several good introductory histories of Spanish America in the colonial period: Salvador de Madariaga, *Rise of the Spanish American Empire* (1947); Charles Gibson, *Spain in America* (1966); Hubert Herring, *A History of Latin America from the Beginnings to the Present* (3d ed., 1968), parts I, II; John H. Parry, *The Spanish Seaborne Empire* (1966); and James Lockhart and Stuart B. Schwartz, *Early Latin America* (1983). An equivalent history of the Portuguese-American empire is C. R. Boxer, *The Portuguese Seaborne Empire, 1415–1825* (1969). On the French empire in America, see George M. Wrong, *The Rise and Fall of New France* (2 vols., 1928), and William J. Eccles, *Canada Under Louis XIV* (1964) and *Canadian Frontier, 1534–1760* (1969). On population recruitment in Canada: Peter Moogk, "Reluctant Exiles: Emigrants from France in Canada before 1760," *William and Mary Quarterly,*[*] 46 (1989), 463–505. The classic account of the administrative and constitutional history of Spanish America is Clarence H. Haring, *The Spanish Empire in America* (1947). For a theoretical analysis of the same subject in sociological terms, see Margali Sarfatti, *Spanish Bureaucratic-*

---

[*]This journal will be referred to hereafter as *Wm. and Mary Q.*

Patrimonialism in America (1966). The underlying ideas of empire are described in John H. Parry, *The Spanish Theory of Empire in the Sixteenth Century* (1940), and on the interpenetration of Spain and its colonies: J. H. Elliott, *The Old World and the New, 1492–1650* (1970).

On economic history, there are two classic works: Clarence H. Haring, *Trade and Navigation Between Spain and the Indies . . .* (1918), and Earl J. Hamilton, *American Treasure and the Price Revolution in Spain, 1501–1650* (1934). In addition, see Peter J. Bakewell, *Silver Mining and Society in Colonial Mexico* (1971); Woodrow W. Borah, *New Spain's Century of Depression* (Ibero-Americana, 35, 1951); and relevant chapters in John Lynch, *Spain Under the Hapsburgs* (2 vols., 1964–69).

There are several studies that concentrate on the particular topics emphasized in this chapter. On Spanish migration to America: essays by Magnus Mörner, Woodrow Borah, and Peter Boyd-Bowman, in Fredi Chiappelli, ed., *First Images of America* (1976), Vol. II; and Ida Altman, *Emigrants and Society* (1989). On race relations in Spanish America: Magnus Mörner, *Race Mixture in the History of Latin America* (1967); Charles Gibson, *The Aztecs Under Spanish Rule* (1964); John H. Rowe, "The Incas Under Spanish Colonial Institutions," *Hispanic American Historical Review,* 37 (1957), 156–91; C. E. Marshall, "The Birth of the Mestizo in New Spain," *Hispanic American Historical Review,* 19 (1939), 161–84; James Lockhart, *Spanish Peru, 1532–1560, A Colonial Society* (1968), and his *Men of Cajamarca* (1972); Lewis Hanke, *The Spanish Struggle for Justice in the Conquest of America* (1949); Anthony Pagden, *The Fall of Natural Man* (1982); and Silvio Zavala, *New Viewpoints on the Spanish Colonization of America* (1943). Nathan Wachtel, *The Vision of the Vanquished* (1977), is an attempt to portray the trauma of the Spanish conquest from the Indians' point of view. On the dominance of native Spaniards in high office and the slow rise of Creoles through purchase of public office, see M. H. Burkholder and D. S. Chandler, *From Impotence to Authority* (1977), and J. H. Parry, *The Sale of Public Office . . .* (1953). For an extended comparison of the Spanish American and the British North American colonial empires, see James Lang, *Conquest and Commerce: Spain and England in the Americas* (1975). Comparisons of slavery in North and South America have been worked out in books by Frank Tannenbaum (*Slave and Citizen*), Carl N. Degler (*Neither Black nor White*), Herbert S. Klein (*Slavery in the Americas*), and most comprehensively by David B. Davis (*The Problem of Slavery in Western Culture*).

The essential writings on England's involvement in geographic discovery, imperial rivalries, and overseas settlement in the sixteenth century are by David B. Quinn. His *Roanoke Voyages, 1584–1590* (2 vols., 1955) contains every document related to that enterprise, a subject he has summarized in an excellent brief account, *Raleigh and the British Empire* (1947) and discussed in broader context in *England's Sea Empire, 1550–1642* (with A. N. Ryan, 1983). In addition, Quinn has edited the documents of the colonizing efforts of Sir Humphrey Gilbert (2 vols., 1940), written a biography of Gilbert, and edited Hakluyt's writings. His essays are brought together in *England and the Discovery of America, 1481–1620* (1974) and summarized in his *North America,* cited above. Quinn's *Set Fair for Roanoke* (1985) is an excellent history of the lost colony; a briefer account is Karen Kupperman's *Roanoke* (1984). The priceless watercolors and other drawings of the natives and their environment that John White made during his stay on Roanoke are reproduced in Paul Hulton's *America 1585* (1984). Samuel E. Morison's *The European Discovery of America: The Northern Voyages, A. D. 500–1600* (1971) covers in the same vivid fashion as *The Southern Voyages* the Cabots' voyages and all of the Elizabethan explorations, and it contains in addition an excellent account of the Roanoke expeditions. Kenneth R. Andrews, *Trade, Plunder, and Settlement* (1984) relates the origins of Britain's empire to the maritime enterprises of the sixteenth century.

The important role of Ireland in the origins of Elizabethan colonization and the connections between Irish and American settlement are best described in David B. Quinn, *The Elizabethans and the Irish* (1966) and in the essays in K. R. Andrews et al., eds., *The Westward*

Enterprise (1978). See also James Muldoon, "The Indian as Irishman," *Essex Institute Historical Collections,* III (1975), 267–89; and Nicholas P. Canny, "The Ideology of English Colonization: from Ireland to America," *Wm. and Mary Q,* 30 (1973), 575–98.*

The masterwork on the financial history of sixteenth- and seventeenth-century English exploration and colonization is W. R. Scott, *The Constitution and Finance of English, Scottish and Irish Joint Stock Companies to 1720* (3 vols., 1912). Theodore K. Rabb, *Enterprise and Empire . . . 1575–1630* (1967), demonstrates statistically the broad social basis of investment in colonization.

---

*This essay and several mentioned in the references to the chapters that follow have been reprinted in an excellent collection, *Colonial America: Essays in Politics and Social Development* (Stanley N. Katz and John M. Murrin, eds., 3d ed., New York, 1983). Essays and selections from books that appear in this volume are indicated by a dagger (†).

2

Transplantation

⟨ornament⟩

$\mathscr{I}$N 1600 the eastern coastal region of mainland North America, some 362,000 square miles from Maine to Georgia and west to the Appalachian Mountains, was largely uncultivated, but it was by no means an unbroken wilderness. A native Indian population, some in loosely organized village bands, some in well-organized tribes, lived settled lives there, and had for countless centuries. Linguistically and culturally they were Algonquians along the coastal plain, Iroquoians in the lower Great Lakes area. Some sustained their lives with hunting and gathering the natural products of the land, but most alternated cycles of agricultural production (largely corn, squash, and beans) in the spring and summer with game hunts in the fall and winter. Their villages, scattered through the vast woodlands, were mostly semipermanent and could house as many as one or two thousand inhabitants, although most contained a few hundred. Surrounded by cultivated fields and forest clearings, these settlements of lightly built pole and bark houses were easily moved when the local soils were exhausted. As a result, after innumerable generations, the landscape the Europeans encountered was an uneven patchwork of fresh grass and meadowlands, fields of low shrubs, and stretches of new forests developing in terrain the Indians had deliberately burnt over, alongside ranges of dense woods untouched for centuries.

By modern demographic measures the natives' numbers in this huge east coast territory were very small: a probable average density of just over one person per square mile, rising perhaps to four or five per square mile in the most fertile regions of New England and New York. But the "emptiness" of the land was deceptive, and led to devastating conflicts with the European settlers. For the unpopulated areas, which Europeans could only assume were wastelands open to conquest by right and law, were as vital to the Indians' survival as the cultivated fields that produced their stable diet of corn and squash and the streams in which they fished. For only in these unpopulated hunting regions could the game flourish that provided vital nutrients and clothing for people who had no domesticated animals and produced no textiles. The native Americans could not conceive of these great hunting ranges as property that could be parceled out to individuals in outright ownership. The concept of individual possession of sections of land or of legally defined "rights" in land was utterly foreign to them. Land was a common resource inherited from ancestors, held in trust by tribal chiefs for future generations, and used by all members of the tribe for their daily needs.

Nor did the Indians think of warfare in European terms. Deadly struggles between individuals and tribes were common, and enemies were treated brutally (war captives were commonly tortured to death). But the Indians did not go to war to annihilate enemy tribes, to create utter devastation, or to engage in wholesale massacres. They fought for revenge and for prestige—to demonstrate valor and manliness, and to replace tribal members lost in raids or abductions. But there was no uniformity in any of this. The Indians' world was as varied as the Europeans'. Some lived lives of marginal subsistence, others were secure in well-organized tribes, moving with the seasons to maximize their advantages; some were monogamous, others were polygamous; some lived in large tribes with highly structured hierarchies, others in elemental groupings of nuclear families; some were warlike, others were peaceable; some were familiar with trade, others had few outside contacts—and they differed widely in the languages of daily discourse. The cultural and political differences between the natives in the two main areas of contact with Europeans are particularly striking.

The Virginia coastal plain, stretching from the Potomac River to the northern border of the present North Carolina, was dominated by an unusually well-organized political structure under the rulership of a single paramount chief, Powhatan. He controlled approximately thirty tribes or territorial units through a cadre of lesser chiefs, the *werowances,* each of whom held life-and-death power over their subjects. Although despotic, the rulers at each level were bound by custom and the advice of counselors and priests, and they helped inculcate a culture of manliness, reckless courage, physical endurance, and pride in warlike accomplishments. The Powhatan Indians were proud people, extremely sensitive to slights, resentful, and aggressive. Fearful of the humiliation of defeat and of showing weakness of any kind, the warriors were suspicious of all outsiders, tested their enemies' bravery constantly, and probed their weaknesses. For the Powhatans the ultimate defeat was not death, which could be proudly and courageously endured, but the loss of independence that led to humbling subordination to others. So life for them was dangerous, tense, and full of heroic drama.

The natives the English encountered in New England were also proud, courageous, and, when necessary, warlike people. But they shared a more egalitarian culture that stressed communal bonds within their tribes and among rival tribes. Neighboring bands peacefully exchanged material goods and provided marriage partners for each other; they participated in common harvest festivals and religious rites. They hunted together, forged intertribal alliances, and lived independently, resisting the creation of a centralized power such as Powhatan's in Virginia. As with the Indians to the south, reciprocity was a dominant theme in all their dealings, but stability was the goal of their politics. So they would approach the Europeans, as they did other strangers, in a spirit of accommodation, seeking not domination but reciprocal exchanges and alliances, hoping to maintain the stable balance they had sought for untold generations.

Into this world of native peoples, living in close harmony with the natural environment, polytheistic and uncompetitive in religion, unsophisticated in weaponry although sufficiently effective for their own needs, unlettered but rich in oral traditions, and eager to maintain the life they had known—into this world the Europeans entered when they established their first permanent settlement in 1607.

A century later the entire coastal region had been transformed. Almost the entire Indian population had been eliminated from the seaboard lands—devastated by epidemics, destroyed by the invading English and Dutch in savage local wars, and driven back beyond the western fringes of European settlement. The area now contained a quarter of a million transplanted Europeans and their children and grandchildren, all attempting to re-create the familiar pattern of European life in this undeveloped land. The settlers had come principally from England and the Netherlands, two of the most dynamic and economically advanced nations of Europe. They lived in communities that were parts of a commercial network spread across the entire Atlantic basin and that directly or indirectly involved all the nations of western Europe. Within this transplanted European population, mainly in Virginia and Maryland, there were also more than 20,000 African slaves, who were bound in lifelong, hereditary, and debased servitude.

The transplanted population of 1700 was organized into eleven provinces loosely controlled by the English government, which was only beginning to understand the full importance of the colonial world it had acquired. A small proportion of the settlers, perhaps 8 percent, lived in the five main port towns (Boston, Newport, New York, Philadelphia, and Charleston) through which flowed most of the commerce and communications that linked this world to Europe. The rest lived in village communities of a few hundred people or on isolated family farms or "plantations" that were modeled on European agricultural establishments but that differed from them in fundamental ways.

These tens of thousands of transplanted Europeans and Africans had arrived in no concentrated stream, under no centralized direction, and in no limited span of years. Rather, they had arrived—and in 1700 were continuing to arrive—irregularly and under various circumstances. Migration and settlement were organized by individuals or by private organizations, and the history of this process forms not one story, but many. Yet for all their variety these stories of colonization have a common pattern. They begin with high hopes and great plans—often visions of utopian societies or of great wealth quickly acquired. But contact with reality brought frustration and the failure of original high hopes. Those who survived, however, learned to adapt creatively to their new environment. This was the persistent pattern of European colonization in the seventeenth century: soaring expectations, disappointment, and frustration, disaster or near disaster, and then a slow adjustment to the realities of life on the wilderness edge of the North American continent. New forms of society gradually emerged from this process, forms made far more complex by their superficial similarities to the familiar patterns of European life.

Virginia: Squalor, Struggle, and a New Way of Life

The settlement of Virginia is a classic case of high hopes shattered and a new world rescued from the ruins. It began in 1606 when the English crown chartered two Virginia companies, one based in Plymouth, England, and the other in London. These two companies incorporated the interests of the two main groups that had already been involved in western exploration and the planning of American settlements—the gentry and merchants of the West Country, and the London merchants to whom Sir Walter Raleigh had transferred his colonizing rights. The companies were given separate although overlapping portions of the North American coast for settlement and were instructed to appoint their own resident governments. In 1607 the Plymouth group, which had been assigned the northern area between the Potomac River and present-day Bangor, Maine, attempted a settlement (called Sagadahoc) on the Maine coast near the mouth of the Kennebec River. But everything went wrong. No signs of quick profits appeared, disease and Indian attacks decimated the small band of settlers huddled in the tiny fort, and within a year the effort was permanently abandoned.

Jamestown　　The Virginia Company of London, which had been assigned the southern sector, was more ambitious and better financed. Its leaders, under Sir Thomas Smith, England's most powerful merchant, were vigorous, hard-driving men. In December 1606 they sent out three ships, the *Susan Constant,* the *Godspeed,* and the *Discovery.* These tiny vessels were scarcely able to hold the 144 people they carried, let alone survive a midwinter crossing of the Atlantic. Not until April 1607 did they reach Chesapeake Bay. In May the 104 survivors of the voyage disembarked on a low-lying island thirty miles upstream in the James River. The spot, close to the riverbank, was so soaked with stagnant water that no homesite could be chosen farther than 800 feet from malarial swamps, but the location was safe from attack and was believed to be close to passages through the continent to the Pacific. This unlikely place, which came to be called Jamestown, was the first permanent English settlement in North America.

The colony survived, but only barely. During the eighteen years of the Virginia Company's existence (1606–24), Jamestown, the main settlement, was a

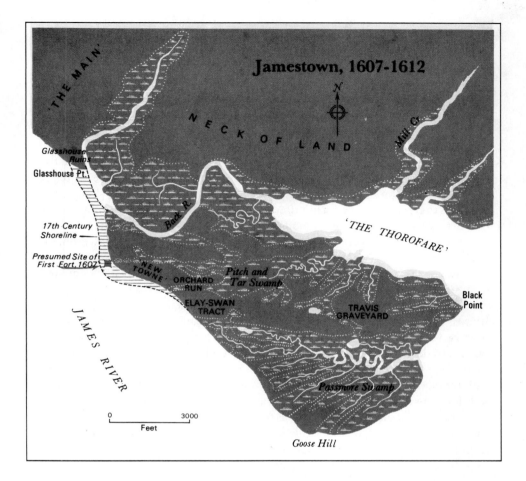

disaster for everyone in any way connected with it. Death was everywhere in the colony. Four out of five of the "planters" died of disease or in Indian attacks. The Virginia Company in London survived beyond its first two years only because of its leaders' persistence in pursuing empty dreams of profits and because of the financial support they were able to mobilize. Seldom has good money been thrown so extravagantly after bad; seldom have hard-headed businessmen been so mistaken in their expectations of success.

It quickly became clear that in Virginia the settlers would discover neither easily mined minerals nor a passage through the continent. Nor would they find a useful native labor force. Hope came to rest on the new idea of giving the colony enough settlers and secure financing to produce more ordinary goods—grapes, sugar, tobacco, cotton, and dye woods. These products could be sold with substantial, although not sensational, profits in England. Once the colonists created this kind of firm economic foundation, they could look into more dramatic and profitable ventures.

To establish Jamestown on this permanent basis, the company in London obtained a revised charter and launched a new effort that gave the endangered colony hope for the future. Without this renewed effort of 1609, Jamestown would have disappeared like Roanoke—and it almost did in any case.

By the terms of the new charter, the company was transformed into a public joint-stock company for a period of seven years. (Previously it had been financed by the contributions only of its incorporators and their friends.) In February 1609 the company staged an elaborate publicity campaign and began to sell public shares. One popular way to purchase shares was to pledge personal service in the colony as a settler. Such an "adventurer of person" received one or more shares of stock depending on his "quality" (that is, social standing) or special skills. Each share was to be worth at least a hundred acres of land in 1616, when the company's total assets would be divided among the stockholders. At the same time, the London stockholders were given more authority, and a new form of government was drawn up for the colony.

Under the first charter the resident government of the colony had consisted of an appointed council that elected its own president. The result had been wrangling among the leaders until Captain John Smith seized power. Smith was a shrewd, stubborn, commanding war veteran, a romantic but intelligent adventurer. By forceful leadership he had prevented the forlorn band of colonists from starving to death. Combining cleverness and brutality, he had kept the neighboring Indian tribes cordial or at least intimidated. Smith had also made important explorations of the Chesapeake region and had surveyed its economic possibilities. The lesson of his leadership was not forgotten. Under the new regulations of 1609, all colonial authority was to be exercised by an appointed governor who was to be advised, not controlled, by a council. The governor's power was to be limited only by the "liberties, franchises, and immunities" accorded all Englishmen and by instructions issued to him by the company.

The publicity campaign of 1609 was sensational. Colonization was preached in the churches of London, and the price of the company's stock rose. For the moment, support of the Virginia Company became a national cause. As a result, in June 1609 the company was able to send to Virginia a fleet carrying five hundred men, one hundred women, and large quantities of equipment and supplies. But the whole expedition seemed doomed. The vessel that carried the newly appointed officers of the colony was blown off course and was wrecked in Bermuda. (News of the shipwreck helped inspire Shakespeare's play *The Tempest.*) The four hundred leaderless settlers who arrived at Jamestown were exhausted by the long voyage and weakened by the putrid shipboard food. Disease was already spreading among them when they landed. They were too feeble at first to work and then became deeply discouraged by the miserable prospects they found. They had been shaken out of their normal sense of social discipline and were confused by the disordered life around them. They fell into fierce factional struggles, lethargy, and despair, and they failed to plant the crops they would need for the coming year. In the midst of a rich land they starved, and, unable to withstand disease, they died in droves, miserably. When the fearful winter of 1609–10 was over, only about sixty of the settlers were still alive. In May 1610 the new leaders of the colony finally arrived from Bermuda. They found a scene of utter desolation: Jamestown's palisade was in ruins, its houses had been burned for firewood, the last scraps of food (including cattle and domestic animals) had been eaten, and people spoke secretly of cannibalism.

The ravaged settlement, still lacking the supplies that had been paid for by the stock sale of 1609, seemed hopeless. On June 7, 1610, it was abandoned. The settlers sailed down the James River in four small vessels, intending to go home to England by way of Newfoundland.

The Settlement Restored   The colony was saved by a coincidence, which people of the time saw as an act of God. By chance the departing settlers were met near the mouth of the James River by a longboat from a fleet just arriving that carried three hundred men and the new governor, Lord De la Warr. The despairing and fearful settlers were ordered back, and De la Warr began the slow process of restoring discipline and confidence, creating a sound agriculture, and establishing profitable relations with the Indians. In England the company, with somewhat despairing vigor, continued its fund-raising and sent further reinforcements of more than six hundred men with hundreds of domestic animals and shiploads of equipment. By now the emphasis was entirely on developing Virginia's agricultural, industrial, and commercial possibilities. A satellite settlement was founded at Henrico on the upper James (the site of present-day Richmond), and two others were located at the mouth of the James. Harsh social discipline was imposed by a new code of laws that was published in 1612. Called *Lawes Divine, Morall, and Martiall,* this code organized the community into a kind of military corps. The settlers were required to perform service on common projects, and they were subjected to severe penalties for failure to work or to share military obligations.

Thus reinforced and disciplined, the colony made slow, painful progress toward self-sufficiency. Humble products—furs, timber, sassafras, some experimentally produced iron, and (beginning in 1614) small quantities of tobacco—began to fill the holds of vessels returning to England. But although the settlers had made an encouraging start, these early cargoes were not profitable enough to stimulate sizable new investments in the company, whose expenses were rising dangerously with each lifesaving supply ship that had to be sent to Virginia. More funds had to be raised. Subscribers were dunned for further contributions, unfulfilled pledges were pursued in the law courts, a public lottery was launched, more pamphlets were written describing Virginia's glowing promise, and more sermons were preached on the people's moral obligation to support this "New Britain." But even these intensified efforts did not generate the necessary aid. To popularize the organization further and to broaden its base, the company obtained a third charter in 1612 that again increased the ordinary shareholders' voice in the company's management. Still, the company's finances remained weak, and despite all the recent reinforcements, the colony's population in 1616 was still a mere 350.

One last, great effort had to be made if the London company was to be saved and any profit realized from the tens of thousands of pounds that had been invested. In 1618 a new group headed by Sir Edwin Sandys took over control of the company from Sir Thomas Smith and initiated the final phase of its history.

Under Sandys's influence the company drew up a uniform and generous policy of land inducements for the established colonists ("ancient planters") and for prospective investors and settlers. It devised the "headright" system, under which anyone who transported a settler to Virginia (either another person or himself) won the right to fifty acres of land. More important, the system allowed shareholders to pool their landholdings into jointly owned tracts, and it granted minor governmental powers to the holders of these tracts and of certain other large personal estates.

The creation of these "private plantations," or "hundreds," began the uncontrolled expansion of settled territory. By 1663 seventy such units were authorized. The lower James valley became dotted with self-contained subcolonies. At the same time, the rigid military discipline of the *Lawes* of 1612 was replaced by a more normal system of civil courts operating under English common law. A representative assembly—the first in American history—was provided for. This assembly consisted of the governor and his council, together with representatives of the private jurisdictions and of four projected urban communities, or "boroughs." At its first meeting in 1619, the assembly made clear that it would not only express popular grievances, as Parliament had been doing for centuries in England, but also protect the fundamental rights of Englishmen as these rights were known "at home."

In addition the company sent another 4,500 settlers to Virginia, who, it was hoped, would establish profitable agricultural enterprises. Expert craftsmen began to manufacture pitch, tar, ships, and other timber products, as well as iron, salt, and glass. And the settlers experimented with growing tropical and semi-tropical crops and with producing salable wine and marketable silk.

It was all a colossal gamble by the energetic entrepreneurs who had taken over the company—and it was hopeless. Simply launching these enterprises drained all the company's cash, most of which had been raised by a public lottery. By 1621 the lottery had become a nuisance, and Parliament stopped it. Only a miraculous parlaying of small successes into basic security could rescue the company; but a single disaster would mean its collapse.

Collapse and Legacy of the Virginia Company

In March 1622 the final catastrophe struck, a fearful culmination of hostilities with the Indians that had begun in the earliest years of settlement. The tense, sensitive, aggressive Powhatans, at first accommodating, had attempted to include the small English "tribe" into their overall political structure, formally adopting John Smith as a tribal member and enlisting the settlers in attacks on their enemies. But as the English, reduced to starvation, repeatedly seized stores of corn supplies and took possession of more and more of the Indians' land, tensions grew and led to an intermittent guerrilla war that lasted from 1609 to 1614. Atrocities multiplied on both sides (the Indian women

Martin's Hundred, One of the "Particular Plantations" Along the James River

A modern artist's sketch, based on archaeological excavations. Founded in 1619 by a company of London investors, the plantation of 21,500 acres was located 10 miles east of Jamestown and originally housed over 200 settlers. By 1622 it was reduced by famine and disease to 20 inhabitants and then almost completely destroyed in the Indian massacre. Depicted here: in the foreground, the company's compound, consisting of a longhouse on the right joined to a stable and a storehouse; in the background, the fort to which the settlers fled when attacked. The excavations have unearthed grisly remains of the massacre, including a corpse whose skull had been broken by a blow with a cleaver or tomahawk and then smashed to pieces by further blows when the body had fallen to the ground.

skinned one English captive alive with mussel shells), and Jamestown was sieged almost to the point of annihilation. But the military regime imposed by the Virginia Company in 1610 together with the arrival of small contingents of experienced, well-armed soldiers, turned the tide, and in 1614 an informal truce was reached, secured by the marriage of Powhatan's daughter Pocahontas to John Rolfe. But in the years of relative peace that followed, the English steadily extended their settlements. By 1622 there were forty-six plantations on the James River alone, and in that year Powhatan's successor, his brother Opechancanough, despairing of ever attaining a just peace with the invaders, led a massacre of the English in which 347 men, women, and children were slaughtered within a few hours. Thereafter all thoughts of a peaceful accommodation were abandoned, and the English began a war of reprisal that amounted to full-scale genocide. Not a year went by thereafter, scarcely a month, in which bloody battles, small and large, were not fought between the races. A second massacre of five hundred colonists in 1644 led to such savage revenge that the Indians had no alternative to surrendering all the land claimed by the English and accepting a small reservation and the status of clients. In the early years of conflict Powhatan's Indians had outnumbered the English 30 to 1; by the 1660s the numbers were reversed.

By then the original Virginia Company had long since failed. It had never succeeded as a commercial enterprise. When in 1624 the company's bankruptcy was acknowledged, the crown annulled the charter and Virginia became a royal colony. In terms of its original purpose, the company was a complete failure.

Yet in a larger sense the Virginia Company had been successful. It had opened the North American mainland to British settlement. It had peopled a small portion of the region, although at a fearful cost in English and Indian lives. It had experimented with the economic possibilities of the Chesapeake, and it had left behind a heritage of the rule of law (at least within the English settlement) and of the practice of self-government, however rudimentary. Above all, the company had set the pattern for Virginia's development.

The general assembly, which the company had created to rally support among the settlers, continued to exist when Virginia became a royal colony. Governor, council, and representatives of the boroughs, or "burghs" (hence the name *burgesses* for the representatives), met together as a single group until the 1660s. By then the burgesses' interests had become distinct enough from those of the council to justify their meeting as a separate body. This central government, along with the county courts that were created in 1643, was the basic public authority in this frontier community, whose everyday life was an unregulated response to the raw Chesapeake environment. By 1642, when Sir William Berkeley first arrived as governor (a position he would occupy for most of the next thirty-four years), the essential character of life in the first permanent English colony in America was clear.

Seventeenth-century Virginia did not offer elegant, easy living on gracious, aristocratic "plantations." True, in the first years, when all sorts of exotic rewards were expected, the leadership of the colony had included intellectuals and the sons of noblemen and other prominent people. But this early leadership had disappeared by 1624, casualties of the environment, the Indians, disease, and discouragement. The new leaders established themselves by their sheer capacity to survive on rough, half-cleared tobacco farms and to produce material gains from the raw wilderness. These men were former servants, yeoman farmers, and adventurers of little social status or wealth. They lacked the outward signs of social authority, but they managed to prosper by brute labor and shrewd manipulation.

The leaders of Virginia in the generation after the company was dissolved were tough, unsentimental, quick-tempered, crudely ambitious men who were concerned with making money from the land and with increasing their landholdings. They cared little for the grace of life. They roared curses, drank heavily, and gambled extravagantly, sometimes betting their servants when they had little else to wager. They asserted their interests fiercely. They wanted an aggressive expansion of settlement and of trading enterprise, and unrestricted legal access to land, no matter what the Indians' objections. But it was cleared and cultivated land that counted—and there was little of that to be had. Labor, not land, was in critically short supply, and every effort was made to entice over from England workers whose labor could be counted on for at least a set period of time. This period was specified in "indentures"—contracts that bound immigrants to service for a number of years in return for payment of their passage to Virginia. Although an average of 1,500 indentured servants arrived in the Chesapeake annually through most of the seventeenth century, their terms of bonded service were short—normally four years for adults and five years or more for minors. After completing their service, most of them joined the general population of free tobacco farmers seeking to expand production and competing for hired labor.

Black "slave" labor (the meaning of the term *slave* was at first ambiguous) was known in Virginia as early as 1619. But black slaves were more expensive, at least in the short run, than white indentured servants. The absolute foreignness of the blacks—their appearance, behavior, language, and skills—offended the English, who were suspicious of all foreigners. A black labor force came into being only gradually. In 1640 a mere 150 blacks were reported in Virginia, and not all of them were slaves. In 1650 there were 300; in 1680, 3,000; in 1704, when the white population may have reached 75,600, there were roughly 10,000 blacks. As the number of black laborers rose and as their importance to the developing economy became clear, a new status of bondage took shape—that of "chattel slavery." This kind of slavery was previously unknown under English law. As servitude for whites became progressively more limited in duration and less rigorous in demands, the laws began to specify that blacks would serve for life. Moreover, their offspring would automatically become the property of their masters. Conversion to Christianity would not lead to slaves' freedom; nothing but their masters' discretion could limit the severity of punishment that could be inflicted on them; and racially mixed marriages were forbidden. Finally, the laws specified that a "slave" was no longer simply the lowest-ranking kind of servant, but rather something absolutely different in the eyes of the law. He or she was a form of property to be bought and sold. This was "chattel slavery," a status applicable only—and necessarily—to blacks and to all their descendants.

These were the main provisions of the "slave codes," so devastating in their consequences for the whole of American history. The codes originated in the latter half of the seventeenth century in response to an acute need for labor, an elemental fear of foreignness, and an insensitivity to cruelty remarkable even for that callous age. But however unique the conditions that gave rise to these codes, once devised they became a fundamental part of the legal fabric of community life, and they intensified and perpetuated the racial fears and hostilities that had helped shape them. By 1700 it was becoming clear, to some at least, that chattel slavery, rising like some terrible germ-laden cloud, was poisoning the very soil and roots of human relations.

The Pilgrims' "Sweet Communion"

It is difficult for twentieth-century Americans to recapture fully the state of mind of those who led the settlement of New England. The Puritans and the Pilgrims are easily caricatured: the Puritans as God-intoxicated demons of self-righteousness, endlessly contemplating the fine points of their theology, and the

Pilgrims as simple, innocent Christians, spotless in their devotion to the Bible. Both groups were products of the attempted reformation of the church in England that had followed Martin Luther's break with the Catholic church in 1517. In the 1530s England's Henry VIII had severed all ties with the Roman Catholic church and had established the Church of England, making himself its supreme head. Although under Henry and his daughter, Elizabeth I, the church had undergone considerable change in both theology and organization, the Puritans and the Pilgrims were among those who felt that the church was still too "Catholic," too ceremonial and formal in its practice, too ecclesiastical, and too closely involved in politics. They sought a more direct experience of God than the existing church provided.

Although the Puritans and the Pilgrims shared this common disillusionment with the state church, otherwise they were different. Their aims, their styles, and their accomplishments were different, and their ultimate contributions to American life lay in different spheres. The Pilgrims were one of many radical "separatist" groups that first appeared in England in the 1570s. While remaining loyal to the English state, they set up their own "purified" churches—often primitive cells where their conventicles (secret religious assemblies) could conduct services that were stripped bare of all ritual. Unaffiliated with each other except for the members' shared aspirations, the conventicles attracted only true believers, who gathered together voluntarily in covenanted brotherhoods. Defiant of the persecution they were suffering at the hands of the government and the state church, and without hope of forcing their views on the world at large, these religious radicals were naturally drawn to America, where in isolation on the far margins of the English world they hoped to find freedom of worship while retaining the protection of the English state.

The Separatists   One such band of pious, humble, and stubborn believers had gathered in the village of Scrooby in east central England. This group, whose members eventually came to be known as the Pilgrims, at first had no desire to settle in America. To escape the corrupting English way of life, they fled, in 1609, to the Netherlands—first to Amsterdam and then to the nearby city of Leyden. Although the Separatists were free to practice their religious beliefs openly among the tolerant Dutch, they became increasingly concerned that their children were being attracted to the evils and "dangerous courses" that the liberal Dutch environment seemed to foster. Fearful that their children would lose their faith, the Separatists decided to move again, hoping to find a place better suited to the establishment of a pure church of Christ. After considering sites elsewhere in the Netherlands, on the northern coast of South America, and on islands at the mouth of the St. Lawrence River in present-day Canada, they decided on Virginia. They had several contacts with the leaders of the Virginia Company, which at the time was offering partially self-governing plantations to groups such as theirs.

By 1619 the Virginia Company had granted the Separatists the right to settle within its jurisdiction, and the English government promised not to molest them there. Financial help came from an investment group headed by an English merchant, Thomas Weston. After many hesitations those Separatists willing to go to America sold their property to purchase shares in the joint undertaking with Weston, with each settler's labor being counted as a single share of stock. In July 1620, 35 of the 238 members of the Leyden congregation took leave of their brethren in a scene so poignant, so prayerful and tearful, that even casual Dutch onlookers wept. They sailed to Southampton, England, on their own small vessel, the *Speedwell,* to join an English contingent of Separatists and the 180-ton *Mayflower,* which the merchant-investors had rented for them. After two false starts and the ultimate abandonment of the unseaworthy *Speedwell,* many were discouraged from going on with the voyage. But the remaining Pilgrims, along with laborers who had been hired by the merchants, crowded into the *Mayflower,* which had been packed high with furniture, equipment, food, and animals. On September 16, 1620, they set sail for Virginia.

Of the 101 passengers on board the crowded vessel, perhaps 87 were Separatists or members of Separatist families. During more than nine weeks at sea, two children were born; remarkably, only one person died. But by the time the voyagers sighted Cape Cod, on November 9, and two days later disembarked at what is now Provincetown on the tip of the cape, they were ridden with disease, primarily scurvy,* and weakened by malnutrition. They had lost the strength and the will to continue on to the land in Virginia to which they had title. At Provincetown they "fell upon their knees and blessed the God of Heaven who had brought them over the vast and furious ocean and delivered them from all the perils and miseries thereof."

An exploring party found Plymouth Harbor on December 11. There, on a slope rising westward from the shore, probably the site of an abandoned Indian cornfield, the Pilgrims built the simple village of their desires. Although the weather during this first winter, 1620–21, was quite mild for New England, the early months of the settlement proved to be one of the worst "starving times" recorded anywhere in British America. When spring arrived, half of those who had crossed on the *Mayflower* were dead.

Plymouth Plantation   Plymouth's history up to 1691, when it was absorbed into the Puritans' more powerful Massachusetts Bay Colony, is a tale of both modest triumphs and shattered dreams. The trials, the victories, and the defeats are all recorded in Governor William Bradford's magnificent history, *Of Plymouth Plantation,* which he began writing in 1630. Bradford's work opens with a review of the settlement's early years and continues as a documentary journal and commentary covering the next sixteen years. It is one of the most moving and eloquent documents in the entire literature of American history. Its vivid imagery and biblical rhythms blend perfectly to

---

*Scurvy is a disease caused by vitamin C deficiency. Its symptoms include weakness, anemia, and bleeding gums.

express Bradford's hopes and struggles, and finally his sense of tragedy and failure.

The Pilgrims' foremost blessing, wrote Bradford, was "to see, and with much comfort to enjoy, the blessed fruits of their sweet communion." Their triumph was that they had finally succeeded in establishing the purified church they had so long sought. But there were troubles from the start, and the first and most pressing problem was financial. For several years the colonists failed in business ventures. The merchants back in England, bickering among themselves and fearful of mounting costs if they continued to resupply the settlers, sold out their shares or simply abandoned their investments. By 1626 the company was bankrupt, but the Pilgrims, more honest than shrewd, continued to honor their original obligations. For years they struggled to squeeze enough profit from fur trading, fishing, and the sale of lumber, Indian corn, and wampum to pay off their debts. But progress came slowly. By the time the colony settled its debts, in 1648, many of Plymouth's founders were dead.

More threatening than debt were the spreading-out of the settlement and the weakening of purpose that grew with the passage of years. After the *Mayflower* a series of vessels had made the long journey to Plymouth, and the population had risen steadily. By 1657, the year of Bradford's death, there were more than 1,360 inhabitants, and Plymouth had changed from a single covenanted community* into a colony of eleven towns. As a result of the growth and scattering of the population, the feeling of singleness of purpose had faded. Even if the gentle Pilgrim leaders had sought to impose discipline and control, they would have lacked the legal means to do so. Their original settlement contract with the Virginia Company was worthless in New England, and a document they had received in 1621 from the Council for New England (the English body that had taken over the legal rights of the defunct Virginia Company of Plymouth) was only a vague land grant and an equally vague license to establish a local government. The colony's government developed slowly and uncertainly, authorized neither by charter nor by the English crown.

The starting point was the Mayflower Compact, a document devised to control the restless non-Pilgrims while the *Mayflower* was still at sea. It was simply an agreement—signed on November 21, 1620, by forty-one Pilgrims, hired laborers, and sailors—to obey whatever laws and officers the community would create. The signing of the Mayflower Compact in the cabin of the Pilgrims' rocking vessel was a dramatic event. But the document was not a constitution. The unauthorized government that in fact developed in Plymouth was primitive in organization. The freemen simply came together annually to choose a governor (Bradford was elected thirty times) and a few assistants to support him. Otherwise the electors convened only on extraordinary occasions, as directed by the governor. The feeble political structure, combined with the second- and third-

---

*A covenanted community is one that has been established by a covenant, or formal binding agreement, especially one with strong religious overtones.

generation colonists' weakened loyalty to the settlement, spelled disaster for Plymouth's continued independence. When in 1691 the more powerful colony to the north, the Puritans' Massachusetts Bay, received its second charter, Plymouth was included within its boundaries. The Pilgrims' colony slipped without a ripple into the larger jurisdiction. By then the erosion in original purposes and in piety was so advanced that Governor Bradford's successors were at least relieved that the government would remain in the hands of religious men—even if they were not of the Separatists' own persuasion.

William Bradford's "sweet communion" in its fullest form had depended for its success on deeply shared aspirations and on isolation from the corrupting influence of the changing outside world. But as towns and churches multiplied to accommodate the waves of new settlers, life in Plymouth eventually came to be shaped by new generations who did not share their predecessors' unshakable faith. Lacking all instinct for power, and tolerant of the errors of others in their humble pursuit of personal piety, the Pilgrims responded to the changes as they always had—by retreating from the world rather than by trying to reform it. They were incapable of perpetuating the community they had built, and their ultimate impact on American life was confined to the realm of ideas. Their unselfish pursuit of an unattainable ideal, and their rejection of wealth, power, comfort, and self-glory in favor of deeper, spiritual rewards, are part of America's collective memory and essential culture. But although the Pilgrims' model of life has been emulated in various ways throughout American history, it has never been dominant. Far more vital in American culture has been the very different legacy of the Puritans.

The Puritans: Power in the Service of God

The Puritans shared with the Pilgrims a desire for a direct religious experience free from an elaborate church organization. The two groups also shared certain theological views and a stubborn moral dignity.* But the Puritans, in America as in England, were proud and driving, and as demanding of themselves as they were of the world about them. They sought power—not for its own sake, to be sure, but for Christian purposes—and they sought it untiringly, intolerantly, and successfully.

The decisions that brought the Puritans to America were made in stages during a hectic three-year period in the late 1620s. In 1628 a group of about ninety active nonconformists, deeply troubled by the repressive steps of the English government and church against dissidents, and well aware of the value of overseas settlements as refuges for people of their persuasion, formed the New England Company. They obtained a land patent covering most of present-day Massachusetts and New Hampshire, and sent out an advance party to rebuild a small

---

*For Puritanism as a religious movement, see chapter 3, pp. 105–109.

settlement on Cape Ann, north of Boston, that had recently been abandoned by a Puritan fishing company. In 1629, increasingly concerned about the future of nonconformity, they sought and obtained a crown charter that created the Massachusetts Bay Company. This elaborate document empowered the company not only to trade and settle within the lands already given to the New England Company, but also "to govern and rule all of His Majesty's subjects that reside within the limits of our plantation." The charter proved to be a legal bulwark behind which a powerful social movement could organize and develop.

The new corporation quickly demonstrated its efficiency. Within weeks of its creation it sent off five vessels bearing more than two hundred settlers to join the advance party that was by then living in thatched cottages on the shores of Cape Ann. But far greater enterprises were stirring. In the spring and summer of 1629, conditions in England continued to worsen for critics of the Church of England. The Puritans also learned of the defeat of Protestant forces in the international war then raging in Europe. Moreover, the English king, Charles I, dissolved Parliament, and with this action all hope of political remedies seemed lost. On top of all this, an economic depression was creating great distress in the very districts of England that were most prone to religious dissent.

The Great Migration In this atmosphere of social, political, and economic panic in the spring and summer of 1629, Puritans of experience, ability, and established position turned their thoughts not merely to creating a religious refuge for their fellow Puritans, but to their own personal escape from England to a world apart, a safe, fresh, and uncorrupted world. Within six months of the creation of the Massachusetts Bay Company, a coalition of merchants, landed gentlemen, lawyers, and minor officials, alienated from their own society, turned to the company. They found in it a means of escaping from England and of serving their own—and Puritanism's—higher purpose.

Only some of the gathering group of substantial Englishmen who were thus attracted to Massachusetts Bay had been directly involved in the company before. Chief among the newcomers was John Winthrop, an intensely pious, well-connected forty-one-year-old Puritan landowner and lawyer who had recently been dismissed from his government position. Faced suddenly with unemployment and with the prospect of continuing harassment, and convinced that England was being overwhelmed by corruption, he came to see the hand of God in the work of the Massachusetts Bay Company. Winthrop and the other leaders of the Massachusetts Bay Colony were no mild and reclusive Pilgrims. They were men of affairs, self-confident, determined, and used to exercising authority. But their love of action in the ordinary world was disciplined by a strong religious commitment. Unlike the Pilgrims, they did not want to separate from the Church of England: they wanted to seize control of it, cleanse it of its corruption, and reconstruct it, at home or abroad, in a pure and unadorned form. And far from withdrawing from society, they sought to seize and transform that, too. By persuasion if possible, but by force if necessary, they hoped to create a society

Governor John Winthrop
The leader of Puritan New England in its heroic age, a devout, able, and strong-willed leader, Winthrop directed his energies and talents to creating a pure version of the Church of England and a society directed to God's will. The set jaw, full but tightly drawn lips, and raised brows suggest intense self-discipline and resolution.

likely to gain God's approval. They were separatists only with respect to the English state, not with respect to the Church of England. Their goals became clear in the conclusion they reached at a momentous secret meeting in Cambridge, England, late in August 1629.

The twelve leaders who assembled at Cambridge pledged themselves "ready in our persons" to join the migration to New England, taking with them their families and whatever supplies they could gather, and "to inhabit and continue in New England." But they agreed to this plan only on condition that the company officially transfer itself—its charter, and the government—to the colony. Three days later the company agreed—in effect voting itself out of existence as a commercial organization and transforming itself into the basis of a simple civil government. In October 1629 Winthrop was elected governor, and five months later, in March 1630, the great Puritan migration began. Before the year was over, a fleet of seventeen ships had carried well over 1,000 settlers to Massachusetts. In all during the years of the Puritan exodus (1630–43), some two hundred vessels transported more than 20,000 Englishmen to the Bay Colony.

No one community could contain all these settlers. The original settlement, Salem on Cape Ann, became a staging area for groups moving south along the coast. First Charlestown and then Boston became the central settlement. From Boston, groups moved on quickly to settle a ring of satellite towns immediately around the bay. Subsequently other parties founded a secondary ring of towns some twenty or thirty miles inland—among them, Haverhill, Concord, and Sudbury. Finally, beginning in 1636, small migrating groups of Puritans broke contact altogether with the central settlement around Boston and established an independent cluster of towns on the Connecticut River, more than one hundred miles from Boston. These towns, to which immigrants soon came directly from England, included Hartford, Wethersfield, and Windsor. By banding together politically, they became the colony of Connecticut, which formed its own government in 1639 and was chartered by the crown in 1662.

Church and Community　　The Puritans, fanning out into towns all over New England with remarkable speed, carried forward their original purpose. They did not scatter randomly. Groups that wished to establish towns sought the approval of the colony's legislature, the General Court. Once granted, this approval carried with it the legal right to create a limited governmental jurisdiction and to send representatives to the General Court. It also embraced control over a large parcel of land—a township—that was to be divided up among the original heads of households in proportion to their wealth or status. Consequently town founders not only owned their individual shares of land, but also collectively controlled the undistributed land. As the founding members of their local church, the same men dominated the vital area of religion. They also constituted the initial voting membership of the town's political assembly (the "meeting"), which regulated the everyday affairs of the community.

The founders' rights were not automatically granted to others who later joined the town. Therefore it was the town founders and their direct heirs who controlled all the main spheres of life. Their power was not resented, at least in the early years. Later there would be opposition and factionalism as newcomers found their way into these small farming villages and as the Puritans' fierce passion to reform the world faded into austerity. But while the fires of the original faith burned brightly, and while the Puritans still thought in terms of reforming the world, these villages—oligarchic in form, but democratic for those who enjoyed full rights of participation—remained cohesive bodies closely bound into the overall colony.

The unity of the Massachusetts colony—the "Bible Commonwealth"—as a whole is remarkable when one considers the rapid and wide dispersal of the settlers. This unity reflected not only a deep general commitment to a particular way of life and to certain beliefs, but also the founders' skill in self-government and their refusal to tolerate dissent.

The Massachusetts charter had simply created a commercial organization: it contained no provision for an independent civil government. However, the structure of the Massachusetts Bay Company was in fact similar to that of a self-governing English town, and the government that developed in Massachusetts emerged along the lines of that model. John Winthrop, the Massachusetts Bay Company's chosen leader, became the colony's governor. The seven or eight members of the company's board of directors who had come to Massachusetts formed the council of magistrates (the governor's assistants and advisers). The adult male heads of household were the "freemen," or voters, necessary to complete the membership of the transformed General Court. Soon a permanent government along these lines was established and the basic rules for its procedures were set down in writing. In 1632 the freemen were given the power to choose not only the governor's assistants, but also the governor himself and the deputy governor. In 1634 it was agreed that taxes could be levied on the towns only by vote of the entire General Court and that in the future the entire body of freemen need not assemble in person for General Court meetings; instead the freemen could select representatives. These representatives—two or three from each town—had the authority to make laws, grant land, levy taxes, and transact whatever other business might come before the General Court.

Thus a civil government evolved from the organization of a commercial corporation. It was quickly completed. Because the representatives to the General Court (called deputies) met together with the council of magistrates, they could conclude no business without the magistrates' approval. Hence the representatives had no distinct voice of their own and no incentive to develop their own rules and procedures. This problem was overcome by 1644. In a sensational case in law that pitted popular emotions against strict legality, the magistrates vetoed the proposals of the more numerous representatives. A great uproar resulted, and the two groups drew apart to form two separate houses. This division proved to be permanent. Each house now could express itself independently, although the agreement of both was needed to enact laws. The lower house thereupon organized itself separately, electing a Speaker and working out parliamentary rules, a committee system, and other procedures modeled on those of the English House of Commons.

During these same years the colony set up a court system, which it largely copied from the local court system of England, and established a code of laws. This code, *The Lawes and Libertyes* of 1647, expressed not only the English common law in terms appropriate for life in the wilderness, but also the Puritans' devotion to the precepts of the Bible.

Puritan Control and Dissent

Massachusetts remained a Bible commonwealth despite all the secular pursuits that were undertaken: clearing the wilderness; organizing towns, courts, and a general government; and expanding coastal and transatlantic commerce. Puritan domination was legally secured not by the clergy's control of the government—in fact, the clergy did not hold public office—but by the fact that only church members could vote. This rule was introduced in 1631. As a result of this measure, the colony's central government would continue to represent primarily those loyal to the original Puritan purposes, no matter how the town populations might change, how the sources of immigration might shift, or how the people themselves might drift away from the church.

This arrangement did not go unchallenged. But the opposition to the Puritan leadership that did arise in these early years challenged not the basic religious character of the Puritan colony, but specific points of doctrine. It resulted not

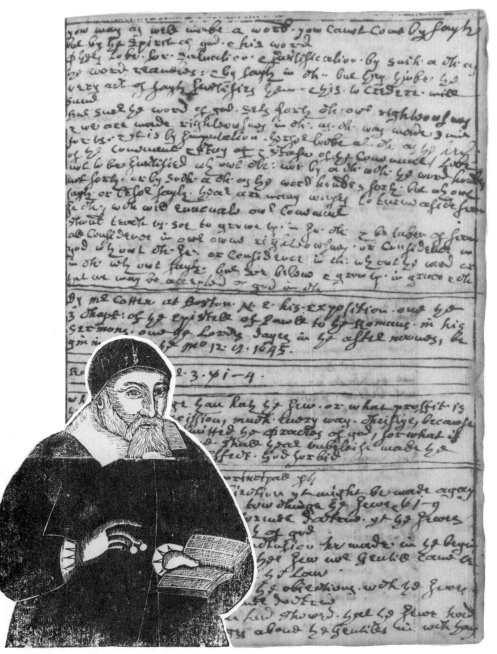

Richard Mather

Founder of a virtual dynasty of New England preachers and intellectuals, Mather is shown here in a woodcut by John Foster (c 1670), which is probably the first print made in British America. Mather preached an austere Calvinism in Massachusetts for thirty-four years. In the background, notes taken on sermons heard in Boston by a spiritually tormented merchant, Robert Keayne. Convicted of overcharging and hence of greed and unchristian behavior, Keayne fell into an agony of protest and recrimination, which he expressed in an extraordinary 50,000-word will.

from a lack of religious commitment, but from radical passions in religion that threatened to reduce the essentially moderate Puritan world to anarchy. For among the religious leaders in the migration were radical sectarians of all kinds: antinomians, separate Baptists, spiritists, familists, and extreme millenarians. These opponents of the Puritan regime were even more fanatical in their pursuit of religious truth, more relentless in their theology, and more single-minded in their beliefs than were the Puritan leaders themselves. In one way or another they went to extremes on religious issues that the colony's leaders felt obliged to keep in balance.

Anne Hutchinson, for example, challenged the Puritan leaders within a few years of the founding of the Bay Colony. She was passionate and rigid in her convictions and brilliant in her arguments. "Justification"—the mysterious gift of divine grace, by which a sinful person becomes one of God's elect—was for her all that essentially mattered in religion. "Sanctification"—that is, moral conduct, Christian behavior, piety, even prayer—was to her only the dry outer shell of religion. Rejecting "works" and in the end all worldly discipline and responsibility, she stood only for the "ravishment" of the soul by God. The band of followers she gathered constituted a church within a church; the Puritan leaders felt that unless they defeated her, they would destroy themselves by tolerating her. But she was not disposed of easily. In the dramatic heresy trial held by the Boston church in 1637, she held off the assembled preachers and elders with astonishing skill, and defended herself learnedly and wittily. But at last, in exhaustion and perhaps also in exaltation, she blurted out that her knowledge of God was "an immediate revelation"—that is, free of all institutions, independent of all earthly authority. This was the worst heresy, condemned as "antinomianism," an arrogance of such dimensions that she was excommunicated by the church and banished from the colony by the General Court.

Roger Williams, a minister at Salem, Massachusetts, was more learned and more respectable than Anne Hutchinson, but he was at least as "divinely mad" as she, and as passionate in his beliefs. He could never accommodate himself to what he regarded as the halfway reforms of the nonseparatist Puritans who had established Massachusetts Bay Colony, nor could he accept the colony's unique constitutional foundation. Not only did he attack the validity of the colony's charter, but he challenged the mingling of church and state that was the essence of the "Bible Commonwealth." Civil officials, he insisted, should have power only over individuals' civil affairs and outward behavior, not over matters of conscience and religion. Only in later years in England and in banishment in Rhode Island did Williams develop the doctrine of religious toleration for which he would become famous. But in Massachusetts he was already heading in the direction of toleration, and the mere approach to this position was intolerable to the rulers of the colony. Moreover, Williams condemned the colony's churches for their refusal to break completely with the polluted Church of England. Church reform, he insisted, was not enough; purification was not enough. Perfection was the goal—a church of absolute purity, even more pure than the church of the Separatists in Plymouth Colony. This kind of church was not to be had in Massachusetts. The Bay Colony's leaders realized that Williams was a fine intellect and a true Christian in his way. They tried to correct him, but when they failed they reluctantly banished him too from the colony.

And there were other deviants from the Puritan way, other challengers, who were either silenced or ejected from the colony. Some of these religious dissidents moved south to Narragansett Bay in what is today Rhode Island. Here Roger Williams, certain followers of Anne Hutchinson, a few Quakers, and other religious outcasts from Massachusetts attempted to form communities in which they would be completely free to pursue their own special version of truth. But the scattered Narragansett villages were torn by discord. They splintered and regrouped repeatedly. Only in the late 1640s did four or five stable communities emerge. Although the prosperous merchants who founded and dominated Newport were the most worldly of the Rhode Islanders, it was Roger Williams, the founder of Providence, who recognized that only a confederation of the towns and legal authorization from England would preserve the freedom of these tiny refugee settlements. And it was he who secured the refugee towns' independence by extracting from the English government in 1644 a patent creating "The Incorporation of Providence Plantations." Finally, in 1663, Williams obtained a crown charter that legalized the permanent existence of the colony of Rhode Island.

Connecticut and Rhode Island were both products of the Massachusetts Bay Colony. Connecticut was a reproduction of the Puritans' culture; Rhode Island was a rejection of it. But throughout New England lay the determination, expressed in these various ways, to wipe out the corruptions of an oppressive world and to create a new Jerusalem, in which power would not be rejected or despised, but mobilized and devoted to the service of the Lord.

A Catholic Refuge on the Chesapeake

Religion was a pervasive force in the establishment of English overseas settlements, and America profited greatly by England's willingness to allow its colonies to become refuges for religious minorities. These points can be seen with special clarity in the founding of Maryland.

In this case the refugees were not radical Protestants but Roman Catholics, a group that the Church of England regarded as even more obnoxious than reforming Protestants. The dynamic force in launching the Maryland colony was a single family, the Calverts, who were ennobled in 1625 as the Lords Baltimore. The Calverts, well connected with the rulers of England, were recent converts to Catholicism. They had long been involved in overseas enterprises. In 1628–29 the first Lord Baltimore had traveled to the Chesapeake to investigate a possible place of refuge for English Catholics, and upon his return he began the elaborate process of obtaining the necessary royal charter. He died just as the charter was being approved, and his twenty-six-year-old son, Cecilius Calvert, the second Lord Baltimore, carried out his father's project.

Cecilius Calvert, Second Lord Baltimore (1605–75)
Baltimore, who devoted his life to developing the colony that his father had planned, was never able to visit Maryland himself, governing instead through deputies. He is pictured here with his grandson, who had been born in Maryland and died at the age of fourteen, holding a "new map of Maryland" ("Nova Terrae-Mariae Tabula") dated 1635 and attended by a handsomely dressed black servant. The boy's father, Charles, governor since 1661, succeeded as proprietor and third Lord Baltimore upon Cecilius' death in 1675.

The key to much of what subsequently happened lies in the terms of the remarkable charter that was issued to the young Lord Baltimore in 1632 and in the use that the Calvert family made of the powers it bestowed. The charter granted Lord Baltimore the entire territory from the Potomac River north to the latitude of present-day Philadelphia and west hundreds of miles to the Appalachian sources of the Potomac. The charter also gave him extensive governmental powers: the colony's government was his to shape as he chose. In this case too, as in so many others, the barrenness and openness of America challenged people's imaginations and inspired them to project their desires and fantasies in elaborate but unrealistic plans for new communities.

Toleration and Proprietary Plans

Success came quickly at first. The young Lord Baltimore, who was the proprietor (overlord) of Maryland until his death in 1675, sent his brother Leonard to the colony as governor. Leonard Calvert took with him detailed instructions on the management of the colony. Lord Baltimore had made it clear that Maryland was to be a Catholic refuge. But he knew that Catholics could survive in the English world only as a tolerated minority; they were in no position to impose their will on others. Further, he knew that the success of the colony would depend on the flow of immigrants into it, and most of these prospective settlers would be Protestants. At the very start, therefore, Lord Baltimore prohibited discrimination of any sort against Protestants. He also forbade Catholics from engaging in public controversies over religion. They were ordered to make every effort to live at peace not only with the Virginians to the south, but also with the Puritans and Dutch to the north.*

These conditions were all necessary and realistic. Fantasy entered Lord Baltimore's thinking only as he contemplated his personal proprietorship of the land and his extensive powers of government. How was he to use his vast domain and these extensive powers? Feudalism, and its economic foundations in manorialism, provided a model of sorts for the Calverts to follow. Thus proprietary manors (landed domains) of 6,000 acres, complete with private law courts, were created and reserved for the blood relatives of the Lord Proprietor. Ordinary manors were limited to 3,000 acres. It was expected that tenants would settle on these manors and that their labor would produce the rents and other dues necessary to support the lords. The rest of the population would be landowning farmers and their dependents, all appropriately submissive to the domination of the provincial nobles. It was a rational but hopelessly outdated and unrealistic design, yet it nevertheless helped shape the community that developed in Maryland.

In 1632 the Calverts set up on the outskirts of London a recruiting office for settlers, advertised their colony (but not their religion) widely, and convinced more than two hundred settlers to join the first expedition. The prospective colonists arrived in the Chesapeake in March 1634, in good time for the year's planting and well equipped to survive the inevitable rigors of the first winter in a new colony. The Calverts located their main settlement, St. Mary's, on a creek just north of the Potomac River. There they constructed a palisaded fort similar to that of early Jamestown. After the first winter in the fort it became clear that the colony would have supplies sufficient for its survival and that the neighboring Indians were friendly. The distribution of land and the spreading-out of the population then began.

Distribution of Land   As planned, the proprietor's relatives were given title to 6,000-acre tracts, and lesser manors were distributed to other persons. The recipients of manors also received rights to private law courts and other privileges. In turn the manorial lords and the proprietor himself began selling pieces of land to those who could afford to pay for them. Other property was rented out. Manorial lords reserved farms on their tracts for their own use ("demesne" farms) and retained all the undivided property. But none of the manorial arrangements survived. The settlement of the countryside was in fact shaped by virtually the same forces already at work in Virginia.

As in Virginia, the primary cash crop in Maryland was tobacco, and the central difficulty in expanding production was similarly the shortage of labor. Every effort was made to stimulate the importation of laborers for the farms that spread out from several centers on the mainland and on the eastern shore of

---

*For religious toleration in Maryland, see chapter 3, pp. 103–104.

Chesapeake Bay. A series of laws required prospective manorial lords to import at first five workers, then ten, then twenty. Virginia's headright system was introduced in Maryland in 1640, and independent householders who settled in the colony received special land grants for themselves and the members of their families. The population rose rapidly, partly because transatlantic migration continued and partly because the availability of fresh tidewater land attracted farmers from Virginia and other neighboring areas. By 1660 the population had probably reached 8,000 and was beginning to grow by natural increase.* The colony had more than 13,000 inhabitants in 1670, and by then—forty years after the initial settlement—it was clear that Maryland had become something different from the feudal-manorial regime that Lord Baltimore had envisioned. Maryland was indeed dominated by a landholding oligarchy, largely Catholic, with an almost monopolistic control of public offices.

But their large estates meant little because the labor shortage allowed the cultivation of only small segments of their properties. As a result indentured servants were brought in on generous terms, and freed servants easily acquired land and established themselves as independent farmers. Property values rose as the more fertile and accessible land came under cultivation and as a growing population competed more intensely for the best of the undistributed land. Freed servants found it increasingly difficult to establish independent property-owning households. More and more they tended to serve, for a time at least, as tenants; and their labor further raised the value of the land they worked. Landlords, of course, benefited greatly. In this situation the original "manorial" grants became valuable simply as land, quite apart from the legal privileges that were supposed to accompany them. The original grantees and their heirs—especially those closely related to the Calverts—found themselves not manorial lords, with ancient, largely archaic, powers, but well-to-do landowners in a world of tobacco farms.

The same men controlled the central offices in Maryland's government, which remained in Lord Baltimore's power except during the years 1655–58. Baltimore filled these offices with members of his own family and their close associates. As in Virginia, the governor's council quickly became the central governing body. But in Maryland membership on the council was less the result of having achieved local prominence than of being a personal ally or a relative of the proprietor. Therefore the earliest political struggles in Maryland were not between the governor and the council (as they were in Virginia), but rather between the governor and council on the one hand and the local representatives on the other. Fiercely competitive politics was part of Maryland life almost from the first years of settlement.

Governor Leonard Calvert had instructions to convene an assembly of freemen and to submit all laws to it for approval. But he retained the right to

---

*Natural increase means the predominance of births over deaths in accounting for a rising population—as opposed to population increase caused by immigration.

summon, adjourn, and dismiss the assembly, and he alone could initiate legislation. The proprietor in England, Baltimore, reserved the power to veto any action taken by the assembly. The first full meeting of the assembly in 1638 was, like the first assembly meetings of Massachusetts and Virginia, a confused affair. Any freemen who chose to appear were seated. From the outset the representatives sought to free themselves from control by the proprietor's friends on the council. Thus they insisted that the assembly model itself on the House of Commons, adopt parliamentary rules, and take over the power of convening and adjourning. Gradually the representatives won these demands, although the proprietor never gave up the theoretical rights granted in the charter. While civil war between the king and the supporters of Parliament raged in England in 1640–49, the Maryland assembly took advantage of the confusion to seize the power of initiating legislation. The representatives also forced the proprietor to allow them to meet independently of the council. Thereafter the representatives formed a separate lower house of the assembly.

By 1650 the political structure of seventeenth-century Maryland was fully evolved. The colony was ultimately governed by an absentee proprietor and by his resident governor and appointed council. Almost all of these leaders were Catholics. Together they monopolized the important public offices and the profits of officeholding, and they were also the major landlords. But the majority of the population, largely Protestant, had a legitimate voice in government through the lower house. In the assembly and outside it, the people fought continuously to force the proprietor and his followers to give up their special privileges. By the middle of the seventeenth century, in no other colony was politics so sophisticated and so bitter as it was in the colony that at first had been planned as an oasis of manorial harmony.

The Failure of the Dutch

The founding of the colony that was later known as New York differed radically from the pattern of the other British colonies. The Dutch, not the English, established this colony, and originally it was not conceived of as a fully developed community at all. From the start its population was culturally diverse. No legal system was effectively established, and no government evolved that was comparable to the assemblies of Virginia and Maryland and to the General Court of Massachusetts Bay.

New Netherland, as the colony was called until the English conquered it in 1664, was an almost accidental creation of the Dutch West India Company. This complex commercial organization, which had been founded in 1621, was originally conceived of as an instrument in the endless war against Spain, from which the Dutch had only recently won a precarious independence after decades of conflict.

The company, organized as a highly decentralized five-chamber structure modeled on the successful Dutch East India Company, devoted its resources to piracy and other high-risk enterprises in Brazil, West Africa, and the Caribbean, and left its monopoly of the commercial and territorial rights in New Netherland almost entirely to the erratic control of the Amsterdam chamber. These Amsterdam merchants, ignoring the welfare of the company as a whole, plunged into a series of experimental efforts to profit from the company's monopoly. First they took control of the rich fur trade of the colony, then opened it, for a fee, to the profiteering of the settlers; at the start they restricted settlement, but then, conceding that an agricultural base had to be created, threw it open to a motley population of colonists they actively recruited. In all these twists and turns, they gradually found ways to profit, until in the end, while the company, buffeted by defeats elsewhere in the Western Hemisphere, was going bankrupt, the Amsterdam merchants were prospering in their private exploitation of the colony.

New Amsterdam Under these conditions the central settlement grew very slowly. In 1624 the company sent thirty Dutch and Walloon (French-speaking Belgian) families to begin settlements at Fort Orange and Esopus on the upper Hudson River and at several points on the Delaware River. Supplies, equipment, and a total of perhaps two hundred people followed in 1625. In that year too a fort was built at the tip of Manhattan Island, which lies at the mouth of the Hudson River, to protect Dutch shipping and to serve as a convenient transfer point for shipments to and from the Hudson and Delaware river posts. The next year, 1626, colonists set about building a village around the fort on Manhattan Island—windmills to power the sawing of wood and grinding of corn, and about thirty log houses spread along the west side of the island. At the same time, an ambitious company official, Peter Minuit, purchased the whole island from the native Manhates Indians. He began to consolidate the main force of the scattered Dutch settlers in this central village, called Fort Amsterdam or New Amsterdam. Minuit withdrew some of the settlers from the distant and exposed posts on the upper Hudson and the Delaware rivers and left only skeleton forces there to channel furs to New Amsterdam and to defend the Dutch claims. The population of New Amsterdam grew slowly, at first, then rose rapidly toward the end of the Dutch period, to a total of perhaps 9,000 by 1664.

By midcentury the village of New Amsterdam consisted of the original blockhouse and windmills and a number of houses, all enclosed within a palisade, or wall, along what is now known as Wall Street. Through Broad Street, the central avenue of the enclosed village, ran a canal—"a befouled and stinking sewer in the warm months," one historian has written, "and a treacherous ice floe in the winter." Scattered in the open area beyond the wall were about fifty small farms, called *bouweries*. The whole settlement formed a tumultuous frontier community in which people of all sorts mingled, traded, and brawled. Men and women of many nationalities—Dutch, Walloons, French, Germans, English, Portuguese, Swedes, Finns, and Brazilian blacks—flocked to the settlement, looking for a chance to profit from trading in furs, manufactured goods, produce, and land. There were reports that eighteen different languages were in use, and

New Amsterdam, c. 1650
This view appeared as a miniature inset in a large map of New Netherlands issued by Nicholas Visscher in 1655. Legend: A: *Fort;* B: *Church of St. Nicholas;* C: *Jail;* D: *Governor's House;* E: *Gallows;* G: *West India Company's Stores.*

that virtually every religious persuasion from Catholicism to Anabaptism was represented. It was as quarrelsome and disorderly a village as could be found in North America.

Contention and Indian Wars

At least one of the company's directors in the Netherlands, however, had a broad and constructive vision of the colony's future, and his strenuous efforts made a difference. Kiliaen Van Rensselaer, a wealthy Amsterdam jeweler, argued for the creation of large-scale private agricultural estates like the proprietary manors in Maryland. These farming establishments, he claimed, would not only help stabilize the colony, but also provide food, cattle, and necessary supplies for the Dutch ships heading for the West Indies and elsewhere in the Western Hemisphere. His efforts resulted in the Charter of Freedoms and Exemptions, issued by the company and confirmed by the Dutch government in 1629. This charter authorized the creation of "patroonships," large estates that would be financed by groups of investors. The investors would share in the profits but not in the management of these plantations, which would be controlled solely by the "patroons," the estate proprietors.

Ten of these investment groups were created. However, only the patroonship of Rensselaerswyck, which was situated on both sides of the Hudson surrounding Fort Orange (present-day Albany), developed in the form that had been provided for in the charter and survived to the end of the seventeenth century. Van Rensselaer, the patroon, sent to this huge estate a flow of goods, cattle, and equipment. At his own expense he also dispatched farmers and other workers to populate the land. By 1655 he had leased sixteen farms on the estate and had developed his personal manor efficiently despite all the confusions and difficulties of managing the property through deputies. And although it is doubtful that in the end Van Rensselaer recovered his heavy investment in the estate, he did establish a prosperous agricultural community on the upper Hudson.

On the whole, however, the province of New Netherland remained (as a contemporary wrote) "a wild country." It was ill organized, ill managed, and contentious. The continuing disorder was partly the result of the uncontrolled multiplication of thinly populated villages that were poorly organized and incapable of defending themselves. They appeared on all sides: on upper Manhattan Island (New Haarlem); across the Harlem River in present-day Westchester County, New York, and across the Hudson in present-day Bergen County, New Jersey; on Staten Island; and especially on Long Island, where five Dutch towns had appeared by the 1640s. The confusion in these border towns was worsened by trouble with the neighboring English who had moved into New Netherland from the surrounding colonies. These newcomers had been attracted by the company's offer of freedom of worship, local self-government, and free land that would remain tax-exempt for ten years. Although the English settlers helped populate the company's lands, they created difficult administrative problems for the Dutch officials. In addition, these alien and discontented groups began to agitate against the Dutch rule and to call for English conquest of the border areas and even of the whole colony. So acute were these border conflicts that New Netherland and the New England colonies finally drew up a formal treaty. The Treaty of Hartford (1650) set the Dutch-Connecticut boundary ten miles east of the Hudson River and eliminated Dutch claims beyond that line. But the New Englanders who had settled on Long Island continued to resist the Dutch authorities. To the south, on the Delaware River, Maryland colonists challenged the Dutch openly. In the years preceding the English conquest of New Netherland, the English settlers in the border areas moved to open revolt.

None of these difficulties was eased by skillful management on the part of the Dutch officials or by the effectiveness of the colony's political institutions. Of the directors-general (governors) who had been sent over by the company, only Peter Minuit (1626–31) was reasonably capable. His two immediate successors were hopelessly inefficient, and they made more enemies than friends in the colony. Both were finally removed from office in response to repeated charges that they were ruining the colony by their arrogance, corruption, laziness, and constant drunkenness. The second of them, Willem Kiefft (1638–47), personally began a savage war against the neighboring Indians.

Competition for land lay behind this war, which began in 1642 after Indians raided a number of outlying farms that had been settled in the natives' territory. In retaliation 110 unsuspecting and peaceful Indians who were encamped near New Amsterdam were killed. These murders were so brutal that even contemporary observers were shocked ("Some came running to us from the country having their hands cut off; some lost both arms and legs; some were supporting their entrails with their hands, while others were mangled in other horrid ways, too horrid to be conceived"). The pattern was thus set for a conflict that tore New Netherland apart for three years. Finally the Dutch hired a veteran English Indian fighter, Captain John Underhill, who led 150 men in a midnight raid on an Indian village. Some 500 Indians were shot or burned alive in Underhill's victory. At that point, in 1646, the Dutch and the Indians concluded a peace treaty, but it was the result only of mutual exhaustion and fear of annihilation. "Our fields lie fallow and waste," New Amsterdam's leading citizens wrote; "our dwellings and other buildings are burnt; not a handful can be planted or sown this fall . . . we have no means to provide necessaries for wife and children; and we sit here amidst thousands of Indians and barbarians, from whom we find neither peace nor mercy." When the next and last director-general, Peter Stuyvesant, arrived in 1647, New Netherland was badly reduced in size, hard-pressed by its competitive neighbors, and profitable only to a few of the more persistent Amsterdam merchants.

Stuyvesant, formerly the governor of the Dutch West Indies island of Curaçao, was commissioned to supervise all Dutch interests in the Caribbean as well as to rule New Netherland. He was a bitter and stubborn man, given to fits of rage. The company had granted him almost dictatorial powers, and he made savage efforts to wipe out all dissent from the official religion of the colony, Reformed Calvinism.* But he made little headway in solving the colony's multiplying problems. When in 1654 the Dutch lost Brazil to the Portuguese and the West India Company's fortunes crumbled, all that remained in New Amsterdam were a few wharves and bridges, a neglected fort, a cluster of houses, and a run-down town hall and market area. In 1655 the Indians took delayed vengeance and launched a new campaign of terror on the faltering and battered settlements. At the same time, the English settlers in Connecticut laid plans to seize the Dutch colony and began more determined encroachments on Dutch-claimed territory. By 1664 New Netherland, while still profitable to a few Amsterdam merchants, was helpless, and an English fleet conquered the colony easily. The strangely mixed population could look to the new English authorities with hopes that had never been stirred by the neglectful Dutch West India Company, the profiteering Amsterdam merchants, or such storming, hard-drinking rulers as Willem Kiefft and Peter Stuyvesant.

Royal Rewards: Carolina and the Jerseys

By the 1640s—within a single generation of the chartering of the Virginia Company—large-scale, permanent colonies with a total population of more than 50,000 had been established along Chesapeake Bay and the rivers of northern Virginia, at the mouth and along the banks of the Hudson River, and in central and southern New England. But no one had yet made a claim to two great

---

*For religion in New Netherland, see chapter 3, pp. 104–105.

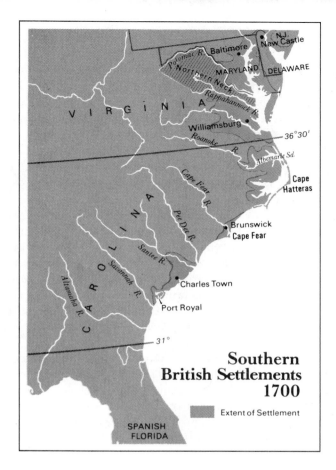

Southern
British Settlements
1700

Extent of Settlement

territories that bordered these earliest European settlements: the mid-Atlantic region between New Netherland and Maryland, and the land south of Virginia, as far as the Spanish settlement at St. Augustine, Florida. The settlement of these two major coastal regions—out of which would eventually be carved Pennsylvania, New Jersey, North and South Carolina, and Georgia—took place in circumstances very different from those operating in the settlement of the first colonies. Yet in these later colonies the same general pattern prevailed: initial high hopes and imaginative designs, followed by failure and disillusionment and then by the slow emergence of communities in unexpected forms.

Before these territories were settled, however, the political world in England had been transformed. In the two decades after 1640 England was convulsed by a civil war, by the execution of Charles I and the exile of Charles II, and by the creation of Oliver Cromwell's republican regime, which in the end became an autocratic "protectorate." In the midst of these domestic convulsions England engaged in two international wars: with the Dutch in 1652–54, largely fought at sea, and with Spain in 1656–59, mainly fought in the Caribbean. By 1658, when Cromwell died and was briefly succeeded as "lord protector" by his son, England was exhausted by the turmoil and was eager for stability and reconciliation. Disillusioned defectors from the republican regime turned to Charles I's son, who had spent many years in exile. The son, Charles II, was welcomed back to England by Parliament in May 1660, having declared amnesty for all, promised liberty of conscience, and recognized existing land titles.

The Carolina Charter   The main flow of colonization had been interrupted during the tumultuous 1640s and 1650s, but it was quickly resumed in the reign of the enterprising Charles II (1660–85). While still in exile in France, he and his followers, deprived of all other properties and prospects, had eyed the colonies as a rich field for profit. In 1649 the exiled king had rewarded the loyalty of seven of his close followers with the proprietorship of the Northern Neck of Virginia, a domain of 5 million acres between the Potomac and Rappahannock rivers. Once the monarchy had been reestablished in England, the royal court turned its attention more fully to the colonies. In the competitive, high-spirited atmosphere of Charles II's court, the most powerful of his followers joined forces to promote the colonization designs of a well-connected royalist, Sir John Colleton.

The exceptionally enterprising Colleton was the owner of a plantation on Barbados, the most profitable of England's Caribbean islands. He knew that the growth of large-scale slave plantations on Barbados was displacing an increasing number of land-hungry English farmers who had settled on that island. He also knew that Virginians and a few New Englanders were already attempting small experimental settlements in the lands just south of Virginia. Colleton proposed to advance the settlement of this region, and he quickly drew into his enterprise seven of the most powerful figures in England. Among them were his kinsman the Duke of Albemarle, who had managed Charles II's return to the throne; the Earl of Clarendon, Charles II's chief minister; Lord Berkeley, the brother of the governor of Virginia; and above all Sir Anthony Ashley Cooper, who as the Earl of Shaftesbury would become an important political power. These imaginative and ambitious men found Colleton's proposal irresistible: no funds, time, or effort seemed to be required of them. Since settlement was already proceeding by spillovers from the older colonies, the proprietors had merely to design a system of government and land distribution, open a land office, appoint officials, and collect the rents.

The charter of Carolina that was issued to the eight partners in 1663 (extended in 1665) granted them title to all the land lying between Virginia and northern Florida and across the continent from sea to sea, with full rights to govern it. The direct management of this immense territory did not interest them; they were not territorial imperialists who wished to acquire and govern more and more land. Rather, they had their eyes on the commercial possibilities of three tiny spots on the coastal fringe. The first was a northern settlement safe behind the long spits of land that formed Albemarle Sound. The second was a middle settlement at the mouth of the Cape Fear River, where a cluster of New

Englanders had already gathered. The third was a community at Port Royal in the deeper South, close to what would later become Georgia. The proprietors hoped that three well-populated, land-buying, rent-paying communities would develop from these sites. They therefore divided the grant into three huge counties that centered on these projected settlements. Then, in "A Declaration and Proposals to All That Will Plant in Carolina," they designed governments that were patterned after those of the older English colonies, with veto powers retained by the proprietors. They guaranteed both freedom of religion and a system of land distribution based on headrights of various dimensions. Large estates were reserved for the proprietors themselves in every settlement.

It was a typical project of enthusiastic colonial entrepreneurs, and it was typically unrealistic. The few Virginians who had been living around Albemarle Sound in the proposed northernmost settlement were disturbed enough by the proprietors' actions to organize an assembly to protest the terms of land allotment. But their settlement, from which would eventually develop the colony of North Carolina, was isolated from transoceanic commerce by coastal sand dunes and yielded not a penny of profit. And nothing, it seemed, could induce settlers in any numbers to remain on the swampy, sandy coastal land of Cape Fear, the proposed middle settlement, which was surrounded by hostile Indians. By 1669 the entire enterprise of Carolina was on the verge of extinction, when Ashley suddenly took it over and rescued it from failure—although not in the way he had planned.

With the assistance of the philosopher John Locke, who was his secretary, physician, and legal adviser, Ashley reorganized the undertaking. He decided that funding would have to come from the sponsors themselves, that settlers would have to be sent directly from England, and that the focal point of colonization would be the third, most southerly location, Port Royal, the site that the settlers from Barbados most favored. With new capital that had been raised from the original proprietors, Ashley was able to send out from England three vessels with about a hundred colonists and a large supply of equipment. But the expedition suffered misfortunes of every kind. Only a handful of colonists survived to establish a settlement, which they located not where one had been planned, but much farther inland, out of the reach of the Spanish. In 1670 that community, isolated from principal transportation routes, was still only a fort surrounded by a few small subsistence farms. More vessels followed, however, especially from Barbados, and the leaders undertook a search for town sites suitable for the grand design of land distribution that the proprietors had drawn up. One of the promising sites they discovered, never considered by the proprietors, was Oyster Point, where the Ashley and Cooper rivers meet, some sixty miles north of the original Port Royal. Gradually the superior attractions of this location, safe from coastal raids yet open to ocean commerce and at the hub of a network of river routes into the interior, prevailed over the proprietors' original plans for concentrated settlements. Family groups and individual farmers from the older mainland settlements and from Barbados began to move into this unplanned center of the colony and to establish claims to the rich land along the riverbanks. By 1683 Oyster Point had been renamed Charles Town (a century later it would be called Charleston), and its population of a thousand had become the center of a quickly growing colony. It was altogether different from the community at Albemarle, three hundred miles to the north. It was also totally different from anything that the Carolina proprietors had contemplated.

Fundamental Constitutions   Ashley's and Locke's hopes and plans for Carolina after the reorganization of 1669 were described in great detail in one of the most remarkable documents of the age, the "Fundamental Constitutions of Carolina," which the two men wrote in collaboration. It presented an elaborate blueprint for a hierarchical manorial world that was to be dominated by three orders of nobility—proprietors, "landgraves," and "caciques." In this intricate utopian system landowners were to be magistrates; laws were to be made by a Council of Nobles, and law courts were to be maintained by the owners of manors. But this plan—like the Calverts' earlier scheme for Maryland—was a dream that could never be put into effect. The government that in fact emerged in the first decades of settlement soon came to resemble that of the other proprietary colonies. In the early eighteenth century, when the original Carolina charter was annulled, the colony's public institutions easily fell into the standard pattern of royal governments. Yet although the romantic notions in Ashley and Locke's "Constitutions" never took hold, some of the document's provisions did become effective and helped shape the emerging community. The provisions that survived were those that conformed to patterns of life that were in fact developing in America.

One of these provisions was for religious toleration, which the original Carolina charter had also established, and which contributed significantly to the development of the Carolinas. Another enduring provision of the "Constitutions" made the naturalization of aliens a simple matter. Further, the "Constitutions" required that two-fifths of all the land in each county be granted in large estates to the nobility—a ruling that paved the way not so much for the creation of a landed nobility as for large-scale land speculation. Finally, the "Constitutions" established the rule of English law and outlined a structure of local administration similar to that of England. These latter provisions would remain fundamental to the distinctive variant of British society that was developing at the end of the seventeenth century in the southern part of the Carolina grant.

Carolina: Society and Economy   Unusual communities were springing up elsewhere in mainland British America, but the settlement that in time would become South Carolina was truly exotic. Its quickly growing population—still a mere 5,000 to 7,000 by the end of the seventeenth century—was peculiarly complex. It included not only New Yorkers, Puritan New Englanders, and Virginians, but also more than five hundred English Presbyterians and Baptists and also a group of Presbyterian Scots.

Moreover, from the colony's earliest years, and increasingly after 1685, the French Protestants known as Huguenots had been induced to immigrate to South Carolina from the Netherlands, where they had taken refuge after being expelled from France; by 1700 at least five hundred Frenchmen were settled in the colony. But from the start the dominant element was the settlers from the West Indies: several thousand experienced frontier farmers who had been displaced by the growth of the plantation economy in the sugar-producing islands, and who were determined to prosper in this hot, fertile, unexplored land.

The West Indian settlers were well acquainted with the production of semitropical crops and took an experimental approach to agriculture. They also knew how to run a slave-labor system. Thus they were able to help the colony through the typical "starving times" of the early years and to lead it in the search for commercially profitable crops. The first marketable products were familiarly British and held no great promise: timber, cattle, and foodstuffs, all of which had to be exchanged for sugar in the West Indies, which in turn could be sold in the British markets. But gradually more exotic and more lucrative possibilities became clear. The first was the fur trade, which remained a crucial element in the economic and social life of South Carolina for half a century. As early as the 1680s pack horses could be seen hauling into Charles Town and the other coastal villages animal skins that had been bought through a series of exchanges with traders and Indian hunters ranging deep in the interior. The Carolina fur traders were anything but squeamish. Not limiting themselves to tracking down animals, they also overpowered and brought back human captives: troops of Indians taken from hostile tribes, who were sold into slavery at home and abroad.

Slavery was a basic fact of life from the earliest days of South Carolina. Africans, West Indian blacks, and Indians alike were enslaved. There is evidence that in the arduous early years, when basic survival was at stake, whites and blacks, freemen and slaves, worked together—"slaved" together—in conditions of relative equality. But by the 1690s the condition of the blacks was reduced to that of absolute degradation. At this time the first successful experiments were made in rice cultivation, which along with indigo* production and the fur trade would ultimately be the basis of South Carolina's economy. These industries required an ever-increasing work force of slaves. As early as 1708 blacks outnumbered whites in South Carolina, and by then the colony's "black code," based on the savage slave laws of Barbados, had been drawn up and was rigorously enforced.

These were the results of the enterprise of Charles II's courtiers who had been granted the great gift of Carolina in 1663. By the beginning of the eighteenth century, South Carolina's survival was assured. The colony would prosper and grow—but not as the utopia of balanced social orders of which Locke and Ashley had dreamed. Rather, it was a competitive world of rice plantations, brutal race

---

*Indigo is a blue dye obtained from various plants.

relations, land speculation, and commerce. As their fortunes rose, its most prominent families were increasingly eager for leisure and the grace of life; but even more than the leaders of the other colonies, they were directly exposed to the wildness of the frontier and the savagery of chattel slavery.

Settlement of the Jerseys

The Jerseys were founded at the same time as the Carolinas, and under similar circumstances. In 1664 Lord John Berkeley and Sir George Carteret—both of whom were also among the proprietors of Carolina—were granted a tract of approximately 5 million acres between the Delaware and Hudson rivers by the Duke of York, overlord of the territory just conquered from the Dutch. But although these first proprietors of what is now called New Jersey issued grandiose plans modeled on the first Carolina designs, they had even less interest in managing this province than they had in governing the Carolinas. The proprietors' powers and claims almost immediately dissolved into a confusing maze of divisions and subdivisions that left New Jersey open to largely unregulated settlement.

In 1674 Berkeley sold his rights to a group of English Quakers. This transaction set in motion a bewildering exchange of shares, in the course of which, in 1676, New Jersey was formally divided into two provinces, East Jersey and West Jersey. In East Jersey Carteret's heirs attempted vainly to organize a coherent government out of the scattered settlements that had been founded by squatters. Meanwhile, amid paralyzing legal complications, the new Quaker proprietors of West Jersey tried to establish a refuge for their fellow Quakers who were being persecuted in England and New York. In 1677 the Quaker leaders, among them William Penn, issued an extraordinarily liberal and humane document, "The Concessions and Agreements of the Proprietors, Freeholders, and Inhabitants of . . . West New Jersey in America." This document guaranteed a democratically elected popular assembly; absolute freedom of conscience, among other individual rights; and adult male participation in both local and provincial government. In the early 1680s the first West Jersey assemblies attempted, with uneven success, to enact these provisions into law. But although groups of settlers appeared and began the cultivation of West Jersey, the Quakers' interests in colonization soon shifted to Pennsylvania. West Jersey thereafter followed the pattern already set in East Jersey, where control was in the hands of land speculators interested primarily in the financial value of the proprietors' claims. The mixture of peoples in East Jersey became even more complex when Scottish entrepreneurs led a migration of Scots Presbyterians into the province. Gradually, as farms and towns were built in both East and West Jersey, a familiarly English pattern of local government emerged, in which the proprietors played only a minor role. Yet the proprietors retained title to the undistributed land, even when the crown took temporary control of the two governments between 1688 and 1692 and permanent control in 1702. In that year East Jersey and West Jersey were rejoined to form the single crown colony of New Jersey.

By 1702 the territory that the Duke of York had so casually bestowed on his two followers contained a population of approximately 14,000, almost all of whom lived on one-family farms of between 50 and 150 acres. The ethnic and religious diversity was extraordinary, even for a British North American colony. Only New York had a more complex population, and there a single group, the Dutch, predominated. In New Jersey no one group was dominant. There were Africans, West Indians, Dutch, Germans, French, English, Scots, and Irish. Religious groups in the colony included Congregationalists, Baptists, Quakers, Anglicans, Presbyterians, Huguenots, and Dutch and German Reformed. The colony had no particular cultural character or social organization, and its mixed farming economy was in no way distinctive in the agricultural world of the northern colonies.

Pennsylvania: A Godly Experiment and a Worldly Success

Of all the colonies perhaps Pennsylvania most vividly shows the contrast between soaring aspirations and modest accomplishments. The vividness of the contrast was in part a consequence of the speed with which everything happened in Pennsylvania, as well as a reflection of the fame of the original plans and the force of the original hopes. The contrast also reflected the mixture of conflicting elements in William Penn's personality.

Quaker Immigrants   The founding of Pennsylvania was the accomplishment of one of the most radical religious sects of the seventeenth century, the Quakers. As religious extremists, they had suffered severe persecution during their thirty years of existence as a group before the founding of Pennsylvania. The Quakers devoted themselves to finding the divine "inner light" within each soul and practiced their religion without the burdens of church, clergy, and formal ritual. They were proud and courageous people who defied state authority to the point of refusing to take ordinary oaths of loyalty. They advocated absolute freedom of conscience and were pacifists and political reformers.

By 1680 there were some 50,000 Quakers in Britain, most of them poor people, and smaller numbers were scattered throughout continental Europe and North America. In the late 1670s the English government, fearful of Catholic conspiracies and hoping to protect the established Church of England, had launched savage attacks on all religious dissidents, especially such extremists as the Quakers. Some 1,400 of these gentle but stubborn nonconformists were thrown into jail, and they were fined heavily for attending Quaker meetings and for failing to attend Church of England services. If they could not pay these fines (and most could not), their goods—including their means of earning a living— were seized and either destroyed or carted away. This treatment severely injured the Quakers, not only economically, but also spiritually: they regarded work a

IAMES NAYLOR

Of all the Sects that Night, and Errors own
And with false Lights possesse the world, ther's none
More strongly blind, or who more madly place
The light of Nature for the light of Grace

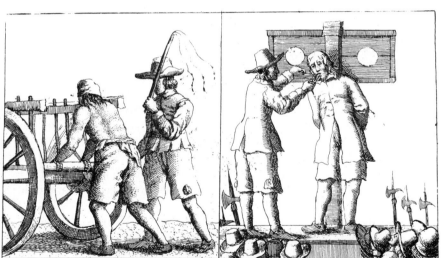

Iames Nailor Quaker, sot 2 howers on the Pillory at Westminster, whiped by the Hang
man to the old Exchainge London, Som dayes after, Stood too howers more on the Pillory
in at the Exchainge, and there had his Tongue Bored throug with a hot Iron, &
Stigmatized in the Forehead with the Letter:B: Decem: 17. anno Dom: 1656:

The Punishment of James Nayler, The Most Notorious Quaker

*His disciples' cries of "Holy, holy, holy, Lord God of Israel" as Nayler rode into Bristol were
interpreted as signs of worship of the man himself. The result was a Parliamentary trial (1656),
conviction for "horrid blasphemy," and the punishment described in the caption. The letter B
branded on his forehead was for "blasphemer."*

"Armor Portrait"
*This portrait of William Penn,
painted when he was a young
man in military service in
Ireland, is the only probable
likeness of the Quaker leader.*

divine calling, and so their inability to pursue their occupations was a further obstacle to their achievement of a full religious life.

William Penn was the well-educated son of one of England's most influential naval officers and a familiar, respected figure at the court of Charles II. But he had joined the Quakers as a young man, and he suffered his share of religious persecution. His outlook was curiously complex. Convinced of the truth of the Quakers' teachings, he brought to the movement great energy, high-level contacts, a lawyer's shrewdness in argument, and a businesslike approach to the endless controversies in which the group was embroiled. He was a radical in religion and also in politics: he sought every means of protecting the individual from arbitrary governmental power and believed that government existed to improve the welfare of the masses. But he remained an aristocrat all his life. Despite being a political reformer and a religious extremist, he was also a monarchist. He continued to believe that well-educated and highly placed men should have the decisive voice in public affairs, and he managed to keep contact with the sources of political favors at Charles II's court despite the suffering he had to endure because of his Quaker views.

Why Charles II granted so vast a territory in America to this outspoken religious dissident has never been fully explained. No doubt one factor was the crown's long-standing debt to Penn's father. The king may also have thought the grant a convenient way of getting rid of the Quakers. But Penn's personal relationship with the royal family was probably the decisive factor, and of that very little is known. In any case, in 1681 Charles II bestowed on Penn the last unassigned portion of the North American coast south of Massachusetts. The grant included the entire area between New York and Maryland, stretching west almost three hundred miles from the New Jersey border at the Delaware River— a total of 29 million acres, almost the size of England.

Penn was the outright owner of this territory. Furthermore, he had been granted the authority to form a government, to appoint most public officials, and to make laws subject only to the approval of an assembly of freemen and the crown's right of veto. The charter specified that England's commercial regulations* be observed, but otherwise Penn was free to govern as he wished. He immediately drew up a Frame of Government—the first in a series of such documents, as it turned out. It was a strange constitution. In part it was a code of moral principles, but it was also a detailed plan for a very traditional civil administration and a blueprint for a remarkably undemocratic government. A governor and a large council were to initiate and execute all laws, which the assembly (elected only by property owners) might accept or reject, but not amend. Thus, amid striking statements of private and public morality and appeals to humanity and decency, Penn gave power not to the people at large but to their "natural" rulers. From this fusing of benevolence and paternalism Penn expected a community of brotherly love to emerge—tolerant, free, secure, and above all peaceful. With these hopes in mind he turned with passion and skill to making his dreams come true.

In the end Penn was deeply disillusioned. Simply maintaining the legal title to his colony was an endless struggle, and his relations with the settlers were profoundly embittering. His efforts to bring settlers to Pennsylvania, however, were extraordinarily successful, especially at the start.

Growth of the Colony

Pennsylvania was the best advertised of all American colonies. Recruitment pamphlets urging emigration to Pennsylvania circulated throughout Britain and, in translation, in western Europe. A central "city of brotherly love," Philadelphia, was founded at an excellent site at the junction of the Delaware and Schuylkill rivers, and a well-designed street plan was laid out. A generous system of land distribution was set up. Land along the Delaware River south of Philadelphia was added to Pennsylvania by the Duke of York to ensure the colony's access to the sea. Quaker merchants contributed heavily to meet the colony's expenses, and within a year an assembly met and composed a "Great Law" that served as a temporary code of legislative and administrative principles and procedures. Above all, settlers arrived in large numbers.

By 1682, when Penn visited the province, the population was already 4,000— a remarkable swarming of people within a few months. There were Dutch, Swedes, and Finns from earlier settlements on the Delaware River; West New Jerseyites; a large and influential influx of Welsh Quakers; Germans from the

---

*For the growth of England's commercial legislation, see chapter 4, pp. 114–116.

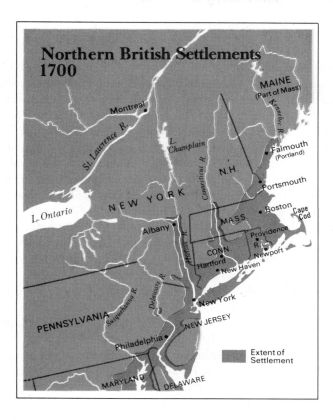

Northern British Settlements 1700

Rhineland who settled Germantown, near Philadelphia; and above all English Quakers who flocked to the refuge Penn had provided for them. Fifty vessels brought 3,000 more settlers in 1683. By 1700 the colony's population was a remarkable 21,000. But by then Penn knew all the difficulties that his proprietorship entailed.

He was embroiled in a bitter struggle with Lord Baltimore over Pennsylvania's southern boundary. (This dispute would be finally settled only with the drawing of the Mason-Dixon line on the eve of the American Revolution.) He was faced with stiff resistance to his authority by the settlers in the newly acquired "lower counties," a district that would ultimately form the state of Delaware; in 1701 he was forced to allow the dissidents to establish their own assembly. Penn was unfortunate in his choice of deputy governors and suffered from their inefficiency. Above all, his concept of government evoked fierce opposition, led by some of the most deeply committed Quakers among the settlers.

From the beginning the colonial leaders had insisted that the representatives—not Penn or his deputy governors—have the deciding voice in government. The house of representatives seized the power of initiating legislation, and in 1696 it forced Penn to agree to its action. Against Penn's will it insisted on amending the bills that he presented, and it challenged his title to the undistributed land. Bitter struggles continued year after year in the 1690s, until finally Penn agreed to an altogether new Frame of Government. Written in 1701 by a joint committee of the council and the house, this charter of liberties marked the final defeat of Penn's political ideals. It would serve as Pennsylvania's constitution until the Revolution. The new Frame of Government completely eliminated the council from the legislative process, thus making the Pennsylvania assembly the only unicameral (one-house) legislature in British America. The king could still veto legislation, but Penn could not, and the inhabitants were freed from any special allegiance to Penn or his descendants. What remained beyond dispute were the founder's and his heirs' title to the undistributed land, and their authority to appoint the resident governors. All other powers that had been granted to the Penn family in the charters were either abolished or challenged. This resistance to Penn's authority did not stem from a democratic, populist majority of the population. Rather, it came from an oligarchy of Quaker politicians and representatives who had been elected on a limited franchise—a quarrelsome, opinionated, ambitious clique that would dominate the colony's politics for the next half-century.

Penn had lost control of the province. But although Pennsylvania had failed to develop into the utopia of its founder's dreams, it was a fabulous worldly success. Its politics were contentious, but it was populous and prosperous from the start, open and attractive to all. Pennsylvania was the distribution center for a mass population of laborers, but also a center of provincial high culture. Within a single generation the colony became the dynamic heart of British North America. With a sure instinct, the eager seventeen-year-old Benjamin Franklin left Boston to seek his fortune in Philadelphia in 1723. William Penn was only five years dead then, but his City of Brotherly Love had become a vigorous, thriving community of 10,000 people, a vital part of a colonial world that was evolving in unexpected ways.

CHRONOLOGY

1607	Virginia Company of London establishes settlement at Jamestown.	**1620**	Mayflower Compact signed; Pilgrims establish Plymouth Colony.
1609	Pilgrims flee to Holland to avoid religious persecution.	**1621**	Dutch West India Company chartered.
1609	Second charter of Virginia Company.	**1622**	Indian rebellion in Virginia.
1612	Third charter of Virginia Company.	**1624**	Virginia Company charter annulled; English crown takes control of Virginia. First settlements in New Netherland.
1619	First Africans arrive in Virginia. First North American representative assembly meets in Virginia.	**1625–1649**	Reign of Charles I.

1626	Dutch settle Manhattan.	**1642**	Basic literacy law passed in Massachusetts Bay.
1629	Massachusetts Bay Company chartered.	**1642– 1648**	Civil war in England.
1630	Puritan emigration from England begins; continues until 1643.	**1643**	Confederation of New England colonies.
1632	Cecilius Calvert, Lord Baltimore, receives charter for Maryland colony.	**1644**	Rhode Island receives patent.
1634	First settlements in Maryland.	**1647**	Law requiring towns to maintain schools passed in Massachusetts Bay Colony.
1635	Roger Williams banished from Bay Colony.	**1649**	Northern neck of Virginia granted to courtiers in exile.
1636	Harvard College founded. First permanent English settlements in Connecticut and Rhode Island.	**1663**	Carolina charter granted to eight proprietors; Rhode Island granted charter.
1638	Anne Hutchinson convicted of heresy in Massachusetts; flees to Rhode Island.	**1664**	English conquest of New Netherland; grant of New Jersey to two proprietors.
1639	Fundamental Orders adopted in Connecticut.	**1681**	Charles II issues Pennsylvania charter to William Penn.

SUGGESTED READINGS

There are two general summaries of the English background of seventeenth-century colonization: Wallace Notestein, *The English People on the Eve of Colonization, 1603–1630* (1954), and Carl Bridenbaugh, *Vexed and Troubled Englishmen, 1590–1642* (1968). Other writings make clear the disarray, mobility, and vitality of English society that underlay the extraordinary exodus of English men and women overseas: Peter Laslett, *The World We Have Lost* (1965); Peter Clark and Paul Slack, eds., *Crisis and Order in English Towns 1500–1700* (1972); John Patten, *English Towns, 1500–1700* (1978); and the writings of W. G. Hoskins on English local history, most of which are listed in his *Local History in England* (1959). The best introduction to the economic history of preindustrial England is Charles Wilson, *England's Apprenticeship, 1603–1763* (1965), two-thirds of which is on the seventeenth century.

The most detailed, technical survey of the native North American population is the massive Volume 15 (1978) of the Smithsonian Institution's new series, *Handbook of North American Indians.* This volume, subtitled *The Northeast,* summarizes the available information—historical, anthropological, and archaeological—concerning all the native tribes from Maine to North Carolina and west to the Great Lakes. Writings on the extremely difficult subject of the size, distribution, and decline of the Indian population are summarized and interpreted in Russell Thornton, *American Indian Holocaust and Survival: A Population History since 1492* (1987). In recent years there has been an outpouring of books on the native Americans in the seventeenth century, among them Neal Salisbury, *Manitou and Providence* (1982); Helen C. Rountree, *The Powhatan Indians of Virginia* (1989); the essays in James Axtell's *After Columbus* (1988) and *The European and the Indian* (1981). William Cronon, *Changes in the Land* (1983) explains the Indians' relation to their environment and the ecological changes that resulted from European settlement. There are detailed accounts of the conflicts of races in Karen O. Kupperman, *Settling with the Indians* (1980); William W. Fitzhugh, ed., *Cultures in Contact* (1985); and J. Frederick Fausz, "The Invasion of Virginia" and "An 'Abundance of Blood Shed on Both Sides,'" *Virginia Magazine of History and Biography*, 95 (1987), 133–156, and 98 (1990), 3–56. Other important works on culture contacts and conflicts are Allen W. Trelease, *Indian Affairs in Colonial New York: The Seventeenth Century* (1960); Alden W. Vaughan, *New England Frontier: Puritans and Indians, 1620–1675* (1975); Douglas E. Leach, *Flintlock and Tomahawk: New England in King Philip's War* (1958); Nancy O. Lurie, "Indian Cultural Adjustment to European Civilization," in James M. Smith, ed., *Seventeenth-Century America* (1959); Stephen S. Webb, *1676: The End of American Independence* (1984); and Francis Jennings, *The Invasion of America* (1975). Jennings's book is a bitter outcry against the wrongs done the North American Indians by the Puritans (and in this, a criticism of Vaughan's more even-handed treatment) and a boiling polemic against historians' characterization of the Indians as sparse in numbers, hostile to Europeans, savage, heathen, and unsophisticated in agriculture, trade, and politics.

The most detailed and comprehensive single narrative of the English settlements in the seventeenth century is Charles M. Andrews, *The Colonial Period of American History* (Vols. I–III, 1934–37), which concentrates on constitutional history and the development of public institutions. A more up-to-date and broad-ranging account of the planting and early growth of the southern colonies is Wesley F. Craven, *The Southern Colonies in the Seventeenth Century, 1607–1689* (1949). The settlement stories are retold in briefer scope in John E. Pomfret, *Founding the American Colonies, 1583–1660* (1970), and Wesley F. Craven, *The Colonies in Transition, 1660–1713* (1968), both of which contain extensive bibliographies.

On the founding of Virginia, there are, besides the relevant chapters of Andrews's *Colonial Period,* Vol. I, and Craven's *Southern Colonies,* a detailed narrative of public events in Richard L. Morton, *Colonial Virginia* (2 vols., 1960); a short summary in Alden T. Vaughan, *American Genesis* (1975); an account of the high culture of the initiators of settlement, in Richard B. Davis, *George Sandys* (1955); biographies of Pocahontas and John Smith by Philip L. Barbour; and two collections of documents: L. G. Tyler, ed., *Narratives of Early Virginia, 1606–1625* (1907), and Warren M. Billings, ed., *The Old Dominion in the Seventeenth Century* (1975). Sigmund Diamond's essay, "From Organization to Society: Virginia in the Seventeenth Century," *American Journal of Sociology,* 63 (1958), 457–75, interprets the founding as the transformation of a quasi-military organization into a fully formed society of multiple relationships. Bernard Bailyn, "Politics and Social Structure in Virginia," in Smith, ed., *Seventeenth-Century America,* pp. 90–115, considers the development of politics in its relation to the evolving social structure. Edmund Morgan considers the human cost of the colony's success in terms of the exploitation of labor in "The First American Boom: Virginia 1618–1630," *Wm. and Mary Q.,* 18 (1971), 169–98, a topic discussed in a broader context in his *American Slavery, American Freedom* (1975).

The labor problem in Virginia involves the difficult question of the origins of chattel slavery. The modern debate on that question was initiated and framed by a brilliant article by Oscar and Mary F. Handlin, "Origins of the Southern Labor System," *Wm. and Mary Q.,* 7 (1950), 199–222,* reprinted as chap. 1 of Oscar Handlin's *Race and Nationality in American Life*

---

*See footnote on p. 30.

(1957). The Handlins' view is that chattel slavery in British America was a unique institution, different from slavery elsewhere; that the concept of "slavery" in its American meaning was created in the seventeenth-century Chesapeake; and that it arose as a legal condition, in response not so much to race prejudice as to an effort to attract voluntary white labor by debasing the condition of involuntary black labor. A more recent study is Russell Menard, "From Servants to Slaves," *Southern Studies,* 16 (1977), 355–90. For differing views, emphasizing race prejudice, the fear of foreignness, and religious differences, see Winthrop Jordan, *White over Black* (1968), Part I,† and Carl N. Degler, "Slavery and the Genesis of American Race Prejudice," *Comparative Studies in History and Society,* 2 (1959), 49–66. For a comprehensive study of all the writing on this controversial subject, see Alden T. Vaughan, "The Origins Debate: Slavery and Racism in Seventeenth-Century Virginia," *Virginia Magazine of History and Biography,* 97 (1989), 311–354.

On the Pilgrims and Plymouth, see George D. Langdon, Jr.'s, general account, *Pilgrim Colony* (1966), and John Demos's social analysis, *A Little Commonwealth* (1970). George F. Willison's *Saints and Strangers* (1945) is a breezy, amusing interpretation. Bradford's great history, *Of Plymouth Plantation,* is available in a modern edition prepared by Samuel E. Morison (1952).

On the founding and early development of the Puritan colonies in New England, see, besides Andrews's chapters in *The Colonial Period,* Edmund S. Morgan's short biography of John Winthrop, *Puritan Dilemma* (1958); Darrett Rutman's *Winthrop's Boston* (1965); Samuel E. Morison's *Builders of the Bay Colony* (1930); Raymond P. Stearns, *The Strenuous Puritan: Hugh Peter* (1954); and above all, Winthrop's own *Journal . . . 1630–1649* (J. K. Hosmer, ed., 2 vols., 1908). Virginia D. Anderson, "Migrants and Motives," *New England Quarterly* 58 (1985), 339–383, is a notable interpretation of the Great Migration, and differs from the view of David Cressy, *Coming Over* (1987). For a theatrical and psychological account of Anne Hutchinson's career, see Emery Battis, *Saints and Sectaries* (1962), and on Roger Williams there are books by S. H. Brockunier, Perry Miller, and Edmund S. Morgan. On seventeenth-century Connecticut, besides Andrews, see Isabel M. Calder, *The New Haven Colony* (1934), and Mary J. A. Jones, *Congregational Commonwealth* (1968). On Rhode Island, see Sydney V. James, *Colonial Rhode Island* (1975), and on Maine and New Hampshire, Charles E. Clark, *The Eastern Frontier* (1970), Part I.

The settlement of Maryland is well covered in Andrews's and Craven's general books, and there is an excellent account of the Dutch founding of New York in Oliver A. Rink, *Holland on the Hudson* (1986); Thomas J. Condon, *New York Beginnings* (1968); and Van Cleaf Bachman, *Peltries or Plantations* (1969) are also useful. M. Eugene Sirmans, *Colonial South Carolina* (1966), and Peter H. Wood, *Black Majority* (1974), are essential on South Carolina. Hugh T. Lefler and Albert R. Newsome, *North Carolina* (1954), is a good summary of that colony's early history. Wesley F. Craven, *New Jersey and the English Colonization of North America* (1964), is the best short book on that colony, though there are a number of more detailed studies by John E. Pomfret. The most recent history of the founding of Pennsylvania is Edwin B. Bronner's *William Penn's "Holy Experiment"* (1962); on the colony's early political history, see Gary B. Nash, *Quakers and Politics . . . 1681–1726* (1968). Mary M. Dunn, *William Penn, Politics and Conscience* (1967), is an excellent study of Penn's ideas and religious beliefs.

---

†See footnote on p. 32.

3

The Colonists' World

American Society in the Seventeenth Century

⤳

By 1700 the native population in the eastern coastal region of North America had largely been destroyed—by diseases introduced by Europeans and by devastating warfare with the European settlers. From New England to North Carolina the native populations had decreased by as much as 90 percent—in some areas none were left—and the remnants of what had once been distinctive communities drifted westward and merged with others. The westward migration of these displaced peoples set in motion a new pattern of inland population movement and a new configuration of tribal relationships stretching back to the Great Lakes and into the trans-Appalachian west. The surviving east-coast natives, decimated in numbers and abandoning their familiar territories, knew that their ancient world was being destroyed. The cycles of their social and economic life had been disrupted, their spiritual values and religious practices were deteriorating, and their folkways were becoming confused. Above all, their relationship to the natural environment—crucial to their cultural as well as their physical existence—had been lost forever.

As the native societies in the coastal regions crumbled, the colonies of Europeans and Africans expanded and took on distinctive characteristics. By the end of the seventeenth century these settler communities formed an irregular line along the Atlantic coast stretching from New Hampshire to South Carolina and inland as much as a hundred miles to the first falls of the coastal rivers. The population of these settlements, totaling some 250,000 people of European and African birth or descent, clustered along river valleys to take advantage of fertile soil and easy lines of communication. Although large pockets of land seized from the natives remained unsettled, and although this was still a frontier world, there were areas that were populated by the native-born children of native-born parents—a third generation in America. For them, home was the colony, however much they might realize that their ancestors had come from a greater "home" overseas. Although they did not think of themselves as "American," they lived settled lives in communities familiar to them from birth.

Immigration continued in all areas, although least in New England. Newcomers to the colonies in 1700 no longer faced the bewildering disorder that earlier settlers had known. But neither did they find themselves in communities quite like any seen before. There were great variations from one region or one settlement to another; but despite the differences, common elements of a reordering of European life could be found everywhere.

This reordering of life was not the result of design, planning, or intent. As we have seen, there had been an abundance of planning—elaborate designs and soaring dreams. But none of the original plans had been fulfilled. All had been quickly destroyed or had slowly dissolved on contact with the harsh reality of America and constant conflict with the natives. The deviations from European life that had developed in the colonies by 1700 were products of the impact of circumstance on the culture of essentially conservative immigrants. Most of these settlers sought personal satisfactions, personal freedoms, and security within the familiar patterns of life. Many felt that the changes they were aware of were backward, not forward, steps. Change was resisted more often than pursued. Only later would the alterations in community life be seen as advances toward an ideal—the ideal, expressed in the goals of the American Revolution, of a freer, simpler, less burdensome, more fulfilling way of life.

Growth and Structure of the Settling Population

European society in seventeenth-century North America was shaped in large part by demographic characteristics. Because the European population consisted originally of immigrant settlers, and because life in the colonies was known to be harsh, the society that resulted was no evenly balanced re-creation of Europe's social structure. The upper classes of traditional society were absent from the start. There were no nobles, who composed the ruling class in Europe. There were few of what might loosely be called aristocrats, and few who had been landowning gentlemen; there were even few of what we would today call upper-middle-class professionals. For in 1700, just as at present, society's leaders and well-established people did not easily tear up their roots, migrate, and struggle to secure themselves in an undeveloped land.

The Free Population Most of the free population in mainland North America was recruited from the lower working population of England and northern Europe. Generally these people did not come from the lowest class—that of penniless vagrants and social outcasts. Rather, they were farm workers, industrial laborers, and artisans. In the lists of immigrants compiled at the time, the two most commonly mentioned occupations were "yeoman," or "husbandman" (a farm worker, usually with some degree of independence), and artisan, or tradesman. Outside New England, between 70 percent

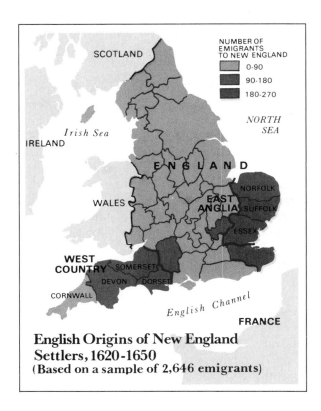

English Origins of New England Settlers, 1620-1650
(Based on a sample of 2,646 emigrants)

and 85 percent of all white immigrants were or had been indentured servants: people who were bound, for four years or more, to serve their masters faithfully in exchange for transatlantic passage, care, and protection. On gaining their liberty they received "freedom dues," which included some clothes, food, and in some places a small piece of land. Somewhat more than 1,000 of these indentured servants, bound in various conditions of servitude, arrived in the Chesapeake region yearly between 1607 and 1700; approximately 100,000 had come by 1700.

Further, the free population in America by 1700 was unusually mobile. The population was originally recruited, and continued to be recruited, from groups that were already on the move in the mother country. For many of them resettlement in America was a second or third uprooting. And institutional and legal restraints on mobility—important factors in traditional European life—scarcely existed outside of New England. The large majority of indentured servants in the Chesapeake area survived servitude and eventually entered the community as free people, free to seek the security, profit, or congenial surroundings they desired and could afford.

More important still, the free population of the northern colonies in the seventeenth century—and of the southern colonies after about 1700—grew unusually quickly. In this era most European populations were hardly growing at all—perhaps 1 percent a year over extended periods—but the population increase in the fastest-growing American communities was extraordinary. In New

England, once the initial immigration was completed, the population grew during the seventeenth century at an average rate of 2.6 or 2.7 percent a year, a statistic that shows that, quite aside from further immigration, the settled population was doubling approximately every twenty-seven years. On the other hand, until the 1650s Virginia and Maryland were death traps of disease. A random list of ninety-nine adults (mostly men) who transacted business in a Virginia court shows an average age at death of forty-eight between 1637 and 1664. The life expectancy for women aged twenty in the same region was only forty. In Maryland the population began to grow on its own, independently of immigration, only in the 1680s; before then only the constant flow of immigrants accounted for population growth, and these immigrants were highly vulnerable to the diseases common in the Chesapeake region. But the death rate in the Chesapeake colonies fell rapidly in the later seventeenth century. This drop occurred as the proportion of native-born people in the population—who early in life had developed immunities to the prevalent diseases—increased. By the late seventeenth century the population of Virginia was growing rapidly, supplemented by constant immigration. It stood at 8,000 in 1644, quadrupled to 32,000 in the next thirty years, and more than doubled again in the next thirty years, to reach an estimated 75,600 in 1704.

Whatever else may be said about the spectacular population growth, this phenomenon meant that all other social changes were intensified by sheer population pressure.

How can this extraordinary growth rate be explained? Not, apparently, by an unusual birthrate. The birthrates available for selected American communities are similar to those in French and English villages of this period. The root of the difference apparently lies in the lower death rate in the American colonies, once the initial "starving times" were over and once the deadly "seasoning" times in the southern colonies came to an end. In Plymouth, Massachusetts, the life expectancy of men who survived to the age of twenty-one was 69.2 years. In Andover, Massachusetts, the average age of death of the first settlers was 71.8 years; for their sons the average was 65.2. The life expectancy at birth for males in seventeenth-century Andover was longer by 12.6 years than it would be for men in England two hundred years later.

This rapidly growing population was also unusual in its age structure, which is associated with rapid population growth. The American population was youthful. Most of the tens of thousands of indentured servants were between eighteen and twenty-four years of age when they arrived. In Bristol, Rhode Island, 54 percent of the population were children; in seventeenth-century England the equivalent figure was 42.6 percent. Because of its youthful composition, the American population was less vulnerable to the ravages of disease than a population more evenly distributed by age would have been. The survival rate also reflects a higher proportion of women in their childbearing years (between fifteen and forty-five), as well as a younger average age at marriage, at least in the northern colonies, especially for women. In England, where 10 percent to 15

Elizabethan London
London was a bustling, crowded, commercial metropolis whose rapid population growth in the 16th century was the major source of recruitment for the North American settlements.

percent of the population were servants who usually could marry only in later life, if at all, and where circumstances made it difficult for those without an inheritance to establish a household, it appears that the average age at first marriage was twenty-eight for men and twenty-four for women. In one Massachusetts community that has been closely studied, Dedham, the equivalent figures are 25.5 and 22.5. In Plymouth, Massachusetts, the average age at first marriage for women at the end of the seventeenth century was 22.3; in Bristol, Rhode Island, before 1750, the average age for women's first marriages was 20.5. As a result of these younger marriages, women commonly bore children from their very early twenties until their mid-forties. Younger marriages also ensured a higher survival rate of children because in preindustrial societies the offspring of younger marriages seem to have been more resistant to disease.

Finally, sex ratios in the emerging American communities differed from those of the parent communities in Europe. In England through these years, as in most settled societies, there were more women than men. (The figures in England for the period 1574–1821 are 91.3 men to every 100 women.) In the early years of American settlement, the figures are wildly inverted. In Virginia in 1625, more than 75 percent of the settlers were men, and by midcentury the proportion was still grossly unequal at approximately six to one. Even in New England, where the immigration of entire families was more common, there were three men to every two women in the middle of the seventeenth century (a ratio reached in Virginia

only in 1700); and although the proportion of men to women tended to equalize over the course of the century, the traditional preponderance of women was by no means reached by 1700.

The Black Population

These data pertain to the free white population; there are no such precise figures for the growing black population. We know only that of the 250,000 inhabitants of British North America in 1700, perhaps 10 percent were blacks, and almost all of them were slaves. Most had arrived from Barbados or elsewhere in the West Indies. Only in 1674 did the Royal African Company bring the first contingent directly from Africa; thereafter shipments of African slaves rose steadily. This increase paralleled a decline in the flow of white indentured servants from Britain, which was the result of changes in the English labor market and of the growing attractions of the nonplantation colonies. The decisive turning point—a landmark in American history—was in the mid-1680s, when black slaves for the first time outnumbered white servants in the southern labor force. In 1698 the Royal African Company lost its monopoly, and a flock of small operators entered the grim but profitable trade in human lives. This development opened the floodgates: 10,000 slaves arrived in the Chesapeake colonies in the years 1698–1709.

In seventeenth-century America, however, the number of blacks was still small. Partly for that reason, the blacks lived lives of extreme degradation on the southern plantations. Family life—any kind of dignified existence—was impossible for the slave population, whose members, predominantly male, had been torn from their homes and brutalized in the utterly alien world of the South. Disease devastated infants and childbearing women. The plantations were so small, isolated, and primitive that the only tasks to be done were the most degrading kinds of field labor. Often slaves lived not even in small huts or sheds, where they might have maintained a semblance of family life or familiar culture, but in laborers' barracks. A measure of relief would come only a generation later, when the American-born black population was settled long enough to develop a more balanced sex ratio. By that time too, plantation life had evolved to the point where the need for artisanship and household help allowed some of the slaves to escape the worst kind of field drudgery. Furthermore, by then stable communities of blacks had arisen in the Chesapeake region that were large enough to nourish a distinctive subculture, blending African and American traditions—a subculture that would develop and in the end help to shape the national culture of the American people.

Economic Instability

In the Euro-American society that had emerged by 1700, economic life, social organization, and the practice of religion varied greatly from region to region and from colony to colony. But a common characteristic ran through all these major areas. There was a glaring difference between the realities of American life and the colonists' assumptions, ideals, and expectations. In studying each of these areas, one should start by isolating the colonists' assumptions and expectations—the ideals by which they would instinctively measure reality. Against this background the unique features of American life stand out most sharply. And in this context one can most clearly assess the impact of these features on the inner experiences of settlers seeking to re-create a familiar and controllable world.

Assumptions and Expectations　　The dominant view of economic life that the colonists brought with them was that of a stable system through which a more or less constant supply of goods and services flowed for the benefit of a population with relatively unchanging needs and desires. In such a system the object of individual effort was to achieve security and to help preserve the system's organization. If difficulties arose, they were assumed to be disturbances in the established relations among the producers, distributors, and consumers; and remedies were sought that would bring these elements back to their established and proper proportions. The object of primary concern was the consumer, not the producer—and a consumer of fixed, not growing, wants. It was assumed that controls were necessary to keep the economy in proper working order, especially to prevent greed or accidents from disturbing the system. And these controls did not necessarily have to be only those of the state. Lesser bodies that stood between the individual and the state, such as guilds and municipal governments, were assumed to be proper agencies of economic regulation.

These were the ordinary assumptions and ideal expectations of the colonists, who were still close to late medieval culture, still far removed from the modern world of dynamic economic systems in which an ever-rising production and the manipulation of consumption are essential to success. How well did the developing colonial economies conform to these traditional assumptions? Both the northern and the southern colonial economies violated these expectations on every point. Because expectations were violated, a sense of jarring disorder arose, and it prevailed until the American economic system became established and familiar—and until Americans learned to accommodate themselves to the instability that lay at the heart of this new system.

New England's Economy

In New England there had originally been little desire to create a commercial system that would link the Bay Colony's small port towns to an intricate network of Atlantic commerce and involve the Puritans in the greater world they had left behind. The original goal had been economic self-sufficiency: the Puritans had expected that the "Bible Commonwealth" would have the best chance of remaining free of corruption and contamination by being self-sufficient. But by the late 1650s circumstances had led the Puritans to create the uniquely complex economic system, closely involved with Atlantic commerce, that would continue essentially unchanged until the American Revolution.

Once the original settlers had exhausted their capital, their unsuccessful efforts to maintain the Bay Colony's economic independence took two main forms. First, Puritan entrepreneurs, with the active support of the colony's government, sought to produce locally the supplies that were needed by the colonists. The manufacture of iron goods and cloth was the key. An elaborate scheme that was launched by John Winthrop, Jr., the governor's son, resulted in the establishment of a complete ironworks at Saugus, Massachusetts. The project involved tremendous efforts by a few devoted entrepreneurs, the investment of more than £12,000 by English businessmen, and the General Court's gifts of land, tax exemption, and a monopoly of the local markets. But the Saugus Works flourished only briefly and then collapsed into bankruptcy, the victim of a destructive squeeze between inescapably high costs and low income.

The colony's effort to establish a local cloth industry was similarly ineffective. A Massachusetts law of 1656 hopefully but quite unrealistically ordered all idle persons to busy themselves with spinning and weaving; and it assessed every family an amount of cloth in proportion to the number of available "spinners" in the household. But there were no "idle hands" in the labor-short Bay Colony. Every available "hand" could find more than enough employment in the fields surrounding the newly established towns. There was no effective response to the government's demands and appeals.

But if neither of the two basic industrial manufactures—iron goods and cloth—could be locally produced, some kind of self-sufficiency might yet be achieved through the discovery of a small, lightweight, and highly valuable commodity that might be exchanged directly in England for the needed goods. For a few years in New England's early economic history, it seemed as though this sort of commodity would be the ultimate solution. The settlers found a rich supply of fur-bearing animals in the coastal region and just beyond, and they began a quick exploitation of this highly profitable resource. The easily available beavers, otters, and raccoons were taken by the hundreds, and their pelts were shipped back to England in direct exchange for manufactured goods. But furs proved to be a limited resource. The animals reproduced themselves far more slowly than they were killed, and by the 1650s trappers had exhausted the supply in the immediate coastal region. The New Englanders then pressed westward to the Hudson but were blocked by the Dutch from contact with fur sources in the Great Lakes region and what is today northern New York. Some furs continued to flow into Boston from trading posts on the Maine coast and on the upper Connecticut River; but after a decade of wonderful promise, the idea of basing New England's economy on the fur trade faded.

After this failure to create economic independence or to establish a direct exchange with England, a generation of small merchants in the Bay Colony worked out a system of exchanges throughout the Atlantic world that would produce the needed imports of manufactured goods. As New England's population multiplied, foodstuffs, fish, and timber products grew increasingly available, and the commercial possibilities they created became clear. These products could not be sold in England, which itself produced them, but in Catholic Europe— France, Spain, and the "Wine Islands" of Madeira, the Azores, and the Canaries. These markets could use all the fish that could be sent; and the West Indies could absorb not only fish and other food supplies needed to feed the labor force, but also timber for building and horses to help work the sugar mills. From the West Indies, in turn, sugar products could be obtained for sale elsewhere in America and in the English markets; and from Madeira, the Azores, and the Canary Islands, wine could be procured for sale in the Atlantic ports. And other contacts could be made. Tobacco could be picked up in the Chesapeake, fish in Newfoundland, and various agricultural products in New York and later in Pennsylvania. An intricate circuit of exchanges could be created—horses and fish for sugar, and sugar for bills of exchange,* wine, tobacco, or locally produced goods.

These exchanges might go on for months or even years before they reached their conclusion—the establishment of credits with some merchant in a leading British port. These credits would finance the purchase of manufactured goods to be imported for profitable sale in the colonies. The profits would in turn make possible bigger shipments in the next cycle, and perhaps investment in shipbuilding as well.

So the commercial system evolved in New England, to be re-created with variations in all the northern colonies. Each colony's system was distinctive, but

---

*A bill of exchange is an order written by a merchant, authorizing the bearer to receive payment from an associated merchant.

Cod Fishing on the Grand Banks and the North American Shore
*This French print of 1705 shows all stages of the fishing industry, from catching the fish (C) to
gutting and scaling (D, E) and drying and packing (M, H). Fish at the upper left are being
carted away for salting (F), and the press at lower left (I) is extracting oil from the cod livers,
the waste draining into the tub (K), the oil into the barrel (L).*

all were interlocked and had common characteristics. These flows of commodities were not stable and easily controllable. They were highly unstable,
driven by uncertainty and inescapable risks. All factors combined to make this
commercial world dynamic and unpredictable.

In the first place, the local production of salable commodities was unreliable
and irregular. Not only were there ordinary crop failures, but on the backcountry
farms that were just coming under cultivation, production was unreliable. Even
less reliable were the West Indian and Atlantic island markets, which might easily
be glutted by a few shipments and from which it was impossible to obtain reliable
market information before cargoes were sent. Further, this commerce was managed not by a few big firms whose decisions and agreements might stabilize the
system, but by many small and highly competitive merchants. Finally, it was
virtually impossible for any of these small merchant entrepreneurs to specialize, if
only because a chronic money shortage made it necessary for them to pay for
goods by bartering other goods. Thus every merchant had to be prepared to
sell—or barter—almost any commodity at any time in any market he could find.

As a result of these conditions, it was nearly impossible to match available goods to available markets. Between the initial shipment of goods and their arrival at an ultimate destination, the entire commercial picture could change. Merchants operated largely in the dark and were victims of sudden gluts, unpredictable shortages, and sharp price fluctuations. Trade patterns did not follow any fixed geometrical form. There was no rigid "triangular" trade in the seventeenth century or later. There were only constantly shifting polygons that formed and reformed as merchants undertook what were in effect peddling voyages up and down the North American coast and in the Caribbean and Atlantic commercial lanes.

As a result of all this, overseas trade proved to be a highly competitive, risky business in which success was the result of speculative venturing, intelligent risk taking, and driving entrepreneurship. The principle of success was not the completion of safe, carefully planned exchanges, but the almost limitless accumulation of exchanges of all sorts of commodities in a great variety of markets. It was a dynamic system propelled by powerfully expansive forces.

For more than a century this commercial system provided the northern colonies with essential goods and helped produce the material basis for a flourishing provincial culture. And from this system important social consequences flowed. In this commercial world there could be no hard and clear definition of a merchant "class." The situation encouraged the participation of newcomers starting with very little—men who would have been rejected as interlopers in English commercial towns. There were no effective institutional barriers that might confine the group. Neither guilds nor municipal corporations developed to restrict the merchant community or to regulate its activities. Anyone's contribution to the struggling commercial economy was valuable, and the government intervened only to stimulate innovation, not to limit it. A dynamic, unstable, unpredictable, yet successful commercial system produced a fluid merchant group, continually recruiting newcomers from among successful tradesmen and farmers, and seeking security and wealth in a system whose essence was risk.

The Southern Economy

The economic system that developed in the Chesapeake region was no less risky, competitive, and unstable. It centered on the production and marketing of a single staple crop, tobacco. The details are of course altogether different from those of the northern commercial system, but here too success was not won by sharing in regular production and a stable process of distribution. To be successful one had to contend with runaway cycles of production and a lurching, unpredictable distribution system. And in the South as in the North, a dynamic economy produced uncontrollable social consequences.

Originally there had been little enthusiasm for producing tobacco, which in the early seventeenth century was considered harmful to health and was associated with general immorality. King James I of England in 1604 wrote a pamphlet condemning smoking, entitled *A Counterblaste to Tobacco,* and during his reign tobacco pipes were used as door signs of brothels. But then as now, however harmful it was to health, tobacco sold—and it sold extremely well in England, originally as an expensive import from Spain. Once Americans began to sell tobacco in England, they worked hard to exploit the market, and they quickly flooded it. By the late 1630s the price of tobacco had dropped sharply, to a point less than the cost of production. There was a mild recovery of prices in the early 1640s, but prices collapsed again in the 1660s as production rose even further in the Chesapeake colonies. By the end of the century, prices were still low, and a pattern of recoveries and collapses had emerged that would persist throughout the colonial period.

The low prices and the uncontrollable cycles were symptoms of deep problems in the tobacco economy. The primary problem was overproduction. By the end of the 1630s—little more than a decade after the first marketable crop had reached England—the Chesapeake colonies were producing 1.5 million pounds of tobacco a year. By 1700 the figure had risen to about 38 million pounds annually. In addition the Chesapeake industry suffered from serious competition. Spain continued to export the best-quality crop, which commanded the highest prices, and the Caribbean islands also shipped sizable amounts. There were competitors too in England itself: tobacco was a well-established crop in Gloucestershire. To compound the troubles further, as production rose American tobacco deteriorated in quality, and the middlemen assumed that it would sell at the lowest prices. And on top of all of this were the technical difficulties of marketing this product of scattered Chesapeake farms.

The tobacco specialists who appeared quickly within the London merchant community worked out a marketing procedure that survived for a century. In this "consignment" system the English merchants acted primarily as selling agents. The Maryland and Virginia tobacco planters sent their crops to these merchants, usually on the merchants' vessels, for sale through them in the English and European markets. The English merchants lent money to the tobacco farmers to cover all the necessary charges—freight, fees, taxes, storage, and so on. They repaid themselves, with profit, when the crop was sold. In addition they provided goods to the planters that they charged against the eventual tobacco sales, and so became the planters' bankers and creditors as well as their merchandisers. There was a rough efficiency in this system, but it victimized the tobacco planters by involving them in endless debt cycles. Any given crop was in effect mortgaged long before it was sold. Further, the planters had no control whatever over the sale of their crops; they had no choice but to rely on the merchants' goodwill. Finally, the system made it impossible ever to adjust production to demand. Often two years would go by between shipment and news of eventual sale, by which time several new crops would have been produced and shipped. The net result of the system was constant debts and an unmanageable rigidity in the economic process that governed the planters' lives.

As if overproduction, keen competition, deteriorating quality, and a rigid marketing system were not enough, there was the all-important problem of breaking into the markets of continental Europe. England could absorb relatively little of the enormous production of the Chesapeake region. Of the approximately 38 million pounds of tobacco exported to England in 1700, 25 million pounds were reexported to the continent. Thus these ultimate European markets were crucial to the prosperity of the American tobacco farmers.

At first the continental countries banned American tobacco altogether. Later they imposed high duties, and finally they established government-controlled or government-owned-and-operated monopolies of imports. These monopolies determined how much tobacco would be imported, what grades would be accepted, and what prices would be charged. As this system matured and the political complexities of tobacco marketing in Europe multiplied, Dutch middlemen became increasingly important in sending the commodity to the ultimate European markets. And so still another burden was added to the already complicated trade.

These were the problems that developed in the seventeenth century as the southern economy took shape. Throughout the century strong efforts were made to overcome them, with only partial success. The English government taxed Spanish tobacco out of the English markets and eliminated tobacco raising in Gloucestershire. At the same time, the West Indian producers withdrew from the increasingly competitive tobacco business. But Dutch shippers were shrewd competitors, and until the end of the seventeenth century they remained effective participants in the shipping trade.* And neither the English government nor the colonial governments could force individual American tobacco growers to limit their production. Quite the contrary. Most planters were convinced that the more they produced, the greater would be their income. Consequently, production continued to expand, and so too did the area of land under cultivation.

The social consequences of this risky and unstable economy were far-reaching. The area of settlement was continually extended without regard for the Indians, who were driven back behind ever-expanding frontiers. As the planters pressed deeper into the interior in search of fresh lands, they forced even the friendly Indians into hostility. There were frontier skirmishes long before the full-scale race war broke out that touched off Bacon's Rebellion in 1676.†

Further, the tobacco economy generated a desperate need for a large labor force. Hired or indentured servants were never available in sufficient numbers, and as a result the tobacco farms remained relatively small (an average of 250 acres). Slavery was an obvious solution to the labor problem, even if its capital costs were greater than those of a free-labor system. By the end of the seventeenth century, it was clear that the demands of the tobacco economy were constantly enlarging the slave labor force and thereby worsening one of the greatest evils of American life.

---

*Dutch competition ended because of the enforcement of England's navigation acts; for the navigation acts, see chapter 4, pp. 114–15.

†For Bacon's Rebellion, see chapter 4, pp. 133–34.

Finally, the tobacco economy eliminated the possibility that an urban society would develop south of Pennsylvania. The way in which the tobacco trade was organized prevented local merchants from developing into independent entrepreneurs, because the commercial processes were provided for in England. As a consequence the secondary activities (shipbuilding, service trades, brokerage, and shopkeeping) that ordinarily develop around "entrepreneurial headquarters" were frustrated from the start. On the eve of the American Revolution, Williamsburg, Virginia, had a total population of only 2,000; and even that small population was largely the result of the Virginia colonial government's residence in the town. Baltimore and Norfolk, each with a population of 6,000, developed not in the heart of the tobacco country, but at the borders of more varied economies.

Social Instability

No aspect of community life came under more intense pressure than did social organization. The mentality of the generation that settled in America in the years before 1660 was still close to that of late-sixteenth-century Englishmen of Queen Elizabeth I's time. Both the Elizabethans and their colonizing descendants assumed that society was not a miscellaneous collection of people who were pursuing their separate goals and relating to each other haphazardly. Rather, Elizabethans and the first English settlers in America thought of society as a disciplined organism, a fabric closely "knit together," as they liked to say. The overall character of society, they thought, was more important than any of the separate parts that composed it. Specifically, they assumed that society would display at least three essential characteristics.

First, they expected that the parts of a community would complement each other and fit together harmoniously to compose the "commonwealth" as a whole. Second, they believed that the structure of society would be essentially hierarchical—that is, organized into distinct levels of inferiority and superiority. These levels did not reflect what we today call "class," but rather status and dignity—characteristics that were related to occupation and wealth but not defined by them. Third, they assumed that the hierarchy of society was a unified structure in which people of superior status in one aspect of life would be superior in all other aspects as well. Thus the rich would be politically powerful, well educated, and dignified. Leadership in public and private affairs would belong to the highborn, the firstborn—the natural leaders, who had the social superiority that was necessary to rule.

Elizabethans believed that these were the characteristics of all well-organized societies, and those who came to America had no intention of changing or rejecting such fundamental notions. But in fact the world that emerged in mainland North America did not conform to these ideals. To be sure, there was no total breakdown, once the horrors of the "starving times" were overcome. There was no instant transformation into a different kind of life. But from the first years of settlement, there were sharp stresses and strains that made social life in the colonies tense, strange, and difficult.

The sources of these problems were obvious. The colonists were well aware that the political and economic leadership of the communities was being taken over by people who, although capable of dealing with the harsh circumstances of life in America, lacked the traditional social qualities of proper leaders. These qualities included a sense of natural superiority, habitual dignity, and personal authority. As a result the respect due to the leading figures was not automatically forthcoming. Political and economic leaders were vulnerable to criticism and were challenged in ways their social·superiors would not have been.

Puritanism and Social Order   In New England this general problem was compounded in a special way. Within the Puritans' distinctive status system, purity of religion, piety, and upright behavior were major factors in establishing differences among individuals. At the same time, every effort was made to keep alive the traditional social structure. For example, the Puritans agreed that in the newly established townships, persons of wealth, position, and professional training should receive the larger allotments of land. Even so vague a distinction as "ability" was materially rewarded. But the conflict with religious values could not be avoided.

At least the problem was clearly understood. One of the Puritans' most influential English leaders, Lord Say and Sele, considered joining the Great Migration in 1636; but he paused. Was it not true, he wrote the Reverend John Cotton in Boston, that men could vote in Massachusetts simply by being accepted into the church, no matter what their social status? If so, what certainty was there that people like himself would be able to play their proper roles? Cotton tried to reassure him. Everyone knew that "monarchy and aristocracy are both of them clearly approved and directed in scripture" and that God never considered democracy "a fit government either for church or commonwealth." So His Lordship need have no fear of finding New England a world turned upside down. Still, Cotton had to admit, the Puritans were committed to the service of the Lord: in the end religious considerations would and should prevail. For is it not better, he asked, "that the commonwealth be fashioned to the setting forth of God's house, which is his church, than to accommodate the church frame to the civil state?" The noble lord read the message correctly and stayed home. The Bay Colony's turmoil in the founding years continued to reflect the strange confusion and the mingling of religious and social distinctions.

Social Structure and Family Life   Everywhere in the colonies there were difficulties and confusions in maintaining a traditional European social order. On the farms in the northern, middle, and southern colonies alike, it was physically impossible to maintain the expected differences in styles of life. Masters and servants had no choice but to labor side by side, and so the differences between them came to rest only on a legal formality, a scrap of paper that established the servants' dependency. There were few luxuries anywhere, and nowhere was there the material basis for leisure. The few people with professional training lived far more primitive lives than their education and occupational role would traditionally have assured them.

The problems of maintaining traditional social distinctions were especially dramatic in the towns. Throughout the seventeenth century there were constant complaints that the free workers—the handicraftsmen, shipwrights, carpenters, shoemakers, and tailors—had lost all respect for traditional roles and social distinctions. It was commonly said that they demanded astronomical wages and that their pretense to social superiority was unbearable. They flaunted their prosperity and aped their superiors in ways that offended the traditional sense of decency and social order. By eliminating the causes of this alleged misbehavior or by limiting its effects, the authorities made every effort to contain the social disorder that the free workers were creating. Occasionally, when the problem became acute, the colonial assemblies voted to keep wages down in order to restrict the workers' ambitions and to protect the public against their apparent greed. But such laws could not be enforced. The workers' services were indispensable; people would pay almost any price they demanded. And the workers' arguments were convincing too: costs, they said, were rising; they had expenses to meet. Let prices be fixed if wages were. But price fixing was as futile as wage fixing, and what a later generation would call "escalator clauses" were tried with only temporary effect on the demands and behavior of the free, self-employed workers.

By 1660 the effort to eliminate the source of the workers' extravagance had clearly failed. The colonial assemblies resorted to the idea of disciplining behavior itself—trying to confine dress and social interaction to appropriate forms of decency. Laws restricted the wearing of fine clothing, limited display, and lectured the supposedly disordered population on the confusion of the times. A law passed in the Massachusetts Bay Colony in 1651 is perhaps the most eloquent testimony of the age to the founders' widespread sense of social confusion. The General Court declared its

> utter detestation and dislike, that men or women of mean [low] condition should take upon them the garb of gentlemen, by wearing gold or silver lace, or buttons, or points at their knees, or to walk in great boots, or women of the same rank to wear silk or tiffany hoods or scarves which, though allowable to persons of greater estates or more liberal education, yet we cannot but judge it intolerable in persons of such like [low] condition.

So, given this disordered condition of society, the legislature ordered

> that no person within this jurisdiction . . . whose visible estates shall not exceed the true and indifferent value of £200 shall wear any gold or silver lace, or gold or silver buttons, or any bone lace above 2 shillings per yard, or silk hoods or scarves, upon the penalty of 10 shillings for every such offense.

John Freake and His Wife Elizabeth and Child, 1674
Freake was one of the successful merchants who arrived in Boston well after the original Puritan migration and brought with him a "corrupting" luxuriance of style. His buttons are silver, his collar fine lace, his sleeves puffed muslin, and his gold brooch studded with precious stones. His wife's embroidered petticoat is carefully revealed.

And then, in a devilishly clever provision, the General Court decreed that if the town selectmen found anyone they judged "to exceed their ranks and abilities in the costliness or fashion of their apparel," they were to increase the offender's tax rate to the level of wealth he or she pretended to. But the General Court added—in an afterthought that brilliantly illuminates the unstable social landscape—that the law would *not* apply to any of the colony's magistrates or their families, to any regular military officers or soldiers on active duty, or to anyone else *"whose education and employment have been above the ordinary degree, or whose estates have been considerable, though now decayed."*

"Though now decayed"—the phrase expresses an extreme sense of disorder, of a decline of standards. And in no aspect of life was this more profoundly felt than in the family.

To understand the problems in family life that arose in the earliest years and persisted through most of the century, it is necessary to note that in this era families were considered to be the basic model of all social order. People believed that at this primary level all order began, and all patterns of inferiority and superiority took shape. The political commonwealth was seen as an enlargement of the family. Rulers were conceived of as patriarchs whose dominance as heads of the commonwealth was justified by God, the father of all. These ideas were

The Patriarchal Family, a Woodcut of 1563

clichés of the age, but—like most clichés that pass unchallenged—they were essentially realistic. For most Englishmen experienced a larger, more highly structured, more complex, and more disciplined family unit than now exists in the Western world.

The reason is not that the nuclear family—parents and children—was significantly larger than it is today. In seventeenth-century England most completed families contained only two or three children, although many more were born and died young. The sense of complexity, structure, and discipline grew from the fact that the word *family* meant or implied the *household*—all those who lived together under one roof. Almost all Englishmen at some time in their lives had experienced the household-family as a complex and disciplined institution. For servants were traditionally considered part of this artificially extended family, and servitude was remarkably widespread. About a third of all English families had servants. At any one time, between 10 percent and 15 percent of the entire English population were serving in someone else's household—and serving not merely as day workers who exchanged limited services for wages, but as family members who were committed to total employment in exchange for maintenance, protection, and to some extent education. In addition, free children of other families circulated as guests, often for long periods, in more affluent households or even in households of equivalent social position. As a result, at least 45 percent of all English people, it has been estimated, lived in households of six or more members. Consequently, most people, at least in their youth, had experienced families as complex, and to some extent patriarchal, units.

Alice Mason, 1670
This forthright, unpretentious portrait by an unknown artist illustrates not only the appearance of children in the seventeenth century, but attitudes toward children and childhood. Although parents did not consider children to be simply miniature adults, as the dress and appearance of this child suggests, and although they were aware that the individual's understanding develops gradually, they had no concept of childhood as such. They expected children to behave like adults, to be capable of religious experience, and to take responsibility for their actions at what seems now to be very early ages.

In traditional settings material circumstances reinforced and helped preserve these household-families. With most of the land of England owned by great landlords, young people found it difficult to break away and establish new independent households by purchasing or leasing plots of farmland. As a result many servants had to remain in service beyond the time of their contractual obligations. Marriages were delayed because married couples were expected to live in their own establishments, not within other households. In these constrained circumstances, family discipline developed naturally and remained a familiar, accepted fact of life.

In contrast, in the colonies of seventeenth-century America, these material reinforcements of traditional family life were either greatly weakened or eliminated—while at the same time families, in the absence of established community and kinship networks, became even more important than they were in traditional settings. Land was far more freely available than in England, and therefore the establishment of independent households was relatively easy economically, although it involved the difficult physical work of clearing new farms. Under these circumstances, it is remarkable not that the average age of first marriage fell, but that it did not fall even lower and faster than it did, and that there was not more pressure against traditional family organization than in fact there was.

But the availability of land was only one of the factors that weakened the reinforcements of traditional family life in the colonies. The acute and continuing labor shortage, which shifted the dependency relations within the family and household, meant that parents and masters depended on their children and servants as never before. They needed them, sometimes desperately, to provide critically necessary labor. In this sense the parents became dependents of their children—but not only in this sense. For the young learned more rapidly than their seniors to cope with the unfamiliar environment. The young adapted to change more easily, and in the end they became their elders' lifelines to the world. In effect they became their parents' teachers, despite the unquestioned and continuing assumption of parental superiority.

In the Chesapeake region through most of the seventeenth century this loss of reinforcement was most severe. Circumstances there made the re-creation of traditional family life almost impossible. The fearful death rate greatly increased the common disorder within families. Only half the children born in that region during the first half-century would live to age twenty, and two out of three marriages were broken by the premature death of one of the partners, more often the husband. Few children ever knew their grandparents, and most knew their parents for very few years. (Grandparents, one historian has remarked, were invented in New England.) Family and household life in the Chesapeake was therefore chaotic. Women, in short supply and married young, often became young widows; left with several children in a rough frontier society, they remarried quickly, if only for survival. Often their husbands, much older than themselves, brought children from earlier marriages, and households were crowded with half-siblings and stepchildren. And there were orphan children everywhere. Only gradually did informal community networks spread throughout the sparsely settled tobacco lands, and only very late in the century did life expectancy extend sufficiently and the sex ratio come close enough to a normal balance to introduce a measure of stability to family life.

Even in New England there was an intense awareness of disarray in family life, despite the fact that conditions there strongly favored the re-creation of traditional forms. For New England was settled largely by family groups, and low mortality, a relatively even sex ratio, long parental survivals, and remarkably tight community controls existed there from the start. Yet Puritan lawmakers repeatedly denounced the loosening of family ties and the defiance of authority in this most intimate and fundamental of all social units. Repeatedly they commanded parents to do their duty to their children and to themselves, and they ordered children to obey their parents and fulfill their family obligations. The laws grew harsher as the years went by. In New Hampshire, Massachusetts, and Connecticut, laws were passed that revived the biblical provision that children who struck or cursed their parents were to be put to death. (These laws were invoked at least once, although the punishment was never carried out.) In Massachusetts, church members called *tithingmen* were made responsible for the good behavior of groups of ten families. A meeting of church leaders in 1679 blamed the evils of the time on "defects of family government" and ordered the tithingmen to increase their efforts to reinforce the failing discipline of weak-willed parents.

The consequences of the tensions and of the widespread disarray ran deep, and in various ways the law responded. Primogeniture—the legal requirement that real estate be inherited only by the eldest son so that the family property would remain intact—was commonly ignored where land was plentiful. Instead the common practice was to divide property among the members of a family, perhaps with double portions for the wife and the eldest son. Orphan courts appeared in the South to protect children who were otherwise uncared for. And the status and role of women were particularly affected. In the confused households of the South wives acquired greater importance and authority than was customary in an age when the law normally made them entirely subordinate to their husbands. And they acquired the legal right to challenge the property provisions of their husbands' wills. In New England, laws were passed that prohibited a husband from striking his wife—"unless it be in his own defense." And there the dominance of religion, in which men and women could participate equally, tended in some degree to equate the status of the sexes. North and south, women acquired new rights to own, administer, and legally protect property; to conduct business; and to represent themselves in court. And the courts treated them more fairly than before in divorce proceedings, and granted widows more favorable treatment. Women's lives were not transformed. Traditional expectations and practices persisted. But significant alterations in their legal status and family roles were made in response to the altered conditions.

The legal position of indentured servants also improved. In some places the severity of punishment was limited by law; in others, working conditions were improved. In all the colonies every effort was made to use the law to keep servants at work despite the liberating forces that surrounded them. A case is recorded in which a servant ran away after being punished for attempting to rape his master's ten-year-old daughter—the suit was filed not to punish the culprit, but to get him back and to force him to complete his term of service! Everywhere the conditions of contractual obligations grew lighter as the ease of transition to personal freedom was recognized.

These were significant changes. But social order was not destroyed in the seventeenth-century colonies. On this western fringe of European civilization, however, society had acquired new instabilities, along with new freedoms for traditionally subordinated elements in the nonslave population. In calmer years and in more settled circumstances, some of these changes would fade back into more traditional forms, but most would become part of a permanently altered way of life.

Religion

Religion inevitably played a major role in the larger social changes in early America, for the colonists' culture was deeply Christian. The churches were still the preeminent cultural institutions, as well as vital social agencies. Everywhere in

Western civilization, the seventeenth century was a period of intense religious controversy as individuals and whole nations struggled savagely over differences in religious opinion. Yet a few basic ideas were shared by almost all religious groups—presumptions that illuminate the history of religion in early America particularly well.

Except for the most extreme radicals, Christians generally assumed that there was one true religion and that differences of belief should not be encouraged. Seventeenth-century Christians disagreed over what doctrines were orthodox, but most assumed that *some* doctrines were absolutely right and others wrong. Efforts to eliminate or at least strongly discourage heresy and to extend orthodoxy were therefore accepted as legitimate. Most Christians also thought that religion was not simply a spiritual matter or something of concern only to the church. They believed that governments should have a major responsibility for supervising religion and enforcing correct belief. Finally, when migration to the New World began, most people assumed that colonial churches would be organized along familiar European lines and would fit into some larger pattern of religious institutions.

The history of religion in the first two or three generations of colonial America can be seen as the story of the violation of these assumptions, and of the struggle to retain them in the face of adversity. Of course, Christianity survived in more or less familiar outward form. However, significant changes occurred—not because the leaders (except in New England) wanted change, but because they had to adapt to difficult circumstances. The churches did not fully accept and incorporate these changes until the eighteenth century. But the seeds of what later grew into the distinctive pattern of what has been called American denominationalism were planted in the seventeenth century.

The Anglican Church in Virginia The way in which circumstances shaped the development of Christianity in America is best illustrated by the history of the Church of England, the Anglican church, in Virginia. Here the sense of orthodoxy was strong, and here no doctrinal conflicts or pressures for reform existed. In Virginia stronger attempts were made to re-create the traditional English church institutions than in any other colony, and here hopes of maintaining these traditions met with particularly severe disappointment.

The Virginia Company—as well as the English government, when it took over direct control of Virginia in 1624—assumed that the settlers would simply reproduce the Church of England in its established form in the colony. But there were serious problems from the start, most of which grew out of the difficulty of putting the new church institutions on a workable financial foundation. In England, churches were usually supported by gifts of income-producing property donated by patrons. In Virginia the company (and later the English government) served as patron to the newly created parishes. In 1618 the company set aside as church land one hundred acres (which the English government later increased to two hundred acres) in each of the "boroughs" into which Virginia

St. Luke's Church, Isle of Wight County, Virginia (Late Seventeenth Century)
A typical Anglican parish church, with its bell tower, arched windows, and buttresses.

was divided.* Tenants were to be settled on this land, and the rent they paid was to support a minister and maintain the local church. However, every free man in Virginia wanted to own property, not to rent it, and thus it proved difficult to find tenants. Yet without someone to rent the land, it was worthless. Two alternative means of supporting the church remained. First, the ministers themselves could become almost full-time, self-supporting farmers on the church land and produce the expected income. But this prospect discouraged the recruitment of well-trained clergy: no self-respecting minister in England had to live in such a manner. The second alternative was to put the financial support of Virginia's ministers on a new basis—taxation. The Virginia Company anticipated this solution when it ordered parish members to supplement whatever income the church land produced until a sum of £200 a year was available to pay the minister and maintain the church. Supplements of this kind quickly became common, and then universal. It was soon standard practice for the governing body of the parish, the vestry, to vote an annual tax for support of the church.

Once taxation was made the financial basis of the church, the physical size of the parish became a major problem. Virginia was still thinly populated. If the parish included as many people as was customary in England, its territory would

---

*For the boroughs, see chapter 2, p. 42.

be so large that proper ministrations would be impossible. On the other hand, if the parish area remained small, so that members could gather easily and the minister could keep in close touch with them, there would be too few members, and the cost per person of maintaining the church would be extremely high. In practice, because of Virginia's underdeveloped and struggling economy, parishes remained unworkably large. Furthermore, because of differences in population density and wealth, there were great variations in the support of the clergy.

The dilemma of how to finance the church was officially recognized by the end of the first generation of settlement in Virginia. In 1662 the colony's assembly tried to make all church salaries uniform at £80 a year. But this figure had to be translated into set amounts of tobacco, which served as a substitute for money in early Virginia. When the market value of tobacco fell, so did the real worth of the ministers' salaries. Because they were paid in tobacco, the ministers were in any case at the mercy of local variations in quality—and they were also dependent on the goodwill of the parish members, who selected the tobacco they were to receive.

This simple but fundamental economic problem had extremely important consequences for the clergy and indeed for religion in general. By English standards almost all of Virginia's ministers were grossly underpaid, and they had to work under what Englishmen considered next-to-impossible conditions. Further, they were stripped of economic independence because of their reliance on annual gifts of the parish. Nor were their jobs secure. In England the patrons who gave the parish churches income-producing land also nominated the ministers for lifetime appointments as rectors, and the bishops confirmed them in office. In Virginia the place of the patrons was taken by the vestries—self-perpetuating bodies that were made up of the leading members of the parish. The church officials in England instructed the vestries to present their nominees to the governor of Virginia, who in turn would formally appoint these candidates as ministers. But in most cases the vestries refused to nominate; only 10 percent of the Virginia clergy in the seventeenth century were ever formally appointed by the governor. The vestries gave as the reason for the scarcity of nominees the fact that available candidates were of such low quality that they did not deserve lifetime appointments.

Thus a vicious circle existed. The vestries named few candidates for permanent positions because they felt that the general quality of the clergy was too low to justify the confidence and respect implicit in a nomination. But the vestries' refusal to nominate for permanent positions was one reason why well-qualified candidates were reluctant to settle in Virginia. Although there had been many excellent young clergymen in Virginia in the colony's early years, there were very few by the end of the seventeenth century. Recruitment seemed to come from the bottom of the barrel. The problem of course was noticed by the English church authorities, who sent over missionaries in an effort to remedy matters. Later, missionary work was undertaken by the Society for the Propagation of the Gospel in Foreign Parts, which was founded in England in 1701. A series of proposals to improve conditions resulted, including one that led to the chartering of the College of William and Mary in 1693, to provide a means of educating Virginians locally for the ministry. But it was extremely difficult to improve the situation. By 1724 the reputation of the clergy in Virginia had fallen so low that the following almost farcical proposals were included in a broad plan of reform that was submitted to the bishop of London, who had jurisdiction over the church in the American colonies:

> And to prevent the scandals of bad life in the clergy, let it be enacted that whatsoever minister shall be found guilty of fornication, adultery, blasphemy, ridiculing of the Holy Scriptures, or maintaining . . . any doctrine contrary to the 39 Articles shall . . . lose his living [income] and be suspended from all exercise of the ministerial function for three years. . . . And because drunkeness is one of the most common crimes and yet hardest to be proved . . . let it be enacted that the following proof shall be taken for a sufficient proof of drunkeness, viz., first, let the signs of drunkeness be proved such as sitting an hour or longer in the company where they were a drinking strong drink and in the meantime drinking of healths or otherwise taking his cups as they came around like the rest of the company; striking, challenging, threatening to fight, or laying aside any of his garments far till that purpose; staggering, reeling, vomiting, incoherent, impertinent, obscene, or rude talking. Let the proof of these signs proceed so far till the judges conclude that the minister's behavior at such time was scandalous, indecent, and unbecoming the gravity of a minister.

The worsening quality of the clergy was one aspect of the general change taking place in the Church of England in Virginia. Another development, in the long run equally important, was the collapse of the church's hierarchical structure—that is, its chain of command, extending from the bishops down to the parish clergy—which was an essential aspect of the Church of England. This breakdown occurred because Virginia was so distant from the higher controls in England, and also because the vestries in Virginia had gained absolute power over the parishes. Officially the church in Virginia was part of the Church of England, which was governed by bishops and archbishops. But in practice the Virginia church was a congregational institution, with each parish responsible for its own affairs.

Furthermore, the practice of religion in Virginia was greatly simplified, even secularized to some extent. Because few ministers could reach all areas of their large parishes, ordinary church members, called lay readers, were appointed to fulfill certain ministerial duties. The general simplicity of life and the lack of funds meant that the church sacraments were administered without what the Church of England regarded as the proper ritual, minister's robes, and communion vessels. The dead were buried in private cemeteries more often than in parish burial grounds. Holy days were neglected, and marriages were performed in private residences without the participation of ministers.

Finally, the church in Virginia came to play a far less significant role as the regulator of community morals than did the Anglican church in England, which

WATERSTONE'S
BOOKSELLERS

DUBLIN

7 DAWSON STREET

DUBLIN 2

TEL: 010 353 16 791260

CORK

69 PATRICK STREET

CORK

TEL: 010 353 21 276522

BOOLE LIBRARY BASEMENT

UNIVERSITY COLLEGE

CORK

TEL: 010 353 21 276575

BELFAST

QUEEN'S BUILDING

8 ROYAL AVENUE

BELFAST BT1 1DA

TEL: 0232 247 355

maintained a system of church courts. In Virginia the same people were often members of the vestry and the local civil court. In view of the weakness of the church, it seemed more reasonable for persons who were accused of moral offenses to be brought before the civil courts than before church courts. Vital statistics—the records of births, baptisms, marriages, and deaths—likewise came to be kept by the civil courts rather than by the weak parish organizations.

No one, of course, doubted that the Church of England had been established in Virginia, but it was a strange establishment indeed. Conditions had led the church as an institution toward what might be called nonseparating Congregationalism—the position adopted in New England—not as a matter of doctrine, but as a matter of social and institutional fact.

Toleration in Catholic Maryland Geographical, social, and economic conditions were similar in Maryland and Virginia, and Maryland's religious institutions would have been similar to Virginia's except for two basic facts. First, the government of Maryland was controlled by a Catholic proprietor who wanted the colony to be a place of refuge for English Catholics. Second, the colony would be successful only if it attracted an adequate number of settlers, but the great majority of the potential settlers of Maryland were Protestants. Thus the proprietor had to treat religious matters very carefully.

At first the proprietary family, the Calverts, gave the colony's governors instructions that they thought would satisfy both the Catholic and the Protestant settlers. They ordered government officials to give no offense to Protestants because of their religion. Catholicism was to be practiced as privately as possible, and all Christians were to be allowed to worship in any form they wished. But this vague, pragmatic liberalism satisfied neither side. The Jesuit priests who had accompanied Maryland's first Catholic settlers demanded that the colony be much more openly Catholic, and Protestant Marylanders rebelled against the colony's Catholic proprietor during the early years of the English Civil War of the 1640s. To stabilize the situation in the face of these conflicting pressures—as well as to protect Maryland's status as a chartered colony—in 1649 the Calverts issued their famous Act Concerning Religion.

Although this document was remarkably liberal for the seventeenth century, it did not provide for full religious freedom. In fact it began by ordering the death penalty for nontrinitarian Christians (those who denied that God was a Trinity of Father, Son, and Holy Spirit) who insisted on professing their religion in Maryland. But the Act Concerning Religion went on to say that in order to ensure public tranquility—and for that reason only—all Christians who accepted the Trinity were guaranteed the right to profess and practice their religion freely.

This document remained in effect for the rest of the seventeenth century. It offered no challenge to what most people of the era thought to be correct Christian doctrine. It contained no hint of the principle of the separation of church and state, or of freedom of conscience and worship as good in themselves—no hint of the soaring ideals of liberty of thought and conscience that would later inspire Thomas Jefferson's great Act for Establishing Religious Freedom. The Calverts' act kept toleration as narrow as possible. It offered religious freedom only to those groups that it was necessary to tolerate: Catholics, Anglicans, and moderate Protestant dissenters. Yet, although it was quite limited and pragmatic, the act represented a significant advance over the policies that were typically followed by European governments of the time. It also fitted in well with the decentralized kind of church organization that was developing in Maryland. For just as in Virginia, in Maryland the churches had to be supported by taxes—and so they came under the full control of local authorities, generally the vestries. This local control, as well as the official toleration of Catholics and of moderate Protestants, meant that a multidenominational Christianity was emerging in Maryland, whose form was essentially congregational.

The Dutch Church in New York   A decentralized church system emerged in an even more extreme form in New York—or, as the Dutch called it, New Netherland. Here the original Dutch settlers assumed that the national church of the Netherlands, officially known as the Dutch Reformed Calvinist church, would be re-created in America and would be supervised by the church's ruling body in Amsterdam. But their expectations were not fulfilled. From the colony's earliest years its religious life was quite complex, and there were no effective controls from the home country. The policy of the Dutch West India Company, which controlled New Netherland, was to permit private worship of any kind, as long as the Dutch Reformed church was officially recognized and was supported by taxes paid by all the colony's residents. Besides Dutch Calvinists, Jews, and the members of many radical sects, New Netherland's population included Lutherans, who insisted on the right to public worship. The Lutherans' demands led to their severe persecution by the colony's governor, Peter Stuyvesant. But the challenge they raised continued to generate fierce arguments until after the English conquered the Dutch colony. Then, in 1665, the qualified voters, called freeholders, of each community were ordered to choose a single Protestant denomination that would become the local established church. Once chosen, this church would be supported by general taxation, although members of other faiths could worship privately.

Under this "local option" plan adopted in 1665, the Dutch Reformed church remained dominant, of course, because most of the colonists were of Dutch background and sought to perpetuate their religious heritage and mode of worship. But in New York, as in Virginia and Maryland, settlements were widely scattered. It was extremely difficult to recruit qualified clergymen, and ministers found it impossible to keep in regular contact with all the members of their congregations. New York's solution was similar to Virginia's and Maryland's: ordinary members of the congregations presided when ministers could not be present to fulfill their duties. The outward quality of religious life declined drastically. Worse still, after they had conquered New York, the English regarded the Dutch Reformed church as a branch of an alien national church. How did this

American branch relate to the home church body in the Netherlands? If the Dutch settlers in New York fully acknowledged the supremacy of the Dutch Reformed church, they would in effect be challenging the supremacy of the English crown; if they did not make that challenge, they would not be entirely true to their own faith. This dilemma could not be resolved, but it might be endured if the issue was never pressed.

New England Puritanism   In view of these unexpected developments elsewhere in the colonies, the outward form of religion that was established in New England may not, perhaps, be considered unique. Everywhere in colonial America, the hierarchy of church organization had failed to take shape, ritual had become simplified, the church's role in dispensing the sacraments had been reduced, and members of the congregations shared the pulpits with ordained ministers. But in most colonies these adaptations had resulted in response to the conditions of life in America, not to doctrine or belief or intent. In New England, however, the same developments were based on religious doctrine and had been intended from the start.

The development of New England's decentralized church system was part of a general plan of religious reform that was pursued almost fanatically and fortified by a theological outlook that was constantly being refined by men of subtle mind and great intellectual energy. But Puritanism was not simply an intellectual system, and it did not satisfy the needs of theologians alone. It was a social movement as well as an intellectual movement, and in both New England and Old England it performed an important social function.

New England Puritanism was one specific offshoot of a broad movement in late-sixteenth-century England that challenged the religious conservatism of the Church of England under Elizabeth I. Those who eventually came to be known as Puritans felt that England's break with the Roman Catholic church in Henry VIII's time had not gone far enough. Puritan reformers and conservative Anglican churchmen did not disagree on central points of theology. Both sides believed in predestination—that is, the idea that human salvation depended not on an individual's efforts, but on the mysterious decisions of God alone. The differences between the Puritans and the conservatives of the Church of England concerned the nature and function of the church as an institution.

Debate over the nature of the church focused on how effective the church could be in assisting people in their search for salvation. The Anglican churchmen, like their Roman Catholic counterparts, believed that the church could help bridge the gap between the world of ordinary, physical humanity and that of people in a state of God's grace. The Church of England insisted that there was not an absolute difference between ordinary physical existence and true holiness, a difference bridgeable only by God's gift of spiritual rebirth. It maintained that qualified priests performing the church's rituals could assist in the great search for salvation. The Puritans disagreed. For them the gap between ordinary natural existence on the one hand, and holiness, or "grace," on the other, was absolute

First Parish Meeting House, Hingham, Mass., 1681
This famous building, whose exterior is largely the work of the eighteenth century, retains much of the original seventeenth-century interior. Lacking models for the spacious but austere building they had in mind, and spurning all architectural embellishments, the ship carpenters hired for the occasion simply built a ship's keel in reverse to form the interior roof.

and total. This gap could not be closed by human efforts of any kind, but only by God entering into direct contact with an open, willing soul—a contact, the Puritans believed, that could be facilitated through study of the Bible, which contained God's actual words. The Puritans considered the church's institutions and rituals to be mere outward "works" that interfered with the central experience of religion. For them the essence of religion was an individual's private, inner struggle for contact with a mysterious God.

Puritans and conservative Anglicans also differed over the question of whether the members of God's church were "visible"—that is, whether those Christians who had been saved could be identified in this life. Orthodox Anglicans felt that it was impossible to tell truly which persons God had saved. The church therefore existed for everyone, in the hope that it would help some achieve a better life and would be a natural home for those whom God had already chosen for salvation as his "elect." For Anglicans, therefore, the membership of the "visible" church (that is, the actual institutions of the church) should include the whole of society. People should be born into the church as a fact of life. The Puritans completely rejected this idea. They felt that it was possible—although difficult—to identify the elect by using various tests and signs. Therefore they believed that church membership could and should be limited to those who were saved: the church should be a "gathering of saints," a congregation of the visibly saved members. As far as possible the visible church should be the same as "God's church" of the elect. Thus not everyone in society should be a church member.

These key issues defined the protest movement of the late sixteenth century that in the broadest sense was Puritanism. But Puritanism in this broadest sense includes a wide range of positions on the question of the church's relation to society. The Puritans who controlled the Bay Colony in Massachusetts believed with the others that church membership should be limited to the elect, but they also thought that the church (even though it excluded many people in the community) should control society as a whole and should create conditions favorable to the search for salvation. They believed that the visibly saved church members—the "saints"—must somehow be active and controlling in the affairs of those who had not been saved.*

Puritans in England and New England alike discussed endlessly how such a program could be put into effect. But in early-seventeenth-century England the Congregational Puritans were wholly engaged simply in the struggle to survive in the face of the hostility of the Anglican church. In Massachusetts and Connecticut, however, they were protected by charters giving them self-government, as well as by distance from England, and they therefore had the opportunity to put into practice their view of how the church should be organized. Believing very strongly that the "visible church" must consist only of God's elect, they concen-

---

*Unlike the Pilgrims of Plymouth Colony, the Puritans who settled Massachusetts Bay Colony were not separatists and did not consider themselves *formally* withdrawn from the Church of England.

trated their attention on the process of becoming full church members. In England only deeply committed and utterly sincere people were willing to run the risks of belonging to the persecuted Congregationalist Puritan groups. In New England, however, the situation was completely different. Here the Congregationalist leaders held all the powers; they were the government, and the communities' available resources and power were at their disposal. Where the Congregational church was fully established and where social rewards were attached to membership in the church, entry into full church membership became an important issue for the society. Therefore the church leaders had to devise procedures that allowed everyone to apply for membership but that permitted only those persons to join who demonstrated their superior spirituality.

Candidates for membership in the New England churches were required to make a public "profession"—that is, to give an account before the entire congregation of how God had saved them, and in that way to justify their membership in the church. They were then publicly interrogated by ministers and experienced members of the congregation. Often this formal questioning was sophisticated and intense: the truthfulness of candidates' public statements could be challenged, and they had to respond to all challenges. If the "profession" and defense were successful, church membership was conferred through a formal ritual of acceptance.

Joining the church was thus no casual matter. Gaining entrance to the church was the central event in the religious life of the Puritan communities. The later history of the church in New England would be shaped by what happened to these procedures.*

Besides defining the process of joining the church, the other major problem that faced the New England Puritan community was that of justifying the rule of the "saints" to those people who were not church members. The *intellectual* justification of the rule of the elect was never in doubt. A central Puritan idea was the doctrine of the "covenant"—the agreement between God and the saved. According to this doctrine, the saved were obliged to do what they could to help those who were not saved to attain salvation—to expose ordinary people to the truth contained in the Bible, to remove obstacles to their salvation, and to urge them to seek salvation. But intellectual justifications for a minority's rule over a majority are never enough to maintain control over a society for any extended period of time. Yet there is every reason to believe that the mass of the settlers, most of whom were probably not church members, accepted—indeed, welcomed—the rule of the saints.†

---

*See chapter 5.

†We do not know exactly how many New Englanders reached full church membership during the first two generations after settlement. One historian estimates that 47 percent did, but this figure is probably too high. In any case the majority of New England's seventeenth-century population remained outside the church and thus under the rule of the saints.

To understand in psychological and sociological terms the reasons for the Puritans' success, it is necessary to know what kinds of people joined the Great Migration. The mass of the settlers were farmers and artisans who were drawn from two regions of England, East Anglia and the Southwest. These regions were the chief centers not only of English Puritanism but also of the seventeenth-century English cloth industry. They were hard hit by severe economic troubles in the 1620s and 1630s: great discontent and social unrest were created by crop failures and by an extended economic depression in the cloth industry. Under these troubled conditions, Puritanism gained many followers. Puritan teachings offered a convincing *moral* explanation of what was happening in the lives of the frightened, uprooted people of these two regions. The Puritans' social views were not modern—the Puritans were basically medieval in their suspicion of trade and moneymaking. They feared the effects of greed and urged individuals to put the welfare of the community above their own ambitions. It is true that the personality traits encouraged by Puritanism—diligence, accountability, self-denial, and the careful use of every God-given moment of time—eventually helped stimulate capitalism. But the seventeenth-century Puritans did not think that a competitive, capitalistic economy was ideal. They believed that diligence and self-denial should be directed toward the welfare of the entire group. Greed and self-satisfaction were not good things in themselves, and they should be strictly controlled.

The thousands of "unsaved" people who joined the Great Migration found in Puritanism not tyranny, but a source of the security. In England they had been uprooted and buffeted by economic distress and social change. They found in New England a society that officially restrained economic activity and explained the mysterious workings of the marketplace in familiar moral language. Moreover, ordinary people were glad to find in the close-knit New England village communities a system of group controls that would effectively eliminate the threat of arbitrary economic fluctuations. Thus New England promised—and in many ways created—the kind of security that was one of the chief goals of life of early-seventeenth-century Englishmen.

By the end of the seventeenth century, however, Puritanism was losing its power. The third generation of New Englanders, American natives who had been born to relative security, lost touch with the original aims of the Great Migration. But for two generations, Puritanism for many had been a comfort, not an affliction. Ordinary victims of social change had found it a source of security that was otherwise unattainable.

No more in religion than in social organization or economic life was this a world transformed. Changes were still in motion. Everywhere in New England's small but rapidly growing communities, there were instabilities, uncertainties, and transitions. The changing world of Puritan New England had not yet settled into permanent new forms.

SUGGESTED READINGS

There is no single comprehensive and detailed history of American society in the seventeenth century. The subject has only recently been conceived of in the terms discussed in this chapter, and the student must draw for details on a scattering of publications. This is especially true of the first topic discussed in this chapter: population. Recent writings on historical demography, especially for the seventeenth century, were in large part stimulated by innovative studies of the French and English populations of the same period. Their influence on early American history is summarized in Philip J. Greven, Jr., "Historical Demography and Colonial America," *Wm. and Mary Q.,* 24 (1967), 438–54. For a general overview of the migration process principally from England, see Bernard Bailyn, *The Peopling of British North America: An Introduction* (1986). Two books concentrate on the flow of indentured servants: Abbot E. Smith, *Colonists in Bondage* (1947), and David Galenson, *White Servitude in Colonial America* (1981). David H. Fischer, *Albion's Seed* (1989), is an effort to trace the persistence of English folkways in the North American colonies.

A summary of New England's extraordinary growth rate appears in Daniel S. Smith, "The Demographic History of Colonial New England," *Journal of Economic History,* 32 (1972), 165–83. Other important writings on population growth in the North are Philip J. Greven, Jr., *Four Generations . . . Andover, Massachusetts* (1970); John Demos, "Notes on Life in Plymouth Colony,"† *Wm. and Mary Q.,* 22 (1965), 264–86, and the same author's *A Little Commonwealth* (1970); and Herbert Moller's occasionally fanciful "Sex Composition and Correlated Culture Patterns of Colonial America," *Wm. and Mary Q.,* 2 (1945), 113–53. On migration to early New England, see Virginia D. Anderson, "Migrants and Motives," *New England Quarterly,* 58 (1985), 339–83; David Cressy, *Coming Over* (1987); and David G. Allen, *In English Ways* (1981). On the spread of population, see Lois K. Mathews, *The Expansion of New England* (1909), chaps. 2–3. See also, on a variety of themes, David D. Hall and David G. Allen, eds., *Seventeenth-Century New England* (1984).

There is a wealth of new and detailed writing on the population history of the seventeenth-century Chesapeake region, of which the most important are Edmund S. Morgan, *American Slavery American Freedom* (1975); Gloria L. Main, *Tobacco Colony* (1982); Paul G. E. Clemens, *The Atlantic Economy and Colonial Maryland's Eastern Shore* (1980); Darrett B. Rutman and Anita H. Rutman, *A Place in Time* (1984); and three excellent collections of essays: A. C. Land et al., eds., *Law, Society, and Politics in Early Maryland* (1977); T. W. Tate and D. L. Ammerman, eds., *The Chesapeake in the Seventeenth Century* (1979); and Lois G. Carr, et al., eds., *Colonial Chesapeake Society* (1988). Essays in J. M. Smith, ed., *Seventeenth-Century America* (1959), and Wesley F. Craven, *White, Red, and Black* (1971), are also useful. For a valuable summary of Maryland's population history, see Russell R. Menard, "Population, Economy and Society in Seventeenth-Century Maryland," *Maryland Historical Magazine,* 79 (1984), 71–92. On the complexity of New York's population: David S. Cohen, "How Dutch Were the Dutch in New Netherland?" and Oliver A. Rink, "The People of New Netherland . . . ," *New York History,* 62 (1981), 5–42, 42–60.

The economic history of early America in all its aspects is covered comprehensively in John J. McCusker and Russell R. Menard, *The Economy of British America, 1607–1789* (1985); the book is a master synthesis, which lists some 1,500 items in its bibliography.

Traditional ideals of social organization are depicted in E. M. W. Tillyard, *Elizabethan World Picture* (1943), and in Gordon J. Schochet, *Patriarchalism in Political Thought* (1975); the latter has an excellent chapter on the ideals and actuality of the family in seventeenth-century England, a subject discussed at length by Peter Laslett in *The World We Have Lost* (1965) and in

---

†See footnote on p. 32.

his introduction to *Household and Family in Past Time* (1972). Many of the new community-demographic studies cited above make clear the difficulty of maintaining traditional social forms in the wilderness setting. See Helena M. Wall, *Fierce Communion: Family and Community in Early America* (1990); Sumner C. Powell, *Puritan Village* (1963); and Edmund S. Morgan, *Puritan Family* (1944). Kenneth A. Lockridge, *New England Town: Dedham* ... (1970), locates the disarray at the end of the seventeenth century. On social mobility there are several important writings: William A. Reavis, "The Maryland Gentry and Social Mobility, 1637–1676," *Wm. and Mary Q.,* 14 (1957), 418–28; Russell R. Menard, "From Servant to Freeholder," ibid., 30 (1973), 37–64;† Linda A. Bissell, "From One Generation to Another," ibid., 31 (1974), 79–110; and Menard et al., "Opportunity and Inequality," *Maryland Historical Magazine,* 69 (1974), 169–84. The political consequences of social mobility and conflict are depicted in Bernard Bailyn, "Politics and Social Structure in Virginia,"† in James M. Smith, ed., *Seventeenth-Century America* (1959). On the role of women in seventeenth-century America, see Mary Beth Norton, "The Evolution of White Women's Experience in Early America," *American Historical Review,* 89 (1984), 593–619; Laurel T. Ulrich, *Good Wives* (1982); and Roger Thompson, *Women in Stuart England and America* (1974). On children and childhood, see Linda A. Pollock, *Forgotten Children . . . 1500 to 1900* (1983). Philip Greven has sketched the history of child rearing in early America in terms of shifting patterns of family life, religious experience, and self-identity in *The Protestant Temperament* (1977).

On religion, Sydney E. Ahlstrom, *Religious History of the American People* (1972), surveys generally the European background as well as the transplantation of European institutions, ideas, and beliefs to the North American continent. For a thoughtful overall interpretation, see Sidney E. Mead, *The Lively Experiment* (1963). For the seventeenth century, the subject has been dominated by the prolific scholarship on Puritanism. The master scholar in that subject has been Perry Miller. His two-volume *New England Mind* (*The Seventeenth Century,* 1939; *From Colony to Province,* 1953); his essays, collected in *Errand into the Wilderness* (1956) and *Nature's Nation* (1967); and his and Thomas H. Johnson's anthology of sources, *The Puritans* (1938), have made New England Puritanism one of the most absorbing subjects of modern historiography. Miller's books set in motion a flood of writing on Puritanism, which is surveyed in Michael McGiffert, "American Puritan Studies in the 1960s," *Wm. and Mary Q.,* 27 (1970), 36–67. For new approaches to Puritanism, see Charles E. Hambrick-Stowe, *The Practice of Piety* (1982), which emphasizes devotional practice; Philip E. Gura, *A Glimpse of Sion's Glory* (1984), which argues that Puritan orthodoxy was a product of pressures exerted by a variety of radical sects that too were "Puritan"; David D. Hall, *Worlds of Wonder, Days of Judgment* (1989), which shows the persistent influence of popular superstitions and magical beliefs and practices; and Andrew Delbanco, *The Puritan Ordeal* (1989), which stresses attitudes and feelings as well as ideas and the transforming effect of migration and resettlement. Sacvan Bercovitch, *The Puritan Origins of the American Self* (1975), shows the enduring impact of Puritan ideals on American self-imagery and culture.

No other religious community of the seventeenth century has received even remotely comparable study. On Anglicanism, see George M. Brydon, *Virginia's Mother Church* (1947); Elizabeth H. Davidson, *Establishment of the English Church in the Continental American Colonies* (1936); and Parke Rouse, Jr., *James Blair of Virginia* (1971). On the Catholics, see John T. Ellis, *Catholics in Colonial America* (1965); on the Dutch Reformed, Frederick J. Zwierlein, *Religion in New Netherland* (1910); and on the Baptists, William G. McLaughlin, *New England Dissent, 1630–1833* (2 vols., 1971).

---

†See footnote on p. 32.

4

Elements of Change

1660–1720

$\mathcal{T}$HUS the founding of British North America is the story of the efforts of private groups and individuals to profit in some way from the exploitation of the North American continent. The leading organizers of settlement had various motives. For some the predominant goals were economic; for others they were religious. For most, however, religious, economic, and patriotic interests were combined, stimulated by discontent at home, the lure of adventure, and the hope of improved fortunes. The scattering of privately organized settlements in British North America, some of them protected in their independence by royal charters, had developed without any overall plan or general organization. By 1660 there was little sense on either side of the Atlantic that these settlements together formed an effective empire.

In the two generations that followed the restoration of the Stuarts to the throne of England (1660), there were determined efforts to draw these scattered colonial settlements into an overall governmental organization, to impose regulation and control of some sort over this miscellaneous collection of towns, villages, and farms. The way this was done, and the way in which these efforts at regulation interacted with the natural growth and maturing of the European communities in America, permanently affected the character of American life.

Empire

Three interest groups, dominant at the Restoration court of Charles II (1660–85), account for the extension of the authority of the English government to America. The first of these was the courtiers, the most active of them the proprietors of the new colony of Carolina, who had helped restore Charles II to the English throne and remained his key advisers. Their stake in America deepened as the possibilities of profiting from the settlements became more realistic. And to advance their interests in the colonies, most of these courtiers were willing to help create and serve in an appropriate administrative system.

A second and ultimately more influential group was that of the merchants and their allies in the English government who marketed American products and sold manufactured goods to the colonists. These merchants knew that an important part of the British economy would in time be involved in the colonies. Therefore, they became the leaders in the growing movement to assert greater English control over the American settlements, for the sake of trade and England's economic prosperity.

A third influential pressure group was the royal family itself—particularly Charles's brother James, the duke of York, and his personal following. James became proprietor of New York when it was seized from the Dutch in 1664. An expert in naval affairs and an unusually forceful administrator, James made it clear soon after the Stuart restoration that he would be a leading figure in designing an empire out of the scattered American settlements.

It was the combination of these three groups—courtiers, merchants, and the royal family, particularly James—all with stakes in the colonies, that accounts for the creation of the British Empire at the end of the seventeenth century. Their goals were not identical, and there was no coordinated planning, but their interests converged in efforts at three levels.

Administration   Together they created, through a fumbling, pragmatic process of evolution, a network of administrative controls. Immediately after the Restoration, the Privy Council began appointing committees of its own members, and occasionally of outside experts, to deal with colonial problems as they arose. Soon, in 1675, enough important business came before these committees that a permanent committee of the Privy Council, called the Lords of Trade, was appointed. This committee met irregularly and had an inadequate staff, but it served as a forerunner of the better-organized permanent supervisory body, the Board of Trade and Plantations, which was created in 1696.

The Board of Trade was an independent agency of eight high state officials and eight paid members. It remained the central pivot of the British imperial administration throughout the eighteenth century. But it had notable weaknesses. First, the range of its activities was unrealistically broad. Besides colonial matters, it was expected to supervise all the trade of Great Britain, the British fishing industry, and the care of the poor throughout Britain. In dealing with the colonies it was given special responsibility for reviewing all royal appointments in America and all laws that the colonists enacted for themselves. Yet despite these broad responsibilities, the board's actual power proved to be severely limited. Other, better-established branches of the British government took over control of some aspects of colonial affairs, and the board's power failed to mature.

The greatest conflict lay between the Board of Trade and the secretary of state for the Southern Department. This secretary of state was one of the chief executive officers of the government, with particular responsibility for international relations. Although this responsibility included the affairs of the Western Hemisphere, the secretary of state's main attention was focused on Europe— especially on the powerful court of Louis XIV of France. Nevertheless by 1704 the secretary of state for the Southern Department successfully challenged the Board of Trade for executive authority over the colonies. As a result, a fundamental weakness arose at the heart of the British overseas administration. The Board of Trade remained an information-gathering body, in charge of the flow of information between the colonies and the mother country, but it had no power to enforce regulations, make appointments, or otherwise control events. It could advise, counsel, and admonish; but orders came from the secretary of state's office, which might or might not be acting on the basis of the Board of Trade's stores of information. Moreover, the secretary of state tended to view colonial affairs from the standpoint not of trade, but of western European diplomacy.

Administrative confusion did not stop there. Almost every major branch of the British government discovered that it had an interest in the colonies, and managed to assert control over some sphere. The Treasury took over the colonial customs administration. The Admiralty successfully claimed jurisdiction over the North American sources of timber and other products vital to the British navy. It also patrolled the coastal waters to enforce the growing body of commercial regulations. The War Office took charge of army operations on the North American mainland during the many years when European international conflicts spilled over to the colonial territories. The army's contracting, like that of the navy, powerfully influenced the economic development of the colonies, and British strategic planning involved American manpower as well. Weaving through all of these ill-assorted jurisdictions was the legitimate authority of such important British officials as the attorney general, the solicitor general, and the various auditors and collectors of royal revenues.

By the early eighteenth century an imperial administration had taken shape in the British world. But it was very different in structure from that of the Spanish-American empire. There was no British equivalent of Spain's Council of the Indies—a central authority that combined information gathering and executive authority and drew together all other governmental agencies that had an interest in colonial matters. British imperial administration was a maze of conflicting offices, with overlaps in jurisdiction and significant gaps in authority. As a result, there was a minimum of effective central control.

Yet this administrative inefficiency was not disastrous for Britain. The British Empire did not need tight administrative control before 1760. The colonies could largely be left alone, as long as certain minimal expectations were met, mostly centering on the regulation of commerce.

Mercantilism and Trade Regulation   Britain's was a mercantilist empire. It arose as an extension of England's commercial growth. Its basic principles of economic organization were derived from mercantilism, a name modern historians have given to the age-old doctrine that the state must regulate economic activity for the public welfare. In seventeenth-century Europe most governments accepted mercantilist ideas, and the continent was torn by intense commercial rivalries among the great powers.

The mercantilists who designed the economic policy of the British Empire made two basic assumptions. First, they believed that the world consisted of competing nation-states. Second, they assumed that there was a fixed amount of wealth available in the world economy. Mercantilists therefore advocated the regulation of commerce by the government in order to make the state economically self-sufficient and, by maintaining a favorable balance of trade, to avoid becoming dependent on rival nations. Colonies were of fundamental importance in this competition among nations. English mercantilists pointed out that if Britain did not obtain necessary products from its own colonies, it would have to buy them from other nations; and thus its wealth would be drained off by rival states. Therefore every effort had to be made to direct the flow of valuable colonial products to Britain alone. Further, Britain had to monopolize the sale of manufactured goods to the colonies, for every purchase of goods from a rival state meant some small drain on the nation's wealth.

To put these ideas into effect, Parliament passed the famous navigation acts in the years after the Restoration. Under the first of these acts, which was passed in 1660, only British subjects could ship and market colonial goods. It was decreed that England alone would enjoy the profits of shipping colonial goods and of reexporting them to other nations. Further, a special list was prepared of "enumerated" commodities—those that the colonies could ship only to England or to British colonial ports. The basic list included all the goods that England would otherwise have had to buy from competing imperial powers, principally France, Spain, and the Netherlands: sugar, tobacco, cotton, indigo, ginger, certain dyes, and special wood products. Later other commodities were added to the original list: rice and molasses in 1704, naval stores in 1705 and 1729, and copper and furs in 1721.

The act of 1660 was the basic law governing colonial trade. Two other acts completed the pattern of mercantilist regulation. First, the so-called Staple Act of 1663 gave England a monopoly of the sale of European manufactured goods to the American colonies. European goods, the law stated, could not be shipped directly to America from Europe, even if the ships that carried them were British. These goods would first have to be sent to England and unloaded there, and then could be reshipped to the colonies. Under this law the English Treasury would collect valuable customs duties, and at the same time foreign merchants would be put at a disadvantage. Certain exceptions were made. Salt was exempted because it was necessary for the American fishing industry. Servants, horses, and provisions from Scotland and Ireland, as well as wines from the Portuguese islands of Madeira and the Azores, were all exempted because they involved no competition with English production. Finally, the third act, a supplementary law of 1673, tried to plug the gaps that had been created by the wording of the earlier legislation. This quite technical law caused endless confusion.

Thus, out of the converging interests of courtiers, merchants, and the royal family had come the foundations of an imperial system. This system operated at three levels: as an administrative apparatus, as a doctrine (mercantilism), and as a set of commercial regulations. By 1700 the British Empire was of world importance, but it was ineffectively governed by a poorly coordinated jumble of agencies. Colonial rule was also limited by the theory of mercantilism, which demanded not the direct governing of the colonies in depth, but only the regulation of their external trade. Finally, colonial rule was limited by the complexity of British commercial laws and by the great difficulty of enforcing these laws 3,000 miles from home. By the early eighteenth century no one could doubt that the American colonies were part of an empire. But neither could anyone think of the poorly managed, superficial colonial administration as a centralized empire. The passion for territorial rule was not there, nor the drive of royal ambition.

James II and the Dominion of New England   The limits of the British imperial system become particularly clear when one considers the efforts that were undertaken in the late seventeenth century to make the British Empire in mainland North America more powerful than it was—more effective than it ever in fact became. For there was one person at the center of the English government who *did* have ambitions similar to those of the continental European monarchs and who also had the instincts of an able administrator and a group of close followers capable of managing an efficient system of government.

This man was the duke of York, who eventually became James II (1685–88). His urge to expand and deepen the controls of empire can be traced back to his childhood training as a military leader at the court of the powerful king of France, and to his desire, during the Stuarts' exile between 1649 and 1660, to exercise the power that had been denied him. He finally got his chance to exert authority when his brother, Charles II, returned to the throne. As lord high admiral with a loyal following of war-seasoned officers, James took command of military garrisons all over England and put those power-hungry veterans in charge of them. For him the colonial world was only an extension of England, another place where he could reward his followers. Soon these men turned up as governors and other high officials in the Caribbean and North American governments. James's base on the mainland of North America was New York, which he ruled as proprietor from the time it was captured from the Dutch. Slowly he expanded this center into a larger imperial dominion. His efforts coincided with the more general efforts that the English government was undertaking in the late seventeenth and early eighteenth centuries to cut back on the powers of the private jurisdictions that had been created in the early years of colonization.

Progress toward the goal of restricting the chartered colonies' authority was slow, erratic, and in the end incomplete. Virginia had become a crown colony when the Virginia Company failed in 1624; New York became a crown colony when its proprietor, James II, acceded to the throne of England in 1685. In 1680 New Hampshire was separated from Massachusetts with little difficulty and was given a royal governor. But in the other colonies the charters created serious problems, and they had to be attacked directly. Between 1684 and 1691 the crown confiscated the charters of Massachusetts, Connecticut, Rhode Island, New Jersey, Pennsylvania, Maryland, and Carolina. The king's grand but ill-fated plans began to unfold during these early years of his campaign against the chartered colonies.

James II's ultimate ambition seems to have been to create two centralized viceroyalties in America that would be ruled by crown-appointed governors and councils. Apparently the boundary between the two viceroyalties was to have been drawn along an east–west line just north of Philadelphia—the division between the grants that had been given to the two Virginia companies at the beginning of the seventeenth century. During his short and tumultuous reign James focused his attention on the northern section, which became known as the Dominion of New England.

In a legal sense the Dominion came together easily after 1685. To the core colony of New York were added New Hampshire, Massachusetts, Connecticut, Rhode Island, and New Jersey as each of these colonies' charters was annulled or suspended. James sent over Edmund Andros, one of his closest allies and a former military associate, to rule the Dominion. Andros had already served James well in several other positions, particularly as governor of New York from 1674 to 1681. To assist Andros at his headquarters in Boston, James appointed a royal council, on which the majority of seats were held by merchants who had recently arrived in America and who had been struggling with little effect against the Puritan establishment. Together, Andros and the new royal council moved to create a centralized system of government similar to that of the Spanish in Latin America.

To the horror of the Puritans throughout New England, Andros declared toleration for all religious groups and confiscated Boston's Old South Church for use by the Church of England in conducting its services. Equally offensive to the colonists was his disregard of the customary principles of English self-government. By mere executive declaration he continued collecting taxes that had originally been levied by the colony's representative General Court. The colonists were even more outraged by his land policy. He commanded that all town lands be regranted in the king's name, and that holders of these grants pay annual taxes ("quitrents") to the crown; also, the towns' undistributed lands (which were held in common by all town members) were to come under the council's control. And to complete the destruction of the local authorities' powers, he ordered the town meetings to limit themselves to electing officials who would help collect taxes.

Andros's efforts never extended beyond Massachusetts; in fact, they scarcely reached beyond Boston and the coastal towns. But their implications were widely known, and they stimulated ferocious opposition. In the town of Ipswich his tax policy provoked an open rebellion, led by the outspoken Reverend John Wise, who was imprisoned along with four of his followers. Resistance grew among the Puritan leaders and the landholders throughout New England.

William III and Mary
The accession of William and Mary marked the beginning of the modern liberal state in Britain, but the benefits of the Glorious Revolution did not extend automatically to the colonies.

Meanwhile, in England, James II's high-handed policies led to his downfall. In the Glorious Revolution of 1688–89, Parliament overthrew James and recognized as his successors the Dutchman, William III, and his wife Mary, James II's daughter. Andros's royal regime in Boston had become so universally hated and so isolated that a rebellion against it in April 1689 succeeded almost without a struggle. Andros and his closest allies were imprisoned.

All of James's colonial plans disappeared with his fall from power. English imperial ambitions had reached their high tide and had receded. The more permanent forms of Anglo-American relations emerged as the colonial charters were restored, although with qualifications. There was a return to the limited and superficial empire that had existed before 1685, modified by the reduction of chartered privileges in several colonies. East and West Jersey were reunited into the single royal colony of New Jersey in 1702. In Carolina a popular rebellion against the proprietors in 1719 and constant pressure against them in England led in 1729 to the formal separation of North and South Carolina into two royal colonies.* The charters of Pennsylvania and Maryland were restored to the Penn and Calvert families; but in both cases the selection of the governor had to be approved by the crown, and all legislation was subject to review by the crown's legal officers.

---

*One aspect of the Carolinas' proprietary origins remained: the diplomat and politician, the Earl Granville, heir of Sir George Carteret, one of the original eight proprietors, retained his ancestor's shares. When it was consolidated in 1745, his inheritance, the so-called Granville District, gave him title to the undistributed land of fully half of North Carolina, on which lived perhaps two-thirds of the colony's population.

The British-American Empire

In its decentralization and inefficiency Britain's empire was far different from Spain's; but it was still a visible, extensive empire. By the early eighteenth century its visibility appeared most dramatically to Americans not so much in law enforcement or in new institutions as in the increasing number of officials sent to America to manage the new system. In most port towns there were customs collectors, appointed by the Treasury, who brought with them small teams of assistants. There were auditors and surveyors of the king's revenues. And there were officers of the vice-admiralty courts that had been created in 1696 as subordinate agencies of the admiralty court system that in Britain held jurisdiction over maritime law. The judges and clerks of these "prerogative" courts (operating without juries and under rules different from those of the common-law courts) were part of an imperial presence. So too—although indirectly, and for the limited purpose of enforcing the navigation laws—were the governors and lieutenant governors of all the royal colonies.

The importance of these officials, most of whom were newcomers to America at the end of the seventeenth century, cannot be exaggerated. They represented—indeed, they embodied—the empire. The way they approached their work, the attitudes they brought to Anglo-American relations, and the manner in which they related to the local communities became matters of importance in the lives of the American people. They affected not only the day-to-day workings of government, but also the popular image of government and of political authority more generally.

These officials were not efficient imperial bureaucrats, and they were seldom committed to promoting the strength of the empire. The positions they held were minor parts of the patronage system of the English government. Hence these offices were seen as a kind of private property that political leaders doled out to their deserving followers. Appointees were expected to profit by their positions through the fees, gifts, and various benefits they received, as well as through their salaries. Appointments were made almost randomly with respect to administrative ability or interest in public affairs. What counted were political connections and the applicants' capacity to force their patrons to reward loyalty and previous service.

At times the appointments, even those at the highest levels, were bizarre. The governor of New York from 1701 to 1708 was Lord Cornbury, a destitute member of the powerful Clarendon family, whose behavior was so strange that the local political opposition could successfully lampoon him as a greedy transvestite who traipsed around in women's clothes. The governor of Virginia from 1705 to 1737 was the earl of Orkney, who never had the slightest intention of setting foot in America, and never did. He had been a war companion of King William III and was the leading infantry commander of the duke of Marlborough. Orkney's appointment was also a reward for somewhat less heroic service: he had made what may have been a supreme sacrifice by marrying William III's mistress, Elizabeth Villiers.

Orkney's career as the absentee governor of Virginia is revealing in many ways. The official salary of the position was £2,000 a year. Orkney in effect sold the office for £1,200 to a series of lieutenant governors who served in his place, with the understanding that they were entitled to make as much out of the job as they could. As it happened, Orkney selected some able men. In 1706 he appointed Robert Hunter—who, because of accidents at sea and his wife's connections, ended up as the governor not of Virginia, but of New York, a post he filled with distinction. Alexander Spotswood, appointed in 1709, and William Gooch, appointed in 1727, were also capable officials. These three men had in common only the fact that they all had fought as army officers under Orkney and Marlborough. No fewer than nine veterans of Marlborough's famous victory in the battle of Blenheim (1704) received colonial governorships for their services.

Under these conditions it is hardly surprising that colonial offices were occasionally filled by avaricious incompetents or by psychological cripples like Sir Danvers Osborn, who hanged himself in a fit of melancholy a week after his arrival in New York to serve as that colony's governor. Nor is it surprising that lesser posts were frequently held by altogether unqualified hacks. What is remarkable is that some appointees were in fact conscientious and honest, and dutifully sought to serve the interests of the empire and of the local population.

Still, it is the randomness of these appointments and the disregard of the incumbents' ability and experience, and hence the arbitrariness of the system, that had the deepest effect on American life. The long-term consequences were profound.

First, these appointments to offices in the colonies served to increase the existing superficiality of the British imperial system. Officeholders, always inse-cure in tenure, realized that the same arbitrary movements of the patronage system that had put them in office could easily remove them. Sooner or later, they knew, they would be replaced by men who were closer to the levers of power, although not necessarily more qualified. Consequently, incumbents were open to compromises and vulnerable to local pressures. If the situation required speed in making a profit from office, they would be quick about it—at the expense of the strict execution of their duties if need be.

Further, as it emerged in these formative years, British officialdom gave Americans the sense that government was far from being a seamless web that united high and low through a series of responsible links. Instead, they learned to see it as a structure that was essentially composed of two antagonistic levels: local, internal government that expressed the dominant interests of the local com-munity; and a superior, external authority that was by nature hostile to local interests. Often the external power became identified with executive authority, and the local and benevolent authority with legislative power. This sharp distinc-tion between the functions of government was extraordinary for the time, and it was destined to have a continuing importance in American history.

An even more general consequence of the character and behavior of British officialdom was the growth among politically active Americans of a kind of anti-authoritarian cynicism about all government. These officeholders represented a nation that was revered by most colonists; but in themselves these officers were often incompetent, poor, and arrogant, a bad enough combination made worse by their easy corruptibility. Americans could only wonder whether the government these officials represented deserved automatic obedience.

Beyond all of this lay the sense, as the imperial officialdom developed, that the social and political worlds were far from unified—that there was a gap between social and political leadership at the highest level. The native-born social leaders of the colonies did not represent the state. In fact, when local leaders competed with outsiders for high office in their own colonies, they competed on unequal terms, and their failures were embittering. Thus William Byrd II, a second-generation American who spent fifteen years being educated and making contacts in England before taking over the family property in Virginia, failed in his bid to buy the lieutenant governorship of his native colony from Orkney. Byrd spent years struggling with his successful rival, Spotswood, who had no original stake in the colony and no knowledge of it when he arrived on the scene. Byrd finally acquired a seat on the colony's council, but only after years of diligent effort.

These consequences of the growth of officialdom were especially important because they coincided with the natural emergence of local elites in the mainland colonies. The dominance of these local leaders within the maturing American communities could not be doubted, and their demands for recognition—in politics as well as in other spheres of life—could not easily be ignored.

Anglo-American Aristocracy

The rise of a provincial aristocracy toward the end of the seventeenth century and in the early eighteenth century was the result of the exploitation, by skillful, energetic, and ambitious men, of opportunities that suddenly became available. These opportunities were created by basic developments in social and economic life.

Land as the Basis of Aristocracy In the colonies as in England, the ownership or control of land was the material basis for most social distinctions. In the thirty years that bridged the end of the seventeenth century, 1690–1720, there was a significant shift in this basic relationship in the American colonies. Between these two dates the land area under active cultivation remained approximately the same because of Indian wars and the difficulty of overcoming natural barriers in the way of westward expansion. But during these same years the population more than doubled, rising from approximately 210,000 to 460,000. Land was still far easier to acquire in the colonies than it was in England; but the increasing population pressure created significant changes in social relations and in itself accounts for the rise of new social elites.

In New England the emergence of a landowning aristocracy in the long-settled towns was marked by dramatic conflicts almost everywhere. In its original form the New England town had been a kind of democracy of male heads of households, all of whom were full church members, voting members (freemen) in the town meeting, and landowners with shares in the undivided land. As time passed, migration among towns grew and immigration into the colonies continued. Questions arose as to how newcomers would share in these original privileges. Certain answers came quickly. Access to membership in the church was controlled by a procedure that was calculated to make the entry of newcomers possible but still highly selective. Access to participation in the town meeting was less easily determined, but in the end the meeting was opened to all respectable male inhabitants. There was no easy way, however, to resolve the question of control of the undivided land. The heirs of the original grantees had no desire to share their inheritances with newcomers, and they closed ranks against the claimants.

Without originally intending to do so, these second- and third-generation colonists began to form exclusive groups of landholders. Challenged in the town meeting by those who were excluded from sharing in the common land, they drew apart and met separately, only to have their rights to the undivided land challenged at law. In certain towns they sought compromises by allocating plots of land to the more prominent opponents or to those with special claims. Most often, confrontation could not be avoided. The challenges were decided by the General Court, which, after a period of uncertainty, favored the heirs of the original grantees.

As a result, the fortunate heirs not only continued to enjoy the increasingly valuable property, but also shared control of the still undivided common land. With this inherited capital, they were in the best possible position to build fortunes out of real estate. Those who were shrewd or enterprising enough to take full advantage of the available opportunities broadened their operations from small local transactions to large-scale land speculation. Some moved into trade after making money at commercial farming; the more industrious engaged in both commerce and farming. The most successful landowners in Connecticut became known as River Gods because of their valuable property along the colony's main waterway, the Connecticut River. Everywhere in New England, land claims proved to be a rich source of money, prestige, and power.

The same was true in the South. But there, as tobacco cultivation spread westward, profits from the land were intimately bound up with the problem of labor, and that increasingly meant slavery. It was in the later seventeenth century that slavery first emerged as a critical problem in southern society. Its spread, and the growth of the black population, created a great revolution in social relations as well as in the economy. Not only did slavery introduce a major element into the American population; it also became a basic source of social stratification among the whites. The logic of this development quickly became clear.

Profits from tobacco production were small and at times nonexistent. Therefore it seemed increasingly important to plant extensively. Land was available for

Indigo Culture in South Carolina
The plants of the blue dyestuff are being carried to fermenting vats, and the resulting liquid flows down the sluice at left into containers.

expansion, but labor was not. The immigration of white indentured servants from England declined sharply after 1660 because of a slowing of England's population growth and an improved English labor market, especially in the London area. Slaves alone, it seemed, provided an answer to the labor problem. And slaves were increasingly available as the British slave trade entered a period of expansion and increasing efficiency.

Slaves in the long run were cheap. Their upkeep, averaged over a lifetime of labor, was perhaps £1 per year, as opposed to an indentured servant's annual maintenance cost of £2–£4. But if slaves were cheaper in the long run, they were more costly in the short run because they required a higher initial investment. And costs were rising constantly. Average slave prices doubled between 1660 and 1750, and by the time of the American Revolution they tripled. In 1700 a newly imported "prime field hand" cost £20 in Virginia; in 1750, £30. Nevertheless, the number of slaves continued to rise as their importance in the expanding tobacco culture became clearly understood. An estimated 20,000 slaves were brought to British North America in the two decades after 1700; 50,000 arrived in the subsequent two decades. In 1715 blacks formed a quarter of Virginia's total population; by the 1730s, 40 percent. In South Carolina blacks outnumbered whites by 1708; by 1720 the ratio was almost two to one, and the black population was growing at a faster rate than the white.

The growth of the slave labor force, which made possible a significant increase in tobacco cultivation and eventually in rice and indigo production, created a deepening social distinction within the white population. Profits depended on the extent of cultivation, and that in turn depended on slave labor, which required high capital outlays. The white population became sharply divided into those who had capital available or could acquire it, and those who did not. Those with greater assets formed a new class of "great planters" in a society that as late as 1700 consisted almost entirely of small and medium-sized farm operations. For example, in Lancaster County in northern Virginia in 1716, a majority of taxpayers owned slaves, but few had more than 2 or 3; only four owned more than 20; one, however—Robert Carter—had 126. Carter was a landowner and above all a land agent and speculator, the son of a settler who in 1649 had brought capital with him and had accumulated the land claims of no less than five wives. At his death in 1732, Carter was said to possess 300,000 acres of land and £10,000 in cash. In a world of steeply rising land values, capital and inherited land claims determined who would succeed and who would not. Those who succeeded would live like princes on the land—bourgeois, enterprising princes, to be sure, desperately concerned with markets, prices, and the humblest details of farming, but princes nevertheless.

Trade as the Basis of Aristocracy

In the main commercial centers the merchant community as a whole remained open—free of the formal limitations of guilds and of other artificial barriers to entrance. Nevertheless, significant differences within the merchant group appeared toward the end of the seventeenth century and increasingly in the early eighteenth century. A merchant aristocracy of sorts began to appear.

As the commercial system settled into a complex pattern of oceanic routes covering the North Atlantic basin, certain portions of the network, especially the direct trade from England to America, proved crucial and dominated the others. It became more and more difficult to enter the trade of these primary routes, and the colonial merchants who controlled them developed into powerful figures. As imports from England increased, and as the handling of ever-larger quantities of colonial products made greater demands on colonial entrepreneurs, the English specialists in North American trade began to concentrate their shipments to a few ports and to a relatively few merchants. They sought commercial correspondents in America who could be relied on to send payments quickly, either in good bills of exchange or in salable commodities. The American merchants who became involved in these primary circuits of trade, through which flowed the all-important "dry goods" (primarily iron products and textiles), had a growing advantage over competitors. The main profits of the commercial system tended to go to these major importers, while the smaller merchants, confined to local, secondary routes, fell more and more clearly into subordinate roles.

Thus a merchant aristocracy of sorts developed in the large port towns. Its members were the dominant entrepreneurs who had gained direct contact with the English merchants and were in control of the critical colonial exports. It was an aristocracy that was still limited in affluence, changing in membership, and insecure; but it was a visible elite nevertheless, whose fortunes depended on the primary flows of commerce.

Political Influence as the Basis of Aristocracy

Native elites thus arose in America on the basis of economic changes: in the ownership of land in New England, in the expansion of the tobacco economy in the Chesapeake region, and in the maturing of commerce in the main centers in the North. But the forces behind this rise of American elites were not merely economic; they were political as well. As the colonial governments took firm shape in the middle and later years of the seventeenth century, the value of political patronage and the yields of officeholding became unmistakably clear. The possibilities were first seen in Virginia, where what might be called the first American "court house gang" formed during the long governorship of Sir William Berkeley (1642–52, 1659–77).

The appointments that Berkeley could make gave him power over many aspects of the colony's life. He appointed justices of the peace, sheriffs, and tax collectors. He also nominated members of the council, who not only enjoyed considerable prestige, but also benefited materially from the privileges that were available to them. During the twenty-nine years of his administration, Berkeley used his power of appointment to create a clique of loyal officials, to whom he channeled these benefits. Similarly, a little group of rich and influential men developed around the proprietors' associates in Maryland.

But it was in New York that the possibilities of becoming wealthy through political connections were most dramatically revealed. A new landowning elite was created in New York almost overnight in the 1690s, largely through the actions of a single governor who was attempting to make his fortunes and the fortunes of his followers as quickly as possible. In New York's tumultuous and competitive politics at the end of the seventeenth century, the ruthless partisanship of Governor Benjamin Fletcher (1692–97) was extraordinarily effective. Fletcher himself was personally greedy, and he was surrounded by a gang of petty plunderers whom he had brought over from England. Like his successor Cornbury, Fletcher proceeded to buy the loyalty of the dominant group of local influential men by bestowing on them enormous grants of land and by confirming other grants that had previously been made.

Fletcher did not invent this procedure. One patroonship from the Dutch period had survived and in fact flourished—Rensselaerswyck, a manor of close to a million acres on both sides of the Hudson surrounding present-day Albany. Several other great estates had been granted subsequently, and of these the most important was Livingston Manor. This grant of 160,000 acres had been extracted from the government of the Dominion of New England by Robert Livingston, a particularly clever politician of Scottish, English, and Dutch ancestry. Fletcher fed the appetites of just such sharp-eyed opportunists and hustling politicians scrambling in the bonanza land grab of late-seventeenth-century New York. The estates he handed out in Dutchess and Westchester counties varied in size and in

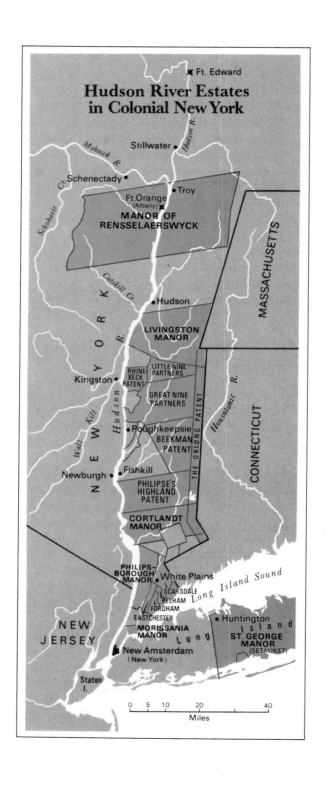

Hudson River Estates in Colonial New York

Johannes De Peyster, III (artist unknown, 1718)
Merchant, mayor of New York City 1698–99, and a prominent member of the colony's legislature, De Peyster was the son of one of the wealthiest Dutch settlers who successfully made the transition to English rule and, despite his faulty English, held several public offices. By Johannes' time the De Peyster family formed a large and influential network within the Anglo-Dutch aristocracy, linked to the Watts, Schuyler, Van Cortlandt, Livingston, and DeLancey families.

legal and political privileges, but almost all exceeded 100,000 acres. Some grants were literally open-ended. Commonly stretching for sixteen miles along a river-bank, they ran back indefinitely into the unsurveyed countryside.

Profits from the French Wars

The results of political influence were not limited to landholding: politics also affected the development of trade and the establishment of the merchant leadership. For at the end of the seventeenth century, government contracting—political in its essence—became a prime source of economic advancement. The colonies were involved in both of the international wars in which England fought during these years. The first was the inconclusive War of the League of Augsburg (1689–97), in which England led a coalition of European states resisting France's effort to dominate central Europe. The second was the War of the Spanish Succession (1702–13), a more decisive conflict, in which England and the Netherlands joined to block the French king Louis XIV's claim to the crown of Spain.

Both of these European wars led to hostilities between the English colonies and the French settlements in southern Canada. The slow-growing French colony of New France had been settled at the same time as the English colonies. But the growth of New France had been limited by religious restrictions on immigration, by rigid systems of land distribution and of social relations, and by a tightly controlled colonial bureaucracy. Its population was only 6,000 in 1660 and perhaps 15,000 in 1700. Nevertheless, from the beginning the French had been aggressive fur traders, trappers, and fishermen, and for years there had been minor clashes between them and the English settlers, especially in Nova Scotia. These clashes escalated into savage border warfare and extended struggles for inland territories during the two international wars that spanned the years 1689–1713.

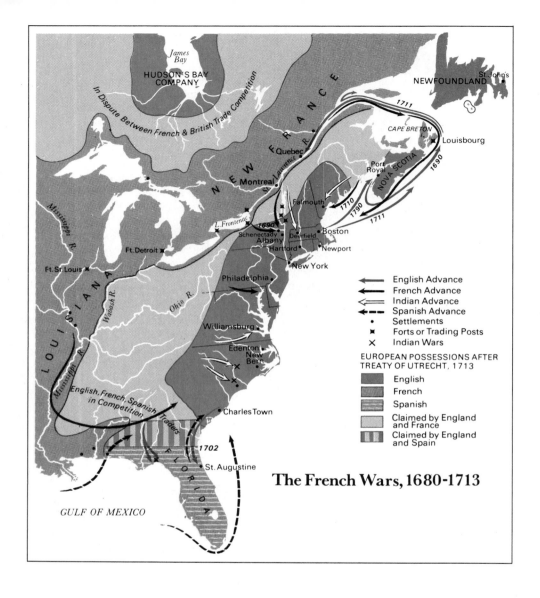

The French Wars, 1680-1713

In the first war, of 1689–97, which was known in the colonies as King
William's War, the French and their Indian allies fought the English for control of
Hudson Bay and in 1690 attacked the exposed northern borders of English
settlement in devastating raids on an arc of towns from Portland, Maine, to
Schenectady, New York. The British and American forces concentrated on
capturing the French fortress of Port Royal in Nova Scotia, which Massachusetts
troops took but then lost in 1690–91. An elaborate Anglo-American attack on the
center of French Canada failed miserably.

The same pattern was repeated in the second of these wars, that of 1702–13,
which the American colonists knew as Queen Anne's War. Once again the Maine

settlements were raided by the French and Indians, and Deerfield, Massachusetts, was destroyed. In retaliation the colonists burned down French villages in Nova Scotia and attacked Port Royal twice before finally taking it. Far to the south a force of Carolinians and Indians burned the Spanish town of St. Augustine, Florida, and destroyed the string of Spanish missionary outposts that linked the Spanish coastal settlements to French Louisiana. The war ended in 1713 with the Treaty of Utrecht, whose main terms marked a significant victory in Europe for Britain. In the Western Hemisphere, Britain obtained permanent title to Newfoundland, Nova Scotia, and Hudson Bay, although not all the boundaries were clear. The British also won a thirty-year contract to supply Spanish America with 4,800 slaves and a cargo of goods annually.

The American efforts in these European wars had made great demands on the fragile American economies and had accounted for significant inflows of money. Troops had to be mobilized, housed, transported, and fed. Ships had to be built, equipped, and manned. Native sources of naval supplies had to be exploited. The management of these efforts during the two decades of war fell into the eager hands of a few colonial merchants. Some were experienced in the business of supplying war materiel. Andrew Belcher, once an innkeeper in Cambridge, Massachusetts, had made his first success in trade as a supplier to the Massachusetts government during King Philip's War (1675–76), a brief but bloody clash between the colonists and the local Indians. In the international conflicts that followed, Belcher became the colony's principal military contractor. With the profits he made, he established a family that would rise to the governorship and to other important offices and would enjoy grand tours of Europe and the acquaintance of monarchs. The Faneuil family, Huguenot refugees from France, also established itself partly through wartime contracting. In New York another Huguenot, Stephanus DeLancey, and the Schuyler brothers in Albany used government contracting as a major source of profits. Through the contracting business, political in its origins, these merchants established families as important in New York as the Belchers and Faneuils were in Massachusetts.

The Limits of Social Distinction

Thus in these many ways toward the end of the seventeenth century, the situation made possible the growth of American elites—a leadership group that was distinguished by wealth or substantial claims to wealth, by political influence, and by a superior style of life. But if these elites constituted an aristocracy, it was a limited aristocracy indeed. The limitations of their distinctions, the basic weakness of their positions, and the instability of their membership were as important as the eminence they had achieved.

To begin with, they formed no "class"—that is, no body with group interests, known and recognized, that were felt to be more important than individual or family concerns. These striving merchants, hustling land speculators, and hardpressed planters were driven by personal, local, and immediate interests. They did not identify themselves with the stable concerns of a particular social group that had existed before them and would exist after them—a group that each individual member recognized as essential to his own welfare. Their interests were their own. Only occasionally and erratically did they merge their concerns with those of other men in similar situations, forming common commitments and a joint program of public action.

Further, these emerging elites were distinguished from most of their contemporaries only by their wealth. In education, in ancestry, in cultural outlook, in speech, and in personal style, they were largely indistinguishable from many others who competed with them openly. They had simply achieved wealth—but wealth in the American colonies was fragile and insecure. There was almost no way to invest a fortune securely. "Urban" properties provided perhaps the steadiest yields, but were limited in scale and availability. Most capital was tied up in daily trading or farming operations or in land that had been bought on speculation. Momentary upsets could be disastrous, and bankruptcies were common. Repeatedly men rose from obscurity only to disappear back into the population at large.

Even if an individual's wealth remained secure, it could provide no institutional protection for the distinctions he had won. No legal barriers or institutions existed to protect the fragile American aristocracy—no nobility, no House of Lords, no legal institution of any kind in which membership, once achieved, could be passed on from generation to generation. The colonial councils were political bodies; although membership in them bestowed enviable status, seats could not be inherited. Membership in them remained open not merely to ambitious local competitors—merchants, farmers, and landowners—but also to officials sent from abroad.

Of all the limitations in the distinctions of the new elites, however, the most striking was the lack of a visible distance between them and the bulk of the population from which they had emerged. In the short time in which these men had risen, they had not been able to create for themselves a world that was set far apart from the world of ordinary prosperous people. They built manor houses, town houses, and plantation "seats" (residential estates) that had some style, and they made other efforts to establish the outward forms of a superior way of life. But as yet their material achievements were relatively modest—lavish, perhaps, by the standards of frontier tobacco farmers and petty shopkeeper-merchants, but not comparable to the magnificent establishments of European aristocrats. The Van Cortlandts' manor house on their estate on the Hudson was a modest one-and-a-half-story wooden building, a pleasant farmhouse that had been improved for middle-class comfort; an affluent country gentleman in early-eighteenth-century England would hardly have considered it a suitable residence. "Westover," the Byrds' estate in Virginia, was more elegant and more substantial, with pretensions to a higher, more sophisticated style in its carved interior woodwork and up-to-date exterior brick facades. But much of its ultimate beauty was acquired gradually, in successive additions and refinements. In its original form it was a square house of eight main rooms. Like so many other

"Westover" (top), Estate of William Byrd II; Byrd and His Wife Maria
Son of a successful Virginia trader and planter, Byrd spent fifteen years in England before settling down to his inheritance. The present house was the third erected on that site, and became one of the showpieces of colonial Virginia.

proud houses of the time, it was solidly middle class. The most elegant and famous house in Boston in this period also seemed an immense achievement by the standards of the place and time. But this house, built by the merchant John Foster between 1689 and 1692 and destined to be inherited by the Hutchinson family, would have been indistinguishable from the ordinary town houses of prosperous tradesmen in any of the major cities of Europe. There was nothing in America to compare with the great urban residences and magnificent country houses of Europe's very rich, or even fairly rich.

The heights that the Van Cortlandts, the Hutchinsons, the Belchers, and the Byrds achieved were within the reach of many, and never free from competition. At the same time, the ordinary people in the colonies enjoyed a relatively high level of general well-being. To be sure, there was poverty in early-eighteenth-century America, as there has been in almost every society that has ever existed; but among the ordinary free population there was a degree of affluence that was unique for the time. Land remained available, even if it was increasingly difficult for freed servants to rise to full independence and public influence. Entrance to wholesale trade, although more difficult than before, remained open to competition. If there were a few great landlords, there were a great many independent farmers. If there were a few merchants who had suddenly become quite rich, there were many others who had some share in the profits of trade. During Queen Anne's War one-third of the entire adult male population of Boston (544 individuals) were part owners of some seagoing vessel. And no fewer than 207 of these investors—12 percent of the adult male population of the town—called themselves merchants.

Rebellion: The Measure of Social Strain

It is the sudden emergence of these new elites—proud but still striving and well within the range of rivals close behind—that explains the intensity of the rash of rebellions that broke out in the American colonies in the late seventeenth century. These rebellions are extremely small events in the scale of Western history, but they are revealing within the context of the rapidly maturing Anglo-American society. They show the inner strains and tensions of communities whose social structure was still forming and in which no group's dominance and no individual's eminence were safe from effective competition.

There were five outbreaks, and their dates are significant:

Virginia	Bacon's Rebellion	1676
Carolina	Culpeper's Rebellion	1677
Massachusetts	Rebellion against Andros and the Dominion of New England	1689
New York	Leisler's Rebellion	1689
Maryland	The Protestant Association	1689

The origins of three of these rebellions—those in Massachusetts, New York, and Maryland—coincided with the arrival in the colonies of news of the Glorious Revolution of 1688 in England. In all three cases the rebels explicitly associated themselves with that uprising in England, which forced James II into exile and destroyed the threat of his authoritarian rule. But the parallels between these American uprisings and the Glorious Revolution are superficial, although not altogether fanciful. The revolution in England deposed a king and showed that sovereignty lay not in a monarch appointed by God, nor in popular mobs, but rather in Parliament and the consensus of political and social leaders. Further, in England the supremacy of law—the statutes of Parliament and the common law—had been placed above any action of the crown, and judges had been made independent of the monarch's wishes. Finally, Parliament had declared that it had an independent existence: its elections and its sessions were fixed on regular schedules, free of dictation by the crown. None of these basic accomplishments of the Glorious Revolution were duplicated in America. Sovereignty was in no way an issue in the colonial upheavals. The American governors retained the arbitrary powers that were eliminated in England. American judges remained subordinate to the crown's will, and the existence and convening of the representative assemblies remained subject to executive decree.

The colonial revolts differed greatly in their immediate causes. But whatever the colonists' original motivations, once under way their uprisings expressed the strains within communities in which social controls and political dominance were both subjects of controversy, objects of challenge and of continuous struggle.

Bacon's Rebellion   In a period of economic distress, Bacon's Rebellion began as an unauthorized war against the Indians on Virginia's northwestern frontier. Governor Berkeley's policy had been to stabilize the boundaries between Indians and whites and to protect the native Americans from land-hungry settlers. Although a sincere attempt to deal with a difficult problem, it was also a conservative policy that favored the well-established farmers, and especially Berkeley's supporters and beneficiaries. As such it was offensive to newcomers like Nathaniel Bacon and the latter's chief ally, Giles Bland. Bacon had quarreled with the governor and had been denied the monopoly of the Indian trade he sought; Bland, who had arrived in the colony in 1671 as a customs collector, had been fined by the governor for "barbarous and insolent behaviors," then arrested, and finally dismissed from his post.

Around Bacon and Bland an opposition group gathered that was increasingly resentful of the benefits that Berkeley's clique had acquired. The challengers demanded land without regard to the rights or needs of the border Indians, who were being squeezed between the double pressure of rival tribes behind them and white settlers before them. A violent clash between the Indians and the settlers in the border area that Bacon sought to control provided an excuse to launch a full-scale war. This conflict became a civil war in 1676 when Berkeley repudiated Bacon and his allies and tried to bring them to justice. Having suppressed the border Indians in bloody battles, the rebels turned back on the colony. They seized the government, defeated and scattered Berkeley's forces, and burned Jamestown to the ground. But they could not sustain the revolt. Bacon died of exposure and exhaustion in the midst of a confused military campaign. Deprived of his leadership, the rebellion faded out, and Bacon's chief allies were soon hanged for treason.

But in all this turmoil the Baconites' voice rose loud and clear. Who are these men "in authority and favor," they demanded to know in their "Manifesto," to whose hands the control of the country's wealth had been committed? Note, they cried,

> the sudden rise of their estates compared with the mean quality in which they first entered the country, . . . and let us see whether their extractions and education have not been vile, and by what pretense of learning and virtue they could [enter] so soon into employments of so great trust and consequence; let us . . . see what sponges have sucked up the public treasure and whether it hath not been privately contrived away by unworthy favorites and juggling parasites whose tottering fortunes have been repaired and supported at the public charge.

But these challengers were themselves challenged. For another element in the upheaval was the discontent among the ordinary settlers over the local privileges of some of the newly risen, powerful men in the counties—the Baconites—who had attacked the privileges of Governor Berkeley's inner clique. The ordinary settlers expressed their grievances in the laws of "Bacon's Assembly," which met in 1676. Thus at both the local and the central levels, the rebellion challenged the stability of newly secured authority.

The wave of rebellion in Virginia, which had risen suddenly and spread quickly, soon subsided. By the end of the seventeenth century, the most difficult period of adjustment had passed: the colonists generally accepted the fact that certain families were indeed distinguished from others in riches, in dignity, and in access to political authority—and were likely to remain so. There had never been a challenge to British supremacy as such or to the idea that some people would inevitably be "high and eminent in power and dignity; others mean and in subjection." Protests and upheavals had resulted from the discomforts of discovering who in fact were "high" and who were "mean," and what the particular consequences were of "power and dignity."

Culpeper's Rebellion   More confused than Bacon's Rebellion was the almost comic-opera uprising that took place in 1677 in Albemarle, the northern sector of Carolina. There some 3,000 farmers struggled to survive in the swampy, sandy coastal lands and to profit from smuggling tobacco with the help of a few enterprising New England merchants. When the Carolina proprietors' clique—men no less hard-drinking, ill-tempered, and profiteering than their opponents—attempted to collect customs duties, they were attacked by a gang of rivals. The leader of this gang, a belligerent malcontent named John Culpeper, accused the clique of corruption and treason. Culpeper seized the government, jailed his enemies, and sent charges against them to England. After endless confusion and an almost farcical series of attacks between the two groups, the Carolina proprietors managed to restore order. But the rebellion died slowly, partly because the legal proceedings in England were drawn out over a long period, and even more because there was ongoing uncertainty over who had legitimate leadership in the rough, tumultuous backwoods community.

Leisler's Rebellion In New York the struggle between an emerging group of influential men and a resentful opposition was clearer than it was in the South; and it was also more bitter and had more permanent political consequences.

When word of the Glorious Revolution arrived in New York, the colony's lieutenant governor, Francis Nicholson, decided to strengthen Manhattan's garrison with militia troops. One of the militia captains was a well-to-do, quarrelsome merchant, Jacob Leisler. Relations between the militia and Nicholson's regular troops grew difficult, then explosive, especially because Nicholson's legal status was unclear after the king who had appointed him, James II, had been deposed. In June 1689 the militia, led by Leisler, seized the fort at Manhattan in the name of the new English monarchs, William and Mary. Nicholson sailed for England. In December a message from William III arrived, instructing the chief officer of New York's government to retain his post. Leisler, in control of the fort, interpreted this message as being addressed to himself as the colony's acting governor. He drew around him what was at first a large group of supporters, who proceeded to parcel out the colony's offices and run New York's government, including its feeble effort in King William's War. In 1691 a new, officially appointed royal governor arrived, Henry Sloughter, whose name soon proved to be appropriate. Sloughter demanded that Leisler surrender the city and the government. Leisler's support had steadily eroded in two years of erratic rule, and he scarcely controlled any of the colony outside the city walls. Nevertheless he refused to give up. Sloughter's superior power prevailed. Leisler and his followers surrendered; and after a legally dubious trial he and his chief assistant, his son-in-law Jacob Milbourne, were hanged for treason and their property was confiscated.

But these savage sentences, which Parliament legally annulled in 1695, hardly ended the struggle. By the time Leisler's regime had ended, the political leadership of the colony was broken into two violently opposing parties, the Leislerians and the anti-Leislerians. Thereafter the two parties alternated in power as successive governors arrived, each side attempting literally to annihilate the other when the opportunity arose—or, failing that, to crush the opposition politically so that it would never regain power. Again, the social background of the turmoil is crucial. Behind the see-sawing political conflict in New York lay a background struggle that had been under way since the English had conquered the colony from the Dutch. In the years that followed the English takeover, an Anglo-Dutch leadership group had taken form under governors sent to the colony by the duke of York. The colony's official patronage had come to center on this small group of families, whose ultimate rewards would come in the land grants of Benjamin Fletcher. Gradually this Anglo-Dutch clique—the Bayards, Van Cortlandts, Philipses, Livingstons, and Schuylers—had made arrangements that satisfied its members' interests. They had gained a monopoly of the milling and exporting of flour for New York City, in effect giving them control of that vital industry; a New York City monopoly of shipping on the Hudson; and an Albany monopoly of the colony's Indian trade.

The Anglo-Dutch clique had thus gained control of the colony's offices, and its members had also begun to control New York's economy. But those excluded from power had grown increasingly resentful. Gradually a combination of alienated factions had taken shape. This opposition was led by the merchants (especially those of Dutch origin) who had been denied access to these privileges. It included the city artisans, who were indirectly the victims of the monopolies, and the Long Island townsmen, most of whom had migrated from Connecticut. Increasingly, Jacob Leisler had assumed the leadership of this rising discontent. Leisler had fought the Anglo-Dutch leaders on several issues, had been jailed in a religious controversy in Albany, had thereafter refused to pay customs duties, and had defied all efforts to bring him to court. His associates had had similar careers.

This group of alienated, resentful, and enterprising men—many of whom had been in positions of authority under the Dutch—had sparked the opposition to Nicholson and turned it into a rebellion against the new Anglo-Dutch establishment. In principle Leisler and his followers were no more "democrats" than were the Baconites in Virginia. But they found in the language of the Glorious Revolution a "Protestant" program—against monopolies, against arbitrary power, in favor of open access to benefits and a broad sharing of them—that served their own interests well.

The Protestant Association

In Maryland, resentment had been building for a long time against the domination of the colony by the Calverts and their Catholic associates. This resentment had erupted into open violence as early as 1676 in an obscure rebellion in Calvert County. When news of the Glorious Revolution arrived, the same group of insurgents, further antagonized by a particularly obnoxious governor, led 250 settlers to seize the colony's government. Calling themselves the Protestant Association, the rebels issued a declaration condemning the proprietor's party for excessive fee taking, for resisting royal authority, and for arbitrary taxation. They also identified telltale signs of a secret papal plot, and they petitioned the crown to take over the colony's government from the Calverts, which was promptly done.

Only in 1715 was control of Maryland restored to the Calvert family, whose members by that time had turned Protestant. By that time too, Maryland had been drawn into the general pattern of colonial governance: the crown had to approve executive appointments and the colony's legislation. The rebellion in Maryland had been the product of the instability created by the conflict of opposing groups in the colony. Although the proprietors' clique thereafter still dominated the executive branch of the colony's government, it could no longer block the advance of the planter aristocracy or ignore the legislative assembly, whose influence was built into the government.

The Downfall of Andros

Although in Massachusetts there were special, local factors in the rebellion that took place, there was also an underlying conflict similar to that found in other colonies. The characteristic struggle of social groups had been delayed in the Bay Colony by the continuing dominance of the Puritan regime, protected by the original Massachusetts charter. But when the colony's charter was taken away by the English government in 1684 and the Dominion of New England was established, the pattern already seen in the other colonies quickly developed. Almost immediately, the favors of patronage and power began to flow to a small group of speculators and merchant insiders. Some of those who were favored had come over with Andros; some of them were ambitious native-born Americans who

Increase Mather (portrait by Jan van der Spriett, London, 1688)
Son of Richard Mather (see p. 52), Increase Mather, the most powerful Puritan of his generation, was the minister of Boston's influential second, or North Church, from 1664 until his death. He served also as president of Harvard College (largely in absentia) from 1685 to 1701. A bitter opponent of Andros and the Dominion of New England, Mather was in England from 1688 to 1692 and negotiated Massachusetts' second charter, which was a compromise between British rule and the colony's independence.

were drawn to the newly established group. For four years the members of this clique collected numerous privileges—and in the process generated resentment among others that found expression in an uprising made especially bitter by the Puritan outrage that fueled it.

These rebellions were obscure and confused events—especially those in New York, Maryland, and Massachusetts, where the insurgents claimed association with the successful revolutionaries in England. Everywhere the rebels sought to identify themselves with the struggle for English liberty and against various forms of tyranny. None, however, questioned the basis of public authority; all submitted to legitimate royal power when it appeared; and none fought for the full range of liberties that were achieved by the Glorious Revolution—liberties that were spelled out in the English Bill of Rights of 1689 and the Act of Settlement of 1701, which concluded the revolution in England. The American rebels did not question the nature, structure, and essential character of government; rather, they challenged the personnel of government—those in control. In short, the issue was not a question of "what?" or "how?" but one of "who?" Enclosed in their provincial world, the rebels sought, above all, fairness in the actions of government that properly reflected the balance of society as it had emerged from a period of rapid growth and change.

Provincial Culture

These uprisings of the late seventeenth century were not only relatively obscure events in the scale of Western history; they were also—significantly—provincial events. And as such they were characteristic of early-eighteenth-century Anglo-American culture. That culture had changed significantly from the parental European, and specifically English, culture from which it had developed.

In the earliest years of settlement the new English colonies in America may have been small, distant, and isolated, but they had been part of a vital movement prominent in western European life. The key figures in the American colonies had been products of the European world. In America they had been isolated physically but not psychologically, intellectually, or spiritually. They never lost the sense of being involved in something that mattered in an important way to the world they had left behind. They felt that they could easily return to that world; and when they did in fact return, they found themselves enhanced, not diminished, by having spent time in the exotic American frontier land. Thus George Sandys, an English poet, traveler, and scholar (and the son of the archbishop of York), easily slipped back into English literary circles after his stay in Virginia (1621–25), having made good progress on his translation of Ovid's *Metamorphoses.* So Roger Williams returned to England from America to join the Council of State during the English Civil War. And John Winthrop's nephew George Downing, who had been sent to Harvard College for his education, became the chief intelligence officer to Oliver Cromwell, the head of England's revolutionary government in the 1650s; ultimately knighted, Downing in 1657 became England's ambassador to the Netherlands. The American settlements had thus been relevant and vital to some of the most forward-looking minds of the time.

By 1700 circumstances had changed drastically. As the colonies had grown, they had grown apart, into a separate world of their own. The colonial world was still connected with the greater world beyond, but it was fundamentally removed from it. The success or failure of the colonists' daily affairs no longer mattered very much in England. The settlers no longer made news in the larger world; they listened for it, intently, from abroad, and they imitated as best they could what they could learn of proper fashions in thought and patterns of behavior. They knew themselves to be provincials in the sense that their culture was not self-contained; its sources and superior expressions were to be found elsewhere than in their own land. They must seek the higher forms of their culture from afar, and maintain them according to standards externally imposed, in the creation of which they themselves had not shared. The most cultivated of the colonists read much, and they read purposefully, determined to retain contact with a world greater than their own. The diary of William Byrd II, with its record of daily stints of study, testifies to the virtues of regularity and effort in maintaining standards of civilization set abroad.

This basic transformation can be seen particularly well in the later career of John Winthrop, Jr., the gifted and learned son of the first governor of Massachusetts Bay Colony. John, Jr., was educated at Trinity College, Dublin, and in London at the lawyers' Inner Temple. As a young man he had helped manage an English overseas military expedition, and he had traveled in the Mediterranean and Middle East. He was a physician, an amateur scientist, and an imaginative entrepreneur, and for eighteen years he served as governor of Connecticut. He struggled to maintain contact with the Royal Society in London, of which he was the first American member. There was "a current of loneliness, almost pathos," the younger Winthrop's most recent biographer writes, "in his anxiety to stay in touch. He wrote letter after letter to the society's secretary. He sent over scientific specimens—rattlesnake skins, birds' nests, plants, crabs, strange pigs. He studied the society's *Transactions* so as not to fall too far behind. And to those in England who were concerned with the spreading of Christianity, he sent back the Indian-language translation of the Bible by the Massachusetts minister John Eliot, and two essays written in Latin by Indian students at Harvard. But these were failing efforts. In the end loneliness and isolation overcame Winthrop. By the time of his death in 1676, he was venerated in the villages along the Connecticut River—themselves changing like autumn leaves from vital, experimental religious communities to sere, old-fashioned backwoods towns. But he was forgotten by the greater world in England. His sons, however, provincial land speculators and petty politicians, had no such memories as their father had had, and no such aspirations; they suffered, therefore, none of his disappointments. They were native to the land, and their cultural horizons had narrowed to its practical demands.

The silent drama of a high culture being transplanted to America and becoming permanently provincial was played out most vividly in the field of education. For in its broadest sense, education, more than any other social process, liberates people from narrow local origins and brings them into contact with larger worlds and broader horizons. Education is perhaps the most sensitive index of the changing character of American life as it developed in the transitional years of the late seventeenth century. It is also one of the most difficult subjects to interpret. For there were great accomplishments in colonial education, but there were also great defeats; soaring ambitions, but serious neglect.

Education   Certain things, however, are clear. In New England the founding generation made a remarkable effort not only to perpetuate education as it was then known, but to improve it. They wanted to spread it more widely and more effectively throughout the entire population than it had been extended even in England, where formal education was unusually widespread for the time. The Puritans' efforts in education stemmed primarily from their religious convictions—specifically, from their insistence that every person, saint or sinner, have personal access to the Holy Scriptures, which meant that everyone must be able to read. But the ability to read was only the beginning, for to the Puritans the truly religious person was a student not only of the Bible, but also of commentaries on the Bible, including those enormously long, intricate sermons preached from every pulpit in the land. Keeping alive this biblical culture among the entire population required that much more schooling be provided than was considered normal by Elizabethan Englishmen, who assumed that the goal of formal education was training in vocational roles. For the Puritans there was only one important vocation, and that was spiritual. Although true salvation was in the end a God-given grace, the preparation for grace—the opening of the mind and soul to such a possibility—required education, knowledge, and will.

It was not this central religious commitment alone, however, that led the Puritans to their remarkable efforts in education. Partly too they were driven by a sense that in their wilderness situation the family, which traditionally had carried so much of the burden of transmitting culture from one generation to the next, had weakened and was failing in its duties. This fear bore heavily on the minds of the founding elders.* They looked ahead and noted that if extraordinary precautions were not taken in time, they would leave behind not a "Bible Commonwealth," but a society of rural barbarians. If family discipline were loose, if parents did not take their responsibilities seriously, the government would have to provide for the future.

When they founded the New England colonies, the Puritans therefore hoped not merely to provide education, but to extend it. Instinctively they relied on the

---

*For pressures on family life in the seventeenth century, see chapter 3, pp. 94–98.

willingness of people voluntarily to establish and support facilities for formal education. They knew that in England numerous primary and secondary schools had recently been founded by private donations—by gifts from such institutions as guilds and universities and even more often from individual donors. Such gifts were usually in the form of grants of land to support a school. In the first fifteen years after settlement, a number of relatively rich inhabitants in six New England towns did attempt to establish schools by making such traditional grants of land. But the land was uncultivated and tenants were scarce. Gifts of land were worthless if they produced no rents. Other ways of financing education would have to be found. Instead of pleading with the rich, the government would have to command. The towns ordered the wealthy to volunteer their help, and later some of the towns' undivided common land was set aside for the support of schools. But the hoped-for income could not be raised for lack of reliable tenants. In the end, there remained only one resource: taxation. It began as a supplement to private gifts and ended as almost the sole and universal basis of elementary education.

In the 1640s, after struggling for more than ten years with the problem of financing education, the Puritans decisively enacted what would become two famous laws. In 1642 the Massachusetts General Court ordered all parents and ministers to assume responsibility for the "calling and employment of their children, especially of their ability to read and understand the principles of religion and the capital laws of this country." Five years later, in 1647, the legislature ruled that all towns of fifty families must provide for the maintenance of elementary schools, and all towns of one hundred families must support secondary (Latin grammar) schools. These laws became models for the rest of Puritan New England. Connecticut enacted similar provisions in 1650, and Plymouth did so in two stages, in 1658 and 1677. Wherever these laws remained on the books, they were innovative and creative. But they are easily misunderstood.

The laws of the 1640s did not provide for public education as it has been known since the nineteenth century. No strict distinction between "private" and "public" existed in the seventeenth century. Neither of these laws specified that "public" money would be the financial basis of a community's schools; neither made formal schooling obligatory at any level. What the laws did do was, first, to establish a minimum level of educational accomplishment (not schooling) by spelling out the obligations of parents toward their children and of masters toward their servants, and by reinforcing these obligations with threats of fines and of removing children to other households. Second, the laws required that, at both the elementary and the secondary levels, schooling be made universally available to those who wished to take advantage of it. Third, the laws established a communitywide obligation to support formal institutions of education without reference to the benefits any individual or family derived from these schools. Finally, the laws made clear that the government's role in the area of education would not be merely supplementary or supportive or supervisory, but positive and compelling.

All the provisions written into these innovative American laws on education were highly creative. But these famous laws stand at the beginning, not at the end, of the historical development of education in Puritan New England. The question is not merely what was hoped for or what was provided for, but what happened to these hopes and these provisions in later years. What effect did these remarkable provisions have on the lives of the people?

By the end of the seventeenth century, it was clear that the hopes of the Puritans were not being evenly and satisfactorily fulfilled. Many towns failed to provide for schools and were fined. Later amendments to the laws complained of continuing neglect of education by masters, parents, and towns. The old fears that New England's younger generation would grow up without a proper education not only remained, but seemed to grow more intense. In 1671 Massachusetts doubled the fines on towns that neglected to maintain grammar-school instruction. In a sermon in 1689, Cotton Mather, the third-generation member of a great line of ministers and the self-appointed guardian of the old Puritan hopes, bemoaned his people's fate. He doubted, he declared, whether New England suffered "under an iller [worse] symptom than the too general want of education in the rising generation." If not overcome, this neglect would "gradually and speedily dispose us to that sort of Creolean degeneracy observed to deprave the children of the most noble and worthy Europeans when transplanted into America."

But even Mather's authoritative voice could not halt the movement of change. In 1718 the General Court, again increasing the delinquency fines, condemned the "many towns that not only are obliged by law but are very able to support a grammar school, yet choose rather to incur and pay the fine and penalty than maintain a grammar school." As settlements spread throughout the countryside, as contact with the centers of high culture grew thin, and as the original Puritan enthusiasms cooled, people increasingly tended to favor modifying the law or adjusting it to the realities of everyday life. The laws remained on the books, and the colonial magistrates sought to enforce them, but sometimes there was outright evasion. A town would obey by hiring a teacher who knew no Latin, telling him to teach the subject "as far as he was able." More commonly, a new institution was used, the "moving school," which satisfied the law by providing a schoolmaster and his equipment but distributed his services on a circuit through the town's lands in proportion to the spread of population. Thus Gloucester, Massachusetts, had a Latin grammar school, but the teacher and his books moved about in a cycle of three years, settling in seven places in the following monthly proportions: 9, 7, 5½, 5½, 4½, 3, 1½. Even the most remote corner of the township had contact with the "moving school," but it was available for children in that most isolated area only one and a half months every three years.

Finally, by the mid-eighteenth century the towns found a permanent solution: the district school. The towns were now formally divided into school districts, each district drawing its proportionate share of the available funds and using the money as the district school committee decided. Schools thus existed in almost every town, although variations were great. For the management of the schools was now entirely in local hands, and some localities were limited, isolated places, incapable of and uninterested in rising above their narrow horizons. Some schools were excellent, some poor, some dismal. Often the Latin grammar school proved to be a one-room schoolhouse in which children of all ages were taught at their own levels. Uniformity was lost, but there was no "Creolean degeneracy" that Mather had feared. New England in fact emerged in the eighteenth century still a literate culture, still open to a high level of cultural attainment.

All of this was a flame, sparked by the original creators of the "Bible Commonwealth," that sputtered at times but never went out. It is a remarkable accomplishment when it is contrasted with the slow and irregular development of education elsewhere in the colonies, where the churches and a few generous individuals sought to provide for schooling. In 1671 Governor Berkeley of Virginia wrote about his colony, "I thank God there are no free schools nor printing," these being sources, he declared, of "disobedience and heresy and sects." By 1689 there were still only six schools of various kinds in Virginia. In that same year Maryland had one school. New York, mainly through the efforts of the Dutch church, may have had eleven.

The Colleges   In New England the remarkable development of education at the elementary and secondary levels was in part the result of the reinforcement it received from higher education, which too became closely bound to the immediate needs of these provincial communities.

There can be little doubt about the Puritans' primary reason for founding in 1636 the institution that became Harvard College (named after its first private benefactor, John Harvard). They dreaded, they said, "to leave an illiterate ministry to the churches when our present ministers shall lie in the dust." There were other motives too. Some Puritans hoped that the institution would help

Colonial Colleges

College	Colony	Founded
Harvard College	Massachusetts	1636
College of William and Mary	Virginia	1693
Yale College	Connecticut	1701
College of New Jersey (Princeton University)	New Jersey	1746
College of Philadelphia (University of Pennsylvania)	Pennsylvania	1754
King's College (Columbia University)	New York	1754
College of Rhode Island (Brown University)	Rhode Island	1764
Queen's College (Rutgers University)	New Jersey	1766
Dartmouth College	New Hampshire	1769

College of William and Mary, Pictured in the 1730s
Founded in large part to educate Virginians for the Anglican ministry, it was built to the plans of Christopher Wren. The central building was erected by the end of the century but had to be rebuilt after a fire of 1705.

spread Christianity to the Indians by training preachers who would go out to deliver the word. But although the gospel mission failed miserably amid the general breakdown of relations between Indians and whites, the effort to maintain a college primarily for training preachers and secondarily for educating gentlemen in the liberal arts took root and flourished. Harvard College was a stable institution by the time the second English colonial college, William and Mary, was chartered in 1693 as part of the effort to improve the quality of the Anglican ministers in Virginia. Through its graduates, Harvard College exerted a great influence; and its continued existence, written into the terms of the Bay Colony's second charter of 1691, was firmly guaranteed.

Yet like so much else in American life, this college, and those that would follow it, became something different from the models on which they were based. The Puritan founders had intended to create an institution similar to the English college—a residential establishment that would be owned and directed by the tutors and professors who lived and taught there. But the colonial colleges did not develop in that way. Instead, the ownership of a college's property, and ultimately its government, came to rest not with the teachers, but with boards of trustees outside the educational process. These trustees hired the teachers and supervised the work of the college on behalf of the founding community. This development arose from the central motivation for the founding of the college: the community's desire to ensure a continuing supply of educated ministers and to advance learning in the American wilderness. Later in American history, the nature of the communities that founded colleges would shift. Colleges would be founded by religious denominations serving their particular concerns, and by state governments recognizing the need for experts in technical fields and seeking to provide for the public's general education. But ever since the establishment of the first college in 1636, the motivation and the resources have come from groups outside the teaching profession. The governance of higher education has reflected the insistence by these groups that the colleges fulfill these community mandates.

In this sense all the American colleges and universities have been community schools—products not so much of the world of education and learning as of desires and decisions of the community at large. Control has therefore rested with the founding communities; and as, in the colonial period, the horizons of the communities narrowed, the mandates of the colleges narrowed too. Educated ministers were indeed trained, and higher education was indeed made generally available, not only in Massachusetts, Virginia, and Connecticut, but also in New Jersey, Pennsylvania, New York, Rhode Island, and New Hampshire. Through the institutions of higher education, the pursuit of learning and the cultivation of the arts were advanced and passed on from generation to generation. But the primary reason for their foundation was not so much a love of learning for its own sake as it was the local concerns of communities with limited horizons— communities that were determined to sustain their founders' commitments to serving local, provincial needs.

CHRONOLOGY

1660	Restoration of Stuart monarchy (Charles II, 1660–85). Basic navigation law, monopolizing colonial trade and shipping for Britain, passed by Parliament; includes "enumeration" clause.	**1673**	New navigation act imposes "plantation duties."
1662	Massachusetts Bay ministers sanction the Halfway Covenant. Colony of Connecticut chartered by crown.	**1675**	Lords of Trade appointed as committee of Privy Council.
		1675–1676	King Philip's War in New England.
1663	New royal charter issued to Rhode Island. New navigation act (Staple Act) passed, channeling colonies' importation of European goods through England. Charter of Carolina given to eight courtiers.	**1676**	Bacon's Rebellion in Virginia. New Jersey divided into East and West New Jersey.
		1677	West New Jersey's Concessions and Agreements issued. Culpeper's Rebellion in Carolina.
1664	England conquers New Netherland, which becomes proprietary colony of Duke of York. New Jersey charter issued to two courtiers.	**1680**	New Hampshire given royal charter.
		1681	Pennsylvania charter granted to William Penn; first settlements in 1682.
1665	Duke's Laws for New York promulgated.	**1684**	Massachusetts Bay charter annulled by crown (charters of Connecticut, Rhode Island, New Jersey, Pennsylvania, Maryland, and Carolina abrogated in following years, to 1691).
1669	Fundamental Constitutions of Carolina issued.	**1685–1688**	Duke of York becomes James II; his accession makes New York a royal colony.

1686 Dominion of New England established.

1688 Glorious Revolution in England drives out James II in favor of William and Mary.

1689 Successful rebellion in Boston against Dominion of New England.
The Protestant Association in Maryland rebels.

1689– Leisler's Rebellion in New York.
1691

1689– King William's War (colonial phase
1697 of Europe's War of the League of Augsburg).

1691 Massachusetts Bay Colony gets new charter.

1692 Witchcraft hysteria in Salem, Massachusetts; twenty "witches" executed.

1693 College of William and Mary founded.

1696 English government establishes Board of Trade and Plantations.

Passage of comprehensive navigation act, extending admiralty court system to America.

1699 Woolen Act passed by Parliament.

1701 Yale College founded.
New and permanent Frame of Government adopted in Pennsylvania.

1702– Queen Anne's War (colonial phase
1713 of Europe's War of the Spanish Succession) concluded in Treaty of Utrecht.

1702 East and West New Jersey formed into single royal colony.

1702– Reign of Queen Anne.
1714

1708 Saybrook Platform adopted in Connecticut.

1714– Reign of George I, beginning
1727 Hanoverian dynasty.

1719 Rebellion against proprietors in Carolina.

Suggested Readings

The fullest account of the origins of the British imperial system, in both theory and institutions, is Charles M. Andrews, *The Colonial Period of American History,* IV (1938); for the system in its fully evolved form, see Leonard Labaree, *Royal Government in America* (1930). On the theory of empire, see also Richard Koebner, *Empire* (1961), chap. 3; on the all-important customs administration in the colonies, Thomas C. Barrow, *Trade & Empire* (1967); and on the difficulty in the late seventeenth century of imposing regulations on the scattered settlements, Michael G. Hall, *Edward Randolph and the American Colonies* (1969). On the influence of the Duke of York (James II) and his entourage on the evolution of empire and the importance of his and his lieutenants' military background, see Stephen S. Webb, " . . . The Household of James Stuart in the Evolution of English Imperialism," *Perspectives in American History,* 8 (1974), 55–80. On the patronage sources of colonial appointments and other aspects of the politics of the early empire, see Webb's "Strange Career of Francis Nicholson"† and "William Blathwayt, Imperial Fixer," *Wm. and Mary Q.*, 23 (1966), 513–48; 26 (1969), 373–415—a subject presented in full in Webb's *The Governors-General* (1979). On James II's ill-fated effort to organize a territorial government, see Viola F. Barnes, *The Dominion of New England* (1923).

The emergence of a native Anglo-American aristocracy is traced generally, in the case of Virginia, in Bernard Bailyn, "Politics and Social Structure in Virginia,"† James M. Smith, ed., *Seventeenth-Century America* (1959), and Louis B. Wright, *First Gentlemen of Virginia* (1940); in the case of Maryland, where socioeconomic differences grew very slowly, in Gloria L. Main, *Tobacco Colony* (1982); in the case of commercial New England, in Bernard Bailyn, *New England Merchants in the Seventeenth Century* (1955), and Christine L. Heyrman, *Commerce and Culture* (1984); in the case of New York, in Thomas Archdeacon, *New York City, 1664–1710* (1976); and in the five main port towns, in Carl Bridenbaugh, *Cities in the Wilderness* (1938). The origins of rural aristocracies in New England, rooted in the shifting relations between population and land, are described in Roy H. Akagi, *The Town Proprietors of the New England Colonies* (1924), and probed analytically in Richard L. Bushman, *From Puritan to Yankee* (1967), and in the individual community studies listed in the references to chapter 3. For case studies of the emergence of the southern aristocracy, see the essays on social mobility in the Chesapeake area cited for the previous chapter; Kenneth A. Lockridge, *The Diary, and Life, of William Byrd II of Virginia, 1674–1744* (1987); and Richard B. Davis, ed., *William Fitzhugh and His Chesapeake World, 1676–1701* (1963). The political aspects of a rising aristocracy are analyzed in the case of New York in Patricia U. Bonomi, *A Factious People* (1971), chaps. 2–3; in Archdeacon's *New York City;* and in Lawrence H. Leder, *Robert Livingston* (1961).

The late-seventeenth-century wars (the subject of Francis Parkman's dramatic classics, *Count Frontenac and New France Under Louis XIV,* 1877, and *A Half-Century of Conflict,* 1892) are sketched briefly in Howard H. Peckham, *The Colonial Wars, 1689–1762* (1964); their significance for the development of Anglo-American politics, trade, and society is suggested in G. M. Waller, *Samuel Vetch, Colonial Enterpriser* (1960).

The colonial rebellions of the late seventeenth century are described, insofar as they relate to the English rebellion against James II, in David S. Lovejoy, *The Glorious Revolution in America* (1972). But as social events these uprisings are to be associated with Bacon's Rebellion, which is described generally in Wilcomb E. Washburn, *The Governor and the Rebel* (1957), and analyzed in social terms in Bailyn, "Politics and Social Structure"†; in Wesley F. Craven, *Southern Colonies in the Seventeenth Century* (1949); and in Edmund S. Morgan, *American Slavery, American Freedom* (1975). Stephen S. Webb, *1676: The End of American Independence* (1984), sees the rebellion as an "imperial revolution" that led to the imposition of royal rule over the once semi-independent colonies. For the social background of Leisler's Rebellion, see Archdeacon's book cited above and Jerome R. Reich, *Leisler's Rebellion* (1953), which exaggerates the "democratic" impulses of the rebels. On Boston's rebellion and its aftermath, see Barnes, *Dominion of New England,* and Michael G. Hall, *The Last American Puritan: The Life of Increase Mather* (1988). The most exhaustive study of the social background of any of these rebellions, however, is Lois G. Carr and David W. Jordan, *Maryland's Revolution of Government 1689–1692* (1974).

The deepening provincialism of American culture in the late seventeenth century emerges in the colonists' writings, analyzed in the opening chapter of Kenneth S. Lynn, *Mark Twain and Southwestern Humor* (1959); in the careers of third-generation Anglo-Americans such as the Winthrops (Richard S. Dunn, *Puritans and Yankees,* 1962, Bk. III) and the Mathers (Robert Middlekauff, *The Mathers,* 1971, Bk. III and Kenneth Silverman, *The Life and Times of Cotton*

---

†See footnote on p. 32.

Mather, 1984); in travelers' accounts (Jasper Danckaerts [1679–80], pub. 1867; the Frenchman Durand [1687], pub. 1923; Sarah Knight [1704], latest pub. 1972); and above all in education.

For a comprehensive, detailed, and broadly conceived account of early American education, see Lawrence A. Cremin, *American Education: The Colonial Experience, 1607–1783* (1970), parts I–III; for a general interpretation of the social role of colonial education, see Bernard Bailyn, *Education in the Forming of American Society* (1960); and for the deepening localization of standards, described in the text, Harlan Updegraff, *Origin of the Moving School in Massachusetts* (1907). Robert Middlekauff has traced the persistence of the classical tradition in the face of provincial difficulties in *Ancients and Axioms* (1963). James Axtell, *The School upon a Hill* (1974), shows through education in the broadest sense how New England's culture was transmitted across the generations. For the efforts to extend formal education to the Indians, see Mary Szasz, *Indian Education in the American Colonies* (1988). The blending of theology, conversion, and education in the famous missionary activity of the Rev. John Eliot is traced in detail in James Holstun, "John Eliot's Empirical Millenarianism," *Representations,* 4 (1983), 128–53.

On the origins of higher education, see Samuel E. Morison's magisterial works, *The Founding of Harvard College* (1935) and *Harvard College in the Seventeenth Century* (2 vols., 1936), both summarized in his *Three Centuries of Harvard: 1636–1936* (1936). Although these learned and readable books remain fundamental, Morison's general interpretation has been challenged by Winthrop S. Hudson, "The Morison Myth Concerning the Founding of Harvard College," *Church History,* 8 (1939), 148–59, and by Jurgen Herbst, *From Crisis to Crisis* (1982), in which parallels are drawn between Harvard, Yale, and William and Mary on the one hand and the "gymnasia illustria, academics, or Gelehrtenschulen on the Continent" on the other. Yale's origins are detailed in Richard Warch, *School of the Prophets: Yale College, 1701–1740* (1973), and William and Mary's in Parke Rouse, Jr., *James Blair of Virginia* (1971). All aspects of education and artistic expression are discussed in Richard B. Davis, *Intellectual Life in the Colonial South, 1585–1763* (3 vols., 1978).

5

American Society in the Eighteenth Century

≈

HE END of the War of the Spanish Succession in 1713 and the creation of a stable political regime in England under Sir Robert Walpole, prime minister from 1721 to 1742, introduced a period of great expansion in all spheres of Anglo-American life. In the two generations that followed the war, the American settlements, despite minor involvements in other international conflicts and repeated cycles of commercial recession, grew so rapidly and matured so fully that they came to constitute an important element in British life and in the life of the Atlantic world generally. From scattered seventeenth-century foundations the colonies, even as they were drawn more and more elaborately into the ill-organized structure of the British Empire, were becoming increasingly distinctive, although outwardly they sought to conform to traditional European ways of life. During this period they acquired characteristics that would remain permanent features of American society.

The New Population: Sources and Impact

Fundamental to all aspects of eighteenth-century American history was the phenomenal growth of the population. By 1700 the population of the mainland colonies was approximately 250,000; by 1775 it had grown tenfold, to 2.5 million, which was more than a third the size of the population of England and Wales (6.7 million). A fifth of the American people were black, almost all of them slaves. Nine-tenths of the slaves lived south of Pennsylvania. They constituted two-fifths of the population of Virginia and almost two-thirds of the population of South Carolina.

By the 1760s the settled areas formed an almost unbroken line down the coast from Maine to Florida, and they reached deep into the interior. In New England, groups moving up the Connecticut River and the coastal streams penetrated into New Hampshire and Vermont. In New York, settlements spread through the rich Hudson, Mohawk, and Schoharie valleys, and in Pennsylvania and the Carolinas they extended back to the Appalachians. In a few places, especially southwestern Pennsylvania, the Appalachian mountain barrier had been breached by frontiersmen who were actively opening fresh lands to cultivation in Indian territories.

The population was almost entirely rural. Of the towns, the most populous was Philadelphia, with approximately 35,000 inhabitants. The five largest communities (Philadelphia, New York, Boston, Charleston, and Newport, Rhode Island) had a combined population of 90,000—3.6 percent of the total population. Fifteen smaller towns, ranging from New Haven, Connecticut (with 8,000), to Savannah, Georgia (with 3,200), account for another 77,500. But very few of the total town population of approximately 167,500 lived in circumstances that can be called "urban" in a modern sense.

The rapid increase in the size of the population—it almost doubled every twenty-five years—was in large part the result of natural growth, that is, the excess of births over deaths. But new flows of immigration also contributed to population growth. The basic recruitment from England continued, although at a somewhat reduced rate, supplemented by the forced transportation to the colonies of some 50,000 British convicts, who were disposed of as indentured servants. And between 250,000 and 300,000 Africans were imported. New groups also began to arrive in significant numbers. Religious persecution in France led to the immigration of several thousand Huguenots (forced to flee from France after 1685, when the tolerant Edict of Nantes was revoked); and from Scotland came groups of Jacobites (those faithful to the exiled James II and his son) after their military defeat by the English in 1715. But the main new flows of immigration came from two quite different sources, which together supplied approximately 20 percent of the total American population when the first national census was taken in 1790.

The Irish   The first new source was Ireland—not Catholic Ireland but Protestant northern Ireland, which had been the first overseas colony of the English people. The efforts of the English in the early seventeenth century to colonize a great "plantation" in Ulster, the six northern counties of Ireland, had attracted to that region a large migration from Scotland, where social and religious conditions throughout the seventeenth century were unsettled. By 1715 perhaps 150,000 Scots had crossed the Irish Sea to settle on Irish estates, where rents were originally low. During the eighteenth century there was a large migration of these "Scotch-Irish" Presbyterians to America. We do not know exactly how many came, but the best estimate is a yearly average of 3,500–4,000 from the first wave of Irish immigration in 1717 until the Revolution, totaling approximately 200,000. It was said by Ireland's great historian, W. E. H. Lecky, that the loss of so many Irish Protestants to America in the eighteenth century ended forever the hope of balancing the religious communities on that tormented island.

German Pietist Emigrants
The man carries in one hand the orthodox Lutheran "Augsburg Confession" and in the other Johann Arndt's classic of pietistic devotion, Vom Wahren Christentum *(1605; republished in Philadelphia in 1751). His pack bears the motto, "God is with us in need," hers, "God has done great things for us"; and between the two is the caption "Nothing but the gospel drives us into exile. Though we leave the fatherland, we remain in God's hand."*

The Germans The other new source of the American population was the upper Rhine Valley in southwestern Germany. This region, especially the area known as the Rhenish Palatinate, had been badly ravaged in the religious wars of the seventeenth century and then, in 1688–89, devastated by French armies. In addition Catholic princes had begun to persecute the region's increasingly numerous Protestant sects. Further troubles beset the area in 1708 and 1709, when crop disasters reduced much of the population to beggary. A new English naturalization law enacted at this time made England an attractive refuge, and a movement of people into British territory began that ended in furnishing a major component of the American population. As early as the 1680s William Penn had begun recruiting settlers in the Rhineland, and the greatest number of German-speaking settlers came to his colony. These "Pennsylvania Dutch" (from Deutsch—that is, Germans, not Hollanders) composed one-third of Pennsylvania's population by 1775. In all, from the original settlement of Pennsylvania to the Revolution approximately 100,000 German-speaking immigrants arrived. The census of 1790 showed almost as many German-born or German-descended Americans (9 percent of the nation's population) as there were Scotch-Irish, and the German influence was at least as important in the development of American society.

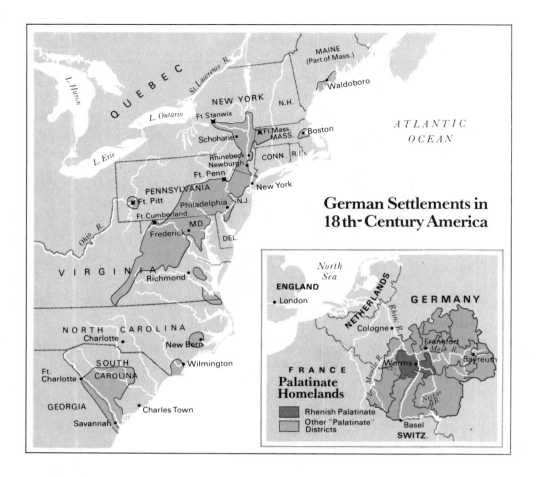

German Settlements in 18th-Century America

Palatinate Homelands

- Rhenish Palatinate
- Other "Palatinate" Districts

Attitudes of the New Immigrants

In the end numbers alone do not account for the importance of migrations like these. More significant are the attitudes, aptitudes, and ambitions of the immigrants, and their influence on the development of the community's life. In the case of the Scotch-Irish and the Germans, the impact was profound. Both groups were alienated from civil and church authority; both were hostile to all establishments, stubborn in defense of their rights, and eager to gain economic security. Both contributed powerfully to the shaping of American social and political life.

For the Scotch-Irish, resentment, if not hatred, of the British establishment had long been a way of life. Britain had excluded Irish products from sale elsewhere in British territory and thereby had crippled Ireland's economic growth. Further, the Anglo-Irish landlords, often absentees, had increased rents when leases fell due. Moreover, the Scotch-Irish, being Presbyterians, were outside the official Anglican church, hence "nonconformist"; as such they were victimized by the Anglican religious establishment, which they had to support by paying special taxes. In 1704 a religious test excluded Presbyterians from all public offices, and marriages performed in their churches were declared invalid.

As a result of this harassment, the first wave of Scotch-Irish immigrants, arriving in Boston and in the Delaware ports between 1717 and 1720, carried with them a burning resentment of the British establishment in all its forms. Those who followed, attracted by enthusiastic letters from America promising "liberty and ease as the reward of...honest industry," freedom from escalating rents, and access to public office, shared these attitudes in varying degrees and carried these resentments throughout the colonies.

The Germans had no natural affinity with the British establishment and no political contacts to help protect them in this exploitative world. Further, since they were aliens, their legal position was weak. Before 1740 they could become British subjects only through specific deeds of "denization" (grants of residency) or through naturalization conferred by the colonial governments. Important rights were bestowed by such actions, but they could be revoked, and they did not bind the British government. Hence locally naturalized Germans could not qualify as "British" subjects under the navigation acts, and naturalization by one colony was not automatically recognized in the other colonies. Many of these problems were eliminated by Parliament's general Naturalization Law of 1740, which permitted aliens who had resided continuously for seven years in any of the British colonies to become naturalized subjects of all colonies. But naturalization by this process was time-consuming. Moreover, it excluded Catholics; it involved an oath offensive to Jews, Quakers, and certain other Protestants; and it did not carry over fully to Britain itself, where naturalized colonists were not automatically entitled to own land or to hold crown office.

Alienated from, if not actively hostile to, the British government, these Scotch-Irish and German newcomers had little reason to feel close to the separate colonial governments either, or to the groups that dominated these governments. They often settled in backcountry areas remote from the colonial capitals; sometimes they did not even know which colony they belonged to as they moved through the hinterland. Often they settled an area before the arrival of the local government, whose agents therefore appeared as exploiters. In addition, the immigrants were often deliberately victimized, not merely by land speculators and managers of the infamous trade in "redemptioners" (those who found on their arrival that they had to sell their labor for a term of years to pay for their transportation), but almost officially by the colonial governments themselves.

The Black Population and Slavery

If the Scotch-Irish and the Germans were alienated in various ways from the Anglo-American establishment, they at least had access to the processes of law and ultimately of politics by which to express their grievances. For the black population there were no possibilities of relief and assimilation. Their separateness was rigidly fixed by the alienation of race and by the debasement of slavery.

We do not fully know—and probably never will know—how this large population of black people accommodated themselves to North American life, the fearful human cost of that accommodation, and the character of their resistance to the brutal system that dominated their lives. There are no documents that directly record their feelings and the intimate details of their personal lives. But from the indirect evidence that has been assembled, one catches glimpses not only of degradation, but also of bewildering ambiguities and paralyzing tensions in human relations. There were also heroic efforts to maintain some measure of human dignity.

As it developed in the eighteenth century, slavery had many shadings and variations. Only 10 percent of the slave population lived north of Maryland, constituting a mere 4 percent to 5 percent of the population of the northern colonies. Slaves were spread thinly throughout the North; their highest concentration in that region was in New York City, where they may have formed as much as 17 percent of the population. Slaves in the North worked side by side with white field servants in the countryside and as laborers in the towns. They mingled with the poorest elements among the whites, formed stable families, and even managed to accumulate small sums on the side when they were "hired out" by their masters to work for others. These northern blacks—field hands, town laborers, and factory workers—were mostly native-born Americans, and they formed part, although a severely deprived part, of the general Anglo-American world.

The opposite was true of the tens of thousands of transplanted Africans (a third of all the North American blacks) who lived in the Carolinas and Georgia. The worst conditions were those on the rice and indigo plantations of South Carolina. There, in tropical heat, laboring half the year knee-deep in the muck of the rice fields, the slaves lived unspeakably wretched lives. They were isolated from the dominant society and alienated from the roots of their own culture. The death rate in this disease-ridden environment was appalling. The black population increased only because of the continuous addition of new arrivals—thousands upon thousands of newly enslaved Africans who had survived the 15–20 percent death rate on the transatlantic voyage and had been sold like animals in the great Charleston slave market. On these isolated plantations in the Deep South, the blacks' culture remained closer to that of West Africa than it did anywhere else in British North America.

The tobacco plantations of the Chesapeake region, on which more than half of the black population lived, were quite different. By the 1760s some of the plantations had become large enough to support slave quarters that constituted well-organized communities. Family life was relatively stable, and the population grew by natural increase. Further, the need for house servants and artisans of all kinds relieved a sizable percentage of the black population from the worst kind of field work. Here, in this long-established tobacco world, where black kinship groups of second- and third-generation American natives spread across groups of plantations, a stable Afro-American culture, distinctive in religion, music and dance, and social institutions, developed most fully. But the decency of the slaves' lives, where it existed at all, was extremely superficial. However assimilated they

Slave Auction, 1769

Virginia Tobacco Wharf
*This realistic dockside scene in
the Chesapeake tobacco country
is a decorative design from the
first accurate map of Virginia
(1751) made by Joshua Fry and
Peter Jefferson, Thomas's father,
who was a surveyor as well as a
planter.*

R UN A W A Y from the subscriber in *Norfolk*, about the 20th of *October* last, two young Negro fellows, *viz.* WILL, about 5 feet 8 inches high, middling black, well made, is an outlandish fellow, and when he is surprised the white of his eyes turns red; I bought him of Mr. *Moss*, about 8 miles below *York*, and imagine he is gone that way, or some where between *York* and *Williamsburg*. PETER, about 5 feet 9 inches high, a very black slim fellow, has a wife at *Little Town*, and a father at Mr. *Philip Burt's* quarter, near the half-way house between *Williamsburg* and *York*; he formerly belonged to Parson *Fontaine*, and I bought him of Doctor *James Carter*. They are both outlawed; and **TEN POUNDS** a piece offered to any person that will kill the said Negroes, and bring me their heads, or **THIRTY SHILLINGS** for each if brought home alive.

JOHN BROWN.

Advertisement for the Return of Runaway Slaves, Virginia, 1767
Such ads were common in the southern newspapers (at least 1,500 appeared in Virginia newspapers, 1736–1801). But this ad, offering a higher reward for the execution of a slave than for his return, was unusual, and relates to the slave's having been "outlawed"—a legal status imposed by justices of the peace that defined a chronic runaway as "incorrigible" and a public liability, available for execution by any citizen. Anyone who killed an "outlaw" was not only rewarded by the owner but also given a fee by the government. According to the Virginia slave code, if returned, an "outlawed" slave could be legally punished "either by dismembering, or any other way…for the reclaiming any such incorrigible slaves, and terrifying others from the like practices."

may have been in the North, and however involved they may have been in kinship networks in Virginia and Maryland, slaves everywhere were debased by the bondage that confined them. Humane masters might create plantations resembling biblical patriarchies, and wise masters might discover the economic value of allowing blacks to enjoy a little leisure and independent activity, as well as the dignity of family life. But everywhere brutality was never far below the surface. And everywhere there was resistance of some sort.

On the plantations in the South, untrained slaves fresh from Africa were most often sent off to outlying plots of land, where they spent their lives in unending field work. Frequently they still bore the ritual face scars of their earlier life in African tribes, where they had learned companionship and cooperation, and where they had thought of time not in terms of hourly routines but of seasonal cycles. Thus they found it extremely difficult, at times impossible, to adjust to the grueling labor. Some ran off in the hope of returning to Africa or of setting up villages to re-create the life they had known. In the early years a few found refuge in "maroon" (fugitive) encampments in the Carolina swamps and deep in frontier forests; but most of the runaways were returned—exhausted, half-starved, and in rags after long exposure in the woods and swamps—to continue their inescapable "seasoning." In time, however, these field hands found effective means of resistance, not in hopeless efforts to escape, but in deliberately slowing down in their work, in wasting equipment, in damaging crops, and in silently disobeying. Their rebelliousness, directed at the plantation and only occasionally at their overseers or master, could have no long-term results, but at least it gave immediate relief to their feelings.

More complex and more self-damaging was the resistance of the American-born slaves employed as personal servants in and around the planters' houses. Enclosed within households of patriarchal discipline, they were forced into continuous close contact with their masters, who were made tense and insecure by the blacks' constant presence, and whose domestic lives were poisoned by the helpless availability of slaves of both sexes. Commonly the slaves perfected techniques of petty harassment that increased their masters' insecurity. Convenient personality disguises (the seemingly obedient "Sambo") minimized for slaves the likelihood of clashes with masters whose tensions could be released in sadistic rages.

The most openly rebellious of the eighteenth-century slaves were the thoroughly assimilated and highly skilled artisans, whose talents gave them a measure of independence and who could deal with the environment as effectively as the whites. They were the most likely to survive as fugitives, and the most capable of easing their everyday burdens by shrewd manipulation. Closest to the white man's world, these skilled workmen understood the full meaning of their bondage; and although they lived more comfortably than the majority of blacks, they may have suffered even more. Everywhere slavery meant profound degradation and constant fear—for the whites as well as for the blacks.

A Maturing Economy and a Society in Flux

The single most distinctive fact of the American economy as a whole in the eighteenth century was the broad spread of freehold tenure—the outright ownership of land—throughout the free population. In contrast, all the land in England in the mid-eighteenth century was owned by only one-tenth of all heads of household. Between 20 percent and 25 percent of England's land was owned by four hundred great landlords, representing a mere $\frac{3}{100}$ of 1 percent of all families. More than 80 percent of this land was worked by tenants, whose rent constituted the income on which the landowners lived. The social experience of the great majority of the English people was based on tenancy; it shaped the structure of English society and the organization of politics, for both rested on the existence of a leisured aristocracy supported by the income that others produced from the land. And the force behind all agrarian enterprise was the unspoken assumption that the more land one owned, the greater one's income would be, an assumption based on the scarcity of arable land relative to the available labor.

The situation in the American colonies was entirely different. From the beginning the great attraction had been the availability of free or cheap land, and that attraction had not proved false. Although there were important regional variations and although tenancy increased, especially in the oldest settlements of the upper South, the majority of the nonslave farm workers owned the land they worked, even if only at the end of their working lives and even if not in the form and amount they desired. This dominant fact of eighteenth-century American life created conditions different from those that existed elsewhere. How unusual the resulting situation was may perhaps best be seen by examining the apparent *exceptions*—situations in which a re-creation of the traditional life of landlords would appear to have taken place.

The Great Landowners The population growth and the resulting increase in land values led the descendants of the seventeenth-century proprietors to cash in, if possible, on their claims to large tracts of land. Four such claims were particularly imposing. The Penn family claimed the undistributed land of Pennsylvania. The Calvert family asserted its rights to Maryland's unsettled land. Earl Granville, the heir of Sir George Carteret, took up his right to one share of the original Carolina grant, a claim that was calculated to cover most of the northern half of the present state of North Carolina. And Lord Fairfax was the heir to the Northern Neck of Virginia, the 5 million acres between the Potomac and the Rappahannock rivers that had originally been granted by Charles II in 1649. By the mid-eighteenth century these colossal properties were no longer wild lands, but territories being opened to cultivation, and they were suddenly becoming valuable to their owners. But with the exception of Fairfax, who lived in Virginia after 1753, none of these great landowners were resident landlords, and none were personally engaged in managing and developing landed estates worked by permanent tenants in the familiar European pattern. The landlords' greatest profits came less from steady rents than from sales in rising land markets.

The operations of these great proprietary landowners were not essentially different from those of lesser land speculators throughout the colonies. Because the lands were originally uncultivated, the owners had the choice either of making a high capital investment to clear the land, to erect buildings on it, and otherwise to make it rentable at a profit; or of renting it out at low or no rent, and benefiting from the increased value created by the labor of tenants as they worked the land. The former of these choices was distinctly uneconomic: many other kinds of investments were more profitable than preparing wild land for lucrative rentals. The best strategy was to rent out the land cheaply to tenants who would open it to cultivation and who looked forward eventually to buying the land themselves. Profits from such land sales, based on the initial labor of tenants, could be large, and also continuous, since the purchasers often bought the farms from the original landowners on loans secured by mortgages on the land itself.

In a few places in the colonies, however, there were landowners who did seek to establish themselves as landlords in the traditional sense, and they encountered sharp and at times even violent opposition. On a few estates along the Hudson River, and in New Jersey to a lesser extent, many of the traditional forms of landlordism were re-created: high perpetual rents imposed on a population of tenants, incidental taxes and fees, and insecurity of tenure. These burdens could be enforced because the landlords had political influence, because their land claims were carefully protected in law, and because they controlled the courts through which tenants would normally have sought relief. But in the end the system produced more trouble than could easily be handled. Many of the tenants simply refused to accept the burdens. They protested continually, and they resorted to all sorts of devices to destroy the landlords' control. From Indians or from New England land speculators, they commonly acquired titles of one sort or another to the land they worked, and they sought to validate these claims legally.

By the 1750s the situation on the tenanted estates in eastern New York and in New Jersey was becoming explosive. The tenants refused to pay rents and duties; and when the courts tried to extract the payments due, the tenants rose up in armed rebellion. The climax came in 1766 in a wave of rioting. Tenants simply renounced their leases and refused to get off the land when ordered to do so. In Westchester County in New York, rebellious farmers formed mobs, opened the jails, and stormed the landlords' houses. It took a regiment of regular troops with militia auxiliaries to put down the uprising. Yet even after the rebellion had been forcibly put down, tenancy could not be uniformly enforced. Many of the farmers simply moved off to the nearest vacant land. One of their chief destinations was Vermont, which as a result of this exodus from the Hudson River estates, and of a parallel migration of discontented New Englanders, was opened to settlement for the first time.

Plantations in the South Thus as an exception to the general American pattern of landownership, landlordism on the Hudson River estates could be maintained only with great difficulty. A more glaring exception to the rule of freehold tenure was in the South, where plantations worked by slave labor would seem, in some measure at least, to have created the economic basis of a landed aristocracy. But the southern aristocrats of the eighteenth century lived in a completely different world from that of the English gentry and aristocracy whose lifestyle they tried to emulate. There were large estates in the South, although not many: in Maryland only 2 percent to 4 percent of all estates were worth over £1,000 in the years before 1760. And these large estates did support an aristocracy of sorts. But the plantation estates in the South were far different from the tenanted estates of the English aristocracy, quite aside from the obvious fact that the labor force was composed of slaves rather than of legally free tenants.

An English estate was not a single unit of production: it was a combination of many separately producing farms managed by individual tenants. A plantation in the eighteenth-century American South, on the other hand, was a single unit of

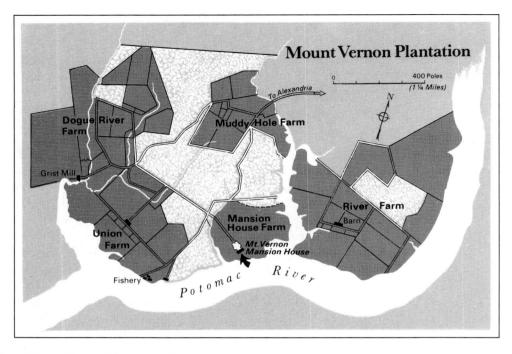

Mount Vernon Plantation, About 1787
The plantation, which occupied about 10,000 acres, consisted of four working farms and the mansion house property. It was a largely self-sufficient community, containing, besides the slave quarters and agricultural buildings on the farms, a coach house and stables, a smoke house, a spinning house, a spring house, a wash house, carpenter's, tailor's, shoemaker's, and blacksmith's shops, and vegetable gardens.

production—a large, unified agricultural organization under a single management. The whole enterprise was operated as a unit in directing labor and in planning production. From these basic conditions flowed the central characteristics of the life of the southern gentry.

The eighteenth-century southern planters were not leisured landlords living comfortably on profits produced by others, any more than the seventeenth-century plantation owners had been. They were closely involved in the process of crop management, land use, and labor direction, and they thus became active producers of their own income. Even if overseers were the immediate supervisors of work on the plantations, the planters discovered at their cost that they themselves had to exercise managerial control. The eighteenth-century British politician and political thinker Edmund Burke said that the basis of any true aristocracy was "uncontending ease, the unbought grace of life." But a glance at such vivid documents as the diaries of the Virginia planter Landon Carter shows the worried concerns of hard-pressed agrarian businessmen, absorbed in ledgers, profit margins, and the endless difficulties of farm production and labor management. The plantation owners did attain a certain graciousness in style of living. But that elegance was a light veneer over a rough-grained life of land dealing, of physically caring for and disciplining a partially dehumanized and potentially rebellious slave labor force, and of trying to make a profit in a commercial world over which the planters could exercise little influence.

Plantations in the South differed from European estates in that an increase in the size of the unit of ownership did not increase the income available to the owner. The larger the plantation, the more exposed the owner was to economic dangers, and the more uncertain the profits he might earn; for the larger the estate, the greater the fixed costs of maintaining slaves and equipment. These expenses remained constant or increased no matter what the marketing situation might be, and in bad years debts could rise drastically. Indeed, once started, a marketing depression tended to deepen rapidly and uncontrollably as unsold goods carried over from one season to the next, enlarging the glut to catastrophic size.

In such periods of downturn, the planter, far from enjoying the "unbought grace of life," struggled desperately to cut overhead costs or otherwise compensate for the marketing losses. Some concentrated on attaining self-sufficiency in the production of food and clothing to reduce the effects of indebtedness. Others turned to crop diversification. Starting on the eastern shore of the Chesapeake in the 1720s and continuing west rapidly, planters began partially converting to the production of grains and livestock, although the emphasis on tobacco production remained. Still other planters took what benefit they could from a new form of marketing introduced by Scottish entrepreneurs, whose investments in the southern American economy in the eighteenth century were a significant development.

The Scottish merchants and bankers, principally in Glasgow, concentrated on developing the interior of the Chesapeake region. In this backcountry, the units of tobacco production tended to be smaller than they were in the coastal regions; there was very little capital to start with; and there was no direct contact with ocean shipping. The old consignment system of marketing tobacco was therefore inappropriate for the development of this region.* In an effort to reduce freight charges and to increase efficiency, the Scottish firms established stores in the backcountry. The agents, or "factors," who managed these stores bought tobacco crops outright, stored them, and shipped them to central distribution points where vessels sent from Scotland could take up cargoes as fast as they could load.

From the merchants' point of view, this system had the advantage of eliminating the waiting time that vessels otherwise would have in collecting a cargo. Hence it provided a considerable reduction in shipping costs. For the tobacco growers it offered somewhat greater control, since they could oversee the actual sale of their crops without having to account for the complexities of the European tobacco markets. Like the tidewater planters, these inland tobacco growers also accumulated debts to the merchants, but their debts were less for consumer

---

*For the consignment system, see chapter 3, p. 89.

goods than for items needed for production: they took the form of loans for the purchase of slaves, equipment, and the other costs of initiating production. In organizing this trade and in making these investments, the Scots became the financiers of the development of the western tobacco lands. It was estimated that in 1765, Glasgow firms had £500,000 of credits outstanding in the Chesapeake region. And by then their "factors" had become prominent figures—usually unpopular figures—in the region's society.

In none of this was there a reproduction of the economic basis of a traditional landlord class. In all areas and in every subcategory of the agricultural economy, something new had evolved. The few vast properties of the heirs of the original proprietary families were less tenanted estates than the assets of personal land companies whose greatest profits came from the sale of the land. The southern planters did not form a traditional, leisured aristocracy, but rather were active, hard-pressed farm and labor managers whose profits could be endangered by an increase in their holdings. In this world of widespread freehold tenure, attempted re-creations of traditional landlord systems led not to reliable incomes and a life of agrarian ease, but often to controversy, or even violent conflict. It is true that there were peaceable tenants in many areas, and their numbers were growing in the late colonial period. But, especially in the middle and northern colonies, tenancy was not the normal, permanent pattern of life for those who worked the land. Most tenants in New England, one historian has written, "would eventually acquire a small estate of their own by migration, savings, or inheritance." In most places tenancy was an exceptional and temporary condition, and its economic function was ordinarily different from what it traditionally had been in Europe. Often it was voluntary—the result of economic strategies that minimized capital investments, an arrangement that benefited the tenants at least as much as the landowners. Above all, land speculation—the use of land as a salable commodity rather than as a source of steady income—was an almost universal occupation in rural America.

The World of Commerce

The commercial sector of the economy was equally distinctive. Its focus lay in the larger port towns, comparable in size to the second- and third-rank English provincial cities. Except for Boston, whose population was stable at around 16,000, all of these towns continued to grow quickly. Although visitors often noted the towns' outward resemblance to such cities as Edinburgh and Bristol, they also observed some of the differences, which resulted from the fact that the American towns were products of a frontier economy. In all these towns there was, of course, a laboring population, but most of the urban workers were self-employed artisans or workmen in small-scale, often family-sized, businesses. There was a small, though growing, number of casual laborers—dock hands, workers in shipbuilding enterprises, and others—who picked up what employment they could in menial tasks around the towns. They formed a volatile element in these communities, and they suffered in times of depression. But while social

18th-Century Atlantic Trade Routes

Glasgow

ENGLAND

Bristol London

Linens, Horses

NORTH AMERICA

EUROPE

Fish, Furs, Raw Materials, Naval Stores →
← Manufactured Products
← Manufactured Products
Silks, Furs, Raw Materials →
← Manufactured Products
Tobacco → ← Manufactured Products
← Meat, Fish, Rum, Lumber, Grain →
← Manufactured Products
Wine Fruit, Salt
Fruit, Wine
PORT. SPAIN
Lisbon
Cadiz
Wine
Salt

Boston
New York
Philadelphia
ENGLISH COLONIES
Charleston

MADEIRA IS.

Molasses, Fruit, Sugar

European Products

Fish, Livestock, Flour, Lumber

Slaves, Molasses

Slaves, Molasses

Slaves, Molasses

Slaves, Coin

CUBA
WEST
JAMAICA
HISPANIOLA
INDIES
Guadeloupe
Martinique
Barbados

Rum
Slaves
Rum → Slaves →

AFRICA

IVORY, GOLD, SLAVE COASTS

← Slaves

SOUTH AMERICA

———— Major Trade Route   - - - - Intercoastal Trade Route

and economic inequality probably increased as the commercial societies matured, there is no evidence of mass poverty before the Revolutionary years. The number of those who received charity grew, but even in the increasingly crowded port towns, it never approached the figures of the dependent poor in Europe. In England, at times, one-third of the entire population was impoverished; and in the cities, where beggars crowded the cellars and attics, massed in back alleys, and overwhelmed the charitable institutions, another third was poor enough to be rendered destitute by the repeated economic crises. But Philadelphia did not even build an almshouse until 1732; New York built one only in 1736. Rarely before 1760 did more than 1 percent of the population of New York and Philadelphia receive public poor relief in any form. Even in Boston only 1 percent to 2 percent of the population was in the almshouse or workhouse at midcentury.

A series of detailed statistical studies of the British mainland North American colonies in the 1700s reveals a level of living that "was probably the highest achieved for the great bulk of the population in any country up to that time."

Sea Captains Carousing in Surinam, by John Greenwood (1758)
Surinam (Dutch Guiana) on the northern coast of South America was a favorite port of call for American merchants who exchanged horses and tobacco there for sugar products. Greenwood, a Bostonian who lived in Surinam, painted in the faces of several well-known Rhode Island merchants.

Rural Connecticut, it has been shown, ended the colonial period as it had begun: "a land of plenty for some and of sufficiency for most people." Although a relatively small part of the urban population controlled an increasing proportion of the total wealth, and although the gap between rich and poor probably deepened, "the fact remains that not only were the rich getting richer but the poor were too, albeit at a slower rate." There was poverty in the pre-Revolutionary towns (towns which in any case contained only 7 percent to 8 percent of the population as late as 1776), but no mass starvation. There were riots, but no "bread riots" such as frequently broke out in European towns at times of food shortages and high prices. The town "mobs" that became highly visible were not spearheads of a desperate proletariat inflamed by utopian aspirations and seeking to transform the structure of society. Rather, they were crowds of young apprentices, dock workers, and seamen temporarily idle between voyages, usually led by lesser merchants or independent craftsmen.

These conditions are not surprising, for the society of the commercial towns retained the characteristics of a pioneer world. Because labor was still relatively scarce, wages remained high enough to make small savings possible. Day laborers in Boston were paid twice as much as their counterparts in London. Furthermore, in the typical small-scale enterprise the distance between employer and employee remained narrow, both objectively (in terms of lifestyle and function) and subjectively (in terms of feelings of superiority or alienation). The typical artisan worked closely with his employer, and their activities were not unbridgeably different. Labor troubles were quite unlike those in modern society. Strikes were not protests by urban workers against conditions or wages. They were either protests by master workers, employers, and independent artisans against price levels set by the community for the sale of their products, or efforts to stop widespread infiltration by outsiders into licensed trades. Town workers periodically experienced hardships because of changes in the economy, which lurched through repeated phases of boom and bust, but there was no permanently alienated "proletariat."

The urban communities were dominated by the merchants, who in this period became important figures throughout the Atlantic world. Two conflicting tendencies shaped the development of the merchant group. During the early and middle years of the eighteenth century, there were forces that tended to limit and stabilize the mercantile leadership—to make of these leading figures an elite merchant aristocracy. But at the same time other forces, related to the deepest elements of the developing economy, were tending to upset the dominance of all would-be merchant elites.

In part, political stability in England created a significant degree of stability in the early-eighteenth-century merchant group. The secure arrangement of politics, patronage, and influence devised by the prime minister Robert Walpole in the 1720s helped stabilize the organization of Atlantic commerce, which was involved with politics and government contracting. At the same time, specialization increased within the English merchant establishment throughout the period, and the specialist wholesalers who controlled shipments to the colonies restricted their trade to selected American associates. And there were also technical improvements in trade and finance, particularly the development of marine insurance, that helped make possible a growing concentration of commercial capital and entrepreneurial control.

All these developments, along with the general fact that large operators could create economies of scale, tended to produce elitist characteristics within the commercial community. Yet despite the emergence of dominant groups, the merchant community as a whole, and commerce as a whole, remained competitive and changeable in membership. For, first, as raw frontier areas matured into settled agricultural producing regions, successful farmers branched out into marketing, becoming inland traders and ultimately merchants. Prosperous market farmers, particularly those located at transfer points on the rivers or inland trade routes, parlayed their advantages in goods and location into trading operations and drifted into commercial pursuits, often combined with land speculation.

But it was not only a matter of old settled areas producing surpluses from which market farmers could build careers in commerce. Wholly new hinterlands developed almost overnight, and from them emerged new men who proved effective competitors indeed.

In 1720 the chief agricultural producing areas were located northeast of the Hudson River and in the Chesapeake region. Thereafter the area between the Hudson River and Chesapeake Bay became the dominant agricultural region. Into the swiftly growing port of Philadelphia poured surplus goods, chiefly grain, from the Pennsylvania backcountry, from New Jersey, and from parts of Maryland; and this flow enriched a new merchant aristocracy in Philadelphia, many of whose members were Quakers. By the 1760s the value of their trade with England exceeded that of all of New England. Similar developments took place in other regions. Within only ten years in the 1740s and 1750s, Baltimore rose from a wilderness village to a thriving urban center serving the marketing needs of a new backcountry area, and within a single generation Baltimore's merchants became important figures in the commercial world.

The result of all these movements in agriculture and trade was a highly dynamic mercantile world. Conditions had made possible the stabilization of a merchant leadership group. But the rapid development of the economy in long-settled areas and the constant opening of new areas of agricultural production created a steady recruitment of new merchants and a continuous competition between established figures and newcomers. There was a widespread sense that certain merchant families, established by the 1760s for two, three, or even four generations, were forming an elite; but there were always new faces, new families, capable of taking the same successful risks that had once served to establish the older families.

Religion: The Sources of American Denominationalism

The tensions within the commercial world were moderate compared with those that developed in religion. Because American culture in the mid-eighteenth century was still largely religious in its orientation, these tensions lay at the heart of the social world everywhere in the colonies, north and south, seaboard and inland.

The central event in the history of religion in America in the eighteenth century was the Great Awakening, a series of outbreaks of revivalism in the late 1730s and the 1740s. The Great Awakening roared through the colonies like a sheet of flame and left behind it a world transformed. In part this wave of passionate evangelicalism was a typical expression of a general religious movement that swept through much of the Western world in the eighteenth century. The Great Awakening coincided with an outpouring of Anglican evangelicalism—which would become Methodism—in England and Wales, and with a wave of Pietism in the German-speaking world. There were direct connections between the American revivalists and their European counterparts; but there was also something unique in the American evangelical movement, and it produced quite distinctive results.

Religion and Society in New England   In New England the background and sources of the Awakening came closest to the European pattern of such evangelical waves. By the early eighteenth century the Congregationalist churches had experienced the draining away of inner fervor and of emotional commitment that is typical of all long-established churches and that characteristically produces searchings for religious renewal and outbursts of evangelical enthusiasm. Puritan Congregationalism had itself originated as a protest against a formal church establishment, the Church of England, and in its original form it contained two essential characteristics that clearly distinguished it from any established church. First, membership in the Congregationalist churches was not an automatic consequence of birth: that is, people were not "born into" the church. Rather, membership resulted from individual acts of voluntary commitment based on an inner experience. Second, church institutions in New England had been decentralized into Congregational units.

But these original characteristics of New England Puritanism did not survive unchanged into the eighteenth century, and their erosion helps explain the background of the Awakening in New England. By the mid-seventeenth century the New England churches had faced a crisis that arose from the failure of the second and third generations to duplicate the spiritual experiences of the founders and to join the churches through an act of saving grace. The founders' children had been baptized in the church because their parents had been members and it was felt that ultimately they too would experience a conversion. But until that "calling" came, these children could not become full members. In fact many were never converted. Should, then, the children of these baptized but unconverted persons also be baptized?

This was the agonizing problem that had faced the Puritans in the mid-seventeenth century. If the answer had been Yes, then the church as a body of converted Christians would have been destroyed. But if the answer had been No, then, as conversions became fewer and fewer, the church would have grown apart from the society as a whole; it would have become a mere sect, without the basis for social control that was so fundamental a part of Puritan life. The solution came from a convention of ministers that met in 1657, whose decision was confirmed by a synod of 1662. The arrangement that was devised became known as the Halfway Covenant. Unconverted members could transmit membership in the church automatically to their children, but only a halfway membership. These children would be baptized, but they would not be offered the sacrament of communion, nor would they be entitled to vote as members of the church. As halfway members, they would be required to make a public pledge to obey the rulings of the church and to bring up their children as proper Christians. Still, they were members, if only partial, and the distinction between them and the full members who sat with them in church week after week was thin and grew thinner and more technical as the years passed.

The Halfway Convenant was an unstable compromise that deeply eroded the Puritans' original concept of the church as a body of proven saints. Conservatives and liberals alike found the halfway distinction illogical and unmanageable. Some of both factions began baptizing all, and sought to bring everyone to communion who was willing to accept it.

It was partly in an effort to control such permissive innovations that the more orthodox Puritan churches moved toward centralization of church government and away from congregational autonomy. In Massachusetts regional associations of ministers were formed, which sought to impose certification and disciplinary powers over the clergy and over the general management of church affairs. Although an attempt to give these organizations legal force was defeated in 1705, informal communication among the churches was strengthened. In Connecticut a parallel effort succeeded completely. There, the so-called Saybrook Platform of 1708 became public law. County "consociations" of the Congregationalist churches with disciplinary powers were created, together with regional associations of ministers and a colonywide general association of delegates of the ministers.

By all of these developments—a slackening in religious fervor, a growing identity of church and society, and the spread of general controls over originally independent congregations—the Puritan churches increasingly approached the condition of a traditional church establishment. But the process had obvious limits. In the eyes of British law, Congregational churches were nonconformist, and therefore they could never have the full sanction of law behind them. In New England the Anglican church (here, paradoxically, a "dissenting" body) led all opposition groups in demanding that its members enjoy the privileges granted to nonconformists in England. And in this the opposition groups were successful. In the 1720s Anglicans, Quakers, and Baptists gained full rights of worship in Congregationalist New England and of using their church taxes to support their own churches. Members of these groups were free, too, to hold office and to attend all institutions of learning. But they still remained tolerated groups, obliged to register with the authorities. No one was free of the obligation to support religion, and no group but these three was allowed the privileges of dissent.

New England Congregationalism was thus an establishment, but it was a loose establishment, in which religion as an intense inner experience tended to fade, and in which formal observance and institutional ritual had grown increasingly important. Less and less did the churches satisfy people's inner yearnings; more and more were these churches vulnerable to the charge of excessive formalism and of a deadening complacency.

Religion and Society South of New England

In the other colonies the churches were even less capable of satisfying the deeper needs of their societies. In the middle colonies, swarming with competitive religious groups, the Presbyterian, Lutheran, and German Reformed churches lacked clergy who could command respect and stir religious feelings, and they failed to provide adequate institutions for worship. Their religion became so slack and coldly formal that some would-be worshipers drifted away into indifference while others sought deeper satisfactions in the passionate worship of the many small sectarian groups whose numbers swelled while the churches declined. In Virginia the Church of England had long been unable to serve the deeper needs of the community, and the situation there was now worsened by the church's uncertain relationship to the new settlers, almost all non-Anglicans, who had moved into the backcountry in the 1720s and 1730s. Maryland too, after 1702, had an established Anglican church, but the Anglican community in that colony was numerically small, and its hold on the population at large was even looser than that of the Church of England in Virginia.

Everywhere the Anglican church was overwhelmed by competition in situations so volatile that they cannot be clearly described. There were Anglican establishments of sorts in the Carolinas and Georgia—the latter colony having been settled in 1732 by Anglicans as a refuge for England's paupers and as a buffer against Spanish Florida. But nonconformists were welcomed in these colonies, and little effort was made to regulate religious life as a whole, which in many areas was overwhelmingly non-Anglican. And in New York, where non-Anglicans outnumbered Anglicans by at least fifteen to one, the only flourishing Anglican institution was New York City's Trinity Church, which Governor Fletcher had endowed with an independent source of income.

Amid the institutional confusion of religion in eighteenth-century America, the overwhelming fact was that the dominant churches, no matter what their definition, were failing to minister effectively to the needs of a people for whom religion continued to be a primary emotional and cultural experience. It is significant that the most vigorous branch of the Church of England in eighteenth-century America was its missionary organization, the Society for the Propagation of the Gospel in Foreign Parts, or SPG. Originally formed to bring Christianity to the Indians, it had instead devoted itself to guaranteeing the survival of the Anglican church in America and strengthening it in every possible way. Under its first leader, the Reverend Thomas Bray (1656–1730), the SPG launched missionary expeditions to likely points throughout the colonies, helped maintain existing parishes and establish new ones, and functioned as the Anglican church's only effective organization above the parish level.

The Great Awakening

Into this increasingly formal, ill-served, parched, and questing religious world the fervor of the Great Awakening fell like a blazing torch. The revival did not begin all at once. There had been premonitions as early as the 1670s, and in the 1730s a major explosion took place in the Connecticut River valley, touched off by the remarkable young minister of Northampton, Massachusetts, Jonathan Edwards.

He was heir to a famous ecclesiastical tradition. Edwards's grandfather had been the influential "Pope" Solomon Stoddard of Northampton, whom he eventually succeeded. From the time of his graduation from Yale at the age of seventeen, Edwards had devoted himself to the central philosophical and theological problems of the age. While preaching and fulfilling his other duties as a minister, he worked out a system of ideas so subtle and so original that it has established him as one of the most powerful thinkers of the eighteenth century. His chief professional task, however, was more ordinary: it was to bring the sinful

Jonathan Edwards, by Joseph Badger
Painted a few years before Edwards was expelled from his Northampton pulpit for insisting on conversion as a basis for church membership and for attempting to discipline children of leading families. After seven years as a missionary to the Indians, Edwards was chosen president of the College of New Jersey (Princeton) but died after a few months in office, at the age of fifty-five.

to a knowledge of God and to the experience of spiritual rebirth. Stoddard had stirred local revivals in the 1720s. In 1734 and 1735 Edwards, to his great surprise and gratification, suddenly found his own people responding overwhelmingly to his carefully reasoned sermons on justification by faith. Northampton was overcome with religious enthusiasm. Dozens of once-complacent parishioners experienced tumultuous passions of religious rebirth.

Word of the God-inspired revival spread swiftly through the farming hamlets of the Connecticut River valley and then eastward along Long Island Sound, touching off similar outbreaks as it went. By the time Edwards published an account of his local revival, his *Faithful Narrative of the Surprising Work of God* (1737), the wave had passed, but already the surge of religious fervor had become famous throughout the colonies and in Great Britain as well. It had inspired ministers everywhere to new efforts in bringing uninspired people to an experience of God's grace, and it had created a great sense of expectation that some vast outpouring of religious zeal—perhaps even the actual establishment of God's Kingdom on earth—was about to take place. Such anticipation was spilling over into fulfillment by 1740. In that year George Whitefield, the brilliant English preacher who had already stirred successful revivals on two tours through the middle and southern colonies, appeared in New England. It was Whitefield, following in the wake of Edwards's revival, who finally threw open the floodgates and let loose an outpouring of soul-shaking evangelicalism that flooded New England for four tumultuous years.

Whitefield's tour of New England was spectacular. In Boston he preached first to hundreds who jammed the churches until they could hold no more, and then to thousands at open-air meetings. The young, impassioned orator deeply

George Whitefield Preaching, by John Wollaston (1741, when Whitefield was 27)

He appeared, a Connecticut farmer recalled, "almost angelical; a young, slim, slender youth before thousands of people with a bold, undaunted countenance,…he looked as if he was clothed with authority from the Great God,…and my hearing him preach gave me a heart wound." "What a spell he casts over an audience," Jonathan Edwards's wife wrote, "by proclaiming the simplest truths of the Bible. I have seen upwards of a thousand people hang on his words with breathless silence, broken only by an occasional half-suppressed sob."

stirred listeners used to hearing scholarly sermons read to them from carefully prepared texts. He was equally successful in a series of meetings in northern New England, and then in the West. In Northampton his preaching was so moving that Jonathan Edwards, Whitefield reported, "wept during the whole time of exercise." After stops south in the Connecticut River valley towns that had already experienced the revival, Whitefield ended his tour in New York.

His preaching, Whitefield correctly reported, had made a significant impact in the North. So too did the preaching of the second great leader of the Awakening, Gilbert Tennent. For a decade this second-generation Scotch-Irish minister had led the "New Light" (evangelical) party within the growing Presbyterian communities of New Jersey and New York. He had been educated in his father's "Log College" in Neshaminy, Pennsylvania, which had been devoted to spreading the principles of "experimental" religion—that is, religion that was deeply experienced rather than intellectual and doctrine-bound. Tennent's tour through southern New England lasted three months in the fall and winter of 1740–41. Where his influence was felt it was a time of mass excitement, profound emotional upheaval, and inner transformation.

Elsewhere too the revival continued its blazing progress. It tore through the Presbyterian and Dutch Reformed communities of the middle colonies, splitting them into conservative and evangelical wings. The "New Side"—evangelical—Presbyterians of Pennsylvania and New Jersey formed their own governing body in 1741 and sent out traveling preachers to invade districts dominated by the conservative "Old Side." These revivalist Presbyterians moving southward from

Pennsylvania had the greatest impact in Virginia; in Hanover County in that colony, their most successful preacher, Samuel Davies, produced the most important of the southern revivals. In the process Davies spurred the Anglican authorities to take repressive measures against nonconformity by fining preachers who had no official license to preach. Even more influential in the southern colonies were the evangelical Baptists. They reached out more effectively than any other church or sect to the unchurched common people in the backcountry, especially the new settlers on the southern frontier. And at the end of the colonial period, evangelicals within the Church of England, led by the Reverend Devereux Jarratt, who would soon organize the Methodist church, also began to share in the work of extending the Awakening to the settlers on the expanding frontier.

Effects of the Great Awakening   Such was the greatest event in the history of religion in eighteenth-century America. Its effects were more revolutionary by far than those of the parallel developments in Europe—Pietism in Germany and Methodism in England and Wales. The differences are revealing. The revivals in America were not, as elsewhere, distinctively lower-class movements that gave new voice to the aspirations of the socially deprived. Nor were they limited to any particular geographical group: they were as successful in the large towns as in the countryside. Their impact could not be confined. The great revivalist wave deeply affected at least four areas of American social life.

First, the authority and status of the established clergy were permanently weakened. The revivalists cared little for offices, formal status, education, learning, or even, within reasonable limits, outward behavior. For the revivalists, qualification for religious leadership was gained only by force of inner experience and by the ability to stimulate parishioners' spiritual aspirations. It followed naturally that the revivalists would challenge the authority of established educational institutions like Yale and Harvard, whose methods of training ministers seemed to them dry and merely intellectual. The government of Connecticut became alarmed at the progress of the Great Awakening and barred from the ministry anyone not trained at Yale, Harvard, or a foreign Protestant university. The Presbyterian "New Lights" responded not only by setting up their own church organization, but also, in 1746, by creating a new college. This institution, the College of New Jersey, later renamed Princeton, was intended to emphasize religion of the emotions, of the spirit, as well as of the mind. Rutgers, Brown, and Dartmouth were also founded in response to the revival movement. For the Awakening, which challenged all preachers to justify their authority by their own spiritual gifts and by their power to reach into other souls, could not tolerate merely formal qualifications.

Second, the Awakening tended to destroy the identification of churches with specific territorial boundaries. The revivalists believed that their call extended not only to the few people who had employed them as preachers, but to anyone anywhere who would heed their word, and especially to all those whose ministers were unconverted. They therefore naturally became "itinerants," wandering ministers who moved into established congregations. If welcomed, they preached officially as visiting ministers; if not, they set up in barns or open fields and preached to anyone who would listen. The official churches angrily protested against such invasions, and "itinerancy" became one of the central controversies of the revival. But it could not be stopped, and where it occurred it tended to free the churches from specific territorial foundations—to release them into a universe of competing groups.

Related to this was a third effect of the Awakening: nothing less, where its impact was strong, than the near destruction of institutional religion as the organizing framework of small-group society. For throughout the new settlements, and especially on the disorganized frontiers, the church had provided a vital center for society itself. When the Awakening and its aftershocks hit the more vulnerable communities, a series of splits—separations of dissident, New Light factions from the established churches—frequently occurred. No less than 147 have been recorded, mainly in New England, between 1740 and 1770, 87 in the 1740s alone. A split-off of a "New Light" faction from a stubborn "Old Light" majority ruptured a community; and even if the splinter group eventually returned, it would be more or less free of the original church community's control. At times there was no point at which the disintegration could be stopped. Whole units could simply disappear in the course of successive splinterings, ending in mere clusters of family-sized factions, free of all constraints of church organization.

Finally, the Awakening put unsupportable pressures on what remained of church-state relations, not in doctrine, but in practice. The revivalists did not consider their beliefs to be unorthodox: quite the contrary. They claimed that they alone represented the true orthodoxy in Protestant Christianity and denounced the established churches for their deviations. In doing so they created new grounds for challenging the practical right of any church to claim a privileged place in the eyes of the law. They thereby moved closer to thinking that the very notion of an established church was false, and that the only safe and correct course was to deny all state privileges to any religious group.

Denominationalism   Religion in America acquired a new character as a result of the developments that had been in motion from the time of the first English settlements in North America, developments that had been greatly intensified by the Great Awakening. American religion became essentially voluntaristic—that is, an activity that one was free to join or not to join. Such voluntarism came to apply even to the older established churches, whose official doctrines assumed a close bond between church and society, enforced by the state. Organized religion in America had also developed an emphasis on persuasion as its essential activity. The churches, lacking the sanction of the state to guarantee membership, as well as secure institutional structures and effective group discipline, swung their efforts toward promotion and outward activity and away from the purification of doctrine and the maintenance of internal order. Finally, the role of individual decision shifted. In traditional societies involvement with a dominant religion was automatic, and it was a significant decision to break with the religious association into which one had been born. As a consequence, religious indifference could go hand in hand with extensive, though merely formal, church membership. In the colonies the opposite became true: to do nothing was likely to mean having no religious affiliation at all, and the significant decision involved joining, not withdrawing from, a religious association. As a result, broad waves of religious enthusiasm could go hand in hand with low church membership.

By the end of the colonial period, these characteristics were taking on a patterned and stable form, which would later be called Denominationalism. Products of the fundamental realities of colonial life, these characteristics would find expression in theory, law, and formal doctrine during the American Revolution and in the years that followed.

The Origins of American Politics

A key to understanding much in eighteenth-century America, as in the earlier years, is the gap that developed between expectation and reality. This discordant pattern was particularly important in politics and government. Not only did the discrepancy between theory and expectation on the one hand and reality on the other shape the character of American public life; it also laid the basis for the transformation of the relations between Britain and the colonies.

The Structure of British Politics   All formal notions of public life in the British world rested on the belief that the British political system of the mid-eighteenth century was the freest and best that existed. And the colonial governments and political systems, it was also believed, were more or less imperfect copies of the world-famous British model.

In theory, the heart of the unwritten British constitution was balance. From classical antiquity had come the notion, reaffirmed in the Renaissance and in seventeenth-century England, that there were three pure forms of government. Any one of these, if properly maintained, could serve the people well; but all three tended to degenerate into evil forms that created oppression. Thus monarchy, rule by one person, tended to degenerate into tyranny; aristocracy, rule by a few, became oligarchy (corrupt government by a group of self-serving, all-powerful leaders); and democracy, the rule of the whole political population, declined into the rule of the mob. The challenge to political thinkers had long been the problem of devising a balance among these forms that would stabilize government and bring the degenerative processes to a halt. The British constitution, it was generally agreed, had achieved precisely such a stable balance of pure forms. This balance was embodied in the competition among the crown (monarchy), the House of Lords (aristocracy), and the House of Commons (democracy). This theory was almost universally believed to explain the stability and freedom that Britain had attained.

Yet the theory was misleading as a description of the actual working of the British government. The balance of these three elements was more apparent than real. In theory, each element stayed in its proper sphere; in practice, each thoroughly infiltrated the others' spheres. Moreover, each element functioned differently from the idealized description. In fact the source of the political stability of mid-eighteenth-century Britain did not lie in the supposed balance of these three elements, a balance that Americans sought to emulate. Rather, stability came from two sets of special conditions, both highly relevant, by contrast, to the unique form of politics that developed in eighteenth-century America.

The main underlying condition that made Britain's political stability possible was the fact that the great constitutional issues of the seventeenth century had been settled in the Glorious Revolution of 1688. These issues had centered on the extent of the crown's authority and on the problem of the relationship between church and state.

First, as to the crown's authority, Parliament had concluded the Glorious Revolution by stipulating that the monarch could neither create courts without a law approved by Parliament nor dismiss judges without Parliament's formally indicting them for misconduct, that is, without a formal impeachment. Furthermore, the monarch could not impose taxes, maintain a standing army in peacetime, or engage in wars for foreign territory without Parliament's consent. The crown had also been forced to agree not to limit unduly or extend the existence of a Parliament or interfere with its regular meetings. Parliamentary elections and convenings were put on a regular calendar schedule. In addition, at least after 1707, it was understood that the monarch would not veto acts of Parliament.

Second, as to the church-state relationship after the Glorious Revolution, the Church of England continued to be the established church and, as such, to enjoy the privileges and benefits of the state; and all persons who did not openly reject it were considered to be among its members. But the desire for an enforced uniformity was abandoned. Dissent was tolerated, although it was penalized. The great majority of nonconformists were permitted to worship as they pleased; they enjoyed almost full civil rights, and in the course of the eighteenth century they gained most political rights as well.

These underlying conditions made political stability possible in Britain. The stability that was actually attained was the result of the informal agreement worked out between the crown and the House of Commons. A working relationship between the two was achieved by a set of rules of operation so fundamental that they constituted, in effect, an informal constitution. Under these rules the ministry acted in the crown's behalf to discipline and manipulate the House of Commons, in part by managing elections to the House through the control or outright ownership of easily dominated election districts and "rotten boroughs,"* and in part by distributing crown favors (patronage) to the members so

*For a discussion of rotten boroughs and the unreformed House of Commons in general, see chapter 7, p. 241.

as to ensure safe majorities on controversial issues. In the mid-eighteenth century about 200 of the 558 members of the House of Commons held crown appointments or gifts of one sort or another, and another 30 or 40 were more loosely tied to the government by awards of profitable contracts. A varying number of other members was bound to the administration less directly, particularly by the gift or promise of one or more of the 8,000 excise (tax-collecting) offices that were available for distribution.

Together with the settlement of the main policy questions—those of the crown's powers and of church-state relations—it was this use of "influence" in managing elections and in controlling votes in the two houses of Parliament that explains the stability of English political life in the mid-eighteenth century. There were certain underlying technical conditions for such stabilizing control. The ministry had to have at its command an abundance of patronage that it could distribute. The electorate had to be small, for the larger the voting population, the greater the difficulty of controlling it. And the system of representation had to be unrelated to the shift and growth of the population and not closely bound to the wishes of a broad electorate.

Differences in the Colonies
None of these conditions existed in anything like the same measure in the mainland colonies of British North America. Yet the similarity between the formal structure of the British government and that of the separate colonial governments was a basic principle of political thought in eighteenth-century America. The colonial governments, it was assumed, were miniatures of the British government, and politics too should be similar. Dr. William Douglass of Boston explained in his *Summary, Historical and Political . . . of the British Settlements in North America* (1749–51) that by the governor's

> representing the King, the colonies are monarchical; by the Council, they are aristocratical; by a House of Representatives or delegates from the people, they are democratical: these three are distinct and independent of one another . . . the several negatives being checks upon one another. The concurrence of these three forms of government seem to be the highest perfection that human civil government can attain to in times of peace.

Such irregularities and exceptions as there were in the American replicas of the perfect British government, Douglass said, "doubtless in time will be rectified."

But while in Britain the mixed and balanced constitution produced a high degree of political stability, similar institutions in the colonies produced the opposite. Factional conflict, bitter and intense at times, was common in American politics. First, there was contention between the branches of government— between the executive on the one hand and the legislatures on the other. But it was not only a matter of conflict between branches of government. There was also a milling factionalism that went beyond institutional boundaries and at times reduced the politics of certain colonies to a chaos of competing interest groups.

Some were personal groups—small clusters of relatives and friends that rose suddenly at particular moments and faded quickly, merging into other equally unstable arrangements. Others were economic, regional, and more generally social interest groups; and some of these quickly rose and fell, while some were durable, persisting through a generation or more, although with continual changes in membership. There also were a few groups formed to defend and advance programs that went beyond immediate personal and group interests.

Most of these competing groups were vocal and difficult to control. It is true that in certain colonies at certain times, political life attained the hoped-for balance and tranquility. But most eighteenth-century governors at one time or another echoed the weary question and the anguished plea of William Penn to the political leaders of the City of Brotherly Love soon after it was founded: "Cannot more friendly and private courses be taken to set matters right in an infant province? . . . For the love of God, me, and the poor country, be not so govern-mentish!"

But Pennsylvania remained, in Penn's words, "noisy and open in [its] dissatisfactions," and so did most of the other colonies during the three genera-tions that preceded the Revolution. For beneath the apparent similarities in the formal systems of government in Britain and America, there were basic dif-ferences in the informal structure of politics. The similarities in government were superficial; the differences in politics were so profound as to make the colonies seem almost the reverse of the universally admired British model.

The political settlement that had been made in England at the end of the Glorious Revolution had not extended to the colonies. In all but the chartered colonies of Rhode Island and Connecticut, the governors had the executive authority to veto legislation, which could also be disallowed by the Privy Council or the proprietors in Britain. In addition, the royal governors had the authority to delay sittings of the lower houses of the colonial assemblies and to dissolve them at will, and they quickly became accustomed to using those powers. As a result, the lower houses were as dependent on executive wishes for their existence as the House of Commons had been before the Glorious Revolution. Nor was the judiciary in the colonies protected as it was in Britain. Judges at all levels, from justices of the peace to the chief justices of the supreme courts, were appointed by nomination of the governors and could be dismissed by the executives' wishes. Similarly, the governors in all but the three chartered colonies (Massachusetts, Rhode Island, and Connecticut) could create courts without the agreement of the legislature. Indeed, the governors did so repeatedly, especially chancery courts, in which there were no juries and which were concerned with such unpopular matters as collecting arrears of quitrents. Associated with these "prerogative courts" in the colonists' minds were the vice-admiralty courts, also without juries, which decided maritime cases and had broader jurisdiction than did the equiv-alent courts in England. Lesser powers that had been eliminated in Britain were also given to the executive in America: power over the election of the Speakers of the House; power over church appointments; power over fees.

It was primarily in the more important areas—vetoing colonial legislation, dismissing and dissolving legislative bodies, and firing judges and creating courts—that the legal power of the executive was felt by the colonists to be most threatening and a source of danger to liberty and to the free constitution. But even more than the greater power of the executive, an array of other circumstances distinguished the American colonial governments from the British government. These factors radically reduced and sometimes eliminated the "influence" by which the executive in England disciplined dissent and conflict in the political community and maintained its supremacy in government.

The colonial executives lacked the flexibility they needed for successful political maneuver. The royal governors arrived in the colonies with instructions that spelled out their duties in great detail and left little room for compromise. Thus in some of the most controversial and sensitive public issues, the executive was politically immobilized. Further, in the colonies there was nothing to match the powerful political weapons that the British government had at its disposal and that were so essential to governing. Very little political patronage—gifts of public office, contracts, honors, or other benefits of government—was available to the colonial governors by which to buy off opposition and maintain their dominance over the legislatures. Furthermore, the American electoral system was not like the highly irregular, corrupt, and hence easily manipulated British system.

There were no rotten boroughs in the colonies. No assembly seats were owned outright by the government, and there were no defunct constituencies that the administration could easily manipulate. In Britain the House of Commons was frozen in composition throughout the eighteenth century, but most of the colonial assemblies had been created on the principle of so many delegates per unit of local government, and the number of such units was continually expanding as settlement spread. By the mid-eighteenth century the governors, fearing a total loss of their influence in the legislatures, tried to stop the multiplication of election districts. But the governors' efforts to keep the legislatures from growing involved them in serious political struggles, so normal had the expectation by this time become that assemblies would continue to expand with the spread of settlement. It scarcely matters that by enlightened twentieth-century standards the distribution of seats in the colonial legislatures was at certain times and in certain places disproportionate to the population. What is important is that by normal eighteenth-century standards apportionment was remarkably well adjusted to the growth and spread of population and thus insensitive to pressure from embattled governors.

Other practices created additional problems for the governors. From the earliest years of settlement, it had been common in Massachusetts for towns to instruct their representatives on how to vote in the General Court on controversial issues. This practice continued irregularly in the eighteenth century, and not only in Massachusetts. It was used when localities were committed to particular views that they wished their representatives to defend no matter what influence was brought to bear against them. And often when delegates were not instructed, they themselves postponed acting until—as in New York in 1734—"they had taken the sentiments of their constituents." Further, delegates were often required to be residents of the communities they represented at the time of their incumbency—something that was not required in eighteenth-century Britain and indeed is still not required there. Residential requirements were not universal in eighteenth-century America, but they were common enough to contribute measurably to the weakening of "influence." The result, wrote the eighteenth-century historian William Smith, was that the assemblies seemed to be composed "of plain, illiterate husbandmen, whose views seldom extended farther than to the regulation of highways, the destruction of wolves, wildcats, and foxes, and the advancement of the other little interests of the particular counties which they were chosen to represent."

But of all the underlying factors that distinguished politics in America from the British model, perhaps the most dramatic was the sheer number of those who could vote. Originally there had been no plan or desire to permit large numbers of men to vote. Most colonies sought to do no more than re-create, or adapt with minor variations, the property qualification that had prevailed in English county districts for three centuries. That requirement was the forty-shilling freehold qualification, the ownership of real estate worth forty shillings a year in rents. But if this was a restrictive qualification in England, it permitted a great many men to vote in the colonies, where freehold tenure was widespread among the white population. So ineffective was this traditional franchise limitation that most colonies went on to create their own specific restrictions. But the effect everywhere was to broaden the voting population rather than restrict it. To the disgusted governor Thomas Hutchinson in Massachusetts, it seemed that "anything with the appearance of a man" was allowed to vote.

One can safely generalize the situation in the various colonies by saying that 50 percent to 75 percent of the adult male white population was entitled to vote. This was far more than could do so in Britain—and, it seems, also far more than wished to do so in the colonies themselves. Apathy in elections was common. Yet however neglected, the widespread right to vote was potentially a powerful weapon, certain to work against the ability of colonial governors to control elections and the voting in the assemblies.

The Pattern of Colonial Politics

Overall, early American politics was a patchwork of contradictions. There was a firmly rooted belief that the colonial constitutions corresponded in their essentials to the English model of mixed government. That assumption was violated, however, by two factors. First, it was believed that too much power was exercised by the governors. Second, in the colonies there were none of the devices by which in Britain the executive maintained discipline, control, and stability in politics. Swollen claims and shrunken powers, especially when they occur together, are always sources of trouble, and the political confusion that resulted from this combination can be traced through the history of eighteenth-century American politics.

But the structure of American politics in the eighteenth century is not wholly revealed in this. The nature of leadership was also a source of controversy. Americans, like all Britons—indeed, like all Europeans of the eighteenth century—assumed that political leadership was only one of a number of expressions of leadership in a society. They believed that those who were superior in one sphere would attain and exercise superiority in other spheres as well. Hence in a society of ranked "dignities" (if not classes), political leadership was expected to rest with the natural social leaders of the community. And so indeed it was in America—in some of the colonies, in certain respects, at certain times.

In Virginia, in the three generations that followed Bacon's Rebellion, a hierarchy of the plantation gentry emerged in stable form, dominated by social and economic leaders whose roots could be traced back to the 1650s and whose preeminence in politics was largely unquestioned. So too in Connecticut, a landed gentry of "ancient" families consolidated its control in the early eighteenth century and came to dominate the political life of the colony. But even in these extreme examples there were signs of trouble to come. In Virginia, settlement expanded in the west, where potentially powerful new men with distinctive religious interests established themselves. In Connecticut the danger sign was the growth of religious radicalism, especially in the eastern counties, which were already disturbed as a result of a poor agricultural economy and a frustrated desire for the expansion of settlement.

Yet Virginia and Connecticut were among the most stable colonies. In most of the colonies, the identity of the natural political leaders remained as it had been in the late seventeenth century—a matter of controversy, at times the source of political struggles. New figures appeared overnight everywhere in the colonies, and always there were alien elements introduced into the top of the political hierarchy in the form of officials sent from England in positions of high authority.

These were the shaping elements of those "noisy dissatisfactions" that so plagued the tranquility of governors in eighteenth-century America. The political system was full of conflict—a factional system in which the will and dignity of the ill-organized imperial state were openly attacked by opposition groups. American politics was freely competitive—the very opposite of the immobile, bureaucratized state system that prevailed in the Spanish-American colonies.

Such was American society in the eighteenth century. It was a strange society, caught between traditional institutions and ways of thinking on the one hand, and unexpected circumstances on the other. Its population, drawn from many sources in Europe, Africa, and the West Indies, lived in communities that did not recognize cultural pluralism or conceive of ways by which an alien race could coexist with the dominant British element except in constant conflict or absolute subjection. While one-fifth of the population was held in slavery and enjoyed no more of the world's goods than well-cared-for animals, and while the decimated native population has been pushed back beyond the borders of European settlement, the free population enjoyed a level of affluence unknown to any other large population in the Western world. Land was widely distributed in freehold

The Virginia House of Burgesses
As in the British House of Commons, the speaker's chair and table separated the facing benches. Both the smallness of the room and the closeness of the seating arrangements encouraged intimate discussion.

tenure, although efforts were repeatedly made to re-create a traditional landlord class. Tenancy, which grew throughout the period, was more likely to foster land speculation than to provide income for a leisured landed gentry. Transoceanic commerce was increasingly dominated by a merchant class tied securely to a traditional mercantile elite in Britain, but the established merchants always had to contend with competition they could not eliminate, generated by the swift, uneven growth of an uncontrolled economy. Religious organization, still traditional in concept and doctrine, was so deeply eroded by altered circumstances that it seemed transformed even before the Great Awakening reduced much of what remained of familiar forms of religion to an almost unrecognizable disorder. Politics was an open competition for place, profit, and power. But it was fought out within a culture that condemned factionalism as seditious and that assumed that the state was in some sense sanctified and above mere factional contention.

It was a strange world, full of contradictions, but it was moving toward a resolution of its most glaring inconsistencies.

Suggested Readings

The most valuable survey of American society in the 1700s remains James T. Adams, *Provincial Society, 1690–1763* (1927); although out of date on certain matters, it touches on all major topics, includes a great deal of basic information, and conceives of society in structural terms. Lawrence H. Gipson, *British Empire Before the American Revolution,* vols. II and III (1936), provides a comprehensive description of the colonies in the years 1748–54; vols. IV and V (1939–1942) survey the frontier areas in dispute with Spain and France and also the Caribbean colonies. An effort to bring together into a general picture the recent findings on social organization is James A. Henretta, *The Evolution of American Society, 1700–1815* (1973), chaps. 1–4. Max Savelle, *Seeds of Liberty* (1948), is a survey of intellectual history and the fine arts, carried forward into the 1760s in Kenneth Silverman, *A Cultural History of the American Revolution* (1976), parts 1 and 2.

On the eighteenth-century population, see Robert V. Wells, *The Population of the British Colonies in America Before 1776* (1975), which analyzes the surviving censuses. Henry A. Gemery, "European Emigration to North America, 1700–1820," *Perspectives in American History,* n.s. 1 (1984), 283–342, estimates the overall migration figures, and Bernard Bailyn discusses migration generally in *The Peopling of British North America: An Introduction* (1986), carried forward in greater detail for the 1760s and 1770s in *Voyagers to the West* (1986). Of the new immigrations, the Irish are described in R. J. Dickson, *Ulster Immigration to Colonial America* (1966), and James G. Leyburn, *The Scotch-Irish* (1962), part 3. On the Germans, Albert B. Faust, *The German Element in the United States* (2 vols., 1909), is still useful, but altogether new material is available in Marianne Wokeck, "The Flow and the Composition of German Immigration to Philadelphia, 1727–1775," *Pennsylvania Magazine of History and Biography,* 105 (1981), 249–78, and "Promoters and Passengers," in Richard S. Dunn and Mary M. Dunn, eds., *World of William Penn* (1986). Wokeck compares Irish and German indentured servants in *The Report (Journal of German-American History),* 40 (1986), 57–76. See also A. G. Roeber's essays in *Perspectives in American History,* n.s. 3 (1986), and in Bernard Bailyn and Philip D. Morgan, eds., *Strangers within the Realm* (1991), and particularly Gillian L. Gollin, *Moravians in Two Worlds* (1967). E. G. Alderfer, *The Ephrata Commune* (1985), is a vivid account of one of the most extreme of the German sects.

The Scots are discussed in Ian C. C. Graham, *Colonists from Scotland* (1956), and Ned C. Landsman, *Scotland and Its First American Colony, 1683–1765* (1985); and the Huguenots in Jon Butler, *The Huguenots in America* (1983). The influx of indentured servants from Britain is analyzed statistically in David Galenson, *White Servitude in Colonial America* (1981), and in Abbot E. Smith, *Colonists in Bondage* (1947). The transportation to America of a large convict population is described in A. Roger Ekirch, *Bound for America* (1987). On the legal incorporation of foreign peoples into British America, see James H. Kettner, *The Development of American Citizenship, 1608–1870* (1978).

A detailed picture of the life of the black population and of slavery in the eighteenth century has recently begun to appear. An excellent description of the regional varieties of slavery is Ira Berlin, "Time, Space, and the Evolution of Afro-American Society on British Mainland America," *American Historical Review,* 85 (1980), 44–78. Philip D. Morgan, "British Encounters with Africans...1600–1780," in Bailyn and Morgan, eds., *Strangers within the Realm,* cited above, probes the interaction of blacks with white society throughout the first British empire. Allan Kulikoff, *Tobacco and Slaves* (1986), is a comprehensive study of slavery in the Chesapeake area, in the context of white society and the evolving tobacco economy. Peter Wood, *Black Majority* (1974), is an excellent account of slavery in South Carolina to 1739. Philip D. Morgan, "Black Life in Eighteenth-Century Charleston," *Perspectives in American History,* n.s. 1 (1984), 187–232, reveals a surprising degree of occupational autonomy on the part of the city's slaves. Winthrop D. Jordan, *White over Black* (1968), parts I and II, scrutinizes white attitudes toward blacks. On the slave trade, see Philip D. Curtin, *The Atlantic Slave Trade* (1969), and H. A. Gemery and J. S. Hogendorn, eds., *The Uncommon Market* (1979).

All aspects of eighteenth-century economic history are analyzed fully in John J. McCusker and Russell R. Menard, *The Economy of British America* (1985). Its vast bibliography lists everything of any importance ever written on the subject. For a general interpretation, see Stuart Bruchey, *Enterprise* (1990), chaps. 1–3. Alice H. Jones has published a masterful interpretation of American affluence on the eve of the Revolution in her *Wealth of a Nation to Be* (1980). For an exceptionally detailed study of the social life and economic condition of one colony, see Jackson T. Main, *Society and Economy in Colonial Connecticut* (1985).

A broad survey of the opening of new frontier lands in the tradition of Frederick Jackson Turner is Ray A. Billington, *Westward Expansion* (1949), chaps. 5–8, which contains an exhaustive bibliography of writings on the westward movement. A case study of the opening of new townships in New England, contradicting the Turner view on many points, is Charles S. Grant, *Democracy in the Connecticut Frontier Town of Kent* (1961). On the New England town and village life, see Main, *Society and Economy in Colonial Connecticut,* cited above; Edward M. Cook, Jr., *The Fathers of the Towns* (1976); Michael Zuckerman, *Peaceable Kingdoms* (1970); and Christine L. Heyrman, *Commerce and Culture* (1984). On settlements in Pennsylvania, see James T. Lemon, *The Best Poor Man's Country* (1972); on land utilization in North Carolina, see Harry R. Merrens, *Colonial North Carolina* (1964); on land and population in Virginia, see Carville V. Earle, *The Evolution of a Tidewater Settlement System* (1975).

Of the exceptions to freehold tenure discussed in this chapter, there is an excellent essay on the old proprietary estates: Rowland Berthoff and John M. Murrin, "Feudalism, Communalism, and the Yeoman Freeholder...," in Stephen G. Kurtz and James H. Hutson, eds., *Essays on the American Revolution* (1973). On tenancy, see Willard F. Bliss, "Rise of Tenancy in Virginia," *Virginia Magazine of History and Biography,* 58 (1950), 427–41; Clarence P. Gould, *Land System in Maryland, 1720–1765* (1913); Gregory A. Stiverson, *Poverty in a Land of Plenty* (1977); Sung Bok Kim, *Landlord and Tenant in Colonial New York* (1978); and Patricia U. Bonomi, *A Factious People* (1971), chap. 6. Lucy Simler, "Tenancy in Colonial Pennsylvania," *Wm. and Mary Q.,* 43 (1986), 542–69, together with Kim's book, shows the general profitability of tenancy where it existed in the North and the economic strategies that made it attractive.

Plantation life and the harassed role of the large planters are vividly revealed in Jack P. Greene, ed., *Diary of Colonel Landon Carter* (2 vols., 1965), and interpreted in Daniel Blake Smith, *Inside the Great House* (1980), and in T. H. Breen, *Tobacco Culture* (1985). The condition of ordinary planters is described in Aubrey C. Land, "Economic Behavior in a Planting Society..." *Journal of Social History,* 33 (1967), 469–85, and "Economic Base and Social Structure...," *Journal of Economic History,* 25 (1965), 639–54.† Rhys Isaac, *The Transformation of Virginia 1740–1790* (1982), contains an interpretation of Virginia society and culture viewed as an anthropologist would view a strange and alien world whose "meanings" are not what the people of the time thought they were, but what the historian interprets them to be. On the role of the Scottish merchants in transforming the marketing of tobacco, see Jacob M. Price, "The Rise of Glasgow in the Chesapeake Tobacco Trade," *Wm. and Mary Q.,* 11 (1954), 179–99, and T. M. Devine, *The Tobacco Lords* (1975). On marketing in general, see Price's "Economic Growth of the Chesapeake and the European Markets, 1697–1775," *Journal of Economic History,* 24 (1964), 496–511, and *France and the Chesapeake* (2 vols., 1973).

On commerce, besides the excellent summary in McCusker and Menard, *Economy of British America,* cited above, there are a number of particularly important specific studies: Thomas M. Doerflinger, *A Vigorous Spirit of Enterprise* (1986), is a masterful analysis of Philadelphia's merchants. Richard Pares, *Yankees and Creoles* (1956), and Richard B. Sheridan,

---

†See footnote on p. 32.

Sugar and Slavery (1974), cover the Caribbean trade; on the timber trade and fisheries, see Joseph J. Malone, *Pine Trees and Politics* (1964), and Harold A. Innis, *The Cod Fisheries* (1940), and on the relation of commerce to social life in two New England fishing towns, see Heyrman, *Commerce and Culture,* cited above. There are valuable insights into the working of commerce in studies of individual merchants: the Hancocks of Boston by W. T. Baxter, the Beekmans of New York by Philip L. White, the Pepperrells of Maine and New Hampshire by Byron Fairchild, and the Browns of Rhode Island (a particularly vivid example of social and occupational mobility) by James B. Hedges. Life in the port towns is described in Carl Bridenbaugh, *Cities in the Wilderness* (1938), *Cities in Revolt* (1955), and *Rebels and Gentlemen* (1942); and in Gary B. Nash, *Urban Crucible* (1979). Nash, and Billy G. Smith, *The "Lower Sort"* (1990) and "Poverty and Economic Marginality in Eighteenth-Century America," *Proceedings of the American Philosophical Society,* 132 (1988), 85–118, argue that poverty was high at times in the eighteenth-century cities, although their data largely relate to the period after 1760.

Eighteenth-century religion is summarized in Sydney E. Ahlstrom, *Religious History of the American People* (1972), part III. Sidney E. Mead, *The Lively Experiment* (1963), skillfully traces the development of American denominationalism, and Jon Butler, *Awash in a Sea of Faith* (1990), argues that most of what historians have said about eighteenth-century religion is wrong, including the idea that there was in fact a Great Awakening. Patricia U. Bonomi, *Under the Cope of Heaven* (1986), is a less strained and less argumentative interpretation, and brings the story up to the Revolution. Major religious currents in New England are described in Perry Miller, *New England Mind: From Colony to Province* (1953); Robert Middlekauff, *The Mathers* (1971); James W. Jones, *The Shattered Synthesis* (1973); and Harry S. Stout, *The New England Soul* (1986). There is a large literature on the Great Awakening, much of it brought together into a single brief book, J. M. Bumsted and John E. Van de Watering, *What Must I Do to Be Saved?* (1976), which contains a good bibliography of the major regional studies. Alan Heimert, *Religion and the American Mind* (1966), part 1, is a comprehensive interpretation of the theology of the revival and of its opponents; part 2 carries those divisions forward into the politics of the early Revolutionary years. C. C. Goen, *Revivalism and Separatism* (1962), is an excellent account of the social and ecclesiastical splintering that resulted from the revival. Evarts B. Greene, *Religion and the State* (1941), and William G. McLaughlin, "Isaac Backus and the Separation of Church and State," *American Historical Review,* 72 (1968), 1392–1413, show the colonial origins of American church-state relations.

The operation of the imperial government is described in Leonard W. Labaree, *Royal Government in America* (1930), and Jack P. Greene, *The Quest for Power* (1963); the constitutional relationship between Britain and the colonies is discussed in Greene's *Peripheries and Center* (1986). But politics, though intimately related to government, is a different matter. Bernard Bailyn, *Origins of American Politics* (1968), is an effort at a general interpretation, stressing the relations between formal and informal organizations and between political activities and political beliefs. The role of colonial offices in the British patronage system is explained from the British point of view in James A. Henretta, *"Salutary Neglect"* (1972), and in Alison G. Olson and Richard M. Brown, eds., *Anglo-American Political Relations, 1675–1775* (1970), and from the American point of view in Stanley N. Katz, *Newcastle's New York* (1968). Michael Kammen, *Empire and Interest* (1970), is an imaginative effort to show the changing ways in which the British political system accommodated the interests of economic and political groups in Britain and America.

Of the many thorough studies of the politics of individual colonies, several are outstanding; see especially Bonomi, *A Factious People;* Robert Zemsky, *Merchants, Farmers, and River Gods* (1971); Charles Barker, *Background of the Revolution in Maryland* (1940); and M. Eugene Sirmans, *Colonial South Carolina* (1966). J. R. Pole, *Political Representation* (1966), covers both England and America throughout the eighteenth century.

6

The Enlightenment's New World

~

*I*N 1760 the young George III ascended the throne of Great Britain. Like Britons everywhere, Americans joined in the celebrations enthusiastically. Along with the people of Britain, the nonslave population of the colonies enjoyed the freest political conditions in the Western world, and the colonists shared, although unevenly, in Britain's rising prosperity. Moreover, the American colonists had participated in Britain's recent military victories over its perennial enemy, France. The colonists now felt a sense of release from the pressure of war on their frontiers, and they were aware as never before of the richness of the land that lay to the west. They glimpsed a future that could be free and prosperous beyond all earlier expectations. In 1759 the Boston preacher Jonathan Mayhew wrote that one could easily imagine in British North America "a mighty empire (I do not mean an independent one) in numbers little inferior perhaps to the greatest in Europe, and in felicity to none." One could picture, he continued, cities "rising on every hill . . . happy fields and villages . . . [and] religion professed and practiced throughout this spacious kingdom in far greater purity and perfection than since the times of the apostles."

In varying degrees, many others shared Mayhem's optimism about America's prospects as part of the British world. But beneath the glowing surface there were tensions—dark undertones in Anglo-American relations. These tensions had been building through all the years of mutual growth and accommodation, but they had no predictable or inevitable outcome. They could as reasonably have grown into a pattern of stable and peaceable relations as become sources of serious disruption. The future would depend on the ability of men in power to understand and manage the complex problems that faced them. In retrospect, however, one thing is clear. These antagonisms, rooted at three levels in the subsoil of Anglo-American life, were like buried traps: to ignore them was to risk disaster.

"Rule Britannia"

At the most obvious level were the antagonisms generated by the war efforts of the mid-eighteenth century.

War of Jenkins' Ear   During the years after 1713, Britain fought three wars with European powers, and the colonies were involved in varying degrees in all of them. The first, the so-called War of Jenkins' Ear (1739–42), was fought with Spain over trading rights in the Caribbean and Central America.

In the peace treaty of 1713 that had ended the War of the Spanish Succession, Britain had been granted the privilege of selling a limited number of slaves and a specified quantity of goods in the Spanish West Indies. The legitimate presence of British trading vessels in these otherwise closed markets had encouraged smuggling, which was countered by mutual rights of search. Spain's brutal handling of shipboard searches had been no more improper or illegal than British smuggling, but it had outraged British public opinion. When a certain Captain Robert Jenkins presented to a parliamentary committee one of his ears, which he said had been cut off by the Spanish seven years earlier as a punishment for smuggling, Parliament demanded a war of revenge for such atrocities. The head of the government, Robert Walpole, wished to avoid a conflict but could not refuse.

The war, which spread over a wide area, was fought at first in the Western Hemisphere. A makeshift army of South Carolina and Georgia troops invaded Spanish Florida but failed to capture St. Augustine or to relieve the pressure on the southern frontier, and the action turned to the Caribbean. There the main effort was an assault in 1740 on the Spanish town of Cartagena, on the coast of what is today Colombia. For this campaign an American regiment of 3,500 men was recruited, serving under British commanders. Most of the money for the expedition was also raised in America. But the campaign was a ghastly failure. A hopelessly slow and poorly mounted attack on Cartagena's fort led to the butchery of the American troops, followed by an epidemic of yellow fever and a loss of supplies. After further failures in Cuba, the remains of the expedition staggered home. The losses were shocking. Only six hundred Americans survived, and they brought back with them a bitter resentment of the callousness, incompetence, and arrogance of the British military commanders. Years later Americans still recalled the agonies their countrymen had endured in this senseless campaign, and the appalling waste of lives and goods.

King George's War   In 1740 the Spanish war had broadened into a general European conflict when Prussia seized the province of Silesia from Austria. To maintain the balance of power, Britain went to Austria's aid, and France joined Spain—already at war with Britain. The British feared above all that a single continental power would control Europe, and so in 1742 they made peace with Spain, and in 1744 declared war on France. This complicated series of struggles was known in Europe as the War of the Austrian Succession (1740–48) and in America as King George's War (1744–48). The agreement that ended the war, the Treaty of Aix-la-Chapelle, was merely a truce to allow the combatants to recuperate. In accepting the treaty the British abandoned an important American victory and thus created another source of resentment between Britain and the colonies.

The focus of conflict in the Western Hemispere during King George's War was the French naval station at Louisbourg. This was a massive fortification on Cape Breton Island, just northeast of Nova Scotia. Louisbourg guarded the entrance to the St. Lawrence River, sheltered French privateers, and controlled the rich fishing waters between mainland North America and Newfoundland. When Governor William Shirley of Massachusetts heard that Louisbourg's garrison was undermanned and in poor spirits, and that its fortifications were in disrepair, he rallied support from the Massachusetts merchant community and persuaded the General Court to finance an expedition to capture the fortress. Equipment and troops were gathered from all over New England and from colonies as far south as Pennsylvania. Arrangements were made for British naval support under a New Yorker, Commodore Peter Warren, and the troop command was given to a popular Maine merchant and militia colonel, William Pepperrell.

As the transports, warships, supplies, and men gathered in Boston, the campaign, in the aftermath of the Great Awakening, took on the air of a festive crusade. Ministers preached fire and destruction to the French Catholics and their Indian allies. In April 1745, 4,000 New England troops landed safely near Louisbourg, turned captured French cannons against the central fortification, and attacked. The assault came not from the sea (as the French had expected), but by weakly defended land approaches. The French held off the attackers through all of April and May while the New Englanders—who were not soldiers but undisciplined farmers, fishermen, and town workers—bumbled and stumbled their way to control of the harbor islands. Just as Warren was preparing to land an untrained amphibious force to take the partly demolished fortress, the French surrendered. They were hopelessly outnumbered and lacked food supplies and naval support. On June 17 the "Gibraltar of the New World" was handed over to Pepperrell.

For New England, indeed for all of America, it was a glorious victory. Warren, who made a fortune from his capture of French merchant ships, was promoted to admiral; Pepperrell was knighted. But the war was far from over. Disease decimated the troops occupying Louisbourg, and the frontiers from Maine to New York were set aflame in savage raids. Border garrisons in Vermont, western Massachusetts, and New York were attacked, captured, retaken, and attacked again. Massachusetts, which had been promised repayment by Parliament for its expenses in capturing Louisbourg, planned a massive assault on Quebec but then abandoned it when news arrived of a large French expedition moving to recover Louisbourg. That French fleet was scattered by storms and swept by disease, and it never made contact with the fortress; another French fleet on the same mission was captured by Warren. But the border raids continued. The war degenerated into random violence. Isolated towns and farmhouses were burned and their inhabitants slaughtered, even though such butchery could make no possible difference in the end. Prisoners were taken and then exchanged. Grand campaigns were hatched with Indian allies but then, for reasons that could not be clearly explained, dissolved before any action could be taken. Spain's raids on several forts along the coast of the southern British mainland colonies were equally inconclusive and equally ill designed to affect the outcome of the war.

Beyond the capture of Louisbourg, nothing substantial had been accomplished when in December 1748 news arrived that peace had been concluded in Europe. It brought relief from bloodshed; but in exchange for the return of Madras in India, which France had taken, England returned Louisbourg, the symbol of American military pride, to the French. Five hundred Americans had died in action to accomplish nothing, and twice that many had been killed by disease, exposure, and accidents. The return of Louisbourg would be recalled along with bitter memories of the Cartagena expedition—and with memories of another famous episode in King George's War.

In 1747 the "press gangs" of the British naval commander, Charles Knowles, had attempted to seize likely recruits for the royal navy on the streets of Boston.* But Boston, he discovered, was not London. To his amazement, his men were fought off by an angry mob in one of the most violent town riots in the pre-Revolutionary years. The townsmen's rampage against this flagrant although traditional violation of civilian rights lasted for four days and remained a living memory for a generation to come.

The French and Indian War The third and last of these pre-Revolutionary wars in part followed the pattern of the others. This time, however, America was the central theater of war, not a marginal one. And this time the military outcome was conclusive, and the resentment generated between Britain and the colonies was much greater.

The conflict that in America was called the French and Indian War was known in Europe as the Seven Years' War; it lasted from 1756 to 1763. As was true of earlier eighteenth-century wars, Britain became involved in order to maintain the balance of power in Europe, which the British government thought was threatened by the aggressive policies of France. This time Britain's ally in continental Europe was Prussia, and France's allies were Austria and Russia. The Seven Years' War was also a struggle for supremacy overseas—not only in the Western Hemisphere, but in Asia and Africa as well.

In America the immediate cause of the conflict was a series of clashes between French army units on the one hand and Virginians on the other. The

---

*"Press gangs" were frequently and legally used in the 1700s to round up the manpower needed for naval vessels.

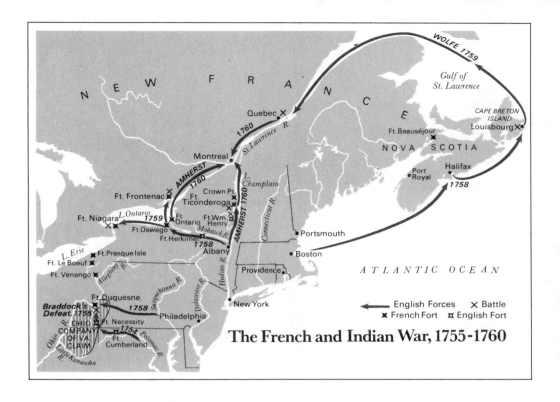

The French and Indian War, 1755-1760

French units were trying to secure the Ohio River valley for France by establishing a string of forts there. The Virginians had claims to this territory going back to the original charter, and these claims were now being advanced by a powerful group of land speculators. The French repulsed the Virginians' efforts to set up a British fort at the strategic junction of the Ohio, Allegheny, and Monongahela rivers (the site of present-day Pittsburgh). Early in 1754 the French established their own Fort Duquesne there. A small British force under the twenty-two-year-old Major George Washington failed to dislodge the French and was itself defeated at a stockaded encampment called Fort Necessity.

The colonies anticipated a conflict larger than any of the previous wars. Shortly after the engagement at Fort Necessity, the representatives of seven colonies met at Albany, New York, to try to work out defense plans among themselves and with their Indian allies. But this effort did not succeed. While in principle the delegates adopted Benjamin Franklin's proposal for a political and military union of the colonies, they could not convince a single colonial assembly to ratify a suggested plan for a general government of all the colonies. Meanwhile the British government moved ahead with a design for a large-scale war that involved dispatching a sizable army to America, enlisting colonial troops, and collecting quantities of provisions and equipment in America. Early in 1755 the British commander, Major General Edward Braddock, arrived with the first regiments. He was an arrogant disciplinarian with little sympathy for difficult colonials and no sense of how to handle them. Even before war was formally

Hendrick (or, Hendrick Peters; Indian name Theyanoguin), Sachem of the Mohawks
Shown in this English print in European dress but with a painted face, Hendrick, eloquent and commanding in manner, had visited England in 1710 and had worked for many years to keep the powerful Iroquois Six Nations in close collaboration with British frontier policy. In a famous speech at the Albany Congress of 1754, he abused the British for exploiting the natives and for failing to protect them from the French. He died the next year leading a force of Mohawks in battle with the French and their Indian allies.

declared in May 1756, Braddock fought the first engagement of the conflict in the wilderness of western Pennsylvania. Once declared, the conflict spread quickly to all points of contact among the major European powers—not only in Europe, America, and the Caribbean, but also in Africa, India, and the Philippines.

For two years the British suffered defeat after defeat. Braddock's army, moving west to eliminate Fort Duquesne, fell into confusion at its first, accidental contact with the enemy and was almost annihilated by a small French and Indian force hidden along the sides of the road. There were 1,000 casualties in an army of 1,400; only 23 of 86 officers survived. Washington, who helped lead the pell-mell retreat, buried Braddock in the road to keep his grave from being discovered. To the north the British had to retake Nova Scotia, whose boundaries were disputed and whose French-speaking inhabitants, the Acadians, were either pro-French or unreliably neutral. Thereafter, 6,000 of the Acadians were rounded up and deported south to the thirteen colonies. But although this action isolated Cape Breton Island and its fortress, Louisbourg, the effort by the new British commander in chief, Lord Loudoun, to capture that stronghold in 1757 failed. So too did Governor Shirley's ambitious attempt to force the French out of the arc of forts that formed the northwest boundary of the British colonies. Instead of the British taking the two French forts, Frontenac and Niagara, on Lake Ontario, the French, under the able commander Montcalm, captured the British fort, Oswego, on the eastern side of Lake Ontario. Secure at Crown Point on Lake Champlain, the French moved deeper into New York by establishing Fort Ticonderoga, ten miles to the south on Champlain. In August 1757 they seized Fort William Henry even farther to the south, on Lake George, capturing 2,000 British troops along with it. Later the French on the western American frontier penetrated northern New York as far as Fort Herkimer on the Mohawk River, murdering noncombatant German farmers along the way. The whole of central New York and western New England was exposed; Albany seemed doomed. In Europe, meanwhile, the allied armies of France and Austria overran Britain's dependent German state, Hanover,* and threatened Britain's ally, Prussia.

It was at this absolute low point in British fortunes that the planning of the great British statesman William Pitt began to have its effect. Pitt was a strange, brilliant, imaginative, and neurotic war minister. Appointed secretary of state in 1757, he possessed a vision of imperial greatness that was unique for the time. He also intended to fight what today would be called a total war. He demanded huge government expenditures, heavy subsidies for the European allies to neutralize the continental theater of war, and large commitments by the colonies, to be financed by Parliament. Pitt planned an American army of 24,000 British regulars and 25,000 colonial troops—a very large force for the time.

Passing over established but ineffective generals in favor of younger and more energetic commanders, Pitt launched a series of efforts to break the arc of French forts north and west of the mainland colonies. The first of his plans—an attack on Ticonderoga in July 1758—failed miserably. But that was his only failure. Later the same month a force of 9,000 regular army troops and 500 colonials under the young general Jeffrey Amherst and the thin, sickly, but tigerish brigadier James Wolfe, only thirty-one years old, took Louisbourg. A month later a swift British raid overran the critical supply depot of Fort Frontenac, the link between the St. Lawrence River and the French posts farther to the west and south. With the capture of Fort Frontenac, the British gained control of Lake Ontario. In November 1758 a mixed force led by three excellent commanders, including Colonel Washington, finally avenged Braddock's defeat by seizing Fort Duquesne from the French, thereby securing British control of the entire upper Ohio River valley.

By early 1759, the year of Britain's greatest victories, the iron ring around the northern British colonies had been broken at three critical points. In the east, Louisbourg and Nova Scotia were in British hands; in the west Fort Frontenac and Lake Ontario were secured; and in the south Fort Duquesne had been captured. Successes had also been won in India, in Africa, and at sea. Then Pitt, riding the crest of great popularity at home, planned the kill. Canada was to be sealed off in the far west by the capture of Fort Niagara; General Amherst was to invade Canada by way of Lake Champlain and the St. Lawrence River valley; and Wolfe was to take Quebec in an amphibious expedition moving west up the St.

---

*Hanover was the small state in northern Germany whose rulers, beginning with George I in 1714, occupied the British throne. Hanover was governed independently of Great Britain.

Lawrence River. For all of this, a fortune in supplies, transports, and firearms, in addition to three large armies with substantial naval support, was required.

Somehow these great demands were met. In July 1759 Fort Niagara, which linked New France with the far west, was captured. At the same time, the French withdrew from Ticonderoga and Crown Point, leaving them to Amherst. By the time his troops had rebuilt these forts, it was too late for Amherst to proceed with the planned thrust into Canada from the south. But Wolfe, in one of the best-organized, most daring, and luckiest exploits in British military history, succeeded in his assigned task in Pitt's strategy.

Moving almost 10,000 men in more than 200 warships and transports through the St. Lawrence to Quebec without serious loss, Wolfe fumbled for more than seven weeks, seeking a way to attack the heavily fortified city, which had been built atop cliffs rising 150 feet above the St. Lawrence. Finally, on the night of September 12, 1759, he led 4,500 men up the cliff along a diagonal roadway he had discovered. A battle began on the Plains of Abraham, just west of the city. The French did not wait for reinforcements but charged the carefully arranged British troops rather wildly. They were met with a disciplined and efficient barrage that broke their ranks, and they were driven from the field defeated. Among the relatively few British casualties (60 dead, 600 wounded) was Wolfe; among the French, Montcalm. On September 17 Quebec surrendered. A year later Amherst's army moved north and east from the lakes, converged on Montreal, and, with the aid of British troops sent from Quebec, forced the French governor to surrender the whole of New France.

The war ended in 1763. In the final peace treaty Britain gained undisputed possession of all of North America east of the Mississippi River except for New Orleans, including all of Nova Scotia and all of Canada. Spain, which had entered the war on the French side in 1762, was forced to give Florida to Britain in exchange for the return of Cuba, captured by a British expedition in 1762. Spain's compensations were New Orleans and the vast lands west of the Mississippi, which France had rashly pledged to Spain as a reward for its entry into the war. Britain had won a great military triumph, and its gains in North America were matched by other British successes all over the world.

But there were serious hidden costs in the British victory. The most obvious was the huge debt that Britain had acquired in fighting the war. This financial burden set off a political reaction in Britain against grand and costly overseas adventures and eventually forced the government of George III to consider new forms of taxation. A less obvious cost was the immediate effect of the war on Anglo-American relations. On the one hand Americans rejoiced in the victory. For the first time in their history, they were relieved of the threat that the French and Spanish would stir up the Indians to attack the frontiers. But in the course of the war, they had learned to fear the presence of large professional armies, and they insisted that the only military forces compatible with liberty were militias. They learned, too, something that they had not fully realized before: although they were British, they were somehow a separate people, yet not an inferior people as the army commanders under whom they fought seemed so often to assume. For through all these wars—from the catastrophe at Cartagena to the triumph on the Plains of Abraham—they experienced the arrogance, the indifference, and often the stupidity of an officer class that was a traditional part of European life but was alien, abrasive, and in the end intolerable in America.

Above all, Americans resented the imperial regulations—some of them newly devised, some newly enforced during the French and Indian War. As part of his program for a total national effort, Pitt sought to eliminate all violations of the navigation acts, all smuggling, and indeed all commercial contact with the enemy that might bolster the enemy's economy or help supply enemy troops. It was not an altogether new effort. As early as 1756 the Privy Council had ordered the colonial governors to enforce the laws strictly and to eliminate the trade with the enemy that was well known to be taking place in neutral ports. In pursuit of these goals and in support of the efforts of the customs officials, the highest colonial courts had issued writs of assistance to customs officers—general warrants authorizing the officers to command court officials to assist them in searching for smuggled goods. Such writs of assistance were granted by the high court of Massachusetts in 1755, 1758, 1759, and 1760, and they were valid through the lifetime of the reigning king. They served their purpose well, but they were deeply resented by the merchant community, which was determined to seek relief when the opportunity arose.

Pitt's insistence on enforcing the letter of the law raised all these efforts to a new level. In the course of his brief but powerful ministry (he was forced to resign in 1761), he issued strict orders that closed the loopholes in the regulations, brought the complex rules together into a unified whole, and imposed punishment for negligence. Governors were drawn directly into the business of imperial law enforcement, and the navy became a more effective police arm than ever before. All this made conflict likely. Well before 1763 certain colonial merchants and politicians who were antagonistic to the imperial establishment were beginning to question the value of the connection with Britain, of which they seemed to be the victims.

Yet all of this was only the tip of an iceberg. Attempts to enforce the mercantilist system during the last colonial war stirred up public controversy over other conflicts in imperial relations that had hitherto been submerged.

The Alienation of the State

Long before Pitt became involved in public affairs, three problems had arisen in Anglo-American relations that had not been solved but merely put off, patched up with makeshift solutions, and then ignored. They could be ignored because they had developed largely as a consequence of the mercantilist system, and as long as that system was not rigidly enforced the pressure of these problems was slight. The problems remained, nevertheless, and there was a price to be paid for evading and neglecting them. Even in their moderate form they created a distance, and alienation, between Britain and America. That alienation was as much a part of the Anglo-American world in 1760 as the universal rejoicing for the new British monarch, the young George III.

Smuggling and the Balance of Payment

The first of these problems arose from the fact that the rapidly increasing American population created an expanding market for British goods that was not matched by an equivalent growth of a market within Britain itself for the products that the colonies could sell. By the 1730s American consumption of British goods rose well beyond the colonists' capacity to pay for them through direct exchanges with Britain. By the late 1760s the colonists were running a trade deficit with Britain of £1,800,000 a year, more than 90 percent of it incurred by the northern and middle colonies.

The deficit had largely been paid for by "invisible earnings" (such as shipping services) and by the profits of trade with southern Europe and the West Indies. The West Indies trade was particularly important in keeping the colonies from falling into debt. Exchanges with the non-British islands in the West Indies—especially with the French sugar-producing islands of Guadeloupe, Martinique, and Santo Domingo—had become a vital part of that trade. Dealings with the French islands, where the American merchants could buy cheaply and sell at unusually high rates, were particularly important in making up the deficits in payments to Britain and thus in keeping the commercial colonies solvent. But that trade was increasingly resented by the British West Indian planters and their merchant associates in Britain. They recognized that the more successful this foreign trade was, the higher the cost of provisions would be on their own plantations and the lower the price they could obtain for their own products.

The issue flared up as early as 1730. The British planters and merchants moved to protect themselves against French competition by seeking to establish high duties on foreign sugar products imported into the mainland colonies. The American merchants and the colonial agents in London rose in opposition, claiming that such duties were more than the trade could bear and that they would wreck the Anglo-American commercial system and bankrupt the northern colonies. A fierce debate raged in the press and in the House of Commons. But there was no question of the result, given the power of the West Indian lobby in London. In 1733 Parliament passed the so-called Molasses Act, which imposed prohibitively high import duties on foreign sugar products.

The problem as it existed in 1760 had thus been created in 1733. Passage of the Molasses Act set in motion the development of a network of illegal importations. Customs officers in the North American ports were systematically bribed. They became accustomed to ignoring the strict letter of the law and to settling for a certain percentage of the legal dues. Techniques for smuggling were perfected, and gradually a large part of the northern commercial economy developed a stake in the systematic breaking of the law—law that seemed arbitrary, the product of a distant, alien, and hostile government.

Sugar Cane and the Art of Making Sugar, from a Print of 1749

**Restricting
Manufactures**
A similar sense of alienation developed from the second problem in Anglo-American economic relations that arose during these years. The mercantile system was based on the assumption that colonial areas were producers of exotic goods and raw materials and that they were consumers, not producers, of finished goods. It was expected that large-scale manufacturing would be confined to the home country, and the law reflected that assumption by prohibiting the manufacture of certain basic goods in the colonies. English statutes from the end of the seventeenth century forbade the export from England of machines or tools used in the clothing industry. The Woolen Act (1699) prohibited the export of American wool or woolen products from any one colony to another. A law of 1718 forbade the free emigration of skilled artisans from Britain, and the Hat Act (1732) barred the exportation of American-made hats from the colony where they were manufactured.

But gradually investments in at least small-scale manufactures seemed attractive as minor accumulations of capital appeared in various areas. The sums were not large by British standards, but other outlets were limited. Some profits of the developing economy could be plowed back into further expansion of commerce and of the fishing industry, and investment could be made in extractive enterprises like processing timber products. Small surpluses could also be invested in urban properties, land speculation, British government bonds, and personal loans. But most such investments were limited to face-to-face transactions; there were no institutions that could broaden the range and size of the investment market. In a society not prone to extravagant consumption, those who controlled the slowly growing surplus began to turn to manufactures. Adverse conditions— a continuing labor shortage, relatively scarce capital, a poor overland transportation system, and limited local markets—restricted what could be done. But wherever these difficulties were to some degree overcome, the results were impressive.

In shipbuilding the problems of both transportation and markets were eliminated, since England had a continuous and heavy need for merchant vessels. By the late colonial period almost 40 percent of all British-owned merchant vessels were built in the thirteen colonies. About one hundred vessels were sold to Britain annually, worth at least £140,000. Iron production presented greater difficulties, which were only partly overcome by dispersal into small producing units and by the use of slave labor. Nevertheless iron production too rose remarkably, not only in the large Principio works in Maryland and the Hasenclever plants in New Jersey, but also in dozens of smaller establishments scattered throughout the colonies. At the end of the colonial period there were 82 blast furnaces and 175 forges in the colonies (more than existed in England and Wales), and they produced 30,000 tons of crude iron a year. This was less than half of Britain's output, but it was an imposing achievement nevertheless.

Of the goods manufactured in the colonies, only ships, other timber products, and rum were produced in such quantities that the colonists' needs were filled. But the manufacture of other products was increasing steadily, and British authorities recognized the danger that this growth posed to the principles of mercantilism. Britain's restrictive legislation grew more elaborate. In 1750 the colonies' manufacture or export of specific textiles was outlawed. And in that year too the most famous restrictive law, the Iron Act, was passed. Although it removed duties on the importation of pig iron and bar iron into Britain, this act prohibited the erection of finishing plants for iron goods in all the colonies.

It is difficult to gauge the effect of these laws in economic terms. There was never a large amount of surplus capital available in the colonies for investment in manufactures, labor continued to be expensive, and local markets were small. But in the less measurable area of attitudes toward the government that passed such laws, these restrictions had a significant impact. To those directly concerned they became what Adam Smith later called them, "impertinent badges of slavery imposed upon them . . . by the groundless jealousy of the merchants and manufacturers of the mother country." They further heightened the colonists' awareness of hostile interests in the government "at home" and deepened Americans' feelings of alienation.

Currency and Banking

The same kind of hostility and alienation resulted from the handling of the money problem, which remained a major issue through most of the mid-eighteenth century. The problem was created by the virtual absence of specie, or coined money, in America as a medium of exchange. The coinage of money was a prerogative of the king and hence was prohibited in the colonies after the confiscation of the original Massachusetts charter in 1684. (Massachusetts had been minting a coin, the "pine tree shilling," during the seventeenth century.) In the eighteenth century the colonists made every effort to attract Spanish coin to the British colonies, but the negative balance of trade made these efforts unsuccessful. The solution was paper money—unusual in the eighteenth century—which entered the American economy in two ways.

The first form of paper money was bills of credit that were issued by the colonial governments to repay debts the governments owed to merchant contractors. Massachusetts began this practice in 1690, and between 1690 and 1760 almost every other colony did the same. These bills were in effect IOUs to be redeemed eventually by the governments. Because they were declared legally valid as payment for taxes, they entered into general circulation, and their value was maintained by the expectation that the governments would eventually redeem them. But these bills were generally not made full legal tender (that is, valid payment of all debts, public and private), and they continued to be thought of as wartime expedients. The quantity available depended less on the needs of the economy than on the occasional demands for public expenditure.

The second form of paper money was the bills issued by land banks, which were in effect public loan agencies. These banks were created to issue money to individuals at 5 percent interest. The loans were repayable gradually, and they were secured against default by mortgages on land or other real estate. By 1750 land banks existed in every colony except Virginia, and their success was striking. They injected a badly needed flow of currency into the colonies' economies. They reduced taxation through the income produced from the interest on the loans. They created a source of low-interest credit needed for agricultural development. And they built up purchasing power that may have helped soften the effects of periodic depressions. Further, unlike bills of credit, the land banks put funds at low interest directly into the hands of the farmers; bills of credit went first to the merchants, who in turn lent to the farmers at higher rates of interest. Both forms of paper money, however, provided a needed medium of exchange and, despite their experimental character, were on the whole successful. Bills of credit were especially sound in the middle colonies, where both merchants and officials backed the issues and limited them carefully.

But in parts of New England and the South, too much paper money was issued, and its value depreciated seriously. In these areas creditors feared that they would be repaid in paper money that had lost value since the time the debts had been incurred. The English merchants were even more apprehensive. They

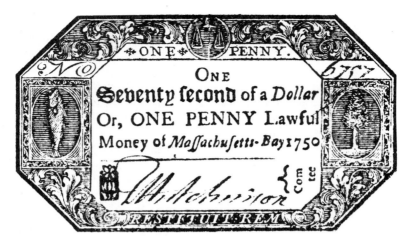

Colonial Paper Money
The Massachusetts paper penny bears the signature of Thomas Hutchinson, the future loyalist governor, then a member of a committee in charge of issuing bills of credit. The issue of 1750 was a victory for Hutchinson's hard money policy. Based on £180,000 of silver that Parliament sent in repayment of wartime expenses, it replaced all of the colony's inflated currency in circulation.

feared severe losses if their credit were in any way affected by the cheapening of the currency. Together, creditors in the colonies and in England pressured the British government to send the colonial governors strict orders not to allow bills to be issued as full legal tender and to insist that the colonial currency laws state clearly when these bills would be redeemed. The governors were to make sure that these requirements were honored to the letter.

Such tight controls were difficult to enforce, however, and a crisis arose in New England in the 1730s. Rhode Island's bills flooded the region (that colony issued £100,000 worth of paper bills in 1733 alone), and Boston merchants refused to honor them. But the pressure for more issues continued, and in 1739 a group of Massachusetts merchants formed a *private* land bank, which was authorized by the General Court to issue £150,000 worth of bills at 3 percent interest. Many members of the business community were greatly alarmed at this development, especially because debtors were allowed to repay in commodities of uncertain value. The opponents of the new land bank formed what was called a silver bank, which would issue notes redeemable in silver, not in commodities. The two groups fought bitterly, and in the end the governor and council declared the land bank's bills invalid, although £50,000 had already been placed in circulation. The leading land bankers organized public protests, which became riotous. There were arrests and jailings, and in the end the British government adopted repressive measures. In 1741 the so-called Bubble Act, already in force in Britain, was extended to the colonies: it outlawed all joint-stock companies not authorized by Parliament. In effect this measure outlawed all private banks. Years of litigation followed in Massachusetts, as creditors who had already accepted payment in the bank's bills demanded repayment in valid money. It was the worst upheaval in the Bay Colony between the establishment of the Dominion of New England in the 1680s and the early years of the Revolution. The father of Samuel Adams, the man who would be a leader of the Revolution in Massachusetts, was one of the local officials removed from office for continuing to support the land bank.

But the more traditional *public* land banks remained in existence, and the value of their issues continued to fluctuate. In Massachusetts paper money was discounted from par (face value) at a ratio of nine to one. In Rhode Island nine issues of paper money were in circulation in 1750, representing a par value of £465,000, and in addition there was £60,000 worth of bills of credit legally available. But by then more comprehensive legislation was being drafted. In 1751 Parliament passed the Currency Act, which applied only to the New England colonies. Under this act no new land banks could be created in New England; no paper money could thereafter be made full legal tender; all bills were to be withdrawn from circulation on the strict schedule that had been specified at the time of issue; and bills could be issued to pay for government expenses only if provisions were made for their redemption out of tax revenues within two years.

Although the Currency Act applied only to New England, it constituted a warning and a threat to all colonial governments against allowing any looseness in the management of paper money. Orders from London severely restricted the use of this currency in all the colonies. But paper money had become an essential part of the American economy, and those who issued it were by no means wildcat inflationists. Every knowledgeable merchant knew the value of sound paper money, and many, like Benjamin Franklin, correctly saw that its controlled expansion could be a stimulus to the entire economy.

In this case, as in the case of the prohibitive taxation of the trade with the foreign West Indies and in the case of the restriction of American manufactures, the action of the British government was seen by Americans as not merely unfairly competitive, but hostile. The legislation and orders seemed arbitrary and unreasonable—impositions that called into question the grounds of loyalty. To obey such laws as these was a form of humiliation at the hands of a government that seemed distant, alienated from the people it governed, and unresponsive to their needs.

The American and the Enlightenment

Thus tensions arose between Britain and the colonies as a result of their uneasy collaboration in wartime and of the resentments created by Britain's seemingly arbitrary and hostile legislation. These were problems largely of policy and management. Potentially, at least, they could be controlled by wise political action. A deeper and less manageable source of distance and alienation between

Britain and America lay in the area of cultural perceptions—the sense Americans had of who they were in relation to the other peoples of the world, of what their life was like, and of who, in contrast, the British were within the same set of considerations. These attitudes and perceptions are facts that in the end are as important as battles, laws, and political campaigns. But they are more difficult to describe and to measure.

Through the two generations of growth and expansion that preceded the accession of George III, Americans had gradually acquired a sense of themselves as a separate people—separate not only in law or politics or constitution, but also in character and culture. Theirs was a complex self-image composed of many strands, and it could be seen as positive or negative depending on the context or point of view. It was an image of a simple, rustic, innocent, uncorrupted, and unsophisticated people, an appropriate self-image for a colonial people, perhaps, but no simple reflection of reality. For it was, first, a blending of several intellectual traditions and influences. It was in addition a reflection of the ideas and attitudes of eighteenth-century Europe's most enlightened thinkers; and it was, finally, a product of certain specific political ideas of great potential power.

The origins of this image can be traced back to the ambiguous picture of the American Indians that Europeans formed soon after their first contact with the Western Hemisphere. This picture combined simplicity and savagery, vigor and barbarism, innocence and paganism. By the eighteenth century this mingled image began to be applied as much to the Creoles—that is, North Americans of European descent—as to the Indians, whom the English had long since come to think of as hopelessly savage, if not satanic. This transfer of traits from the native Americans to the colonists of European background was facilitated by the common belief that the colonists had deliberately copied various practices and skills from the Indians and as a result had acquired from them certain peculiar characteristics. Infants strapped to boards, for example, were thought to develop like Indians whatever their race or culture. American women, like Indian women, were believed to be taller than European women and to suffer fewer miscarriages. This notion was reinforced by the "scientific" arguments of the environmentalists, an influential group of continental European thinkers who held that life in all its forms was shaped by the material conditions in which it was lived. From this point of view it seemed reasonable to believe that what was true of the Indians in the great American laboratory of nature would eventually apply, if it did not already, to the colonists too.

But more practical and immediate influences were also at work detailing the Americans' simplicity, innocence, and rural virtues. The image of the American colonists—their own view of themselves as well as the view that others had of them—was also shaped by the recruiting propaganda that had circulated throughout Europe and America for more than a century. All these publications had stressed the wonders of a simple, loosely institutionalized, benign society where land was free, where government scarcely existed, and where religion was practiced in absolutely uncontested freedom.

Perhaps the greatest influence of all in spreading the image of British North America as a land of simple, innocent, independent, and virtuous folk was the widespread knowledge of the kinds of people who had in fact gone there. Europeans were aware that immigrants to America had been self-respecting servants, ambitious artisans, sturdy yeoman farmers, Puritans, and—above all, and most sensationally—Quakers.

The symbolic importance of the Quakers to the world at large was overwhelming. In the seventeenth century they had been thought of principally as exotic radicals. They were famous throughout Britain and France for their fanatical independence of mind and for their absolute refusal to respect mere earthly authorities (hence their practice of addressing people of all ranks with the familiar "thee" and "thou"). In the more tolerant atmosphere of the early eighteenth century, the Quakers' reputation had shifted from that of defiant and fanatical seekers of religious freedom to that of gentle advocates of pacifism, toleration, simplicity in religion, and ordinary human rights in the face of aristocratic and authoritarian power. These traits had impressed Voltaire, the best known of the enlightened thinkers of the eighteenth century, during his stay in England from 1726 to 1729, and had led him to praise them extravagantly again and again.

For Voltaire, the Quakers as a group were the embodiment of civic virtue. And, he believed, the essence of their virtue could be seen in Pennsylvania, where their dreams and the dreams of all humanity, he thought, had reached fulfillment. Here, Voltaire stated, an enlightened republican lawgiver had created a human paradise. Philadelphia, he wrote in one of his *Philosophical Letters* (1734), was so prosperous that people flocked to it from all over America. Penn's laws were so wise that not one of them had ever been changed. The Indians had been won over to friendship; there was equality and religious freedom without priests; and there was peace everywhere. "William Penn might glory," he wrote, "in having brought down upon the earth the so much boasted golden age, which in all probability never existed but in Pennsylvania."

The world, it seemed, agreed with Voltaire. Montesquieu, perhaps the most widely respected and influential political analyst of the age, called Penn the greatest lawgiver since classical antiquity. The French *Encyclopédie*, the monumental collection of enlightened ideas published in the mid-eighteenth century, included Penn among the cultural heroes of Europe. And in addition to all this, every informed person in the Western world knew something about Pennsylvania and about America in general through the extraordinary figure of Benjamin Franklin.

Franklin and the Image of America   Franklin, the most celebrated American of the eighteenth century and one of the most famous and influential Americans who has ever lived, was born in Boston in 1706, the son of a candle- and soap-maker. At the age of seventeen he ran away to Philadelphia, where he eventually prospered as a printer and an organizer of

"Franklin Drawing Electricity from the Sky," by Benjamin West, c. 1805–15
Based on West's recollection of Franklin and his imagination, this painting idealizing Franklin's genius as a natural American scientist shows him assisted by various cherubs, two of whom are playing with Franklin's scientific equipment, the others (one in Indian headdress) are helping with the famous kite string. Franklin's right hand draws the electric power from the wet key struck by lightning.

printing businesses in several colonies. At the age of forty-two he retired from business to devote himself to public causes, writing, and scientific experimentation. He corresponded with English scientists and intellectuals, particularly Peter Collinson, a Quaker merchant and a member of the Royal Society, on the problems of electricity. It was in the form of letters to Collinson that he published the results of his studies, *Experiments and Observations on Electricity* (1751). This book was one of the great sensations of the eighteenth century. Before 1800 it went through five editions in English, three in French, one in Italian, and one in German, and it raised Franklin to the highest ranks among Western thinkers. The Count de Buffon, the greatest French naturalist of the age, himself arranged for the French edition; Denis Diderot, the editor of the *Encyclopédie*, declared Franklin to be the very model of the modern experimental scientist.

And who was Franklin? A simple, unsophisticated product of the primitive society of British North America—yet he had outdone the most sophisticated intellectuals of Europe in their own fields of endeavor. The implications were sensational. In the context of the great wave of reform thinking that is called the Enlightenment, Franklin's mere existence as a successful intellectual conveyed a powerful message. It reinforced the arguments of reformers everywhere and demonstrated conclusively the validity of their challenge to the establishment.

Although Enlightenment thought was complicated in its details, in its essence it was clear and simple. At its heart lay discontent with the condition of life as it was known in Europe, and a general approach to improvement. All enlightened thinkers in one way or another pictured human nature as good—or if not good, then at least capable of great improvement and of far more happiness than was commonly experienced. The evils of the world that reduced people to misery were seen mainly as artifacts, things that men and women themselves had created. To Voltaire, the chief evils of life were the great public institutions, especially the church and a corrupt and dogmatic priesthood. To the physiocrats, the French economic reformers who believed that agriculture alone produced wealth, the great evil was the irrational controls on agricultural production and marketing that the European governments imposed. To John Locke, the primary evil was the arbitrary, authoritarian state. To Jean-Jacques Rousseau, the primary evil was civilization itself. For all, the cruelties and miseries of life were products of institutions and practices that people themselves had made. The solution was to reform these structures so that human nature would be released to attain the happiness of which it was capable.

But there were powerful counter-arguments to these visions of the Enlightenment. The great imposing institutions—the state, the church, the regulated economy, and the social structures that gave power to a hereditary aristocracy—were, after all, the guardians of social order and stability. They were also the carriers of high culture and the sponsors of the finest human achievements. To eliminate or change them radically might create not freedom, but anarchy; not a higher civilization, but barbarism. To answer these arguments, the enlightened thinkers needed to be able to point to an example of civilized simplicity—a Christian society free of the hindrances of rigid and powerful institutions, a society in which reason had been used in shaping public institutions and in which, despite the simplicity of life, high culture was maintained and advanced. They found the example they wanted in British North America generally, in Pennsylvania more specifically, and above all in the figure of Franklin—apparently an untutored genius, a simple and unaffected but accomplished man of

Franklin, The Enlightenment Philosopher
This engraving by Augustin de Saint Aubin, based on a drawing by Charles Cochin, was made in early 1777, shortly after Franklin arrived in France to represent the United States. It expresses perfectly the image of Franklin as nature's philosopher and as the embodiment of Enlightenment ideals.

28 Letters *concerning*

different perfuafion, embrac'd him ten-
derly. *William* made a fruitlefs exhor-
tation to his father not to receive the fa-
crament, but to die a Quaker; and the
good old man intreated his fon *William*
to wear buttons on his fleeves, and a
crape hatband in his beaver, but all to no
purpofe.

William Pen inherited very large
poffeffions, part of which confifted in
crown-debts due to the vice-admiral for
fums he had advanc'd for the fea-fervice.
No monies were at that time more fe-
cure than thofe owing from the king.
Pen was oblig'd to go more than once,
and *Thee* and *Thou* king *Charles* and his
minifters, in order to recover the debt;
and at laft inftead of fpecie, the government invefted him with the right and fo-
vereignty of a province of *America*, to
the fouth of *Maryland.* Thus was a
Quaker rais'd to fovereign power. *Pen*
fet fail for his new dominions with two
fhips freighted with Quakers, who follow'd his fortune. The country was
then call'd *Penfilvania* from *William
Pen*, who there founded *Philadelphia*,
now

the English Nation. 29

now the moft flourifhing city in that
country. The firft ftep he took was to
enter into an alliance with his *American* neighbours; and this is the only
treaty between thofe people and the
Chriftians that was not ratified by an
oath, and was never infring'd. The
new fovereign was at the fame time the
legiflator of *Penfilvania*, and enacted ye-
ry wife and prudent laws, none of
which have ever been chang'd fince his
time. The firft is, to injure no perfon
upon a religious account, and to confider as brethren all thofe who believe in
one God.

He had no fooner fettled his government, but feveral *American* merchants
came and peopled this colony. The natives of the country inftead of flying
into the woods, cultivated by infenfible
degrees a friendfhip with the peaceable
Quakers. They lov'd thefe foreigners as
much as they detefted the other Chriftians who had conquer'd and laid wafte
America. In a little time, a great number of thefe favages (falfely fo call'd)
charm'd with the mild and gentle dif-
pofition

30 Letters *concerning*

pofition of their neighbours, came in
crowds to *William Pen*, and befought him
to admit them into the number of his
vaffals. 'Twas very rare and uncommon for a fovereign to fee *Thee'd* and
Thou'd by the meaneft of his fubjects,
who never took their hats off when
they came into his prefence; and as
fingular for a government to be without
one prieft in it, and for a people to be
without arms, either offenfive or defen-
five; for a body of citizens to be abfo-
lutely undiftinguifh'd but by the public:
employments, and for neighbours not to
entertain the leaft jealoufy one againft
the other.

William Pen might glory in having brought down upon earth the fo
much boafted golden age, which in all
probability never exifted but in *Penfilvania.* He return'd to *England* to fettle
fome affairs relating to his new dominions. After the death of king *Charles*
the fecond, king *James*, who had lov'd
the father, indulg'd the fame affection
to the fon, and no longer confider'd him
as an obfcure Sectary, but as a very great
man,

The European Image of America: Voltaire on Pennsylvania and the Quakers

Voltaire's account of Anglo-American life, which first appeared in English translation in 1733, was published in France in 1734 as Lettres Philosophiques *and was promptly condemned to be burnt by the hangman as "likely to inspire a license of thought most dangerous to religion and civil order." The book nevertheless circulated widely. This passage on Penn as a great lawgiver, on Pennsylvania as a utopia, and on the Quakers as humble people of civic virtue and peace was taken over almost verbatim into the great French* Encyclopédie *(1751–80), the massive summary of European liberal thought, and hence entered the mainstream of the Enlightenment.*

science, letters, and statecraft. If Franklin had never existed, it would have been necessary for the philosophers of the Enlightenment to invent him. Franklin understood this perfectly, shrewdly played upon it, and expressed it most clearly in his *Autobiography,* which he wrote in the later years of his life.

To much of the Western world, Franklin *was* America. Caught up in the imagery of simplicity and natural gifts demanded by Enlightenment aspirations, Franklin demonstrated the meaning of the New World to the Old. He thereby helped shape Americans' self-awareness, as well as Europe's perception of the provincial society beyond the sea.

America and the Grounds of Political Freedom

Inevitably, Franklin played up the theme of the social and moral grounds of political freedom, for it was in this area that American self-imagery came into its sharpest focus and acquired its greatest relevance for everyday affairs. Informed people universally agreed that in the end the success of

Britain's famous unwritten constitution—indeed, the success of any constitution that protected the people's liberties—depended on the virtue of the politically active population. Eternal vigilance was needed to maintain in government the balance of forces that prevented the misuse of power. Freedom from oppression rested on the ability of the people to resist the encroachments of a privileged and arrogant aristocracy; it also required the aristocracy to resist the temptations of profit and power and to use its privileges for the good of the entire society. If the people's will to protect their own liberties weakened, or if the British aristocracy gave in to laziness and self-indulgence as had the aristocracies of continental Europe, freedom would be destroyed by the predictable growth of arbitrary power.

The signs, for Americans of the late colonial period, were worrisome. Repeatedly, the colonists found reason to question the moral qualities of English society, to doubt the independence of "the democracy" in Britain and the impartiality and responsibility of the British aristocracy. American visitors to England sent back disturbing reports. John Dickinson of Pennsylvania, in England in the election year 1754, wrote home that he was "filled with awe and reverence" by his contact with scenes of ancient greatness and by the sophistication and variety of life in London. But he was also shocked by the corruption of English politics. More than £1 million, he reported to his father, was spent in efforts to manipulate the election.

> If a man cannot be brought to vote as he is desired, he is made dead drunk and kept in that state, never heard of by his family or friends till all is over and he can do no harm. The oath of their not being bribed is as strict and solemn as language can form it, but is so little regarded that few people can refrain from laughing while they take it.... Bribery is so common that it is thought there is not a borough in England where it is not practiced.... We hear every day in Westminister Hall leave moved to file information for bribery, but it is ridiculous and absurd to pretend to curb the effects of luxury and corruption in one instance or in one spot without a general reformation of manners, which everyone sees is absolutely necessary for the welfare of the kingdom. Yet Heaven knows how it can be effected. It is grown a vice here to be virtuous.

This was not simply provincial prudery. English writers too deplored the loss of virtue, warning of its implications for politics, and their voices were clearly heard in America. James Burgh's *Britain's Remembrancer* (1746) denounced "our degenerate times and corrupt nation." The British people, he said, were wallowing in "luxury and irreligion...venality, perjury, faction, opposition to legal authority, idleness, gluttony, drunkenness, lewdness, excessive gaming, robberies...a legion of furies sufficient to rend any state or empire...to pieces." Burgh's pamphlet was reprinted first by Franklin in 1747, then by another Philadelphia printer in 1748, and again in Boston in 1759. So too Dr. John Brown's blistering attack on English corruption, *An Estimate of the Manners and Princi-*

ples of the Times (1757), found an eager audience in America—an audience convinced of the superiority and virtue of its own uncorrupted manners and of its own moral capacity to satisfy the demands of freedom if freedom were ever challenged.

So the American people entered the age of George III. Their prospects were excellent despite the troubles that lay beneath the surface of Anglo-American life and the doubts they had about the moral quality of the British people and the responsibility of the British leaders. Conscious of their characteristics as a colonial people—provincial but vigorous, unsophisticated but uncorrupted, quarrelsome but free, undeveloped in all the main institutions of society but more prosperous than any large group in the Western world—they saw themselves growing powerful and mature as part of an enriching imperial connection.

Chronology

1727–1760	Reign of George II.	1739–1742	War of Jenkins' Ear, fought with Spain principally in Caribbean and Central America.
1729	Separate royal colonies, North and South Carolina, created.	1740–1741	Private land bank created in Massachusetts; outlawed by Parliament.
1732	Georgia established as buffer against Spanish and as philanthropic effort to relocate England's paupers.	1744–1748	King George's War (colonial phase of Europe's War of the Austrian Succession, 1740–48); concluded in Treaty of Aix-la-Chapelle.
1733	Molasses Act restricts colonial importation of sugar goods from French West Indies.	1745	New England troops take fortress of Louisbourg on Cape Breton Island (returned to France at end of war).
1734–1735	Jonathon Edwards touches off evangelical revival in Northampton, Massachusetts, and throughout Connecticut River valley.	1750	Iron Act, limiting production of finished iron goods in colonies, passed by Parliament.
1735	New York jury acquits John Peter Zenger of charge of seditious libel on ground that printing truth can be no libel.	1751	Currency Act, restricting issuance and currency of paper money in New England colonies, passed by Parliament.
1739–1740	George Whitefield tours America and ignites major phase of Great Awakening.		

1751	Publication of Franklin's *Experiments and Observations on Electricity.*	**1754– 1763**	French and Indian War (colonial phase of Europe's Seven Years' War, 1756–63).
1754	Albany Congress and Plan of Union.	**1759**	Quebec falls to British army.
		1760	George III accedes to throne.

Suggested Readings

The eighteenth-century colonial wars were the subject of Francis Parkman's most dramatic narratives—still immensely readable—in his nine-volume series, *France and England in North America.* His *Half-Century of Conflict* (2 vols., 1892) covers King George's War, and his *Montcalm and Wolfe* (2 vols., 1884) the French and Indian War. A modern, technical, scholarly work covering the same ground in greater detail but lacking Parkman's narrative style is Lawrence H. Gipson's *British Empire Before the American Revolution,* vols. VI–VIII (1946–53). Howard H. Peckham, *The Colonial Wars, 1689–1762* (1964), provides a brief introduction to the main events. On the British army in pre-Revolutionary America, see John Shy, *Toward Lexington* (1965), chaps. 1–3. Fred Anderson, *A People's Army: Massachusetts Soldiers and Society in the Seven Years' War* (1984), is a masterful study of the life of local militiamen under British command in the last colonial war and the meaning of war in their deeply Christian world view.

All three of the economic problems of Anglo-American relations discussed in the second section of the chapter (balance of payments, manufactures, and the money supply) are analyzed, with references to all the relevant writings on the subjects, in John J. McCusker and Russell R. Menard, *The Economy of British America* (1985).

On cultural relations between the colonies and Europe, see, besides the Savelle and Silverman books cited for chapter 5, Michael Kraus, *The Atlantic Civilization: Eighteenth-Century Origins* (1949); Durand Echeverria, *Mirage in the West . . . the French Image of American Society to 1815* (1957); Howard M. Jones, *O Strange New World* (1964); Henry F. May, *The Enlightenment in America* (1976); and Bernard Bailyn, *Ideological Origins of the American Revolution* (1967), chaps. 2–3. On Franklin's extraordinary role in cultural relations between Europe and America, see Alfred O. Aldridge, *Franklin and His French Contemporaries* (1957); Antonio Pace, *Franklin and Italy* (1958); I. Bernard Cohen's edition of *Benjamin Franklin's Experiments* (1941), his *Franklin and Newton* (1956), and his collected papers on Franklin's science (1990); and Charles C. Sellers, *Benjamin Franklin in Portraiture* (1962). The standard biographies are by Carl Van Doren (1938) and Esmond Wright (1986). A shorter but well-rounded account is Verner W. Crane, *Benjamin Franklin and a Rising People* (1954). Ronald W. Clark's biography (1983) concentrates on Franklin's early career and his achievements in science. There is a subtle interpretation of Franklin as publicist and writer, and especially of his manipulation of his public image in his autobiography, in R. Jackson Wilson, *Figures of Speech* (1989).

PART TWO

Framing the Republic
1760–1820

Gordon S. Wood

$\mathscr{T}$HE American Revolution is the single most important event in American history. Not only did it create the United States, but it defined most of the persistent values and hopes of the American people. The noblest ideals of Americans—the commitments to freedom, equality, constitutionalism, and the well-being of ordinary people—were first defined in the Revolutionary era. The Revolution gave Americans the belief that they were a people with a special destiny to lead the world toward liberty. The Revolution, in short, gave birth to whatever ideology Americans as a whole have had. The United States was the first nation in the modern world to make political and social principles the foundation of its existence. A society that was composed of so many different races and of people from so many different places could not be a nation in any traditionally understood sense of the term. It is the Revolutionary experience and the ideals and beliefs flowing from it that have held Americans together and made them think of themselves as a single people.

The origins of such a great event lie deep in America's past. A century and a half of dynamic developments in the British mainland colonies of North America had fundamentally altered inherited European institutions and patterns of life and had created the basis for a new society. Suddenly in the 1760s Great Britain thrust its imperial power into the changing world of North America with a thoroughness that had not been felt in a century. Its policies touched off a crisis within the loosely organized empire, and American resistance turned into rebellion. As the colonists searched for a way to make sense of the unique qualities of their society, this rebellion became for them a justification and idealization of American life as it had gradually and unintentionally developed over the previous century and a half. In this sense, as John Adams later said, "The Revolution was effected before the war commenced." It was a change "in the minds and hearts of the people."

But this change was not the whole American Revolution. The Revolution was also part of the great transforming process that carried America into modernity. By 1760 the different circumstances of life in the North American wilderness had fundamentally altered the institutions and lives of the colonists. But along with powdered wigs and knee breeches, mid-eighteenth-century society still retained many traditional habits of behavior and social relationships. These traditional patterns of life separated colonial America from the more rapidly changing, bustling, individualistic world of the early nineteenth century. Much had changed by 1760, but more remained to be changed.

Although the Revolution began as a political and constitutional struggle, its deepest roots and its most far-reaching results were social. The Revolution released and intensified forces that, by the early years of the nineteenth century, helped create a society unlike any that had existed before. The society that emerged from the Revolution was almost as different from the America of 1760 as colonial America had been from eighteenth-century England.

The Revolution's origins went back to the seventeenth-century settlements, and its consequences are still felt by the American people. Yet the Revolution itself took place essentially between 1760 and 1820. Some Americans thought that the Revolution was over in 1776 with the Declaration of Independence and the creation of new state governments. Others believed that the Revolution ended only with the reconstruction of the national government in 1787. Still others thought it was not finished until the new central government gathered strength and energy in the 1790s. Yet many other Americans saw these later centralizing developments—the creation of a strong national government—as a betrayal of the original Revolution and thus sought to recover the spirit of 1776. For them the election of Thomas Jefferson as president of the United States in 1800 was the real fulfillment of the Revolution, a fulfillment that required confirmation in another war against Great Britain in 1812.

By the end of that second war against Britain, the central impulses of the Revolution had run their course. At last the future and stability of the Republic seemed secure. Democracy and equality were no longer issues to be debated; they had become articles of faith to be fulfilled. The ideological antagonisms that the Revolution had aroused had finally petered out. In 1760 the colonists were provincial Britons living on the edges of civilization; by 1820 they were Americans leading what they thought was a world revolution on behalf of liberty. In place of a collection of little more than 2 million monarchical subjects huddled along the Atlantic coast, America by 1820 had become a huge, expansive nation of nearly 10 million republican citizens, active, energetic, and filled with the great possibilities that lay before them.

7

Sources of the Revolution

⧽

N 1763 Great Britain straddled the world with the greatest and richest empire since the fall of Rome. From India to the Mississippi River, its armies and navies had been victorious. The Peace of Paris that concluded the Seven Years' War—or the French and Indian War, as the Americans called it— gave Britain undisputed dominance over the northern and eastern half of North America. From the defeated powers, France and Spain, Britain acquired huge chunks of territory in the New World—all of Canada, East and West Florida, and millions of fertile acres between the Appalachian Mountains and the Mississippi River. France turned over to Spain the territory of Louisiana in compensation for Spain's loss of Florida; and thus this most fearsome of Britain's enemies removed itself altogether from the North American continent.

Yet at the moment of Britain's supremacy there were powerful forces at work that would soon, almost overnight, change everything. In the aftermath of the Seven Years' War, British officials found themselves having to make long-post-poned decisions concerning the colonies that set in motion a chain of events that ultimately shattered the empire.

The Changing Empire

Ever since the formation of the British Empire in the late seventeenth century, royal officials and bureaucrats had been interested in reforming the awkwardly imposed imperial structure and in expanding royal authority over the American colonists. But most of their schemes had been blocked by English ministries more concerned with the patronage of English politics than with colonial reform. These ministries were anxious to keep troublesome colonial issues out of Parlia-ment, where they might be readily exploited by opposition politicians. Under such circumstances, the empire had been allowed to grow haphazardly, without much control from London. People from all countries had been allowed to settle in the colonies, and land had been given out freely.

Although few imperial officials had ever doubted that the colonies were supposed to be inferior to the mother country and dependent on it, in fact the empire had not worked that way. The relationship that had developed reflected the irrational and inefficient nature of the imperial system—the variety of offices, the diffusion of power, and the looseness of organization. Even in trade regulation, which was the empire's main business, inefficiency, loopholes, and numerous opportunities for corruption prevented the imperial authorities from interfering substantially with the colonists' pursuit of their own economic and social interests.

By the middle of the eighteenth century, however, new circumstances began forcing changes in this irrational but working relationship. The British colonies—there were twenty-two of them in the Western Hemisphere in 1760—were becoming too important to be treated as casually as the mother country had treated them in the first half of the eighteenth century. Dynamic developments throughout the greater British world demanded that England pay more attention to its North American colonies.

Population Growth and Movement

The most basic of these developments were the growth and movement of people. In the middle decades of the eighteenth century, the population throughout the whole English-speaking world—in Britain and the colonies alike—was increasing at unprecedented rates and redistributing itself in massive movements of people. During the 1740s the population of England, which had hardly grown at all for half a century, suddenly began to increase. The populations of Ireland and Scotland had been rising steadily since the beginning of the eighteenth century. The population of the North American colonies was growing even faster—virtually exploding—and had been doing so almost since the beginning of the settlements. Indeed, the North American colonists continued to multiply more rapidly than any other people in the Western world. Between 1750 and 1770 they doubled in number, from a million to more than 2 million, and thereby became an even more important part of the British world. In 1700 the American population had been only one-twentieth of the British and Irish populations combined; by 1770 it was nearly one-fifth, and such farsighted colonists as Benjamin Franklin were predicting that sooner or later the center of the British Empire would shift to America.

Everywhere the expanding British population was in motion, moving from village to village and from continent to continent. In Britain growing numbers of migrants in a few decades created the new industrial cities of Birmingham, Manchester, and Leeds and made London the largest urban center in the Western world. A steady stream moved from the British Isles across the Atlantic to the New World. The migration of Protestant Irish and Scots that had begun early in the century increased after the French and Indian war. Between 1764 and 1776

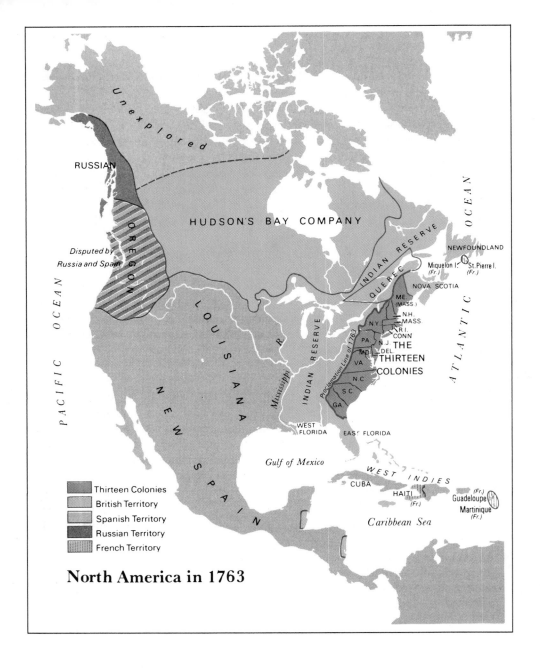

North America in 1763

Legend:
- Thirteen Colonies
- British Territory
- Spanish Territory
- Russian Territory
- French Territory

some 125,000 people left the British Isles for the American colonies. From the colonial port towns, particularly Philadelphia, British migrants and Germans from the Rhine Valley joined with increasing numbers of uprooted colonists to spread over half a continent, along a variety of routes.

For nearly a century and a half the colonists had been confined to a several-hundred-mile-wide strip of territory along the Atlantic coast. But in the middle decades of the eighteenth century, the pressures of increasing population density began to be felt. Overcultivated soil in the East was becoming depleted. Particularly in the Chesapeake areas the number of tenants was visibly growing. Older towns now seemed overcrowded, especially in New England, and young men coming of age could no longer count on obtaining pieces of land as their fathers had done. Throughout the colonies more and more people were on the move; many drifted into the small colonial cities, which were ill equipped to handle them. By 1772 in Philadelphia, the percentage of poor was eight times greater than it had been twenty years earlier, and almshouses were being constructed and filled as never before. Most of these transient poor, however, saw the cities only as way stations in their endless search for land on which they might recreate the stability they had been forced to abandon.

With the defeat of the French, people set out in all directions, eager to take advantage of the newly acquired land in the interior. In 1759 speculators and settlers moved into the area around Lake Champlain and westward along the Mohawk River into central New York. Between 1749 and 1771 New York's population grew from 73,348 to 168,007. Tens of thousands of colonists and new immigrants pushed into western Pennsylvania and southward into the Carolinas along routes on each side of Virginia's Blue Ridge. Along these roads strings of towns—from York, Pennsylvania, to Camden, South Carolina—quickly developed to service the travelers and to distribute produce to distant markets. The growth of settlement was phenomenal. In Pennsylvania twenty-nine new localities were created between 1756 and 1765—more in these few years than in the colony's entire previous history. North Carolina increased its population sixfold between 1750 and 1775 to become the fourth largest colony.

New frontiers appeared everywhere simultaneously throughout British North America. By the early 1760s hunters and explorers such as Daniel Boone began opening up paths westward through the Appalachians. Settlers, mostly small farmers, soon followed. Some moved southward to the valley of the Holston River and to the headwaters of the Cumberland and Tennessee rivers, and others spread northwest into the Ohio Valley and the Kentucky basin. Some drifted down the Ohio and Mississippi rivers to join overland migrants from the southern colonies in the new province of West Florida, and thus completed a huge encirclement of the new western territory.

During the decade and a half before Independence, New England throbbed with movement. New towns were created by the founding of new settlements and the division of existing ones. By the early 1760s the number of transients drifting from town to town throughout the region multiplied dramatically, in some counties doubling or even more than tripling the numbers of the previous decade. Many farmers gave up searching for opportunities within established communities and set out for distant places on the very edges of the expanded empire. Massachusetts and Connecticut colonists trekked not only to northern New England and Nova Scotia, but to areas as far away as the Susquehanna River in Pennsylvania and the lower Mississippi River. Indeed the largest single addition to the population of West Florida came from the settlement of four hundred

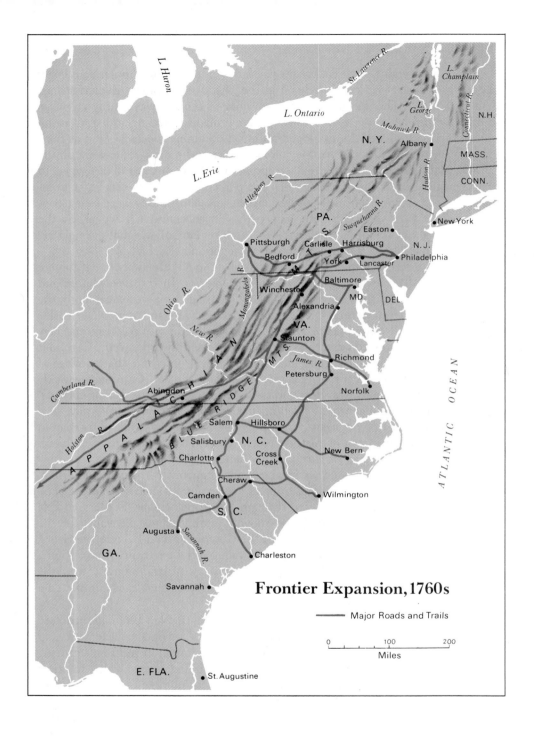

Frontier Expansion, 1760s

—— Major Roads and Trails

0   100   200
Miles

families from Connecticut in 1773–74. In the late 1760s the migration of people from Connecticut to the Wyoming Valley in Pennsylvania was so massive that Connecticut in 1774 annexed these Pennsylvania settlements and made them part of one of the province's counties. Between 1760 and 1776 some 20,000 people from southern New England moved up the Connecticut River into New Hampshire and into what would later become Vermont. In that same period migrants from Massachusetts streamed into Maine and founded 94 towns. A total of 264 new towns were established in northern New England during the years between 1760 and 1776.

British and colonial authorities could scarcely comprehend the meaning of this enormous explosion of peoples in search of land. The colonists, one astonished official observed, were moving "as their avidity and restlessness incite them. They acquire no attachment to place: but wandering about seems engrafted in their nature; and it is a weakness incident to it that they should forever imagine the lands further off are still better than those upon which they are already settled." Land fever infected all levels of society. While Ezra Stiles, a minister in Newport, Rhode Island, and later the president of Yale University, bought and sold small shares in places all over New England and in Pennsylvania and New York, more influential figures like Benjamin Franklin were concocting huge speculative schemes in the vast unsettled lands of the West.

All this movement had far-reaching effects on American society and its place in the British Empire. The fragmentation of households, churches, and communities increased, and the colonial governments lost control of the mushrooming new settlements. In the backcountry, lawlessness and vagrancy became common, and disputes over land claims and colonial boundaries increased sharply. But the most immediate effect of this rapid spread of people—and the effect that was most obvious to imperial officials in the 1760s—was the pressure that the migrations placed on native Americans.

Indians   At the beginning of the Seven Years' (or French and Indian) War, the problem of native Americans in the West compelled the British government for the first time to take over from the colonies the direct control of Indian affairs. Two British officials, one each for the northern and southern regions, now had the task of pacifying tribes of Indians, whom one of the superintendents described as "the most formidable of any uncivilized body of people in the world." New England had few Indians left, but in New York there were 2,000 warriors, mostly fierce Senecas, left from the once-formidable Six Nations of the Iroquois. In the Susquehanna and Ohio valleys dwelled a variety of tribes, mostly Delawares, Shawnees, Mingos, and Hurons, who claimed about 12,000 fighting men. On the southern frontiers the Indian presence was even more forbidding. From the Carolinas to the Yazoo River were some 14,000 warriors, mainly Cherokees, Creeks, Chocktaws, and Chickasaws. Altogether this native American population formed an imposing barrier to British western expansion.

After French authority had been eliminated from Canada and Spanish authority from Florida, the native Americans were no longer able to play one European power off against the other. Britain now had sole responsibility for regulating the profitable fur trade and for maintaining peace between whites and Indians. The problems were awesome. Not only were many whites prepared to

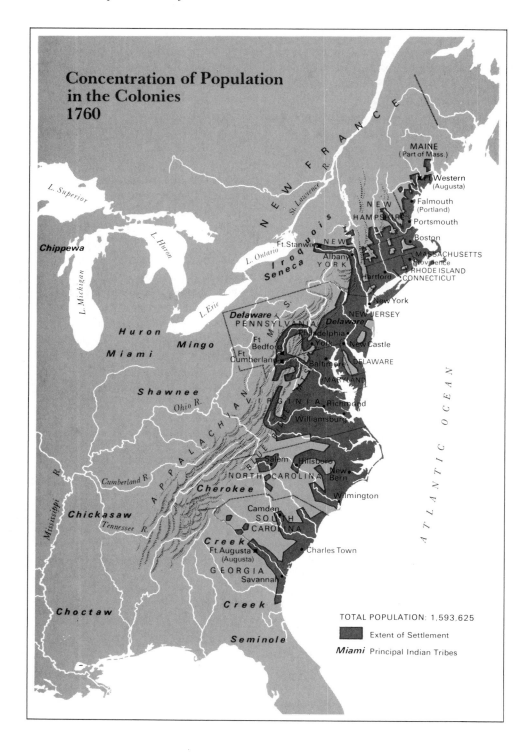

Concentration of Population in the Colonies 1760

TOTAL POPULATION: 1,593,625

Extent of Settlement

Miami Principal Indian Tribes

use brandy and rum to achieve their aims, but they had conflicting interests. Traders competed among themselves: some favored regulation of the fur trade, although most did not. But all traders favored the establishment in the West of Indian reservations that settlers would not be permitted to invade, and they drew on the support of humanitarian groups who were concerned with the Indians' fate. Land speculators, however, wanted to push back the Indians and open the West for settlement. Confused, lied to, and cheated of their land and their furs by greedy white traders and land-hungry migrants, the Indians retaliated with atrocities and raids. Some tribes attempted to form coalitions and wage full-scale war.

Thus the end of the Seven Years' War did not end violence on the frontier. From the devastating Cherokee War of 1759–61 in South Carolina to the assault on the Shawnees in 1774 by Lord Dunmore, the royal governor of Virginia, British officials repeatedly had to resort to troops to put down the Indians' revolts over white encroachments on their lands and to curb the dishonest practices of the traders. The biggest Indian uprising of the period occurred in 1763 following the British takeover of the former French forts in the West. In just a few weeks Indians from several tribes that had joined under the leadership of an Ottawa chief named Pontiac surprised and destroyed all but three of the British posts west of the Appalachians. Before they were defeated by British troops, the angry warriors had penetrated eastward into the backcountry of Pennsylvania, Maryland, and Virginia and had killed more than 2,000 colonists. It is no wonder that many royal authorities in the 1760s concluded that only the presence of regular troops of the British army could maintain peace in the American borderlands of the empire.

Backcountry Disorder

The rapid growth and spread of people in the mid-eighteenth century affected more than white-Indian relations on the frontier. Thousands of migrants flowed into the backcountry, beyond the reach of the colonial governments. These backcountry settlers were so distant from authority that sometimes vigilante groups had to be relied on to impose order. In the 1760s backcountry people in South Carolina organized vigilante "Regulators" to put down roving gangs of thieves, but illegal posses of this kind often turned raiders themselves. By the early 1770s the Green Mountain Boys of Vermont, under the leadership of Ethan Allen and his brother, were terrorizing all who submitted to New York's jurisdiction, and Connecticut Yankees were fighting Pennsylvanians for control of the settlements along the Susquehanna River. Sometimes frontiersmen in these trans-Appalachian areas had to form compacts of government for their raw societies, which often consisted of little more than "stations"—primitive stockaded forts surrounded by huts.

Everywhere in the backcountry the sudden influx of people weakened the legitimacy of existing authority. In the rapidly growing interiors of both Pennsylvania and North Carolina, settlers in the 1760s rose in arms against what they believed was exploitation by remote eastern governments. In western Pennsylvania Scotch-Irish settlers led by the Paxton Boys rebelled against the Quaker-dominated, pacifist-minded colonial legislature, in which they were underrepresented. In 1763–64 they killed Indians who were under the government's protection and then marched on Philadelphia. The rebels turned back only after mediation by Benjamin Franklin and the promise of a greater voice in the colonial assembly. In North Carolina not only was the backcountry underrepresented in the provincial legislature, but its local government was under the corrupt management of officials and lawyers from the eastern part of the colony. In 1767 a group of western vigilantes, assuming the familiar title "Regulators," erupted in violence. They took over the county courts and petitioned the North Carolina government for greater representation, lower taxes, and local control of their affairs. Two thousand of these "Regulators" were dispersed by the North Carolina governor and his force of eastern militia at the so-called battle of the Alamance in 1771. But royal officials could not so easily dispel the deeply rooted fears among many Americans of the dangers of unfair representation and distant political power. Indeed, these Westerners were only voicing toward their own colonial governments the same attitudes that Americans in general had about British power.

Economic Expansion   All these consequences flowing from the increased numbers and movement of people in North America were bound to raise Britain's interest in its colonies. But population pressures were not the only factor in the reshaping of British attitudes toward the colonies and in the transforming of American society. Equally important was the related expansion of the Anglo-American economy that took place in the middle years of the eighteenth century.

By 1750 the immediate origins of what would soon become the industrial revolution were already visible in Britain. British imports, exports, and industrial production of various sorts—all the major indicators of economic growth—were rapidly rising. Americans were deeply involved in this sudden British economic expansion, and by the 1760s they were feeling its effects everywhere.

In the years after 1745, colonial trade with Great Britain grew dramatically and became an increasingly important segment of the English and Scottish economies. Nearly half of all English shipping was engaged in American commerce. The North American mainland was absorbing 25 percent of English exports, and Scottish commercial involvement with the colonies was growing even faster. From 1747 to 1765 the value of colonial exports to Britain doubled, from about £700,000 to £1,500,000, while the value of colonial imports from Britain rose even faster, from about £900,000 to more than £2 million. For the first time in the eighteenth century, Britain's own production of foodstuffs could not meet the needs of its suddenly rising population. By 1760 Britain was importing more grain than it exported.

This increasing demand for foodstuffs—not only in Great Britain, but in southern Europe and the West Indies as well—meant soaring prices for American exports. Between the 1740s and the 1760s, the price of American wheat that was exported to the Caribbean increased nearly 60 percent, flour 54 percent, and pork 48 percent. Even tobacco prices went up 34 percent in the same period. Seeing the greater demand and rising prices for American exports, more and more ordinary farmers began to produce foodstuffs and other goods for distant markets. By the 1760s remote trading centers in the backcountry such as Staunton, Virginia, and Salisbury, North Carolina, were shipping large quantities of tobacco and grain eastward to the sea along networks of roads and towns. Port cities like Baltimore, Norfolk, and Alexandria grew up almost overnight to handle this swelling traffic.

Soaring prices for agricultural exports meant rising standards of living for more and more Americans. It was not just the great planters of the South and the big merchants of the cities who were getting richer. Now ordinary Americans were also buying luxury items that traditionally had been purchased only by the well-to-do—items that were increasingly called conveniences and that ranged from Irish linen and lace to matched sets of Wedgwood dishes.

Although nineteen out of twenty Americans were still engaged in agriculture, the rising levels of taste and consumption drew more colonists into manufacturing—at first, mostly the production of crude textiles and shoes. Transportation and communications rapidly improved as roads were built and regular schedules established for stagecoaches and packet boats. In the 1750s the post office, under the leadership of Benjamin Franklin, the colonial deputy postmaster general, instituted weekly mails between Philadelphia and Boston and cut delivery time in half, from six to three weeks. The growing population, better roads, more reliable information about markets, and the greater variety of towns all encouraged domestic manufacturing for regional and intercolonial markets. By 1768 colonial manufacturers were supplying Pennsylvania with 8,000 pairs of shoes a year. Areas of eastern Massachusetts were becoming more involved in manufacturing: in 1767 the town of Haverhill, with fewer than three hundred residents, had forty-four workshops and nineteen mills. By this date many colonial artisans and would-be manufacturers were more than eager to support associations to boycott English imports.

But most colonists still preferred British goods. Since the mid-1760s Americans were importing from Britain about £500,000 worth of goods more than they were exporting to the mother country, and thus they continued to be troubled by a trade deficit with Britain. Part of this deficit in the colonists' balance of payments with Britain was made up by the profits of shipping, by British wartime expenditures in America, and by increased sales to Europe and the West Indies. But a large part was also made up by the extension to the colonists of large amounts of English and Scottish credit. By 1760 colonial debts to Britain amounted to £2 million; by 1772 they had jumped to more than £4 million. After 1750 a growing proportion of this debt was owed by colonists who earlier had been excluded from direct dealings with British merchants. Small tobacco farmers in the Chesapeake gained immediate access to British credit and markets through the spread of Scottish "factors" (stores) in the backcountry of Virginia and Maryland.* By 1760 it was not unusual for as many as 150 petty traders in a single port to be doing business with a London merchant company.

These demographic and economic forces undermined the traditional structure of colonial society. The ties of kinship and patronage that held people together, which had never been strong in America, were now further weakened. Even in Virginia, one of the most stable of the colonies, the leading plantation owners found their authority challenged by small farmers who had been cut loose from older dependent economic relationships. During the middle decades of the eighteenth century, ordinary people in Virginia left the official Church of England in growing numbers. They formed new evangelical religious communities that rejected the high style and luxury of the dominant Anglican gentry. Within a few years succeeding waves of New Light Presbyterians, Separate Baptists, and finally Methodists swept up new converts from among the common farmers of the Chesapeake region. Between 1769 and 1774 the number of Baptist churches in Virginia increased from seven to fifty-four.

The Virginia gentry blamed the growth of religious dissent on the long-existing incompetence of the Anglican ministers. In turn the ministers accused the lay vestries, which were composed of Anglican gentry, of not supporting them. Amid these mutual accusations the Virginia House of Burgesses passed acts in 1755 and 1758 that fixed at two pence a pound the standard value of tobacco used to meet debts and public obligations. Since tobacco prices were rising rapidly, these so-called Two Penny Acts penalized creditors and those public officials (including ministers) who were used to being paid in tobacco. British merchants and the ministers of the Virginia established church protested and were able to get the king's Privy Council in England to veto the Burgesses' 1758 act. In 1763 a rising young lawyer, Patrick Henry, first made his reputation in a court battle over one of the Virginia ministers' legal suits for the recovery of wages lost by the Two Penny Act. In his defense of the Virginia planters against this "Parson's Cause," Henry argued that, because the king had disallowed the act, he "from being the father of his people [has] degenerated into a Tyrant, and forfeits all rights to his subjects' obedience." In similar ways in all the colonies, local and imperial authority was being placed under increased pressure.

It is doubtful whether anyone anywhere in the mid-eighteenth century knew how to control the powerful social and economic forces at work in the Anglo-American world. Certainly the flimsy administrative arrangement that governed the British Empire was unable to manage this dynamic world. By midcentury many British officials realized that some sort of overhaul of this increasingly important empire was needed. But few understood the explosive energy and the sensitive nature of the people they were tampering with. The British Empire,

---

*For the Scottish "factors," see chapter 5, p. 161.

Benjamin Franklin warned, was like a fragile Chinese vase that required delicate handling indeed.

The Reorganization of the Empire

After 1748 various imperial reforms were in the air. The eye-opening experience of fighting the Seven Years' War amid the colonists' evasion and corruption of the navigation laws had provoked William Pitt and other royal officials into vigorous, though piecemeal, reforms of the imperial system. But these beginnings might have been suppressed, as others had been, if it had not been for the enormous problems that were created by the Peace of Paris, which ended the Seven Years' War in 1763.

The most immediate of these problems was the reorganization of the territory that had been acquired from France and Spain. New governments had to be organized. The Indian trade had to be regulated, land claims had to be sorted out, and something had to be done to keep the conflicts between land-hungry white settlers and restless native Americans from exploding into open warfare.

Even more disturbing was the huge expense confronting the British government. By 1763 the war debt totaled £137 million; its annual interest alone was £5 million, a huge figure when compared with an ordinary yearly British peacetime budget of only £8 million. There was, moreover, little prospect of military costs declining. Since the new territories were virtually uninhabited by Englishmen, the government could not rely on its traditional system of local defense and police to preserve order. Lord Jeffrey Amherst, commander in chief in North America, estimated that he would need 10,000 troops to keep the peace among the French and Indians and to deal with squatters, smugglers, and bandits. Thus at the outset of the 1760s, the British government made a crucial decision that no subsequent administration ever abandoned—the decision to maintain a standing army in America. This peacetime army was more than double the size of the army that had existed in the colonies before the Seven Years' War, and the costs of maintaining it quickly climbed to well over £400,000 a year.

Where was the money to come from? The landowning gentry in England felt pressed to the wall by taxes; a new English cider tax of 1763 actually required troops to enforce it. Meanwhile returning British troops were bringing home tales of the prosperity Americans were enjoying at the war's end. Under the circumstances it seemed reasonable to the British government to seek new sources of revenue in the colonies and to make the navigation system more efficient in ways that royal officials had long advocated. A half-century of "salutary neglect" had come to an end.

George III and British Politics
Disruptions within the delicate balance of the empire were therefore inevitable. But the coming to the throne in 1760 of a new monarch, the young and impatient George III, worsened the changing Anglo-American relations. George III was only twenty-two years old at the time, shy and inexperienced in politics. But he

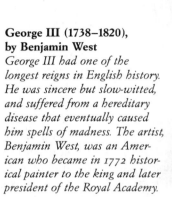

George III (1738–1820),
by Benjamin West
George III had one of the
longest reigns in English history.
He was sincere but slow-witted,
and suffered from a hereditary
disease that eventually caused
him spells of madness. The artist,
Benjamin West, was an Amer-
ican who became in 1772 histor-
ical painter to the king and later
president of the Royal Academy.

was stubbornly determined to rule personally, in a manner distinctly different from that of George I and George II, the first of the Hanoverian kings. After the disastrous failure in 1745–46 of the Stuart heir, "Bonnie Prince Charlie," to reclaim the English throne, the Whigs' repeated cry that they were the only real defenders of the Hanoverian crown against the Tories and the Stuarts tended to lose its power and meaning.* By 1760 George III felt little of the loyalty to the old Whigs that his grandfather and great-grandfather had felt. Instead, influenced by his inept Scottish tutor and "dearest friend," Lord Bute, George aimed to purify English public life of its corruption and factionalism. He wanted to replace former Whig-Tory squabbling and party intrigue with duty to crown and country. The results of George's good intentions were the greatest and most bewildering fluctuations in English politics in a half-century—all at the very moment the long-postponed reforms of the empire were to take place.

---

*In eighteenth-century British politics the Whigs, especially under the leadership of Sir Robert Walpole (1721–42), were those who controlled the crown offices; they upheld the supremacy of Parliament and the 1714 settlement of the British crown on George I and the Hanoverian line of kings. The Tories were good royalists and good believers in nonresistance to legitimate authority; they tended to look backward to an earlier time when the king and the Church of England together dominated English life. Because after 1714 many of the Tories were suspected of being supporters of the Stuart line (the so-called Jacobites), the Tories were effectively excluded from crown offices through the reigns of George I (1714–27) and George II (1727–60).

Historians no longer depict George III as a tyrant seeking to undermine the English constitution by choosing his ministers against Parliament's wishes. But there can be little doubt that men of the time felt that George III, whether he intended to or not, was violating the political customs of the day. When he chose Lord Bute, his Scottish favorite, who had little strength in Parliament, to head his government, thereby excluding such Whig ministers as William Pitt and the Duke of Newcastle, who did have political support in Parliament, the new king may not have been acting unconstitutionally; but he certainly was violating customary political realities. Bute's retirement in 1763 did little to ease the opposition's fears that the king was seeking the advice of Tory favorites "behind the curtain" and was attempting to impose decisions on the leading political groups in Parliament rather than governing through them. By diligently attempting to shoulder what he thought was his constitutional responsibility for governing in his own stubborn, peculiar way, George III helped to increase the political confusion of the 1760s.

A decade of short-lived ministries in the 1760s contrasted sharply with the stable and long-lasting Whig governments of the previous generation. It almost seemed as if the stubborn king trusted no one who had Parliament's support. After Pitt and Newcastle had been dismissed, and after Bute had failed, the king in 1763 turned to George Grenville, Bute's protégé, only because he found no one else acceptable to be his chief minister. Although Grenville was responsible for the first wave of colonial reforms, his resignation in 1765 resulted from a personal quarrel with the king and had nothing to do with colonial policy. Next, a government was formed by Whigs who were connected with the Marquess of Rockingham and for whom the great orator and political thinker Edmund Burke was a spokesman; but this Whig coalition never had the King's confidence, and it lasted scarcely a year. In 1766 George at last called on the aging Pitt, now Lord Chatham, to head the government. But Chatham's illness (gout in the head, critics said) and the bewildering parliamentary factionalism of the late 1760s turned his ministry into a hodgepodge that Chatham scarcely ruled at all.

By 1767 no one seemed to be in charge. Ministers shuffled in and out of offices, exchanging positions and following their own inclinations even against their colleagues' wishes. Amid this confusion only Charles Townshend, chancellor of the exchequer, gave any direction to colonial policy, and he died in 1767. Not until the appointment of Lord North as prime minister in 1770 did George find a politician whom he trusted and who also had Parliament's support.

Outside of Parliament, the huge portion of the British nation that was excluded from active participation in politics was stirring as it never had before. Ireland was restless under Britain's continual interference in its affairs. Political corruption and Parliament's failure to extend either the right to vote or representation created widespread resentment and led to many calls for reform. Mob rioting in London and elsewhere in England increased dramatically in the 1760s. In 1763 George III noted that there were "insurrections and tumults in every part of the country." The situation was worse at the end of the decade. Lord North

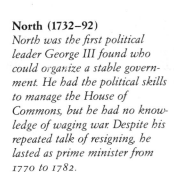

North (1732–92)
North was the first political leader George III found who could organize a stable government. He had the political skills to manage the House of Commons, but he had no knowledge of waging war. Despite his repeated talk of resigning, he lasted as prime minister from 1770 to 1782.

was attacked on his way to Parliament; his coach was destroyed and he barely escaped with his life. Rioting had long been common in England, but many of the popular uprisings of the 1760s were different from those in the past. Far from being limited to particular grievances such as high bread prices, much of the rioting was now directed toward the whole political system. The most important crowd leader was John Wilkes, one of the most colorful demagogues in English history. Wilkes was a member of Parliament and an opposition journalist who in 1763 was arrested and tried for seditiously libeling George III and the government in No. 45 of his newspaper, the *North Briton.* Wilkes immediately became a popular hero, and the cry "Wilkes and Liberty" spread on both sides of the Atlantic. The House of Commons ordered the offensive issue of the newspaper publicly burned, and Wilkes fled to France. In 1768 he returned and was several times elected to the House of Commons; but each time Parliament denied him his seat. London crowds, organized by substantial shopkeepers and artisans, found in Wilkes a symbol of all their pent-up resentments against Britain's corrupt and oligarchic politics. The issue of Wilkes helped to bring together a radical reform movement that shook the foundations of Britain's narrow governing class.

Thus in the 1760s and early 1770s, the British government was faced with the need to overhaul its empire and gain revenue from its colonies at the very time when the political situation in the British Isles was more chaotic, confused, and disorderly than it had been since the early eighteenth century. No wonder that it took only a bit more than a decade for the whole shaky imperial structure to come crashing down.

The Proclamation of 1763 and the West

The government began its reform of the newly enlarged empire by issuing the Proclamation of 1763. This crown proclamation created three new royal governments—East Florida, West Florida, and Quebec—and enlarged the province of Nova Scotia. It turned the vast trans-Appalachian area into an Indian reservation and prohibited all private individuals from purchasing Indian lands. The aim was to maintain peace in the West and to channel the migration of people northward and southward into the new colonies. There, it was felt, the settlers would be in closer touch with both the mother country and the mercantile system—and more useful as buffers against the Spanish and the remaining French.

But circumstances destroyed these royal blueprints. Not only were there bewildering shifts of the ministers in charge of the new policy, but news of Pontiac's Indian rebellion in the Ohio Valley in 1763 forced the government to rush its program into effect. The demarcation line along the Appalachians that closed the West to white settlers was hastily and crudely drawn, and some colonists suddenly found themselves living in the Indian reservation. The new trading regulations and sites were widely ignored and created more chaos in the Indian trade than had existed earlier. So confusing was the situation in the West that the British government could never convince the various contending interests that the Proclamation was anything more than, in the words of George Washington, who had speculative interests in western lands, "a temporary expedient to quiet the minds of the Indians." Scores of speculators and lobbyists pressured the unsteady British governments to negotiate a series of Indian treaties shifting the line of settlement westward. But each modification only whetted the appetites of the land speculators and led to some of the most grandiose land schemes in modern history. The climax of this speculative frenzy was reached in 1769, when a huge conglomerate, the Grand Ohio Company, whose membership involved prominent figures on both sides of the Atlantic, petitioned the crown for the rights to millions of acres in the Ohio Valley.

In the Quebec Act of 1774, the British government, with Parliament's help, finally tried to steady its dizzy western policy. This act transferred to the province of Quebec the land and the control of the Indian trade in the huge area between the Ohio and Mississippi rivers and allowed Quebec's French inhabitants French law and Roman Catholicism. As enlightened as this act was toward the French Canadians, it managed to anger all American interests—speculators, settlers, and traders alike. This arbitrary alteration of provincial boundaries threatened the security of all colonial boundaries and frightened American Protestants into believing that the British government was trying to erect a hostile Catholic province in the North and West.

The Sugar and Stamp Acts

The new colonial trade policies were more coherent than Britain's western policy, but no less dangerous in American eyes. The Plantation Act, or Sugar Act, of 1764 was clearly a major successor to the great navigation acts of the late seventeenth century. The series of regulations that it established were designed to

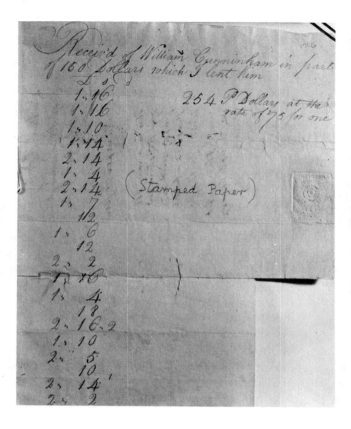

Revenue Stamp

This is an example of the revenue-producing stamp instituted by the British government in 1765. Similar stamps are used by the United States government even today, for example, on playing cards.

tighten the navigation system and in particular to curb the colonists' smuggling and corruption. Absentee customs officials were ordered to return to their posts and were given greater authority and protection. The jurisdiction of the vice-admiralty courts in customs cases was broadened.* The navy was granted greater power in inspecting American ships. The use of writs of assistance (or search warrants) was enlarged. To the earlier list of "enumerated" colonial products that had to be exported directly to Britain, such as tobacco and sugar, were added hides, iron, timber, and others.† And finally the requirements of American shippers for posting bonds and for obtaining certificates of clearance were so greatly increased that nearly all colonial merchants, even those involved only in the coastwise trade, found themselves enmeshed in a bureaucratic web of bonds, certificates, and regulations.

To these frustrating rigidities that were now built into the navigation system were added new customs duties, which raised the expenses of American importers in order to increase British revenue. The Sugar Act imposed duties on foreign

---

*For the vice-admiralty courts, see chapter 5, p. 177.

†For the "enumerated" colonial goods, see chapter 4, p. 115.

cloth, sugar, indigo, coffee, and wine imported into the colonies, and eliminated the refunds of duties that had been previously made in England on foreign goods reexported to America. Most important, the Sugar Act reduced the supposedly very high duty of sixpence a gallon on foreign molasses, set by the Molasses Act of 1733, to threepence a gallon; in 1766 the duty was further reduced to one penny a gallon on all molasses. The government assumed that with the smaller duty it would be cheaper for American merchants to import molasses legally than to resort to smuggling and bribery. The lower duty would thus earn money for the crown.

These British reforms, which threatened to upset the delicately balanced patterns of trade that had been built up in the previous generations, could be regarded as part of Britain's traditional authority over colonial commerce. But the next step in Britain's new imperial program could not be thus regarded; it was radically new. Grenville's ministry, convinced that the customs reforms could not bring in the needed revenue, was determined to try a decidedly different method of getting at American wealth. In March 1765 Parliament by an overwhelming majority passed the Stamp Act, which levied a tax on legal documents, almanacs, newspapers, and nearly every form of paper used in the colonies. Like all duties the tax was to be paid in British sterling, not in colonial paper money. Although stamp duties had been used in England since 1694 and in several colonies in the 1750s, this parliamentary tax, which directly touched Americans' everyday affairs, exposed the nature of political authority within the empire in a way no other issue in the eighteenth century ever had.

American Resistance

The atmosphere in the colonies could not have been less receptive to these initial efforts by the British government to reorganize the empire. In the early 1760s, with the curtailing of wartime spending, the commercial boom collapsed. Between 1760 and 1764 American markets were glutted with unsold goods. At the same time, bumper tobacco crops (in part the result of new independent producers) drove tobacco prices down by 75 percent. These developments threatened the entire credit structure, from London and Scottish merchant companies to small farmers and shopkeepers in the colonies. As a result business failures and bankruptcies multiplied. The collapse was worsened by the large number of small merchants who had entered the market during the boom in the previous decade.

It is not surprising that the victims of the collapse sought to blame their shifting fortunes on the distant government in England. In fact the British government's response to the financial crisis could not have been more clumsy and irritating to the Americans. In 1764 Parliament passed a new Currency Act, which extended to all the colonies the 1751 prohibition against New England's issuing of paper money as legal tender. This sweeping and simpleminded attempt to solve a complicated problem was only one of the many ways in which British power in these years brought to the surface the deep-rooted antagonisms between the colonies and England.

The Sugar Act, coinciding with this postwar depression, created particularly severe problems for all those who depended on trade with the French and Spanish West Indies. The colonists feared that an added duty on foreign molasses would make it too expensive to import. Yet a lack of foreign sugar products would ruin the northern rum industry, which in turn would curtail the export trade in fish and foodstuffs to the Caribbean and endanger America's ability to pay for its British imports. These fears, together with hostility to all the new trade regulations accompanying the Sugar Act, stirred up opposition and provoked the first deliberately organized intercolonial protest. In 1764 the assemblies of eight colonies drew up and endorsed formal petitions claiming that the Sugar Act was causing economic injury, and sent them to the royal authorities in England.

Britain's next step, however—Grenville's stamp tax of 1765—excited not a protest, but a firestorm that swept through the colonies with amazing force. This parliamentary tax, however justifiable it may have been in fiscal terms, posed such a distinct threat to the colonial legislatures' jurisdictions and the colonists' liberties that Americans could no longer contain their opposition within the traditional channels of complaints and lobbying.

When word reached America that Parliament had passed the Stamp Act without even considering any of the colonial petitions against it, the colonists reacted angrily. Merchants in the principal ports formed protest associations and pledged to stop importing British goods in order to bring economic pressure on the British government. Newspapers and pamphlets, the number and like of which had never appeared in America before, carried articles that seethed with resentment against what one New Yorker called "these designing parricides" who had "invited despotism to cross the ocean, and fix her abode in this once happy land." At hastily convened meetings of towns, counties, and legislative assemblies, the colonists' anger boiled over into fiery declarations.

The Pennsylvania Journal
Newspapers were important in spreading resistance sentiments. By the time of the Revolution, Philadelphia alone had five newspapers, but each had a circulation of only about 1500 copies a week.

Patrick Henry (1736–99)
Unlike most of the other Revolutionary leaders, Henry left almost no writings. What he did leave were vivid memories of his impassioned oratory. He introduced to the political world of the Virginia gentry the fervor and style of an evangelical preacher.

This torrent of angry words could not help but bring the constitutional relationship between Britain and its colonies into question. In the spring of 1765, the Virginia House of Burgesses adopted a series of resolves denouncing the parliamentary taxation and asserting the colonists' right to be taxed only by their elected representatives. These resolves were introduced by Patrick Henry, who at age twenty-nine had just been elected to the legislature. Henry had made a name for himself in a county courthouse two years earlier during the Parson's Cause, the legal suits over the payment of Anglican ministers. Now, in the more dignified setting of the House of Burgesses, Henry dared to repeat his earlier challenge to crown authority. He declared that, just as Julius Caesar had had his Brutus and King Charles I his Oliver Cromwell, so some American would undoubtedly stand up for his country. The Speaker of the House stopped him for suggesting treason; and some of his resolves (including one proclaiming the right of Virginians to disobey any law that had not been enacted by the Virginia assembly) were too inflammatory to be accepted by the legislature. Nevertheless colonial newspapers printed the resolves as though they had all been endorsed by the Virginia assembly, and many Americans were convinced that Virginians had virtually asserted their legislative independence from Great Britain.

Henry's boldness was contagious. The Rhode Island assembly declared the Stamp Act "unconstitutional" and authorized the colony's officials to ignore it. In October 1765 thirty-seven delegates from nine colonies met in New York in the Stamp Act Congress and drew up a set of formal declarations and petitions denying Parliament's right to tax them. But as remarkable as this display of colonial unity was, the Stamp Act Congress, with its opening acknowledgment of "all due Subordination to that August Body the Parliament of Great Britain," could not fully express American hostility.

Anti-Stamp Act Riot, 1764
The vehemence with which Americans of all social classes protested the Stamp Act as the opening wedge for arbitrary government is captured in this contemporary drawing.

Ultimately it was violence that destroyed the Stamp Act in America. On August 14, 1765, a crowd tore apart the office and attacked the home of Andrew Oliver, the stamp distributor for Massachusetts. The next day Oliver promised not to enforce the Stamp Act. Twelve days later a mob burned down the home of the person who seemed to be responsible for defending the Stamp Act in Massachusetts, Oliver's brother-in-law, Lieutenant Governor Thomas Hutchinson. As news of the rioting spread to other colonies, similar violence and threats of violence spread with it. From Newport, Rhode Island, to Charleston, South Carolina, local groups organized for resistance. In many places fire and artillery companies, artisan associations, and other fraternal bodies formed the basis for these emerging local organizations, which commonly called themselves Sons of Liberty. Led mostly by members of the middle ranks—shopkeepers, printers, master mechanics, small merchants—these Sons of Liberty burned effigies of royal officials, forced stamp agents to resign, compelled businessmen and judges to carry on without stamps, developed an intercolonial network of correspondence, and generally enforced nonimportation and managed antistamp activities throughout the colonies.

British Reaction In England the Rockingham Whigs (who had been critical of the policies of George III and Grenville) were now in charge of the ministry, and the government was prepared to retreat. Not only were these Whigs eager to disavow Grenville's policies, but they had close connections with British merchants who had been hurt by American economic boycotts. In February 1776 Parliament repealed the Stamp Act. Yet British anger over the rioting in the colonies, and the constitutional issue that had been raised by colonial protests, forced the Rockingham Whigs to couple the repeal with a Declaratory Act stating that Parliament had the right to legislate for the colonies "in all cases whatsoever."

Despite the British government's attempt to offset its repeal of the Stamp Act by this declaration of parliamentary supremacy, after 1765 the imperial relationship and American respect for British authority—indeed, for all authority—would never be the same. The crisis over the Stamp Act aroused and unified Americans as no previous political event ever had. It stimulated bold political and constitutional writings throughout the colonies, deepened the colonists' political consciousness and participation, and produced new forms of organized popular resistance. In their mobs the people learned that they could compel both the resignation of royal officials and obedience to other popular measures. Through "their riotous meetings," Governor Horatio Sharpe of Maryland observed in 1765, the people "begin to think they can by the same way of proceeding accomplish anything their leaders may tell them they ought to do."

The British government could not rely on a simple declaration of parliamentary supremacy to satisfy its continuing need for more revenue. Since the colonists evidently would not stomach a "direct" and "internal" tax like the stamp tax, British officials concluded that the government would have to gather revenue through the more traditional "indirect" and "external" customs duties. After all, the colonists were already paying duties on molasses, wine, and several other imported products as a result of the Sugar Act. Consequently, in 1767, led by Chancellor of the Exchequer Charles Townshend, Parliament imposed new levies on glass, paint, paper, and tea imported into the colonies. Although all the new customs duties, particularly the lowered molasses duty of 1766, began bringing in an average yearly revenue of £45,000—in contrast to only £2,000 a year collected before 1764—the yearly sums that were raised were scarcely a tenth of the annual cost of maintaining the army in America.

Convinced that something more drastic had to be done, the British government reorganized the executive authority of the empire. In 1767–68 the government created the American Board of Customs, located in Boston and reporting directly to the Treasury. It also established three new superior vice-admiralty courts—in Boston, Philadelphia, and Charleston—to supplement the one already in operation in Halifax, Nova Scotia. In belated recognition of the importance of the colonies, it created a new secretaryship of state exclusively for American affairs, an office that would cap the entire structure of colonial government. At the same time, the government decided to economize by pulling back much of its army from its costly deployment in the West and by closing many remote posts. The army was now to be stationed in the coastal cities, where, according to Parliament's Quartering Act of 1765, the colonists would be responsible for its housing and supply. Not only did this withdrawal of the troops

"Attempt to Land a Bishop in America"
By 1768 proposals for establishing an Anglican bishop in America had become identified with British efforts to deprive the colonists of their liberties.

eastward away from the French and Indians contribute to the chaos in the western territory, but the concentration of a standing army in peacetime amid a civilian population blurred the army's original mission in America and raised the colonists' fears of British intentions.

By 1768 there was a new determination among royal officials to put down the unruly forces that seemed to be loose. Amid the ministerial squabbling of the late 1760s, some officials were suggesting that British troops be used against American rioters. Revenue from the Townshend duties was earmarked for the salaries of royal officials in the colonies so that they would be independent of the colonial legislatures. The colonial governors were instructed to maintain tighter control of the assemblies and not to agree to acts that would increase popular representation in the assemblies or the length of time the legislatures sat. Royal officials toyed with more elaborate plans for remodeling the colonial governments: some proposed that the Massachusetts charter be revoked; others, that royal councils be strengthened. Some even suggested introducing a titled nobility into America to sit in the colonial upper houses.

The Townshend Crisis in America

In the atmosphere of the late 1760s, these measures and proposals were not simply irritating; they were explosive. After the Stamp Act crisis, American sensitivities to all forms of English taxation were thoroughly aroused. With the passage of the Townshend duties, the earlier pattern of resistance reappeared and expanded. Pamphleteers and newspaper writers again leapt to the defense of American liberties. The cultivated Philadelphia lawyer John Dickinson, in his *Letters from a Farmer in Pennsylvania* (1767–68), the most popular pamphlet of the 1760s, rejected all parliamentary taxation. According to Dickinson, Parliament had no right to impose either "internal" or "external" taxes levied for the sole purpose of raising revenue. He called for the revival of the nonimportation agreements that had been so effective in the resistance to the Stamp Act. Following Boston's lead in March 1768, merchants in colonial ports again formed associations to boycott British goods. Despite much competition among different groups of merchants and jealousy among the ports, by 1769–70 these nonimportation agreements had cut British sales to the northern colonies by nearly two-thirds. The wearing of homespun cloth was encouraged, and in New England villages "Daughters of Liberty" held spinning bees. By now more Americans were involved in the resistance movement. Extralegal groups and committees, usually but not always restrained by popular leaders, emerged to intimidate tobacco inspectors in Maryland, punish importers in Philadelphia, mob a publisher in Boston, or harass customs officials in New York.

Nowhere were events more spectacular than in Massachusetts. There the situation was so inflammatory that every move triggered a string of explosions that widened the gap between the colonists and royal authority. Forty-six-year-old Samuel Adams, with his puritanical zeal, organizational skill, and deep hatred of crown authority, soon became a dominant political figure. It was later said that 1768 was the year Adams decided on independence for America. Given the events in Massachusetts during that year, it is easy to see why.

In February 1768 the Massachusetts House of Representatives issued to the other colonial legislatures a "circular letter" that denounced the Townshend duties as unconstitutional violations of the principle of no taxation without representation. Lord Hillsborough, the secretary of state of the newly created American Department and a hard-liner on controlling the colonies, ordered the Massachusetts House to revoke its circular letter. When the House defied this order by a majority of 92 to 17 (thereby enshrining the number 92 in patriot rituals), Governor Francis Bernard dissolved the Massachusetts assembly. With this legal means for dealing with grievances silenced, mobs and other unauthorized groups in the colony broke out in violence. Boston, which was rapidly becoming a symbol of colonial resistance, ordered its inhabitants to arm and called for a convention of town delegates—a meeting that would have no legal standing. Attacked by mobs, customs officials in Boston found it impossible to enforce the navigation regulations and pleaded for military help. When a British warship arrived at Boston in June 1768, customs officials promptly seized

**Samuel Adams (1722–1803),
by John Singleton Copley**
*Of all the American leaders, Sam
Adams came closest to being a
professional revolutionary, self-
lessly devoted to the cause. As
"one of Plutarch's men," Adams
took seriously the spartan
severity of classical
republicanism.*

John Hancock's ship *Liberty* for violating the trade acts. Since the wealthy
Hancock was prominently associated with the resistance movement, the seizure
was intended to be an object lesson in royal authority. Its effect, however, was to
set off one of the fiercest riots in Boston's history.

Hillsborough, believing that Massachusetts was in a state of virtual anarchy,
dispatched two regiments of troops from Ireland. They began arriving in Boston
on October 1, 1768, and their appearance marked a crucial turning point in the
escalating controversy: for the first time the British government had sent a
substantial number of soldiers to enforce British authority in the colonies. By 1769
there were nearly 4,000 armed redcoats in the crowded seaport of 15,000 inhabitants. Since the colonists shared traditional English fears of standing armies,
relations between townspeople and soldiers deteriorated. On March 5, 1770,
British troops fired on a threatening crowd and killed five civilians. The "Boston
Massacre," especially as it was depicted in Paul Revere's engraving, aroused
American passions and inspired some of the most sensational rhetoric heard in
the Revolutionary era.

"The Boston Massacre," Engraved by Paul Revere
This print was scarcely an accurate depiction of the "Massacre." It aimed for rhetorical and emotional effect and became perhaps the most famous piece of antimilitary propaganda in American history.

This resort to troops to quell disorder was the ultimate symptom of the ineffectiveness of the British government's authority, and many Britons knew it. The use of force, it was argued in Parliament and in the administration itself, only destroyed the goodwill on which the colonists' relation to the mother country must ultimately rest. Indeed, throughout the escalation of events in the 1760s, many British ministers remained confused and uncertain. "There is the most urgent reason to do what is right, and immediately," wrote Lord Barrington to Governor Bernard in 1767, "but what is that right and who is to do it?" English officials advanced and retreated, pleaded and threatened, in ever more desperate efforts to enforce British authority without aggravating the colonists' hostility. In the winter of 1767–68 the British responded to the disorder in Massachusetts with a series of parliamentary resolutions and addresses to the king, in which they condemned Massachusetts's denial of parliamentary supremacy and threatened to bring the colonial offenders to England for trial. Yet strong minority opposition in the House of Commons and the ministry's unwillingness to bring on further crises made these resolutions empty gestures: the government was now only waging what one Englishman called "a paper war with the colonies."

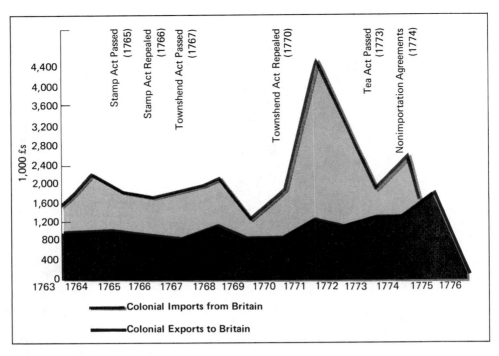

Trade Between the Colonies and Britain, 1763–76

By the end of the 1760s, British plans for reorganizing the empire were in shambles. Colonial legislatures and royal governors were at loggerheads. Colonial papers daily denounced Britain's authority, and mobs were becoming increasingly common in the countryside as well as in city streets. Customs officials, under continuous intimidation, quarreled with merchants, naval officers, and royal governors. The customs officials' entanglement in local politics made efficient or evenhanded enforcement of the trade acts impossible. What enforcement there was thus appeared arbitrary and discriminatory, and drove many merchants, such as the wealthy South Carolinian Henry Laurens, who had earlier been contemptuous of the Sons of Liberty, into bitter opposition.

The financial returns to the British government from the customs reforms seemed in no way worth the costs. By 1770 less than £21,000 had been collected from the Townshend duties, while the loss to British business because of American nonimportation movements during the previous year was put at £700,000. It was therefore not surprising that the British government now abandoned the hope of securing revenue from the duties and labeled the Townshend program, in Lord Hillsborough's words, "contrary to the true principles of commerce." In 1770, after years of chaos in the British government, the reorganization of the king's ministry under Lord North prepared the way for repeal of the Townshend duties. Only the duty on tea was retained, to serve, as Lord North said, "as a mark of the supremacy of Parliament, and an efficient declaration of their right to govern the colonies."

Yet the stabilization of English politics that came with the formation of North's ministry and the repeal of the Townshend duties could scarcely undo what had already been done. Whatever ties of affection had earlier existed between the colonists and Great Britain were fast being destroyed by irritation and suspicion. Many Americans were coming to believe that their interests and their hopes, their rights and their liberties, were threatened by British power. Although politicians on both sides of the Atlantic were by the early 1770s calling for a return to the conditions that had existed before 1763, going back was clearly no longer possible.

For two years there was a superficial tranquility. Then the struggle began again. In 1772 Rhode Islanders, angry at the heavy-handed enforcement of the navigation acts, boarded the British naval schooner *Gaspée,* which had run aground in Narragansett Bay, sank it, and wounded its captain. A royal commission, empowered to send all suspects to England for trial, was dispatched from England to inquire into the sinking. This authority seemed to fulfill earlier British threats to bypass regular judicial procedures, and it provoked Virginia into calling for the creation of legislative committees of correspondence, to which five assemblies responded.

Under Boston's and particularly Samuel Adams's leadership, Massachusetts towns had already begun organizing committees of correspondence. In the fall of 1772 Bostonians published a fiery document, *The Votes and Proceedings* of their town meeting, which listed all the British violations of American rights. These included taxing and legislating for the colonists without their consent, introducing standing armies in peacetime, extending the powers of vice-admiralty courts (which did not use jury trials), restricting colonial manufacturing, and threatening to establish Anglican bishops in America. The publication was sent to the 260 towns of Massachusetts, and more than half responded positively in the greatest outpouring of ordinary local opinion the resistance movement had yet seen. By the end of 1773, independence was being discussed freely in colonial newspapers. Since the North government was determined to uphold the sovereignty of Parliament, an eventual confrontation seemed unavoidable.

The Climax: The Tea Act and the Coercive Acts

In 1773 Parliament provided the occasion for a confrontation, by granting the East India Company the exclusive privilege of selling tea in America. Although the North government intended this Tea Act only to be a means of saving the East India Company from bankruptcy, it set off the final series of explosions. For the act not only allowed colonial radicals to draw attention once again to the unconstitutionality of the existing tax on tea, but it also permitted the company to grant monopolies of selling tea to particular colonial merchants—a provision that angered those American traders who were excluded. The Tea Act spread an alarm throughout the colonies. In several ports colonists stopped the ships from landing the company's tea. When tea ships in Boston were prevented from unloading their cargoes, Governor Thomas Hutchinson, whose merchant family had been given the right to sell tea, refused to allow the ships to leave without landing the tea. In response, on December 16, 1773, a group of patriots disguised as Indians dumped about £10,000 worth of tea into Boston harbor. "This is the most magnificent movement of all," exulted John Adams, an ambitious young lawyer from Braintree, Massachusetts. "This destruction of the tea is so bold, so daring, so firm, intrepid, and inflexible, and it must have so important consequences, and so lasting, that I can't but consider it an epocha in history."

Adams was right. To the British the Boston Tea Party was the ultimate outrage. Angry officials and many of the politically active people in Great Britain clamored for a punishment that would squarely confront America with the issue of Parliament's right to legislate for the colonies. "We are now to establish our authority," Lord North told the House of Commons, "or give it up entirely." In 1774 Parliament passed a succession of laws that came to be known as the Coercive Acts. The first of these closed the port of Boston until the destroyed tea was paid for. The second altered the Massachusetts charter and reorganized the government: council members were now to be appointed by the royal governor rather than elected by the legislature, town meetings were restricted, and the governor's power of appointing judges and sheriffs was strengthened. The third act allowed royal officials who had been charged with capital offenses to be tried in England or in another colony to avoid a hostile jury. The fourth gave the governor power to take over private buildings for the quartering of troops instead of using barracks. At the same time, Thomas Gage, commander in chief of the British army in America, was made governor of the colony of Massachusetts.

These Coercive Acts were the last straw. They convinced Americans once and for all that Parliament had no more right to make laws for them than to tax them.

The Imperial Debate

The colonists had been groping toward this denial of Parliament's power from the beginning of the controversy. For a decade they had engaged in a remarkable constitutional debate with the British over the nature of the empire. This debate exposed for the first time just how divergent America's previous political experience had been from that of the mother country. By the 1770s the colonists had arrived at a very different understanding of the empire from most Englishmen.

Virtual Versus Actual Representation With the passage of the Stamp Act, Parliament's first unmistakable tax levy on Americans, American intellectual resistance was immediately raised to the highest plane of principle. "It is inseparably essential to the freedom of a people, and the undoubted rights of Englishmen," the Stamp Act Congress declared in 1765, "that no taxes should be imposed on them, but with their own consent, given personally, or by their representatives." And since "the people of these colonies are not, and from their local circumstances, cannot be represented in the House of Commons in Great Britain," the colonists would be represented and taxed only by persons who were known and chosen by themselves and who served in their respective legislatures. This statement defined the American position at the outset of the controversy, and despite subsequent confusion and stumbling the colonists never abandoned this essential point.

Once the British ministry sensed a stirring of colonial opposition to the Stamp Act, a number of English government pamphleteers set out to explain and justify Parliament's taxation of the colonies. Although the arguments of these writers differed, they all eventually agreed that Americans, like Englishmen everywhere, were subject to acts of Parliament through a system of "virtual" representation. These writers argued that it was this concept of virtual representation, as distinct from actual representation, that gave Parliament its supreme authority—its sovereignty. One government pamphleteer wrote that even though the colonists, like "nine-tenths of the people of Britain," did not in fact choose any representative to the House of Commons, they were undoubtedly "a part, and an important part of the Commons of Great Britain: they are represented in Parliament in the same manner as those inhabitants of Britain are who have not voices in elections."

During the eighteenth century the British electorate made up only a tiny proportion of the nation; probably only one in six British adult males had the right to vote, compared with two out of three in America. In addition Britain's electoral districts were a confusing mixture of sizes and shapes left over from past centuries. Some of the constituencies were large, with thousands of voters, but others were virtually in the pocket of a single great landowner. Many of the electoral districts had few voters, and some so-called rotten boroughs had no inhabitants at all. One town, Dunwich, continued to send representatives to Parliament even though it had long since slipped into the North Sea. At the same time, some of England's largest cities, such as Manchester and Birmingham, which had grown suddenly in the mid-eighteenth century, sent no representatives to Parliament. Although radical reformers, among them John Wilkes, increasingly criticized this political structure, parliamentary reform was slow in coming and would not begin until 1832. Many Englishmen justified this hodgepodge of representation by claiming that each member of Parliament represented the whole British nation, and not just the particular locality he came from. (In 1774 Edmund Burke, the famous political philosopher and member of Parliament, offered the classic expression of this concept of virtual representation.) According to this view, virtual representation in England was proper and effective not because of the process of election, which was incidental, but rather because of the mutual interests that members of Parliament were presumed to share with all Englishmen for whom they spoke—including those, like the colonists, who did not actually vote for them.

The Americans immediately and strongly rejected these British claims that they were "virtually" represented in the same way that the nonvoters of cities like Manchester and Birmingham were. In the most notable colonial pamphlet written in opposition to the Stamp Act, *Considerations on the Propriety of Imposing Taxes* (1765), Daniel Dulany of Maryland admitted the relevance in England of virtual representation, but he denied its applicability to America. For America, he wrote, was a distinct community from England and thus could hardly be represented by members of Parliament with whom it had no common interests. Others pushed beyond Dulany's argument, however, and challenged the very idea of virtual representation. If the people were to be properly represented in a legislature, many colonists said, they not only had to vote directly for the members of the legislature but had to be represented by members whose numbers were proportionate to the size of the population they spoke for. What purpose is served, asked James Otis of Massachusetts in 1765, by the continual attempts of Englishmen to justify the lack of American representation in Parliament by citing the examples of Manchester and Birmingham, which returned no members to the House of Commons? "If those now so considerable places are not represented, they ought to be."

In the New World, electoral districts were not the products of history that stretched back centuries, but rather were recent and regular creations that were related to changes in population and the formation of new towns and counties. As a consequence many Americans had come to believe in a very different kind of representation from that of the English. Their belief in "actual" representation made election not secondary but central to representation. Actual representation stressed the closest possible connection between the local electors and their representatives. For Americans it was only proper that representatives be residents of the localities they spoke for and that people of the locality have the right to instruct their representatives. Americans thought it only fair that localities be represented in proportion to their population. In short the American belief in actual representation pointed toward the fullest and most equal participation of the people in the process of government that the modern world had ever seen.

The Problem of Sovereignty

Yet while Americans were denying Parliament's right to tax them because they were not represented in the House of Commons, they knew that Parliament had exercised some authority over their affairs during the previous century. They therefore tried to explain what that authority should be. What was the "due subordination" that the Stamp Act Congress admitted Americans owed Parliament? Could the colonists accept parliamentary legislation but not taxation—"external" customs duties for the purpose of regulating trade, but not "internal" stamp taxes for the purpose of raising revenue? In his famous *Letters from a Farmer in Pennsylvania*, John Dickinson rejected the idea that Parliament could rightly impose "external" or "internal" taxes and made clear that the colonists opposed *all* forms of parliamentary taxation. Dickinson recognized nevertheless that the empire required some sort of central regulatory authority, particularly for commerce, and conceded Parliament's supervisory legislative power so far as it preserved "the connection between the several parts of the British empire." The empire, it seemed to many colonists, was a unified body for some affairs but not for others.

To counter all these halting and fumbling efforts by the colonists to divide parliamentary authority, the British offered a simple but powerful argument. Since they could not conceive of the empire as anything but a single, unified community, they found absurd and meaningless all these American distinctions between trade regulations and taxation, between "external" and "internal" taxes, and between separate spheres of authority. If Parliament even "in one instance" was as supreme over the colonists as it was over the people of England, wrote a sub-cabinet official, William Knox, in 1769, then the Americans were members "of the same community with the people of England." On the other hand, if Parliament's authority over the colonists was denied "in any particular," then it must be denied in "all instances," and the union between Great Britain and the colonies must be dissolved. "There is no alternative," Knox concluded; "either the colonies are part of the community of Great Britain or they are in a state of nature with respect to her, and in no case can be subject to the jurisdiction of that legislative power which represents her community, which is the British Parliament."

What made this British argument so powerful was its basis in the widely accepted doctrine of sovereignty—the belief that in every state there could be only one final, indivisible, and uncontestable supreme authority. This was the most important concept of eighteenth-century English political theory, and it became the issue over which the empire was finally broken.

This idea that, in the end, every state had to have one single supreme undivided authority had been the basis of the British position from the beginning. The British expressed this concept of sovereignty officially in the Declaratory Act of 1766, which, following the repeal of the Stamp Act, affirmed Parliament's authority to make laws binding the colonists "in all cases whatsoever." But now in the early 1770s, the implications of this argument were drawn out fully. In 1773 Massachusetts Governor Thomas Hutchinson was provoked into directly challenging the radical movement and its belief in the *limited* nature of Parliament's power. In a dramatic and well-publicized speech to the Massachusetts legislature, Hutchinson attempted once and for all to clarify the central constitutional issue between America and Great Britain and to show the colonists how unreasonable their views were. "I know of no line," he declared, "that can be drawn between the supreme authority of Parliament and the total independence of the colonies, as it is impossible there should be two independent legislatures in one and the same state."

By 1773 many Americans despaired of trying to divide what royal officials told them could not be divided. The Massachusetts House of Representatives had a simple answer to Hutchinson's position. If, as Governor Hutchinson had said, there was no middle ground between the supreme authority of Parliament and the total independence of the colonies from Parliament, the House members felt that there could be no doubt that "we were thus independent." The logic of sovereignty therefore forced a fundamental shift in the American position. By 1774 the leading colonists, including Thomas Jefferson and John Adams, were arguing that only the separate American legislatures were sovereign in America. According to this argument Parliament had no final authority over America, and the colonies were connected to the empire only through the king. The most the colonists would concede was that Parliament had the right to regulate their external commerce—"from the necessity of the case, and a regard to the mutual interest of both countries," as the Declarations and Resolves of the First Continental Congress put it. But the British government remained committed to the principle of the Declaratory Act, which no leader of the Revolution could any longer take seriously.

It was now only a matter of time before these irreconcilable positions would be brought to the point of conflict.

CHRONOLOGY

1760 George III accedes to throne.

1763 Treaty of Paris ends Seven Years' War between Great Britain, and France and Spain.
Pontiac's rebellion, uprising of Indians in Ohio Valley.
Proclamation line drawn along Appalachians by British forbids settlement in West by whites.
Parson's Cause, resulting from efforts by Anglican clergy in Virginia to recover salaries lost from Two Penny Acts.
Paxton uprising by Scotch-Irish settlers in western Pennsylvania.

1764 Sugar Act passed by Parliament, reducing duty on foreign molasses.
Currency Act prohibits issues of legal-tender currency in the colonies.
Brown University founded.

1765 Stamp Act passed.
Stamp Act Congress meets in New York.

1766 Stamp Act repealed by Parliament, which adopts Declaratory Act asserting its authority to bind the colonies "in all cases whatsoever."
Antirent riots by tenant-farmers in New York.

1767 Townshend duties passed.
American Board of Customs established.
John Dickinson's *Letters from a Farmer in Pennsylvania.*
Organization of the Regulators in backcountry of South Carolina.

1768 Secretary of State for the Colonies established in England—first executive department with exclusively colonial concerns.
Circular letter of Massachusetts House of Representatives.
John Hancock's ship *Liberty* seized.
British troops sent to Boston.

1769 American Philosophical Society reorganized, with Benjamin Franklin as president.

1770 Lord North's ministry formed.
Townshend duties repealed,
except for duty on tea.
Boston Massacre.

1771 Benjamin Franklin begins his
Autobiography.
Battle of the Alamance, North
Carolina, between western
Regulators and eastern militia
led by the governor.

1772 British schooner *Gaspée* burned in
Rhode Island.
Boston Committee of
Correspondence formed.

1773 Tea Act imposed.
Boston Tea Party.

1774 Coercive Acts.
Continental Congress meets in
Philadelphia.
Galloway's Plan of Union.
Continental Association.

Suggested Readings

A convenient guide to the historical literature on the American Revolution can be found in Jack P. Greene, ed., *The Reinterpretation of the American Revolution, 1763–1789* (1968). Although there are many short accounts of the Revolution, including Edmund S. Morgan, *The Birth of the Republic, 1763–1789* (1956), and Robert Middlekauff, *The Glorious Cause: The American Revolution, 1763–1789* (1982), the student ought to begin with R. R. Palmer's monumental *The Age of the Democratic Revolution: A Political History of Europe and America, 1760–1800* (2 vols. 1959, 1964), which places the American Revolution in a Western perspective. Stephen G. Kurtz and James H. Hutson, eds., *Essays on the American Revolution* (1973); Alfred F. Young, ed., *The American Revolution* (1976); and the five volumes from the Library of Congress, *Symposia on the American Revolution* (1972–76), are collections of original essays on various aspects of the Revolution.

Among the early attempts to treat the coming of the Revolution from an imperial viewpoint, George Louis Beer, *British Colonial Policy, 1754–1765* (1907), is still informative. Charles M. Andrews summarized his ideas on the causes of the Revolution in *The Colonial Background of the American Revolution* (1931). The most detailed narrative of the political events leading up to the Revolution, written from an imperial perspective, is Lawrence H. Gipson, *The British Empire Before the American Revolution* (15 vols., 1936–70). Gipson has summarized his point of view in *The Coming of the Revolution, 1763–1775* (1954). Merrill Jensen, *The Founding of a Nation* (1968), is the fullest single volume of the pre-Revolutionary years written from an American perspective; it is especially rich in its description of the factional struggles within the separate colonies. An ingenious but sound study that combines the views of a British and an American historian on the causes of the Revolution is Ian R. Christie and Benjamin W. Labaree, *Empire or Independence, 1760–1776* (1976).

The appropriate chapters of James A. Henretta, *The Evolution of American Society, 1700–1815* (1973), discuss American society on the eve of the Revolution. Jackson T. Main, in *The Social Structure of Revolutionary America* (1965), has attempted to describe the distribution of wealth and the nature of "classes" in American society. Rhys Isaac, *The Transformation of Virginia, 1740–1790* (1982), uses anthropological techniques to describe popular challenges to the Virginia aristocracy. Carl Bridenbaugh, *Cities in Revolt* (1955), attributes the Revolutionary impulse to the cities. Gary B. Nash, *The Urban Crucible: Social Change, Political Consciousness, and the Origins of the American Revolution* (1979), stresses urban class conflict in bringing on the Revolution. Stimulating overviews of the mid-eighteenth-century Atlantic world in motion are Bernard Bailyn, *The Peopling of British North America: An Introduction* (1986), and Bailyn, *Voyagers to the West: A Passage in the Peopling of America on the Eve of the Revolution* (1986). The extent of westward migration is ably recounted in Jack M. Sosin, *Revolutionary Frontier, 1763–1783* (1967). Carl Bridenbaugh, *Mitre and Sceptre* (1962), describes the growth of Anglicanism and the effort to establish an American episcopacy in the decades leading up to the Revolution. For the American reaction to these efforts, see Charles W. Akers, *Called unto Liberty: A Life of Jonathan Mayhew, 1720–1766* (1964).

The opening years of the reign of George III have been the subject of some of the most exciting historical scholarship in the twentieth century—largely the work of Sir Lewis Namier and his students. Namier and his followers have exhaustively demonstrated that George III was not seeking to destroy the British constitution, as nineteenth-century historians had argued, and that in 1760 party government with ministerial responsibility to Parliament lay very much in the future. Namier's chief works include *The Structure of Politics at the Accession of George III* (2d ed., 1957), and *England in the Age of the American Revolution* (2d ed., 1961). For detailed studies of British politics in the Revolutionary era, see P. D. G. Thomas, *British Politics and the Stamp Act Crisis* (1975); Paul Langford, *The First Rockingham Administration: 1765–1766* (1973); John Brooke, *The Chatham Administration, 1766–1768* (1956); and Bernard Donoughue, *British Politics and the American Revolution: The Path to War, 1773–1775* (1964). The best biography of George III is John Brooke, *King George III* (1972). An excellent summary of British politics is George H. Guttridge, *English Whiggism and the American Revolution* (2d ed., 1963); but for a more recent study that reconciles the Whig and Namierite interpretations, see John Brewer, *Party Ideology and Popular Politics at the Accession of George III* (1976).

Other important studies of British imperial policy in the period 1760–1775 include Jack M. Sosin, *Whitehall and the Wilderness . . . 1763–1775* (1961); Michael Kammen, *A Rope of Sand: The Colonial Agents, British Politics, and the American Revolution* (1968); and Franklin B. Wickwire, *British Subministers and Colonial America, 1763–1783* (1966). On the military in America, see John Shy, *Toward Lexington: The Role of the British Army in the Coming of the American Revolution* (1965), and Neil R. Stout, *The Royal Navy in America, 1760–1776* (1973).

On American resistance, see especially Edmund S. Morgan and Helen M. Morgan, *The Stamp Act Crisis* (1953), which emphasizes the colonists' appeal to constitutional principles. Pauline Maier, *From Resistance to Revolution* (1972), stresses the limited and controlled character of American opposition. But see Dirk Hoerder, *Crowd Action in Revolutionary Massachusetts, 1765–1780* (1977). Oliver M. Dickerson, *The Navigation Acts and the American Revolution* (1951), argues that Americans accepted the navigation system until "customs racketeering" was introduced in the late 1760s. For a more balanced view of the navigation system, see Thomas C. Barrow, *Trade and Empire: The British Customs Service in Colonial America, 1660–1775* (1967).

On other irritants and incidents in the imperial relation, see Joseph A. Ernst, *Money and Politics in America, 1755–1775* (1973); Carl Ubbelohde, *The Vice-Admiralty Courts and the American Revolution* (1960); M. H. Smith, *The Writs of Assistance Case* (1978); Hiller Zobel, *The Boston Massacre* (1970); Benjamin W. Labaree, *The Boston Tea Party* (1964); and David Ammerman, *In the Common Cause: American Response to the Coercive Acts of 1774* (1974). Arthur M. Schlesinger, *The Colonial Merchants and the American Revolution, 1763–1776* (1918), traces the responses of an important social group.

Among the many local studies of American resistance are Carl Becker, *The History of Political Parties in the Province of New York, 1760–1776* (1909); David S. Lovejoy, *Rhode Island Politics and the American Revolution, 1760–1776* (1958); Theodore Thayer, *Pennsylvania Politics and the Growth of Democracy, 1740–1776* (1954); Richard Ryerson, *The Revolution Is Now*

Begun: The Radical Committees of Philadelphia, 1765–1776 (1978); Patricia Bonomi, *A Factious People:... New York* (1971); Jere R. Daniel, *Experiment in Republicanism: New Hampshire Politics and the American Revolution, 1741–1794* (1970); Richard D. Brown, *Revolutionary Politics in Massachusetts* (1970); Stephen E. Patterson, *Political Parties in Revolutionary Massachusetts* (1973); and Ronald Hoffman, *A Spirit of Dissension: Economics, Politics, and the Revolution in Maryland* (1973). For biographies of some leading Revolutionaries, see John C. Miller, *Sam Adams* (1936); Richard R. Beeman, *Patrick Henry* (1974); Merrill Peterson, *Thomas Jefferson and the New Nation* (1970); Eric Foner, *Tom Paine and Revolutionary America* (1976); Peter Shaw, *The Character of John Adams* (1976); and John R. Howe, Jr., *The Changing Political Thought of John Adams* (1966).

On the imperial debate see Bernard Bailyn, *The Ideological Origins of the American Revolution* (1967), and Randolph G. Adams, *Political Ideas of the American Revolution* (1922).

8

Independence and War

⁓

$\mathcal{B}$Y 1774, within the short span of a decade following the introduction of the imperial reforms, Americans who had celebrated George III's coronation were in virtual rebellion against Great Britain. During the two years after the Coercive Acts of 1774, events moved rapidly, and reconciliation between Britain and its colonies became increasingly unlikely. By this time the crisis had become something more than a simple breakdown in the imperial relationship. The colonists' extraordinary efforts to understand what was happening transformed their resistance and ultimately their rebellion into a world-shattering revolution. The Americans' 1776 Declaration of Independence turned their separation from Britain into an event that Americans thought rivaled anything that had happened before in history. Americans saw themselves striving not only to make themselves free, but also to bring freedom to the whole world. To do so, however, they would have to wage war against the greatest power of the eighteenth century.

The Coming of Independence

The Coercive Acts of 1774 provoked open rebellion in America. Whatever royal authority was left in the colonies now dissolved. Many local communities, with a freedom they had not had since the seventeenth century, attempted to put together new popular governments from the bottom up. Mass meetings that sometimes attracted thousands of aroused colonists endorsed resolutions and called for new political organizations. Committees of different sizes and various names—committees of safety, of inspection, of merchants, of mechanics, of Fifty-One, of Nineteen, of Forty-Three—competed with one another for political control. In the various colonies royal government was displaced in different ways, depending on how extensive and personal previous royal authority had been. In Massachusetts, where the crown's authority had reached into the villages and towns through the royally appointed justices of the peace, the displacement was greater than in Virginia, where royal influence had scarcely touched the control of the counties by the powerful landowners. But everywhere there was a fundamental transfer of authority that opened new opportunities for new men to assert themselves.

By the end of 1774 in many of the colonies, local associations were controlling and regulating various aspects of American life. Committees manipulated voters, directed appointments, organized the militia, managed trade, intervened between creditors and debtors, levied taxes, issued licenses, and supervised or closed the courts. Royal governors stood by in helpless amazement as new informal governments gradually grew up around them. These new governments ranged from town and county committees and the newly created provincial congresses to a general congress of the colonies—the First Continental Congress, which convened in Philadelphia in September 1774.

The First Continental Congress

In all, fifty-five delegates from twelve colonies (all except Georgia) participated in the First Continental Congress. Some colonists, and even some royal officials, hoped that this Congress might work to reestablish imperial authority. Those who were eager to break the bond with Great Britain, however, won the first round. Led by the cousins Samuel and John Adams from Massachusetts, and by Patrick Henry and Richard Henry Lee from Virginia, the Congress endorsed the fiery Resolves of Suffolk County, Massachusetts, which recommended outright resistance to the Coercive Acts. But the Congress was not yet ready for independence. It came very close—failing by the vote of a single colony—to considering further and perhaps adopting a plan of union between Britain and the colonies, which had been proposed by Joseph Galloway, leader of the Pennsylvania assembly and spokesman for the conservative congressional delegates from the middle colonies. Galloway's plan was radical enough: it called for the creation of a grand colonial council along the lines that the Albany Congress had proposed in 1754. Laws passed by either the American grand council or the British Parliament were to be subject to mutual review and approval.

By 1774, however, it was unlikely, even if Galloway's plan had been adopted, that the Congress could have reversed the transfer of authority that was taking place in the colonies. In the end the Continental Congress simply recognized the new local authorities in American politics and gave them its blessing by establishing the Continental Association. This continentwide organization put into effect the nonimportation, nonexportation, and nonconsumption of British goods that the Congress had agreed on. Committees in all the counties, cities, and towns were now ordered by the Congress "attentively to observe the conduct of all persons," to condemn publicly all violators as "enemies of American liberty," and to "break off all dealings" with them.

Thus with the Congress's endorsement through the association, the local committees, speaking in the name of "the body of the people," proceeded with the political transformation that was taking place. Groups of men, from a few dozen to several thousand, marched through villages and city streets searching out enemies of the people. Suspected enemies were often forced to take back unfriendly words or designs against the public, to sign confessions of guilt and repentance, and to swear new oaths of friendship to the people. In all the colonies there were signs of an emerging new political order.

The Popularization of Politics

These remarkable political changes were not simply the product of the colonists' resistance to British imperial reform. Britain's attempts to reorganize its empire took place not in a vacuum, but in complicated, highly charged situations existing in each colony. In some cases these local political conditions had as much to do with the escalation of the controversy between the colonies and the mother country as did the steps taken by the British government 3,000 miles away. Everywhere in the 1760s various members of the colonial gentry were eager to exploit popular resentment against the British reforms in order to gain local political advantage—with, however, little understanding of the ultimate consequence of their actions.

In New York, for example, political factions that were led by the well-to-do Livingston and DeLancey families vied with each other in whipping up opposition to the imperial legislation and in winning the support of popular extralegal groups such as the Sons of Liberty. Thus these gentry generally helped expand the rights and participation of the people in politics—not with the aim of furthering electoral democracy, but only for the tactical purpose of gaining control of the elective assemblies. While this sort of unplanned popularization of politics had gone on in the past, particularly in urban areas, the inflamed atmosphere that the imperial crisis generated gave it a new cutting edge with new and unpredictable implications.

In colony after colony local quarrels, often of long standing, became so entangled with imperial antagonisms that they reinforced one another in a spiraling momentum that brought all governmental authority into question. Even those colonial authorities that were not directly controlled by Great Britain, such as the proprietary governments of Pennsylvania and Maryland, were victimized by the imperial crisis. Thus in Maryland in 1770, a proclamation by the proprietary governor setting the fees that were paid to government officials seemed to violate the principle of no taxation without representation that had been made so vivid by the imperial debate. This executive proclamation provoked a bitter local struggle that forced Daniel Dulany, a wealthy member of the colony's council and former opponent of the Stamp Act, into defending the governor. In the end the controversy destroyed the governor's capacity to rule and made Dulany a loyalist to the British cause.

By the 1770s all these developments, without anyone's clearly intending it, were revealing a new kind of politics in America. The rhetoric of liberty now quickened long-existing popular political tendencies. Ordinary people were no longer willing to trust only wealthy and learned gentlemen to represent them in government. Various artisan, religious, and ethnic groups now felt that their particular interests were so distinct that only people of their own kind could speak for them. In 1774 radicals in Philadelphia demanded that seven artisans and six Germans be added to the revolutionary committee of the city. Americans today are used to such "coalition" and "interest-group" politics, but their eighteenth-century counterparts were not. Educated gentlemen such as the prominent Oxford-trained landowner William Henry Drayton of South Carolina therefore complained of having to participate in government with men who knew only "how to cut up a beast in the market" or "to cobble an old shoe": "Nature never intended that such men should be profound politicians, or able statesmen." In 1775 the royal governor of Georgia noted in astonishment that the committee in control of Savannah consisted of "a Parcel of the Lowest People, chiefly carpenters, shoemakers, Blacksmiths etc. with a Jew at their head." In some colonies politicians called for an expanded suffrage, the use of the ballot rather than the customary oral voting, the opening of legislative meetings to the public, the printing of legislative minutes, and the recording of votes that were taken in the legislatures. All these proposals involved enlarging the political arena and limiting the power of those who clung to the traditional ways of private arrangements and personal influence.

Everywhere in the colonies "incendiaries" (as royal officials called them) used fiery popular rhetoric and competed openly for political leadership. More and more "new men" took advantage of the people's resentments of the British regulations and actively campaigned for popular election in order to bypass the traditional narrow and patronage-controlled channels of politics. The political atmosphere in America was now charged as never before with both deep animosities and new hopes for bettering the world. Americans told themselves they were "on the eve of some great and unusual events," events that "may form a new era, and give a new turn to human affairs."

Men who, like Thomas Hutchinson, had been reared in the old ways and had benefited from them stood bewildered and helpless in the face of these popularizing developments. They possessed neither the psychological capacity nor the political sensitivity to understand—let alone to deal with—this popular politics and the moral outrage and fiery zeal that lay behind it. They intrigued and schemed, and they tried to manipulate those who they thought were the important people in the opposition. (In 1768, for example, John Adams was offered the office of advocate-general in the Massachusetts admiralty court.) When they could not buy them off, they accused those individuals of demagoguery or ridiculed them as upstarts. Frightened by the increased violence, they struck out furiously at the kinds of popular politics they believed were undermining authority and causing the violence. Traditional and prudent men of this sort could not accept a new and different world, and soon they either fell silent or became loyalists, determined to remain faithful to the king and to support the society that had bred them.

The Declaration of Independence

By the beginning of 1775, the British government was already preparing for military action. In February, Lord North got Parliament to pass what he regarded as a conciliatory measure. He proposed that any colony contributing its proportionate share to the common defense would not be subject to parliamentary taxation. But since the British government had done nothing to resolve the issues that had been raised by the Coercive Acts and by the declarations of the Continental Congress, the colonists regarded North's efforts at reconciliation as an underhanded attempt to divide them. By this date North's supporters and the king himself saw no choice but force to bring the colonists back into line. As early as November 1774, George III had told North that "blows must decide whether they are to be subject to the Country or Independent." The British government thus built up its army and navy and began restraining the commerce first of New England and then of the other colonies.

The Second Continental Congress In May 1775 delegates from the colonies met in Philadelphia for the Second Continental Congress, to take up where the first Congress had left off. Outwardly the Congress continued the policy of resolves and reconciliation. In July, at the urging of John Dickinson, the Congress approved the Olive Branch Petition, which claimed loyalty to the king and humbly asked him to break with his "artful and cruel" ministers, whom the Congress blamed for the oppressive measures. At the same time the Congress issued the Declaration of the Causes and Necessities of Taking Up Arms (largely the work of Dickinson and Thomas Jefferson), in which the colonies denied that they had any "ambitious design of separating from Great Britain, and establishing independent states." As this superb summary of the American case against Britain demonstrated, the time for paper solutions had passed.

In April 1775 fighting had broken out in Massachusetts. The British government had long assumed that Boston was the center of the disturbances in America: the collapse of colonial resistance would follow simply from isolating and punishing the port. The Coercive Acts of 1774 had rested on this assumption, and the British military actions of 1775 were simply a logical extension of the same assumption. The British government, thinking that it was dealing only with mobs led by a few seditious instigators, therefore ordered its commander in Massachusetts, General Gage, to arrest the rebel leaders, to break up their bases, and to reassert royal authority in the colony. On April 18–19 Gage's army attempted to seize rebel arms and ammunition stored at Concord, a town northwest of Boston. Colonial scouts, including the silversmith Paul Revere, rode ahead of the advancing redcoats, warned patriot leaders John Hancock and Samuel Adams to flee, and roused the farmers of the countryside—the minutemen—to arms. No one knows who fired first at Lexington, but shots between the colonial militia and British troops were exchanged there and later at Concord, where the British found only a few supplies. During their long march back to Boston, the strung-

The Battle of Concord, Massachusetts
In their march to and from Concord on April 19, 1775, 73 British soldiers were killed and 200 wounded out of a total force of 1,800. Of the nearly 4,000 colonial militia who fought sometime during the day, 49 were killed and 46 were wounded.

out British columns were repeatedly harassed by patriot militia. By the end of the day, 273 redcoats and 95 patriots had been killed, wounded, or lost, and the countryside was aflame with revolt. From positions in Charlestown and Dorchester, the colonists quickly surrounded the besieged British in Boston and thus raised doubts that police action would be enough to quell the rebellion.

Two months later, in June 1775, British soldiers attempted to dislodge the American fortification on a spur of Bunker Hill in Charlestown, overlooking Boston. The British assumed, as one of their generals, John Burgoyne, put it, that no numbers of "untrained rabble" could ever stand up against "trained troops." Under General William Howe British forces attempted a series of frontal assaults on the American position. These attacks were eventually successful, but only at the terrible cost of 1,000 British casualties—more than 40 percent of Howe's troops. At Bunker Hill—the first formal battle of the Revolution—the British suffered their heaviest losses in what would become a long and bloody war.

When news of the fighting reached Philadelphia, the Second Continental Congress had to assume the responsibilities of a central government for the colonies. The Congress created a Continental army, appointed George Washington of Virginia as commander, issued paper money for the support of colonial troops, and formed a committee to negotiate with foreign countries.

"The Battle at Bunker's Hill"
This engraving of a painting by John Trumball, though scarcely an accurate depiction of the battle, captures the heroic patriot view of what happened.

By the summer of 1775 the escalation of actions and reactions was out of control. On August 23, George III, ignoring the colonists' Olive Branch Petition, proclaimed the colonies in open rebellion. In October he publicly accused them of aiming at independence. By December the British government had declared all American shipping liable to seizure by British warships. As early as May 1775, American forces had captured Fort Ticonderoga at the head of Lake Champlain. Out of a desire to bring the Canadians into the struggle against Britain, the Congress ordered makeshift forces under Richard Montgomery and Benedict Arnold to invade Canada, but the colonists were badly defeated in Quebec in the winter of 1775–76. With all this fighting between Britain and its colonies taking place, it was only a matter of time before the Americans formally cut the remaining ties to Great Britain. Although no official American body had as yet endorsed independence, the idea was obviously in the air.

It was left to Thomas Paine, a onetime English corsetmaker and school-master and twice-dismissed excise officer who had only arrived in the colonies in late 1774, to express in January 1776 the accumulated American rage against George III. In his pamphlet *Common Sense* Paine dismissed the king as the "Royal Brute" and called for American independence immediately. *Common Sense* was the most incendiary and popular pamphlet of the entire Revolutionary era; it went through twenty-five editions in 1776 alone. In it Paine rejected the traditional and stylized forms of persuasion designed for educated gentlemen and reached out for new readers among the artisan- and tavern-centered worlds of the cities. Unlike more genteel writers, Paine did not decorate his pamphlet

**Thomas Paine (1737–1809),
by John Wesley Jarvis**
*Paine was probably the first
detached "intellectual" in
American history. He belonged
to no country, lived by his pen,
and saw his role as the
stimulator of revolutions.*

with Latin quotations and learned references to the literature of Western culture, but instead relied on his readers' knowing only the Bible. Although Paine was criticized for using ungrammatical language and coarse imagery, he showed the common people, who in the past had not been very involved in politics, that fancy words and Latin quotations no longer mattered as much as honesty and sincerity and the natural revelation of feelings.

In the early spring of 1776 the Congress threw open America's ports to the world and prepared for independence. On July 4, 1776, the delegates formally approved the Declaration of Independence, a thirteen-hundred-word document largely written by the graceful hand of Thomas Jefferson of Virginia. In the Declaration the king, who was now regarded as the only remaining link between the colonists and Great Britain, was held accountable for every grievance that the Americans had suffered since 1763. The reign of George III, Americans declared "to a candid world," was "a history of repeated injuries and usurpations, all having in direct object the establishment of an absolute Tyranny over these States."*

The Declaration of Independence was a brilliant expression of Enlightenment ideals—ideals that still reverberate powerfully in the lives of Americans and

---

*For the full text of the Declaration of Independence, see Appendix.

"The Declaration of Independence," by John Trumbull
The committee that drafted the Declaration of Independence included, from left to right, John Adams, Roger Sherman, Robert R. Livingston, Thomas Jefferson, and Benjamin Franklin.

other peoples today. "That all men are created equal; that they are endowed by their Creator with certain inalienable rights; that among these are life, liberty, and the pursuit of happiness"—these "truths" seemed "self-evident" even to an eighteenth-century American society that was divided by classes and by the glaring contradiction of black slavery. Jefferson later recalled that his draft of the Declaration aimed "not to find out new principles, or new arguments, never before thought of," but rather "to place before mankind the common sense of the subject, in terms so plain and firm as to command their assent." The Declaration of Independence set forth a philosophy of human rights that could be applied not only to Americans, but to peoples everywhere. It was essential in giving the American Revolution a universal appeal.

An Asylum for Liberty

It was a strange revolution that Americans had begun, one that on the face of it is not easily comprehended. A series of trade acts and tax levies does not seem to add up to a justification for independence. And although by 1776 most Americans agreed with John Adams that they were "in the very midst of a revolution, the most complete, unexpected and remarkable of any in the history of nations," their revolution has always seemed to have had an unusual conservative cast to it.

Throughout the imperial crisis American patriot leaders insisted that they were rebelling not against the principles of the English constitution, but on behalf of them. In order to express continuity with the great struggles for political liberty

in England, they invoked historic English party designations and called themselves "Whigs," and branded the supporters of the crown "Tories." By emphasizing that it was the letter and spirit of the English constitution that justified their
resistance, Americans could easily believe that they were simply preserving what
Englishmen had valued from the beginning of their history.

Yet the colonists were mistaken in believing that they were struggling only to
return to the essentials of the English constitution. The historical traditions of
that constitution were not the principles that were held by English officials in the
mid-eighteenth century. In fact the Americans' principles were, as the Tories and
royal officials tried to indicate, "revolution principles" outside the mainstream of
English thought. Since the colonists seemed to be reading the same literature as
other Englishmen, they were hardly aware that they were seeing the English
tradition differently. Despite their breadth of reading and references, however,
they concentrated on a set of ideas that ultimately gave them a peculiar conception of English life and an extraordinarily radical perspective on the English
constitution they were so fervently defending.

**The Country
Tradition of
Opposition**

The heritage of liberal thought that the colonists drew
on was composed not simply of the political treatises of
notable philosophers like John Locke but also of the
writings of such influential eighteenth-century pamphleteers as John Trenchard and Thomas Gordon. Indeed, many of England's
leading intellectuals, such as Alexander Pope and Jonathan Swift, wrote in the
first half of the eighteenth century out of a deep and bitter hostility to the great
political, social, and economic changes they saw taking place around them. These
critics thought that traditional values were being corrupted and that England was
being threatened with ruin by the general commercialization of English life, as
seen in the rise of such institutions as the Bank of England, powerful stock
companies, stock markets, and the huge public debt. Believing that the crown
was ultimately responsible for these changes, such writers championed a so-
called country opposition to the deceit and luxury of the "court," which they
associated with the crown and its networks of influence.

This country opposition had a long and complicated history in England. It
stretched back at least to the early seventeenth century, to the Puritan opposition
to the established church and the courts of the early Stuart kings, James I and
Charles I. The English Civil War of the mid-seventeenth century can in part be
understood as an uprising of the local gentry, representing the counties or the
"country" of England in the House of Commons, against the court surrounding
the Church of England and the king. Such localist and grassroots opposition to
the far-removed central authorities was a recurring theme in English history, as it
would continue to be in American history.

In the eighteenth-century Anglo-American world, writers in this country-
opposition tradition were especially fearful that executive or state power—
particularly as it operated under the ministries of Sir Robert Walpole—was

corrupting Parliament and English society. Throughout the first half of the eighteenth century, these defenders of political liberties made ringing proposals to reduce and control what seemed to be the enormously expanded powers of the crown. Their goal was to recover the rights of the people and the original principles of the English constitution.

Many of the reforms they proposed were ahead of their time for England—reforms that advocated the right to vote for all adult males and not just the well-to-do property holders, more liberty for the press, and greater freedom of religion. Other suggested reforms aimed at prohibiting salaried government puppets ("placemen") from sitting in the House of Commons, at reducing the public debt, and at obtaining such popular rights as equal representation for more people, the power to instruct members of Parliament, and shorter Parliaments. All these reform proposals combined into a widely shared conception of how political life in England should ideally be organized. In this ideal nation the parts of the constitution would be independent of one another, and members of Parliament would be independent of any "connection" or party. In other words there would exist a political world in which no one would be controlled by anyone else.

The American colonists had long felt the relevance of these "country" ideas more keenly than the English themselves. These ideas had not only explained the simple character of American life in contrast with the sophistication of England. They had also justified the colonists' antagonism to royal power. In the conflicts between the colonial assemblies and the royal governors in the first half of the eighteenth century, Americans had invoked these ideas off and on. Now, however, in the years after 1763, the need to explain the growing controversy with Britain gave this country-opposition ideology a new and comprehensive importance. It not only prepared the colonists intellectually for resistance, but also offered them a powerful justification of their many differences from a decayed and corrupted mother country.

A Conspiracy Against Liberty
These inherited ideas contained an elaborate set of rules for political action by the people. How were the people to identify a tyrant? How long should the people put up with abuses? How much force should they use? The answers to these questions came logically as events unfolded, and led the colonists almost irresistibly from resistance to rebellion. Step by step the colonists became convinced that the obnoxious efforts of crown officials to reform the empire were not simply the result of insensitivity to unique American conditions or mistakes of well-meant policy. Instead Americans saw these as the intended consequences of a grand tyrannical design. In Thomas Jefferson's words the British reforms were nothing less than "a deliberate systematical plan of reducing us to slavery."

America, the colonists believed, was the primary object of this tyrannical conspiracy, but the goals of the conspiracy ranged far beyond the colonies. Americans were involved not simply in a defense of their own rights, but in a

COMMON SENSE;

ADDRESSED TO THE

INHABITANTS

O F

A M E R I C A,

On the following interesting

S U B J E C T S.

I. Of the Origin and Design of Government in general,
with concise Remarks on the English Constitution.

II. Of Monarchy and Hereditary Succession.

III. Thoughts on the present State of American Affairs.

IV. Of the present Ability of America, with some miscellaneous Reflections.

Man knows no Master save creating HEAVEN,
Or those whom choice and common good ordain.

THOMSON.

PHILADELPHIA;

Printed, and Sold, by R. BELL, in Third-Street.

MDCCLXXVI.

Common Sense
Common Sense *was the first
powerfully written, direct assault
on hereditary monarchy and the
famous balanced English constitution to appear in the resistance
literature.*

worldwide struggle for the salvation of liberty itself. The crucial turning point came in the late 1760s. Americans earlier had read of the prosecution of the English radical John Wilkes for criticizing His Majesty's government in his *North Briton* No. 45 and had made Wilkes and the number 45 part of their political symbolism. Then in 1768 Wilkes's four successive expulsions from the House of Commons, despite his repeated reelection by the voters of Middlesex, outside London, for many Americans marked the twilight of representative government in Great Britain. Everywhere liberty seemed to be in retreat before the forces of tyranny. The struggles of "sons of liberty" in Ireland to win constitutional concessions from Britain were suppressed. The attempts of the freedom fighter Pascal Paoli and his followers to establish the independence of Corsica from France ended in failure. As Americans learned of these setbacks, they became convinced that America was the only place where a free popular press still existed and where the people could still elect representatives who spoke for them and them only.

By 1776 their picture of the immense struggle they were involved in was complete. And they could respond enthusiastically, as lovers of humanity and haters of tyranny, to the passionate appeal of Thomas Paine's *Common Sense* to stand forth for liberty:

> Every spot of the old world is overrun with oppression. Freedom hath been hunted round the globe. Asia and Africa have long expelled her. Europe regards her like a stranger, and England hath given her warning to depart. O! receive the fugitive, and prepare in time an asylum for mankind.

The War for Independence

However necessary were ideas such as Paine's in making events meaningful and in mobilizing people into revolution, ideas by themselves could not achieve independence. Once Britain had determined to enforce its authority with troops, Americans knew that they had to take up arms to support their beliefs. For over a year before the Declaration of Independence, American and British forces had been at war. It was a war that would go on for nearly eight years—the longest conflict in American history until the Vietnam War two centuries later.

The war for independence passed through a series of distinct phases, growing and widening until what had begun in British eyes as a breakdown in governmental authority in a section of the empire became a worldwide struggle. For the first time in the eighteenth century, Great Britain found itself diplomatically isolated; at one point in 1779 it was even threatened with French invasion. The war for American independence thus eventually became an important episode in Britain's long struggle with France for global supremacy, a struggle that went back a century and would continue for another generation into the nineteenth century.

The War in the North, 1775–1776 British troops had suffered heavy losses in their first clashes with the American militia in Massachusetts in the spring of 1775—at Lexington and Concord and especially in the bloody battle of Bunker Hill. This initial experience convinced the British government that it was not simply dealing with a New England mob, and it swept away almost every objection the members of the ministry had to a conquest of the colonies. The appointment of generals by the Second Continental Congress, the organization of a Continental field army under George Washington in the summer of 1775, and the American invasion of Canada only confirmed the British government's realization that it was now involved in a military rather than a police action. This new understanding of what Britain was up against dictated a conventional eighteenth-century military policy of maneuver and battle.

This change of strategy required that the British evacuate Boston and transfer their main forces to New York, with its presumably more sympathetic population, its superior port, and its central position. Accordingly, in the summer of 1776 Sir William Howe, who replaced Gage as commander in chief of the British army in North America, sailed into New York harbor with a force of more than 30,000

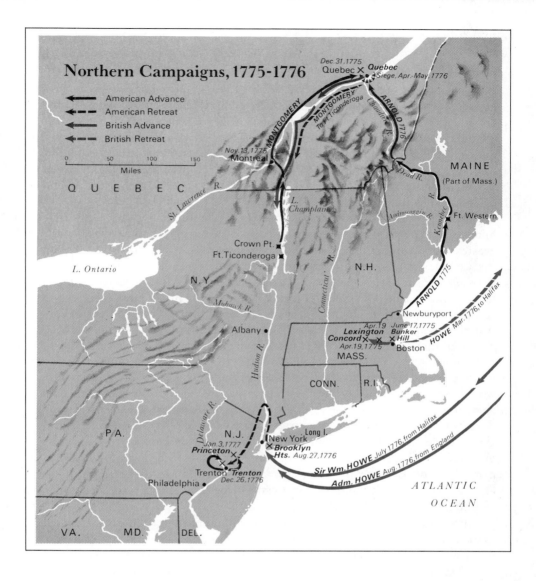

Northern Campaigns, 1775-1776

← American Advance
←-- American Retreat
← British Advance
←-- British Retreat

men. Howe aimed to cut New England off from the other rebels and to defeat Washington's army in a decisive battle. He was to spend the next two frustrating years trying to succeed at this plan.

On the face of it, a military struggle seemed to promise all the advantage to the British. Britain was the most powerful nation in the world with a population of about 11 million, compared with only 2.5 million colonists. The British navy was the largest in the world, with nearly half its ships initially committed to the American struggle. The British army was a well-trained professional force, having at one point in 1778 nearly 50,000 troops in North America alone; and more than 30,000 hired German mercenaries were added to this force during the war. To confront this military might the Americans had to start from scratch. Eventually they created a small Continental army, numbering at times less than 5,000 troops, supplemented by state militia units of varying sizes. In most cases inexperienced, amateur officers served as the American military leaders. For example, the commander in chief, Washington, had been only a regimental colonel on the Virginia frontier and had little firsthand knowledge of combat. Not surprisingly, then, most British officers thought that the Americans would be no match for His Majesty's troops. A veteran of many North American campaigns told the House of Commons in 1774 that with 5,000 regulars he could easily march from one end of the country to the other.

Yet this contrast of numbers was deceptive. The British disadvantages were immense and perhaps overwhelming—even at the beginning, when they had the greatest opportunities to put down the rebellion. Great Britain had to carry on the war 3,000 miles across the Atlantic with consequent problems of communications and logistics. It also had to wage a different kind of war from any other it had fought in the eighteenth century. A well-trained army might have been able to conquer the American forces, but, as one French officer observed at the end, America itself was unconquerable. The great breadth of territory and the wild nature of the terrain made conventional maneuverings and operations difficult and cumbersome. The fragmented and local character of authority in America inhibited decisive action by the British. There was no nerve center whose capture would destroy the rebellion. In these circumstances the Americans' reliance on amateur militia forces and the weakness of their organized army made them more dangerous than if they had had a trained professional army. The British never clearly understood what they were up against—a revolutionary struggle involving widespread support in the population. Hence they continued to underestimate the staying power of the rebels and to overestimate the strength of the loyalists. And in the end independence came to mean more to the Americans than reconquest did to the English.

From the outset the English objective could never be as simple and clear-cut as the Americans' desire for independence. Conquest by itself could not restore political relations and imperial harmony. Many people in England were reluctant to engage in a civil war, and several officers actually refused on grounds of conscience to serve in America. Although the British ministry and most members of Parliament were intent on subjugating America by force, the British commanders appointed in 1775 never shared this overriding urge for outright coercion. These commanders—Sir William Howe and his brother Admiral Richard, Lord Howe, who was in charge of the navy—saw themselves not simply as conquerors, but also as peacemakers. They interrupted their military operations with peace feelers to Washington and the Continental Congress, and they tried to avoid plundering and ravaging the American countryside and ports out of fear of destroying all hope for reconciliation. This "sentimental manner of waging war," as Lord George Germain, head of the American Department, called it, weakened the morale of British officers and troops and left the loyalists confused and disillusioned.

George Washington (1732–99), by Charles Willson Peale
Washington's genius lay not in his military expertise in the field, but in his coolness, determination, and extraordinary political skills. Although he lost most of his battles, he never lost the support of his officers or the Congress.

The Howes' policy was not as ineffectual initially as it later appeared. After defeating Washington at Brooklyn Heights on Long Island in August 1776 and expelling him from New York City, General Howe drove Washington into pell-mell retreat southward. Instead of pursuing Washington across the Delaware River, Howe resorted to a piecemeal occupation of New Jersey. He extended his lines and deployed brigade garrisons at a half-dozen towns around the area with the aim of gradually convincing the rebels that the British army was invincible. Loyalist militiamen emerged from hiding and through a series of ferocious local struggles with patriot groups began to assume control of northern New Jersey. Nearly 5,000 Americans came forward to accept Howe's offer of pardon and to swear loyalty to the crown. American prospects at the end of 1776 were as low as they ever would be during the war. These were, as Thomas Paine wrote, "times that try men's souls."

The Howes' policy of leniency and pacification, however, was marred by plundering by British troops and by loyalist acts of vengeance against the rebels. But even more important in undermining the British successes of 1776 were Washington's brilliant strokes in picking off two of General Howe's extended outposts, at Trenton on December 26, 1776, and at Princeton on January 3, 1777. With these victories Washington forced the British to withdraw from the banks of the Delaware and to leave the newly formed bands of loyalists to fend for themselves. American morale soared, oaths of loyalty to the king declined, and patriot militia regained local control in areas that had been vacated by the withdrawing British troops. The British again had to reconsider their plans.

Burgoyne and Saratoga, 1777

The British strategy for 1777 involved sending an army of 8,000 under General John Burgoyne southward from Canada by way of Lake Champlain to recapture Fort Ticonderoga. Near Albany Burgoyne was to join a secondary force under Lieutenant Colonel Barry St. Leger, moving eastward through the Mohawk Valley, and General Howe, advancing northward from New York City through the Hudson Valley. The ultimate aim of the campaign was to isolate New England and break the back of the rebellion. It was assumed in England that General Howe would join with Burgoyne. But Howe continued to believe that there was widespread loyalist support in the middle states and decided to capture Philadelphia, the seat of the Continental government. He moved on Philadelphia by sea and after much delay landed at the head of Chesapeake Bay in late August 1777. Washington, believing that he should not give up the Continental capital without a struggle, confronted Howe at Brandywine and later at Germantown. He was defeated in both battles. But his defeats were not disastrous: they proved that the American army was capable of organized combat, and they prevented Howe from moving north to help Burgoyne. Howe's capture of Philadelphia demonstrated that loyalist sentiment reached only as far as the British army could advance, and it scarcely justified what happened to Burgoyne's army in the north.

After St. Leger's force was turned back at Oriskany, New York, in the summer of 1777, Burgoyne and his huge slow-moving army from Canada increasingly found their supply lines stretched thin and their flanks harassed by patriot militia from New England. While Burgoyne's slow advance gave the American forces in the Hudson Valley needed time to collect themselves, the British army was diminishing. When 900 of Burgoyne's men attempted to seize supplies from a patriot arsenal in Bennington, Vermont, they were defeated by 2,000 New England militia under John Stark. Another 900 British redcoats were detached to garrison Ticonderoga. Burgoyne decided to press on. On September 13–14 he crossed to the west side of the Hudson River, cutting off communications with his rear. When he reached Saratoga, he confronted a growing American force of more than 10,000 men under General Horatio Gates. Two bloody battles convinced Burgoyne of the hopelessness of his situation, and in October 1777 he surrendered his entire army to the Americans.

Saratoga was the turning point. It suggested that the reconquest of America might be beyond British strength. It brought France openly into the struggle. And it led to changes in the British command and a fundamental alteration in strategy.

From the beginning of the rebellion, France had been secretly supplying money and arms to the Americans in the hope of avenging its defeat by Britain in the Seven Years' War. Benjamin Franklin had gone to Paris in 1776 to serve as the unofficial American ambassador. By 1777 French ports had been opened to

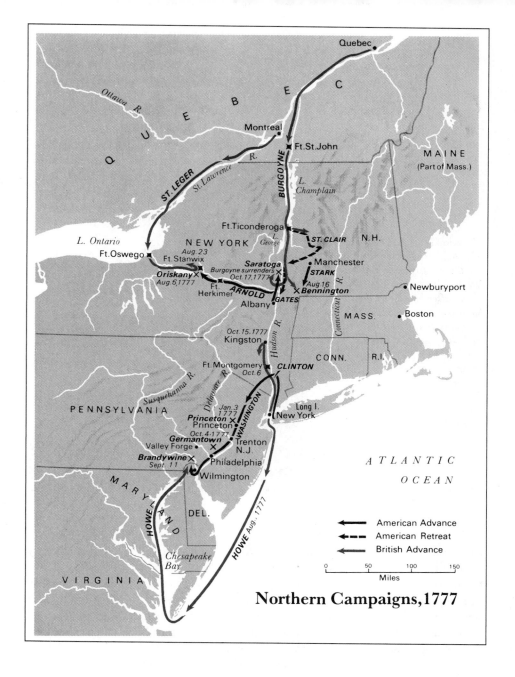

Northern Campaigns, 1777

American privateers, and French officers were joining Washington's army. It seemed only a matter of time before France would recognize the new republic. The British ministry realized at once the significance of Burgoyne's surrender, and by appointing the Carlisle Commission early in 1778 made new efforts to negotiate a settlement. The British government now offered the rebels a return to

Horatio Gates (1728–1806)
This lowborn former officer in the British army was appointed Washington's adjutant-general in 1775. After his victory at Saratoga, some members of Congress and several officers, including General Thomas Conway, thought about replacing Washington with Gates. These suggestions, which became known as the "Conway Cabal," were stifled by Washington's political shrewdness.

the imperial status before 1763—indeed, everything that the Americans had originally wanted. These British overtures, which Franklin skillfully used in Paris to play on French fears of an Anglo-American reconciliation, led the government of King Louis XVI in February 1778 to sign two treaties with the United States: one a commercial arrangement, the other a military alliance that was pledged to American independence. In 1779 Spain became allied with France in the hope of recovering earlier losses from England, especially Gibraltar. And in 1780 Russia formed the League of Armed Neutrality, which nearly all the maritime states of Europe eventually joined. For the first time in the eighteenth century, Britain was diplomatically isolated.

The War in the South, 1778–1781   After 1778 putting down the rebellion became secondary to Britain's global struggle with France and Spain. The center of the war effort in America shifted seaward and southward as Britain sought to protect its possessions in the West Indies.

General Howe was replaced by Sir Henry Clinton, and a more ruthless policy was adopted, including the bombardment of American ports, and raids on the countryside. The British abandoned Philadelphia and assumed a defensive position in New York and Rhode Island. Concentrating their forces in the West Indies, they now aimed to secure military control of ports in the American South, restore civil royal government with loyalist support, and then methodically move the army northward as a screen behind which local loyalists would gradually pacify the rebel territories. This strategy was based on the assumption that the South, with its scattered, presumably more loyalist population living in fear of Indian raids and slave uprisings, was especially vulnerable to the reassertion of British authority.

At the end of 1778 the British captured Savannah. On May 12, 1780, with the surrender of General Benjamin Lincoln and an American army of 5,500, the British took Charleston. It was the greatest American loss of soldiers in the entire war. A new, hastily assembled American southern army under General Gates— the victor at Saratoga—rashly moved into South Carolina to stop the British advance. On August 16, 1780, at Camden, South Carolina, Gates suffered a devastating defeat, which destroyed not only his new American army but his military reputation as well. But the British were not able to consolidate their gains and give the loyalists the military protection they needed to pacify the countryside. Loyalist retaliations against patriots for past harsh treatment, along with British plunder of the backcountry, particularly by Colonel Banastre Tarleton, drove countless Georgians and Carolinians into support of the Revolution. Colorful leaders such as Francis Marion, "the Swamp Fox," organized bands of patriots outside of the regular army to harass the loyalists and the British forces. The war in the South became a series of guerrilla skirmishes.

Now in command of the British forces in the South, Lord Cornwallis was impatient with the gradual policy of pacification. He was eager to demonstrate British strength by dramatically carrying the war into North Carolina. With his army constantly bedeviled by patriot guerrillas, he had just begun moving northward when he learned of the destruction of his left flank at King's Mountain on October 7, 1780. The news forced him to return to South Carolina. In the meantime the Americans had begun organizing a third southern army under the command of a thirty-eight-year-old ex-Quaker from Rhode Island, Nathanael Greene, recently quartermaster general of the Continental army. Shrewdly avoiding direct confrontation with Cornwallis, Greene compelled the British to divide their forces. On January 17, 1781, at Cowpens in western South Carolina, a detached corps of Greene's army under Daniel Morgan defeated "Bloody" Tarleton's Tory Legion and changed the course of British strategy in the South. Cornwallis cut his ties with his base in Charleston and set out after the elusive American army. After an indecisive battle with Greene at Guilford Courthouse on March 15, 1781, Cornwallis's tired and battered soldiers withdrew to Wilmington on the North Carolina coast with the intention of moving the seat of war northward into Virginia. Thus ended the British experiment with a thorough program of pacification. During the spring and summer of 1781, patriot forces

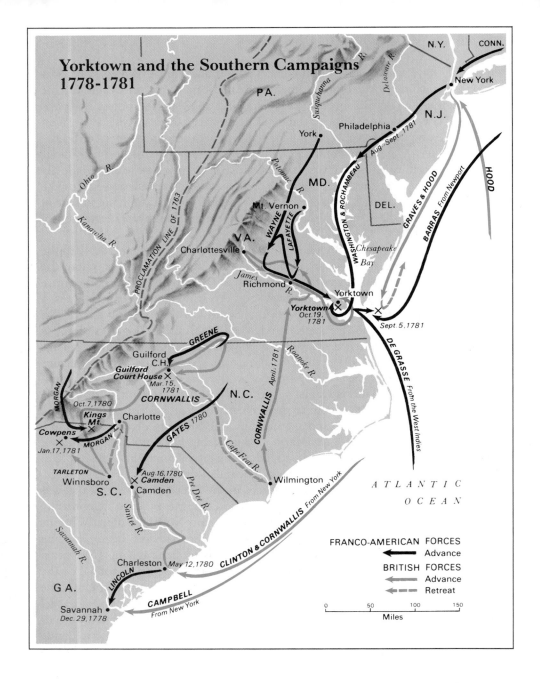

Yorktown and the Southern Campaigns 1778-1781

N.Y.
CONN.
New York
PA.
Susquehanna R.
York
Philadelphia
Aug.-Sept. 1781
N.J.
Delaware R.
MD.
DEL.
HOOD
GRAVES & HOOD
BARRAS From Newport
Potomac R.
Mt. Vernon
WAYNE
LAFAYETTE
WASHINGTON & ROCHAMBEAU
Chesapeake Bay
VA.
Charlottesville
PROCLAMATION LINE OF 1763
Ohio R.
Kanawha R.
James R.
Richmond
Yorktown
Yorktown
Oct. 19, 1781
Sept. 5, 1781
DE GRASSE From the West Indies
GREENE
Guilford C.H.
Guilford Court House
Mar. 15, 1781
CORNWALLIS
Roanoke R.
CORNWALLIS April 1781
N.C.
MORGAN
Oct. 7, 1780
Kings Mt.
Charlotte
GATES 1780
Cowpens
Jan. 17, 1781
MORGAN
Cape Fear R.
TARLETON
Winnsboro
Aug. 16, 1780
Camden
Camden
S.C.
Wilmington
ATLANTIC OCEAN
Santee R.
Pee Dee R.
CLINTON & CORNWALLIS From New York
Charleston May 12, 1780
LINCOLN
G A.
Savannah R.
CAMPBELL From New York
Savannah
Dec. 29, 1778

FRANCO-AMERICAN FORCES
Advance
BRITISH FORCES
Advance
Retreat

0   50   100   150
Miles

regained control of the entire Lower South except for a narrow strip between Charleston and Savannah.

Although raids by British forces in the summer of 1781 frightened Virginians and humiliated Governor Thomas Jefferson, Cornwallis could not convince his commander in chief, Clinton, in New York to make Virginia the center of British military operations. The haggling between the two generals enabled the Amer-

Cornwallis's Surrender Following the Yorktown Siege, 1781
*A French engraving of the British surrender at Yorktown, October 19, 1781. Since Cornwallis
did not himself present his sword to the American forces, Washington, always punctilious
about his status as commander in chief, had General Benjamin Lincoln receive the surrender.*

icans to bolster their Virginian troops under the command of the dashing French
nobleman, the Marquis de Lafayette, who had been in the struggle since 1777.
Cornwallis's withdrawal to the Virginia coast and his eventual isolation at York-
town gave the combined American and French army of nearly 17,000 men under
Washington and the Comte de Rochambeau the opportunity it was looking for.
The French fleet under Admiral de Grasse moved into Chesapeake Bay and
blocked Cornwallis's planned escape by sea. Thus surrounded and bombarded at
Yorktown, Cornwallis was forced to surrender his army of 8,000 troops to
Washington in October 1781. Britain's policy since 1778 of spreading its control
along the entire Atlantic coastline had depended on maintaining naval superi-
ority; and when this superiority was temporarily lost in 1781, the entire plan
collapsed. Although the war dragged on for several months, everyone knew that
Yorktown meant American independence.

The Peace Treaty   Nevertheless the peace still had to be won. The main
objective of the new nation—independence from
Great Britain—was clear and straightforward. But this objective and others
concerning America's territorial boundaries and its rights to the Newfoundland
fisheries had to be reconciled with the aims of America's ally, France, and with
those of France's ally, Spain, which had been at war with Great Britain since 1779.

The United States and France had pledged in 1778 not to make a separate peace with Britain. But since France was bound to Spain against Britain until Gibraltar was recovered, there was great danger of American interests getting lost in the maneuverings of the European powers. Despite the desire of France and Spain to humiliate Britain, neither monarchy really wanted a strong and independent American republic. Spain in particular feared the spread of republicanism among its South American colonies and sought to protect its interests in the Mississippi Valley.

Although Franklin, John Adams, and John Jay, the American negotiators in Europe, were only "militia diplomats," in Adams's words, they wound their way through the intricate problems of international politics with professional diplomatic skill. Despite instructions from the Continental Congress to do nothing without consulting France, the American diplomats decided to negotiate with Britain alone. By hinting at the possibility of weakening the Franco-American alliance, they persuaded Great Britain to recognize the independence of the United States and to agree to much more generous boundaries than the French and particularly the Spanish had been willing to support. On the west, United States territory reached to the Mississippi River; on the south, to the thirty-first parallel; and on the north, roughly to the present boundary with Canada. The American negotiators then presented this preliminary Anglo-American treaty to France and persuaded the French to accept it by suggesting that the allies must conceal their differences from their enemies. The prospect of American peace with Britain now compelled Spain to abandon its demands for Gibraltar and to settle for the Mediterranean island of Minorca (lost to Britain early in the eighteenth century) and for East and West Florida. In the final treaty, signed in Paris on September 3, 1783, the United States, by shrewdly playing off the mutual fears of the European powers, gained both independence and concessions that stunned the French and indeed all Europeans.

CHRONOLOGY

1774 Coercive Acts.
Continental Congress meets in Philadelphia.
Galloway's Plan of Union.
Continental Association.

1775 Battle of Lexington and Concord.
Fort Ticonderoga taken by American forces.
Second Continental Congress meets in Philadelphia.
George Washington appointed commander in chief of Continental army.

Battle of Bunker Hill.
Congress adopts its "Declaration of the Causes and Necessities of Taking Up Arms."
George III proclaims colonists in open rebellion.
American forces fail to take Quebec; General Montgomery killed.
Pennsylvania Quakers form first antislavery society in world.

1776 Thomas Paine's *Common Sense.*
British troops evacuate Boston.

1776 Congress calls on colonies to suppress all crown authority and establish governments under authority of the people.
Declaration of Independence.
Battle of Long Island, New York; Americans defeated by General Howe.
British take New York City.
Battle of Trenton.
New Hampshire, New Jersey, Pennsylvania, Delaware, Maryland, Virginia, North Carolina, and South Carolina write state constitutions.
Rhode Island and Connecticut change their colonial charters.

1777 Battle of Princeton.
Battle of Brandywine, Pennsylvania; Washington defeated.
British occupy Philadelphia.
Battle of Germantown, Pennsylvania; Howe repulses Washington's attack.
Burgoyne surrenders at Saratoga.
Articles of Confederation adopted by Continental Congress, but not ratified by all states until 1781.
Washington retires to Valley Forge for winter.
New York and Georgia write state constitutions.

1778 United States concludes military alliance and commercial treaty with France. First and only military alliance by United States until North Atlantic Treaty Organization, 1949.
British evacuate Philadelphia.
Battle of Monmouth, New Jersey. Although outcome indecisive, Washington's troops stand up to British regulars.
British seize Savannah, Georgia.

1779 Spain enters the war against Britain.
George Rogers Clark captures Vincennes and ends British rule in Northwest.

1780 Americans surrender 5,500 men and the city of Charleston, South Carolina.
Battle of Camden, South Carolina; Gates defeated by Cornwallis.
Battle of King's Mountain, South Carolina; British and Tories defeated.
Creation of Massachusetts constitution.

1781 Battle of Cowpens, South Carolina; British under Tarleton defeated by Morgan.
Battle of Guilford Courthouse, North Carolina; outcome indecisive, but Cornwallis withdraws to coast.
Cornwallis surrenders to Washington at Yorktown, Virginia.

1783 Treaty of Peace with Britain signed.

SUGGESTED READINGS

Modern interest in the ideas of the Revolution dates back to the 1920s and 1930s with the studies of constitutional law and natural rights philosophy by Carl Becker, *The Declaration of Independence* (1922); Charles H. McIlwain, *The American Revolution: A Constitutional Interpretation* (1923); William S. Carpenter, *The Development of American Political Thought* (1930); and Benjamin F. Wright, Jr., *American Interpretations of Natural Law* (1931). While these books emphasized formal political theory, others explicitly treated the ideas as propaganda. See Philip Davidson, *Propaganda and the American Revolution, 1763–1783* (1941); and Arthur M. Schlesinger, *Prelude to Independence: The Newspaper War on Britain, 1764–1776* (1958).

In the 1950s serious attention was paid to the determinative influence of ideas in Clinton Rossiter, *Seedtime of the Republic* (1953); and especially in Edmund S. Morgan and Helen M. Morgan, *The Stamp Act Crisis* (1953). The Morgan book focuses on parliamentary sovereignty.

Only in the 1960s, however, did historians comprehend the Revolutionary ideas as ideology and begin to recover the distinctiveness of the late-eighteenth-century world. The starting point now for analyzing the ideology of the Revolution—as a configuration of ideas giving meaning and force to events—is Bernard Bailyn, *The Ideological Origins of the American Revolution* (1967). Bailyn's book, which appeared initially as the introduction to the first of a four-volume edition of *Pamphlets of the American Revolution, 1750–1776* (1965–), was partly based on the rediscovery of the radical Whig tradition by Caroline Robbins, *The Eighteenth-Century Commonwealthmen* (1959). J. G. A. Pocock, *The Machiavellian Moment* (1975); J. R. Pole, *Political Representation in England and the Origins of the American Republic* (1966); Trevor H. Colbourn, *The Lamp of Experience: Whig History and the Beginnings of the American Revolution* (1965); and Isaac F. Kramnick, *Bolingbroke and His Circle* (1968), have further contributed to an understanding of the sources of the Revolutionary tradition. Pauline Maier, *From Resistance to Revolution* (1972), details the escalation of American fears of British policy between 1765 and 1776. For detailed analyses of the Americans' legal positions in the imperial debate see the many books of John Phillip Reid. Jack P. Greene, *Peripheries and Center* (1986) sets the constitutional issues of federalism in perspective.

The loyalist reaction is analyzed in William H. Nelson, *The American Tory* (1961); Robert M. Calhoon, *The Loyalists in Revolutionary America: 1760–1781* (1973); and Bernard Bailyn, *The Ordeal of Thomas Hutchinson* (1974). A vitriolic account by a loyalist of the causes of the Revolution is Peter Oliver, *Origin and Progress of the American Rebellion,* ed. Douglass Adair and John A. Schutz (1961).

On the military actions of the Revolutionary War, the best brief account is Willard M. Wallace, *Appeal to Arms* (1951). Don Higginbotham, *The War of American Independence* (1971), and John Shy, *A People Numerous and Armed: Reflections on the Military Struggle for American Independence* (1976), best appreciate the unconventional and guerrilla character of the war. Two books edited by George A. Billias, *George Washington's Generals* (1964) and *George Washington's Opponents* (1969), contain excellent essays written by various historians on the military leaders of both sides. Eric Robeson, *The American Revolution in Its Political and Military Aspects, 1763–1783* (1955), has some penetrating chapters on the conduct of the war. For naval operations, see Gardner W. Allen, *A Naval History of the American Revolution* (2 vols., 1913). The fullest account of British strategy is Piers Mackesy, *The War for America, 1775–1783* (1964). On the British commanders in chief, see Ira Gruber, *The Howe Brothers and the American Revolution* (1972), and William Willcox, *Portrait of a General: Sir Henry Clinton in the War of Independence* (1964). Paul H. Smith, *Loyalists and Redcoats* (1964), describes British attempts to mobilize the loyalists. A particularly imaginative study is Charles Royster, *A Revolutionary People at War: The Continental Army and American Character, 1775–1783* (1979).

On diplomacy the standard account is Samuel Flagg Bemis, *The Diplomacy of the American Revolution* (1935). See also William C. Stinchcombe, *The American Revolution and the French Alliance* (1969), and Jonathan Dull, a *Diplomatic History of the American Revolution* (1985). Richard B. Morris, *The Peacemakers* (1965), is a full study of the peace negotiations.

9

Republicanism

~

$\mathcal{A}$MILITARY victory over Great Britain may have been essential for the success of the Revolution, but for Americans it was scarcely the whole of the Revolution. Although the Revolution had begun as a political crisis within the British Empire, by 1776 it was no longer merely a colonial rebellion. The imperial debate had released a flood of American writings that ultimately made the Revolutionary era the most creative period in the history of American political thought. From 1775, when independence and hence the formation of new governments became imminent, and continuing throughout the war, nearly every piece of writing about the future was filled with extraordinarily visionary hopes for the transformation of America. Americans had come to believe that the Revolution meant nothing less than the remaking of eighteenth-century politics and society—a remaking that was summed up in the concept of republicanism.

Republican Idealism

This republicanism was in every way a radical ideology—as radical for the eighteenth century as Marxism was to be for the nineteenth century. It meant more than simply eliminating a king and establishing an elective system of government. It added a moral, idealistic, and indeed utopian dimension to the political separation from Britain—a dimension that promised a fundamental shift in values and a change in the very character of American society.

Republicanism intensified the radicalism of the "country" ideology that Americans had borrowed from opposition groups in English society, and linked it with older and deeper European currents of thought that went back to antiquity. Indeed, classic republican ideas had their ultimate origin in ancient Greece and Rome. They had been revived by Renaissance writers, particularly by the early-sixteenth-century Italian philosopher Niccolò Machiavelli, and had been carried into seventeenth-century English thought by such writers as James Harrington, the poet John Milton, and Algernon Sidney. It was under the influence of these classical republican ideas that England in the seventeenth century had executed its king, Charles I, and had tried its brief experiment in republicanism, the Commonwealth (1649–53). By the eighteenth century these classical republican ideals had spread through western Europe; indeed they had become a kind of counterculture for many dissatisfied Europeans. In countless writings and translations eighteenth-century European and English intellectuals evoked the utopian image of an earlier Roman republican world of simple farmer-citizens enjoying liberty and rural virtue. They viewed this idealized ancient world as an alternative to the sprawling monarchies, with their hierarchies, luxury, and corruption, that they had come to despise in their own time.

In the excitement of the Revolutionary movement, these classical republican values came together with the long-existing image of Americans as simple liberty- and equality-loving people to form one of the most coherent and powerful ideologies the Western world had yet seen. Many of the ambiguities Americans had felt about the rural, provincial character of their society were now clarified. What some people had seen as the crudities and limitations of American life could now be viewed as advantages for republican government. Independent American farmers who owned their own land were no longer regarded as primitive folk living on the edges of European society and in the backwaters of history. Rather, they were now perceived as citizens naturally equipped to realize the republican values that intellectuals had advocated for centuries.

Independent Citizens   Inevitably the new American states in 1776 became republics. Everyone knew that these new republics with their elective systems had not only political but also moral and social significance. Republicanism struck directly at the traditional society, in which heredity, patronage, and dependency were essential. Republican liberals believed that the social evils of the Old World—entrenched privilege, inflated aristocracy, and ever-present poverty—all flowed from the abuses of government. Therefore they aimed to reduce, if not destroy, government's overarching power. They were determined that government would no longer be able to squeeze money from the people, create titles of distinction, grant monopolies, shore up religious establish-ments, give out offices, and do all those other things that ate away at the moral vitality of the people. In place of strong government, republicanism promised a society in which relations would be based on natural merit and the equality of independent citizens who were linked to one another in affection and harmony. Although republicanism was based on individual property holding, it rejected a narrow, selfish individualism and stressed a morality of social cohesion and devotion to the common welfare. Several of the states—Massachusetts, Pennsyl-vania, and Virginia—in 1776 even adopted the name "commonwealth" to express better this new dedication to the public good.

VENERATE THE PLOUGH

These new republican communities of independent citizens were an inspiring ideal. But history had shown republics to be the most unstable kind of state, highly susceptible to faction and internal disorder. Theorists thus concluded that republics had to be small in territory and of essentially uniform character. The only existing European republican models—the Netherlands, and the Italian and Swiss city-states—were small and compact. According to the best political science of the day, when a large country attempted to establish a republic, as England had tried to do in the seventeenth century, the experiment was sure to end in some sort of dictatorship, like that of Oliver Cromwell. Unlike monarchies, whose executive power and numerous dependent ranks maintained public order even over a large and diverse population, republics had to be held together from below, by the people themselves.

The Need for Virtue   Republicanism was radical precisely because it demanded an extraordinary degree of moral virtue— unselfish devotion to the public good—in the people. If only the society could be organized so as to allow the moral strength of people to express itself, then there would be little need for excessive central or royal government. But if the society developed in such a manner as to lessen the people's virtue, if the people became selfish and luxury-loving as the ancient Romans had, then the society would lose its ability to keep the republic alive and the degeneration of the republican state into a monarchy or dictatorship would be inevitable.

Americans, however, believed themselves to be naturally virtuous and thus ideally suited for republican government. Did they not possess the same hardy equality-loving character that the ancient republican citizens of Greece and Rome had had? Were not the remarkable displays of popular order in the face of disintegrating royal government in 1774–75 evidence that the American people

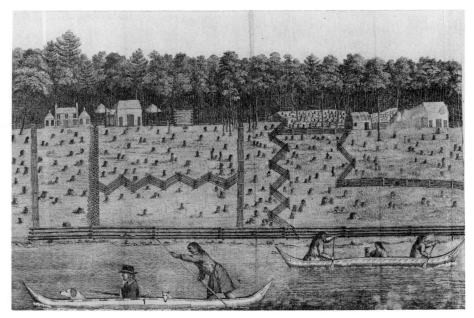

Frontier Farm in 1793
Even at the end of the eighteenth century, many American farmers continued to grow their crops Indian style, girdling and burning trees, planting between tree stumps, and allowing the fields to revert to forest when their fertility gave out. Such wasteful and shifting methods of agriculture shocked foreign observers but made sense where land was so abundant.

would obey their governments without coercion? The Revolutionary leaders appealed to the American people to act patriotically, telling them, as Samuel Adams did, that "a Citizen owes everything to the Commonwealth." The citizen was, in fact, as the Philadelphia physician Benjamin Rush said, "public property. His time and talents—his youth—his manhood—his old age—nay more, life, all belong to his country."

In short, republican citizens had to be patriots, and patriots were not simply those who loved their country but those who were free from the control of others. As Jefferson wrote in his *Notes on Virginia,* "Dependence begets subservience and venality, suffocates the germ of virtue, and prepares fit tools for the designs of ambition." Hence the sturdy independent yeoman-farmers, Jefferson's "chosen people of God," were regarded as the most incorruptible and the best citizens for a republic.

The individual ownership of property, especially land, was essential for a republic, both as a source of independence and as evidence of a permanent attachment to the community. Those who were propertyless and dependent, like women and servants, thus could justifiably be denied the vote because they could have no wills of their own. In Europe corruption and dependency were thought to be common because only a few people possessed property. But, as one Carolinian wrote in 1777, "the people of America are a people of property; almost every man is a freeholder." Jefferson was so keen on this point that he proposed in

1776 that the new commonwealth of Virginia grant fifty acres of land to every citizen who did not have that many.

Equality   At the heart of this republican emphasis on virtue and independence lay equality, the most powerful and influential concept in American history. Equality was the necessary basis for the anticipated harmony and public virtue of the New World. Many felt that the endless squabbling over position and rank and the bitter factional politics in the colonies had been the result of the artificial inequality of colonial society. This inequality, republicans said, had been created and nourished largely through the corrupting influence and patronage of the British crown. In a republic individuals were no longer doomed to be what their fathers had been. Ability, not birth, was what mattered. But republican egalitarianism did not mean the elimination of distinctions. Republics would still have an aristocracy, said Jefferson, but it would be a natural, not an artificial, one. A republican elite would resemble not the luxury-loving, money-mongering lackeys of the British court, but the stern and disinterested heroes of antiquity—men like George Washington, who seemed to Americans to embody perfectly the classical ideal of a republican leader.

Obviously these ideals of Revolutionary republicanism could not be wholly fulfilled. Much of republicanism's emphasis on the common good contradicted the surging individualism of American life. Yet whatever the practical results, republicanism as it was idealized by Jefferson's generation colored the entire Revolutionary movement. Eventually it would come to shape much of what Americans believe and value.

State Constitution Making

"How few of the human race have ever enjoyed an opportunity of making an election of government," rejoiced John Adams, like many others in 1776. Indeed, it was in the spirit of being able to control their own destinies that the Revolutionaries approached the immense task ahead of them. They knew very well that the entire world was watching to see how they would put their republican ideals into practice when they established governments for the new country. Their investigations into the abuses of power and the protection of liberty that had begun during the imperial debate now shaped the new constitutions they formed.

From the time royal authority had begun to disintegrate, Americans began thinking about creating new governments. During the summer of 1775, Samuel Adams and John Adams of Massachusetts, together with the Virginia delegation to the Continental Congress, led by Richard Henry Lee, worked out a program of independence. They made plans to negotiate foreign alliances, to create a confederation—a union for common purposes—and, most important, to establish new state governments. The climax of their efforts came with the congressional resolutions of May 1776, advising the colonies to adopt new governments "under the authority of the people" and declaring "that the exercise of every kind of authority under the . . . Crown should be totally suppressed." Even before the Declaration of Independence, the Congress had created a committee to form a confederation, and some of the states—New Hampshire, South Carolina, and Virginia—had begun working on new constitutions. With the May resolves and the Declaration of Independence, the other states also began to form new governments. By the end of 1776, new constitutions had been adopted in New Jersey, Delaware, Pennsylvania, Maryland, and North Carolina. Because they were corporate chartered colonies, Rhode Island and Connecticut were already republics in fact, and they simply confined themselves to eliminating all mention of royal authority in their existing charters. War conditions forced Georgia and New York to delay their constitution making until 1777. Massachusetts had recovered its old charter, which the British had abolished, and was busy preparing to write a more permanent constitution.

In 1776–77 Americans concentrated much of their attention and energy on establishing these new state constitutions. The states, not the central government or the Congress, were to test the Revolutionary hopes. In fact, forming new state governments, as Jefferson said in the spring of 1776, was "the whole object of the present controversy." For the aim of the Revolution had become not simply independence from British tyranny, but the prevention of future tyrannies.

Constitutions as Written Documents
It was inevitable that Americans would draw up written constitutions. By the word *constitution* most eighteenth-century Englishmen meant not a written document, but the existing arrangements of government—that is, laws, customs, and institutions, together with the principles they embodied. Americans, however, had come to view a constitution in a different way. Ever since the seventeenth century they had repeatedly used their colonial charters as defensive barriers against royal authority. During the imperial debate with Britain, they had been compelled to recognize that laws made by Parliament were not necessarily constitutional or in accord with fundamental principles of rightness and justice. If the constitutional principles were to be asserted against a too powerful government, then somehow they had to be lifted out of the machinery of day-to-day government and set above it. The Americans' new state constitutions would therefore have to be fixed plans—written documents, as the English constitution never had been—outlining the powers of government and specifying the rights of citizens.

Fear of Executive Power
As they wrote these new state constitutions, the Americans set about to institutionalize all that they had learned from their colonial experience and the recent struggle with England. Although they knew they would establish republics, they did not know precisely what forms the new governments should take. Their central aim was to prevent power, which they identified with the rulers or governors, from encroaching on liberty, which they identified with the people or their representatives in the legislatures. This aim was basic to the Anglo-Amer-

ican "country" ideology. Only the Americans' deep fear of executive power can explain the radical changes they made in the authority of their now elected governors.

In their desire to root out tyranny once and for all, the members of the state congresses who drafted the new constitutions reduced the elected governors' powers to a pale reflection of those that had been exercised by the royal governors. No longer would governors have the authority to create electoral districts, control the meeting of the assemblies, veto legislation, grant lands, establish courts of law, issue charters of incorporation to towns, or—in some states—pardon crimes. All the new state governors were surrounded by controlling councils whose members were elected by the assemblies. These governors were to be elected annually (generally by the assemblies), limited in the number of times they could be reelected, and subject to impeachment.

However radical these changes in executive authority may have been, many Americans believed that they did not get to the heart of the matter. They did not destroy the most subtle and dangerous source of despotism—the executive's power of appointment to office. Since in a traditional, monarchical society the distribution of offices, honors, and favors affected the social order, American republicans were determined that their governors would never again have the capacity to dominate public life. Exclusive control over appointments to executive and judicial offices was now taken from the traditional hands of the governors and shared with the legislatures. This change in the new state constitutions of 1776 was justified by the familiar principle of "separation of powers." The idea behind maintaining the executive, legislative, and judicial parts of the government separate and distinct was not to protect each power from the others, but to keep the judiciary and particularly the legislature free from executive manipulation—the very kind of manipulation that, Americans believed, had corrupted the English Parliament. Hence the new constitutions absolutely barred all executive officeholders and those receiving government salaries from sitting in the legislatures. As a consequence, parliamentary cabinet government of the kind that existed in England was forever prohibited in America, and constitutional development moved off in a direction independent of Great Britain—a direction that American government still follows.

Strengthening of the Legislatures

The powers and rights that the new state constitutions of 1776 took from the governors were granted to the legislatures. This action marked a radical shift in the responsibility of government. In English history the "government" had traditionally been identified mainly with the executive. Representative bodies had generally been confined to voting taxes and passing corrective legislation on special occasions. But the new American state legislatures, in particular the lower houses of the assemblies, were no longer merely to be secondary units of governmental power or checks upon it. They were now given powers that had formerly been reserved for the magistrates—the executive and judicial leaders of government. These powers included making alliances and granting pardons.

To ensure that the state legislatures fully embodied the people's will, the ideas and experiences behind the Americans' view of representation were now drawn out and implemented. The Revolutionary state constitutions put a new emphasis on actual representation and explicit consent. They did so by creating equal electoral districts, requiring annual elections, enlarging the suffrage, imposing residence requirements on both electors and the persons elected, and granting constituents the right to instruct their representatives. The royal governors' former attempts to resist extending representation to newly settled areas was now dramatically reversed. Towns and counties, particularly in the backcountry, were granted either new or additional representation in the state legislatures. Thus Americans belatedly recognized the legitimacy of the western uprisings of the 1760s. Some of the new constitutions even explicitly stated the principle that population was the basis of representation. Five states wrote into their constitutions specific plans for periodic adjustments of their representation, so that (as the New York constitution of 1777 stated) it "shall for ever remain proportionate and adequate."

In light of what would happen in the coming decade, the Revolutionaries' confidence in 1776 in their representative legislatures was remarkable. Except for some dissatisfied Tories, few people expected these state legislatures to become tyrannical—in the Whig theory of politics, it did not seem possible for the people to tyrannize over themselves. Of course the people were apt to be rowdy or impatient; hence the republics needed not only governors, but also upper houses in the legislature to counterbalance the popular lower houses of representatives. All the states except Pennsylvania, Georgia, and the new state of Vermont therefore provided for upper houses, or senates, the designation taken from Roman history. The senators in these bicameral, or two-chamber, state legislatures were not to be a legally defined nobility but the wisest and best members of the society, who would revise and correct the well-intentioned but often careless measures of the people represented in the lower houses.

This Revolutionary state constitution making was an extraordinary achievement. Nothing quite like it had occurred before in modern history. Foreign intellectuals considered the new American state constitutions concrete realizations of Enlightenment ideas. In the decade following Independence the state constitutions were translated, published, and republished in France and other European countries, and their features were eagerly examined and debated. More than anything else in 1776, these new written state constitutions gave people everywhere a sense that a new era in history was beginning.

The Articles of Confederation

At the same time that the Revolutionaries were creating their state constitutions, they also set up a central government. Yet in marked contrast to the rich and exciting public explorations of political theory accompanying the formation of the state constitutions, there was little discussion of the plans for a central government. In 1776 most people's loyalties were still concentrated on their particular provinces. The Declaration of Independence, drawn up by the Continental Congress, was actually a declaration by "thirteen united States of America" proclaiming that as "Free and Independent States, they have full Power to levy War, conclude Peace, contract Alliances, establish Commerce, and to do all other Acts and Things which independent States may of right do." Despite all the talk of union, few Americans in 1776 could conceive of creating a single full-fledged Continental republic.

Still, the Congress needed some legal basis for its authority. Like the various provincial conventions, it had been created in 1774 simply out of necessity, and it was exercising an extraordinary degree of political, military, and economic power over Americans. It had adopted commercial codes, established and maintained an army, issued a Continental currency, laid down a military law code, defined crimes against the Union, and negotiated abroad. With the approach of Independence it was obvious to many leaders that a more permanent and legitimate union of the states was necessary. Although a draft of confederation was ready for consideration by the Congress as early as mid-July 1776, not until November 1777, after heated controversy, did the Congress present a document of union to the states for each of them to approve or reject. It took nearly four years, until March 1781, for all the states to accept this document and thereby legally establish the Articles of Confederation.

The Nature of the Union

The Articles created a confederation, "The United States of America," that was essentially a continuation of the Second Continental Congress. Delegates from each state were to be sent annually to the Congress, and each state delegation was to have only a single vote. In Article 9 the Congress was granted authority to control diplomatic relations, requisition soldiers and money from the states, coin and borrow money, regulate Indian affairs, and settle disputes between the states. Although a simple majority of seven states was needed to settle minor matters, a larger majority, nine states, was required to resolve important issues, including engaging in war, making treaties, and coining and borrowing money. There was no real executive, but only congressional committees with fluctuating memberships.

The Union was stronger than many people expected. The states were specifically forbidden to conduct foreign affairs, make treaties, and declare war. The citizens of each state were entitled to the privileges and immunities of the citizens of all states. All travel restrictions and discriminatory trade barriers between the states were eliminated. The judicial proceedings of each state were honored by all the states. These provisions, together with the substantial powers granted to the Congress, made the United States of America as strong as any similar republican confederation in history. The Articles marked a big step toward a genuine national government.

Nevertheless the Americans' fear of distant central authority, intensified by century of experience in the British Empire, left no doubt that this Confederation would remain something less than a full national government. Under the Articles the crucial powers of commercial regulation and taxation—indeed, all final lawmaking authority—remained with the states. Congressional resolutions continued to be, as they had been under the Continental Congress, only recommendations; the states, it was assumed, would enforce them. And should there be any doubts of the decentralized nature of the Confederation, Article 2 stated bluntly that "each State retains its sovereignty, freedom and independence, and every power, jurisdiction, and right, which is not by this confederation expressly delegated to the United States, in Congress assembled."

The phrase "United States of America" thus possessed a literal meaning that is hard to appreciate today. The Confederation, based on the equal representation of each state, was more like a treaty among closely cooperating sovereign states than a single government. It was intended to be and remained, as Article 3 declared, "a firm league of friendship" among states jealous of their individuality. Not only ratification of the Articles of Confederation, but any subsequent changes in them, required the consent of all states.*

State Rivalries and the Disposition of the Western Lands   The local self-interests of the states prolonged the congressional debates over the adoption of the Articles and delayed the required unanimous ratification until 1781. The major disputes—over representation, the share each state should contribute to the Union, and the disposition of the western lands—involved concrete state interests. Virginia and other populous states argued for proportional representation in the Congress, but these larger states had to give way to the smaller states' determination to maintain equal representation. The original draft of the Articles provided that each state's financial contribution to the general treasury would be based on its population, including slaves. Strong opposition from the southern states, however, forced the Congress to shift the basis for a state's financial contribution to the value of its land. This change was made against the wishes of the New England states, where land values were high.

The states' rivalries were most evident in the long controversy over the disposition of the western lands between the Appalachian Mountains and the Mississippi River. The Articles sent to the states in 1778 for ratification gave the Congress no authority over the unsettled lands of the interior, and this omission delayed their approval. States like Virginia and Massachusetts with charter claims to this western territory wanted to maintain control over the disposal of their land. But states without such claims, like Maryland and Rhode Island, wanted the western land pooled in a common national domain under the authority of the Congress. By March 1779, however, all but Maryland had ratified the Articles. Maryland, under the influence of land speculators, refused to join the Union until all the states had ceded their western lands to the central government. When

---

*For the Articles of Confederation, see Appendix.

State Claims to Western Lands and Cessions

Western Claims
Western Reserve, Ceded 1800

Virginia, the state with charter rights to the largest amount of western territory, finally agreed on January 2, 1781, to surrender its claims to the United States, the way was prepared for other land cessions and for ratification of the Articles of Confederation by all the states. But the Confederation had to promise, in return for the cession of claims by Virginia and the other states, that this huge national domain in the West would "be settled and formed into distinct republican states."

Ordinances for the West

The Congress drew up land ordinances in 1784 and 1785, and in 1787 it adopted the famous Northwest Ordinance. This act acknowledged—as the British had not done in the 1760s—the settlers' destiny in the West. The land ordinances of 1784 and 1785 provided for the land north of the Ohio River and west of the

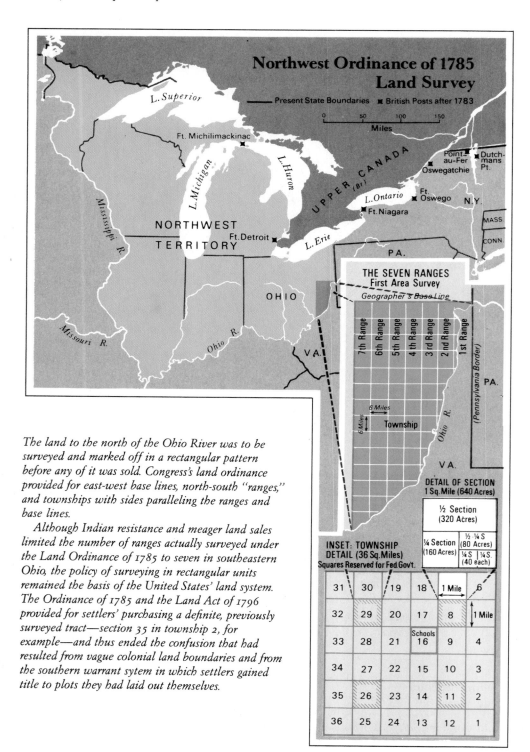

Northwest Ordinance of 1785 Land Survey

—— Present State Boundaries ■ British Posts after 1783

0   50   100   150
Miles

L. Superior

Ft. Michilimackinac

L. Michigan

L. Huron

UPPER CANADA (Br.)

Point-au-Fer
Oswegatchie
Dutch-mans Pt.

L. Ontario

Ft. Oswego   N.Y.

Ft. Niagara

MASS.

CONN.

NORTHWEST TERRITORY

Ft. Detroit

L. Erie

Mississippi R.

PA.

OHIO

Ohio R.

Missouri R.

V.A.

THE SEVEN RANGES
First Area Survey

Geographer's Base Line

7th Range | 6th Range | 5th Range | 4th Range | 3rd Range | 2nd Range | 1st Range

(Pennsylvania Border)

PA.

6 Miles

6 Miles

Township

V.A.

Ohio R.

DETAIL OF SECTION
1 Sq. Mile (640 Acres)

½ Section (320 Acres)		
¼ Section (160 Acres)	½ · ¼ S (80 Acres)	
	¼ S (40 each)	¼ S (40 each)

INSET: TOWNSHIP DETAIL (36 Sq. Miles)
Squares Reserved for Fed. Govt.

31	30	19	18	1 Mile	6
32	29	20	17	8	1 Mile
33	28	21	Schools 16	9	4
34	27	22	15	10	3
35	26	23	14	11	2
36	25	24	13	12	1

The land to the north of the Ohio River was to be surveyed and marked off in a rectangular pattern before any of it was sold. Congress's land ordinance provided for east-west base lines, north-south "ranges," and townships with sides paralleling the ranges and base lines.

Although Indian resistance and meager land sales limited the number of ranges actually surveyed under the Land Ordinance of 1785 to seven in southeastern Ohio, the policy of surveying in rectangular units remained the basis of the United States' land system. The Ordinance of 1785 and the Land Act of 1796 provided for settlers' purchasing a definite, previously surveyed tract—section 35 in township 2, for example—and thus ended the confusion that had resulted from vague colonial land boundaries and from the southern warrant sytem in which settlers gained title to plots they had laid out themselves.

Appalachians to be surveyed and formed into townships of six miles square along lines running east–west and north–south. Each township was to be divided into thirty-six numbered lots (called sections) of 640 acres each. The Confederation favored speculators and large groups by providing for the sale of the land by auction and by requiring that a section was to be the smallest unit purchased, at a price of no less than a dollar an acre. In each township the Congress retained four sections for future sale and set aside one other for the support of public education. The Ordinance of 1787 dealt with the political organization of the Northwest. It guaranteed to the settlers basic political and legal rights and arranged for the area to be divided into not less than three nor more than five territories. When a territory reached a population of 60,000, it was to be admitted to the Union on equal terms with the existing states.

Outside of winning the war, these remarkable ordinances were the Confederation's greatest achievement. They solved at a stroke the problem, which Britain had been unable to solve, of relating "colonies" or other dependencies to the central government. In succeeding decades the Land Ordinance of 1785 and the Ordinance of 1787 remained the bases for the surveying, sale, and political evolution of America's western territories. Settlers could leave the older states with the assurances that they were not losing their political liberties and that they would be allowed eventually to form new republics as sovereign and independent as the other states in the Union. Thus even the organization of this great national landed resource by the Congress was immediately devoted to the dispersion of central authority through the anticipated creation of more states—the only political units most Americans seemed to value.

Republican Society

At the same time that Americans were trying to establish new governments and constitutions, disturbing changes in American society were taking place. To be sure, there was no immediate collapse of the social order and no abrupt and wholesale destruction of familiar social institutions. But everywhere there were alterations in the way people related to government, to the economy, and to each other. Many of these changes were the results of deeply rooted forces long in motion, some dating back to the beginning of the colonial period. But others were the recent and direct results of the Revolution itself.

The Departure of the Loyalists One sudden effect was the departure of tens of thousands of loyalists—or Tories, as the patriots called them. The loyalists may have numbered close to half a million, or 20 percent of white Americans. Nearly 20,000 of them fought for the crown in the regiments of His Majesty's army, and thousands of others served in local loyalist militia bodies. As many as 60,000 to 80,000 loyalists, it is estimated, left America for Canada and Great Britain during the Revolution, although many of these returned after the war and were reintegrated into American society.

Although the loyalists came from all ranks and occupations, a large proportion belonged to the upper political and social levels. Many had been officeholders and overseas merchants involved in government contracting; in the North, most were Anglicans. Their regional distribution was likewise uneven. The loyalists were a tiny minority in New England and Virginia; but in western frontier areas, where hostility to eastern encroachment went back to pre-Revolutionary times, they were numerous. The loyalists also made up a considerable part of the population in the regions of New York, New Jersey, Pennsylvania, and the Deep South where the British army offered them protection. Their flight, displacement, and retirement created a vacuum at the top of society that was rapidly filled by patriots. The effects were widespread. Crown and Tory property and lands valued at millions of pounds were confiscated by the Revolutionary governments and almost immediately thrown onto the market. The resulting speculation contributed to the sudden rise and fall of fortunes during the Revolutionary years.

Economic Effects of the Revolution   Economic disruptions created most of the social disorder. Suddenly Americans found themselves outside the protective walls of the British mercantile empire that had nurtured their commercial life for more than a century. Exports dropped drastically. Traditional markets in Britain, and especially in the British West Indies, were closed. Bonuses or bounties that formerly had been paid on particular colonial products were now gone. Colonial ships could no longer be sold to Britain, and prewar sources of credit were upset. These changes were devastating to particular groups and individuals, but overall the results of the break from Britain were beneficial and stimulating. Simply by destroying old encrusted habits and relationships, the Revolution released new energies.

The South suffered the greatest upheavals from the war. Not only did it lose established markets for its tobacco and other cash crops, but the British freed tens of thousands of its slaves to fight for the crown; at the end of the war, the British settled these former slaves in Canada, the West Indies, and other parts of the world. Indeed, the British army was perhaps the greatest single instrument of emancipation in America until the Civil War. But these dislocations only accelerated an agricultural diversification that had begun before the Revolution. The Upper South in particular recovered rapidly. Tobacco production in the 1780s equaled prewar levels, and it involved many new participants and new marketing arrangements.

Within the merchant communities in the North, divisions that had been apparent before the Revolution now widened, and merchants who had previously been on the fringe of economic activity found new opportunities at the center of things. In Massachusetts, provincial families like the Higginsons, Cabots, and Lowells moved into Boston and quickly formed the basis of a new Massachusetts elite. The same process was duplicated less notably but no less importantly elsewhere. New merchants pushed out in all directions in search of fresh markets, not only into the restricted colonial areas of the West Indies and South America, but also throughout Europe and even as far away as China.

"View of Bridge Over Charles River," 1789
*Building a bridge across the Charles River and linking Boston with Cambridge, Massachusetts,
in the 1780s was only one of many such encouragements to internal commerce in post-
Revolutionary America. This chartered toll bridge was the one later challenged by a rival
bridge, a challenge that eventually resulted, in 1837, in one of the great Supreme Court
decisions of American history.*

Postwar trade with Great Britain quickly reached its earlier levels. By the
1780s the overall figures show an amazing recovery of commerce. Yet gross
statistics do not do justice to the extent of change that was involved. In all the
states there were new sources of supply, new commercial patterns, and new and
increased numbers of participants in the market. Although exports soon sur-
passed their prewar levels, they now represented a smaller part of America's total
economic activity. The wartime collapse of British imports had encouraged
domestic manufacturing; and although the purchase of British goods resumed
with the return of peace, societies were now formed to promote protective
legislation for American manufacturing. Already the economy was beginning to
turn inward: a remarkable spread of interstate and interregional trade would
soon generate demands for new roads and canals. In these changing circumstances towns without hinterlands to exploit began a relative decline. Newport,
Rhode Island, for example, had been a flourishing colonial port. But without an
inland area for supply and marketing, it rapidly slipped into insignificance.

The Revolutionary War itself was both a disruptive and a creative force. It
touched nearly everyone in one way or another. Like all wars, it destroyed familiar
channels of trade and produced new sources of wealth. During the eight long
years of the war, perhaps as many as 100,000 men bore arms in the Continental
army and the state militias. All these soldiers had to be clothed, fed, housed,
armed, and moved about. Thus for years the Congress and the state governments
were involved in gigantic mobilization efforts that had powerful and far-reaching
effects on the American economy. Hundreds of military and government

officials, ranging from quartermasters and commissary generals down to a variety of local purchasing agents, bought millions of dollars' worth of goods, from food and wagons to blankets and uniforms—anything and everything needed to wage war. Some military supplies were imported from abroad; but because of the scarcity of foreign credit and the British blockade of American shipping, most goods had to be grown or made by Americans. Consequently, American farmers and artisans were drawn into producing for these huge new government markets on a scale never before experienced in America. Although in the past Americans had thought of commerce mostly in terms of international or overseas trade, as a result of this wartime experience they now began to realize the tremendous significance of trading with each other in their own domestic markets. Therefore military purchasing agencies became important new centers of economic activity and breeding grounds for both petty entrepreneurs and powerful postwar capitalists. Moreover, countless farmers and artisans became used to the idea that they could expand their productivity and their wealth by working harder and selling goods in impersonal domestic markets. No wonder that by the 1780s many ordinary Americans were enthusiastic about the possibility of raising their standard of living.

Because the Revolutionary states were reluctant to tax their citizens, and because the Congress did not even have the legal authority to tax, the American governments had to rely on borrowing to pay for all the goods they needed for the war effort. But government borrowing could scarcely raise the needed sums. Both the Congress and the state governments therefore resorted to the extensive printing of noninterest-bearing paper currency. These bills of credit, which the governments promised to redeem by taxes at some future date, were given to citizens in payment for supplies and services.

The currency that was issued by the congressional and state governments eventually totaled nearly $400 million in paper value and led to a socially disintegrating inflation. By 1781, $167 of congressional paper money was worth only $1 in specie (gold and silver), and the depreciation of the states' bills was nearly as bad. While creditors, wage earners, and those on relatively fixed incomes were hurt by this inflation, many of those who were most active in the economy—those who bought and sold goods rapidly—were able to profit. These circulating government bills enabled countless commodity farmers and traders to break out of a simple barter economy and to specialize and participate more independently in the market than they had in the past. The war thus fundamentally altered the American economy.

Long-Range Social Change These were the immediate social and economic effects of the war. But there were other, deeper, and more long-lasting forces that were greatly affected by the Revolution and by republicanism. Despite a slowing-down of immigration and the loss of tens of thousands of loyalists who emigrated, the population continued to grow. The 1780s saw the fastest rate of population growth of any decade in

American history. This swelling population resumed its movement westward after being delayed for several years in the late 1770s by intermittent warfare against the British and Indians. By the early 1780s there were more than 20,000 inhabitants in the Kentucky territory; within a decade it had become more populous than most of the colonies had been at the time of the Revolution.

This spectacular growth and movement of people further weakened the traditional forms of social organization. Such a mobile population, one Kentuckian told James Madison in 1792, "must make a very different mass from one which is composed of men born and raised on the same spot.... They see none about them to whom or to whose families they have been accustomed to think themselves inferior." And the ideology of republicanism intensified these tendencies. In a republic, declared a writer in 1787 in the *American Museum* (the most important of several new American magazines that were founded in the postwar years), "the idea of equality breathes through the whole and every individual feels ambitious to be in a situation not inferior to his neighbour."

This republican equality became a rallying cry for people in the aspiring middle ranks who were now more openly resentful than before of those who presumed to be their social superiors. In 1783 Revolutionary army officers formed the hereditary Order of the Cincinnati, named after the legendary Roman republican leader Cincinnatus, who retired from war to take up his plow. Although Washington was asked to lead the organization, the Cincinnati aroused bitter hostility. Old patriots such as Samuel Adams thought that the order represented "as rapid a Stride towards an hereditary Military Nobility as was ever made in so short a Time." This sort of ferocious criticism forced the army officers to deny some of their pretensions, and the Cincinnati soon became just another one of the many pressure groups emerging in a country that, as the governor of South Carolina said in 1784, had gone "Society mad."

Some fervent equality-minded citizens attacked distinctions of all kinds, including membership in private social clubs and the wearing of imported finery. Gentlemen in some areas of the North found that the traditional marks of social authority—breeding, education, good manners—were becoming liabilities for political leadership. In this new republican society no one would admit being dependent on anyone else. Ordinary citizens now claimed the right to the titles— "Mr." and "Mrs."—that had once belonged only to the members of the gentry. Foreign visitors were stunned by the unwillingness of American servants to address their masters and mistresses as superiors and by the servants' refusal to admit that they were anything but "help." For many Americans, living in a free country meant never having to tip one's cap to anyone.

This growing egalitarianism did not mean that wealth was distributed more evenly in post-Revolutionary America. On the contrary: the inequality of wealth was greater after the Revolution than before. What it did mean was that the way people related to one another was being transformed. Relationships came to be based on money rather than on social position. Towns, for example, stopped assigning seats in their churches by age and status and began auctioning the pews

"Accident in Lombard Street, Philadelphia, 1787," by Charles W. Peale
Even Philadelphia, as the new country's largest city, was by today's standards only a small town. Its population of 30–40,000 could easily fit into a present-day football stadium.

to the highest bidders. Self-earned wealth gave men the independence that republicans celebrated; it seemed a more appropriate source of achievement than patronage or influence. For many Americans wealth soon became the sole means and—in the new republican society—the proper means of distinguishing one person from another.

By the end of the eighteenth century, the character of all sorts of former paternalistic dependencies was changing. Apprentices were no longer "children" in the master's family; rather, they were considered trainees in a business that was now often conducted outside the household. Paternalism in labor relations was now replaced by impersonal cash payments, and journeymen moved more frequently from one master to another.* In many crafts both masters and journeymen saw themselves less as members of a common household and more as employers and employees. Their interests were more distinct and conflicting than they had been before; and they formed new class-conscious organizations to protect these interests. Between 1786 and 1816 at least twelve major strikes by various craftsmen occurred—the first major strikes by employees against employers in American history. Meanwhile masters resorted more and more to the courts to enforce what had once been seen as a mutual and personal relationship.

---

*A journeyman was a craftsman who had ceased to be an apprentice but was not yet willing or able to set himself up as an independent master.

The Destruction of Corporate Privilege Many of the individual and face-to-face relationships that had characterized the older society gradually gave way to larger and more impersonal business associations. Although only a half-dozen business charters had been granted in the entire colonial period, corporate grants multiplied after the Revolution. The republican state legislatures created private banks, insurance companies, and manufacturing concerns, and they licensed entrepreneurs to operate bridges, roads, and canals.

The states issued 11 charters of incorporation between 1781 and 1785, 22 between 1786 and 1790, and 114 between 1791 and 1795. Between 1800 and 1817 they granted nearly 1,800 corporate charters; Massachusetts alone had more corporations than existed in all of Europe. If one town had an incorporated bank, it seemed that every town wanted one, and the annually elected popular state legislatures, beset by hosts of new interests, were readily pressured into granting them.

This rapid creation of corporations typified the increasingly fragmented nature of the public interest under popularly elected governments. As far back as the Virginia Company at the time of the original settlements, chartered corporations had been instruments by which the government harnessed private enterprise to carry out such desirable public goals as founding a colony, maintaining a college, or building a bridge. In the new republican society, however, not only were these forms of legal privilege beginning to be regarded with suspicion, but it was no longer clear to whom the states ought to grant legal authority. So mistrusted was legal privilege in the egalitarian atmosphere of the early republic that these corporate monopolies could be justified only if the states made them available virtually to everybody. This practice, of course, destroyed their exclusiveness. If nearly everybody had access to the corporate powers granted by the states, then what had once been a privilege now became a right. And as rights, these corporate charters, even though issued by state legislatures, were immune from future legislative tampering. Eventually this view was endorsed by the United States Supreme Court in the *Dartmouth College* case of 1819.

In this famous case the Court decided that the charter of Dartmouth College, although it was originally granted by the New Hampshire legislature and had a public purpose, was a private contract that the legislature could not violate. The states in the post-Revolutionary years therefore not only parceled out their legal authority to individuals and groups in the society, but at the same time lost control of what they dispersed. Unexpected and disturbing as these disintegrating developments were to Jefferson and other devout republicans, they were only the logical consequence of the Revolution's promise to break up politically supported privilege in order to allow free rein to individual talent and energy.

The Betterment of Humanity

The republicanism of the Revolutionary era was not just exhilarating; it was contagious as well. Its optimistic liberalism, its promise of beginning everything anew, could not be confined to governmental reform or to the stimulation of manufacturing and commerce. Inevitably it spilled out into all areas of American life.

Following the Revolution there was a suddenly aroused enthusiasm for putting the humanitarian hopes of the Enlightenment into practice. Drawing on the thoughts of the great seventeenth-century English philosopher John Locke, eighteenth-century liberals stressed the capacity of human nature to be shaped by experience and external circumstances. Placed in a proper republican environment, people could develop in healthy ways that the rigid Old World society had not permitted. From these enlightened assumptions flowed the reforming liberalism that would affect the Revolutionary era and all subsequent American history as well.

Educational and Social Reform　　Since republicanism depended on a knowledgeable citizenry, the Revolution immediately inspired educational efforts of every conceivable sort. American leaders formed numerous scientific organizations and medical societies and produced many scholarly magazines. Gentleman-scientists and amateur philosophers gave lectures and wrote essays on everything from raising Merino sheep to expelling noxious vapors from wells. They compiled geographical and historical studies of the states. And they prepared elaborate plans for educational structures ranging from elementary schools to a national university.

Although by 1776 there were only nine colleges in America, sixteen more had been founded by 1800. By the early nineteenth century, colleges—mostly religiously inspired and short-lived—were being created by the dozens. Yet in the decades immediately following the Revolution, most of the high hopes of the Revolutionary leaders for the establishment of publicly supported educational systems were not fulfilled largely because of penny-pinching legislatures and religious jealousies. Even in New England, which had a long tradition of public education, privately supported academies sprang up in the post-Revolutionary years to replace the older town-supported grammar schools. Nevertheless, the republican ideal of the state's fundamental responsibility to educate all its citizens remained alive and was eventually realized in the educational reform movement of the second quarter of the nineteenth century.*

All social institutions were affected by this Revolutionary idealism. Americans grasped at the possibility that they might change their environment, even their natural environment, and thus their character. When the fast-growing cities were struck by epidemics of yellow fever, Americans cleaned the streets and built public waterworks for sanitation. If the heat and cold of America's climate were too extreme, they cleared forests and drained marshes—and congratulated themselves on having moderated the weather. They now regarded virtually every sort of social victim as salvageable. Societies for assisting widows, immigrants,

---

*See chapter 13, pp. 412–17.

Abigail Adams (1744–1818)
Though unschooled, the wife of John Adams was a confident, intelligent, and widely read woman. Occasionally she expressed her resentment at the circumscribed role allowed to women in the eighteenth century, playfully urging John in 1776 to "remember the ladies" in his plans for enhancing liberty. But generally she was very willing to sacrifice herself for her husband and to accept her femininity "as a punishment for the transgressions of Eve."

debtors, and other distressed groups were formed in the cities. More charitable organizations were established in the decade and a half following Independence than in the entire colonial period. Jefferson and other Revolutionary leaders drew up plans for liberalizing the harsh penal codes inherited from the colonial period. Pennsylvania led the way in the 1790s by abolishing the death penalty for all crimes except murder. Instead of—as in the past—publicly punishing criminals by such bodily penalties as whipping, mutilation, and execution, that state began the experiment of confining criminals in private cells in penitentiaries that were designed to work on the criminals' minds.

The Family and Women

Republicanism even affected the transformation of the family that was taking place in many parts of the Western world at the end of the eighteenth century. In a republican society children could no longer be regarded simply as a means of making money for the family and bringing honor to it. Everyone in the family had to be treated individually and equally. Thus the new Revolutionary state governments repealed aristocratic colonial laws that had confined the inheritance of property to the eldest son (primogeniture) and to special lines of heirs (entail). Family-arranged marriages increasingly gave way to ties that were based on romantic love, and novelists and others writing in the post-Revolutionary years stressed the importance of raising children to become rational and independent citizens.

Republicanism also raised the status of women. It was now said that women as wives and mothers had a special role: that of cultivating in their husbands and children the moral feelings—virtue and social affection—necessary to hold a sprawling and competitive republican society together. Although some American leaders, among them the physician and humanitarian Benjamin Rush, concluded that republicanism required women to be educated along with men, others feared that female education would lead only to vanity and an affected gentility. Besides, asked Timothy Dwight, president of Yale, if women were educated, "Who will make our puddings?"

At the same time that women were being urged to make themselves useful in a distinct domestic sphere, they were becoming more economically important and independent. Economic developments made it possible for women to earn their own incomes by working in handicrafts at home, hence enabling them to purchase more and more luxury items and conveniences. Once they had gained increased independence by earning money at home, women found it easier to work outside the household, as factory workers and later as teachers. Although the development of a new sphere of domestic usefulness for women may seem a step backward by modern standards, it was at the time liberating, and it intensified the advance, which had begun in the colonial period, over the dependent, inferior position that women had traditionally held.

Antislavery   Perhaps the institution that was most directly and substantially affected by the liberalizing spirit of republicanism was slavery. To be sure, the enslavement of nearly half a million blacks was not ended at the Revolution, and in modern eyes this failure, amid all the high-blown talk of liberty and equality, becomes the one glaring and hypocritical inconsistency of the Revolutionary era. Nevertheless the Revolution did suddenly and effectively end the social and intellectual climate that had allowed black slavery to exist in the colonies for more than a century without substantial questioning. The colonists had generally taken slavery for granted as part of the natural order of society and as one aspect of the general brutality and cheapness of life in those premodern and prehumanitarian times. Bondage and servitude in many forms had continued to exist in pre-Revolutionary America, and the colonists had felt little need to question or defend slavery any more than other forms of debasement. Now, however, republican citizenship suddenly brought into question all kinds of personal dependency. For the first time Americans were compelled to confront the slavery in their midst. They had to recognize that it was a deviation, a "peculiar institution," and that if they were to retain it they would have to explain and justify it.

Even before the Declaration of Independence, the colonists' struggle against what they called political "slavery" had exposed the contradiction of their toleration of chattel slavery. The initial efforts to end the contradiction were directed at the slave trade. In 1774 the Continental Congress urged the abolition of this trade, and a half-dozen states quickly complied. In 1775 the Quakers of Philadelphia formed the first antislavery society in the world, and soon similar societies were organized elsewhere, even in the South. During the war the

Congress and the northern states, as well as Maryland, gave freedom to black slaves who enlisted in their armies. In various ways the Revolution worked to weaken slavery.

In the North, where slavery of a less harsh sort than existed in the South had been widespread but not deeply rooted in the society or economy, the institution was open to political pressure, and it slowly began to disappear. In the decades following the Revolution, most northern states moved to destroy slavery. By 1830 there were fewer than 3,000 slaves out of a northern black population of more than 125,000. The Revolutionary vision of a society of independent freeholders led the Congress in the 1780s to forbid slavery in the newly organized Northwest Territory between the Appalachians and the Mississippi River. The new federal Constitution of 1787 promised an end to the slave trade after twenty years—that is, in 1808—and many hoped that this action would cripple the institution of slavery.

In the South, however, despite initial criticism by Jefferson, Madison, and other enlightened social thinkers, slavery was too deeply entrenched to be abolished by legislative or judicial action. Southern whites who had been in the forefront of the Revolutionary movement and among the most fervent spokesmen for its liberalism now began to realize for the first time that the South was different from the rest of America. In the 1790s slave insurrections on the French West Indian island of Santo Domingo, together with the tales of horror brought by thousands of fleeing white refugees to American ports, created fears about the future stability of America's slave society. By this time the South had to live with a growing realization that the American claim that people everywhere had a right to seek their freedom meant *all* people, blacks as well as whites. Liberalism in the South was now on the defensive.

SUGGESTED READINGS

For a summary of the history writing covering the eighteenth-century tradition of republicanism, see Robert E. Shalhope, "Toward a Republican Synthesis: The Emergence of an Understanding of Republicanism in American Historiography," *Wm. and Mary Q.,* 3d. ser., 29 (1972). Studies emphasizing the peculiar character of this tradition include Bernard Bailyn, *The Ideological Origins of the American Revolution* (1967); J. G. A. Pocock, *The Machiavellian Moment* (1975); Franco Venturi, *Utopia and Reform in the Enlightenment* (1971); Gerald Stourzh, *Alexander Hamilton and the Idea of Republican Government* (1970); and Gordon S. Wood, *The Creation of the American Republic, 1776–1787* (1969). Garry Wills, *Inventing America: Jefferson's Declaration of Independence* (1978), stresses the importance of Scottish moral sense philosophy and the natural sociableness of people in Jefferson's thought. On the origins of the Americans' conception of the individual's relationship to the state, see James H. Kettner, *The Development of American Citizenship, 1608–1870* (1978). For the influence of antiquity, see Richard Gummere, *The American Colonial Mind and the Classical Tradition* (1963), and Meyer Reinhold, ed., *The Classick Pages* (1975). For the way in which many Europeans viewed the New World in the eighteenth century, see Durand Echeverria, *Mirage in the West* (1957).

The fullest account of state constitution making and politics is Allan Nevins, *The American States During and After the Revolution, 1775–1789* (1924). Elisha P. Douglass, *Rebels and Democrats* (1955), is important in emphasizing the radical and populist impulses in the states. Among the most significant of the state studies are Philip A. Crowl, *Maryland During and After the Revolution* (1943); Richard P. McCormick, *Experiment in Independence: New Jersey in the Critical Period, 1781–1789* (1950); Irwin H. Polishook, *Rhode Island and the Union, 1774–1795* (1969); Robert J. Taylor, *Western Massachusetts in the Revolution* (1954); and Alfred F. Young, *The Democratic Republicans of New York: The Origins, 1763–1797* (1967). Jackson T. Main, *The Sovereign States, 1775–1783* (1973), describes state affairs during the war. J. R. Pole, *Political Representation in England and the Origins of the American Republic* (1966), has some excellent chapters on state politics during the Revolutionary and immediate post-Revolutionary years. Merrill Jensen, in *The Articles of Confederation . . . 1774–1781* (1940) and *The New Nation . . . 1781–1789* (1950), describes the political and social conflicts within the Confederation government and stresses the achievements of the Articles. H. James Henderson, *Party Politics in the Continental Congress* (1974), emphasizes a sectional rather than a social division among the delegates to the national government. The best history of the Congress is Jack N. Rakove, *The Beginnings of National Politics* (1979). Peter S. Onuf, *The Origins of the Federal Republic* (1953) deals with jurisdictional controversies among the states and the Confederation between 1775 and 1787.

The starting point for appreciating the social changes of the Revolution is the short essay by J. Franklin Jameson, *The American Revolution Considered as a Social Movement* (1926). The last two chapters of James A. Henretta, *The Evolution of American Society, 1700–1815* (1973), summarize the social effects of the war and the Revolution. J. Kirby Martin, *Men in Rebellion: Higher Government Leaders and the Coming of the American Revolution* (1973); Jackson T. Main, *The Upper House in Revolutionary America, 1763–1788* (1967); and Main, "Government by the People: The American Revolution and the Democratization of the Legislatures," *Wm. and Mary Q.,* 3d ser., 28 (1966), document the displacement of elites in politics during the Revolution. Chilton Williamson, *American Suffrage from Property to Democracy, 1760–1860* (1960), describes the expansion of voting rights. A neat account of Concord, Massachusetts, in the Revolution is Robert A. Gross, *The Minutemen and Their World* (1976).

A helpful survey of American social history is Rowland Berthoff, *An Unsettled People* (1971). But it has not replaced the encyclopedic History of American Life Series edited by Arthur M. Schlesinger and Dixon Ryan Fox. The two volumes covering the Revolutionary era are Evarts B. Greene, *The Revolutionary Generation, 1763–1790* (1943), and John Allen Krout and Dixon Ryan Fox, *The Completion of Independence, 1790–1830* (1944). Population developments are summarized by J. Potter, "The Growth of Population in America, 1700–1860," in David Glass and D. E. Eversley, eds., *Population in History* (1965). An important social history that goes well beyond its title is David J. Rothman, *The Discovery of the Asylum: Social Order and Disorder in the New Republic* (1971). *The Press and the American Revolution,* ed. Bernard Bailyn and John B. Hench (1980), is an important collection. See also the relevant chapters in Richard D. Brown, *Knowledge Is Power: The Diffusion of Information in Early America, 1700–1865* (1989).

Two surveys of economic life are useful: Stuart Bruchey, *The Roots of American Economic Growth, 1607–1861* (1965), and Douglass C. North, *The Economic Growth of the United States, 1790–1860* (1961). See also the appropriate chapters in John J. McCusker and Russell R. Menard, *The Economy of British America, 1607–1789* (1985). To understand the interrelated nature of the social, economic, and political processes in this period, the student can find no better work than Oscar Handlin and Mary Handlin, *Commonwealth: A Study of the Role of Government in the American Economy: Massachusetts, 1774–1861* (rev. ed., 1969). It is especially important for its analysis of the changing nature of the corporation.

On the commercial effects of the Revolution, see Curtis P. Nettles, *The Emergence of a National Economy, 1775–1815* (1962), Robert A. East, *Business Enterprise in the American Revolutionary Era* (1938), Ronald Hoffman, ed., *The Economy of Early America: The Revolutionary Period, 1763–1790* (1988), and Cathy Matson and Peter S. Onuf, *A Union of Interests* (1989). On the plight of the loyalists, see Wallace Brown, *The Good Americans* (1969), and Mary Beth Norton, *The British-Americans: The Loyalist Exiles in England, 1774–1789* (1972).

On the Enlightenment, see Henry May, *The Enlightenment in America* (1976), and Henry S. Commager, *Empire of Reason* (1977). The standard survey is Russel B. Nye, *The Cultural Life of the New Nation, 1776–1830* (1960). See also Joseph J. Ellis, *After the Revolution: Profiles of Early American Culture* (1979), and Robert E. Shalhope, *The Roots of Democracy: American Thought and Culture, 1760–1800* (1990). A particularly important study of education is Carl F. Kaestle, *The Evolution of an Urban School System* (1973). See also Rush Welter, *Popular Education and Democratic Thought in America* (1962), and Douglas Sloan, *The Scottish Enlightenment and the American College Ideal* (1971), and David W. Robson, *Educating Republicans: The College in the Era of the American Revolution* (1985). On women, see Mary Beth Norton, *Liberty's Daughters: The Revolutionary Experience of American Women, 1750–1800* (1980), Linda Kerber, *Women of the Republic: Intellect and Ideology in Revolutionary America* (1980), and Nancy Cott, *The Bonds of Womanhood* (1977). Benjamin Quarles, *The Negro in the American Revolution* (1961), is the best study of the contribution of blacks to the Revolution. On slavery and opposition to it, see Winthrop Jordan, *White over Black: American Attitudes Toward the Negro, 1550–1812* (1968), and David Brion Davis, *The Problem of Slavery in the Age of Revolution, 1770–1823* (1975). On the abolition of slavery in the North, see Arthur Zilversmit, *The First Emancipation* (1967).

10

The Federalist Age

⁓

*T*HE AMERICAN Revolution, like all revolutions, could not fulfill every high hope of its leaders. Within a decade after the Declaration of Independence was signed, many Revolutionary leaders had come to doubt the way America was going. Not only were they eager to lessen the power of the state legislatures, but at the same time they were becoming increasingly aware that the Confederation Congress was too weak to accomplish its tasks, both at home and abroad. In the mid-1780s frustration with piecemeal changes in the Articles of Confederation came together with mounting concern over examples of democratic despotism and other political and social conditions in the states to produce a powerful momentum for drastic constitutional change. The result was the federal Constitution of 1787.

This new national Constitution, which replaced the Articles of Confederation, limited the authority of the states and created an unprecedented concentration of power at the federal level. Many Americans could only conclude that the new Constitution represented as radical a change as the Revolution itself. At last, in the eyes of some, the inauguration of a new federal government promised the harmony and stability that would allow America to become a great and glorious nation.

The Critical Period

For some Americans the 1780s had become a very critical period, a point at which the Revolution and the entire experiment in republicanism seemed to be in danger. The very success of the Revolution in opening up opportunities for economic prosperity to new and lower levels of the population helped to create a sense of crisis among certain members of the Revolutionary elite.

Too many ordinary people, some felt, were distorting republican equality, defying legitimate authority, and blurring those natural distinctions that all gentlemen, even republican gentlemen, thought essential for social order. Everywhere, even among the sturdy independent yeoman-farmers—Jefferson's "chosen people of God"—private interests, selfishness, and moneymaking seemed to be destroying social affection and public spirit—the very qualities of virtue that were required of republicans. The expressions of democratic despotism by the state legislatures seemed to be evidence that the people were too self-interested to be republicans. Some feared, therefore, that America was doomed to share the fate that had befallen the ancient republics, Britain, and other corrupt nations. Americans, Governor William Livingston of New Jersey concluded in 1787, "do not exhibit the virtue that is necessary to support a republican government." Many thought that this unrepublican character of the people was most clearly revealed in the behavior of the greatly strengthened state legislatures.

The Democratization of the State Legislatures The radical changes in representation that accompanied the Revolution had democratized the state assemblies by increasing the number of members and by altering their social character. Men of more humble and more rural origins—and less educated than those who had sat in the colonial legislatures—now became representatives. In New Hampshire, for example, in 1765 the colonial house of representatives had contained only thirty-four members, almost all well-to-do gentlemen from the coastal region around Portsmouth. By 1786 the state's house of representatives had increased to eighty-eight members. Most of these were ordinary farmers or men of moderate wealth, and many were from the western areas of the state. In other states the change was less dramatic but no less important. It was reflected in the shifts (or attempted shifts) of many of the state capitals from their former colonial locations on the eastern coastline to new sites in the interior—from Portsmouth to Concord in New Hampshire, from New York City to Albany in New York, from Williamsburg to Richmond in Virginia, from New Bern to Raleigh in North Carolina, from Charleston to Columbia in South Carolina, and from Savannah to Augusta in Georgia.

Everywhere, electioneering and the open competition for office increased, along with demands for greater public access to governmental activities. The number of contested elections and the turnover of legislative seats multiplied. Assembly proceedings were opened to the public, and a growing number of newspapers (which now included dailies) began to report legislative debates. Self-appointed leaders, speaking for newly aroused groups and localities, took advantage of the enlarged suffrage and the annual elections of the legislatures (a radical innovation in most states) to seek membership in the assemblies. New petty entrepreneurs like Abraham Yates, a part-time lawyer and shoemaker of Albany, and William Findley, a Scotch-Irish ex-weaver of western Pennsylvania, bypassed the traditional hierarchy and vaulted into political leadership in the states.

Local Factionalism Under these circumstances a number of the state legislatures could scarcely fulfill what many Revolutionaries in 1776 had assumed was their republican responsibility to promote the general good. In every state decisions had to be made about what to do with the loyalists and their confiscated property, about the distribution of taxes among the citizens, and about the economy. Yet with the general political instability, the common welfare in the various states was increasingly difficult to define. By the 1780s James Madison concluded that "a spirit of *locality*" in the state legislatures was destroying "the aggregate interests of the community." This localist spirit, he thought, was a consequence of having small districts and towns elect members of the state legislatures. Each representative, said Ezra Stiles, president of Yale College, was concerned only with the special interests of his electors. Whenever a bill was read in the legislature, "every one instantly thinks how it will affect his constituents."

Narrow-minded politics of this kind was not new to America. But the multiplication of economic and social interests in the post-Revolutionary years, along with the greater sensitivity of the enlarged popular assemblies to the conflicting demands of these interests, now dramatically increased its intensity and importance. Farmers in debt urged low taxes, the suspension of court actions to recover debts, and the printing of paper money. Merchants and creditors called for high taxes on land, the protection of private contracts, and the encouragement of foreign trade. Artisans pleaded for the regulation of the prices of agricultural products, the abolition of mercantile monopolies, and tariff protection against imported manufactured goods. And entrepreneurs everywhere petitioned for legal privileges and corporate grants.

All this political scrambling among contending interests made lawmaking in the states seem chaotic. Laws, as the Vermont Council of Censors said in 1786 in a common complaint, were "altered—realtered—made better—made worse; and kept in such a fluctuating position, that persons in civil commission scarce know what is law." As James Madison pointed out, more laws were enacted by the states in the decade following Independence than in the entire colonial period. Many of them were simply private acts for individuals or resolutions that satisfied minor grievances. But every effort by the legislatures to respond to the excited pleas and pressures of all the various groups alienated as many people as it satisfied and brought lawmaking itself into contempt.

By the mid-1780s many American leaders had come to believe that the state legislatures, not the governors, were the political authority to be most feared. Some of the legislatures were violating the individual rights of property owners through their excessive printing of paper money and their various acts on behalf of debtors. Furthermore, in all the states the assemblies pushed beyond the generous grants of legislative authority of the 1776 Revolutionary constitutions and were absorbing numerous executive and judicial duties. It began to seem that the legislative power of the people was no more trustworthy than the detested royal power had been. Legislators were supposedly the representatives of the people who annually elected them. But "173 despots would surely be as oppressive as one," wrote Jefferson in 1785 in his *Notes on Virginia*. "An *elective despotism* was not the government we fought for."

Revision of the State Constitutions

These growing fears of tyrannical legislatures forced many leaders to have second thoughts about their popularly elected assemblies. Indeed, the ink was scarcely dry on the Revolutionary state constitutions before some were suggesting that they needed to be revised. Beginning with the New York constitution in 1777 and proceeding through the constitutions of Massachusetts in 1780 and New Hampshire in 1784, constitution makers now sought a very different distribution of powers of government from that made in 1776.

Instead of placing all power in the legislatures, particularly in the lower houses, and draining all power from the governors, as the early state constitutions had done, these later constitutions strengthened the executives, senates, and judiciaries. The Massachusetts constitution of 1780 especially seemed to many to have recaptured some of the best characteristics of the English constitutional balance, which had been forgotten during the popular enthusiasm of 1776. The new Massachusetts governor, with a fixed salary and elected directly by the people, had more of the independence and some of the powers of the old royal governors, including those of appointing to offices and vetoing legislation.

With the Massachusetts constitution as a model, reformers from other states worked to revise their constitutions. The popular legislatures were reduced in size, and their authority was curbed. Senates, or upper houses, were instituted where they did not exist, as in Pennsylvania, Georgia, and Vermont. In states where senates did exist, they were made more stable by lengthening their terms and by requiring higher property qualifications for their members. The governors were freed of their dependence on the legislatures, and they were given a clearer responsibility for government. And judges became independent guardians of the constitutions. By 1790 Pennsylvania, South Carolina, and Georgia had reformed their constitutions along these more conservative lines. New Hampshire, Delaware, and Vermont soon followed in the early 1790s.

At the same time that political leaders were trying to restrengthen the authority of governors, senators, and judges, they were also trying to limit the powers of the legislatures by appealing to the "fundamental law" that was presumably embodied in these written documents. Since many of the constitutions had been created by simple legislative act, it was not easy to draw a line between "fundamental" and ordinary law. At first several of the states had grappled with various devices to ensure that their constitutions remained "fundamental" law. Some simply declared their constitutions to be "fundamental"; others required a special majority or successive acts of the legislature for amending the constitution. But none of these measures proved effective against repeated legislative encroachments.

Out of these kinds of pressures, both logical and political, Americans gradually moved toward institutionalizing the belief that if the constitution was to be truly immune from legislative tampering, it would have to be created, as Jefferson said in 1783, "by a power superior to that of the ordinary legislature." For a solution Americans fell back on the institution of the convention. In 1775–76 the convention had been merely an ad hoc legislative assembly, lacking legal sanction but made necessary by the crown's refusal to call together the regular representatives of the people. Now, however, the convention became a special alternative institution representing the people and having exclusive authority to write or amend a constitution. When Massachusetts and New Hampshire came to write new constitutions in the late 1770s and early 1780s, the proper pattern of constitution making and constitution altering had become clear. Constitutions were formed by specially elected conventions and then submitted to the people for ratification.

With the idea growing that a constitution was fundamental law, immune from legislative changes, some state judges during the 1780s began cautiously moving in isolated cases to impose restraints on what the assemblies were enacting as law. In effect they said to the legislatures, as George Wythe, judge of the Virginia supreme court, did in 1782, "Here is the limit of your authority; and hither shall you go, but no further." These were the hesitant beginnings of what would come to be called judicial review.* But as yet many leaders were unwilling to allow appointed judges to set aside laws that had been made by the people represented in democratically elected legislatures. It appeared obviously unrepublican.

As vigorously as all these state reforms were tried in the 1780s, however, to many they did not seem sufficient. By the mid-1780s some reformers were thinking of shifting the arena of constitutional change from the states to the nation and were considering a modification of the structure of the central government as the best and perhaps only answer to America's political and social problems.

Domestic Weakness of the Confederation Even before the Articles of Confederation were ratified in 1781, the experiences of war had exposed the weakness of the Congress and had encouraged some Americans to think about making changes in the central government. By 1780 the war was dragging on longer than anyone had expected, and the skyrocketing inflation of the paper money that was being used to finance it was unsettling commerce and business. Congressional delegates were barred from serving more than three years in any six-year period, and leadership in the Confederation was unstable and confused. The states were ignoring congressional resolutions and were refusing to supply their allotted contributions to the central government. The Congress stopped paying interest on the public debt. The Continental army was smoldering with resentment at the lack of pay and was falling apart through

---

*For judicial review, see chapter 11, pp. 350–54.

desertions and even outbreaks of mutiny. All these circumstances were forcing merchant and creditor interests, especially those that were centered in the mid-Atlantic states, to seek to add to the powers of the Congress. They tried to strengthen the Congress by broadly interpreting the Articles, by directly amending the Articles (which required the consent of all the states), and even by threatening military force.

A shift in congressional leadership in the early 1780s demonstrated the increasing influence of these concerned groups. Older popular radicals such as Richard Henry Lee and Arthur Lee of Virginia and Samuel Adams of Massachusetts were replaced by such younger men as James Madison of Virginia and Alexander Hamilton of New York. These new leaders were more interested in authority and stability than in popular liberty. Disillusioned by the Confederation's ineffectiveness, these nationalists in the Congress set about reversing the localist and power-weakening emphasis of the Revolution. They strengthened the regular army at the expense of the militia and promised pensions to the Continental army officers. They reorganized the departments of war, foreign affairs, and finance in the Congress and replaced the committees that had been running them with individuals.

The key man in the nationalists' program was Robert Morris, a wealthy Philadelphia merchant who was made superintendent of finance and virtual head of the Confederation in 1781. Morris undertook to stabilize the economy and to involve financial and commercial groups with the central government. He persuaded the Congress to recommend to the states that paper-money laws be repealed and to require that the states' contributions to the general expenses be paid in specie—gold or silver. And he sought to establish a national bank and to make the federal government's bonds more secure for investors.

Carrying out this nationalist program depended on amending the Articles so as to grant the Confederation the power to levy a 5 percent duty on imports. Once the Congress had adequate revenues independent of the states, the Confederation could pay its debts and would become more attractive to prospective buyers of its bonds. Although Morris was able to get the Congress to charter the Bank of North America, the rest of the nationalists' economic proposals narrowly failed. Not only did the states ultimately refuse to approve the tax amendment, but many were slow in supplying money that had been requested of them by the Congress. Nor was the Congress able to get even a restricted authority to regulate commerce.

After the victory at Yorktown in October 1781 and the opening of peace negotiations with Great Britain, the states lost interest in the Congress. Some individuals became desperate. The prospect of the Congress's demobilizing the army without fulfilling its promises of back pay and pensions created a crisis that brought the United States as close to a military coup d'état as it has ever been. In March 1783 the officers of Washington's army that were encamped at Newburgh, New York, on the Hudson River, issued an address to the Congress concerning their pay. They actually considered some sort of military action against the

Confederation. Only when Washington personally intervened and refused to support a movement that was designed, he said, "to open the floodgates of civil discord, and deluge our rising empire in blood" was the crisis averted.

News of the peace treaty shattered much of the unionist sentiment that had existed during the war. By December 1783 the Congress, in Jefferson's opinion, had lost most of its usefulness. "The constant session of Congress," he said, "can not be necessary in time of peace." After clearing up the most urgent business, the delegates should "separate and return to our respective states, leaving only a Committee of the states," and thus "destroy the strange idea of their being a permanent body, which has unaccountably taken possession of the heads of their constituents."

Congressional power, which had been substantial during the war years, now began to disintegrate. The delegates increasingly complained of how difficult it was even to gather a quorum. The Congress could not even agree on a permanent home for itself: it wandered from Philadelphia to Princeton, New Jersey; to Annapolis, Maryland; to Trenton, New Jersey; and finally to New York City. The states reasserted their authority and began taking over the payment of the federal debt that many had earlier hoped to make the cement of union. By 1786 nearly one-third of the Confederation's securities had been converted into state bonds, thus creating a vested interest among public creditors in the sovereignty of the individual states. Under these circumstances the influence of those, in Hamilton's term, "who think continentally" rapidly declined, and the chances of amending the Confederation piecemeal declined with them. The only hope of reform now seemed to lie in some sort of convention of all the states.

International Weakness of the Confederation

In Europe the reputation of the United States dwindled as rapidly as did its credit. The Dutch and French would lend money only at extraordinary rates of interest. Since American ships now lacked the protection of the British flag, many of them were seized by corsairs from the Muslim states of North Africa, and their crews were sold as slaves. The Congress had no money to pay the necessary tribute and ransoms to these Barbary pirates.

It was even difficult for the new republican confederacy to maintain its territorial integrity in the late-eighteenth-century world of hostile empires. Britain refused to send a diplomatic minister to the United States and ignored its treaty obligations to evacuate its military posts in the Northwest, claiming that the United States had not honored its own commitments. The treaty of peace had specified that the Confederation would recommend to the states that loyalist property confiscated during the Revolution be restored, and that neither side would make laws obstructing the recovery of prewar debts. When the states flouted these treaty obligations, the impotent Confederation could do nothing.

Britain was known to be plotting with the Indians and encouraging separatist movements in the Northwest and in the Vermont borderlands, and Spain was doing the same in the Southwest. Spain in fact refused to recognize American claims in the territory between the Ohio River and Florida. In 1784, in an effort to influence American settlers moving into Kentucky and Tennessee, Spain closed the Mississippi River to American trade. Many Westerners were ready to deal with any government that could ensure access to the sea for their agricultural produce. As Washington noted in 1784, they were "on a pivot. The touch of a feather would turn them any way."

In 1785–86, John Jay, a New Yorker and the secretary of foreign affairs, negotiated a treaty with the Spanish minister to the United States, Diego de Gardoqui. By the terms of this agreement, Spain was opened to American trade in return for America's renunciation of its right to navigate the Mississippi for several decades. Out of fear of being denied an outlet to the sea in the West, the southern states prevented the necessary nine-state majority in the Congress from agreeing to the treaty. But the willingness of a majority of seven states to sacrifice western interests for the sake of northern merchants aroused long-existing sectional jealousies and threatened to shatter the Union.

Toward the Phila-delphia Convention The Confederation's inability to regulate commerce finally brought about reform of the Articles. Jefferson, Madison, and other leaders with agrarian interests feared that if American farmers were prohibited from selling their surplus crops freely in Europe, not only would the industrious character of the farmers be undermined, but the United States would be unable to pay for manufactured goods imported from Europe, and would therefore be compelled to begin large-scale manufacturing for itself. These developments in turn would eventually destroy the farmer-citizenry on which republicanism was based and would create in America the same kind of corrupt, rank-conscious, and dependent society that existed in Europe.

Yet the mercantilist empires of the major European nations remained generally closed to the new republic in the 1780s. John Adams in Britain and Jefferson in France made strong diplomatic efforts to develop new international commercial relationships based on the free exchange of goods, but these efforts failed. The French were unwilling to take as much American produce as had been expected, and Britain effectively closed its markets to competitive American goods while recapturing American consumer markets for its own goods. The Confederation lacked the authority to retaliate with its own trade regulations, and several attempts to grant the Congress a restricted power over commerce were lost amid state and sectional jealousies. The Confederation Congress watched helplessly as the separate states attempted to pass conflicting navigation acts of their own. By the mid-1780s, for example, Connecticut was laying heavier duties on goods from Massachusetts than on those from Great Britain.

By 1786 these accumulated pressures made some sort of revision of the Articles inevitable. Virginia's desire for trade regulation led to a convention of several states at Annapolis, Maryland, in September 1786. Those who attended this meeting quickly realized that commerce could not be considered apart from other problems and called for a larger convention in Philadelphia the following year. After several states agreed to send delegates to Philadelphia, the Confederation Congress belatedly recognized the approaching convention and in February 1787 authorized it to revise and amend the Articles of Confederation.

Although by 1787 nearly all of America's political leaders agreed that some reform of the Articles was necessary, few expected what the Philadelphia Convention eventually created—a new Constitution that utterly transformed the structure of the central government and promised a radical weakening of the power of the states. The extraordinarily powerful national government that emerged from Philadelphia had far more than the additional congressional powers that were required to solve the United States' difficulties in credit, commerce, and foreign affairs. Given the Revolutionaries' loyalty to their states and their deep-rooted fears of centralized governmental authority, the formation of the new Constitution was a truly remarkable achievement. It cannot be explained simply by the obvious weaknesses of the Articles of Confederation.

In the end it was the problems within the separate states during the 1780s that made possible the constitutional reform of the central government. The confusing and unjust laws coming out of the state legislatures, Madison informed Jefferson in 1787, had become "so frequent and so flagrant as to alarm the most stedfast friends of Republicanism." These popular abuses by state legislatures, said Madison, "contributed more to that uneasiness which produced the Convention, and prepared the public mind for a general reform, than those which accrued to our national character and interest from the inadequacy of the Confederation to its immediate objects."

In 1786 a rebellion of nearly 2,000 debtor farmers who were threatened with foreclosure of their mortgaged property broke out in western Massachusetts. This rebellion, led by a former militia captain, Daniel Shays, confirmed many of these anxieties about state politics. The insurrection, which temporarily closed the courts and threatened a federal arsenal, occurred in the very state that was considered to have the best-balanced constitution. Although Shays's rebels were defeated by militia troops, his sympathizers were victorious at the polls early in 1787. The newly chosen state representatives soon enacted debtor relief legislation that added to the growing fears of legislative tyranny.

Thus by 1786–87 the reconstruction of the central government was being sought as a means of correcting not only the weaknesses of the Articles, but also the democratic despotism and the internal political abuses of the states. A new central government, some believed, could save both the Congress from the states and the states from themselves. And new groups joined those already working to invigorate the national government. Urban artisans hoped that a stronger national government would prevent competition from British imports. Southerners, particularly in Virginia, wanted to gain representation in the national government proportional to their growing population. And most important, members of the gentry up and down the continent momentarily submerged their sectional and economic differences in the face of what seemed a threat to individual liberty from the tyranny of legislative majorities within the states. Creating a new

Daniel Shays and Jacobb Shattucks
Shays and Shattucks, former militia officers, were leaders of the uprising of aggrieved western Massachusetts farmers in 1786. The farmers, calling themselvees "Regulators," protested the shortage of money and the foreclosures of mortgages and imprisonments for debt. Shays's Rebellion had a powerful effect on conservative leaders and helped compel reform of the national government.

central government was no longer simply a matter of cementing the Union, or of standing up strong in foreign affairs, or of satisfying the demands of particular creditor, merchant, and army interests. It was now a matter, as Madison declared, that would "decide forever the fate of republican government."

The Federal Constitution

The meeting of the Philadelphia Convention that drafted the federal Constitution in the summer of 1787 was very much a revolutionary action. Yet such were the circumstances and climate of opinion of the post-Revolutionary years in America that the sudden calling of a constitutional convention and the creation of an entirely new and different sort of federal republican government in 1787 seemed remarkably natural and legitimate.

Fifty-five delegates representing twelve states attended the Philadelphia Convention. (Rhode Island, which feared any national regulation of its trade, refused to have anything to do with efforts to revise the Articles.) Although many of the delegates were young men—their average age was forty-two—most were well educated and experienced members of America's political elite. Thirty-nine had served in the Congress at one time or another, eight had worked in the state constitutional conventions, seven had been state governors, and thirty-four were lawyers. One-third were veterans of the Continental army, that "great dissolvent of state loyalties," as Washington once called it. Nearly all were gentlemen, "natural aristocrats," who took their political superiority for granted as an inevitable consequence of their social and economic position. Washington was made president of the Convention. But some of the outstanding figures of the Revolution were not present: Samuel Adams was ill; Thomas Jefferson and John Adams were serving as ministers abroad; and Richard Henry Lee and Patrick Henry, although selected by the Virginia legislature, refused to attend the Convention. "I smelt a rat," said Henry. The most influential delegations were those of Pennsylvania and Virginia, which included Gouverneur Morris and James Wilson of Pennsylvania, and Edmund Randolph, George Mason, and James Madison of Virginia.

The Virginia Plan   The Virginia delegation took the lead and presented the Convention with its first working proposal. This, the Virginia Plan, was largely the effort of the thirty-seven-year-old Madison, who more than any other person deserves the title "father of the Constitution." He was a short, shy, and soft-spoken man who habitually dressed in black. Madison had not trained for a profession, but he was widely read, possessed a sharp and questioning mind, and had devoted his life to public service. He understood clearly the historical significance of the meeting of the Convention; and it is because he decided to make a detailed private record of the Convention debates that we know so much of what was said that summer in Philadelphia.

Madison's initial proposals for reform were truly radical. As he pointed out, they were not mere expedients or simple revisions of the Articles; they promised "systematic change" of government. Madison wanted to create a general government that would be not a confederation of independent republics but a national republic in its own right. It would exercise direct power over individuals and be organized as most of the state governments were organized, with a single executive, a bicameral legislature, and a separate judiciary.

This national republic would be superimposed on the states. The states, in John Jay's words, would now stand in relation to the central government "in the same light in which counties stand to the state of which they are parts, viz., merely as districts to facilitate the purposes of domestic order of good government." Thus the radical Virginia Plan provided for a two-house national legislature with the authority to legislate "in all cases to which the states are incompetent" and to veto, or negative, "all laws passed by the several states, contravening in the opinion of the national legislature, the articles of union." If the national government had the power to veto all state laws, Madison believed, it could then play the same role the English crown had been supposed to play in the British Empire— that of a "disinterested umpire" over clashing interests.

The New Jersey Plan   For many in the Philadelphia Convention, however, this Virginia Plan was much too extreme. Most delegates were prepared to grant substantial power to the federal government, including the right to tax, regulate commerce, and execute federal laws. But many

James Madison (1751–1836)
*Madison was the greatest political
thinker of the Revolutionary era and
perhaps of all American history. His
was the most critical and undogmatic
mind of the Revolutionary leaders.
More than anyone else, he formulated
the theory that underlaid the new
expanded republic of 1787.*

refused to allow such a weakening of state authority as the Virginia Plan proposed. Opponents of the nationalists, led by the delegates from New Jersey, Connecticut, New York, and Delaware, countered with their own proposal, the New Jersey Plan (so-called because it was introduced by William Paterson of New Jersey). This plan essentially amended the Articles of Confederation by increasing the powers of the Congress, but at the same time it maintained the basic sovereignty of the states. With two such opposite proposals before it, the Convention approached a crisis in the middle of June 1787.

Provisions of the Constitution

During the debate that followed, the nationalists, led by Madison and Wilson, were able to retain the basic features of the Virginia Plan. Although the Convention refused to grant the national legislature a blanket authority "to legislate in all cases to which the separate States are incompetent," it granted the Congress (in Article I, Section 8, of the Constitution) a list of enumerated powers, including the powers to tax, to borrow and coin money, and to regulate commerce. Instead of giving the national legislature the right to veto harmful state laws, as Madison wanted, the Convention forbade the states to exercise certain sovereign powers whose abuse had helped to create the crisis of the 1780s. In Article I, Section 10, of the final Constitution, the states were barred from carrying on foreign relations, levying tariffs, coining money, issuing bills of credit, passing ex post facto laws (which punished actions that were not illegal when they were committed), and doing anything to relieve debtors of the obligations of their contracts.*

---

*For the Constitution, see Appendix.

In contrast to the Congress, which was given extensive fiscal powers, the state governments were rendered nearly economically impotent. Not only did the new federal Constitution prohibit the states from imposing customs duties—the eighteenth century's most common and efficient form of taxation—but it denied the states the authority to issue paper money, and thus succeeded in doing what the British government's various currency acts had earlier tried to do.

The Convention decided on a single strong executive. The president was to stand alone, unencumbered by an executive council except one of his own choosing—his group of cabinet officers. With command over the armed forces, with the authority to direct diplomatic relations, with power over appointments to the executive and judicial branches, and with a four-year term of office and perpetual eligibility for reelection, the president was a high official who, as Patrick Henry later charged, could "easily become a king."

To ensure the president's independence, he was not to be elected by the legislature, as the Virginia Plan had proposed. Since the framers of the Constitution believed that few presidential candidates in the future would enjoy wide popular recognition throughout the country, they provided for local elections of "electors," equal in number to the representatives and senators from each state. These electors would cast ballots for the president. If no candidate received a majority—which in the absence of political parties and organized electioneering was normally expected—the final selection from the five candidates with the most votes would be made by the House of Representatives, with each state delegation having one vote.

The Virginia Plan's suggestion of a separate national judiciary to hold office "during good behavior" was accepted without dispute. The structure of the national judiciary was left to the Congress to devise. However, the right of this judiciary to nullify acts of the Congress or of the state legislatures was as yet by no means clearly established.

The nationalists in the Convention reluctantly gave way on several crucial issues, particularly on the national legislature's authority to veto state legislation. But they fought longest and hardest to hold on to the principle of proportional representation in both houses of the legislature, and this dispute almost stalemated the Convention. It was decided at last that both taxation and representation, at least in the House of Representatives, would be based not on the states as such or on landed wealth, but on population, with the slaves each counting as three-fifths of a person. The nationalists like Madison and Wilson, however, wanted representation in the Senate also to rest on population. Any suggestion that the separate sovereignty of the states might be represented smacked too much of the Articles of Confederation. Hence the nationalists came to regard as a defeat the eventual adoption of the "Connecticut Compromise," by which each state was given two senators in the upper house of the legislature.

Thus Madison and Wilson lost the battles over the congressional veto of state laws and proportional representation in both houses. But the Federalists (as those who supported the Constitution came to call themselves) had won the war even before the Convention adjourned. Once the New Jersey Plan, which preserved the essentials of the Articles of Confederation, was rejected in favor of the Virginia Plan, the opponents of the Constitution, or Antifederalists, found themselves forced, as Richard Henry Lee complained, to accept "this or nothing."

The Articles of Confederation required that amendments be made by the unanimous consent of the state legislatures. But the delegates to the Philadelphia Convention decided to bypass the state legislatures and to submit the Constitution to specially elected state conventions for ratification. Approval by only nine of the thirteen states was necessary for the new government to take effect. This violation of earlier political principles was only one of many to which the Antifederalists objected.

The Federalist-Antifederalist Debate   The federal government that was established by the Philadelphia Convention seemed severely to violate the ideals of 1776 that had guided the Revolutionary constitution makers. The new Constitution provided for a strong government, with an extraordinary amount of power given to the president and the Senate. It also created a single republican state that would span the continent and encompass all the diverse and scattered interests of the whole of American society—an impossible thing to expect of a republic, according to the best political science of the day.

During the debates over ratification in the fall and winter of 1787–88, the Antifederalists focused on these Federalist violations of the earlier Revolutionary assumptions. They charged that the new federal government resembled a monarchy in its concentration of power at the expense of liberty. Because the society it was to govern was extensive and heterogeneous, the Antifederalists asserted, the federal government would have to act tyrannically. Inevitably America would become a single consolidated state, with the individuality of the separate states sacrificed to a powerful government. And the source of this development, the Antifederalists argued, would be the logic of sovereignty. That powerful principle of eighteenth-century political science, on which the British had relied in the imperial debate, held that no society could long possess two legislatures: it must inevitably have one final, indivisible lawmaking authority. The Antifederalists argued that if the new national government was to be more powerful than the state governments—and if the Constitution was to be "the supreme law of the land"—then, according to the doctrine of sovereignty, the legislative authority of the separate states would eventually be annihilated.

Despite these formidable Antifederalist arguments, the Federalists did not believe that the Constitution repudiated the Revolution and the principles of 1776. In the decade since Independence had been declared, the political world had been transformed. Americans, it now appeared clear, had effectively transferred this final lawmaking authority, called sovereignty, from the institutions of government to the people at large.

In the years since the Revolution many Americans had continued to act outside of all official institutions of government. During the 1780s they had organized various committees, conventions, and other extralegal bodies of the people in order to voice grievances and to achieve political goals. By so doing they had continued a common practice of the Revolution itself. Vigilante actions of various kinds had done quickly and efficiently what the new state governments were often unable to do—control prices, prevent profiteering, and punish Tories. Everywhere people had extended the logic of "actual" representation and had sought to instruct and control the institutions of government. By 1787–88 all this activity by the people at large tended to give reality to the idea that sovereignty in America resided in the people, and not in any specific institution of government. Only by believing that sovereignty was held by the people outside of government could Americans make theoretical sense of their recent remarkable political inventions—their conception of a written constitution that was immune from legislative tampering, their special constitution-making conventions, and their unusual ideas of "actual" representation. This new concept of sovereignty residing in the people rather than in any institution of government now made the traditional logic of having ultimate power in one legislature or another irrelevant.

To meet the Antifederalist arguments against the Constitution, the Federalists were now determined to use this new understanding of the ultimate power of the people. True, they said, the Philadelphia Convention had gone beyond its instructions to amend the Articles of Confederation. It had drawn up an entirely new government, and it had provided for the new Constitution's ratification by special state conventions. But had Americans not learned during the previous decade that legislatures were not competent to create or change a constitution? If the federal Constitution were to be truly a fundamental law, then, argued the Federalists, it had to be ratified "by the supreme authority of the people themselves." Hence it was "We the people of the United States," and not the states, that ordained and established the Constitution.

By locating sovereignty in the people rather than in any particular institution, the Federalists could now conceive of what had previously been a contradiction in politics—two legislatures operating simultaneously over the same community. Thus they could answer the principal objection to the Constitution: the logic of legislative sovereignty. Only by making the people themselves the final lawmaking authority could the Federalists explain this emerging conception of federalism, that unique division of legislative responsibilities between the national and state governments that still amazes the world.

This new understanding of the relation of the society to government now enabled the Federalists to explain the expansion of a single republican state over a large continent of diverse groups and interests. The Federalists—especially Madison—took up the Scottish philosopher David Hume's radical suggestion that a republican government might operate better in a large territory than in a small one, and ingeniously used it to turn upside down the older assumption that a republic must be small and compact.

The Federalists argued that American experiences since 1776 had demonstrated that no republic could be made small enough to avoid the clashing of rival parties and interests. (Tiny Rhode Island was the most faction-ridden of all.) The extended territory of the new national republic was actually its greatest source of strength, Madison wrote in a series of publications, especially in his most famous piece, *The Federalist* No. 10.* In a large society, Madison concluded, there were so many interests and parties that no one faction could triumph, and thus the threat of tyranny by the majority would be eliminated. Furthermore, representatives to the national Congress would have to be elected from relatively large districts—a fact that Madison hoped would inhibit demagogic electioneering. If the people of a particular state—New York, for example—had to elect only ten men to the federal Congress, in contrast to the sixty-six they elected to their state legislature, they would be more likely to pass over ordinary men and to elect those who were experienced, well educated, and well known. In this way the new federal government would avoid the problems that had plagued the states in the 1780s.

The Antifederalists provided little match for the arguments and the array of talents that the Federalists gathered in support of the Constitution in the ratifying conventions that were held in the states throughout the fall, winter, and spring of 1787–88. Many Antifederalists were state-centered men with local interests and loyalties. They tended to lack the influence and education of the Federalists, and often they had neither social nor intellectual confidence. The Antifederalists had difficulty making themselves heard because they had very few influential leaders and because much of the press was closed to them; out of a hundred or more newspapers printed in the late 1780s, only a dozen supported the Antifederalists.

Many of the small states—Delaware, New Jersey, Connecticut, and Georgia—commercially dependent on their neighbors or militarily exposed, ratified immediately. The critical struggles took place in the large states of Massachusetts, Virginia, and New York. The Constitution was accepted in these states only by narrow margins and with the promise of future amendments. North Carolina and Rhode Island rejected the Constitution, but after New York's ratification in July 1788 the country was ready to go ahead and organize the new government without them.

Despite the difficulties and the close votes in some states, the country's eventual acceptance of the Constitution was almost inevitable. The alternative was governmental chaos. Yet in the face of the great number of wealthy and influential people who supported the Constitution, what in the end remains extraordinary is not the political weakness and disunity of Antifederalism, but its strength. The fact that large numbers of Americans could actually reject a plan of government that was backed by George Washington and nearly the whole of the country's "natural aristocracy" said more about the changing character of American politics and society than did the Constitution's acceptance. It was indeed a sign of what was to come.

The Federalist was a series of eighty-five essays in defense of the Constitution, published in New York in the winter of 1787–88. They were written under the pen name "Publius," largely by Madison and Alexander Hamilton, with five essays contributed by John Jay. The essays were quickly published as a book and became the most famous work of political philosophy in American history, labeled by Jefferson in 1788 as "the best commentary on the principles of government, which ever was written."

314

Edward Savage's "Liberty"
*This 1796 engraving combines
the two most important symbols
of the early Republic, the goddess
"Liberty" and the eagle, the
latter representing power and
unity. The print was very
popular and for years appeared
in a wide variety of adaptations,
including embroidery. Note the
liberty cap on the flagstaff in the
background.*

The Hamiltonian Program

The Constitution created only the outline of the new government. Americans still had to fill in the details of the government and make something of it. During the 1790s the government leaders—that is, the Federalists, who clung to the name used by the supporters of the Constitution—sought to build a large consolidated nation that few Americans had envisioned in 1776. The consequence of their efforts was to make the 1790s the most awkward decade in American history, a decade that bore little relation to what went on immediately before or after.

Because the Federalists stood in the way of democracy as it was emerging in the United States, everything seemed to turn against them. They despised political parties, yet parties nonetheless emerged, shattering the remarkable harmony of 1790 and producing one of the most divisive and passionate eras in American history. They sought desperately to avoid conflict with England, to the point of appearing to compromise the new nation's independence. But in 1812 the war with Great Britain that they sought to avoid had to be fought anyway. By the early nineteenth century Alexander Hamilton, the brilliant Federalist leader who more than anyone else pursued the heroic dreams of the age, was not alone in his despairing conclusion "that this American world was not made for me."

Organizing the Government

There was more consensus when the new government was inaugurated in 1789–90 than at any time since the Declaration of Independence. Regional differences were temporarily obscured by a common enthusiasm for the new Constitution. And the unanimous election of Washington as the first president gave the new government an immediate respectability. Washington, with his tall, imposing figure, Roman nose, and stern, thin-lipped face, was already at age fifty-eight an internationally famous classical hero. Like the Roman conqueror Cincinnatus, he had returned to his farm at the moment of military victory. He was understandably reluctant to take up one more burden for his country and thus risk shattering the reputation he had so painstakingly earned as commander in chief. Yet his deep sense of duty made refusal of the presidency impossible. He possessed the dignity, patience, and restraint that the untried but potentially powerful office needed at the outset. Despite the strong-minded, talented people around him— particularly Secretary of the Treasury Hamilton and Secretary of State Jefferson—Washington was very much the leader of his administration.

Madison, the government's leader in the House of Representatives, immediately sought to fulfill earlier promises to the Antifederalists and to quiet their fears by proposing amendments to the Constitution. He beat back Antifederalist efforts to change fundamentally the character of the Constitution and extracted from the variety of suggested amendments those that were least likely to drain the new government's energy. To the disappointment of some former Antifederalists, the ten amendments that were ratified in 1791—the amendments known collectively as the Bill of Rights—were mostly concerned with protecting from the federal government the rights of *individuals* rather than the rights of the *states.* They included the guarantees of freedom of speech, press, religion, petition, and assembly, as well as a number of protections for accused persons. Only the Tenth Amendment, which reserved for the states or for the people those powers not delegated to the United States, was a concession to the main Antifederalist fear.*

With the inauguration of Washington and the establishment of the new government, many Americans began to feel a sense of beginning anew, of putting the republican experiment on a new and stronger foundation. They talked of benevolence, glory, and heroism, and they foresaw the inevitable westward movement of the arts and sciences from Europe to the New World. The outlook was cosmopolitan, liberal, and humanitarian; America was entering a new age.

Yet despite all this optimism, the Americans of the 1790s never lost their Revolutionary sense of the novel and fragile nature of their boldly extended republican government. Except in the epic poems of a few excited patriots such as Joel Barlow and Timothy Dwight, America was far from being a consolidated nation in any modern sense. Already separatist movements in the West threatened to break up the new country. Some westerners even considered giving their

---

*For the first ten amendments, see Appendix.

allegiance to Spain in return for access to the Gulf of Mexico. The entire Mississippi River basin was open to exploitation by ambitious adventurers willing to sell their services to European nations. These included William Blount, a senator from Tennessee, and George Rogers Clark, a frontier hero during the Revolution. Fear of this kind of intrigue and influence led to the hasty admission of Vermont, Kentucky, and Tennessee into the Union during the 1790s. But the danger of splintering remained.

The Federalist aims and the conflicting passions they aroused can be properly understood only if one takes into account this context of uncertainty and awesome responsibility for the future of republican government. The very character of America's emerging republican state was at issue in the 1790s. The Federalist leaders sought to maintain the momentum that had begun in the late 1780s when the Constitution was formed. In place of the impotent confederation of chaotic states, they envisioned a strong, consolidated, commercial state that would be led by an energetic government composed of the best men in the society.

Many Federalists were interested in bolstering the dignity of the new republic by adopting some of the ceremony and majesty of monarchy. Led by Vice-President John Adams, some Federalists in the Senate tried to make "His Highness" the proper title for addressing the president. Because the future of the new republic was so unformed and doubtful, this issue seemed loaded with significance, and it occupied the Congress in a month of debate. The attempt to give the president a royal-sounding title failed, and the republican simplicity of "Mr. President" was adopted. But the Federalists did draw up elaborate rules concerning government receptions and the proper behavior at what soon came to be called the "republican court," located in New York and, after 1790, in Philadelphia. At the same time, plans were begun for erecting a monumental "federal city" as the permanent capital. Always strongly sensitive to the precedents being established, the Federalists also worked out the relations between the president and Congress. Before the end of the first session of Congress in 1789, the bare outlines of government that had been provided by the Constitution had been filled in. Congress created the executive departments of state, war, and treasury, as well as a federal judiciary consisting of the Supreme Court and a pyramid of lower courts.

Hamilton's Financial Program

Alexander Hamilton, then thirty-five years old, was the moving force in the new government. As a military aide to Washington during the Revolutionary War, he had earned the president's admiration. In fact, despite his short stature, Hamilton impressed everyone who met him. Unlike Washington, he was quick-witted, excitable, and very knowledgeable about public finance. Born in the West Indies an illegitimate son of a Scottish merchant, Hamilton longed to enter and enjoy the polite world of the rich and wellborn. But despite his concern for the commercial prosperity of the United States, he cannot be regarded simply as a capitalist

**Alexander Hamilton
(1757–1804)**
*Hamilton is the most
controversial of the Founding
Fathers. Certainly he was the
least taken with radical Whig
ideology and the most
adventurous and heroic. As
Gouverneur Morris said, "He
was more covetous of glory
than of wealth or power." His
talents, his energy, and his
clear sense of direction awed
his contemporaries, friends and
enemies alike.*

promoter of America's later business culture. He was willing to allow ordinary men their profits and property, but it was fame and honor he wanted for himself and for his country. As the secretary of the treasury, he was now in a crucial position to put his ideas into effect.

Since British "country-opposition" groups had traditionally considered the treasury a source of political corruption, the first Congress regarded the new secretary of the treasury with some suspicion—and with good reason. The treasury was by far the largest department, with dozens of officers and well over 2,000 customs officials, revenue agents, and postmasters. Although Congress limited the capacity of these officials to engage in business and trade and to buy public lands and government securities, the treasury offices were an important source of patronage and influence. Hamilton, in fact, saw his role in eighteenth-century English terms—as a kind of prime minister to President Washington. Hamilton felt justified in meddling in the affairs of other departments and of Congress and in taking the lead in organizing and administering the government. He denied that he was creating a "court" party, but he set out to duplicate the great financial achievements of the early-eighteenth-century English governments that had laid the basis for England's stability and commercial supremacy.

Hamilton worked out his program in a series of four reports to Congress in 1790–91: on credit (including duties and taxes), on a national bank, on a mint, and on manufactures. Nearly everyone admitted that the new government needed to put its finances in order and to settle the Revolutionary War debts of the United States. Hamilton was determined to establish the public credit of the United

States. In 1790 the amount owed to foreigners totaled $12 million, and no one had any quarrel with Hamilton's desire to pay this off in full. Of the domestic public debts—that is, the amount due Americans—the federal government owed $42 million, and the various state governments owed an estimated $25 million. In the boldest and most controversial part of his plan, Hamilton proposed that the United States government assume the obligation of paying all the state debts. But then instead of paying off either these assumed state debts or the Confederation's debts, he urged that the United States government "fund" them. That is, he wanted the new national government to collect into a single package all the federal and state bonds and loan certificates left over from the Revolutionary War and to issue new federal securities in their place with the same face value as the old debts. Although Hamilton, in order to maintain the value of the government's new bonds, had to promise to pay off the principal of the debt, he actually had no intention of doing so. Retirement of the public debt would only destroy its usefulness.

By these proposals Hamilton hoped to create a consolidated and permanent national debt that would strengthen America in the same way that the British national debt had strengthened Great Britain. Regular interest payments on the refunded debt were to be backed by the new government's revenues from customs duties and excise taxes. Indeed, more than 40 percent of these revenues in the 1790s went to pay interest on the debt. These interest payments not only would make the United States the best credit risk in the world, but would create a system of investment for American moneyed groups that had lacked the stable alternatives for speculation and investment that Europeans had.

Besides giving investors a secure stake in the new national government, these new bonds would become the basis of the nation's money supply. Not only would the securities themselves be negotiable instruments in business transactions, but Hamilton's program provided for their forming three-fourths of the privately subscribed capital of a new national bank that would be patterned on the Bank of England. This Bank of the United States and its branches (to be established in selected cities) would serve as the government's depository and fiscal agent and would act as a central control on the state banks, of which there were thirty-two by 1801. But most important, the Bank of the United States would create paper money.

The Bank would issue its notes as loans to private citizens, and these notes, along with those of the banks chartered by the states, would become the principal circulating medium of money for a society that lacked an adequate supply of specie, gold and silver coin. Above all, Hamilton wanted a paper money that would hold its value in relation to specie. By guaranteeing that the federal government would accept the Bank's notes at face value in payment of all taxes, holders of the notes would be less likely to redeem them in coin. The notes would pass from hand to hand without depreciating, even though only a fraction of their value was available in specie at any one time. Many American leaders continued to believe, as John Adams did, that "every dollar of a bank bill that is issued

First Bank of the United States, Philadelphia
Designed by an unsuccessful businessman from New Hampshire, Samuel Blodget, this building was essentially a three-story New England brick house with a classical portico, decorated, the Gazette of the United States *reported excitedly, in the style of "Palmyre and Rome when architecture was at its zenith in the Augustan age."*

beyond the quantity of gold and silver in the vaults, represents nothing, and is therefore a cheat upon somebody." Nevertheless, these multiplying bank notes quickly broadened the foundation of the nation's economy.

In his final report, the report on manufactures, Hamilton laid out plans for eventually industrializing the United States. He and some other Federalists hoped to transform America from an agricultural nation into precisely the complicated and rank-organized country that agrarians like Jefferson and Madison feared. He proposed incentives and bounties for the development of large-scale manufacturing that would be very different from the small household industry that most Americans were used to. Yet because the Federalist government needed the revenue from customs duties on imported manufactures, and because most businessmen's energies were still absorbed in overseas shipping and land speculation, these proposals for stimulating manufacturing went unfulfilled. The rest of Hamilton's extraordinary financial program, however, was adopted by Congress early in the 1790s.

Hamilton's Political Program

As much as Hamilton and other Federalist leaders planned for and celebrated the commercial prosperity of the United States, their ultimate goals were more political than economic. Like many other Federalists, Hamilton had no faith in the idealistic Revolutionary hopes that American society could be held together solely by "virtue," by the people's willingness to sacrifice their private interests for the sake of the public good. Instead of virtue and the natural sociability of man, Hamilton saw only the ordinary individual's selfish pursuit of his own private happiness. Social stability therefore required the harnessing of this self-interest. The Federalists thus tried to use the new economic and fiscal measures to re-create in America traditional kinds of eighteenth-century "connections" that would knit the sprawling society together.

In effect, Hamilton sought to reverse the egalitarian thrust of the Revolutionary movement. He and other Federalists believed that the national government could influence and manipulate the economic and social leaders of the country. These leaders in turn would use economic self-interest to gain support for the new central government among the groups and individuals dependent on them. Not only did the Federalists expect the new national financial program to draw people's affections away from the now economically weakened state governments, but they deliberately set out to "corrupt" the society (as eighteenth-century "country-opposition" writers put it) by tying people's interests to the central government. In local areas they built up a following among Revolutionary War veterans and among members of the Society of the Cincinnati, the organization of Revolutionary War officers. They appointed important and respectable local figures to the federal judiciary and other federal offices. They carefully managed the Bank of the United States and other parts of the national economic program. And in 1791 they had President Washington make an elaborate tour of the country in the manner of a king.

By 1793, through the shrewd use of these kinds of influence or "corruption" on key individuals, the Federalists had formed groups of "friends of government" in most of the states. The lines of connection of these centers of economic and political patronage ran from the federal executive through Congress down to the various localities. Thus was created a vested interest in what opponents called "a court faction"—the very thing that Madison in *The Federalist* No. 10 had believed unlikely in an expanded republic.

Hamilton ultimately believed, as he declared in 1794, that "government can never [be] said to be established until some signal display has manifested its power by military coercion." From the beginning many Federalists, including Secretary of War Henry Knox, regarded a cohesive militia and a regular army as "a strong corrective arm" necessary for the federal government to meet all crises "whether arising from internal or external causes." In 1791 the Federalists imposed a federal excise tax on whiskey—a profitable and transportable product for many inland grain farmers—to ensure that all citizens, however far removed from the seaports, felt the weight of the new national government. When in 1794 some western Pennsylvania farmers rebelled against this hated internal tax, they seemed to fall into the government's plans (as Madison charged) to "establish the principle that a standing army was necessary for enforcing the laws." The national government raised nearly 15,000 militia troops to meet this Whiskey Rebellion. This excessive show of force was essential, President Washington declared, because "we had given no testimony to the world of being able or willing to support our government and laws."

Dealing with external problems was not as easy as putting down internal rebellions. Both Great Britain and Spain maintained positions on the borderlands of the United States. There they traded and plotted with the Indians, who still occupied huge areas of the trans-Appalachian West. From its base in Canada, Britain encouraged the Indians to join forces and resist American encroachments. In the South, Spain, which held the Floridas, New Orleans, and the Louisiana territory, refused to recognize American boundaries, controlled navigation down the Mississippi River, and offered protection to the Creek and Cherokee Indians of the Southwest. Much of the diplomacy of the early Republic was devoted to the removal of these barriers to western expansion.

Major breakthroughs came in 1795. In 1790–91 the Indians of the Northwest had inflicted several defeats on American soldiers, mostly militia, in the area along the present boundary between Ohio and Indiana. The worst came in November 1791, with the annihilation of a motley collection of troops under the command of Arthur St. Clair, the territorial governor of the Northwest. These devastating defeats gave the Federalists the opportunity to overhaul the War Department and to create the regular standing army that many of them wanted. With a reorganized professional army, General Anthony Wayne in 1794 smashed the Indians at Fallen Timbers, near present-day Toledo, Ohio, and temporarily broke Indian resistance and British influence in the Old Northwest. In the Treaty of Greenville in 1795, the Indians ceded much of the Ohio territory to the United States. In turn, this cession now made inevitable Britain's evacuation of the Northwest posts it had been occupying since the Revolution. In a treaty negotiated by John Jay and ratified in 1795,* Britain finally agreed to get out of American territory.

In another treaty, negotiated by Thomas Pinckney in the same year, Spain finally recognized American claims to the Florida boundary and to navigation of the Mississippi River. Both Jay's Treaty and Pinckney's Treaty thus secured the territorial integrity of the United States in a way the diplomacy of the Confederation had been unable to do.

But the United States was still far from being a world power. Measuring American strength by European standards, the Federalists were strongly aware of the country's weakness in the world, and this awareness largely determined their foreign policy. Unlike England and France, the United States as yet lacked the

---

*For Jay's Treaty, see p. 326.

essential elements that made a nation powerful and great—commercial strength and military might. Since to build the United States into a strong and prosperous nation rivaling the powers of Europe might take fifty years or more, the Federalists thought that the new nation had to buy time by maintaining harmonious relations with Great Britain.

Britain was the only power that could seriously hinder American development. Duties on British imports supplied the national revenue on which Hamilton's entire financial program depended. Until the United States could stand up to Great Britain, the Federalists believed that the country ought to concentrate on acquiring or controlling the New World possessions of a weakened Spain and on dominating the Western Hemisphere. The Federalists' policy of reconciliation with Britain thus became another means toward the ultimate fulfillment of their grandiose dreams of American glory.

The Republican Opposition

Opposition to the Federalist program was slow in developing. Since the only alternative to the new national government was the prospect of disunity and anarchy, Alexander Hamilton and the Federalists were in a position to build up their system without great difficulty. During the first year of the new government (1789–90), James Madison acted as congressional leader of those who were eager to counteract Antifederalist sentiment and to build a strong and independent executive. Not only did Madison write President Washington's first inaugural address, but he argued for the president's exclusive power to remove executive officials, and worked hard to create a Treasury Department with a single head. Indeed, Hamilton, thinking of the cooperative atmosphere of 1787–88 in which he and Madison had written the *Federalist* papers, was so confident of Madison's nationalism and of the nationalism of the southern representatives in Congress that he felt betrayed when they did not unquestioningly support his program.

But Madison broke with the administration on the issues of refunding the debt and the federal government's assumption of the states' debts. On the refunding issue he urged that some sort of distinction be made between the original purchasers of the federal bonds and their present, often northern, speculative holders who had bought them cheaply. Madison was also convinced that national assumption of the existing state debts would penalize those states, particularly Virginia, that had already paid off a large portion of their debts. Yet in 1790 congressmen who were opposed to these measures were still capable of compromising for the sake of federal union. Jefferson, Madison, and other southern representatives were even willing to support national assumption of state debts in return for locating the new federal capital on the Potomac River on the border between Virginia and Maryland.

With the government's effort to charter the Bank of the United States in December 1790, the opposition began to assume a more strident and ideological character. Madison in the House of Representatives and Jefferson in the cabinet (as secretary of state) both urged a strict interpretation of the Constitution as a defense against what seemed to be the dangerous consolidating implications of Hamilton's program. They argued that the Constitution had not expressly granted the federal government the authority to charter a bank. Washington, after asking the opinions of his cabinet members on the constitutionality of the Bank, rejected Jefferson's view in favor of Hamilton's broad "construction," or interpretation, of the Constitution. Hamilton argued that Congress's authority to charter a bank was implied by the clause in the Constitution that gave Congress the right to make all laws "necessary and proper" to carry out its delegated powers. But this presidential decision in favor of the Bank did not quiet the opposition.

By 1791 a "republican interest" was emerging in Congress and in the country, with Madison and Jefferson as its spokesmen. By 1792 this "interest" had begun to form into a Republican "party." This Republican party now saw itself representing the "country opposition" of the people against the corrupt influence of the Federalist "court." It was the 1760s and 1770s all over again.

The Republican Party The Republican party was composed of and supported by a variety of social elements. Foremost were the southern landowners, who were becoming increasingly conscious of the distinctiveness of their section of the country and more and more estranged from the business world that Hamilton's system seemed to be promoting. Unlike Federalist gentlemen in the North, these members of the southern gentry retained the earlier Whig confidence in what Jefferson called the "honest heart" of the common man. Part of this faith in democracy that Jefferson and his southern colleagues shared came from their relative isolation from it. With the increasing questioning of black slavery in the North and throughout the world, small white farmers in the South found a common identity with large plantation owners. Most of the leading landowners therefore did not feel threatened by the democratic electoral politics that was eating away people's deference to "the better sort" in the North.

In the North, especially in the rapidly growing middle states, ambitious individuals and new groups without political connections were finding that the Republican party was a means by which they could challenge entrenched leaders. Therefore the Republican party in the North was very different from what it was in the South. In the South the Republican opposition to the Federalist program was largely the response of rural gentry who were committed to a nostalgic image of independent freeholding farmers. In the North, however, the Republican party was the political expression of new equality-minded social forces released and intensified by the Revolution—particularly ambitious artisans, tradesmen, and second- and third-level merchants who were resentful of the pretensions and privileges of the Federalist elites. These rising northern entrepreneurs were in fact the principal contributors to the very world the southern Republicans were coming to fear.

These diverse and ultimately incompatible sectional and social elements were brought together in a national Republican party by a comprehensive and common ideology. This Republican ideology, involving a deep hatred of overgrown central power and of the political and financial mechanisms that created such power, had been inherited from the English "country-opposition" tradition that had been sharpened and Americanized during the Revolutionary years. Now, during the 1790s, it was given a new and heightened relevance by the policies of the federal administration.

To those who deeply believed in country-Whig ideology, Hamilton's system threatened to re-create the kind of government and society that Americans had presumably destroyed in 1776. It was feared that such a society, based on patronage connections and artificial privilege and supported by executive power, would in time destroy the independence of the republican citizenry. Hamilton appeared to be another Sir Robert Walpole, using the new economic program to corrupt Congress and the country and to create a swelling army of "stock-jobbers and king-jobbers" (in Jefferson's words) in order to build up executive power at the expense of the people.*

Once the Republicans grasped this ideological pattern, all the Federalist measures fell into place. The high-toned pageantry of the "court," the aristocratic talk of titles, the defense of corporate monopolies, the enlargement of the military forces, the growth of taxes, the reliance on the monarchical president and the aristocratic Senate—all these pointed toward a systematic plan, as Caroline

---

*For Walpole's "system" in Great Britain, see chapter 8, pp. 257–58.

County of Virginia declared in 1793, of "assimilating the American government to the form and spirit of the British monarchy." Most basic and dangerous of all was the Federalist creation of a huge perpetual federal debt, which, as George Clinton, the Republican governor of New York, explained, not only would poison the morals of the people through speculation, but would also "add an artificial support to the administration, and by a species of bribery enlist the monied men of the community on the side of the measures of the government.... Look to Great Britain."

The French Revolution
The outbreak of the French Revolution in 1789, and its subsequent expansion in 1792 into a European war pitting monarchical Britain against republican France, added to the quarrel Americans were having among themselves over the direction their society and government were taking. The meaning of the American Revolution, and the capacity of the United States to sustain its grand republican experiment, now seemed tied to the fate of Britain and France.

President Washington proclaimed America's neutrality in the spring of 1793. The United States quickly tried to take advantage of its position and to gain the warring countries' recognition of its neutral rights. Unable to control the seas, France threw open its empire in the West Indies to American commerce, and American merchants soon developed a profitable shipping trade between the French and Spanish West Indies and Europe. Britain retaliated by invoking what was called the Rule of 1756. This rule, which had been first set forth during the Seven Years' War, enabled British prize courts (that is, courts that judged the legitimacy of the seizure of enemy ships or goods) to deny the right of neutral nations in time of war to trade with ports in belligerent countries that had been closed to them in time of peace. During 1793 and 1794 Britain seized more than three hundred American merchant ships.

Although Washington had proclaimed the United States' neutrality, both the Federalists and their Republican opponents sought to favor whichever power— Britain or France—they thought would better promote American interests. The Federalists made strong attempts to overcome the natural sympathy most Americans had for France, their former ally in the Revolutionary War and now a sister republic. Citizen Genêt, the new French minister to the United States, in 1793 began arming privateers in the United States for use against the British and seemed to be appealing over the head of the government to the American people for support. These clumsy actions helped the Federalists win over many Americans who were otherwise sympathetic to the French Revolution. In addition the Federalists recruited to their cause a growing number of Protestant ministers and conservative groups who were alarmed by the social upheaval and antireligious passion that they thought were being spread by the French Revolution. Britain seemed to the Federalists to be a bastion of stability in the midst of worldwide chaos. While the Republicans were calling for stiff commercial retaliation against Britain for its seizing of American ships and sailors and for its continued occupation of posts in the Northwest, the Federalists hoped to head off war with Britain by negotiation. In the spring of 1794, Washington appointed John Jay, chief justice of the Supreme Court, to be a special minister to Great Britain.

Jay's Treaty
The treaty that Jay negotiated with Britain in 1794 demonstrated both the Federalists' fears of France and their reliance on the British connection. In the treaty Britain finally agreed to evacuate the Northwest posts, to open parts of its empire to American commerce, and to set up joint arbitration commissions to settle the unresolved issues of prewar debts, boundaries, and compensation for illegal seizures. The United States was compelled to abandon principles concerning freedom of the seas and broad neutral rights that it had been supporting since 1776. In effect the treaty recognized the British Rule of 1756. Moreover, by granting Britain more favorable trade conditions than it gave to any other nation, the United States surrendered the power to make any future commercial discrimination against Britain, the one great weapon that the Republicans were counting on to weaken the former mother country's hold on American commerce.

The Republicans were greatly shocked and angered by the treaty. Jay was burned in effigy. When the Senate reluctantly ratified the treaty in 1795 after a bitter struggle, the Republicans in the House tried to prevent its implementation. Although the Republicans thought that Britain had conceded to the United States little more than peace, peace was enough for most Federalists. War with Britain, they thought, would be disastrous for America. It would end the imports of British goods and the customs revenues on which Hamilton's financial program depended and would only increase the influence of what the Federalist senator George Cabot of Massachusetts called "French principles [that] would destroy us as a society."

The Quasi-War with France
Washington's decision to retire from the presidency at the end of his second term created an important precedent for the future. The New Englander and vice-president John Adams was widely regarded as Washington's natural successor, but he was elected in 1796 by only a narrow margin of electoral votes, 71 to 68, over the Republican leader, Thomas Jefferson. Under the constitutional rule then in force, Jefferson as runner-up became vice-president.

Before Washington left office, with Hamilton's help he prepared his Farewell Address. By laying the basis for later American "isolationism," the address became one of the most important political documents in American history. In it Washington urged Americans "to steer clear of permanent alliances" with any foreign power. Republicans saw this neutralism as anti-French: they rightly thought that Washington was rejecting the idea that the United States and France were naturally linked in the common cause of bringing revolutionary republicanism to the world.

The Federalist government's pro-British policies as expressed in Jay's Treaty now drove the embattled French into a series of attacks on American shipping;

they even refused to treat with the United States until the new American connection with Britain was broken. President Adams dealt with the crisis in 1797 by sending a special mission to France. The French government, using agents whom they designated as X, Y, and Z, tried to extort a payment from the American diplomats as a precondition for negotiations. This humiliating "XYZ Affair" further aroused American antagonism to France and led to the American revocation of the Franco-American treaties of 1778. In 1798 an undeclared "quasi-war" with France broke out on the seas. All this in turn created an opportunity for some extreme Federalists, led by Hamilton, to call for a strengthening of the central government once and for all.

As leader of the Republican party, Jefferson saw the world differently. Whether in or out of office, he never let the growing anti-French atmosphere weaken his faith in the cause of the French revolutionary republic. Although he supported the outward neutrality of the United States in the European war between Britain and France, he and other Republicans were bitterly opposed to Jay's Treaty; they were convinced that they could not remain impartial in the French revolutionary cause, on which "the liberty of the whole earth was depending." Jefferson was aware of the bloody excesses of the French Revolution, including the Reign of Terror, in which thousands of aristocrats, priests, and others were guillotined for political offenses; but his enthusiasm for the Revolution was not dampened. "Rather than it should have failed," he wrote in 1793, the year of the Terror, "I would have seen half the earth desolate; were there but an Adam and Eve left in every country, and left free, it would be better than it is now."

Because Federalists and Republicans alike were convinced that the very meaning of the United States as a republic was directly related to the conflict between Britain and France, some American public officials of both parties were led into extraordinarily improper diplomatic behavior during the 1790s. Hamilton as secretary of the treasury secretly passed on information about United States plans to the British government. Jefferson as secretary of state under Washington, his successor Edmund Randolph, and James Monroe as minister to France all indiscreetly tried to undermine the pro-British stand of the administration they were serving and came very close to becoming unwitting tools of French policy.

The Crisis of 1798–1799

In this inflamed atmosphere political passions ran as high as they ever have in American history. Every aspect of American life—business groups, banks, dance assemblies, even funerals—became politicized. People who had known each other their whole lives now crossed streets to avoid meeting. As personal and social ties fell apart, differences easily spilled into violence, and fighting broke out in the state legislatures and even in the Congress.

Amid these passions the political parties that emerged in the 1790s were unlike any later American parties. Although by 1796 the Federalists and the Republicans had organized to win the presidency for their respective candidates,

Adams and Jefferson, both parties saw themselves in an increasingly revolutionary situation. The Federalists thought of themselves as the most enlightened and socially established members of the natural aristocracy, who were best able to carry out the responsibility of running the country. Thus they claimed that they were the government, not a "party." Parties, as Washington warned in his Farewell Address, were equivalent to factions and could lead only to sedition and the disruption of the state.

Although Jefferson and many other Republicans shared this traditional eighteenth-century abhorrence of parties, they considered that the extraordinary circumstances of the 1790s justified the formation of an organized opposition. The Republicans thought that the normal processes of American politics had become corrupted and poisoned by a Federalist government that had detached itself from the people. Hence it was necessary to create popular organizations of political opposition similar to those that the American Whigs had formed during the pre-Revolutionary crisis. Their goal in forming caucuses, corresponding committees, and Democratic-Republican societies was to band people together and use what they increasingly called "public opinion" to influence elections and counteract the influence of prominent Federalists in national politics. The extralegal opposition of the Republican party, they believed, would be a temporary but necessary instrument that would save the people's liberties from Federalist monarchism.

In mobilizing the people into political consciousness, nothing was more important than the press. Newspapers multiplied dramatically, from fewer than 100 in 1790 to more than 230 by 1800. By 1810 Americans were buying more than 22 million copies of 376 papers annually, the largest circulation of newspapers anywhere in the world. By the late 1790s these papers, many of them Republican, were lowering their prices and adopting eye-catching typography and cartoons in order to reach new readers. By popularizing political affairs as never before and by relentlessly criticizing Federalist officials, the press seemed to be single-handedly shaping American political life.

Although the Federalists began to adopt some of what they called the "petty electioneering arts" of the Republican opposition, they were not comfortable with the new democratic politics. They saw themselves in traditional eighteenth-century terms as gentlemen leaders to whom ordinary people, if they were only left alone, would naturally defer. The Federalists attributed the difficulties and disorder of the 1790s to the influence of newspapers, demagogues, and extralegal political associations. Republican upstarts and factions, they believed, were stirring up the people against their natural rulers. They spread radical French principles, interfered with the electoral process, and herded the people, including recent immigrants, into political activity. New kinds of writers and publishers, including the former indentured servant and now congressman and editor Matthew Lyon of Vermont, were reaching out to influence an audience as obscure and ordinary as themselves. Through the coarse language and slander of their publications, thought the Federalists, these writers and editors were destroying

Cartoon Lampooning the Lyon-Griswold Tangle in Congress in 1797
With the wrestling on the floor of the House of Representatives in 1797 between Republican Matthew Lyon of Vermont and Federalist Roger Griswold of Connecticut, followed by Lyon's "outrageous" and "indecent" defense (he was reported in the Annals of Congress *to have said, "I did not come here to have my——kicked by everybody"), some members concluded that Congress had become no better than a "tavern," filled with "beasts, and not gentlemen," and contemptible in the eyes of all "polite or genteel" societies.*

the governing gentry's personal reputation for character on which popular respect for the entire political order was presumably based.

By the late 1790s, amid an economic depression and the "quasi-war" with France, all these Federalists' fears climaxed in their desperate repressive measures of 1798. These measures more than anything else have tarnished the historical reputation of the Federalists. In control of both the presidency and Congress, the Federalists contemplated various plans for strengthening the Union. They sought to broaden the power of the federal judiciary, to increase the transportation network throughout the country, and to enlarge the army and navy. Above all, the Federalists aimed to end the Republicans' political exploitation of new immigrants and to stop the flow of Republican literature that was poisoning the relations between the rulers and the ruled.

In 1798 the Federalist-dominated Congress passed the Alien and Sedition Acts. These acts lengthened the naturalization process for foreigners, gave the president extraordinary powers to deal with aliens, and provided the central government with the authority to punish as crimes seditious libels—derogatory remarks tending to incite disobedience to the law—against federal officials. At the same time Congress ordered the immediate enlistment of a new regular army of 12,000 and laid plans for provisional armies numbering in the tens of thousands. Washington was to be called out of retirement as commander in chief of the new army, but Hamilton was to be actually in command. Presumably all these measures were designed to meet the threat of a French invasion, but some people believed that their purpose was actually to deal with domestic disorder in the United States. When the United States army quickly suppressed an armed rebellion of several northeastern Pennsylvania counties, led by John Fries, in protest against the new federal tax on houses, land, and slaves, the advantages of federal strength were confirmed in some Federalist eyes.

For their part, the Republicans in 1798–99 thought the very success of the American Revolution was at stake. In response to the Federalist repression, particularly the Alien and Sedition Acts, the Virginia and Kentucky legislatures issued resolutions that were drawn up by Madison and Jefferson respectively. These resolutions proclaimed the right of the states to judge the constitutionality of federal acts and to interpose themselves between the citizenry and the unconstitutional actions of the central government. Although the other states declined to support Virginia and Kentucky, the stand taken by these two states opened a question about the nature of the Union that would trouble the country for many decades, leading up to the Civil War.

By the end of the 1790s, several developments brought a measure of reconciliation. Both Madison and Jefferson were unwilling to resort to force to support their resolutions. British Admiral Horatio Nelson's naval victory over the French at the Battle of the Nile in October 1798 lessened the threat of a French invasion of either England or America. But most important in calming the crisis was the action of President John Adams.

Adams's presidency had been contentious, and he was never in command of his own cabinet, let alone the government. This short, puffy, and sensitive man, who wore his heart on his sleeve, was much too honest, impulsive, and independent-minded to handle the growing division among the Federalists over the military buildup. But he had an abiding fear of standing armies and a stubborn courage. In 1799, against the wishes of his advisers, he decided to send another peace message to France despite the humiliating failure of his earlier effort in the XYZ Affair. France, now headed by First Consul Napoleon Bonaparte, who would soon make himself emperor, agreed to make terms and in 1800 signed an agreement with the United States that brought the quasi-war to a close.

Adams's independent action fatally divided the Federalist leadership between the moderates who supported the president and the High Federalists who supported Hamilton. This split crippled Adams's chances of winning the presidential election of 1800. Adams, always ready to bemoan his country's neglect of his achievements, considered his decision to negotiate with France "the most disinterested, most determined and most successful of my whole life." His controversial decision ended the war crisis and undermined the attempts of the

John Adams (1735–1826)
*Adams is perhaps the most
neglected of the Founders; he
certainly felt himself to be. He
seemed to court unpopularity
with his displays of jealousy,
vanity, and pomposity. Yet as his
diaries reveal, he was at heart
vulnerable and amiable.*

extremist Federalists to strengthen the central government and the military forces of the United States. Although the worst was over, that was not yet clear to everyone at the time. In 1800 the British ambassador still thought the "whole system of American Government" was "tottering to its foundations."

Chronology

1781 Articles of Confederation ratified. Congress establishes Bank of North America.

1782 Fall of Lord North's ministry.

1783 Newburgh conspiracy of American army officers.
Society of the Cincinnati founded.
Pennsylvania Evening Post, first daily newspaper in the United States, begins publication.
Treaty of Peace with Britain signed.

1785 Land Ordinance for Northwest Territory adopted by Congress.

1786 Jay-Gardoqui Treaty; rejected by Congress.

Virginia Act for Establishing Religious Freedom.
Shays's Rebellion in western Massachusetts.
Annapolis Convention; adopts plan to meet in Philadelphia to revise Articles of Confederation.

1787 Federal Constitutional Convention meets in Philadelphia and drafts Constitution.
Northwest Ordinance enacted by Congress.
The Federalist papers begun by Madison, Hamilton, and Jay.

1788 Ratification of United States Constitution by all states except Rhode Island and North Carolina.

1789 First session of Congress meets.
Washington inaugurated as first
president.
Capitol at Richmond, Virginia,
built from model of Maison
Carrée supplied by Jefferson.
Outbreak of French Revolution.

1790 Hamilton's Report on Public
Credit; Funding Bill;
Assumption Bill.
Father John Carroll made first
Roman Catholic bishop of
United States with see in
Baltimore.

1791 Bank of the United States
established.
First ten amendments to
Constitution (Bill of Rights)
adopted.
Defeat of General Arthur St. Clair
by Ohio Indians.

1793 Execution of Louis XVI of France;
outbreak of European war.
Washington inaugurated for
second term.
Proclamation of Neutrality by
Washington.
Citizen Genêt Affair.
Samuel Slater erects first U.S.
cotton mill, at Pawtucket, Rhode
Island.
Eli Whitney applies for patent on
cotton gin.
Yellow fever epidemic in
Philadelphia.

1794 Whiskey Rebellion in western
Pennsylvania.
Battle of Fallen Timbers, Ohio;
General Anthony Wayne defeats
Indians.
Philadelphia-Lancaster turnpike
completed.

1795 Jay's Treaty with Britain.
Treaty of Greenville, between
United States and Indians of
Northwest.
Pinckney's Treaty with Spain.

1796 Washington's Farewell Address,
warning against foreign
entanglements and domestic
factionalism.
John Adams elected president.

1798 XYZ Affair reported by Adams to
Congress.
Quasi-war with France on high
seas.
Alien and Sedition Acts enacted by
Federalists in Congress.
Virginia and Kentucky resolutions.
Eleventh Amendment to
Constitution ratified.

1799 *American Review and Literary
Journal,* first quarterly literary
review in America, established
by the novelist Charles
Brockden Brown.
Fries uprising in Pennsylvania.

Suggested Readings

John Fiske, *The Critical Period of American History* (1888), popularized the Federalist view of the Confederation for the nineteenth century. Merrill Jensen, *The New Nation* (1950), minimizes the crisis of the 1780s and explains the movement for the Constitution as the work of a small but dynamic minority. E. James Ferguson, *The Power of the Purse . . . , 1776–1790* (1961), also stresses the nationalists' efforts to strengthen the Confederation. Clarence L. Ver Steeg, *Robert Morris, Revolutionary Financier* (1954), is the major study of that important figure.

Forrest McDonald, *E Pluribus Unum: The Formation of the American Republic, 1776–1790* (1965), describes the commercial scrambling by the Americans in the 1780s. The best account of the army and the Newburgh Conspiracy is Richard H. Kohn, *Eagle and Sword: The Federalists and the Creation of the Military Establishment in America, 1783–1802* (1975). Frederick W. Marks III, *Independence on Trial* (1973), analyzes the foreign problems contributing to the Constitution. The best short survey of the Confederation period is still Andrew C. McLaughlin, *The Confederation and the Constitution, 1783–1789* (1905).

Charles Beard's *An Economic Interpretation of the Constitution* (1913) sought to explain the Constitution as something other than the consequence of high-minded idealism. It became the most influential history book ever written in America. Beard saw the struggle over the Constitution as a "deep-seated conflict between a popular party based on paper money and agrarian interests and a conservative party centered in the towns and resting on financial, mercantile, and personal property interests generally." While Beard's particular proof for his thesis—that the Founders held federal securities that they expected would appreciate in value under a new national government—has been demolished, especially by Forrest McDonald, *We the People* (1958), his general interpretation of the origins of the Constitution still casts a long shadow. Jackson T. Main, *Political Parties Before the Constitution* (1974), finds a "cosmopolitan"-"localist" split within the states over the Constitution. Gordon S. Wood, *The Creation of the American Republic, 1776–1787* (1969), working through the ideas, discovers a similar social, but not strictly speaking a "class," division over the Constitution.

For a different emphasis on the origins of the Constitution, see Robert E. Brown, *Reinterpretation of the Formation of the American Constitution* (1963), and Benjamin F. Wright, Jr., *Consensus and Continuity, 1776–1787* (1958). The best history of the Convention is still Max Farrand, *The Framing of the Constitution of the United States* (1913), which sees the Constitution as "a bundle of compromises" designed to meet specific defects of the Articles. Irving Brant's third volume of his biography of *James Madison* (6 vols., 1941–61) has a sure-footed description of the Convention. The best brief biography of the "father of the Constitution" is Jack N. Rakove, *James Madison and the Creation of the American Republic* (1991).

Max Farrand, ed., *The Records of the Federal Convention of 1787* (4 vols.; 1911, 1937); and Jonathan Elliot, ed., *The Debates in the Several State Conventions on the Adoption of the Federal Constitution* (5 vols., 1876), are collections of the important documents. Jacob Cooke, ed., *The Federalist* (1961), is the best edition of these papers. Two sympathetic studies of the Antifederalists are Jackson T. Main, *The Antifederalists . . . , 1781–1788* (1961); and Robert A. Rutland, *The Ordeal of the Constitution* (1966). See also Robert A. Rutland, *The Birth of the Bill of Rights, 1776–1791* (1955). The papers of the Founders—Jefferson, Franklin, Hamilton, John Adams, Madison, and others—are currently being published in mammoth scholarly editions.

Politics in the 1790s is ably summarized in John C. Miller, *The Federalist Era, 1789–1801* (1960). Richard Buel, Jr., *Securing the Revolution: Ideology in American Politics, 1789–1815* (1972), however, better recaptures the distinctiveness of the age and the problematical character of the new national government. John C. Miller, *Alexander Hamilton, Portrait in Paradox* (1959), is the fullest biography; but Gerald Stourzh, *Alexander Hamilton and the Idea of Republican Government* (1970), better places this leading Federalist in an eighteenth-century context. In this respect, see also the collected essays of Douglass Adair, *Fame and the Founding Fathers* (1974). A concise study is Forrest McDonald, *The Presidency of George Washington* (1974). For single-volume biographies of Washington, see Marcus Cunliffe, *George Washington: Man and Monument* (1958), and James Thomas Flexner, *Washington: The Indispensable Man* (1974). See also Garry Wills, *Cincinnatus: George Washington and the Enlightenment* (1984).

Leonard D. White, *The Federalists: A Study in Administrative History* (1948), is the standard account of the creation of the governmental bureaucracy. See also Carl Prince, *The Federalists and the Origins of the U.S. Civil Service* (1978). Lisle A. Rose, *Prologue to Democracy*

(1968), describes the formation of Federalist influence in the South during the 1790s. Richard H. Kohn, *Eagle and Sword: The Federalists and the Creation of the Military Establishment in America, 1783–1802* (1975), is important for understanding the Federalist goals. On foreign policy, see Samuel Flagg Bemis, *Jay's Treaty* (1923) and *Pinckney's Treaty* (1926). Jerald A. Combs, *The Jay Treaty* (1970), is broader than its title would suggest. A good survey is Lawrence S. Kaplan, *Colonies into Nation: American Diplomacy, 1763–1801* (1972).

Much of the literature on the history of the 1790s treats the opposition of the Republicans as ordinary party activity. See William N. Chambers, *Political Parties in a New Nation . . . , 1776–1809* (1963), and Noble E. Cunningham, Jr., *The Jeffersonian Republicans: The Formation of Party Organization, 1789–1801* (1957). Notable exceptions are Richard Buel, Jr., *Securing the Revolution* (1972); Lance Banning, *The Jeffersonian Persuasion* (1978); and Ronald Formisano, *The Transformation of Political Culture: Massachusetts Parties, 1790s–1840s* (1983). See also John Zvesper, *Political Philosophy and Rhetoric: A Study of the Origins of American Party Politics* (1977). Joyce Appleby, *Capitalism and a New Social Order* (1984) captures the progressive optimism of many of the Republicans. On the formation of extralegal organizations, all we have is Eugene P. Link, *Democratic Republican Societies, 1790–1800* (1942). There are a number of studies of the growth of the Republican party in the separate states. See especially Paul Goodman, *The Democratic Republicans of Massachusetts* (1964); Alfred F. Young, *The Democratic Republicans of New York* (1967); Sanford W. Higgenbotham, *The Keystone in the Democratic Arch: Pennsylvania Politics 1800–1816* (1952); Carl E. Prince, *New Jersey's Jeffersonian Republicans* (1967); and Norman K. Risjord, *Chesapeake Politics, 1781–1800* (1978). On the Whiskey Rebellion, see Leland D. Baldwin, *Whiskey Rebels* (1939), and Thomas P. Slaughter, *The Whiskey Rebellion* (1986).

On the foreign crisis of the late 1790s, see Alexander De Conde, *The Quasi-War: Politics and Diplomacy of the Undeclared War with France, 1797–1801* (1966). Manning J. Dauer, *The Adams Federalists* (1953), captures some of the desperation of the Federalists in 1798. The fullest study of the Alien and Sedition Acts is James Morton Smith, *Freedom's Fetters* (1956); but for a proper appreciation of the special eighteenth-century context in which freedom of speech and of the press has to be viewed, see Leonard W. Levy, *Legacy of Suppression* (1960). Stephen G. Kurtz is solid on *The Presidency of Adams . . . , 1795–1800* (1957).

11

The Jeffersonian Revolution

~

*T*HE FEDERALIST world had been born in reaction to the popular excesses of the Revolution, and it could not endure. It ran too much against the grain of fast-moving social developments. The Federalists of the 1790s refused to recognize that the people's position in American politics was no longer a debatable issue. Convinced that people feared disunion so much that almost any sort of strong national government within a republican framework would be acceptable, the Federalists tried to revive some of the energy and authority of executive government that had been lost in the turbulence of the Revolution. America was increasingly prosperous, and the Federalists counted on this prosperity to justify both their program and their reliance on rule by a traditional gentlemanly elite. But they were so out of touch with the rapid developments of American life, and their program was so counter to the basic principles of American republican ideology, that they provoked a second revolutionary movement that threatened to tear the Republic apart.

Only the electoral victory of the Republicans in 1800 ended this threat and brought, in the eyes of many Americans, the entire revolutionary venture of two and a half decades to successful completion. Indeed, "the Revolution of 1800," as the Republican leader and third president of the United States, Thomas Jefferson, described it, "was as real a revolution in the principles of our government as that of 1776 was in its form."

The Revolution of 1800

Thomas Jefferson was an unlikely popular radical. He was a well-connected and highly cultivated southern landowner who never had to scramble for his position in Virginia. The wealth and leisure that made possible his great contributions to liberty were supported by the labor of a hundred or more slaves. He was tall,

Thomas Jefferson (1743–1826)
*Jefferson is surely the American
founder most closely identified
with democracy. No one more
fully embodied the hopes and
promise of the Enlightenment
and, indeed, of America itself.*

gangling, red-haired; and unlike his fellow Revolutionary John Adams, whom he both fought and befriended for fifty years, he was reserved, self-possessed, and incurably optimistic. He disliked personal controversy and was always charming in face-to-face relations with both friends and enemies. But at a distance he could hate, and thus many of his opponents concluded that he was two-faced. He was undeniably complicated. He mingled the most lofty visions with astute back-room politicking. He was a sophisticated man of the world who loved no place better than his native Virginia. This complex slaveholding aristocrat became the most important apostle for democratic idealism in American history.

Thomas Jefferson's narrow victory in the presidential election of 1800 confirmed the changing course of national developments. Jefferson received 73 electoral votes to the 65 of the Federalist candidate, John Adams, who was opposed by the Hamiltonians within his own party. For a moment even that close victory was in doubt. Because the Constitution did not state that the electors had to distinguish between their votes for president and those for vice-president, both Jefferson and the Republican vice-presidential candidate, Aaron Burr, had received the same number of electoral votes. Thus the election was thrown into the House of Representatives. After thirty-five deadlocked ballots, Hamilton and other Federalist leaders allowed Jefferson, the acknowledged Republican leader, to become president. They preferred Jefferson to Burr and thought that they had assurances from Jefferson that he would continue Federalist policies.* To avoid a

---

*This was one of the causes of the feud between Burr and Hamilton that led to a duel between the two men in 1804, in which Hamilton was killed.

repetition of this electoral impasse, the country adopted the Twelfth Amendment to the Constitution, which allowed the electors to designate their presidential and vice-presidential choices separately in their ballots.*

In this confused electoral maneuvering it is difficult to see the bold and revolutionary character of Jefferson's election. It was one of the first popular elections in modern history that resulted in the peaceful transfer of power from one "party" to another. At the outset Jefferson himself struck a note of concilia-tion: "We are all republicans—we are all federalists," he said in his inaugural address. Many Federalists were soon absorbed into the Republican cause. And the Republican administration did subsequently deviate from strict Republican principles. Thus the continuities are impressive, and the Jeffersonian "revolution of 1800" has blended nearly imperceptibly into the main democratic currents of American history. However, when compared to the consolidated state that the Federalists tried to build in the 1790s, what the Republicans did after 1800 proved that a real revolution—as real as Jefferson said it was—took place.

Government Without Power

Believing that most of the evils afflicting humanity in the past had flowed from the abuses of political estab-lishments, the Republicans in 1800 deliberately set about to carry out what they rightly believed was the original aim of the Revolution: to reduce the overawing and dangerous power of government. They wanted to form a national republic that would be based on the country-opposi-tion ideology and modeled on the Revolutionary state governments of 1776. They envisioned a central government whose authority would resemble that of the old Articles of Confederation more than that of the European type of government the Federalists had thought essential. In fact, they wanted to create a general govern-ment that would rule without the traditional characteristics of power.

From the outset Jefferson was determined that the new government would lack even the usual rituals of power. At the very beginning he purposefully set a new tone of republican simplicity that was in sharp contrast to the stiff formality and regal ceremony with which the Federalists, in imitation of European court life, had surrounded the presidency. The Federalist presidents, like the English monarchs, had personally delivered their addresses to the legislature "from the throne," but Jefferson chose to submit his in writing. Unlike Washington and Adams, he made himself easily accessible to visitors, all of whom, no matter how distinguished, the British government's representative to the United States reported, he received "with a most perfect disregard to ceremony both in his dress and manner." Much to the shock of foreign dignitaries, at American state occasions Jefferson replaced the protocol and distinctions of European court life with the egalitarian rules of what he called "pell-mell."

Although Jefferson's dignity and gentlemanly tastes scarcely allowed any actual leveling in social gatherings, his transformation of manners at the capital

---

*For the Twelfth Amendment, see Appendix.

Earliest-Known Engraved View of Washington, D.C.

In the early nineteenth century Washington, D.C., the nation's capital, was such a primitive, desolate village that, as a British diplomat remarked, "one may take a ride of several hours within the precincts without meeting a single individual to disturb one's meditations." Its streets were muddy and filled with tree stumps, its climate was swampy and mosquito-infested, and its unfinished government buildings stood like Greek temples in a deserted ancient city.

harmonized with changes that were occurring in American society. For the Republican revolution soon brought to the national government men who, unlike Jefferson, did not have the outward manner of gentlemen, who did not know one another, and who were decidedly not at home in polite society. During the early years of the nineteenth century, life in the national capital became steadily vulgarized by the growing presence in drawing rooms of muddy boots, unkempt hair, and the constant chawing and spitting of tobacco.

Even the removal of the national capital in 1800 from Philadelphia, the bustling intellectual and commercial center of the country, to the rural wilderness of the "federal city" on the Potomac accentuated the transformation of power that was taking place. It dramatized the Republicans' attempt to separate the national government from close involvement in the society and their aim to erect the very kind of general government that Hamilton, in *The Federalist* No. 27, had warned against, "a government at a distance and out of sight" that could "hardly be expected to interest the sensations of the people." The new and remote capital, Washington, D.C., utterly failed to attract the population, the commerce, and the social and cultural life that were needed to make it what its original planners had boldly expected, the Rome of the New World. By 1820 Washington was an out-of-the-way village of less than 10,000 inhabitants whose principal business was keeping boardinghouses. Situated in a marsh, the federal city fully deserved the gibes of the visiting Irish poet Thomas Moore:

> *This embryo capital*
> *where Fancy sees*
> *Squares in Morasses,*
> *obelisks in trees.*

Political Reform   The Republicans in fact meant to have an insignificant national government. The federal government, Jefferson declared in his first message to Congress in 1801, was "charged with the external and mutual relations only of these states." All the rest—the "principal care of our persons, our property, and our reputation, constituting the great field of human concerns"—was to be left to the states. Such a limited national government required turning back a decade of Federalist policy. The Sedition Act of 1798 was allowed to lapse; a new, liberal naturalization law was adopted; and strict economy was ordered, to root out Federalist corruption.

The inherited Federalist governmental establishment was minuscule by modern standards and was small even by eighteenth-century European standards. In 1801 the headquarters of the War Department, for example, consisted of only the secretary, an accountant, fourteen clerks, and two messengers. The attorney general did not have even a clerk. Nevertheless, in Jefferson's eyes, this tiny federal bureaucracy had become "too complicated, too expensive," and offices under the Federalists had "unnecessarily multiplied." Thus the roll of federal officials was severely cut back. All tax inspectors and collectors were eliminated. The diplomatic establishment was reduced to three missions—in Britain, France, and Spain. The Federalist dream of creating a modern army and navy in imitation of Europe disappeared, and the military budget was cut in half. The army, stationed in the West, was left with 3,000 regulars and only 172 officers. The navy had but a half-dozen frigates, and by 1807 these were replaced with several hundred gunboats, which were designed only to defend the coast and to deal with the Barbary pirates in the Mediterranean. The benefits of a standing military establishment, the Jeffersonians believed, were not worth the cost either in money or in the threat to liberty that this kind of establishment posed.

Since Hamilton's financial program had formed the basis of the heightened political power of the federal government, it above all had to dismantled. All the internal excise taxes the Federalists had designed to make the people feel the energy of the national government were eliminated. For many citizens the federal presence was now reduced to the delivery of the mails.

Although Jefferson's extremely able secretary of the treasury, Albert Gallatin, persuaded the reluctant president to keep the Bank of the United States, the government was under continual pressure to reduce the Bank's influence. The growing numbers of state banking interests resented the privileged and restraining authority of the national Bank. Eventually, in 1811, state bankers, along with southern landowners, who hated all banks, prevented a renewal of the Bank's charter. The federal government then distributed its patronage among twenty-one state banks and thus effectively diluted its authority to control either the society or the economy. It was in fact the proliferation of these state-chartered banks and their issuing of notes that enabled the states to have paper money after all, despite the Constitution's prohibition against the states' issuing bills of credit.

Precisely because Hamilton had regarded the permanent federal debt as a principal source of support for the federal government, the Republicans were determined to pay off the debt—and quickly. By 1810 the federal debt had been reduced to nearly half of the $80 million it had been when the Republicans took office. Jefferson's lifelong desire to reduce the government's debt was not simply a matter of prohibiting a present generation from burdening its descendants. He wanted also to destroy what he considered an insidious and dangerous instrument of political influence. His aim was to create a new kind of government, one without privilege or patronage.

Perhaps nothing illustrates Jefferson's radical conception of government better than his problems with patronage. Jefferson was reluctant to dismiss or appoint men to office for political reasons. But not all Republicans took his dislike of using patronage as seriously as he did, and many Republicans hesitated to join a government in which they would have no sources of influence. Time and again Jefferson found himself caught between his conscientious determination to avoid anything resembling Hamilton's political patronage, or "corruption," and the pressing demands of his fellow Republicans that he give them a share in the government and oust the enemy. Once the Federalists were replaced by Republicans, however, there was no further need for Republicans to compromise on this issue; and removals from office for political reasons came to an end. By the end of the administrations of Jefferson's Republican successors, James Madison (1809–17), James Monroe (1817–25), and John Quincy Adams (1825–29), the holders of government appointments had become a permanent officialdom of men grown old in their positions. Until the Jacksonian revolution of 1828, patronage as a means of influence in government virtually ceased.

Republican Politics   Jefferson was able personally to direct Congress and the Republican party to an extraordinary degree. He used a combination of this initial patronage and some improvised forms of political influence—in particular, his nightly legislative dinner parties and his use of confidential legislative agents. Yet Jefferson's personal strength and his notable achievements as president cannot hide the remarkable transformation in the traditional meaning of government that the Republican revolution of 1800 created. During the opening three decades of the nineteenth century, particularly after Jefferson retired from the presidency, the United States government was weaker than at any other time in its national history.

The alignments of politics became increasingly confused. The Federalists in 1800–1801 surrendered the national ruling authority without a fight. Because the Federalist leaders considered themselves gentlemen for whom politics was not an exclusive concern, they were prepared to retire to their businesses and private lives and await what they assumed would soon be the people's desperate call for the return of the "wise and good" and the "natural rulers." But the popular reaction against the Republican revolution did not come. Some, like John Jay and John Adams, retired to their country estates. Others, like John Quincy Adams, the son of the former president, eventually joined the Republican movement. Others, like Robert Goodloe Harper of South Carolina, clung to their principles and their minority status in politics. And still others, like Timothy Pickering, secretary of state under John Adams, dreamed of revenge and encouraged separatist plots in New England. But as a national party, Federalism slowly withered under the relentless democratization of American society.

Although the Federalists and Republicans continued to compete for election and worked successfully to increase voter participation, neither was a party in any modern sense; that is, neither recognized the other as a necessary and permanent part of the political process. It is therefore probably anachronistic to call their electoral competition "the first party system," as some historians have done. Although the Federalists continued to put up presidential candidates, their electoral strength was generally very weak and was confined primarily to New England. By 1807 even in Massachusetts there were more Republican than Federalist congressmen. During the administration's Republican crises over foreign policy and the embargo in 1808–09 and the War of 1812, the Federalists did manage to rally and to win major victories—not only in New England, but also in New York, Maryland, and Delaware. But elsewhere the Federalists' power at the polls rarely approached that achieved in 1800, and the party slowly declined. It was much too tainted with aristocracy and New England sectionalism to persist as a national party. By 1820 it was too weak even to nominate a presidential candidate.

While the declining Federalist gentlemen regarded themselves less as a party than as rightful rulers who had been driven from power, the Republicans saw themselves as leaders of a revolutionary movement and were eager to incorporate the bulk of the opposition into their fold. Only as long as the Federalists posed a threat to the principles of free government could the Republicans remain a unified party. Thereafter, as the possibility of a Federalist comeback faded, the Republican party gradually fell apart. A variety of Republican factions and groups arose in Congress and in the country. These were organized around particular individuals (the "Burrites," the "Clintonians"), around states and sections (the "Pennsylvania Quids," the "Old Republicans" of Virginia), and sometimes around ideology ("the Principles of '98," the "Invisibles," the "War Hawks"). Individual politicians continued to pride themselves on their independence from influence of any sort, and *party* remained a disrespectful word. In fact, until the Jacksonian era nothing approaching a stable party system developed in Congress.

By the end of Jefferson's presidency in 1809, the balance of governmental power had slipped to Congress, which was unequipped to exercise it. Because of the great increase in the size of Congress and its growing disintegration into diverse voting blocs, neither Madison nor Monroe was able to use any of the personal charm and influence that Jefferson had used. By 1808 caucuses of Republicans within Congress had taken over nomination of the party's candidates for the presidency, and Republican presidential aspirants soon became dependent on the legislature in the way governors in the Revolutionary state constitutions of 1776 had been.

With Jefferson's private blessing, Secretary of State James Madison was able to secure the Republican nomination in 1808 and again in 1812 against only some divided opposition. But in 1816, Madison's secretary of state, James Monroe, had to contend strenuously with Secretary of War William H. Crawford of Georgia for the nomination. By the early 1820s Secretary of State John Quincy Adams, Secretary of War John C. Calhoun, and Secretary of the Treasury Crawford were all feuding with one another and seeking support in Congress for the presidential nomination. If such political realities did not dictate that presidents defer to the legislature, Republican ideology did. Except in foreign affairs, presidents Madison and Monroe, the second and third members of the so-called Virginia Dynasty, considered that Congress had the right to determine the public will, free of executive influence.

As Congress gathered up the power draining away from the executive in the Madison and Monroe administrations (1809–25), it sought to organize itself into committees in order to initiate and supervise policy. But the rise of the committee system only further fragmented the government into contending interest groups. The executive authority itself broke apart into competing departments, with each member of the cabinet seeking his own support in Congress and becoming a rival of the president. Congress now fought with the president for control of the cabinet and connived with executive department heads behind the president's back. At one point Congress actually forced Madison to accept a secretary of state who was plotting against him, and its meddling drove Monroe into bitter hostility against his secretary of the treasury, with whom he stopped speaking. Until the congressional caucus system of presidential nomination collapsed in 1824 and a new kind of democratic presidency emerged in 1828 with the election of Andrew Jackson, the energy of the national executive remained weak.

But despite this concentration on strict republican principles, by the second decade of the nineteenth century many Americans sought to reclaim and reenact some of the abandoned Federalist measures. A new generation of politicians, less attached to the ideology and fears of the eighteenth century and with none of Hamilton's dream to create a consolidated state in the European manner, now began urging a new national bank, protective tariffs, and a federally sponsored system of "internal improvements"—canals, turnpikes, and the like. By 1814 the nation had grown faster than anyone had expected, and new states, new interest groups, and new outlooks had to be taken into account. By then it was becoming clear that the future of the country lay in the West.

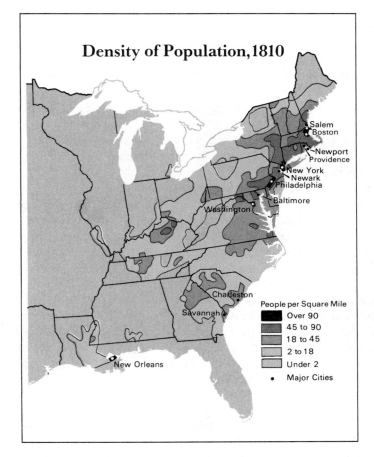

Density of Population, 1810

People per Square Mile
- Over 90
- 45 to 90
- 18 to 45
- 2 to 18
- Under 2
- • Major Cities

An Empire of Liberty

While Hamilton and the Federalists had looked eastward across the Atlantic to Europe for their image of the destiny of the United States, the Republicans from the beginning had had their eyes on the West. Only by moving westward, Jefferson thought, could Americans maintain their republican society of independent yeoman-farmers and avoid the miseries of the concentrated urban working classes of Europe. Jefferson was indeed the most expansion-minded president in American history. He dreamed of Americans with republican principles eventually swarming over the continent and creating an "empire of liberty." Yet even Jefferson did not anticipate how suddenly and chaotically Americans would scatter westward.

The population grew from almost 4 million in 1790 to more than 7 million in 1810 and nearly 10 million by 1820, and much of it was moving west. By the 1790s the population in some of the tidewater counties of the Chesapeake region was declining. The advance over the Allegheny Plateau that had been a trickle before the Revolution and had swelled during the 1780s now became a flood. Within a single generation after the Revolution, more territory was occupied than during the entire colonial period. By 1810 westward-moving Americans had created a great triangular wedge of settlement reaching to the Mississippi River. The northern side of the triangle ran from New York along the Ohio River, the southern side extended from east Georgia through Tennessee, and the two sides met at the tip of the wedge at St. Louis. Within this huge triangle of settlement, people were distributed haphazardly, and huge pockets remained virtually uninhabited.

National leaders had expected westward migration, but not the way it happened. The massive and chaotic movement of people simply overwhelmed the carefully drawn plans of the 1780s for the orderly surveying and settlement of the West. Many settlers ignored land ordinances and titles, squatted on the land, and claimed rights to it. For decades beginning in 1796, the federal government steadily lowered the price of land, reduced the size of purchasable tracts, and relaxed the terms of credit in ever more desperate efforts to bring the public land laws into line with the speed with which the West was being settled. There was more land than people could use, and still they kept moving. Some moved three and four times in a lifetime. Speculators and land companies that had counted on land values rising through neat and orderly settlement, as in colonial days, were now wiped out. Many of the most prominent and wealthy Revolutionary leaders, including Robert Morris, the financier of the Confederation, Henry Knox, Washington's secretary of war, and James Wilson, justice of the Supreme Court, speculated heavily in land and ended their careers in bankruptcy. Even Washington died with his estate tied up in speculative land that no one would pay for.

The Louisiana Purchase   Nothing in Jefferson's administration contributed more to this astonishing expansion than his sudden acquisition in 1803 of the entire territory of Louisiana. This territory extended from the Mississippi River to the Rocky Mountains, and its acquisition doubled the size of the United States. For decades Jefferson and other American leaders had foreseen that the young and thriving nation would expand naturally and "piece by piece" would take over the feebly held Spanish possessions in North America. Some even thought that British-held Canada would eventually pass to the United States. When the Revolutionary War ended in 1783, Jefferson was already dreaming of explorations to the Pacific. And when he became president, well before he had any inkling that America would purchase all of Louisiana, he laid plans for scientific—and also military and commercial—expeditions into the foreign-held trans-Mississippi West. The most famous of these expeditions was that of Lewis and Clark, eventually undertaken in 1803–06.

In 1800 these dreams of expansion were suddenly placed in doubt when, in the Treaty of San Ildefonso, a weak Spain ceded back to a powerful France the territory of Louisiana, including New Orleans, that France had once held west of the Mississippi River. The livelihood of the western farmers depended on the free navigation of the Mississippi, and Jefferson was determined to maintain it. He immediately began strengthening fortifications in the West and preparing for the worst. "The day that France takes possession of New Orleans," he informed the American minister to France, Robert Livingston, in April 1802, "we must marry

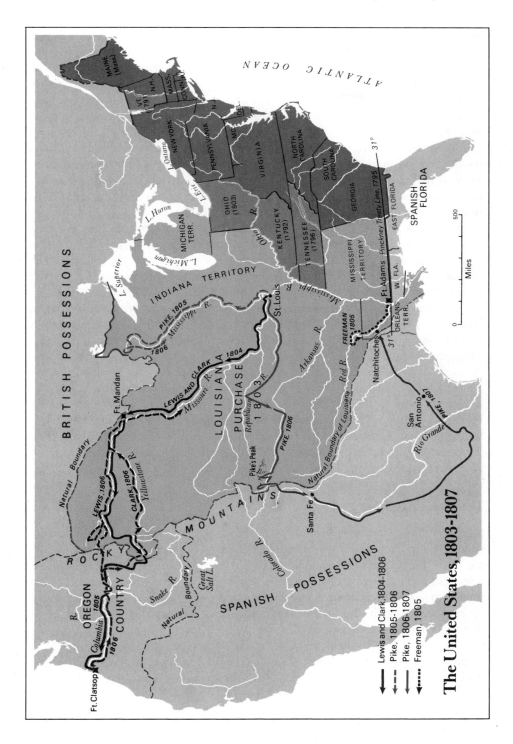

The United States, 1803-1807

ourselves to the British fleet and nation." This prospect of an American-British alliance threatened the French. Napoleon Bonaparte—soon to become Emperor Napoleon I—was already calculating the difficulties of reestablishing the French empire in the New World if war should break out again in Europe. As a result, in 1803 the French government decided to sell to the United States not just New Orleans, which Jefferson had sought to purchase, but all of Louisiana, for $15 million.

Jefferson hesitated over what to do. He feared that the purchase of Louisiana by the federal government would exceed the limited powers that had been granted to the government by the Constitution. He considered amending the Constitution in order to acquire this new territory. But finally and regretfully, under intense pressure, he allowed his constitutional scruples to be passed over in silence. Despite the fact that the Louisiana Purchase fulfilled his grandest dreams for America, Jefferson's agonized decision did not suggest that he was conceding in any way to a broad Federalist interpretation of the Constitution. His hesitation only showed the extreme seriousness with which he took his strict construction of the Constitution.

The purchase of Louisiana was the most popular and important event of Jefferson's presidency. It ended the long struggle for control of the Mississippi River's outlet to the sea. It also, as Jefferson exulted, freed America from Europe's colonial entanglements and prepared the way for the eventual dominance of the United States in the Western Hemisphere. Its most immediate consequence, however, was to raise new fears of the country's splitting apart. The borders of the new territory were so vague, the Spanish hold on Mexico and the Floridas so weak, and the rough and unruly frontier inhabitants so captivated by the dreams of America's continued expansion that adventurers, filibustering expeditions,* and rumors of plots and conspiracies flourished throughout the South and the West.

The Burr Conspiracy　The most grandiose of these schemes was that of 1806–07. It involved Aaron Burr, Jefferson's former vice-president, and (until he turned state's evidence) General James Wilkinson, commanding general of the United States Army. Wilkinson was secretly in the pay of the Spanish government and was one of the most unscrupulous and skillful adventurers in American history. In the summer of 1806, Burr and sixty men floated in flatboats down the Ohio and Mississippi rivers toward New Orleans to make contact with the Spanish. When Burr learned that Wilkinson had denounced him, he fled toward Florida, probably on his way to Europe, but he was captured and brought east to be tried for treason. Although Burr was acquitted because no overt act of treason could be constitutionally proved, he undoubtedly had had in mind some sort of conspiracy, involving a number of

---

*In nineteenth-century America *filibustering* meant stirring up or attempting to carry out revolutions in Central American or Caribbean nations. Those who led expeditions for this purpose were called filibusters.

From the Journal of Lewis and Clark

The Lewis and Clark expedition (1804–06) was the greatest expedition of exploration in American history. Lewis and Clark led a party of fifty from St. Louis to the Pacific with instructions from President Jefferson to keep detailed records of everything they saw.

American civil and military officials, directed toward an attack on Mexico or a separation of the western areas of the United States.

These kinds of activities and the danger of the country's splintering caused Congress to incorporate into the Union as fast as possible the underdeveloped frontier territories of Ohio (1803), Louisiana (1812), Indiana (1816), Mississippi (1817), Illinois (1818), and Alabama (1819). These new western states were firmly Republican, and they created constitutions that were more democratic than those of the older eastern states. Most provided for weak executives, white male suffrage, annually elected legislatures, no property qualifications for officeholders, and popular election for a host of officials, including judges.

Indians

The native Americans in these western territories were no match for the hordes of advancing settlers. By 1800 Ohio had 45,000 inhabitants; by 1810 it had more than 230,000 and was already bursting its boundaries. Although the Greenville Treaty of 1795 had drawn a definite line between Indians and whites, most Americans, including President Jefferson, assumed that the vast Indian hunting grounds between the Ohio and Mississippi rivers must sooner or later belong to the advancing Americans. Jefferson expected the native Americans willingly to cede their lands to the United States and either become farmers and share the blessings of republican civilization or move west beyond the Mississippi.

American pressure on the Indians to surrender their lands was immense, and under presidents Jefferson and Madison fifty-three treaties of land cession were

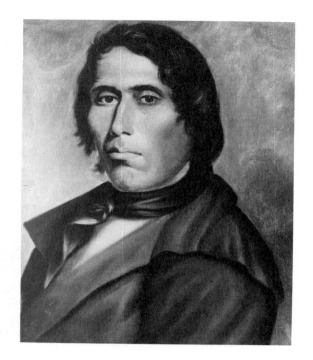

Tecumseh (c. 1768–1813)
*Tecumseh, a Shawnee chief, was
perhaps the most extraordinary
Indian leader in American history. Together with his brother,
The Prophet, he attempted in
the early nineteenth century to
organize a huge confederation of
Indians in the Northwest. The
Indians were to refuse to cede
any more lands to the Americans
and were to abandon the white
man's ways and goods. But after
the battle of Tippecanoe in 1811,
organized Indian resistance
gave way to sporadic warfare.
Tecumseh was killed fighting for
the British at the battle of the
Thames (1813).*

made. Finally in 1805 the Shawnee chief Tecumseh and his brother The Prophet
attempted to halt this steady American encroachment by forming an Indian
confederacy. This tribal effort at organized resistance was broken by the governor
of the Indiana Territory, General William Henry Harrison, in a battle between six
hundred Indians and a mixed force of a thousand American army troops and
Kentucky frontiersmen at Tippecanoe in 1811. Sporadic Indian fighting and
raiding in the Old Northwest continued, however it did not stop the wave of
settlers. By 1815 the Indiana Territory had nearly 60,000 settlers.

In the southwestern territories the Indian presence was even more formidable. Still, by 1810 the Mississippi Territory (much of present-day Alabama and
Mississippi) had more than 40,000 people, including 17,000 slaves, mainly clustered along the Mississippi River counties south of Natchez, which was fast
becoming a bustling trade center. In 1810 the Territory of Orleans (modern
Louisiana) had more than 76,000 inhabitants, more than half of whom were
slaves. New Orleans, with its mixture of Spanish, French, and other nationalities
in a population of more than 10,000 was by far the largest and most flamboyant
city of the Mississippi Valley and was on its way to becoming one of the greatest
ports of the country. By 1810 pioneers were rapidly pushing beyond the
Mississippi River into what are now the states of Arkansas and Missouri, leaving
behind huge pockets of native Americans—Creeks in Georgia and Cherokees in
Tennessee. By 1815 the Missouri Territory had more than 20,000 people.

All the while, eastern Federalists expressed alarm at this expanding "empire
of liberty." With their vision of the United States as a homogeneous and inte-

Creek House in 1791
The Creek Indians, numbering perhaps 20,000, lived in towns in parts of Georgia and present-day Alabama.

grated nation-state like those of Europe, the Federalists found it inconceivable that such a gigantic republic could long hold together. To the Republicans, however, who thought of the United States as a loosely bound confederation of states, the huge expanse of territory posed no problems. "Who can limit the extent to which the federative principle may operate effectively?" asked Jefferson in his second inaugural address. Jefferson always conceived of his "empire of liberty" in terms of like principles, not of like boundaries. At times he was remarkably indifferent to the possibility that a western confederacy might break away from the eastern United States. What did it matter? he asked in 1804. "Those of the western confederacy will be as much our children and descendants as those of the eastern."

The Federalists called this idea of a nation bound together only by principles "a most visionary theory," and they believed that the consequence would eventually be anarchy. But Republicans considered that Americans were creating new bonds of social cohesion—not the patronage and coercion of the Federalists, and not even the virtue of classical republicanism, but, as Jefferson said, "that progress of opinion which is tending to unite them in object and in will."

The Origins of Judicial Review

At the time of Jefferson's election in 1800, no institution of the national government was more detested by the Republicans than the judiciary. The appointed federal judges were less susceptible to popular rule than were other government officials, and during the 1790s the Federalists had consciously tried to strengthen the federal courts in order to extend the central government's presence among the people. Since there was not a single Republican judge in the entire national judiciary during the 1790s, Republican newspaper editors had often been brought before the federal courts on charges of sedition. Moreover, Federalist land speculators with interests that spanned state lines had used the more sympathetic federal courts to resolve their conflicting claims, often to the anger of Republican-controlled state courts. Even after the Federalists had lost the election of 1800, the lame-duck Congress dominated by Federalists had passed a new judiciary act creating a system of circuit courts and broadening the jurisdiction of the federal courts. And before surrendering the presidency to Jefferson, John Adams had hastily appointed a number of judges, including John Marshall as chief justice of the United States. Jefferson was convinced that "the remains of federalism" had "retired into the judiciary as a stronghold . . . , and from that battery all the works of republicanism are to be beaten down and erased."

To complete "the revolution," therefore, as a fellow Virginian told Jefferson, "the enemy" had to be routed from "that strong fortress." After a bitter debate in Congress, the Republicans repealed the Federalist Judiciary Act of 1801. They thus destroyed the newly created circuit courts and for the first and only time in United States history revoked the tenure of federal judges as well. In order to bring the entire judicial establishment under greater congressional control, some Republicans proposed amending the Constitution. Others, however, fixed on impeachment for "high crimes and misdemeanors" as the best constitutional device for removing obnoxious Federalist judges. The Republicans in the House of Representatives first impeached and the Senate then convicted John Pickering, an alcoholic and insane judge of the federal district court of New Hampshire, even though he had committed no crimes or misdemeanors.

Having thus broadly interpreted the criminal meaning of impeachment, the most rabid Republicans, under the leadership of John Randolph of Virginia, next attempted to bring down Supreme Court Justice Samuel Chase, the most overbearing Federalist on the Court. However, this perversion of the impeachment process into a means of simply removing unpopular judges from office was too much for some Republicans. Although a majority of the Senate in 1805 found Chase guilty, the Republicans could not muster the necessary two-thirds majority. Not only did Chase's acquittal hurt Randolph's reputation, driving him to the extremist edges of the Republican party, but it ended any further direct assault by the Republicans on the national judiciary.

John Marshall (1755–1835), by Cephas Thompson
Marshall is the most famous Chief Justice of the Supreme Court in American history. During his long tenure on the Court from 1801 to his death, this Virginia Federalist participated in more than 1,000 decisions, writing over half himself. In effect Marshall created for America what came to be called constitutional law and transformed the meaning and role of the Supreme Court.

Marbury v. Madison   In the meantime John Marshall, who was to become the most important chief justice of the Supreme Court in American history, used his position to drain some of the bitterness from the controversy over the judiciary. During his long career (1801–35), which spanned the administrations of five presidents, he laid the foundations both for the Court's eventual independence and for the constitutional supremacy of the national government over the states.

In 1801, however, the Court was very weak. Although Marshall solidified the Court by making one justice's opinion (usually his own) stand for the decision of the whole Court, he had to move very cautiously. Many Federalists urged him to confront the Republicans head-on by declaring unconstitutional Congress's repeal of the Judiciary Act of 1801. But Marshall chose to act indirectly. In the case of *Marbury* v. *Madison* (1803), the Marshall Court decided that Marbury, one of the "midnight judges" whom President Adams had appointed as his own term was ending, was entitled to his commission, which Secretary of State Madison had withheld. Yet if unenforced by the president, such a bold decision would obviously have discredited the Court. Marshall avoided a losing clash with the executive by going on to state that, although Marbury deserved his commission, the Court had no authority to order the president to grant it. He ruled that the provision of the earlier, Federalist-enacted Judiciary Act of 1789, which had given the Supreme Court such original authority, was unconstitutional. Thus Marshall indirectly asserted the Court's role in overseeing the Constitution without the serious political repercussions involved in openly opposing the Republicans. Since the American people regarded their written Constitution as "the fundamental and paramount law of the nation," wrote Marshall for the Court, then it followed that "a law repugnant to the Constitution," such as part of the Judiciary Act of 1789, "is void; and that courts, as well as other departments, are bound by that instrument."

Although Marshall's decision in *Marbury* v. *Madison* has since taken on immense historical significance as the first assertion by the Supreme Court of its right to declare acts of Congress unconstitutional, few in 1803 saw its far-reaching implications. This right of judicial review was nowhere explicitly recognized in the Constitution. To be sure, some, like Hamilton in *The Federalist* No. 78, had tried to justify this ultimate judicial authority by invoking the supremacy of the Constitution as created by the sovereignty of the people and as protected by the courts. But it was by no means established in American culture at the end of the eighteenth century.

By asserting in the *Marbury* decision that the Supreme Court had a right and a duty to declare what the fundamental law was, Marshall obviously drew on this earlier thinking. But he did not say explicitly that the Court was the only part of the national government that had this right and duty. Indeed, Marshall's assertion of judicial authority in the *Marbury* decision was limited and ambiguous. Consequently it allowed the other branches of the government, the executive and legislative, to claim an equal right with the judiciary to interpret the Constitution. Jefferson, for one, always denied the "exclusive" authority of the judiciary to decide what laws were constitutional. Such a monopoly of interpretative power, he said in 1804, "would make the judiciary a despotic branch." *Marbury* v. *Madison* in fact marked the only time in Marshall's long tenure in which the Supreme Court declared an act of Congress unconstitutional.

Constitutional Nationalism

What the Marshall Court did do in its long career, however, was bring the exposition of the Constitution within the routine business of the courts and declare a large number of *state* judicial interpretations and *state* laws invalid because they violated the federal Constitution. In a series of decisions beginning with *United States* v. *Peters* (1809) and proceeding through *Martin* v. *Hunter's Lessee* (1816) and *Cohens* v. *Virginia* (1821), the Supreme Court established its right to review and reverse decisions of state courts involving interpretations of federal law and the federal Constitution. At the same time, following the first test in *Fletcher* v. *Peck* (1810), the Court overturned a series of state laws that interfered with private contracts and hence violated the Constitution.

Marshall, however, was not content merely with these negative restraints on the states' powers. He sought positively to enhance the supremacy of the national government. In the greatest decision of his career, *McCulloch* v. *Maryland* (1819), Marshall upheld the right of Congress to charter a national bank even though that right was not specifically mentioned in the Constitution. The power to charter a bank, said Marshall, was implied by the "necessary and proper" authority that the

Constitution granted to Congress to carry its delegated powers into effect. Hence the attempt by the Maryland legislature to destroy the Bank of the United States by taxation was unconstitutional. No decision of Marshall's was more important to the future of America, and none asserted the supremacy of the Constitution more clearly. By 1820 the Court had already become—even for James Madison— something resembling that "disinterested umpire" that in 1787 he had wanted the entire federal government to be.

The Manipulative Tradition of American Law
Yet as important as Marshall's decisions were in establishing the Supreme Court's final authority over the states to interpret the Constitution, they do not by themselves explain the origins of the extraordinary authority that has been wielded by all American judges. Judicial review has deeper roots than simply the Marshall court. Nineteenth-century Americans inherited from the colonial period an unusually manipulative attitude toward law. Since the colonists had derived their law haphazardly both from their colonial legislature and courts and from various English sources, they tended to equate law not with what English judges and legal authorities said it was, but with what made sense in America's local circumstances. Time and again eighteenth-century Americans had justified minor deviations and irregularities in their laws in the name of reason, justice, or utility. They thus developed a particularly pragmatic attitude toward law that became stronger in the decades that followed the Revolution.

In the emerging business society of early-nineteenth-century America, the desired predictability of law came not from strict adherence to the decisions of the past, but rather from rapid adaptability to changing commercial circumstances. To mold the law to fit the needs of America's expanding enterprise, both state and federal judges increasingly abandoned the customs and technicalities of the inherited English common law and replaced them with useful and prudent regulations. The idea of the sovereignty of the people that had been emphasized by Revolutionary ideology only confirmed and further justified the independent manipulative power of the judges; the judges were now seen as just another kind of agent of the people with a responsibility equal to that of the legislatures or executive to carry out the people's will. By the second decade of the nineteenth century, American law was coming to be thought of as a man-made creative instrument of social policy. And under fast-moving economic pressures, judges were becoming the chief agents of legal change. The judicial interpretative power that from the beginning was present in the flexibility of American law was now starkly revealed and greatly expanded.

Despite continued efforts in the early nineteenth century to weaken this remarkable judicial authority, law in America maintained its flexible quality. Although judges continued to deny that they made law in the way legislatures did, it was obvious that they did something more than simply discover it in the precedents and customs of the past. Law in America, rooted in the consent and sovereignty of the people, was designed to serve the needs of that people; and when it did not, it was the obligation of judges to interpret it in such a way that it did. In fact, if neither legislatures nor judges could act fast enough to shape the law to changing circumstances, then, some Americans thought, the people themselves, in extralegal groups and "mobs," had the right to take the law into their own hands and mold it as their situation demanded. The uniquely American practices of judicial review and vigilantism were actually two sides of the same legal coin.

Republican Religion

Although politics and constitutionalism dominated the Revolutionary era, most ordinary Americans still conceived of the world in religious terms. Hence the Revolution and even republicanism had a religious dimension. Indeed, the Revolution marked an important point in the history of American religion. It endorsed the Enlightenment's faith in liberty of conscience, cut the already weak connection between church and state, and advanced America into a religious world of competing denominations that was unique to Christendom.

Religious Liberty in the Revolution

From the outset of the Revolutionary controversy, Americans had argued that the dark forces of civic tyranny and religious tyranny were linked. All the new Revolutionary constitutions of 1776 in some way affirmed religious freedom. Yet the constitutional declarations "that all men have a natural and unalienable right to worship Almighty God according to the dictates of their own consciences" did not necessarily mean that the government would abandon its traditional role in religious matters. To be sure, the official establishment of the Church of England that existed in several of the colonies was immediately eliminated. But the Maryland, South Carolina, and Georgia Revolutionary constitutions authorized their state legislatures to create in place of the Anglican church a kind of multiple establishment of a variety of religious groups, using tax money to support "the Christian religion."

Virginians especially were divided over the meaning of their 1776 declaration of religious liberty. Liberals like Jefferson and Madison joined growing numbers of Presbyterian and Baptist dissenters to oppose the Anglican clergymen and landowners in a fierce but eventually successful struggle for the complete disestablishment of the Church of England. In 1786 this Virginia struggle was climaxed by the passage of Jefferson's memorable Act for Establishing Religious Freedom. Many of the states, however, retained some vague or general religious qualifications for public office, and both Connecticut and Massachusetts continued to recognize the modified but still official status of the Congregational church.

In short, unlike the church in Europe, the American churches, developing as they had in the colonial period, perceived no threat from revolution or republicanism. Except for the Anglicans, Protestant ministers were in the forefront of the Revolutionary movement. In fact, it was the clergy who made the Revolution meaningful for most common people. For every gentleman who read a scholarly pamphlet and delved into Whig theory and ancient history for an explanation of events, there were dozens of ordinary people who read the Bible and looked to their ministers for an interpretation of what the Revolution meant. Evangelical Protestantism blended with republicanism in a common effort to rid America of sin and luxury and to build a new society of goodness and virtue.

Despite these hopes, however, the immediate effect of the Revolution on church organization was devastating. The Revolutionary War destroyed churches, scattered congregations, and led to a sharp decline in church membership. By the 1790s perhaps only one in twenty Americans was affiliated with a church. The earlier revivalistic enthusiasm receded under the pressure of a spreading religious rationalism, called deism, which sought to substitute nature and reason for revelation, and the science of Sir Isaac Newton for the mysteries of traditional Christianity. In 1784, the Vermont Revolutionary Ethan Allen published his book *Reason the Only Oracle of Man,* which boldly attacked the Bible and the clergy and defended natural religion. This was followed by other works, such as Thomas Paine's *Age of Reason* (1794) and the French Comte de Volney's *Ruins of Empire* (1791), which together with Elihu Palmer's attempts to organize deistic societies among urban workingmen in the 1790s, frightened many religious leaders into concluding that republicanism was breeding disbelief in traditional Christianity.

As long as the enlightened deism of Jefferson and other Revolutionary leaders had been confined to the drawing rooms of the gentry and was not publicized, it had posed little threat to traditional Protestantism. But the spreading of rational and natural religion among ordinary people at the time of the French Revolution alarmed American clergymen, particularly those of the older Calvinist churches. These ministers thus began a countermovement on behalf of orthodox Christianity. For many people, rational deism became so deeply identified with the anti-Christian excesses of the French Revolution and hence with the Republican party that even Hamilton toyed with the idea of enlisting Christianity on behalf of the politically beleaguered Federalists. In the end this countermovement by conservative Congregationalists and Presbyterians in the 1790s went beyond its creators. It became an eastern version of the revivalism that had continued throughout the South and West during the Revolutionary era, and it eventually fused into the early-nineteenth-century evangelical movement that is known as the Second Great Awakening.

The Second Great Awakening

The Second Great Awakening was a radical expansion and extension of the earlier eighteenth-century revivals. It did not simply intensify the religious feeling of existing church members. More important, it mobilized unprecedented numbers of people who previously had belonged to no church and made them members of religious groups. By popularizing religion as never before and by extending Christianity into the remotest areas of America, this great revival marked the beginning of the republicanizing and nationalizing of American religion. Thousands upon thousands of ordinary people found in evangelical religion new sources of order and community.

In the decades following the Revolution, the various Protestant churches reorganized themselves nationally and entered a period of denominational rivalry. Among the gentry the number of college graduates willing to enter the ministry was declining, and the older Calvinist churches—the Presbyterians and Congregationalists—were forced to form separate colleges and seminaries for the professional education of ministers. They also had to recruit increasing numbers of ministers from lower social levels. The newer denominations—the Methodists and the Baptists—recruited their preachers even more informally. Rejecting the idea of a settled and learned ministry, this new breed of preachers was more capable than the ministers of the older churches of speaking the language of the common people it sought to convert. By 1820 the Baptists and Methodists had become the largest denominations in America.

Although evangelism spread throughout America, it was most successful in the West, where the dynamic process of revivalism was better able to deal with a mobile population than were the traditional churchly institutions. In the first twelve years of the nineteenth century, the Methodists in Tennessee, Kentucky, and Ohio grew from less than 3,000 to well over 30,000. In the short period between 1800 and 1802, the Baptists in Kentucky alone increased from 4,700 to 13,500. In these fast-growing new territories, the need for some kind of community, however loose and voluntary, among isolated men and women was most intense. And there the need for building barriers against barbarism and sinfulness was most keenly felt.

In the summer of 1801 at Cane Ridge, Kentucky, unbelievable numbers of these Westerners, together with dozens of ministers of several denominations, came together in what some thought was the greatest outpouring of the Holy Spirit since the beginning of Christianity. Crowds that were estimated at 12,000–15,000 participated in a week of frenzied conversions. The heat, the noise, and the confusion were overwhelming. Ministers shouted sermons from wagons and tree stumps; people fell to the ground moaning and wailing in remorse, and they sang, laughed, barked, rolled, and jerked in excitement. This gigantic camp meeting at Cane Ridge immediately became the symbol of the promises and the excesses of the new kind of evangelical Protestantism spreading throughout the South and West. Although the conservative Presbyterians and Congregationalists in the East did not hold camp meetings, they too were compelled to adopt some of the new revivalistic methods. By 1820 there were already clearly revealed a number of basic, interrelated characteristics of American religious life whose roots went back to the colonial period and which underlay the emerging Evangelical Age.

Evangelical Denominationalism　First, the number of religions multiplied, and any lingering sense that there was one true religion disintegrated. What was left of the official establishment of Congregationalism was eliminated in Connecticut in 1818 and in Massachusetts in 1833. American religions became denominations and abandoned once and for all the traditional belief that any of them could be the true and exclusive church for

Fundamentalist Prayer Meeting
The new untrained evangelical preachers were better able to meet the emotional needs of the tens of thousands of ordinary people cut loose from traditional authorities in the early decades of the nineteenth century.

the society. Each religious association, called or *denominated* by a particular name, now saw itself simply as one limited and imperfect representative of the larger Christian community. Each denomination was equal to and in competition with the others. No other society in the world had ever conceived of religion in this way.

By abandoning all expectation of maintaining any special identity with the society, religion in America became an entirely personal and voluntary affair in which individuals who wished to could bring about their own salvation. Even the Calvinists, who believed that God had already chosen those who were to be saved, nevertheless managed to stress the responsibility of each individual for his or her own conversion. Sin was no longer thought of as inherent in human beings but as a kind of failure of individual will. Thus each person was fully capable of eliminating sin through his or her individual exertion. With such an assumption the numbers who could be saved were no longer limited by God's election, and all the denominations began to sound remarkably like the new denomination, the Universalists, who democratically promised salvation for everyone.

Since religion was now clearly personal and voluntary, people were free to join and change religious associations whenever they wished. Consequently, the churches were less capable than they had been in the eighteenth century of reflecting the variety of social ranks within their own community. Particular denominations were identified with particular social classes. For example, the Episcopalians (as the Anglicans were now known) and the Unitarians (liberal Congregationalists) became largely the preserve of social elites. If the role of the denominations was to contend with one another for souls in the religious marketplace, then it was important that each denomination be as united, tightly organized, and homogeneous in its membership as possible. Dissenters were thus allowed to go their separate ways without the struggles that had marked earlier American religious life. The result was a further splintering of religion and the multiplying of new, unique religious groups, like the Stonites and Campbellites, with no connection whatever to the Old World.

The divisive effects of this fragmentation were offset by a curious blurring of theological distinctions among the competing denominations. Some extreme evangelicals urged the creation of a simple Christian religion based only on the gospel. In the name of the Revolution, they denounced all the paraphernalia of organized Christianity, including even the ministry, and claimed the right of each individual to be his own theologian. Within a few decades some of these fundamentalist Christians came together as the Disciples of Christ, which soon emerged as the fifth largest Protestant religious group in nineteenth-century America.

Despite the competition among them, all the denominations identified them-selves with the nation and worked to unify American culture under evangelical Protestantism. Clergymen were determined to prove that America's separation of church and state would not result in the infidelity and religious neglect that most Europeans expected. Evangelicals emphasized over and over that America, although without a state-supported church, was nonetheless a nation of God. Throughout the early nineteenth century, religious groups resisted the seculariz-ing effects of the Enlightenment and the First Amendment, which had forbidden the federal government from establishing any religion. Instead they urged the Republic to recognize its basis in Christianity by providing chaplains in Congress, proclaiming days of fasting and prayer, and ending mail delivery on the Sabbath. Ministers, said Nathaniel William Taylor of Connecticut, the most important theologian of the Second Great Awakening, had no intention of creating a new church establishment or of denying the rights of conscience. "We only ask for those provisions in law . . . in behalf of a common Christianity, which are its due as a nation's strength and a nation's glory."

By 1800 the fate of Christianity and the fate of the nation were tied together by a belief in millennialism. Many evangelical ministers had come to believe that America was leading humanity into the millennium—the earth's final thousand years of glory and happiness before the Second Coming of Christ and the Day of Judgment that had been predicted in the Bible. The hopes of these ministers focused on contemporary historical events occurring in America as signs of the approaching age of perfection. The millennium thus became more than a vague promise of Christian theology; it was to be an actual phase in the history of the

American republic. Every advance in America's worldly progress—even new inventions and canals—was interpreted in millennial terms. By giving the millennium such a concrete temporal and material character and by identifying the Kingdom of God with the prospects of the United States, the Protestant ministry contributed greatly to nineteenth-century Americans' growing sense of mission. By improving and prospering, the United States—it was thought—was destined to redeem the world.

Republican Diplomacy

The dramatic culmination of the Republican revolution of 1800 came in the War of 1812. It was an unusual war, a war on which the entire experiment in free government seemed to rest. It was a war that few wanted but that many had made inevitable. It was a war that in the end solved nothing but that was widely regarded as a glorious American victory.

The origins of the War of 1812 lay in the American principles of foreign relations that were first expressed at the time of the Revolution. The American Revolution had been centrally concerned with power—not only power within a government, but power among governments in their international relations. Throughout the eighteenth century, liberal intellectuals had looked forward to a rational world in which corrupt monarchical diplomacy and secret alliances, balances of power, and dynastic conflicts would be eliminated. In short, they had dreamed of nothing less than an end of war and a new era of peace based on natural commercial relations among nations. If the people of the various nations were left alone to exchange goods freely among themselves, it was believed, then international politics would become republicanized and pacified.

Suddenly in 1776, with the United States isolated outside the European mercantile empires, the Americans had an opportunity and a need to put into practice these liberal ideas about international relations and the free exchange of goods. Thus commercial interest and Revolutionary idealism blended to form the basis for American thinking about foreign affairs that lasted until well into the first half of the twentieth century. America first expressed these principles during discussions over the proposed treaty with France at the time of Independence. Many in the Congress in 1776 attempted to work out a model treaty that would be applied to France and eventually to other nations—a treaty that would avoid the traditional kinds of political and military commitments and focus instead on exclusively commercial connections. Although in the treaties of 1778 with France the United States was unable to implement its desired commercial plan—and in fact had to settle for a customary European kind of military alliance—many Americans never lost their enlightened hope that international politics might be transformed by new liberal commercial relationships.

By the 1790s, however, the Federalists had rejected many of these Revolutionary enlightened dreams for international relations. Hamilton in particular denied the liberal assumptions that republics were naturally peaceful and that commerce was an adequate substitute for the power politics of traditional diplomacy. He put no stock in the idealistic Republican conviction that Britain's great power could be dealt with solely by a policy of commercial discrimination and economic coercion.

The Republicans therefore emerged as the preservers of the visionary principles of diplomacy that were identified with the Revolution of 1776. In contrast to the Federalists, who thought that the only way to prepare for war was to build up the government and armed forces in a European manner, the Republicans believed that the United States did not need, nor could safely afford, enlarged national power and a traditional army and navy. It did not even need an elaborate diplomatic establishment: some Republicans in the 1790s urged eliminating all American diplomatic posts except those in London and Paris; others favored replacing the entire American representation abroad with consuls, who were all that were required to handle matters of international trade. At times Jefferson even talked wistfully of abandoning all international commerce so that the United States might "stand, with respect to Europe, precisely on the footing of China." More often, however, he and other Republicans saw American commerce not simply as something to be protected by national policy, as the Federalists did, but as a political weapon to be used as an alternative to war in the way the colonists had used nonimportation in the pre-Revolutionary crisis with Great Britain.

Republicans and the War in Europe

When the conflict between Britain and France resumed in 1803, the Republicans, now in control of the national government, at last had an opportunity to put their policies to a test. Since Britain was unable to oppose on land Napoleon's domination of the continent of Europe, it was determined to exploit its supremacy on the seas to blockade France into submission.

American commerce, once again caught between these two Goliaths, prospered magnificently. Ever since the outbreak of the European war in the early 1790s, American merchants had gained access to the European mercantile empires that had formerly been barred to them and had made the United States the largest neutral carrier of goods in the world. Between 1793 and 1807 American ship tonnage tripled, and the value of American exports increased fivefold. America's expanding wartime shipping between the Spanish and French possessions in the New World and Europe was particularly profitable. The value of this trade increased from $300,000 in 1790 to nearly $60 million by 1807. This commerce, however, violated the British Rule of 1756, which prohibited neutrals in time of war from trading within a mercantile empire closed to them in time of peace. To protect this carrying trade, therefore, American merchants developed a legal fiction. For example, by carrying goods from the French West Indies to American ports, unloading and paying duties on them, and then reloading and getting a rebate on the duties before taking them on to France, American traders broke their voyage and thus technically conformed to the British Rule of 1756. The British now resolved to put a stop to this reexport trade. The *Essex* decision of 1805, in which a British admiralty court held that enemy goods reexported in

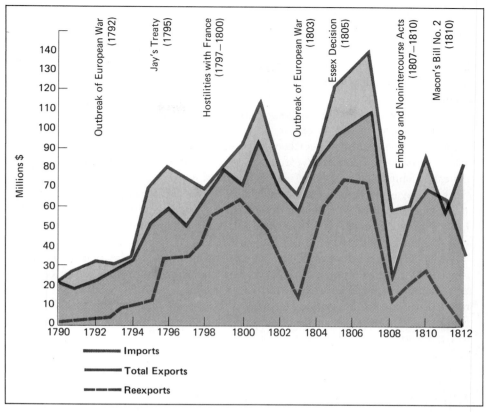

American Foreign Trade, 1790–1812

this fictitious manner were liable to seizure, opened the way to increased British attacks on American ships.

At the same time, Britain expanded its impressment, or forcible removal, of seamen from American vessels on the grounds that they were British subjects. Many of these seamen were deserters from the British navy; and since Great Britain refused to recognize the right of expatriation (or changing citizenship), which was an essential right for a nation of immigrants, conflict over the nationality of American seamen was inevitable. "This authorized system of kidnapping upon the ocean," as John Quincy Adams called it, continued until it was ended by the general European peace of 1815. It resulted in an estimated 10,000 sailors being forcibly taken from American ships. These provocative practices dissolved the cordial relations between Britain and America that had begun with Jay's Treaty in 1795.

Napoleon responded to the British blockade with commercial restrictions of his own—a "continental system" that was designed essentially to deprive England of markets in Europe. In his Berlin Decree of 1806, he ruled that any neutral vessel stopping at an English port would be denied access to all European ports under French control. The British retaliated by requiring all neutral ships trading in the blockaded zones of Europe to stop at British ports to secure licenses. Napoleon then countered with his Milan Decree of 1807, which declared that all neutral ships submitting to British search or entering British ports to secure licenses would be confiscated by the French. The net effect of these regulations by the warring parties was to render all neutral commerce illegal and liable to seizure by one power or the other. Although by 1807 the French were rigorously confiscating American ships in European ports, Britain's greater ability to capture American vessels (it was plundering about one of every eight American ships that put to sea) and its humiliating practice of impressment made Britain appear the greater culprit in American eyes. British regulations seemed to strike at the heart of American independence. "They assume the principle," said John Quincy Adams in 1808, "that we shall have no commerce in time of war, but with her dominion, and as tributaries to her."

The Jefferson administration's immediate response to the British seizures was the Nonimportation Act of 1806, which threatened a prohibition of certain British imports unless an Anglo-American agreement could be reached. Jefferson refused to send to the Senate for ratification a treaty with Britain that William Pinkney and James Monroe had negotiated in December 1806. Jefferson objected to the treaty not only because its commercial provisions scarcely went beyond Jay's Treaty in opening the British Empire to American trade, but, more important, because it did not renounce the British practice of impressment.

Almost immediately thereafter, in June 1807, the British man-of-war *Leopard* fired on the American warship *Chesapeake* as it sailed out of Norfolk, Virginia. Several seamen were killed. The British then boarded the American ship and impressed four sailors, including three Americans who were alleged to be deserters from the British navy. Waves of patriotic indignation swept through the United States and brought Anglo-American relations to the breaking point. "Never since the battle of Lexington," said President Jefferson, "have I seen the country in such a state of exasperation as at present." Although the United States was emotionally primed for war, the Republican leaders were reluctant as yet to abandon their idealistic principles of diplomacy.

The Embargo   All the strains of idealism and utopianism in American Revolutionary thinking were now brought to a head with the Republicans' resort to a general embargo. In 1807 Congress passed a sweeping prohibition of all American shipping with the outside world. Jefferson was determined to see this "candid and liberal experiment" in "peaceful coercion" through to the end. From December 1807 to March 1809, in the face of mounting opposition (particularly from New England), Jefferson's government desperately stuck by its embargo policy. In fact, it used ever harsher measures to enforce it.

Although Britain and France showed few ill effects from this self-imposed stoppage of American shipping, American commerce was thrown into chaos. The American export and reexport trade, which between 1805 and 1807 had doubled to more than $108 million in value, suddenly fell to $22 million during 1808; and American imports declined in value from $138 million to $56 million. Some places were especially hard hit. Although many areas of the United States could fall back on their domestic overland and coastwise trade to replace losses in international commerce, the New England ports, such as Boston, Salem, and Providence, had relatively meager backcountries and unusually heavy investments in the carrying and reexport trade; these ports thus could not easily adjust to the embargo. Yet the economic effects of the embargo on the nation as a whole were far from disastrous. Not only did numerous loopholes and violations— especially toward the end of 1808—lessen the embargo's depressing impact on the economy, but America's growing reliance on its domestic manufactures and its internal markets was strengthened by the cutbacks in international trade.

Still, everywhere in the North but especially in New England, the embargo had the political effect of temporarily reviving Federalism. Hundreds of New England petitions flooded in on the government. Some New Englanders were on the verge of rebellion, and the Federalist governor of Connecticut claimed the right of his state to interpose its authority between the federal government and its citizens. Thus some sort of retreat from the embargo was inevitable. Hopeful of salvaging something from their policy of peaceful coercion, the Republicans on March 1, 1809, replaced the embargo with the Nonintercourse Act, which prohibited trade with France and Britain alone and provided that if either warring side canceled its blockade against American shipping, then nonintercourse would be maintained only against the other.

President Madison was just as determined as Jefferson had been to maintain this Republican experiment in commercial warfare. But difficulties in enforcing the Nonintercourse Act and growing governmental deficits from the loss of duties on trade forced the Madison administration to turn its commercial restrictions inside out. Macon's Bill No. 2, which passed Congress in May 1810, once again opened American shipping with both Britain and France, with the provision that if either side revoked its restrictions on neutral commerce, nonintercourse would be restored against the other. Signs of a change in Napoleon's policy against American shipping, coupled with Madison's eagerness to prove the workability of the experiment in peaceful coercion, led the Republican administration in March 1811 into a hasty invocation of nonintercourse against Great Britain.

If the United States had to go to war, the Republicans thought, then better to fight Britain, the country that from the beginning had symbolized resistance to the experiment in popular self-government. Despite some strong misgivings over Napoleon's dictatorship and some weak suggestions that America fight both belligerents simultaneously, it was virtually inconceivable that the Republicans would have gone to war against France. The threat of Federalist "monarchism" tied to Great Britain was still so real to Republicans that war with Britain became a necessary product of the Republican revolution of 1800, and thus of the original Revolution itself. "We are going to fight for the re-establishment of our national character," declared Andrew Jackson.

The War of 1812 – Major Campaigns

American Forces
British Forces
✕ Battles

CANADA
(British)

War in the South

The War of 1812

War was declared in June 1812, and it was strictly a Republican party war. The congressional vote for war was solidly opposed by the Federalists, and it temporarily unified the splintered Republican party. A number of Republican congressmen who were newly elected in 1810, such as Henry Clay of Kentucky, Felix Grundy of Tennessee, and John C. Calhoun of South Carolina, were so eager to fight that they earned the label "War Hawks." Although many of the Republican congressmen came from areas that were far removed from the eastern trading ports, they represented farmers who were interested in commerce and in the marketing of their agricultural produce. Moreover, such backcountry dwellers tended deeply to resent British and Spanish scheming among the native Americans of the Northwest and Southwest, and they were convinced, especially by the recent battle with Tecumseh's Indians at Tippecanoe in November 1811, that the frontier would never be at peace until the British and Spanish bases in Canada and Florida were eliminated. War offered them the opportunity to do just that.

Yet in the end the war came because the Republicans' foreign policy left no alternative. America had been engaged in a kind of war with both Britain and France since 1806. The actual fighting of 1812 was only the logical consequence of the failure of "peaceful coercion." Still, many Republicans hesitated to commit the United States to a traditional sort of military conflict. They realized, as Jefferson had warned in 1806, that "our constitution is a peace establishment—it is not calculated for war." War, they feared, would lead to a Hamiltonian enlargement of taxes, debt, military forces, and the executive branch. Far from saving the Jeffersonian revolution of 1800, war might ultimately destroy republican principles. Therefore, even as the Republicans moved inevitably toward war, many of them opposed all efforts to strengthen the government's capacity to wage it. For example, Nathaniel Macon of North Carolina reluctantly conceded the necessity of war, but like other Republicans he urged reduction of the navy and even abolition of the army, opposed raising taxes, and resisted all efforts to add two assistant secretaries to the War Department. Not only was the regular army cut back in favor of the militia, but the Bank of the United States, the government's chief financial agency, was allowed to expire in 1811 on the eve of hostilities. With such a deliberate lack of preparation, the war was bound to be very different from any known before.

The Invasions of Canada

Although woefully unprepared for war, many Americans in 1812 were confident of victory. Since two out of every three persons in Upper Canada (present-day Ontario) came from America, Canada seemed ripe for American "liberation." It would be, said Jefferson, "a mere matter of marching." But the American militia campaigns against Canada in 1812 were all dismal failures. General William Hull surrendered his entire army at Detroit without a fight. William Henry Harrison, the hero at Tippecanoe, was then made commander of the northwestern army; but before he could get very far, part of his army was wiped out at Frenchtown, near Detroit, in January 1813.

In April 1813 invading Americans captured York (present-day Toronto), the capital of Upper Canada, and burned its public buildings. But within two months the American forces were in retreat once again. After Oliver Perry secured naval control of Lake Erie, Harrison finally defeated combined British and Indian forces on the Thames River north of Lake Erie in October 1813. Although this victory broke up the Indian confederacy, American leaders thought it was too far west to have any strategic significance and did not follow it up. During the summer of 1814, Americans tried to invade Canada again but withdrew after several tough but indecisive battles in the Niagara region. After two years of repeated forays, the American position on the Canadian frontier remained what it had been at the beginning.

"*Constitution* and *Guerrière*" by Peter Cobbaugh
This patriotic primitive watercolor celebrates the famous victory of the American frigate,
Constitution, *over her British opponent, the* Guerrière, *southeast of Halifax on August 19,*
1812. Note the triumphant eagle dominating the inverted British national symbol.

On the sea American frigates, including the USS *Constitution,* initially won some notable single-ship engagements, and American privateers, the naval equivalent of the militia, captured more than 1,300 British merchant vessels. Eventually, however, Britain's great naval superiority made itself felt: by 1813 most of the American warships were bottled up in their ports and American commerce was effectively blockaded. When Napoleon abdicated early in 1814, Britain was able to concentrate its military attention on America. It planned several major assaults: one was designed to move down the Lake Champlain route that Burgoyne had followed in the Revolutionary War, and another was aimed at New Orleans. During the summer of 1814, a British marauding force landed in Chesapeake Bay, entered Washington, and burned the Capitol building and the White House. The government's credit collapsed and the nation's finances were thrown into chaos. Without a national bank the government was unable to transfer funds across the country or pay its mounting bills.

The Treaty of Ghent   Despite these humiliating circumstances, however, the American peace commissioners who had been sent to negotiate with the British in August 1814 in Ghent, Belgium, were unwilling to make any concessions. The British, learning that their invasion from Canada had turned back as a result of an American naval victory on Lake Champlain in

September 1814, and increasingly anxious about the shifting situation in Europe, came to realize once again that a decentralized government and a spacious continent were not easily conquered. The peace that was signed on Christmas Eve, 1814, restored the status quo as it was before the war and said nothing about impressment and maritime rights. Andrew Jackson's smashing victory over the British invasion at New Orleans at the beginning of 1815 came after the treaty was signed, and clinched it. Although the Americans had gained nothing tangible from the peace, the war was widely and rightly regarded as a great success for the Republican party and the nation.

The Hartford Convention and the End of the Federalists

The peace effectively destroyed Federalism as a national movement. The northeastern Federalists had repeatedly obstructed the war, refusing to comply with federal militia call-ups and discouraging loans to the United States government. Some New England extremists talked of separating from the Union. Other Federalists were convinced that the Republican failures in the war would justify their opposition and that a disillusioned people would catapult the Federalists back into national dominance.

Hence the Federalist convention that met in Hartford, Connecticut, at the end of 1814 was hopeful for the future; it rejected secession and contented itself with proposing a series of amendments to the Constitution. These amendments were designed to curb the power of the South in the federal government by eliminating the three-fifths representation of slaves; to prevent the admission of new states, future embargoes, and declarations of war without a two-thirds majority of Congress; and to end Virginia's dominance of the executive by prohibiting the president from serving two terms and the same state from providing two presidents in succession. But the national exuberance following the Treaty of Ghent and Jackson's victory discredited these Federalist hopes and led to the enthusiastic election in 1816 of still another Republican and Virginian president, James Monroe. The Republicans' remarkable experiment in governing a huge country and fighting a war without the traditional instruments of power was thus vindicated.

Although the war seemed to settle nothing, actually it settled everything. "Notwithstanding a thousand faults and blunders," John Adams told Jefferson in 1817, Madison's administration had "acquired more glory, and established more Union than all his three predecessors, Washington, Adams, Jefferson, put together." The Revolution, which had begun nearly a half-century earlier, at last seemed to be over and to have succeeded. The Federalist attempt to build a strong central government had been halted. The new national government that the Republicans had created was unlike any other government known to the age. Its capital was isolated from the main social and economic centers of the country; its influence was diffused throughout a rapidly expanding geographical sphere; and its effect on the daily lives of its citizens was negligible.

By 1818 Jefferson was exultant. "Our government," he wrote to his old French ally, the Marquis de Lafayette, "is now so firmly put on its republican tack, that it will not be easily monarchised by forms." The War of 1812 and the disgrace of the Federalists, he said, had ended the need for his revolutionary party, and had in fact resulted in the "complete suppression of party." In the new so-called Era of Good Feelings, symbolized by Monroe's uncontested reelection to the presidency in 1820, the ideological passions and divisions that had been aroused by the Revolution could at last subside. Americans could begin celebrating their own common national identity.

CHRONOLOGY

1800	Washington, D.C., becomes capital. Library of Congress established. Convention of 1800, supplanting treaties of 1778 with France. Thomas Jefferson elected president.	**1805**	Pennsylvania Academy of Fine Arts formed. *Essex* decision by British prize court increases British seizures of American neutral ships.
1801	Plan of Union between Presbyterians and Congregationalists to bring religion to frontier. War with Barbary states. Cane Ridge, Kentucky, revival meeting. John Marshall becomes chief justice.	**1806**	Monroe-Pinkney Treaty with Britain, which Jefferson refuses to send to Senate for ratification. Burr conspiracy.
		1807	*Chesapeake-Leopard* affair. Embargo Act. Robert Fulton's steamboat *Clermont* travels on Hudson River from Albany to New York City in 30 hours.
1802	Republican Congress repeals Judiciary Act of 1801.		
1803	*Marbury* v. *Madison,* Supreme Court upholds right of judicial review. Louisiana Purchase. War resumed in Europe. Lewis and Clark expedition begun.	**1808**	Congress prohibits Americans from participating in African slave trade. James Madison elected president.
		1809	Embargo repealed; Nonintercourse Act passed, prohibiting trade with Britain and France.
1804	Hamilton killed by Vice-President Aaron Burr in duel. Impeachment of judges Pickering and Chase. Twelfth Amendment to Constitution ratified. Jefferson elected for second term.	**1810**	Macon's Bill No. 2 passed, restoring trade with Britain and France, but providing for trade restrictions to be reimposed on one of the powers if the other should abandon its seizure of American ships.

1810   Connecticut Moral Society formed to combat infidelity and drinking.

West Florida annexed by Madison.

American Board of Commissioners for Foreign Missions formed.

In *Fletcher* v. *Peck,* Supreme Court invalidates state law regarding *Yazoo* land claims because of impairment of contracts.

1811   Madison, believing Napoleon has removed restrictions on American commerce, prohibits trade with Britain.

Battle of Tippecanoe, Indiana, in which William Henry Harrison defeats Tecumseh and prevents formation of Indian confederacy.

Charter of the Bank of the United States allowed to lapse by Congress.

1812   Congress declares war against Britain.

Americans surrender Detroit to British.

Madison elected for second term.

1813   Battle of Lake Erie, in which Captain Oliver Perry defeats British naval forces.

Battle of the Thames, in which General Harrison defeats British and their Indian allies.

1814   Battle of Horseshoe Bend, Alabama; General Andrew Jackson defeats Creek Indians fighting for British.

British burn Washington, D.C.

Commander Thomas Macdonough defeats British fleet on Lake Champlain; invading British turned back at Plattsburgh, New York.

Hartford Convention of Federalist delegates from New England states meets.

Treaty of Ghent signed between United States and Great Britain.

1815   Battle of New Orleans; Jackson defeats British.

North American Review founded in Boston; soon becomes leading literary review in America.

1816   Second Bank of the United States chartered by Congress.

American Bible Society founded.

Protective tariff passed.

James Monroe elected president.

1817   Bonus Bill establishing fund for building roads and canals vetoed by Madison.

American Tract Society formed to circulate religious literature in the West.

Seminole War on Georgia-Florida border.

1818   General Jackson invades Florida to end Seminole War.

Rush-Bagot convention between Britain and United States establishes American fishing rights and boundary between United States and Canada.

1819   Commercial panic with many bank failures.

Adams-Onís Treaty signed between United States and Spain; Spain cedes Florida to the United States and recognizes the western limits of the Louisiana Purchase.

Dartmouth College case.

McCulloch v. *Maryland.*

1820   Missouri Compromise.

James Monroe reelected president.

SUGGESTED READINGS

The classic account of the Republican administrations is Henry Adams, *History of the United States of America During the Administration of Thomas Jefferson [and] of James Madison* (9 vols., 1889–1891). It is artful, but its obsession with the ironic turn of Jeffersonian policies subtly distorts the period. Marshall Smelser, *The Democratic Republic, 1801–1815* (1968), is a one-volume survey. Daniel Sisson, *The American Revolution of 1800* (1974), tries to recapture the radical meaning of Jefferson's election; but it does not succeed as well as James S. Young, *The Washington Community, 1800–1828* (1966), which despite an unhistorical focus rightly stresses the Republicans' fear of power. On the Republican party, see Noble E. Cunningham, Jr., *The Jeffersonian Republicans in Power: Party Operations, 1801–1809* (1963). Richard Hofstadter, *The Idea of a Party System: The Rise of Legitimate Opposition in the United States, 1740–1840* (1969), is a lucid essay that tries but does not quite break from the party conception of the secondary sources on which it is based. David Hackett Fischer, *The Revolution of American Conservatism: The Federalist Party in the Era of Jeffersonian Democracy* (1965), is an important book that compels a new look at the Republicans as well as the Federalists. A tough-minded study is Forrest McDonald's *The Presidency of Thomas Jefferson* (1976). See also James H. Broussard, *The Southern Federalists, 1800–1816* (1979). Howard B. Rock, *Artisans of the New Republic: The Tradesmen of New York City in the Age of Jefferson* (1979), describes the rise of an important social and economic group. On the Republicans' dismantling of the Federalist bureaucracy, see Leonard D. White, *The Jeffersonians: A Study in Administrative History, 1801–1829* (1951). See also Noble E. Cunningham, Jr., *The Process of Government Under Jefferson* (1979), and Robert M. Johnstone, Jr., *Jefferson and the Presidency* (1979). On Jefferson and Madison, see the monumental multivolumed biographies by Dumas Malone and Irving Brant.

Daniel Boorstin, *The Lost World of Thomas Jefferson* (1948), describes the rigidities of intellectual life in Republican circles, while Linda K. Kerber analyzes the Federalists' cultural problems in *Federalists in Dissent* (1970).

On the development of the West, see Reginald Horsman, *The Frontier in the Formative Years, 1783–1815* (1970). On the new cities of the West, see Richard C. Wade, *The Urban Frontier* (1959). Beverley W. Bond, *The Civilization of the Old Northwest: A Study of Political, Social and Economic Development, 1788–1812* (1934), is a good compilation. Land policy and land laws are covered in Malcom J. Rohrbough, *The Land Office Business . . . 1789–1837* (1968).

On the Louisiana Purchase, see Alexander De Conde, *The Affair of Louisiana* (1976), and the appropriate chapters of George Dangerfield, *Chancellor Robert R. Livingston of New York, 1746–1803* (1960). On Indian affairs, see Reginald Horsman, *Expansion and American Indian Policy, 1783–1812* (1967). For the tragic irony in the story of American relations with the Indians, see Bernard W. Sheehan, *Seeds of Extinction: Jeffersonian Philanthropy and the American Indian* (1973). A good, short, though unsympathetic, account of the Burr conspiracy can be found in Thomas Abernathy, *The South in the New Nation, 1789–1819* (1961).

On the politics of the judiciary, see Richard E. Ellis, *The Jeffersonian Crisis* (1971). The best biography of Marshall is still Albert J. Beveridge, *The Life of John Marshall* (4 vols., 1919). The origins of judicial review are treated in Edward S. Corwin, *The "Higher Law" Background of American Constitutional Law* (1955), Charles G. Haines, *The American Doctrine of Judicial Supremacy* (1932), and Sylvia Snowiss, *Judicial Review and the Law of the Constitution* (1990). But despite all that has been written, the sources of judicial review remain perplexing. Understanding the problem requires less work on the Supreme Court and more on colonial jurisprudence. For a significant study of changes in law during the Revolution, and after, see William E. Nelson, *Americanization of the Common Law: The Impact of Legal Change on Massachusetts Society, 1760–1830* (1975), and Morton J. Horowitz, *The Transformation of American Law, 1780–1860* (1977).

On religion and the Revolution, see William W. Sweet, *Religion in the Development of American Culture, 1765–1840* (1952). On the varying definitions of the American Enlightenment and its relation to Protestantism, see the superb study by Henry F. May, *The Enlightenment in America* (1976). The opening chapters of Perry Miller, *The Life of the Mind in America* (1965), are very helpful for understanding the emergence of evangelicism. The essays collected in Elwyn A. Smith, ed., *The Religion of the Republic* (1971), are important in relating evangelical Protestantism and republicanism. More important is Nathan Hatch, *The Democratization of American Christianity* (1989). Older studies that need updating are Catherine C. Cleveland, *The Great Revival in the West, 1797–1805* (1916), and Oliver W. Elsbree, *The Rise of the Missionary Spirit in America, 1790–1815* (1928). See also John Bole, *The Great Revival in the South, 1787–1805* (1972); Howard Miller, *The Revolutionary College: American Presbyterian Higher Education, 1707–1837* (1976); and especially Donald G. Mathews, *Religion in the Old South* (1977). For secular-minded approaches to evangelicism, see Charles I. Foster, *An Errand of Mercy: The Evangelical United Front, 1790–1837* (1960), and Clifford S. Griffin, *Their Brothers' Keepers: Moral Stewardship in the United States, 1800–1865* (1960). On the changing role of the ministry, see Donald M. Scott, *From Office to Profession: The New England Ministry, 1750–1850* (1978). On deism, see Gustav A. Koch, *Republican Religion* (1933), and Herbert M. Morais, *Deism in Eighteenth-Century America* (1934). On millennialism, see Ernest Lee Tuveson, *Redeemer Nation: The Idea of America's Millennial Role* (1968); James W. Davidson, *The Logic of Millennial Thought* (1977); Nathan O. Hatch, *The Sacred Cause of Liberty* (1977), and Ruth M. Bloch, *Visionary Republic* (1985).

The underlying eighteenth-century liberal assumptions about international politics are explored in Felix Gilbert, *To the Farewell Address: Ideas of Early American Foreign Policy* (1961). Lawrence S. Kaplan, *Jefferson and France: An Essay on Politics and Political Ideas* (1967), captures the idealism of Jefferson. A tough-minded critique of that idealism is Robert Tucker and David C. Henderson, *Empire of Liberty: The Statecraft of Thomas Jefferson* (1990). The best discussion of the diplomatic steps into war is Bradford Perkins, *Prologue to War: England and the United States, 1805–1812* (1961). Burton Spivak, *Jefferson's English Crisis: Commerce, Embargo and the Republican Revolution* (1979), is the best study of the embargo. Julius W. Pratt, *Expansionists of 1812* (1925), stresses how the desire of Westerners and Southerners for land caused the war. However, A. L. Burt, *The United States, Great Britain and British North America* (1940), emphasizes the issues of impressment and neutral rights. Roger H. Brown, *The Republic in Peril: 1812* (1964), and Norman K. Risjord, *The Old Republicans* (1965), and J. C. A. Stagg, *Mr. Madison's War: Politics, Diplomacy, and Warfare in the Early American Republic, 1783–1830* (1983), offer the best perspective on the logic of the Republicans' foreign policy that led to war.

Harry L. Coles, *The War of 1812* (1965), and Reginald Horsman, *The War of 1812* (1969), are good brief surveys. Irving Brant, *James Madison: The Commander in Chief, 1812–1836* (1961), defends Madison's wartime leadership, but Ralph Ketcham, *James Madison* (1971), is better in recovering the peculiar character of Madison's republican aims. On the Treaty of Ghent, see Bradford Perkins, *Castlereagh and Adams: England and the United States, 1812–1823* (1964). James M. Banner, *To the Hartford Convention: The Federalist and the Origins of Party Politics in Massachusetts, 1789–1815* (1970), superbly describes the Federalists' attitudes and stresses their conservative purposes in calling the Convention. Steven Watts, *The Republic Reborn: War and the Making of Liberal America, 1790–1820* (1987), imaginatively interprets the meaning the war of 1812 had for Americans.

PART THREE

Expanding the
Republic
1820–1860

David Brion Davis

THE END of the American Enlightenment and of the Revolutionary period also marked the end of attempts to model American society on European blueprints. By the 1820s it was becoming clear that the American people would quickly leap across restraints and limits of every kind. They were expansive, self-assertive, and extravagantly optimistic, and they believed that they had a God-given right to pursue happiness. In a nation of supposedly infinite promise, there could be no permanent barriers to the people's aspirations toward wealth and self-improvement.

This absence of barriers, of distinctions of rank, and of prescribed identities was what the famous French social critic Alexis de Tocqueville meant by "the general equality of condition among the people." When he visited the United States in 1831, nothing struck Tocqueville more forcibly than this leveling of ancient and inherited distinctions of rank. He took it to be "the fundamental fact" about American society; all other facts seemed "to be derived" from it. Tocqueville was aware of the economic and racial inequalities of American society. Indeed, he suggested that precisely the lack of traditional restraints, such as those associated with a landed aristocracy, opened the way for racial oppression and for a new kind of aristocracy created by business and manufacturing. A racial minority, such as the African Americans, seemed more vulnerable in a society where all white males were eager to assert their own equality.

All societies require a system of rules, restraints, and limits. In a traditional, premodern society, such as the European feudal regime to which Tocqueville looked back with some nostalgia, there was a certain stability to the territorial boundaries of a kingdom, an estate, or a people. Similarly, few people in such a traditional society questioned the customary rules that defined social rank, the rights and duties of lords and peasants, the inheritance of land, the limits of political power and economic enterprise, and the expectations appropriate for each individual. Men and women knew what they had been born to, what place they had been assigned by fate. There was a close relation between the narrow boundaries of the physical environment and the social boundaries that political, legal, and religious institutions imposed.

The United States, as Tocqueville repeatedly emphasized, had thus far managed to avoid anarchy while greatly expanding most people's possibilities of life. From the time of the first colonial settlements, Americans had evolved institutions that had ensured a degree of order and stability in social life, protecting the public good from the worst excesses of acquisitive self-interest. This protection of the public good had been the preeminent goal of republican political culture. By the early nineteenth century, however, there was a growing faith that the public good would best be served by allowing maximum freedom to the individual pursuit of self-interest.

In the period 1820–60 this drive for individual self-betterment led to an unprecedented economic and territorial expansion, to the migration of millions of Europeans to America, and to the settlement of millions of Americans in the new states and territories of the West. Much of the nation's foreign policy was devoted to extending territorial boundaries and to preventing European attempts to impose future barriers to American influence and expansion in the Western Hemisphere. Federal land policy encouraged rapid settlement of the West. Both national and state governments committed a large share of public resources to the construction of roads, canals, and railroads to overcome the barriers of mountains and increasing distance. Government at all levels actively sought to stimulate growth and economic opportunity. Much of the political ideology of the period was directed against forces and institutions, such as the Second Bank of the United States, that could be portrayed as restricting individual opportunity.

But for many thoughtful Americans, reformers as well as conservatives, there was a danger that these expansive energies would erode all respect for order, balance, and community purpose. The fear arose that the competitive spirit would lead to a fragmented society ruled by the principle "every man for himself and the devil take the hindmost." Some worried that the American people would become enslaved to money, success, and material gratification, and that the centrifugal forces of expansion would cause the nation to fly apart.

Most of the proposed remedies to social problems centered on the critical need to shape and reform individual character. Rather than looking to constitutional reforms or governmental programs, most Americans sought social change through the moral reformation of individuals. They believed that if self-interest could be enlightened by a sense of social responsibility, the nation could be saved from the dehumanizing effects of commercialism and competitive strife. This improvement of the individual was the great goal of the public schools, the religious revivals, and most of the new reform movements. It was a mission that gave a new importance and an educational role to mothers and to the middle-class home. In one sense these efforts at shaping character embodied a nostalgic desire to restore a lost sense of community and united purpose. But the crusades for moral improvement also served to modernize society, for they encouraged predictable and responsible behavior and moreover aimed at giving moral legitimacy to a market-oriented society—that is, to a society governed by the standards of economic exchange, of supply and demand.

The issue of black slavery—the South's "peculiar institution"—finally dramatized the conflict between self-interest and the ideal of a righteous society, a society that could think of itself as "under God." And it was the westward expansion of black slavery that ultimately became the testing ground for defining and challenging limits—the territorial limits of slavery, the limits of federal power, and the limits of popular sovereignty and self-determination. For most of the period, these matters remained ambiguous. This ambiguity allowed the North and South to expand together and resolve periodic conflicts by compromise.

By the 1850s, however, southern leaders were insisting that the equal rights of slaveholders would be subverted unless the federal government guaranteed the protection of slave property in the common territories. Northern leaders, eventually including many moderates who had always favored compromise, drew a firm line against imposing slavery on a territory against the wishes of the majority of settlers. To paraphrase the twentieth-century poet Robert Frost, the territorial question came down to what Americans were willing to wall in or wall out. In one form or another, Americans had to face the question of whether, in a free society, any limits could be imposed on the total domination of one person over another.

12

Population Growth and Economic Expansion

$\rightharpoonup$

$\mathcal{T}$O UNDERSTAND the American experience during the four decades preceding the Civil War, one must grasp the dimensions of demographic and economic change that occurred during this period. Other nations have undergone periods of rapid growth and industrialization, accompanied by painful cultural adjustment and social conflict. In general, however, this modernizing experience has occurred in long-settled communities with traditions, customs, and class interests that served simultaneously as barriers to change and stabilizers of society. What distinguished American history in the period 1820–60 was that a modern market economy emerged in conjunction with the rapid settlement of "virgin land" and the unprecedented expansion of the western frontier.

There were few barriers to this double process, and the American people were determined to overcome what barriers there were. The American economy showed a remarkable freedom in the flow of goods, people, and capital in response to market forces. The ease with which resources were shifted from region to region and from agriculture to commerce or industry accounted for much of the economic growth in the early and mid-nineteenth century. No laws restricted the influx of European and Asian laborers. The Constitution ruled out any taxes on American exports. Thanks largely to southern pressure, the federal government gradually lowered protective tariffs on imports. The federal government's sale and donation of immense tracts of public land were intended to encourage individual enterprise in a free and unregulated market. Political stability, even in the rapidly created new states, helped to guarantee the security of private property and the legal enforcement of contracts. The states themselves actively promoted economic growth, but no other society had imposed so few fiscal, political, religious, and social restraints on the marketplace. No other society had been so confident that market forces constituted the "invisible hand" that kept the competitive economy in balance. No other society had become so

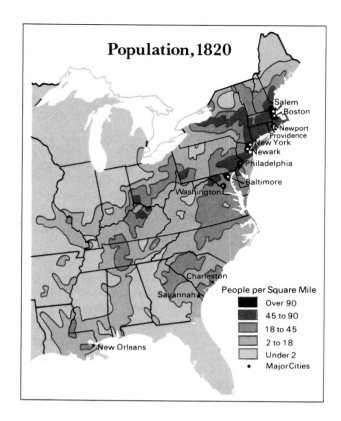

committed to the goals of maximizing individual profits by increasing productivity and lowering costs.

The result of this extraordinary freedom from limitations, along with the availability of land and the somewhat lagging availability of labor and capital, was extremely rapid economic growth. As perceived and experienced by living human beings, however, this growth was both liberating and extremely disruptive. "While trade is destined to free and employ the masses," Henry W. Bellows pointed out in 1845, "it is also destined to destroy for the time much of the beauty and happiness of every land.... We are free.... But the excitement, the commercial activity, the restlessness, to which this state of affairs has given birth, is far from being a desirable or a natural condition." Commercial expansion destroyed family self-sufficiency, pride in craftsmanship, and personal and family ties that unified residential communities with local economic markets. "We learn to live within ourselves," Bellows lamented, "we grow unsocial, unfraternal in feeling; and the sensibility, the affection, the cordiality, the putting forth of graces of a warm and virtuous heart, die or disuse... the domestic and social virtues languish."

Although the growth of national markets broadened the range of individual choice for businessmen, there was little choice for native Americans, slaves, unskilled laborers, landless farmers, and domestic servants: in short, for all those who were excluded by force or circumstance from the benefits of the market.

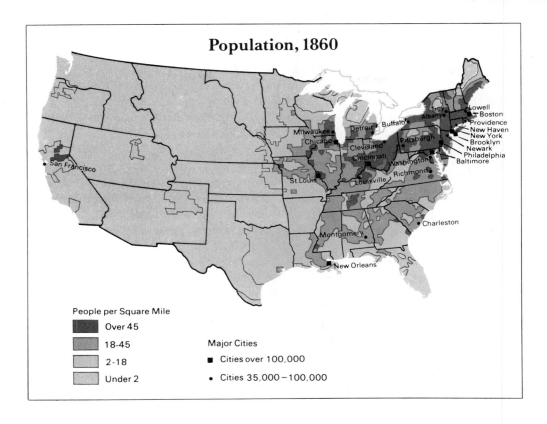

Population, 1860

People per Square Mile

- Over 45
- 18–45
- 2–18
- Under 2

Major Cities

- Cities over 100,000
- Cities 35,000–100,000

Despite a generally rising standard of living, Americans in the pre–Civil War decades witnessed growing economic inequalities. Moreover, the nation's triumphs in economic and territorial expansion depended on two forms of outright racial exploitation: the forcible removal of the Indian people from rich lands east of the Great Plains; and the forced labor of black slaves who produced invaluable exports, mainly cotton, that helped finance America's economic growth.

Population Growth, Immigration, and Urbanization

From 1820 to 1860, America's population maintained the extraordinary rate of growth that had characterized the colonial and post-Revolutionary periods. The population increased by an average of 35 percent every decade, and the total population continued to double every twenty-five years. The United States sustained this high rate of growth until the 1860s. During the nineteenth century no European nation achieved a growth rate one-half as high as America's for even two decades.

America's population growth cannot be attributed to any single, consistent cause. Before the mid-1840s most of the population growth resulted from the remarkable fertility—the rate of reproduction—of the American people, reinforced by a relatively low rate of infant mortality. Like many countries in modern Africa and South America, the United States literally swarmed with children. In

1830 nearly one-third of the total white population was under the age of ten. Yet in most parts of the country the birthrate had actually begun to decline before 1810, and it continued to fall throughout the century. By the 1840s it was only the influx of European immigrants, who accounted for one-quarter of the total population increase in that decade, that maintained the previous rate of national growth.

The Immigrants Immigration was partly the result of economic distress in Europe. Few Europeans would have left for America if population growth in their homelands had not pressed hard on available supplies of land, food, and jobs, and if they had not been displaced and made expendable by technological change in a capitalist, industrializing economy. In 1845 the Irish potato crop—which provided most ordinary Irish with their basic food supply—failed disastrously. Five years of famine followed. Many Irish thus had little choice but to emigrate or starve. As an Irish newspaper put it in 1847: "The emigrants of this year are not like those of former ones; they are now actually running away from fever and disease and hunger, with money scarcely sufficient to pay passage for and food for the voyage." And the British landlords who controlled Ireland helped to subsidize emigration in the hope of reducing taxes that were being levied for the support of workhouses, which were spilling over with starving laborers who had been evicted from the land. In parts of Germany and Scandinavia, governments encouraged emigration as a way of draining off unemployed farmers and artisans, who had been displaced by the modernization of agriculture and by competition from imported machine-made goods.

But the most important stimulus to immigration was the promise of jobs in the United States. Immigration soared during America's years of greatest prosperity, and it lagged during America's years of economic recession. Mass emigration from Europe was a direct response to the sudden demand in America for labor in construction and manufacturing, and to the supposedly limitless opportunity for landownership in the West. American promoters, representing shipping firms, labor contractors, manufacturers, and even the governments of western states, enticed Europeans with glowing accounts of the United States. More persuasive were the reports of fellow villagers or family members who had already crossed the Atlantic. "A poor man in Ireland could not do better than come here," one immigrant wrote to his father, "for it is the truth of a good country." Another recent Irish immigrant reported to his sister in 1841: "It would give me greate pleasure to think that you Come here, for i think you would do verry well in this Country.... And my sister Bridget do what she can to come here. Let my sister Ellen know that she would get five shillings to six for making one dress here." In the 1830s, when northwestern Europe became aware of America's economic boom, of the North's shortage of labor, and of the opening of vast tracts of farmland in the West, the number of immigrants rose to nearly 600,000—approximately a fourfold increase over the previous decade. In the 1840s the number soared to about 1.5 million, and in the 1850s to about 2.8 million.

Emigration Agent's Office
By the 1840s the expansion of transatlantic commerce had greatly reduced the westbound steerage fare from Europe to America. Nevertheless, many emigrants, such as the Irish portrayed here, had to depend on loans, charitable gifts, or funds sent from relatives in America.

The swelling stream, although it originated almost entirely from north-western Europe, was anything but homogeneous. It included illiterate peasants from Germany and Ireland; highly skilled artisans from England, Germany, Belgium, and Switzerland; political refugees escaping the repression that followed the abortive European revolutions of 1830 and 1848; and Jews and other victims of religious discrimination. The Germans amounted to about 1.3 million immigrants, and many had sufficient funds to purchase farms in the West or at least to make their way to thriving German communities in Cincinnati, St. Louis, and Milwaukee. The Irish, numbering some 1.7 million, had few skills and often arrived penniless, traveling in the holds of westbound ships that had carried American lumber, grain, cotton, and other bulk products to Europe.

Cast off by Britain as an unwanted population, the Irish peasants were in effect dumped in the northeastern port cities or sometimes in Canada, from which they migrated southward. Many Irish immigrants grew so discouraged by the "overstocked" labor market that they returned to Ireland. Others gradually found employment in heavy construction work, in foundries and factories, and in domestic service. But for a while they swelled enormously the ranks of the recipients of public and private welfare.

Before the Civil War the proportion of foreign-born in the population as a whole never rose above 15 percent, but in Boston and New York City by the 1850s the figure had climbed to more than 50 percent. Over half the foreign-born lived in Ohio, Pennsylvania, and New York. This concentration of immigrants greatly accelerated the growth of cities in the Northeast and of the towns and villages along the Great Lakes and in the Ohio and Mississippi river valleys.

**Urban Growth and
Population Mobility**
In 1860 four out of five Americans still lived in rural environments—that is, on farms or in settlements of less than 2,500. Nevertheless, by 1850 more than half the populations of Massachusetts and Rhode Island lived in urban centers; the United States as a whole did not become so urbanized until the 1920s. By 1860 eight American cities (three of them west of the Appalachian Mountains) had more than 150,000 inhabitants, a population that was exceeded at the time by only seven cities in industrial England. Although America could boast no metropolis equivalent to London, in 1860 the combined populations of Manhattan and Brooklyn exceeded 1 million. New York City, endowed with a superior harbor and with the Hudson River, which provided deep-water navigation into the interior, had won a further competitive advantage over other East Coast cities when in 1818 its merchants established the first regular scheduled sailings to Europe. Seven years later the Erie Canal opened cheap access to the Great Lakes and to the markets of the West. The success with which New Yorkers consolidated commercial capital and expanded transport routes led one observer to assert: "The great city of New York wields more of the destinies of this great nation than five times the population of any other portion of the country." Many immigrants, after crossing the Atlantic, simply settled where they landed. Philip H. Bagenal, an English traveler, noted that newcomers "blocked up the channels of immigration at the entrance, and remain like the sand which lies at the bar of a river mouth." Immigrants arrived and stayed in New York because it was America's great seaport and commercial center, a crucible of risk and opportunity.

Overall, the declining birthrate resulted in a slightly higher average age for the American population, but the influx of immigrants greatly enlarged the number of northeasterners between the ages of twenty and thirty. In 1850 more than 70 percent of the American people were still under thirty, a figure that takes on greater meaning when compared with the 63 percent for England and the 52 percent for France. Before the Civil War the Americans remained an extraordinarily youthful people, a circumstance that helps to account for their restlessness, their venturesomeness, and their impatience with boundaries of any kind.

Alexis de Tocqueville echoed the amazement of many Europeans at the "strange unrest" of a people who could be seen "continually to change their track for fear of missing the shortest cut to happiness":

> In the United States a man builds a house in which to spend his old age, and he sells it before the roof is on . . . he brings a field into tillage and leaves other men to gather the crops; he embraces a profession and gives it up; he settles in a place, which he soon afterwards leaves to carry his changeable longings elsewhere . . . and if at the end of a year of unremitting labor he finds he has a few days' vacation, his eager curiosity whirls him over the vast extent of the United States, and he will travel fifteen hundred miles in a few days to shake off his

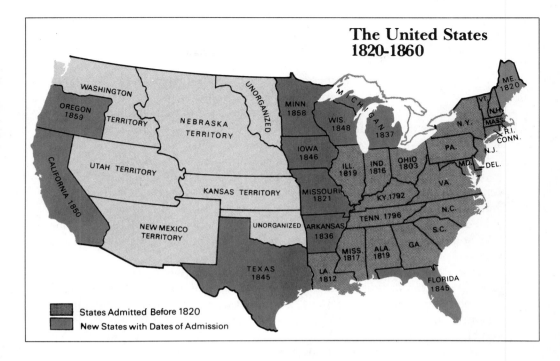

**The United States
1820-1860**

WASHINGTON

OREGON
1859

TERRITORY

UNORGANIZED

NEBRASKA
TERRITORY

MINN.
1858

WIS.
1848

MICHIGAN
1837

ME.
1820

VT.

N.H.

N.Y.

MASS.

R.I.
CONN.

CALIFORNIA 1850

UTAH TERRITORY

IOWA
1846

ILL.
1819

IND.
1816

OHIO
1803

PA.

N.J.

MD.

DEL.

KANSAS TERRITORY

MISSOURI
1821

KY. 1792

VA.

NEW MEXICO
TERRITORY

UNORGANIZED

ARKANSAS
1836

TENN. 1796

N.C.

S.C.

TEXAS
1845

LA.
1812

MISS.
1817

ALA.
1819

GA.

FLORIDA
1845

■ States Admitted Before 1820
■ New States with Dates of Admission

happiness. Death at length overtakes him, but it is before he is weary of his bootless chase of that complete felicity which forever escapes him.

This sense of limitless possibility helps explain the feverish westward rush of population. By 1860 the settled area of the United States was five times what it had been in 1790, and nearly half the people lived beyond the 1790 boundaries of settlement. As late as 1820 many Americans had thought it would take at least a century to settle the vast territory west of the Mississippi River. In 1860 the United States had firmly established its present continental boundaries, except for Alaska. No other nation had populated so much new territory in so short a time or had absorbed so many immigrants. No other had combined rapid urbanization with the dramatic expansion of an agricultural frontier and a transportation network.

Agriculture

Before the Civil War the majority of American families made their livings by supplying the primary human needs for food and clothing. Agriculture dominated the economy and provided the commodities for most of the nation's domestic and foreign trade. Even in towns and cities, families customarily kept a vegetable garden and perhaps a pig, a cow, and chickens. Many of the most seasoned urbanites could at least remember the smell of a barnyard from their childhoods.

Agricultural Expansion

The period 1820–60 was distinguished by two trends that might at first seem contradictory. On the one hand, the quickening pace of urbanization and industrialization brought a decisive shift toward nonagricultural employment. This shift had actually begun in the late eighteenth century, but it had started to slow before 1820, when approximately 71 percent of the labor force was gainfully employed in agriculture. By 1850, however, the proportion of farmers had fallen to 55 percent. This was the most rapid structural change in the economy during the entire nineteenth century. On the other hand, the same period saw a phenomenal expansion of agriculture into the "virgin lands" of the West and the Old Southwest, accompanied by revolutionary changes in transportation and marketing.

But these two trends were actually intimately related. The urban East provided the capital and markets that made the agricultural expansion possible. The food and fiber of the West and Old Southwest were indispensable for the industries and urban growth of the East. Western farming, fur trapping, mining, and lumbering were the spearheads of an expansive capitalist economy that was increasingly integrated with the great markets of the world.

A nation of farmers is almost by definition a nation at an early stage of economic development. "Despite the increasing availability of threshing, harvesting and reaping machines," the historian Jonathan Prude has noted, "many New England farmers continued to cling to familiar methods of cultivation, like the time-consuming hill method of planting Indian corn." Nevertheless, in nineteenth-century America, agriculture did not suggest a conservative way of life limited by the entrenched customs of a feudalistic past. "Let our farmers study their true interests," an agricultural reform journal advised: "Let them not stand while others are getting ahead. Let them be up and doing something to supply the wants of the towns and cities in their vicinity; and not the necessities only, but the tastes also. Let them raise flowers, even, if it will pay a profit. Why not?" Farming increasingly took on the characteristics of a speculative business.

The very isolation of individual farms, posted like sentries along lonely country roads, indicated that Americans placed efficiency above the community solidarity that was characteristic of tight-knit European peasant villages. The individual American farm family, practically imprisoned near the fields it worked and usually owned, had proved to be the most effective unit of production.

Four central conditions shaped America's unprecedented expansion of cultivated land. First, public policy continued to favor rapid settlement of the immense public domain, amounting to a billion acres if one includes the territorial acquisitions of the 1840s. There was no opposing interest in conserving natural resources and future revenue. Second, despite population growth, agricultural labor remained scarce and expensive, especially in frontier regions. Most

A Plank Road Contrasted with Mud
Wagons laden with lumber and hay speed along on the high and dry plank road, while the woman driving the team to the left struggles with the traveler's traditional nightmare: mud. Although improved roads made it easier for farmers to carry produce to local urban markets, they could not compete with canals and railroads in longer distance trade.

farm owners had to rely on an occasional hired hand to supplement the labor of their own families or of tenant families. In the South the price of slaves continued to rise. Third, the dispersion of settlement made farmers heavily dependent, for many decades, on navigable rivers and waterways for transportation. Fourth, the real-estate mentality of earlier periods burgeoned into a national mania as the westward movement and the mushrooming of towns brought spectacular rises in land values. Great land companies and private investors, representing eastern and European capital, purchased virtual empires of western land and then used every possible device to promote rapid settlement. Even the small farmers saw that it was more agreeable to make money by speculating in land than by removing stumps or plowing up the resistant blue-stem grass of the prairies. When Harriet Martineau, a famous British writer and popular economist, visited frontier Chicago in 1837, she exclaimed over the wild speculation in building lots: "I never saw a busier place than Chicago was at the time of our arrival. The streets were crowded with land speculators, hurrying from one sale to another .... [It] seemed as if some prevalent mania infected the whole people.... As the gentlemen of our party walked the streets, store-keepers hailed them from their doors, with offers of farms, and all manner of land-lots, advising them to speculate before the price of land rose higher."

From one point of view the pioneering outlook was progressive. There can be no doubt that Americans who moved were inventive, hardy, and willing to take risks. Often pushing forward ahead of roads and organized government, the frontier farmers engaged in a struggle by trial and error to succeed in the face of unfamiliar climate, insects, soil conditions, and drainage. In time they experimented with different crops, livestock, and transportation routes, searching for the commodity and market that would bring a predictable cash return. Although the federal government supplied little direct information to farmers, it continued Jefferson's tradition of promoting land surveys and sending expeditions into land west of the Mississippi River to collect information on flora and fauna, geology, watersheds, and Indians. This enterprising spirit, evident in both public and private endeavors, led to the discovery and exploitation of undreamed-of resources, confirming Tocqueville's judgment that "Nature herself favors the cause of the [American] people."

But the quest for immediate returns also led to a ruthless stripping of natural resources. In the absence of national legislation and national power, the timber, grasses, and minerals of the public domain invited a headlong scramble by the pioneers to cut trees, graze their cattle, and dig for ore. The government actually bought gold and silver that miners took from public property. European visitors were astonished at the American conviction that forests were a hostile element to be destroyed without regard for need. Trees, like the buffalo and beaver of the West, seemed so plentiful that few Americans could foresee a time of diminishing supply.

The soil itself, the most valuable of all resources, fared no better. Americans generally lacked the incentives and patience to conserve the soil by using fertilizers and by carefully rotating crops. They tended to look on land as a temporary and expendable resource that should be mined as rapidly as possible. This attitude, which was especially prevalent in the South and the West, reflected the common need to produce the most profitable single crop—wheat, corn, rice, tobacco, or cotton—in order to pay for land that had been purchased on credit. As one historical geographer has concluded, American farmers "earned well their reputation as 'soil killers'" as they speculated in land and pushed cultivation ever westward.

The entrepreneurial character of American agriculture owed much to the way new lands were originally settled. It is difficult for Americans of the late twentieth century to grasp the significance of the fact that before the Civil War the chief business of the federal government was the management and disposal of public land. Seeking revenue as well as rapid settlement, the government hastily surveyed tracts of western land and sold them to the highest bidder at public auction; the remainder was offered at the minimum price of $1.25 per acre. Because there was no limit on how many acres an individual or company might buy, investors eagerly bought blocks of thousands of acres. The great peaks of speculation coincided with the expansion of bank credit in the early 1830s and the mid-1850s. The profitable resale of western land depended on promoting settlement.

Speculators and Squatters

Speculators had always helped to shape the character of American agriculture. The great theme of American settlement was the continuing contest of will between absentee owners and the squatters who first developed the land and who often had some partial claim to it. Although squatters frequently sold their own claims to the succeeding waves of immigrants, they tended to picture wealthier speculators as greedy vampires. Yet the large speculators played a key role in financing the rapid settlement of the public lands. Pooling private capital, they lent money to squatters, often at illegally high interest rates, to finance the purchase of tools, livestock, and supplies. They extended credit for buying farms. They pressured local and national governments to subsidize canals and railroads. This speculation often involved considerable risk; the returns on investment depended on the speculators' ability to predict business conditions accurately and on how fast settlement took place.

Squatters for their part yearned for economic independence. They successfully agitated for state "occupancy laws" favoring the claims of actual settlers and guaranteeing them compensation, if evicted, for their cabins, fences, outbuildings, and other improvements. Squatters also pressed for a lowered minimum in the amount of public land that could be purchased—a restriction that by 1832 fell to forty acres. Above all, squatters called on the federal government to sanction squatting, formally allowing settlers to clear and cultivate tracts of public land prior to purchase. This policy of "preemption," which was developed in limited acts in the 1830s and finally established in a general law of 1841, gave squatters the right to settle land and then purchase as much as 160 acres at the minimum price in advance of public sale.

In practice the federal land system was a compromise between the interests of farmers and those of speculators. Government measures did nothing to curb speculators, who were in fact favored by the requirement, beginning in 1820, of full cash payment for public land. Speculators were also favored by lavish government donations of public land to military veterans, railroad companies, and state governments, as well as by the eventual pricing, at as little as 12.5 cents an acre, of land that had long been unsold. Federal land policy allowed speculators to amass great private fortunes by acquiring valuable tracts of the public domain. Yet the wide dispersion of freehold farms gave a grain of substance to the myth that any American could become an owner of property and an independent producer for the capitalist market.

Demand for Better Transportation

Access to growing markets was the overriding concern of the commercial farmer. Yet the craze during the early nineteenth century for building turnpikes, bridges, and plank roads failed to reduce significantly the cost of long-distance freight. The teams of horses that hauled wagons of freight over the nation's turnpikes averaged no better than two miles an hour. Not until canals began to link together other inland waterways could northern farmers think of concentrating on the production of corn and wheat for distant markets.

Steamboat on the Hudson
*After Robert Fulton's first steamboat sailed the Hudson River in 1807, as pictured above,
Americans quickly took advantage of their unparalleled system of navigable rivers. The
steamboat revolutionized transport, especially in the Mississippi valley and southern states.*

The Erie Canal, which was completed in 1825, united Northeast and West by
providing a continuous waterway from Lake Erie to the Atlantic. It was by far the
longest canal in the world, and it dramatically lowered shipping costs. In 1817 it
had cost 19.2 cents per mile to ship a ton of freight overland from Buffalo to New
York City. By the late 1850s the cost per mile, via the canal, had dropped to 0.81
cents. New York State had directed and financed this enormous undertaking, and
it soon reaped spectacular rewards. Foreign capital quickly flowed into the
country to meet the demand of other state and municipal governments, setting
off a canal-building mania that soon linked Pittsburgh with Philadelphia, and the
Ohio River with the Great Lakes. The high cost of building this network of
waterways, undertaken for the most part by the states themselves, severely
strained the credit of Ohio, Pennsylvania, and Indiana. But by sharply lowering
the costs of transport, the most successful canals had an enormous effect on
northern agriculture and industry.

By the mid-1830s the basic pattern of internal transportation began to shift
away from the traditional routes that had led from the Ohio and upper
Mississippi valleys to New Orleans and ocean shipment via the Gulf of Mexico.
Ohio Valley farmers would continue to ship grain and pork down the Mississippi
by flatboat. The richest markets, however, lay east of the Great Lakes, and for a
time the richest commercial agriculture developed in regions accessible by canal
to Lake Erie. By 1840 Rochester, New York, had become the leading flour-milling
center in the country. The marketing of grain became more efficient as brokers
and other middlemen began to arrange for storage, transport, sale, and credit.

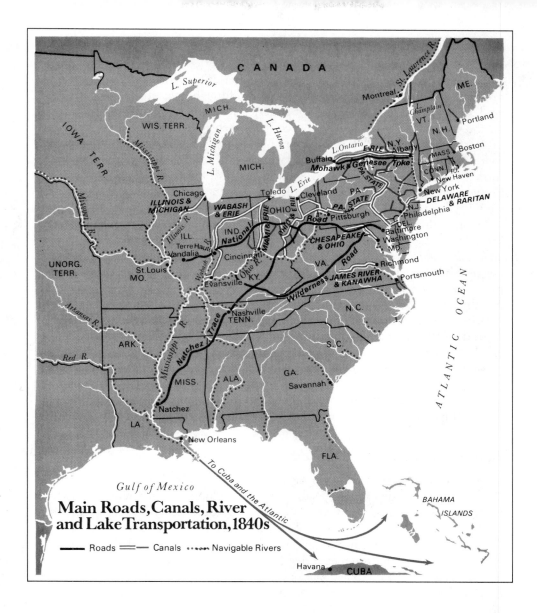

Main Roads, Canals, River and Lake Transportation, 1840s

—— Roads ═══ Canals ·····• Navigable Rivers

This transformation preceded the East–West railroad connections of the early 1850s.

The Commercialization of Agriculture In both North and South, the expansion and commercialization of agriculture provided the impetus for the economy's accelerated growth and modernization. During the 1840s the United States began to export an increasing proportion of its agricultural output, partly in response to poor harvests in Europe and to Britain's repeal of its Corn Laws, which had excluded American and other foreign grain, even during the worst of the Irish famine. This new outflow of wheat and other foodstuffs helped pay for America's imports of manufactured products and the immense interest charges on foreign investment in American land, cotton, and railroads. Much of America's economic expansion depended on the country's ability to attract such investment from Europe. By diverting produce from domestic markets, agricultural exports also had the effect of sharply raising the price of domestic farm products. While this encouraged the further expansion of cash crops, the soaring price of food between 1848 and 1855 brought great hardship to nonagricultural workers in the Northeast and Midwest.

Continuing improvements in transportation enabled agricultural regions to specialize in the search for competitive advantages in response to the pressures of an increasingly national market. In the Midwest, north of the Ohio River, farmers began to buy trademarked tools and machines from authorized distributors. Steel plows, invented in the 1830s but widely accepted only in the 1850s, made it possible to break the tough sod and cultivate the rich but sticky soil of the prairies. Mechanical reapers had also been invented in the 1830s, but only in the 1850s did Cyrus McCormick's Chicago factory begin large-scale production and employ modern techniques of advertising and promotion. As the Midwest proved its superiority in producing wheat and other grains, along with wool, corn, pork, and beef, farmers in the East found it increasingly difficult to compete with their western counterparts. Instead eastern farmers began to specialize in the production of hay for horses and perishable foodstuffs for urban markets.

Industrialization and Railroads

There is still much controversy over the stages of America's economic growth. The best recent evidence suggests that a pattern of long-term accelerated growth in per-capita real income (income measured by purchasing power) preceded significant industrialization and probably originated in the 1820s or earlier from the interaction between urbanization and western agriculture. In those years manufacturing still mostly meant that goods were made by hand in households and in small shops or mills. Blacksmiths, coopers (barrel makers), cobblers, curriers (leather workers), hatters, tailors, weavers—these and other artisans and apprentices worked in central shops, mills, and stores, or traveled through the more sparsely settled countryside. Yet the independent artisans' world began to disintegrate in the 1820s as merchant capitalists expanded and reorganized markets and gradually gained control of the means of production.

Manufacturing   As had happened in England, cotton textiles became the leading industrial innovation. Although Britain tried to guard industrial know-how by strictly banning the export of cotton technology, the New Englander Francis Cabot Lowell memorized the design of textile machinery he saw in Lancashire. After returning to Waltham, Massachusetts, during the War of 1812, Lowell helped form the Boston Manufactur-

Mule Spinning in Lowell

The spinning of thread or yarn, traditionally done at home on a spinning wheel, became almost wholly mechanized when gigantic power-driven machines called mules not only drew and twisted fiber into thread or yarn but wound it for future use on a cylindrical quill or tube. In this view of a textile mill in Lowell, Massachusetts, the two workers, sweeper, and supervisor seem dwarfed by the machines.

ing Company and succeeded in constructing spinning machinery and an improved power loom. This technological triumph enabled Lowell and his associates to build a textile mill at Waltham in which spinning and weaving were all integrated under a single roof. Aided somewhat by protective tariffs, a group of wealthy Boston merchants pooled their capital and in the 1820s extended large-scale factory production to the new manufacturing centers like Lowell (named after Francis Cabot) and Chicopee, in Massachusetts. This so-called Waltham system of centralized factories owed much to the investment capital of New England merchants, who turned to manufacturing when the War of 1812 had curtailed international trade. It exploited the latest British technology, such as the power loom, and it continued to draw upon the expertise of immigrant British artisans.

If their products were to compete successfully with imported British textiles, New England manufacturers had to lower the cost and increase the efficiency of labor. American manufacturers had traditionally cut costs by employing children or families including children, who increased the labor force without increasing wages. Despite attempts to romanticize this kind of family employment, a young Connecticut worker voiced a common protest that "manufacturing breeds lords and Aristocrats, Poor men and slaves. . . . I am for Agriculture. . . . I cannot bear the idea, that I, or my children, . . . should be shut up 16 or 18 hours every day all our life like Slaves and that too for a bare subsistence!" It soon became apparent that children could not handle the frequent breakdowns of the new machinery or conform to the routine that was necessary for increased labor productivity.

By the late 1840s immigrants had begun to ease the general shortage of cheap factory labor. But for a few decades the Boston merchants relied on the unique expedient of employing adult young women, who were attracted to the factories by the provision of chaperoned dormitories and various cultural and educational amenities. Amazed by the interest of these "factory girls" in intellectual self-improvement, a visiting Harvard professor exclaimed: "I have never seen any-where so assiduous note-taking. No, not even in a college class, as in that assembly of young women, laboring for their subsistence." The merchant-manufacturers desired, no doubt sincerely, to avoid the moral degradation that had been a black mark on the British factory system. As economy-minded entrepreneurs, they also hoped to control their employees' leisure time, preventing the binges and self-proclaimed holidays that had always led to irregular work habits and absenteeism among preindustrial people. New England farm girls could also be hired for less than half the wages of male factory hands because they saw their employment as a temporary stage of independence between childhood and marriage and because the factory represented for them virtually the only possible liberation from the farm. As one young woman expressed her newfound sense of economic independence in a letter sent home to her sister on a New Hampshire farm: "Since I have wrote you, another pay day has come around. I earned 14 dollars and a half, nine and a half beside my board. . . . I like it as well as ever and Sarah don't I feel independent of everyone! The thought that I am living on no one is a happy one indeed to me."

From 1815 to 1833 the cotton textile industry increased average annual output at the phenomenal rate of 16 percent. Slackening demand soon reduced the annual rate of growth to about 5 percent, but textile producers, including wool and carpet manufacturers, continued to pioneer in mechanization, in efficiency, and in the use of steam power.

New England also gave birth to the so-called American system of manufacturing. This innovation depended on the imaginative adaptation of a machine-tool technology that had first been developed in England. Unlike the British, however, American manufacturers could not draw on a plentiful supply of highly skilled craftsmen with many years of training in an established craft tradition. Therefore American manufacturers encouraged the perfection of light machine tools that not only eliminated many hand operations but also allowed ordinary mechanics to measure within one-thousandth of an inch and to mill or cut metal with great precision. At the British Crystal Palace exhibition of 1851—a great international show of industrial techniques and products—American machinery astonished European experts. In 1854 one of the British commissions that had

The Working Woman
The woman pictured above is tending a power loom, weaving cloth from machine-spun thread. She typifies the industrial work force that led New England through the first stage of the industrial revolution.

been sent to study American achievements exclaimed over "the extraordinary ingenuity displayed in many of their labour-saving machines, where automatic action so completely supplies the place of the more abundant hand labour of older manufacturing countries."

The British investigators understood the significance for the future of such a seemingly ordinary device as a machine that produced 180 ladies' hairpins every minute. As early as 1853 an exuberant writer for the *United States Review* could predict that within a half-century machines would liberate Americans from the burdens of work: "Machinery will perform all work—automata will direct them. The only tasks of the human race will be to make love, study, and be happy."

But in 1860 American industry was still at an early stage of transition. There were sharp contrasts in the degree of industrialization with respect to different products and different regions. For example, despite an impressive expansion of output, the American iron industry was not nearly as successful as the cotton industry in adopting and improving the latest British technology. The continued use of small blast furnaces that used charcoal to produce malleable iron has been explained by the cheapness and availability of wood for charcoal, by the absence of bituminous coal east of the Allegheny Mountains, by the belated discovery and use of anthracite coal, and by the particular needs of local blacksmiths. Whatever the reasons, and American iron producers increasingly blamed political opponents of protective tariffs, American industry in the 1850s depended heavily on imported British wrought iron and railroad rails, and it lagged far behind Britain in exploiting coal, iron, and steam.

In the West manufacturing often reverted to preindustrial methods that had almost disappeared in the East. But even in the Northeast many goods were produced not in factories but by merchants who still relied on the "putting-out" system—that is, distributing raw materials to laborers who often owned their own tools and worked at home. Other merchant capitalists hired laborers essentially as instruments of production, for the workers had no share in the ownership of tools and machines, in managerial decisions, in the risks of marketing, or in the industrial product.

In 1860 American manufacturing still depended largely on water power, not steam. The typical firm employed a handful of workers, was unincorporated, and engaged in the small-scale processing of raw materials. Few industries processed the products of other industries. The nation's largest industries included some that were thoroughly mechanized, such as the production of cotton goods, flour, and meal. Some, however, were only partly mechanized, such as the manufacture of boots and shoes. And some were characterized by premodern technology and low labor productivity, such as lumbering and the making of men's clothing.

Railroad Building   The great railroad boom of the late 1840s and 1850s dramatized the growing links between industry and agriculture. Although the nation's railroads equaled the canals in mileage as early as 1840, canal barges and river steamboats were usually less expensive than railroads and continued to carry a significant proportion of freight throughout the antebellum period, the years before the Civil War. But by providing speedy access to isolated farms and distant markets, railroads extended the risks and promises of a commercial society and also opened the interior to port cities like Baltimore, Boston, and Charleston, which lacked major inland waterways.

While the smoke and roar of steam trains evoked thoughts of progress and prosperity, the locomotive also became a symbol of the monstrous forces of industry invading the serenity of rural America. In the summer of 1844, for example, the writer Nathaniel Hawthorne recorded a sudden disruption as he tried to commune with nature in a grove of woods known as "Sleepy Hollow": "But hark! There is the whistle of the locomotive—the long shriek, harsh, above all other harshness. . . . It tells a story of busy men, citizens, from the hot street, men of business; in short, of all unquietness; and no wonder that it gives such a startling shriek, since it brings the noisy world into the midst of our slumbering peace."

The development of railway networks was long delayed by primitive technology, a high incidence of breakdowns and accidents, and construction costs

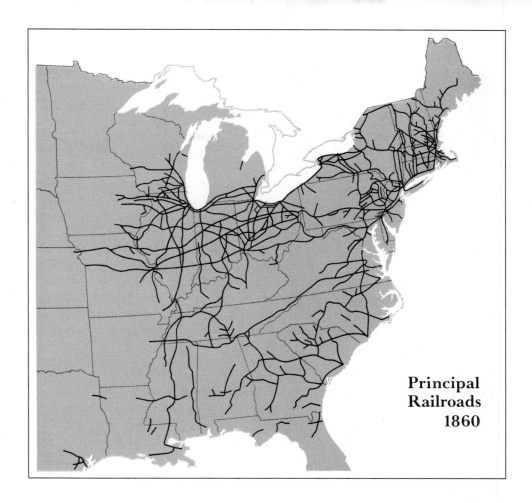

The First Steam Railroad Passenger Train in America.

Dawn of the Railroad Age

In 1831, five years after the Mohawk and Hudson Railroad Company received its charter, an English engineer piloted two carloads of passengers from Albany to Schenectady, New York. Within the next twenty years railroads had linked the Northeast to the Midwest, immensely lowering the cost of shipping farm produce and manufactured goods, and profoundly influencing every aspect of American society and culture.

that required unprecedented amounts of capital investment. As early as 1828, Baltimore promotors began building the first trans-Appalachian railroad to compete with New York's Erie Canal, which threatened to channel much of the western trade toward New York City. But not until 1853 did this Baltimore and Ohio Railroad reach the Ohio River. As late as 1860 there were still hundreds of small, independent lines with different widths of track. Nevertheless, by the early 1850s construction engineers were improving rails, roadbeds, bridges, and locomotives. Railroad corporations had amassed immense reserves of capital, and their managers were learning how to administer complex bureaucracies that employed thousands of workers and required instant interstate communication by means of the recently perfected electric telegraph. By 1854 tracks extended from New York City to the Mississippi River, and by 1860 to the Missouri River at St. Joseph, Missouri. This burst of western railroad construction led to the beginning of consolidation into main lines that further cemented economic ties between the West and the Northeast. By 1860 railroads had become the nation's first billion-dollar industry, spawning the first giant corporations and linking cash-crop farming with the production of iron, coal, lumber, and machine tools.

Population Distribution and Opportunity

There can be no doubt that the nation's overall economic growth brought impressive gains in income and standard of living. By 1860 the United States was well ahead of western Europe in per capita income; even the South, which lagged behind the Northeast, was richer than most nations of Europe. But historians still have much to learn about the actual distribution of wealth in the pre–Civil War decades, to say nothing of the people's opportunity to acquire property or to rise in status and occupation.

Discussions of America's economic opportunities generally omit three groups: the Indians; the black slaves; and the free blacks in both North and South, whose small economic gains in various skilled trades and service industries were severely damaged by competition from white immigrants. Even excluding these oppressed minorities, one finds many indications that economic inequality increased substantially from 1820 to 1860.

The Rich Grow Richer, 1820–1860 According to the best recent estimates, by 1860 the upper 5 percent of families owned over half the nation's wealth. The disparity was far greater in parts of the South, where the wealth of the average slaveholder was growing far more rapidly than that of the average nonslaveholder. The typical slaveholder was not only more than five times as wealthy as the average Northerner, but more than ten times as wealthy as the average nonslaveholding southern farmer. Even in the farming country of the eastern North Central states, where there was greater economic equality, the upper 10 percent of landholders owned nearly 40 percent of the taxable wealth. The national centers of inequality, however, were the growing urban regions from Boston to New Orleans. Although much statistical research remains to be done, it is clear that between 1820 and 1860 the big cities led the nation toward the increasing domination of the very rich. By 1860, according to one estimate, Philadelphia's richest 1 percent of the population owned half the city's wealth; the lower 80 percent of the city's population had to be content with 3 percent of the wealth. A relatively modest estimate concluded that the richest 5 percent of American families in 1860 received between 25 percent and 35 percent of the national income. Although these figures indicate an inequality far greater than that estimated for modern America, they are roughly comparable to the inequalities in northern Europe in the late nineteenth century.

This conclusion would not be so startling if America's pre–Civil War decades had not once been described and almost universally accepted as "the age of the common man." American politicians and journalists of the era eagerly expanded on the theme of "equality of condition," supposedly confirmed by the observations of Alexis de Tocqueville and other European visitors. On closer inspection, however, it is clear that Tocqueville and others claimed only that American fortunes were "scanty" compared with fortunes in Europe; that in America "most of the rich men were formerly poor"; and that in America "any man's son may become the equal of any other man's son." In other words, American inequalities were thought to be temporary and to enhance the incentives of a race to success in which all were free to compete.

This belief in America's unique capacity for avoiding permanent inequalities was especially reassuring by 1850, when European industrialism had produced undeniable evidence of misery, class conflict, and seething revolution. By that date American leaders could not hide their alarm over similar contrasts of wealth and extreme poverty in their own country, particularly when the urban poor congregated in slums beyond the reach of traditional religious and social discipline. Yet affluent Americans persuaded themselves that the poor were free to climb the ladder of success. They also firmly believed that the wealthiest citizens were, in the words of the powerful Kentucky senator Henry Clay, "enterprising self-made men, who have whatever wealth they possess by patient and diligent labor."

In truth, however, the fortunes of the John Jacob Astor family and of other leading American families compared favorably with the fortunes of the richest Europeans. Notwithstanding a few astonishing examples of rags-to-riches achievement, the great majority of America's rich and successful men had benefited from inherited wealth, an affluent childhood, or a prestigious family tradition. Between 1820 and 1860 there was a marked persistence of family wealth. In effect, the rich grew richer. In the cities, at least, they constituted an elite that became increasingly segregated by exclusive clubs, high social life, intermarriage, foreign travel, and business alliances.

At the other end of the spectrum was the mass of unskilled day laborers, who took what temporary jobs they could find and whose wages, even if regular, could not possibly support a family unless supplemented by the income of wives and children. No one knows the size of this unskilled, propertyless population, which drifted in and out of mill towns, flocked to the construction sites of canals and railroads, or gravitated to urban slums. In the 1840s and 1850s the largest cities attracted the chronic failures and castoffs who had no other place to turn. In 1849 New York City's first chief of police warned of "a deplorable and growing evil" in the city, "the constantly increasing number of vagrants, idle and vicious children of both sexes, who infest our public thoroughfares." The poor jammed themselves into the attics and dank, windowless basements of Boston's Half Moon Place, where as many as one hundred people might share the same overflowing privy; or into New York's notorious Old Brewery, a foul tenement that supposedly housed over a thousand beggars, pickpockets, whores, robbers, alcoholics, and starving children. Boston investigators described one such dwelling as "a perfect hive of human beings, without comforts and mostly without common necessaries; in many cases, huddled together like brutes, without regard to sex, or age, or sense of decency." In contrast with the society of mid-nineteenth-century England, the relatively unstructured society of America provided very few public agencies that could begin to enforce minimal standards of health, welfare, and safety.

Urban poverty was immensely aggravated by the arrival of so many immigrants that no conceivable public works program, even if nineteenth-century America had thought in such "New Deal" terms, could have provided the poor with adequate housing, sanitation, and safe water. More immigrants poured into the United States in the ten years between 1841 and 1851 than in the entire previous history of two and a half centuries. From 1848 to 1850 German immigrants ignited a raging cholera epidemic in New York and from New Orleans up the Mississippi and Ohio rivers. Cholera was compounded by new risks of typhus, typhoid, tuberculosis, and other diseases. Although the northern states had become by the late eighteenth century the healthiest region on earth, life expectancy fell 25 percent by 1850. In New York and Philadelphia life expectancy at birth plummeted to age twenty-four.

Social Mobility The extremes of wealth and poverty tell little about the amount of upward movement from one class to another. The available evidence indicates that the odds were heavily against an unskilled laborer's acquiring a higher occupational status. The overwhelming majority of unskilled workers remained unskilled workers. It is true that in the 1850s many of the sons of unskilled workers were moving into semiskilled factory jobs. But this generational advance was almost always limited to the next rung on the ladder. It was extremely rare for the children of manual workers, even skilled manual workers, to rise to the level of clerical, managerial, or professional employment.

Despite growing signs of semipermanent boundaries between occupational groups in the pre–Civil War decades, there were remarkably few expressions of class conflict or class interest. The rarity of such expressions is underscored by the temporary radicalism of lone figures like Orestes A. Brownson, who in 1840 published an eloquent analysis of the plight of the working classes. "Our business is to emancipate the proletaries," Brownson proclaimed, "as the past has emancipated the slaves. This is our work. There must be no class of our fellow men doomed to toil through life as mere workmen at wages." In 1844 Brownson converted to Roman Catholicism and thenceforth became a leading conservative theorist and defender of the church. Historians have sometimes been misled by the labor rhetoric of the Jacksonian period, a time when the rich felt it necessary to prove their humble origins and when politicians and even successful entrepreneurs proudly claimed to be "workingmen."

The labor leaders of the era were typically artisan proprietors and small businessmen who were intent on fixing prices and reducing the hazards of interregional competition. This is not to deny the importance of British artisans who, displaced by the British factory system, had migrated to the United States. These men, who reinforced the preindustrial craft traditions in America, were schooled in the techniques of secret organization and industrial warfare. Nor can one deny the courage of union organizers who faced conspiracy trials in the 1820s and 1830s, who saw their gains wiped out by the depression of 1837–42, and who finally formed city federations of craft unions and national trade unions in the 1850s. Yet the great strikes for higher wages and for the ten-hour day were staged by skilled printers, typographers, hatters, tailors, and other artisans. Employers, who were mostly supported by the courts and who benefited from fresh supplies of cheap immigrant labor, had little difficulty in breaking strikes. Although the Massachusetts Supreme Court led the way, in the case *Commonwealth* v. *Hunt* (1842), in ruling that trade unions were not in themselves conspiracies in restraint of trade, in 1860 only 0.1 percent of the American labor force was organized.

Even by the 1840s America's relative freedom from class consciousness and class conflict evoked considerable comment. According to Karl Marx and other European observers, the explanation could be found in the fresh lands of the American frontier, which provided an outlet for surplus population. In America, George Henry Evans's National Reform Association referred to the West as a "safety valve" that could and should provide an escape for workers whose opportunities were limited in the East. Evans contended in the 1840s that the nation owned enough land in the West to guarantee every family a farm. In the 1850s Horace Greeley, editor of the enormously influential *New York Tribune,* popularized the Republican party's slogan, "Vote yourself a farm." More than a generation later, the historian Frederick Jackson Turner and his followers developed a detailed theory that pictured the frontier as both a safety valve for the pressures of the industrializing East and a constant source of new opportunity.

The "safety-valve" theory, in its simplest and crudest form, has been thoroughly demolished. The eastern laborer, earning a dollar a day or less, could not afford to travel to the frontier and borrow funds for a farm and tools, even if he possessed the skills for western farming. The evidence shows that western land sales lagged in hard times, when a safety valve would be most needed, and

"Go Westward, Young Man!"
*The lure of upward mobility and improving one's condition led thousands of young people,
such as this young Vermont man depicted above, to abandon rural regions in the northeast and
strike out for a supposedly better life in the west.*

increased when prosperity drove up the prices of wheat and cotton. Except for a
few cooperative settlement associations and a few hundred wage earners sent by
antislavery groups to settle Kansas in the 1850s, there are no records to show that
industrial workers were transformed into frontier farmers.

On the other hand, the westward surge of millions of Americans intensified
and dramatized the central fact of American life: physical mobility. Wages in the
Northeast might well have been lower if the farmers, shopkeepers, artisans, and
small businessmen who did go West had stayed put. Some of these aspiring
adventurers might have been forced to seek factory employment. Some might
have become America's counterparts of Europe's labor organizers. Ironically,
since young males predominated in the migration away from industrial New
England, an increasing number of women there had no prospect for marriage
and thus became part of a permanent industrial labor force. These women found
themselves living permanently on the low wages from jobs they had taken while
awaiting marriage.

Intense geographical mobility reinforced the myth of America's bound-
lessness, of its infinite promise. By 1850 one-quarter of the entire population born

in New England states had moved to other states. The South Atlantic states experienced a no less striking westward drain of whites and of black slaves. In each decade the northern cities, towns, and factories witnessed an extraordinary inflow and outflow of population. Although few of these mobile Americans had a chance to acquire farms, they moved because they had hopes of finding life better somewhere else. And the hope may have been more significant than the reality they found. The reality was often grim for unskilled laborers, but the factories and towns they left behind had no need to worry about their accumulating grievances. The more fortunate and competitive movers could not doubt that Illinois was preferable to Ohio, or that New York City offered more opportunities than the rocky hillsides of Vermont.

It was obvious that the economic condition of most white Americans, except for the floating population of impoverished laborers, was improving. Even the lowliest Irish laborers in a factory town like Newburyport, Massachusetts, found that they could accumulate more property if they stuck to their jobs for a decade or longer. To maintain a savings account or eventually to buy a house required discipline, frugality, and multiple incomes; for some, additional incomes came at the expense of family members' education and leisure time. The Irish put a greater premium on home ownership than on education or occupational achievement. The Jews, on the other hand, tended to make every sacrifice for their family's education. Particularly for the families of manual workers, the gains were extremely limited. But these gains engendered pride in achieving what others had not achieved, and they were sufficient to prevent even a permanent working class from becoming a permanent and propertyless proletariat.

The incessant turnover of population and the lack of physical roots also gave force to the ideology of an open and boundless society—an ideology that was repeatedly stressed in newspaper articles, sermons, and political speeches. Who could tell what had become of all one's former neighbors and fellow workers? No doubt, some had hit it rich. The mystery of everyone's past made it believable that most men's positions had been won according to talent and performance—that in America, where the only limits were individual will and ability, most men got what they were worth. If in time a manual worker could finally boast of a savings account of $300, of owning the roof over his head, or of a son who had moved up to the next rung on the ladder, why should he doubt the common claim, "This is a country of self-made men," where most of the rich had once been poor?

The Cost of Expansion: The Indians

The rapid expansion of agriculture, North and South, depended initially on the displacement of the native population. The white Americans, determined to go where they pleased and to seize any chance for quick profit, regarded the millions of acres of western land as a well-deserved inheritance that should be exploited as quickly as possible. But in 1820 the prairies and forests east of the Mississippi River still contained approximately 125,000 native Americans. Although millions of acres had been cleared of Indian occupancy rights in accordance with Anglo-

American law, the physical presence of the Indians blocked the way to government sale of much public land that could lead to increased revenues, to profits from land speculation, and to the creation of private farms and plantations.

The Indians, hopelessly outnumbered by an invader with superior technology, had little room to maneuver. Although they had long sought trade and alliances with whites, native Americans had learned that advancing white settlements undermined tribal culture and destroyed the fish and game on which their economy depended. The Indians had little understanding of the whites' conceptions of private property and competitive individualism. But the whites were just as blind to the diversity and complexity of Indian cultures, to the native Americans' traditions of mutual obligation and communal ownership of land, and to the peculiarly advanced position of Indian women (Iroquois women, for example, played a crucial role in political and economic decisions). These cultural barriers made it easier for whites to think of Indians in terms of negative stereotypes as deceitful and blood-thirsty savages or as a weak and "childlike" race doomed to extinction. Even the more humane and well-meaning Christian missionary groups considered the destruction of Indian culture before the white advance as "the natural course of things." "There is no place on earth to which they can migrate, and live in the savage and hunter state," reported the Congregationalist Board of Commissioners for Foreign Missions in its 1824 address to Congress. "The Indian tribes must, therefore, be *progressively civilized* or *successively perish.*" In fact, the Indian response to white advances was complex, ranging from skillful warfare and stubborn negotiation to resigned submission in the face of treachery and superior force.

The native Americans had proved to be the major losers in the War of 1812. By ending the long conflict between Western settlers and European empires, this war had removed the Indians' last hope of finding white allies who could slow the advance of white Americans. The decisive victories of William Henry Harrison over the Shawnees in the Old Northwest, and of Andrew Jackson over the Creeks in the Old Southwest, had also shattered the hope of a union between northern and southern Indian confederations. These triumphs opened the way for the whites' exploitation of tribal divisions and for their abandonment of what Jackson termed "the farce of treating with Indian tribes" as units. Jackson thought that all Indians should be required as individuals to submit to the laws of the states, like everyone else, or to migrate beyond the Mississippi River, where they could progress toward civilization at their own pace.

Federal Indian Policy   The land-hungry frontiersmen faced controls on their actions in the form of a federal Indian policy that had evolved from imperial, colonial, and post-Revolutionary precedents. This makeshift policy rested on four premises that in time became increasingly contradictory.

First, in line with European legal concepts, the federal government continued to acknowledge that the Indian tribes were in some sense independent nations that had acquired rights of possession by prior occupancy of the land, even though they lacked many of the usual characteristics of sovereign countries. The federal government's continuing efforts to negotiate treaties, to purchase land, and to mark off territorial boundaries demonstrated that legitimate settlement by whites required at least symbolic consent from the native Americans. The same European model allowed the United States to punish "aggressor" tribes by demanding the cession of land as a legal compensation for the damages of war.

The second premise, a product of New World experience, was that Indian "occupancy" must inevitably give way to white settlement. White Americans, like the heirs of a dying relative, had an eventual right—an "expectancy," to use Jefferson's phrase—to the property that native Americans held. In theory this claim did not interfere with the existing property rights of Indians. It simply gave the American government an exclusive right to purchase Indian lands, thereby blocking any future imperial designs by European powers.

In practice, however, this doctrine led to the third premise—that of supreme federal authority over Indian affairs. Knowing the dangers of alliances between hostile Indians and foreign nations, the federal government had from the beginning assumed powers that would have been unthinkable in any other domestic sphere. It subjected all trade with the native Americans to federal licensing and regulation. It invalidated the sale or transfer of Indian lands, even to a state, unless made in accordance with a federal treaty. It guaranteed that the native Americans would be protected from white advances on lands that they had not ceded to the federal government. But unfortunately no federal administration had the will or military power to protect Indian rights while supervising the fair acquisition of land by whites. In a government that was increasingly inclined to listen to the voice of the people, the native Americans had no voice of their own.

The fourth premise, which Jefferson had stated and which gained momentum after the War of 1812, was that Indian culture, which whites called savagery, could not permanently coexist with American civilization. President James Monroe expressed the common conviction in a letter of 1817 to Andrew Jackson: "The hunter or savage state requires a greater extent of territory to sustain it, than is compatible with the progress and just claims of civilized life, and must yield to it." The government actively promoted schools, agriculture, and various "useful arts" among the native Americans, hoping to convert supposed nomadic hunters into settled farmers. This hope was nourished by the progress of the more populous southern tribes, particularly the Cherokees, whose achievements in agriculture, in developing a written alphabet, and in adopting white technology seemed to meet the American tests of capability. But the government also pressured the Cherokees into ceding tracts of valuable eastern land in exchange for lands west of the Mississippi River. By 1824 it was becoming clear that the five southern confederations—Cherokees, Creeks, Choctaws, Chickasaws, and Seminoles—could not survive even as temporary enclaves without federal protection against white exploiters. The southern tribes occupied western Georgia and North Carolina, as well as major portions of Tennessee, Florida, Alabama, and Mississippi. Thus their lands covered the heart of the future Cotton Kingdom. In

1825 President Monroe officially proposed that these and all other remaining tribes be persuaded to move west of the Mississippi River, a plan that Jefferson and others had long regarded as the only way of saving America's original inhabitants from ultimate extinction.

Conflict of Federal and State Laws

In Georgia white speculators, squatters, and gold miners had no desire to see civilized Indians living on choice land, and the fact that it was ancestral Indian land made little difference. In 1828, when the Cherokees adopted a constitution and claimed sovereign jurisdiction over their own territory, Georgia declared them to be mere tenants on state land, subject to the state's laws and authority. In 1832, in the case of *Worcester* v. *Georgia,* Chief Justice John Marshall ruled against the state. Georgia, he said, had no right to extend state laws to the Cherokees or their territory. "The several Indian nations," he maintained, were "distinct political communities, having territorial boundaries, within which their authority is exclusive, and having a right to all lands within those boundaries, which is not only acknowledged, but guaranteed by the United States." But President Jackson, who had already withdrawn the federal troops that had earlier been sent to protect Cherokee land from intrusion, had no intention of enforcing the Supreme Court's decision.

Jackson firmly believed that the native Americans should be subject to state law and to the forces of a free-market economy, in which individuals bought and sold commodities according to the laws of supply and demand. To deal with tribes as privileged corporate groups, he thought, was simply to reinforce the power of corrupt chiefs and cunning half-breeds, who prevented tribesmen from following their own best interest. Jackson had no doubt that the vast majority of Indians, when liberated from tribal tyranny, would willingly emigrate to the West. The civilized few would be free to cultivate modest tracts of land and would become responsible citizens of state and nation.

Jackson's denial of federal protection provided the needed incentives for a supposedly voluntary migration. Following Georgia's lead, other southern states harassed native Americans with laws that few tribesmen could comprehend. White traders and lawyers descended like locusts on Indian lands, destroying tribal unity and authority. In 1830 Congress supported Jackson's policy by voting funds that would enable the president to negotiate treaties for the removal of all the Indian tribes then living east of the Mississippi River. The government still considered it necessary to purchase title to Indian land and to grant allotments of land to individual tribal leaders who could prove a legitimate claim. Federal officials even sought to protect native Americans by supervising private contracts for the sale of land. The majority of Indians, however, had no concept of land as a measurable and salable commodity. A few of the more experienced Chickasaws and other tribesmen secured good prices for rich cotton land, but white speculators, who swiftly cornered between 80 and 90 percent of southern allotments, reaped windfall profits.

"Trail of Tears"
In this painting by Robert Lindneux, the dispossessed Cherokee are depicted in their forced exodus to Oklahoma, struggling to transport the few belongings they can carry to a bleak and unfamiliar homeland.

The government thus furthered its goal of removal by dispossessing the native Americans of their land. Victims of wholesale fraud, trickery, and intimidation, the great mass of southern Indians had no choice but to follow the so-called Trail of Tears to the vacant territory of what is today Oklahoma. Subjected to disease, starvation, and winter cold, thousands died along the way. Military force gave a cutting edge to removal deadlines: in 1838 federal troops herded 15,000 Cherokees into detention camps. "They are dying like flies," various witnesses reported. As one Cherokee recalled many years later: "Long time we travel on way to new land. People feel bad when they leave old Nation. Women cry and make sad wails. Children cry and many men cry, and all look sad like when friends die, but they say nothing and just put heads down and keep on towards West. Many days pass and people die very much." Meanwhile Indians north of the Ohio River had earlier been demoralized as whites had cut down the supply of game, negotiated treaties with factions of certain tribes that had accepted more of white civilization, and ensnared primitive societies with unfamiliar mechanisms of debt and credit. In 1832 the government crushed the resistance of Sac and Fox Indians in Illinois and Wisconsin, and in 1835 it launched a long and costly war against the Seminoles in Florida. By 1844, except for a few remaining pockets mainly in the backcountry of New York, Michigan, and Florida, removal had been accomplished.

In his Farewell Address of March 4, 1837, Jackson applauded this brutal policy of Indian removal as a great humanitarian achievement that had also happily removed the main block to America's economic growth:

> While the safety and comfort of our own citizens have been greatly promoted by their removal, the philanthropist will rejoice that the remnant of that ill-fated race has been at length placed beyond the reach of injury or oppression, and that paternal care of the General Government will hereafter watch over them and protect them.

The Beginning of Indian Reservations   Ten years later, however, the government had recognized the impossibility of a "permanent Indian barrier" west of the Mississippi River. Having defeated all Indian attempts to resist the pressure of westward white migration, the government now began moving toward a policy of fencing native Americans within specified "reservations" and opening the otherwise boundless territory of the great West to wagon trains, cavalry, miners, farmers, surveyors, and railroad builders. Even in the 1820s a few perceptive Indian chieftains had foreseen that western lands would be no more invulnerable than the lands in the East. This conclusion was soon confirmed by the destruction of tribal game reserves and by the purchase of remaining Indian lands in Missouri and Iowa. The Anglo-Saxon settlers in Texas, who won independence from Mexico in 1836, asserted the unprecedented claim that Indians had no right whatever to possession of the land. Texas reaffirmed this doctrine after being annexed as a state in 1845, and even demanded that some 25,000 Apaches and other tribesmen be removed or face extermination. Years of border warfare finally led in 1854 to the Texans' acceptance of Indian reservations under federal jurisdiction. But the federal government found that it could not protect Texas tribes from being slaughtered by marauding whites and therefore authorized their removal to the territory north of the Red River, in what later became Oklahoma.

Meanwhile, between 1846 and 1860 government policy began to settle the fate of the strong western tribes that had previously been free to roam prairies and intermountain grasslands without concern for the conflicting claims of white nations. The American invasion and occupation of New Mexico in the Mexican War led to brutal punitive expeditions against the Navajo. In 1851 Congress passed the critically important Indian Appropriations Act, which was designed to consolidate western tribes on agricultural reservations, thereby lessening the danger to the tens of thousands of emigrants streaming toward California and Oregon and also to the proposed transcontinental railroad.

The degradation reached its climax in the 1850s in California, where federal restraints on white aggression disappeared. Whites molested the Diggers and other primitive native Americans, shooting the males for sport and enslaving the women and children. Farther east, the Apaches and powerful Plains tribes offered occasional and sometimes spectacular resistance. The famed encounters

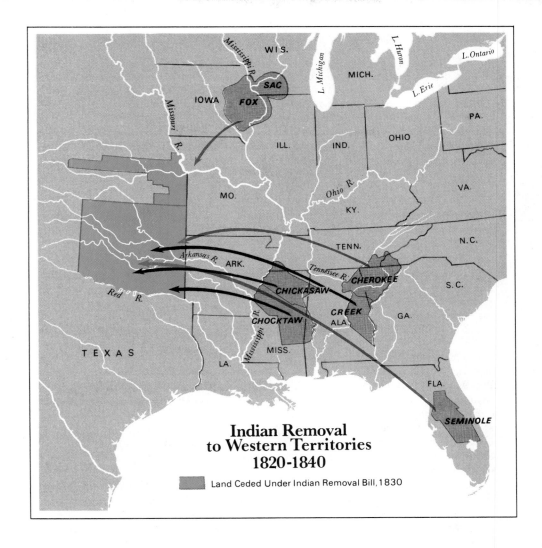

**Indian Removal
to Western Territories
1820-1840**

Land Ceded Under Indian Removal Bill, 1830

between Indians and the United States Cavalry came after the Civil War. But even by 1860 the western tribes had been demoralized, their economy had been fatally weakened when buffalo and other game became depleted, and increasing numbers of native Americans had been herded into compounds with boundaries that moved only inward.

SUGGESTED READINGS

For informative surveys and syntheses, often with detailed bibliographies, see George Dangerfield, *The Awakening of American Nationalism, 1815–1828* (1965); Robert H. Wiebe, *The Opening of American Society: From the Adoption of the Constitution to the Eve of Disunion* (1984); Charles G. Sellers, *The Market Revolution, 1815–1848* (1992); Edward Pessen, *Jacksonian America: Society, Personality, and Politics,* rev. ed. (1978); Steven Hahn and Jonathan

Prude, eds., *The Countryside in the Age of Capitalist Transformation* (1985), and Russel B. Nye, *Society and Culture in America, 1830–1860* (1974). Lawrence A. Cremin, *American Education: The National Experience, 1783–1876* (1980), is a sweeping study not only of formal education, but of the transmission of knowledge in a democratic society. Many interpreters of the period draw heavily on Alexis de Tocqueville's classic work *Democracy in America,* of which there are many editions. Daniel I. Boorstin's *The Americans: The National Experience* (1965) emphasizes America's uniqueness, although more recent work has reversed this trend. The period is illuminated in different ways by Yehoshua Arieli, *Individualism and Nationalism in American Ideology* (1964); Rowland Berthoff, *An Unsettled People: Social Order and Disorder in American History* (1971); and Fred Somkin, *Unquiet Eagle: Memory and Desire in the Idea of American Freedom, 1815–1860* (1967). An anthology of primary source material, accompanied by extensive commentary, is David B. Davis, ed., *Antebellum American Culture: An Interpretive Anthology* (1979).

Population growth is analyzed by J. Potter, "The Growth of Population in America, 1700–1860," in *Population and History . . . ,* eds. D. V. Glass and D. E. C. Eversley (1965); and Richard A. Easterlin, *Population, Labor Force and Long Swings in Economic Growth: The American Experience* (1968). Maldwyn A. Jones, *American Immigration* (1960), is a useful introduction to the subject; it should be supplemented by Marcus L. Hansen, *The Atlantic Migration, 1607–1860* (1940); Oscar Handlin, *Boston's Immigrants* (1959); Robert Ernst, *Immigrant Life in New York City, 1825–1863* (1949); Kathleen N. Conzen, *Immigrant Milwaukee, 1836–1860* (1977); Kerby A. Miller, *Emigrants and Exiles: Ireland and the Irish Exodus to North America* (1985); and Carl Wittke, *The Irish in America* (1956). For urbanization and urban problems, see Sam Bass Warner, Jr., *The Urban Wilderness* (1972); Elizabeth Blackmar, *Manhattan for Rent, 1785–1850* (1989); Thomas Bender, *Toward an Urban Vision: Ideas and Institutions in Nineteenth-Century America* (1975); Richard C. Wade, *The Urban Frontier* (1964); and Paul Boyer, *Urban Masses and Moral Order in America, 1820–1920* (1978). Anthony F. C. Wallace, *Rockdale: The Growth of an American Village in the Early Industrial Revolution* (1978), is an imaginative but controversial interpretation of the way industrialization affected the entire life and culture of an American community.

For overviews of antebellum economic growth, see Thomas C. Cochran, *Frontiers of Change: Early Industrialism in America* (1981); W. Elliot Brownlee, *Dynamics of Ascent* (1974), and Stuart Bruchey, *Growth of the Modern American Economy* (1975). For a fascinating discussion of the economic thought of the pre–Civil War period, see Joseph Dorfman, *The Economic Mind in American Civilization,* vol. 2 (3 vols., 1946–49). Douglass C. North, *The Economic Growth of the United States, 1790–1860* (1961), stresses the importance of international trade. For the international impact of textile technology, see David J. Jeremy, *Trans-Atlantic Industrial Revolution: The Diffusion of Textile Technology Between Britain and America, 1790–1830* (1981). Peter Temin, *The Jacksonian Economy* (1969), challenges many of the traditional beliefs of historians. The best treatment of early American science is Robert V. Bruce, *The Launching of Modern American Science, 1846–1876* (1987).

Ray A. Billington, *Westward Expansion* (1974), presents an excellent survey of the history of the American West as well as a comprehensive bibliography. For the magic symbolism of California, see Kevin Starr, *Americans and the California Dream, 1850–1915* (1973). The fullest histories of agriculture are Percy W. Bidwell and John I. Falconer, *History of Agriculture in the Northern United States, 1620–1860* (1925), and Lewis C. Gray, *History of Agriculture in the Southern United States to 1860* (2 vols., 1933). A briefer and outstanding survey is Paul W. Gates, *The Farmer's Age: Agriculture, 1815–1860* (1960), which can be supplemented by Clarence H. Danhof, *Change in Agriculture in the Northern United States, 1820–1870* (1969).

The classic study of transportation is George R. Taylor, *The Transportation Revolution, 1815–1860* (1951). A monumental work, confined to New England, is Edward Kirkland, *Men,*

Cities, and Transportation (2 vols., 1948). For canals, see Harry N. Scheiber, *Ohio Canal Era* (1969), and R. E. Shaw, *Erie Water West* (1966).

For railroads, see Albert Fishlow, *American Railroads and the Transformation of the Ante-Bellum Economy* (1965); John F. Stover, *Iron Road to the West: American Railroads in the 1850s* (1978); Alfred D. Chandler, Jr., ed., *The Nation's First Big Business* (1965); and Thomas C. Cochran, *Railroad Leaders, 1845–1890* (1953). Christopher T. Baer, *Canals and Railroads of the Mid-Atlantic States, 1800–1860* (1981), is especially valuable for its detailed maps and tables. The organization and management of railroad corporations is masterfully analyzed in Alfred D. Chandler, Jr., *The Visible Hand: The Managerial Revolution in American Business* (1977). The role of government is treated in Carter Goodrich, *Government Promotion of American Canals and Railroads, 1800–1890* (1960); Louis Hartz, *Economic Policy and Democratic Thought* (1954); and Oscar Handlin and Mary F. Handlin, *Commonwealth: A Study of the Role of Government in the American Economy* (1969).

The best works on maritime trade are Robert G. Albion, *The Rise of New York Port* (1939), and Samuel E. Morison, *Maritime History of Massachusetts, 1789–1860* (1921). For the clipper ships, see C. C. Cutler, *Greyhounds of the Sea* (1930), and A. H. Clark, *The Clipper Ship Era* (1910). L. H. Battistini, *The Rise of American Influence in Asia and the Pacific* (1960), treats an important aspect of America's commercial expansion.

On manufacturing, Victor S. Clark, *History of Manufactures in the United States, 1607–1860* (3 vols., 1929), remains indispensable. Thomas C. Cochran, *Frontiers of Change: Early Industrialism in America* (1981), synthesizes the results of recent research and casts new light on the factors leading to rapid industrialization in Pennsylvania and New York. For New England's pioneers in modernization, see Robert F. Dalzell, Jr., *Enterprising Elite: The Boston Associates and the World They Made* (1987). The impact of industrialization on a rural and small-town culture is treated in Jonathan Prude, *The Coming of Industrial Order: Town and Factory Life in Rural Massachusetts, 1810–1860* (1983). The best specialized studies are Peter Temin, *Iron and Steel in Nineteenth Century America* (1964); Caroline F. Ware, *The Early New England Cotton Manufacture* (1931); Arthur H. Cole, *The American Wool Manufacture* (2 vols., 1926); and Otto Mayr and Robert C. Post, eds., *Yankee Enterprise: The Rise of the American System of Manufactures* (1981). Siegfried Giedion, *Mechanization Takes Command* (1948), contains a fascinating account of American technological innovation. A brilliant study of the significance of the new technology is Merritt R. Smith, *Harpers Ferry Armory and the New Technology: The Challenge of Change* (1977). H. I. Habakkuk, *American and British Technology in the Nineteenth Century* (1962), places American invention in a larger context, as does Carroll W. Pursell, Jr., *Early Stationary Steam Engines in America: A Study in the Migration of Technology* (1969). For a comprehensive reference work, see Melvin Kranzberg and Carroll W. Pursell, Jr., eds., *Technology in Western Civilization* (2 vols., 1967). The ideological impact of technology is imaginatively treated in John F. Kasson, *Civilizing the Machine: Technology and Republican Values in America, 1776–1900* (1976).

A pioneering study of social and economic mobility is Stephan Thernstrom, *Poverty and Progress* (1964). For disparities in the distribution of wealth and income, see Edward Pessen, *Riches, Class, and Power Before the Civil War* (1973), and Lee Soltow, "Economic Inequality in the United States in the Period from 1790 to 1860," *Journal of Economic History*, 31 (December 1971), 822–39. The discovery of poverty is analyzed in Robert H. Bremner, *From the Depths* (1956), and Raymond A. Mohl, *Poverty in New York, 1783–1825* (1971). On working-class culture and ideology, the best guides are Alan Dawley, *Class and Community: The Industrial Revolution in Lynn* (1977); Christine Stansell, *City of Women: Sex and Class in New York, 1789–1860* (1986); Paul G. Faler, *Mechanics and Manufacturers in the Early Industrial Revolution: Lynn, Massachusetts, 1780–1860* (1981); Bruce Laurie, *Working People of Philadelphia, 1800–1850* (1980); Bruce Laurie, *Artisans into Workers: Labor in Nineteenth-Century America* (1989); Herbert G.

Gutman, *Work, Culture, and Society in Industrializing America* (1976); Howard M. Gitelman, *Workingmen of Waltham* (1974); Peter R. Knights, *The Plain People of Boston* (1971); and Norman Ware, *The Industrial Worker, 1840–1860* (1959). For labor movements and protests, see David Montgomery, *Workers' Control in America: Studies in the History of Work, Technology, and Labor Struggles* (1979); Sean Wilentz, *Chants Democratic: New York City and the Rise of the American Working Class, 1788–1850* (1984); Joseph Rayback, *A History of American Labor* (1966); and Walter Hugins, *Jacksonian Democracy and the Working Class* (1960). For a richly informative analysis of women's experience in the most famous New England mill town, see Thomas Dublin, *Women at Work: The Transformation of Work and Community in Lowell, Massachusetts, 1826–1860* (1979). Two good studies of the ideology of the self-made man—Irvin G. Wyllie, *The Self-Made Man in America* (1954), and John G. Cawelti, *Apostles of the Self-Made Man* (1965)—should be supplemented by Daniel T. Rodgers, *The Work Ethic in Industrial America, 1850–1920* (1978). Although dealing with a later period, Richard Weiss, *The American Myth of Success* (1969), also sheds light on the earlier history of the subject.

A good introduction to Indian removal is Wilcomb E. Washburn, *The Indian in America* (1975). Francis P. Prucha, *American Indian Policy in the Formative Years* (1962), is sympathetic to government policymakers. Ronald N. Satz, *American Indian Policy in the Jacksonian Era* (1975), provides an informative account of the subsequent period. The most comprehensive studies of the so-called civilized tribes are William G. McLoughlin, *Cherokee Renascence in the New Republic* (1986) and Charles Hudson, *The Southeastern Indians* (1976); for the Far West, see Sherburne F. Cook, *The Conflict Between the California Indian and White Civilization* (1976). An outstanding work that corrects the mythology regarding the relation between the native Americans and western pioneers is John Unruh, *The Plains Across: The Overland Emigrants and the Trans-Mississippi West* (1979). There are three valuable related works in intellectual history: Roy H. Pearce, *The Savages of America* (1965); Richard Slotkin, *Regeneration Through Violence: The Mythology of the American Frontier, 1600–1860* (1973); and Roderick Nash, *Wilderness in the American Mind* (1967).

13

Shaping the American Character

Reform, Protest, Dissent, Artistic Creativity

*T*HE DESIRE to transform character lay at the heart of American reform in the mid-nineteenth century. In line with republican tradition, reformers rejoiced that the nation was free from kings and nobles, from aristocratic institutions, and from status and roles defined at birth, with the flagrant exception of black slavery. Like other Americans, reformers were cheered by the absence or removal of traditional barriers to human progress. But in pursuing the good life that had supposedly been made accessible by the sacrifices of the Founders, Americans had somehow created a society of astounding moral and physical contrasts—a society of luxury and of squalor, of spiritual uplift and of degradation, of freedom and of bondage. In the eyes of dissenters and reformers, it often seemed that America was ruled only by the principles of ruthless self-interest and power.

During the pre–Civil War decades, political and religious leaders repeatedly warned that the fate of free institutions, both in the United States and in the rest of the world, depended on the moral and intellectual character of the American people. If the American people betrayed their high mission, the very idea of popular self-government would be discredited for centuries to come. Religious beliefs continued to differ about humanity's sinfulness or inherent capacity for love and social harmony. But Americans of various outlooks agreed that human nature was much like clay that can be molded to any shape before it hardens. And the American people were still at a highly plastic stage of development.

This conviction could be inspiring. In 1823, for example, Charles Jared Ingersoll, a Philadelphia lawyer and former congressman, delivered an influential *Discourse Concerning the Influence of America on the Mind.* Ingersoll was confident that the average American, as a result of the free and republican environment, stood far above the average European in both intelligence and virtue. He promised that American achievements in the arts and sciences would soon show the world the full potentialities of human nature when it was not crippled by despotism and aristocratic privilege.

But a capacity for infinite improvement might also be a capacity for infinite corruption. Even the optimists tended to worry over the growing inadequacy of local religious and social institutions in the face of America's sensational expansion. The need to shape or change individual character gave a new social importance to educators, religious revivalists, popular essayists, phrenologists, and other promoters of self-improvement.

The spirit of reform and dissent was centered in the Northeast, and particularly in New England. During the years before the Civil War, this region spawned numerous crusades to regenerate the social order—to substitute love, harmony, and cooperation for what a leading religious reformer, William Ellery Channing, termed the "jarring interests and passions, invasions of rights, resistance of authority, violence, force" that were deforming the entire society. Whether these movements were religious or secular, most of them sought to bring American culture into harmony with a "higher law"—"the moral government of God"—as a means of preventing anarchy. Although reformers differed in their specific objectives, they shared a common desire to channel spiritual aspirations into the secular world of power.

The character of the reform movement of the pre–Civil War period was unique. Throughout history religious reformers had sent out missionaries to convert heathens and had sought to provide the world with models of saintly life, including dietary discipline and selfless commitment. But they had never created the kind of highly professional reform organizations that began to spring up in both Britain and America in the early nineteenth century.* These organizations were devoted to various goals—to building model penitentiaries, to persuading people to abstain from alcoholic drinks, and above all to abolishing slavery. The objectives were uncompromising, and the systematic techniques for mobilizing public opinion and exerting pressure on public officials were altogether novel.

Nevertheless these reform movements usually embodied a nostalgia for a supposedly simpler and more harmonious past. Members of the movements believed that the evils they combated had multiplied because of an alarming disintegration of family authority, of community cohesiveness, and of traditional morality. The various programs, therefore, had a dual objective for change and improvement. On the one hand, they attacked institutions, lifestyles, and traditional social roles that seemed to limit individual opportunity and to block the path of progress. On the other hand, they attempted to restore and revitalize the sense of purity, simplicity, and community that had been lost in the headlong pursuit of modernity and material improvement.

---

* Although Britain was still ruled by a monarch, a landed aristocracy, and an established church, a popular political culture had begun to emerge alongside vocal and dynamic minorities of religious dissent; consequently, there were strong similarities and lines of influence between reformers in Britain and the United States. See pp. 436–37.

"We Must Educate or Perish"

Shaping character, whether by school, church, prison, or asylum, seemed to be the only means of ensuring moral stability in an expansive and increasingly individualistic society. Lyman Beecher—best known today as the father of the novelist Harriet Beecher Stowe but in his own day the most prominent Protestant minister in the North—viewed the rapid settlement of the West with a mixture of exhilaration and alarm. By 1835 the states west of the Appalachian Mountains had grown so rapidly that he could predict a population of 100 million by 1900, "a day which some of our children may live to see." The West, Beecher believed, was a "young empire of mind, and power, and wealth, and free institutions." It contained the potential for nothing less than "the emancipation of the world." Beecher had no doubts about the West's material progress. The danger was "that our intelligence and virtue will falter and fall back into a dark minded, vicious populace—a poor, uneducated reckless mass of infuriated animalism." Beecher was aroused particularly by the supposed threat of Catholic immigrants, whom he pictured as the agents of foreign despots intent on subverting republican institutions. For Beecher, the hands-off policy of laissez-faire liberalism had erased the old republican concern for the common good. He therefore urged an immediate crusade to evangelize and educate the West: "For population will not wait, and commerce will not cast anchor, and manufacturers will not shut off the steam nor shut down the gate, and agriculture, pushed by millions of free men on their fertile soil, will not withhold her corrupting abundance. We must educate! We must educate! or we must perish by our own prosperity."

The State of Education

Educational reformers had some reason for alarm. Even Massachusetts, which in 1837 established the nation's first state board of education, suffered from broken-down school buildings, untrained and incompetent teachers, and dependence on unequal and unpredictable local funding. The one-room country schoolhouse, often idealized in later years, not only was dirty, drafty, and overheated in winter, but was commonly packed with children of all ages—some old and rowdy enough to inflict beatings on male teachers and to prompt some women teachers to hide a pistol in a desk drawer. The soaring growth of eastern cities made middle-class citizens suddenly aware of begging street urchins, teenage prostitutes, gangs of juvenile delinquents, and vagrant children, who, like Mark Twain's Huckleberry Finn, had little desire to be "civilized."

Until the second quarter of the nineteenth century, the education of Americans was informal, unsystematic, and dependent on parental initiative and ability to pay. Even so, compared with most Europeans, white American males had always enjoyed a high rate of literacy, especially in New England. During the 1790s a surprising number of artisans and skilled laborers had sent their children to the "common pay schools" in New York City, where children of rich and poor backgrounds mingled. By the early nineteenth century, illiteracy was rapidly disappearing among white females. Boys and girls frequently attended the same schools, despite prejudices against gender integration. Some free schools expected parents to pay a small fee, and most tax-supported schools were intended only for the children of the very poor. Aside from school attendance, apprenticeship long served as a noteworthy means of education, providing the vocational skills that could not be learned in any school. Not until the mid-nineteenth century—and in the South not until after the Civil War—did education become increasingly confined to specialized institutions segregated from the mainstreams of adult social life.

Working-Class Demands   Middle-class religious reformers were not alone in demanding educational reform. In 1828 the organized mechanics and journeymen of Philadelphia, most of whom were skilled artisans and craftsmen who had served their apprenticeship, began to protest. As in other northeastern cities, these workers were angered by low wages, by the substitution of temporary child "apprentices" for skilled adult laborers, and by the erosion of the traditional craft system that had allowed apprentices and journeymen to rise within a given trade. The Philadelphia Working Men's party pressed for a broad range of economic and social reforms. One of these was for better educational opportunities. "The original element of despotism," proclaimed a party committee in 1829, "is a monopoly of talent, which consigns the multitude to comparative ignorance, and secures the balance of knowledge on the side of the rich and the rulers."

The demand for free tax-supported schools became a rallying cry for the workingmen's parties and associations that sprang up in New York, Boston, and dozens of small towns throughout the country. A group of New York workers expressed the typical rhetoric when they asked in 1830 "if many of the monopolists and aristocrats of our city would not consider it disgraceful to their noble children to have them placed in our public schools by the side of poor yet industrious mechanics." Although many of the leaders of these groups were not manual laborers, the short-lived workingmen's movement reflected an authentic desire for equal educational opportunity on the part of skilled laborers whose economic and social condition had begun to deteriorate.

For most workingmen economic grievances soon took precedence over education. The economic growth of the pre–Civil War decades called for more and more unskilled laborers, but not for a significant increase in the number of skilled and nonmanual workers who might benefit materially from an education beyond the "three Rs." In New York City, where the proportion of nonmanual and professional jobs changed very little from 1796 to 1855, many working-class parents questioned whether they should sacrifice family income in order to educate children for jobs that did not exist.

As early as 1832 the New York Public School Society pointed out: "The labouring classes of society will, to a great extent, withhold their children from school, the moment they arrive at an age that renders their services in the least available in contributing to the support of the family." Later evidence indicated that children under fifteen earned as much as 20 percent of the income of working-class families in Newburyport, Massachusetts. For such families compulsory attendance laws often threatened an unbearable drop in already subsistence level income. Not surprisingly, 40 percent of Newburyport's laborers admitted to the census takers in 1850 that their school-age children had not been enrolled in any school during the previous year. And many children who were enrolled could not attend regularly.

Moreover, by the 1840s the working class in the Northeast was becoming increasingly Roman Catholic. Although the public schools were theoretically secular—in New York and elsewhere, denominational schools had been deprived of public funding—the values and teachings of the schools were unmistakably Protestant. Most Americans of the mid-nineteenth century still thought that Americanism meant Protestantism. Protestant clergymen played a critical role on school committees and in school reform. They saw nothing sectarian about public school teachers' reading aloud from the King James Bible or teaching that the sixteenth-century Protestant Reformation had represented a liberation from Catholic despotism. Bishop John Hughes and other Catholic leaders saw the matter differently. In 1840 New York Catholics launched a political offensive against the Protestant monopoly of public education. As a result of this conflict, the Catholic church decided to construct its own separate system of schools, a costly program that took many decades to complete.

For many immigrants, Catholics, and working-class parents, the Protestant school reformers threatened to impose a uniform set of values on all segments of American society—a flagrant instance of violating minority rights. Resistance also arose from local authorities who feared any centralizing interference from a state board of education. Many conservatives insisted that parents should pay for education, if they could afford it, just as they would pay for any other service or commodity. Others, brought up on the tradition of church schools, feared that the teaching of moral values would be dangerously undermined if guided only by a vaguely Protestant and nondenominational spirit.

Educational Reformers

These obstacles to the expansion of public education were finally overcome by reformers like Horace Mann, who as the chief officer of the Massachusetts Board of Education from 1837 to 1848 became the nation's leading champion of public schools. Mann was a severe, humorless puritan who denounced intemperance, profanity, and ballet dancing along with ignorance, violence, and black slavery. Having personally struggled with the terrors of his New England Calvinist heritage, he had finally concluded that children were capable of infinite improvement and goodness. As a kind of secular minister, still intent on saving souls, he insisted that there must have been a time in the childhood of the worst criminal when, "ere he was irrecoverably lost, ere he plunged into the abyss of infamy and guilt, he might have been recalled." Mann offended traditional Christians by winning the fight in Massachusetts against specific religious instruction in the public schools. He outraged conservatives by asserting that private property is not an absolute right but rather a trusteeship for society and future generations. Trained as a lawyer, he decided as a young man that "the next generation" should be his clients. In pleading the cause of generations to come, he held that school taxes were not a "confiscation" from the rich, but rather a collection of the debt the rich owed to society.

Reformers placed a stupendous moral burden on the public schools. Horace Mann proclaimed the common school to be "the greatest discovery ever made by man." "Other social organizations are curative and remedial," he said; "this is a preventive and antidote." This characteristic argument suggests that the schools were to be a defense against undesirable change, preserving the cherished values of a simpler, more homogeneous America. Educators spoke of the frenzied pace of American life, of the diminishing influence of church and home. They held that the school should thus serve as a substitute for both church and home, preventing American democracy from degenerating into what Mann called "the spectacle of gladiatorial contests." The school, representing the highest instincts of society, could alone be counted on for cultivating decency, cooperation, and a respect for others. Women, reformers believed, were best suited as teachers because they exemplified the noncombative and noncompetitive instincts. Because they could also be employed for lower wages than men, women teachers soon predominated in New England's elementary schools.

The character traits most esteemed by educational reformers were precisely those alleged to bring material success in a competitive and market-oriented society: punctuality, cheerful obedience, honesty, responsibility, perseverance, and foresightedness. Public schools seemed to promise opportunity by providing the means of acquiring these traits. In the words of one school committee, the children "entered the race, aware that the prize was equally before all, and attainable only by personal exertion." The famed McGuffey's "Eclectic" series of readers, which after 1836 became the basic reading textbooks in countless schoolrooms and of which well over 100 million copies were eventually sold, taught young students that no possession was more important for getting on in the world than reputation—"a good name." On the other hand, the readers held out little hope of rags-to-riches success. When the good little poor boy sees other children "riding on pretty horses, or in coaches, or walking with ladies and gentlemen, and having on very fine clothes, he does not envy them, nor wish to be like them." For he has been taught "that it is God who makes some poor, and others rich; that the rich have many troubles which we know nothing of; and that the poor, if they are but good, may be very happy."

From a present-day viewpoint the educational reformers were often insensitive to the needs of non-Protestants, non-Christians, nonwhites, and women. Throughout the North, except in a few scattered communities, the public schools excluded black children. Many localities made no provision for blacks to be educated. Other towns and cities, including New York and Boston, distributed a small portion of public funds to segregated and highly inferior schools for blacks. By 1850 blacks constituted no more than 1.5 percent of Boston's population, but to achieve local desegregation still required a prolonged struggle on the part of militant blacks and white abolitionists. In 1855 Massachusetts became the single state in which no applicant to a public school could be excluded on account of "race, color or religious opinions." In marked contrast to the public schools, Oberlin, Harvard, Bowdoin, Dartmouth, and some other private colleges opened their doors to a few black students. In 1837 Oberlin also became America's first coeducational college. In general, however, American women had no opportunities for higher education except in female seminaries and, by the 1850s, a few western state universities.

By the 1850s Massachusetts had acquired all the essentials of a modern educational system: special "normal schools" for the training of female teachers; the placement of pupils in grades according to age and ability; standardized procedures for advancement from one grade to another; uniform textbooks; and a bureaucracy extending from the board of education down to superintendents, principals, and teachers. Although Massachusetts led the nation, by the 1850s it was possible for a New York City male child to proceed from an "infant school" to a college degree without paying tuition. Educational reformers, many of them originally New Englanders, had helped to create state-supported and state-supervised school systems from Pennsylvania to the new states of the Upper Mississippi Valley. In the 1850s the same cause made some headway in the South, particularly in Virginia and North Carolina.

Whatever prejudices and blind spots the public school movement may have had, it aroused the enthusiasm of hundreds of idealistic men and women who devoted time and energy to the cause. Northern legislators committed an impressive proportion of public spending to the education of succeeding generations. Particularly in the 1850s the movement trained a young generation of teachers inspired with missionary zeal. After the Civil War they would descend on the devastated South, equipped with an ideology for "reconstruction." Above all, the movement reinforced the American faith that social problems could be solved by individual enterprise, a diffusion of knowledge, and a reconstruction of moral character.

The Evangelical Age

Americans continued to look on the church, no less than on the public school, as a decisive instrument for shaping the national character. As in the post-Revolutionary period, religion became more widely accepted and democratic the more it achieved independence from the government. (In 1833 Massachusetts became the last state to give up an established church.) Despite the officially secular stance of American governments, evangelical Protestantism became increasingly identified with patriotism, democracy, and America's mission in the world. And despite the continuing division and competition among religious denominations, Americans increasingly appealed to religion as the only force in American life that could preserve a sense of community and united purpose.

Religious Revivals Between 1820 and 1860 religious revivalism became a powerful organizing and nationalizing force that reached into all parts of American life and all corners of the vast nation—the South as well as the North, the cities as well as the western frontier. Church membership figures can be misleading since many people who regularly attended church could not meet the religious or financial obligations that were required for formal membership. But it has been estimated that by 1835 as many as three out of four adult Americans maintained some nominal relationship to a church. Most foreign observers agreed with Tocqueville that by the 1830s there was no country in the world in which the Christian religion retained "a greater influence over the souls of men."

For the majority of adults, evangelical Protestantism provided a common language and a common frame of reference. It explained not only the nature and ultimate destiny of human beings, but also the meaning of democracy and of American nationality. In the words of a non–church member, a young self-made man and future president of the United States, Andrew Johnson, "Man can become more and more endowed with divinity; and as he does he becomes more godlike in his character and capable of governing himself." Like millions of other Americans, Johnson believed that Christianity and political democracy were together elevating and purifying the people, working toward the day when it could be proclaimed: "The millennial morning has dawned and the time has come when the lion and the lamb shall lie down together, when the glad tidings shall be proclaimed . . . of man's political and religious redemption, and there is 'on earth, peace, good will toward men.'"

In some ways this evangelical vision transcended boundaries of class and section. Although it is possible to think of America as undergoing a single Great Revival during the six decades preceding the Civil War, the revival's social significance differed according to time and place. Some socioeconomic groups were more susceptible to religious enthusiasm than others. Some personality types were likely to view revivalists as self-righteous zealots who threatened to remove all fun from life. Others were likely to seize the chance to profess faith in Christ crucified, to announce repentance for their sins, to experience the liberation of rebirth, and as the popular hymn put it, to "stand up, stand up for Jesus!" For many Americans religion provided the key to social identity. It was not that people flocked to churches to meet the right kind of people, although some no doubt did. It was rather that the "right" kind of religion, as defined by employers, slaveholders, and other wielders of power, was often considered to bestow the "right" kind of character.

Religious revivalism depended on sensitivity to the community's norms and vital interests. In the South leaders of various denominations discovered that any open criticism of slavery could threaten the very survival of a church. The Baptist and Methodist churches thus gradually retreated from their cautious antislavery views of the late eighteenth century, which had supposedly bred discontent if not rebellion among black slaves. By the 1830s the most influential southern churches had begun to deny that there was any moral contradiction between slavery and Christianity. They also insisted that Christianity, rightly understood, posed no danger to "the peculiar institution."*

Civilizing the West Revivalism also served as a socializing force in the nonslaveholding West, but the context and consequences were different. Easterners tended to think of the West as both lawless and sinful. From the lumber camps of Wisconsin to the mining camps of California, easterners' image of westerners was essentially the same: rough, dirty men who swore, gambled, got drunk, frequented houses of prostitution, and relished savage eye-gouging, knife-slashing fights. Although the stereotypes were exaggerated, there was no doubt that frontier communities strained nineteenth-century notions of decency and civilization.

The challenge of the West could not be met simply by building churches where none had existed before. When Theron Baldwin, a member of a Yale missionary group, arrived in Illinois in 1830, he was horrified by the ignorance of the settlers. Even in Vandalia, then the state's capital, Baldwin discovered that most of the pupils in his Sunday school class were illiterate. Nor could he find a literate adult in more than half the families he visited in the region. Religion, Baldwin concluded, could make no headway without education and an institutional rebuilding of society. Appealing for funds from the East, he expressed the New England ideal: "We wish to see the school house and church go up side by side and the land filled with Christian teachers as well as preachers." He added, significantly, that young men could come there "and in a short time get enough by teaching to purchase a farm that would ever after fill their barns with plenty and their hands with good things." Baldwin himself worked to secure from the legislature a charter for the first three colleges in the state. As a result of the labors of Baldwin and other young missionaries, the Old Northwest became dotted with academies, seminaries, and small denominational colleges.

Easterners who still thought of churches as fixed institutions within an ordered society did not understand that religious revivals were an effective instrument for shaping and controlling character. The frank emotionalism and homespun informality of the western and southern revivals disguised the fact that even the camp meetings were soon stabilized by rules, regulations, and the most careful advance planning. And camp meetings were by no means the most important tools of the revivals. The power of the revival movement flowed from the dynamic balance between popular participation and the control of leaders. According to the evangelical message, every man and woman, no matter how humble or trapped in sin, had the capacity to say "Yes!" to Christ's offer of salvation—to reject what was called "cannot-ism," and along with it an

---

*For the impact of Christianity on the slaves' culture and on plantation life, as well as among the free blacks, see chapter 14, pp. 467–68.

Where Character Ultimately Leads
This fanciful diagram of values and human destiny dramatizes the connections between religion and education, and between behavior and one's ultimate fate. "The College" is significantly close to the path of virtues that lead to heaven. But out of the schoolhouse, with its disobedience to parents and teachers, come those who move from fighting and profanity to the "House of Sin," gambling, intemperance, cheating, and on to prison, the gallows, and hell. Such imagery was designed to impress—and frighten—young minds.

unsatisfying identity. Even for the poor and uneducated, consent opened the way for participation and decision making.

Peter Cartwright, for example, grew up in one of the most violent and lawless regions of Kentucky. His brother was hanged for murder, and his sister was said to have "led a life of debauchery." At the age of sixteen, Cartwright repented his sins at a Methodist camp meeting; at seventeen he became an "exhorter"; at eighteen, a traveling preacher; at twenty-one, a deacon; and at twenty-three, a presiding elder of the church. Each upward step required a trial period, followed by an examination of his conduct, ability, and purity of doctrine. The Methodists showed particular skill in devising a system that encouraged widespread participation and upward mobility in the church's organizational structure. But all the evangelical churches displayed the great American gift for organization. Revivals, they believed, could not take place by waiting for God to stir human hearts. Revivals required planning, efficient techniques, and coordinated effort. The need was not for educated theologians, but for professional promoters.

Christianity and the Social Order

Although revivalism was an organizing and socializing movement, it was also by definition selective. The people most likely to be converted were those who had had some Christian upbringing or those who were already disturbed by excessive drinking, gambling, fighting, disorder, and irresponsibility. Conversion itself reinforced crucial social distinctions. For one part of the community, religion became more than a matter of going to church on Sunday. The obligations of a new religious life required sobriety and responsibility from friends, family, employees, and business associates. The weekly "class meetings" and "love feasts" provided fellowship and helped to prevent backsliding. No doubt the solidarity of the converted individuals brought order and discipline to the community at large. But if the evangelicals always insisted that every man and woman could say "Yes!" there were always those who said "No!" The congregations that loved to hear their preachers "pouring hot shot into Satan's ranks" knew that Satan's ranks were concentrated on the other side of the tracks.

Religious revivals could accentuate social distinctions by forging an alliance among the more ambitious, self-disciplined, and future-oriented members of a community. In the fall of 1830, for example, the leaders of Rochester, New York, invited Charles Grandison Finney to save that booming town from sin. By far the most commanding and influential evangelist of the pre–Civil War period, Finney was a tall, athletic spellbinder, a former lawyer who had undergone a dramatic religious conversion in 1823. Although he lacked formal seminary training, Finney had been ordained as a Presbyterian minister and in 1825 had begun a series of highly unusual and spectacular revivals along the route of the newly constructed Erie Canal.

In 1831 Finney's triumphs in Rochester stunned Christian America. Communities from Ohio to Massachusetts appealed to him to save their collective souls. Finney's converts in Rochester were largely housewives, manufacturers, merchants, lawyers, shopkeepers, master artisans, and skilled journeymen. He appealed to people who had profited from the commercial revolution initiated by the building of the Erie Canal but who had become deeply disturbed by the immense influx of young transient laborers looking for work. Rochester's leaders had no control over the behavior of these youths. Significantly, during Rochester's revival years church membership declined among the hotel proprietors and tavern keepers who catered to the floating population of young males traveling the Erie Canal. Rochester's Protestant churches, interpreting the revival as a sweeping popular mandate, launched a crusade to purge the city of its dens of vice and unholy amusement. They also offered a "free church"—free of pew rents and other financial obligations—to the workers on the canal. Increasingly Rochester became divided between a Christian minority dedicated to education and upward advancement and an essentially nonpolitical, free-floating majority of disoriented and unskilled young men.

Philadelphia differed from Rochester in important respects, but there too religious revivals eventually redefined the boundaries of respectable and "modern" behavior. Unlike Rochester, which grew by 512 percent in the 1820s, Philadelphia was not a new boom town. An old city by American standards, Philadelphia was relatively resistant to religious enthusiasm. Revivalism had little appeal to the wealthy Quakers and conservative Presbyterian clergymen who dominated the city's religious life. Evangelical morality was even less appealing to

Philadelphia's workingmen, who preserved and cherished a traditional artisan, preindustrial culture. Largely because of irregular and undeveloped transportation to interior markets, Philadelphia workers suffered periodic layoffs. This forced leisure allowed them to enjoy traveling circuses, cockfights, drinking and gambling at the local taverns, and above all the boisterous comradeship of volunteer fire companies. Until 1837 neither the revival nor the closely related temperance movement made much headway among Philadelphia's manual workers. The people who reformed their drinking habits and who joined the reform-minded wing of the Presbyterian church were the professional and business groups who were ushering in the new industrial order. But in 1837 the financial panic and subsequent depression began to undermine the traditional habits and culture of the working class. Waves of religious revivalism, often Methodist in character, reached working-class neighborhoods. A new and more powerful temperance movement developed spontaneously from the ranks of master craftsmen, journeymen, shopkeepers, and the most ambitious unskilled laborers. In Philadelphia, as in Rochester, the decision to abstain from all alcohol was the key symbol of a new morality and of a new commitment to self-improvement. By the 1840s the evangelical workingmen could contrast their own sobriety and self-discipline with the moral laxity of mounting numbers of Irish immigrants. Not surprisingly, the revivalism that bolstered the self-respect of blue-collar native workers and their wives also contributed to passionate anti-Catholicism and to old-stock prejudice against a population that seemed to threaten the newly won dignity of manual labor.

Revivalism and Economic Prosperity
Revivals appeared to be the only hopeful counterforce against rampant individualism, self-serving politics, and corrupting luxury. As Finney put it, "the great political and other worldly excitements" of the time distracted attention from the interests of the soul. He held, accordingly, that these excitements could "only be counteracted by religious excitements." Only revivals could prevent the United States from sliding into the decay and collapse of ancient Greece and Rome. Only revivals could prepare the nation "to lead the way," in Lyman Beecher's phrase, "in the moral and political emancipation of the world."

Revivalism was fed by the moral doubts that inevitably accompanied rapid economic growth, the disruption of older modes of work and responsibility, the sudden accumulation of wealth, and the appearance of new class differences. Revivalist preachers denounced atheism far less than "Mammonism," the greedy pursuit of riches. They voiced repeated concern over the frantic pace of American life, the disintegration of family and community, and the worship of material success.

But revivalism seldom led to saintly withdrawal or to spiritualistic contemplation. Evangelical religion was above all activist, pragmatic, and oriented toward measurable results. The fame of Finney and the other great exhorters depended on the body count, or soul count, of converts. Finney proclaimed: "The results justify my methods—a motto that could as well have come from

John Jacob Astor or other entrepreneurs in more worldly spheres. Finney confidently predicted: "If the church will do her duty, the millennium may come in this country in three years." He knew, however, that a millennium would require no revivals, and that as a revivalist, although dedicated to virtue, he needed sin as much as a soldier needs war.

There was a close relation between the revivals and America's expansive economy. The exuberant materialism of American life furnished revivalists with continuing targets for attack and with vivid signs of community strife and moral shortcoming. Without moral crises there would be no cause for national rededication, and calls for rededication have long been America's way of responding to social change. But on another level the revivalists had merged their cause with America's secular destiny. They had repeatedly warned that without religion, American democracy would speedily dissolve into "a common field of unbridled appetite and lust." Yet instead of dissolving, the nation continued to prosper, expand, and reveal new marvels. Sometimes clergymen hailed the achievements as signs of national virtue and divine favor. More important, as a reflection of their increasing respect for efficient methods and material results, they applauded technological improvements as the instruments that God had provided for saving the world.

The telegraph, railroad, and steamship all quickened the way for spreading the gospel around the world, and thus they could be interpreted as signs of the coming millennium. But America's technology and rapid westward expansion could be justified only if Americans took the burdens of a missionary nation seriously. Samuel Fisher, the president of Hamilton College in upstate New York, elaborated on this message in an address to the American Board of Commissioners for Foreign Missions:

> Material activity, quickened and guided by moral principle, is absolutely essential to the development of a strong and manly character. . . . The product of this devotion to material interests is capital diffused through the masses; and capital is one of the means God uses to convert the world.

The diffusion of capital through the masses seemed to falter in 1857, when a financial crash brought a severe depression and unprecedented unemployment among factory workers. Economic insecurity formed the backdrop of what many took to be "the event of the century," the great urban revival of late 1857 and 1858. What distinguished this event from earlier religious revivals was the absence of revivalists. In Philadelphia and New York thousands of clerks and businessmen began to unite spontaneously for midday prayer. The New York *Herald* and the New York *Tribune* devoted special issues to the remarkable events—wealthy stockbrokers praying and singing next to messenger boys; revivals in the public high schools; joint services by Methodists, Episcopalians, Presbyterians, Baptists, and even the traditionally antirevivalist Unitarians. The spirit rapidly spread to manufacturing towns throughout the Northeast. Unscheduled and unconventional religious meetings sprang up in small towns and rural areas from Indiana to

Quebec. "It would seem," wrote one enthusiast, "that the mighty crash was just what was wanted...to startle men from their golden dreams." Americans had become too overbearing, too self-confident, too complacent in their success. Yet if God had shown his displeasure, as countless interpreters maintained, he had also chosen means that underscored America's promise. He had punished Americans with economic loss, which even the hardest head among the business community could understand.

The great revival of 1858 gave a new sense of unity to northerners, who had become increasingly divided by class and religious conflict, to say nothing of the issue of slavery. It also signified the maturity of an urban, industrial Protestantism that was committed to material progress and self-improvement. For good or for ill, the revivals reinvigorated America's official ideal of *Novus Ordo Seclorurm*—a New Order for the World—the phrase today stamped on every dollar bill, conveying the message that a new social order is to exist, that Americans carry the high burden of helping to create a better world.

The Cult of Self-Improvement

What made public schools and religious revivals seem so indispensable by the 1830s was the relative absence of authoritative institutions that could define social roles, rules of conduct, and models of character. There was no standing army, for example, that could train a military class or enforce unpopular public policy. The abolition of public support for established churches gave semiliterate evangelists the same official status as college-trained theologians. Some states guaranteed any citizen, regardless of training, the right to practice law in any court. Americans showed less and less respect for any intellectual elite, religious or secular, or for any group of self-perpetuating masters who claimed to preserve and monopolize a body of knowledge that the public at large could not understand.

Not only had American law rejected European notions of privileged social orders, but as time went on the courts swept away most of the legal barriers that had restrained individuals from entering into certain kinds of risky or unfair agreements. In other words, the law assumed that all society was a marketplace of competitive exchange in which each individual calculated the probable risks of a given choice of action. As a result of this new burden of individual freedom and responsibility, Americans began to place enormous importance on acquiring effective skills and up-to-date knowledge. Continuous self-improvement became the great ideal of the age.

Lyceums and Learning   To Americans of the late twentieth century, there is nothing novel about fads, cults, and nostrums that promise the solution to life's problems. But in the 1830s and 1840s the cult of self-improvement was unprecedented in both the boldness and the variety of its appeals. Some conservatives expressed alarm over the credulity of public opinion, assuming that fads and quackery posed a threat to public order. But in general the people desired not the restructuring of society, but self-knowledge and self-advancement. In the 1820s numerous respectable societies and institutes for adult education and "mutual improvement" began to spread from England to the United States. Tens of thousands of adults, first in New England and then in the Old Northwest, grew accustomed to attending lectures, concerts, and various cultural events at lyceums (public halls). Lyceum lectures covered a vast range of subjects, but in the early years of the movement they tended to concentrate on "useful knowledge" associated with moral improvement and popular science.

Americans generally equated the advance of science with the advance of human liberty, a linkage that was part of the heritage of the European Enlightenment. They believed that everyone could benefit from the scientific method, that the marvels and secrets of nature were open to all. But what most impressed and fascinated American audiences were lectures and books on the applications of science, demonstrating the ingenious ways that human beings could master nature. As early as 1829, Jacob Bigelow's *Elements of Technology* not only helped to popularize a new word, but gave impetus to the general public's growing inclination to see invention as the key to national progress. Excitement over the uses of technology and steam power was matched by a new curiosity about the human mind, which had shown that it could unlock nature's secrets.

Mind Control and Phrenology The gap between public ignorance and the achievements of science could be bridged if someone invented the supreme technology, a technology for controlling the human mind. The quest for this power united many of the popular cults and fads. Mesmerists, for example, claimed to have discovered the laws of magnetic attraction and repulsion that governed relations between people. Spiritualists convinced hundreds of thousands that they had found techniques and apparatus for communicating with the dead and probing the laws of the occult. Even the manuals on self-improvement and character building, directed mainly at the young, presumed definitive knowledge of the mechanics of the brain. The Reverend John Todd's *Student's Manual* (1835), which sold by the hundreds of thousands, maintained that mental power depends on a strict conservation of bodily and especially sexual energies. Todd's thesis, repeated by countless physicians and other experts, was that masturbation and sexual excess posed the gravest threats to sanity, social order, and individual achievement. Self-improvement thus required the rigorous avoidance of unwholesome thoughts and tempting situations.

The most ambitious and institutionalized science of the mind, however, was phrenology, the invention of Franz Joseph Gall, a Viennese physician. Phrenology identified the supposed physical location in the brain of a large assortment of human "faculties," such as firmness, benevolence, acquisitiveness, destructiveness, and platonic love. Phrenologists claimed that they could precisely measure character from the form and shape of a head. Americans first responded to phrenology as a promising medical breakthrough. Gall's leading disciple, Johann Gaspar Spurzheim, became the first spreader of the cause. On a visit to

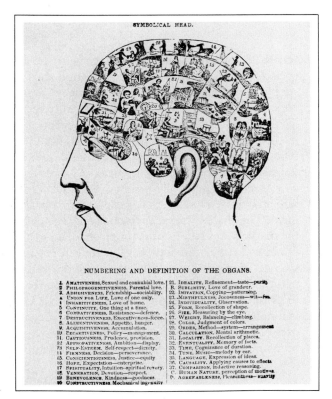

SYMBOLICAL HEAD.

NUMBERING AND DEFINITION OF THE ORGANS.

1. AMATIVENESS, Sexual and connubial love.
2. PHILOPROGENITIVENESS, Parental love.
3. ADHESIVENESS, Friendship—sociability.
4. UNION FOR LIFE, Love of one only.
5. INHABITIVENESS, Love of home.
6. CONTINUITY, One thing at a time.
7. COMBATIVENESS, Resistance—defence.
8. DESTRUCTIVENESS, Executiveness—force.
9. ALIMENTIVENESS, Appetite, hunger.
10. ACQUISITIVENESS, Accumulation.
11. SECRETIVENESS, Policy—management.
12. CAUTIOUSNESS, Prudence, provision.
13. APPROBATIVENESS, Ambition—display.
14. SELF-ESTEEM, Self-respect—dignity.
15. FIRMNESS, Decision—perseverance.
16. CONSCIENTIOUSNESS, Justice—equity.
17. HOPE, Expectation—enterprise.
18. SPIRITUALITY, Intuition—spiritual revery.
19. VENERATION, Devotion—respect.
20. BENEVOLENCE, Kindness—goodness.
21. CONSTRUCTIVNESS, Mechanical ingenuity

21. IDEALITY, Refinement—taste—purity
B. SUBLIMITY, Love of grandeur.
22. IMITATION, Copying—patterning.
23. MIRTHFULNESS, Jocoseness—wit—fun.
24. INDIVIDUALITY, Observation.
25. FORM, Recollection of shape.
26. SIZE, Measuring by the eye.
27. WEIGHT, Balancing—climbing.
28. COLOR, Judgment of colors.
29. ORDER, Method—system—arrangement
30. CALCULATION, Mental arithmetic.
31. LOCALITY, Recollection of places.
32. EVENTUALITY, Memory of facts.
33. TIME, Cognizance of duration.
34. TUNE, Music—melody by ear.
35. LANGUAGE, Expression of ideas.
36. CAUSALITY, Applying causes to effects
37. COMPARISON, Inductive reasoning.
C. HUMAN NATURE, perception of motives
D. AGREEABLENESS, Pleasantness—suavity

"Symbolical Head"
This diagram illustrates the assortment of abilities, emotions, inclinations, and character traits that phrenologists claimed to identify as "organs" of the brain.

America in 1832, he was ushered around as a celebrity by New England dignitaries, including Supreme Court Justice Joseph Story and the Yale chemist Benjamin Silliman. For a time phrenology enjoyed intellectual prestige through the support of Horace Mann, the famous Unitarian preacher William Ellery Channing, and a number of business leaders, among them Abbott Lawrence. As usual, however, the American public displayed far more interest in practical application than in theory. Two skillful promoters, Orson and Lorenzo Fowler, helped to convert phrenology into a major business enterprise. In the cities audiences of thousands paid fees for lengthy lectures expounding the new science. Thousands more flocked to salons to have their characters analyzed. Traveling lecturers and mail-order courses enlightened the countryside. By the mid-1850s the *American Phrenological Journal* had a circulation of more than 50,000.

In many ways phrenology perfectly suited the needs of a population that was devoted to technique and uncertain of its own character. In an expansive and socially disruptive economy, phrenology provided a new set of guidelines that reduced the fear of risk. For example employers, who could no longer rely on long-term apprenticeships, on personal knowledge of an employee's family, or even on a worker's reputation in the community, could request a phrenological examination. Young men who dreamed of many careers but could decide on none welcomed a science that would measure their talents and capabilities. The great message of phrenology was individual adjustment. In a world of confusing and changing expectations, it furnished boundaries and specific identities. It told the individual which traits to cultivate and which to restrain. Criminologists not only found a physical explanation for deviant behavior, but also discovered a new hope for preventing crime by identifying potential criminals and by teaching convicts to control their overdeveloped antisocial faculties. Although Americans gradually came to realize that the results of phrenology could not substantiate its high promise, they had expressed an ardent desire—which would continue to our own time—for a popular science of human behavior.

Emerson   Ralph Waldo Emerson came closer than anyone else to being America's "official" philosopher of the nineteenth century. Like phrenology, Emerson's essays and lyceum lectures offered something for everyone and thus nourished hope for reducing friction and creating social harmony. There is no way of knowing how much influence Emerson actually had on American thought and culture, but he certainly helped to stimulate the great literary renaissance of the 1850s. For decades to come his writings were a source of inspiration for reformers, businessmen, and countless ordinary folk. It can be argued that Emerson's worship of power and of self-improvement provide the spiritual backdrop for the entire progressive era of the early twentieth century.

Yet Emerson's thought escapes all attempts at classification or categorization. His words awakened reformers, but he wrote the most penetrating critiques of reform of his generation. Although homespun and down-to-earth, at the same time he was among the most abstract American thinkers. An ardent champion of cultural independence, he defined the mission of native artists and writers, yet he exploited his knowledge of the newest currents of German and English thought. He was the leading figure in a group that introduced to America German idealist philosophy, usually referred to by the awkward term *Transcendentalism,* taken from the work of the great German philosopher of the late eighteenth century, Immanuel Kant. But Emerson advocated an extreme form of individualism and never felt comfortable as a member of any association. His brief, pointed sayings on self-reliance were later quoted by anarchists and yet were framed on the walls of the nation's business leaders.

Emerson's spongelike capacity to absorb ideas and the common attitudes of his time, as well as his empathy for all sides and commitment to none, had much in common with America's greatest weaknesses and strengths. To various audiences he proclaimed that "who so would be a man, must be a nonconformist." To the youth of America he delivered the reassuring thought: "We but half express ourselves, and are ashamed of the divine idea which each of us represents. Trust thyself: every heart vibrates to that iron string." He criticized Americans for their single-minded pursuit of wealth and fame, for their obsession

Ralph Waldo Emerson
(1803–82)

with material things. But the point of this protest against materialism and conformity—which became clearer as both Emerson and his audiences grew older—was the need for a continuing reshaping and reinvigoration of the American character.

To Emerson the great peril that threatened the American people was not injustice, but a fragmentation of soul: "The reason why the world lacks unity and lies broken and in heaps, is because man is disunited with himself." The essential problem, then, was one of reconstituting character, of recovering a sense of the whole. By self-reliance Emerson really meant a detachment from society in order to achieve the sense of wholeness that flowed from unity with God—or, as Emerson put it, "the Oversoul." This notion that every "private man" possesses infinite and godlike capacities was an inspiring ideal, perfectly suited to the fantasies and aspirations of many Americans. At times, however, this doctrine meant that Emerson had no standard beyond power and success: "Power is, in nature, the essential measure of right."

Dissent: The Mormons as a Test Case

The history of the Mormons is seldom included in discussions of American dissent and reform. Yet Mormonism was not only America's first truly native religion; it began as a radical expression of dissent. This dissent was so extreme that Mormons found that they could survive only by building their own refuge in the remote deserts of the Far West. Because the early history of Mormonism exemplifies so many of the aspirations and difficulties of other dissenters—who also wished to live in their own ways in accordance with a higher moral law, free from the religious and political contaminations of their time—the Mormon experience can serve as an introduction, or a "test case." Essentially, the Mormons tested the outermost limits of permissible dissent, as well as the ability of any minority group or subculture to withstand the pressures of American secular society.

Joseph Smith, Founder

In 1830 Joseph Smith, Jr., published the Book of Mormon in Palmyra, New York. He said that the work was a translation of mysterious golden plates containing the history of an ancient Christian civilization in the New World. It portrayed the American Indians as the degenerate but saveable descendants of an ancient Hebrew tribe, and it foresaw a new American prophet who would discover the lost history and reestablish Christ's pure Kingdom in the New World. Smith in 1830 was an athletic, friendly, cheerful, intensely imaginative man of twenty-four, who claimed he had long had religious visions and revelations. He was the son of one of America's many families of drifters, debtors, and habitual losers, whose poverty worsened as they drew closer to the belts of commercial prosperity. Smith had been born in the hills of Vermont, and his parents had migrated to that caldron of progress and poverty—of religious revivalism and new social movements—in upstate New York that was soon to be known as the Burned-Over District. Shortly after the publication of the Book of Mormon, Smith organized the Church of Christ, which in 1834 would be renamed the Church of Jesus Christ of Latter-day Saints.

Faced at the outset with religious persecution, Smith knew that the saints must ultimately move westward and build their city of God at some divinely appointed spot near the Indian tribes they were commissioned to convert. As he was told to do in his revelations, he dispatched missionaries to scout out the Missouri frontier. In 1831 a few Mormons established an outpost near Independence, Missouri, which Smith designated as the site of the New Jerusalem, and which was then the eastern end of the Santa Fe Trail. During the same year, Smith and his New York followers migrated to Kirtland, Ohio, where Mormon missionaries had converted an entire community.

Persecution of the Mormons

By 1839 the Mormons had met defeat in both Ohio and Missouri and were fleeing to a refuge of swampy Illinois farmland that Smith had bought along the eastern shore of the Mississippi River. In Ohio the Mormons had experimented with communal ownership of property and with an illegal wildcat banking venture that had brought disaster during the Panic of 1837. In Missouri proslavery mobs, hostile to any group of nonslaveholding Yankees and inflamed by reports that Mormons intended to bring free blacks into the state, had destroyed the settlements around Independence. A series of armed encounters, beginning with an attempt to bar

Mormons from voting, led to outright warfare and to Governor L. W. Boggs's proclamation that the Mormons had to be treated as enemies—that they "had to be exterminated, or driven from the state." At Haun's Mill a band of Missourians massacred nineteen Mormon men and boys. Smith himself was convicted of treason and sentenced to be shot. But he managed to escape, and in Illinois some 12,000 to 15,000 Mormons finally built their model city of Nauvoo, which the legislature incorporated in 1840 as a virtually independent city-state. The Mormons' political power derived from the decisive weight they could throw in state elections that were fairly evenly balanced between Whigs and Democrats. Beginning in 1840 their numbers grew as the result not only of missionary work in the East, but also of the immigration of thousands who had been converted to Mormonism in the manufacturing districts of England. The English converts' route to the American Zion was eased by the church's highly efficient planning authority, which took care of the details of travel.

By the early 1840s visitors to Nauvoo marveled at the city's broad streets, carefully laid out in neat squares, and at the steam sawmills and flour mill, the factories, hotel, and schools. Although the Nauvoo temple, supported by thirty gigantic pillars and walls of hewn stone, was not yet complete, it promised to be, in the words of the poet John Greenleaf Whittier, "the most splendid and imposing architectural monument in the new world." Dressed in the uniform of a lieutenant general, Smith commanded the Nauvoo legion of 2,000 troops. In 1843 he dictated the official revelation, which he never made public, justifying the practice of plural marriage, or polygamy. The next year he established the secret Council of Fifty, a secular authority independent of the church, and gave it the mission of building a world government that would prepare the way for Christ's Kingdom.

But Smith felt the American world closing in on him and his fellow Mormons. Sensing that the surrounding society would not long tolerate Mormon power and that dissident Mormons were rebelling against his institution of plural marriage and his being secretly crowned king, Smith unsuccessfully tried to persuade the new Republic of Texas to sponsor an independent Mormon colony along the contested border with Mexico. While also sending secret diplomatic missions to Russia and France, he tried to influence the established order through normal political channels. But neither the federal government nor the 1844 presidential candidates would defend the Mormons' claims against Missouri outlaws who had seized thousands of Mormon farms and buildings. As a gesture of protest, Smith finally announced his own candidacy for the highest office in the land. But well before the election, he ordered the destruction of a printing press that had been set up by Mormon dissidents, who had declared: "We will not acknowledge any man as king or lawgiver to the church." Illinois then charged Smith with treason and locked him and his brother in the Carthage jail. On June 27, 1844, a "mob" made up of a state militia group including many prominent non-Mormon citizens stormed the jail and killed them both.

To the Mormons the Prophet's martyrdom brought shock, division, and a struggle over what kind of religion Mormonism should become. It also tem-

Brigham Young (1801–77)
*Despite his lack of formal
education, Brigham Young—
popularly known as "The Lion
of the Lord"—proved to be one
of the most effective executives
and organizers of the nineteenth
century.*

porarily appeased the aggression of anti-Mormons and gave Smith's followers time to plan an exodus. Brigham Young, like Smith, a man of humble Vermont origin, soon emerged as the leader of the Mormon majority and as one of the nineteenth century's greatest organizers. Although dissenting factions trekked off to northern Michigan, Texas, Pennsylvania, and parts of the Midwest, Young received indispensable support from the elite Quorum of the Twelve Apostles and the Council of Fifty. He succeeded in preserving order and morale while considering and rejecting possible refuges in British and Mexican territory. Before the end of 1845 the Mormon leadership had decided to send an advance company of 1,500 men to the valley of the Great Salt Lake, then still part of Mexico. As a result of mounting persecution and harassment, the Mormons soon concentrated their energies on evacuating Nauvoo, on selling property at tremendous sacrifice, and on setting up refugee camps stretching from eastern Iowa to Winter Quarters, a temporary destination in eastern Nebraska. The last refugees crossed the Mississippi River at gunpoint, leaving Nauvoo a ghost town. During the summer of 1846 some 12,000 Mormons were on the road; 3,700 wagon teams stretched out across the prairies of Iowa.

In the summer of 1847, Brigham Young led an advance party of picked men across the barren wastes of Nebraska and Wyoming to the Great Salt Lake Valley of Utah. In September a second band of 2,000 weary Mormons found a home in the new Zion. During the same year the American defeat of Mexico brought Utah

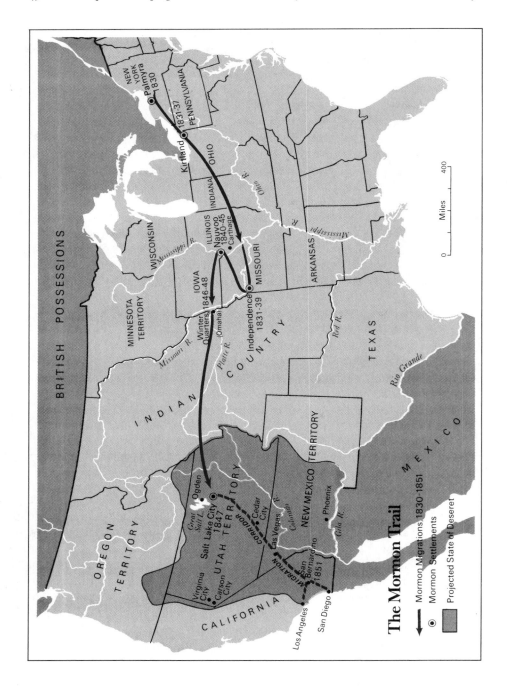

The Mormon Trail

→ Mormon Migrations 1830–1851
⊙ Mormon Settlements
▨ Projected State of Deseret

within the boundaries of the United States. The Mormons had contributed a battalion of five hundred men who had marched with the American army across New Mexico to southern California, and whose pay had helped to finance the migration to Utah. Yet by 1848 the Mormons occupied an inland mountain fortress, a thousand miles beyond the Kansas frontier, and seemed at last to be the masters of their own destiny. When federal judges and other officials arrived in the territory, they found that the Mormons had held a census, adopted a constitution, elected Young governor, and established what they called the State of Deseret, complete with its own currency and army. The religiously run government was responsible for the remarkably rapid and orderly settlement of the valley, for the collective labor and central economic planning that brought irrigation to the dry but fertile land, and for the coordinated expansion that in ten years established ninety-six colonies, extending in a corridor from Salt Lake City to San Diego.

Ten years before the time when South Carolina defied federal authority by firing on Fort Sumter and thus beginning the Civil War, federal officials fled from Utah, denouncing Young's government as a church-state fundamentally disloyal to the United States. Although the Mormons claimed to be loyal to the Constitution and acknowledged their status as an American territory, they intended to pay little attention to the authorities who had been sent from Washington. When Young publicly proclaimed the sacred doctrine of polygamy, which Mormon leaders had privately practiced for more than a decade, he presented a ready-made issue to outraged reformers, ministers, and politicians. President Buchanan felt the need for appeasing this popular clamor and of forcibly establishing federal authority in Utah. In 1857 he dispatched a regular army force of 2,500 men to impose federal law on the Mormons. In an irony of history, they were led by Albert Sidney Johnston, who would soon be a Confederate general resisting an invasion by the United States.

Fortunately for the Mormons, winter storms trapped the expedition in the Rocky Mountains, allowing time for behind-the-scenes negotiations. Governor Young proclaimed martial law and threatened to burn Salt Lake City to the ground and "to utterly lay waste" the land if Utah were invaded. States' rights Democrats had little enthusiasm for setting precedents that might be turned against southern slavery, and although Buchanan had sworn that he would "put down the Mormon rebellion," he decided early in 1858 to proclaim a "pardon" to the inhabitants of Utah if they would obey United States laws and cooperate with federal officials. To prove their strength, however, the Mormons evacuated Salt Lake City. Johnston's army entered a deserted city, greeted only by squads of tough police, "glowering from beneath their hat-brims, with clubs in their hands, and pistols ready slung at their belts." The later withdrawal of federal troops concluded the so-called Mormon War, which brought no change in the actual government of Utah. When Buchanan's successor, Abraham Lincoln, was asked what he proposed to do about the Mormons, he answered, "I propose to let them alone." Lincoln, of course, had other problems on his hands.

No story in American history is more incredible. From the outset Mormonism embodied the longings and hopes of people who had not shared in the growing prosperity and social modernization of the early nineteenth century. After listening to a Mormon service in Massachusetts, the poet Whittier observed that "they speak a language of hope and promise to weak, weary hearts, tossed and troubled, who have wandered from sect to sect, seeking in vain for the primal manifestation of the divine power." The new church recruited most of its members from the more remote and isolated parts of New England; from the sparsely populated southern districts of New York and the adjacent parts of northern Pennsylvania; from the rural backcountry of the Upper South and frontier Midwest; and eventually from both rural and manufacturing districts of Wales, Lancashire (in northern England), and Scandinavia. Few of these converts were well-to-do, well educated, or well established in settled communities. They were mainly small farmers who had been displaced by commercial agriculture, and footloose tradesmen and artisans who had been bypassed by expanding markets. All were people already uprooted and highly mobile, long engaged in a search for communal and religious security.

The Meaning of Mormon Dissent

Because the Mormon search for authority took religious form, it is easy to miss its radical challenge to American secular values and institutions. Against a pluralistic, permissive, and individualistic society, the Mormons pitted a higher authority that rested on a rock of unswerving certainty and conviction. Their institutions, based on divine authority, cast doubt on the legitimacy of popular sovereignty, secular law, and established government. The claim that divine revelation sanctioned such a practice as polygamy challenged the basic premises of secular law and morality. And according to their enemies, the Mormons' communal economy subverted private property, encouraged wholesale theft, and excluded non-Mormon enterprise from Utah. Far worse, the Mormons had shown little Christian patience in response to persecution. If like the earliest Christians they had looked for strength from the blood of their martyrs, they had also promised retaliation, or "blood atonement," to their enemies.

But the Mormons were not revolutionaries. Despite many points of dissent, Mormonism had much in common with the developing culture of pre–Civil War America. No other American denomination so fully incorporated the so-called Protestant ethic of work, or the rule of abstaining from tobacco and all alcoholic drinks as a symbol of their own self-discipline and modernizing values. In many respects the Mormons' ideal of a religious state was an extreme version of the ideal of Lyman Beecher, the New England revivalist reformer, and of countless other evangelists who insisted that rampant democracy must be guided by a higher moral force.

In sum, Mormonism was both a radical protest against the values of an individualistic, competitive, uprooting, and disinheriting world, and a way of achieving solidarity and authority that enabled its members to adjust to that world. During the pre–Civil War decades no other movement—with the exception of the movement among southerners to defend black slavery—posed so serious a challenge to the ideology of the industrializing, urbanizing, and modernizing North. The Mormons probed the outermost limits of tolerance, the violent limits where dissent verged on treason, and finally established their own fragile refuge beyond—but soon within—America's geographical frontiers. Unlike southerners, they escaped the major confrontation of civil war. But their unique success required a prolonged accommodation with and ultimate surrender to the civilization against which the South finally waged civil war.

The Benevolent Empire

Like the founders of Mormonism, the reformers of the early nineteenth century were responding to the breakdown of social rules and moral authority associated with a traditional society. To restore "the moral government of God" was the supreme goal of the so-called Benevolent Empire—an informal coalition of home and foreign missionary societies, the American Tract Society, the American Sunday School Union, the American Society for the Promotion of Temperance, the American Colonization Society, the Prison Discipline Society, and the General Union for Promoting the Observance of the Christian Sabbath. Even William Lloyd Garrison, who later came to symbolize radical abolitionism and a defiance of church and state, began his career in the 1820s as a lowly but ardent champion of these seemingly conservative reform organizations. Like many ministers and wealthy humanitarians, young Garrison deplored the rising "mobocracy," the "lawless multitude" who enjoyed liquor, violence, profanity, sexual vice, and vulgar entertainment. American social reform originated in the crusade to purify public morals and find new means, such as the asylum and penitentiary, for instilling habits of regularity, sobriety, obedience, and responsibility.

The Reform of Society

Ideals of purification and the exclusion of undesirables dominated the activities of the Benevolent Empire. Having already provided for the abolition of slavery in the northern states, many antislavery reformers wanted to send the free blacks back to Africa, an idea that gained increasing support during the early nineteenth century, especially among missionary groups who assumed that American blacks would help to Christianize the land of their ancestors. Drunkards were to be banished from the sight of respectable society. Criminals and deviants of various kinds were to be walled off in prisons and asylums, where "their stubborn spirits are subdued, and their depraved hearts softened, by mental suffering," as some New York reformers put it in 1822. When deviants were institutionalized, they could neither disturb nor contaminate a society that needed to concentrate on business and on moral virtue. Some enthusiastic prison reformers even argued that society itself should be modeled on "the regularity, and temperance, and sobriety of a good prison."

Unlike the Mormons, these reformers aspired to lead and transform the dominant secular society. Although they sought to gather together like-minded promoters of virtue, they originally gave no thought to withdrawing from a sinful society in order to practice virtue. Most of the leaders of the Benevolent Empire were men of economic and educational attainment. They could think of themselves, under "normal" circumstances, as the natural leaders of their communities. They tended to idealize the New England heritage of ordered and homogeneous communities governed by educated ministers and political leaders. Above all, they looked increasingly to Britain for models of "practical Christianity" and organized reform.

Organized humanitarianism had a long history in Britain, but during the Napoleonic wars (1798–1815) it grew dramatically. A vast campaign was undertaken in Britain to reform public morals, to Christianize the world, and to unite rich and poor by an affectionate bond of humanitarianism that would replace the traditional deference to the upper classes, which had begun to decay even in England. The British and Foreign Bible Society, founded in 1804, became the model for nonsectarian organizations committed to the ideal of "Christian unity." The Bible Society also became a pioneer in highly specialized organization as it acquired women's auxiliaries, skilled professional agents, and teams of "visitors" assigned to specific towns, districts, and streets to collect funds, interview poor families, and distribute Bibles. This kind of systematic division of labor was soon adopted by hundreds of British societies and was eventually copied by the Mormons to organize their community in Utah.

British societies were formed to promote Christianity among the Jews, observance of the Christian Sabbath, universal peace, and the abolition of slavery. There were societies to suppress immorality, antireligious publications, juvenile delinquency, and cruelty to animals; societies to aid the poverty-stricken blind, the industrious poor, orphans of soldiers and sailors, and "Poor, Infirm, Aged Widows, and Single Women, of Good Character, Who Have Seen Better Days." The English, who seem to have outdone the Americans as a nation of joiners, even launched the Society for Returning Young Women to Their Friends in the Country.

By the 1820s Britain appeared suddenly to have moved into the forefront of humanitarianism. The evangelical reformers won particular prestige by taking the lead in the successful campaign to abolish the African slave trade. Most Americans, however, remembered the British invasions of the United States during the War of 1812 and continued to think of England as a nation of tyranny and political corruption. Thus they remained suspicious of any alleged humanitarian change of heart in Britain. But the New England clergy welcomed news of England's moral transformation. Confronted by the collapse of Federalist political power, by the growing political force of public opinion, and by irresistible demands for the separation of church and state, many New England clergymen adopted the organizational apparatus of British benevolence as a means of securing control of American culture. With the aid of allies from the other parts of the Northeast, these New England ministers and reformers succeeded in

capturing and Americanizing the British evangelical spirit and in institutionalizing it in New York City, Philadelphia, and regions stretching west to Illinois.

From about 1810 to 1830 the Benevolent Empire developed gradually as local
societies for the reformation of morals enlarged their objectives through various
interstate and interlocking personal networks. A remarkable number of the
original promoters of benevolent societies were students or recent graduates of
Andover Theological Seminary in Massachusetts, founded by Congregationalists
in 1809 in opposition to Harvard's drift toward the liberal, rationalistic creed of
Unitarianism. Andover was a seedbed for missionary work in Asia, Africa, and
the American West. Many of the seminary's alumni took up such secular causes as
black colonization, prison reform, and the suppression of intemperance. Louis
Dwight, for example, who traveled the country as an agent for the American
Bible Society, was so shocked by the squalor and disorder of jails that he became a
leading crusader for the penitentiary system of total silence, close surveillance,
and solitary confinement at night used in the Auburn, New York, prison. This
Auburn system, Dwight maintained, "would greatly promote order, seriousness,
and purity in large families, male and female boarding schools, and colleges."

These Andover reformers worked closely with serious-minded young ministers and laymen who had attended Yale or Princeton, as well as with rich and
pious businessmen like Edward C. Delavan, Gerrit Smith, and the Tappan
brothers. Delavan, a former wine merchant and Albany real estate magnate,
contributed a fortune to the temperance cause. The reform movements nourished by the Benevolent Empire moved in radical as well as conservative directions. Gerrit Smith, a land baron in upstate New York, promoted innumerable
reforms ranging from Sunday schools, penitentiaries, and temperance to radical
abolitionism, women's rights, and world peace. Arthur and Lewis Tappan, who
were wealthy importers and retail merchants in New York City, contributed
money and leadership to a whole galaxy of local and national reform societies,
especially those devoted to the abolition of slavery.

The Sabbatarian Movement
The movement to enforce the Christian Sabbath reveals
some of the basic concerns of the Benevolent Empire,
as well as the obstacles that prevented the emergence of
a much-hoped-for "Christian party in politics." In 1810 Congress had passed a law
requiring the mail to flow seven days a week, in order to meet the critical business
demands for faster communication. Sunday mail service immediately drew fire
from Lyman Beecher and other New Englanders, and subsequently it provoked
national debate. For devout Christians the Sabbath evoked memories of a less
hurried, agrarian past. Even merchants, although wrapped up in their own
success and totally involved in worldly pursuits, found the silent Sabbath a
reassuring symbol of spiritual goals that justified the previous six days of earthly
cares and ambition.

It is significant that Sabbatarian reform originated in the boom town of
Rochester, not in the long-settled urban areas along the coast. Rochester's
established ministers had come from New England and New Jersey, where a quiet

Sabbath had been enforced by custom and law. But the Erie Canal passed directly under the windows of Rochester's First Presbyterian Church, and the rowdy boatmen made no effort to lower their voices during the hours of Sunday prayer. In 1828 the town's leading ministers, real estate magnates, and entrepreneurs enlisted Lyman Beecher and Lewis Tappan in a national crusade to persuade Congress to enforce the laws of God. Although unsuccessful, the movement was historically important because it polarized "serious Christians" against the multitude; because it prepared the way for collaboration between wealthy New York humanitarians and social activists, inspired by the revivals of Charles Grandison Finney; and because it marked the transition between merely distributing Bibles and resorting to direct political and economic action. It should also be emphasized that Rochester lay at the heart of the Burned-Over District and that the Sabbatarian movement coincided with the Anti-Masonic crusade,* Finney's revivals, the perfection and extension of the Auburn penitentiary system, and the birth of Mormonism.

Although the various causes taken up by the Benevolent Empire appear conservative when compared with later abolitionism, feminism, and perfectionism, they too challenged vested interests and provoked immediate and furious resistance. The Sabbatarian movement, for example, threatened loss to owners of boat lines, ferries, taverns, theaters, and stores, much as the temperance movement threatened not only brewers, distillers, and distributors, but also thousands of grocers and storekeepers whose customers expected a free pick-me-up as a sign of hospitality. Like the more militant temperance reformers, the Sabbatarians urged true Christians to boycott offending proprietors. Between Buffalo and Albany they also established their own six-days-a-week Pioneer Stage Line, a counterpart of the special temperance hotels and of the abolitionist shops that sold only produce made by free labor. These "anti"-institutions, which were almost uniformly unsuccessful, were intended to be sanctuaries—virtuous, disciplined environments set off from a chaotic and corrupting society—and models for the world to imitate. But like other reformers, the Sabbatarians were also committed to an imperial mission. Setting a precedent for later abolitionists, they organized a great petition campaign to persuade Congress to stop the Sunday mails. Like the abolitionists, they warned that unless Congress acknowledged a "higher law," the nation had little chance for survival:

> If this nation fails in her vast experiment, the world's last hope expires; and without the moral energies of the Sabbath it will fail. You might as well put out the sun, and think to enlighten the world with tapers...as to extinguish the moral illumination of the Sabbath, and break this glorious mainspring of the moral government of God.

---

*For Anti-Masonry, see chapter 15, pp. 514, 516.

But as the Mormons later discovered, many Americans were suspicious of people who claimed to stand for the moral government of God. By 1831 the Benevolent Empire had failed in its most daring and secular missionary efforts to regenerate society. Lyman Beecher had early defined the supreme goal of the missionary and benevolent societies: to produce "a sameness of views, and feelings, interests, which would lay the foundation of our empire upon a rock." But this purpose smashed against the rocklike resistance of people who refused to be homogenized, especially under Yankee direction. In response to the Sabbatarians' petitions, Congress agreed with a Kentucky senator who drafted a report stating that the national legislature was not "a proper tribunal to determine the laws of God." The colonization movement—the movement to send free blacks to Africa—did much to unite northern urban blacks in opposition to the idea. These blacks angrily affirmed that they would not accept a foreign refuge as a substitute for justice: "We will never separate ourselves voluntarily from the slave population of this country. Let not a purpose be assisted which will stay the cause of the entire abolition of slavery." Ironically, resistance to the Benevolent Empire also appeared in the South and Southwest, where an antimission movement appealed to so-called Hard-Shell Baptists and rural Methodists. These groups found no biblical support for benevolent societies and bitterly resisted any attempts to bring religious instruction to the blacks. Further, as one Baptist declared, "our backwoods folks" simply could not understand the pretentious talk of the "young men come from the eastern schools."

The Benevolent Empire solved no social problems. It received no credit for legislative triumphs of the magnitude of Britain's abolition of the slave trade (1807) and gradual emancipation of West Indian slaves (1833). By 1837, moreover, internal conflicts had shattered all hope of a united front among evangelical reformers. Growing divisions over slavery simply intensified suspicions and grievances that had long been festering on every level. Rivalry between religious groups weakened the supposedly nondenominational societies that northern Presbyterians and Congregationalists had always controlled. In 1837, when the Presbyterian church separated into conservative Old School and liberal New School camps, the economic depression also sharply reduced humanitarian gifts and thus further weakened the various organizations of the Benevolent Empire. The major Protestant churches, however, continued much of the work under denominational auspices.

Waging the War   It can be argued that the true revolution in American reform began in the 1820s with the militancy, the dedication, the towering expectations, and the phenomenal organization of the nonsectarian, evangelical societies. It began, that is, when an agent of the Sunday School Union, addressing the well-to-do members of the Bible Society, repeated the British motto: "Not by exactions from the opulent but by the contributions from all"; it began when the organizer of foreign missions called for a "vast body like a host prepared for war"; it began when the benevolent societies developed the techniques of modern fund-raising campaigns. The real revolution began with the mass production of literally millions of moralistic tracts, priced cheaply enough to undersell all commercial publications and marketed by discounts and other techniques that were far ahead of commercial practice. By 1830, in short, the evangelicals had devised all the apparatus needed for a massive conquest of American culture.

Although the conquest had ethnic, class, and geographical boundaries, few invading armies or political revolutions have had such a far-reaching effect on an entire society as the Benevolent Empire did. In 1834 the Temperance Society estimated that it had more than 1.25 million members; in 1836 the American Tract Society alone sold more than 3 million publications. In 1843, in response to the depression that had filled New York City's streets with thousands of beggars and vagrants, the New York Association for Improving the Condition of the Poor imitated the earlier models and sent teams of agents to gather information district by district and to distribute food, fuel, and clothing. The needy recipients could not help but be influenced, one way or another, by the association's links with the temperance movement, its conviction that poverty was a problem of individual morality, and its commitment to making the poor "respectable." If the reformers harbored little sympathy for sinners who refused to be saved, their ideology rested on a belief in human perfectibility, strongly laced with hopes for an American millennium.

The reformers' confidence in human perfectibility inspired a multitude of efforts, especially in the 1840s, to liberate individuals from all coercive forces and institutions. Perfectionism—the belief that people are capable of unlimited moral improvement—took both religious and secular forms. Suddenly, new things seemed possible, new ways of thinking and acting seemed worth trying. The nation had never before witnessed such frothy experimentation, such gusty defiance of traditional wisdom, or such faith in spontaneous love and harmony. Some reformers won fame for their success in emancipating individual victims of deafness, blindness, and insanity. Samuel Gridley Howe, best known for his pioneering work with the blind and deaf-blind, expressed the growing view that even criminals were "thrown upon society as a sacred charge." "Society," Howe said, "is false to its trust, if it neglects any means of reformation." Prison reformers tried, with little success, to transform penitentiaries into communities of rehabilitation and to persuade society of the need for parole, indeterminate sentences, and sympathetic care for discharged convicts. Nativists, who were alarmed by the increasing number of Catholic immigrants, publicized cases of Catholic women who had escaped from supposedly tyrannical and immoral nunneries, and demanded laws that would liberate Catholic laymen from the control of their priests.

Temperance   The temperance movement, a direct outgrowth of the Benevolent Empire, illustrates this mixture of humanitarianism, intolerance, progressivism, and self-righteousness. Although sometimes portrayed as religious cranks and killjoys, the temperance reformers were

Temperance
The worst evil of alcohol, according to temperance reformers, was its destruction of family harmony and the sanctity of the home. Innumerable storybooks and illustrations pictured a husband and father inflamed by spiritous liquor, attacking his helpless wife and children.

responding to a genuine social problem. During the early 1800s, per capita consumption of hard liquor far exceeded even the highest twentieth-century levels. Alcohol abuse undoubtedly contributed to family discord and child abuse, to public disorder, and to lowered productivity and rising social costs. By the mid-1830s various groups of urban artisans and northern free blacks endorsed temperance as a prerequisite for self-improvement. At the same time, middle-class champions of total abstinence became embroiled in bitter disputes over biblical approval or disapproval of drinking wine.

In 1840 the movement took a new direction when groups of reformed alcoholics began organizing "Washingtonian Societies," which appealed to working-class people and to members of subcultures that had not been reached by the traditional temperance organizations. At society meetings former drunkards told rapt audiences what hell was really like, sometimes reenacting the agonies of the delirium tremens that their excessive drinking had induced. Old-guard temperance leaders tried to use and patronize the Washingtonians, much as some white abolitionists tried to use and patronize fugitive slaves. But the middle-class societies never felt comfortable with the former victims of intemperance or with the boisterous showmanship that induced thousands of disreputable looking people to pledge themselves, at least temporarily, to total abstinence.

Faith in "moral suasion"—individual conversion to abstinence—disintegrated in the face of hundreds of thousands of German and Irish immigrants who had little taste for Yankee moralism. The celebrated "Maine law" of 1851, which outlawed the manufacture and sale of alcoholic beverages, marked the maturing of a new campaign for legal coercion in the form of statewide prohibition. On both local and state levels, bitter political conflicts erupted over the passage, repeal, and enforcement of prohibition laws. For temperance reformers of the 1850s, it was no longer safe to rely on the individual's mastery of temptation. The crucial act of will was now to be made by the state, which would attempt to remove the temptation. In less than thirty years, one of the supreme goals of the Benevolent Empire had been handed over to the realm of political power. Faith in moral influence and liberation had yielded to what the *American Temperance Magazine* hailed as the only force that drunkards could comprehend—"the instrumentality of the law."

Feminism and Perfectionism

By the second quarter of the nineteenth century, a broad protest movement, with strong religious undercurrents, was unfolding against forms of oppression and inequality that had long been accepted as inevitable. A major—and bitterly controversial—part of this protest movement attacked slavery.* But by the 1830s abolitionism had become intertwined with attacks against the traditional subordination of women. The founders of the feminist movement, like the male abolitionists, had mostly served apprenticeships in the moral-reform and temperance societies of the Benevolent Empire. Hundreds of female benevolent societies provided women with invaluable experience in fund-raising, organization, and public speaking. As women increasingly defied traditional restraints on engaging in public activities, they increasingly demanded equal educational and employment opportunities.

Women were not only deprived of higher education, barred from the professions, and denied the right to vote. Upon marriage, most women also surrendered any legal right to their own earnings and property. Harriet Robinson, who began working in a Massachusetts textile mill at age eleven and who in 1836 participated in one of the first women's strikes against wage cutting, recalled that many workers were "fugitives" from oppressive husbands and had thus assumed false names in order to prevent their husbands from legally seizing their wages. These conditions evoked a mounting protest from writers like Catharine Beecher, a daughter of Lyman Beecher and sister of Harriet Beecher Stowe. While conceding that women should not infringe on the "male sphere" of business and politics, Catharine Beecher exposed the oppression of mill girls, fought for improved female education, and attempted to enlist thousands of American women as teachers in a great crusade "to secure a proper education to the vast multitude of neglected American children all over our land." This

---

*For abolitionism, see chapter 14, pp. 472–83.

Making Fun of Feminists' Complaints
A favorite tactic of antifeminists was to spoof the reversal of gender roles. If rights were equalized, this cartoon suggests, men could expect to find themselves washing clothes, sewing, and tending babies while women ventured out into the world in carriages driven by other women.

agitation focused attention on women's collective interests, problems, and responsibilities, and thus contributed to a new feminist consciousness.

Female Abolitionists   Abolitionism provided female reformers with an egalitarian ethic and with a public forum for attacking entrenched injustice. From the outset the radical abolitionist movement led by William Lloyd Garrison attracted a group of exceptionally talented writers such as Maria Weston Chapman, Lydia Maria Child, Abby Kelley, and Lucretia Mott. Among Garrison's most important converts were Sarah and Angelina Grimké, two outspoken sisters who had abandoned their father's South Carolina plantation and had then been converted to Quakerism and abolitionism in Philadelphia. Because they could speak of southern slavery from personal experience, the Grimkés had a striking effect on New England audiences. In 1837 they boldly lectured to mixed audiences of men and women, an offense that outraged ministers and conservative reformers who believed that women should move within a precisely limited "sphere." The Grimkés attacked the hypocrisy of conservative abolitionists who scoffed at the biblical justifications for slavery advanced in the South but who then invoked the Bible when defending female subservience. The Garrisonians convinced the Grimkés that the Christian "principles of peace" were at the root of all reform; the Grimkés helped to convince the Garrisonians that the same principles applied to the "domestic slavery" of women to men.

Sarah Grimké was especially penetrating when she criticized the way most American girls were trained and conditioned to accept a separate sphere, or what later historians have termed "the cult of domesticity":

> During the early part of my life, my lot was cast among the butterflies of the fashionable world; and of this class of women, I am constrained to say, both from experience and observation, that their education is miserably deficient; that they are taught to regard marriage as the one thing needful, the only avenue to distinction; hence to attract the notice and win the attentions of men, by their external charms, is the chief business of fashionable girls. They seldom think that men will be allured by intellectual acquirements, because they find, that where any mental superiority exists, a woman is generally shunned and regarded as stepping out of her "appropriate sphere," which, in their view, is to dress, to dance, and to set out to the best possible advantage her person....
>
> There is another and much more numerous class in this country, who are withdrawn by education or circumstances from the circle of fashionable amusements, but who are brought up with the dangerous and absurd idea, that marriage is a kind of preferment; and that to be able to keep their husband's house, and render his situation comfortable, is the end of her being.... For this purpose more than for any other, I verily believe the majority of girls are trained....

In 1840 the issue of women's participation in abolitionist conventions caused a final split in the national abolitionist organization, the American Anti-Slavery Society. The more conservative faction, led by Arthur and Lewis Tappan, abandoned the society to the Garrisonian radicals. Female abolitionists increasingly stressed the parallels between their own powerlessness and the legal status of slaves. At Seneca Falls, New York, in 1848, Elizabeth Cady Stanton and Lucretia Mott finally organized the first convention in history devoted to women's rights. The convention's Declaration of Sentiments, modeled on the Declaration of Independence, proclaimed that "the history of mankind is a history of repeated injuries and usurpations on the part of man toward woman, having in direct object the establishment of an absolute tyranny over her." Among the list of specific grievances Stanton insisted on mentioning the exclusion of woman from "her inalienable right to the elective franchise."

Despite this demand for political rights, the National Women's Rights conventions of the 1850s devoted the greatest attention to legal and economic disabilities and to challenging ministers' insistence that the Bible placed the "weaker sex" in a subordinate "sphere." "Leave woman," Lucy Stone, a radical feminist leader, demanded, "to find her own sphere."

Although abolitionism provided the feminists with a sympathetic audience and with ready-made channels of communication, the relationship was also limiting in the sense that women's rights were always subordinate to the seemingly more urgent cause of slave emancipation. This dependence is evident even in the rhetoric of the radical feminists who compared the prevailing system

Lucy Stone (1818–93)
After rebelling as a girl against the subordination of her sex, Lucy Stone taught school and finally earned her way through Oberlin College. A radical abolitionist and lecturer on women's rights, she chose to keep her maiden name after she married Henry B. Blackwell, a businessman who fully supported her feminist views. Lucy Stone continued to fight for women's suffrage during and after the Civil War.

of marriage to a private plantation in which every woman was a slave breeder and a slave in the eyes of her husband.

Communitarianism   The quest for social equality led some reformers including abolitionists to join experimental communities where they could escape from the coercions and frustrations of competitive labor and of the private, isolated family. Some of these communities were inspired by secular social theories. In the 1820s, for example, the socialist experiment at New Harmony, Indiana, was based on the doctrines of Robert Owen, a wealthy Scottish industrialist turned radical humanitarian. In the 1840s a wide scattering of projects drew on the theories of Charles Fourier, a French social philosopher. The most successful communities, however, were those of religious sects like the Rappites and Shakers or those disciplined by the authority of extraordinary leaders such as John Humphrey Noyes.

Noyes had studied theology at Andover and Yale. He was a perfectionist who believed that the millennium had already begun and that the time had arrived for "renouncing all allegiance to the government of the United States, and asserting the title of Jesus Christ to the throne of the world." Garrison's rejection of all coercive government owed much to the influence of Noyes, who had proclaimed that "as the doctrine of temperance is total abstinence from alcoholic drinks, and the doctrine of antislavery is immediate abolition of human bondage, so the doctrine of perfectionism is the immediate and total cessation from sin." For Noyes and his followers there was no point in attacking a single sin like slavery when all Americans were enslaved by the bonds of private property and monogamous marriage, both of which imprisoned the human spirit behind walls of sinful possessiveness. At Putney, Vermont, and then at Oneida, New York, Noyes and his growing group of disciples developed a cohesive community based on a nonexclusive form of plural marriage, the collective ownership of property, and the discipline of "mutual criticism." The Oneida experiment, which flourished from 1847 to 1879, posed a radical alternative to the economic, sexual, and educational practices of the surrounding society.

The Tensions of Democratic Art

The continuing democratization of American culture produced a profound uneasiness about the artistic standards and precedents of European culture. On the one hand, American writers and artists felt the need to proclaim their independence from Europe and to create a genuinely native art, stripped of aristocratic associations. On the other hand, by the 1820s it was becoming clear that political independence did not guarantee cultural independence and that republican institutions would not automatically give birth to the Great American Masterwork. Improved transportation, coupled with a prolonged period of peace in Europe after the end of the Napoleonic wars in 1815, made it easier for Americans to cross the Atlantic in search of inspiration and training.

Even the more ardent cultural nationalists viewed Europe with awe and fascination. Often shocked by European contrasts between elegance and squalor, they were also dazzled by the great cathedrals, castles, spacious parks, monumental public buildings, museums, and villas. From Washington Irving's *Alhambra* (1832) to Nathaniel Hawthorne's *Marble Faun* (1860), American writers expressed their enchantment with castles and ruins, with places that had been steeped in centuries of history. Whatever its evils, Europe teemed with associations that fed the imagination. It was the continent of mystery, of beauty, of romance—in short, of culture. For many American artists it was also at least a temporary refuge from the materialism, vulgarity, and hurried pace of life they found in the United States. It is significant that Washington Irving was living in England when he created the classic American tales "Rip Van Winkle" and "The Legend of Sleepy Hollow" (1819–20). James Fenimore Cooper was living in Paris when he wrote *The Prairie* (1827). Horatio Greenough, America's first professional sculptor and a champion of democratic artistic theory, completed his gigantic, half-draped statue of George Washington—a statue that had been commissioned by the United States government—in his studio in Florence.

It would be a mistake, however, to think of American art of the period as slavishly imitative. Although Americans tended to express native subject matter in conventional artistic forms, they became increasingly skilled and sophisticated in their mastery of the forms. The choice of native material also affected the total character of a work. For example, space, nature, and the wilderness took on new qualities as Thomas Cole, Asher B. Durand, and other painters of the Hudson River School sought to idealize the American landscape. Cooper's five "Leatherstocking Tales"—*The Pioneers* (1823), *The Last of the Mohicans* (1826), *The Prairie* (1827), *The Pathfinder* (1840), and *The Deerslayer* (1841)—were far more than American versions of Sir Walter Scott's "Waverley novels." Like William Gilmore

Horatio Greenough's Washington

Horatio Greenough catered to popular neoclassical taste when he depicted the nation's first president in a Roman toga, seated in a pose resembling Zeus as carved by the great Greek sculptor Phidias. Commissioned by Congress, this gigantic statue was originally intended for the Capitol's rotunda, but when the lighting failed, Congress had it moved to the eastern front of the Capitol, where it became the butt of numerous jokes. Undiscouraged, Greenough wrote in a letter of 1847: "When...the true sculptors of America shall have filled the metropolis with beauty and grandeur, will it not be worth $30,000 [the staggering cost of his sculpture] to be able to point to the figure and say: 'There was the first struggle of our infant art'?"

Simms's tales of the southern frontier and backcountry, they gave imaginative expression to a distinctively American experience with Indians, violence, the law, and the meaning of social bonds in a wilderness setting. The popular New England poets and men-of-letters chose homey, everyday subjects that disguised both their literary skill and learnedness. Thus Henry Wadsworth Longfellow, a translator of Dante and a master of meter, celebrated the village blacksmith. John Greenleaf Whittier sang of the barefoot boy. And the highly cultivated James Russell Lowell delivered political satire in the homespun Yankee dialect of an imaginary Hosea Biglow.

Art as Product   By the 1820s it was becoming clear that art in America would have to be marketed like any other commodity, and that the ideal of the dabbling gentleman amateur would have to give way to the reality of the professional who wrote, carved, or painted for a living. Federal, state, and local governments did award a few commissions for patriotic and historical subjects, but political squabbles over art (including the seminudity of Greenough's Washington) dampened artists' desire for government patronage. The need to compete for middle-class customers and audiences helps to explain the dominant patriotic, lesson-teaching, and sentimental themes of popular American culture.

Thomas Cole's *The Voyage of Life, Childhood*
In 1839 and 1849 Thomas Cole, America's leading landscape painter, depicted the four stages of human life, "Childhood," "Youth," "Manhood," and "Old Age," as parts of a "Voyage" in a small boat set against a melodramatic landscape of cliffs, peaks, and stormy or radiant skies. In "Childhood," pictured here, a smiling angel guards a baby cushioned in a bed of flowers. "The rosy light of the morning," Cole wrote, "the luxuriant flowers and plants, are emblems of the joyousness of early life." Cole associated life's stages both with the earth's seasons and with the course of a nation's history.

Art as Character Shaper

A self-consciously democratic art, as opposed to the remnants of folk art that it began to replace, had to justify itself by serving such an essentially nonartistic need as the shaping of character. Before the Civil War both literature and the so-called fine arts claimed to perform educational, quasi-religious functions. They provided models to imitate, they trained and refined the emotions, and they taught that sin is always punished and virtue rewarded. Art promoted patriotism by glorifying the American Revolution and deifying George Washington. It defined idealized sex roles by identifying the American male as the man of action and the conqueror of nature—hunter, trapper, scout, mountain man, seafaring adventurer—while at the same time associating the American female with confinement in a home and with refinement of emotions—physical frailty, periods of melancholy, and a sensitivity expressed by sudden blushing, paleness, tears, and fainting. Above all, art furnished models of speech, manners, courtship, friendship, and grief that helped establish standards of middle-class respectability.

A few writers achieved the imaginative independence to interpret character and sensibility in new ways. Edgar Allan Poe, who strove for commercial success while remaining committed to the ideal of art as an independent craft, gave a dark coloring to the stock themes of sentimental poetry and fiction. In a different way

**Henry David Thoreau
(1817–62)**
*Although Thoreau published
only two books in his own
lifetime, including the classic*
Walden: or, Life in the Woods
*(1854), he came to be regarded in
the twentieth century as one of
the greatest writers America has
produced.*

Nathaniel Hawthorne subtly went beyond the conventions of sentimental moral-ism in *The Scarlet Letter* (1850), *The House of the Seven Gables* (1851), and *The Blithedale Romance* (1852). This period of creativity, later termed the American Renaissance, included Walt Whitman's *Leaves of Grass* (1855), which not only celebrated the boundless potentialities of American experience but took joy in defying the conventional limits of poetic language. Herman Melville's *Moby-Dick* (1851), one of the world's great novels, also fused native subject matter with new and distinctively American artistic forms. Henry David Thoreau's *Walden* (1854) stated a goal that could be applied to many of the best works of the period. Thoreau had nothing but contempt for the conventional efforts to shape character in the interest of social conformity. But his decision to live by himself on Walden Pond was an experiment in self-improvement. The goal of his experi-ment, and of the art it produced, was to break free from the distractions and artificialities that disguised "the essential facts of life"—"to drive life into a corner, and reduce it to its lowest terms." "For most men, it appears to me," he said, "are in a strange uncertainty about it, whether it is of the devil or of God."

Suggested Readings

An excellent collection of source material on children can be found in the first volume of Robert H. Bremner, ed., *Children and Youth in America: A Documentary History* (1970–71). Two important studies of the history of juvenile delinquency are Joseph M. Hawes, *Children in Urban Society* (1971), and Robert M. Mennel, *Thorns and Thistles* (1973).

    Lawrence A. Cremin, *American Education: The National Experience, 1783–1876* (1980), is the most comprehensive account of American education in antebellum America. Michael Katz, *The Irony of Early School Reform* (1968), sharply challenges the self-congratulatory tradition of educational history. Three important studies, also critical but more balanced, are Carl F. Kaestle, *Pillars of the Republic: Common Schools and American Society, 1780–1860* (1983); Carl Kaestle, *The Evolution of an Urban School System: New York City, 1750–1850* (1973); and Stanley K. Schultz, *The Culture Factory: Boston Public Schools, 1789–1860* (1973). Rush Welter, *Popular Education and Democratic Thought in America* (1962), presents a more traditional approach, and so does the excellent biography by Jonathan Messerli, *Horace Mann* (1972). Among the special studies of note are Bernard Wishy, *The Child and the Republic: The Dawn of Modern American Child Nurture* (1968); Marianna C. Brown, *The Sunday School Movement in America* (1961); Ruth Elson, *Guardians of Tradition: American Schoolbooks of the Nineteenth Century* (1964); Vincent P. Lannie, *Public Money and Parochial Education* (1968); and Merle Curti, *The Social Ideas of American Educators* (1935). The best introduction to higher education is Frederick Rudolph, *The American College and University* (1962), which can be supplemented by Theodore R. Crane, ed., *The Colleges and the Public, 1767–1862* (1963), and by Richard Hofstadter and Wilson Smith, *American Higher Education: A Documentary History* (2 vols. 1961). For the origins of women's higher education, see Barbara Miller Solomon, *In the Company of Educated Women: A History of Women and Higher Education in America* (1985).

The most imaginative treatment of revivalism is the first section of Perry Miller, *The Life of the Mind in America* (1965). William G. McLoughlin, Jr., *Modern Revivalism* (1959), gives a more detailed and systematic account of individual revivalists, and more recently McLoughlin has written a stimulating interpretive essay, *Revivals, Awakenings, and Reform: An Essay on Religion and Social Change in America, 1607–1977* (1978). A recent biography of the king of early revivalists is Keith J. Hardman, *Charles Grandison Finney, 1792–1875: Revivalist and Reformer* (1987). Two bold and sweeping reinterpretations of nineteenth-century religion are John Butler, *Awash in a Sea of Faith: Christianizing the American People* (1990), and Nathan O. Hatch, *The Democratization of American Christianity* (1989). Charles A. Johnson, *The Frontier Camp Meeting* (1955), is the standard history of the subject. The wider social impact of revivalism in New York State is brilliantly traced in Whitney R. Cross, *The Burned-Over District* (1950), but this must now be supplemented by Paul E. Johnson's *A Shopkeeper's Millennium: Society and Revivals in Rochester, New York, 1815–1837* (1978) and Mary P. Ryan's indispensable *Cradle of the Middle Class: The Family in Oneida County, New York, 1790–1865* (1981). No less insightful for an understanding of religion, politics, regional variation, and reform is Randolph A. Roth, *The Democratic Dilemma: Religion, Reform, and the Social Order in the Connecticut River Valley of Vermont, 1791–1850* (1987).

The fullest general history of American religion is Sydney E. Ahlstrom, *A Religious History of the American People* (1972), which should be supplemented on special topics by Charles H. Lippy and Peter W. Williams, eds., *Encyclopedia of the American Religious Experience* (3 vols., 1988). A provocative study analyzing the cultural alliance between Protestant ministers and middle-class women is Ann Douglas, *The Feminization of American Culture* (1977). A different and no less valuable perspective is provided by Lori D. Ginzberg, *Women and the Work of Benevolence: Morality, Politics, and Class in the Nineteenth-Century United States* (1990). Among the special studies of unusual interest are Henri Desroche, *The American Shakers from Neo-Christianity to Pre-Socialism* (1971); Nathan Glazer, *American Judaism* (1957); Daniel W. Howe, *The Unitarian Conscience* (1970); Martin Marty, *The Infidel: Freethought in American Religion* (1961); William G. McLoughlin, Jr., *The Meaning of Henry Ward Beecher* (1970); Theodore Maynard, *The Story of American Catholicism* (1960); Ernest L. Tuveson, *Redeemer Nation: The Idea of America's Millennial Role* (1968); D. H. Meyer, *The Instructed Conscience: The Shaping of the American National Ethic* (1972); T. D. Bozeman, *Protestants in an Age of Science: The Baconian Ideal and Antebellum American Religious Thought* (1977); Colleen McDannell, *The Christian Home in Victorian America, 1840–1900* (1986), and Winton U. Solberg, *Redeem the Time: The Puritan Sabbath in Early America* (1977).

Perry Miller, *Life of the Mind in America* (1965), contains a brilliant analysis of legal thought in America. A masterly interpretive work is James W. Hurst, *Law and Social Order in the United States* (1977), which should be contrasted with the challenging and highly innovative work by Morton I. Horwitz, *The Transformation of American Law, 1780–1860* (1977). An important aspect of constitutional development is traced in Bernard Schwartz, *From Confederation to Nation: The American Constitution, 1835–1877* (1973). Leonard W. Levy, *The Law of the Commonwealth and Chief Justice Shaw* (1957), is an outstanding study of a leading jurist. The standard biographies of Marshall and Taney are Albert I. Beveridge, *The Life of John Marshall* (4 vols., 1916–19), and Carl B. Swisher, *Roger B. Taney* (1936).

On science, the last section of Perry Miller's *Life of the Mind* contains important insights. The best general works are Robert V. Bruce, *The Launching of Modern American Science, 1846–1876* (1987) and George Daniels, *American Science in the Age of Jackson* (1968). For medicine, see Richard H. Shryock, *Medicine and Society in America* (1960), and Martin Kaufman, *Homeopathy in America: The Rise and Fall of a Medical Heresy* (1971). Among the best biographies of individual scientists are Edward Lurie, *Agassiz: A Life of Science in America* (1960), and Frances Williams, *Matthew Fontaine Maury* (1963).

John D. Davies, *Phrenology: Fad and Science* (1955), is highly informative. Carl Bode treats the popularization of knowledge in *The American Lyceum* (1956), and reveals popular taste and culture in *The Anatomy of American Popular Culture* (1959). Stephen Nissenbaum, *Sex, Diet, and Debility in Jacksonian America: Sylvester Graham and Health Reform* (1980), is a fascinating study of a popular but neglected aspect of self-improvement. Lewis O. Saum, *The Popular Mood of Pre–Civil War America* (1980), disputes the belief that most Americans were dedicated to progress and self-improvement. Various aspects of self-improvement and changing views of gender roles are examined in Steven Mintz, *A Prison of Expectations: The Family in Victorian Culture* (1983); James C. Whorton, *Crusaders for Fitness: The History of American Health Reformers* (1982); and Carroll Smith-Rosenberg, *Disorderly Conduct: Visions of Gender in Victorian America* (1985).

The most illuminating studies of Emerson's thought are Joel Porte, *Representative Man: Ralph Waldo Emerson in His Time* (1979), and Stephen Whicher, *Freedom and Fate: An Inner Life of Ralph Waldo Emerson* (1953). Anne C. Rose, *Transcendentalism as a Social Movement, 1830–1850* (1981), succeeds in rooting Transcendentalism in the concrete needs and aspirations of New England society. Perry Miller, ed., *The Transcendentalists* (1950), is a difficult but magnificent anthology. Walter Harding's *Thoreau: Man of Concord* (1960), and Joseph W. Krutch, *Henry David Thoreau* (1948), can be supplemented with profit by Robert D. Richardson, Jr., *Henry Thoreau: A Life of the Mind* (1986) and Richard Lebeaux, *Young Man Thoreau* (1977). F. O. Matthiessen, *American Renaissance* (1941), is a brilliant and unsurpassed study of Emerson, Thoreau, Hawthorne, Melville, and Whitman. For connections between such major writers and the penny press, trial reports, and sensational fiction, see David S. Reynolds, *Beneath the American Renaissance: The Subversive Imagination in the Age of Emerson and Melville* (1988). For the theme of masculinity, see David Leverenz, *Manhood and the American Renaissance* (1989).

Whitney R. Cross, *The Burned-Over District* (1950), analyzes the origins of secular reform as well as of Mormonism and other religious movements. Leonard J. Arrington and Davis Bitton, *The Mormon Experience: A History of the Latter-day Saints* (1979), Jan Shipps, *Mormonism: The Story of a New Religious Tradition* (1985), and Klaus I. Hansen, *Mormonism and the American Experience* (1981), are the best introductions to Mormonism. Fawn M. Brodie, *No Man Knows My History: The Life of Joseph Smith* (1945), Leonard J. Arrington, *Brigham Young: American Moses* (1985), and Linda K. Newell and Valeen T. Avery, *Mormon Enigma: Emma Hale Smith, Prophet's Wife, "Elect Lady," Polygamy's Foe* (1984), are readable and extremely valuable biographies. Klaus I. Hansen, *Quest for Empire* (1967), is a valuable account of the Mormons' efforts to prepare for a worldly Kingdom of God. Some of the best specialized studies are D. Michael Quinn, *Early Mormonism and the Magic World View* (1986); Lawrence Foster, *Religion and Sexuality: Three American Communal Experiments of the Nineteenth Century* (1981); and Robert B. Flanders, *Nauvoo: Kingdom on the Mississippi* (1965). A dramatic and authoritative narrative of the westward migration is Wallace Stegner, *The Gathering of Zion: The Story of the Mormon Trail* (1964). Leonard I. Arrington's two works *Great Basin Kingdom* (1958) and *Building the City of God: Community and Cooperation Among the Mormons* (1976) are masterly accounts of the Mormon settlement of Utah. Norman F. Furniss, *The Mormon Conflict, 1850–1859* (1960), covers the so-called Mormon War.

There are no satisfactory general works on the relation between religion and secular reform, although much can be learned from the previously cited books by Randolph Roth, Mary P. Ryan, Lori D. Ginzberg, Paul E. Johnson, and Whitney R. Cross. Important aspects of the subject are examined in Carroll Smith-Rosenberg, *Religion and the Rise of the American City: The New York Mission Movement* (1971); Charles I. Foster, *An Errand of Mercy: The Evangelical United Front* (1960); Nancy A. Hewitt, *Women's Activism and Social Change* (1984); Clifford S. Griffin, *Their Brothers' Keepers: Moral Stewardship in the United States* (1960); and Timothy L. Smith, *Revivalism and Social Reform* (1957). The temperance movement, a critical link between evangelical religion and secular reform, is well described in Ian R. Tyrrell, *Sobering Up: From Temperance to Prohibition in Antebellum America* (1979). See also Barbara Leslie Epstein, *The Politics of Domesticity: Women, Evangelism, and Temperance in Nineteenth-Century America* (1981). For American drinking habits, see W. I. Rorabaugh, *The Alcoholic Republic: An American Tradition* (1979).

An original work that is indispensable for understanding the changing status of women and the origins of feminism is Nancy F. Cott, *The Bonds of Womanhood: "Woman's Sphere" in New England, 1780–1835* (1977), which should be supplemented by Barbara I. Berg, *The Remembered Gate: Origins of American Feminism—The Woman and the City, 1800–1860* (1978), and Keith M. Melder, *Beginnings of Sisterhood: The American Woman's Rights Movement, 1800–1850* (1977). William Leach, *True Love and Perfect Union: The Feminist Reform of Sex and Society* (1980), is an original and provocative study of feminism and women's position in antebellum and postbellum society. A helpful overall survey of both family history and women's changing aspirations is Carl N. Degler, *At Odds: Women and the Family in America from the Revolution to the Present* (1980). Other useful works are Ellen C. DuBois, *Feminism and Suffrage: The Emergence of an Independent Women's Movement in America, 1848–1869* (1978); W. L. O'Neill, *Everyone Was Brave: The Rise and Fall of Feminism in America* (1970); and Page Smith, *Daughters of the Promised Land* (1970). For individual biographies, see Elisabeth Griffith, *In Her Own Right: The Life of Elizabeth Cady Stanton* (1984); Otelia Cromwell, *Lucretia Mott* (1971); Celia Morris Eckhardt, *Fanny Wright: Rebel in America* (1984); and Gerda Lerner, *The Grimké Sisters from South Carolina: Rebels Against Slavery* (1967). For the changes in state laws relating to women's ownership of property and other legal rights, see Peggy A. Rabkin, *The Legal Foundations of Female Emancipation* (1980).

David S. Rothman, *The Discovery of the Asylum* (1971), is a brilliant interpretation of reformatory institutions. The most imaginative study of early prisons is W. David Lewis, *From Newgate to Dannemora: The Rise of the Penitentiary in New York* (1965). Blake McKelvey, *American Prisons* (1936), is a more comprehensive reference. On the insane, the best guides are Ellen Dwyer, *Homes for the Mad: Life Inside Two Nineteenth-Century Asylums* (1987); Helen E. Marshall, *Dorothea Dix: Forgotten Samaritan* (1937); and Gerald N. Grob, *Mental Institutions in America: Social Policy to 1875* (1973). For the reformer who did most for the deaf and blind, see Harold Schwartz, *Samuel Gridley Howe* (1956).

The classic work on the peace movement is Merle Curti, *The American Peace Crusade, 1815–1860* (1929), which should be supplemented by Peter Brock, *Pacifism in the United States: From the Colonial Era to the First World War* (1968).

On communitarian settlements, the best general works are Mark Holloway, *Heavens on Earth* (1951), and the relevant chapters in Lawrence Foster, *Religion and Sexuality: The Shakers, the Mormons, and the Oneida Community* (1984), and Donald D. Egbert and Stow Persons, *Socialism and American Life* (2 vols., 1952). The communitarian phase inspired by Robert Owen is masterfully covered by I. F. C. Harrison, *Quest for the New Moral World: Robert Owen and the Owenites in Britain and America* (1969). For the New Harmony experiment, see also William Wilson, *The Angel and the Serpent* (1964), and Arthur Bestor, *Backwoods Utopias: The Sectarian and Owenite Phases of Communitarian Socialism in America, 1663–1829,* 2d enl. ed. (1970). The best introduction to the Oneida community is Maren L. Carden, *Oneida: Utopian Community to Modern Corporation* (1969). For Noyes himself, see Robert D. Thomas, *The Man Who Would Be Perfect: John Humphrey Noyes and the Utopian Impulse* (1977). Three other studies of unusual importance are Lawrence Veysey, ed., *The Perfectionists: Radical Social Thought in the North, 1815–1860* (1973); Michael Fellman, *The Unbounded Frame: Freedom and Community in Nineteenth-Century Utopianism* (1973); and William H. Pease, *Black Utopia: Negro Communal Experiments in America* (1963).

Of the numerous studies of important literary figures, the following have special value for the historian: Richard Chase, *The American Novel and Its Tradition* (1957); Joel Porte, *The Romance in America: Studies in Cooper, Poe, Hawthorne, Melville, and James* (1969); A. N. Kaul, *The American Vision: Actual and Ideal Society in Nineteenth-Century Fiction* (1963); R. W. B. Lewis, *The American Adam: Innocence, Tragedy and Tradition in the Nineteenth Century* (1955); and David Levin, *History as Romantic Art* (1959). For Whitman, see Gay Allen, *The Solitary Singer* (1967). An informative introduction to Poe is Edward Wagenknecht, *Edgar Allan Poe: The Man Behind the Legend* (1963). Newton Arvin has written two fine literary biographies: *Herman Melville* (1950), and *Longfellow: His Life and Work* (1963). For Hawthorne, see Edward Wagenknecht, *Nathaniel Hawthorne: Man and Writer* (1961).

Van Wyck Brooks, *The Flowering of New England, 1815–1865* (1936), is still highly readable and informative. On the South, the best guide is Jay B. Hubbell, *The South in American Literature, 1607–1900* (1954). Henry Nash Smith, *Virgin Land: The American West as Symbol and Myth* (1950), is a brilliant study of the imaginative portrayal of the West. The early publishing industry is analyzed in William Charvat, *Literary Publishing in America, 1790–1850* (1959). For popular literature, see Mary Kelly, *Private Woman, Public Stage: Literary Domesticity in Nineteenth-Century America* (1984); Herbert R. Brown, *The Sentimental Novel in America, 1798–1860* (1940); and Frank L. Mott, *Golden Multitudes: The Story of Best Sellers in the United States* (1947). Mott, *American Journalism* (1962), is the standard source on newspapers. The first volume of Mott's monumental *A History of American Magazines* (5 vols., 1957) is a mine of information. For folk songs, see Alan Lomax, *The Folk Song in North America* (1969).

Oliver W. Larkin, *Art and Life in America* (1949), is a comprehensive study of the early history of art and architecture. On painting it should be supplemented by Barbara Novak's superb study, *Nature and Culture: American Landscape and Painting, 1825–1875* (1980), as well as by David C. Huntington, *Art and the Excited Spirit: America in the Romantic Period* (1972), and James T. Flexner, *That Wilder Image: The Painting of America's Native School from Thomas Cole to Winslow Homer* (1962). Neil Harris, *The Artist in American Society: The Formative Years, 1790–1860* (1966), is a sensitive study of art as a profession. Arthur H. Quinn, *American Drama* (2 vols., 1955), is a comprehensive introduction to the theater. A more imaginative work is David Grimstead, *Melodrama Unveiled* (1968). On architecture, see Roger G. Kennedy, *Greek Revival America* (1989) and Wayne Andrews, *Architecture in America* (1960). The best guides to early American music are Gilbert Chase, *America's Music* (1955); H. Wiley Hitchcock, *Music in the United States* (1969); and Dena I. Epstein, *Sinful Tunes and Spirituals: Black Folk Music Through the Civil War* (1977).

14

The Peculiar Institution

≈

*H*ISTORIANS still debate the importance of similarities and differences between the antebellum North and South. Was the South simply a variant form of American society and culture, or was it becoming a separate and indigestible nation within a nation? Clearly the two regions shared much in common: the American Revolutionary heritage; a commitment to constitutional government and to English laws and judicial procedure; a loyalty to national political parties and a growing acceptance of universal suffrage for white males; a widespread hunger for evangelical religion combined with an insistence on the separation of church and state. The typical southerner, like the typical northerner, was a small farmer who tried to achieve both relative self-sufficiency and a steady income from marketable cash crops. Nor was the South distinctive in its dedication to white supremacy. As slavery gradually disappeared in the North during the first decades of the nineteenth century, antiblack racism became more intense. Free blacks were barred from schools, colleges, churches, and public accommodations. Excluded from all but the most menial jobs, they were also deprived of the most elemental civil rights. But racism did not necessarily mean an approval of human slavery. As the North moved rapidly toward an urban and industrial economy, northerners celebrated the virtues and benefits of free labor, which they hailed as the keystone of free institutions. Having earlier assumed that slavery was a "relic of barbarism" that the forces of social and economic progress would gradually destroy, they looked on the South with dismay as black slavery became the basis for a vigorous, expanding economy and as southerners took the lead in the rush for western land.

Rise of the Cotton Kingdom

From 1820 on, southerners benefited from three advantages unavailable in the North. First, the climate and soil of large parts of the South were ideally suited to growing cotton, the indispensable raw material for the industrial revolution, which was well under way in Great Britain and was already beginning in New

Eli Whitney's First Cotton Gin
When Eli Whitney, the brilliant Yankee inventor, applied in 1793 for a patent on his first cotton gin, American cotton production was limited to high-quality "sea-island" cotton grown only on the coast of South Carolina and Georgia. Whitney's invention, which was soon improved and enlarged, efficiently separated the hard seeds from the lint of short-staple cotton, which could be cultivated inland on wide belts of land extending from Georgia and South Carolina to Texas. Since this technological breakthrough coincided with a soaring demand for cotton in the industrializing regions of Europe and New England, it became the foundation for the South's famous "Cotton Kingdom."

England. The perfection of the cotton gin and screw press, devices for extracting cotton from the plant and compressing it into bales, gave southerners benefits of technological innovation that northerners did not begin to approximate until the late 1850s. Second, the rapid improvement and wide use of steamboats opened the way to upriver navigation of the Mississippi and of the rich network of other southern rivers, thereby lowering transportation costs even more dramatically than the northern canals did. Third and most important, southern agriculture could exploit the forced labor of black slaves, whose numbers increased from 1.5 million in 1820 to nearly 4 million in 1860. A self-reproducing labor force had long distinguished the South from other slave societies in the New World. These included Brazil and Cuba, which until the mid-nineteenth century remained dependent on the continuing importation of slaves from Africa. The unprecedented natural increase of the slave population in the South enabled white southerners to clear and settle the vast Cotton Kingdom, extending from Georgia to Louisiana, Arkansas, and eventually eastern Texas.

Scholars still dispute important questions relating to the economics of slavery. But one must begin by emphasizing the shortage of white labor as a crucial condition affecting both northern and southern agriculture. All American farmers wanted the independence and relative security of owning their own land. Since land was generally accessible, especially in the West, it was difficult for farmers to hire nonfamily labor in order to expand production, specialize, and take advantage of a rising demand for cash crops, such as wheat, cotton, and corn.

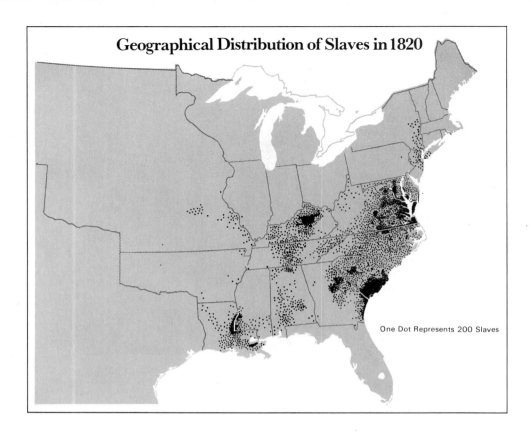

Geographical Distribution of Slaves in 1820

One Dot Represents 200 Slaves

In the North this labor shortage led to improved transportation, labor-saving machinery, and promotional schemes to attract immigrants. Between 1820 and 1860, for example, these three developments wholly transformed the New England labor market for the textile industry. Labor shortages were so severe in the early part of this period that factory owners and supervisors had to scramble for recruits just to keep the mills in operation. As railroad and highway networks expanded, however, local labor markets became more regional. As mills drew employees from the entire Northeast, immigrants from Ireland and Canada further expanded the potential labor supply. Moreover, the gradual mechanization of previously hand-powered processes, such as those in weaving, drove many outworkers from their farms or shops into the mills. By the 1850s, then, owners and supervisors of New England's textile mills virtually ceased to complain that they were "short of hands." Throughout this period the situation was entirely different in the South, where black slaves provided a highly mobile and flexible supply of labor. Large planters and speculators could quickly transport an army of involuntary workers to clear rich western land or could sell slaves to meet the labor demands of expanding areas. Even prospering family farmers could buy or rent a few slaves to increase their output of cotton or other cash crops. The flexibility of the system also enabled planters to allocate needed labor to raising

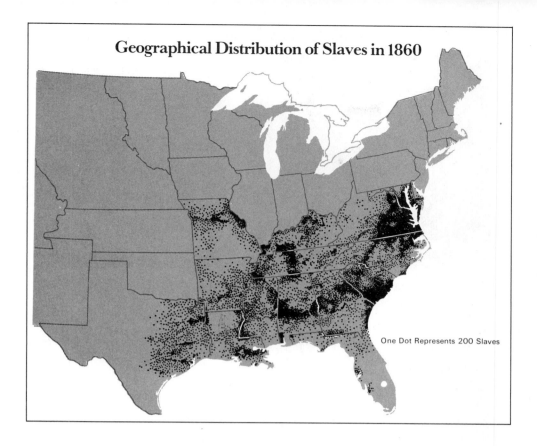

Geographical Distribution of Slaves in 1860

One Dot Represents 200 Slaves

livestock and growing foodstuffs for domestic consumption. And when market conditions improved, slaveholders could increase the proportion of work time devoted to cotton or other cash crops.

These various advantages also meant that slaves became the major form of southern wealth, and slaveholding became the means to prosperity. Except for the bustling port of New Orleans, great urban centers failed to appear, and internal markets declined. European immigrants, having no wish to compete with slave labor, generally shunned the region. Investment flowed mainly into the purchase of slaves, whose soaring price reflected an apparently limitless demand. The large planters, who profited from the efficiency of mobilizing small armies of slaves in specialized working groups or "gangs," soon ranked among America's richest men. In 1860, indeed, two-thirds of the richest Americans—men with estates of $100,000 or more—lived in the South.

There can be no doubt that investment in slaves brought a considerable return, or that the slave economy grew rapidly throughout the pre–Civil War decades. Yet essentially the system depended on the world's demand for cotton as it entered the age of industrialization, led by the British textile industry. At times the South's production of cotton exceeded international demand, and cotton prices fell sharply in the economic depressions known as the Panics of 1819 and

Sugar Manufacture

For over two hundred years sugar was the preeminent commodity produced by slaves in the West Indies; Europe's demand for sugar was the driving force behind most of the slave trade between Africa and the New World. In the United States, however, sugar production developed relatively late and was confined to southern Louisiana and a few other regions with a suitable climate. Slave labor was applied not only to the cultivation of sugarcane but also to the stages of manufacture needed to extract and refine sugar, molasses, and related products.

1837. But until the Civil War the world market for cotton textiles grew at such a phenomenal rate that both southern planters and British manufacturers thought only of infinite expansion. By 1840 the South grew more than 60 percent of the world's cotton; during the pre–Civil War boom more than three-fourths of the South's cotton was exported abroad. Much of it went to Britain, amounting to more than 70 percent of that country's cotton imports. In addition the South shipped cotton to the rising industries of continental Europe, including Russia. Throughout the antebellum period cotton accounted for over half the value of all American exports, and thus it paid for the major share of the nation's imports. A stimulant to northern industry, cotton also contributed to the growth of New York City as a distributing and exporting center that drew income from commissions, freight charges, interest, insurance, and other services connected with the marketing of America's number-one commodity.

Neither American sellers nor British buyers felt comfortable about their dependence on a single source of prosperity. British manufacturers searched unsuccessfully for alternative sources of high-grade cotton. Although the South continued to export large quantities of rice, tobacco, and other cash crops, southern business conventions unsuccessfully called for a more balanced economy. In Louisiana wealthy sugar growers expanded production by using new technology for the processing of cane. Plantation owners effectively applied slave labor to cultivating hemp, corn, and grain; to mining and lumbering; to building canals and railroads; and even to manufacturing textiles, iron, and other industrial products. Yet the South's economic growth and prosperity depended ultimately on foreign markets.

No other American region contained so many farmers who merely subsisted on their own produce; yet in no other region had agriculture become so speculative and commercial—for small cotton farmers who could not afford slaves, as well as for the planter elite. A typical farmer cultivating sixty-five acres in the Georgia Upcountry, for example, might devote most of his soil to growing corn, wheat, oats, fruit, and vegetables to cover his own family's subsistence needs and give over only an acre or two to cash crops like cotton intended for sale in the market. In such settlements, "habits of mutuality" among neighbors and kin, rather than competition in the marketplace, governed social relations. Yet by the 1850s an increasing number of voices arose, even in the Georgia Upcountry, imploring farmers to speculate in cash crops "to extend the cotton planting area...until every foot of land throughout the cotton growing region shall be brought into cultivation." Like some of the later Third World regions where involuntary labor produced raw materials for industrial nations, the South was intimately connected with industrial capitalism and yet cut off from its liberalizing and diversifying influences.

The Slave Masters In theory the southern slaveholder possessed all the power of any owner of chattel property. This power was limited only by state laws (which were generally unenforceable) that protected slaves from murder and mutilation; that set minimal standards for food, clothing, and shelter; and that prohibited masters from teaching slaves to read or allowing them to carry firearms or roam about the countryside. These slave codes acknowledged that bondsmen were human beings who were capable of plotting, stealing, fleeing, or rebelling, and who were likely to be a less "troublesome property" if well cared for under a program of strict discipline. Yet the laws also insisted that the slave was a piece of property that could be sold, traded, rented, mortgaged, and inherited. They did not recognize the interests and institutions of the slave community, or the slave's right to marry, to hold property, or to testify in court.

In practice it proved impossible to treat human beings as no more than possessions or as the mere instruments of an owner's will. Most masters were primarily motivated by the desire for profit. They wanted to maximize their slaves' productivity while protecting the value of their capital investment, a value that kept rising with the generally escalating trend in slave prices. Accordingly, it made sense to provide a material standard of living that would promote good health and a natural increase in the size of slave families, and thus increase capital gains. It also made sense to keep the slaves' morale as high as possible and to encourage them to do willingly and even cheerfully the work they would be forced to do in the last resort. Convinced of the moral legitimacy of the system, most slaveowners sincerely believed that their own best interests were identical with their slaves' best interests. "The master should never establish any regulation among his slaves," cautioned *DeBow's Review,* "until he is fully convinced of its

Slave Cabins in Georgia
Because the material conditions of slave life depended on the wealth, self-interest, and good will of individual owners, slave housing ranged from relatively comfortable cabins to overcrowded shanties whose occupants had little protection from the elements. Southern apologists had some grounds for claiming that American slaves were better housed and fed than were the laboring classes of Europe. Most abolitionists wisely insisted that the moral evil of slavery had nothing to do with the material standard of life.

propriety and equity.... The negro should feel that his master is his lawgiver and judge; and yet is his protector and friend, but so far above him, as never to be approached save with in the most respectful manner." Masters therefore sought to convince the slaves of the essential justice of slavery, and they expected gratitude for their acts of kindness, indulgence, and generosity, and even for their restraint in inflicting physical punishment.

But slaves were not passive, agreeable puppets who could be manipulated at will. As human beings they had one overriding objective: self-preservation at a minimal cost of degradation and of loss of self-respect. To avoid punishment and win rewards, they carried out their owners' demands with varying degrees of thoroughness. But black slaves became cunningly expert at testing their masters' will. They learned how to mock while seeming to flatter; how to lighten unending work with moments of spontaneity, song, intimacy, and relaxation; how to exploit the whites' dependence on black field drivers and household servants; and how to play on the conflicts between their masters and white overseers. In short, they learned through constant experiment and struggle how to preserve a core of dignity and self-respect. Sarah Gayle, the young wife of an Alabama governor, recorded in her diary the frustrations she felt over the "insubordination" of a slave named Hampton:

> I never saw such a negro in all my life before—he did not even pretend to regard a command of mine, and treated me, and what I said, with the utmost contempt. He has often laughed in my face and told me that I was the only mistress he ever failed to please, on my saying he should try another soon [a threat to sell Hampton], he said he could not be worsted, and was willing to go.

Although slavery "worked" as an economic system, its fundamental conflict of interests created a highly unstable and violent society. The great sugar planters in Louisiana and cotton growers in the delta country of Mississippi, often employing more than one hundred slaves on a productive unit, tried to merge Christian paternalism with a kind of welfare capitalism. They provided professional medical care, offered monetary rewards for extra productivity, and granted a week or more of Christmas vacation. Yet these same plantations were essentially ruled by terror.

Even the most humane and kindly masters knew that only the threat of violence could force gangs of field hands to work from dawn to dusk "with the discipline," as one contemporary observer put it, "of a regular trained army." Frequent public floggings reminded every slave of the penalty for inefficient labor, disorderly conduct, or refusal to accept the authority of a superior. Bennet H. Barrow, a particularly harsh Louisiana slaveowner, maintained discipline by ordering occasional mass whippings of all his field hands, by chaining offenders or ducking them under water, and even by shooting a black who was about to run away. Barrow also distributed generous monetary bonuses to his slaves and bought them Christmas presents in New Orleans. The South could point to far gentler masters who seldom inflicted physical punishment. Slaves understood, however, that even the mildest of whites could become cruel despots when faced with the deception or ingratitude of people who, regardless of pretenses to the contrary, were kept down by force.

Masters also uneasily sensed that circumstances might transform a loyal and devoted slave into a vengeful enemy. It is true that white southerners could congratulate themselves on the infrequency of serious slave uprisings, especially when the South was compared with Brazil and most of the Caribbean. Yet in the French colony of Saint Domingue (Santo Domingo), which at one time had enjoyed at least as secure a history as the American South, the greatest of all slave revolts had begun in 1791 and had led to the creation of the black republic of Haiti, after the mobilized slaves had defeated the best armies of Spain, England, and France. And indeed the South had no immunity from slave revolts. In 1822 South Carolinians hanged thirty-five blacks after uncovering Denmark Vesey's plot for a full-scale uprising, a plot that involved some of Charleston's most trusted household servants. Nine years later Nat Turner led some seventy slaves on a bloody rampage through Southampton County, Virginia. To the outside

Identifying Marks of Ownership
*Illustrations of slave branding were usually of British origin and referred to the West Indies,
where Africans had long been systematically branded after disembarking from the slave ships.
In the early nineteenth century, southern states tried to prohibit branding (although not until
1833 in South Carolina), but some advertisements for runaway slaves continued to refer to
brands, which were sometimes inflicted as a punishment. Abolitionists exploited the theme,
along with the slaves' semi-nudity, as a way of dramatizing the excesses of slaveholder power.*

world southerners presented a brave facade of self-confidence, and individual
masters reassured themselves that their own slaves were happy and loyal. But
rumors of arson, poisoning, and suppressed revolts continued to flourish. Alarmists frequently warned that outside agitators were secretly sowing discontent
among the slaves. This widespread fantasy at least hinted at the truth: not only did
slavery have little approval in the outside world, but the institution ultimately
depended on the sheer weight of superior force.

The difficulties in generalizing about the slave's world are compounded by
the geographic, climatic, and cultural diversities of the "South"—a region in
which mountain highlands, pine forests, and swampy lowlands are all frequently
encountered within a few hundred miles of one another.

Almost half of the southern slaveholders owned fewer than five slaves; 72
percent owned fewer than ten. The typical master could thus devote close
personal attention to his human property. Many small farmers worked side by
side with their slaves, an arrangement that might have been far more humiliating
for the slaves than working in a field gang under black "drivers." From the slave's
viewpoint, much depended on an owner's character, on the norms of a given

locality, on the accidents of sale, and on the relative difficulty of harvesting cotton, rice, tobacco, or sugar.

Slave experiences covered a wide range—from remarkable physical comfort and a lack of restraint to the most savage and unrelieved exploitation. But to dwell on contrasting examples of physical treatment is to risk losing sight of the central horror of human bondage. As the Quaker John Woolman pointed out in the eighteenth century, no human is saintly enough to be entrusted with total power over another. The slave was an inviting target for the hidden anger, passion, frustration, and revenge from which no human is exempt. A slave's work, leisure, movement, and daily fate depended on the will of another person.

Moreover, despite the numerical predominance of small slaveholders, most southern slaves were concentrated on large farms and plantations. Over half belonged to owners who held twenty or more slaves; one-quarter belonged to productive units of more than fifty slaves. In the South slave ownership was the primary road to wealth, and the most successful masters cornered an increasing share of the growing but limited human capital. Therefore most slaves experienced fairly standardized patterns of plantation life.

Life on the Plantation

By sunrise black drivers herded gangs of men and women into the fields. Slave women, including pregnant women and nursing mothers, were subjected to heavy field labor. Even small children served as water carriers or began to learn the lighter tasks of field work. Slaves too old for field work took care of small children and also worked in the stables, gardens, and kitchens. This full employment of all available hands was one of the economies of the system that increased the total output from a planter's capital investment. Nevertheless slaves often succeeded in maintaining their own work rhythm and in helping to define the amount of labor a planter could reasonably expect. Bursts of intense effort required during cotton picking, corn shucking, or the eighteen-hours-a-day sugar harvest were followed by periods of festivity and relaxation. Even in relatively slack seasons, however, there were cattle to be tended, fences to be repaired, forests to be cleared, and food crops to be planted.

Black slaves were saved from becoming mere robots in the field by the strength of their own community and evolving culture. There has long been controversy over the degree to which African cultural patterns were able to survive in North America. In contrast to Brazil, where continuing slave importations sustained for blacks a living bond with African cultures, the South had a black population in which the vast majority were removed by several generations from an African-born ancestor. Some research has uncovered striking examples of African influence in the southern slaves' oral traditions, folklore, songs, dances, language, sculpture, religion, and kinship patterns. The question at issue is not the purity or even the persistence of distinct African forms. In the New World all imported cultures underwent blending, adaptation, and combination with other elements. The point is that slaves, at least on the larger plantations,

A Slave Family
Although slave marriages were not recognized or protected in any way by state law, slaves observed their own traditions of courtship, marriage ceremony, naming children after ancestors or relatives, and burying deceased family members. This 1862 photograph of a slave family on a Beaufort, South Carolina plantation shows that generational continuity could sometimes be maintained despite the threat of separate sale of family members. Note the absence, however, of a single young adult male.

created their own African-American culture, which helped to preserve the most crucial areas of life and thought from white domination. Within such a culture, sustained by strong community ties, slaves were able to maintain a sense of apartness, of pride, and of independent identity. Plantations with more than fifty slaves contained an average of fewer than two adult white males, a fact that dramatizes the relative weakness of white surveillance and the reliance on a hierarchy of black managers, artisans, and mechanics.

African kinship patterns seem to have been the main vehicle for the maintenance of cultural identity. As in West Africa, children were frequently named for grandparents, who were revered even in memory. Kinship patterns survived even the breakup of families, although mother-headed families and family fragmentation were far commoner on plantations with fewer than fifteen slaves. On larger plantations black strangers often took on the functions and responsibilities of grandparents, uncles, and aunts. Many younger slaves were cared for and protected by "aunts" and "uncles" who were not blood kin. These older teachers and guardians passed on knowledge of the time when their ancestors had not been slaves, before the fateful crossing of the sea. This historical awareness inspired hope in a future time of deliverance—a deliverance that slaves associated with the Jews' biblical flight from Egypt, with the sweet land of Canaan, and with the Day of Jubilee. In the words of one spiritual:

> *Dear Lord, dear Lord, when slavery'll cease*
> *Then we poor souls will have our peace;—*
> *There's a better day a-coming,*
> *Will you go along with me?*
> *There's a better day a-coming,*
> *Go sound the jubilee!*

Historians have recently recognized how important the slave family was as a refuge from the dehumanizing effects of being treated as chattel property. The strength of family bonds is suggested by the thousands of slaves who ran away from their owners in search of family members separated through sale. The myth of weak family attachments is also countered by the swarms of freedmen who roamed the South at the end of the Civil War in search of their spouses, parents, or children, and by the eager desire of freedmen to legalize their marriages.

Nevertheless the slave family was a highly vulnerable institution. Although many slaveowners had moral scruples against separating husbands from wives or small children from their mothers, even the strongest scruples frequently gave way in times of economic need. The forced sale of individual slaves in order to pay a deceased owner's debts further increased the chances of family breakups. In some parts of the South, it was common for a slave to be married to another slave on a neighboring or even distant plantation, an arrangement that left visitation at the discretion of the two owners. At best, slave marriage was a precarious bond, unprotected by law and vulnerable to the will of whites.

In sexual relations there was a similar gap between moral scruples and actual practice. White planter society officially condemned miscegenation—interracial sexual unions—and tended to blame lower-class whites for fathering mulatto children. Yet there is abundant evidence that many slaveowners, sons of slaveowners, and overseers took black mistresses or sexually exploited the wives and daughters of slave families. This abuse of power was not as universal as northern abolitionists claimed, but it was common enough to humiliate black women, to instill rage in black men, and to arouse shame and bitterness in white women. No one conveyed this message more poignantly than Sarah Grimké, the abolitionist daughter of a wealthy South Carolina slaveholding family:

> [T]he virtue of female slaves is wholly at the mercy of irresponsible tyrants, and women are bought and sold in our slave markets, to gratify the brutal lust of those who bear the name of Christians. In our slave States, if amid all her degradation, and ignorance, a woman desires to preserve her virtue unsullied, she is either bribed or whipped into compliance, or if she dares resist her

Auctioning Slaves
Nothing revealed the basic inhumanity of slavery more than the slave auction, an institution that was allowed even in the nation's capital. Because state laws defined them as chattel property, slaves were openly traded and sold on the market. Even the most sheltered or privileged slave could face the auction block as the result of an owner's indebtedness or the settlement of his estate. On such occasions mothers were sold separately from their children, husbands were separated from wives, human beings were examined, probed, and bid for like cattle.

seducer, her life by the laws of some of the slave States may be, and has actually been sacrificed to the fury of disappointed passion. . . .

Nor does the colored woman suffer alone: the moral purity of the white woman is deeply contaminated. In the daily habit of seeing the virtue of her enslaved sister sacrificed without hesitancy or remorse, she looks upon the crimes of seduction and illicit intercourse without horror, and although not personally involved in the guilt, she loses that value for innocence in her own, as well as the other sex, which is one of the strongest safeguards to virtue.

The larger slave communities provided some stability and continuity for the thousands of blacks who were sold and shipped to new environments. On the larger plantations one could find conjurers whose alleged magic powers were thought to ward off sickness, soften a master's heart, or hasten the success of a

An African Church in Cincinnati
In northern cities like Cincinnati, Ohio, blacks created and patronized their own African churches for two reasons: in white churches they were treated as inferiors and often forced to sit in a balcony or in special pews; in their own churches they could give uninhibited expression to a blend of African and Christian traditions that formed the core of African-American culture. Black churches became centers of antislavery activism and trained a large proportion of the leaders of the free black community.

courtship. There were black preachers who mixed Christianity with elements of West African religion and folklore. In the slave quarters particular prestige was attached to those who excelled at the traditional memorizing of songs, riddles, folktales, superstitions, and herb cures—who were carriers, in short, of African-American culture. These forms of oral communication allowed free play to the imagination, enabling slaves to comment on the pathos, humor, absurdity, sorrow, and warmth of the scenes they experienced. Together with the ceremonial rituals, especially at weddings and funerals, the oral traditions preserved a sanctuary of human dignity that enabled slaves to survive the humiliations, debasement, and self-contempt that were inseparable from human bondage.

As a result of the evangelical revivals,* southern planters increasingly promoted the religious conversion of their slaves. Even by the first decades of the nineteenth century, a growing number of churchmen and planters had argued

---

*On nineteenth-century revivalism in the South, see chapter 13, pp. 418–19.

that religious instruction would make slaves more obedient, industrious, and faithful. The ideal Christian master would treat his slaves with charity and understanding. The ideal Christian slave would humbly accept his assigned position in this world, knowing that his patience and faithfulness would be rewarded in heaven. Servitude, in short, could be softened, humanized, and perfected by Christianity. The reality of slavery fell short of the ideal, as indicated, for example, by the ghastly infant mortality and malnutrition of slave children. Religion may have induced many masters to take a sincere interest in their slaves' welfare, but it could not eliminate the cruelty and injustice inherent in the system.

No white preachers could entirely purge Christianity of overtones that tended to oppose slavery. Nor could whites prevent black preachers from converting Christianity into a source of self-respect, dignity, and faith in eventual deliverance—the longed-for Day of Jubilee. In both North and South free blacks responded to growing racial discrimination by forming what they called African churches, usually Baptist or Methodist. And despite the efforts by whites to control every aspect of their slaves' religion, the slaves created their own folk religion and shaped it to their needs and interests. As one ex-slave from Texas recalled, "The whites preached to the niggers and the niggers preached to theyselves."

The South as a "Slave Society"

By the 1830s black slavery had come to dominate all aspects of southern society. Old-fashioned defenses of slavery as an unfortunate although necessary evil were beginning to give way to aggressive self-justification. Ironically, as the South became increasingly isolated from the free-labor ideology of the Western world, the expansion of cotton cultivation helped assure southern leaders that slavery was indispensable to northern and British industry, which promoted the idealization of free labor. Accordingly, slaveholders regarded their critics as ungrateful hypocrites who would bite the hand that fed them.

The meaning of the phrase *slave society* is best illustrated by the West Indian colonies of the eighteenth and early nineteenth centuries. There black slaves typically made up 90 percent or more of an island's population. Political and social life was wholly dominated by large plantation owners, their managers and agents, and the merchants who lived off the system. There was almost no dissent over the question of black slavery.

Parts of the South almost approximated this model: the swampy lowcountry of South Carolina and the adjoining Sea Islands; the fertile Black Belt, extending from Georgia to Mississippi; the delta counties of Mississippi and the sugar parishes (counties) of Louisiana. But unlike the small and isolated West Indian islands, the sprawling South was in no way a solid and uniform society. In 1860, out of a white population of some 8 million, roughly 10,000 families belonged to the planter "aristocracy." Fewer than 3,000 families owned over one hundred slaves. Barely one out of four white southerners owned a slave or belonged to a

Florida "Crackers"
The term "cracker" referred originally to frontier outlaws and "great boasters" and braggarts, but in the nineteenth century it was applied to southern backwoodsmen and "poor whites" in general. This Florida family, guarding their palm-frond hut, lived in a subsistence-level economy that was far removed from the great market-oriented plantations.

family that did. There were extensive regions of eastern Tennessee and western Virginia where blacks, slave or free, were a rarity. Slavery had declined sharply in most of the Upper South—most dramatically of all in Delaware, where fewer than 2,000 slaves remained by 1860. Nor could most of the nonslaveholding majority be classed as hillbillies and poor whites. In addition to artisans, factory workers, and professionals, there were millions of small farmers in the South who worked their own land or who grazed herds of cattle, pigs, and horses in the forests and open range of the public domain.

Nevertheless, except for a few isolated pockets, the South did become a slave society dominated politically and ideologically by a plantation-owning elite. Throughout the pre–Civil War period, slaveholding remained the most widespread and obvious road to wealth and status. By 1860 millions of nonslaveholders believed that any serious threat to slavery was sufficient justification for southern independence; many of them, especially in the Southwest, had reasonable hopes of acquiring land and becoming planters even though the cost of buying slaves was soaring. Others, such as the yeoman farmers of the Georgia Upcountry, recognized that black slavery served their own interests by limiting their participation in market wage relations. "It is a well-known fact in the South," reported the Atlanta *Daily Intelligencer* in 1856, "that it is to preserve their own independence that non-slaveholding voters of the South have ever been staunch supporters of slavery." And small farmers often depended on a neighboring slaveowner's cotton gin or political patronage—and knew that in turn he depended for security on their services as armed patrols that searched the countryside for any unauthorized movement of blacks.

Dominance of the Planter Class The planter class could also draw on a rich tradition of political leadership. In the South—but not in the North—the eighteenth-century connection between wealth and personal political power had endured. Political leadership sprang directly from the ownership of slaves, which was supposed to provide leisure, a concern for public order, and a certain paternalistic self-assurance in exercising authority. The southern planter elite demonstrated skill in commanding the loyalty of nonslaveholding whites and also in disciplining dissent within the white population. The southern code of honor also sanctioned an open resort to violence. According to South Carolina's chief apologist for dueling, such formalized combat "will be persisted in as long as man's independence, and a lofty personal pride in all that dignifies and ennobles the human character, shall continue to exist." By the 1830s numerous southern abolitionists and southerners with simply a strong distaste for slavery had emigrated to the North or West after abandoning hope of challenging the entrenched idea that black slavery was a necessary evil that should be discussed as little as possible. They left behind them a plantation-owning elite that was solidified in its defense of slavery and militantly intolerant of dissent.

Southern white unity centered on race. Southern society was dedicated to the ideal of equality of opportunity as long as the ideal applied only to whites. It was also a region that depended economically on a system of labor exploitation that was difficult to square with republican and liberty-loving principles. Racial doctrine—the supposed innate inferiority of blacks—became the primary instrument for justifying the persistence of slavery, for rallying the support of nonslaveholding whites, and for defining the limits of dissent. In 1837 Chancellor William Harper of South Carolina summed up the prevailing dogma: "That the African negro is an inferior variety of the human race, is, I think, now generally admitted, and his distinguishing characteristics are such as peculiarly mark him out for the situation which he occupies among us."

Southern Free Blacks The key to racial policy was the status of free blacks. Before the nineteenth century this status had been ambiguous, and the number of free blacks was insignificant. By 1810, however, as a result of the emancipations that had accompanied and followed the Revolution, there were 100,000 free blacks and mulattoes in the southern states. This group, the fastest-growing element in the southern population, was beginning to acquire property, to found "African" churches and schools, and to assert its independence, especially in the Upper South. In response, white legislators tightened restrictions on private acts of freeing slaves in an effort to curb the growth of an unwanted population. A rash of new laws, similar to the later Black Codes of Reconstruction,* reduced free blacks almost to the status of slaves without masters. The new laws regulated their freedom of movement, forbade them to associate with slaves, subjected them to surveillance and discipline by whites, denied them the legal right to testify in court against whites, required them to work at approved jobs, and threatened them with penal labor if not actual reenslavement. Ironically, in parts of the Deep South free blacks continued to benefit from a more flexible status because there were fewer of them in the population than elsewhere in the South and they could serve as valued intermediaries between a white minority and a slave majority, as in the West Indies. Racial discrimination was worse in the Upper South, precisely because slavery was economically less secure in that region.

Decline of Antislavery in the South

From the time of the Revolution, a cautious, genteel distaste for slavery had been fashionable among the planters of the Upper South. This Jeffersonian tradition persisted even after the more militant abolitionists had been driven from the region and after Methodist and Baptist leaders had backtracked on various resolutions encouraging gradual emancipation. The desire to find some way of ridding the South of its "burden" or "curse," as the Jeffersonian reformers called it, was kept alive by some of the sons of affluent plantation owners who went to the North or to Europe to study.

The hope of removing the South's burden also won support from a few broad-minded plantation owners, mostly Whigs,† who were troubled by the economic decline of eastern Virginia and Maryland, and by the continuing loss of population to the Southwest. In 1832 the belief that slavery was "ruinous to the whites" received unexpected support in the Virginia legislature from non-slaveholders who lived west of the Blue Ridge Mountains and who had various motives for challenging the political control of tidewater planters. But in the end their arguments, advanced in a notable legislative debate of 1832 in response to Nat Turner's revolt,‡ demonstrated the power of racism. Even the non-slaveholding dissenters acknowledged that bondage had benefits for blacks and that its destructive effects on white society could be ended only by gradually freeing and deporting the entire black population. The antislavery delegates failed even to carry a resolution that would have branded slavery as an evil to be dealt with at some future time.

---

*For the Black Codes, see chapter 20, pp. 674, 684.

†For southern Whigs, see chapter 15, pp. 509–16.

‡For Nat Turner's revolt, see pp. 461, 473.

The Proslavery Argument

By the early 1840s—less than a decade later—such a public debate would have been inconceivable in any southern state. By then regional loyalty, intensified by sectional conflict, required that southerners believe slavery to be a "positive good." The proslavery argument ranged from appeals to ancient Greek and Roman precedents to elaborate biblical interpretations designed to prove that slavery had never been contrary to the laws of God. Drawing on the romantic and chivalric literary fashions of the time, southern writers represented the plantation as a feudal manor blessed with human warmth, mutual duties, knightly virtues, and loyalty to blood and soil.

The most striking part of the proslavery ideology was its indictment of liberalism and capitalism—its well-documented charge that the prevailing rule in so-called free societies, as George Fitzhugh put it, was "every man for himself, and the devil take the hindmost." In his *Sociology for the South* (1854) and *Cannibals All!* (1857), Fitzhugh sharply criticized the philosophic premises of an individualistic, egalitarian society. He also examined the destructive historical consequences of dissolving the social and psychological networks that had once given humanity a sense of place and purpose. Fitzhugh, the most rigorous and consistent proslavery theorist, presented the master-slave relation as the only alternative to a world in which unlimited self-interest had subjected propertyless workers to the impersonal exploitation of "wage-slavery." He was consistent enough to renounce *racial* justifications for actual slavery and to propose that the benefits of the institution he boasted of be extended to white workers. But these arguments, however interesting theoretically, only showed how far Fitzhugh had moved from social reality. Racism lay at the heart of the South's unity. The enslavement of whites was unthinkable, and in the 1850s the South even rejected extremist proposals for expelling or reenslaving a quarter of a million free blacks. Fitzhugh's theories did more to expose the moral dilemmas of free society than to illuminate the actual complexities and contradictions of the South.

It is true that moral doubts persisted, especially in the Upper South. But after the 1830s these doubts were more than counterbalanced by the conviction that emancipation in any form would be a disaster, for blacks as well as for whites. Southerners channeled their moral concern into dedicated efforts to reform, improve, and defend what they called the peculiar institution. It was almost universally accepted that to own slaves meant to have a sense of duty and a burden—a duty and a burden that defined the moral superiority of the South. This duty and burden was respected by nonslaveholding southerners, who were prepared to defend it with their lives. That, perhaps, was the ultimate meaning of a "slave society."

Radical Abolitionism

Black slavery was the first issue to expose the limitations of the Benevolent Empire. Even by 1830 there was a striking gap between the public optimism of the evangelical humanitarians and their whispered despair concerning black slavery.

Harsh realities made the gap increasingly noticeable. Despite the fact that federal law prohibited slave imports from Africa, the natural increase of the American slave population exceeded all earlier expectations. The number of slaves in the United States increased from approximately 1.5 million in 1820 to more than 2 million in 1830. This figure represented almost one-sixth of the total United States population and more than twice the number of slaves in the British and French West Indies. The number of free blacks grew during the 1820s from about 234,000 to 320,000.

The Failure of Black Colonization
In 1830 the American Colonization Society transported a total of only 259 free blacks to Liberia, the West African colony that the society had established as a refuge for American blacks. Yet most reformers still regarded colonization as the only solution: "We must save the Negro," as one missionary put it, "or the Negro will ruin us." Racial prejudice was pervasive in the Benevolent Empire, and it was by no means unknown among later radical abolitionists. But the new and significant fact was the rising tide of virulent racism among the working classes of the North. Prejudiced as they may have been, many leaders of the colonization movement were sincere opponents of slavery who abhorred the growing racism of the northern masses and who saw black emigration as the only realistic means for preventing racial war in the North and for inducing southern masters to free their slaves.

A series of events reinforced the realization that white America could not solve its racial problem by shipping a few hundred free blacks each year to Liberia. In 1829 David Walker, a Boston black who belonged to the Massachusetts General Colored Association, published his revolutionary *Appeal to the Colored Citizens of the World,* which justified slave rebellion and warned white Americans that if justice were delayed blacks would win their liberty "by the crushing arm of power." The pamphlet created an uproar, and copies smuggled by sailors soon appeared among blacks in the Deep South. Then in 1831 Nat Turner, a trusted Virginia slave, led the bloodiest slave revolt the South had yet experienced. At the end of the same year a far larger uprising rocked the British colony of Jamaica. In Britain mass demonstrations continued to demand the immediate and unconditional emancipation of West Indian slaves. When Parliament responded in 1833 with generous monetary compensation to slaveowners to cover part of the financial loss of emancipation, and with an apprenticeship plan to prepare slaves for freedom, a few Americans concluded that effective political action of any kind required a mammoth mobilization of public opinion.

The Ethical Basis of Abolitionism
To the young abolitionists who began to appear in the early 1830s, black slavery was the great national sin. The fusion of American religious revivalism with the influence of the British antislavery movement was symbolized by Theodore Dwight Weld, the son of a Connecticut minister. Weld was a convert and close associate of

the famous evangelist Charles Grandison Finney in upstate New York. Weld's closest friend and religious model was Charles Stuart, a visiting British reformer who worked with Finney's disciples in the Burned-Over District and then in 1829 returned to England to throw himself into the battle for slave emancipation. After being urged by Stuart to take up the cause in America, Weld shifted from temperance and educational reforms to abolitionism, becoming one of the most fearless and powerful lecturers in the area from Ohio to Vermont. Early in 1833 he wrote a letter to William Lloyd Garrison, whom he knew only by reputation. In it he illuminated the meaning of slavery as sin:

> That no condition of birth, no shade of color, no mere misfortune of circum-stances, can annul the birth-right charter, which God has bequeathed to every being upon whom he has stamped his own image, by making him a free moral agent, and that he who robs his fellow man of this tramples upon right, subverts justice, outrages humanity, unsettles the foundations of human safety, and sacrilegiously assumes the prerogatives of God; and further, tho' he who retains by force, and refuses to surrender that which was originally obtained by violence or fraud is joint partner in the original sin, becomes its apologist and makes it the business of every moment to perpetuate it afresh, however he may lull his conscience by the vain plea of expediency or necessity.

Weld's statement sums up a moral command that sprang from three funda-mental convictions. He believed that all men and women have the ability to do what is right and therefore are morally accountable for their actions; that the intolerable social evils are those that degrade the image of God in human beings, stunting or corrupting people's capacities for self-control and self-respect; and that the goal of all reform is to free individuals from being manipulated like physical objects. As one follower of William Lloyd Garrison put it, the goal of abolitionism was "the redemption of man from the dominion of man."

The fact that Weld and other abolitionists were almost wholly concerned with ideals was both their greatest strength and their greatest weakness. America was supposedly a nation of doers, of practical builders, framers, drafters, organizers, and technicians. The overriding question, in abolitionist eyes, was whether the nation would continue to accommodate itself to a social system that was based on sheer violence. To propose rational plans or to get embroiled in debates over the precise means and timing of emancipation would only give slavery's defenders an advantage. What the times required, therefore, was "an original motive power" that would shock and awaken public opinion, create a new moral perspective, and require legislators to work out the details, however imperfectly, of practical emancipation. In 1831 William Lloyd Garrison admitted: "Urge immediate abolition as earnestly as we may, it will alas! be gradual abolition in the end. We have never said that slavery would be overthrown by a single blow; that it ought to be we shall always contend."

**William Lloyd Garrison
(1805–79)**
*Raised by an indigent mother
abandoned by his alcoholic
father, Garrison began his career
as a printer and a conservative
supporter of the Benevolent
Empire before moving on to
become the most famous and
controversial American abolitionist. Courageous and supreme-
ly confident of the rectitude of
his own moral views, Garrison
owed much of his prominence to
the anger and outrage he
provoked among slaveholders,
northern clergymen, ordinary
citizens, and even other
abolitionists and reformers. As
an agitator determined to expose
the sins of slavery, racism, and
all forms of coercive authority,
Garrison continues to arouse
controversy among historians.*

The Abolitionists On one level the abolitionists realistically saw that the
nation had reached a dead end on slavery. Instead of
gradually withering away, as earlier optimists had hoped, the evil had grown and
had won increasing acceptance among the nation's political leaders and most
powerful institutions. Therefore the abolitionists took on the unpopular role of
agitators, of courageous critics who stood outside the popular refuges of delu-
sion, hypocrisy, and rationalization. In 1830 Garrison went to jail for writing
libelous attacks against a New England merchant who was shipping slaves from
Baltimore to New Orleans. After his fine was paid and his release was secured by
the wealthy supporter of reform groups, Arthur Tappan, Garrison in 1831
founded his newspaper *The Liberator* in Boston. In the first issue he hurled out his
famous pledge: "I will be as harsh as truth, and as uncompromising as justice.... I
am in earnest—I will not equivocate—I will not excuse—I will not retreat a
single inch—AND I WILL BE HEARD."

Although *The Liberator* had an extremely small circulation and derived most
of its support from black subscribers in the Northeast, Garrison succeeded in
being heard. In the South especially, newspaper editors seized the chance to
reprint specimens of New England's radicalism, accompanied by their own
furious rebuttals. Even before the end of 1831, mere months after *The Liberator* first appeared, the Georgia legislature proposed a reward of $5,000 for
anyone who would kidnap Garrison and bring him south for trial. Garrison also

championed the free blacks' grievances against the Colonization Society, which he had once supported, and mounted a blistering attack against the whole concept of colonization. He pointed out that the hope for colonization confirmed and reinforced white racial prejudice and that racial prejudice was the main barrier the abolitionists faced in the North. Largely as a result of Garrison's early and independent leadership, the American Anti-Slavery Society, founded in 1833, committed itself to at least a vague legal equality of whites and blacks, and totally rejected colonization.

Even though they had practically declared war against the values, institutions, and power structure of Jacksonian America, the abolitionists continued to think of their reform societies as simple extensions of the Benevolent Empire. They assumed that they could quickly win support from churches and ministers—that they could persuade the pious, influential, and respectable community leaders that racial prejudice was as harmful as intemperance. Then, after mobilizing righteous opinion in the North, they could shame the South into repentance. Abolitionists did not think of themselves as provokers of violence and disunion. Rather, it was slavery that had brought increasing violence and threats of disunion. A national commitment to emancipation, they believed, would ensure harmony and national union.

Like the wealthy British supporters of humanitarian causes (including antislavery), Arthur Tappan and his brother Lewis moved from various benevolent causes to that of immediate emancipation. By 1833 humanitarians in Great Britain had won the support of the established order, as well as of middle-class public opinion. But in America, precisely because the Tappans had wealth and prestige, they were viciously attacked for encouraging Garrison and other radicals and for betraying the common interests that had allowed leaders in different sections to do business with one another. Mass rallies in the South pledged as much as $50,000 for the delivery of Arthur Tappan's body, dead or alive. In New York City, business leaders vainly pleaded with the Tappan brothers, whose lives were being repeatedly threatened by 1834, to give up their radical activities. In that year prominent New Yorkers cheered on a mob of butcherboys and day laborers who smashed up Lewis Tappan's house and burned the furnishings. Only the unexpected arrival of troops prevented an armed assault on the Tappans' store.

Antiabolitionists played on popular suspicions of England, charging that men like George Thompson, an English friend of Garrison, had been sent "to foment discord among our people, array brother against brother...to excite treasonable opposition to our government...to excite our slave population to rise and butcher their masters; to render the South a desert, and the country at large the scene of fraternal war." Abolitionists continually invoked the ideals of the Declaration of Independence and portrayed themselves as fulfilling the Revolution's promise. But their enemies styled themselves as minutemen defending American liberties. The mob riots of the Revolutionary periods appeared to legitimize the antiabolitionist riots that spread across the North in the 1830s. For the most part this mob violence was carefully planned, organized, and directed toward specific goals, such as the destruction of abolitionist printing presses and the intimidation of free blacks. The leaders were "gentlemen of property and standing"—prominent lawyers, bankers, merchants, doctors, and local political leaders of both the Democratic and Whig parties. In most towns and cities the white abolitionists and free blacks received little protection from the forces of law and order. The colonizationists, already weakened by financial difficulties and internal division, took the lead in accusing the abolitionists of being "amalgamationists" who would not stop short of encouraging black men to woo the daughters of white America.

Abolitionism and Freedom of Speech
This racist bugaboo brought the northern crowds into the streets and also lay behind the abolitionists' most dramatic break with the Benevolent Empire. Lane Theological Seminary in Cincinnati was meant to be one of the empire's crowning achievements—a beachhead of benevolence on the Ohio River, a staging ground for the missionary conquest of the West. Arthur Tappan paid the salary of the president of the seminary, Lyman Beecher. He also paid the way for Theodore Weld, then thirty-one, to study there. Early in 1834 Weld conducted at Lane an eighteen-day soul-searching revival on the question of slavery. After converting many students and nonstudents to the doctrine of immediate emancipation, Weld led his band into the slums where the black residents of Cincinnati lived. There they set up libraries, conducted evening classes, and fraternized with the city's "untouchable" caste, the blacks. In Weld's view educational institutions had a duty to train minds for the new "era of disposable power and practical accomplishment."

But to the Tappans' dismay, Lane's board of trustees voted to silence Weld and the other antislavery leaders, and Lyman Beecher—who was still a supporter of colonization—went along with the decision.

Various leaders of American higher education agreed that antislavery agitation endangered the fundamental purposes of American colleges. In response, almost all the Lane students walked out of the seminary with Weld. Some ended up in Arthur Tappan's newly financed college, Oberlin. But many joined Weld as traveling agents for the American Anti-Slavery Society, of which Arthur Tappan was president, braving showers of rotten eggs and stones in order to address the American people.

As a product of the Benevolent Empire, abolitionism drew on and perfected techniques of mass communication that gave the nation its first taste of modern "public relations." By 1835 the new steam printing press and other technological improvements had reduced the cost and increased the volume of mass publication. In 1834 the Anti-Slavery Society distributed 122,000 pieces of literature; in 1835 the figure rose to 1.1 million. President Jackson and various national and local authorities expressed alarm over this attempt to apply the methods of the Bible Society and Tract Society to a revolutionary purpose—a purpose that threatened one of the nation's chief capital investments as well as a national system for racial

The Killing of an Abolitionist
A woodcut illustration of the anti-abolitionist mob attacking the printing office of Elijah P. Lovejoy in Alton, Illinois on November 7, 1837. Lovejoy's death dramatized the issue of free speech and public repression.

control. But although the government encouraged the destruction of abolitionist mail, it could do nothing about the traveling abolitionist lecturers in the North, the "antislavery bazaars" held to raise funds and distribute literature, the auxiliary societies for ladies and children, or the flood of propaganda in the forms of medals, emblems, posters, bandannas, chocolate wrappers, songs, and children's readers.

The rapid growth of abolitionist societies, coupled with violent efforts to suppress them, led to sharp divisions of opinion over abolitionist principles and tactics. One turning point was the celebrated martyrdom in 1837 of Elijah P. Lovejoy, a New England abolitionist who, like the Mormons, had been driven out of Missouri and had established a refuge in Illinois. While trying to defend a new printing press from an antiabolitionist mob, Lovejoy was shot and killed. His violent death dramatized the issue of civil liberties and won new support for the abolitionists; and it also forced abolitionists to debate the proper response to violence, since Lovejoy and his men had used arms in self-defense.

Nonresistance Garrison, who had nearly been lynched in 1835 by a Boston mob, had become convinced that violence was a disease infecting the entire body of American society. He came to believe that whenever the nation faced any issue of fundamental morality, such as the treatment of Indians, blacks, or dissenters, it resorted to the principle that might

478

makes right. The only Christian response, Garrison maintained, was to renounce all coercion and adhere to the perfectionist ideal of absolute nonresistance. If abolitionists tried to oppose power with power, as Lovejoy had done, they were certain to be crushed. They would also dilute their moral argument, since the essence of slavery was the forcible dominion of man over man. In 1838 Garrison and his followers formed the New England Non-Resistance Society. This group condemned every kind of coercion—not only defensive war and capital punishment, but lawsuits, prisons, and insane asylums, unless designed solely for "cure and restoration."

Thus there began to emerge in New England abolitionism a radical repudiation of all limits imposed on the individual by the threat of force. Black slavery and racial oppression were merely extreme manifestations of an evil embodied in the male-dominated family, the criminal law, and the police power of the state. By 1843 Garrison concluded that the majority rule was simply the rule of superior power, with no protection for human rights. The Union, he asserted, had always been a compact for the preservation of slavery, and the Constitution was therefore "a covenant with death, and an agreement with Hell." The Garrisonians demanded withdrawal from corrupt churches and from all connection with the corrupt government. They refused to vote or engage in any political activities. Calling for disunion with the South, they also crossed the threshold of symbolic treason and declared themselves enemies of the Republic.

In interesting ways the Garrisonians' rhetoric paralleled the rhetoric of the Mormons. "The governments of the world," Garrison announced in 1837, "are all anti-Christ." Yet by 1845 he also cast off the Old Testament, arguing that God could never have approved of slavery and violence. Instead of moving beyond the geographic frontiers to establish the Kingdom of God, as the Mormons had done, Garrison defended his own fortress of moral independence within a hostile society.

Political Antislavery: From the Liberty Party to Free Soil
By the 1840s, however, most abolitionists expressed new hopes for transforming the dominant society by means of the political process. There were various indications of this growing involvement in political action. During the late 1830s thousands of antislavery petitions poured into Congress as a popular challenge to the "gag rule," which prevented congressional discussions of slavery.* Former president John Quincy Adams, then a Whig congressman from Massachusetts, used every parliamentary trick to defend the petitioners' rights. Antislavery Whigs like congressmen Joshua Giddings and Salmon P. Chase, both of Ohio, capitalized on their constituencies' resentment of the "gag rule" and other sectional compromises that sacrificed moral principle. Liberal Democrats, such as senators Thomas Morris of Ohio and John P. Hale of New Hampshire, voiced growing dissatisfaction with their party, which professed

*For the "gag rule," see chapter 15, pp. 503–04.

to attack economic privilege while serving the interests of wealthy slaveowners. And after 1842, when the Supreme Court ruled that the Fugitive Slave Law of 1793 applied solely to the federal government's responsibility in helping to recover fugitives, five northern states enacted "personal liberty laws" prohibiting state officials from assisting in the recapture of runaway slaves.

For the most part, political abolitionists hoped to pursue their goals by promoting antislavery candidates and by bringing well-organized public pressure on the two major parties to prohibit the interstate slave trade, to abolish slavery in the District of Columbia, and to prevent any further expansion of slavery in western states and territories—the only antislavery measures that the Constitution seemed to allow. In 1839, however, Alvan Stewart, a lawyer and president of the New York State Anti-Slavery Society, drew most of the non-Garrisonian abolitionists into a temporary third party. It was hoped that this Liberty party, which ran James G. Birney for president in 1840, would win a balance of power in closely contested regions of the North and would thus free Whigs and Democrats from the stranglehold of what abolitionists called the Slave Power—an alleged conspiratorial alliance of southern slaveowners and their northern supporters.* By 1855 the judicious Charles Francis Adams could confidently assert that the Slave Power, consisting of "three hundred and fifty thousand men, spreading over a large territorial surface, commanding the political resources of fifteen states, was also in undisputed possession of all the official strongholds in the general government."

The Libertymen blamed the Slave Power for the economic depression that had begun in 1837, for the undermining of civil liberties, and for most of the other ills that the nation had suffered. Although Birney captured only a small fraction of the potential antislavery vote in the elections of 1840 and 1844, the Liberty party succeeded in popularizing the belief in a Slave Power conspiracy. By offering voters an abolitionist alternative to even moderately antislavery Whigs and Democrats, the Libertymen also stimulated figures like Giddings, Chase, and Hale to make a bolder appeal for antislavery votes.

By 1848 the more extreme political abolitionists had come to the conclusion that the Constitution gave Congress both the power and the duty to abolish slavery in the southern states. But in that year most abolitionists looked to the more moderate, broadly coalitionist Free-Soil party, which promised only to remove all federal sanctions for slavery by abolishing the institution in the District of Columbia, by excluding it from the territories, and by employing all other constitutional means to deprive it of national support.

The Free-Soil platform of 1848, unlike the platform of the Liberty party, ignored the legal discriminations that free blacks suffered. Many of the dissident northern Democrats who helped form the party had consistently opposed black

---

*The politics of the 1840s, in which debate over the expansion of slavery played a central role, is discussed more fully in chapter 16.

suffrage and had exploited white racist prejudice. And indeed abolitionism in general became more acceptable in the North by accommodating itself to white racism. Many blacks increasingly resented the attention given to such other interests of white reformers as women's rights, nonresistance, and communitarian experiments, to say nothing of the hypocrisy of many reformers regarding racial equality in the North. They also resented the patronizing attitudes of white abolitionists who might defend abstract ideals of equality while in practice treating blacks as inferiors who had to be led.

Black Abolitionists   From the outset black abolitionists had worked closely with the antislavery societies in New England and New York. Beginning with Frederick Douglass's celebrated escape from slavery in 1838 and his enlistment as a lecturer for Garrison's Massachusetts Anti-Slavery Society in 1841, fugitive slaves performed the indispensable task of translating the abolitionists' abstract images into concrete human experience. The lectures and printed narratives of Douglass, William Wells Brown, Ellen Craft, Henry Bibb, Solomon Northup, and other escaped slaves did much to undermine whatever belief there was in the North that slaves were kindly treated and contented with their lot. The wit and articulate militancy of black abolitionists like Henry Highland Garnet, James McCune Smith, Sarah Parker Remond, and Charles Lenox Remond, coupled with the towering dignity of Douglass, also helped to shake confidence in the popular stereotypes of black inferiority.

Yet black abolitionists faced barriers and physical dangers that made the difficulties of white abolitionists seem like child's play. When Douglass and Garrison traveled together on lecture tours, it was Douglass who experienced constant insult, humiliation, and harassment. Black vigilance committees could help a small number of fugitives find their way to relative security in Canada— and blacks were the main conductors on the so-called Underground Railroad— but except in Massachusetts black abolitionists had little leverage for loosening the rocklike discriminatory laws. Instead white abolitionists kept pressuring blacks to keep a low profile, to act the part assigned to them by white directors (who presumably knew the tastes of an all-white audience), and to do nothing that might spoil the show.

In the 1840s black leaders gradually cast off the yoke that had bound them to a white man's cause, and tried to assert their own leadership. In 1843, at the Convention of the Free People of Color held at Buffalo, Garnet openly called for a slave rebellion, arguing that it was a sin to submit voluntarily to human bondage. Douglass adhered to his own version of nonresistance until 1847, when he broke with Garrison over the idea of founding a black abolitionist newspaper, *The North Star.* In the same year Garrison sadly reported that Charles Lenox Remond had proclaimed that "the slaves were bound, by their love of justice, to RISE AT ONCE, en masse, and THROW OFF THEIR FETTERS."

But speeches were one thing, action another. Black abolitionists had always looked to voting—a right few blacks possessed—as the most promising route to

Frederick Douglass (1818–95)
*The greatest black leader of the
nineteenth century, Frederick
Douglass was born into slavery
in Maryland (he never knew his
birth date), and as a house
servant learned to read and
write. In 1838 he escaped to the
North, and in 1841 he began to
lecture for the Massachusetts
Anti-Slavery Society. After
publishing his masterful*
Narrative of the Life of
Frederick Douglass, *he lectured
widely in Britain. Returning to
the United States in 1847, he
edited his own newspaper,* The
North Star. *An eloquent and
prolific reformer, Douglass fought
for women's rights as well as
racial equality.*

power. For the most part, therefore, they supported the Liberty party in 1840 and 1844, and the Free-Soil party in 1848. The drift of antislavery politics, however, was away from black civil rights in the North and emancipation in the southern states. Rather, the drift was now toward walling off of the western territories—a walling off, in all probability, of free blacks as well as slaves. It is not surprising that by 1854 Martin Delaney and a few other black leaders were talking of a separate black nation, or that blacks who had proudly defended their American heritage and right to American citizenship were beginning to reconsider voluntary colonization in Africa or Haiti.

By 1854, however, many northern whites had also concluded that the Slave Power had seized control of America's Manifest Destiny, thereby appropriating and nullifying the entire evangelical and millennial mission.* Moreover, the Fugitive Slave Law of 1850, requiring federal agents to recover fugitive slaves from their sanctuaries in the North, directly challenged the North's integrity and its new self-image as an asylum of liberty. The arrival of federal "kidnappers" and the spectacle of blacks being seized in the streets invited demonstrations of defiance and civil disobedience. Increasing numbers of former moderates echoed Garrison's rhetoric of disunion, and an increasing number of former nonresistants called for a slave uprising or predicted that the streets of Boston might "yet run with blood." Wendell Phillips, a Boston aristocrat and the most powerful of all abolitionist orators, rejoiced "that every five minutes gave birth to a black baby," for in its infant wail he recognized the voice that should "yet shout the war

---

*For Manifest Destiny, see chapter 16; for the contest over admitting Kansas as a slave state, chapter 17.

cry of insurrection; its baby hand would one day hold the dagger which should reach the master's heart."

In the 1850s northern abolitionists finally concluded that if the Slave Power were not crushed by rebellion or expelled from the Union, it would cross every legal and constitutional barrier and destroy the physical ability of northerners to act in accordance with the moral ability that had been the main legacy of religious revivals. The western territories were thus the crucial testing ground that would determine whether America would stand for something more than selfish interest, exploitation, and rule by brutal power. All the aspirations of the Benevolent Empire, of evangelical reformers, and of perfectionists of every kind could be channeled into a single and vast crusade to keep the territories free, to confine and seal off the Slave Power, and thus to open the way for an expansion of righteous liberty and opportunity that would surpass all worldly limits.

SUGGESTED READINGS

The best general guides to sectional conflict and the coming of the Civil War are David M. Potter, *The Impending Crisis, 1848–1861* (completed and edited by Don E. Fehrenbacher, 1976), and James M. McPherson, *Battle Cry of Freedom: The Civil War Era* (1988). Allan Nevins, *Ordeal of the Union* (2 vols., 1947), is a highly readable and informative survey of the same subject. William W. Freehling, *The Road to Disunion: Secessionists at Bay, 1776–1854* (1990), contains many valuable insights. A short and imaginative reinterpretation is James Oakes, *Slavery and Freedom: An Interpretation of the Old South* (1990).

A comprehensive picture of the South as a slave society can be found in Clement Eaton's *A History of the Old South: The Emergence of a Reluctant Nation* (1975) and *Freedom of Thought in the Old South* (1940). The growth of sectional feeling is outlined in more detail in Charles S. Sydnor, *The Development of Southern Sectionalism, 1819–1848* (1948); Richard E. Ellis, *The Union at Risk: Jacksonian Democracy, States' Rights and the Nullification Crisis* (1987); Alison Goodyear Freehling, *Drift Toward Dissolution: The Virginia Slavery Debate of 1831–1832* (1982); Drew Gilpin Faust, *The Creation of Confederate Nationalism: Ideology and Identity in the Civil War South* (1988); and Avery O. Craven, *The Growth of Southern Nationalism, 1848–1861* (1953). Carl N. Degler, *The Other South: Southern Dissenters in the Nineteenth Century* (1974), traces the decline of antislavery protest. H. Shelton Smith, *In His Image, But . . .* (1972), is a fine study of the growing racism in the southern churches. Two valuable studies of non-slaveholding southern whites are Steven Hahn, *The Roots of Southern Populism: Yeoman Farmers and the Transformation of the Georgia Upcountry, 1850–1890* (1983), and J. William Harris, *Plain Folk and Gentry in a Slave Society: White Liberty and Black Slavery in Augusta's Hinterlands* (1985). For the story of a remarkable slaveholding black family in South Carolina, see Michael P. Johnson and James L. Roark, *Black Masters: A Free Family of Color in the Old South* (1984). A penetrating study of the mythology of the Old South, often northern in origin, is William R. Taylor, *Cavalier and Yankee* (1961). C. Vann Woodward's essays in *The Burden of Southern History* (1960) and *American Counterpoint* (1971) are indispensable for understanding the South. The mind of the planter class is brilliantly illuminated by two accounts contemporary with the period: C. Vann Woodward, ed., *Mary Chesnut's Civil War* (1981), and Robert M. Myers, ed., *The Children of Pride: A True Story of Georgia and the Civil War* (1972). James Oakes, *The Ruling Race: A History of American Slaveholders* (1982), is a provocative interpretation of slaveholders as calculating capitalists. George M. Fredrickson, *White Supremacy: A Com-*

parative Study in American and South African History (1981), brilliantly compares the development of slavery and racism in the United States and South Africa. A lucid analysis of slavery, race, and class in a crucial border state, which sheds light on broader sectional divergence, is Barbara Jeanne Fields, *Slavery and Freedom on the Middle Ground: Maryland During the Nineteenth Century* (1985).

Eugene D. Genovese, *Roll, Jordan, Roll* (1974), is a monumental study of black slavery in the South. It is beautifully complemented, with respect to black and white women, by Elizabeth Fox-Genovese, *Within the Plantation Household: Black and White Women of the Old South* (1988). The most comprehensive study of the economics of slavery, which includes discussions of slave culture, antislavery, and the political and social conditions that led to a victorious antislavery coalition, is Robert William Fogel, *Without Consent or Contract: The Rise and Fall of American Slavery* (1989). A different and no less valuable perspective on the southern economy can be found in Gavin Wright, *The Political Economy of the Cotton South: Households, Markets, and Wealth in the Nineteenth Century* (1978). An excellent survey of the more traditional literature on this subject is Harold D. Woodman, ed., *Slavery and the Southern Economy* (1966). For the use of slaves in nonagricultural employment, see Robert S. Starobin, *Industrial Slavery in the Old South* (1970). Gang labor in the fields depended on black supervisors, a subject well treated by William L. Van Deburg, *The Slave Drivers: Black Agricultural Labor Supervisors in the Antebellum South* (1988). Herbert G. Gutman, *The Black Family in Slavery and Freedom, 1750–1925* (1976), is a pioneering work on a fundamental aspect of slave culture. For black women, the student should also consult Jacqueline Jones, *Labor of Love, Labor of Sorrow: Black Women, Work, and the Family from Slavery to the Present* (1985), and Deborah Gray White, *Ar'n't I a Woman? Female Slaves in the Plantation South* (1985). A model study of free women in a key Virginia town is Suzanne Lebsock, *Free Women of Petersburg: Status and Culture in a Southern Town, 1784–1860* (1984). For an illuminating discussion of the slaves' society, based mainly on slave narratives, see John W. Blassingame, *The Slave Community* (rev. ed., 1979). Two rich collections of source material are Willie Lee Rose, ed., *A Documentary History of Slavery in North America* (1976), and John W. Blassingame, ed., *Slave Testimony* (1977). As an overall survey of slavery as an institution, Kenneth Stampp's *The Peculiar Institution* (1956) has not been superseded. Willie Lee Rose, *Slavery and Freedom* (1982), is a collection of essays that combine wide-ranging interests with insightful wisdom. David B. Davis, *Slavery and Human Progress* (1984), places southern slavery and emancipation within a context of world history from antiquity to modern times.

The synthesis of African and Christian religious forms is carefully studied in Albert J. Raboteau, *Slave Religion: The "Invisible Institution" in the Antebellum South* (1978). A rich and comprehensive study of black folklore and culture is Lawrence W. Levine, *Black Culture and Black Consciousness: Afro-American Folk Thought from Slavery to Freedom* (1977). The origins in slave culture of black national consciousness are traced in Sterling Stuckey, *Slave Culture: Nationalist Theory and the Foundations of Black America* (1987).

The standard work on proslavery thought is William S. Jenkins, *Pro-Slavery Thought in the Old South* (1935), which should be supplemented by Harvey Wish, *George Fitzhugh* (1943); Drew Gilpin Faust, *A Sacred Circle: The Dilemma of the Intellectual in the Old South, 1840–1860* (1977); and Drew Gilpin Faust, *James Henry Hammond and the Old South: A Design for Mastery* (1982). A fresh and highly original reinterpretation of southern society and culture is Bertram Wyatt-Brown, *Southern Honor: Ethics and Behavior in the Old South* (1982). For the evangelical revival in the South, see Anne C. Loveland, *Southern Evangelicals and the Social Order, 1800–1860* (1980). Ira Berlin, *Slaves Without Masters* (1975), is a superb analysis of free blacks in the South. John H. Franklin, *From Slavery to Freedom* (1974), is the best introduction to African-American history. George M. Fredrickson, *The Black Image in the White Mind: The Debate on Afro-American Character and Destiny, 1817–1914* (1971), is a brilliant study of racism in

America. More specialized works of importance are Eugene H. Berwanger, *The Frontier Against Slavery: Western Anti-Negro Prejudice and the Slavery Extension Controversy* (1967), and William Stanton, *The Leopard's Spots: Scientific Attitudes Toward Race in America, 1815–1859* (1960).

The literature on abolitionism is voluminous. The historical precedents and background are covered in David B. Davis, *The Problem of Slavery in Western Culture* (1966), and *The Problem of Slavery in the Age of Revolution, 1770–1823* (1975). The best brief account of later abolitionism is James B. Stewart, *Holy Warriors: The Abolitionists and American Slavery* (1976), which should be supplemented by Ronald G. Walters's more interpretive study, *The Antislavery Appeal: American Abolitionism After 1830* (1976). An innovative study of the motivations and inner dynamics of abolitionism is Lawrence J. Friedman, *Gregarious Saints: Self and Community in American Abolitionism, 1830–1870* (1982). Gilbert H. Barnes, *The Anti-Slavery Impulse* (1933), is a dramatic and readable study, emphasizing the role of Theodore Weld and the Lane Seminary rebels. For an opposing and brilliantly argued view, see Aileen S. Kraditor, *Means and Ends in American Abolitionism: Garrison and His Critics on Strategy and Tactics* (1967). A similarly powerful and creative work is Lewis Perry, *Radical Abolitionism: Anarchy and the Government of God in Antislavery Thought* (1973). Robert H. Abzug, *Passionate Liberator: Theodore Dwight Weld and the Dilemma of Reform* (1980), is a probing biography of one of the most fascinating abolitionists. Other informative biographies include Bertram Wyatt-Brown, *Lewis Tappan and the Evangelical War against Slavery* (1969); Betty Fladeland, *James Gillespie Birney: Slaveholder to Abolitionist* (1955); John L. Thomas, *The Liberator: William Lloyd Garrison* (1963); Gerda Lerner, *The Grimké Sisters from South Carolina: Rebels Against Slavery* (1967); David Donald, *Charles Sumner and the Coming of the Civil War* (1960); and Hugh Davis, *Joshua Leavitt: Evangelical Abolitionist* (1990). The connection between antislavery and feminism is imaginatively explored by Jean Fagan Yellin, *Women and Sisters: The Antislavery Feminists in American Culture* (1989). Provocative approaches can be found in Lewis Perry and Michael Fellman, eds., *Antislavery Reconsidered: New Perspectives on the Abolitionists* (1979). Leonard L. Richards, *"Gentlemen of Property and Standing": Anti-Abolition Mobs in Jacksonian America* (1970), keenly analyzes antiabolition violence. Concerning civil liberties, see Russel B. Nye, *Fettered Freedom: Civil Liberties and the Slavery Controversy* (1963), and Thomas O. Morris, *Free Men All: The Personal Liberty Laws of the North, 1780–1861* (1974). Abolitionists' disillusion with the compromising stand taken by America's churches is set forth insightfully in John R. McKivigan, *The War against Proslavery Religion: Abolitionism and the Northern Churches, 1830–1865* (1984). For the conflict between conscience and "positive law" as judges struggled with issues related to slavery, see the brilliant study by Robert M. Cover, *Justice Accused: Antislavery and the Judicial Process* (1975).

For the politics of antislavery, see Richard H. Sewell, *Ballots for Freedom* (1976). For slavery and theories of constitutional law, see William M. Wiecek, *The Sources of Antislavery Constitutionalism in America, 1760–1848* (1977). Benjamin Quarles, *Black Abolitionists* (1969), is a pioneering study of a subject long neglected by historians. For the important role played by black American abolitionists who toured and lectured in Britain, see R. J. M. Blackett, *Building an Antislavery Wall: Black Americans in the Atlantic Abolitionist Movement, 1830–1860* (1983). The dilemma of black abolitionists is also illuminated by Jane H. Pease and William H. Pease, *They Who Would Be Free: Blacks' Search for Freedom, 1830–1861* (1974). For Frederick Douglass, the preeminent black leader of the nineteenth century, the best biography is William McFeely, *Frederick Douglass* (1991).

15

Politics

Cohesion and Division
1820–1840

⤳

THE GENERATION of Americans who came to maturity in the early nineteenth century carried a unique burden. As "children of the Founding Fathers," they could not achieve immortal fame by winning independence from British tyranny. Instead their assigned mission was vigilant preservation—the preservation of what the famous lawyer Rufus Choate called the "beautiful house of our fathers" against divisive ambition, corruption, sectional jealousy, and arbitrary power.

For a time it seemed that Liberty and Union could be preserved by patriotic rhetoric honoring hallowed figures like Thomas Jefferson and John Adams (who both died on July 4, 1826, exactly fifty years after the adoption of the Declaration of Independence), and by the election of presidents from the so-called Virginia Dynasty. The last in that succession, James Monroe, still appeared in public dressed in his Revolutionary War uniform. After the War of 1812, the collapse of the Federalist party fostered the illusion of an Era of Good Feelings in which a single national party would guarantee republican simplicity, order, and self-restraint. In his second inaugural address in 1821, President Monroe invoked the image of harmony. The American people, he affirmed, constituted "one great family with a common interest." Four years later President John Quincy Adams, also a Republican, voiced similar sentiments and happily observed that "the baneful weed of party strife" had been uprooted. Most Americans still associated political parties with the self-serving, aristocratic factions that had dominated British politics. In a republican nation, as in a republican family, no room could be allowed for selfish alliances representing separate interests.

This ideal of family unity was, however, far removed from social and economic realities. In chapter 12 we have already considered the revolutionary expansion and triumph of a market economy in the decades following the War of 1812. The sudden burgeoning of cities and towns, the construction of vast new transportation networks, the rise of manufacturing and the influx of tens of thousands of immigrants, the collapse of local markets and traditional patterns of self-sufficiency, the alarming growth in economic inequalities—all these transformations signaled an abrupt departure from the world of the Founders. Precisely because Americans were so fearful of betraying their Revolutionary and republican heritage, politicians often disguised innovation behind rhetorical appeals to preserve or return to the genuine spirit of the Founders.

This mythology of *continuity* obscured the sheer novelty of the two-party political system that emerged from the turmoil of the 1820s, a decade characterized by increasing sectional tension, class conflict, and democratization of politics. Between 1819 and 1821 Congress faced the most dangerous crisis it had yet experienced when northern and southern representatives deadlocked over the admission of Missouri as a new slave state. Simultaneously, the financial panic of 1819, followed by a severe depression, aroused widespread hostility toward banking corporations and other groups that had used political influence to gain economic privilege. Economic recovery and expansion only intensified demands for equality of opportunity, as various competing classes, localities, and social groups became increasingly aware of the unequal effects of government policies concerning tariffs, banking and currency, and public land sales. By the mid-1820s it was becoming painfully clear that widening opportunities for some Americans meant narrowing opportunities for others. Ironically, the post-Revolutionary generation finally found a way of containing the many factions that had arisen by institutionalizing division in the form of political parties.

In the national election of 1824 candidates still represented factions of a single Republican (or Democratic Republican) party. By 1828 a new Democratic party had emerged under the leadership of Andrew Jackson; their opponents, whom the Democrats tried to identify with the old, discredited Federalists, were first called National Republicans and then in the early 1830s adopted the name Whigs. The Democrats and their National Republican or Whig opponents were national coalitions of sectional, class, economic, ethnic, and religious interests, held together by compromise and cooperation. To maximize votes, politicians had to find ways of arousing apathetic citizens on more than immediate local issues. The basic political style that emerged in antebellum America—in the South and West as well as in the North—centered on the portrayal of some self-serving, privileged interest that had secretly consolidated power and had begun to shut off from others equal access to the rewards of national growth. In an era of relative security from foreign dangers, politicians continued to portray their opponents as heirs of the British and Tories who were seeking to undermine American liberties and betray the heritage of the Founders. From the early 1830s to the early 1850s, the two-party system helped preserve national cohesion. The Democrats and Whigs survived as national coalitions as long as they drew significant support from *both* the slaveholding and nonslaveholding states. But when black slavery, the institution that most flagrantly subverted liberty and opportunity, was seriously questioned in a national forum, the unifying force of the parties was destroyed.

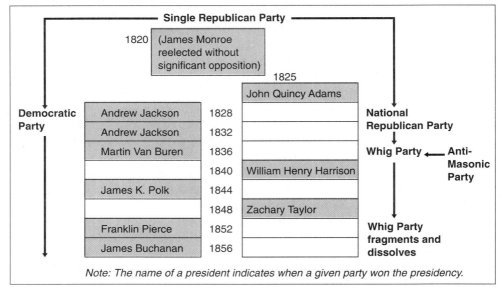

Note: The name of a president indicates when a given party won the presidency.

The Two-Party System

"A Fire Bell in the Night": The Missouri Compromise

From the time of the Continental Congress, American leaders had recognized that a serious dispute over slavery could jeopardize their bold experiment in self-government. Beginning with the Constitutional Convention, the entire structure of national politics had been designed to prevent any faction from directly threatening southern slaveholders and thereby subverting common national interests. It is therefore not surprising that before 1819 slavery never became a central issue in national politics. But it was an issue that sat like an unactivated bomb in the minds of the foremost political leaders.

The agreement to keep the bomb unactivated rested on two unwritten understandings: that the North would recognize the property rights of southern slaveholders, and that the South would recognize slavery as an evil that should be discouraged and eventually abolished whenever it became safe and practicable to do so. Changing circumstances, including the shifting balance of sectional power, forced repeated challenges to these understandings. The challenges took the form of clashes in Congress, during which representatives from the Lower South threatened to dissolve the Union and even hinted at the possibility of civil war. On each occasion the resulting compromise strongly favored the South. This political process demonstrated the Americans' remarkable ability to make pragmatic adjustments in the interest of national stability. Yet these successful compromises depended on the dangerous assumption that southern threats of disunion would always be met by northern concessions.

The militancy of the Lower South's congressional leaders was based on a realistic estimate of the future. For a time the North could afford to make concessions because slavery seemed to endanger no vital northern interests. But after 1815 humanitarian causes had increasing appeal in the North, and more and more northerners expressed moral and patriotic misgivings over the westward expansion of slavery. Sooner or later, as southerners like John Randolph predicted, these northern antislavery sentiments would become strong enough to create new sectional parties. Even by 1820, as a result of rapid population growth in the North, the major slaveholding states held only 42 percent of the seats in the House of Representatives. Only the Senate could provide a firm defense against potential northern encroachments, and the key to the Senate was new slave states. In the Senate, following the admission of Mississippi and Alabama (1817, 1819), eleven slave states balanced eleven free states.

Sectional Conflict The Missouri crisis erupted in February 1819, when the House was considering a bill that would enable the people of Missouri to draft a constitution and be admitted as a slave state. Slaves constituted nearly one-sixth of the territory's population. James Tallmadge, Jr., a New York Jeffersonian Republican, offered an amendment that prohibited the further introduction of slaves into Missouri and provided for the emancipation, at age twenty-five, of all children of slaves born after Missouri's admission as a state. During the prolonged and often violent debate, Senator Jonathan Roberts of Pennsylvania urged his colleagues not to admit Missouri "with her features marred as if the fingers of Lucifer had been drawn across them." Nathaniel Macon of North Carolina responded that restricting slavery necessarily implies eventual emancipation and even racial equality: "Are you willing to have black members of Congress? . . . There is no place for free blacks in the United States." The House approved Tallmadge's amendment by an ominously sectional vote. The Senate, after equally violent debates, passed a Missouri statehood bill without any restrictions on slavery. The issue seemed hopelessly deadlocked.

Virginia now took the lead in militancy, trying to arouse a generally apathetic South to a common peril. "This momentous question," Jefferson announced from Monticello, where he had retired, "like a fire bell in the night, awakened and filled me with terror." Along with Madison and other Virginia statesmen, Jefferson was convinced that the attempt to exclude slavery from Missouri was part of a Federalist conspiracy to create a sectional party and destroy the Union.

The Missouri crisis was aggravated by a sense that understandings had been broken, veils torn off, and true and threatening motives exposed. The congressional debates rekindled the most divisive issues that supposedly had been settled in the Constitutional Convention, and thus raised the hypothetical question of disunion. This reenactment of 1787 was underscored by the prominence in the congressional debates of two of the Constitutional Convention's surviving antagonists—Charles Pinckney of South Carolina, who now insisted that Congress had no power to exclude slavery from even the unsettled territories; and Rufus King of New York, the alleged leader of the Federalist conspiracy, who now announced that any laws upholding slavery were "absolutely void, because [they are] contrary to the law of nature, which is the law of God."

It was a new generation of northerners, however, who had to reaffirm or reject the kind of compromises over slavery that had created the original Union. Like the Founders, the northern majority in Congress could do nothing about slavery in the existing states. But there had been an understood national policy, these northerners believed, enshrined in the Northwest Ordinance, committing the government to restrict slavery in every feasible way. This understanding had seemingly been confirmed by southern statements that slavery was an evil inherited from the past. The North had accepted the original slave states' expectations that migrating slaveholders would not be barred from bringing their most valuable property—their slaves—into the territories south of the Ohio River and east of the Mississippi River. But Missouri occupied the same latitudes as Illinois, Indiana, and Ohio (as well as Kentucky and Virginia). To allow slavery to become legally entrenched in Missouri might thus encourage its spread throughout the entire West, harming free labor and industry. Southerners had long argued, however illogically, that if slavery were diffused over a large geographical area, it would weaken as an institution, and the likelihood of slave uprisings would diminish. In 1820 Daniel Raymond, a prominent northern political economist, gave the obvious reply: "Diffusion is about as effectual a remedy for slavery as it would be for the smallpox, or the plague."

Southerners were particularly alarmed by the argument of some northern congressmen that the constitutional guarantee to every state of "a republican form of government" meant that Missouri could not be admitted as a slave state. The argument implied that Virginia and other southern states fell short of having "a republican form of government" and therefore would not be admissible to a new Union. If this argument prevailed, the southern states would be reduced to a second-class status. If they accepted the northern definition of a republican form of government, they had no choice but to take steps toward abolishing slavery or to face, like colonies, the punitive measures of an imperial authority.

The Terms of Compromise

Henry Clay, the Speaker of the House of Representatives, exerted all the powers of his office and of his magnetic personality in order finally to achieve a compromise. A small minority of northern congressmen agreed to drop the antislavery provision for Missouri, while a small minority of southerners agreed that slavery should be excluded from the remaining and unsettled portions of the Louisiana Purchase north of latitude 36°30', the same latitude as the southern border of Missouri. In effect, this measure limited any further expansion of slavery within the Louisiana Purchase to Arkansas and what would later become Oklahoma. Given the sectional balance of power, the swing vote favoring these concessions was sufficient to carry the compromise. The way was now opened for admitting Maine as a free state, since the Senate had refused to accept Maine's statehood until the House had abandoned efforts to restrict slavery in Missouri.

The press and legislatures of the North generally interpreted the Missouri Compromise as a victory for the South. A new hope arose that public pressure

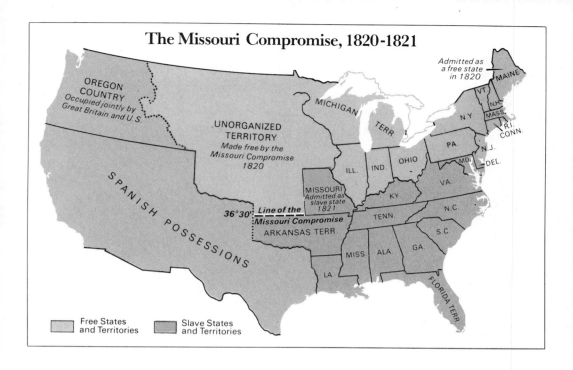

The Missouri Compromise, 1820-1821

OREGON COUNTRY
Occupied jointly by Great Britain and U.S.

MICHIGAN

Admitted as a free state in 1820
MAINE

VT

N.H.

N.Y.

MASS.

R.I.

CONN.

UNORGANIZED TERRITORY
Made free by the Missouri Compromise 1820

SPANISH POSSESSIONS

36°30' Line of the Missouri Compromise

ARKANSAS TERR.

MISSOURI
Admitted as slave state 1821

TERR.

PA.

N.J.

ILL. IND. OHIO

MD.

DEL.

VA.

KY

TENN.

N.C.

S.C.

MISS. ALA. GA.

LA

FLORIDA TERR.

Free States and Territories
Slave States and Territories

could force Missouri to adopt a constitution providing for gradual emancipation. But the defiant Missourians drafted a constitution that prohibited the state legislature from emancipating slaves without the consent of their owners and that barred free blacks and mulattoes from entering the state. Since free blacks had been recognized as citizens by some of the eastern states, this second provision violated the constitutional guarantee that "the citizens of each State shall be entitled to all privileges and immunities of citizens in the several States." Northern congressmen now stood firm in rejecting the Missouri constitution and, in effect, the entire compromise. Eventually, in 1821, Clay's skillful manipulation of committees produced a second compromise prohibiting Missouri from discriminating against the citizens of other states—an abstract resolution that still left citizenship undefined. The country applauded Clay for saving the Union.

But the Union would never be the same. In southern eyes the uninhibited debates on slavery had opened a Pandora's box of dangers. The free blacks of Washington had packed the galleries of the House and had listened intently to antislavery speeches. In 1822, during the trial of the conspirators associated with Denmark Vesey, the free black leader of a planned racial insurrection in South Carolina, a Charleston slave testified that Vesey had shown him an antislavery speech delivered by Rufus King, "the black man's friend." The link between the Missouri debates and a sizable slave conspiracy stunned South Carolina, confirming its worst fears. The cumulative effect was twofold: to unite all whites in the suppression of dangerous discussion, and to strengthen the hand of states' rights extremists and of the defenders of slavery as a positive good.

Henry Clay (1777–1782)
Henry Clay's campaign posters stressed national economic growth and public welfare, goals to be directly fostered by protective tariffs and a national bank.

The End of Republican Unity

The Missouri crisis alerted politicians to the perils of sectional division. The North's unexpected outrage over the admission of a new slave state convinced many southerners that they needed to cultivate rising northern leaders. One such leader was Martin Van Buren, whose faction of young "Bucktails" had captured control of the New York Republican party by 1820. Van Buren, whose shrewdness, ambition, and personal charm made up for his lack of family prestige and connections, viewed the clamor over slavery as evidence of a dangerous breakdown in party loyalty. New national organizations were needed that could prevent sectional conflict. Party distinctions, he said, were infinitely safer than geographical ones. If party distinctions were suppressed, their place would inevitably be taken by "geographical differences founded on local instincts or what is worse, prejudices between free and slaveholding states."

The Van Buren faction also stated a new conception of political parties as agencies of the people. When the Bucktails were attacked by their opponents as the Albany Regency, a label suggesting the oppressive British regency of the Prince of Wales (1811–20) that had governed in place of the insane George III, Van Buren's faction replied with a strong defense of political parties—a defense that later Democrats and Whigs would echo. In America, Van Buren's followers claimed, political parties drew their power from the people instead of from kings or aristocratic cliques; therefore the American people could safely extend their loyalty to parties. American parties, far from being self-serving, required a selfless submission to the will of the organization. This respect for party discipline was later summed up by a prominent Whig who declared that he "would vote for a dog, if he was the candidate of my party." In theory, the excesses of one party would inevitably be exposed by the other party, and public opinion would decide between them. Responsiveness to the people would thus be ensured as each party strove to win the largest possible mandate from the people.

Van Buren's appeal for disciplined national parties came at the right moment. As early as 1821 it was evident that the Virginia Dynasty of presidents would end in 1825 with Monroe's second term. The Republicans, no longer confronted by Federalist opponents, were splitting into personal and sectional factions. One group responded to the vibrant nationalism of Henry Clay's so-called American System—a policy for direct government encouragement of economic expansion by such means as protective tariffs, a national bank, and federal aid for internal improvements. But other "Old Republicans," including Van Buren, viewed government intervention in the economy in terms of the old "country opposition" ideology—as a revival of the kinds of alliances between political power and special privilege that had corrupted Britain. By the early 1820s many Americans, especially in the South and West, had ample grounds for fearing that a northeastern business elite would gain economic control of the nation's banks and system of credit.

The Election of 1824   Monroe's second administration was dominated by political maneuvering to determine who would be his successor. Three of the leading contenders—William H. Crawford, John Quincy Adams, and John C. Calhoun—were nationally distinguished members of Monroe's cabinet. A Georgian born in Virginia, Crawford was secretary of the treasury during several administrations and had won prestige as America's minister to France during the War of 1812. He was an advocate of states' rights and limited federal power, was supported by the aged Thomas Jefferson and other influential Virginians, and would be heavily favored in any congressional party caucus. Van Buren led the Crawford forces in Congress. But the skeleton congressional caucus that nominated Crawford carried little weight, and an incapacitating illness further diminished his chances.

The other leading candidates bypassed the established procedure of nomination by congressional party caucus and sought support from state legislatures. Three of the remaining aspirants were closely associated with the economic nationalism that had alienated the Old Republicans. John Quincy Adams, the secretary of state and the nation's most experienced diplomat, could easily expect solid support from his native New England but would always be aloof from the rough-and-tumble campaigning of the South and West. John C. Calhoun, the secretary of war, had little support outside his own state, South Carolina. A graduate of Yale and a product of America's first small law school, Calhoun was one of the few political leaders of his time who could be described as an intellectual. He withdrew from the presidential race before the election, assuming that his almost certain choice as vice-president would help him win the highest office in 1828. Henry Clay, the popular "Harry of the West," had won national prestige as a parliamentarian and engineer of compromise in the House of Representatives.

The fifth candidate, Andrew Jackson, entered the contest unexpectedly and at a later stage. Unlike the other candidates, he had taken no clear stand on the controversial issues of the day, and his brief terms in the House and Senate had been undistinguished. Jackson's national fame arose from his victory over the British at the Battle of New Orleans in the War of 1812, as well as from his unswerving efforts to clear the West of Indians, thus promising unlimited opportunities for white Americans. But "Old Hickory," as Jackson was widely known, was a good bit more than a military hero and an Indian fighter. Born on the Carolina frontier and orphaned at age fourteen, Jackson had studied law and had finally emigrated to Nashville, Tennessee, where he became attached by marriage and business connections to the local network of leading families. Far from remaining aloof from the rising market economy, he prospered as an attorney, land speculator, and planter, and became the master of more than one hundred slaves. The Tennessee leaders who originally promoted Jackson for the presidency did not take his candidacy seriously, hoping only to use his popularity as a military hero for their own local purposes. But in 1823 Jackson's backers were astonished when the movement caught fire in Pennsylvania and other states. Old Hickory turned out to be an astute politician who perfectly gauged the national temper and who, once launched on the road to the presidency, skillfully managed his own campaign.

Jackson won a plurality of both the popular and the electoral votes in the election of 1824, and therefore he could legitimately claim to be the choice of the people. But because no candidate had won an electoral majority, the responsibility of electing a president fell to the House of Representatives. It had been expected that if no candidate should win the electoral majority, the House would elect Clay. But despite his appeal in Kentucky and other western states, Clay had run fourth in electoral votes and was therefore excluded by the Twelfth Amendment from further consideration. Clay threw his decisive support behind Adams, who was elected president and who soon appointed Clay secretary of state. This so-called corrupt bargain deeply embittered Calhoun, who, although he became vice-president, was already beginning to defect from his former colleagues' economic nationalism. It also infuriated Jackson, who almost immediately launched a campaign to unseat Adams in 1828.

J. Q. Adams (1767–1848)
*John Quincy Adams personified
the intellectual as statesman. A
man of learning and of wide
diplomatic experience, he was
more at home in the courts and
capitals of Europe than in the
caucuses and public forums of
American politics.*

**John Quincy Adams
as President**

This final collapse of Republican unity proved to be a
disaster for Adams's presidency. Adams inaugurated his
administration by proposing a sweeping program of
federal support for internal improvements, science, education, and the arts. "The
great object of the institution of civil government," Adams told Congress, "is the
improvement of the condition of those who are parties to the social compact....Roads and canals, by multiplying and facilitating the communications
and intercourse between distant regions and multitudes of men, are among the
most important means of improvement. But moral, political, intellectual
improvement are duties assigned by the author of Our Existence to social no less
than to individual man." Adams hoped that Congress would subsidize western
explorations and an astronomical observatory. He soon discovered, however,
that he lacked the mandate and the power for even the simple tasks of government. One of the most intelligent and farseeing presidents, Adams was also one of
the least successful, in part because he had no taste for the kind of political
maneuvering needed to build a base of support. Unfairly accused of being a
monarchist with an arrogant contempt for the people, he had the misfortune of
inheriting the presidency when it had fallen into decay. His own inexperience
with the realities of American political life helped to make him the unmourned
victim, in 1828, of the first modern presidential contest.

Jackson's Rise to Power

Andrew Jackson, the leader of the rising Democratic coalition, precisely fitted the need for a popular national political leader. His stately bearing and natural dignity befitted one of "nature's noblemen," someone who had risen to greatness without benefit of family connections, formal education, or subservience to any faction. Jackson's promoters spread the romantic mythology and stimulated voter activism by every conceivable means: ballads, placards, barbecues, liberty pole raisings, local committees, and militia companies marching in torchlit parades. In contrast to the office-grubbing politicians and to the coldly dignified, highly cultivated John Quincy Adams, here was a frontiersman, a truly self-made man, a soldier of iron will who personified the will of the people, a man without disguises or pretension who moved decisively in the light of simple moral truths. The Jackson image, in short, was an image of reassuring stability in the face of bewildering social and economic change.

Jackson also fitted the need for a leader who understood the new meaning of party politics. Against the Adams-Clay alliance, he molded a coalition that included among other groups the followers of Calhoun (who became his running mate in 1828), Virginia's Old Republicans, influential westerners who had become disillusioned with Clay, former Federalists who had lost office in New Jersey, and Van Buren's powerful Albany Regency. This new Democratic party appealed to many urban workers and immigrants, to frontier expansionists and Indian haters, to many southern planters, and to various northeastern editors, bankers, and manufacturers who built local Democratic machines as the means of gaining or preserving power.

The "Tariff of Abominations" Looking ahead to the election of 1828, Jackson's state organizers bypassed the local ruling gentry and concentrated for the first time on mobilizing the necessary popular vote to capture the full electoral vote of critical states. Because the new coalition contained Pennsylvanians who clamored for higher tariffs and South Carolinians who detested tariffs, keeping unity required delicate manipulation. In 1828 Jackson's leaders in Congress helped to pass the so-called Tariff of Abominations, an opportunistic bill that made arbitrary concessions to various groups that were demanding protection against foreign competition. These leaders assumed that southern support for Jackson was secure, that the new duties on raw materials would win votes from northern and western protectionists, and that the most objectionable provisions could be blamed on the Adams administration. The subsequent outrage in the South suggested that Jackson as president could no longer get by with vague statements favoring a "judicious" tariff. Yet southerners knew that a Jackson-Calhoun alliance was far more promising than the economic nationalism of Adams and Clay, who were now known as National Republicans.

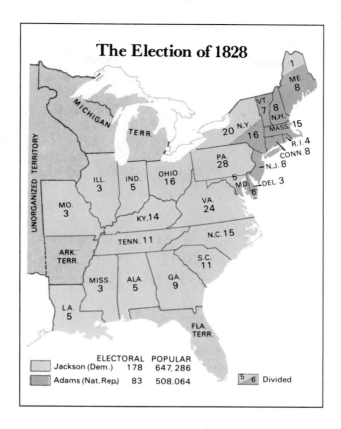

The Election of 1828

ELECTORAL	POPULAR
Jackson (Dem.) 178	647,286
Adams (Nat. Rep.) 83	508,064

5 6 Divided

The Election of 1828   In a general sense the election of 1828 affirmed the people's rejection of policies that seemed to encourage special privileges for the business classes as a result of the government's direct involvement in the market economy. Yet the Jacksonian Democrats, for all their talk of liberty and equality, never questioned the privilege of owning slaves and counting three-fifths of the slave population for purposes of representation. In the South, Jackson's 200,000 supporters, accounting for 73 percent of that section's vote, gave him 105 electoral votes; in the North, where he won only slightly more than half the popular vote, his 400,000 supporters gave him only 73 electoral votes. The election also proved the effectiveness of campaign organization and of the promotional techniques that Jackson's managers, particularly Van Buren, had perfected.

Once in power the Democrats soon adopted two instruments that solidified popular support for party rule. The first was a system of patronage, called the spoils system, that continued practices begun during previous administrations and tried to give them legitimacy. Jackson ardently defended the theory that most

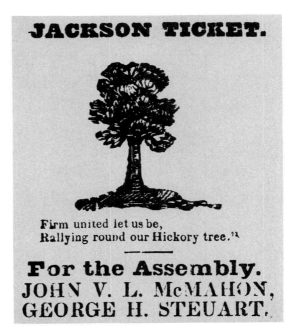

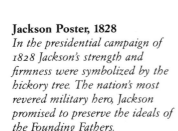

Jackson Poster, 1828
In the presidential campaign of 1828 Jackson's strength and firmness were symbolized by the hickory tree. The nation's most revered military hero, Jackson promised to preserve the ideals of the Founding Fathers.

public offices required no special abilities or experience, that they should frequently rotate among loyal deserving party workers, and that party rule should prevent the establishment of a permanent and parasitic class of civil servants. In fact, however, Jackson actually removed no more than one-fifth of the surviving federal officeholders.

The second mechanism was the national party convention. This, like various other Jacksonian measures, had earlier been initiated by anti-Jackson forces. As an alternative to nomination by legislative caucus, the "convention" suggested by its very name a return to fundamental law—to the direct voice of the people assembled in a constitution-making body. Although party conventions could do no more than frame partisan platforms and nominate partisan candidates, they pretended to represent the true interests of the people. In theory, since they drew representatives from a broad spectrum of society, they were more democratic than legislative caucuses. In practice, they were more subject to manipulation by political machines. But like the partisan spoils system, the party convention symbolized the central appeal of Jackson's party. It promised to break the rigid crust of privilege and eliminate all institutional barriers to individual opportunity. It also provided the assurance of solidarity with a party headed by a man of the people, a man who magnified the idealized self-image of millions of Americans.

Certain principles and aspirations distinguished the Jacksonian Democrats from their National Republican (and later Whig) opponents. Jackson had long given voice to the West's demand for territorial expansion as a way to ensure economic opportunity. As the first westerner elected to the presidency, he symbolized a geographical shift of political power. Of course, not all westerners

Andrew Jackson (1767–1845)
Sixty-two years old when he became president, Andrew Jackson was one of the strongest and most vigorous chief executives in American history. Despite his dedication to states' rights, he expanded the power of the presidency and affirmed the supremacy of the federal union.

supported Jackson. Those who understood that western economic expansion depended on access to eastern markets and on investment capital from the East and Europe favored federal aid for internal improvements, a program that Henry Clay sponsored. But although Jackson vetoed the Maysville Road Bill (which would have authorized funds to build a road in Kentucky), suggesting that federal support for internal improvements was unconstitutional, he did not lose the majority of western voters. Many westerners had come to view federally supported internal improvements as sources of waste and corruption. Others learned that, despite Jackson's pronouncements, federal support for roads and canals continued to pour in from a Congress that was less concerned with constitutional theory than with constituents' needs. On the whole, the West cheered for Jackson because it had come to see itself as the home of the values that Jackson fought for: a rural society of independent farmers, committed to individual enterprise and local self-determination.

To say that Jacksonian Democrats were advocates of minimal government and laissez-faire policies is accurate but insufficient.* They knew that on the local

---

*Laissez-faire means the government's refusal to intervene in economic matters beyond the minimum needed to maintain peace and property rights.

and state levels, economic opportunity hinged on political power. And Jackson was the most forceful and aggressive president since Washington. During the preceding administrations the chief executive's powers had been siphoned off by cabinet rivals and a jealous Congress. With the aid of party discipline, Jackson soon exerted his dominance over Congress by an unprecedented use of vetoes and pocket vetoes (the refusal to sign a bill during the last ten days of a congressional session). Except for Van Buren, whom he chose as secretary of state, Jackson treated his cabinet in the manner of the army's commander in chief. Unlike his predecessors, Jackson escaped the coercion of disloyal and powerful cabinet members by relying on a group of informal advisers, the so-called Kitchen Cabinet, who could be trusted or dismissed at will.

The Threat of National Division: Tariffs, Nullification, and the Gag Rule

Protective Tariffs   Tariffs and fiscal policy were obvious testing grounds for defining the federal government's role in national economic life. The economy was still more regional than national, and the national government had few functions. The critical issues of the day therefore grew out of the commitment to protective tariffs and a national bank that had resulted from the War of 1812. The Middle Atlantic states, which were the most vulnerable to competition from European manufactured goods, had long been the political stronghold of protectionism. During the 1820s, as New England's economy became increasingly dependent on the production of wool and on textile manufacturing, Daniel Webster and other New England leaders abandoned their traditional defense of free trade and portrayed protective tariffs as the key to economic growth and individual opportunity. Simultaneously, however, the Lower South became increasingly hostile to tariffs that threatened to raise the price of manufactured goods and to curtail foreign markets for rice and cotton exports. For a time the Democrats successfully arranged compromises among the various interests and regions that were represented in the party. But in 1832 Congress passed a tariff bill that was unresponsive to the demands of the Lower South. South Carolina thereupon defied federal authority and sought to arouse the rest of the slaveholding South to the dangers of being victimized economically by the federal government. The tariff, South Carolina's state legislature charged, was essentially "intended for the protection of domestic manufactures, and the giving of bounties to classes and individuals engaged in particular employments, at the expense and to the injury and oppression of other classes and individuals," namely, the agricultural producers of the South. South Carolinians believed that acceptance of this dependence would reduce their state to the status of a colony and deprive it of any effective protection against antislavery ideas. "[W]e will not submit to the application of force, on the part of the Federal Government," the legislature warned, "to reduce this State to obedience." Such an attempt at coercion, it announced, would be considered "inconsistent with the longer continuance of South Carolina in the Union."

South Carolina's sudden threat of disunion severely tested the American political system, and it involved issues that went far beyond the protective tariff. In no other state had a planter elite succeeded so well in commanding the allegiance of small farmers, both slaveholding and nonslaveholding, and in preventing the development of an effective two-party system. Despite continuing conflicts between the coastal and upcountry regions, there were few checks on states' rights extremists who were able to exploit fears of a slave uprising and anger over persisting agricultural depression, high consumer prices, and sagging prices for rice and cotton in foreign markets.

Moreover, of all the southern states South Carolina had the closest historical, geographical, and cultural ties with the British West Indies. Like those British colonies, South Carolina had a dense concentration of slaves, and its merchants and plantation owners had continued to import African slaves until 1808, when the Atlantic slave trade was forbidden by federal law. South Carolinians were acutely aware that in Britain a seemingly harmless movement to end the slave trade had been transformed, by 1823, into a crusade for slave emancipation. And they knew that the West Indians, although still a powerful faction in Parliament, had found no way of countering commercial policies that had hastened their economic decline. The lesson was clear. The West Indian colonies had once been far richer and more valued than Canada or New England. But at Christmas 1831 a massive slave revolt had broken out in Jamaica. By 1832 the West Indians' representatives in England were beginning to accept the inevitability of slave emancipation even though they were convinced this would lead to certain economic ruin.

Theory of Nullification

South Carolina's leaders believed that their state could escape a similar fate only by reasserting state sovereignty and insisting on the strict limitation of national power. The tariff issue made an ideal testing ground for the defense of slavery without risking the explosive effects of debating the morality of slaveholding. Because the power to tax and regulate trade could also be used to undermine slavery, the two questions had been linked in the Constitutional Convention of 1787 and in the Missouri debates. Conversely, a state's power to nullify a tariff would be a guarantee not only against economic exploitation but also against direct or indirect interference with slavery. Calhoun anonymously wrote the South Carolina *Exposition* on behalf of that state, refining the theoretical arguments that were being put forward by South Carolina's most militant leaders. According to Calhoun, in any dispute between federal and state interests the ultimate appeal must be directed to a state convention—the same body that had originally enabled the state to ratify the Constitution. Otherwise, a national majority, controlling the federal courts as well as Congress, would have unlimited power. The tyranny of the majority could be curbed only if each state retained the

John C. Calhoun (1782–1850)
Although Calhoun never realized his lifelong ambition to become president, he served in the House of Representatives, in the Senate, as secretary of war, secretary of state, and vice-president of the United States. An ardent nationalist in his youth, he became the foremost defender of southern slavery and states' rights.

right to either accept or nullify, within its own jurisdiction, the national majority's decisions. Calhoun carefully distinguished nullification from secession. He looked for means by which states might exercise an authentic, although limited, sovereignty while remaining within the Union.

The nullification controversy was complicated by the shifting pressures of state, sectional, and national politics. Calhoun, the vice-president, hoped to succeed Jackson as president, and many South Carolinians still believed they could achieve their goals through the Democratic party. Calhoun did not disclose his authorship of the *Exposition* until 1831, when he had split with Jackson over various personal and political issues. When Jackson purged Calhoun's followers from his cabinet and administration, Van Buren became in effect the president's chosen successor and the nation's vice-president during Jackson's second term. Nevertheless Calhoun continued to aspire to the presidency. He believed that nullification would be a means of satisfying South Carolina's "fire-eater" extremists and of establishing the Union on a more secure basis, while still preserving his own national following.

By 1832, however, South Carolina had become increasingly isolated from the rest of the South and had also failed to unite the West against an alleged northeastern conspiracy to discourage western settlement. Although many southerners detested protective tariffs and maintained that states had a right to secede from the Union, southern legislatures turned a stony face to nullification. As a result there was no regional convention of southern delegates that might have moderated South Carolina's suicidal course by reinforcing the hand of the South

Carolina unionists who risked their lives and reputations in a violent and losing struggle with the extremists. In the fall of 1832 South Carolina held a state convention that directly challenged federal authority by making it unlawful after February 1, 1833, to collect tariff duties within the state.

South Carolina chose the wrong president to test. Andrew Jackson was a wealthy slaveholder, but he was also a shrewd politician. Although his maturing views on tariffs and internal improvements were close to those of the South Carolina elite, he had fought for the military supremacy of the United States, crushing British and Indian armies; he had hanged English meddlers in Spanish Florida; and he had ordered the execution of an unruly teen-age soldier. He was probably the toughest of America's presidents. When South Carolina nullified the tariff of 1832, the old general privately threatened to lead an invasion of the state and have Calhoun hanged. In a public proclamation to the people of South Carolina, Jackson warned: "To say that any state may at pleasure secede from the Union is to say that the United States are not a nation, because it would be a solecism to contend that any part of a nation might dissolve its connection with the other parts, to their injury or ruin, without committing any offense. . . . Disunion by armed force is *treason.*" Jackson sent reinforcements to the federal forts in Charleston harbor but publicly sought to avoid armed conflict by relying on civilian revenue agents to enforce the law and by warning that armed resistance would be punished as treason.

As in 1820, the crisis ended in a compromise that failed to resolve fundamental conflicts of interest and ideology. In an attempt to head off civil war, Henry Clay, assisted by Calhoun, secured the passage of a compromise bill that would gradually reduce tariff duties over a period of nine years. But this measure was accompanied by a "force bill," reaffirming the president's authority to use the army and navy, when necessary, to enforce federal laws. South Carolina's fire-eaters continued to call for armed resistance; the governor himself recruited a volunteer army. Early in 1833, however, the state convention repealed its earlier nullification of the tariff and, to save face, nullified the force bill. Jackson ignored this defiant gesture. He had already branded as unlawful and unconstitutional the claim that any state could annul the laws of the United States. In effect he had told rebellious states that secession was their only escape, and that secession would be met with armed force.

"Gag Rules"

The compromise did not relieve South Carolina's suspicions and anxieties. The nullification controversy had failed to provide the assurance of constitutional safeguards against a hostile national majority. Southern extremists demanded ironclad guarantees that would permanently bar the abolitionists' "incendiary publications" from the mails and prevent Congress from receiving petitions calling for the abolition of slavery in the District of Columbia. In actuality, the Democratic party fulfilled these objectives in a less formal way. The Jackson and Van Buren administrations, dependent on the large Democratic vote in the South, encouraged federal postmasters to stop abolitionist literature at its point of origin. Despite continuing protest from northern Whigs, northern Democrats also provided southern congressmen of both parties with enough votes to maintain "gag rules" from 1836 to 1844, a procedure that automatically tabled abolitionist petitions in Congress and helped prevent explosive debates on the subject of slavery. Many northerners were outraged by these infringements on civil and political liberties. But South Carolinians were also dissatisfied with pragmatic mechanisms for security that depended on the continuing support of the national Democratic party. Without further constitutional protections, they feared that a shift in northern opinion might induce Congress to withdraw all federal sanction and protection of slavery.

The Bank War, the Panic of 1837, and Political Realignments

The Bank War   Meanwhile, President Jackson had extended his national popularity by declaring "war" on the Second Bank of the United States (BUS). Jackson had long harbored a mistrust of banks in general, especially of the BUS. Van Buren, Senator Thomas Hart Benton of Missouri, Amos Kendall of the Kitchen Cabinet, and other key presidential advisers shared these sentiments. To understand their "hard-money" position, it is important to realize that the national government issued no "paper money" like that in circulation today. Payment for goods and services might be in gold or silver coin (specie) or, more likely, in paper notes issued by private commercial banks. The value of this paper currency fluctuated greatly, which meant that wages or other payments might suddenly decline in purchasing power. The hard-money Democrats realized that large commercial transactions could not be carried on with specie. But they believed that the common people, including small businessmen as well as farmers and wage earners, should not be burdened with the risk of being cheated by a speculative currency. They also knew that a policy favoring the greater circulation of gold and silver coin, which seemed magically endowed with some fixed and "natural" value, would win votes for the party.

To a large degree, however, the nation's reserves and transfers of gold and silver were controlled by the BUS. The BUS performed many of the functions of a truly national bank. Its own notes could be exchanged for specie, and they were accepted by the government as legal payment for all debts to the United States. The BUS had large capital reserves, and it limited the issue of its own highly stable notes. It was therefore a creditor to the hundreds of state-chartered banks throughout the country. It also served as a clearinghouse and regulatory agency for their money, refusing to accept notes that were not backed by sufficient reserves of specie. By promoting monetary stability, the BUS helped to improve the public reputation of banks in general and eased the difficulties of long-distance transfers of goods and credit. Moreover, it mobilized a national reserve of capital on which other banks could draw. Consequently, most state banks favored congressional renewal of the BUS charter, which was scheduled to expire in 1836.

Opponents of the bank feared the concentration of so much economic power in a few hands and worried that the federal government had practically no control over the bank, although the government provided one-fifth of the bank's capital. The bank's critics complained that, even under the expert management of the bank's president, Nicholas Biddle, this partly public institution was far more oriented to the interests of its private investors than to the interests of the general public. Senator Daniel Webster, the main lobbyist for rechartering the BUS, not only was the director of the Boston branch but also relied heavily on Biddle for private loans and fees for legal and political services. To Jackson the BUS had become a "monster institution," unconstitutionally diverting public funds for private profit. The central issue, then, was how far the government should subsidize and become allied with private business interests in order to promote the regulated growth of a national market economy.

The famous "Bank War" erupted into open conflict in 1832, when Webster and Clay launched a legislative offensive, partly to prevent Jackson's reelection. They knew that they could win support from many Democrats for the passage of a bill rechartering the BUS. Therefore they were confident that the president could not veto the measure without fatally damaging his chances for reelection in the fall. But Jackson took up their challenge. In a masterful veto message he spelled out the principles that would be the basis for "Jacksonian democracy" and for populist politics in the decades to come. Jackson denounced the BUS as a privileged monopoly. He vowed to take a stand "against all new grants of monopolies and exclusive privileges, against any prostitution of our Government to the advancement of the few at the expense of the many." Jackson in no way favored equalizing wealth or otherwise removing distinctions derived from "natural and just advantages." He insisted that "equality of talents, of education, or of wealth cannot be produced by human institutions." But he believed that government should provide "equal protection, and, as heaven does its rains, shower its favors alike on the high and the low, the rich and the poor." The BUS, he declared, represented a flagrant example of government subsidy to the privileged—of laws that made "the rich richer and the potent more powerful." Jackson also warned of the dangerous provisions that allowed foreigners to buy BUS stock and thus to acquire influence over American policy. In defiance of the Supreme Court's decision in *McCulloch* v. *Maryland* (1819), the president argued that the BUS was unconstitutional.

Webster and other conservative leaders immediately cried that the president was trying "to stir up the poor against the rich." But the election of 1832 decisively vindicated Jackson's political shrewdness and bold leadership. Old Hickory would have won a sweeping victory even if the opposition votes had not been divided between Henry Clay, the National Republican candidate, and William Wirt, the reluctant leader of the Anti-Masons, a party based on the widespread fear that free institutions were endangered by the secret society of Freemasons.

Having been reelected, Jackson was confident that the supporters of the BUS could never override his veto. He vowed to pull out the fangs of the "monster institution" by removing all of the deposits placed in the bank by the federal government.

Many of the president's advisers opposed this aggressive and arguably illegal policy, since the BUS already seemed doomed. Jackson had to rid himself of two secretaries of the treasury before he found in Roger B. Taney a secretary who would carry out his will. The removal policy also raised new problems. According to Jackson's plan, federal funds would be dispersed among chosen state-chartered banks that were soon dubbed "pet" banks. For the policy to succeed, Jackson had to persuade the banking community that decentralization would not bring economic disaster. On the other hand, the BUS's president, Nicholas Biddle, needed to produce a minor financial panic to underscore the powerful role of the BUS in maintaining financial stability. Biddle could not exert his full financial powers, however, without adding to popular hostility to the bank. In the winter of 1832–33 Biddle instituted a tight-money policy, but the limitation on credit was not serious enough to shake Jackson's resolution. Jackson also gained political leverage through his careful choice of pet banks to which federal funds were to be transferred. Many bankers who had earlier hoped to keep clear of the political struggle were eager to receive interest-free federal funds that would enable them to expand their loans and other commercial operations. Jackson's victory was fairly complete by the spring of 1834. Two years later, when the charter of the BUS terminated, the United States was left without a central banking agency of any kind.

Jackson's Hard-Money Policy

Like many triumphs, the destruction of the BUS caught the victors in a web of problems. The Democrats claimed that by slaying the "monster," they had purged the nation of a moral evil. Yet the deposit of federal funds in pet banks encouraged the expansion of credit, and in the mid-1830s the nation reeled from the intoxication of a speculative boom. As the volume of bank notes soared, it became so easy to purchase federal land on credit that the value of land sales jumped nearly tenfold in four years. The General Land Office made so many sales in this period that the phrase "doing a land office business" became synonymous with reaping huge profits from speculation. The federal surplus grew—an unimaginable phenomenon for twentieth-century generations, who have known only federal deficits and mounting public debts. Some of the more obstinate Jacksonian advisers even bemoaned this surplus because there seemed to be no place to put the funds that would not corrupt the Republic. Whatever the administration did invited trouble. On the one hand, if it distributed funds to the states, it would feed the speculative boom by encouraging further construction of roads and canals and other kinds of "improvements." On the other hand, if it kept the funds in the pet banks, these banks clearly had to be regulated by the federal government: otherwise they too might feed inflation by issuing vast quantities of paper money based on the new reserves of federal funds they had received.

Slowly Jackson and his successor, Van Buren, who was elected in 1836, moved toward a policy of hard money. They tried to reduce or eliminate the circulation of small-denomination bank notes and to set a minimal requirement for the pet banks' specie reserves. In 1836 Jackson also issued an executive order, the so-called Specie Circular, requiring payment in specie for purchase of public land. The specie circular represented a direct federal effort to curb speculation and thus to control economic fluctuations. This controversial measure was a sign of the growing dominance of the antibank and hard-money factions in the Democratic party. The subsequent nomination and election of Van Buren strengthened the hand of those Democrats who found hostility to all banks politically effective.

The Panic of 1837 In 1837 a banking panic brought an abrupt end to the speculative boom. By 1839 a severe depression had developed that persisted to the mid-1840s. This painful downturn in investment, prices, and employment was primarily the product of a business cycle still tied to agriculture (mainly cotton) and related to British demand, British investment, and the international flow of silver. In many respects the American economy still resembled the economy of a colony or underdeveloped nation dependent on

Jackson over the Cliff
An anti-Democratic cartoon portrays Thomas Hart Benton—the Democratic senator from Missouri who favored gold and silver coinage to paper money and who led the fight in the Senate to "expunge" the Bank of the United States—encouraging Jackson to pursue the "Gold Humbug" even though this policy leads to disaster. Van Buren, meanwhile, has decided "to deviate a little." A "shin plaster" was a contemptuous term for small-denomination currency issued during the depression of 1837 when banks were suspending specie payment.

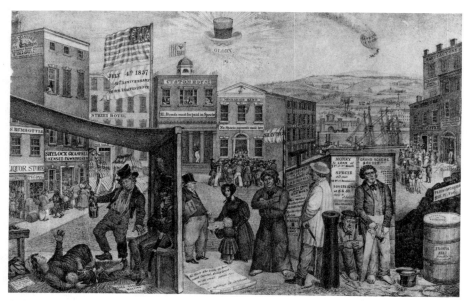

"The Times"

This complex cartoon portrays the allegedly disastrous results of the Democratic rule: the government's hard money policy leads to a run on the bank, which has suspended specie payments; the custom house is deserted; debtors are herded into the sheriff's office; beggars and unemployed artisans crowd the streets; scenes of drunkenness are linked with the unruliness of immigrants and Locofoco radicals.

foreign investment and on raw material exports. Hence the American economy was vulnerable to sudden contractions of British credit coupled with temporary drops in the British demand for cotton.

As bankruptcies multiplied, the business community blamed the widespread suffering on Jacksonian fiscal policies. These policies, they charged, had first fueled reckless expansion by destroying the BUS and then had suddenly limited credit by requiring specie for the purchase of public land. But as bankers and businessmen deserted the Democratic party, the dominant hard-money, laissez-faire faction argued that the economic collapse proved the folly of government partnership with even pet banks.

After three years of bitter Democratic-Whig struggle, President Van Buren finally achieved a "divorce of bank and state" with the passage of the Independent Treasury Act (1840). But this measure probably prolonged the depression. It locked federal funds into "independent" subtreasuries of the United States government that were insulated from the banking community, thereby depriving the banking system of reserves that might have encouraged loans and aided economic recovery.

The Democrats' Legacy

The ambiguity of the Democrats' program can be illuminated by pointing to two inconsistencies. First, their economic policies did little to aid the groups of farmers and artisans whom the Democrats claimed to represent. The political attacks on privilege may have strengthened an abstract commitment to equality, embodied in a new democratic ideology that built on older republican traditions. Yet the Democrats' ultimate beneficiaries were southern planters who were aided by Indian removal, lowered tariffs, and the suppression of antislavery literature and petitions. Moreover, the policy of economic laissez-faire seemed to offer the South assurances that the federal government would not interfere with the interstate movement of slave labor. By 1838 Calhoun and his followers returned to the Democratic party, which they had earlier left in protest against Jackson's authoritarian style. As it turned out, Calhoun's return paved the way for southern domination of the Democratic party in the two decades to come.

Second, the nation's banking system continued to grow into an integrated system, and the nation's economy continued to grow with serene disregard for the fluctuation of power between the Democrats and Whigs. Jackson's and Van Buren's attempts to withdraw the government from what they saw as a corrupting economy had little effect on the general trends of economic development.

Whigs and the Two-Party System

The Democrats controlled the White House for most of the thirty years following Jackson's 1828 victory. Between 1828 and 1856 their presidential nominees defeated every opposition candidate except William Henry Harrison in 1840 and Zachary Taylor in 1848, both of whom died in office. John Tyler, the vice-president who succeeded Harrison only a month after the latter's inauguration, soon returned to his original Virginia Democratic loyalties and principles. Millard Fillmore, Zachary Taylor's successor, was a genial but colorless Whig party hack who had begun his political career as an Anti-Mason and ended it by running for president in 1856 on the nativist and anti-Catholic "Know-Nothing" (or American) party ticket.

But the Democrats' dominance of the presidency is deceptive. By the late 1830s Whigs could match Democratic strength in most parts of the country. Although the South has commonly been pictured as a preserve for states' rights Democrats, Whigs predominated as the South's representatives in three out of five Congresses elected between 1832 and 1842. Whig strength was particularly evident on local, county, and state levels.

The viability of the two-party system depended essentially on vigorous local conflict—on the ability of a second party to challenge incumbents by convincing voters that a genuine alternative was available. To maintain party loyalties, leaders tried to exploit or manufacture conflicts, to dramatize party differences, and to be responsive enough to public demands to convince voters that their grievances

"King Andrew the First"
*The Whig image of Jackson as an
autocratic king, brandishing the
veto and trampling the
Constitution under foot.*

could be resolved through the ballot. The Whigs, like the Democrats, claimed to represent the interests of the *excluded* people against a privileged and self-serving "power." In 1844 the Whig journalist Calvin Colton characterized the Jackson administration as a "ONE MAN POWER" where "the long-established, simple, and democratic habits of the people, social and political, were superseded by the dictation of a Chief, and by the aristocratic assumptions of his menials." Since no incumbent party could possibly avoid patronage, the game of two-party politics consisted of proving that the incumbents were partial to their friends and thus insincere in claiming to serve the common good. In effect, both parties were torn between a desire to battle for the special interests of their permanent followers and a need to advocate bland, lofty goals that would attract the widest possible national following. From the mid-1830s to the early 1850s both Democrats and Whigs were remarkably successful in cultivating partisan loyalty: once voters had acquired a party identity, they persisted over the years in voting for Whig or Democratic candidates; state legislators and congressmen generally exhibited the same party loyalty in roll-call votes on divisive measures.

Webster, Clay, and Calhoun

Like the Democrats, the Whigs were a wholly new coalition. They were not, as the Democrats charged, simply Federalists in disguise—the Democrats themselves recruited an impressive number of ex-Federalist leaders. In Congress the Whigs first began to emerge in a legislative rebellion against Jackson's so-called Executive Usurpation. During the summer of 1832, Jackson's veto of the bill rechartering the BUS led to the temporary coalition of three of the most formidable senators in American history. All longed for the presidency. By 1832 they had won fame as godlike deliverers of majestic oratory that dazzled aspiring young men.

Daniel Webster, "a steam engine in trousers" in the words of the Englishman Sydney Smith, struck the keynote when he attacked "King Andrew" as a reincarnation of the French monarch Louis XIV, who had declared, "I am the State." A man of humble New Hampshire origins and aristocratic Boston tastes, Webster had risen in the legal profession by emulating and paying deference to New England's commercial elite. Many years after Webster's death, Henry Cabot Lodge voiced the common conclusion that his "moral character was not equal to his intellectual force." Webster was a heavy drinker, given to extravagant living and continual debt. His rich, booming voice and commanding physical presence could never quite convey the moral sincerity that most northeastern Whigs expected of their leaders. Yet Webster upheld their traditional mistrust of divisive parties and their traditional ideal of government by "disinterested gentlemen." He succeeded in blending this conservative tradition with a celebration of material and moral progress. As the agent of commercial and manufacturing interests in Massachusetts, he was flexible enough to shift his style of argument from the forums of the Supreme Court and the Senate to the stump of popular politics. Always, however, he pleaded for the natural harmony of interests that, he claimed, the Democratic party threatened to undermine.

Henry Clay joined Webster's assaults on Jackson's alleged despotism. He considered himself a Jeffersonian Republican and the leader of the National Republicans, the label originally applied to Jackson's opponents. Clay's program, which he called the American System, was designed to maximize federal support for industry, economic growth, and national self-sufficiency. He was a Kentuckian born in Virginia, and he had also risen from humble origin. Like Webster, he was notorious for extravagant living, although Clay's self-indulgence took the typically southern forms of gambling, dueling, and horse racing. A slaveowner and brilliant courtroom lawyer, Clay assumed two contradictory political roles. He competed with Jackson as a western man of the people, a coonskin man of nature. But Clay had also helped to negotiate the Treaty of Ghent, which had ended the War of 1812; he had been John Quincy Adams's secretary of state; and he had represented the western business and commercial interests that demanded federal aid for internal improvements. One of the greatest political manipulators in nineteenth-century America, Clay had unequaled talents in caucuses, committee rooms, and all-night boardinghouse negotiations.

John C. Calhoun was the most unpredictable of the three anti-Jackson leaders. Calhoun had originally been a militant nationalist, but in the 1820s he had become a militant defender of slavery and states' rights. He had been Jackson's nominal ally until personal conflicts had provoked a fatal split. Despite Calhoun's dramatic turnabouts, contemporaries admired the clarity and logical force of his arguments and respected his earlier distinguished service as secretary of war. But Calhoun's role in the nullification controversy made him a dangerous ally in the developing Whig coalition. Most southern Whig leaders shared the economic and nationalist views of the northern Whigs; Calhoun did not.

Whig Philosophy   The Whig outlook on the world was almost too diffuse to be termed an ideology. Like the Democrats, Whigs dreamed of a glorious future for America as the greatest nation the world had ever seen, and they found confirmation of that dream in the measurable growth of the country's population, wealth, and power. Far more than the Democrats, they associated the "spirit of improvement" with concrete technological and social inventions, which would allow "conservatism and progress," as Millard Fillmore put it, "to blend their harmonious action." They assumed that steam power, the telegraph, railroads, banks, corporations, prisons, factories, asylums, and public schools all contributed to an advancing civilization and to an increasing equality of opportunity. For individuals and the nation alike, Whigs advocated saving from income, capital accumulation, budgetary planning, and fiscal responsibility. Whigs opposed aggressive territorial expansion as a cure-all for economic problems. As the Whig newspaper editor Horace Greely observed in 1851: "Opposed to the instinct of boundless acquisition stands that of Internal Improvement. A nation cannot simultaneously devote its energies to the absorption of others' territories and the improvement of its own. In a state of war, not law only is silent, but the pioneer's axe, the canal digger's mattock, and the house-builder's trowel also." Whigs insisted that America's expansion and power should be harnessed to social objectives and stabilized by publicly acknowledged moral boundaries. Alarmed by the excesses of uncontrolled individualism, they expressed continuing and sometimes hysterical concern over the loss of community—over what they saw as demagogues who won support by inciting the poor against the rich, children against parents, wives against husbands, and geographic section against geographic section.

Whigs thought of themselves as conservatives, and they often invoked European theories that stressed the organic unity of society and the necessity of balancing human rights with social duties. Yet the Whig ideal of government was essentially optimistic and progressive. In 1825, long before the Whig party began to take shape, John Quincy Adams advanced the central Whig idea that the Constitution had given the central government both the duty and the necessary powers to promote "the progressive improvement of the condition of the governed."

The Whig party began to appear on a popular level by 1834. At that time it was essentially a loose coalition of state and local groups opposed to Jacksonian

Democrats. Because they were reluctant to allow the Jacksonians a monopoly of the popular label "democrat," the anti-Jacksonians sometimes called themselves Democratic Whigs. The final acceptance of the term *Whig* was significant. Superficially the label suggested an identity with the British "country-opposition" that had allegedly defended the British constitution against the despotism of the pro-Catholic Stuart kings in the late seventeenth century and against the encroachments of George III in the eighteenth century. This imagery linked "King Andrew" with the various arbitrary and despotic European monarchs. These parallels may seem farfetched, but the very act of drawing parallels with Europe contained a deeper significance. Unlike the Democrats, the Whigs tended to deny the uniqueness of the American experience and to place less faith in political institutions than in economic and cultural progress. They also tended to look on Britain, despite its monarchical and aristocratic institutions, as a model of economic and cultural progress. The most thoughtful Whig spokesmen considered America less a revolutionary departure from the rest of the world than a testing ground for progressive forces that were universal and that depended essentially on moral character.

The Whig Constituency

In all parts of the country, Whigs attracted a broad cross section of the electorate. This cross section was often weighted in favor of the wealthy, the privileged, and the aspiring. But it also included the victims of overt discrimination. In the North this constituency included most of the free blacks; British and German Protestant immigrants; manual laborers sympathetic with their employers' interests; business-oriented farmers; educators, reformers, and professional people; well-to-do merchants, bankers, and manufacturers; and active members of the Presbyterian, Unitarian, and Congregationalist churches. In the South the party had particular appeal to urban merchants, editors, bankers, and those farmers and planters who associated progress with expanding commerce, capital accumulation, railroads, and economic partnership with the North.

During their initial stages of organization the Whigs faced three formidable problems. First, in the populous northern states like New York, Pennsylvania, and Massachusetts they had to find strategies for uniting the economic interests of the National Republicans with the moral and cultural aspirations of various groups alienated by the incumbent Democrats. Second, they had to get rid of the elitist stigma that had been fastened first on John Quincy Adams and then on the defenders of the BUS. Thus they had to prove somehow that they were better democrats than the Democrats. Finally, they had to find delicate maneuvers for bypassing senatorial prima donnas like Webster and Clay and selecting less controversial presidential candidates who could appeal to the nation without arousing dissension and jealousy among the various state party organizations.

The way these problems were met is well illustrated by the career of Thurlow Weed of New York, who became the model of the nineteenth-century political boss and manipulator. A self-made man, Weed first acquired a voice in New York politics as editor of the *Rochester Telegraph* and a bitter foe of Van Buren's Albany

Regency. In 1827 Weed and his young protégé William H. Seward took up the cause of Anti-Masonry as a means of embarrassing the ruling Van Buren machine. In western New York Anti-Masonry had suddenly become a kind of religious crusade after the abduction and probable murder of William Morgan, a former Freemason who wanted to disclose the secrets of the fraternal society. The crusade expressed widespread popular resentment against the Masonic fraternity, which knit many of the wealthier and more powerful urban leaders of the state into a secret brotherhood that was pledged to mutual aid and support. Weed and Seward succeeded in portraying the Van Buren regime as the agent of Freemasonry—a "monster institution"—intent on suppressing legal investigation and prosecution of the alleged murder and on disguising statewide links between Masonic political influence and economic privilege. This antielitist rhetoric helped to counteract the Democrats' claims of being the true champions of the people against the unpopular Adams administration in Washington. By 1830 Anti-Masons had captured approximately one-half the popular vote in New York State. When the movement showed increasing signs of strength in other northern states, Weed and other strategists worked to absorb the National Republicans into a new anti-Jackson coalition.

Although the Anti-Masons organized the first national political convention in American history, Weed began to sense that the movement could be no more than a springboard for a successful national party. Weed launched his powerful *Albany Evening Journal* as an Anti-Masonic newspaper, but he increasingly downplayed Masonry and combined blistering attacks on the Albany Regency with the advocacy of various social reforms. To his political cronies and businessmen backers, Weed kept insisting that the Jacksonians could never be beaten so long as they continued to convince the people that they alone represented "the principle of democracy...the poor against the rich." By 1834 Weed had abandoned Anti-Masonry and had succeeded in organizing a New York Whig coalition.

In 1836 the Whigs tried to broaden their appeal by nominating various regional candidates for president, including Daniel Webster of Massachusetts and Hugh White of Tennessee. But it was Weed's candidate, William Henry Harrison of Ohio, who won the most electoral votes (by running three strong regional candidates, the Whigs hoped to deprive Van Buren of an electoral majority and thus let the outcome be decided, as in 1824, in the House of Representatives). Harrison, or "Old Tippecanoe," famous for his military defeat of the Shawnee Indians at Tippecanoe in 1811, appealed to many former Anti-Masons and won strong support in the South as well as in New York, Ohio, and Pennsylvania.

After years of patient organizing, wire-pulling, and passing out cigars, Weed finally came into his own in 1838 when he succeeded in getting William Seward elected governor of New York. As the master of patronage, the official state printer, and the "dictator" of the New York machine, Weed was now in a position to challenge his old archrival Van Buren, who claimed to be the president of the common people.

Whig Campaign Tactics in 1840
One of the political gimmicks used by the Harrison and Tyler campaign to attract public attention was to parade behind a huge ball as enthusiasts rolled it from one city to another. This particular procession moved across the entire state of Ohio and part of Kentucky.

The Election of 1840
In 1840 Weed played a key role in blocking the Whigs' nomination of Clay and in opening the way for Harrison. Weed's young follower, Horace Greeley, edited the Whigs' most influential newspaper, *The Log Cabin,* which set the pace for the campaign by attacking President Van Buren as an affected dandy who had transformed the White House into a palace of effeminate luxury. Greeley and others portrayed Harrison as a frontiersman of simple tastes. His symbols were a barrel of cider (whether hard or soft depended on the locality) and a log cabin with a welcoming coonskin at the door. Because Harrison was popularly known as "Old Tippecanoe" from his victory in 1811 over Tecumseh's Indian confederacy in the Northwest, Whigs adopted the triumphant campaign slogan, "Tippecanoe and Tyler too!" Harrison's victory seemed to show that Weed and fellow strategists had overcome the Whigs' political liabilities. They could rival the Democrats in populistic appeals, in carnival-style hucksterism, and, above all, in grassroots organization.

Nevertheless the Whigs never found a magnetic national leader who, like Jackson for the Democrats, could become a unifying symbol for their party. Harrison died of pneumonia a month after his inauguration. John Tyler, the vice-president who succeeded him after some debate over Tyler's constitutional status, soon betrayed the economic principles of the party. In 1844 the Whigs nominated Clay, but he went down to defeat for the third time. Thereafter the Whigs returned to the tested expedient of nominating apolitical military heroes—Zachary Taylor in 1848 and Winfield Scott in 1852.

The Whigs' difficulties went beyond the weaknesses of their presidential candidates. Despite their political pragmatism and impressive party discipline,

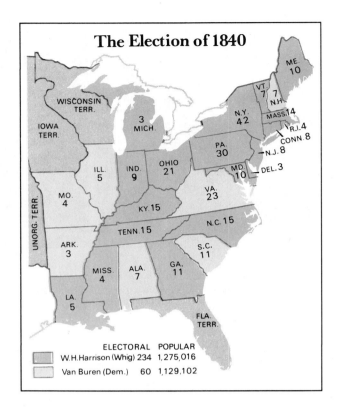

The Election of 1840

ELECTORAL POPULAR
W.H.Harrison (Whig) 234 1,275,016
Van Buren (Dem.) 60 1,129,102

the Whigs contained a militant, reform-minded element that resented the compromises necessary for a national party. Anti-Masonry had been one of the early expressions of such reformist and issue-oriented politics, and many of the Anti-Masons who had joined the Whigs had never been comfortable with the opportunism of the Weed school of leaders, who placed victory above principle. In addition to the Anti-Masons, the Whig party became the uneasy home for people who wanted laws enforcing a stricter Sabbath, laws prohibiting the sale of alcohol, laws barring slavery from the territories and abolishing slavery in the District of Columbia, and laws prolonging the time before an immigrant could be naturalized or allowed to vote. These causes were nourished by the spread of Protestant religious revivals in the North. They had little appeal among southern Whigs and hardheaded supporters of Clay's American System.

Limitations of the Two-Party System   Nevertheless, although a national party's strength depended on a continuing sensitivity to the needs of its constituent groups, it also served as a disciplining and educational force, imposing definite limits to individual, local, and regional self-assertion. The political issues of the 1840s tended to reinforce such party loyalty.

The majority of state legislators voted a strict Whig or Democratic line even when a different position might have harmonized better with local or personal interests. Whig or Democratic nerve centers were established at the grassroots level through the appointment of loyal party men to positions in local land offices, post offices, and customhouses. Until the early 1850s, when voters became disillusioned with traditional alternatives and when the Whig party began to fall apart, the two-party system worked as a powerful cohesive force in American society. Unfortunately, this political stability depended on the illusion of constant and sharply defined differences between two parties—parties that were intended to represent the interests of white Americans alone. The existence of national parties succeeded in moderating sectional conflict, but it did so at the cost of suppressing alternatives to the expansion of slavery and of stifling national debate over America's most dangerous conflict of interest.

Jacksonian Democracy

The limitations of the two-party system should not obscure the extraordinary fact that a functioning democracy had emerged in the United States. While historians continue to ponder and debate the contradictions of the so-called Age of Jackson, particularly the simultaneous expansion of slavery and democracy, one needs to recognize the utter novelty of popular sovereignty in action. The United States was the first nation in the world in which the great majority of free adult males not only possessed the vote but also cast their ballots (some 78 percent of adult white males voted in the election of 1840, and this level of turnout persisted until the Civil War). In contrast to the republicanism of the Federalist and Jeffersonian periods, the political system did not promote "natural aristocrats" who could supposedly preserve the public good. On the contrary, politicians deferred frankly and unashamedly to the people—or to interest groups among the people—and a revered leader like Jackson became charismatic precisely because he was thought to embody the wisdom of the common man.

What amazed Alexis de Tocqueville and other European observers, who were sensitive to the seething, volcanic upheavals of Europe, was the realization that America's "great social revolution" had almost "reached its natural limits . . . in a simple, easy fashion, or rather one might say that that country sees the results of the democratic revolution taking place among us [i.e. in Europe], without experiencing the revolution itself." In America, where the ideal of equality had never been pitted against an entrenched aristocracy, there had been no mass exterminations, no coups d'état, no secret police, no repressive armies or controlling bureaucracy. Conservatives might complain that farmers, artisans, and even women no longer knew their "place," that society had become so "leveled" that distinctions of rank had lost all meaning. As cheap newspapers and protest movements proliferated, no institution, tradition, or class remained invulnerable from attack. Despite widening disparities in wealth, America's political culture became profoundly antielitist and suspicious of privilege.

Democracy, as Tocqueville came to understand, had as much to do with a state of mind, with expectations of the future, as with political institutions:

> When citizens are classified by rank, profession, or birth, and when all are obliged to follow the career which chance has opened before them, everyone thinks that he can see the ultimate limits of human endeavor quite close in front of him, and no one attempts to fight against an inevitable fate. It is not that aristocratic peoples absolutely deny man's capacity to improve himself, but they do not think it unlimited. . . .
>
> But when castes disappear and classes are brought together, when men are jumbled together and habits, customs, and laws are changing, when new facts impinge and new truths are discovered, when old conceptions vanish and new ones take their place, then the human mind imagines the possibility of an ideal but always fugitive perfection.

Writing a new preface to his *Democracy in America* in 1848, when revolutions convulsed most of Europe, Tocqueville cautioned against turning to America "in order slavishly to copy the institutions she has fashioned for herself." But "where else," he asked, "can we find greater cause of hope or more valuable lessons?"

CHRONOLOGY

1820	Missouri Compromise. Maine admitted as twenty-third state. Reelection of James Monroe without opposition symbolizes "Era of Good Feelings."	**1828**	John C. Calhoun's anonymous South Carolina Exposition and Protest. Congress passes "Tariff of Abominations." Election of Andrew Jackson as president brings triumphant victory to new Democratic party.
1821	Henry Clay effects "Second Missouri Compromise." Missouri admitted as twenty-fourth state.	**1830**	Jackson vetoes Maysville Road Bill. Anti-Masonic party holds first national party convention.
1822	Denmark Vesey's conspiracy to lead massive slave uprising in South Carolina exposed.	**1832**	Beginning of Jackson's "war" against Second Bank of the United States (BUS). Special convention in South Carolina nullifies new protective tariff. Jackson reelected president.
1824	John Quincy Adams elected president by House of Representatives after failure of any candidate to win electoral majority.	**1833**	Congress provides for a gradual lowering of tariffs but passes Force Bill authorizing Jackson to
1827	Thurlow Weed takes up cause of Anti-Masonry.		

	enforce federal law in South Carolina.		to widespread bankruptcies and default of several states.
1836	Jackson's "specie circular." Martin Van Buren elected president.	**1840**	Congress passes Van Buren's Independent Treasury Act. William H. Harrison elected president; Whigs in power.
1837	Financial panic brings many bank failures and suspension of specie payment.	**1841**	John Tyler becomes president upon Harrison's death.
1839	A major depression begins, leading	**1844**	James K. Polk elected president.

SUGGESTED READINGS

Arthur M. Schlesinger, Jr., *The Age of Jackson* (1945), should be used with caution but is still an indispensable introduction to political democratization. The best recent syntheses and reinterpretations are Edward Pessen, *Jacksonian America: Society, Personality, and Politics* (rev. ed., 1978); Robert H. Wiebe, *The Opening of American Society: From the Constitution to the Eve of Disunion* (1984); Charles G. Sellers, *The Market Revolution, 1815–1848* (1992); and Harry L. Watson, *Liberty and Power: The Politics of Jacksonian America* (1990).

Other studies that illuminate various aspects of democratization, including rent wars and local rebellions, are Shaw Livermore, Jr., *The Twilight of Federalism* (1962); Chilton Williamson, *American Suffrage: From Property to Democracy* (1960); Henry Christman, *Tin Horns and Calico: A Decisive Episode in the Emergence of Democracy* (1945); David M. Ludlum, *Social Ferment in Vermont* (1939); Marvin E. Gettleman, *The Dorr Rebellion* (1973); and John Ashworth, *"Agrarians" and "Aristocrats": Party Political Ideology in the United States, 1837–1846* (1983).

Lee Benson, *The Concept of Jacksonian Democracy: New York as a Test Case* (1961), challenges the traditional historical categories of liberalism and conservatism. Richard P. McCormick, *The Second American Party System: Party Formation in the Jacksonian Era* (1966), also deemphasizes political issues and ideology. These pioneering works should be supplemented by Richard Hofstadter, *The Idea of a Party System* (1969); Ronald P. Formisano, *The Birth of Mass Political Parties: Michigan, 1827–1861* (1971); Formisano, *The Transformation of Political Culture: Massachusetts Parties, 1790s–1840s* (1983); Joel Silbey, ed., *Transformation of American Politics, 1840–1860* (1967); Jean H. Baker, *Affairs of Party: The Political Culture of Northern Democrats in the Mid-Nineteenth Century* (1983); Douglas T. Miller, *Jacksonian Aristocracy: Class and Democracy in New York, 1830–1860* (1967); and Michael F. Holt, "The Antimasonic and Know-Nothing Parties," and Holt, "The Democratic Party," in *History of U.S. Political Parties,* ed. Arthur M. Schlesinger, Jr., vol. 1 (*1789–1860: From Factions to Parties*) (4 vols., 1973). For fascinating studies of the Anti-Masonic party, see William Preston Vaughn, *The Antimasonic Party in the United States, 1826–1843* (1983), and Paul Goodman, *Towards a Christian Republic: Antimasonry and the Great Transition in New England, 1826–1836* (1988). Michael F. Holt, *The Political Crisis of the 1850s* (1978), points to important connections between political ideology and the working of the party system.

For the election of 1828, see Robert V. Remini, *The Election of Andrew Jackson* (1963). Two imaginative studies of Jacksonian ideology are Marvin Meyers, *The Jacksonian Persuasion* (1957), and John W. Ward, *Andrew Jackson: Symbol for an Age* (1955). For the most comprehensive biography of Jackson, see Robert V. Remini, *Andrew Jackson and the Course of American Empire, 1767–1821* (1977); *Andrew Jackson and the Course of American Freedom, 1822–1832* (1981); and *Andrew Jackson and the Course of American Democracy, 1833–1845* (1984). Jackson's presidency is also ably covered by Richard B. Latner, *The Presidency of Andrew Jackson: White House Politics, 1829–1837* (1979). John Niven, *Martin Van Buren and the Romantic Age of American Politics* (1983), and Donald B. Cole, *Martin Van Buren and the American Political System* (1984), bring out the central importance of a much underrated political leader. Informative essays on all the presidential elections can be found in Arthur M. Schlesinger, Jr., ed., *History of American Presidential Elections, 1789–1968,* vol. 1 (4 vols., 1971). See also Richard P. McCormick, *The Presidential Game: The Origins of American Presidential Politics* (1982), and Lawrence Frederick Kohl, *The Politics of Individualism: Parties and the American Character in the Jacksonian Era* (1988).

The standard work on the tariff issue is Frank W. Taussig, *The Tariff History of the United States* (1931). The best introduction to the banking controversy is Robert V. Remini, *Andrew Jackson and the Bank War* (1967). The main authorities on the history of banking are Bray Hammond, *Banks and Politics in America from the Revolution to the Civil War* (1957); J. Van Fenstermaker, *The Development of American Commercial Banking 1782–1837* (1965); and Fritz Redlich, *The Molding of American Banking* (2 vols., 1947–51). Thomas P. Govan, *Nicholas Biddle* (1959), presents a strong defense of the president of the Bank of the United States. The wider political ramifications of the controversy are examined in William G. Shade, *Banks or No Banks: The Money Question in Western Politics* (1972), and John M. McFaul, *The Politics of Jacksonian Finance* (1972).

On the Missouri crisis of 1820, Glover Moore, *The Missouri Controversy* (1953), is still the most thorough and convincing account. William W. Freehling, *Prelude to Civil War* (1966), presents a masterful interpretation of South Carolina's growing militancy and of the nullification and gag-rule controversies. For the general question of sectionalism, see William J. Cooper, *The South and the Politics of Slavery, 1528–1856* (1978). The most penetrating and informative study of politics in a southern state is J. Mills Thornton III, *Politics and Power in a Slave Society: Alabama, 1800–1860* (1978).

There is still no adequate history of the Whig party and its antecedents, but Daniel W. Howe, *The Political Culture of the American Whigs* (1980), brilliantly illuminates the Whig ideology. See also Lynn L. Marshall, "The Strange Stillbirth of the Whig Party," *American Historical Review,* 62 (January 1967), 445–68; and Thomas H. O'Connor, *Lords of the Loom: The Cotton Whigs and the Coming of the Civil War* (1968). Political history is always enriched by the biographies of influential figures. The transition from the era of the Founders is imaginatively analyzed in Drew R. McCoy, *The Last of the Fathers: James Madison and the Republican Legacy* (1989). A fine study of Jackson's three towering opponents is Merrill D. Peterson, *The Great Triumvirate: Webster, Clay, and Calhoun* (1987). For Calhoun, see also John Niven, *John C. Calhoun and the Price of Union: A Biography* (1988). An older and more comprehensive biography is Charles M. Wiltse, *John C. Calhoun: Nationalist, 1782–1828* (1944), *Nullifier, 1829–1839* (1949), and *Sectionalist, 1840–1850* (1951). For Henry Clay, see Clement Eaton, *Henry Clay and the Art of American Politics* (1957); for Webster, see Irving H. Bartlett, *Daniel Webster* (1978), and Robert F. Dalzell, Jr., *Daniel Webster and the Trial of American Nationalism, 1843–1852* (1973).

Other fine biographies that shed much light on the political history of this period include Martin Duberman, *Charles Francis Adams, 1807–1886* (1961); Samuel F. Bemis, *John Quincy Adams and the Foundations of American Foreign Policy* (1949) and *John Quincy Adams and the Union* (1956); William Nisbet Chambers, *Old Bullion Benton: Senator from the New West* (1956); William E. Smith, *The Francis Preston Blair Family in Politics* (2 vols., 1933); Harry

Ammon, *James Monroe: The Quest for National Identity* (1971); Charles G. Sellers, Jr., *James K. Polk: Jacksonian, 1795–1843* (1957) and *Continentalist, 1843–1846* (1966); Robert Dawidoff, *The Education of John Randolph* (1979); Glyndon G. Van Deusen, *William Henry Seward* (1967); K. Jack Bauer, *Zachary Taylor: Soldier, Planter, Statesman of the Old Southwest* (1985); Frederick J. Blue, *Salmon P. Chase: A Life in Politics* (1986); David H. Donald, *Charles Sumner and the Coming of the Civil War* (1960); Carl B. Swisher, *Roger B. Taney* (1935); Holman Hamilton, *Zachary Taylor* (1951); William Y. Thompson, *Robert Toombs of Georgia* (1966); James P. Shenton, *Robert John Walker: A Politician from Jackson to Lincoln* (1961); Glyndon G. Van Deusen, *Thurlow Weed: Wizard of the Lobby* (1947); and John W. DuBose, *The Life and Times of William Lowndes Yancey* (2 vols., 1892). Richard Hofstadter, *The American Political Tradition* (1948), provides brilliant sketches of a number of pre–Civil War leaders.

16

Expansion and New Boundaries

～

$\mathcal{T}$HE 1840s marked the beginning of a new era. In the North recovery from a long depression was accompanied by rapid urban growth, the extension of machine production and of the factory system, the influx of hundreds of thousands of immigrants, and the construction of vast railway networks linking western farms with eastern markets. In the South the remarkable profitability of cotton and sugar plantations confirmed a whole region's unapologetic commitment to slave labor. The moral discomforts that had troubled Jefferson's generation of southerners had finally given way to a proud and self-conscious identity as a "progressive slave society." This sectional confidence was bolstered not only by the world's demand for cotton but also by the American annexation of Texas. The resulting Mexican War, which extended America's boundaries to the Pacific, led some southern leaders to dream of a vast tropical empire based on the slave labor of an "inferior race." These spectacular fulfillments of trends and aspirations that had been developing since the War of 1812 posed grave challenges to governmental policy and to the nation's sense of its own character.

There were other dark shadows in this overall picture of growth and economic integration. In the mid-1850s investment and industrial production both underwent a slowdown, which culminated in the financial panic of 1857. For the first time the business cycle seemed to be primarily geared to the fluctuations of *nonagricultural* forces in the domestic economy, among them speculative investment in railroads. Significantly, the South suffered little from the essentially industrial depression of the late 1850s. Southern leaders could not refrain from gloating over the economic vulnerability of northern industry and the insecurities of "wage slavery." Northern leaders angrily accused the South of contributing to the depression by defeating northern moves for protective tariffs and free homesteading in the West. Slave-grown cotton remained an important contributor to the North's industrial growth. But many northerners perceived the South as a holdover of colonial dependency—a dependency on British markets that blocked the way to national self-sufficiency.

Foreign Dangers, American Expansion, and the Monroe Doctrine

America's foreign policy had always presupposed the national government's commitment to protect and support the South's "peculiar institution." However, the nation's foreign policy reflected many other interests and motives, and protecting slavery was not explicitly acknowledged as a vital objective until 1844. The overriding objective in the early nineteenth century, as in the post-Revolutionary period, was to prevent Britain or France from acquiring a foothold in the increasingly vulnerable Spanish territories of North America. But those territories, including Cuba, East and West Florida, and Texas, were a threat mainly to the slaveholding South. The War of 1812 made clear that possession of the Floridas was essential for the security of the entire Lower South. From bases in supposedly neutral Spanish Florida, the British had incited Indian raids, had encouraged slave desertions, and had originally planned to launch an invasion to cut off New Orleans from the rest of the United States. The revolution of 1791–1804 in the French colony of Saint Domingue (which became the Republic of Haiti) had also shown that war could ignite a massive slave uprising and totally destroy a slaveholding society.

Decline of New World Slavery One of the consequences of the Napoleonic wars at the beginning of the nineteenth century was the fatal weakening of slaveholding regimes in most parts of the New World. Not only did France lose Haiti, the most valuable sugar colony in the world, but Napoleon's seizure of Spain opened the way for independence movements in the immense Spanish territories from Mexico to Chile. The prolonged wars of liberation undermined the institution of slavery and committed the future Spanish-American republics to programs of gradual emancipation. After the British abolished the slave trade in their own colonies at the beginning of the nineteenth century, they embarked on a long-term policy of suppressing the slave trade of other nations. By 1823, when little remained of the former Spanish, Portuguese, and French New World empires, slavery was a declining institution except in Brazil, Cuba (still a Spanish colony), and the United States.

This wider context of New World slavery dramatizes a momentous irony of American foreign policy from the time of Jefferson's presidency to the Civil War. The extension of what Jefferson called an "empire for liberty" was also the extension of an empire for slavery and thus a counterweight to the forces that threatened to erode slavery throughout the hemisphere. Jefferson himself initiated the policy of trying to isolate Haiti economically and diplomatically in order to end the spread of black revolution. In 1820, in the midst of the Missouri crisis and in response to Spain's delay in ratifying the Transcontinental Treaty of 1819, ceding East Florida, Jefferson privately assured President Monroe that the United States could soon acquire not only East Florida but also Cuba and Texas. Cuba was at the time becoming the world's greatest producer of slave-grown sugar, and Jefferson confidently predicted that Texas would be the richest state in the Union, partly because it would produce more sugar than the country could consume.

There is no reason to think that American statesmen consciously plotted to create a vast empire for slavery—at least until the 1840s. From the annexation of Florida in 1821 to the annexation of Texas in 1845, the United States acquired no new territory that could upset the balance between free states and slave states achieved by the Missouri Compromise. The Old Southwest contained immense tracts of uncleared and uncultivated land, and many southerners feared that reckless expansion would lead to excessive production, which would lower the price of cotton and other cash crops.

Slavery and Territorial Expansion The connections between slavery and national expansion were more indirect. They involved two basic and continuing assumptions that governed foreign policy. The first assumption was that territorial expansion was the only means of protecting and extending the principles of the American Revolution in a generally hostile world. "The larger our association," Jefferson had predicted, "the less will it be shaken by local passions." According to this nationalist view, Americans could deal with domestic imperfections once the nation had achieved sufficient power to be secure. Thus ardent nationalists like John Quincy Adams felt that personal misgivings over slavery had to give way to the need for a united front against the monarchical despots of Europe. During the Missouri crisis the antislavery forces could never overcome the unfair charge that they were serving Britain's interests by fomenting sectional discord and blocking the westward expansion of the United States.

The second assumption, held with passionate conviction by every president from Jefferson to Polk, was that Great Britain was America's "natural enemy." These presidents saw Britain as a kingdom ruled by selfish interest, filled with a deep-rooted hatred for everything America represented, and committed to the humiliation and subjugation of its former colonies. Anglophobia had much to do with the swift death of the Federalist party. This hatred of England was nourished by contemptuous anti-American essays in British periodicals and by unflattering descriptions by English travelers that were widely reprinted in the United States. According to Mrs. Frances Trollope's *Domestic Manners of the Americans,* published in 1832, "the theory of equality may be very daintily discussed by English gentlemen in a London dining room . . . but it will be found less palatable when it presents itself in the shape of a hard greasy paw, and is claimed in accents that breathe less of freedom than of onions and whiskey. Strong, indeed, must be the love of equality in an English breast, if it can survive a tour through the Union." Many Americans blamed Britain for the economic depressions of 1819 and 1837.

Irish immigrants regarded the English as their hereditary enemies. No American politician could risk even the suspicion of being an unintentional agent of British interests. It was thus an unhappy coincidence that British interests veered increasingly toward antislavery—which some American leaders interpreted, not without some reason, as a cloak for new forms of economic and ideological imperialism.

The American takeover of Florida established precedents for the future and also coincided with the dramatic southwestward expansion of cotton and slavery. As early as 1786 Jefferson had warned against pressing "too soon on the Spaniards." For the time being, he believed, it was best that East and West Florida be in Spanish hands. He feared, however, that the Spanish were "too feeble to hold them [the Floridas] till our population can be sufficiently advanced to gain it [the Floridas] from them piece by piece." By 1810 there were enough American settlers in the Baton Rouge district of West Florida to stage an armed rebellion against Spanish rule. President Madison, claiming that West Florida was part of the Louisiana Purchase, promptly annexed the section of the Gulf coast extending eastward to the Perdido River. To prevent any possible transfer of West Florida to Great Britain, Congress sanctioned Madison's annexation. But it balked at plans to seize East Florida during the War of 1812.

The Transcontinental Treaty of 1819

Negotiations with Spain after the War of 1812 involved not only Florida but also the entire western boundary of the United States. Spain had never recognized the validity of Napoleon's sale of Louisiana, a sale prohibited by the treaty that had earlier transferred the territory from Spain to France. Luis de Onís, the Spanish minister to the United States, tried to limit American claims to the narrowest strip possible west of the Mississippi River. But as the negotiations dragged on, the South American wars of independence increasingly undermined Spain's position. Secretary of State John Quincy Adams proved to be a tough and skillful bargainer, and in 1818 Andrew Jackson, then the American military commander in the South, immensely strengthened Adams's hand. Without official authorization Jackson invaded East Florida, captured the main Spanish ports, deposed the governor, and hanged two English troublemakers. The excuse was that Florida had become a refuge for fugitive slaves and a base for Seminole Indian raids on American settlements.

Thus Onís was faced with the temporary seizure of his main bargaining card, and he feared that the United States would begin aiding the rebellious Spanish colonies. He therefore agreed to the Transcontinental Treaty of 1819, which ceded the Floridas to the United States in return for American acknowledgment that Texas was not part of the Louisiana Purchase—a questionable claim that the Americans had already put forward. In fact, Onís had been desperate enough to give up most of Texas. But as President Monroe assured General Jackson, "We ought to be content with Florida, for the present, and until the public opinion ... [in the Northeast] shall be reconciled to any further change."

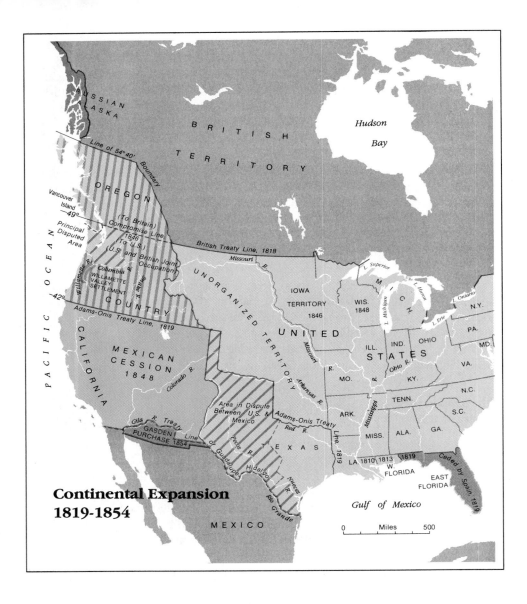

**Continental Expansion
1819–1854**

For Adams the Transcontinental Treaty (also known as the Adams-Onís Treaty), which was ratified in 1821, was "a great epoch [turning point] in our history." Not only did it transfer the Floridas to the United States, but it extended American territorial claims to the Pacific Ocean. The rather weak Spanish claims to the Pacific Northwest were ceded to the United States. Spain also agreed to an international boundary that extended northward from the Sabine River (which divided Louisiana from Texas) to the Red River, westward along the Red and Arkansas rivers to the Rocky Mountains, and then along the forty-second parallel to the Pacific.

At the time the Transcontinental Treaty was being negotiated, Spain was reasserting its control in Mexico, which had revolted for the first time in 1808–15.

But the revival of Spanish rule proved temporary. In 1820 a revolution in Spain itself permitted the Mexicans to declare their independence once again. By 1822 the burden of defending the boundaries that had been established by the Transcontinental Treaty had fallen on an independent but weak and war-torn Mexico.

Events Leading to the Monroe Doctrine   The collapse of the Spanish Empire led directly to the Monroe Doctrine. By 1823 it was clear that Spain could never force its rebellious colonies to return to their former status. Moreover, Britain and the United States had a common interest in preventing the autocratic monarchies of continental Europe from intervening in Latin America in Spain's behalf. Under pressure from the Russian tsar, France was about to invade Spain to put down its revolution, which aimed at establishing a constitutional monarchy. It was known that the French foreign minister had grandiose schemes for imposing on Latin America the kind of reactionary monarchical government that predominated in continental Europe. Although Great Britain was not willing to risk war, it was strongly opposed to French intervention in Spain. And while not a promoter of independent republics, the British government had no intention of allowing the continental powers' anti-revolutionary zeal to interfere with Britain's growing commercial dominance in the former Spanish Empire. George Canning, the British foreign minister, therefore proposed a joint Anglo-American declaration that would assert that neither Britain nor the United States had designs on former Spanish territory, and would warn other nations against intervention.

The British offer presented the Monroe administration with a serious dilemma. The United States was the only nation that had begun to recognize the independent republics of Spanish America, but only Britain had the power to deter France and Spain from trying to reconquer them. Moreover, Russia— which was leading the reactionary crusades in Europe and which already occupied Alaska—in 1821 claimed a monopoly over the North Pacific. Russian traders were becoming more active in the Oregon country, a region that Britain and the United States had agreed to occupy jointly at least until 1828. Accepting the British offer of a joint declaration would have the drawback of temporarily preventing the American annexation of Cuba. Despite this disadvantage, the idea appealed to the elder statesmen Jefferson and Madison, as well as to Monroe and most of his cabinet.

But the question of accepting the British offer was complicated by the forthcoming presidential election of 1824. The nationalist, anti-English vote was much on the minds of the leading candidates. Secretary of State John Quincy Adams was already being portrayed by his rivals as a former Federalist and as secretly pro-British. Despite his proved nationalism and loyal service to Republican administrations, Adams was vulnerable to these charges because of his New England and Federalist background. He was also the only candidate who was not a slaveowner. He knew that as secretary of state he would bear the largest share of political liability resulting from any Anglo-American alliance. He had long gone out of his way to publicize his resistance to British pressure for an anti-slave-trade treaty. Therefore Adams now insisted on a unilateral American declaration against European intervention in the New World, much as he insisted on a unilateral policy against the slave trade. It would be more candid and dignified, Adams pointed out, to declare the United States' principles directly to Russia and France than "to come in as a cock-boat in the wake of the British man-of-war."

Adams's arguments prevailed. Monroe sent to Congress a message, largely written by Adams, setting forth what has become known as the Monroe Doctrine. By stating that America would not intervene in the "internal concerns" of European states, Monroe in effect repudiated the popular clamor in the United States for aiding the various revolutionary struggles against despotism in Europe, including the Greek war for independence from Turkey. But America's warning to Europe against its future colonization of the New World extended to Britain as well as to Russia and France. And the Monroe Doctrine in no way prevented America's own expansion in the New World.

For some time the Monroe Doctrine had little practical consequence, except perhaps in proving Adams to be a nationalist and thus in helping him to win the presidency. Regardless of American pronouncements, it was British naval power that ensured the independence of Spanish America. Yet by rejecting an Anglo-American alliance, the Monroe administration also set a precedent for opposing any foreign attempts to limit the expansion of slavery. No doubt Monroe was thinking only of monarchical institutions when he warned that the United States would consider as dangerous to America's peace and safety any attempt by Europeans to extend "their system" to the Western Hemisphere. By the 1830s, however, antislavery was an integral part of the British "system," and many southerners regarded the expansion of slavery as vital to America's "peace and safety."

Annexation of Texas   The Texas issue eventually tested this point and led to a proslavery reformulation of the Monroe Doctrine. For abolitionists in both Britain and the United States, it was not inevitable that Texas should become a slave state. In 1829 Mexico had abolished slavery in all its provinces (including California), and it provided loopholes only for the stubborn Anglo-American settlers in Texas. By 1830 the Mexican government had become alarmed by the growing autonomy of the Anglo-American settlements in Texas, by the intrigue accompanying the United States government's secret efforts to purchase Texas, and by the Jacksonian press's agitation for annexation. Consequently, in 1830 the Mexican government tried to prohibit the further immigration of Anglo-Americans and the further importation of slaves. It also sought to promote European settlements in Texas, which would be a buffer against encroachments from the United States. Since black slavery had only begun to take root in Texas, British reformers were beginning to look on the province as a promising site for cultivating cotton with free labor. Benjamin Lundy, an Amer-

The Fall of the Alamo
After the Anglo-Texans declared their independence on March 2, 1836, General Santa Anna led a large army into the province and on March 6 wiped out a small garrison of Americans, including David Crockett, at the Alamo mission in San Antonio. The martyrdom of these heroes did much to inflame anti-Mexican sentiment in the United States.

ican Quaker abolitionist, even tried in the early 1830s to establish a refuge in Texas for free blacks from the United States.

But during his travels in Texas, Lundy found evidence of growing proslavery sentiment and of various plots to throw off Mexican rule and annex Texas to the United States. The Mexican government was in fact capable of neither governing the Anglo-Texans nor satisfying their needs. In 1836, after President Antonio López de Santa Anna had abolished Mexico's federal constitution and had imposed centralized rule, the Texans proclaimed their independence. Their new constitution, modeled on the United States Constitution, specifically legalized black slavery. Meanwhile Santa Anna's army had wiped out a small band of Texas rebels at San Antonio's Alamo Mission, and cries for revenge resounded in the American press. A great influx of volunteers from the officially neutral United States went to the aid of the Texans. Led by General Sam Houston, Texan forces crushed the Mexican army at San Jacinto and captured Santa Anna. Soon thereafter the Texans voted overwhelmingly to join the United States.

As late as 1835 President Jackson had tried to buy not only Texas but all the Mexican territory stretching northwestward to the Pacific. His main object was to secure "within our limits the whole bay of St. Francisco." By then Americans had long been engaged in trade along the Santa Fe trail, and settlers were beginning to arrive by sea in sparsely populated California. After the Texan revolution, however, Jackson knew that a premature attempt at annexation would in all likelihood bring on a war with Mexico, which refused to acknowledge Texan independence. It would also arouse the fury of the Northeast and lead to a

Sam Houston (1793–1863)
Leader of the badly outnumbered Texans whose spectacular victory at San Jacinto in 1836 secured Texas's independence from Mexico, Houston went on to become president of the new republic, then senator from the new state. In 1861 as governor, Houston's stand against Texas's secession from the Union forced him out of office.

sectional division within the Democratic party in the election year of 1836. But Jackson knew that California was important to the whaling and maritime interests of the Northeast. New England whalers and cargo ships had begun to make portions of the Pacific an American preserve. Jackson therefore secretly advised the Texans to bide their time and to establish a claim to California, "to paralyze the opposition of the North and East to Annexation." He assumed that this opposition would fade as soon as northerners concluded that annexing Texas would lead to the acquisition of California.

The passage of time, however, encouraged the hopes of American and British opponents of slavery. Jackson's Democratic successor, Martin Van Buren, was too dependent on northeastern support to risk taking a role himself in agitating the public with the question of annexation. John Quincy Adams's eloquent speeches in the House of Representatives, in which he served for seventeen years after he retired as president, popularized the view that the southern Slave Power had engineered the Texas Revolution and the drive for annexation. In 1838 Adams carried on a three-week filibuster, presented hundreds of antislavery petitions, and finally defeated a move to annex Texas by joint resolution. The rebuffed Texan leaders withdrew their formal proposal for annexation and began to think seriously of building an independent empire. As time went on, they looked to Britain and France for financial support and for diplomatic aid in ending the dangerous state of war with Mexico.

The spring and summer of 1843 marked a decisive turn of events. John Tyler, who had been elected as Harrison's vice-president in 1840 and had then become president after Harrison's death, had been disowned by the Whig party. He was therefore courting southern Democrats and searching for an issue that would win him reelection. Daniel Webster, the last of his Whig cabinet members, finally resigned as secretary of state after negotiating with Britain the Webster-Ashburton Treaty, which settled disputed borders with Canada and provided for cooperative measures in suppressing the Atlantic slave trade. The treaty was immediately attacked by Democrats for betraying American interests. Through Calhoun's influence, Webster was replaced by Abel P. Upshur, a Virginian who had defended slavery as a "positive good." For the first time, an entire administration was in the hands of ardent proslavery southerners who saw territorial expansion as the key to southern security.

Britain and Texas   Although British leaders did not want to antagonize the South, on which Britain depended for cotton, they were sensitive to one abolitionist argument. An independent Texas might begin importing slaves from Africa, thereby adding to Britain's difficulties in suppressing the Atlantic slave trade. The British had evidence that American officials in Cuba were conniving with slave smugglers and that American ships participated in the illegal slave trade to Cuba. Texas might open another rich market for the same interests. Therefore, when Britain offered Texas a treaty of recognition and trade, it included a secret agreement to outlaw the slave trade. Otherwise, under close questioning from a delegation of abolitionists, Foreign Secretary Lord Aberdeen conceded only two points: first, that in serving as mediator between Texas and Mexico, Britain hoped that any peace agreement would include a commitment to slave emancipation; and second, that as everyone knew, the British public and government hoped for the abolition of slavery throughout the world.

These words caused anger and alarm in Washington. The Tyler administration was convinced that West Indian emancipation had proved to be an economic and social disaster. According to the prevailing southern theory, the British were now determined to undermine slavery in other nations in order to improve the competitive advantage of their own colonies, including India. But southerners never comprehended the depth of antislavery sentiment among the British middle class. Having subsidized West Indian emancipation by paying £20 million in compensation to former slaveowners, British taxpayers wanted assurance that Britain's short-term sacrifices would not lead to the expansion of plantation slavery in neighboring regions of the Caribbean and the Gulf of Mexico.

Regardless of the truth, however, southerners had long been inclined to believe that British antislavery was part of a long-term diplomatic plot to seal off and contain the United States within an arc of British influence extending from Cuba and Texas to California, Oregon, and Canada. In 1843 this conviction was seemingly confirmed by the exaggerated reports of Duff Green, President Tyler's secret agent in Britain and France and a friend of Calhoun. According to Green, the British government was about to guarantee interest on a loan to Texas on the condition that Texans abolish slavery. The plan would make Texas a British satellite and a place of refuge, like Canada, for fugitive slaves from the United States. Green claimed that, by erecting a barrier of freedom across the southwestern flank of the slaveholding states, the British could effectively join northern abolitionists in destroying both slavery and the federal Union.

Like many myths, this elaborate fantasy rested on a thin foundation of truth. It interpreted every event as part of a master plan, and it justified national desires that were otherwise difficult to justify. It furnished the pretext for the grand strategy that would govern American expansionist policy for the next five years. In response to an appeal for advice from Secretary of State Upshur, Calhoun in 1843 secretly spelled out the steps for implementing this policy. He called for private assurances to Texas that as soon as a propaganda campaign had been launched to soften northern opposition, the administration would secure annexation. In order to win support from the land-hungry farmers of the Old Northwest, Calhoun also suggested linking Texas annexation with the assertion of American claims to Oregon. As a preliminary step in carrying out this plan, he wanted to demand a formal explanation from Britain for policies that threatened "the safety of the Union and the very existence of the South."

Calhoun himself soon had the power to begin implementing this grand design. Early in 1844 Upshur was killed in an accident, and Calhoun succeeded him as secretary of state. Soon afterward a Whig newspaper revealed that the administration had been engaged for months in secret negotiations with Texas and that Tyler was about to sign an annexation treaty. In response to a growing northern uproar, Calhoun seized on and made public the British government's private statement that Britain "desires, and is constantly exerting herself to procure, the general abolition of slavery throughout the world." By skillfully distorting and publicizing the British diplomatic notes, Calhoun tried to identify the antiannexation cause with a British plot to destroy the Union. He lectured the British on the blessings of black slavery, employing faulty statistics from the census of 1840 to argue that emancipation in the North had produced black insanity, crime, suicide, and degeneracy. He also informed Mexico that because of the British conspiracy to subvert southern slavery, the United States was forced to annex Texas in self-defense.

The Expansionist Issue and the Election of 1844

This open defense of slavery by an American secretary of state marked the beginning of a sectional conflict over slavery and expansionism that severely tested the party system. President Tyler's defection from the Whigs, in addition to Calhoun's presidential ambitions and independence from party discipline, complicated the political maneuvering that set the stage for the 1844 campaign. With an eye to northern votes, both Henry Clay and Martin Van Buren, the leading Whig and Democratic contenders, felt compelled by April 1844 to express their opposition to the immediate annexation of Texas.

James K. Polk (1795–1849)
As Speaker of the House of Representatives, Polk served President Andrew Jackson as a loyal lieutenant. In 1844 Jackson, as the retired elder statesman of the Democratic party, supported Polk's candidacy for president after Martin Van Buren had taken a public stand against annexing Texas. As a young "dark horse" in the race, Polk defeated the veteran Van Buren for the Democratic nomination. Polk's election as president helped the outgoing Tyler administration to secure Texas's annexation and led directly to the Mexican War and to the acquisition of Oregon as well as California and the southwest.

In the Senate the Missouri Democrat Thomas Hart Benton led the attack against the trickery of Tyler and Calhoun. Seven other Democratic senators, all northerners, joined the Whigs in decisively rejecting the annexation treaty. Yet the Whig opposition to expansion encouraged the Democratic party to close ranks and rally behind patriotic demands for the "reannexation of Texas" and the "reoccupation of Oregon." (These demands assumed that Texas had been part of the Louisiana Purchase and that Britain had never had legitimate claims to the region south of 54°40′, the border of Russian Alaska.) The issue of expansion diverted attention from the Democrats' internal disputes over banking and fiscal policy, and it also enabled a southern-dominated coalition to defeat Van Buren and nominate James K. Polk, a Jacksonian expansionist from Tennessee, as the Democratic candidate for the 1844 election.

As Calhoun had predicted, the Oregon question became an ideal means for exploiting national Anglophobia and winning northern support for national expansion. For decades the British Hudson's Bay Company had ruled the region north of the Columbia River, although the United States had strong claims to the Columbia itself and to the territory extending southward to latitude 42°. New England ships had long frequented the entire Pacific Northwest in search of sea otter furs for the China trade, and since the 1820s American trappers had developed a thriving trade in beaver and other furs within the region west of the Rockies. As American traders challenged the political and judicial authority of the powerful Hudson's Bay Company, it became more difficult to resolve conflicting Anglo-American claims. Moreover, in 1827, when the two nations had

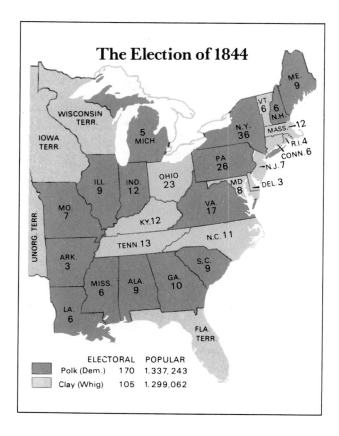

The Election of 1844

	ELECTORAL	POPULAR
Polk (Dem.)	170	1,337,243
Clay (Whig)	105	1,299,062

renewed a "joint occupation" agreement that simply deferred any settlement of national boundaries, no one could foresee the future appeal of Oregon's fertile Willamette Valley to farmers in the Old Northwest. American missionaries working with the Indians sent back glowing reports of the rich farmland in the Willamette Valley, and these helped spread the "Oregon fever" of the 1840s. Thousands of families risked the perils of overland travel to the Pacific. In 1843 the first of the great overland wagon migrations along the Oregon Trail took place, and the resulting claims to "All Oregon" including what later became Washington state, Idaho, and southern British Columbia, acted as a political balance wheel for the annexation of Texas.

In the 1844 election, as in other elections of the time, voter preference depended less on issues than on ethnic, religious, and party loyalty. And so, concerned about the crucial swing vote, Clay, the Whig candidate, retreated from his earlier stand against Texas annexation. His last-minute gestures for southern support persuaded thousands of northern Whigs to vote for James G. Birney, the Liberty party candidate, who stood firm against annexation. More popular votes were actually cast against Polk than for him. Although Polk barely won the election, he would certainly have lost it if Birney's 15,000 votes in New York State had gone to Clay.

Nevertheless the incumbent President Tyler and the triumphant Democrats interpreted the election as a mandate for the immediate annexation of Texas. The

Democrats in Congress united in championing the new expansionism, allowing the outgoing Tyler administration to secure annexation by joint resolution of both houses of Congress. After a tense period of international intrigue, the Republic of Texas rejected offers of peace from Mexico and mediation from Britain. In December 1845, having bypassed territorial status, Texas entered the Union as a new slave state.

The Mexican War and Manifest Destiny

The admission of Texas coincided with President Polk's aggressive reformulation of the Monroe Doctrine. In his annual message of December 2, 1845, Polk warned that henceforth the United States would not tolerate any kind of European interferences designed to limit the spread of the American form of government or the right of any peoples of North America "to decide their own destiny." By this Polk meant the right to be annexed to the United States. In the case of Texas, whose boundaries were still extremely controversial, annexation meant a federal commitment to the restoration of slavery in a region in which it had earlier been outlawed by Mexico. Only the future could determine the fate of Cuba, California, and Oregon—provinces that Polk very much had in mind. And the future too would determine precisely how the people would "decide their own destiny," an ideal soon to be known as "popular sovereignty."

Oregon and California
President Polk's warnings about European interference were directed mainly at Britain. He emphasized that the danger of British economic or political interference, even apart from physical colonization, justified an indefinite expansion of America's boundaries. He also rejected further negotiation with Britain over the Oregon question and asked Congress to give notice of the termination of the 1827 joint occupation agreement. The dismayed British government ignored the belligerent rhetoric, but it commissioned new steam warships and ordered a naval force to the northeast Pacific.

Although Polk hoped to force British concessions regarding Oregon, his primary objective was California, a Mexican province that contained no more than 10,000 white, mostly Hispanic inhabitants. In 1845 a British consul correctly observed that California was at the mercy of whoever might choose to take possession of it. Polk feared that the British might seize the province as compensation for money owed by Mexico. Months before Polk's December message, the government had ordered the commodore of the American Pacific Squadron to take San Francisco and other ports if he could "ascertain with certainty" that Mexico had declared war against the United States.

Polk's secretary of state, James Buchanan, also sent secret instructions to Thomas Larkin, the American consul at Monterey, California, telling him to foil British plots and to foment, as cautiously as possible, a spirit of rebellion among the Spanish Californians. Finally, only days after Polk's belligerent message, America's dashing "Pathfinder," Captain John C. Frémont, arrived in California

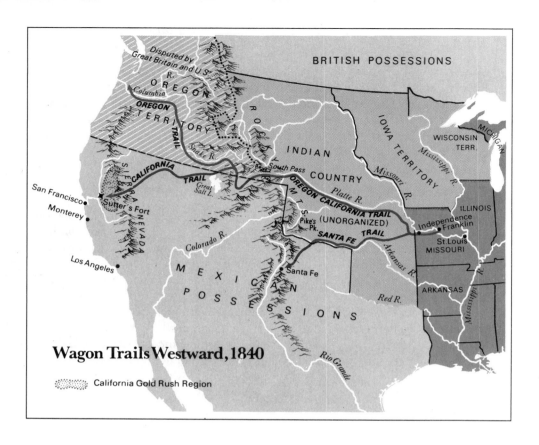

Wagon Trails Westward, 1840

California Gold Rush Region

at the head of a "scientific expedition" of heavily armed engineers. Frémont had been exploring the Mexican West without permission from Mexico, and he would soon defy the Mexican authorities in California and encourage the small population of Anglo-American settlers in an uprising, supposedly in their own self-defense.

Slidell's Mission   December 1845 also marked the arrival in Mexico City of Polk's secret minister, John Slidell, who had orders to win Mexican acceptance of the Rio Grande River as the new border with the United States, as well as to purchase as much of New Mexico and California as possible. His instructions emphasized the determination of the United States to prevent California from becoming a British or French colony, and authorized Slidell to extend to Mexico as much as $25 million for the territories desired. The Americans also offered to assume the debts owed by Mexico to American citizens.

The Mexican government had previously been willing to settle the Texas dispute. But one of Mexico's numerous revolutions was about to erupt, and the unstable government could not dare recognize an American envoy who made such sweeping demands—demands that had already been leaked to the American press. Mexican nationalists considered Texas a "stolen province," and they especially resented the wholly unfounded claim that Texas extended to the Rio Grande. In 1816 Spain had designated the Nueces River, 130 miles north and east of the Rio Grande, as the boundary between the provinces of Tamaulipas and Texas; this was the boundary that appeared on American and European maps. In 1836, however, when the Texans had captured the Mexican president, Santa Anna, he had been forced to agree to the Rio Grande boundary as a condition for his release. The Mexican government had promptly rejected this extortionary agreement. By the end of 1845, Mexican nationalists hoped for European support and were eager for a war of revenge against American imperialists.

War with Mexico On learning of Slidell's failure, the Polk administration was also eager for war but wanted a pretext that would justify seizing California. In January 1846 the president ordered General Zachary Taylor, who had been poised for the move, to march to the Rio Grande. Without opposition, American ships blockaded that river and Taylor took up a position across the Rio Grande from the Mexican town of Matamoros, toward which he aimed his cannons. By early May, however, Washington had heard no news of hostilities, and the impatient president and cabinet decided that Mexico's unpaid debts and the rebuff to Slidell were sufficient grounds for war. Then, just as Polk had drafted a war message to Congress, news arrived of a minor skirmish between Mexican and American patrols. Polk could now indignantly inform Congress that war already existed. He said, "Notwithstanding all our efforts to avoid it [war] exists by the act of Mexico herself. [Mexico] has passed the boundary of the United States, has invaded our territory and shed American blood upon the American soil."

By any objective interpretation, Americans had crossed the Mexican boundary and had shed Mexican blood on Mexican soil. American expansionists, however, believed that the protests from Europe simply confirmed that the growth of the United States was a blow to political and religious tyranny. It was America's mission, expansionists assumed, to liberate the peoples of California, Mexico, Cuba, Central America, and even Canada, allowing them to share in the blessings of republican government, religious freedom, and modern technology. In 1845 an influential Democratic editor had coined the electric phrase "Manifest Destiny," at the same time denouncing the policy of other nations of "hampering our power, limiting our greatness and checking the fulfillment of our manifest destiny to overspread the continent allotted by Providence for the free development of our yearly multiplying millions."

But the crusade to prevent Europe from imposing a "balance of power" in North America strained the fragile balance on which the Union had always depended—the balance of power between North and South. In the Northeast and particularly in New England, the Mexican War provoked thunderous outrage. It was denounced from press and pulpit as a war of brutal aggression, plotted by the Slave Power to extend slavery and secure permanent control over the free states. The Massachusetts legislature went so far as to proclaim the president's war-inciting acts unconstitutional. The war remained unpopular with

Major Campaigns of the Mexican War

the great majority of Whig leaders, even in the South, who objected to Polk's devious tactics and to the way in which Congress had been stampeded into a declaration of war in order to "rescue" Zachary Taylor's army, which had falsely been said to be endangered. Typical of Whig opposition to the war were Representative Abraham Lincoln's "spot resolutions," which incisively questioned whether the spot at which hostilities had commenced was really, as Polk claimed, on *"our own soil."* Lincoln described Polk's justifications for war as "half insane mumbling" and declared that "the blood of Abel is crying to heaven against him."

Settlement of the Oregon Controversy

By June 1846, a month after the war had begun, even the prowar western Democrats were angered when Polk allowed the Senate to assume full responsibility for approving a treaty that gave to Britain Vancouver Island and all of the Oregon country north of the forty-ninth parallel. As the western expansionists rightly suspected, southerners had never been enthusiastic about adding probable free states in the Pacific Northwest, and Polk had no wish to risk war with Britain when he was intent on dismembering Mexico.

Yet the nation as a whole supported the war. Remembering that opposition to the War of 1812 had split and destroyed the Federalist party, Whigs in Congress dutifully voted for military appropriations and congratulated themselves on the fact that the army's two leading generals, Zachary Taylor and Winfield Scott, were also Whigs. Taylor was the first to win glory. Within a few months, and with few American casualties, he defeated Mexican armies much larger than his own, crossed the Rio Grande, and captured the strategic town of Monterrey, thereby commanding northeastern Mexico. According to Democratic critics, he then settled down to prepare for the presidential campaign of 1848, which he won. In February 1847, however, Taylor crushed another Mexican army more than three times the size of his own in the battle of Buena Vista. The Mexican army was led by Santa Anna, who had earlier been exiled from Mexico. Polk had allowed Santa Anna to enter Mexico from Cuba because he believed that this self-styled "Napoleon of the West" would persuade Mexico to sue for peace.

By early 1847 Polk's professed objectives had been achieved. Mexico's defense of California collapsed so suddenly that the only serious conflict stemmed from the rival and uncoordinated American onslaughts: Consul Larkin's

The Way They Go to California
The discovery of gold in California followed closely on the heels of the American conquest of this Mexican territory. Would-be prospectors were so eager to rush to California from all parts of the country that cartoonists made much sport of imaginary air vehicles supplementing the overcrowded ships bound for Central America or the Pacific.

efforts to mobilize the dissatisfied Spanish Californians; Frémont's leadership of the Anglo-American settlers; the American navy's capture of the port towns; and the arrival of an overland force, led by Colonel Stephen W. Kearny, which conquered New Mexico on the way to San Diego.

But the war was far from over. What the Mexicans lacked in leadership and modern armament, they made up for in national pride and determination. The United States could hardly claim an efficient military machine, but the army sparkled with talent. The roster of young officers read like a gallery of later Union and Confederate heroes: Lee, Grant, Sherman, Meade, McClellan, Beauregard, Stonewall Jackson, and even Jefferson Davis. For Europeans, whose memories of Napoleonic battles had receded into more than thirty years of romantic haze, the American military triumphs were stupendous. The Manchester *Guardian* wrote that the American victories were without parallel, "except in that of Alexander the Great through Persia, Hannibal from Spain to the gates of Rome, or Napoleon over the Alps into Italy." Instead of one Napoleon, America had them "by the dozen."

Treaty of Guadalupe Hidalgo

The events that astonished even hostile Europeans began with General Scott's invasion of central Mexico in March 1847. In the United States Americans were becoming increasingly divided over the meaning of Manifest Destiny. As the American army pushed toward Mexico City, "our Destiny higher an' higher kep' mountin'," in the caustic words of the New England poet James Russell Lowell. By September, after winning a series of hotly contested battles, American troops had captured Mexico City and were resting in the halls of the Montezumas. The Mexicans still refused to surrender. Some southerners believed that slavery could be extended at least into the northern states of Mexico; some antislavery northerners believed that Mexico would be a force for freedom, and therefore they favored annexing the whole country. In general, however, the Democratic leaders—Polk, Buchanan, Lewis Cass, Stephen Douglas, Sam Houston, Jefferson Davis—demanded and expected to get no less than a third of the country south and west of the Rio Grande. They were therefore outraged when Nicholas Trist, America's negotiator whom Polk had angrily ordered to return from Mexico, proceeded to conclude the unauthorized Treaty of Guadalupe Hidalgo. Instead of capitalizing on America's conquests, Trist settled for the same terms that Slidell had been prepared to offer before the war: the United States was to pay Mexico $15 million and assume up to $3.25 million in Mexican debts to American citizens. In return the United States obtained California, New Mexico, and the Rio Grande boundary for Texas, a vast territory containing about 75,000 Spanish-speaking people who had no say about falling under United States rule. Polk would have liked to reject the treaty for being too favorable to Mexico, but he feared that further war and prolonged negotiations would split the already divided Democratic party in an election year. Alarmed by the growing antiwar and Free-Soil movement among northern Democrats, he reluctantly submitted

"The Occupation of the Capital of Mexico by the American Army," by P. S. Daval
Americans enter the historic square, or Zocalo, of Mexico City, March 1847.

PLUCKED:
OR.
THE MEXICAN EAGLE BEFORE THE WAR!   THE MEXICAN EAGLE AFTER THE WAR!

The Triumph of the American Eagle
This cartoon displays the sense of triumphant pride most Americans felt over Mexico's humiliating defeat in 1848.

the treaty to the Senate, which approved it in March 1848. Although the results of the war disappointed the more ardent United States expansionists, the conquests left a legacy of bitterness in Mexico, which continued to view its northern neighbor as a hypocritical aggressor.

Attempts to Acquire Cuba
President Polk also had other cards up his sleeve. In 1848 the Democratic expansionists launched an intensive propaganda campaign to annex the Yucatán Peninsula, a rebellious province that had seceded from Mexico and whose white inhabitants were in danger of being exterminated by hostile Indians. Polk feared British intervention and realized that the American army in Mexico was virtually unemployed, and thus he invited Congress to act. But enthusiasm waned when news arrived that the Yucatán racial crisis had subsided.

Polk was actually far more interested in acquiring Cuba. Like the Yucatán Peninsula, Cuba guarded access to the Gulf of Mexico. Its traditional strategic importance would be increased by any future canal connecting the Gulf of Mexico with the Pacific—something that was already much discussed. Britain, being on the verge of war with Spain in 1848, might at any time gain control of Cuba. Many of Cuba's sugar growers, resenting Britain's increasing interference with their slave-labor system and fearing the continuing spread of emancipation in the West Indies, believed that annexation to the United States was their only guarantee of remaining a prosperous slave society.

The Polk administration knew, however, that the North would not approve the use of military force to acquire more than one-third of a million additional black slaves. Polk's only alternative was to try, with the utmost caution and secrecy, to persuade Spain that $100 million was a good price for a colony that was about to rebel or to be lost to Britain. But Spain greatly prized the only rich remnant of its once-great empire and contemptuously rejected the bungled overtures of Polk's minister. The prospects for annexing Cuba were further dashed when Lewis Cass, the Democratic presidential candidate who favored the purchase of Cuba and the annexation of Yucatán, was defeated in the fall of 1848 by the nonexpansionist Zachary Taylor.

Southern hopes for acquiring Cuba now turned to encouraging a Cuban revolution against Spain. Groups of Cuban emigrés, aided by American expansionists, planned a series of filibustering invasions to liberate the Cuban people. By 1850, however, the anxieties of Cuban planters had subsided and their desire to be taken over by the United States had faded. In 1851, in an episode that strangely anticipated the Bay of Pigs disaster of 1961, Cubans captured the entire expedition of Narciso López, a southern hero, and executed him and fifty of his American followers.

Schemes for further expansion revived under the Democratic administration of Franklin Pierce (1853–57). Members of Pierce's cabinet gave encouragement to John A. Quitman, a filibuster from Mississippi who spent years waiting for the opportune moment to lead a gigantic invasion of Cuba. The invasion never took place, and in 1854 President Pierce warned that the government would prosecute Americans who violated the laws ensuring the nation's neutrality in foreign conflicts. Yet in 1856 Pierce's administration accorded diplomatic recognition to a regime established in Nicaragua by another American filibuster, William Walker. Walker, a native of Tennessee, had earlier led an invasion of Lower California (part of Mexico), where he had unsuccessfully proclaimed an independent republic. Having won acquittal for this violation of America's neutrality laws, Walker became involved in a revolution in Nicaragua. In 1856, aided by a small army of American volunteers, he emerged as president of the Central American nation.

Because Nicaragua occupied a strategic location as a transit point between the Atlantic and Pacific oceans, it became the site of intense Anglo-American rivalry. In the Clayton-Bulwer Treaty of 1850, both nations agreed not to take over any territory in Central America and to ensure that any future interoceanic canal would be unfortified and open to vessels of all countries. But the Clayton-Bulwer Treaty was extremely unpopular, especially in the South, and Walker appealed to American Anglophobia to win support for his dream of a Caribbean empire. He also reestablished slavery in Nicaragua but was soon driven out of the country by the armed forces of neighboring Central American nations that were supported by powerful American shipping interests.

Except for some ardent expansionists in the South, Americans were cooling toward proposals for further territorial acquisitions. In 1854 the Senate almost defeated a treaty that provided for the purchase from Mexico of a parcel of land south of the Gila River in what is now southern New Mexico and Arizona. The land was considered essential for building a railroad that would connect the southeastern states with southern California. But although James Gadsden, Pierce's negotiator with Mexico, had originally sought to obtain the northern part of five Mexican provinces and all of Lower California, the Senate insisted on cutting 9,000 square miles from the modest segment of desert that Mexico had been willing to sell.

In 1854 the expansionist intrigues of Pierce's administration culminated in the secret meetings of America's ministers to Spain, France, and Great Britain, who drafted a long memorandum to the State Department justifying the forcible seizure of Cuba if the island could not be purchased from Spain. Labeled the Ostend Manifesto, the secret memorandum was leaked to the American public at a moment of explosive sectional conflict. It confirmed many northerners' belief that the Slave Power would continue to expand unless checked by political might. One of the authors of the manifesto was James Buchanan, the minister to Britain. In 1856 Buchanan became the Democratic presidential candidate, and his platform openly called for annexing Cuba. By this time, however, the heated controversy over legalizing slavery in Kansas had diverted attention from further national expansion.

CHRONOLOGY

1819	Transcontinental (Adams-Onís) Treaty. Spain renounces claims to the Floridas and Pacific Northwest; United States renounces claims to Texas.
1823	President issues Monroe Doctrine.
1829	Mexico abolishes slavery.
1836	Texas proclaims its independence from Mexico. Martin Van Buren elected president.
1838	John Quincy Adams's filibuster defeats move to annex Texas.
1841	John Tyler becomes president on death of Harrison.
1842	Webster-Ashburton Treaty settles disputed U.S.–Canada boundary; provides for extradition of fugitives.
1843	"Oregon Fever"; first overland caravans to Oregon.
1844	Senate rejects Calhoun's Texas annexation treaty. James K. Polk elected president.

1845	Texas enters Union as slave state. Polk gives aggressive reformulation to Monroe Doctrine. John Slidell's unsuccessful mission to Mexico to negotiate purchase of New Mexico and California.
1846	Beginning of Mexican War. General Zachary Taylor invades Mexico from the north. Treaty with Britain divides Oregon Territory along forty-ninth parallel.
1847	General Winfield Scott captures Vera Cruz and Mexico City.
1848	Treaty of Guadalupe Hidalgo ends Mexican War and establishes Rio Grande as border. Secret attempts to purchase Cuba from Spain. Zachary Taylor elected president.
1854	Ostend Manifesto favors U.S. purchase or annexation of Cuba. Railroads link New York City with the Mississippi River.
1857	Financial panic and depression.

SUGGESTED READINGS

Ray A. Billington and Martin Ridge, *Westward Expansion* (1982), covers every aspect of America's westward expansion and contains an encyclopedic bibliography. Albert K. Weinberg, *Manifest Destiny* (1935), is a fascinating study in intellectual history, but it should be supplemented by Edward M. Burns, *The American Idea of Mission: Concepts of National Purpose and Destiny* (1957). For American expansionism and Manifest Destiny, see Thomas R. Hietala, *Manifest Design: Anxious Aggrandizement in Late Jacksonian America* (1985), and Reginald Horsman, *Race and Manifest Destiny: The Origins of American Racial Anglo-Saxonism* (1981). In three outstanding revisionist studies, Frederick W. Merk reemphasizes the importance of slavery and the fear of British encroachments on the West: *Manifest Destiny and Mission in American History: A Reinterpretation* (1963); *The Monroe Doctrine and American Expansionism 1843–1849* (1966); and *Slavery and the Annexation of Texas* (1972). For a detailed treatment of western diplomatic history, see D. M. Fletcher, *The Diplomacy of Annexation: Texas, Oregon and the Mexican War* (1973).

The fullest history of the origins of the Monroe Doctrine is Dexter Perkins, *The Monroe Doctrine, 1823–1826* (1927). Ernest R. May, *The Making of the Monroe Doctrine* (1975), stresses the importance of domestic politics preceding the presidential election of 1824. For the European background, see E. H. Tatum, Jr., *The United States and Europe, 1815–1823* (1936), and C. C. Griffin, *The United States and the Disruption of the Spanish Empire* (1937). For a general introduction to American foreign policy, see Lloyd C. Gardner et al., *Creation of the American Empire* (1973); for a more traditional view, see Samuel F. Bemis, *A Diplomatic History of the United States* (1965). The standard work on Asia is A. Whitney Griswold, *The Far Eastern Policy of the United States* (1938).

On Texas two of the standard works are by William C. Binkley: *The Texas Revolution* (1952) and *The Expansionist Movement in Texas, 1836–1850* (1925). Much can still be learned from the older, nationalistic studies: J. H. Smith, *The Annexation of Texas* (1911), and E. C. Barker, *Mexico and Texas, 1821–1835* (1928). For a meticulous portrayal of the Mexican point of view, see Gene M. Brack, *Mexico Views Manifest Destiny, 1821–1846* (1976).

The best study of the American settlement of Oregon is Malcolm Clark, Jr., *Eden Seekers: The Settlement of Oregon, 1812–1862* (1981). Frederick W. Merk has written several superb essays on the Anglo-American diplomacy regarding Oregon: *Albert Gallatin and the Oregon Problem* (1950), and *The Oregon Question: Essays in Anglo-American Diplomacy and Politics* (1967). For general histories of the Northwest, see Norman A. Graebner, *Empire on the Pacific* (1955); Oscar O. Winther, *The Great Northwest* (1947); and Earl Pomeroy, *The Pacific Slope: A History* (1965).

By far the best account of the overland emigration to the Far West is John D. Unruh, Jr., *The Plains Across: The Overland Emigrants and the Trans-Mississippi West, 1840–1860* (1979). For the experience of women and the division of sex roles, see John Mack Faragher, *Women and Men on the Overland Trail* (1979); Sandra L. Myres, *Westering Women and the Frontier Experience, 1800–1915* (1982); and Julie Roy Jeffrey, *Frontier Women: The Trans-Mississippi West, 1840–1860* (1979). Two outstanding studies of the earlier, midwestern frontier are John Mack Faragher, *Sugar Creek: Life on the Illinois Prairie* (1986), and Malcolm J. Rohrbough, *The Trans-Appalachian Frontier: Peoples, Societies, and Institutions, 1775–1850* (1978). The fascinating story of government exploration of the West is described with admirable care in William H. Goetzmann, *Army Exploration in the American West, 1803–1863* (1959). Gloria G. Cline, *Exploring the Great Basin* (1963), is also an invaluable study. For the all-important fur trade, see David J. Wishart, *The Fur Trade of the American West, 1817–1840* (1979), which can be supplemented by H. M. Chittenden, *The American Fur Trade of the Far West* (3 vols., 1935). Although sometimes scorned by professional historians, Bernard DeVoto's *Across the Wide Missouri* (1947), which deals with the Mountain Men and the fur trade, and DeVoto's *The Year of Decision, 1846* (1943), which considers the political, social, and cultural events surrounding America's war with Mexico, are exciting, readable, and basically accurate accounts of the early West.

J. H. Smith, *The War with Mexico* (2 vols., 1919), is still useful as a comprehensive source of information, but students should turn first to Robert W. Johannsen, *To the Halls of the Montezumas: The Mexican War in the American Imagination* (1985). The best recent account of the military campaigns is K. Jack Bauer, *The Mexican War, 1846–1848* (1974). Gene M. Brack, *Mexico Views Manifest Destiny* (1976), deserves special mention for its insight into the Mexican motives for war. For the conquest of California, see Neal Harlow, *California Conquered: The Annexation of a Mexican Province, 1846–1850* (1982). For an understanding of the Mexican provinces before American annexation, see David J. Weber, *The Mexican Frontier, 1821–1846:*

The American Southwest Under Mexico (1982). John H. Schroeder, *Mr. Polk's War: American Opposition and Dissent, 1846–1848* (1973), is an excellent study of antiwar sentiment. Much relevant information on these years of decision can also be found in Paul H. Bergeron, *The Presidency of James K. Polk* (1987), which presents a more moderate portrayal of Polk than does Charles G. Sellers's standard biography, *James K. Polk: Continentalist, 1843–1846,* vol. 2 (1966). See also William R. Brock, *Parties and Political Conscience: American Dilemmas, 1840–1850* (1979). For American involvement in Cuba and Central America, see William O. Scroggs, *Filibusters and Financiers: The Story of William Walker and His Associates* (1916), and Robert E. May, *The Southern Dream of a Caribbean Empire, 1854–1861* (1973).

17

Compromise and Conflict

≈

O N THE surface the two-party system resolved the dangerous sectional conflicts that had been unleashed by the annexation of Texas, the Mexican War, and the acquisition of a new continental empire. By the early 1850s cohesion and compromise seemed to have triumphed over division. Middle-class Americans were more prosperous than they ever had been before, and for the most part they were able to ignore or rationalize evidence of continuing injustice and exploitation. Public interest in further empire building faded, despite attempts by Democratic leaders to revive the people's enthusiasm. There was sufficient challenge, it seemed, in settling a continent, constructing more miles of railroad track in the 1850s than could be found in the rest of the world combined, and extending American commerce. In 1854, for example, Commodore Matthew Perry used diplomatic tact and a display of naval power to help break down the Japanese government's already crumbling resistance to Western trade and influence. In view of such global as well as domestic opportunities, political realists believed that the North did not desire to interfere with slavery in the South. In the eyes of moderates, there was no reason for the North to fear that slavery would expand beyond its "natural limits" in Missouri, Arkansas, and Texas.

There were hazards, however, in this triumph of moderation. The stormy passions that culminated in the Compromise of 1850 gave way to political apathy and disenchantment. Voters complained that Whigs and Democrats had the same self-serving lust for office, mouthed the same stale rhetoric on such stale issues as banks and tariffs, and were equally unresponsive to public needs and fears. For reasons that varied in each state and locality, significant numbers of voters abandoned their former party allegiance. One consequence of this broad realignment was the rapid disintegration of the Whigs, especially in the South. By 1855 the anti-Catholic Know-Nothing party had replaced the Whigs as the dominant alternative to the Democrats in the Northeast. In all sections of the country, the weakening of balanced national parties opened the way for new and more extreme appeals to resist the encroachments of some supposedly anti-republican "power."

The American fear of unchecked power and special privilege was deeply rooted in the colonial and Revolutionary past. The fear acquired new dimensions, however, as the restraints of local customs and traditions gave way to individual enterprise and unrestrained capitalism. For a time the party system had succeeded in channeling and moderating public alarm over the rise of various "powers," such as the Freemasons, the "Monster Bank," the "Money Power," Jackson's "monarchical" presidency, and the alleged British conspiracy to block American expansion. In each case, alarmist rhetoric was ultimately balanced by the political realities of a two-party system. By the mid-1850s, however, the national Whig party had collapsed and the controversy over slavery in the territories began to distract attention from anti-Catholic nativism. At this ominous juncture, the Americans' fear of unchecked power became grounded in the concrete conflict of interests between free and slave societies.

Like a magnetic field, black slavery polarized opposing clusters of values, interests, and aspirations. "Are you for Freedom, or are you for Slavery?" Senator Charles Sumner asked a crowd at Boston's Faneuil Hall: "Are you for God, or are you for the Devil?" Echoing the theme that there could be no peace between slavery and democracy, Theodore Parker, Boston's famous Unitarian minister, affirmed that "the idea which allows Slavery in South Carolina will establish it also in New England." Southerners believed that any withdrawal of federal sanction and protection for slavery would expose private property to the tyranny of a national majority, undermine the equal sovereignty of the states, and lead America in the direction of European "wage-slavery" and class warfare—to say nothing of race mixing and black revolt.

By the mid-1850s a growing number of northerners had become convinced that black slavery, by supporting "idle planters" and by associating work with servility, undermined the dignity of labor. As an alternative to the whips and chains of the South, the North offered an idealized vision of prosperity and progress without exploitation—a vision of industrious farmers and proud artisans, of schoolhouses, churches, town meetings, and self-made men. The vast territories of the West, unfenced and held in common by the American people, would thus become the critical testing ground for two competing versions of the American dream.

Free Soil and the Challenge of California

Once the United States had acquired the vast Mexican territories from Texas to California, national decisions had to be made. All the constitutional issues and the political and moral arguments of the Missouri crisis of 1819–21 were revived. Would the South be able to maintain its balance of power in the Senate? What was the precise nature of congressional power over territories and the creation of

Poster for a Free Soil Rally

new states? Would the government limit the future expansion of slavery? Would it adopt a policy of noninterference? Or would it perhaps openly sanction slavery by recognizing black slaves as a form of property entitled to federal protection in the western territories?

The Wilmot Proviso It was predictable that a move would be made in Congress to prohibit slavery in the territories acquired during the Mexican War; similar moves had been made since 1784 concerning the trans-Appalachian West, Mississippi, Louisiana, Arkansas, and Missouri. In 1846 the motion came from David Wilmot, a Pennsylvania Democrat who disavowed any sympathy for the southern slaves and who wished to exclude free blacks as well as slaves from the new western territories. The Wilmot Proviso, a proposed amendment to an appropriation bill, was extraordinarily significant because it was used to challenge what protesters called "Mr. Polk's War" and all that it meant. The legislatures of fourteen free states eventually endorsed the proviso's principle of barring slavery from any territories obtained from Mexico. The House of Representatives several times approved the measure, which antislavery members continued to offer, but enough northern senators ignored the instructions of their states to bring defeat in the Senate.

From 1847 to 1850 this sectional insistence that the territories ceded by Mexico remain "free soil" challenged Whig and Democratic party unity. "There can be no compromise between right and wrong," proclaimed Joshua R. Giddings, the antislavery Whig congressman from Ohio. Many southern Whigs denounced any proposal for excluding slavery from the territories as a direct violation of southern rights and of state equality. "The North is insolent and unyielding," declared Georgia Whig Alexander Stephens. "My southern blood...is up and...I am prepared to fight at all hazards and to the last extremity in vindication of our honor and our rights." The more extreme Calhounites tried to erode national party loyalties by uniting all southerners in defense of sectional rights and in opposition to any candidate who failed to oppose the Wilmot Proviso. In the North in the election of 1848, both Whigs and Democrats suffered losses to the new Free-Soil party, which endorsed the Wilmot Proviso and which nominated Martin Van Buren for president. So-called Conscience Whigs, centered in Massachusetts, refused to vote for Zachary Taylor, the former general and Louisiana slaveholder nominated by the Whigs. The Conscience Whigs claimed that moral protest against the further expansion of slavery should take precedence over the material and political advantages of a united Whig party. Free-Soil Democrats were led by the so-called New York Barnburners, politicians who had been angered when the Democrats rejected Van Buren in favor of Polk in 1844 and who then had been further alienated when Polk's administration had favored rival Democratic factions in distributing patronage.

But this upsurge of sectional politics proved to be temporary and quite unsuccessful in undermining the two-party system. Both the Whig and the Democratic parties evaded official commitment on the territorial issue and unashamedly made contradictory appeals to northern and southern voters. In the election of 1848, Van Buren received only 14 percent of the popular vote in the North and won no electoral votes for his Free-Soil party. Taylor carried even Massachusetts, where the Whig defections seemed most threatening; Whigs actually gained strength in the South. As a result of this defeat, Van Buren and most of his Free-Soil Democratic followers returned to the national Democratic party that now shared common interests in opposing a new Whig administration. The Conscience Whigs mostly returned to their uneasy alliance with the so-called Cotton Whigs, led by such powerful New England textile manufacturers as Abbott Lawrence and Nathan Appleton, who desired a continuation of their profitable trade relations with the cotton-producing South. And early in 1849 it became clear that the Calhounites had little hope of winning support for a new southern rights coalition. The nation's voters appeared to have subdued sectionalism's threat to federal union.

The survival of national parties did nothing, however, to resolve the territorial issue or to break the congressional deadlock over the Wilmot Proviso. Northern Democrats had favored either extending the Missouri Compromise line of 36°30′ to the Pacific or leaving the question of slavery to territorial legislatures without congressional interference. The latter alternative was known as popular sovereignty. President Taylor, on the other hand, tried to prevent further sectional confrontations by urging California and New Mexico to draft constitutions and to apply for immediate statehood. This strategy would have avoided congressional action either sanctioning or banning slavery. Both Taylor and his southern opponents recognized that the inhabitants of the Far West, if

California Gold Diggers
Gold mining was an arduous and usually unsuccessful enterprise that was both exhausting and disheartening to many of the migrants who streamed to California from Australia, Europe, and Latin America as well as from the eastern states. Nevertheless, there was always the hope of striking pay dirt and becoming rich almost overnight.

allowed to organize state governments, would almost certainly vote to exclude black slavery (and perhaps free blacks as well). These settlers, most of whom had lived in the intensely racist states of the Old Northwest, cared little about the fate of the slaves in the South, but they feared the competition of slave labor in a "land of promise" that was supposedly reserved for aspiring whites.

Suddenly antiblack feeling became acute in California. Gold was discovered in the American River in 1848, and the great gold rush of 1849 brought tens of thousands of settlers who resented the prolongation of ineffective military government and who clamored for instant statehood. It also brought a small number of southern masters and slaves—and of free black prospectors who, according to hostile whites, were "proverbially lucky." White miners considered it unfair to compete with slave labor, and they also considered it degrading "to swing a pick side by side with the Negro," whether free or slave. Fear and hatred of blacks, particularly in the mining regions, led the California constitutional convention of 1849 to copy the sections of the newly written Iowa constitution that prohibited slavery.

In Oregon, which was organized as a separate territory south of the Columbia River, the fusion of racism with antislavery was even more clear-cut. Although few blacks had arrived in the region by 1844, the provisional government followed the models of the Old Northwest and ordered the removal of both slaves and free blacks. The South succeeded in delaying Oregon's elevation to territorial status until 1848, and as late as 1857 there was a strong drive to legalize slavery in the Oregon Territory. After heated public debate, a referendum decisively rejected slavery but approved even more decisively the constitutional exclusion of free black settlers—a measure that Congress accepted as part of the state's constitution.

By 1849, however, southerners tended to interpret even these dubious forms of antislavery as abolitionism in disguise. Most southern leaders, whether Whig or Democrat, had moved from a defensive policy of censorship and gag rules to an aggressive hostility to any barrier, however theoretical, to the expansion and legitimation of slavery. They feared that enactment of the Wilmot Proviso would swing the full weight of the federal government against the institution of slavery, which it had always protected. By 1849 Free-Soil and antislavery congressmen had already linked the Wilmot Proviso with demands for abolishing slavery in the District of Columbia, which, like the territories, was subject to federal legislation. The new personal liberty laws of the northern states also raised the prospect that the North would become as secure a refuge for runaway slaves as British Canada, to which a small number of blacks had successfully escaped.

Indeed, for a growing number of southern diehards, the Northeast was by the late 1840s becoming a perfect replica of the British enemy. Britain, these southerners believed, had first exploited its own slave colonies, then ruined them under the influence of misguided humanitarianism, and finally used antislavery as a mask of righteousness in assuming commercial and ideological domination of the world. According to a typical proslavery editorial printed in a Democratic newspaper in 1860, the West Indian blacks freed by the British had "degenerated into a barbarism not much in advance of their race in Africa. . . . It is altogether useless to say that the negro has a right to liberty, when it can be conclusively demonstrated that he is physically unadapted for it. . . . The British experiment of emancipation . . . in the West Indies . . . proves it beyond a doubt." Furthermore, the Northeast, like England, was attracting millions of immigrant wage earners, was developing vast urban centers, and was gaining mastery over the mysterious sources of credit and investment capital. Unless Dixie made its stand, it would therefore share the fate of the exploited, debt-ridden, and ravaged West Indies. If the South were deprived of land and labor for expansion, its boundaries pushed back from the west and the Gulf of Mexico as well as from the north, it would then be subjected by a tyrannical government to slave emancipation and race mixing.

The Crisis of 1850

The Taylor administration faced a succession of problems that exposed irreconcilable divisions within the Whig party. Zachary Taylor was a recent convert to the Whig party (previously, he had never even voted); he had run for president as a military hero and as a man "above party." As president he aggravated the mistrust of the so-called Old Whigs when, seeking to broaden the administration's national support, he bypassed party faithfuls in distributing patronage. Taylor also seemed to betray traditional Whig principles when he tried to build a broad coalition that could compete with the Democrats, who were gaining enormous strength from the votes of recent immigrants.

The preceding administration, that of the Democrat Polk, had reestablished the Independent Treasury, reaffirming the Democrats' opposition to any alliance between government and banks.* It had also enacted the Walker Tariff, which had drastically reduced the duties the Whigs had established in 1842. To the dismay of Old Whigs, Taylor balked at proposals to repeal both these Democratic measures, and he advocated compromises that would avoid unnecessary conflict. Simultaneously, southern Whigs, who had thought they could trust a Louisiana planter, were shocked to discover that Taylor had no objection to admitting California as a free state. In fact Taylor even dumbfounded his powerful Georgia backer Robert Toombs by saying that if Congress saw fit to pass the Wilmot Proviso, "I will not veto it."

When the Thirty-first Congress convened in December 1849, there was a prolonged and ominous conflict over electing the Speaker of the House. It soon became clear that Taylor's program for immediately admitting California and New Mexico as states would receive no support from southern Whigs or even from such party chieftains as Clay, Webster, and Seward. Even one new free state would break the balance of fifteen free states and fifteen slave states represented in the Senate. Tensions were heightened by the knowledge that all northern legislatures, with one exception, had instructed their senators to insist on the Wilmot Proviso in any agreement concerning the territories. Also, a growing number of southern legislatures were appointing delegates to attend a convention at Nashville in June 1850 to consider potentially revolutionary measures for the defense of southern rights.

Clay's Resolutions   In January 1850 the aging Henry Clay temporarily recovered leadership of the Whig party by offering the Senate a series of compromise resolutions. An adept and skillful bargainer, Clay had been credited with saving the Union in 1820 and 1832, at the time of the Missouri and nullification crises, and he now sought a permanent solution to sectional strife. As an alternative to the Wilmot Proviso and to the popular southern plan that would extend the Missouri Compromise line to the Pacific, Clay favored admitting California as a free state, in accordance with the clear wishes of its settlers. He proposed that no restrictions on slavery be imposed in the rest of the vast territory that had been acquired from Mexico (New Mexico and Utah territories included most of present-day Colorado, Arizona, and Nevada). Clay also attempted to resolve the critical Texas issue. Texas claimed a

---

*For the Independent Treasury, see chapter 15, p. 508.

Countering the Fugitive Slave Law

This abolitionist broadside dramatizes the ways in which the Fugitive Slave Law impinged upon the lives of the people of Boston while also warning the black population about the danger of being kidnapped by conniving public officials and shipped off to the South as a slave.

CAUTION!!

COLORED PEOPLE

OF BOSTON, ONE & ALL,

You are hereby respectfully CAUTIONED and advised, to avoid conversing with the

Watchmen and Police Officers of Boston,

For since the recent ORDER OF THE MAYOR & ALDERMEN, they are empowered to act as

KIDNAPPERS

AND

Slave Catchers,

And they have already been actually employed in KIDNAPPING, CATCHING, AND KEEPING SLAVES. Therefore, if you value your LIBERTY, and the *Welfare of the Fugitives* among you, *Shun* them in every possible manner, as so many *HOUNDS* on the track of the most unfortunate of your race.

Keep a Sharp Look Out for KIDNAPPERS, and have TOP EYE open.

APRIL 24, 1851.

western boundary that included more than half of the present state of New Mexico and parts of Oklahoma and Colorado. As a result there was an imminent danger of border conflict between the armed forces of Texas and the United States, a conflict that could easily escalate into civil war. Further, when Texas had become an American state it had lost its former customs revenue, which was a matter of considerable concern to the influential holders of Texas bonds. To resolve these problems, Clay proposed that the United States government assume the Texas debt—which promised windfall profits to Texas bondholders as compensation for Texas's acceptance of New Mexico's territorial claims.

In a gesture to northern feelings, Clay recommended that Congress prohibit professional slave trading in the District of Columbia, to rid the national capital of the moral eyesore of slave pens and public auctions. But he also urged that Congress ease southern fears of abolitionists' intentions by formally denying that it had authority to interfere with the interstate slave trade and by promising that slavery would never be abolished in the District of Columbia without the consent of its citizens, as well as the consent of neighboring Maryland. Finally, in this so-called Omnibus Bill, Clay proposed that Congress adopt a fugitive-slave law that would severely punish anyone who obstructed slaveholders' efforts to recover runaway slaves in any part of the United States.

The Compromise of 1850

The ensuing congressional struggle to achieve the so-called Compromise of 1850 took place on two distinct levels. On the loftier level the Senate became a public forum for some of the most famous and eloquent speeches in American history—speeches that clarified conflicting principles, conflicting political philosophies, and conflicting visions of America's heritage, mission, and destiny. Calhoun, so ill and so near death that he had to listen as a colleague read his farewell address to the nation, argued that a tyrannical northern majority had gradually excluded southerners from 1.25 million square miles of territory. No further compromises could save the South from a continuing loss of power or prevent the day when a hostile and increasingly centralized government would carry out the demands of the abolitionists. The Union, he declared, might be saved if the North agreed to open all the territories to slaveholders and to restore, by constitutional amendment, an equal and permanent balance of sectional power. Otherwise self-preservation would require the South to separate—and to fight if the North refused to accept secession in peace.

Daniel Webster, in his famous reply on March 7, 1850, insisted: "There can be no such thing as a peaceable secession." Recoiling in horror from the prospect of disunion and civil war, he pleaded for compromise and for a charitable spirit toward the South. He agreed with southern complaints against the abolitionists and supported Clay's demand for an effective fugitive-slave law. The territorial issue, he claimed, should be no cause for further discord. Convinced that slave labor could never be profitable in the western territories, Webster saw no need for a further legal exclusion that could only antagonize the South.

On March 11 the growing antislavery audience in the Senate found a spokesman in William H. Seward, the New York Whig leader who had helped engineer Taylor's candidacy but who now refused to support the president's plan. Seward, whom Webster described as "subtle and unscrupulous" and dedicated "to the one idea of making himself president," gave political force to the traditional abolitionist doctrine concerning the territories: "There is a higher law than the Constitution, which regulates our authority over the domain...the common heritage of mankind."

These and other great speeches raised momentous issues, but it is unlikely that they changed many votes. The second level of struggle involved political infighting that ranged from bribes and lobbying by speculators in Texas bonds to patient and tireless work by committees of experts faithful to American political procedures and to the technicalities of constitutional law. Apart from the moderating influence of powerful banking and business interests, which stood to gain by national unity, four circumstances contributed to the final congressional approval of the Compromise of 1850.

First, despite signs of an ominous sectional division of parties, Stephen Douglas rallied a core of Democrats, particularly from the Old Northwest and border states, who could counteract the combined pressures of southern and northern extremists. Second, Douglas's drive to win southern support for a

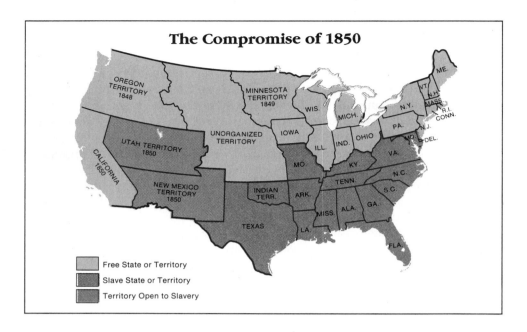

railroad connecting Chicago with the Gulf of Mexico (soon known as the Illinois Central Railroad) demonstrated the rewards that could be gained through sectional cooperation. Third, under Douglas's leadership the Senate wisely abandoned the Omnibus Bill that combined most of the compromise in one package. This move allowed both houses of Congress to form sectional alliances that were just barely strong enough to carry each measure—the North overcoming southern resistance to the admission of California as a free state and the abolition of the slave trade in the District of Columbia; the South, thanks to many northern abstentions, having its way in enacting the new Fugitive Slave Law. Finally, President Taylor, who had shown no sympathy for the compromise, died suddenly in July. Millard Fillmore, his successor, was close to Webster and Clay and threw the full weight of his administration behind the compromise. Fillmore also skillfully defused the explosive crisis over the Texas–New Mexico boundary. In September 1850 much of the nation sank back in relief, assuming that the adoption of Clay's and Douglas's proposals marked the end of serious sectional conflict.

Thus the Compromise of 1850 was made up of the following points: (1) the admission of California as a free state; (2) the organization of the rest of the Mexican cession into two territories, New Mexico and Utah, without a federal restriction on slavery; (3) the adjustment of the Texas–New Mexico boundary; (4) the award of $10 million to Texas as compensation for the land yielded to New Mexico; (5) the prohibition of the slave trade but not of slavery itself in the District of Columbia; and (6) a stringent fugitive-slave law. This complex con-

Blacks Resist the Fugitive Slave Law
When Edward Gorsuch and his son tried to recover four escaped slaves at Christiana, Pennsylvania, in September 1851, they provoked a battle with a community of blacks who had given shelter to the fugitives. The blacks killed Gorsuch and wounded his son. Some thirty blacks and whites, including two Quakers who had refused to join a posse to round up the blacks, were arrested and charged with treason against the United States. After a trial that attracted national attention, the jury acquitted all of the defendants.

gressional agreement created an illusion of peace, but there was no real consensus on any of the critical issues. In the District of Columbia, trading and selling of slaves continued, although not as openly as before. Blacks, and particularly Indians, continued to be held as slaves on the supposedly free soil of California. The Fugitive Slave Law, which deprived accused blacks of a jury trial and of the right to testify in their own defense, dramatized the agonizing consequences of enforcing a national compromise for which the North had little taste.*

One of the northern responses to this law was the serial publication in 1851 of Harriet Beecher Stowe's *Uncle Tom's Cabin,* a novel that soon reached millions in book form and in stage presentations. Mrs. Stowe's popular classic, today often underrated as a literary work, interpreted the moral and psychological evils of slavery in terms that were perfectly attuned to the culture of northern evangelical Protestantism, especially to its belief in the sanctity of the family. *Uncle Tom's Cabin* vividly demonstrated the ability of slavery to destroy or corrupt the family unit. And it encouraged every reader who sympathized with the fictional fugitives, in their terrible ordeal of escape, to share the guilt of a compromise that gave national sanction to slave catchers.

---

*For northern reactions to the Fugitive Slave Law, see chapter 14, p. 482.

Harriet Beecher Stowe (1811–96)
The daughter of Lyman Beecher, Harriet Beecher Stowe suddenly became not only the most famous member of an illustrious family, but also the world's most admired and hated woman. Bitterly attacked in the South, she was lionized in England and soon became an international literary celebrity.

Popular Sovereignty   It was on the territorial issue that the Compromise of 1850 seeded the worst storm clouds of the future. The compromise was deliberately ambiguous concerning the territories. Congress appeared to reaffirm its authority to prohibit slavery in the territories, for it delegated this authority to the legislatures of Utah and New Mexico, subject to the possible veto of a federally appointed governor or of Congress itself. To appease the South, however, Congress publicly expressed doubts about the constitutionality of this authority, which could be determined only by the Supreme Court. In effect Congress invited slaveholders to challenge the constitutionality of any restrictions that territorial governments might make on their property rights before the state governments had been established. Most southerners reluctantly accepted "popular sovereignty" because it at least left the doors open to slavery. Northern moderates—called "doughfaces" by their antislavery enemies—were convinced that popular sovereignty would ultimately guarantee free states but would avoid a congressional showdown that would lead to the South's secession.

To pragmatists like Daniel Webster and Stephen Douglas, it seemed inconceivable that national policy of any kind could reverse the dominant western pattern of free-labor settlement. Cultivating cotton was too profitable and the value of slaves too great to encourage risky experiments in the semiarid West. It is true that in 1852 Utah legally recognized slavery and that in 1857 New Mexico adopted a slave code. Yet neither territory acquired more than a handful of black slaves. Southerners, long accustomed to the security of slave patrols and local law enforcement agencies, were fearful of taking valuable human property into a region where courts might invoke the old Mexican law prohibiting slavery and where legislatures might at any time be swayed by the convictions of the free-soil and antiblack majority. Moderates like Douglas claimed that the Compromise of

1850 was a "final settlement," but in fact it narrowed the area of future acceptable compromise. The belief grew in the South that disunion would be the inevitable—and the only honorable response to any further northern threats.

Destabilizing the Two-Party System

Despite the occasional appearance of parties oriented to special issues, American political history has been dominated by a two-party system inclined toward compromise and addressed to a wide range of local and national interests. The more historians have learned about American political behavior, the more they have marveled over the unique events of the early and mid-1850s: the destabilization of the traditional party system, the sudden collapse of the Whig party, and the unlikely rise to power of a sectional third party, the Republicans. Imagine the surprise people would feel today if in the space of six years the Democrats or Republicans were to disappear and be replaced by an "extremist" regional party that actually succeeded in electing a president! The political transformation of the mid-1850s is all the more significant since it opened the way for the election of Abraham Lincoln, the secession of the southern states, and the Civil War.

Immigration and Nativism   It is important to recall that the Whig and Democratic parties both claimed to defend republican traditions against various kinds of privilege or threatening "powers," and also relied on state and local issues for their high voter turnouts. The period from 1844 to 1860 was characterized by vigorous economic growth that evaporated many of the concerns that had risen to the fore after the Panic of 1819 and the depression of 1837–43. Many voters grew bored with debates over banking, fiscal policy, tariffs, and internal improvements. What did shock many native-born Americans between 1845 and 1854 was the largest influx of immigrants, as a percentage of the nation's total population, in all American history. The nearly 3 million immigrants who arrived in those brief years equaled the total 1850 population of nine of the North's sixteen states! Although it is easy in retrospect to take pride in America's heritage as a nation of immigrants and a haven for the oppressed, one should not underestimate the physical disruption and revolutionary cultural impact produced by the disembarkation of armies of foreigners, many of them destitute, who differed in religion, customs, language, and ethnic values from most native-born Americans.

Because the immigrants, although usually of peasant origin, tended to congregate in the larger cities of New York, Massachusetts, Pennsylvania, and Ohio, nativists predictably blamed them for overcrowded tenements, the collapse of sanitary facilities, and an escalation of street crime and violence. The most explosive conflicts, however, arose from the fact that the great majority of the Irish and many of the German newcomers were Roman Catholics. Anti-Catholicism had been deeply embedded in colonial America, and the religious revivals of the 1820s and 1830s had cultivated the belief that the survival of republican government depended on the liberating and unifying force of Protestantism.

Protestant revivalists had repeatedly attacked any cohesive group, such as the Freemasons or the Mormon or Catholic churches, that supposedly put institutional loyalty above individual moral choice. Prominent northern clergymen, mostly Whigs, had saturated the country with lurid and often hysterical anti-Catholic propaganda. Their actions had contributed to mob violence and church burning, which culminated in a bloody Philadelphia riot in 1844. On one occasion, however, a group of nativists actually protected a Catholic church against a rival mob.

Fortunately, bigotry was partly counterbalanced by the political self-interest of the two-party system. Even a prejudiced politician understood that immigrants cast votes, at least after the five years' wait required for naturalized citizenship. While the Irish in particular flocked to the Democratic banner, Whig leaders like Governor William H. Seward of New York knew that their own political fortunes depended on capturing part of the immigrant and Catholic vote. Seward offended many of his fellow Whigs by advocating public support for Catholic schools. Until 1853 the need to attract at least some immigrant voters in closely contested elections kept nativism from acquiring a political focus.

Even by 1850, however, it was becoming clear that the hundreds of thousands of newcomers, with their divergent values and lifestyles, threatened the Whig dream of an ordered, morally progressive, and homogeneous society—what one nativist congressman referred to as "a unity of character and custom." And Catholic leaders, among them Archbishop John Hughes of New York, made no apologies for their own mobilization of political power or for their own vision of a Catholic America. As Hughes launched a counteroffensive against tax support for public schools, which he considered seedbeds of Protestant indoctrination, the nativists warned that immigrant voters slavishly obeyed the orders of their priests who, as agents of European despotism, sought to undermine America's republican institutions. The fact that the Catholic church had opposed the European revolutionary movements of 1848—and supported the subsequent restoration of repressive government in France, Austria-Hungary, and the Italian and German states—reinforced many Americans' fear of antirepublican subversion. Paradoxically, nativists concluded that America's very commitment to freedom of speech and representative institutions had made it that much easier for an authoritarian church to subvert those institutions: "[T]his Church," a prominent nativist wrote in 1856, "relying on the 'profligacy of our politicians,' has freely declared its intentions (being an alien), to substitute the mitre for our liberty cap, and blend the crozier with the stars and stripes! and to subvert 'the very Citadel of Republican strength in the free education of youth and the consequent independence of mind.'"

The "Hidden Depression" An economic crisis, which is only beginning to be understood by historians, greatly reinforced the popular appeal of nativism, especially to urban craftsmen, tradesmen, and petty merchants. Although the period 1848–55 has generally been interpreted as a time of prosperity, especially for farmers and planters, it brought acute distress to millions of northern manual workers. For nonfarm workers, who made up approximately one-fourth of the North's electorate, real wages—that is, wages adjusted for the cost of living—plummeted. Skilled workers of various kinds were replaced by casual day laborers; in the Midwest as well as Northeast, layoffs multiplied in the iron, construction, and lumber industries. This so-called hidden depression was partly the result of unprecedented immigration and a rapidly expanding labor force, which put downward pressure on wages and, because of the shortage of housing, upward pressure on rents. Simultaneously, food prices soared as American merchants exported grains and other foodstuffs to meet European demand.

While the disastrous hardships of native-born workers were the result of complex shifts in national and international markets, which also encouraged the massive westward flow of immigrant workers, it was easy to scapegoat the immigrants themselves as the source of all evil, as the corrupters of a once pure and prosperous America. Employers helped this process along by recruiting immigrant workers as strikebreakers. The early 1850s witnessed the rapid growth of trade unions and the outbreak of numerous strikes. Yet when faced with hungry mouths to feed, foreign-born workers were generally willing to take the place of strikers, at much lower pay. And by 1860 some 69 percent of New York City's labor force was foreign-born.

As early as the mid-1840s nativist workers in Philadelphia and New York City had begun organizing various secret fraternal orders to advance their own interests. Although hostile toward the temporizing and elite leadership of the Whig and Democratic parties, groups like the Order of United Americans were less concerned with politics than with providing mutual aid, insurance, and other kinds of assistance to native-born workers. Secrecy was in part a shield against the legal actions taken to prevent workers from unionizing or "conspiring" to present a united front to employers. Increasingly angered by the way politicians of both parties catered to the immigrant vote, the Order of United Americans mounted a drive in 1851 to defend New York's public schools against politicians who accepted the position of the Catholic church. The nativists also merged traditional working-class demands—such as an end to imprisonment for debt—with appeals for more police control of public drunkenness, prostitution, and rioting, all of which they associated with immigrants. As "the Know Nothing fever" reached "epidemic" proportions, as one Pennsylvanian reported, the nativists proclaimed that "Americans must rule America; and to this end native-born citizens should be selected for all State, Federal and municipal offices of government employment, in preference to all others."

The Election of 1852   The election of 1852 was the last "normal" election, preceding the disintegration of the two-party system. And the contest revealed the strains of trying to mitigate or conceal the nativist and sectional controversies. Despite the moderating efforts of most politicians, the "ethnocultural" issues raised by immigrants and nativists overlapped and competed for public attention with the sectional hostility engendered by the debates and decisions of 1850.

In 1852 the Whigs were still seriously divided over the Compromise of 1850. In deference to southern demands, the party's 1852 platform endorsed this essentially Democratic "final settlement" of the slavery issue. Southern Whigs, however, were infuriated by the party's refusal to renominate Fillmore, whom many northerners saw as a puppet of the Slave Power. Winfield Scott, the military hero whom the Whigs finally nominated for president, showed signs of becoming a Seward protégé, like Zachary Taylor. Because southerners no longer trusted northern Whigs as reliable allies in the defense of slavery, the party suffered a devastating defection of southern voters in the election of 1852. The Whig party was already beginning to die in the South. In the North, simultaneously, a distinctive Whig identity became blurred. The Whig platform was very similar to the Democratic platform, which led to widespread cynicism and apathy. Moreover, northern Whigs made clumsy and unsuccessful attempts to compete with the Democrats for the votes of immigrant Catholics. This strategy alienated the growing number of Whig nativists—as well as many native-born Democrats of Protestant background—who believed that the professional politicians' hunger for votes had betrayed America's heritage of republicanism, Protestantism, and independence from foreign influence, including that of the Catholic pope.

On a superficial level, the decisive victory in 1852 of Franklin Pierce (pronounced "Purse"), a bland northern Democrat from New Hampshire, could be interpreted as confirmation of a national desire for compromise and mediocrity. Pierce was the kind of president who appeared to agree with all factions and with the arguments of anyone who happened to have his ear. On a deeper level, however, the results of state and local elections in 1852 showed that voters felt that the existing parties were unresponsive to the people's needs. Anti-Catholic nativism suddenly became the way of asserting previously vague grievances. The Order of United Americans took over a small organization called the Order of the Star-Spangled Banner and enlarged it into an effective political machine. In the state elections of 1853 Whigs were challenged and badly damaged in various parts of the North by independent tickets that went by various names. Democrats and especially Whigs suffered from the militancy of the temperance movement, whose leaders, associating Catholic immigrants with an alcohol-loving culture, demanded state prohibition laws like the one enacted in Maine in 1851.

The Know-Nothing Upsurge

The remarkable upsurge of political nativism, manifested in 1854 by the Know-Nothing or American party, indicated a widespread popular hostility toward the traditional Democrats and Whigs. The name Know-Nothing came from the fact that party members, when asked by outsiders about the party's organization, were supposed to say they "knew nothing." The Order of the Star-Spangled Banner, which was the nucleus of the Know-Nothing party, remained an obscure secret society until the local spring elections of 1854, when entire tickets of secret Know-Nothing candidates were swept into office by write-in votes. Local digni-

Singing with the Know-Nothings

The nativist Know-Nothings publicized their cause with popular songs such as this "Quick Step," which appealed to patriotism with an image of marching Minute Men preparing to fight alien forces.

taries of the traditional parties, often confident that they were unopposed, found themselves thrown out of office by men they had never heard of. In Massachusetts the Know-Nothings won 63 percent of the popular vote. In the congressional election of 1854 seventy or more Know-Nothings were sent to the House of Representatives, where for a time they held the balance of power.

By 1855 the Know-Nothings, now officially called the American party, had captured control of most of New England and had established roots in every state of the Union. They had become the dominant party opposing the Democrats in New York, Pennsylvania, California, and the border states. They had also made striking inroads in Virginia, North Carolina, Georgia, Kentucky, and Texas. Ironically, while northern Know-Nothings often merged nativism with antislavery, attacking the Catholic church as a proslavery institution, southern nativists pictured immigrants themselves as potential abolitionists and pointed out that immigrants, by avoiding the slaveholding states, were increasing the political power of the tyrannical North. In the South and in the border states, people also hoped that the Know-Nothing movement would distract attention from abolitionism and finally end the "needless" sectional disputes over slavery.

As we have seen, nativism had special appeal for artisans and manual workers who associated immigrants with a new and threatening America—an America of increasing urban poverty, of factories and railroads, and of rising prices and abruptly changing markets. The Know-Nothing movement began to subside after 1855, when the number of immigrants arriving in the country had declined and improved economic conditions had lessened the fear of competition for jobs. Nevertheless in two years the Know-Nothings had replaced the Whigs as a national political force. And in much of the Northeast the Know-Nothings had defeated or prevented the spread of the new Republican party, which had been founded in 1854 to prevent the extension of slavery into the western territories. In 1855 it appeared that the Know-Nothings, rather than the Republicans, would become the dominant national party challenging the Democrats.

In 1856 Millard Fillmore ran as the candidate of the combined American (Know-Nothing) and Whig parties and received nearly 44 percent of the popular vote in the slaveholding states. Nativism was weaker in the Old Northwest, where there was a greater tolerance of immigrants. Yet there the Republican party capitalized on a similar disenchantment with the old parties, often at the expense of the Democrats. Moreover, in 1854 the Democrats had suffered irretrievable losses throughout the North; in that section their representation in Congress had fallen from ninety-one seats to twenty-five. These sudden defections to the Know-Nothing and Republican parties meant that, henceforth, northern Democrats would have little leverage within their restructured national party, which became increasingly southern-dominated.

The Know-Nothing movement is significant because it helped to destroy the existing party system. Once in power, the Know-Nothings failed to restrict immigration or to lengthen the traditional five years' residence required for naturalized citizenship. Like other parties, the short-lived American party proved to be vulnerable to political ambition and compromise. But before being absorbed by the Republicans, the Know-Nothings brought about a massive shift in voter alignments, undermined national party discipline, and hastened the total disappearance of the Whigs. The importance of this ominous development cannot be exaggerated. When the discipline of the party system was swept away, sectional conflict could no longer be suppressed or safely contained.

The Confrontation over Kansas

From 1854 to 1856 northern politics displayed a dramatic shift in the perception of adversaries: the southern Slave Power, in its lawless attempts to seize the virgin lands of Kansas, replaced Roman Catholic immigrants as the primary threat to republican institutions and the promise of American life. Yet for a time it appeared that Know-Nothings had the upper hand over their Republican rivals. They were better organized and were the dominant power in most of the northern states. It was not until June 1855 that a national council of the Know-Nothings divided along sectional lines over the controversial Kansas-Nebraska Act of 1854. And it was the continuing storm over Kansas that enabled the Republicans to smother or absorb the nativists and become the major political force in the North.

The Kansas-Nebraska Act

Stephen Douglas, the northern Democratic leader, had long been interested in the organization and settlement of the Nebraska Territory—the vaguely defined region west and northwest of Missouri and Iowa. This immense portion of the Louisiana Purchase had been reserved for Indians, and there were few white settlers in the region. As a senator from Illinois, Douglas had a frank interest in the transcontinental railroad routes, which, he expected, would make Chicago the hub of mid-America. He was also an ardent patriot and expansionist, convinced that America should free the world from despotism. He thought the only serious obstacle to this mission was England, which, Douglas believed, had instigated the subversive activities of the American abolitionists, who in turn had provoked the militancy of the southern extremists. These southerners had then blocked the organization of the territories north of the Missouri Compromise line of 36°30′.

By 1854, when Douglas was chairman of the Senate Committee on Territories, he had concluded that the Missouri Compromise must be modified to overcome southern fears. This course of action, he thought, was the only way to open the Nebraska country to settlement, to bind the nation together with transcontinental railroads and telegraph, to fulfill the American mission of driving Great Britain from the continent, and to reunite the fractured Democratic party under his own leadership. He therefore drafted a bill that applied to Nebraska the popular sovereignty provision that Congress had already applied to Utah and New Mexico under the terms of the Compromise of 1850. This unexpected move destroyed nearly four years of relative sectional peace.

At first Douglas tried to play down the contradiction between popular sovereignty and the slavery prohibition of 1820, which applied to all the Louisiana Purchase territory north of the present state of Oklahoma. In 1850 Congress had left it to the courts to resolve any conflicts between popular sovereignty and the unrepealed Mexican law prohibiting slavery in Utah and New Mexico. Douglas hoped to bypass the Missouri Compromise in the same way. But William Seward and other antislavery Whigs plotted to make the Nebraska bill as objectionable as possible. At the same time, a powerful group of southern senators, the disciples of Calhoun, conspired to make repeal of the Missouri Compromise a test of Democratic party loyalty.

After a series of caucuses Douglas recognized that the Nebraska bill would not pass unless southerners were assured that *all* territories would be legally open to slaveholders. Aided by his southerner allies, Douglas helped to persuade President Pierce to throw administration support behind a new proposal that would declare the Missouri Compromise "inoperative and void" because it was "inconsistent with the principles of nonintervention by Congress with slavery in the States and Territories, as recognized by the legislation of 1850." This new bill would also provide for the organization of two separate territories, Kansas and Nebraska. By simply affirming that the rights of territorial governments were "subject only to the Constitution of the United States," Douglas's new bill evaded the critical question of whether popular sovereignty included the right to exclude

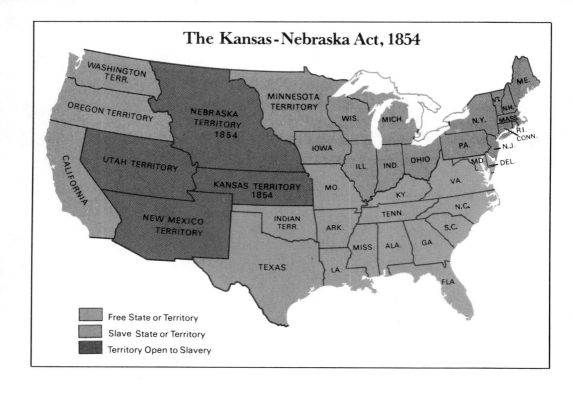

The Kansas-Nebraska Act, 1854

Free State or Territory

Slave State or Territory

Territory Open to Slavery

slavery before a state was constituted. In this form the Kansas-Nebraska bill of 1854 won almost unanimous support from southern Whigs and Democrats and from enough northern Democrats to pass both houses of Congress.

Southern leaders, no less than Stephen Douglas, were astonished by the outrage that exploded across the North. Opponents interpreted the bill as the violation of a "sacred compact," the Missouri Compromise, and as a shameless surrender to the Slave Power. The legislatures of five northern states passed resolutions condemning the Kansas-Nebraska Act. Thousands of northern workingmen, who had traditionally been hostile to abolitionists, condemned the attempt to repeal "the Missouri Compromise, in order to introduce Slavery into *our* free territory of Nebraska and Kansas." These rallies of laborers, who had once looked to the Democratic party for land reform, called the Kansas-Nebraska Act "a crime, a breach of plighted faith," and "a violation not only of our just rights but of the rights of man." When Douglas was traveling by train, he saw so many figures of himself hanging from trees and burned in effigy that he joked, "I could travel from Boston to Chicago by the light of my own effigy." According to the law's defenders, the cries of betrayal were sheer hypocrisy, for antislavery northerners themselves had rejected the principle of the Missouri Compromise by refusing to extend the compromise line to the Pacific coast. Yet the breach of faith, however interpreted, led to a rapid dissolution of other shared understandings and political restraints. For the first time, the two sections became sharply polarized, and antislavery and proslavery moderates began to perceive each other as more dangerous than the extremists.

**Rise of the
Republican Party**

What most alarmed proslavery moderates was the sudden appearance of a new and wholly sectional party, which they scornfully termed the "Black Republicans." In the eyes of its enemies, this party professed moderation but tried to use the goal of excluding slavery from the territories as a means of capturing control of the federal government. Even moderate southerners believed that, instead of being satisfied that California was free and that the number of free states was bound to increase, the self-styled Republicans (who had resurrected Jefferson's old party label) were intent on humiliating the South and on reducing the slaveholding states to colonial status.

The Republicans actually represented a coalition of various groups of Free-Soilers, antislavery Democrats, Conscience Whigs, and nativists who shared a common fear of Slave Power aggression, symbolized by the move to legitimize slavery in Kansas. While most Republican leaders disavowed any ties with the abolitionists, they popularized the abolitionist portrait of the South as a land in which the absolute personal power of slaveholders had nourished tyrannical behavior, arrogance, drunken indolence, sexual depravity, and a contempt for wholesome labor. Republican newspapers, such as Horace Greeley's influential New York *Tribune,* dwelled particularly on the economic liabilities of the slave system, stressing that it was the Slave Power and not immigrants who actually threatened the living standard of northern workers. Slave labor, according to Republican dogma, was not only inefficient and nonproductive, but degraded the very meaning of manual work. "Enslave a man," Greeley explained, "and you destroy his ambition, his enterprise, his capacity. In the constitution of human nature, the desire of bettering one's condition is the mainspring of effort." Slavery also diverted capital from investments that would benefit the entire nation; it stunted the growth of southern markets, to say nothing of cities and internal improvements. The evils of slavery therefore reached into the pocketbook of every northerner. To allow the westward expansion of such a cancerous system would destroy the hopes and values on which America had been built.

By the mid-1850s southerners were keenly aware of the growing contrast between their own rural economy and the economy of the urbanizing Northeast. The great cotton boom of the 1850s seemed to prove that even unparalleled southern prosperity could not narrow the gap in wealth. Picturing themselves as the nation's true producers of wealth, slaveholders blamed northern middlemen—epitomized by Wall Street bankers and merchants—for siphoning off their just rewards. The new Republican party represented the final and fatal spearhead of a conspiracy that allied abolitionists, renegade Democrats, and the remnants of powerful Whig combines, such as the Seward and Weed machine of New York. The earlier Liberty and Free-Soil parties had never had a chance of success. But in 1856 the Republicans, hardly two years after their appearance, carried eleven of the sixteen free states. Colonel John C. Frémont, the Republican presidential candidate, amassed an astonishing popular vote and would have defeated James Buchanan, the Democratic candidate, if he had carried Pennsylvania and Illinois.

The Crisis over Kansas

Even for antislavery moderates, the events in Kansas following passage of the Kansas-Nebraska Act seemed to prove that compromise had only encouraged pro-slavery conspirators to take over the western territories. In 1854 and 1855 some 1,700 proslavery Missourians had crossed the Kansas border in order to cast fraudulent votes, intimidate election judges, and ensure that "popular sovereignty" would exclude any fair debate on the desirability of slavery. The Republicans believed that unless drastic countermeasures were taken, America's free white workers would be deprived of the land and opportunity that was their birthright. By failing to provide definite legal measures for excluding slavery from the territories, Congress had guaranteed that the issue would be decided by numerical and physical force.

The crisis over Kansas was actually the result of complex rivalries and aspirations. The government opened the territory to settlement before Indian treaties had been ratified and before Indian tribes—many of them recently moved to Kansas from the East—had been dispossessed and pushed onto reservations. In 1854 thousands of white settlers began the scramble for Kansas land, searching for the best town sites and the most likely railroad routes of the future. Even without the slavery issue Kansas would have been the scene of a speculative mania and a shameless defrauding of the Indians.

But the passions that were generated by slavery swept aside the last fragile restraints, including the frontier's customary rules against jumping (disregarding) prior land claims. According to Missouri's fiery ex-senator David R. Atchison, a free Kansas would inevitably lead to the end of slavery in Missouri: "We are playing for a mighty stake; if we win we carry slavery to the Pacific Ocean; if we fail we lose Missouri, Arkansas, and Texas and all the territories; the game must be played boldly." Atchison thus helped to organize bands of so-called Border Ruffians to harass settlers from the free states. On the opposite side, opponents of slavery organized a New England Emigrant Aid Company with the purpose of colonizing Kansas with free-state settlers. Although Stephen Douglas referred to the Emigrant Aid Society as "that vast moneyed corporation," the movement was in fact poorly financed, and it succeeded in transporting barely 1,000 settlers to Kansas. But the movement's sensational promotion fed the fantasies of Missourians and southerners that eastern capitalists were recruiting armies of abolitionists and equipping them with Sharps rifles. "We will before six months rolls round," promised Atchison, "have the Devil to play in Kansas and this State [Missouri], we are organizing to meet their organization, we will be compelled to shoot, burn & hang, but the thing will soon be over. We intend to 'Mormanise' the abolitionists."

The acts of terrorism reached a climax in May 1856, both in Kansas and on the floor of the United States Senate. Antislavery newspapers declared that a civil war had actually begun in Kansas when a large proslavery force sacked the free-state town of Lawrence. "The War Actually Begun," ran a headline in the New York *Tribune*: "Triumph of the Border Ruffians—Lawrence in Ruins—Several

"Border Ruffians" Heading for Kansas
A group of armed proslavery Missourians on their way to cast ballots in Kansas.

Persons Slaughtered—Freedom Bloodily Subdued." Although free-state migrants greatly outnumbered the settlers from Missouri and other slave states, the federal government sanctioned only the proslavery government that had been elected by fraud. On May 21 a federal marshal led a large body of armed men into Lawrence for the purpose of arresting members of the antislavery government who had been charged with high treason. After the arrests had peacefully been made and the marshal had disbanded his posse, a zealous sheriff took unauthorized command of the group, which proceeded to bombard and burn the hotel that sheltered the Emigrant Aid Society, destroy the presses of two antislavery newspapers, and destroy other buildings in the town.

The revenge for such proslavery outrages was even more savage. Even fervid southern alarmists had not imagined anything as brutal as John Brown's retaliatory massacre at Pottawatomie Creek. Brown, a fanatical ne'er-do-well with an abolitionist background and abolitionist connections, thought of himself as an agent of God's vengeance. He led four of his sons and two followers in a night attack on an unprotected settlement, brutally executing five men and boys who were vaguely associated with the proslavery party.

Even in the nation's capitol, all pretense of civility collapsed. Speakers became inflamed, personal, malicious, even before news arrived of the proslavery attack on Lawrence. Senator Charles Sumner of Massachusetts, after denouncing

Violence in the United States Senate

Note that in this depiction of Preston Brooks attacking Senator Charles Sumner on the Senate floor, some southern senators are laughing or protecting Brooks from interference after Sumner has fallen away from his desk.

"the crime against Kansas" and "the rape of a virgin territory, compelling it to the hateful embrace of slavery," delivered studied insults to the elderly Andrew Butler, a senator from South Carolina. On the Senate floor Butler's cousin, Preston Brooks, a young congressman from South Carolina, later savagely attacked the seated Sumner with a cane, leaving him unconscious, bleeding profusely, and seriously injured. This triumph of "Bully" Brooks won applause from much of the South—indeed, Brooks was deluged with souvenir canes and invited to celebratory dinners. For many northerners, Sumner's Senate seat, which remained empty for more than three years during his prolonged recovery, was a silent warning that southerners could not be trusted to respect any codes, agreements, or sets of rules. Nothing could have been more favorable for the Republican party. "The outrage upon Sumner & the occurrences in Kansas," Abraham Lincoln wrote to Senator Lyman Trumbull, "have helped us vastly."

"Occurrences in Kansas" continued to aid Republican aspirations in the North. By 1857 there could be no doubt that the overwhelming majority of Kansas settlers opposed admitting the territory as a slave state. Like the white settlers in California and Oregon, they wanted to exclude free blacks along with slaves. For most Kansans these were minor matters compared to other issues, among them squatter rights, rival railroad routes, the disposal of Indian lands, and the desirability of free homesteads. What made slavery an explosive question in Kansas—and what made Kansas a detonating fuse for the nation—was the federal government's effort to bypass the people's will.

The Pierce and Buchanan administrations made a series of miscalculations. In the first tumultuous stage of settlement, as we have seen, the Pierce administration had legally recognized a proslavery territorial legislature established by wholesale fraud. Many moderates hoped that the flagrant acts of this provisional legislature—such as making it a felony to question the right to hold slaves in Kansas—would soon be repealed by a more representative body. But the free-state settlers chose to boycott the elections that the "legal" proslavery government authorized and to establish their own extralegal government and constitution.

The Lecompton Constitution

In 1857 the Buchanan administration was thus committed to support the outcome of an official election of delegates to a constitutional convention in Lecompton, Kansas, in preparation for Kansas statehood, even though only one eligible voter in twelve had gone to the polls. By then southerners had become convinced that the security of the slave system hinged on making Kansas a slave state. Buchanan had become equally convinced that the survival of the Democratic party hinged on appeasing the South—in 1856, 119 of his 174 electoral votes had come from slave states. In Kansas there were no moderating influences on the proslavery convention that drafted the so-called Lecompton constitution. In Washington the declining power of the northern Democrats gave a similarly unrestrained hand to the southern Democrats who dominated Buchanan's administration.

Stephen Douglas considered the vote in Kansas on the proslavery Lecompton constitution a total subversion of popular sovereignty. Instead of being allowed to accept or reject the constitution as a whole, voters were asked only to approve the article guaranteeing for the future the right of slave property. If the article were rejected, the Lecompton constitution would still protect the legal status of the slaves already in the territory. Although the free-state majority again protested by abstaining from voting, Buchanan used the powers of his office to pressure Congress into admitting Kansas as a slave state. This policy caused a bitter break with Douglas, who denounced Buchanan's attempt to "force this constitution down the throats of the people of Kansas, in opposition to their wishes." In 1858, as in 1854, Congress became the scene of a violent sectional struggle. But this time Douglas led the antiadministration forces. Buchanan stood firm, sacrificing much of his remaining Democratic support in the North. In the end, in 1858, the Buchanan administration suffered a crushing defeat when advocates of Kansas's admission as a free state forced a popular vote in Kansas on the *whole* of the Lecompton constitution. The territory's electorate rejected the constitution by a vote of nearly 10 to 1, although at the cost of indefinitely postponing statehood. (Kansas ultimately became a free state in 1861.)

Dred Scott and the Lincoln-Douglas Debates

By the stormy 1850s the largest Protestant churches had divided along sectional lines; the Whig party had collapsed. The Democratic party had survived, but the Lecompton struggle helped to split it fatally. Although the Democratic party had given the South disproportionate access to national power, this access depended on winning the support of northern allies. As the number of such allies began to dwindle, they were partly replaced by southern Whigs. Thus as the Democratic party became more southern in character, there were fewer restraints on attempts to test the party loyalty of northern Democrats and to adopt an openly proslavery program. The Lecompton constitution was actually the second such critical test imposed on northern Democrats. The first test was the *Dred Scott* decision.

The *Dred Scott* Decision   The southerners who dominated the Supreme Court decided to use the *Dred Scott* case as a way to resolve critical issues that Congress had long evaded. From the time that the Court had received the case, late in 1854, to the Court's long-delayed decision in 1857, the primary issue was whether Congress had the constitutional right to prohibit slavery in any territory or to delegate such a right to territorial governments, as implied by Stephen Douglas's formula of "popular sovereignty." In the recently disputed territories of New Mexico, Utah, and Kansas, no judicial cases involving the exclusion of slavery had yet arisen.

There had been many previous suits for freedom by slaves who had lived with their masters as temporary residents of free states. Even southern courts had sometimes granted freedom to such slaves, but the decisions had depended on complex technical issues that mostly involved state law. What distinguished *Dred Scott*, a Missouri slave who sued the state for his freedom, was that he and his master, an army surgeon, had lived together for several years not only in the free state of Illinois, but also in a part of the Wisconsin Territory where slavery had been federally prohibited by the Missouri Compromise. Despite this clear violation of federal law, Scott's initial trials in Missouri courts were confined to narrower issues.

In 1854 technical complications allowed Scott's lawyers to transfer his suit for freedom to the United States Circuit Court for the District of Missouri. This first federal trial raised a preliminary question that courts had never resolved and that affected the enforcement of the Fugitive Slave Law of 1850. Were any black persons citizens to the extent of being qualified by the Constitution to bring suit in a federal court? After years of debate and postponement in the United States Supreme Court, this jurisdictional question enabled Chief Justice Roger Taney (pronounced "Tawney") to link Scott's individual claim with momentous constitutional issues. For if blacks were not citizens entitled to constitutional rights and privileges, Dred Scott would be subject only to the laws of Missouri, and blacks seized under the Fugitive Slave Law of 1850 would have no recourse to federal courts. Moreover, the Dred Scott case involved a second question of enormous significance. The Court had to decide whether Congress had exceeded its powers in 1820 when it had outlawed slavery in the Louisiana Purchase north of 36°30′. If so, Dred Scott was still a slave and therefore could not bring suit in federal court.

By the end of 1856 the *Dred Scott* case had received widespread national publicity, with newspapers summarizing the opposing arguments that were delivered before the Court. Although informed observers anxiously awaited a verdict that might have explosive political consequences, they generally expected the Court to deny its jurisdiction on narrow technical grounds, thus confirming the judgment of lower courts that Scott was still a slave. When the decision was finally announced, in 1857, seven of the justices rejected Scott's claim to freedom, but all nine wrote separate opinions. There is still controversy over what parts of the "Opinion of the Court," written by Chief Justice Taney, represented the opinion of a majority of the justices.

Taney's opinion stated three sweeping conclusions. First, Taney held that at the time the Constitution of the United States had been adopted, blacks had "for more than a century been regarded as beings of an inferior order ... so far inferior that they had no rights which the white man was bound to respect; and that the negro might justly and lawfully be reduced to slavery for his benefit." Taney further contended that neither the Declaration of Independence nor the Constitution had been intended to apply to blacks—whether slave or free. Even if free blacks in certain states had later been granted citizenship, Taney said, they were not citizens "within the meaning of the Constitution of the United States." They were not entitled to the rights and privileges of a citizen in any other state, nor could they sue in a federal court.

After thus denying the Supreme Court's jurisdiction over Dred Scott, the second major conclusion of Taney's decision dealt with the substantive issues. As for Scott's residence in Illinois, the Court had already recognized the principle that the status of a slave taken to a free state should be determined by the laws of the slave state to which he had returned. On Scott's residence in the federal territory north of 36°30′, Taney ruled that the Missouri Compromise had been unconstitutional. Congress, he declared, had no more power to take away a citizen's property in a federal territory than it did in a state.

Finally, having argued that slaves could not be differentiated from other forms of property protected by the Fifth Amendment, Taney stated his third major conclusion. Congress, he ruled, could not give a territorial government powers that exceeded those of the federal government: "It could confer no power on any local Government, established by its authority, to violate the provisions of the Constitution." This judgment struck directly at Douglas's interpretation of popular sovereignty, and it upheld the extreme southern view that the people of a territory could not legally discriminate against slave property until they acquired the sovereignty of statehood.

Reaction to the Decision

Both the South and President Buchanan were jubilant. Despite vigorous dissenting opinions from justices John McLean and Benjamin R. Curtis, the highest court in the land had ruled that excluding slavery from the territories—the goal that had brought the Republican party into existence—was unconstitutional. Republican newspapers, among them the New York *Tribune,* scornfully replied that the decision was "entitled to just as much moral weight as would be the judgment of a majority of those congregated in any Washington bar-room." Stephen Douglas, the leading contender for the Democratic presidential nomination in 1860, remained silent for many weeks. He wholly agreed with the denial of black citizenship and took credit for the congressional repeal of the Missouri

Compromise. Yet his relations with Buchanan and the South were already strained, and he knew that his future career hinged on finding a way to reconcile the southern version of limited popular sovereignty, embodied in the *Dred Scott* decision, with his own constituents' demand for genuine self-determination.

Douglas finally presented his response to the *Dred Scott* decision in an important speech at the Illinois statehouse in May 1857. He argued that the constitutional right to take slaves into a territory was a worthless right unless it was sustained, protected, and enforced by "police regulations and local legislation." By contrasting an empty legal right with the necessary public support to enforce such a right, Douglas denied any meaningful contradiction between the *Dred Scott* decision and his own principle of popular sovereignty.

Two weeks later Abraham Lincoln gave his reply to Douglas from the same forum. Terming the *Dred Scott* decision erroneous, Lincoln reminded his audience that the Supreme Court had frequently reversed its own decisions, and he promised that "we shall do what we can to have it to over-rule this."

Elected to Congress as a Whig in 1846, Lincoln had suffered politically from his opposition to the Mexican War. But since 1854, when he had attacked the Kansas-Nebraska Act, he had been making a new career by pursuing Douglas. Lincoln was a self-educated Kentuckian, shaped by the Indiana and Illinois frontier. In moral and cultural outlook, however, he was not far from the stereotyped New Englander. He abstained from alcohol, revered the idea of self-improvement, dreamed of America's technological and moral progress, and condemned slavery as a moral and political evil. He told a Chicago audience in 1858, "I have always hated slavery I think as much as any Abolitionist. . . . I have always hated it, but I have always been quiet about it until this new era of the introduction of the Nebraska Bill began. I always believed that everybody was against it, and that it was in course of ultimate extinction."

The Kansas-Nebraska Act taught Lincoln that men like Douglas did not care whether slavery was "voted *down* or voted *up*." It also allowed him to exercise his magnificent talents as a debater and stump speaker—talents that had already distinguished him as a frontier lawyer, a state legislator, and an attorney and lobbyist for the Illinois Central Railroad and other corporations. Lincoln's humor, his homespun sayings, and his unaffected self-assurance all diverted attention from his extraordinary ability to grasp the central point of a controversy and to compress an argument into its clearest and most striking form. In 1856, after a period of watchful waiting, Lincoln played an important part in the belated organization of the Illinois Republican party. Two years later the Republican state convention unanimously nominated him to run for Douglas's Senate seat.

The Lincoln-Douglas contest was unprecedented in both form and substance. At the time senators were elected by state legislatures,* and no party

---

*Only after 1913, with the adoption of the Seventeenth Amendment, did the direct popular election of senators begin.

convention had ever nominated a candidate. In an acceptance speech on June 16, 1858, Lincoln concisely and eloquently stated the arguments he would present directly to the people, appealing for a Republican legislature that would then be committed to elect him to the Senate. Since Douglas had unexpectedly rejected the proslavery Lecompton constitution and had joined the Republicans in fighting it, Lincoln needed to persuade the electorate that Douglas's own crusade for popular sovereignty had rekindled the agitation over slavery and led directly to the *Dred Scott* decision and the Lecompton constitution. According to Lincoln, Douglas's moral indifference to slavery disqualified him as a leader who could stand firm against the Slave Power. For Lincoln was wholly convinced that the conflict over slavery would continue until a crisis had been reached and passed. As he said in his famous "House Divided" speech of 1858:

> "A house divided against itself cannot stand."
> I believe this government cannot endure, permanently half *slave* and half *free.*
> I do not expect the Union to be *dissolved*—I do not expect the house to *fall*—but I *do* expect it will cease to be divided.
> It will become *all* one thing, or *all* the other.
> Either the *opponents* of slavery, will arrest the further spread of it, and place it where the public mind shall rest in the belief that it is in course of ultimate extinction; or its *advocates* will push it forward, till it shall become alike lawful in *all* the States, *old* as well as *new*—*North* as well as *South.*
> Have we no *tendency* to the latter condition?

The "House Divided" speech signified a turning point in American political history. Lincoln stated that expediency and a moral neutrality toward slavery had undermined the Founders' expectation that slavery was "in course of ultimate extinction." If the North continued to make compromises and failed to defend a boundary of clear principle, the South was certain to dictate "a second Dred Scott decision," depriving every state of the power to discriminate against slave property. In Lincoln's view, Douglas's Kansas-Nebraska Act had been part of a master plan or conspiracy, which Lincoln compared to "a piece of *machinery*" that had been designed to legalize slavery, step by step, throughout the United States. In asserting that "the people were to be left 'perfectly free' subject only to the Constitution, Douglas had provided "an exactly fitted *niche,* for the Dred Scott decision to afterwards come in, and declare the perfect freedom of the people, to be just no freedom at all."

Lincoln was not an abolitionist. He was convinced that prohibiting the further spread of slavery would be sufficient to condemn it to "ultimate extinction," a belief shared by many southern leaders. Yet he insisted on a public policy aimed at that goal—a public policy similar to that of Great Britain in the 1820s or, in Lincoln's eyes, to that of the Founders. For Lincoln, rejecting popular sovereignty was the same as rejecting the moral indifference exemplified by Douglas; and this was the first step toward national redemption.

A Lincoln-Douglas Debate
As Lincoln stands and gestures before an Illinois crowd, Douglas sits quietly to the left of Lincoln, next to his water glass.

The Lincoln-Douglas Debates

Douglas seemed to be the nation's most likely choice for president in 1860. His struggle with Lincoln for reelection to the Senate in 1858 therefore commanded national attention. Making full use of newly constructed railroads, the two candidates traveled nearly 10,000 miles in four months. They crisscrossed Illinois, their tireless voices intermingling with the sounds of bands, parades, fireworks, cannons, and cheering crowds. Each community tried to outdo its rivals in pageantry and in winning the greatest turnout from the countryside. Lincoln and Douglas agreed to participate in seven face-to-face debates, which are rightly regarded as classics in the history of campaign oratory. Douglas tried to make the most of his experience as a seasoned national leader (at forty-five he was four years younger than Lincoln) and to portray his opponent as a dangerous radical. According to Douglas, Lincoln's "House Divided" speech showed a determination to impose the moral judgments of one section on the other. Lincoln's doctrines threatened to destroy the Union and to extinguish the world's last hope for freedom. Douglas also exploited his listeners' racial prejudice, drawing laughter from his sarcastic refusal to question "Mr. Lincoln's conscientious belief that the negro was made his equal, and hence his brother."

Lincoln searched for ways to counteract the image of a revolutionary. Always insisting on the moral and political wrong of slavery, he repeatedly acknowledged that the federal government could not interfere with slavery in the existing states. He opposed repeal of the Fugitive Slave Law. He wholly rejected the idea of "perfect social and political equality with the negro." He did maintain, however, that blacks were as much entitled as whites to "all the natural rights enumerated

Stephen A. Douglas (1813–61)
*This anonymous wooden folk
sculpture is of Stephen A.
Douglas, who beat Lincoln in the
1858 Illinois senatorial election
and lost to Lincoln in the
presidential election of 1860.*

in the Declaration of Independence, the right to life, liberty, and the pursuit of
happiness." If the black was "perhaps" not equal in moral or intellectual
qualities, "in the right to eat the bread, without leave of anybody else, which his
own hand earns, *he is my equal and the equal of judge Douglas, and the equal of
every living man.* [Great applause.]"

The election in Illinois was extremely close. The Republicans did not win
enough seats in the legislature to send Lincoln to the Senate, but the campaign
immediately elevated him to national prominence. Lincoln had expressed and
defended a Republican antislavery ideology that combined fixed purpose with a
respect for constitutional restraints. Lincoln had also magnified the gap that
separated the Republicans from Douglas and other anti-Lecompton Democrats.
He had further isolated Douglas from proslavery southern Democrats who were
already embittered by Douglas's "treachery" with regard to the Lecompton
constitution. They were then outraged by Douglas's response to Lincoln in the
debate at Freeport, Illinois, where Douglas had maintained that regardless of
what the Supreme Court might decide about the constitutionality of slavery in a
territory, the people had the "lawful means to introduce it or exclude it" as they
pleased. Repeating his familiar point that slavery could not exist "a day or an hour

anywhere" unless it was supported by local police regulations, Douglas emphasized that the "unfriendly legislation" of a territorial government could effectively prevent slavery from being introduced. As Lincoln quipped, this was to say, "A thing may be lawfully driven from a place where it has a lawful right to stay."

In 1859 the breach between Douglas and the South could no longer be contained. The people of Kansas ratified a new constitution prohibiting slavery, thereby giving bite to Douglas's so-called Freeport Doctrine. In the Senate, where Douglas had been ousted from his chairmanship of the Committee on Territories, he led the fight against the southern demand for a federal slave code protecting slave property in all the territories. During a tour of the South, Douglas became alarmed by the growing movement, led by young proslavery "fire-eaters," to revive and legalize the African slave trade. Looking ahead to the Democratic convention of 1860, Douglas issued what amounted to an ultimatum about the party platform. Northern Democrats, he insisted, would not allow the party to be used as a means for reviving the African slave trade, securing a federal slave code, or pursuing any of the other new objectives of southern extremists. Douglas warned the South that northerners would not retreat from defending genuine popular sovereignty, even though popular sovereignty was clearly running against the interests of the South.

The Ultimate Failure of Compromise

By 1860 a multitude of previously separate fears, aspirations, and factional interests had become polarized into opposing visions of America's heritage and destiny. Traditional systems of trust and reciprocity had collapsed.

John Brown's Raid   John Brown, who had warred against slavery in Kansas, was a key symbol in this polarization. Since 1857 Brown had been held in high esteem by the most eminent New England reformers and literary figures. Backed financially by a secret group of abolitionists, Brown also cultivated close ties with free black communities in the North. On the night of October 16, 1859, he and some twenty heavily armed white and black followers seized part of the federal arsenal at Harpers Ferry, Virginia (now West Virginia). Brown hoped to begin the destruction of slavery by igniting a slave revolt and creating in the South a free-soil refuge for fugitives. After resisting federal troops for two days, Brown surrendered; he was tried for conspiracy, treason, and murder, and was hanged.

During his trial Brown claimed to have acted under the "higher law" of the New Testament. He insisted that "if I had done what I have for the white men, or the rich, no man would have blamed me." For Brown the higher law was not a philosophical abstraction but a moral command to shed blood and die in the cause of freedom. In the eyes of armchair reformers and intellectuals, Brown's courage to act on his principles made him not only a revered martyr but also a symbol of all that America lacked. Democratic editors and politicians, however,

John Brown (1800–59)
Leader of the Pottawatomie massacre in 1856 and the raid on the Harpers Ferry arsenal in 1859, Brown has often been portrayed as a fanatical and probably insane abolitionist who believed that God had ordained him to destroy slavery. Yet no other white man won such respect from the free black community. Ralph Waldo Emerson, speaking for many Northern intellectuals, called Brown "a pure idealist of artless goodness."

saw Brown's criminal violence as the direct result of the irresponsible preaching of William H. Seward and other so-called Black Republicans. The Democratic New York *Herald* reprinted Seward's speech on the "irrepressible conflict between slave and free states" alongside news accounts from Harpers Ferry. Many southerners came to the stunned realization that Brown's raid could not be dismissed as the folly of a madman, since it had revealed the secret will of much of the North. A Virginia senator concluded that Brown's "invasion" had been condemned in the North "only because it failed." In the words of Jefferson Davis, a Mississippi senator who had been Pierce's secretary of war, the Republican party had been "organized on the basis of making war" against the South.

Ironically, both the Republicans and the southern extremists agreed that slavery must expand under national sanction if it were to survive. They also agreed that if the *Dred Scott* decision was valid, the government had an obligation to protect slave property in all the territories. This denial of any middle ground made it logical for southern fire-eaters to argue that a revived African slave trade would allow more whites to own slaves and would thus help to "democratize" the institution. Above all, both the Republicans and the southern extremists rejected popular sovereignty as Douglas had defined it. For southerners the Constitution prohibited either Congress or a territorial legislature from depriving a settler of his slave property. For the Republicans the Constitution gave Congress both the duty and the power to prevent the spread of an institution that deprived human beings of their inalienable right to freedom.

Because these positions were irreconcilable, the northern Democrats held the only keys to possible compromise in the presidential election of 1860. But like the Republicans, the Douglas Democrats had drawn their own firm limits against further concessions to southern extremists. Early in 1860 Jefferson Davis challenged those limits by persuading the Senate Democratic caucus to adopt a set of resolutions committing the federal government to protect slavery in the territories. For Davis and other southern leaders, a federal slave code was the logical extension of the *Dred Scott* decision. They also agreed that the forthcoming Democratic platform must uphold the principle of federal protection of slave property. The Douglas Democrats knew that such a principle of guaranteed protection would completely undercut their reliance on legislation "unfriendly" to slavery in a territory and that such a plank would guarantee their defeat in the North.

Division of the Democratic Party

In April 1860 the fateful Democratic national convention met at Charleston. When a majority of the convention refused to adopt a platform similar in principle to Davis's Senate resolutions, the delegates from eight southern states withdrew, many of them assuming that this disunionist gesture would force the Douglas faction to compromise. Douglas held firm to his principle of popular sovereignty, and as a result he could not muster the two-thirds majority that was needed for nomination. In a surprise move the northern Democrats then agreed to adjourn the convention and to reconvene six weeks later in Baltimore.

At Baltimore the Democratic party finally destroyed itself as a national force. Delegates from the Lower South again seceded, and this time they adopted an extreme proslavery platform and nominated Vice-President John C. Breckinridge of Kentucky for the presidency. The northern remnants of the party remained loyal to popular sovereignty, however it might be modified in practice by the *Dred Scott* decision, and nominated Douglas.

Meanwhile the division of the Democrats at Charleston had given the Republicans greater flexibility in nominating a candidate. In 1858 Douglas had portrayed Lincoln as a flaming abolitionist, and the South had accepted the image. To the North, however, Lincoln appeared more moderate and less controversial than the better-known Senator Seward of New York. Unlike Seward, Lincoln was not popularly associated with the higher-law doctrines that had led to Harpers Ferry. Although Lincoln disapproved of Know-Nothing nativism, he was more discreet than Seward and thus stood less chance of losing the nativist vote in Pennsylvania and other critical states. If some northerners regarded him as a crude buffoon from the prairies, he appealed to many other northerners as the tall rail-splitter of humble origins, a man of the people, an egalitarian. Lincoln had made few enemies and was associated with few issues, but he had given general endorsement to the proposed Homestead Act, protective tariffs, and a

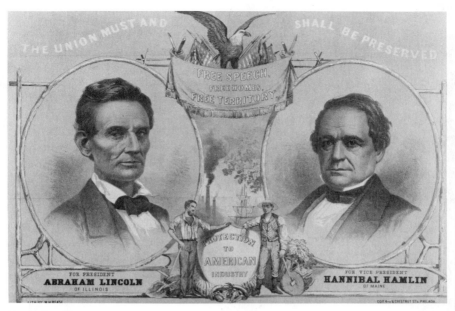

Campaign Poster
The Republican candidates for president and vice-president in 1860.

transcontinental railroad—all programs that were popular in the North and West and that had been blocked in Congress by the South. In May, at the Republicans' boisterous convention in Chicago, Lincoln finally overcame Seward's early lead and received the nomination.

The presidential campaign of 1860 was filled with the noisy hucksterism and carnival atmosphere that had been standard since 1840. The Republicans tended to discount the warnings of serious crisis, and they contemptuously dismissed southern threats of secession as empty bluff. The Breckinridge Democrats tried to play down these threats and to profess their loyalty to the Constitution and the Union. Yet various groups of moderates realized that both the Constitution and the Union were in jeopardy. This was the message of the new Constitutional Union party, which was led largely by former Whigs and which won many supporters in the Upper South. And this was the message that Stephen Douglas repeated bravely and incessantly—in the South as well as in the North—in the first nationwide speaking campaign by a presidential candidate.

The Election of 1860 In November the national popular vote was divided among four candidates, and Lincoln received only 40 percent of the national total. Yet he received 180 electoral votes—57 more than the combined total of his three opponents. He carried every free state except New Jersey, and he won 4 of New Jersey's 7 electoral votes. In ten of the slave states, however, he failed to get a single popular vote. Breckinridge, the southern Democrat, captured all the states of the Lower South as well as Delaware,

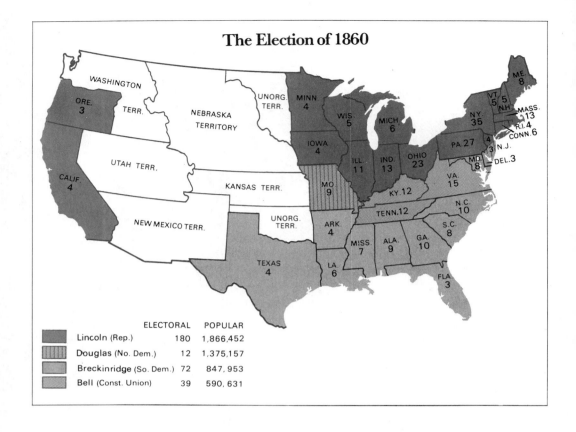

The Election of 1860

	ELECTORAL	POPULAR
Lincoln (Rep.)	180	1,866,452
Douglas (No. Dem.)	12	1,375,157
Breckinridge (So. Dem.)	72	847,953
Bell (Const. Union)	39	590,631

Maryland, Arkansas, and North Carolina. John Bell, the leader of the once-powerful Whig party in Tennessee and the candidate of the Constitutional Union party, carried Tennessee, Kentucky, and Virginia. Although Douglas received approximately 525,000 more popular votes than Breckinridge, and trailed Lincoln by only 491,000, he won a mere 12 electoral votes (9 from Missouri and 3 from New Jersey). In many respects it was not really a national election. In the North it was essentially a contest between Lincoln and Douglas; in the South, between Breckinridge and Bell.

For the South the worst fears and predictions of forty years had come true. The United States had never had an administration that was openly hostile to black slavery. Lincoln's reassurances regarding the constitutional protection of slavery in the existing states could not mitigate the crucial facts. The election had proved that the North was populous enough to bestow national power on a minority party that had no support in the South. The Republican party was committed to free-labor ideology and to the proposition that slavery was morally wrong. Slaveholders would have to take Lincoln's professions of restraint on good faith. If he or his successors should become more militant, they could not be checked by a balance of political power. A dominant sectional party would control federal patronage, the postal service and military posts, and the appointment of federal judges and other officeholders. Considerations of this kind strengthened the hand of secessionists. On December 20, 1860, South Carolina crossed the threshold that had been so closely approached during the nullification crisis. A special convention repealed the state's ratification of the Constitution and withdrew South Carolina from the Union. Unlike Jackson when faced with similar defiance, President Buchanan maintained that the federal government could do nothing to prevent the move.

Unionists mounted stiffer resistance to secession in other states of the Lower South. The chief controversies, however, involved timing—whether to follow the stampede of the fire-eating militants or to wait until Lincoln had shown his true colors. By February 1, 1861, the militants had triumphed in Mississippi, Florida, Alabama, Georgia, Louisiana, and Texas. Inevitably the shock produced reflex actions toward the traditional saving compromise. Senator John Crittenden of Kentucky initiated the first of such moves two days before South Carolina officially seceded. Although Crittenden's proposed amendments to the Constitution were defined as moderate, they matched the most extravagant southern demands of a few years before. Even so, the leaders of the Lower South knew that no "compromise" would be secure unless the Republican party miraculously cast off its antislavery principles. Most Republicans could not publicly approve Crittenden's "unamendable" amendment that would have guaranteed the permanent security of slavery. Nor could they return to the old Democratic proposal for extending the Missouri Compromise line to the Pacific. The 1850s had shown that federal commitment to establishing and protecting slavery south of that line would only encourage southern ambitions in the Caribbean and Latin America. As Lincoln confidentially warned William Kellogg, his spokesman in Congress: "Entertain no proposition for a compromise in regard to the *extension* of slavery. The instant you do, they have us under again; all our labor is lost, and sooner or later must be done over. . . . The tug has to come and better now than later."

By 1860 the North and South had moved beyond the reach of compromise. The United States had originally emerged from an act of secession—from a final rejection of compromise with Britain. Even after independence had been won, Americans continued to perceive Britain as a conspiratorial power that threatened to hold back the nation's expansive energies. But despite this threat, America had continued to prosper and expand. The period from 1820 to 1860 witnessed a continuing extension of limits, an overleaping of boundaries of every kind. History seemed to confirm the people's wish for total self-determination. The American people, like the American individual, seemed to be free from the burdens of their past and free to shape their own character. The one problem that their ingenuity could not resolve was black slavery, which the Founders had seen as an unwanted legacy of British greed. Ironically, the South increasingly came to regard black slavery as the necessary base on which freedom must rest. For the North a commitment to slavery's ultimate extinction was the test of freedom. Each section detected a fatal change in the other—a betrayal of the principles and mission of the Founders. Each section feared that the other had become transformed into a despotic and conspiratorial "power" very similar to the original British enemy. And both sections shared a heritage of standing firm against despotism.

It was not accidental that the greatest American novel of the period, Herman Melville's *Moby-Dick* (1851), tells of the destruction that inevitably flows from denying all limits, rules, and boundaries. The novel concerns Captain Ahab's relentless and stubborn pursuit of a great white whale, a "nameless, inscrutable, unearthly thing" that becomes a symbol for all the opposing, unknown forces of life. Ahab, who commands a crew containing most of the races and types of humanity, thinks that he can become the master of his own fate. Ignoring a series of warnings and portents, he is incapable of admitting that he might be wrong or that there might be forces beyond his control.

Melville's novel is full of rich and universal meaning concerning the heroic yet impossible quest to know the unknowable. Since Americans of the 1850s believed that God would ensure the triumph of democracy in the world, they could not accept Melville's brooding skepticism. Nevertheless there was a lesson for pre–Civil War America in this tale of a highly rational but half-crazed captain—a captain who becomes so obsessed with his mission that he finally throws his navigation instruments overboard so that he can steer only toward the visible spout of the whale. Captain Ahab seeks liberation in an unswerving pursuit and conquest of limits. In the end he dooms himself and his ship to destruction.

CHRONOLOGY

1846 Wilmot Proviso fuses question of slavery's expansion with consequences of Mexican War.
Walker tariff, adopted for revenue only, eliminates principle of protection.

1848 Gold discovered on American River in California.
Van Buren, running for president on Free-Soil ticket, receives 10 percent of popular vote.
Zachary Taylor elected president.

1850 In Congress, violent sectional debate culminates in Compromise of 1850.
Fugitive Slave Law requires federal agents to recover escaped slaves from sanctuaries in the North.
Taylor's death makes Millard Fillmore president.

1851 Herman Melville's *Moby-Dick.*

1852 Franklin Pierce elected president.
Harriet Beecher Stowe's *Uncle Tom's Cabin.*

1853 Upsurge of political nativism, the Know-Nothings.

1854 Spectacular Know-Nothing election victories.
Collapse of Whigs.
New Republican party emerges.
Commodore Perry opens Japan to American trade.
Kansas-Nebraska Act rekindles sectional controversy over slavery.

1856 John Brown's murderous raid at Pottawatomie Creek.
James Buchanan elected president.

1857 *Dred Scott* decision.
In Kansas, proslavery Lecompton constitution ratified as free-state men refuse to vote.

1858	Lincoln-Douglas debates.		Abraham Lincoln elected president.
1859	John Brown's raid on Harpers Ferry.		South Carolina secedes from the Union.
1860	Democratic party, deadlocked at Charleston convention, finally divides along sectional lines at Baltimore.	**1861**	Mississippi, Florida, Alabama, Georgia, Louisiana, and Texas secede.

SUGGESTED READINGS

David M. Potter, *The Impending Crisis, 1848–1861* (1976), continues to be an excellent guide to the topics discussed in the present chapter. But see also James M. McPherson, *Battle Cry of Freedom: The Civil War Era* (1988); William J. Cooper, *The South and the Politics of Slavery 1828–1865* (1978); Cooper, *Liberty and Slavery: Southern Politics to 1860* (1983); and other general survey or interpretive works cited at the end of chapters 12, 15, and 16. The titles on the causes of the Civil War, listed at the end of chapter 18, are also highly relevant.

On California, the best general guide is Andrew F. Rolle, *California: A History* (1969). For the California gold rush and western mining in general, see Rodman W. Paul, *California Gold: The Beginnings of Mining in the Far West* (1947), and Paul, *Mining Frontiers of the Far West, 1848–1880* (1963). Kevin Starr, *Americans and the California Dream, 1850–1915* (1973), presents brilliant vignettes of early California history. For the experiences of blacks in California, see Rudolph M. Lapp, *Blacks in Gold Rush California* (1977). Chinese immigration and anti-Chinese sentiment is admirably treated in Alexander Saxton, *The Indispensable Enemy: Labor and the Anti-Chinese Movement in California* (1975).

Holman Hamilton, *Prologue to Conflict* (1964), is the most detailed and accurate account of the Compromise of 1850. For the preceding presidential election, see Joseph G. Rayback, *Free Soil: The Election of 1848* (1970). Stanley W. Campbell, *The Slave Catchers: Enforcement of the Fugitive Slave Law, 1840–1860* (1968), traces the consequences of the most unpopular provision of the Compromise of 1850. Stephen Douglas's motives for introducing the Kansas-Nebraska Act are judiciously weighed in Robert W. Johannsen, *Stephen A. Douglas* (1973). This definitive biography is also an excellent source on the later Kansas controversy and the Lincoln-Douglas debates. The tangled local conflicts over land and railroad sites are illuminated in Paul W. Gates, *Fifty Million Acres: Conflicts over Kansas Land Policy, 1854–1890* (1954), and James C. Malin, *The Nebraska Question, 1852–1854* (1953). For Harriet Beecher Stowe's world-famous response to the Kansas controversy, see Philip van Doren Stern, *Uncle Tom's Cabin, an Annotated Edition* (1964), and Charles H. Foster, *The Rungless Ladder: Harriet Beecher Stowe and New England Puritanism* (1956).

The political realignment of the 1850s has been reinterpreted in Michael F. Holt, *The Political Crisis of the 1850s* (1978), and also in Joel H. Silbey, *The Partisan Imperative: The Dynamics of American Politics Before the Civil War* (1985). The appalling political corruption of the 1850s is exposed in Mark W. Summers, *The Plundering Generation: Corruption and the Crisis of the Union, 1849–1861* (1987). Robert William Fogel, *Without Consent or Contract: The Rise and Fall of American Slavery* (1989), presents a challenging thesis regarding the effects of immigration on the living standard of native workers and the links between nativism and an antislavery coalition. Ray Billington, *The Protestant Crusade, 1800–1860* (1938), provides an outstanding overview of anti-Catholic nativism. The best studies of political nativism are Michael F. Holt, "The Politics of Impatience: The Origins of Know-Nothingism," *Journal of*

American History, 60 (September 1973), and Holt, *Forging a Majority: The Formation of the Republican Party in Pittsburgh* (1969).

A recent and monumental work that explains the unique conditions that gave rise to the Republican party is William E. Gienapp, *The Origins of the Republican Party, 1852–1856* (1987). See also Hans L. Trefousse, *The Radical Republicans* (1969). Eric Foner, *Free Soil, Free Labor Free Men: The Ideology of the Republican Party Before the Civil War* (1970), is a penetrating study of the Republicans' thought and values. For the Democratic party, see the classic work by Roy F. Nichols, *The Disruption of American Democracy* (1948), and Jean H. Baker, *Affairs of Party: The Political Culture of Northern Democrats in the Mid-Nineteenth Century* (1983). The definitive study of the *Dred Scott* decision is Don E. Fehrenbacher, *The Dred Scott Case: Its Significance in American Law and Politics* (1978). Paul Finkelman, *An Imperfect Union: Slavery, Federalism and Comity* (1981), examines the problem of slaveholders who took their slaves into free states and shows that Lincoln had grounds for fearing a "second Dred Scott decision."

John Brown, a man of violence, has been the subject of violently conflicting interpretations. For traditional and hostile views, see James C. Malin, *John Brown and the Legend of Fifty-Six* (1942), and the brilliant essay by C. Vann Woodward in *The Burden of Southern History* (1960). More sympathetic evaluations can be found in Stephen B. Oates, *To Purge the Land with Blood: A Biography of John Brown* (1970); Benjamin Quarles, *Allies for Freedom: Blacks and John Brown* (1974); and Louis Ruchames, ed., *John Brown: The Making of a Revolutionary* (1969).

Robert W. Johannsen's biography of Douglas, listed above, treats the Lincoln-Douglas debates, and a penetrating analysis can be found in Don E. Fehrenbacher, *Prelude to Greatness: Lincoln in the 1850s* (1962). The debates themselves are presented in an authoritative edition by Paul M. Angle, ed., *Created Equal? The Complete Lincoln-Douglas Debates of 1858* (1958). Harry V. Jaffa, *Crisis of the House Divided: An Interpretation of the Issues in the Lincoln-Douglas Debates* (1959), gives the brilliant, far-reaching, and somewhat eccentric interpretation of a conservative political philosopher.

Most of the biographical studies of Lincoln listed at the end of chapter 18 are relevant here. Fehrenbacher's *Prelude to Greatness* is important, and mention should be made of James G. Randall, *Lincoln, the Liberal Statesman* (1947); Benjamin Quarles, *Lincoln and the Negro* (1962); and, above all, Allan Nevins, *The Emergence of Lincoln* (2 vols., 1950).

The climactic impasse between North and South is imaginatively presented in three major and very different studies: Kenneth M. Stampp, *America in 1857: A Nation on the Brink* (1990); Roy F. Nichols, *The Disruption of American Democracy* (1948); and David M. Potter, *Lincoln and His Party in the Secession Crisis* (1942). Avery O. Craven, *The Coming of the Civil War* (1942), stresses the importance of propaganda and irrationality. For the hopes and fears of contemporaries, see J. Jeffrey Auer, ed., *Antislavery and Disunion, 1858–1861: Studies in the Rhetoric of Compromise and Conflict* (1963). No one has yet written a wholly satisfactory account of the secessionist movements in the South. For conflicting interpretations, see William L. Barney, *The Secessionist Impulse: Alabama and Mississippi* (1974); Daniel W. Crofts, *Reluctant Confederates: Upper South Unionists in the Secession Crisis* (1989); Steven A. Channing, *Crisis in Fear: Secession in South Carolina* (1970); Charles B. Dew, "Who Won the Secession Election in Louisiana?" *Journal of Southern History,* 36 (February 1970), 18–32; Dwight L. Dumond, *The Secession Movement, 1860–1861* (1931); William J. Evitts, *A Matter of Allegiances: Maryland from 1850 to 1861* (1974); and R. A. Wooster, *The Secession Conventions of the South* (1962).

Two works that describe the northern response to secession are Kenneth M. Stampp, *And the War Came: The North and the Secession Crisis, 1860–61* (1950), and Howard C. Perkins, ed., *Northern Editorials on Secession* (2 vols., 1942). For the election of 1860, see Elting Morison, "Election of 1860," in *History of American Presidential Elections, 1789–1968,* ed. Arthur M. Schlesinger, Jr., vol. 2, 1097–1122 (4 vols., 1971). On the futile gestures for compromise, see Albert J. Kirwan, *John J. Crittenden: The Struggle for the Union* (1962), and Robert G. Gunderson, *Old Gentlemen's Convention: The Washington Peace Conference of 1861* (1961).

PART FOUR

Uniting the
Republic
1860–1877

David Herbert Donald

$\mathcal{T}$HESE [Northern] people hate us, annoy us, and would have us assassinated by our slaves if they dared," a Southern leader wrote when he
learned that a "Black Republican," Abraham Lincoln, would certainly be elected
president in 1860. "They are a *different* people from us, whether better or worse
and *there is no love* between us. Why then continue together?" The sectional
contests of the previous decades suggested that Americans had become members
of two distinct—and conflicting—nationalities. By 1860 Northerners and Southerners appeared not to speak the same language, not to share the same moral
code, and not to obey the same law. Compromise could no longer patch together
a union between two peoples so fundamentally different. "I do not see how a
barbarous and a civilized community can constitute one state," Ralph Waldo
Emerson gravely concluded, and many Northerners concurred with him. "The
North and the South are heterogeneous and are better apart," agreed the *New
Orleans Bee.*

On first thought, the four-year civil war that broke out in 1861 seems
powerfully to confirm the view that the Union and the Confederacy were two
distinct nations. Yet the conduct of the war suggests that Northerners and
Southerners were not so different as their political and intellectual leaders had
maintained. At the beginning of the conflict, both governments tried in much the
same ways to mobilize their poorly organized societies for battle. As the war
progressed, both Union and Confederacy adopted similar diplomatic, military,
and economic policies. By the end of the war, both governments were committed
to abolishing slavery, the one institution that had most clearly divided the sections
in 1860.

The Reconstruction era, which followed the Civil War, gives further evidence
that the inhabitants of the North and the South were—as they had always been—
part of the same nationality. There were relatively few, and only limited, social
experiments or political innovations during Reconstruction. Shared beliefs in
limited government, in economic laissez-faire, and in the superiority of the white
race blocked drastic change. Meanwhile common economic interests and
national political parties pulled the sections back into a common pattern of
cooperation.

In the backward glance of history, then, the Civil War takes on a significance
different from its meaning to contemporaries and participants. In retrospect it is
clear that it was less a conflict between two separate nations than a struggle within
the American nation to define a boundary between the centralizing and
nationalizing tendencies in American life and the opposing tendencies toward
localism, parochialism, and fragmentation.

18

Stalemate

1861–1862

⁓

$\mathcal{D}$URING the first two years of the Civil War, as the Union and the Confederacy grappled with each other inconclusively, it seemed that two distinct and incompatible nations had emerged from the American soil. Certainly the aims announced by their leaders were totally inconsistent. President Abraham Lincoln announced that the United States would "constitutionally defend, and maintain itself"; the territorial integrity of the nation must not be violated. For the Confederate States, President Jefferson Davis proclaimed that his country's "career of independence" must be "inflexibly pursued." As the rival governments raised and equipped armies, attempted to finance a huge war, and sought diplomatic recognition and economic assistance abroad, the people of the two sides increasingly thought of each other as enemy nations: Yankees and Rebels. It is easy to understand why Lord John Russell, the British foreign minister, concluded: "I do not see how the United States can be cobbled together again by any compromise. . . . I suppose the break-up of the Union is now inevitable."

A shrewder observer might have noted that the Union and the Confederate governments faced similar wartime problems and tried to solve them with the same wartime solutions. Northerners and Southerners on the battlefields found each other to be not two alien peoples, but kindred peoples. That identity made the conflict truly a brothers' war.

The Rival Governments

The government of the Confederate States was in most respects a duplicate of the United States government from which the Southern states had just withdrawn. Delegates of the six states of the Lower South (South Carolina, Georgia, Alabama, Mississippi, Florida, and Louisiana) met in Montgomery, Alabama, in early February 1861 and promptly drafted a Confederate Constitution; delegates from Texas, which had seceded on February 1, arrived late. The new charter largely followed the wording of the one drawn up in Philadelphia in 1787. To be sure, the Confederate Constitution recognized the "sovereign and independent character" of the constituent states, but it also announced that these states were forming "a permanent federal government," and it listed most of the same restrictions on state action that had been included in the United States Constitution. Unlike that document the Confederate charter used no euphemism about persons "held to Service or Labour" but instead recognized explicitly "the right of property in negro slaves." Otherwise the two documents were substantially and intentionally identical. As the secessionist Benjamin H. Hill of Georgia explained, "We hugged that [United States] Constitution to our bosom and carried it with us."

Inaugurating the Presidents

For president of the new republic, the Montgomery convention chose Jefferson Davis of Mississippi, who had ardently defended Southern rights in the United States Senate but who had only reluctantly come to advocate secession.* If the crowds that thronged the streets of Montgomery on February 18, 1861, hoped to hear a stirring inaugural from the new Southern head of state, they were disappointed. Stepping forward on the portico of the Alabama statehouse, Davis gave a long, legalistic review of the acts of Northern aggression that had led to the formation of the new government. He pledged to use force, if necessary, to "maintain...the position which we have assumed among the nations of the earth." But he spoke in a tone more melancholy than martial. He saw himself as the leader of a conservative movement. "We have labored to preserve the Government of our fathers in its spirit," he insisted.

Just two weeks later, from the portico of the yet unfinished Capitol in Washington, another conservative took his inaugural oath. The capital city was thronged, as Nathaniel Hawthorne wrote, with "office-seekers, wire-pullers, inventors, artists, poets, prosers (including editors, army correspondents, attaches of foreign journals, and long-winded talkers), clerks, diplomatists, mail contractors, [and] railway directors." On public buildings along the route of the inaugural procession, sharpshooters were strategically placed, to prevent any pro-Southern interruption of the proceedings. Abraham Lincoln's inaugural address was similar in tone to Davis's. Lincoln vowed that the Union would be preserved and gave a low-keyed version of the previous sectional quarrels. He explained his

---

*The Montgomery convention drew up a provisional constitution of the Confederacy, established itself as the new republic's provisional legislature, and named Jefferson Davis the provisional president. It also drew up a permanent constitution, which was submitted to the states for ratification. Regular elections were held in the fall of 1861 both for members of the Confederate Congress and for president. Reelected without opposition, Davis was formally inaugurated as the first and only regular president of the Confederate States on February 22, 1862.

Jefferson Davis (1808–89)
*"The hour and the man have
met!" proclaimed William L.
Yancey, presenting Jefferson
Davis to the admiring throngs at
Montgomery in February 1861.
Intelligent, experienced, and
incorruptible, the Senator from
Mississippi seemed the ideal
president for the new
Confederacy.*

personal view on slavery, but he also pledged that he contemplated "no invasion—no using of force" against the seceded states. In a warning softened by
sadness, he reminded his listeners of the oath he had just taken to preserve,
protect, and defend the government of the United States, and he entreated his
Southern fellow citizens to pause before they assailed it. "In *your* hands, my
dissatisfied fellow-countrymen," he concluded, "and not in *mine,* is the momentous issue of civil war."

**Organizing the Two
Administrations**
In the weeks immediately following the two inaugura-
tions, the central problem confronting both Davis and
Lincoln was how to form viable governments. In
Davis's Confederacy everything had to be started afresh. Even the most routine
legal and governmental matters could not be taken for granted. For example,
until the Confederate Congress passed an act that addressed the matter, it was not
certain whether the laws of the United States enacted before 1861, and the
decisions of the United States courts, were binding in the seceded states. The new
nation had to choose a flag—although some purists objected, claiming that the
Confederacy, which represented the true American spirit, ought to retain the
Stars and Stripes and let the Union look for a new banner.

In selecting his cabinet advisers, President Davis theoretically had a free
hand, but his range of choice was severely limited. No man of doubtful loyalty to
the new government could be permitted a place in the cabinet. Thus no Southern
Unionist in the tradition of Henry Clay, John J. Crittenden, and John Bell was

invited. On the other hand, because Davis wanted the world to see that the Confederacy was governed by sober, responsible men, he excluded all the most conspicuous Southern fire-eaters. Then, too, he had to achieve some balance between former Whigs and former Democrats, and he felt obliged to secure a wide geographical spread by appointing one member of his original cabinet from each of the seven Confederate states except Mississippi, which he himself represented. Davis's cabinet thus consisted neither of his personal friends nor of the outstanding political leaders of the South, except for Secretary of State Robert Toombs, a Georgian who served only briefly.

Such a cabinet might have sufficed in a country where administrative procedures and routines were firmly rooted. Instead in the Confederacy there was everywhere a lack of preparation, a lack of resources for running a government. Typical was the Confederate Treasury Department, which initially consisted of one unswept room in a Montgomery bank, "without furniture of any kind; empty . . . of desks, tables, chairs or other appliances for the conduct of business." The secretary of the treasury had to pay for the first rickety furniture out of his own pocket.

Disorganization and improvisation also characterized Lincoln's government in Washington. The Union had the advantage of owning the Capitol, the White House, and the permanent records of the United States government, and it had a recognized flag and a postal system. But in other respects it was thoroughly demoralized. Lincoln's administration had no clear mandate from the people, for the president had received less than 40 percent of the popular vote in the 1860 election. The Union had an army of only 14,657 men, and every day army and navy officers announced that they were defecting to the South. Its treasury was empty. Some of the most experienced clerks in the Washington offices were leaving to join the Confederacy, and many who remained were of suspect loyalty. The confusion was compounded by the presence in the capital of hundreds of office seekers, party workers who had helped elect the first Republican administration and, under the spoils system, expected to oust Democratic incumbents. Accompanied by their representatives or senators and bearing huge rolls of letters of recommendation, the office seekers besieged Lincoln in the White House. Wryly the president compared himself to an innkeeper whose clients demanded that he rent rooms in one wing of his hotel while he was trying to put out a fire in the other.

Not one member of the Lincoln administration had previously held a responsible position in the executive branch of the national government. Many, including the president himself, had no administrative experience of any sort. Like Davis, Lincoln made no attempt to form a coalition government. His cabinet included no leaders of the Douglas wing of the Democratic party or of the Constitutional Union party. Nor, after a few unsuccessful efforts, did he name Unionists from the South. Instead all members of his cabinet were Republicans. That fact, however, scarcely gave his government unity, for several of Lincoln's cabinet appointees had themselves been candidates for the Republican nomina-

Abraham Lincoln (1809–65)
"Probably," wrote Walt Whitman, "the reader has seen physiognomies...that, behind their homeliness or even ugliness, held superior points so subtle, yet so palpable, making the real life of their faces almost as impossible to depict as a wild perfume or fruit taste...such was Lincoln's face—the peculiar color, the lines of it, the eyes, mouth, expression. Of technical beauty it had nothing—but to the eye of a great artist it furnished a rare study, a feast, and fascination."

tion in 1860 and were rivals of Lincoln and of each other. The most conspicuous member was the wily and devious secretary of state, William H. Seward, a man who spoke extravagantly but acted cautiously. Seward felt that he had a duty to save the nation through compromise and conciliation despite its bumbling, inexperienced president. Seward's principal opponent in the cabinet was Secretary of the Treasury Salmon P. Chase, pompous and self-righteous, who had an equally condescending view of Lincoln's talents and who lusted to become the next president. The other members, with whom Lincoln had only limited personal acquaintance, were appointed because they were supposed to have political influence or to represent key states.

Winning the Border States

Desperately needing time to get organized, these two shaky rival administrations immediately confronted a problem and a crisis, which were intimately interrelated. The problem concerned the future of the eight remaining slave states, which had not yet seceded. Although these states were tied to the Deep South by blood and sentiment and feared abolitionist attacks on their "peculiar institution" of slavery, they refused to rush out of the Union. In January 1861 Virginia had elected a convention to consider secession, but it dillydallied and did nothing. In February North Carolinians and Tennesseans voted against holding secession conventions. When the Arkansas and Missouri conventions met in March, they voted not to secede. Up to April 1861, Kentucky, Maryland, and Delaware held neither elections nor conventions. But the loyalty of all these states to the Union clearly depended on the policy Lincoln's government adopted toward the Confederacy.

Crisis over Fort Sumter   The Fort Sumter crisis was the first test of that policy. It concerned the fate of the United States installations in the seceded states that still remained under the control of Washington. At Fort Pickens in Pensacola Bay, an uneasy truce held between the Union troops in the garrison and the Confederate forces on the Florida mainland. The real trouble spot was Fort Sumter, in the harbor of Charleston, South Carolina. Its garrison, which consisted of about seventy Union soldiers and nine officers under the command of Major Robert Anderson, was no serious military threat to the Confederacy, but its presence at Charleston, the very center of secession, was intolerable to Southern pride. Confederates insisted that President Davis demonstrate his devotion to the Southern cause by forcing Anderson and his men out immediately. Many Northerners, who had despairingly watched as fort after fort was turned over to the Confederates during the final months of the Buchanan administration, likewise saw Sumter as a test of the strength and will of the Lincoln administration.

Despite these pressures powerful voices in both governments urged compromise or at least delay. All but two members of Lincoln's cabinet initially thought that Sumter should be evacuated. Davis's secretary of state was equally opposed to hasty action. When the Confederate cabinet discussed attacking Fort Sumter, Toombs solemnly warned: "The firing upon that fort will inaugurate a civil war greater than any the world has yet seen."

But Anderson's situation made some action necessary. When Charleston authorities prohibited further sale of food to the troops in the fort, the garrison faced starvation. On March 5, the day after he was inaugurated, Lincoln learned that Anderson and his men could hold out no longer than April 15 unless they were resupplied. Since Lincoln had just pledged that he would "hold, occupy, and possess" all places and property belonging to the government, he promptly directed his secretary of the navy to outfit an expedition to bring provisions to Fort Sumter. At the same time, recognizing how dangerously explosive the Charleston situation was, he explored alternatives. One possibility was to reinforce Fort Pickens, in the relatively calm area of Florida. Doing so would allow Lincoln to demonstrate his firmness of purpose, even if he had to withdraw Anderson from the Charleston harbor. But the naval expedition sent to Florida miscarried, the Union commander at Pickens misunderstood his orders, and the planned reinforcement could not be completed in time for Lincoln to know about it before Anderson's deadline for surrender. Another possibility was to consent to a peaceable withdrawal from Fort Sumter in return for assurances that the still-undecided border states would remain in the Union. "If you will guarantee to me the State of Virginia, I shall remove the troops," Lincoln confidentially promised a prominent Virginia Unionist. "A State for a fort is no bad business." But the Virginians delayed, and a rainstorm kept a delegation of Unionists from reaching Washington; Lincoln received no firm pledge. Seeing no other possible course, he let the expedition bearing food and supplies sail for Sumter.

President Davis understood that Lincoln was not committing an act of aggression in merely supplying Fort Sumter. Indeed, he predicted that for political reasons the United States government would avoid making an attack so long as the hope remained of retaining the border states. But the Confederate president's hand was forced, too. Hotheaded Governor Francis Pickens and other South Carolina extremists, impatient with Davis's caution, prepared to attack the fort. Rather than let Confederate policy be set by a state governor, Davis ordered General P. G. T. Beauregard, in command of the Confederate forces at Charleston, to demand the surrender of Fort Sumter. Anderson responded that he would soon be starved out, but he failed to promise to withdraw by a definite date. Beauregard's officers felt they had no alternative but to take the fort by force. At 4:30 A.M. on April 12, firing began. Outside the harbor the relief expedition Lincoln had sent watched impotently while Confederates bombarded the fort. After thirty-four hours, with his ammunition nearly exhausted, Anderson had to surrender.

Lincoln promptly called for 75,000 volunteer soldiers to put down the "insurrection" in the South. On May 6 the Confederate Congress countered by formally declaring that a state of war existed. The American Civil War had begun.

Both at the time and later there was controversy about the responsibility for beginning the conflict. Critics claimed that, by sending the expedition to resupply Fort Sumter, Lincoln deliberately tricked the Confederates into firing the first shot. Indeed, some months after the event, Lincoln himself told a friend that his plan for sending supplies to Major Anderson had "succeeded." "They attacked Sumter," he explained; "it fell, and thus, did more service than it otherwise could." That statement clearly reveals Lincoln's wish that if hostilities began the Confederacy should bear the blame for initiating them, but it does little to prove that Lincoln wanted war. It is well to remember that the Confederates took the initiative at Sumter. It was Charleston authorities who cut off Anderson's food supply; it was Confederate authorities who decided that, although the fort offered no military threat, Anderson must surrender; and it was the Southerners who fired the first shot. Writing privately to the Confederate commander at Fort Pickens, President Davis had acknowledged that there would be a psychological advantage if the Southerners waited for the Union government to make the initial attack. But, he added, "When we are ready to relieve our territory and jurisdiction of the presence of a foreign garrison that advantage is overbalanced by other considerations." These other considerations impelled Davis to demand Fort Sumter's surrender.

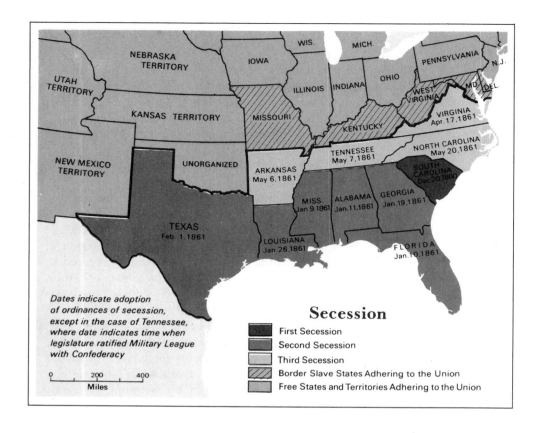

Dates indicate adoption of ordinances of secession, except in the case of Tennessee, where date indicates time when legislature ratified Military League with Confederacy

0   200   400
Miles

Secession

- First Secession
- Second Secession
- Third Secession
- Border Slave States Adhering to the Union
- Free States and Territories Adhering to the Union

Decisions in the Border States

Initially, the Confederacy, not the Union, benefited from the attack on Fort Sumter. The slave states still in the Union now had to make a choice of allegiances, and for a time it seemed that all would join the Confederacy. Virginia governor John Letcher spurned Lincoln's call for troops as a bid "to inaugurate civil war," and on April 17 the state convention hastily passed a secession ordinance. Technically secession was subject to popular ratification. But in fact the convention's action immediately linked to the Confederacy the most populous and influential state of the Upper South, with its long tradition of leadership, its vast natural resources, and its large Tredegar Iron Works.

Other border states acted only a little less quickly. On May 6 the Arkansas convention voted, with only five members dissenting, to withdraw from the Union. When Lincoln's call for troops reached Governor Isham Harris of Tennessee, he replied haughtily, "In such an unholy crusade no gallant son of Tennessee will ever draw his sword," and he began private negotiations with Confederate officials. On May 7 the Tennessee state legislature ratified the arrangements Harris had already made and voted to secede. On May 20 the North Carolina convention, under pressure from pro-Confederate newspapers to withdraw from the "vile, rotten, infidelic, puritanic, negro-worshipping, negro-stealing, negro-equality...Yankee-Union," unanimously adopted a secession ordinance.

Far to the west, the Confederacy scored another victory in the Indian Territory (later to become the state of Oklahoma). Confederate Commissioner Albert Pike had little success with the Plains Indians there, but he won over most of the Five Civilized Nations, many of whom were slaveowners. The Confederacy agreed to pay all annuities that the United States government had previously provided, and it allowed these tribes—the Choctaws, Chickasaws, Creeks, Seminoles, and Cherokees—to send delegates to the Confederate Congress. In return these tribes promised to supply troops for the Confederate army. Most of the tribes loyally supported the Southern effort throughout the war, and the Cherokee chief, Brigadier General Stand Watie, did not formally surrender until a month after the war was over. A rival faction among the Cherokees, headed by Chief John Ross, as well as most of the Plains Indians favored the Union cause.

Elsewhere along the border, the Confederacy fared less well. Delaware, although it was a slave state with sentimental ties to the South, never really contemplated secession. In Maryland, a bitterly divided state, the decision was much more painful. On April 19 a pro-Confederate mob in Baltimore fired on a Massachusetts regiment en route to Washington, and communications were then cut between the Union capital and the rest of the country. For a time it seemed highly probable that Maryland would secede. But Lincoln arranged for further shipments of Union troops to bypass Baltimore until passions could cool. By May Baltimore was back under Union control, and the mayor, along with nineteen members of the state legislature, was unceremoniously arrested and jailed without trial. In the 1861 fall elections, Maryland chose an uncompromising Unionist as governor, and thereafter there was no further question of secession.

In Missouri the Union cause was managed with less skill. Although the pro-Southern governor denounced Lincoln's call for troops as "illegal, unconstitutional, revolutionary, inhuman, [and] diabolical," public opinion was so evenly divided that secession probably would not have occurred except for the Union commander Nathaniel Lyon, who started hostilities by overrunning an encampment of prosecessionist militia near St. Louis. Confederate sympathizers rallied to protect them, and for two days there was bloody street fighting in the city. Open warfare followed. Union forces controlled the area around St. Louis; secessionists commanded by Sterling Price dominated most of the rest of the state. After General John C. Frémont became commander of the department of the West, with his headquarters in St. Louis, the territory under Union control was gradually extended. During the next three years, guerrilla warfare devastated the Missouri countryside as neighbor fought neighbor. The bitterness was further aggravated when free-soil men from Kansas, remembering how Missouri "border ruffians" had once tried to extend slavery into their territory, crossed the border to take revenge on secessionist sympathizers. In turn, Confederate gangs (the most notorious led by the horse thief and murderer William C. Quantrill) preyed on Missouri Unionists.

Far more adroit was Lincoln's handling of Kentucky—his native state, as well as Jefferson Davis's. As in Missouri, the governor was an outright secessionist, but strong Unionist sentiment prevented the calling of a state convention. Thus there was a stalemate, and Kentucky declared itself neutral in any conflict between the United States and the Confederacy. Between May and September 1861, both the Lincoln and the Davis governments claimed to accept this neutrality; but at the same time, each tried to strengthen the hands of its supporters in Kentucky. Finally, suspecting that Union forces were about to seize a position in Kentucky, the Confederates moved first and took Columbus. Federal troops then entered Paducah, and neutrality was dead. But these months of wavering had given Kentucky Unionists a chance to plan and organize, so that the state did not join the Confederacy like Tennessee or become a fierce battleground like Missouri. Lincoln himself played a large role in bringing about this outcome. He gave Kentucky affairs close attention and was careful to assure prominent Kentuckians privately that he "intended to make no attack, direct or indirect, upon the institution or property [meaning slavery] of any State."

Although most Virginians favored the Confederacy, the Union had loyal supporters in the western counties of the state. The people of these counties had long resented the domination of the state by the planters of the tidewater region and had little interest in slavery. When the Virginia convention voted for secession, a sizable minority of the delegates, mostly from these western counties, were opposed, and they went home vowing to keep their state in the Union. A series of exceedingly complex maneuvers followed, including the summoning of several more-or-less extralegal conventions and the creating of a new government for what was termed "reorganized" Virginia, rivaling the secessionist government at Richmond. This "reorganized" government then gave its permission—as required by the United States Constitution—for the counties west of the mountains to form a new and overwhelmingly Unionist state of West Virginia. Not until 1863, when all these steps were completed, was the new state admitted to the Union. Thus by that date there were no fewer than three state governments on Virginia soil: the pro-Confederate government at Richmond; the "reorganized" pro-Union government, which had few supporters and huddled under the protection of Northern guns at Alexandria; and the new Union government of West Virginia.

In summary, then, after Fort Sumter was fired on, the border states divided. Virginia, Arkansas, Tennessee, and North Carolina went with the Confederacy; Delaware, Maryland, Missouri, Kentucky, and, presently, West Virginia remained in the Union.

Importance of the Border States   It is impossible to exaggerate the importance that these decisions, made early in the conflict, had on the conduct of the Civil War. For the Confederacy it was essential that states from the Upper South join the secession. For all the brave talk at Montgomery, the Confederacy was not a viable nation so long as it consisted only of the seven states in the Deep South. The population of these seven states was only one-sixth that of the remaining states of the Union. In all the Gulf States in 1861, there was not a single foundry to roll heavy iron plate or to cast cannon, nor a large powder works, nor indeed a single important factory. But when Virginia, North Carolina, Arkansas, and Tennessee joined the Confederacy, they almost doubled its population. What is more, they brought to the new nation the natural resources, the foundries and factories, and the skilled artisans that made it possible to rival the Union. To recognize the economic and psychological strength added by these states of the Upper South—and also to escape the sweltering summer heat of Montgomery—the Confederacy in May 1861 moved its capital from Montgomery to Richmond.

But if the states of the Upper South brought the Confederacy strength, they also limited its freedom of action. Richmond and Virginia became so important to the South that the Confederate government became obsessed with defending them—at the expense of neglecting the vital western theaters of military operations.

For Lincoln's government, too, the border states were vital. If Maryland had seceded, the capital at Washington would have been surrounded by enemy territory—cut off from the Union states of the North and the West. Confederate control of Kentucky would have imperiled river transportation along the Ohio, and the secession of Missouri would have endangered traffic on the Mississippi and disrupted communication with Kansas and the Pacific coast. Although Lincoln grieved over the secession of the states that joined the Confederacy, he could feel proud that by keeping four slave states in the Union he was preventing the Southern armies from recruiting from a population that was three-fifths as large as that of the original Confederacy.

So important were the border states for the Union that special pains had to be taken not to disturb their loyalty. In particular, Lincoln saw that there must be no premature action against slavery. European nations might fail to understand the nature of the American Civil War, and Northern abolitionists might denounce their president as "the slave-hound from Illinois," but Lincoln knew that to tamper with slavery would result in the loss of the border states, particularly Kentucky. "I think to lose Kentucky is nearly the same as to lose the whole game," he wrote to a friend. "Kentucky gone, we cannot hold Missouri, nor, as I think, Maryland. These all against us, and the job on our hands is too large for us. We would as well consent to separation at once, including the surrender of this capitol."

Raising the Armies

While Lincoln and Davis were moving in parallel fashion to win the support of the border states, ordinary folk in the North and South were rallying around their flags. On both sides the firing on Fort Sumter triggered a rush to enlist. "War! and volunteers are the only topics of conversation or thought," an Oberlin College student reported when the news reached Ohio. "The lessons today have been a mere form. I cannot study. I cannot sleep, I cannot work, and I don't know

Private John Werth, Richmond Howitzer Battalion, C.S.A., and an Illinois Volunteer of 1861

As soon as volunteers were sworn in and received their uniforms and equipment, most rushed to photographers' studios to have pictures made for their loved ones.

as I can write." An Arkansas youth recorded identical emotions: "So impatient did I become for starting that I felt like a thousand pins were pricking me in every part of the body and [I] started off a week in advance of my brothers."

The Rush to Volunteer

Ordinarily a volunteer offered to enlist in one of the regiments that was being raised in his community. Wealthy citizens and prominent politicians usually took the lead in recruiting these companies. Inevitably these regiments displayed a wide variety of arms, ranging from rusty flintlocks to the latest sharpshooting rifles. Often their uniforms bore distinctive insignia. (For example, a Louisiana battalion recruited from the daredevil New Orleans roustabouts called themselves the Tigers, and their scarlet skullcaps bore mottoes like "Tiger on the Leap" and "Tiger in Search of a Black Republican." Perhaps the most colorful—and impractical—uniforms were those of the Northern Zouave regiments,

NO COMPROMISE WITH TRAITORS, AND NO ARGUMENT BUT A KNOCK-DOWN ARGUMENT.

Volunteers Wanted!
FOR COMPANY M,
COLONEL OWEN'S 2d REGIMENT,
BAKER'S BRIGADE!

This is an excellent opportunity for Young Men to serve in this Company. The Officers have been in active service since the commencement of the Rebellion, and understand their duty.

PAY AND RATIONS BEGIN WHEN ENROLLED.

Regim'l Head Quarters, 421 Walnut St.
COMPANY HEAD QUARTERS, Richmond St. above Palmer, Philadelphia.

JOHN DOYLE, 1st Lieut.
JOHN McQUILLIN, 2d " **MARTIN CALLINAN FROST, Captain.**

KING & BAIRD, Printers, No. 607 Sansom Street, Philadelphia.

Recruiting Poster for Zouave Regiment

dressed in imitation of the French troops in North Africa. (These soldiers, wearing their red fezzes, scarlet baggy trousers, and blue sashes, were magnificent in military reviews, but when they had to wade across a stream, their baggy garments ballooned around them and they floated down the current like so many exotic waterlilies.) When a regiment's ranks were filled, there was invariably a farewell ceremony, featuring rousing addresses, lengthy prayers, and the presentation of the regimental flag, often hand-sewn by patriotic wives and sweethearts of the enlisted men. Then, loaded with hams, cakes, and sweetmeats provided by fellow townsmen, the men went off to war.

Wartime Maladministration Neither the Union nor the Confederate War Department knew what to do with the flood of volunteers. Leroy P. Walker, the first Confederate secretary of war, had had no military training and no administrative experience. An amiable Southern gentleman, fond of prolonged conversations with visitors and of writing rambling three-page business letters, Walker was wholly unable to cope with the situation. Complaining that he lacked arms and equipment, he refused the services of regiment after regiment. Perhaps 200,000 Confederate volunteers were thus rejected in the first year of the war.

The Northern war office was equally chaotic. Simon Cameron, the secretary of war, had been forced on Lincoln as part of a political bargain. Cameron's main objective was to become the undisputed boss of Pennsylvania politics. There is no evidence that he used his cabinet position to line his own pockets, but he did employ his huge patronage to strengthen his faction of Pennsylvania Republicans. Lacking administrative talents, Cameron, like Walker, simply could not deal with the flood of volunteers, nor could he supervise the hundreds of contracts his office had to make for arms, ammunition, uniforms, horses, and dozens of other articles for the army. Haste, inefficiency, and corruption inevitably resulted. For example, in October 1861 General Frémont, desperately needing horses for his cavalry in Missouri, contracted to purchase 411 animals. Subsequent investigation proved that 350 of the horses supplied him were undersized, under- or overaged, ringboned, blind, spavined, and incurably unfit for service; 5 were dead. Unable to equip the Union volunteers as they rushed to defend the flag, Cameron thought it was his principal duty "to avoid receiving troops faster than the government can provide for them."

As the war wore on, the initial zeal for volunteering abated. Many of the men rejected by Walker and Cameron in the early months of the conflict were never available again. Soon even those whose services had been accepted began to exhibit less enthusiasm for the war. Most had expected the army to be like the peacetime militia, to which all able-bodied white men belonged; the monthly militia rallies had been the occasion for fun and frolic, punctuated by a little uneven military drill, a considerable amount of political oratory, and a great deal of drinking. Now they discovered that war was not a lark. Belonging to the army meant discipline, spit-and-polish cleaning of equipment, and hours of close-order drill. A soldier's life was one of endless monotony, interrupted occasionally by danger from enemy bullets and more frequently by diseases resulting from inadequate food and clothing, lack of vaccination, filthy drinking water, and open latrines. By the end of 1861, many Union volunteers were beginning to count the weeks until the end of their three-month term of enlistment. Confederate regiments, which had been enrolled for a year, were about ready to disband in the spring of 1862.

Reorganization and Conscription

Of necessity Lincoln and Davis moved almost simultaneously to strengthen their war departments in order to give more central direction to their armies. In January 1862, having persuaded Cameron to become American minister to Russia, Lincoln named a former Democrat, the brusque and imperious Edwin M. Stanton, to the War Department. Stanton quickly reorganized the department, regularized procedures for giving out war contracts, and investigated frauds. Standing behind an old-fashioned writing desk, looking like an irritable schoolmaster before a willful class, Stanton heard all War Department business in public. He curtly dismissed patronage seekers, even when congressmen accompanied them; contractors had to state their prices in loud, clear voices; and even a petitioner bearing a letter of introduction from the president might be abruptly shown to the door. Working incessantly, Stanton saw to it that the Union army became the best-supplied military force the world had ever seen.

It took a bit longer for Davis to find a war secretary to his liking. When Walker, to everyone's relief, resigned in September 1861, Davis replaced him briefly with Judah P. Benjamin and then, after Benjamin became the Confederate secretary of state, with George Wythe Randolph. Randolph did much to see that Robert E. Lee and Thomas J. ("Stonewall") Jackson had the necessary arms and supplies for their 1862 campaigns. But when Randolph and Davis disagreed over strategy, the secretary had to go, and in November 1862 he was succeeded by the sallow and cadaverous James A. Seddon. As one of his clerks remarked, Seddon looked like "an exhumed corpse after a month's interment." Nevertheless he was diligent and efficient. He also had the good sense to give solid support to subordinates of great ability. Perhaps the most competent of these was General Josiah Gorgas, head of the Confederate ordnance bureau. Thanks to Gorgas's efforts, the Confederacy, which in May 1861 had only about 20 cartridges for each musket or rifle, by 1862 had built powder plants capable of producing 20 million cartridges. This was enough ammunition to supply an army of 400,000 men for twelve months.

While both presidents were strengthening their war departments, they also moved, in 1862, to take a more active role in recruiting troops. Because the twelve-month period of enlistment of Confederate troops expired in the spring of 1862, Davis warned that the Southern army would be decimated just as Union forces were approaching Richmond. The Southern Congress felt uncomfortable in ignoring the principle of state sovereignty proclaimed in the Confederate Constitution. But on April 16, 1862, it passed a national conscription act, which made every able-bodied white male between the ages of eighteen and thirty-five subject to military service. This first conscription law in American history, however, exempted numerous groups from military service, ranging from druggists to Confederate government officials; and a subsequent law excused planters or overseers supervising twenty or more slaves. The Confederate conscription act was meant less to raise new troops than to encourage veterans to reenlist. The law provided that if the men stayed in the army, they could remain in their present regiments and elect new officers; but if they left, it threatened, they could be drafted and assigned to any unit that needed them.

Lincoln's government moved toward conscription a little more slowly. Volunteering all but stopped after the bloody campaigns in the summer of 1862,* and the army needed 300,000 new men. Union governors suggested to the president that a draft would stimulate volunteering, and on July 17 the United States Congress passed a loosely worded measure authorizing the president to set quotas of troops to be raised by each state and empowering him to use national

---

*For these military operations, see pp. 612–17.

force to draft them if state officials failed to meet their quotas. This first Union conscription law was intentionally a bogeyman that the governors used to encourage enlistments, and it brought in only a handful of men.

Financing the War

Hard as it was for the Union and Confederate governments to raise troops, it was even harder to supply and pay for them. Although the United States in 1860 was potentially one of the great industrial nations of the world, it was still primarily an agricultural country, with five out of six of its inhabitants living on farms. The factories that would be called on to supply vast armies were mostly small in scale. Some 239 companies manufactured firearms in 1860; their average invested capital was less than $11,000. Textile mills, especially for the manufacture of woolens, were larger, but ready-made clothing was still sewn in small shops. The country produced an abundance of foodstuffs, but there was no effective whole-sale marketing system for meat and grain. According to 1860 maps 30,000 miles of railroads crisscrossed the country, but most of these were short spans, each under its own corporate management. Often they were not connected to other lines at common terminals and had different rail gauges. Sending a boxcar from, say, Baltimore to St. Louis required diplomacy, improvisation, frequent transshipment, long delays, and a great deal of luck. Commercial transactions were impeded because the United States did not have a national bank; indeed, the country did not even have a national currency, for most of the circulating money consisted of bills issued by the numerous state banks, depreciating at various rates.

Problems of the Treasury Departments

Yet Union and Confederate leaders had somehow to mobilize this disorganized economy to support an enormous war effort. Both governments relied primarily on privately owned rather than government-operated factories to supply their armies. Necessity more than a theoretical preference for free enterprise lay behind this choice. If individual businessmen and corporations had little experience in the large-scale production of goods, the civil servants in Washington and Richmond had even less. Where it seemed useful, both governments supplemented the output of private industry with production from government-owned plants. While the Lincoln administration was purchasing firearms from Colt, Remington, and dozens of other manufacturers, it continued to rely on its own armories, especially the one at Springfield, Massachusetts, for some of its best weapons. The South was even more largely rural and agricultural than the North, and thus it had to be more active in establishing government-owned plants, the most successful of which was the huge powder factory at Augusta, Georgia. But both governments contracted with private individuals and corporations for most of the arms, clothing, and other equipment needed for the armies.

It was easier to contract for supplies than to pay for them. Both Union and Confederacy began the war with empty treasuries. When Secretary of the Treasury Chase took up his duties in Washington, he was horrified to discover that between April and June 1861 the expenses of the Union government would exceed its income by $17 million. Chase, who had built his reputation as an antislavery lawyer and politician, was inexperienced in financial matters, and he began casting about desperately for solutions.

But Chase's difficulties were nothing compared with those of his Confederate counterpart, Christopher G. Memminger, who had to make bricks without clay as well as without straw. Like Chase, Memminger had no extensive experience in financial matters, and his neat, systematic mind was troubled by the free and easy ways of government wartime expenses. He did what he could to bring order—by requiring Confederate Treasury employees to keep regular nine-to-five hours, by outlawing drinking on the job, and by insisting that his visitors curb their customary long-windedness and promptly state their business. These measures, however, did little to solve Confederate financial difficulties.

Sources of Revenue   Neither secretary seriously thought of financing the war through levying taxes. For either the Union or the Confederacy to impose heavy taxation in 1861 might well have killed the citizens' ardor for war. Americans were not used to paying taxes to their national government. For thirty-five years before the war, there had been no federal excise duties. In 1860 the United States Treasury had no internal revenue division, no assessors, no inspectors, and no agents. Since tariffs were a more familiar method of raising revenues, both secretaries hoped for large customs receipts. But when the Republicans in the Union Congress passed the high protective Morrill Tariff in 1861 and raised rates even higher in 1862, they effectively killed that source of revenue. At the same time the Union blockade of the South reduced the amount and value of goods brought into Confederate ports and cut the Southern income from tariffs. In desperation the Union government in August 1861 resorted to a direct tax of $20 million, levied on each state in proportion to population; much of it was never collected. That same month, the Confederates imposed a "war tax" of 0.5 percent on taxable wealth. Davis's government, like Lincoln's, had to rely on the states to collect this tax, and most of them preferred issuing bonds or notes to levying duties on their people.

In neither country was borrowing a realistic possibility for financing the war. Americans of the 1860s were products of the Jacksonian era, with its suspicion of paper certificates of indebtedness. Thus Americans preferred to hoard rather than to invest their surplus funds. The rival Union and Confederate governments themselves shared this same suspicion of paper and this trust in hard money, or specie. In the North, Secretary Chase insisted that the banks of New York, Philadelphia, and Boston subscribe to a $150 million federal bond issue, but he was unwilling to take anything but gold or silver in payment. In December 1861 the resulting drain on bank reserves of precious metals, coupled with uncertainty over the course of the war, forced Northern banks to suspend payments in specie for the notes they had issued to the public in past years. Nor was Chase more successful in his early attempts to sell Union bonds directly to small investors. The Confederacy followed much the same course in its borrowing. An initial loan of $15 million was quickly subscribed to, with the result that Southern banks, including the strong institutions of New Orleans, were obliged to give up virtually all their precious metals to the new government. Consequently, they could no longer redeem their notes in gold or silver. Memminger's attempt to sell subsequent Confederate bonds directly to the Southern people ran into the difficulty that nobody had any precious metals. Urged by Vice-President Alexander H. Stephens and other Confederate orators, plantation owners in the fall of 1861 subscribed tobacco, rice, cotton, and other commodities to purchase bonds. But since the Union blockade cut off the market for these products, the Confederate government realized little from the loan.

Recourse to Paper Money   In consequence, by early 1862 both governments began to issue paper money, backed only by the promise that someday they would redeem the paper money in specie. Both treasury secretaries agreed to this policy reluctantly. Memminger, a prominent hard-money advocate before the war, had to resort to the printing presses in 1861. The Confederacy issued $100 million in paper money in August 1861, and the next year it printed millions of dollars more. Having denounced "an irredeemable paper currency, than which no more certainly fatal expedient for impoverishing the masses and discrediting the government of any country, can well be devised," Chase found it even more embarrassing than Memminger to resort to treasury notes. But in January 1862 he had no alternative. Declaring that an issue of paper money was now "indispensably necessary," he persuaded Congress to authorize the printing of $150 million in non-interest-bearing United States treasury notes (which were promptly dubbed "greenbacks" because of their color). Rarely does history provide such a tidy illustration of how huge impersonal forces overrule the preferences and will of individual statesmen.

Wartime Diplomacy

In diplomacy as in economic policy, the Union and the Confederacy moved along parallel paths during the first two years of the war. Neither Lincoln nor Davis had much knowledge of diplomacy or took an active role in the conduct of foreign policy. Both, however, had difficulties with their secretaries of state.

Seward, Lincoln's principal adviser, would ultimately rank as one of the greatest secretaries of state, but in the early stages of the Civil War he gave evidence of eccentricity, coupled with deep personal ambition. At the height of the Sumter crisis, he submitted to Lincoln a private memorandum complaining that the government as yet had no policy for dealing with secession, announcing his readiness to take over the president's function and shape a suitable policy, and suggesting that the administration's proper course was to "change the question before the public from one upon slavery...for a question upon union or disunion." This redefinition of the critical issue was to be accomplished by provoking a confrontation with foreign powers. If allowed, Seward would "seek explanations from Great Britain and Russia"—for what offenses he did not specify; he "would demand explanations from Spain and France, categorically, at once," presumably over their threatened intervention in the affairs of Santo Domingo and Mexico; and if Spain and France did not respond forthwith, he would urge a declaration of war against these powers. Lincoln, to his enduring credit, quietly filed away this memorandum, refrained from dismissing a secretary who planned to bring on a world war, and allowed Seward time to come to his senses.

Despite Lincoln's efforts to keep the matter quiet, word of Seward's aggressive inclinations leaked out in conversations at Washington dinner tables, and diplomats at the capital soon had a pretty good idea of what was in the secretary's mind. Perhaps awareness of Seward's hair-trigger temper did something to make European governments more cautious in their relations with the United States and less eager to recognize the Confederacy.

Davis too had trouble with his state department. Robert Toombs, the first Confederate secretary of state, was as ambitious and overbearing as he was able. Deciding that the path to glory lay on the battlefield rather than in the cabinet, Toombs soon resigned to take a commission in the Southern army. His successor, R. M. T. Hunter, was equally ambitious, and—perhaps with an eye on the 1868 Confederate presidential election—he too promptly resigned, to become senator from Virginia. In March 1862 Davis finally found his man in Judah P. Benjamin, who had already been Confederate attorney general and secretary of war. Serving until the end of the war, Benjamin cleverly reflected the changing moods of his chief, but he was not an innovator in foreign policy. In the words of a critical Northerner who visited Richmond during the war, Benjamin had a "keen, shrewd, ready intellect, but not the stamina to originate, or even to execute, any great good, or great wickedness."

Union and Confederate diplomatic appointments abroad were a rather mixed lot. Perhaps Lincoln lacked tact in appointing the German-born Carl Schurz as minister to conservative, monarchical Spain, for Schurz was considered a "red republican" because of his participation in the German revolution in 1848. But Davis also showed a total failure to understand British antislavery sentiment by sending William L. Yancey, the most notorious Southern fire-eater, as first Confederate commissioner to Great Britain. On the positive side, the Union minister to Great Britain, Charles Francis Adams, exhibited the patience and restraint that were required in his difficult assignment. The dignity of this son of President John Quincy Adams and grandson of President John Adams made him a match even for the aristocratic British foreign minister, Lord John Russell. Of the Confederate emissaries abroad, John Slidell of Louisiana probably proved the ablest. The wily, adroit, and unscrupulous Slidell was perfectly at home in the court of Napoleon III, Napoleon Bonaparte's nephew, who had reestablished the imperial regime in France and was eager to spread French influence in the world.

European Neutrality Much to the disappointment of Americans on both sides, the European powers' attitudes toward the Civil War were not primarily shaped by the actions of American ministers, secretaries of state, or even presidents. Nor, during 1861 and 1862, were they shaped by appeals to economic self-interest. Southerners firmly believed that cotton was king and expected that pressure from British and French textile manufacturers would compel Great Britain and France to recognize the Confederacy and to break the Union blockade. But European manufacturers had an ample stockpile of cotton, purchased before the outbreak of hostilities, and therefore they were not much affected by the cutoff of Southern cotton in 1861. By 1862 cotton mills in both Britain and France were suffering, but Union and Confederate orders for European arms, ammunition, and other equipment counterbalanced these losses. There was great hardship among the workers in the cotton mills, especially in the Lancashire district of England, where unemployment was high. But these work-ers' complaints were relatively ineffectual because Britain still did not allow the workers to vote.

Northerners were equally disappointed by the attitudes of the European governments. Knowing the strength of the antislavery movement abroad, par-ticularly in Great Britain and France, they expected the European powers to condemn the slaveholding Confederacy. Their hope was unrealistic because, during the early years of the war, the Union government took no decisive steps toward emancipation. Indeed, Lincoln pledged that he would not interfere with slavery where it existed, Seward called the abolitionists and "the most extreme advocates of African slavery" equally dangerous to the Union, and Union gener-als helped Southern masters reclaim their runaway slaves. Confused by the mixed signals, European opponents of slavery could do little to influence the attitudes of their governments toward the war in America.

Northerners and Southerners alike failed to understand that the policy of European states toward the Civil War would be determined largely by considera-tions of national self-interest. An uneasy balance of power prevailed in Europe, and no nation was eager to upset it by unilateral intervention in the American conflict. But joint action by the European powers was always difficult because of mutual suspicion, and in the 1860s it was virtually impossible because of the nature of the British government. The British prime minister, Lord Palmerston, who was nearly eighty years old, headed a shaky coalition government that was certain to fall if it undertook any decisive action. With the British government thus immobilized, Russia favoring the Union cause, and Prussia and Austria mostly indifferent to the conflict, the ambitious Napoleon III found his inclina-tions to meddle in favor of the Confederacy effectively curbed.

As a result European nations announced their neutrality early in the war. Queen Victoria's proclamation of May 13, 1861, was typical in recognizing that a state of war existed between the United States and "the states styling themselves the Confederate States of America" and in declaring neutrality. None of the European proclamations recognized the Confederacy as a nation—that is, no one declared that it was a legitimate, independent power, entitled to send ambassadors and ministers abroad and to receive those from other nations, to enter into treaties with other powers, or, in general, to be treated just like any other sovereign state. But the proclamations did recognize the Confederates as belligerents. That acknowledgment meant that the Southerners were not to be considered simply a group of riotous or rebellious individuals, but as participants in a systematic, organized effort to set up their own independent government. Under international law, recognition as a belligerent entitled the Confederacy to send out privateers without their being considered pirate ships. Acknowledgment that a state of war existed in America also meant that the Union government could not declare Southern ports closed to foreign ships. To exclude foreign shipping, the North would have to maintain an effective blockade of the Confederacy. Initially, therefore, these European proclamations of neutrality and recognition of Southern belligerency seemed a great Confederate success. In fact, however, they were both necessary and warranted by international law—and, despite Seward's rantings, they were truly impartial.

The Trent Affair   In November 1861 the rash action of a Union naval officer threatened to upset this neutrality. Union Captain Charles Wilkes learned that President Davis was replacing the temporary commissioners whom he had sent to France and Britain with permanent envoys, John Slidell and James M. Mason. Wilkes decided to capture these diplomats en route. Off the shore of Cuba on November 8, 1861, his warship stopped the British merchant ship *Trent,* Union officers boarded and searched the vessel, and Mason and Slidell were unceremoniously removed, transferred to a Union ship, and sent to Boston for imprisonment. Wilkes's action was a clear violation of international law. When news of the incident reached Europe, hostility toward the Union government flared up. "You may stand for this," Prime Minister Palmerston told his cabinet, "but damned if I will!" The British foreign minister, Russell, drafted a stiff letter demanding the immediate release of the envoys. It was clear that the Lincoln government faced a major crisis if it held its prisoners. After conferring with cabinet members and senators, the president decided on Christmas Day to release the Southern envoys. He would fight only one war at a time.

Even with the firm intention of remaining neutral, European powers found their patience tested as the American war stretched on without apparent chance of ending. International relations were disturbed, commerce was disrupted, textile manufacturing was suffering, and neither North nor South seemed able to achieve its goal. Increasingly, support built up in both France and Britain for offering mediation to the combatants, and such an offer inevitably involved recognition of the Confederacy as an independent nation. In September 1862

"Cotton in the Stocks"
The Union blockade sealed off Southern exports of cotton and helped produce severe hardships in the textile-producing regions of Great Britain and France. This 1862 cartoon shows the French minister to Washington, Henri Mercier, threatening Uncle Sam with European intervention if the blockade is not lifted.

COTTON IN THE STOCKS.

M. Mercier :—" HOW MUCH LONGER IS THIS TO LAST? OR ARE YOU WAITING UNTIL WE INTERFERE?"

Palmerston and Russell agreed to explore a mediation plan involving France and Russia as well as Great Britain, but pro-Union members of the British cabinet, among them the Duke of Argyll and George Cornewall Lewis, replied with strong arguments against mediation. Faced with dissension within his unstable coalition and given no encouragement by Russia, Palmerston by October 1862 had changed his mind and concluded that the European states must continue to be lookers-on until the war took a more decided turn.

Battles and Leaders

But on the battlefields in 1861 and 1862, there were no decided turns. Engagement followed engagement, campaign followed campaign, and neither side could achieve a decisive victory. The stalemate was baffling to both Northern and Southern armchair strategists, who had been sure that the war would be short and decisive and would end in an overwhelming victory for their own side.

Confederate war planners counted among their assets the fact that some of the best graduates of West Point led their armies and that President Davis himself had military training and experience. They believed that Southern men had more fighting spirit than Northerners, and they were probably correct in thinking that Southerners had more experience in handling firearms and were better horsemen. They knew that the Confederacy would generally act on the defensive and assumed that the offensive Union army would have to be at least three times as large as the Southern army. Since Southern forces could operate on interior lines, they could move more quickly and easily than Union forces, which would have to travel longer distances. While recognizing the superiority of the Northern navy, Southerners knew that the Confederacy had 3,500 miles of coastline, with innumerable hidden harbors and waterways through which shipping could escape. When Confederate strategists added to all these assets the fact that Southern soldiers were fighting on their home ground, where they knew every road and byway, they saw no reason to doubt ultimate victory.

But an equally good case could be made for the inevitability of a Union victory. The population of the Union in 1860 was about 20.7 million; that of the Confederacy, only 9.1 million. Moreover, 3.5 million of the inhabitants of the South were blacks—mostly slaves, who, it was presumed, would not be used in the Confederate armies. Along with this superiority in manpower, the North had vastly more economic strength than the Confederacy. The total value of all manufactured products in all eleven Confederate states was less than one-fourth that of New York alone. The iron furnaces, forges, and rolling mills in the United States were heavily concentrated in the North. The North in 1860 built fourteen out of every fifteen railroad locomotives manufactured in the United States. Northern superiority in transportation would more than compensate for Southern interior lines, as only 30 percent of the total rail mileage of the United States ran through the states forming the Confederacy. The Union navy, which experienced few defections to the South, was incomparably superior. And the blockade that President Lincoln announced at the outbreak of hostilities would cut off, or at least drastically reduce, Southern imports from Europe. When Northern planners added to the advantages of their side the possession of an established government, the recognition of foreign powers, and the enormous enthusiasm of the people for maintaining the Union, they could not doubt that victory would be sure and swift.

Jomini's Game Plan   In fact these assets substantially canceled each other during the first two years of the war and produced not victory, but deadlock. As the armies engaged in complex maneuvers and in indecisive battles, Union and Confederate commanders largely employed the same strategic plans, for most had learned the art of war from the same teachers. In fifty-five of the sixty biggest battles of the war, the generals on both sides had been educated at West Point, and in the remaining five, a West Pointer led one of the opposing armies. At the military academy they had studied the theories of the French historian and strategist Baron Henri Jomini. Some had read Jomini's works in the original French or in translation; more, doubtless, had absorbed his ideas from the abridgment and interpretation of his work, *Elementary Treatise on Advance-Guard, Outpost, and Detachment of Service of Troops* (1847), written by Dennis Hart Mahan, who for a generation taught at the academy and greatly influenced his students.

Jomini's military theories constituted a complex body of doctrine, subject to many differing interpretations. But as his theories were understood by American commanders, they stressed the importance of the conquest of territory and emphasized that the seizure of the enemy's capital was, "ordinarily, the objective point" of an invading army. Jomini had pictured a battle situation in which two armies were drawn up in opposing lines, one offensive and the other defensive, and he had even prepared a set of twelve diagrams showing the possible orders of battle. In all twelve, a major determinant of victory was the concentration of force—the bringing to bear of a powerful, united force on the enemy's weakest point. Warfare was thus something like an elaborate game of chess, an art that only professional soldiers could fully master.

Most of the military operations during the first two years of the Civil War can best be understood as a kind of elaborate illustration of Jomini's theories, slightly modified to fit the American terrain. The first big battle of the war occurred on July 21, 1861, when Union General Irwin McDowell, under much pressure from Northern newspapers and much badgered by exuberant politicians in Congress, reluctantly pushed his poorly organized army into Virginia. He expected to encounter the Confederates, under General Beauregard, near Centreville. Numerous sightseers from Washington followed the Union forces, expecting to witness a spectacular victory. In the ensuing battle of Bull Run (or Manassas), both armies tried to apply the same battle plan from Jomini's treatise: each attempted a main attack on the enemy left flank, to be followed by a secondary thrust at his center and right wings. If completely executed, the two plans would have had the amusing result of leaving each army in the opponent's original place. But the Confederates also followed another of Jomini's principles, that of concentration of force. By using the railroad, they rushed General Joseph E. Johnston's troops from the Shenandoah Valley to join Beauregard's main force. The Union troops fought bravely and initially seemed to be carrying the day, but after Johnston's men were in position, the Union army was thrown back and then routed. Weary and disorganized, Northern troops limped back to the Potomac and safety. Panic among the onlookers heightened the confusion. The Confederates were almost equally demoralized by their victory and were unable to pursue. The South thus lost its easiest opportunity to follow Jomini's maxim and seize the enemy's capital.

After this initial engagement it was clear that both armies needed reorganization and training before either could attempt further campaigns. Despite growing impatience for action, there was little significant military engagement during the rest of 1861 except for minor encounters in Kentucky and Missouri. During this period General George Brinton McClellan, who was credited with some overrated small successes in western Virginia, was summoned to Washington to bring order to the Union army. With enormous dash and enthusiasm, the young commander began to whip the Northern regiments into fighting shape. He insisted on careful drill and inspection; he demanded the best of food and equipment for his men; and he refused to move forward until his army was thoroughly prepared.

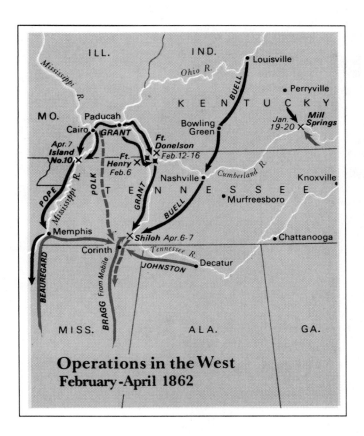

**Operations in the West
February–April 1862**

The War in the West, 1862

By early 1862 Union armies were ready to advance, not only in the East, but in all the theaters of war. Taking advantage of numerical superiority, Union commanders concentrated on a series of weak spots in the Confederate defenses, just as Jomini had directed. In January General George H. Thomas defeated a Confederate force at Mill Springs, Kentucky, and made a significant break in the Southern defense line west of the Appalachian Mountains. The next month General Ulysses S. Grant made an even more important breach in that line. In collaboration with the Union gunboats on the Tennessee and Cumberland rivers, Grant captured Fort Henry and Fort Donelson, requiring the Confederate army in the latter fort to accept his terms of unconditional surrender.

The Southerners now had to abandon Tennessee. Union armies under Grant and Don Carlos Buell pushed rapidly after them until stopped at the battle of Shiloh (April 6–7). General Henry Wager Halleck, the Union commander for the entire western theater, was dissatisfied with Grant's generalship and took personal charge of the army after Shiloh. Halleck was a dedicated disciple of Jomini (whose works he had translated) and concentrated his force for a push on Corinth, Mississippi, in order to break the important rail connection that linked Memphis and the western portion of the Confederacy with the East.

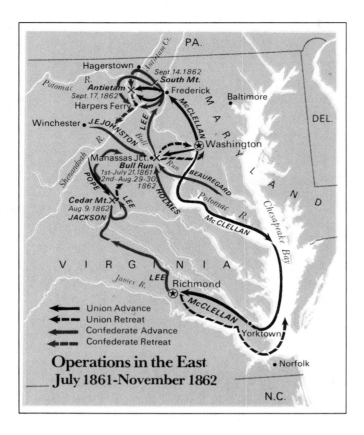

Hagerstown
Sept.14,1862
South Mt.
Antietam
Sept.17,1862
Harpers Ferry
Winchester • J.E.JOHNSTON
Frederick
Baltimore
DEL.
PA.
Potomac R.
LEE
McCLELLAN
MARYLAND
Washington
Manassas Jct.
Bull Run
1st-July 21,1861
2nd-Aug.29-30,
1862
POPE
BEAUREGARD
HOLMES
Potomac R.
McCLELLAN
Chesapeake Bay
Cedar Mt.
Aug.9,1862
JACKSON
LEE
V I R G I N I A
James R.
LEE
Richmond
McCLELLAN
Yorktown
Norfolk
N.C.

Union Advance
Union Retreat
Confederate Advance
Confederate Retreat

Operations in the East
July 1861-November 1862

The Peninsula Campaign

A Union advance in the eastern theater promised to be equally successful. After long delays McClellan began his offensive against Richmond. Instead of attacking overland from the north, he transported his troops to Fort Monroe, on the peninsula between the York and James rivers. McClellan complained bitterly because Lincoln violated the principle of concentration and held back 40,000 troops to defend Washington. Nevertheless McClellan prepared to follow Jomini's advice and seize the Confederate capital.

At this point in the gigantic, synchronized Union offensive, designed to crush the Confederacy, everything began to go wrong. The difficulties stemmed in part from human inadequacies. Although good theoreticians and able administrators, Halleck and McClellan were indecisive fighters. Halleck took nearly two months to creep from Shiloh to Corinth, stopping to fortify his position every night. By the time he reached his destination, the Southern army had moved south with all its provisions. Equally cautious was McClellan's advance on the peninsula, where he allowed 16,000 Confederate soldiers under General John B. Magruder to hold up his magnificent army of 112,000 until the Confederates could bring reinforcements to Richmond. The trouble was partly that these Union campaigns required the coordinated movement of forces larger than any seen before on the American continent, directed by commanding officers who had never led anything larger than a regiment. But the Union failed chiefly because able Confederate generals had read the same books on strategy as the Union commanders and knew how to fight the same kind of battles.

While McClellan slowly edged his way up the peninsula, the Confederate commander, Joseph E. Johnston, who had rushed in with reinforcements, kept close watch until the Union general unwisely allowed his forces to be divided by the flooded Chickahominy River. Applying Jomini's principle of concentration on the enemy's weakest spot, Johnston on May 31–June 1 fell upon the exposed Union wing in battles at Fair Oaks (or Seven Pines), which narrowly failed of being a Confederate triumph. When Johnston was wounded in this engagement, President Davis chose Robert E. Lee to replace him.

Lee quickly revealed his military genius by showing that he knew when to follow Jomini's principles and when to ignore them. Remembering from his days at West Point how slow McClellan was, Lee allowed "Stonewall" Jackson to take 18,000 men from the main army for a daring campaign through the Shenandoah Valley. Jackson defeated and demoralized the Union forces in the Shenandoah and so threatened Washington that Lincoln withheld reinforcements that he had promised McClellan. After Jackson had accomplished this objective, Lee reverted to the principle of concentration and ordered Jackson promptly to rejoin the main army before Richmond. The combined Confederate force fell upon McClellan's exposed right flank at Mechanicsville. Lee failed to crush McClellan; but in a series of engagements known as the Seven Days (June 25–July 1), he forced the Union armies to beat a slow, hard-fought retreat to the banks of the James River, where it lay under the protection of Northern gunboats. Lee had saved Richmond.

The Confederate Counteroffensive

As the Union advances ground to a halt by midsummer 1862, the Confederates planned a grand offensive of their own. In the West two Southern armies under generals Braxton Bragg and Edmund Kirby-Smith swept through eastern Tennessee in August; by September they were operating in Kentucky, where they were in a position to cut the supply line for Buell's army in Tennessee. The early phases of their offensive were brilliantly successful, but the campaign as a whole was fruitless because of a lack of coordination between the two Southern armies and because of Bragg's indecisiveness. After a bloody battle at Perryville (October 8), the Confederate forces withdrew toward Chattanooga, followed by the Union army at a respectful distance.

The more daring part of the Confederate offensive was in the East. While McClellan's army was slowly being withdrawn from the peninsula, Lee turned quickly on the Union forces in central Virginia under the braggart general John Pope. Concentrating his entire strength on this segment of the Union army, Lee scored a brilliant Confederate victory in the second battle of Bull Run (August 29–30) and was now free to push into the North. He crossed the Potomac into

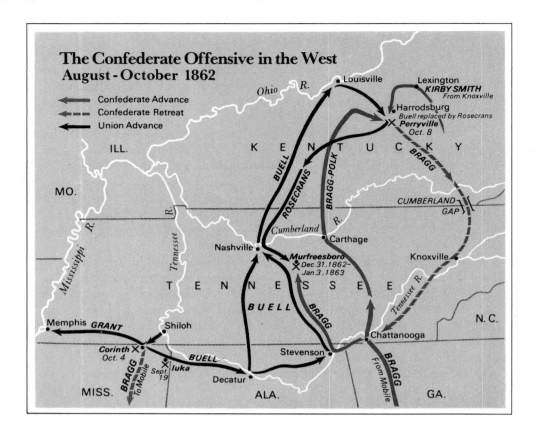

The Confederate Offensive in the West
August - October 1862

→ Confederate Advance
⇢ Confederate Retreat
→ Union Advance

Ohio R.

Louisville

Lexington
KIRBY SMITH
From Knoxville

Harrodsburg
Buell replaced by Rosecrans
✗ **Perryville**
Oct. 8

ILL.

K E N T U C K Y

MO.

BUELL

ROSECRANS

BRAGG-POLK

BRAGG

CUMBERLAND
GAP

Cumberland R.

Carthage

Nashville

✗ **Murfreesboro**
*Dec.31,1862–
Jan.3,1863*

Knoxville

T   E   N   N   E   S   S   E   E

Tennessee R.

N.C.

Mississippi R.

Tennessee R.

BUELL

BRAGG

Memphis **GRANT**

Shiloh

Chattanooga

Corinth ✗
Oct. 4

BRAGG
To Mobile

✗ Iuka
*Sept.
19*

BUELL

Decatur

Stevenson

BRAGG
From Mobile

MISS.

ALA.

GA.

Maryland, where he hoped to supply his ragged army and to rally the inhabitants of that state to the Confederate cause.

Lee's invasion of Maryland ended with the battle of Antietam (September 17), an indecisive engagement whose very inconclusiveness clearly demonstrated the impossibility of ever ending the war as long as it was fought by the conventional rules. McClellan, once again the Union commander, moved slowly to catch up with Lee's army because he wanted to concentrate all his forces for an attack. Lee in turn waited in a defensive position behind Antietam Creek at Sharpsburg, Maryland, because he too needed to concentrate his troops, a portion of whom had been sent on a successful expedition to capture Harpers Ferry. When McClellan was finally ready to take the offensive, he followed one of Jomini's battle plans precisely, and Lee defended his position by the same rules. The result was the bloodiest day of the Civil War. In areas of the battlefield like the cornfield, the Dunker church, the Bloody Lane, and Burnside's bridge, men fell as in a slaughterhouse. By the end of the day there were more than 25,000 casualties, with at least 5,000 dead. The next day an eyewitness noted "the most appalling sights upon the battlefield . . . the ground strewn with the bodies of the dead and the dying . . . the cries and groans of the wounded . . . the piles of dead men, in attitudes which show the writhing agony in which they died—faces

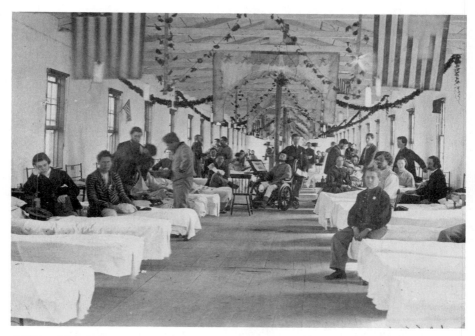

A Union Hospital
The superintendent of the Union nursing corps was Dorothea L. Dix, who had led a movement to improve the lot of the mentally ill. To counteract the general impression that nurses were women of low moral character, she insisted that appointees had to be plain looking and over thirty years old.

distorted . . . begrimed and covered with clotted blood, arms and legs torn from the body or the body itself torn asunder."

Quietly Lee slipped back into Virginia, and McClellan did not pursue him. The Confederate offensive was over, and with it ended an era. If Jomini's strategy could lead only to stalemate, it was time for both Union and Confederacy to experiment with new ways of waging war.

CHRONOLOGY

1861 Secession of remaining states of Deep South (Texas, Louisiana, Mississippi, Alabama, Georgia, and Florida).
Jefferson Davis begins term as president of the Confederate States of America.

Abraham Lincoln inaugurated as president of the United States of America.
Firing on Fort Sumter precipitates war.
Secession of border slave states (Virginia, North Carolina, Tennessee, and Arkansas).

1861	Union army routed at first battle of Bull Run (Manassas). McClellan heads Union forces. *Trent* affair threatens to change European neutrality.
1862	Both Union and Confederacy adopt paper money. Union general U. S. Grant captures Fort Henry and Fort Donelson. Grant's advance checked at Shiloh. Battle of the ironclads: *Virginia (Merrimack)* vs. *Monitor.* McClellan's peninsula campaign

brings Union army to outskirts of Richmond, the Confederate capital. Robert E. Lee becomes commander of Army of Northern Virginia. Confederate victory at second battle of Bull Run. Bloody battle between Lee and McClellan at Antietam. Confederate invasion of Kentucky. Lincoln issues preliminary Emancipation Proclamation. Confederate victory at Fredricksburg.

SUGGESTED READINGS

An excellent guide to the extensive literature on the causes of Civil War is Thomas J. Pressly, *Americans Interpret Their Civil War* (1954).

James M. McPherson, *Battle Cry of Freedom* (1988), is the best narrative history of the Civil War. Other useful one-volume accounts are Peter J. Parish, *The American Civil War* (1975); J. G. Randall and David Herbert Donald, *The Civil War and Reconstruction* (1969); and James M. McPherson, *Ordeal by Fire* (1982). The most complete modern account is Allan Nevins, *The War for the Union* (4 vols., 1959–71). Shelby Foote, *The Civil War* (3 vols., 1958–74), is a spirited narrative, written on a grand scale.

There are several excellent reference works: Mark M. Boatner III, *The Civil War Dictionary* (1988); Patricia L. Faust, ed., *Historical Times Illustrated Encyclopedia of the Civil War* (1986); and Steward Sifakis, *Who Was Who in the Civil War* (1988).

On the Sumter crisis, see David M. Potter, *Lincoln and His Party in the Secession Crisis* (1942); Kenneth M. Stampp, *And the War Came* (1950); and Richard N. Current, *Lincoln and the First Shot* (1963). Daniel W. Crofts, *Reluctant Confederates* (1989), explores the plight of the border states.

The best history of the Confederacy is Emory M. Thomas, *The Confederate Nation, 1861–1865* (1979). The fullest life of the Confederate president is Hudson Strode, *Jefferson Davis* (3 vols., 1955–64). Rembert W. Patrick, *Jefferson Davis and His Cabinet* (1944), is revealing on Confederate administration. Three Confederate diaries are invaluable: *Mary Chestnut's Civil War,* ed. by C. Vann Woodward (1981); John B. Jones, *A Rebel War Clerk's Diary* (2 vols., 1866); and Robert G. H. Kean, *Inside the Confederate Government,* ed. by Edward Younger (1955).

The most recent biography of Abraham Lincoln is Stephen B. Oates, *With Malice Toward None* (1977). Benjamin P. Thomas, *Abraham Lincoln* (1952), has long remained standard. The fullest and most flavorful of the biographies is Carl Sandburg, *Abraham Lincoln: The War Years* (4 vols., 1939). The most scholarly and critical is J. G. Randall and Richard N. Current, *Lincoln the President* (4 vols., 1945–55). A brilliant psychoanalytical interpretation is Charles B. Strozier, *Lincoln's Quest for Union* (1982). Mark E. Neely, Jr., *The Abraham Lincoln Encyclopedia* (1982), is exceptionally useful. The diaries of three of Lincoln's cabinet officers are indispensable: Howard K. Beale, ed., *The Diary of Edward Bates* (1933); David Donald, ed., *Inside Lincoln's*

Cabinet [Salmon P. Chase] (1954); and Howard K. Beale and Alan W. Brownsword, eds., *Diary of Gideon Welles* (3 vols., 1960).

The standard work on Anglo-American relations remains Ephraim D. Adams, *Great Britain and the American Civil War* (2 vols., 1925). Frank L. Owsley, *King Cotton Diplomacy* (1959), David P. Crook, *The North, the South, and the Powers* (1974), and Brian Jenkins, *Britain & the War for the Union* (2 vols., 1974–80), are valuable. See also Glyndon G. Van Deusen, *William Henry Seward* (1967); Martin B. Duberman, *Charles Francis Adams* (1961); and David Donald, *Charles Sumner and the Rights of Man* (1970). Franco-American relations are admirably covered in Lynn M. Chase and Warren F. Spencer, *The United States and France: Civil War Diplomacy* (1970), and Daniel B. Carroll, *Henri Mercier and the American Civil War* (1971).

On social and economic conditions, see Paul W. Gates, *Agriculture and the Civil War* (1965), and Mary E. Massey, *Bonnet Brigades: American Women and the Civil War* (1966). Developments on the Southern home front are sketched in Charles W. Ramsdell, *Behind the Lines in the Southern Confederacy* (1944), and Bell I. Wiley, *The Plain People of the Confederacy* (1943). Emerson D. Fite, *Social and Industrial Conditions in the North During the Civil War* (1910), remains the best survey. For the continuing debate on the effect of the war on American economic growth, see Ralph Andreano, ed., *The Economic Impact of the American Civil War* (1961), and David T. Gilchrist and W. David Lewis, eds., *Economic Change in the Civil War Era* (1965).

Studies dealing with other aspects of the war years are listed at the end of the following chapter.

19

Experimentation
1862–1865

⁓

$\mathcal{A}$T THE outset of the Civil War, both President Lincoln and President Davis assumed that the conflict would be a limited and relatively brief one, waged in conventional fashion by armies in the field and having little impact on the economic, social, and intellectual life of their sections. The events of 1861–62 proved these expectations utterly wrong. It slowly became clear that to carry on the war, Americans in both North and South had to break with tradition and experiment broadly. They had to try new forms of government action, new modes of social and economic cooperation, and new patterns of thought.

Because the Union was ultimately victorious, it would be easy to conclude that Northerners were more willing to experiment, and better able to mobilize all their resources, for what has been called the first modern war. But such a judgment makes the historian the camp follower of the victorious army. The record shows instead that both the Confederacy and the Union attempted innovations that were daringly original for the time. It also shows that both sides resorted to much the same kinds of experimentation during the final years of the war.

Evolution of a Command System

The bloody and indecisive campaigns of 1861 and 1862 made innovators out of both Union and Confederate soldiers. Experience under fire convinced them not to follow Jomini's tactics. The French writer had conceived of a tactical situation in which infantrymen, drawn up in close, parallel lines, blazed away at each other with muskets that could be loaded perhaps twice a minute and that had an effective range of one hundred yards. But Civil War soldiers were equipped with rifles that not only were more quickly loaded, but had an effective range of about eight hundred yards. In Jomini's day the offensive force had the great advantage: rushing forward with bayonets fixed, charging troops could break the defenders' line before they had time to reload. But in the Civil War the advancing force was exposed to accurate fire during the last half-mile of its approach. In consequence, nine out of ten infantry assaults failed, and the Civil War soldier had little use for his bayonet—except perhaps as a spit on which to cook meat.

Soldiers on both sides rapidly learned how to make defensive positions even stronger. At the beginning of the war, most military men were scornful of breastworks and entrenchments, arguing that they pinned down a defending force and made it more vulnerable to a charge. When Lee, on assuming command of the Army of Northern Virginia in 1862, ordered his men to construct earthworks facing McClellan's advancing troops, Confederate soldiers bitterly complained and called their new general the King of Spades. But when they saw how entrenchments saved lives, they changed their tune. Lee became to the Confederate common soldier "Marse Robert," the general who looked after his men's welfare. What Confederate generals started, Union commanders imitated. By the end of 1862, both armies dug in wherever they halted. Using spades and canteens, forks and sticks, soldiers pushed up improvised earthworks and strengthened them with fence rails and fallen logs.

Experience also quietly killed off Jomini's view that warfare was restricted to professionals. In the early days of the conflict, commanders believed that warfare should not do harm to civilians or their property. When McClellan's army pushed up the peninsula, the general posted guards to keep his soldiers from raiding Confederate farmers' cornfields. Similarly, Halleck permitted slaveowners to search his camp in order to reclaim their runaway slaves. By the end of 1862, such practices had vanished. Soldiers joyfully foraged through civilians' watermelon patches, cornfields, and chicken roosts while their officers ostentatiously turned their backs. Northern generals exhibited a growing reluctance to permit the recapture of fugitive slaves who had fled to the Union lines. As early as May 1861 General Benjamin F. Butler at Fort Monroe, Virginia, refused to return three such fugitives on the grounds that they were contraband of war. "Contrabands" became a code name for escaped slaves, and in 1862 the United States Congress showed what it thought of Jomini's notion of limited warfare by prohibiting military officers from returning runaways.

Lincoln Takes Command   The deadlock of 1861–62 also brought about a transformation of the command systems of both the Union and the Confederate armies. Because the Union lost so many battles during the first two years of the conflict, Lincoln was forced to experiment. His initial venture came in mid-1862. Since he distrusted McClellan's capacity to keep an eye on the overall progress of the war while also leading a campaign to capture Richmond, Lincoln brought in Halleck from the West to serve as his military adviser, and gave him the grand title of general in chief. The position was not a viable one, for it placed Halleck in conflict with the other

Reburial of the Dead
After each major Civil War battle, in order to prevent the spread of disease, the dead had to be hastily buried, often in mass graves. Months later, soldiers had the gruesome task of excavating these graves, trying to sort and identify the remains, and giving them a proper burial.

generals, especially McClellan. It also often put him at odds with Secretary of War Stanton and exposed him to what he called the "political Hell" of pressure from congressmen. In addition Halleck's slowness, his indecisiveness, and his rigid adherence to Jomini's principles made him hostile to all innovation, and Lincoln soon concluded that he was of little more use than a clerk.

Seeing no alternative, Lincoln then tried to direct military operations himself. In the eastern theater he replaced McClellan, after his failure to follow up his partial success at Antietam, with the incompetent Ambrose E. Burnside. Burnside led the Army of the Potomac into the battle of Fredericksburg on December 13, 1862, one of the most disastrous—and surely the least necessary—Union defeats of the war. The appointment of "Fighting Joe" Hooker, a boastful egotist who was fond of the bottle, to replace Burnside brought no better luck to the Union cause. The battle of Chancellorsville (May 1–4, 1863) was still another Confederate triumph—but a victory won at a great price, for "Stonewall" Jackson was accidentally fired on by his own Southern soldiers and was mortally wounded.

Still trying to direct military operations himself, Lincoln watched anxiously as Lee in the midsummer of 1863 began his second invasion of the North, this time pushing into Pennsylvania. When Hooker appeared unable or unwilling to

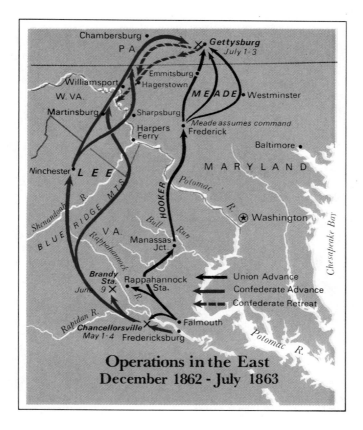

**Operations in the East
December 1862 - July 1863**

Map labels: Chambersburg, PA, Gettysburg July 1-3, Williamsport, Emmitsburg, Hagerstown, W. VA., MEADE, Westminster, Martinsburg, Sharpsburg, Harpers Ferry, Meade assumes command, Frederick, Baltimore, Winchester, LEE, MARYLAND, Shenandoah R., BLUE RIDGE MTS, HOOKER, Potomac, Washington, VA., Bull Run, Manassas Jct., Rappahannock, Brandy Sta., June 9 X, Rappahannock Sta., Falmouth, Chancellorsville May 1-4, Fredericksburg, Rapidan R., Potomac R., Chesapeake Bay

Legend: Union Advance, Confederate Advance, Confederate Retreat

pursue the Confederates, Lincoln replaced him with the shy, scholarly George Gordon Meade, who assumed command of the army only three days before the climactic battle of Gettysburg (July 1–3, 1863). Rushing all available forces to that Pennsylvania town, Meade succeeded in turning back the invaders. At last the Army of the Potomac had won a victory—but Meade failed to pursue, and Lee's army recrossed the Potomac to safety. "We had them within our grasp," Lincoln lamented. "We had only to stretch forth our hands and they were ours. And nothing I could say or do could make the Army move."

Lincoln was no more successful in trying to direct the trans-Appalachian theater of war. After the battle of Perryville in October 1862, it was clear that Don Carlos Buell must be replaced, and the president chose W. S. Rosecrans. Lincoln urged him to push on to Chattanooga, the rail hub of the Confederacy, but en route Rosecrans encountered Bragg's army in the bloody and indecisive battle of Murfreesboro (December 30, 1862–January 2, 1863). Although Rosecrans claimed victory, his army was so badly mauled that he could not advance for another six months. Finally, in June 1863 he maneuvered the Confederates out of Chattanooga, but in pursuing Bragg's army he received a smashing defeat at Chickamauga (September 19–20). Only the rocklike determination of General George H. Thomas prevented the reverse from becoming a rout, and Rosecrans's

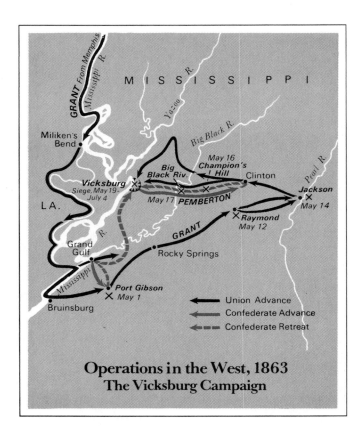

Operations in the West, 1863
The Vicksburg Campaign

army limped back into Chattanooga. Disoriented by defeat, Rosecrans, as Lincoln said, behaved "like a duck hit on the head" and allowed Bragg to besiege the city.

Farther west, Lincoln's personal direction of the Union armies proved equally ineffectual. Here the major objective was Vicksburg, the last major city on the Mississippi River still in Confederate hands; when it fell, the eastern part of the Confederacy would be severed from the trans-Mississippi region.

Grant's Success at Vicksburg

Grant commanded the Union forces in this area after Halleck went to Washington, and William Tecumseh Sherman was his ablest lieutenant. After a frontal assault on the almost impregnable bluffs of Vicksburg failed to drive out the Confederates, commanded by General John C. Pemberton, Grant devised a bold new strategy without aid from Washington. Using the navy's gunboats and transports to run his ammunition and supplies down the Mississippi River past the Vicksburg batteries, Grant marched his army to a point on the west bank south of the city, staged a rapid amphibious crossing, and—before the Confederates could recover from their surprise—pushed rapidly inland. To Lincoln's dismay he thus abandoned his base of supplies, announcing that he planned to live on the countryside. First he struck at Jackson, the capital of Mississippi, to drive back the small Confederate force that General Joseph E. Johnston had collected there. Then he turned on Pemberton's army and forced it into Vicksburg. After two ill-advised assaults, the Union army settled down to besiege the city, while from the river the Union gunboats kept up a constant bombardment. As civilians in the city took to caves for safety, and as starvation made mule meat a delicacy, Pemberton fought back as well as he could, but on July 4, 1863— the day after Gettysburg—he had to surrender his army and the city.

When the news reached Washington, Lincoln, who had distrusted Grant's strategy, wrote the general a handsome apology: "I now wish to make the personal acknowledgment that you were right, and I was wrong." The president was happy to be proved wrong, for Grant's success meant that he finally had a general who knew how to plan a campaign and fight it. Putting Grant in command of all the troops in the West, Lincoln directed him to relieve the army cooped up in Chattanooga. Quickly Grant and Sherman came to the rescue. They opened up a line of communication to the starving Union troops in Chattanooga, now commanded by Thomas instead of the inept Rosecrans, and brought in reinforcements. On November 23–25 the combined forces routed Bragg's encircling army and drove it back into Georgia.

Two New Systems of Command

This further victory gave Lincoln a solution to the problem of command, which had so long troubled him. Early the next year he brought Grant to Washington. Grant became a lieutenant general and was assigned to command all the armies of the United States. Initially, Washington observers thought the burden might be too much for this "short, round-shouldered man," whom they now saw for the first time. One observer reported that the new lieutenant general "had no gait, no station, no manner, rough, light-brown whiskers, a blue eye, and rather a scrubby look withal . . . rather the look of a man who did, or once did, take a little too much to drink." But appearances were deceiving, for in the next few days Grant set forth a broad strategy for winning the war. Taking advantage of Northern superiority in manpower, he planned a simultaneous advance of all Union armies, so that the Confederates must divide their forces or else leave their territory open to invasion. The idea of involving all the Northern forces at once made sense to Lincoln. "Oh, yes! I can see that," he exclaimed. "As we say out West, if a man can't skin he must hold a leg while somebody else does." Accepting Grant's plan, Lincoln created a modern command system for the United States army, with the president as commander in chief, Grant as general in chief, and Halleck as essentially a chief of staff, while Stanton as secretary of war ably supported all the others.

Meanwhile the Confederate command system was also evolving through experimentation. The tremendous victories won by Lee and the Army of Northern Virginia made it unnecessary constantly to change commanders in the East, but by 1863 it was evident that there must be a reorganization of Confederate commanders in the West. Davis instituted what was, in effect, a theater command system. Lee led the forces in Virginia, Joseph E. Johnston (now recovered from his wound) commanded the troops between the mountains and the Mississippi River, and Edmund Kirby-Smith was in charge of all troops in the vast trans-Mississippi region.

The new system was only partially successful. Kirby-Smith became a kind of supercommander of the trans-Mississippi theater (which was becoming increasingly isolated as Union forces captured point after point on the Mississippi) and did an effective job of recruiting and organizing the troops in his region. He stepped up trade with Mexico, so that impressive amounts of European munitions and supplies came in by way of Matamoros, Mexico. So strengthened, "Kirby-Smithdom," as it was popularly called, fared better than most of the rest of the South. But Kirby-Smith did little to make the vast resources of his command available to the government at Richmond.

In the central theater a strong Confederate command system failed to emerge. Johnston claimed that he did not know the extent and nature of his duties. Repeatedly he asked whether he was supposed to take field command of the widely scattered armies of Bragg (near Chattanooga) and of Pemberton (at Vicksburg), or was merely to serve as adviser to those generals. Knowing that both were protégés of President Davis, Johnston did not dare give a positive order to either. In consequence, he made only a feeble effort to replace the unpopular Bragg and diverted a few of his troops to support Pemberton. Johnston could not persuade Pemberton to leave Vicksburg while there was still time, and he watched in impotent impatience as the Confederate army there was cornered and starved into surrender.

In the eastern theater the brilliant successes of Lee and his lieutenants allowed the Army of Northern Virginia to operate essentially as it wished, without much regard for the needs of the Confederacy elsewhere. Lee, who had direct access to President Davis, resisted any attempt to weaken his force. In mid-1863, rather than attempt to relieve Vicksburg, Lee deliberately chose to invade the North again, in the vain hope that this course would relieve pressure on Confederate armies elsewhere. The result was the defeat at Gettysburg and the capture of Vicksburg.

Even so, by 1864 Lee was the only Confederate commander who retained the confidence of the country and of his troops. As Southern defeats became more numerous than victories, a strong demand welled up in the Confederate Congress for coordinated direction of all Southern armies, and men naturally looked to Lee. The general was, however, opposed to accepting these broader responsibilities and did all that he could to discourage the plan. When the Confederate Congress in January 1865 passed an act requiring the appointment of a commander in chief of all the armies, it had Lee in mind, and Davis named him. But Lee made it clear that he would continue to be essentially a theater commander, responsible only to Davis. Thus the Confederacy never developed a truly unified command system like the Union's.

The Naval War

Necessity compelled the Confederacy to take the lead in experimentation in naval warfare. Southerners were not a seagoing people and had no tradition of ship-building. Initially Secretary of the Navy Stephen R. Mallory had not a single ship at his command. He had to improvise, and he did so with imagination and remarkable success.

In the early months of the war, the long Southern coastline seemed to be at the mercy of the Union fleet, which could pick the most vulnerable points for attack. In November 1861 a Union naval force commanded by Flag Officer Samuel F. DuPont routed the weak Confederate defenders of Port Royal Sound, on the South Carolina coast, and Northern troops occupied Beaufort and the adjoining South Carolina Sea Islands. The victory gave the vessels in the Atlantic blockading fleet a much-needed fueling station and also brought freedom to the numerous slaves of the area. In February and March 1862 another Union expedition easily reduced Confederate positions on Roanoke Island and at New Bern, North Carolina, and enabled the Northern blockaders to keep a closer watch on Hatteras Sound. David G. Farragut's fleet in April 1862 helped capture New Orleans, the Confederacy's largest city.

By this time the Confederacy had greatly strengthened its coastal defenses, and further Union successes came slowly and at great cost. In April 1863 the Confederates repelled a vast Union armada, commanded by DuPont, that tried to capture Charleston. That stronghold of secession remained in Confederate hands until nearly the end of the war. Equally effective were the Confederate defenses of Wilmington, North Carolina, which became the main Southern port on the Atlantic through which supplies from Europe were imported. Not until January 1865 could Union troops capture Fort Fisher, the principal defense of Wilmington. The powerfully protected harbor of Mobile remained in Southern hands until August 1864, when the sixty-three-year-old Admiral Farragut, lashed in the rigging of his flagship so that he would not fall to his death if wounded, led his fleet past the defending Confederate forts to seize the last remaining major Southern port on the Gulf of Mexico.

Innovations in Naval Warfare

To supplement the coastal batteries that protected these and other harbors, the Confederate navy experimented with new weapons. They used torpedoes extensively for the first time in warfare. These "infernal machines," constructed of kegs, barrels, and cans filled with explosives, were sometimes anchored at the entrance of Southern harbors. At other times they were turned loose to float with the tide toward attacking Union vessels, and on still other occasions they were propelled at the end of long poles by a small boats whose crews were willing to undertake the suicidal risk. Even more risky were the several Confederate experiments with submarines. The most successful of these novel vessels was the *H. L. Hunley,* propelled under water by a crank turned by its eight-man crew.

After four unsuccessful trials, in which all members of the crews were killed, the *Hunley* in February 1864 sank the Union warship *Housatonic* in Charleston harbor, but the submarine itself was lost in the resulting explosion.

Mallory quickly concluded that the Confederacy could never build as large a fleet as the Union, and early in the war he urged the construction of iron-armored ships, against which the wooden vessels of the North would stand no chance. Despite shortages of iron and a lack of rolling mills, the Confederacy developed a surprising number of these vessels. The most famous of the Confederate iron-clads was the *Virginia,* originally the United States warship *Merrimack,* which had been sunk when Union forces abandoned the Norfolk navy yard at the beginning of the war. Raised and repaired, the *Virginia* had its superstructure covered with four-inch iron plate and carried a cast-iron ram on its prow. On March 8, 1862, just as McClellan began his campaign on the peninsula, the *Virginia* emerged and began attacking the wooden vessels of the Union fleet at Hampton Roads. In the first day's action the ironclad destroyed two of the largest ships in the squadron and ran a third aground. Reappearing on the second day, the *Virginia* found its way barred by a curious Union vessel, the *Monitor,* which looked like a tin can on a raft. Belatedly contracted for by the slow-moving Union navy department, the *Monitor,* designed by John Ericsson, was a low-lying ironclad with a revolving gun turret. The battle between the *Virginia* and the *Monitor* ended in a draw, but the Confederate ship had to return to Norfolk to repair its defective engines. Two days later, when forced to abandon Norfolk, the Southerners ran the *Virginia* ashore and burned the vessel to prevent its capture. The South's most promising hope for breaking the blockade was lost.

Mallory was equally prompt in purchasing or commissioning conventional vessels for the Confederate navy. These ships were designed not to combat Union warships, but rather to harass the United States merchant marine. The most successful of these vessels was the CSS *Alabama,* built to Southern specifications at the Laird shipyards in Liverpool, England, and commanded by Raphael Semmes. Ranging over the Atlantic, Indian, and Pacific oceans, the *Alabama* between 1862 and 1864 hunted down and destroyed sixty-nine Union mer-chantmen, valued at more than $6 million. Not until nearly the end of the war could the Union navy corner and sink the raider. By this time, however, the *Alabama,* along with other Confederate cruisers, had virtually exterminated the United States carrying trade.

But however imaginative and innovative, Confederate navy officials could not keep pace with the growth of the Union navy under the slow but honest direction of Navy Secretary Gideon Welles. Drawing on the vast industrial resources of the North and on the experience of its seagoing population, Welles was able to build up the United States navy from its 42 active vessels in 1861, only 26 of which had steam power, to 671 ships in December 1864, of which 71 were ironclad. Navy personnel rose from 7,400 at the start of the war to 68,000 at its end. Superbly equipped and managed, the Union fleet maintained an ever-tightening blockade of the Southern coast. According to the best—but not wholly reliable—statistics, the Union fleet captured not more than one in ten blockade runners in 1861, and not more than one in eight in 1862. But by 1864 it caught one in three, and by 1865, every other one.

The Wartime Economy

Inevitably these huge military and naval operations put a heavy strain on the economic resources of the combatants. In the Confederacy one result was a sharp shift in the nature of Southern agriculture. When the outbreak of war cut off Northern markets and the blockade increasingly sealed off European outlets for cotton and tobacco, farmers—at the urging of the Confederate and state governments—turned to producing grain and other foodstuffs. Cotton production in the South dropped from 4 million bales in 1861 to 300,000 bales in 1864.

In the North, too, farmers began producing more grain. Partly because of inflation, the price of wheat rose from 65 cents a bushel in December 1860 to $2.26 a bushel in July 1864. Farmers, especially in the Middle West, saw a chance to make money. At first the labor shortage kept them from expanding their acreage, for many farmhands enlisted in the Union army at the outbreak of the war. But machines soon made up for the absent men. One of Cyrus Hall McCormick's reapers could replace from four to six farmhands, and McCormick sold 165,000 of his machines during the war.

Industry also grew in both the Union and the Confederacy. As the Union blockade cut off imports, Southern factories gained a virtual monopoly in that region, and military and civilian needs provided an insatiable market. It is hard to measure Southern industrial growth, both because there was no Confederate census and because inflation affected all prices, yet there are some indications that manufacturing could be very profitable. For example, the 1862 conscription acts exempted the owners of certain basic industries provided that their annual profits were no more than 75 percent. Under the astute management of Joseph Anderson, the Tredegar Iron Works at Richmond, the largest privately owned factory in the South and the primary source of Confederate cannon, made profits of 100 percent in 1861 and of 70 percent in 1862.

Northern manufacturing was equally profitable, especially when it produced items needed for the army. The demand for uniforms enabled woolen mills to pay 25 percent dividends by 1865, compared to the 9 percent dividends they had paid before the war. Moreover, the number of woolen mills more than doubled during the war. Investors were willing to pour money into industry more confidently than before because Congress raised tariffs to levels that virtually excluded competing European products. War demands made the mass production of ready-made clothing profitable, and the army's need for shoes speeded the introduction of Gordon McKay's machine for sewing soles to uppers. Simultaneously, in an unrelated development, the discovery of oil at Titusville, Pennsylvania, in 1859 led to a wartime boom in the new petroleum industry.

Structural Changes in the Two Economies   These changes had an important impact on the structure of the American economy. The increase in the number of factories encouraged entrepreneurship. In the North men like John D. Rockefeller and Andrew Carnegie, who started their fortunes during the war, continued to dominate the industrial scene after 1865. When the South began rebuilding its industry in the 1870s and 1880s, it looked for leadership to its wartime entrepreneurs and to the Confederate commanders who had experience in directing the labor of large numbers of men. The war also encouraged the growth of large, rather than small, factories. Obliged to contract for huge shipments, both the Union and the Confederate governments naturally turned to those manufacturing companies that were financially and physically able to handle them. The selective process was accelerated because larger firms could pay agents in Washington or Richmond who understood the requirements of the army and navy—as well as those of influential congressmen and bureaucrats.

Most important of all, the wartime experience changed attitudes toward the role of the national government in the economy. Since the destruction of the Second Bank of the United States in the Jacksonian era, the national government had done little to regulate or control the economy. But during the war both the Union and the Confederate governments took steps that affected every branch of economic life. In passing the Homestead Act of May 20, 1862, which offered any citizen 160 acres of the public domain after five years of continuous residence on the land, the Union Congress signaled its intention henceforth to give more attention to the nation's farmers—as it did in creating the federal Department of Agriculture that same year. The Morrill Act of 1862, designating vast tracts of the public domain to support agricultural (land-grant) colleges, was further evidence of the same purpose. Both Union and Confederate governments found it necessary to regulate transportation, especially railroads, during the war. Davis, despite his strict interpretation of the Confederate Constitution, urged his Congress to finance the construction of some missing links in the Southern rail system. Lincoln in July 1862 signed the Pacific Railroad Act, giving enormous tracts of the public land to support the construction of a transcontinental rail route.

In both the United States and the Confederate States, private citizens became aware, often for the first time, of the economic impact of their national governments. In the Confederacy, the Impressment Act of March 1863 authorized government agents to seize civilian food, horses, wagons, or other supplies if required for the army, and to set an arbitrary price for the confiscated goods. In the Union the creation of a new national banking system in 1863 (amended and strengthened in 1864) meant, among other things, that a uniform national currency began to replace the dozens of issues by local banks.* Citizens, paying

---

*In return for purchasing government bonds, banks chartered by the national government were allowed to issue national bank notes, which gradually replaced the state bank notes and local scrip hitherto in use. A tax placed on state bank notes in 1865 ensured that this national currency would have no competition in the future.

national taxes in national currency, grew accustomed to the idea that their national government would henceforth play a positive role in the economic life of the country.

Inflation and Its Consequences

During the desperate final years of the Civil War, the Union and Confederate treasury departments had to experiment with new ways to finance the war. Both imposed broad excise duties. The Internal Revenue Act, enacted by the Union Congress on July 1, 1862, has been fairly characterized as an attempt to tax everything. The act imposed duties on all sorts of manufactures, with a fresh duty levied each time the raw material underwent a new process. In a carriage, for example, the leather, the cloth, the wood, and the metal were each taxed; then the manufacturer was taxed for the process of putting them together; the dealer was taxed for selling the carriage; and the purchaser, having paid a sufficient price to cover all these duties, was taxed in addition for ownership. Heavy duties fell on luxuries like billiard tables and yachts, and taxes on professions and occupations covered, as Representative James G. Blaine said, "bankers and pawn brokers, lawyers and horse-dealers, physicians and confectioners, commercial brokers and peddlers." Ultimately these taxes brought in about 21 percent of the total wartime expenditures of the Union government.

The Confederacy moved more slowly, but on April 24, 1863, it too adopted a comprehensive tax measure. This included an income tax, occupational and license taxes ranging from $40 for bowling alleys to $500 for bankers, and what later generations would call an excess profits tax. A unique feature of the Confederate legislation was the tax-in-kind, which compelled producers of wheat, corn, oats, potatoes, sugar, cotton, tobacco, and other farm products to pay one-tenth of their crop each year to the government. A last, desperate attempt in March 1865 to tax all coin, bullion, and foreign exchange was made too late to have any effect. All told, the Confederacy raised only about 1 percent of its income from taxes.

The sale of bonds contributed little more to the Confederate treasury. Values were so uncertain in the wartime South that investors were afraid to tie up their money in such fixed investments, and doubts spread as to when and whether the Confederate government would even pay the interest on its obligations. In the Union, on the other hand, bonds became a major source of revenue. At first Treasury Secretary Chase could not sell bonds, even at a discount, but when he appointed his friend Jay Cooke, the Philadelphia banker who also had an office in Washington, as special agent of the Treasury Department, the story changed. Using high-pressure advertising, Cooke launched an extensive propaganda campaign that extolled the merits of the "five-twenties"—bonds bearing 6 percent interest, which could be paid off after five years and must be redeemed in twenty years. Cooke was so successful that between 600,000 and a million citizens were persuaded to invest in the public debt, and the entire loan of half a billion dollars was oversubscribed. But in 1864, as the war stretched on endlessly and victory appeared nowhere in sight, the market for bonds collapsed. Resigning for political reasons, Chase left office at an opportune moment to preserve his reputation as a financier, and Cooke went with him. Chase's successor, William Pitt Fessenden, could raise money only through short-term loans at an exorbitant rate of interest. Not until the very end of the war, when victory was obviously near, did the sale of Union bonds pick up, and Cooke, reappointed special agent, attracted many additional investors.

The Resort to Paper Money

Thus through necessity both governments continued to depend on paper money. The Union treasury, which had cautiously issued its first greenbacks in 1862, printed more and more during the rest of that year and during 1863 as well, until most of the $450 million authorized by Congress was in circulation. The value of these greenbacks gradually declined. A Union treasury note with a face value of one dollar was worth 99.86 cents in gold in 1862, but by 1864 it was worth only 62.66 cents, and by early 1865, 50.3 cents. In the Confederacy, where the printing presses never stopped, paper money had even less value. Perhaps $2 billion in unredeemable paper was issued in all. A Confederate treasury note for one dollar, worth 82.7 cents in gold in 1862, dropped to 29 cents in 1863 and to 1.7 cents in early 1865. In a desperate attempt to halt the slide, the Confederate Congress in February 1864 undertook a partial repudiation of these notes, but the confusing and complex legislation was badly administered and served further to undermine trust in the government and its money. Having lost the confidence of the country, Treasury Secretary Memminger resigned in the summer of 1864—at about the same time that Chase left the Union Treasury Department. Memminger's successor, the South Carolina banker and businessman George A. Trenholm, could devise no better solution for the Confederacy's financial woes than to urge citizens to donate to the government their money, jewels, gold and silver plate, and public securities.

The excessive amount of paper money was only one of many factors that produced runaway inflation in both the North and the South. With importations largely cut off (in the North by the high protective tariff and in the South by the Union blockade), with the productive labor force sharply reduced because of the number of men in military service, and with a huge portion of all goods required to supply the armies and navies, civilians had to expect shortages and high prices.

Profits and Deprivation

In both sections some people profited from the wartime economy. War contracts helped pull the Union economy out of a sharp depression, and higher prices spurred on manufacturers, who could now look for higher profits. The demand for grain, along with the Homestead Act, encouraged new settlers to begin farming, and the development of petroleum and other new industries made for quick fortunes. The wartime boom in the North had a hectic quality about it, and people spent their easily earned money quickly lest it be worth less in the future. Many of the new rich were extravagant and hedonistic. Angrily the *New York Independent* asked in June 1864:

> Who at the North would ever think of war, if he had not a friend in the army, or did not read the newspapers? Go into Broadway, and we will show you what is meant by the word "extravagance." Ask [A. T.] Stewart [the department-store owner] about the demand for camel's-hair shawls, and he will say "monstrous." Ask Tiffany what kinds of diamonds and pearls are called for. He will answer "the prodigious," "as near hen's-egg size as possible," "price no object." What kinds of carpetings are now wanted? None but "extra." . . . And as for horses the medium-priced five-hundred-dollar kind are all out of the market. A good pair of "fast ones" . . . will go for a thousand dollars sooner than a basket of strawberries will sell for four cents.

But not everyone in the North shared in this wartime prosperity. Wages lagged sadly behind prices, so that in real income a worker between 1861 and 1865 lost 35 percent of his earnings. Women, who composed one-fourth of the nation's manufacturing force in 1860, were especially hard hit. Soldiers could send their wives and mothers only a pittance for support, and as more and more women found it necessary to work, employers actually cut their wages. Even the United States government participated in this practice. At the Philadelphia armory, the government in 1861 paid a seamstress 17 cents for making a shirt; three years later, when prices were at their highest, it cut the wage to 15 cents. Meanwhile private contractors paid only 8 cents.

Suffering in the North was, however, relatively minor when compared to that in the South. To be sure, residents of some parts of the agricultural South who were never disturbed by Union troops had only minor shortages to complain of. As imported goods disappeared from the grocers' shelves, they resorted to sassafras tea and to "coffee" made of parched rye, okra seeds, corn, and even sweet potatoes, the grounds of which were said to be a remarkable cleaning agent for curtains and carpets. Because salt was in short supply, meat could not be preserved, and Southerners ate more chicken and fish. As clothing wore out, they increasingly turned to homespun, and velvet draperies and brocaded rugs found new uses as gowns and overcoats.

But the thousands of Southerners in the path of the armies had to think not just of shortages, but of survival. Hundreds of families fled before the invading Union armies, often attempting to take their slaves with them, but nowhere could these refugees find assurance of safety. Their lives took on a desperate, nightmarish quality, and merely existing from one day to the next was a struggle. There was never enough of anything, including food. Recalling those unhappy days, one writer declared that "the Confederacy was always hungry."

The greatest destitution appeared in towns and cities, where supplies had to be brought in over the rickety Southern railroad system. White-collar workers, especially those on fixed government salaries, were particularly hard hit. The famous diary of J. B. Jones, a clerk in the Confederate War Department at Richmond, is a melancholy record of shortages and high prices. In May 1864 he reported that beans in Richmond were selling for $3 a quart, meal for $125 a bushel, and flour for $400 a barrel. Richmond, he observed, was an astonishingly clean city since "no garbage or filth can accumulate." The citizens of the Confederate capital were obliged to be "such good scavengers" that there was "no need of buzzards."

Deprivation was the more painful because, as in the North, some made enormous profits from the war. The blockade runners, who preferred to bring in compact, expensive items like silks and jewels rather than bulky supplies for the army, often reaped fantastic profits. Speculators flourished. As early as the winter of 1862 the governor of Mississippi learned that the families of volunteers in his state were seriously suffering because of the lack of corn and salt, while rich planters held back their ample supply of both commodities, waiting for the inevitable rise in prices. Trading with the enemy was even more profitable. The practice was completely illegal but tacitly permitted by both Confederate and Union officials. Southern women and men who were initiated into the mysteries of the trade bought up as much cotton as they could find in their neighborhoods and took it to convenient exchange points like Memphis and Natchez to sell to the Yankees for coffee, clothing, and luxuries. Late in the war they accepted payment in United States greenbacks, which Southerners valued more than their own depreciated currency.

Conscription and Conflict

Along with economic grievances, the unfairness of conscription was the source of bitter complaints by Northerners and Southerners alike during the Civil War.

The Confederate conscription act of 1862 theoretically made all able-bodied white males between the ages of eighteen and thirty-five equally eligible for military service, but the Southern Congress promptly began exempting large categories of men. As men rushed to enter "bombproof" occupations and claim exemptions, the outcry against the Confederate conscription system grew louder. One of the strongest critics was Governor Joseph E. Brown of Georgia, who protested, "The conscription Act, at one fell swoop, strikes down the sovereignty of the States, tramples upon the constitutional rights and personal liberty of the citizens, and arms the President with imperial power." After attempting unsuccessfully to induce the Georgia supreme court to declare conscription unconstitutional, Brown proceeded to undermine the policy by naming his supporters to state jobs exempt from military service. According to some estimates he put 15,000 able-bodied Georgians into this exempt category; certainly he created 2,000 justices of the peace and 1,000 constables, none of whom had to serve in the army. Less prominent than Brown but equally potent were the critics who complained that conscription was class legislation that benefited the educated and the wealthy. They objected especially to the so-called "twenty-nigger" provision, which clearly favored plantation owners at the expense of farmers. "Never did a law meet with more universal odium than the exemption of slave owners," wrote Senator James Phelan of Mississippi to President Davis. "It has aroused a spirit of rebellion . . . and bodies of men have banded together to desert."

Despite intense criticism and dubious results, the Davis administration continued conscription, for it saw no other way to raise the needed number of men. Indeed, as the war progressed, the Confederacy was obliged to experiment with even more stringent legislation. In a new conscription act of February 17, 1864, the Confederate Congress declared that all white males between the ages of seventeen and fifty were subject to the draft, with the seventeen-year-old boys and the men above forty-five to serve as a reserve for local defense. As a concession to small planters, the act exempted one farmer or overseer for every plantation with fifteen slaves; but it abolished most other exemptions, on the theory that once skilled laborers were in the army, the government could detail them to the forges and factories where they were most needed. Total mobilization of manpower was, however, far beyond the competence of the shaky Confederate government, and in practice the industrial-detail system never worked. As the Confederacy scraped the bottom of the barrel, more and more white Southerners began thinking about the one group of able-bodied males who did not serve in the armies, the blacks.

In the North, too, conscription evoked bitter criticism. The first effective Northern draft act, passed by the Union Congress on March 3, 1863, was obviously unfair. The act declared that all able-bodied males between the ages of twenty and forty-five (except for certain high governmental officials and the only sons of widows and of infirm parents) were liable to military service. But it promptly contradicted itself by permitting those who could afford to do so to hire substitutes. In an effort to keep the price of substitutes down, it also permitted a man to purchase outright exemption from military service for $300.

As in the South, there was immediate and widespread hostility toward conscription. The system favored the wealthiest citizens and the most prosperous sections of the country. A well-to-do man like George Templeton Strong of New York, for example, did not dream of serving in the army; he paid $1,100 for a substitute, "a big 'Dutch' boy of twenty or thereabouts," who, as Strong remarked complacently, "looked as if he could do good service." Rich towns and counties raised bounty funds to encourage volunteering, so that none of their citizens would have to be drafted; and as the war went on, they offered higher and higher bounties. The volunteers they sought were by no means all local residents who needed a little financial inducement; many of them were professional bounty hunters, who went from place to place enlisting, receiving bounties, and promptly deserting. Perhaps the record for bounty jumping was held by one John O'Connor, who when arrested in March 1865 confessed to thirty-two such desertions.

Part of the outcry against conscription in the North stemmed from the unfairness of the quotas the president was authorized to announce for each state, presumably giving credit for the number of volunteers it had previously supplied.

The Democratic governor of New York, Horatio Seymour, engaged in angry correspondence with Lincoln and finally forced the president to admit that the quota assigned to New York was excessive. This and similar concessions, however, came too late to placate those who were threatened by the draft. In Wisconsin, Kentucky, and Pennsylvania, in Troy, Newark, and Albany, there was outright resistance to the enrolling officers, and in several instances federal troops had to be brought in to quell the uprisings. But none of these outbreaks was as large or ferocious as that in New York City, where the drawing of the first draftees' names triggered a three-day riot (July 13–15, 1863) by a mob of predominantly Irish workingmen. Turning first against the enrollment officers and the police, the rioters then exhibited their hostility toward the rich by plundering fine houses and rifling jewelry stores. The mob acted with hideous brutality toward blacks, whom the rioters feared as economic competitors and blamed for the war and hence for conscription. After sacking and looting a black orphan asylum, the rioters chased down any blacks unwary enough to appear on the streets and left those they could catch hanging from lampposts. The Union government had to rush in troops from the Gettysburg campaign to stop the rioting and disperse the mob.

Despite all resistance, Lincoln's government continued conscription because, as in the Confederacy, there seemed to be no other source of soldiers. Even so, the draft remained cumbersome and often ineffectual. In 1864, for example, 800,000 names were drawn, but so many were exempted because of health or occupation, and so many others hired substitutes or paid the commutation fee, that only 33,000 were actually inducted into the army. As conscription proved both unfair and ineffective, citizens in the North, like those in the South, began to think of the value of black soldiers.

Steps Toward Emancipation

Just as African Americans played a central role in causing the Civil War, so they played a major role in determining its outcome. At the beginning there was an unspoken agreement that the Civil War was to be a white man's fight, and both the Union and the Confederate governments in 1861 refused to accept black volunteers. In the Confederacy during the first two years of the war, virtually nobody questioned the correctness of this decision. After all, as Vice-President Alexander H. Stephens announced, slavery was "the real 'cornerstone'" on which the Confederate States had been erected, and few Southern whites could even contemplate the possibility of arming slaves or of freeing blacks who became soldiers.

In the Union, on the other hand, powerful voices from the beginning urged the emancipation of slaves and the enlistment of blacks. Frederick Douglass, the leading spokesman of blacks in the North, repeatedly insisted: "Teach the rebels and traitors that the price they are to pay for the attempt to abolish this Government must be the abolition of slavery." Abolitionists, white and black,

Black Teamsters near the Signal Tower at Bermuda Hundred, Virginia, 1864
Although there was opposition in both the Confederacy and the Union to the emancipation of slaves, neither side was reluctant to employ blacks in nonmilitary service. For both armies blacks served as teamsters, butchers, drovers, boatmen, bakers, shoemakers, and nurses. Nearly 200,000 blacks performed labor for the Union armies.

again and again instructed Lincoln that he could win the war only if he emancipated the slaves. Senator Charles Sumner of Massachusetts visited the White House almost daily in his efforts to persuade Lincoln that emancipation was the "*one way to safety,* clear as sunlight—pleasant as the paths of Peace."

This antislavery sentiment was so influential that several of the president's subordinates who fell into disfavor with the administration tried to appeal to it. But President Lincoln, aware of the dangerous complexity of the issue, patiently overruled each of these subordinates, declaring that emancipation was a question "which, under my responsibility, I reserve to myself."

Nonmilitary Employment of Blacks

Unwillingness to arm or emancipate the slaves did not signify any reluctance to employ blacks in nonmilitary service. Slaves were the backbone of the Confederate labor force. If blacks had not continued to cultivate and harvest the grain, the Confederacy could never have fielded so large an army. Equally important was the role played by blacks, slave and free, in the industrial production of the Confederacy. In the Tredegar Iron Works, for example, half the 2,400 employees were blacks; they included not merely unskilled workers, but puddlers, rollers, and machinists. Blacks also performed indispensable service for the quartermaster and commissary departments of the Confederacy, laboring as teamsters, butchers, drovers, boatmen, bakers, shoemakers, and blacksmiths; and they were nurses in many Confederate hospitals.

Contrabands Following the Union Army

Wherever Union armies advanced into the South, they attracted throngs of slaves who escaped from their masters and, packing their meager belongings on their backs or in rickety wagons, sought the protection of the federal soldiers.

So essential was black labor to the existence of the Confederacy that President Davis had to ensure that enough blacks were available for this service. From the beginning of the war, Confederate authorities sought to compel slaves to work on fortifications. Some states, notably Virginia, moved promptly to require owners to lease their slaves to the government when needed. But the Confederate government itself did not act until March 1863. At that time the Confederate Congress, despite much opposition from slaveowners, authorized the impressment of slaves, whose owners were to receive $30 a month. In February 1864 the Southern Congress permitted military authorities to impress more slaves, whether or not these officials had obtained the consent of the slaveowners.

Meanwhile the Union was also making full use of black labor. As slaves fled from their masters to the Union army, they were put to use as teamsters, cooks, nurses, carpenters, scouts, and day laborers. Perhaps half a million blacks crossed over to the Union lines, and nearly 200,000 of these performed labor for the army. Many of these "contrabands" brought with them valuable information about the location of Confederate troops and supplies. Occasionally some brought even more valuable assets. Robert Smalls and his brother, who were slaves in Charleston, South Carolina, in May 1862 daringly seized the Confederate side-wheel steamer *Planter,* navigated it out of the harbor ringed with Confederate guns, and delivered it to the blockading Union fleet.

**Debate over
Emancipation
in the North**

When the war seemed to have reached a stalemate, Northern sentiment grew more favorable to freeing and arming the slaves. Republican congressmen were ahead of the president on these questions. As early as August 1861 they had passed an act declaring that slaves who had supported the Confederate military were free. In March 1862 Congress forbade the Union army to return fugitive slaves. And on July 17, 1862, in a far-reaching confiscation act, Congress declared that slaves of all persons supporting the rebellion should be "forever free of their servitude, and not again [to be] held as slaves." These measures were, however, poorly drafted and not readily enforced, so that they had little practical consequence. But Congress's abolition of slavery in the District of Columbia on April 16, 1862, was more effective.

Powerful forces in the North, however, opposed emancipation. The border states, where slavery still prevailed, threatened to break away from the Union if emancipation became a Northern war aim. In the free states antiblack prejudice was rampant, and many feared that emancipation would result in a massive migration of blacks to the North, where they would compete with white laborers for jobs. Belief in black inferiority was general, and the experience of Union soldiers in the South often strengthened this stereotype, for the fugitive slaves who fled to their camps were for the most part illiterate, ragged, and dirty.

Lincoln hated slavery, but during the initial stages of the war he could move toward emancipation only in a roundabout way. In early 1862 he made an earnest, although ultimately unsuccessful, plea to the border states to devise plans of gradual, compensated emancipation, for which he promised federal financial assistance. At the same time, he took antiblack sentiment into account by favoring plans to settle freedmen (ex-slaves) in Central America and Haiti.

By the fall of 1862, however, Lincoln felt able to act decisively against slavery. In failing to adopt his program of gradual emancipation, the border states had lost their chance. Blacks showed little interest in his plans for colonization, which in any case were poorly thought out and could only lead to disaster. As casualties mounted, Northern soldiers came to think that it was time to enroll blacks in the army, although they did not necessarily shed their prejudices against blacks. But most influential in changing Lincoln's mind was his grim recognition that after eighteen months of combat, the war could not be ended by traditional means. "We . . . must change our tactics or lose the war," he concluded.

Waiting only for McClellan to end Lee's invasion at Antietam, Lincoln on September 22, 1862, issued a preliminary emancipation proclamation. This announced that unless the rebellious states returned to their allegiance, he would on January 1, 1863, declare "all persons held as slaves" in the territory controlled by the Confederates to be "then, thenceforward, and forever free." Since the president justified his action on the ground of military necessity, it was appropriate that the definitive Emancipation Proclamation, which was issued at the beginning of the new year, officially authorized the enrollment of black troops in the Union army.

Company E, 4th U.S. Colored Infantry, at Petersburg
General Benjamin F. Butler used black troops in his assault on Petersburg because, he said, "I knew that they would fight more desperately than any white troops, in order to prevent capture, because they knew . . . that if captured they would be returned into slavery."

The War Department promptly began to accept black recruits. These were not, to be sure, the first black soldiers to serve in the war, for without permission from Washington a few blacks had been enrolled in the Union forces on the Sea Islands of South Carolina, in Louisiana, and in Kansas. But large numbers of blacks now joined the army. They were enrolled in segregated regiments, nearly always with white officers, and they received less pay than did white soldiers. By the end of the war there were 178,895 black soldiers in the Union army—more than twice the number of soldiers in the Confederate army at Gettysburg.

At first most Union officials thought that black regiments would be useful only for garrison duty, but in such bitterly contested engagements as Fort Wagner and Port Hudson, Miliken's Bend and Nashville, they demonstrated how well they could and would fight. The battle record of these black troops did much to change popular Northern stereotypes of the black man.

The South Moves Toward Emancipation Meanwhile, and much more slowly, sentiment was growing in the Confederacy for the military employment of blacks. Support for arming the slaves emerged first in those areas devastated by Northern armies. After Grant's successful Vicksburg campaign, the *Jackson Mississippian* boldly called for enrolling slaves in the Confederate army. Although other Mississippi and Alabama newspapers echoed the appeal for black recruits, the most powerful voice for arming the slaves was that of General Patrick R. Cleburne, who witnessed how easily the powerful Union army broke the thin Confederate line at Chattanooga. Seeing no other source of manpower, Cleburne and his aides addressed a long letter to General Joseph E. Johnston, who had succeeded Bragg as commander of the army of Tennessee, urging "that we immediately commence training a large reserve of the most courageous of our slaves, and further that we guarantee freedom within a reasonable time to every slave in the South who shall remain true to the Confederacy in this war."

So drastic a proposal was bound to rouse strong opposition. On learning of Cleburne's letter, President Davis ordered it suppressed. But the subject would not die. As Union armies moved closer to the Confederate heartland, Virginia editors also began to urge arming the blacks, and in October 1864 a meeting of Southern governors proposed "a change of policy on our part" as to the slaves. Finally, on November 7, 1864, President Davis put himself at the head of the movement in a deliberately obscure message to Congress. Urging further impressment of blacks for service with the army, Davis argued that the Confederate government should purchase the impressed slaves.

However ambiguously it was phrased, Davis's proposal clearly looked toward the end of slavery, and it at once encountered powerful resistance. Davis, said his enemies, proposed the confiscation of private property; he was subverting the Constitution. His plan would be a confession to the world of the South's weakness. It would deplete the labor force needed to feed the army. And most frightening of all, it would arm black men, who at best might desert to the Union armies and at worst might take up arms against their masters.

Despite all opposition, the Confederate government pushed ahead with the plan, for it had no other reservoir of manpower. In February 1865 the scheme received the backing of General Lee, who wrote that employing blacks as soldiers was "not only expedient but necessary" and announced plainly that "it would be neither just nor wise . . . to require them to serve as slaves." The next month, by a very close vote, the Confederate Congress passed an act calling for 300,000 more soldiers, irrespective of color. No provision was made to free blacks who enrolled, but the Confederate War Department in effect smuggled emancipation into the measure through the orders it issued for its enforcement. Promptly the recruiting of black troops began, and some black companies were raised in Richmond and other towns. By this time, however, it was too late even for such a revolutionary experiment, and none of the black Confederate soldiers ever saw military service.

Europe and the War

Although the Union and Confederate governments moved toward emancipating and arming the blacks because of military necessity, both recognized how profoundly their actions affected the continuing struggle for European recognition and support. Informed Americans were aware of the intensity of European antislavery sentiment. But so long as neither government took a bold stand against the South's peculiar institution, European antislavery leaders were puzzled and divided by the war. Lincoln's Emancipation Proclamation ended the confusion. European antislavery spokesmen recognized that the proclamation marked a new era. Within three months after the final Emancipation Proclamation was issued, fifty-six large public meetings were held in Great Britain to uphold the Northern cause.

Union diplomacy needed such popular support, for there was still a possibility of European intervention in the war. Although the gravest threat had passed in the fall of 1862, before the full effect of the Emancipation Proclamation could be sensed abroad, Emperor Napoleon III of France continued to contemplate the advantages that might come of meddling in American affairs. Napoleon hoped that the division of the United States would help him establish a puppet empire in Mexico under Archduke Maximilian of Austria. When Northern military fortunes were at their low point in February 1863, after the battle of Fredericksburg, Napoleon offered to mediate between the two belligerents. Shrewdly judging that Great Britain and Russia were not behind the French move, Secretary of State Seward spurned the offer.

The warships being built for the Confederacy in British shipyards were more dangerous to the Union cause than was Napoleon's clumsy diplomacy. Supplying either belligerent in war with armed ships was contrary both to international law and to British statutes, but a loophole in the law made it possible to sell unarmed vessels separately from the armaments that would convert them into men of war. In March 1862 the ship that became the CSS *Florida* sailed from a British shipyard, and in July of that year the more powerful *Alabama* set forth to begin its raids. Even as these raiders swept the Union merchant marine from the high seas, a more formidable Confederate naval threat—this time to the blockade itself— was being forged in the form of two enormous ironclad steam rams under construction at the Laird yards in Liverpool.

The British government wished to observe its neutrality laws, but the legal machinery was slow and cumbersome. When Union minister Charles Francis Adams called the attention of the foreign office to the rams, Lord Russell replied that he could not act to detain them unless there was convincing evidence of Confederate ownership. Adams and his aides rushed to secure proof that the vessels were intended for the Confederacy, but British law officers were unconvinced. Finally, in utter exasperation, Adams on September 5, 1863, sent Russell a final warning against permitting the ships to sail, adding: "It would be superfluous in me to point out to your Lordship that this is war." Fortunately, two days before receiving Adams's ultimatum, Russell had already decided to detain the rams, and the Confederates' final hope of breaking the blockade was lost.

With that crisis, the last serious threat of European involvement in the American war disappeared. So indifferent, or even hostile, to the Southern cause was the British cabinet that late in 1863 Confederate Secretary of State Judah P. Benjamin ordered James M. Mason, his envoy, to leave London on the grounds that "the Government of Her Majesty [Queen Victoria] . . . entertains no intention of receiving you as the accredited minister of this government."

President Davis was keenly aware of the influence that emancipation had exerted in uniting European opinion against the South, and he sought similarly to capitalize on the actions against slavery that the Confederate States took during the final months of the war. In January 1865 he sent Duncan F. Kenner, one of Louisiana's largest slaveholders, on a secret mission to Europe. Kenner was authorized to promise the emancipation of slaves in return for European recognition and aid to the Confederacy. The experiment came too late, for now it was evident that Northern victory was inevitable. Neither the French nor the British government expressed interest in Kenner's proposal.

Wartime Politics in the Confederacy

The military and diplomatic advantages resulting from emancipation were to a certain extent counterbalanced by its political disadvantages. In the Confederacy there had been from the beginning of the war a sizable disloyal element. Unionism was strong in the Upper South, in the mountain regions, and in some of the poorer hill counties. As the war went on, some of the Southern malcontents joined secret peace societies such as the Order of the Heroes, which had its following in the Carolinas and Virginia. Disloyalty extended into the ranks of the Confederate army, especially after conscription was initiated, and desertion was widespread. Some men left because their families needed them at home; some felt a greater loyalty to their states than to the Confederacy as a whole; but many were disillusioned with the whole idea of Southern independence. About one out of every nine soldiers who enlisted in the Confederate army deserted. Sometimes deserters formed guerrilla bands that preyed equally on Confederate and Union sympathizers. When halted by an enrollment officer and asked to show his pass to leave the army, a deserter would pat his gun defiantly and say, "This is my furlough."

Probably no action of the Davis administration could have won over these actively disloyal citizens, but the policies of the Confederate government alienated also a large number of entirely loyal Southerners. Some of these critics complained that President Davis was timid and tardy. He was sickly, neurasthenic, and indecisive, they said; he could not tolerate strong men around him and relied for advice on yes men; he did not know how to rouse the loyalty and passions of the Southern people; he lacked courage to put himself at the head of the Southern armies and lead the Confederacy to victory.

Many more Confederates were bitterly critical of their president for exactly the opposite reasons. Davis's plan to arm and free the slaves reinforced their conviction that he intended to undermine the principles on which the Confederacy had been founded. Conscription, they argued, had begun the subversion of state sovereignty, guaranteed by the Constitution. They found evidence of Davis's dictatorial ambitions in his requests that Congress suspend the writ of habeas corpus, so that disloyal persons could be arrested and imprisoned without trial. Congress grudgingly agreed to the suspension for three limited periods, but late in 1864 it rejected Davis's appeals for a further extension on the ground that it would be a dangerous assault on the Constitution. Although infringements on civil liberties were infrequent in the Confederacy, and no Southern newspaper was suppressed for publishing subversive editorials, the critics warned that Davis was reaching after imperial powers. Leading this group of Davis's critics was none other than the vice-president of the Confederate States, Alexander H. Stephens, who spent most of the final years of the war not in Richmond but in Georgia, stirring up agitation against the president's allegedly unconstitutional usurpation of power, and simultaneously complaining of Davis's "weakness and imbecility."

The congressional elections of 1863, held after Southerners had begun to realize the gravity of their defeats at Gettysburg and at Vicksburg, greatly strengthened the anti-Davis bloc. During the following year the president often could muster a majority in Congress only because of the consistent support of representatives from districts in the upper South overrun or threatened by advancing Northern armies. But by the desperate winter of 1864–65, not even this support could give Davis control of Congress. Now in a majority, the president's critics refused his request for control over the state militias and rejected his plea to end all exemptions from conscription. Even as Sherman's army advanced through the Carolinas,* Congress endlessly debated Davis's plan for arming the slaves. Over presidential opposition, it passed an act creating the position of general in chief, advising Davis to name Lee. Fearful of attacking the president directly, congressional critics began investigations of several of his cabinet officers, and they introduced resolutions declaring that the resignation of Secretary of State Benjamin, Davis's closest friend and most trusted adviser, would be "subservient of the public interest." Secretary of War James A. Seddon also came under fire, and when the Virginia delegation in Congress called for his resignation, he felt obliged to leave the cabinet. In January 1865, for the first and only time, the Confederate Congress overrode a presidential veto.

Wartime Politics in the North

Meanwhile, in the North, Abraham Lincoln and his government were subjected to the same kinds of criticism. Pro-Confederate sympathy was strongest in the states of the Upper South that remained in the Union, in those parts of the Old Northwest originally settled by Southerners, and in cities like New York, where the Irish immigrant population was bitterly hostile to blacks. Northerners joined secret societies, such as the Knights of the Golden Circle and the Order of American Knights, devoted to bringing about a negotiated peace, which inevitably would entail recognizing Confederate independence. Although most members of these secret "Copperhead" organizations intended nothing more subversive than replacing a Republican administration with a Democratic one, certain of the leaders were ready to accept the dissolution of the Union. Some idea of the

---

*For Sherman's advance in 1864–65, see below, pp. 649–50.

extent of unrest in the North can be gained from the figures on desertion: one out of every seven who enlisted in the Union armies deserted.

Much of the criticism of the Lincoln administration came from those who were entirely loyal to the Union but who deplored the measures the president took to save it. They complained bitterly when Lincoln, without waiting for congressional approval, suspended the writ of habeas corpus so that suspected subversives could be arrested without warning and imprisoned indefinitely. Although Chief Justice Roger B. Taney protested against the unconstitutionality of these arrests, Lincoln refused to heed his objections. Several thousand persons were thus arbitrarily imprisoned. Critics also complained when the Lincoln administration curbed the freedom of the press. Because of the publication of allegedly disloyal and inflammatory statements, the *Chicago Times,* and *New York World,* the *Philadelphia Evening Journal,* and many other newspapers were required to suspend publication for varying periods of time.

Lincoln's Emancipation Proclamation, followed by the arming of black soldiers, gave his critics further evidence of his ambition to become dictator and of his diabolical plan to change the purpose of the war. So unpopular was the policy of emancipation that Lincoln's preliminary proclamation, together with the inability of Union generals to win victories, seriously hurt his party in the congressional elections of 1862. In virtually every Northern state there was an increase in Democratic votes. The Republican majority in Congress was now paper-thin, and the administration kept that lead only because the army interfered in the Maryland, Kentucky, and Missouri elections. Just as Jefferson Davis's control of the Confederate Congress after 1863 depended on the votes of border state representatives, so Abraham Lincoln's majority in the Union Congress rested on the support of representatives from the same region.

Republican Criticism of Lincoln If Democrats complained that Lincoln acted arbitrarily and too swiftly, critics within his own party held that he was too slow, too cautious, and too indecisive. His own attorney general, Edward Bates, felt that the president could cope with "neither great *principles* nor great *facts.*" Lincoln lacked "practical talent for his important place," concluded Senator Sumner, who thought that in his slowness to act and his indecisiveness the president resembled the bumbling French king Louis XVI more than any other ruler in history.

Dissatisfaction with Lincoln was so widespread that when Congress reassembled in December 1862, after the fiasco at Fredericksburg, the Senate Republican caucus tried to force the president to change his cabinet. Just as Davis's critics made Benjamin their target, so Republican senators blamed Secretary of State Seward for the weakness of the Lincoln administration and the poor handling of the war. By forcing Seward's resignation, these critics hoped to make Chase (who had fed them stories of Lincoln's incompetence) in effect premier. This maneuver distressed Lincoln deeply, and he thwarted it with great skill. He secured Seward's resignation and forced Chase also to offer his; then he declined both resignations by announcing that either one would leave the cabinet unbalanced. His cabinet remained intact, and the president remained responsible for Union policy.

Such sleight of hand was not enough to make dissent within Lincoln's own party disappear. Gradually two rival Republican factions emerged, the Conservatives, or Moderates, and the Radicals—whom their enemies called Jacobins, comparing them to the extremists of the French Revolution. The Conservatives were represented by Seward in the cabinet and by Senator James R. Doolittle of Wisconsin in Congress. They continued to think that the war could be won by conventional means and opposed such experiments as emancipation, the arming of slaves, and the confiscation of rebel property. The Radicals, on the other hand, represented by Chase in the cabinet and by Sumner and Thaddeus Stevens in Congress, were eager to try more drastic experiments. They demanded that the entire Southern social system be revolutionized, that Southern slaveholders be punished and, increasingly, that blacks be given not merely freedom, but civil and political equality as well.

Lincoln refused to align himself with either faction and tried to be even-handed in distributing federal patronage to both. He shared the Conservatives' desire for a speedy peace and a prompt reconciliation between the sections; but he recognized that in casting about for votes to carry through their plans, they would be "tempted to affiliate with those whose record is not clear," even persons infected "by the virus of secession." As for the Radicals, he conceded that "after all their faces are set Zionwards" but he objected to their "petulant and vicious fretfulness" and thought they were sometimes "almost *fiendish*" in attacking Republicans who disagreed with them. Because of his neutrality, the president gained the distrust and abuse of both factions.

The Election of 1864   The split within the Republican party was the more serious because the presidential election of 1864 was approaching. The Democrats had a handsome, glamorous candidate in General George B. McClellan, and they had a powerful set of issues. They could capitalize on war weariness. They made much of Lincoln's arbitrary use of executive power and the infringement of civil liberties. They objected to the unfairness of the draft. They showed how the Republican Congress had benefited the Northeast by enacting protective tariffs, handing out railroad subsidies, and creating a national banking system. The Democrats endlessly harped on the antiblack theme, charging that the Lincoln administration had changed the war for union into a war for emancipation. If Lincoln was reelected, they charged, Republicans were planning to amalgamate the black and white races. The word *miscegenation* (race mixing) made its first appearance in an 1864 campaign document.

Even in the face of such powerful opposition, the Republicans in the winter of 1863–64 divided sharply when Lincoln in December 1863 announced a plan for reconstructing the Southern states. The president promised amnesty to all Confederates except for a few high government officials. He also proposed to reestablish civilian government in the conquered areas of the South. If in any state 10 percent or more of those who had voted in 1860 would take an oath swearing future loyalty to the United States and pledging acceptance of emancipation, the president promised to recognize the legality of the government these voters set up. Fearing that his program would put the prewar leadership back in control of the South and would leave freedmen in peonage, the Radicals pushed the Wade-Davis bill through Congress. This bill required that more than half the number of 1860 voters in each Southern state swear allegiance and participate in drafting a new constitution before their state could be readmitted to the Union. This measure was passed at the end of the 1864 congressional session, and Lincoln killed it by refusing to sign it after Congress had adjourned. The Radicals were furious. Senator Benjamin F. Wade and Representative Henry Winter Davis, the sponsors of the vetoed bill, issued a public statement accusing the president of "usurpations" and claiming that he had committed a "studied outrage upon the legislative authority of the people."

Lincoln had control of the federal patronage and of the party machinery, and so he was readily renominated in June 1864 by the Republican national convention, which selected Andrew Johnson of Tennessee as his running mate. But the unanimity of the vote was only a facade. After an unsuccessful attempt to run Chase as a rival to Lincoln, some ultra-Radicals had already thrown their support to a third-party ticket headed by General Frémont, who had been hostile to the president since his removal from command in Missouri. Even after Lincoln had been renominated, other Radicals tried to persuade the party to pick a new candidate. As late as September 1864 a questionnaire sent to Republican governors, leading editors, and prominent congressmen drew a virtually unanimous response that if Lincoln could be persuaded to withdraw from the race, Republicans should name another standard-bearer. As Massachusetts Governor John A. Andrew expressed the general sentiment, Lincoln was "essentially lacking in the quality of leadership." So bleak was the outlook that a few weeks before the elections, the president himself conceded that McClellan was likely to win.

Northern Victory

Until the fall of 1864, then, the wartime history of the United States and of the Confederate States moved in parallel lines as each government improvised experiments that might lead to victory. But in the final months of the struggle, the course of the two rivals dramatically diverged. Increasing dissension and unrest marked Jefferson Davis's last winter in office, while Abraham Lincoln won triumphant reelection in November 1864. By April 1865 the Confederacy was dead, and a month later Davis was in irons, like a common criminal, at Fort Monroe, Virginia. The Union was victorious, and Lincoln, killed by the bullet of the mad assassin John Wilkes Booth, lived in memory as the nation's martyred president who had freed the slaves and saved the Union.

Campaigns in the East, 1864–1865

The very different fates of the Lincoln and Davis administrations were decided, in large part, on the battlefield. When Grant became general in chief of the Union armies in 1864, he decided to make his headquarters not in Washington, but with the often-defeated Army of the Potomac. Working closely with Meade, the actual commander of that army, Grant developed a plan for pushing Lee back on the defenses of Richmond. Stopped in the bloody battle of the Wilderness (May 5–7), Grant did not retreat, as other Union commanders had done. Instead he pushed around Lee's right flank, attempting to get between him and the Confederate capital. Stopped again at Spotsylvania (May 8–12), Grant again did not retreat but sent word to Washington: "I propose to fight it out along this line if it takes all summer."

After a disastrous direct assault on the Confederate lines at Cold Harbor (June 3), Grant again skillfully maneuvered around Lee's right flank, crossed the James River, and joined Union troops already there under General Butler. He then began what became known as the "siege" of Petersburg and Richmond—incorrectly so, since the two cities were not fully surrounded and since supplies continued to come in from the South and West. But as Grant's lines constantly lengthened, he cut these access routes one by one. Pinned down before Richmond, Lee remembered "Stonewall" Jackson's brilliant diversionary campaign of 1862 and sent what men he could spare under Jubal A. Early into the Shenandoah Valley. Although Early achieved initial success and even pushed on to the outskirts of Washington, Grant did not loosen his grip on Richmond. Instead he sent brash, aggressive Philip H. Sheridan to the Shenandoah Valley, ordering him not merely to drive out the Confederates, but to devastate the countryside so that thereafter a crow flying over it would have to carry its own rations. Sheridan followed his orders explicitly, and Early's army was smashed. More than ever before, the fate of the Confederacy was tied to Richmond and to Lee's army.

Campaigns in the West, 1864–1865

Meanwhile, on May 7, 1864, Sherman had begun his slow march through northwestern Georgia, opposed by the wily Joseph E. Johnston, who made the Union troops pay for every foot they advanced. But as Sherman neared the railroad hub of Atlanta, President Davis—who had never trusted Johnston—removed the

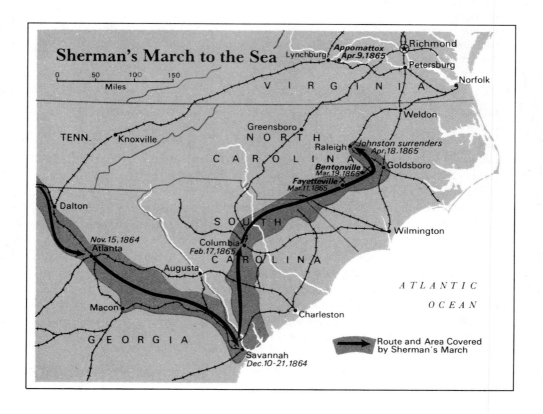

Sherman's March to the Sea

0   50   100   150
Miles

Lynchburg

Appomattox Apr. 9, 1865

Richmond
Petersburg
Norfolk

V I R G I N I A

Weldon

TENN.   Knoxville

Greensboro

N O R T H

Raleigh

Johnston surrenders Apr. 18, 1865

C A R O L I N A

Bentonville Mar. 19, 1865

Goldsboro

Fayetteville Mar. 11, 1865

Dalton

S O U T H

Wilmington

Nov. 15, 1864 Atlanta

Columbia
Feb. 17, 1865

C A R O L I N A

Augusta

A T L A N T I C

O C E A N

Macon

Charleston

G E O R G I A

Route and Area Covered by Sherman's March

Savannah
Dec. 10–21, 1864

The Union Army Entering Richmond, April 9, 1865
Attempting to destroy military supplies as they withdrew from Richmond, Confederate authorities accidently started fires that devastated much of the center of the city. When Union troops entered, whites made a point of staying out of sight, but Richmond blacks joyfully welcomed the federal soldiers who brought them freedom.

general and put John B. Hood in command. In a series of attacks on the overwhelmingly superior Union forces (exactly the sort of engagement Johnston had so skillfully avoided), Hood was defeated. On September 2 Sherman occupied Atlanta. News of the victory reached the North just before the presidential election and made a farce of the Democratic platform's assertion that the war was a "failure."

Next, casually dispatching Thomas to fend off Hood and to hold Tennessee, Sherman turned his back on the smoking ruins of Atlanta and set out on a march toward Savannah and the sea, where he knew that a Union fleet was waiting with supplies.* Meeting only light resistance, Sherman's men cut a swath through central Georgia, destroying railroads, military supplies, and even many private houses. Sherman's objective was as much psychological as military. "I can make the march," he had promised Grant, "and make Georgia howl!"

Offering captured Savannah to Lincoln as a Christmas present, Sherman turned his army north, pushing aside the depleted Confederate forces that again

---

*Attempting to force Sherman back, Hood invaded Tennessee but was stopped in the battle of Franklin (November 30, 1864) and routed in the battle of Nashville (December 15–16).

"General Robert E. Lee Leaving the McLean House After the Surrender at Appomattox, 1865," by A.W. Waud

After accepting Grant's terms of surrender, Lee stepped out to the porch of the McLean House and signaled his orderly to bring up his horse. While the animal was being bridled, one of Grant's aides remembered, Lee "gazed sadly in the direction…where his army lay—now an army of prisoners. He thrice smote the palm of his left hand slowly with his right fist in an absent sort of way." Then he mounted, and Grant saluted him by raising his hat. "Lee raised his hat respectfully, and rode off at a slow trot to break the sad news to the brave fellows whom he had so long commanded."

were under the command of Johnston. His men took Columbia, South Carolina, which was burned either by intention or by accident, and drove on into North Carolina. Grant meanwhile clamped down ever tighter on Richmond. At last, on April 2, 1865, Lee found his position untenable. Warning President Davis and his government to flee, he tried to lead his ragged troops to join Johnston's dwindling force. Cut off by Grant, Lee had no alternative but to surrender, and on April 9 at Appomattox Court House he told his weary, hungry men to lay down their arms. On April 18 Johnston followed by surrendering to Sherman (although the final terms were not agreed on until April 26). When the news reached the trans-Mississippi region, Kirby-Smith surrendered in June. The war had lasted almost precisely four years.

The Union cause and the Lincoln administration were the beneficiaries of these victories. The critics of the government had been most vocal, their opposition most powerful, in the heartbreaking summer months of 1864, when Grant seemed to be getting nowhere in Virginia and Sherman appeared unable to bag his enemy in Georgia. Northern morale and support for the president mounted perceptibly at the news of Sherman's success at Atlanta and of Farragut's victory at Mobile Bay. Conversely, support for Davis's administration dwindled and critical voices became louder as Confederate reverse followed reverse. In a certain sense, then, victory begot victory, and defeat begot defeat.

Why the North Won the War   Yet this is circular reasoning and does not explain the final Union triumph after so many earlier Confederate successes. For a fuller understanding one must turn to the slow but steady mobilization of the North's infinitely superior economic resources and to the gradual erosion of those in the South. The effect of Northern economic and industrial superiority was not fully felt until after more than two years of war; it took time to award contracts, to expand factories, to recruit skilled laborers, and to deliver the products. But observers noted that by 1863 Lee's veterans invading Pennsylvania looked like a gaggle of "barefooted, ragged, lousy, [but] disciplined, desperate ruffians." These troops were so badly supplied and so poorly fed that their line of march was "traceable by the deposit of dysenteric stool the army leaves behind it." By 1863 the Union armies, on the other hand, were so completely equipped that their paraphernalia became a hindrance. When Northern soldiers advanced, they shucked off layers of great-coats, blankets, and other unnecessary supplies. By the end of the war, Union economic superiority was most evident in the Northern transportation system. Southern railroads by that time had worn out. In the Union, on the other hand, some 5,000 more miles of railroad were in operation in 1865 than at the start of the war—a figure that does not include the numerous military railroads operated in the South. Moreover, because they had to link up with the newly authorized Union Pacific Railroad, Northern lines had all converted to a standard rail gauge.

Supplies, however, do not fight wars, nor do trains; men do. From the start the North's overwhelming population advantage counted heavily against the Confederacy. That advantage increased during the conflict. In the course of the four years of war, more than 180,000 male immigrants of military age settled in the North, whereas there was virtually no immigration to the Confederacy. In addition the black population became another vast source of Union manpower. Confederates dared not tap this source until their cause was already lost.

But men, no matter how numerous, fight well only if ably led by their military commanders and inspired by their political leaders. It would be hard to argue that Northern generalship was superior to that of the South. While Grant has his admirers, most students of Civil War military history consider Robert E. Lee the greatest commander. Nor is it easy to maintain that the political leadership of the North was markedly superior. Later generations, recalling the eloquence of the Gettysburg Address and the mystical beauty of the second inaugural address, have found it difficult to remember that for most of his administration Lincoln was considered uninspiring and ineffectual. Had Lincoln been defeated for

A Dead Confederate Soldier at Fort Mahone, Near Petersburg, Virginia, April 2, 1865
In the final bloody battles of the war, the Confederacy lost men who could not be replaced. "Where is this to end?" asked General Josiah Gorgas. "No money in the Treasury—no food to feed Gen. Lee's army—no troops to oppose Gen. Sherman—what does it all mean...? Is the cause really hopeless?"

reelection in 1864, he would doubtless be rated as an honest but unsuccessful president. On the other hand, had the Southern states been able to win their independence, Jefferson Davis would undoubtedly rank as the George Washington of the Confederacy.

There were, of course, important differences between the two wartime presidents, but these were of less significance than the differences in the political systems in which they had to work. Like many more recently emerging nations, the Confederacy tried to present a facade of unity to the world. It was a one-party—or, more properly, a no-party—state. Southerners feared that party divisions would suggest that they were less than unanimous in seeking independence. The most careful analysis of the voting records of Confederate congressmen has been able to show, at most, only the beginnings of party lines. Small temporary factions rather than permanent political parties dominated the Confederate Congress. President Davis had many enemies, and they were constantly attacking him from all directions, like a swarm of bees. His friends were divided, and he could never rally them into a unified group. As with the Congress, so with the people. It is safe to guess that if at any point the voters of the Confederacy had been asked to endorse their president or to topple him, Davis would have received overwhelming support. But lacking political parties, Southerners had no way of making this sentiment felt.

In the Union, on the other hand, the two-party system remained active. The Democrats continued as a formidable, if not always united, force throughout the war. They came close to winning a majority in Congress in the 1862 elections; and even in 1864 McClellan received 45 percent of the popular vote—at a time when the strongest opponents of the Republican party were still out of the Union and, of course, not voting. Such a powerful opposition party compelled the Republican factions, however bitterly at odds with each other, to work together. Conservatives and Radicals might disagree over slavery, emancipation, and reconstruction, but they all agreed that any Republican administration was preferable to a Democratic one.

It was, then, the absence of political machinery in the South that weakened Davis's regime and rendered him unable fully to mobilize the material and spiritual resources of the Confederacy. And it was the much-maligned two-party system that allowed Lincoln, despite quarrelsome and impassioned attacks from fellow Republicans, to experiment boldly and to grow into an effective wartime leader.

CHRONOLOGY

1863   Lincoln issues final Emancipation Proclamation.

Confederates defeat Union army under Hooker at Chancellorsville.

Lee's invasion of the North checked by Union army under Meade at Gettysburg.

Grant captures Vicksburg.

Draft riots in the North.

Confederate army under Bragg defeats Union forces at Chickamauga.

Union victory at Chattanooga (Lookout Mountain and Missionary Ridge).

Lincoln offers lenient reconstruction program.

1864   Grant named Union general in chief.

Grant's direct advance on Richmond checked at the Wilderness, Spotsylvania, and Cold Harbor.

Grant moves south of James River to begin "siege" of Petersburg.

Sherman pushes back Confederates under Joseph E. Johnston and captures Atlanta.

Farragut captures Mobile.

Lincoln reelected president over Democrat McClellan.

Sherman marches from Atlanta to the sea.

1865   Sherman pushes northward through South Carolina and North Carolina.

Lee gives up Petersburg and Richmond, and Confederate government flees.

Lee surrenders at Appomattox.

Johnston surrenders to Sherman.

Kirby-Smith surrenders Confederate forces west of the Mississippi.

Lincoln assassinated; Andrew Johnson becomes president.

SUGGESTED READINGS

Most of the studies listed at the end of the previous chapter also relate to the topics discussed in this chapter.

The best general analysis of military operations is Herman Hattaway and Archer Jones, *How the North Won* (1983). On the Northern armies the most comprehensive work is Kenneth P. Williams's *Lincoln Finds a General* (5 vols., 1949–59). The most readable is Bruce Catton's trilogy on the Army of the Potomac: *Mr. Lincoln's Army* (1951); *Glory Road* (1952); and *A Stillness at Appomattox* (1953). Michael C. C. Adams, *Our Masters the Rebels* (1978), is a provocative interpretation. Among the best biographies of Union generals are Stephen W. Sears, *George B. McClellan: The Young Napoleon* (1988); William S. McFeely, *Grant* (1981); and Lloyd Lewis, *Sherman* (1932).

Grady McWhiney and Perry D. Jamison, *Attack and Die* (1982), is an interpretation of Confederate strategy. Douglas S. Freeman, *Lee's Lieutenants* (3 vols., 1942–44), examines Confederate commanders in the eastern theater, while Thomas Connelly, *Army of the Heartland* (2 vols., 1967–71), is an excellent account of those in the West. Among the most significant biographies of Confederate generals are Douglas S. Freeman, *R. E. Lee* (4 vols., 1934–35); Frank E. Vandiver, *Mighty Stonewall* (1957); Grady McWhiney, *Braxton Bragg and Confederate Defeat* (1969); and Richard M. McMurry, *John Bell Hood and the War for Southern Independence* (1982). Steven E. Woodworth, *Jefferson Davis and His Generals* (1990), analyzes the reasons for Confederate failure in the West, while Alan T. Nolan, *Lee Considered* (1991), offers a negative appraisal of the Confederacy's leading general.

Gerald F. Linderman, *Embattled Courage* (1987), shows how Union and Confederate soldiers found the realities of battle at odds with their expectations. Two books by Bell I. Wiley provide a fascinating social history of the common soldiers of the Civil War: *The Life of Johnny Reb* (1943) and *The Life of Billy Yank* (1952).

The best accounts of Civil War naval operations are Virgil C. Jones, *The Civil War at Sea* (3 vols., 1960–62), and Bern Anderson, *By Sea and by River* (1962). Rowena Reed, *Combined Operations in the Civil War* (1978), is an important study. See also John Niven's fine biography, *Gideon Welles: Lincoln's Secretary of the Navy* (1973). Stephen R. Wise, *Lifeline of the Confederacy* (1988), deals with blockade running.

The story of Confederate politics has to be pieced together from Wilfred B. Yearns, *The Confederate Congress* (1960); Thomas B. Alexander and Richard E. Beringer, *The Anatomy of the Confederate Congress* (1972); and Frank L. Owsley, *State Rights in the Confederacy* (1925). See also Paul D. Escott, *After Secession: Jefferson Davis and the Failure of Confederate Nationalism* (1978).

James A. Rawley, *The Politics of Union* (1974), is the best general study. There are several analyses of Republican factions and leadership: T. Harry Williams, *Lincoln and the Radicals* (1941); William B. Hesseltine, *Lincoln and the War Governors* (1948); Hans L. Trefousse, *The Radical Republicans* (1969); and Allan G. Bogue, *The Earnest Men: Republicans of the Civil War Senate* (1981). On the Democrats, see Joel H. Silbey, *A Respectable Minority* (1977), and Jean H. Baker, *Affairs of Party* (1983).

Benjamin Quarles, *The Negro in the Civil War* (1953), is comprehensive. James M. McPherson, ed., *The Negro's Civil War* (1965), is a valuable set of documents, skillfully interwoven. *Freedom: A Documentary History of Emancipation,* ed. by Ira Berlin and others (1982), is richly rewarding. Bell I. Wiley, *Southern Negroes, 1861–1865* (1938), is a standard account. The early chapters of Leon F. Litwack, *Been in the Storm So Long* (1979), superbly recapture slave life during the war. The authoritative account of Negro troops in the Union army is Dudley T. Cornish, *The Sable Arm* (1956), and Joseph T. Glatthaar, *Forged in Battle*

(1990) tells the dramatic story of black soldiers and their white officers. William S. McFeely, *Frederick Douglass* (1991), is a superior biography of the influential African-American leader.

For explanations of the collapse of the Confederacy, see Henry S. Commager, ed., *The Defeat of the Confederacy* (1964); David Donald, ed., *Why the North Won the Civil War* (1960); and Bell I. Wiley, *The Road to Appomattox* (1956).

20

Reconstruction

1865–1869

"A HOUSE divided against itself cannot stand," Abraham Lincoln prophesied in 1858. The Civil War proved that the United States would stand, not as a loose confederation of sovereign states but as one nation, indivisible. Never again would there be talk of secession. The war also ended slavery, the most divisive institution in antebellum America. Weakened by the advances of the Union armies and undermined by Lincoln's Emancipation Proclamation, slavery received its deathblow in February 1865, when Congress adopted the Thirteenth Amendment, outlawing slavery and involuntary servitude. After three-fourths of the states had ratified it, the amendment became part of the Constitution in December 1865.

But the Civil War did not settle the terms and conditions on which the states, sections, races, and classes would live in the firmly united "house." Those problems formed the agenda of the Reconstruction era, one of the most complex and controversial periods in American history. During these postwar years some basic questions had to be answered. What, if any, punishment should be imposed on Southern whites who had supported the Confederate attempt to break up the Union? How were the recently emancipated slaves to be guaranteed their freedom, and what civil and political rights did freedmen have? When and on what conditions were the Southern states, so recently in rebellion, to be readmitted to the Union—that is, entitled to vote in national elections, to have senators and representatives seated in the United States Congress, and, in general, to become once more full-fledged, equal members of the United States?

The initial moves to answer these questions came from the president, whose powers had grown significantly during the war years. In December 1863 President Lincoln announced a generous program of amnesty to repentant rebels and inaugurated a plan for reorganizing loyal governments in the South when as few as 10 percent of the voters in 1860 were willing to support them. After Lincoln's assassination in April 1865, President Andrew Johnson, his successor, continued the process of Reconstruction under a similar plan. Johnson, like Lincoln, expected Southern whites to take the lead in establishing new state governments loyal to the Union. To begin the process, the president appointed a provisional governor for each of the former Confederate states (except those in which Lincoln had already initiated Reconstruction). Johnson directed these provisional governors to convene constitutional conventions, which were expected to adopt the Thirteenth Amendment ending slavery, to nullify or repeal the ordinances of secession, and to cancel state debts incurred for the prosecution of the war. By early 1866 each of the states that had once formed the Confederacy had completed most of these required steps, and the president viewed the process of Reconstruction as concluded. He recommended that the senators and representatives chosen by these reorganized governments promptly be given their rightful seats in Congress.

Presidential Reconstruction drew criticism from the outset. Having jealously watched executive power grow during the war, Congress was ready to reestablish its political equality with the presidency, and even to reassert its superior influence. Unlike President Lincoln, Andrew Johnson had no popular mandate. Johnson, a Tennessee Democrat and former slaveholder, was an inflexible and aggressive man who did not understand that politics is the art of compromise.

After an initial attempt to cooperate with the new president, Republican leaders in 1866 began to draw up their own plans for Reconstruction. The first congressional plan was embodied in the Fourteenth Amendment to the Constitution, which made it clear that blacks were citizens of the United States and tried to define the rights and privileges of American citizens. When the Southern states refused to ratify this amendment, congressional Republicans moved in 1867 to a tougher program of reorganizing the South by insisting that blacks be allowed to vote. Under this second plan of congressional Reconstruction, every Southern state (except for Tennessee, which had been readmitted to the Union in 1866) received a new constitution that guaranteed to men of all races equal protection of the laws. Between 1868 and 1871, all these states were readmitted to the Union. Republican governments, which depended heavily on black votes, controlled these states for a period ranging from a few months in the case of Virginia to nine years in the case of Louisiana.

Paths Not Taken

Contemporaries called this the period of Radical Reconstruction—or, very often, Black Reconstruction. It is easy to understand why many Americans viewed these changes as little short of revolutionary. No amendments had been added to the Constitution since 1804; but within the five years after the Civil War, three new and far-reaching amendments were adopted. The Thirteenth Amendment ended slavery, the Fourteenth Amendment defined the rights of citizens, and the Fifteenth Amendment (1870) prohibited discrimination in voting because of race or color. The national government, which so recently had tottered on the edge of defeat, was now more powerful than at any previous point in American history.

The Southern ruling class of whites, lately in charge of their own independent government, now had to ask for pardon. More than 3 million blacks, slaves only a few months earlier, were now free and entitled to the same privileges as all other citizens. Americans fairly gasped at the extent and the speed of the changes that had occurred in their society, and it is hardly surprising that most subsequent historians accepted this contemporary view of the Reconstruction era as one of turbulent disorder.

Without denying that real and important changes did occur during the Reconstruction period, it might help to put these changes into perspective by inventing a little counterfactual, or imaginary, history—a recital of conceivable historical scenarios that never in fact occurred. For example, it would be easy to imagine how the victorious North might have turned angrily on the defeated South. In 1865 Northerners had just finished four years of war that had cost the Union army more than 360,000 casualties. Americans of the Civil War era and subsequent generations had to pay at least $10 billion in taxes to destroy the Confederacy. Northerners had reason to believe, moreover, that their Confederate opponents had conducted the war with fiendish barbarity. Sober Union congressmen informed their constituents that the Confederates had employed "Indian savages" to scalp and mutilate the Union dead. Reliable Northern newspapers told how in April 1864 General Nathan Bedford Forrest and his Confederates overran the defenses of Fort Pillow, Tennessee, manned by a black regiment and, refusing to accept surrender, deliberately beat, shot, and burned their prisoners. The influential *Harper's Weekly Magazine* carried apparently authentic drawings of a goblet that a Southerner had made from a Yankee soldier's skull and of necklaces fashioned of Yankee teeth that Southern ladies wore. When Union armies liberated Northern prisoners from such hellholes as Andersonville, Georgia, pictures of these half-starved skeletons of men, clad in grimy tatters of their Union uniforms, convinced Northerners that Jefferson Davis's policy had been "to starve and freeze and kill off by inches the prisoners he dares not butcher out-right."

After the murder of President Lincoln by the Southern sympathizer John Wilkes Booth, an outraged North could easily have turned on the conquered Confederacy in vengeance. The victorious Northerners might have executed Jefferson Davis, Alexander H. Stephens, and a score of other leading Confederates and might have sent thousands more into permanent exile. The triumphant Union might have erased the boundaries of the Southern states and divided the whole region into new, conquered territories. Northerners might have enforced the confiscation acts already on the statute books and seized the plantations of rebels, for distribution to the freedmen.

But nothing so drastic happened. No Confederate was executed for "war crimes" except Major Henry Wirtz, commandant of the infamous Andersonville prison, who was hanged. A few Southern political leaders were imprisoned for their part in the "rebellion," but in most cases they were promptly released. To be sure, Jefferson Davis remained in prison for two years at Fort Monroe, and he was under indictment for treason until 1869, when all charges were dropped. His case was, however, as unusual as it was extreme. One reason for the long delay in bringing him to trial was the certainty that no jury, Northern or Southern, would render an impartial verdict. There was no general confiscation of the property of Confederates, and no dividing up of plantations.

Another scenario—this time featuring the Southern whites—is equally conceivable, but it too did not happen. For four years Confederate citizens had been subjected to a barrage of propaganda designed to prove that the enemy was little less than infernal in his purposes. Many believed the Southern editor who claimed that Lincoln's program was "Emancipation, Confiscation, Conflagration, and Extermination." According to the North Carolina educator Calvin H. Wiley, the North had "summoned to its aid every fierce and cruel and licentious passion of the human heart"; to defeat the Confederacy it was ready to use "the assassin's dagger, the midnight torch, . . . poison, famine and pestilence." Charges of this kind were easy to credit in the many Southern families that had relatives in Northern prison camps, such as the one at Elmira, New York, where 775 of 8,347 Confederate prisoners died within three months for lack of food, water, and medicine. The behavior of Union troops in the South, especially of Sherman's "bummers," members of raiding forces who plundered indiscriminately in Georgia and the Carolinas, gave Southerners every reason to fear the worst if the Confederate government failed.

It would therefore have been reasonable for Confederate armies in 1865, overwhelmed by Union numbers, to disband quietly, disappear into the countryside, and carry on guerrilla operations against the Northern invaders. Indeed, on the morning of the day when Lee surrendered at Appomattox, Confederate General E. P. Alexander advocated just such a plan. He argued that if Lee's soldiers took to the woods with their rifles, perhaps two-thirds of the Army of Northern Virginia could escape capture. "We would be like rabbits and partridges in the bushes," he claimed, "and they could not scatter to follow us." The history of more recent wars of national liberation suggests that Alexander's judgment was correct. At least his strategy would have given time for thousands of leading Southern politicians and planters, together with their families, to go safely into exile, as the loyalists did during the American Revolution.

But again, no such events occurred. A few Confederate leaders did leave the country. For example, General Jubal A. Early fled to Mexico and from there to Canada, where he tried to organize a migration of Southerners to New Zealand. But when he found that nobody wanted to follow him, Early returned to his home and his law practice in Virginia. A few hundred Confederates migrated to Mexico and to Brazil. But most followed the advice of General Lee and General Wade Hampton of South Carolina, who urged their fellow Southerners to "devote their whole energies to the restoration of law and order, the reestablishment of agriculture and commerce, the promotion of education and the rebuilding of our cities and dwellings which have been laid in ashes."

Still another counterfactual historical scenario comes readily to mind. Southern blacks, who for generations had been oppressed in slavery, now for the first time had disciplined leaders in the thousands of black soldiers who had served in the Union army. They also had weapons. The blacks could very easily have turned in revenge on their former masters. Seizing the plantations and other property of the whites, the freedmen might have made the former Confederacy a black nation. If the whites had dared to resist, the South might have been the scene of massacres as bloody as those in Haiti at the beginning of the nineteenth century, when Toussaint L'Ouverture drove the French from that island.

Many Southern whites feared, or even expected, that the Confederacy would become another Haiti. They were frightened by reports that blacks were joining the Union League, an organization that had originated in the North during the war to stimulate patriotism but during the Reconstruction era became the stronghold of the Republican party in the South. The secrecy imposed by the league on its members and its frequent nighttime meetings alarmed whites, and they readily believed reports that the blacks were collecting arms and ammunition for a general uprising. Fearfully, Southern whites read newspaper accounts of minor racial clashes. Indeed, whites were told, racial tension was so great that blacks "might break into open insurrection at any time."

But no such uprising occurred. Although the freedmen unquestionably hoped to obtain the lands of their former masters, they did not seize them. Indeed, black leaders consistently discouraged talk of extralegal confiscation of plantations. Nor did freedmen threaten the lives or the rights of whites. One of the earliest black political conventions held in Alabama urged a policy of "peace, friendship, and good will toward all men—especially toward our white fellow-citizens among whom our lot is cast." That tone was the dominant one throughout the Reconstruction period, and in many states blacks took the lead in repealing laws that disfranchised former Confederates or disqualified them from holding office.

The point of these three exercises in counterfactual history is, of course, not to argue that the Civil War brought no changes in American life. The preservation of the Union and the emancipation of the slaves were two consequences of tremendous importance. Instead, these exercises suggest that conventional accounts of the Reconstruction period as a second American Revolution are inadequate. During these postwar years there were swift and significant changes in Southern society, but the shared beliefs and institutions of the American people—North and South, black and white—set limits to these changes.

Constitutionalism as a Limit to Change

One set of ideas that sharply curbed experimentation and political innovation during the Reconstruction period can be labeled constitutionalism. It is hard for twentieth-century Americans to understand the reverence with which their nineteenth-century ancestors viewed the Constitution. Next to the flag, the Constitution was the most powerful symbol of American nationhood. Tested in the trial of civil war, the Constitution continued to command respect—almost veneration—during the Reconstruction era.

States' Rights   Among the most unchallenged provisions of the Constitution were those that separated the powers of state and national government. Although the national government greatly expanded its role during the war years, Americans still tended to think of it as performing only the specific functions delegated to it in the Constitution. These functions allowed the national government virtually no authority to act directly on individual citizens. For example, the national government could neither prevent nor punish crime; it had no control over public education; it could not outlaw discrimination against racial minorities; and it could not even intervene to maintain public order unless requested to do so by the state government. Virtually everybody agreed, therefore, that if any laws regulating social and economic life were required, they must be the work of state and local, not of national, government.

Consequently, nobody even contemplated the possibility that some federal agency might be needed to supervise the demobilization after Appomattox. Everybody simply assumed that after some 200,000 of the Union army volunteers bravely paraded down Pennsylvania Avenue on May 23–24, 1865, and received applause from President Johnson, the cabinet, the generals, and members of the diplomatic corps, the soldiers would disband and go back to their peaceful homes. This is precisely what they did. Of the more than one million volunteers in the Union army on May 1, 1865, two-thirds were mustered out by August, four-fifths by November. The United States government offered the demobilized soldiers no assistance in finding jobs, purchasing housing, or securing further education. It paid pensions to those injured in the war and to the families of those who had been killed, but assumed no further responsibility. Nor did anyone think of asking the national government to oversee the transition from a wartime economy to an era of peace. By the end of April 1865, without notice the various bureaus of the army and navy departments simply suspended requisitions and purchases, government arsenals slowed down their production, and surplus supplies were sold off.

Hardly anybody thought that the national government might play a role in rebuilding the warworn South. The devastation in the South was immense and ominous. The Confederate dead totaled more than a quarter of a million. In Mississippi, for example, one-third of the white men of military age had been killed or disabled for life. Most Southern cities were in ruins. Two-thirds of the Southern railroads were totally destroyed; the rest barely creaked along on worn-out rails with broken-down engines. But none of these problems was thought to be the concern of the United States government.

Ruins of Charleston
When the Confederate government evacuated Charleston on April 3, 1865, orders were given to burn supplies that might fall into the enemy's hands. There were heavy explosions as ironclads, armories, and arsenals were blown up. The next morning, as the fires spread, a mob of men and women, whites and blacks, began to plunder the city.

    The national government's failure to come to the rescue was not caused by vindictiveness. To the contrary, Union officials often behaved with marked generosity toward Confederates. After Lee's hungry battalions surrendered at Appomattox, Grant's soldiers freely shared their rations with them. All over the South, federal military officials drew on the full Union army storehouses to feed the hungry. But the federal government did not go beyond these attempts to prevent starvation, and very few thought that it should. Not until the twentieth century did the United States make it a policy to pour vast sums of money into the rehabilitation of enemies it had defeated in war.

Rebuilding therefore had to be the work of the Southern state and local authorities, and this task imposed a heavy burden on their meager resources. In Mississippi one-fifth of the entire state revenue in 1866 was needed to provide artificial limbs for soldiers maimed in the war. The resources of the South were obviously inadequate for the larger tasks of physical restoration. Drawing on antebellum experience, Southern governments did the only thing they knew how to—namely, they lent the credit of the state to back up the bonds of private companies that promised to rebuild railroads and other necessary facilities. These companies were underfinanced, and the credit of the Southern states after Appomattox was questionable, to say the least. Therefore these bonds had to be sold at disadvantageous prices and at exorbitant rates of interest. In later years, when many of these companies defaulted on their obligations and southern state governments had to make good on their guarantees, these expenditures would be condemned as excessive and extravagant. Democrats blamed them on the Republican regimes established in the South after 1868. In fact, however, immediately after the war the need for physical restoration was so obvious and so pressing that nearly every government—whether controlled by Democrats or Republicans—underwrote corporations that promised to rebuild the region.

The Freedmen's Bureau

Even in dealing with the freedmen—the some 3 million slaves emancipated as a result of the war—the United States government tried to pursue a hands-off policy. In North and South alike, few influential leaders thought that it was the function of the national government to supervise the blacks' transition from slavery to freedom. Even abolitionists, genuinely devoted to the welfare of blacks, were so accustomed to thinking of the black man as "God's image in ebony"—in other words, a white man in a black skin—that they had no plans for assisting him after emancipation. In 1865 William Lloyd Garrison urged the American Anti-Slavery Society to disband because it had fulfilled its function, and he suspended the publication of *The Liberator.* Sharing the same point of view, the American Freedmen's Inquiry Commission, set up by the Union War Department in 1863, unanimously opposed further governmental actions to protect the blacks. "The negro does best when let alone," argued one member of the commission, Samuel Gridley Howe, noted both for his work with the deaf, dumb, and blind and for his hostility to slavery. "We must beware of all attempts to prolong his servitude, under pretext of taking care of him. The white man has tried taking care of the negro, by slavery, by apprenticeship, by colonization, and has failed disastrously in all; now let the negro try to take care of himself."

But the problem of caring for the freedmen could not be dismissed so easily. Wherever Union armies advanced into the South, they were "greeted by an irruption of negroes of all ages, complexions and sizes, men, women, boys and girls . . . waving hats and bonnets with the most ludicrous caperings and ejaculations of joy." "The poor delighted creatures thronged upon us," a Yankee soldier reported, and they insisted: "We'se gwin wid you all." "What shall be done with them?" commanders in the field plaintively wired Washington.

A Group of Freedmen in Richmond, Virginia, 1865
A central problem of Reconstruction years was the future of the freedmen. Nobody had made any plans for a smooth transition from slavery to freedom. Consequently, when emancipation came, as one former slave recalled, "We didn't know where to go. Momma and them didn't know where to go, you see, after freedom broke. Just like you turned something out, you know. They didn't know where to go."

The administration in Washington had no comprehensive answer. Initially it looked to private humanitarian organizations to rush food, clothing, and medicine to the thousands of blacks who thronged in unsanitary camps around the headquarters of each Union army. The New England Freedmen's Aid Society, the American Missionary Association, and the Philadelphia Society of Friends [Quakers] promptly responded, but it was soon clear that the problem was too great for private charity.

Gradually sentiment grew in the North for the creation of a general Emancipation Bureau in the federal government—only to conflict directly with the even stronger sentiment that the national government had limited powers. Out of this conflict emerged the Freedmen's Bureau Act of March 3, 1865. Congress established the Bureau of Refugees, Freedmen, and Abandoned Lands under the jurisdiction of the War Department. It entrusted to the new agency, for one year after the end of the war, "control of all subjects relating to refugees and freedmen." To head the new organization, Lincoln named Oliver O. Howard, a Union general with paternalistic views toward blacks.

At first glance, the Freedmen's Bureau seems to have been a notable exception to the rule that the national government should take only a minor, passive role in the restoration of the South. Howard had a vision of a compassionate network of "teachers, ministers, farmers, superintendents" working together to

The Freedmen's Union Industrial School, Richmond, Virginia
Freedmen were eager to learn, and both the old and the young flocked to schools sponsored by the Freedmen's Bureau. Most of these schools taught only reading, writing, and arithmetic, but this one, in Richmond, gave instruction in sewing, cooking, and other domestic skills.

aid and elevate the freedmen; and, under his enthusiastic impetus, the bureau appointed agents in each of the former Confederate states. The bureau's most urgent task was issuing food and clothing, mostly from surplus army stores, to destitute freedmen and other Southern refugees. This action unquestionably prevented mass starvation in the South. The bureau also took the initiative in getting work for freedmen. The bureau agents feared on the one hand that Southern landlords would attempt to exploit and underpay the freedmen, but they were also troubled by the widespread belief that blacks, once emancipated, would not work. The agents therefore brought laborers and landlords together and insisted that the workers sign labor contracts.

The bureau's most successful work was in the field of education. The slow work of educating the illiterate Southern blacks had already begun under the auspices of army chaplains and Northern benevolent societies before the creation of the bureau. Howard's bureau continued to cooperate with these agencies, providing housing for black schools, paying teachers, and helping to establish normal (teachers') schools and colleges for the training of black teachers. The freedmen enthusiastically welcomed all these educational efforts. During the day, black children learning the rudiments of language and arithmetic crowded into the classrooms; in the evenings, adults "fighting with their letters" flocked to the schools, learning to read so that they would not be "made ashamed" by their children. "The progress of the scholars is in all cases creditable and in some remarkable," reported one of the teachers condescendingly. "How richly God has endowed them, and how beautifully their natures would have expanded under a tender and gentle culture."

Even more innovative was the work of the bureau in allocating lands to the freedmen. During the war many plantations in the path of Union armies had been deserted by their owners, and army commanders like Grant arranged to have these lands cultivated by the blacks who flocked to their camps. The largest tract of such abandoned land was in the Sea Islands of South Carolina, which Union troops had overrun in the fall of 1861. Although speculators bought up large amounts of this land during the war, many black residents were able to secure small holdings. When General W. T. Sherman marched through South Carolina, he ordered that the Sea Islands and the abandoned plantations along the river-banks for thirty miles from the coast be reserved for black settlement and directed that the black settlers be given "possessory titles" to tracts of this land not larger than forty acres. The act creating the Freedmen's Bureau clearly contemplated the continuation of these policies, for it authorized the new bureau to lease confiscated lands to freedmen and to "loyal refugees." The bureau could also sell the land to these tenants and give them "such title thereto as the United States can convey."

But if the Freedmen's Bureau was an exception to the policy of limited federal involvement in the reconstruction process, it was at best a partial exception. Although the agency did extremely valuable work, it was a feeble protector of the freedmen. Authorized to recruit only a minimal staff, Howard had to rely heavily on Union army officers stationed in the South—at just the time when the Union army was being demobilized. Consequently, the bureau never had enough manpower to look after the rights of the freedmen; toward the end of its first year of operation, the bureau employed only 799 men, 424 of whom were soldiers on temporary assigned duty. Important as the work of the bureau was in black education, its chief function was to stimulate private humanitarian aid in this field. In providing land for the freedmen, the bureau was handicapped because it controlled only about 800,000 acres of arable land in the South, at best enough for perhaps one black family in forty. Moreover, Congress and the president repeatedly undercut its efforts to distribute land to the blacks. The very wording of the act creating the bureau suggested congressional uncertainty about who actually owned deserted and confiscated lands in the South. When President Johnson issued pardons to Southerners, he explicitly called for the "restoration of all rights of property." In October 1865 the president directed Howard to go in person to the Sea Islands to notify blacks there that they did not hold legal title to the land and to advise them "to make the best terms they could" with the white owners. When blacks bitterly resisted what they considered the bureau's betrayal, Union soldiers descended on the islands and forced blacks who would not sign labor contracts with the restored white owners to leave. Elsewhere in the South the record of the bureau was equally dismal.

In short, belief in the limited role to be played by the national government affected the rehabilitation of the freedmen, just as it did the physical restoration of the South and the demobilization in the North. The United States government was supposed to play the smallest possible part in all these matters, and its minimal activities were to be of the briefest duration.

It is certain that most whites in the North and in the South fully approved of these strict limitations on the activities of the national government. It is harder to determine what the masses of freedmen thought. On the one hand stands the protest of the Sea Island blacks when they learned they were about to be dispossessed: "Why, General Howard, why do you take away our lands? You take them from us who have always been true, always true to the Government! You give them to our all-time enemies! That is not right!" On the other is Frederick Douglass's reply to the question "What shall we do with the Negroes?" The greatest black spokesman of the era answered: "Do nothing with them; mind your business, and let them mind theirs. Your doing with them is their greatest misfortune. They have been undone by your doings, and all they now ask and really have need of at your hands, is just to let them alone."

Laissez-Faire as a Limit to Change

Along with the idea of limited government went the doctrine of laissez-faire ("let things alone"), which sharply limited what the government could do to solve the economic problems that arose after the Civil War. Except for a handful of Radical Republicans, such as Charles Sumner and Thaddeus Stevens, most congressmen, like most academic economists, were unquestioning believers in an American version of laissez-faire. Although they were willing to promote economic growth through protective tariffs and land grants to railroads, they abhorred government inspection, regulation, and control of economic activities. These matters, they thought, were ruled by the unchanging laws of economics. "You need not think it necessary to have Washington exercise a political providence over the country," William Graham Sumner, the brilliant professor of political and social science, told his students at Yale. "God has done that a great deal better by the laws of political economy."

Reverence for Private Property   No violation of economic laws was considered worse than interference with the right of private property— the right of an individual or group to purchase, own, use, and dispose of property without any interference from governmental authorities. There was consequently never a chance that most congressmen would support Thaddeus Stevens's radical program to confiscate all Southern farms larger than two hundred acres and to divide the seized land into forty-acre tracts among the freedmen. "An attempt to justify the confiscation of Southern land under the pretense of doing justice to the freedmen," declared the *New York Times,* which spoke for educated Republicans, "strikes at the root of all property rights in both sections. It concerns Massachusetts quite as much as Mississippi."

Experts in the North held that the best program of Reconstruction was to allow the laws of economics to rule in the South with the least possible interference by the government. Obsessed by laissez-faire, Northern theorists failed to consider the physical devastation in the South caused by the war, and they did not recognize how feeble were the South's resources to rebuild its economy. Even excluding the loss of slave property, the total assessed property evaluation of the Southern states shrank by 43 percent between 1860 and 1865.

Southern Economic Adjustments

Northern experts also failed to take into account the psychological dimensions of economic readjustment in the South. For generations Southern whites had persuaded themselves that slavery was the natural condition of the black race, and they truly believed that their slaves were devoted to them. But as Union armies approached and slaves defected, these Southerners were compelled to recognize that they had been living in a world of misconceptions and deceits. So shattering was the idea that slaves were free that some Southern whites simply refused to accept it. Even after the Confederate surrender, some owners would not inform their slaves of their new status. A few plantation owners angrily announced that they were so disillusioned that they would never again have anything to do with blacks, and they sought, vainly, to persuade European immigrants and Chinese coolies to work their fields.

Even those whites who on the surface accepted emancipation betrayed the fact that, on a deeper emotional level, they still could only think of blacks as performing forced labor. "The general interest both of the white man and of the negroes requires that he should be kept as near to the condition of slavery as possible, and as far from the condition of the white man as is practicable," announced one prominent South Carolinian. "Negroes must be made to work, or else cotton and rice must cease to be raised for export." The contracts that in 1865 planters signed with their former slaves under pressure from the Freedmen's Bureau were further indications of the same attitude. Even the most generous of these contracts provided that blacks were "not to leave the premises during work hours without the consent of the Proprietor," that they would conduct "themselves faithfully, honestly and civilly," and that they would behave with perfect obedience" toward the landowner.

Nor did the advocates of laissez-faire take into account the blacks' difficulties in adjusting to their new status. *Freedom*—that word so often whispered in the slave quarters—went to the heads of some blacks. A few took quite literally the coming of what they called Jubilee, thinking that it would put the bottom rail on top. Nearly all blacks had an initial impulse to test their freedom, to make sure that it was real. Thus during the first months after the war there was much movement among southern blacks. "They are just like a swarm of bees," one observer noted, "all buzzing about and not knowing where to settle."

Much of this black mobility was, however, purposeful. Thousands of former slaves flocked to the Southern towns and cities where the Freedmen's Bureau was issuing rations, for they knew that food was unavailable on the plantations. Many blacks set out to find husbands, wives, or children from whom they had been forcibly separated during the slave days. A good many freedmen joined the general movement of the Southern population away from the coastal states, which had been devastated by war, and migrated to the southwestern frontier in Texas. Most blacks, however, did not move so far but remained in the immediate vicinity of the plantations where they had labored as slaves.

The freedmen's reluctance in 1865 to enter into labor contracts, either with their former masters or with other white landowners, was also generally misunderstood. Most blacks wanted to work—but they wanted to work on their own land. Freedmen knew that the United States government had divided up some abandoned plantations among former slaves, and many believed that on January 1, 1866—the anniversary of their freedom under Lincoln's Emancipation Proclamation—all would receive forty acres and a mule. With this prospect of having their own farms, they were unwilling to sign contracts to work on plantations owned by others.

Even when the hope of free land disappeared, freedmen resisted signing labor contracts because, as has been noted, so many white landowners expected to continue to treat them like slaves. The blacks were especially opposed to the idea of being again herded together in the plantation slave quarters, with their communal facilities for cooking and washing and infant care, and their lack of privacy. Emancipation did much to strengthen the black family. Families divided by slave sales could now be reunited. Marital arrangements between blacks, which had not been legally valid during slavery, could be regularized. Freedmen's Bureau officials performed thousands of marriage ceremonies, and some states passed general ordinances declaring that blacks who had been living together were legally man and wife and that their children were legitimate. This precious new security of family life was not something blacks were willing to jeopardize by returning to slave quarters. Before contracting to work on the plantations, they insisted on having separate cabins, scattered across the farm, each usually having its own patch for vegetables and perhaps a pen for hogs or a cow.

When these conditions were met, freedmen in the early months of 1866 entered into labor contracts, most of which followed the same general pattern. Rarely did these arrangements call for the payment of wages, for landowners were desperately short of cash and freedmen felt that a wage system gave landowners too much control over their labor. The most common system was sharecropping. Although there were many regional and individual variations, the system usually called for the dividing of the crop into three equal shares. One of these went to the landowner; another went to the laborer—usually black, although there were also many white sharecroppers in the South; and the third went to whichever party provided the seeds, fertilizer, mules, and farming equipment.

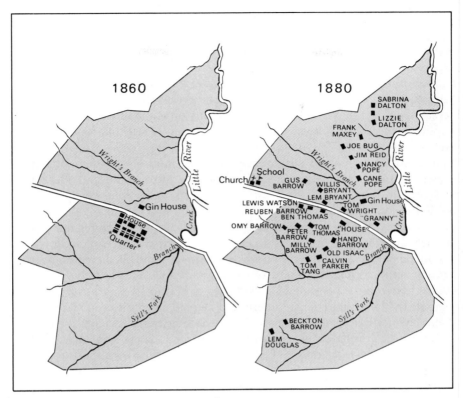

The Same Georgia Plantation in 1860 and 1880
Before the Civil War, slave quarters were located close together, all near the white master's house, so that he could impose order and prevent secret meetings of the blacks. After emancipation, freedmen insisted upon scattering out over the plantation, so that each family could have its own house and some privacy.

This system had several advantages for the landowner. At a time when money was scarce, he was not obliged to pay out cash to his employees until the crop was harvested. He retained general supervision over what was planted and how the crop was cultivated, and he felt he was more likely to secure a good harvest because the freedmen themselves stood to gain by a large yield. Blacks too found the sharecropping system suited to their needs. They had control over how their crops were planted and when they were cultivated and harvested. They could earn more money by working harder in the fields.

The "Breakup" of the Plantation System

To some observers the disappearance of the slave quarters and the resettling of families in individual, scattered cabins seemed to mark a revolution in the character of Southern agriculture. According to the United States census, the number of Southern landholdings doubled between 1860 and 1880, and their average size dropped from 365 acres to 157 acres. But these figures are misleading, because the census takers failed to ask farmers whether they owned their land or were sharecroppers. An examination of tax records, which show landownership, in the representative state of Louisiana helps correct the census distortion. Between 1860 and 1880 in Louisiana, the number of independently owned farms of less than one hundred acres actually dropped by 14 percent, while during the same period the number of plantations increased by 287 percent. By 1900 plantations of one hundred acres or more encompassed half the cultivated land in the state, and more than half the farmers were not proprietors.

If the postwar period did not see the breakup of large plantations, it did bring some significant changes in ownership and control of the land. Hard hit by debt, by rising taxes, and by increasing labor costs, many Southern planters had to sell their holdings, and Northern capital flowed into the region after the war. More tried to cling to their acres by going heavily into debt. Since the postwar Southern banking system was inadequate, the principal source of credit was the local merchant, who could supply both the landowner and his sharecroppers with clothing, shoes, some food, and other necessities to tide them over the lean months between the planting of the tobacco or cotton crop and its harvest. On each sale the merchant charged interest, to be paid when the crop was sold, and he also charged prices ranging from 40 percent to 110 percent higher for all goods sold on credit. It is hardly surprising that those landowners who could afford to do so set up their own stores and extended credit to their own sharecroppers—and quite soon they discovered they were making more profits from mercantile enterprises than from farming. Planters who could not make such arrangements frequently had to sell their lands to the neighborhood merchant. It is not accidental that in William Faulkner's twentieth-century series of novels that constitute a fictional saga of Southern history, the power of landowning families like the Compsons and the Sutpens diminished during the postwar years, while the Snopes family of storekeepers—hard-trading, penny-pinching, and utterly unscrupulous—emerged prosperous and successful.

It would be a mistake, however, to accept without reservation the novelist's hostile characterization of the Southern merchant. The storekeeper insisted on the crop-lien system, which required the farmer legally to pledge that the proceeds from his crop must go first to pay off his obligations to the merchant, because he knew that crops could fail throughout the South, as they did in both 1866 and 1867. And if the merchant urged farmers to forget about soil conservation, diversification, and experimentation with new crops, he did so because he realized that the only way to pay his own debts was to insist that his debtors raise cotton and tobacco, for which there was a ready cash market.

Thus merchants, landowners, and sharecroppers—white Southerners and black Southerners—became locked into an economic system that, at best, promised them little more than survival. At worst, it offered bankruptcy, sale of lands, and hurried nighttime migrations in an attempt to escape from a set of debts in one state but with little more than the hope of starting a new set in another.

By the 1880s, then, the South had become what it remained for the next half-century—the nation's economic backwater. In 1880 the per capita wealth of the South was $376, compared with per capita wealth outside the South of $1,086. Yet this impoverished region had to deal with some of the most difficult political and racial problems that have ever confronted Americans. In attacking these problems, Southerners, black and white, could expect no assistance from the government, because such intervention would violate the unchanging laws of laissez-faire economics.

Political Parties as a Limit to Change

The most influential institutions that blocked radical change during Reconstruction were the national political parties. The fact that both parties were conglomerates of different and often competing sectional and class interests meant that parties had to decide on their policies through compromise and concession. That process nearly always screened out extreme and drastic measures.

Nationally the Democratic party was torn by two conflicting interests during the postwar years. On the one hand, Democrats sought the immediate readmission of the Southern states under the governments President Johnson had set up. Controlled by whites hostile to the Republican party, these states would surely send Democrats to Congress and support Democratic candidates in a national election. Even during the 1850s the South had increasingly become a one-party region; now the goal of a solidly Democratic South appeared within reach. On the other hand, too-enthusiastic advocacy of the Southern cause could hurt Democrats in the North by reviving talk of disloyalty and the Copperhead movement during the war. To blunt such attacks, Democrats had no choice but to urge restraint on their colleagues in the former Confederacy.

Among Republicans, similar constraints dampened any ideas of taking vengeance on the South or of encouraging blacks to seize control of that region. From its beginnings the Republican party had been an uneasy alliance of antislavery men, former Whigs, dissatisfied Democrats, and Know-Nothings. The factional disputes that racked Lincoln's administration showed the weakness of the ties that bound these groups together. It was a bad omen for the party that Republicans disagreed most sharply over Lincoln's plan to reorganize the Southern state governments.

Presidential Reconstruction

During the first year after Lincoln's death, quarrels among Republicans were somewhat muted because practically all members of the party joined in opposing President Johnson's program of Reconstruction. Followed by only a handful of Conservative Republicans, including Secretary of State Seward and Navy Secretary Gideon Welles, Johnson began to work closely with the Democrats of the North and South. He announced that the Southern states had never been out of the Union, and he insisted that, under the provisional governments he had set up, they were entitled to be represented in Congress.

It is easy to understand why almost all Republicans—whether they belonged to the Radical or Moderate faction—rejected the president's argument. Members of both these wings of the party were outraged when the Southern elections of 1865, held at the president's direction, resulted in the choice of a Confederate brigadier-general as governor of Mississippi, and they were furious when the new Georgia legislature named Alexander H. Stephens, the vice-president of the Confederacy, to represent that state in the United States Senate.

Republicans had even more reason to fear these newly elected Southern officials because, although many of the Southerners had been Whigs before the war, they clearly contemplated allying themselves with the Democratic party. However much Republicans disagreed among themselves, they all agreed that their party had saved the Union. They believed, with Thaddeus Stevens, "that upon the continued ascendancy of that party depends the safety of this great nation." Now this ascendancy was threatened. The threat was the more serious because once the Southern states were readmitted to the Union they would receive increased representation in Congress. Before the Civil War, only three-fifths of the slave population of the South had been counted in apportioning representation in the House of Representatives; but now that the slaves were free men, all would be counted. In short, the Southern states, after having been defeated in the most costly war in the nation's history, would have about fifteen more representatives in Congress than they had before the war. And under the president's plan all Southern Congressmen unquestionably would be Democrats.

Republicans of all factions were equally troubled by the fear of what white Southerners, once restored to authority, would do to the freedmen. The laws that the Southern provisional legislatures adopted during the winter of 1865–66 gave reason for anxiety on this score. Not one of these governments considered treating black citizens just as they treated white citizens. Instead the legislatures adopted special laws, known as the Black Codes, to regulate the conduct of the freedmen. On the positive side, these laws recognized the freedmen's right to make civil contracts, to sue and be sued, and to acquire and hold most kinds of property. But with these rights went restrictions. The laws varied from state to state, but in general they specified that blacks might not purchase or carry firearms, that they might not assemble after sunset, and that those who were idle or unemployed should "be liable to imprisonment, and to hard labor, one or both, ... not exceeding twelve months." The Mississippi code prevented blacks from renting or leasing "any lands or tenements except in incorporated cities or towns." That of South Carolina forbade blacks from practicing "the art, trade or business of an artisan, mechanic or shopkeeper, or any other trade, employment or business (besides that of husbandry, or that of a servant)." So clearly did these measures seem designed to keep the freedmen in quasi-slavery that the *Chicago Tribune* spoke for a united, outraged Republican party in denouncing the first of these Black Codes, that adopted by the Mississippi legislature: "We tell the white men of Mississippi that the men of the North will convert the state of Mississippi into a frogpond before they will allow any such laws to disgrace one foot of soil over which the flag of freedom waves."

The Fourteenth Amendment

For these reasons, all Republicans were unwilling to recognize the regimes Johnson had set up in the South; when Congress reassembled in December 1865, they easily rallied to block seating of the Southern senators and representatives. All agreed to the creation of a special joint committee on Reconstruction to handle questions concerning the readmission of the Southern states and their further reorganization. In setting up this committee, congressional Republicans carefully balanced its membership with Radicals and Moderates. Its most conspicuous member was the Radical Stevens, but its powerful chairman was Senator William Pitt Fessenden, a Moderate.

Congressional Republicans found it easier to unite in opposing Johnson's plan of Reconstruction than to unite in devising one of their own. Congressional leaders recognized that it would take time to draft and adopt a constitutional amendment and then to have it ratified by the required number of states. Therefore, early in 1866 they agreed on interim legislation that would protect the freedmen. One bill extended and expanded the functions of the Freedmen's Bureau, and a second guaranteed minimal civil rights to all citizens. Contrary to expectations, Johnson vetoed both these measures. Refusing to recognize that these measures represented the wishes of both Moderate and Radical Republicans, the president claimed that they were the work of the Radicals, who wanted "to destroy our institutions and change the character of the Government." He vowed to fight these Northern enemies of the Union just as he had once fought Southern secessionists and traitors. The Republican majority in Congress was not able to override Johnson's veto of the Freedmen's Bureau bill (a later, less sweeping measure extended the life of that agency for two years), but it passed the Civil Rights Act of 1866 over his disapproval.

While relations between the president and the Republicans in Congress were deteriorating, the joint committee on Reconstruction continued to meet and consider various plans for reorganizing the South. With its evenly balanced membership, the committee dismissed the president's theory that the Southern states were already reconstructed and back in the Union, as well as Thaddeus Stevens's view that the Confederacy was conquered territory over which Congress could rule at its own discretion. It also rejected Charles Sumner's more elaborate argument that the Southern states had committed suicide when they seceded, so that their land and inhabitants now fell "under the exclusive jurisdiction of Congress." More acceptable to the majority of Republicans was the "grasp of war" theory advanced by Richard Henry Dana, Jr., the noted Massachusetts constitutional lawyer who was also the author of *Two Years Before the Mast*. Dana argued that the federal government should hold the defeated Confederacy in the grasp of war only for a brief and limited time, during which it must act swiftly to revive state governments in the region and promptly to restore the constitutional balance between national and state authority. Dana's theory was an essentially conservative one: it called for only a short period of federal domination and looked toward the speedy restoration of the Southern states on terms of absolute equality with the loyal states.

Finding in Dana's theory a constitutional source of power, the joint commit-tee after much hard work produced the first comprehensive congressional plan of Reconstruction—the proposed Fourteenth Amendment to the Constitution, which Congress endorsed in June 1866 and submitted to the states for ratification. Some parts of the amendment were noncontroversial. All Republicans accepted its opening statement: "All persons born or naturalized in the United States, and subject to the jurisdiction thereof, are citizens of the United States and of the State wherein they reside." This provision was necessary in order to nullify the Supreme Court's decision in the *Dred Scott* case (1857), which had denied citizenship to African Americans. There was also no disagreement about the provision declaring the Confederate debt invalid.

All the other provisions of the amendment, however, represented a compro-mise between Radical and Moderate Republicans. For example, Radicals wanted to keep all Southerners who had voluntarily supported the Confederacy from voting until 1870. Indeed, the arch-Radical Stevens urged: "Not only to 1870 but 18,070, every rebel who shed the blood of loyal men should be prevented from exercising any power in this Government." Moderates favored a speedy restora-tion of all political rights to former Confederates. As a compromise, the Four-teenth Amendment excluded high-ranking Confederates from office, but it did not deny them the vote.

Similarly, the Fourteenth Amendment's provisions protecting the freedmen represented a compromise. Radicals like Sumner (who was considered too radical to be given a seat on the joint committee) wanted an outright declaration of the national government's right and duty to protect the civil liberties of the former slaves. But Moderates drew back in alarm from entrusting additional authority to Washington. The joint committee came up with a provision that granted no power to the national government but restricted that of the states: "No State shall make or enforce any law which shall abridge the privileges and immunities of citizens of the United States; nor shall any State deprive any person of life, liberty, or property, without due process of law; nor deny to any person within its jurisdiction the equal protection of the laws."

Finally, another compromise between Radicals and Moderates resulted in the amendment's provision concerning voting. Although Sumner and other Radicals called black suffrage "the essence, the great essential," of a proper Reconstruction policy, Conservatives refused to give the national government power to interfere with the state requirements for voting. The joint committee thereupon devised a complex and, as it proved, unworkable plan to persuade the Southern states voluntarily to enfranchise blacks, under threat of having their representation in Congress reduced if they refused.

The Fourteenth Amendment's feasibility as a program of Reconstruction was never tested because of the outbreak of political warfare between President Johnson and the Republican party, which had elected him vice-president in 1864. During the summer of 1866, Johnson and his friends tried to create a new political party, which would rally behind the president's policies the few Conservative

Republicans, the Northern Democrats, and the Southern whites. With the president's hearty approval, a National Union Convention held in Philadelphia in August stressed the theme of harmony among the sections. The entry into the convention hall of delegates from Massachusetts and South Carolina, arm in arm, seemed to symbolize the end of sectional strife. The president himself went on a "swing around the circle" of leading Northern cities, ostensibly on his way to dedicate a monument to the memory of another Democrat, Stephen A. Douglas. In his frequent public speeches Johnson defended the constitutionality of his own Reconstruction program and attacked Congress—and particularly the Radical Republicans—for attempting to subvert the Constitution. In a final effort to consolidate sentiment against Congress, he urged the Southern states not to ratify the proposed Fourteenth Amendment. With the exception of Tennessee, which was controlled by one of Johnson's bitterest personal and political enemies, all the former Confederate states rejected the congressional plan.

The Second Congressional Program of Reconstruction

When Congress reassembled in December 1866, the Republican majority therefore had to devise a second program of Reconstruction. Cheered by overwhelming victories in the fall congressional elections, Republicans felt even less inclined than previously to cooperate with the president, who had gone into political opposition, or to encourage the provisional regimes in the South, which had rejected their first program. Republican suspicion that Southern whites were fundamentally hostile toward the freedmen was strengthened by reports of a race riot in Memphis during May 1866, when a mob of whites joined in a two-day indiscriminate attack on blacks in that city. An even more serious affair occurred four months later in New Orleans, when a white mob, aided by the local police, attacked a black political gathering with what was described as "a cowardly ferocity unsurpassed in the annals of crime." In New Orleans, 45 or 50 blacks were killed, and 150 more were wounded.

Once again, however, the Republican majority in Congress found it easier to agree on what to oppose than on what to favor in the way of Reconstruction legislation. Stevens urged that the South be placed under military rule for a generation and that Southern plantations be sold to pay the national debt. Sumner wanted to deny the vote to large numbers of Southern whites, to require that blacks be given the right to vote, and to create racially integrated schools in the South. Moderate Republicans, on the other hand, were willing to retain the Fourteenth Amendment as the basic framework of congressional Reconstruction and to insist on little else except the ratification of the amendment by the Southern states.

The second congressional program of Reconstruction, embodied in the Military Reconstruction Act of March 2, 1867, represented a compromise between the demands of Radical and Moderate Republican factions. It divided

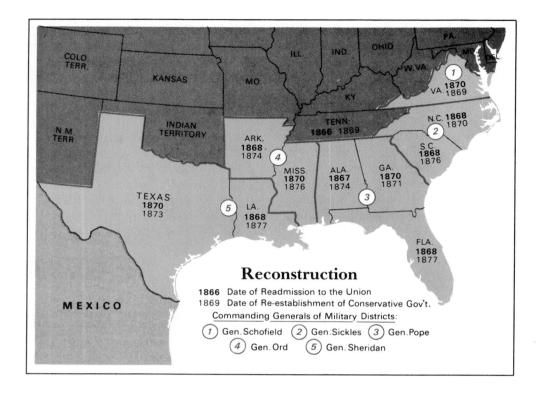

Reconstruction

1866 Date of Readmission to the Union
1869 Date of Re-establishment of Conservative Gov't.
Commanding Generals of Military Districts:
(1) Gen. Schofield (2) Gen. Sickles (3) Gen. Pope
(4) Gen. Ord (5) Gen. Sheridan

the ten former Confederate states that had not ratified the Fourteenth Amendment into five military districts. In each of these states there were to be new constitutional conventions, for which black men were allowed to vote. The task of these conventions was to draft new state constitutions that provided for black suffrage, and they were required to ratify the Fourteenth Amendment. When thus reorganized, the Southern states could apply to Congress for readmission to the Union.

It was easy to recognize the radical aspects of this measure, which Democrats pointed out during the congressional debates and President Johnson denounced in his unsuccessful veto of the act. In particular, the requirement of black suffrage, which Sumner sponsored, seemed to Radicals "a prodigious triumph."

In fact, however, most provisions of the Military Reconstruction Act were more acceptable to Moderate than to Radical Republicans. The measure did nothing to give land to the freedmen, to provide education at national expense, or to end racial segregation in the South. It did not erase the boundaries of the Southern states. It did not even sweep away the provisional governments Johnson had established there, although it did make them responsible to the commanders of the new military districts. So conservative was the act in all these respects that Sumner branded it as "horribly defective."

Intent on striking some kind of balance between the Radical and Con-servative wings of the Republican party, the framers of the Military Reconstruc-tion Act drafted the measure carelessly. As Sumner had predicted, the act promptly proved to furnish "Reconstruction without machinery or motive power." Having to choose between military rule and black suffrage, the Southern provisional governments chose the former, correctly believing that army officers generally sympathized with white supremacy. To get the Reconstruction process under way, Congress therefore had to enact a supplementary law (March 23, 1867), requiring the federal commanders in the South to take the initiative, when the local governments did not, in announcing elections, registering voters, and convening constitutional conventions. During the summer of 1867, as the presi-dent, the attorney general, and Southern state officials tried by legalistic inter-pretations to delay the Reconstruction program, Congress had to pass two further supplementary acts, explaining the "true intent and meaning" of the previous legislation.

With these measures, the congressional Reconstruction legislation affecting the South was substantially completed. Both the first and the second congres-sional plans of Reconstruction were compromises between the Radical and the Moderate factions in the Republican party. The Radicals' insistence on change was essential in securing the adoption of this legislation, but the Moderates blocked all measures that would have revolutionized the social and economic order in the South.

Impeachment   The same need to compromise between the factions of the Republican party dictated Congress's policy toward the president during the Reconstruction years. Almost all Republicans were suspicious of President Johnson and feared that he intended to turn the South over to Confederate rule. Johnson's repeated veto messages, assailing carefully balanced compromise legislation as the work of Radicals and attacking Congress as an unconstitutional body because it refused to seat congressmen from all the states, angered Republicans of both factions. Therefore, most Republicans wanted to keep a close eye on the president and sought to curb executive powers that had grown during the war. In 1867, fearing that Johnson would use his power as commander in chief to subvert their Reconstruction legislation, Republican factions joined to pass an army appropriations bill that required all military orders to the army—including those of the president himself—to go through the hands of General Grant. Suspecting that Johnson wanted to use the federal patronage to build up a political machine of his own, they enacted at the same time the Tenure of Office Act, which required the president to secure the Senate's consent not merely when he appointed officials, but also when he removed them.

The Republicans in Congress were prepared to go this far in impressive unanimity—but no farther. When Radical Republican James M. Ashley in Janu-ary 1867 moved to impeach the president, he was permitted to conduct a half-serious, half-comic investigation of Johnson's alleged involvement in Lincoln's

"Awkward Collision on the Grand Trunk Columbia Railroad"
*This cartoon depicts presidential and congressional Reconstruction as two engines going in
opposite directions on the same rails. Andrew Johnson, driver of the locomotive "President,"
says: "Look here! One of us has got to [go] back." But Thaddeus Stevens, driver of the
locomotive "Congress," replies: "Well, it ain't going to be me that's going to do it, you bet!"*

assassination, his purported sale of pardons, and other trumped-up charges. But
when Ashley's motion reached the House floor, Moderate Republicans saw that it
was soundly defeated.

A subsequent attempt at impeachment fared better, but it also revealed how
the Radical and Moderate factions blocked each other. In August 1867, President
Johnson suspended from office Secretary of War Edwin M. Stanton, who was
collaborating closely with the Radicals in Congress. As required by the Tenure of
Office Act, he asked the Senate to consent to the removal. When the Senate
refused, the president removed Stanton anyway and ordered him to surrender his
office. News of this seemingly open defiance of the law caused Republicans in the
House of Representatives to rush through a resolution impeaching the president,
without waiting for specific charges against him to be drawn up.

The trial of President Johnson (who was not present in court but was represented by his lawyers) was a test of strength not merely between Congress and the chief executive, but also between the Radical and the Moderate Republicans. Impeachment managers from the House of Representatives presented eleven charges against the president, mostly accusing him of violating the Tenure of Office Act but also censuring his repeated attacks on Congress. With fierce joy Radical Thaddeus Stevens, who was one of the managers, denounced the president: "Unfortunate man! thus surrounded, hampered, tangled in the meshes of his own wickedness—unfortunate, unhappy man, behold your doom!"

But Radical oratory could not persuade Moderate Republicans and Democrats to vote for conviction. They listened as Johnson's lawyers challenged the constitutionality of the Tenure of Office Act, showed that it had not been intended to apply to cabinet members, and proved that, in any case, it did not cover Stanton, who had been appointed by Lincoln, not Johnson. When the critical vote came, Moderate Republicans like Fessenden voted to acquit the president, and Johnson's Radical foes lacked one vote of the two-thirds majority required to convict him. Several other Republican Senators who for political expedience voted against the president were prepared to change their votes and favor acquittal if their ballots were needed.

Nothing more clearly shows how the institutional needs of a political party prevented drastic change than did this decision not to remove a president whom a majority in Congress hated and feared. The desire to maintain the unity of the national Republican party, despite frequent quarrels and endless bickering, overrode the wishes of individual congressmen. Throughout the Reconstruction period Moderate Republicans felt that they were constantly being rushed from one advanced position to another in order to placate the Radicals, who were never satisfied. More accurately, Radical Republicans perceived that the need to retain Moderate support prevented the adoption of any really revolutionary Reconstruction program.

Racism as a Limit to Change

A final set of beliefs that limited the nature of the changes imposed on, and accepted by, the South during the Reconstruction period can be labeled racism. In all parts of the country, white Americans looked with suspicion and fear on those whose skin was of a different color. For example, in California white hatred built up against the Chinese, who had begun coming to that state in great numbers after the discovery of gold and who were later imported by the thousands to help construct the Central Pacific Railroad. White workers resented the willingness of the Chinese to work long hours for "coolies" wages; they distrusted the unfamiliar dress, diet, and habits of the Chinese; and they disliked all these things more because the Chinese were a yellow-skinned people. Under the leadership of a newly arrived Irish immigrant, Dennis Kearney, white laborers organized a workingman's party with the slogan "The Chinese must go."

Anti-Chinese Agitation in San Francisco: A Meeting of the Workingman's Party on the Sand Lots
Racism in postwar America took many forms. In California its strongest manifestation was in the hostility toward the Chinese immigrants stirred up by Dennis Kearney's workingman's party.

The depression that gripped the nation in 1873* gave impetus to the anti-Chinese movement. Day after day thousands of the unemployed gathered in the San Francisco sandlots to hear Kearney's slashing attacks on the Chinese and on the wealthy corporations that employed them. In the summer of 1877, San Francisco hoodlums, inspired by Kearney, burned twenty-five Chinese laundries and destroyed dozens of Chinese homes. The movement had enough political strength to force both major parties in California to adopt anti-Chinese platforms, and California congressmen succeeded in persuading their colleagues to pass a bill limiting the number of Chinese who could be brought into the United States each year. Because the measure clearly conflicted with treaty arrangements with China, President Rutherford B. Hayes vetoed it, but he had his secretary of state initiate negotiations leading to a new treaty that permitted the restriction of immigration. Congress, in 1882, passed the Chinese Exclusion Act, which suspended all Chinese immigration for ten years and forbade the naturalization of Chinese already in the country.

---

*For the Panic of 1873, see chapter 21, p. 55.

Northern Views of the Black Race If white Americans became so agitated over a small number of Chinese, who were unquestionably hardworking and thrifty and who belonged to one of the most ancient of civilizations, it is easy to see how whites could consider blacks an even greater danger. There were more than 3 million blacks in the United States, most of them recently emancipated from slavery. The exploits of black soldiers during the war—their very discipline and courage—proved that blacks could be formidable opponents. More than ever before, blacks seemed distinctive, alien, and menacing.

Most American intellectuals of the Civil War generation accepted black inferiority unquestioningly. Although a few reformers like Charles Sumner vigorously attacked this notion, a majority of philanthropic Northerners accepted the judgment of the distinguished Harvard scientist Louis Agassiz concerning blacks. He held that while whites during antiquity were developing high civilizations, "the negro race groped in barbarism and never originated a regular organization among themselves." Many adopted Agassiz's belief that blacks, once free, would inevitably die out in the United States. Others reached the same conclusion by studying Charles Darwin's recently published *Origin of Species* (1859), and they accepted the argument put forward by Darwin's admirers that in the inevitable struggle for survival "higher civilized races" must inevitably eliminate "an endless number of lower races." Consequently, the influential and tenderhearted Congregational minister Horace Bushnell could prophesy the approaching end of the black race in the United States with something approaching smugness. "Since we must all die," he asked rhetorically, "why should it grieve us, that a stock thousands of years behind, in the scale of culture, should die with few and still fewer children to succeed, till finally the whole succession remains in the more cultivated race?"

When even the leaders of Northern society held such views, it is hardly surprising that most whites in the region were openly antiblack. In state after state whites fiercely resisted efforts to extend the political and civil rights of blacks, partly because they feared that any improvement in the condition of blacks in the North would lead to a huge influx of blacks from the South. At the end of the Civil War only Maine, New Hampshire, Vermont, Massachusetts, and Rhode Island allowed blacks to have full voting rights; in New York only blacks who met certain property-holding qualifications could have the ballot. During the next three years in referenda held in Connecticut, Wisconsin, Kansas, Ohio, Michigan, and Missouri, constitutional amendments authorizing black suffrage were defeated, and in New York voters rejected a proposal to eliminate the property-holding qualifications for black voters. Only in Iowa, a state where there were very few blacks, did a black suffrage amendment carry in 1868, and that same year Minnesota adopted an ambiguously worded amendment. Thus at the end of the 1860s, most Northern states refused to give black men the ballot.

In words as well as in votes, the majority of Northerners made their deeply racist feelings evident. The Democratic press constantly cultivated the racial fears of its readers and regularly portrayed the Republicans as planning a "new era of miscegenation, amalgamation, and promiscuous intercourse between the races." From the White House, denouncing Republican attempts "to Africanize the [Southern] half of our country," President Andrew Johnson proclaimed: "In the progress of nations negroes have shown less capacity for self-government than any other race of people. . . . Whenever they have been left to their own devices they have shown an instant tendency to relapse into barbarism." Even Northern Republicans opposed to Johnson shared many of his racist views. Radical Senator Timothy O. Howe of Wisconsin declared that he regarded "the freedmen, in the main . . . as so much animal life," and Senator Benjamin F. Wade of Ohio, whom the Radical Republicans would have elevated to the presidency had they removed Johnson, had both a genuine devotion to the principle of equal rights and an incurable dislike of blacks. Representative George W. Julian of Indiana, one of the few Northern congressmen who had no racial prejudice, bluntly told his colleagues in 1866: "The real trouble is that *we hate the negro.* It is not his ignorance that offends us, but his color. . . . Of this fact I entertain no doubt whatsoever."

Both personal preferences and the wishes of their constituents inhibited Northern Republicans from supporting measures that might have altered race relations. When Sumner sought to remove from the books federal laws that recognized slavery or to prohibit racial discrimination on public transportation in the District of Columbia, his colleagues replied: "God has made the negro inferior, and . . . laws cannot make him equal." Such congressmen were hardly in a position to scold the South for racial discrimination or to insist on drastic social change in that region.

Southern Views of the Black Race

If racism limited the innovation that northerners were willing to propose during the Reconstruction period, it even more drastically reduced the amount of change that white southerners were prepared to accept. Racial bigotry runs through both the private correspondence and the public pronouncements of Southern whites during the postwar era. "Equality does not exist between blacks and whites," announced Alexander H. Stephens. "The one race is by nature inferior in many respects, physically and mentally, to the other. This should be received as a fixed invincible fact in all dealings with the subject." A North Carolina diarist agreed: "The Anglo-Saxon and the African can never be equal . . . one or the other must fall." Or, as the Democratic party of Louisiana resolved in its 1865 platform: "We hold this to be a Government of white people, made and to be perpetuated for the exclusive benefit of the white race; and . . . that people of African descent cannot be considered as citizens of the United States, and that there can, in no event, nor under any circumstances, be any equality between the white and other races." The Black Codes were the legal embodiment of these attitudes.

These racist views shaped the attitudes of most Southern whites toward the whole process of Reconstruction. White Southerners approved of President

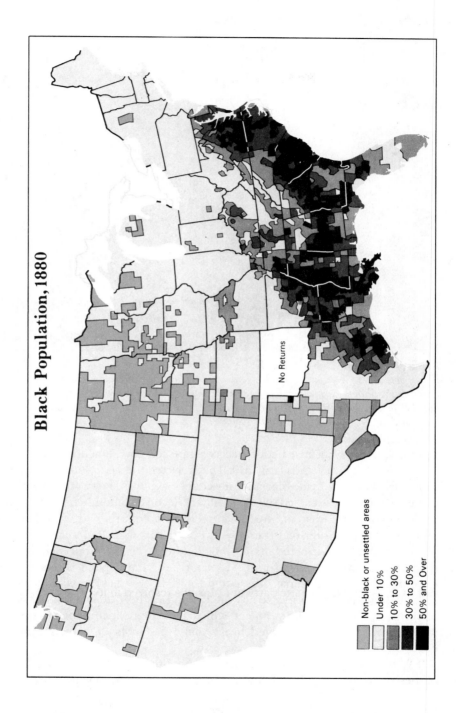

Black Population, 1880

No Returns

Non-black or unsettled areas
Under 10%
10% to 30%
30% to 50%
50% and Over

Blacks in the South Carolina Legislature
Blacks voted and were elected to office under the Radical Reconstruction program. In South Carolina they briefly formed a majority in the House of Representatives. Hostile observers noted that some black members engaged in idle chatter, read the newspapers, and put their feet on their desks while the legislature was conducting business.

Johnson's plan of Reconstruction because it placed government in the Southern states entirely in the hands of whites. They rejected the Fourteenth Amendment primarily because it made blacks legally equal to whites. They watched with utter disbelief as Congress passed the 1867 Military Reconstruction Act, for they simply could not imagine that the freedmen were to vote. Stunned, they saw army officers supervise voter registration—a process that excluded many prominent whites who had participated in the Confederate government but included more than 700,000 blacks, who formed a majority of the eligible voters in South Carolina, Florida, Alabama, Mississippi, and Louisiana. Knowing that these black voters were well organized by the Union League, often with the assistance of agents of the Freedmen's Bureau, whites were more apathetic than surprised when the fall elections showed heavy majorities in favor of convening new constitutional conventions.*

With hostile and unbelieving eyes, most Southern whites observed the work of these conventions, which between November 1867 and May 1868 drafted new

---

*The Texas election was not held until February 1868. Tennessee had no election, because it had already been readmitted to the Union.

Blacks Voting
Under the congressional plan of Reconstruction, Southern states were required to give blacks suffrage. This drawing from Harper's Weekly *shows how both old and young flocked to the polls to exercise their new right. Notable is one young black who is still wearing his US Army uniform.*

constitutions for the former Confederate states. To Southern whites unaccustomed to seeing blacks in any positions of public prominence, the presence of freedmen in these conventions meant that they were black-dominated. In fact, except in the South Carolina convention, in which blacks did form a majority, only between one-fourth and one-ninth of the delegates were blacks. Whites ridiculed the black members' ignorance of parliamentary procedures, and they laughed sarcastically when they read about how the "coal black" temporary chairman of the Louisiana convention put a question by asking those who favored a motion "to rise an stan on der feet" and then directing "all you contrairy men to rise."

Racial prejudice also determined Southern whites' reactions to the constitutions produced by these conventions. Generally the whites denounced these new charters as "totally incompatible with the prosperity and liberty of the people." In reality the constitutions, often copied from Northern models, were generally improvements over the ones they replaced. Besides giving blacks the right to vote (as Congress had directed), they promised all citizens of the state equality before the law. They reformed financial and revenue systems, reorganized the judiciary, improved the organization of local government, and, most important of all, instituted a state-supported system of public education, hitherto notably lacking in most Southern states.

The Reconstruction Governments in the South

Because these constitutions guaranteed racial equality, Southern whites tried, without great success, to block their ratification. In Alabama whites boycotted the ratification election; in Mississippi they cast a majority of votes against the new constitution. In Virginia ratification was delayed because the conservative army commander of that district discovered that there was no money to hold an election, and in Texas all moves toward the creation of a new government lagged several months behind those in the eastern states. But despite all the foot dragging, new governments were set up, and in June 1868 Congress readmitted representatives and senators from Alabama, Arkansas, Florida, Georgia, Louisiana, North Carolina, and South Carolina. Two years later the Reconstruction of Virginia, Mississippi, and Texas was completed, and in early 1870 these states were also readmitted. Meanwhile Georgia experienced one further reorganization after its state legislature attempted to exclude blacks who had been elected to it. But by 1871, when the Georgia senators and representatives again took their seats in Congress, all the states of the former Confederacy had undergone Reconstruction and had been readmitted to the Union.

Most Southern whites were bitterly hostile to this reorganization of their state governments. The name "Black Reconstruction," as they called the ensuing period of Republican domination in the South, reveals the racial bias behind their opposition. In fact, these Southern state governments were not dominated by blacks, and blacks held a smaller proportion of offices than their percentage of the population. Blacks dominated the state legislature only in South Carolina. No black was elected governor, although there were black lieutenant governors in South Carolina, Louisiana, and Mississippi. Only in South Carolina was there a black supreme court justice. During the entire Reconstruction period only two blacks served in the United States Senate—Hiram R. Revels and Blanche K. Bruce, both from Mississippi and both men of exceptional ability and integrity. Only fifteen blacks were elected to the House of Representatives.

Even to the most racist Southern whites, it was obvious that most of the leaders of the Republican party in the South, and a large part of the Republican following as well, were white. Racists called the Northern-born white Republicans carpetbaggers because they allegedly came South with no more worldly possessions than could be packed into a carpetbag (a small suitcase), ready to live on and exploit the conquered region. The term, with its implication of corruption, was applied indiscriminately to men of Northern birth who had lived in the South long before the war, as well as to newly arrived fortune hunters, many of them recently discharged Union army officers.

Southern-born white Republicans were called scalawags, a term that cattle drivers applied to "the mean, lousy and filthy kine [cattle] that are not fit for butchers or dogs." Again the term was used indiscriminately. Southern racists applied it to poor hill-country whites, who had long been at odds with the plantation owners in states like North Carolina and Alabama and now joined the Republican party as a way of getting back at their old enemies. But other scalawags were members of the plantation-owning, mercantile, and industrial classes of the South. Many were former Whigs who distrusted the Democrats, and they felt at home in a Republican party that favored protective tariffs, subsidies for railroads, and appropriations for rebuilding the levees along the Mississippi River. A surprising number of Southern-born white Republicans were former high-ranking officers in the Confederate army, like General P. G. T. Beauregard and General James Longstreet, who knew at first hand the extent of the damage caused by the war and were willing to accept the victors' terms promptly.

Bitterly as they attacked these white Republicans, Southern Democrats reserved their worst abuse for blacks. They saw in every measure adopted by the new state governments evidence of black incompetence, extravagance, or even barbarism. In truth, much that these state governments did supplied the Democrats with ammunition. The postwar period was one of widespread political corruption, and there was no reason to expect that newly enfranchised blacks would prove any less attracted by the profits of politics than anybody else. Petty corruption prevailed in all the Southern state governments. Louisiana legislators voted themselves an allowance for stationery—which covered purchases of hams and bottles of champagne. The South Carolina legislature ran up a bill of more than $50,000 in refurbishing the statehouse with such costly items as a $750 mirror, $480 clocks, and two hundred porcelain spittoons at $8 apiece. The same legislature voted $1,000 to the speaker of the House of Representatives to repay his losses on a horse race.

But these excesses angered Southern Democrats less than the legitimate work performed by the new state governments. Unwilling to recognize that blacks were now equal citizens, they objected to expenditures for hospitals, jails, orphanages, and asylums to care for blacks. Most of all they objected to the creation of a public school system. There was considerable hostility throughout the South to the idea of educating any children at the cost of the taxpayer, and the thought of paying taxes in order to teach black children seemed a wild and foolish extravagance. The fact that black schools were mostly conducted by Northern whites, usually women, who came south with a reforming mission, did nothing to increase popular support. Too many of the teachers stated plainly and publicly their intention to use "every endeavor to throw a ray of light here and there, among this benighted race of ruffians, rebels by nature." Adding to all these hostilities was a fear that a system of public education might someday lead to a racially integrated system of education. These apprehensions had little basis in reality, for during the entire period of Reconstruction in the whole South there were significant numbers of children in racially mixed schools only in New Orleans between 1870 and 1874.

The Ku Klux Klan Not content with criticizing Republican rule, Southern Democrats organized to put an end to it. They made a two-pronged attack. On the one hand, they sought to intimidate or to drive from the South whites who cooperated politically with the Republican regimes. On the other hand, they tried to terrorize and silence blacks, especially those active in

Ku Klux Klan Broadside
A terrorist organization, the Ku Klux Klan pictured itself as a defender not merely of white supremacy but of the nation itself against incendiary blacks.

politics. Much of this pressure was informal and occasional, but much was the work of racist organizations that sprang up all over the South during the postwar years. The most famous of these was the Ku Klux Klan, which originated in 1866 as a social club for young white men in Pulaski, Tennessee. As the Military Reconstruction Act went into effect and the possibility of black participation in Southern political life became increasingly real, racists saw new potential in this secret organization with its mysterious name and its bizarre uniforms of long flowing robes, high conical hats that made the wearers seem unnaturally tall, and white face masks.

In 1867 the Klan was reorganized under a new constitution that provided for local dens, each headed by a Grand Cyclops. The dens were linked together into provinces (counties), each under a Grand Titan, and in turn into realms (states), each under a Grand Dragon. At the head of the whole organization was the Grand Wizard—who, according to most reports, was former Confederate General Nathan Bedford Forrest. Probably this elaborate organizational structure was never completely filled out, and certainly there was an almost total lack of central control of the Klan's activities. Indeed, at some point in early 1869 the Klan was officially disbanded. But even without central direction its members, like those of the Order of the White Camellia and other racist vigilante groups, continued in their plan of disrupting the new Republican regimes in the South and terrorizing the blacks who supported these administrations.

Along with other vigilante organizations, the Klan expressed traditional Southern white racism. White Southerners were willing to accept the defeat of the Confederacy and were prepared to admit that slavery was dead. But they could not bring themselves to contemplate a society that would treat blacks and whites as equals. As a group of South Carolina whites protested to Congress in 1868: "The white people of our State will never quietly submit to negro rule.... We will keep up this contest until we have regained the heritage of political control handed down to us by honored ancestry. That is a duty we owe to the land that is ours, to the graves that it contains, and to the race of which you and we alike are members—the proud Caucasian race, whose sovereignty on earth God has ordained."

The appeal was shrewdly pitched, for the Southern racist knew how to reach his Northern counterpart. Joined together, their fears of men with darker skins helped to undercut the Reconstruction regimes in the South and to halt any congressional efforts at further innovative Reconstruction legislation.

CHRONOLOGY

1865 Lincoln assassinated; Andrew Johnson becomes president.
Johnson moves for speedy, lenient restoration of Southern states to Union.
Congress creates Joint Committee of Fifteen to supervise Reconstruction process.
Thirteenth Amendment ratified.

1866 Johnson breaks with Republican majority in Congress by vetoing Freedmen's Bureau bill and Civil Rights bill. Latter is passed over his veto.
Congress approves Fourteenth Amendment and submits it to states for ratification.
Johnson and Republicans quarrel. Republicans win fall congressional elections.
Ku Klux Klan formed.

1867 Congress passes Military Reconstruction Act over Johnson's veto. (Two supplementary acts in 1867 and a third in 1868 passed to put this measure into effect.)

Congress passes Tenure of Office Act and Command of Army Act to reduce Johnson's power.

1868 Former Confederate states hold constitutional conventions, in which freedmen are allowed to vote, and adopt new constitutions guaranteeing universal male suffrage.
Alabama, Arkansas, Florida, Georgia, Louisiana, North Carolina, and South Carolina readmitted to representation in Congress. Because of discrimination against black officeholders, Georgia representatives are expelled. (State is again admitted in 1870.)
President Johnson impeached. Escapes conviction by one vote.
Republicans nominate Ulysses S. Grant for president; Democrats select Governor Horatio Seymour of New York. Grant elected president.

1869 Congress passes Fifteenth Amendment and submits it to states for ratification.

SUGGESTED READINGS

Reconstruction: America's Unfinished Revolution (1988), by Eric Foner, is a full, eloquent account. Three shorter interpretations are John H. Franklin, *Reconstruction After the Civil War* (1961); Kenneth M. Stampp, *The Era of Reconstruction* (1965); and Rembert W. Patrick, *The Reconstruction of the Nation* (1967).

The best account of steps taken during the Civil War to reorganize the Southern states is Herman Belz, *Reconstructing the Union* (1969). William B. Hesseltine, *Lincoln's Plan of Reconstruction* (1960), argues that Lincoln had not one but many approaches to Reconstruction, all of them unsuccessful. LaWanda Cox, *Lincoln and Black Freedom* (1981), is an important study. Peyton McCrary, *Abraham Lincoln and Reconstruction* (1978), is the authoritative account of developments in Louisiana, where Lincoln's approach to Reconstruction was most fully tested.

The Presidency of Andrew Johnson (1979), by Albert Castel, is a balanced account, and Hans L. Trefousse's *Andrew Johnson* (1989) is the best biography of that president. Favorable versions of Johnson's Reconstruction program include George F. Milton, *The Age of Hate* (1930), and Howard K. Beale, *The Critical Year* (1930). The following accounts are critical: Eric L. McKitrick, *Andrew Johnson and Reconstruction* (1960); LaWanda Cox and John H. Cox, *Politics, Principle, and Prejudice* (1963); and W. R. Brock, *An American Crisis* (1963).

On constitutional changes in the postwar period, see Harold M. Hyman, *A More Perfect Union* (1973); Hyman and William M. Wiecek, *Equal Justice Under Law* (1982); Stanley I. Kutler, *Judicial Power and Reconstruction Politics* (1968); and Charles Fairman, *Reconstruction and the Union* (1971).

George R. Bentley, *A History of the Freedmen's Bureau* (1955), is a standard work, but it should be supplemented by William S. McFeely, *Yankee Stepfather: General O. O. Howard and the Freedmen* (1968). Claude F. Oubre, *Forty Acres and a Mule* (1978), discusses the abortive efforts of the bureau in land distribution.

Leon Litwack, *Been in the Storm So Long* (1979), is a masterful account of the transition from slavery to freedom. See also Peter Kolchin, *After Freedom* (1972), on Alabama; Willie Lee Rose, *Rehearsal for Reconstruction* (1964), and Joel Williamson, *After Slavery* (1965), on South Carolina; and Vernon L. Wharton, *The Negro in Mississippi* (1947).

Fred A. Shannon, *The Farmer's Last Frontier* (1945), and E. Merton Coulter, *The South During Reconstruction* (1972), give good general accounts of economic changes in the postwar South. Recently historians and economists using sophisticated quantitative methods have reexamined these changes: Stephen J. DeCanio, *Agriculture in the Postbellum South* (1974); Robert Higgs, *Competition and Coercion: Blacks in the American Economy* (1977); Roger Ransom and Richard L. Sutch, *One Kind of Freedom: The Economic Consequences of Emancipation* (1977); and Gavin Wright, *Old South, New South* (1986). On the alleged breakup of the plantation system, see Roger W. Shugg, *Origins of Class Struggle in Louisiana* (1939), and on the continuing dominance of the planter class, see Jonathan M. Wiener, *Social Origins of the New South* (1978).

On Radical Reconstruction, see Michael L. Benedict, *A Compromise of Principle* (1974); David Donald, *The Politics of Reconstruction* (1965); and Hans L. Trefousse, *The Radical Republicans* (1969). The best account of Grant's Southern policy is William Gillette, *Retreat from Reconstruction* (1980). Among the fullest biographies of Reconstruction politicians are Fawn M. Brodie, *Thaddeus Stevens* (1959); David Donald, *Charles Sumner and the Rights of Man* (1970); William S. McFeely, *Grant* (1981); and Benjamin P. Thomas and Harold M. Hyman, *Stanton* (1962).

David M. DeWitt, *Impeachment and Trial of Andrew Johnson* (1903), remains the standard account, but it should be supplemented with Michael L. Benedict's book of the same name (1973) and with Hans L. Trefousse, *Impeachment of a President* (1975).

On American racial attitudes, George M. Fredrickson, *The Black Image in the White Mind* (1971), is excellent. On Northern racism, see V. Jacque Voegeli, *Free But Not Equal* (1967), and Forrest G. Wood, *Black Scare* (1967).

Dan T. Carter, *When the War Was Over* (1985), ably traces the failure of presidential reconstruction in the South. For a favorable view of the Reconstruction governments in the South, see W.E.B. DuBois, *Black Reconstruction* (1935). Some excellent accounts of Reconstruction in individual states are Francis B. Simkins and Robert H. Woody, *South Carolina During Reconstruction* (1932); Jerrell H. Shofner, *Nor Is It Over Yet: Florida in the Era of Reconstruction* (1974); James W. Garner, *Reconstruction in Mississippi* (1901); and Joe G. Taylor, *Louisiana Reconstructed* (1974).

On the education of blacks after the war, see Henry A. Bullock, *A History of Negro Education in the South* (1967); William P. Vaughn, *Schools for All* (1974); and Roger A. Fischer, *The Segregation Struggle in Louisiana* (1974). Two useful accounts of the educational work of the Freedmen's Bureau are Ronald E. Butchart, *Northern Schools, Southern Blacks, and Reconstruction* (1980), and Robert C. Morris, *Reading, 'Riting, and Reconstruction* (1981).

Southern white resistance to the Reconstruction process is the theme of Michael Perman, *Reunion Without Compromise* (1973). Allen W. Trelease, *White Terror* (1971), is a harrowing recital of white vigilantism. *The Road to Redemption* (1984), by Michael Perman, traces southern politics from 1869 to 1879.

21

Compromises

1869–1877

*A*N EXCLUSIVE focus on the Southern states during the postwar years obscures the fact that Reconstruction was a national, not just a sectional, process. In the North as well as the South the impulses unleashed by the Civil War portended revolutionary consequences. With nationalism at high tide, many Northerners favored an expansionist foreign policy. Just as some Radical Republicans wished to overturn the entire Southern social system, so other postwar leaders hoped to change the North. Some reformers wanted to expand the role of the federal government in the economy. Civil service reformers sought the end of the spoils system and the professionalization of governmental bureaucracy. Other advocates of change wanted to improve the lot of labor, of women, and of native Americans. But many—perhaps most—Northerners objected to all these changes. To them the reforms proposed for their section were almost as objectionable as Radical Reconstruction was to most white Southerners.

This tension between those who opposed change and those who favored it became a central theme of American history in the decades following the Civil War. When the advocates of change were politically powerful and vigorously led, supporters of the status quo found it necessary to accept compromises. Thus by the 1880s a series of loose, informal, and frequently tacit understandings had evolved, between Democrats and Republicans, between supporters and opponents of expansion, between friends and enemies of the high tariff and "sound" currency. But where the innovators were politically inexperienced, like the leaders of the women's movement in the 1860s, or poorly organized, like the members of the early national labor unions, the powerful conservative majority found it possible to ignore or overrule their wishes.

Compromises Between Equal Forces

Nationalism   In the years after the Civil War one major compromise reconciled divergent views as to the nature and direction of America as a nation. The war strongly encouraged nationalist sentiments among Northerners. The primary Northern war aim was not to guarantee equal rights to all men nor even to end slavery; it was to preserve the Union. By that often repeated phrase, men and women of the war years meant something more than merely maintaining the country as a territorial unit. The idea of union implied an almost mystical sense of the wholeness of the American people. Americans viewed themselves as a chosen people, selected to conduct an experiment in self-government, to be a test case of the viability of democratic institutions. As Lincoln declared, the United States was nothing less than "the last, best hope of earth."

That faith in the special destiny of the United States gave courage and hope to Northerners during the darkest hours of the war. Defeats on the battlefield, properly understood, seemed to them the fire that burned away the impurities in American life. As the Reverend Marvin R. Vincent of Troy, New York, announced: "God has been striking, and trying to make us strike at elements unfavorable to the growth of a pure democracy; and . . . he is at work, preparing in this broad land a fit stage for a last act of the mighty drama, the consummation of human civilization." A similar inspiration moved Julia Ward Howe to draw on the imagery of the Book of Revelation in composing the most powerful and popular battle hymn ever written:

> *Mine eyes have seen the glory of the coming of the Lord:*
> *He is trampling out the vintage where the grapes of wrath are stored;*
> *He hath loosed the fateful lightning of His terrible swift sword:*
> *His truth is marching on.*

Northerners believed that the Union would emerge from the war more powerful, more firmly united, than ever before. They expected that the United States would no longer be a confederation, or union of states, but rather a nation in the fullest sense. A small shift in grammar tells the whole story. Before the Civil War many politicians and writers referred to the United States in the plural—"the United States *are*"—but after 1865 only a pedant or the most unreconstructed Southerner would have dreamed of saying anything but "the United States *is.*"

The word *nation* now came easily to American lips. Unlike his predecessors, who generally avoided the term, Lincoln regularly referred to the United States as a nation. For example, he used the word no fewer than five times in his brief Gettysburg Address, most eloquently in the concluding pledge: " . . . that this nation, under God, shall have a new birth of freedom." In 1865, when Republicans agreed to establish a weekly journal that would reflect their views, they called it, as a matter of course, *The Nation,* and it became, as it has remained, one of the most influential periodicals in the country. When Charles Sumner, in 1867, took to the lecture circuit to supplement his senatorial salary, he chose for his topic, "Are We a Nation?" The answer, he believed, was obvious. Americans were "one people, throbbing with a common life, occupying a common territory, rejoicing in a common history, sharing in common trials." Never again should any "local claim of self-government" be permitted "for a moment [to] interfere with the supremacy of the Nation." He concluded: "Such centralization is the highest civilization, for it approaches the nearest to the heavenly example."

Political theorists as well as public men in the postwar generation exalted American nationalism. In 1865 Orestes Brownson, once a spokesman for Jacksonian ideals, published the first book-length contribution to the bibliography of American nationalism, *The American Republic: Its Constitution, Tendencies, and Destiny.* "Nations are only individuals on a larger scale," Brownson argued. His book was designed to resolve the identity crisis of the Civil War by persuading the American nation to "reflect on its own constitution, its own separate existence, individuality, tendencies, and end." Even more soaring were the claims of the Reverend Elisha Mulford's *The Nation: The Foundations of Civil Order and Political Life in the United States* (1870). Mulford's argument derived from the views of the early-nineteenth-century German philosopher Hegel: the nation was a mystic body, endowed with a spirit and a majesty of its own. "The Nation," he concluded, "is a work of God in history. . . . Its vocation is from God, and its obligation is only to God."

It would be easy to conclude from such statements that Americans of the post–Civil War generation, rejoicing in the newly restored unity of their country, were swept into an ultranationalistic frenzy comparable to that of the Germans, who almost simultaneously achieved national unity under Bismarck, or of the Italians, who were being reunited under Cavour. But a moment's reflection shows the weakness of these historical parallels. After all, the federal structure of the American government survived the Civil War. The government in Washington continued to coexist with the governments of the several states. If there was no further talk of secession, there was frequent invocation of states' rights, and regionalism and localism remained strong forces in American life.

American political theorists sought a formula to express the proper relationship between the nation and its constituent sections and groups. The most influential of these attempts was that of Professor Francis Lieber of Columbia University, whose book *On Civil Liberty and Self-Government,* published before the war, became a bible for statesmen of the postwar era. Lieber understood the power of nationalistic feeling; as a youth in Prussia he had wept when the armies of Napoleon overran his native land, and he had fought against the French at Waterloo. But he also was acquainted with the dangers of excessive nationalism, for the Prussian government had arrested him for harboring dangerous, liberal ideas and he had been obliged to flee to the United States. In this country he realized that nationalism was essential for "the diffusion of the same life-blood through a system of arteries, throughout a body politic." But he sought to check excessive centralization through organically related institutions—the family, the churches, the scientific community, the business community, and the like—which could provide "the negation of absolutism" by supporting "a union of harmonizing systems of laws instinct with self-government." Thus Lieber's theory simultaneously exalted American nationalism and encouraged autonomy for local and particularistic interests. It upheld the Union but sought to prevent its powers from becoming despotic. Lieber's political theory was, in short, typical of the compromises of the postwar period. His formulation allowed Americans to eat their cake and have it too.

American Foreign Policy   American diplomacy during the post–Civil War generation fell into a pattern that Lieber heartily approved. On the one hand, it was vigorously nationalistic, even at times bellicose; on the other, it drew back from conflict with foreign powers, and it refrained from pursuing goals strongly opposed by influential interest groups.

In the decade after the Civil War hardly a year passed without some significant American diplomatic move, either to assert the dominance of the United States in the Western Hemisphere or to annex new territory. These foreign policy

"The Stride of a Century"
Buoyed with nationalist sentiment, the United States celebrated at the Centennial Exposition at Philadelphia of 1876. This Currier and Ives print shows a boastful Uncle Sam bestriding the Western Hemisphere.

initiatives received considerable popular support. After Appomattox there was a general feeling that the United States, with a million seasoned veterans under arms, was in a position to humiliate the French emperor Napoleon III, to have a showdown with Great Britain, and to pick up any adjacent territory that it pleased. The expansionist spirit of Manifest Destiny, which had flourished in the 1840s but had languished during the war, sprang to life again. Even those who feared expansionism expected its triumph. The more optimistic rejoiced in the prospect. Advocating the annexation of both Haiti and the Dominican Republic, and hoping for the future acquisition of the Kingdom of Hawaii, President Johnson concluded in his 1868 annual message to Congress: "The conviction is rapidly gaining ground in the American mind that with the increased facilities for intercommunication between all portions of the earth the principles of free government, as embraced in our Constitution, if faithfully maintained and carried out, would prove of sufficient strength and breadth to comprehend within their sphere and influence the civilized nations of the world."

Even if the accomplishments of American foreign policy did not live up to Johnson's predictions, they were, nevertheless, considerable. From the point of view of national security, the most important feat was Seward's success in getting French troops out of Mexico. Introduced into Mexico during the Civil War, ostensibly to compel the bankrupt Mexican government of President Benito Juarez to pay its debts, French troops in 1864 provided the support for installing Archduke Maximilian of Austria as emperor of Mexico. While the war was going on, Seward could do no more than protest against this violation of the Monroe Doctrine's principle that European powers must not extend their "system" to the New World. But he adopted a more vigorous tone after Appomattox. Yet, knowing that the French emperor was a proud and volatile man, Seward refrained from direct threats and allowed Napoleon to discover for himself how expensive, unpopular, and unsuccessful his Mexican adventure was proving. By 1867 Napoleon finally decided to cut off further financial support for Maximilian's shaky regime and, under steady American pressure, withdrew his troops. Captured by Juarez's forces, Maximilian was shot by a firing squad on June 19, 1867.

A second diplomatic achievement of the Reconstruction years was the settlement of the *Alabama* claims—claims of American shippers against the British government for damages that British-built Confederate raiders had inflicted during the war. Immediately after the war it probably would have been possible to clear up this controversy speedily and inexpensively, had not the British government haughtily denied that it had violated international law by permitting Confederate raiders to be built in its shipyards. American grievances deepened with delay. Sumner, the powerful chairman of the Senate Committee on Foreign Relations, began to argue that the British not only owed repayment for actual damages done by the *Alabama* and other vessels; they also were responsible, he said, for prolonging the war—for the "immense and infinite" cost of the entire last two years of the conflict. Americans were further embittered by the failure of Reverdy Johnson, Seward's special envoy to Great Britain, to secure an apology or an expression of regret from the stubborn British government. A settlement was worked out only when Grant put Hamilton Fish in charge of the American State Department and a new cabinet came to power in Great Britain.

In the Treaty of Washington of 1871, Great Britain admitted negligence in permitting the Confederate cruisers to escape and expressed regret for the damages they had caused; and the United States quietly abandoned the extravagant claims put forward by Sumner and agreed that the amount of damages should be assessed by an arbitration commission representing five nations. Ultimately, damages to American shipping were estimated at $15.5 million, and the British government paid this amount. However, the precedent of settling international disputes by arbitration was more important than any monetary settlement, and the Treaty of Washington paved the way for an improvement in relations between the two greatest English-speaking nations. Not until the two world wars of the twentieth century would the full consequences of this development emerge.

Apart from the almost unnoticed American occupation of the Midway Islands in August 1867, the United States' sole territorial acquisition during the Reconstruction era was the purchase of Alaska. Seward's 1867 treaty to buy Russian America for $7.2 million brought under the American flag new territory one-fifth as large as the entire continental United States, a land of obvious strategic importance for the future of the United States in the Pacific. Nevertheless there was little popular enthusiasm for the purchase. Newspapers called Alaska "a national icehouse" consisting of nothing but "walrus-covered icebergs." Congressmen were equally unenthusiastic. Yet after much grumbling the Senate finally ratified the treaty and the House reluctantly appropriated the money for the purchase. Seward's success in part reflected his ability to convince senators that Alaska had vast hidden natural resources. It was also in part the result of the judicious payment of money to American congressmen by the Russian minister in Washington. The most important factor, however, was the general feeling that rejecting the treaty would alienate Tsar Alexander II, who alone of the leading European rulers had been sympathetic to the Union cause during the Civil War.*

Nothing came of other postwar plans for expansion. Each of them ran into snags that made American diplomats draw back. For example, the desire of many United States politicians, including Grant, Fish, and Sumner, to annex Canada had to be abandoned when it became clear that the British would not withdraw without a fight. Grant's plan to acquire the Dominican Republic aroused the

---

*The tsar's pro-Union policy resulted in part from unrest in the Russian-ruled Polish territories, which revolted in 1863 and were reconquered by military force. Like the Union, Russia feared European intervention in what both regarded as internal matters. After the Civil War, the tsar concluded that Alaska was vulnerable to seizure by the British in the event of a future conflict and that it would be better to sell the territory to the United States.

opposition of Sumner, who considered himself the blacks' senatorial voice and wanted the island to become not an American possession, but the center of "a free confederacy [of the West Indies], in which the black race should predominate." Seward's proposal for the purchase of the Danish West Indies (now the Virgin Islands) was pigeonholed by the Senate when those unfortunate islands were visited by a hurricane, a tidal wave, and a series of earthquake shocks.

It would, however, be a mistake to put too much stress on these special factors that stopped American expansionism. Broader forces were also at work. The American people were exhausted by four years of fighting, and they were not prepared to support a vigorously nationalistic foreign policy if it threatened another war. Northern businessmen felt that it was more important to reduce taxes and to return to a sound monetary policy than to engage in foreign adventures. The difficulties of racial adjustment in the South made increasing numbers of politicians hesitate before agreeing to annex additional dark-skinned populations. During Johnson's administration many Republicans opposed all Seward's expansion plans because they might bring credit to the unpopular president. During Grant's tenure alienated Republicans had similar motives for blocking the president's diplomatic schemes; by 1872, these dissidents had joined the Liberal Republican party and were opposing Grant's reelection. Most important of all, the American people were generally aware that they had plenty of room for expansion closer to home, in the lands still occupied by the Indians.

American foreign policy during the Reconstruction generation, then, was the result of compromise. On issues that clearly touched the national security, such as the presence of French troops in Mexico, there was a consensus sufficiently strong to allow the national government to act. But where there was no clear, overriding national interest, objections to expansion prevailed. Although presidents and secretaries of state often fumed, local, sectional, racial, and class objections blocked expansion.

Politics of the Gilded Age   A similar deadlock marked the politics of the Gilded Age—so called after the novel of that title by Mark Twain and Charles Dudley Warner, which depicted the boom-and-bust mentality of businessmen of the post–Civil War era and the willingness of politicians to serve the needs of these speculators. The two major parties were almost equally balanced during the entire era. Most of the presidents of the period barely squeaked into office. Grant's success in 1868 was a tribute to a great military leader, not an endorsement of the Republican party that nominated him. Even so, he received only 53 percent of the popular vote. Grant's reelection by a huge popular margin in 1872 was due chiefly to his opponents' willingness to commit political suicide. Dissatisfied members of Grant's own party joined the Liberal Republican movement, which agitated for lower tariffs and for reconciliation with the South—and then proceeded to nominate for president the erratic *New York Tribune* editor Horace Greeley, famed as a protectionist and hated for his prewar denunciation of slaveholders. Holding its nose, the Democratic party also endorsed Greeley, but thousands of Democrats and Liberal Republicans stayed away from the polls. In 1876 Republican Rutherford B. Hayes received a minority of the popular vote and was inaugurated only after a prolonged controversy.

Even had these presidents been elected by overwhelming majorities, they would have been frustrated in attempting to implement any programs because their political opponents usually controlled Congress. To be sure, Grant started with safely Republican majorities in both houses of Congress, but Carl Schurz, Charles Sumner, and other leading Republicans soon defected to the Liberal Republican movement, voted with the Democrats, and blocked the administration's favorite measures. In the congressional elections of 1874 the Democrats for the first time since the Civil War won a majority in the House of Representatives which, except for two years, they continued to control until 1889. Given these conditions, it is easy to understand that the few measures enacted by the politicians of the Gilded Age had to be compromises.

Economic Issues of the Gilded Age
For the most part the national government had little to do with the basic economic problems of the Gilded Age. In dealing with economic issues, just as in dealing with those relating to the South and the freedmen, Americans were constrained by the doctrines of constitutionalism—by the belief that the government had only the fixed powers set forth in the Constitution. In the area of economics, only the tariff and the currency seemed to be clearly under the control of the national government. Therefore during the postwar years disagreements over economic issues were usually voiced in connection with these two endlessly troublesome, highly technical questions, so complex that only a handful of congressmen fully understood them.

The Tariff Problem
Debates on the tariff involved basic questions as to whether the industrial sector of the economy should be favored at the expense of the exporting agricultural sector and whether the factories of the Northeast should benefit at the expense of the farmers of the South and West. But these questions did not surface clearly, and during the debates in Congress the issue was rarely put in terms of free trade versus protection. Almost everybody during the Gilded Age recognized that some tariff barrier was needed to protect American industries from cheap foreign imports. The debates in Congress revolved around which industries and how much protection.

By 1865 most informed Americans recognized the need to modify the high tariffs that had been enacted during the Civil War to protect heavily taxed American industry from untaxed foreign competition. A bill intended to make a reasonable adjustment was drafted by the New England economist David A. Wells, who was appointed Special Commissioner of the Revenue in 1866. Wells's bill proposed to reduce duties on imported materials such as scrap iron, coal, and lumber; eliminated arbitrary and unnecessary duties on items like chemicals and spices; and made slight reductions in duties on most manufactured articles. Most lawmakers admitted the theoretical excellence of Wells's bill—and most opposed the provisions that lessened or removed protection from their own constituents' businesses. Consequently, Congress rejected Wells's bill, and during the next fifteen years there was no general revision of the tariff legislation.

The absence of general tariff acts did not mean that discussion of tariff rates had ended. To the contrary, throughout the period there was constant pulling and hauling between economic interests that stood to gain or lose from changes in duties on specific imported items. For example, during the war Boston and Baltimore had developed a considerable copper industry that smelted and refined Chilean ore, which paid a very low tariff duty. But in the late 1860s the great copper mines around Lake Superior began to be worked on a large scale, and their owners asked Congress to protect their product by raising duties on imported ore. After sharp disagreement, in which President Johnson supported the refiners and most congressional Republicans sided with the ore producers, the tariff on copper ore was increased in 1869 to a point at which most of the eastern smelting firms had to go out of business.

Other tariff changes were the consequence of combined efforts by the producers and processors of raw materials. An 1867 act revising the duties on raw wool and on woolen cloth was drafted at a convention of wool producers and manufacturers at Syracuse, and it was lobbied through Congress by the tireless and effective secretary of the Wool Manufacturers' Association, John L. Hayes.

Some of the minor adjustments made in the tariff during the postwar years reflected political pressures. In a general way Republicans, with some notable exceptions, tended to favor high protective tariffs, and Democrats, especially those in the South who needed foreign markets for their cotton, wanted to reduce duties. But the issue was rarely clear-cut, for Democrats in manufacturing states like Pennsylvania were high-tariff men. Moreover, both parties tinkered with the tariff issue at election time. In 1872, for instance, the Republican party faced a split. Many tariff reformers in the Liberal Republican movement were preparing to join the Democrats. Attempting to check the bolt, the Republican-dominated Congress rushed through a bill reducing all duties by 10 percent.

The complex history of tariff legislation during the Gilded Age demonstrates the continuing strength of the highly nationalistic impulse toward protectionism that had manifested itself during the war. At the same time it shows that powerful regional and economic interests adversely affected by high duties were able to secure relief without overturning the general protective framework.

Debates over Currency

The controversies over currency during the post–Civil War generation were more complex, but in general they illustrate the same tension between the needs of a national economy and the desires of local and special economic interests.

Unless a historian is prepared to write a book about these monetary issues, perhaps he ought to confine his account to two sentences: During the generation after the Civil War there was constant controversy between those who wished to continue, or even to expand, the inflated wartime money supply and those who wanted to contract the currency. Most debtors favored inflation because it would allow them to pay debts in money that was less valuable than when they had borrowed it; and creditors favored contraction, so that the money they received in payment of debts would be more valuable than it had been when they lent it.

But these two sentences, accurate enough in a general way, fail to convey the full dimensions of the controversy. They make the whole issue seem a purely economic question of profit and loss. In fact, for many people the resumption of specie payment—that is, the redemption in gold, at face value, of the paper money that had been issued by the United States government—involved the sanctity of contracts, the reliability of the government's pledges, and the rights of private property. Indeed, the return to the gold standard seemed to have an almost religious significance. Probably most economists of the period shared the conviction of Hugh McCulloch, Johnson's secretary of the treasury, that "gold and silver are the only true measures of value.... I have myself no more doubt that these metals were prepared by the Almighty for this very purpose, than I have that iron and coal were prepared for the purposes for which they are being used." On the other hand, the advocates of so-called soft, or paper, money argued that it was downright un-American to drive greenbacks out of circulation and return to the gold standard. "Why," asked the promoter Jay Cooke, "should this Grand and Glorious Country be stunted and dwarfed—its activities chilled and its very life blood curdled—by these miserable 'hard coin' theories, the musty theories of a bygone age?"

That two-sentence summary also ignores the fact that the currency controversy involved economic interests falling into categories more sophisticated than debtors and creditors. Merchants in foreign trade were ardent supporters of resumption because fluctuations in the gold value of United States paper money made the business of these importers and exporters a game of chance. On the other hand, many American manufacturers, especially iron makers, staunchly resisted resumption because they needed an inflated currency to keep their national markets expanding.

Finally, that two-sentence summary does not indicate that attitudes toward these monetary policies changed over time. Throughout the postwar period farmers were mostly debtors, but they were primarily concerned with such issues as railroad regulation and until 1870 showed little interest in the currency. Creditor interests of the Northeast were indeed mostly supporters of resumption, but when a depression began in 1873 they unsuccessfully urged President Grant to sign the so-called Inflation Bill of 1874, which would have slightly increased the amount of paper money in circulation. In other words, they preferred mild inflation to economic collapse. Moreover, by the late 1870s, inflationists were no longer calling for additional greenbacks; instead they joined forces with western mining interests to demand that the government expand the currency by coining silver dollars. When they discovered that, partly by oversight and partly by plan, the Coinage Act of 1873 had discontinued the minting of silver, they were outraged. Protesting the "Crime of '73," they demanded a return to bimetallism (both gold and silver being accepted in lawful payment of all debts) and the free and unlimited coinage of silver dollars.

With so many opposing forces at work, it is scarcely surprising that the history of currency policy and financial legislation in the postwar years is one of sudden fits and starts. Right after the war, Secretary McCulloch assumed that everybody wanted to return to specie payments promptly, and, in order to raise the value of the paper currency, he quietly held back greenbacks paid into the United States treasury for taxes and for public lands. His mild contraction of the currency restricted business expansion, and Congress forced him to stop. Subsequently, the greenbacks that had been taken out of circulation were reissued, and they remained in circulation for the next decade in the total amount of $382 million.

Indirectly the currency became an issue in the presidential election of 1868. During the previous year, what became known as the Ohio Idea gained popularity in the Middle West. Critics of hard money objected to the government's practice of paying interest on the national debt in gold—which was, of course, much more valuable than greenbacks. The critics argued that since the bonds had been purchased with greenbacks, it would be entirely legal and proper to pay their interest in the same depreciated currency. In this way the crushing burden of the national debt on the taxpayer would be reduced. This argument was so attractive that the Democratic national convention incorporated a version of the Ohio Idea in its 1868 platform. However, the party negated the move by nominating Governor Horatio Seymour of New York, an earnest hard-money man, for president. The Republican national convention sternly rejected the Ohio Idea— against the wishes of many western delegates—and nominated Grant with a pledge to reject "all forms of repudiation as a national crime."

Despite this commitment, Grant's administration witnessed the completion of a series of compromises on currency. The new president announced that he favored a return to the gold standard; but at the same time he warned: "Immediate resumption, if practicable, would not be desirable. It would compel the debtor class to pay, beyond their contracts, the premium on gold... and would bring bankruptcy and ruin to thousands." But lest anyone think that this last statement meant that he desired further issues of paper money, Grant vetoed the Inflation Bill of 1874, against the wishes of many of his advisers.

It was within this broad policy of affirmation checked by negation that John Sherman, the Senate expert on finance, persuaded Congress in 1875 to pass the Resumption Act. This law announced the United States government's intention to redeem its paper money at face value in gold on or after January 1, 1879. On the surface this legislation was a victory for hard-money interests, but in fact it was a brilliant compromise. It did commit the United States to resumption—but only after four years' delay. Sherman sweetened this pill for the silver-mining interests by providing that "as rapidly as practicable" silver coins would be minted to replace the "fractional currency"—notes of postage-stamp size in 3-, 5-, 10-, 15-,

25-, and 50-cent denominations—issued during the war. To placate the green-back interests in the South and West, Sherman's measure made it easier to incorporate national banks in those regions and thus increased their supply of treasury notes.

Although efforts were made after 1875 to repeal the Resumption Act, it was such a carefully constructed compromise that all these attempts failed. Sherman, who became secretary of the treasury in President Hayes's cabinet, skillfully managed the transition in 1879 so that resumption took place without fanfare and without economic disturbance. The whole controversy over currency during the Gilded Age thus illustrates the kind of compromises that Americans of this generation hammered out. The national policy of resumption, desired by most businessmen and needed if the United States was to play a part in world trade, was sustained; but local business interests were able to delay and modify imple-mentation of the policy so that it did not impose too sudden or heavy a burden on groups adversely affected by hard money.

Scandals and Corruption   During the Gilded Age neither the Democrats nor the Republicans were able to take a decisive stand, whether on issues relating to the South or those connected with the national economy, and the principal means of cementing party loyalty became patronage and favoritism. As a result the Gilded Age was a period of low political morality in the United States, and many public officials were stained by charges of fraud, bribery, and subservience to special interests. During the 1870s reformers and crusading newspaper editors started to expose shocking scandals. The earliest revelations concerned New York City, which had fallen under the control of "Boss" William Marcy Tweed, who proceeded joyfully to loot the taxpayers. Tweed's ring began construction of a new county courthouse, on which $11 million was spent. Nearly $3 million went to a man named Garvey for plastering; after the amount of his fees leaked out, he became known as the "Prince of Plasterers." Tweed approved the purchase of so many chairs, at $5 each, that if placed in a line they would have extended seventeen miles. In 1871, when the *New York Times* began to expose the ring's padded bills, faked leases, false vouchers, and other frauds, the entire nation's attention was attracted, and when *Harper's Weekly* started carrying Thomas Nast's devastating caricatures of the Boss, Tweed's face became more familiar to Americans than that of any other man except Grant.

Soon revelations about the national government began to make equally fascinating reading. Shortly before the 1872 election, the *New York Sun,* a Democratic paper, exposed the workings of the Crédit Mobilier, the construction company that the Union Pacific Railroad Company paid to build its transconti-nental route. Investigation proved that members of the Crédit Mobilier were also members of the board of directors of the Union Pacific, who were thus paying themselves huge profits. Even more damaging was the revelation that, in order to prevent public inquiry, the Crédit Mobilier offered stock to Vice-President

Schuyler Colfax, Representative (and future President) James A. Garfield, and other prominent politicians. They were allowed to "purchase" the stock on credit, the down payment being "earned" by the high dividends that the stock began to pay.

Although Republicans found it advisable to drop Colfax from their ticket in 1872, scandal did not seriously touch the Grant administration until after the election. Then, in short order, stories of fraud began to appear about practically every branch of the executive offices. In the Treasury Department unscrupulous customhouse officers, especially in New York, preyed on importers. Merchants who failed to pay off the thieves had their shipments delayed; their imported goods subjected to minute, time-consuming inspection; and their crates and boxes that were not immediately removed from the docks stored at exorbitant rates. Corruption was rampant in the Navy Department, where political favoritism dictated everything from the employment of workers in the shipyards to the contracts for the construction of new vessels. Secretary of War William W. Belknap was proved to have accepted bribes from Indian traders, who had the exclusive and well-paying franchise to sell goods to Indians and soldiers at frontier posts. He resigned to avoid impeachment.

Of all these scandals, the closest to the White House was the Whiskey Ring. In order to avoid heavy excise taxes, first levied during the war, whiskey distillers, especially those at St. Louis, had for years been conspiring with officials of the Internal Revenue Service. During Grant's administration the dealers secured the cooperation of none other than Orville E. Babcock, the president's private secretary, who warned the swindlers whenever an inspection team was sent out from Washington. In return for his assistance, Babcock received such favors as a $2,400 diamond shirt stud—which he found defective and asked to have replaced with another, more expensive one—and from time to time the services of a prostitute. When Grant first learned of the scandal, he urged, "Let no guilty man escape." But as it became clear that his close friends and his personal staff were involved, he did everything he could to block further investigation. When Babcock went on trial, the president of the United States offered a deposition expressing "great confidence in his integrity and efficiency." Babcock was acquitted, and Grant retained him on the White House staff.

Civil Service Reform   The desire to reduce political corruption led to the emergence of the civil service reform movement during the Gilded Age. Although the spoils system had been criticized long before the Civil War, an organized reform drive did not appear until after Appomattox. Knowledge of widespread corruption among government officials, fear that President Johnson might convert the government bureaucracy into a tool to promote his renomination, and the example of the British system of appointing civil servants after competitive examinations gave strength to the movement. Early efforts to require federal appointees to pass competitive examinations failed in Congress, but the reformers, led by the politically ambitious George

William Curtis, editor of *Harper's Weekly,* and by E. L. Godkin of *The Nation,* hoped for success under Grant's administration.

The reformers were doomed to disappointment, for on this, as on all other controversial topics, Grant perfectly understood that compromise was the mood of the age, and he straddled. He made no mention of civil service reform in his first message to Congress. The future historian Henry Adams—the son of Lincoln's minister to Great Britain and the grandson and great-grandson of presidents—remarked in his snobbish way that Grant was inaugurating "a reign of western mediocrity." But when angry civil service reformers began to talk loudly about joining the Liberal Republican movement, Grant moved swiftly to head them off. In 1871 he pressured Congress into creating the Civil Service Reform Commission, and he neatly co-opted his chief critic by naming Curtis its chairman. Although the commission had little power and achieved less success, the move kept Curtis and a sizable number of reformers as supporters of Grant's reelection. Once the election was over, Grant lost interest in the commission and so blatantly violated its rules that Curtis had to resign.

Strengthened by news of the scandals that rocked Grant's second administration, civil service reformers claimed some of the credit for the nomination of Rutherford B. Hayes in 1876. But they found him as difficult to manage as Grant had been. On the one hand, the new president did take on the powerful political machine of New York's Senator Roscoe Conkling, and he succeeded in ousting some of Conkling's supporters—a group called Stalwarts, which included the future president Chester A. Arthur—from the New York customhouse. On the other hand, at election time the president wanted his own appointees to contribute to Republican campaign funds and to help organize Republican state conventions, much as their predecessors had done. "I have little or no patience with Mr. Hayes," exclaimed the reforming editor of the *New York Times.* "He is a victim of . . . good intentions and his contributions to the pavement of the road to the infernal regions are vast and various."

Hayes's successor, James A. Garfield, gave civil service reformers little more satisfaction. With cruel accuracy one Massachusetts reformer characterized the new president as a "grand, noble fellow, but fickle, unstable, . . . timid and hesitating." Civil service reform advocates noted suspiciously that Garfield's vice-president was Arthur, named by the Republican national convention in a vain attempt to placate Conkling. Consequently, reformers felt no special sense of victory when Garfield began to remove more of Conkling's Stalwarts from the New York customhouse. Conceited and arrogant, Conkling resigned from the Senate in a huff and rushed to Albany seeking vindication through reelection. To his surprise, the removal of his friends from federal office undercut his support, and the New York legislature failed to send him back to the Senate. Shortly afterward, a crazed office seeker named Charles Guiteau assassinated Garfield, shouting that he was a Stalwart and rejoicing that Arthur was now president. Shocked by Garfield's assassination, Congress in 1883 passed the Pendleton Act, which required competitive examinations of applicants for many federal jobs.

The measure was typical of the compromises of the period. It was a genuine measure of civil service reform and encouraged the emergence of a professional government bureaucracy, but it covered only a fraction of all government employees and permitted the spoils system to continue in the distribution of most federal patronage.

Where Compromise Did Not Work

Thus compromise was usually the outcome of struggles in the post–Civil War era when the rivals for the control of policy and power were relatively evenly balanced. But when the rival forces were unevenly matched, the outcome was very different, as the story of labor, women, and Indians reveals.

Labor Organization in the Gilded Age Industrial laborers in the United States were slow to organize. Factory workers came from many national backgrounds and spoke many languages. In the decade after the Civil War, more than 3.25 million immigrants, mostly from northern Europe, poured into the United States, and from these the labor force was largely recruited. By 1880, 87 percent of the inhabitants of Chicago, 84 percent of those in Detroit and Milwaukee, and 80 percent of those in New York and Cleveland were immigrants or the children of immigrants. Divided along ethnic and religious lines, they had little sense of workers' solidarity. Many members of the work force, moreover, regarded their status as transient. They hoped, unrealistically, to move west as homesteaders or, having made their fortunes, to return to their European homelands.

It was almost impossible for a meaningful national labor movement to emerge from such a fractured work force. One of the earliest efforts was the eight-hour movement, led by Ira Stewart, a Boston machinist who sought legislation to limit the workday to eight hours without reduction of wages. Under this pressure the United States established an eight-hour day for its employees in 1868, and legislatures in six states passed acts to make eight hours a legal day's work. In private industry these laws proved ineffectual because they instituted the eight-hour restriction only "where there is no special contract or agreement to the contrary." Consequently, most businessmen required employees to agree to work longer hours as a condition of employment.

The National Labor Union, created in 1866 at a Baltimore conference of delegates from various unions, proved little more effective. It was headed by William H. Sylvis, a dedicated propagandist and a superb speaker, whose interests, however, were not in conventional labor issues like hours and wages, but rather in cooperatives and currency reform. Sylvis recruited many members for the National Labor Union—it claimed 640,000 in 1868—but whether these were actual workingmen is questionable. A scornful observer remarked that the National Labor Union was made up of "labor leaders without organizations, politicians without parties, women without husbands, and cranks, visionaries, and agitators without jobs." After Sylvis's death in 1869, the organization began to decline, and it disappeared during the depression of 1873.

An ultimately more successful labor movement was the Knights of Labor, founded in 1869 by Uriah Stephens and other garment workers of Philadelphia. It grew slowly at first and, like the National Labor Union, received a serious setback in the depression. By the 1880s, however, its membership increased spectacularly as it attempted to create a broad union of all workingmen, skilled and unskilled.*

Neither the National Labor Union nor the Knights of Labor organized a large segment of the nation's industrial labor forces, and the tactics of both organizations did little to relieve the day-to-day problems of working men and women. Hours were long, wages were miserably low, regular employment was uncertain, health or accident insurance was absent, and there were no pension or retirement programs. Child labor was exploited, and employees who dared to speak out against such abuses found themselves blacklisted by employers.

The Panic of 1873   These labor organizations were even less able to help in the severe depression that followed the Panic of 1873, precipitated by the failure of the financial firm of the Civil War financier Jay Cooke, who had subsequently become deeply involved in speculative ventures. Between 1873 and 1879 business activity in the United States declined by about one-third, and bankruptcies doubled. Thousands of workers lost their jobs. During the winter of 1873–74 about one-fourth of all laborers in New York City were unemployed, and during the following winter the number increased to one-third. In this time of crisis, the National Labor Union virtually collapsed, and many local unions disappeared as well. In New York City, for example, membership in all unions dropped from 45,000 in 1873 to 5,000 in 1877.

Private charities did what they could to relieve distress. But nobody seemed to know how to end the depression. Experts tended to view the panic and the subsequent unemployment and suffering as part of the natural workings of the national economic order, necessary to purge unsound businesses and speculative practices. Economists warned that "coddling" laborers would only retard this inevitable and necessary process. Blaming the depression on the wartime habit of looking to the federal government for leadership, Democratic Governor Samuel J. Tilden of New York called for a return to "government institutions, simple, frugal, meddling little with the private concerns of individuals . . . and trusting to the people to work out their own prosperity and happiness."

Those labor leaders who remained active were little more helpful. Many sought panaceas for the economic crisis. A writer in the *Radical Review* found the cause of the depression in private landownership which, in his words, "begets . . . ground rent, an inexorable, perpetual claim for the use of land, which, like air and light, is the gift of Nature." Later, in 1879, Henry George made that idea the basis for the economic system proposed in his book *Progress and Poverty.*

---

*For the Knights of Labor in the 1880s, see chapter 22, p. 121.

Baltimore and Ohio Railroad Strike
*The 1877 strike on the Baltimore and Ohio Railroad led to the worst labor violence the
United States had experienced. President Hayes called upon federal troops to break the strike
and to restore order.*

Other labor voices supported the Socialist Labor movement, founded in 1874,
which foresaw the ultimate overthrow of the capitalist system through a socialist
revolution. As interim measures to combat the depression, the movement advocated federal aid for education, industrial accident compensation, and women's
suffrage. It attracted only a tiny following.

Some labor spokesmen sought the way out of the depression by supporting
independent political parties pledged to protect labor's position in the national
economy. There was considerable labor support for the Greenback, or National
Independent, party, which was organized in 1874 at Indianapolis. The party's
national program opposed the resumption of specie payments and advocated
further issues of paper money to relieve the country's depressed industries. But
the Greenback party was not exclusively a labor movement: its presidential
candidate in 1876 was the eighty-five-year-old New York iron manufacturer Peter
Cooper. The 80,000 votes Cooper received came mostly from middle western
farm states. In the congressional elections two years later, however, more laborers
supported the National Independent party because it campaigned for governmental regulation of the hours of labor and for the exclusion of Chinese immigrants. Like other advocates of inflation, the party by this time had moved beyond
favoring greenbacks and urged expansion of the currency through silver coinage.
Candidates endorsed by the National Independent party received more than a
million votes in the 1878 congressional elections.

With the collapse of the trade union movement, other laborers during the depression rejected politics in favor of strikes and terrorism.* In July 1877, the worst year of the long depression, labor unrest reached its peak in the Great Railroad Strike, a spontaneous and violent outburst that spread throughout the East and to some of the roads beyond the Mississippi and into Canada. Local and State governments proved unable or unwilling to cope with the crisis. To protect the national system of transportation so essential to the United States economy, President Hayes sent in regular army troops. This action marked the first time in American history that the army had been used on any extensive scale to crush a labor disturbance. The army promptly restored order, and the strike collapsed. Deeply disturbed members of the business community took steps to prevent any recurrence of such labor violence. State legislatures began passing conspiracy laws directed against labor organizations, and the courts began to invoke the doctrine of malicious conspiracy to break strikes and boycotts. Throughout the North the state militia, which had so often proved untrustworthy during the 1877 crisis, was reorganized and given stricter training. The inventor and manufacturer Cyrus Hall McCormick personally purchased equipment for the Second Regiment of Illinois militia because it had, he said, "won great credit for its action during... [labor] disturbances and can be equally relied on in the future."

The Women's Movement

The fate of the women's rights movement during the postwar era offers another illustration of how the conservative forces in society dealt with advocates of change who lacked political power and effective leadership. During the Civil War years the central concern of most women was to house and clothe their families after the men had gone into the army. Great numbers of women entered the teaching profession, and for the first time the number of women workers in the federal bureaucracy—mostly on lower, clerical levels—became significant. Others found new fields of usefulness by becoming army nurses. Dorothea Dix, famed as an advocate of reform of prisons and insane asylums, began a new career as head of the nursing service in the Union hospitals, and Clara Barton, who worked closely behind the lines of the Union armies, distributing medical supplies and nursing the wounded, gained the experience that later led her to found the American Red Cross.

During the war the leaders of the women's suffrage movement reluctantly put aside their crusade in order to give their wholehearted support to the Union cause. Critical of the Lincoln administration for its slowness in moving toward emancipation, both Susan B. Anthony and Elizabeth Cady Stanton sought to rally loyal women in support of a constitutional amendment abolishing slavery. With the motto "Let none stand idle spectators now," they organized the National Woman's Loyal League to secure signatures on a gigantic petition to Congress.

---

*Labor unrest in the 1870s is discussed in detail in volume 2, chapter 22, pp. 121–123.

Ultimately, nearly 400,000 women and men signed the document, which contributed to the adoption of the Thirteenth Amendment.

Quite reasonably, the leaders of the women's rights movement expected their services be recognized when the war was over. They were appalled to discover that in the proposed Fourteenth Amendment to the Constitution, which Congress began debating in the summer of 1866, only males were to be guaranteed the right to vote. Furious, Anthony pledged, "I will cut off this right arm of mine before I will ever work for or demand the ballot for the Negro and not the woman." Women were further outraged when the Fifteenth Amendment prohibited discrimination against voters "on account or race, color, or previous condition of servitude"—but not sex.

They looked for support from their former allies in the antislavery movement, only to be rebuffed. Horace Greeley's reformist *New York Tribune* had no good word for their complaints, and Charles Sumner, while admitting that women's suffrage was "obviously the great question for the future," refused to have the Reconstruction amendments "clogged, burdened, or embarrassed" by provisions for women's suffrage.

Angry, Stanton and Anthony in 1869 formed the National American Woman's Suffrage Association, to promote a proposed Sixteenth Amendment to the Constitution that would provide for women's suffrage, but their movement had little chance against the powerful conservative interests in society. Senator George Williams of Oregon announced that the proponents of women's suffrage were displaying "a spirit which would, if able, convert all the now harmonious elements of society into a state of war, and make every home a hell on earth," while Senator Theodore Freylinghuysen of New Jersey unctuously pronounced that women possessed "a milder, gentler nature, which not only makes them shrink from, but disqualifies them for the turmoil and battle of public life." By invoking women's higher and holier mission of domesticity, conservatives ended hopes for women's suffrage for the next fifty years.

Indian Problems   Equally unsuccessful in bargaining with the dominant forces of society were the Native Americans. Whites called all these diverse peoples Indians—meaning, really, "wild Indians." President Lincoln voiced the general paleface view of the redskin. To leaders of several western Native American nations who visited the White House in March 1863, just after the bloody battle of Fredericksburg, the president announced, with no intentional irony: "We are not, as a race, so much disposed to fight and kill one another as our red brethren."

Union leaders took advantage of the opportunities presented during the Civil War to limit the rights of native Americans and to restrict their territories. The loyalties of the Five Civilized Nations were divided between the Union and the Confederacy, and after the Union victory the treaties governing the Indian Territory were renegotiated. As a result the native Americans were forced to give up huge tracts of land and to grant a right of way to railroads crossing the territory.

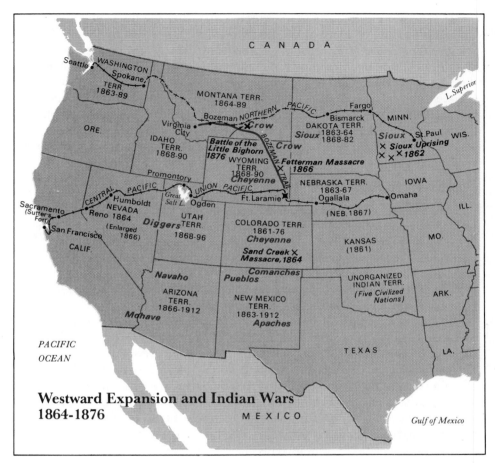

Westward Expansion and Indian Wars 1864-1876

The first date indicates the establishment of the territory with the boundaries shown. In several instances earlier territories were formed with the same names but with different boundaries.

Far to the north, wartime inefficiency and delay, along with the endemic corruption of the federal Indian Bureau, which regulated white–Indian relations, kept promised supplies from reaching the Santee Sioux. In desperation, the Indians took to the warpath and threatened white settlements in Minnesota. Lincoln appointed John Pope, fresh from his defeat at the second battle of Bull Run, to command the armed forces in the Northwest, and the general announced that he would deal with the Sioux "as maniacs or wild beasts, and by no means as people with whom treaties or compromises can be made." When the Sioux surrendered in September 1862, about 1,800 were taken prisoner and 303 were condemned to death. Against the strong objections of local authorities, Lincoln commuted the sentences of most, but he authorized the hanging of 38—the largest mass execution in American history.

In 1864 warfare spread to the Central Plains after the discovery of gold in Colorado and the opening of the Pike's Peak trail led to an influx of whites. Because the regular army was fighting the Confederacy, maintaining the peace was the job of the poorly trained Colorado territorial militia. On November 29, 1864, a group of Colorado volunteers, under the command of a former minister, Colonel John M. Chivington, fell on Chief Black Kettle's unsuspecting band of Cheyennes at Sand Creek in eastern Colorado, where they had gathered under the protection of the governor. "As an act of duty to ourselves and civilization," the militia slaughtered about 150 native Americans, mostly women and children.*

The Restoration of "Home Rule" in the South

The final adjustment of the relationship between the triumphant Union and the conquered South provides yet one more illustration of the process of compromise in the Gilded Age. In this case there were three parties to the compromise: the victorious Northerners, eager to restore the Union but uncertain what constraints to impose on the South; the Southern whites, who had been conquered but not stripped of their economic power; and the Southern blacks, who had been emancipated and enfranchised but not given land.

Within eighteen months after Appomattox, Northern interest in Southern problems began to wane. In the fall elections of 1867, when many Northern states chose governors and legislators and filled vacancies in the House of Representatives, the Democrats made impressive gains. Responding to the popular mood of conservatism, the Republican party in 1868 passed over Radical presidential candidates like Benjamin F. Wade and nominated Ulysses S. Grant, who had only recently affiliated with the Republicans but whose broad popular appeal as a military hero was unrivaled. Shrewdly sizing up the country's changing attitude toward Reconstruction, Grant used his inaugural address to announce his policy: "Let us have peace."

Just what he meant was not immediately clear. Some thought the new president was appealing to the white Ku Kluxers who were trying to overthrow the Reconstruction governments in the South; others believed that he was speaking to Northern Radicals who wanted to bring about further changes in Southern society. As it proved, Grant had both extremes in mind. On the one hand, the president warmly supported the immediate and unconditional readmission of Virginia to the Union, even though Radicals like Sumner warned that the Virginia legislature was "composed of recent Rebels still filled and seething with that old Rebel fire." On the other hand, Grant was outraged by the terrorism rampant in the South, and he insisted that Congress pass a series of Enforcement Acts (1870–71) enabling him to crush the Ku Klux Klan. Under this legislation the president proclaimed martial law in nine South Carolina counties in which white

---

*Further outrages against the native Americans are discussed in volume 2, chapter 22, pp. 103–107.

"One Vote Less"
Thomas Nast's drawing picked up on a statement in the Richmond Whig *that the death of a black man meant one vote less for the Republican ticket in 1868.*

Anti–Ku Klux Klan Propaganda
Thomas Nast, the celebrated Republican cartoonist, suggested that Democrats and the Ku Klux Klan wanted to return African Americans to a condition worse than slavery.

terrorists were most active, and federal marshals arrested many suspected Klansmen in North Carolina, Mississippi, and other Southern states. In brief, then, Grant's policy was to warn Southern whites that the national government would not tolerate open violence and organized military activity—but to let them understand that at the same time they would not be harassed if they regained control of their state governments through less revolutionary tactics.

The "Redemption" of the South   Southern whites quickly accepted the hint. They promptly undertook the restoration of what they called home rule—the rule of native white Democrats. Aware of Northern sensitivities, they now downplayed, when possible, the more brutal forms of terrorism and outright violence. White Republicans had to face social pressure and economic boycott; many fled the South, and others joined the Redeemers (as the advocates of home rule and white supremacy liked to call themselves). Redeemers exerted economic pressure on blacks by threatening not to hire or extend credit to those who were politically active.

In several states whites organized rifle clubs that practiced marksmanship on the outskirts of Republican political rallies. Usually blacks were cowed by these tactics. In a few cases, however, they organized and tried to defend themselves. On such occasions there occurred what Southern newspapers called race riots— a better term would have been "massacres," for the more numerous and better-armed whites overpowered the blacks and slaughtered their leaders. In state after state, Republican governors appealed to Washington for additional federal troops, but Grant refused, convinced that the public was tired of "these annual autumnal outbreaks" in the South.

In consequence of Grant's policy, the Redeemers quickly seized power in Virginia, North Carolina, Tennessee, and Georgia. In 1875 they won control of Alabama, Mississippi, Arkansas, and Texas, and early in 1877 they ended Republican rule in Florida. By the end of Grant's second administration, South Carolina and Louisiana were the only Southern states with Republican governments.

The Election of 1876   The fate of these two remaining Republican regimes in the South became intricately connected with the outcome of the 1876 presidential election. The Democratic nominee, Samuel J. Tilden, undoubtedly received a majority of the popular votes cast—although, equally undoubtedly, thousands of blacks who would have voted for his Republican rival, Rutherford B. Hayes, were kept from the polls. But Tilden lacked one vote of having a majority in the electoral college unless he received some of the votes from South Carolina, Florida, and Louisiana, all of which submitted to Congress competing sets of Democratic and Republican ballots. (There was also a technical question of the eligibility of one Republican elector from Oregon.)

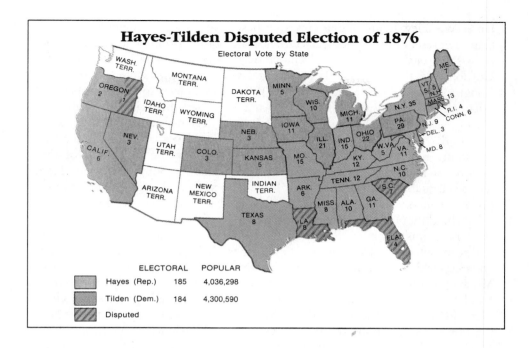

Hayes-Tilden Disputed Election of 1876

Electoral Vote by State

	ELECTORAL	POPULAR
Hayes (Rep.)	185	4,036,298
Tilden (Dem.)	184	4,300,590
Disputed		

Congress therefore confronted a crisis when it assembled in December 1876. If it decided to accept the disputed Democratic electoral votes, Republican control of the White House would be broken for the first time in a quarter of a century and the Reconstruction of the South would be ended. If Congress accepted the Republican electoral votes, that decision would run contrary to the will of a majority of the voters in the country.

Thus to resolve the impasse a compromise was needed—and not just a single compromise, but a complicated, interlocking set of bargains. After elaborate and secret negotiations, several agreements were reached. First, Congress decided that the disputed electoral votes should be referred to a special electoral commission, which should consist of five members from the House of Representatives, five members from the Senate, and five associate justices of the Supreme Court. This body was composed of eight Republicans and seven Democrats, and on every disputed ballot the commission ruled in favor of Hayes by the same 8-to-7 vote. In consequence of these decisions, Tilden's electoral vote remained at 184, while Hayes's slowly mounted to 185. In March 1877, for the fifth time in succession, a Republican president was inaugurated.

Democrats reluctantly accepted Hayes's election because of some other bargaining that took place while the electoral votes were being counted. One set of compromises came to be known as the Wormley agreement because it was negotiated in the luxurious Washington hotel owned by the black restaurateur

James Wormley. Representing Hayes at these sessions were Senator John Sherman, Representative James A. Garfield, and other prominent Republicans. Across the table sat Southern Democratic leaders, including Senator John B. Gordon, the former Confederate general who now represented Georgia in Congress, and L. Q. C. Lamar, once the Confederate envoy to Russia and now a senator from Mississippi. The Republicans promised the Southerners that, if Hayes was allowed to be inaugurated, he "would deal justly and generously with the South." Translated, this statement meant that Hayes would withdraw the remaining federal troops from the South and allow the overthrow of the Republican regimes in South Carolina and Louisiana. The Southerners found the terms acceptable, and they promptly leaked the news of the agreement, so as to protect themselves from charges that they had betrayed their section.

Behind the Wormley agreement lay other, less formal, compromises. Hayes's backers promised that the new president would not use federal patronage in the South to defeat the Democrats. They further pledged that he would support congressional appropriations for rebuilding levees along the flood-ridden Mississippi River and for construction of a transcontinental railroad along a Southern route. In return, Southerners agreed to allow the Republicans to elect Garfield Speaker of the new House of Representatives—a position that gave him the power to determine the membership of congressional committees. More important, the Southerners promised to protect the basic rights of blacks, as guaranteed in the Thirteenth, Fourteenth, and Fifteenth amendments to the Constitution.

Virtually all these informal agreements were ignored by both sides once Hayes was inaugurated. For his part, Hayes did order the removal of federal troops from the South and appointed a Southerner and former Confederate colonel, David M. Key, to his cabinet as postmaster general. But two-thirds of the federal officeholders in the South remained Republicans. Hayes changed his mind about supporting a Southern transcontinental railroad, alleging that federal funding would lead to corruption.

Southern Democrats likewise went back on their promise to support Garfield for Speaker. They eagerly joined in an investigation of alleged fraud in Hayes's election once the House was organized under Democratic leadership. Only a very few Southern Democratic politicians, among them Governor Wade Hampton of South Carolina, remembered their promise to respect the rights of blacks. Instead almost all took the final withdrawal of federal troops from the South as a signal that blacks, already put in a position of economic inferiority, could also be excluded from Southern political life.

Disfranchisement of Blacks Southern whites moved steadily and successfully to reduce black voting, although they had to act cautiously, so as not to offend public opinion in the North or to invite renewed federal intervention. One of the simplest devices was the poll

A Southern Chain Gang
Unwilling to spend much of their revenues to build penitentiaries, state governments instead turned black convicts over to railroads and other businesses, who leased the prisoners for cheap manual labor under brutal and degrading conditions.

tax, adopted in Georgia in 1877 and quickly copied by other Southern states. To Northerners the requirement that a voter pay $1 or $2 a year did not seem unreasonable. Yet because three-fourths of the entire Southern population had an average income of only $55.16 in 1880, the poll tax was a considerable financial drain, especially to poverty-stricken blacks. More imaginative was the "eight box" law adopted by South Carolina in 1882 and imitated by North Carolina and Florida. Under this system ballots for each contested race had to be deposited in separate boxes—one for governor, one for sheriff, and so forth. The system frustrated the illiterate black voter, who could no longer bring to the polls a single ballot, marked for him in advance by a Republican friend. To make the task of semiliterate voters more difficult, election officials periodically rearranged the order of the boxes. Still another device, which did not become popular until the late 1880s, was the secret ballot, also called the Australian ballot. The secret ballot was supposedly introduced in the South, as in the North, to prevent fraud. But actually it discriminated heavily against blacks, for as late as 1900 the number of illiterate black males ranged from 39 percent in Florida to 61 percent in Louisiana.

Despite all these obstacles, Southern blacks continued to vote in surprising numbers. In the 1880 presidential election, for example, more than 70 percent of the eligible blacks voted in Arkansas, Florida, North Carolina, Tennessee, and Virginia, and between 50 percent and 70 percent voted in Alabama, Louisiana, South Carolina, and Texas. These black voters posed a double threat to the Redeemers. Black voters were numerous enough that ambitious Northern Republicans, hoping to break the now solidly Democratic South, might be tempted again to try federal intervention in state elections. Even more dangerous was the possibility that Southern poor whites, whose needs for public education and welfare were consistently neglected by the business-oriented Redeemers, might find common cause with the poor blacks.

The Redeemers saw both these dangers materialize after 1890. Shortly after the Republicans gained control of the House of Representatives in 1889, Representative Henry Cabot Lodge of Massachusetts introduced a strong bill for federal control of elections, which promptly became known as the Force Bill. Although Democrats in the Senate defeated Lodge's bill in January 1891, Redeemers saw in it a threat to renew "all the horrors of reconstruction days." Their fear was doubtless greater because the almost simultaneous rise of the Populist movement threatened, as never before, to split the white voters of the region.* The Populist party appealed to farmers and to small planters and was the enemy of lawyers, bankers, and the rising commercial and industrial spokesmen of the so-called New South. Some of the Populist leaders, like Thomas Watson of Georgia, openly criticized the Redeemers' policy of repressing the blacks and seemed to be flirting with the black voters.

Faced with this double threat, Southern states moved swiftly to exclude the blacks completely and permanently from politics. Mississippi led the way with a constitutional convention in 1890 that required voters to be able to read and interpret the Constitution to the satisfaction of white registration officials. It is not hard to imagine how difficult even a graduate of the Howard University Law School would have found this task. In 1898 a Louisiana constitutional convention improved on the Mississippi example by requiring that a literacy test be passed by all voters except the sons and grandsons of persons who had voted in state elections before 1867. Because no Louisiana blacks had been permitted to vote before that date, this provision allowed illiterate whites to vote, while the literacy test excluded most black voters.

State after state across the South followed, or elaborated on, these requirements. South Carolina held a disfranchising convention in 1895. North Carolina amended its constitution to limit voting in 1900. Alabama and Virginia acted in 1901–02, and Georgia adopted a restrictive constitutional amendment in 1908. The remaining Southern states continued to rely on the poll tax and other varieties of legislative disfranchisement. When opponents of these measures accused their advocates of discriminating against blacks, Senator Carter Glass of

---

*For the rise of the Populist movement, see volume 2, chapter 22.

WHITE SUPREMACY!

Attention, White Men!

Grand Torch-Light Procession

At JACKSON,

On the Night of the

Fourth of January, 1890.

The Final Settlement of Democratic Rule and White Supremacy in Mississippi.

GRAND PYROTECHNIC DISPLAY!
Transparencies and Torches Free for all.

All in Sympathy with the Grand Cause are Cordially and Earnestly Invited to be on hand, to aid in the Final Overthrow of Radical Rule in our State.

Come on foot or on horse-back; come any way, but be sure to get there.
Brass Bands, Cannon, Flambeau Torches, Transparencies, Sky-rockets, Etc.

A GRAND DISPLAY FOR A GRAND CAUSE.

"White Supremacy!"
In 1890, when the Mississippi constitutional convention devised a way to disfranchise virtually all blacks, whites held a "grand pyrotechnic display" to celebrate.

Virginia replied for his entire generation: "Discrimination! Why that is precisely what we propose; that exactly is what this convention was elected for."

It took time, then, for the complete working out of the political compromises of the Reconstruction era. Not until the end of the nineteenth century did white Southerners receive the full price they had demanded in permitting the election of Rutherford B. Hayes. But by 1900 that payment had been made in full. The black man was no longer a political force in the South, and the Republican party was no longer the defender of black rights.

CHRONOLOGY

1866 National Labor Union formed.

1867 Maximilian's empire in Mexico falls. Purchase of Alaska.

1868 Ulysses S. Grant elected president in contest with Democrat Horatio Seymour.

1869 Knights of Labor organized.

1871 Treaty of Washington, settling differences between United States and Great Britain, signed. Tweed Ring scandals in New York City exposed.

1872	Crédit Mobilier scandals revealed. Grant names G. W. Curtis to head Civil Service Commission. Grant reelected over Horace Greeley, candidate of Liberal Republicans and Democrats.	**1876**	Exposure of Whiskey Ring reveals further corruption in Republican administration. Republicans nominate Rutherford B. Hayes for president; Democrats nominate Samuel J. Tilden. Disputed returns leave outcome in doubt.
1873	Coinage Act demonetizes silver in so-called Crime of '73. Panic of 1873 begins long depression.	**1877**	Congress creates electoral commission, which rules that all disputed ballots belong to Hayes, who is inaugurated president.
1874	Grant vetoes Inflation Bill.		Nationwide railroad strike and ensuing violence lead to first significant use of federal troops to suppress labor disorders.
1875	Specie Resumption Act provides for return to gold standard by 1879.		

Suggested Readings

The best general treatment of social and economic change during the post–Civil War period is Allan Nevins, *The Emergence of Modern America, 1865–1878* (1927). Ellis P. Oberholtzer, *History of the United States Since the Civil War,* vols. 1–4 (1929–31), contains an enormous amount of unassimilated data.

Foreign affairs during the Reconstruction era are treated in Glyndon G. Van Deusen, *William Henry Seward* (1967); Allan Nevins, *Hamilton Fish* (1936); and David Donald, *Charles Sumner and the Coming of the Civil War* (1970). Adrian Cook, *The Alabama Claims* (1975), is authoritative. Thomas D. Schoonover, *Dollars over Dominion* (1978), examines Mexican-American relations. On expansionism the standard work is A. K. Weinberg, *Manifest Destiny* (1935).

For a spirited, irreverent, and not entirely accurate account of the politics of the Gilded Age, read Matthew Josephson, *The Politicos, 1865–1896* (1938). Morton Keller, *Affairs of State: Public Life in Late Nineteenth Century America* (1977), is much more judicious and analytical. For balanced studies of three Republican presidents, see William S. McFeely, *Grant* (1981); Harry Barnard, *Rutherford B. Hayes and His America* (1954); and Allan Peskin, *Garfield* (1978). Two full studies of corruption in New York City are Alexander B. Callow, *The Tweed Ring* (1966), and Seymour Mandelbaum, *Boss Tweed's New York* (1965). Ari A. Hoogenboom, *Outlawing the Spoils* (1961), is a model history of the civil service reform movement.

Three modern, sophisticated analyses of the currency controversy are Robert P. Sharkey, *Money, Class, and Party* (1959); Irwin Unger, *The Greenback Era* (1964); and Walter T. K. Nugent, *The Money Question During Reconstruction* (1967).

Wilcomb E. Washburn, *The Indian in America* (1975), and Robert F. Berkhofer, Jr., *The White Man's Indian* (1978), are superior works. On governmental policy toward the Native Americans, see David A. Nichols, *Lincoln and the Indians* (1978); Francis P. Prucha, *American Indian Policy in Crisis* (1975); and Loring B. Priest, *Uncle Sam's Stepchildren* (1942).

Labor organization and unrest are treated in depth in John R. Commons et al., *History of Labor in the United States,* vol. 2 (1918). Norman J. Ware, *The Labor Movement in the United*

States (1929), is especially valuable on the National Labor Union. On the changing character of work and laborers' responses to industrialism, see Herbert G. Gutman, *Work, Culture and Society in Industrializing America* (1976), and Daniel T. Rogers, *The Work Ethic in Industrial America* (1978).

Eleanor Flexner, *Century of Struggle* (1975), is the standard account of the woman's suffrage movement. For two excellent general accounts of the role of women, see Mary P. Ryan, *Womanhood in America* (1979), and Carl Degler, *At Odds: Women and the Family in America* (1980).

Many of the works cited in the previous chapter are also helpful in understanding the restoration of "home rule" in the South. C. Vann Woodward, *Reunion and Reaction* (1951), is an original reexamination of the compromise of 1876–77. Keith I. Polakoff, *The Politics of Inertia* (1973), is a more recent interpretation. For an analysis of the Redeemer regimes, see Woodward's *Origins of the New South* (1951). The best study of the disfranchisement of blacks is J. Morgan Kousser, *The Shaping of Southern Politics* (1974).

APPENDIX

Declaration of Independence

IN CONGRESS, JULY 4, 1776

THE UNANIMOUS DECLARATION OF THE THIRTEEN UNITED STATES OF AMERICA

When, in the course of human events, it becomes necessary for one people to dissolve the political bands which have connected them with another, and to assume, among the powers of the earth, the separate and equal station to which the laws of nature and of nature's God entitle them, a decent respect to the opinions of mankind requires that they should declare the causes which impel them to the separation.

We hold these truths to be self-evident: That all men are created equal; that they are endowed by their Creator with certain unalienable rights; that among these are life, liberty, and the pursuit of happiness; that, to secure these rights, governments are instituted among men, deriving their just powers from the consent of the governed; that whenever any form of government becomes destructive of these ends, it is the right of the people to alter or to abolish it, and to institute new government, laying its foundation on such principles, and organizing its powers in such form, as to them shall seem most likely to effect their safety and happiness. Prudence, indeed, will dictate that governments long established should not be changed for light and transient causes; and accordingly all experience hath shown that mankind are more disposed to suffer, while evils are sufferable, than to right themselves by abolishing the forms to which they are accustomed. But when a long train of abuses and usurpations, pursuing invariably the same object, evinces a design to reduce them under absolute despotism, it is their right, it is their duty, to throw off such government, and to provide new guards for their future security. Such has been the patient sufferance of these colonies; and such is now the necessity which constrains them to alter their former systems of government. The history of the present King of Great Britain is a history of repeated injuries and usurpations, all having in direct object the establishment of an absolute tyranny over these states. To prove this, let facts be submitted to a candid world.

He has refused his assent to laws, the most wholesome and necessary for the public good.

He has forbidden his governors to pass laws of immediate and pressing importance, unless suspended in their operation till his assent should be obtained; and, when so suspended, he has utterly neglected to attend to them.

He has refused to pass other laws for the accommodation of large districts of people, unless those people would relinquish the right of representation in the legislature, a right inestimable to them, and formidable to tyrants only.

He has called together legislative bodies at places unusual, uncomfortable, and distant from the depository of their public records, for the sole purpose of fatiguing them into compliance with his measures.

i

He has dissolved representative houses repeatedly, for opposing, with manly firmness, his invasions on the rights of the people.

He has refused for a long time, after such dissolutions, to cause others to be elected; whereby the legislative powers, incapable of annihilation, have returned to the people at large for their exercise; the state remaining, in the mean time, exposed to all the dangers of invasions from without and convulsions within.

He has endeavored to prevent the population of these states; for that purpose obstructing the laws for naturalization of foreigners; refusing to pass others to encourage their migration hither, and raising the conditions of new appropriations of lands.

He has obstructed the administration of justice, by refusing his assent to laws for establishing judiciary powers.

He has made judges dependent on his will alone, for the tenure of their offices, and the amount and payment of their salaries.

He has erected a multitude of new offices, and sent hither swarms of officers to harass our people and eat out their substance.

He has kept among us, in times of peace, standing armies, without the consent of our legislatures.

He has affected to render the military independent of, and superior to, the civil power.

He has combined with others to subject us to a jurisdiction foreign to our constitution, and unacknowledged by our laws, giving his assent to their acts of pretended legislation:

For quartering large bodies of armed troops among us;

For protecting them, by a mock trial, from punishment for any murders which they should commit on the inhabitants of these states;

For cutting off our trade with all parts of the world;

For imposing taxes on us without our consent;

For depriving us, in many cases, of the benefits of trial by jury;

For transporting us beyond seas, to be tried for pretended offenses;

For abolishing the free system of English laws in a neighboring province, establishing therein an arbitrary government, and enlarging its boundaries, so as to render it at once an example and fit instrument for introducing the same absolute rule into these colonies;

For taking away our charters, abolishing our most valuable laws, and altering fundamentally the forms of our governments;

For suspending our own legislatures, and declaring themselves invested with power to legislate for us in all cases whatsoever.

He has abdicated government here, by declaring us out of his protection and waging war against us.

He has plundered our seas, ravaged our coasts, burned our towns, and destroyed the lives of our people.

He is at this time transporting large armies of foreign mercenaries to complete the works of death, desolation, and tyranny already begun with circumstances of cruelty and perfidy scarcely paralleled in the most barbarous ages, and totally unworthy the head of a civilized nation.

He has constrained our fellow-citizens, taken captive on the high seas, to bear arms against their country, to become the executioners of their friends and brethren, or to fall themselves by their hands.

He has excited domestic insurrection among us, and has endeavored to bring on the inhabitants of our frontiers the merciless Indian savages, whose known rule of warfare is an undistinguished destruction of all ages, sexes, and conditions.

In every stage of these oppressions we have petitioned for redress in the most humble terms; our repeated petitions have been answered only by repeated injury. A prince, whose character is thus marked by every act which may define a tyrant, is unfit to be the ruler of a free people.

Nor have we been wanting in our attentions to our British brethren. We have warned them, from time to time, of attempts by their legislature to extend an unwarrantable jurisdiction over us. We have reminded them of the circumstances of our emigration and settlement here. We have appealed to their native justice and magnanimity; and we have conjured them, by the ties of our common kindred, to disavow these usurpations, which would inevitably interrupt our connections and correspondence. They, too, have been deaf to the voice of justice and of consanguinity. We must, therefore, acquiesce in the necessity which denounces our separation, and hold them, as we hold the rest of mankind, enemies in war, in peace friends.

We, therefore, the representatives of the United States of America, in General Congress assembled, appealing to the Supreme Judge of the world for the rectitude of our intentions, do, in the name and by the authority of the good people of these colonies, solemnly publish and declare, that these United Colonies are, and of right ought to be, FREE AND INDEPENDENT STATES; that they are absolved from all allegiance to the British crown, and that all political connection between them and the state of Great Britain is, and ought to be, totally dissolved; and that, as free and independent states, they have full power to levy war, conclude peace, contract alliances, establish commerce, and do all other acts and things which independent states may of right do. And for the support of this declaration, with a firm reliance on the protection of Divine Providence, we mutually pledge to each other our lives, our fortunes, and our sacred honor.

JOHN HANCOCK [*President*]
[*and fifty-five others*]

The Articles of Confederation and Perpetual Union

BETWEEN THE STATES OF NEW HAMPSHIRE, MASSACHUSETTS BAY, RHODE ISLAND AND PROVIDENCE PLANTATIONS, CONNECTICUT, NEW YORK, NEW JERSEY, PENNSYLVANIA, DELAWARE, MARYLAND, VIRGINIA, NORTH CAROLINA, SOUTH CAROLINA, GEORGIA.*

Article 1.

The stile of this confederacy shall be "The United States of America."

Article 2.

Each State retains its sovereignty, freedom and independence, and every power, jurisdiction, and right, which is not by this confederation expressly delegated to the United States, in Congress assembled.

Article 3.

The said states hereby severally enter into a firm league of friendship with each other for their common defence, the security of their liberties and their mutual and general welfare; binding themselves to assist each other against all force offered to, or attacks made upon them, or any of them, on account of religion, sovereignty, trade, or any other pretence whatever.

Article 4.

The better to secure and perpetuate mutual friendship and intercourse among the people of the different states in this union, the free inhabitants of each of these states, paupers, vagabonds, and fugitives from justice excepted, shall be entitled to all privileges and immunities of free citizens in the several states; and the people of each State shall have free ingress and regress to and from any other State, and shall enjoy therein all the privileges of trade and commerce, subject to the same duties, impositions, and restrictions, as the inhabitants thereof respectively; provided, that such restrictions shall not extend so far as

---

*This copy of the final draft of the Articles of Confederation is taken from the *Journals,* 9:907–925, November 15, 1777.

to prevent the removal of property, imported into any State, to any other State of which the owner is an inhabitant; provided also, that no imposition, duties, or restriction, shall be laid by any State on the property of the United States, or either of them.

If any person guilty of, or charged with treason, felony, or other high misdemeanor in any State, shall flee from justice and be found in any of the United States, he shall, upon demand of the governor or executive power of the State from which he fled, be delivered up and removed to the State having jurisdiction of his offence.

Full faith and credit shall be given in each of these states to the records, acts, and judicial proceedings of the courts and magistrates of every other State.

Article 5.

For the more convenient management of the general interests of the United States, delegates shall be annually appointed, in such manner as the legislature of each State shall direct, to meet in Congress, on the 1st Monday in November in every year, with a power reserved to each State to recall its delegates, or any of them, at any time within the year, and to send others in their stead for the remainder of the year.

No state shall be represented in Congress by less than two, nor by more than seven members; and no person shall be capable of being a delegate for more than three years in any term of six years; nor shall any person, being a delegate, be capable of holding any office under the United States, for which he, or any other for his benefit, receives any salary, fees, or emolument of any kind.

Each State shall maintain its own delegates in a meeting of the states, and while they act as members of the committee of the states.

In determining questions in the United States, in Congress assembled, each State shall have one vote.

Freedom of speech and debate in Congress shall not be impeached or questioned in any court or place out of Congress: and the members of Congress shall be protected in their persons from arrests and imprisonments, during the time of their going to and from, and attendance on Congress, *except for treason,* felony, or breach of the peace.

Article 6.

No State, without the consent of the United States, in Congress assembled, shall send any embassy to, or receive any embassy from, or enter into any conference, agreement, alliance, or treaty with any king, prince, or state; nor shall any person, holding any office of profit or trust under the United States, or any of them, accept of any present, emolument, office or title, of any kind whatever, from any king, prince, or foreign state; nor shall the United States, in Congress assembled, or any of them, grant any title of nobility.

No two or more states shall enter into any treaty, confederation, or alliance, whatever, between them, without the consent of the United States, in Congress assembled, specifying accurately the purposes for which the same is to be entered into, and how long it shall continue.

No State shall lay any imposts or duties which may interfere with any stipulations in treaties entered into by the United States, in Congress assembled, with any king, prince, or state, in pursuance of any treaties already proposed by Congress to the courts of France and Spain.

No vessels of war shall be kept up in time of peace by any State, except such number only as shall be deemed necessary by the United States, in Congress assembled, for the defence of such State or its trade; nor shall any body of forces be kept up by any State, in time of peace, except such number only as, in the judgment of the United States, in Congress assembled, shall be deemed requisite to garrison the forts necessary for the defence of such State; but every State shall always keep up a well regulated and disciplined militia, sufficiently armed and accoutred, and shall provide, and constantly have ready for use, in public stores, a due number of field pieces and tents, and a proper quantity of arms, ammunition and camp equipage.

No State shall engage in any war without the consent of the United States, in Congress assembled, unless such State be actually invaded by enemies, or shall have received certain advice of a resolution being formed by some nation of Indians to invade such State, and the danger is so imminent as not to admit of a delay till the United States, in Congress assembled, can be consulted; nor shall any State grant commissions to any ships or vessels of war, nor letters of marque or reprisal, except it be after a declaration of war by the United States, in Congress assembled, and then only against the kingdom or state, and the subjects thereof, against which war has been so declared, and under such regulations as shall be established by the United States, in Congress assembled, unless such State be infested by pirates, in which case vessels of war may be fitted out for that occasion, and kept so long as the danger shall continue, or until the United States, in Congress assembled, shall determine otherwise.

Article 7.

When land forces are raised by any State for the common defence, all officers of or under the rank of colonel, shall be appointed by the legislature of each State respectively, by whom such forces shall be raised, or in such manner as such State shall direct; and all vacancies shall be filled up by the State which first made the appointment.

Article 8.

All charges of war and all other expences, that shall be incurred for the common defence or general welfare, and allowed by the United States, in Congress assembled, shall be defrayed out of a common treasury, which shall be supplied by the several states, in proportion to the value of all land within each State, granted to or surveyed for any person, as such land and the buildings and improvements thereon shall be estimated according to such mode as the United States, in Congress assembled, shall, from time to time, direct and appoint.

The taxes for paying that proportion shall be laid and levied by the authority and direction of the legislatures of the several states, within the time agreed upon by the United States, in Congress assembled.

Article 9.

The United States, in Congress assembled, shall have the sole and exclusive right and power of determining on peace and war, except in the cases mentioned in the 6th article; of sending and receiving ambassadors; entering into treaties and alliances, provided that no treaty of commerce shall be made, whereby the legislative power of the respective states shall be restrained from imposing such imposts and duties on foreigners as their own people are subjected to, or from prohibiting the exportation or importation of any species of goods or commodities whatsoever; of establishing rules for deciding, in all cases, what captures on land or water shall be legal, and in what manner prizes, taken by land or naval forces in the service of the United States, shall be divided or appropriated; of granting letters of marque and reprisal in times of peace; appointing courts for the trial of piracies and felonies committed on the high seas, and establishing courts for receiving and determining, finally, appeals in all cases of captures; provided, that no member of Congress shall be appointed a judge of any of the said courts.

The United States, in Congress assembled, shall also be the last resort on appeal in all disputes and differences now subsisting, or that hereafter may arise between two or more states concerning boundary, jurisdiction or any other cause whatever; which authority shall always be exercised in the manner following: whenever the legislative or executive authority, or lawful agent of any State, in controversy with another, shall present a petition to Congress, stating the matter in question, and praying for a hearing, notice thereof shall be given, by order of Congress, to the legislative or executive authority of the other State in controversy, and a day assigned for the appearance of the parties by their lawful agents, who shall then be directed to appoint, by joint consent, commissioners or judges to constitute a court for hearing and determining the matter in question; but, if they cannot agree, Congress shall name three persons out of each of the United States, and from the list of such persons each party shall alternately strike out one, in the petitioners beginning, until the number shall be reduced to thirteen; and from that number not less than seven, nor more than nine names, as Congress shall direct, shall, in the presence of Congress, be drawn out by lot; and the persons whose names shall be so drawn, or any five of them, shall be commissioners or judges to hear and finally determine the controversy, so always as a major part of the judges who shall hear the cause shall agree in the determination; and if either party shall neglect to attend at the day appointed, without shewing reasons which Congress shall judge sufficient, or, being present, shall refuse to strike, the Congress shall proceed to nominate three persons out of each State, and the secretary of Congress shall strike in behalf of such party absent or refusing; and the judgment and sentence of the court to be appointed, in the manner before prescribed, shall be final and conclusive; and if any of the parties shall refuse to submit to the authority of such court, or to appear or defend their claim or cause, the court shall nevertheless proceed to pronounce sentence or judgment, which shall, in like manner, be final and decisive, the judgment or sentence and other proceedings being, in either case, transmitted to Congress, and lodged among the acts of Congress for the security of the parties concerned: provided, that every commissioner, before he sits in judgment, shall take an oath, to be administered by one of the judges of the supreme or superior court of the State where the cause shall be tried, "well and truly to hear and determine the matter in question, according to the best of his judgment, without favour, affection, or hope of reward": provided, also, that no State shall be deprived of territory for the benefit of the United States.

All controversies concerning the private right of soil, claimed under different grants of two or more states, whose jurisdictions, as they may respect such lands and the states which passed such grants, are adjusted, the said grants, or either of them, being at the same time claimed to have originated antecedent to such settlement of jurisdiction, shall, on the petition of either party to the Congress of the United States, be finally determined, as near as may be, in the same manner as is before prescribed for deciding disputes respecting territorial jurisdiction between different states.

The United States, in Congress assembled, shall also have the sole and exclusive right and power of regulating the alloy and value of coin struck by their own authority, or by that of the respective states; fixing the standard of weights and measures throughout the United States; regulating the trade and managing all affairs with the Indians not members of any of the states; provided that the legislative right of any State within its own limits be not infringed or violated; establishing and regulating post offices from one State to another throughout all the United States, and exacting such postage on the papers passing through the same as may be requisite to defray the expences of the said office; appointing all officers of the land forces in the service of the United States, excepting regimental officers; appointing all the officers of the naval forces, and commissioning all officers whatever in the service of the United States; making rules for the government and regulation of the said land and naval forces, and directing their operations.

The United States, in Congress assembled, shall have authority to appoint a committee to sit in the recess of Congress, to be denominated "a Committee of the States," and to consist of one delegate from each State, and to appoint such other committees and civil officers as may be necessary for managing the general affairs of the United States, under their direction; to appoint one of their number to preside; provided that no person be allowed to serve in the office of president more than one year in any term of three years; to ascertain the necessary sums of money to be raised for the service of the United States, and to appropriate and apply the same for defraying the public expences; to borrow money or emit bills on the credit of the United States, transmitting, every half year, to the respective states, an account of the sums of money so borrowed or emitted; to build and equip a navy; to agree upon the number of land forces, and to make requisitions from each State for its quota, in proportion to the number of white inhabitants in such State; which requisitions shall be binding; and, thereupon, the legislature of each State shall appoint the regimental officers, raise the men, and cloathe, arm, and equip them in a soldier-like manner, at the expence of the United States; and the officers and men so cloathed, armed, and equipped, shall march to the place appointed and within the time agreed on by the United States, in Congress assembled; but if the United States, in Congress assembled, shall, on consideration of circumstances, judge proper that any State should not raise men, or should raise a smaller number than its quota, and that any other State should raise a greater number of men than the quota thereof, such extra number shall be raised, officered, cloathed, armed, and equipped in the same manner as the quota of such State, unless the legislature of such State shall judge that such extra number cannot be safely spared out of the same, in which case they shall raise, officer, cloathe, arm, and equip as many of such extra number as they judge can be safely spared. And the officers and men so cloathed, armed, and equipped, shall march to the place appointed and within the time agreed on by the United States, in Congress assembled.

The United States, in Congress assembled, shall never engage in a war, nor grant letters of marque and reprisal in time of peace, nor enter into any treaties or alliances, nor coin money, nor regulate the value thereof, nor ascertain the sums and expences necessary for the defence and welfare of the United States, or any of them: nor emit bills, nor borrow money on the credit of the United States, nor appropriate money, nor agree upon the number of vessels of war to be built or purchased, or the number of land or sea forces to be raised, nor appoint a commander in chief of the army or navy, unless nine states assent to the same; nor shall a question on any other point, except for adjourning from day to day, be determined, unless by the votes of a majority of the United States, in Congress assembled.

The Congress of the United States shall have power to adjourn to any time within the year, and to any place within the United States, so that no period of adjournment be for a longer duration than the space of six months, and shall publish the journal of their proceedings monthly, except such parts thereof, relating to treaties, alliances or military operations, as, in their judgment, require secrecy; and the yeas and nays of the delegates of each State on any question shall be entered on the journal, when it is desired by any delegate; and the delegates of a State, or any of them, at his, or their request, shall be furnished with a transcript of the said journal, except such parts as are above excepted, to lay before the legislatures of the several states.

Article 10.

The committee of the states, or any nine of them, shall be authorized to execute, in the recess of Congress, such of the powers of Congress as the United States, in Congress assembled, by the consent of nine states, shall, from time to time, think expedient to vest them with; provided, that no power be delegated to the said committee, for the exercise of which, by the articles of confederation, the voice of nine states, in the Congress of the United States assembled, is requisite.

Article 11.

Canada acceding to this confederation, and joining in the measures of the United States, shall be admitted into and entitled to all the advantages of this union; but no other colony shall be admitted into the same, unless such admission be agreed to by nine states.

Article 12.

All bills of credit emitted, monies borrowed and debts contracted by, or under the authority of Congress before the assembling of the United States, in pursuance of the present confederation, shall be deemed and considered as a charge against the United States, for payment and satisfaction whereof the said United States and the public faith are hereby solemnly pledged.

Article 13.

Every State shall abide by the determinations of the United States, in Congress assembled, on all questions which, by this confederation, are submitted to them. And the articles of this confederation shall be inviolably observed by every State, and the union shall be perpetual; nor shall any alteration at any time hereafter be made in any of them, unless such alteration be agreed to in a Congress of the United States, and be afterwards confirmed by the legislatures of every State.

These articles shall be proposed to the legislatures of all the United States, to be considered, and if approved of by them, they are advised to authorize their delegates to ratify the same in the Congress of the United States; which being done, the same shall become conclusive.

Constitution of the United States of America

PREAMBLE

We the people of the United States, in order to form a more perfect union, establish justice, insure domestic tranquillity, provide for the common defense, promote the general welfare, and secure the blessings of liberty to ourselves and our posterity, do ordain and establish this Constitution for the United States of America.

Article I

Section 1.   All legislative powers herein granted shall be vested in a Congress of the United States, which shall consist of a Senate and a House of Representatives.

Section 2.   The House of Representatives shall be composed of members chosen every second year by the people of the several States, and the electors in each State shall have the qualifications requisite for electors of the most numerous branch of the State Legislature.

No person shall be a Representative who shall not have attained to the age of twenty-five years, and been seven years a citizen of the United States, and who shall not, when elected, be an inhabitant of that State in which he shall be chosen.

Representatives and direct taxes shall be apportioned among the several States which may be included within this Union, according to their respective numbers, *which shall be determined by adding to the whole number of free persons, including those bound to service for a term of years, and excluding Indians not taxed, three-fifths of all other persons.* The actual enumeration shall be made within three years after the first meeting of the Congress of the United States, and within every subsequent term of ten years, in such manner as they shall by law direct. The number of Representatives shall not exceed one for every thirty thousand, but each State shall have at least one Representative; *and until such enumeration shall be made, the State of New Hampshire shall be entitled to choose three, Massachusetts eight, Rhode Island and Providence Plantations one, Connecticut five, New York six, New Jersey four, Pennsylvania eight, Delaware one, Maryland six, Virginia ten, North Carolina five, South Carolina five, and Georgia three.*

When vacancies happen in the representation from any State, the Executive authority thereof shall issue writs of election to fill such vacancies.

The House of Representatives shall choose their Speaker and other officers; and shall have the sole power of impeachment.

NOTE: Passages that are no longer in effect are printed in italic type.

Section 3. The Senate of the United States shall be composed of two Senators from each State, *chosen by the legislature thereof,* for six years; and each Senator shall have one vote.

Immediately after they shall be assembled in consequence of the first election, they shall be divided as equally as may be into three classes. The seats of the Senators of the first class shall be vacated at the expiration of the second year, of the second class at the expiration of the fourth year, and of the third class at the expiration of the sixth year, so that one-third may be chosen every second year; *and if vacancies happen by resignation or otherwise, during the recess of the legislature of any State, the Executive thereof may make temporary appointments until the next meeting of the legislature, which shall then fill such vacancies.*

No person shall be a Senator who shall not have attained to the age of thirty years, and been nine years a citizen of the United States, and who shall not, when elected, be an inhabitant of that State for which he shall be chosen.

The Vice President of the United States shall be President of the Senate, but shall have no vote, unless they be equally divided.

The Senate shall choose their other officers, and also a President *pro tempore,* in the absence of the Vice President, or when he shall exercise the office of President of the United States.

The Senate shall have the sole power to try all impeachments. When sitting for that purpose, they shall be on oath or affirmation. When the President of the United States is tried, the Chief Justice shall preside: and no person shall be convicted without the concurrence of two-thirds of the members present.

Judgment in cases of impeachment shall not extend further than to removal from office, and disqualification to hold and enjoy any office of honor, trust or profit under the United States; but the party convicted shall nevertheless be liable and subject to indictment, trial, judgment and punishment, according to law.

Section 4. The times, places and manner of holding elections for Senators and Representatives shall be prescribed in each State by the legislature thereof; but the Congress may at any time by law make or alter such regulations, except as to the places of choosing Senators.

The Congress shall assemble at least once in every year, and such meeting *shall be on the first Monday in December, unless they shall by law appoint a different day.*

Section 5. Each house shall be the judge of the elections, returns and qualifications of its own members, and a majority of each shall constitute a quorum to do business; but a smaller number may adjourn from day to day, and may be authorized to compel the attendance of absent members, in such manner, and under such penalties as each house may provide.

Each house may determine the rules of its proceedings, punish its members for disorderly behavior, and with the concurrence of two thirds, expel a member.

Each house shall keep a journal of its proceedings, and from time to time publish the same, excepting such parts as may in their judgment require secrecy; and the yeas and nays of the members of either house on any question shall, at the desire of one-fifth of those present, be entered on the journal.

Neither house, during the session of Congress, shall, without the consent of the other, adjourn for more than three days, nor to any other place than that in which the two houses shall be sitting.

Section 6. The Senators and Representatives shall receive a compensation for their services, to be ascertained by law and paid out of the treasury of the United States. They shall in all cases except treason, felony and breach of the peace, be privileged from arrest during their attendance at the session of their respective houses, and in going to and returning from the same; and for any speech or debate in either house, they shall not be questioned in any other place.

No Senator or Representative shall, during the time for which he was elected, be appointed to any civil office under the authority of the United States, which shall have been created, or the emoluments whereof shall have been increased during such time; and no person holding any office under the United States shall be a member of either house during his continuance in office.

Section 7. All bills for raising revenue shall originate in the House of Representatives; but the Senate may propose or concur with amendments as on other bills.

Every bill which shall have passed the House of Representatives and the Senate, shall, before it become a law, be presented to the President of the United States; if he approve he shall sign it, but if not he shall return it with objections to that house in which it originated, who shall enter the objections at large on their journal, and proceed to reconsider it. If after such reconsideration two-thirds of that house shall agree to pass the bill, it shall be sent, together with the objections, to the other house, by which it shall likewise be reconsidered, and, if approved by two-thirds of that house, it shall become a law. But in all such cases the votes of both houses shall be determined by yeas and nays, and the names of the persons voting for and against the bill shall be entered on the journal of each house respectively. If any bill shall not be returned by the President within ten days (Sundays excepted) after it shall have been presented to him, the same shall be a law, in like manner as if he had signed it, unless the Congress by their adjournment prevent its return, in which case it shall not be a law.

Every order, resolution, or vote to which the concurrence of the Senate and House of Representatives may be necessary (except on a question of adjournment) shall be presented to the President of the United States; and before the same shall take effect, shall be approved by him, or being disapproved by him, shall be repassed by two-thirds of the Senate and House of Representatives, according to the rules and limitations prescribed in the case of a bill.

Section 8. The Congress shall have power

To lay and collect taxes, duties, imposts and excises, to pay the debts and provide for the common defense and general welfare of the United States; but all duties, imposts and excises shall be uniform throughout the United States;

To borrow money on the credit of the United States;

To regulate commerce with foreign nations, and among the several States, and with the Indian tribes;

To establish an uniform rule of naturalization, and uniform laws on the subject of bankruptcies throughout the United States;

To coin money, regulate the value thereof, and of foreign coin, and fix the standard of weights and measures;

To provide for the punishment of counterfeiting the securities and current coin of the United States;

To establish post offices and post roads;

To promote the progress of science and useful arts by securing for limited times to authors and inventors the exclusive right to their respective writings and discoveries;

To constitute tribunals inferior to the Supreme Court;

To define and punish piracies and felonies committed on the high seas and offenses against the law of nations;

To declare war, grant letters of marque and reprisal, and make rules concerning captures on land and water;

To raise and support armies, but no appropriation of money to that use shall be for a longer term than two years;

To provide and maintain a Navy;

To make rules for the government and regulation of the land and naval forces;

To provide for calling forth the militia to execute the laws of the Union, suppress insurrections, and repel invasions;

To provide for organizing, arming, and disciplining the militia, and for governing such part of them as may be employed in the service of the United States, reserving to the States respectively the appointment of the officers, and the authority of training the militia according to the discipline prescribed by Congress;

To exercise exclusive legislation in all cases whatsoever, over such district (not exceeding ten miles square) as may, by cession of particular States, and the acceptance of Congress, become the seat of government of the United States, and to exercise like authority over all places purchased by the consent of the legislature of the State, in which the same shall be, for erection of forts, magazines, arsenals, dock-yards, and other needful buildings;—and

To make all laws which shall be necessary and proper for carrying into execution the foregoing powers, and all other powers vested by this Constitution in the government of the United States, or in any department or officer thereof.

Section 9.   *The migration or importation of such persons as any of the States now existing shall think proper to admit shall not be prohibited by the Congress prior to the year 1808; but a tax or duty may be imposed on such importation, not exceeding $10 for each person.*

The privilege of the writ of habeas corpus shall not be suspended, unless when in cases of rebellion or invasion the public safety may require it.

No bill of attainder or ex post facto law shall be passed.

No capitation, or other direct, tax shall be laid, unless in proportion to the census or enumeration herein before directed to be taken.

No tax or duty shall be laid on articles exported from any State.

No preference shall be given by any regulation of commerce or revenue to the ports of one State over those of another; nor shall vessels bound to, or from, one State, be obliged to enter, clear, or pay duties in another.

No money shall be drawn from the treasury, but in consequence of appropriations made by law; and a regular statement and account of the receipts and expenditures of all public money shall be published from time to time.

No title of nobility shall be granted by the United States: and no person holding any office of profit or trust under them, shall, without the consent of the Congress, accept of any present, emolument, office, or title, of any kind whatever, from any king, prince or foreign state.

Section 10.   No State shall enter into any treaty, alliance, or confederation; grant letters of marque and reprisal; coin money; emit bills of credit; make anything but gold and silver coin a tender in payment of debts; pass any bill of attainder, ex post facto law, or law impairing the obligation of contracts, or grant any title of nobility.

No State shall, without the consent of Congress, lay any imposts or duties on imports or exports, except what may be absolutely necessary for executing its inspection laws: and the net produce of all duties and imposts, laid by any State on imports or exports, shall be for the use of the treasury of the United States; and all such laws shall be subject to the revision and control of the Congress.

No State shall, without the consent of Congress, lay any duty of tonnage, keep troops or ships of war in time of peace, enter into any agreement or compact with another State, or with a foreign power, or engage in war, unless actually invaded, or in such imminent danger as will not admit of delay.

Article II

Section 1.   The executive power shall be vested in a President of the United States of America. He shall hold his office during the term of four years, and, together with the Vice-President, chosen for the same term, be elected as follows:

Each state shall appoint, in such manner as the legislature thereof may direct, a number of electors, equal to the whole number of Senators and Representatives to which the State may be entitled in the Congress; but no Senator or Representative, or person holding an office of trust or profit under the United States, shall be appointed an elector.

The electors shall meet in their respective States, and vote by ballot for two persons, of whom one at least shall not be an inhabitant of the same State with themselves. And they shall make a list of all the persons voted for, and of the number of votes for each; which list they shall sign and certify, and transmit sealed to the seat of government of the United States, directed to the President of the Senate. The President of the Senate shall, in the presence of the Senate and House of Representatives, open all the certificates, and the votes shall then be counted. The person having the greatest number of votes shall be the President, if such number be a majority of the whole number of electors appointed; and if there be more than one who have such majority, and have an equal number of votes, then the House of Representatives shall immediately choose by ballot one of them for President; and if no person have a majority, then from the five highest on the list said House shall in like manner choose the President. But in choosing the President, the votes shall be taken by States, the representation from each State having one vote; a quorum for this purpose shall consist of a member or members from two-thirds of the States, and a majority of all the States shall be necessary to a choice. In every case, after the choice of the President, the person having the greatest number of votes of the electors shall be the Vice-President. But if there should remain two or more who have equal votes, the Senate shall choose from them by ballot the Vice-President.

The Congress may determine the time of choosing the electors and the day on which they shall give their votes; which day shall be the same throughout the United States.

No person except a natural born citizen, *or a citizen of the United States at the time of the adoption of this Constitution,* shall be eligible to the office of President; neither shall any person be eligible to that office who shall not have attained to the age of thirty-five years, and been fourteen years a resident within the United States.

In case of the removal of the President from office or of his death, resignation, or inability to discharge the powers and duties of the said office, the same shall devolve on the

Vice-President, and the Congress may by law provide for the case of removal, death, resignation or inability, both of the President and Vice-President, declaring what officer shall then act as President, and such officer shall act accordingly, until the disability be removed, or a President shall be elected.

The President shall, at stated times, receive for his services a compensation, which shall neither be increased nor diminished during the period for which he shall have been elected, and he shall not receive within that period any other emolument from the United States, or any of them.

Before he enter on the execution of his office, he shall take the following oath or affirmation:—"I do solemnly swear (or affirm) that I will faithfully execute the office of the President of the United States, and will to the best of my ability preserve, protect and defend the Constitution of the United States."

Section 2.   The President shall be commander in chief of the army and navy of the United States, and of the militia of the several States, when called into the actual service of the United States; he may require the opinion, in writing, of the principal officer in each of the executive departments, upon any subject relating to the duties of their respective offices, and he shall have power to grant reprieves and pardons for offenses against the United States, except in cases of impeachment.

He shall have power, by and with the advice and consent of the Senate, to make treaties, provided two-thirds of the Senators present concur; and he shall nominate, and by and with the advice and consent of the Senate, shall appoint ambassadors, other public ministers and consuls, judges of the Supreme Court, and all other officers of the United States, whose appointments are not herein otherwise provided for, and which shall be established by law; but Congress may by law vest the appointment of such inferior officers, as they think proper, in the President alone, in the courts of law, or in the heads of departments.

The President shall have power to fill up all vacancies that may happen during the recess of the Senate, by granting commissions which shall expire at the end of their next session.

Section 3.   He shall from time to time give to the Congress information of the state of the Union, and recommend to their consideration such measures as he shall judge necessary and expedient; he may, on extraordinary occasions, convene both houses, or either of them, and in case of disagreement between them, with respect to the time of adjournment, he may adjourn them to such time as he shall think proper; he shall receive ambassadors and other public ministers; he shall take care that the laws be faithfully executed, and shall commission all the officers of the United States.

Section 4.   The President, Vice-President and all civil officers of the United States shall be removed from office on impeachment for, and on conviction of, treason, bribery, or other high crimes and misdemeanors.

Article III

Section 1.   The judicial power of the United States shall be vested in one Supreme Court, and in such inferior courts as the Congress may from time to time ordain and establish.

The judges, both of the Supreme and inferior courts, shall hold their offices during good behavior, and shall, at stated times, receive for their services a compensation which shall not be diminished during their continuance in office.

Section 2. The judicial power shall extend to all cases, in law and equity, arising under this Constitution, the laws of the United States, and treaties made, or which shall be made, under their authority;—to all cases affecting ambassadors, other public ministers and consuls;—to all cases of admiralty and maritime jurisdiction;—to controversies to which the United States shall be a party;—to controversies between two or more States;— *between a State and citizens of another State;*—between citizens of different States;— between citizens of the same State claiming lands under grants of different States, and between a State, or the citizens thereof, and foreign states, citizens or subjects.

In all cases affecting ambassadors, other public ministers and consuls, and those in which a State shall be party, the Supreme Court shall have original jurisdiction. In all the other cases before mentioned, the Supreme Court shall have appellate jurisdiction, both as to law and fact, with such exceptions, and under such regulations, as the Congress shall make.

The trial of all crimes, except in cases of impeachment, shall be by jury; and such trial shall be held in the State where said crimes shall have been committed; but when not committed within any State, the trial shall be at such place or places as the Congress may by law have directed.

Section 3. Treason against the United States shall consist only in levying war against them, or in adhering to their enemies, giving them aid and comfort. No person shall be convicted of treason unless on the testimony of two witnesses to the same overt act, or on confession in open court.

The Congress shall have power to declare the punishment of treason, but no attainder of treason shall work corruption of blood, or forfeiture except during the life of the person attainted.

Article IV

Section 1. Full faith and credit shall be given in each State to the public acts, records, and judicial proceedings of every other State. And the Congress may by general laws prescribe the manner in which such acts, records, and proceedings shall be proved, and the effect thereof.

Section 2. The citizens of each State shall be entitled to all privileges and immunities of citizens in the several States.

A person charged in any State with treason, felony, or other crime, who shall flee from justice, and be found in another State, shall on demand of the executive authority of the State from which he fled, be delivered up, to be removed to the State having jurisdiction of the crime.

No person held to service or labor in one State, under the laws thereof, escaping into another, shall, in consequence of any law or regulation therein, be discharged from such service or labor, but shall be delivered up on claim of the party to whom such service or labor may be due.

Section 3. New States may be admitted by the Congress into this Union; but no new State shall be formed or erected within the jurisdiction of any other State; nor any State be formed by the junction of two or more States, or parts of States, without the consent of the legislatures of the States concerned as well as of the Congress.

The Congress shall have power to dispose of and make all needful rules and regulations respecting the territory or other property belonging to the United States; and nothing in this Constitution shall be so construed as to prejudice any claims of the United States, or of any particular State.

Section 4. The United States shall guarantee to every State in this Union a republican form of government, and shall protect each of them against invasion; and on application of the legislature, or of the executive (when the legislature cannot be convened), against domestic violence.

Article V

The Congress,whenever two-thirds of both houses shall deem it necessary, shall propose amendments to this Constitution, or, on the application of the legislatures of two-thirds of the several States, shall call a convention for proposing amendments, which, in either case, shall be valid to all intents and purposes, as part of this Constitution, when ratified by the legislatures of three-fourths of the several States, or by conventions in three-fourths thereof, as the one or the other mode of ratification may be proposed by the Congress; provided *that no amendents which may be made prior to the year one thousand eight hundred and eight shall in any manner affect the first and fourth clauses in the ninth section of the first article;* and that no State, without its consent, shall be deprived of its equal suffrage in the Senate.

Article VI

All debts contracted and engagements entered into, before the adoption of this Constitution, shall be as valid against the United States under this Constitution, as under the Confederation.

This Constitution, and all the laws of the United States which shall be made in pursuance thereof; and all treaties made, or which shall be made, under the authority of the United States, shall be the supreme law of the land; and the judges in every State shall be bound thereby, anything in the Constitution or laws of any State to the contrary notwithstanding.

The Senators and Representatives before mentioned, and the members of the several State legislatures, and all executive and judicial officers, both of the United States and of the several States, shall be bound by oath or affirmation to support this Constitution; but no religious test shall ever be required as a qualification to any office or public trust under the United States.

Article VII

The ratification of the conventions of nine States shall be sufficient for the establishment of this Constitution between the States so ratifying the same.

Done in convention by the unanimous consent of the States present, the seventeenth day of September in the year of our Lord one thousand seven hundred and eighty-seven and of the Independence of the United States of America the twelfth. In witness whereof we have hereunto subscribed our names.

[Signed by]
G° WASHINGTON
Presidt and Deputy from Virginia
[*and thirty-eight others*]

Amendments to the Constitution

Article I*

Congress shall make no law respecting an establishment of religion, or prohibiting the free exercise thereof; or abridging the freedom of speech, or of the press; or the right of the people peaceably to assemble, and to petition the government for a redress of grievances.

Article II

A well-regulated militia being necessary to the security of a free State, the right of the people to keep and bear arms shall not be infringed.

Article III

No soldier shall, in time of peace, be quartered in any house without the consent of the owner, nor in time of war, but in a manner to be prescribed by law.

Article IV

The right of the people to be secure in their persons, houses, papers, and effects, against unreasonable searches and seizures, shall not be violated, and no warrants shall issue but upon probable cause, supported by oath or affirmation, and particularly describing the place to be searched, and the persons or things to be seized.

Article V

No person shall be held to answer for a capital, or otherwise infamous crime, unless on a presentment or indictment of a grand jury, except in cases arising in the land or naval forces, or in the militia, when in actual service in time of war or public danger; nor shall any person be subject for the same offence to be twice put in jeopardy of life or limb; nor shall be compelled in any criminal case to be a witness against himself, nor be deprived of

---

*The first ten Amendments (Bill of Rights) were adopted in 1791.

life, liberty, or property, without due process of law; nor shall private property be taken for public use without just compensation.

Article VI

In all criminal prosecutions, the accused shall enjoy the right to a speedy and public trial, by an impartial jury of the State and district wherein the crime shall have been committed, which district shall have been previously ascertained by law, and to be informed of the nature and cause of the accusation; to be confronted with the witnesses against him; to have compulsory process for obtaining witnesses in his favor, and to have the assistance of counsel for his defence.

Article VII

In suits at common law, where the value in controversy shall exceed twenty dollars, the right of trial by jury shall be preserved, and no fact tried by a jury shall be otherwise re-examined in any court of the United States, than according to the rules of the common law.

Article VIII

Excessive bail shall not be required, nor excessive fines imposed, nor cruel and unusual punishments inflicted.

Article IX

The enumeration in the Constitution, of certain rights, shall not be construed to deny or disparage others retained by the people.

Article X

The powers not delegated to the United States by the Constitution, nor prohibited by it to the States, are reserved to the States respectively, or to the people.

Article XI
[Adopted 1798]

The judicial power of the United States shall not be construed to extend to any suit in law or equity, commenced or prosecuted against one of the United States by citizens of another State, or by citizens or subjects of any foreign state.

Article XII
[Adopted 1804]

The electors shall meet in their respective States, and vote by ballot for President and Vice-President, one of whom, at least, shall not be an inhabitant of the same State with themselves; they shall name in their ballots the person voted for as President, and in distinct ballots the person voted for as Vice-President, and they shall make distinct lists of all persons voted for as President, and of all persons voted for as Vice-President, and of the number of votes for each, which lists they shall sign and certify, and transmit to the seat of government of the United States, directed to the President of the Senate;—The President of the Senate shall, in the presence of the Senate and House of Representatives, open all the certificates and the votes shall then be counted;—the person having the greatest number of votes for President shall be the President, if such number be a majority of the whole number of electors appointed; and if no person have such majority, then from the persons having the highest numbers not exceeding three on the list of those voted for as President, the House of Representatives shall choose immediately, by ballot, the President. But in choosing the President, the votes shall be taken by States, the representation from each State having one vote; a quorum for this purpose shall consist of a member or members from two-thirds of the States, and a majority of all the States shall be necessary to a choice. And if the House of Representatives shall not choose a President whenever the right of choice shall devolve upon them, before *the fourth day of March* next following, then the Vice-President shall act as President, as in the case of the death or other constitutional disability of the President.

The person having the greatest number of votes as Vice-President shall be the Vice-President, if such a number be a majority of the whole number of electors appointed; and if no person have a majority, then from the two highest numbers on the list the Senate shall choose the Vice-President; a quorum for the purpose shall consist of two-thirds of the whole number of Senators, and a majority of the whole number shall be necessary to a choice. But no person constitutionally ineligible to the office of President shall be eligible to that of Vice-President of the United States.

Article XIII
[*Adopted 1865*]

Section 1.   Neither slavery nor involuntary servitude, except as a punishment for crime whereof the party shall have been duly convicted, shall exist within the United States, or any place subject to their jurisdiction.

Section 2.   Congress shall have power to enforce this article by appropriate legislation.

Article XIV
[*Adopted 1868*]

Section 1.   All persons born or naturalized in the United States, and subject to the jurisdiction thereof, are citizens of the United States and of the State wherein they reside. No State shall make or enforce any law which shall abridge the privileges or immunities of citizens of the United States; nor shall any State deprive any person of life, liberty, or property, without due process of law; nor deny to any person within its jurisdiction the equal protection of the laws.

Section 2.   Representatives shall be apportioned among the several States according to their respective numbers, counting the whole number of persons in each State, excluding Indians not taxed. But when the right to vote at any election for the choice of Electors for President and Vice-President of the United States, Representatives in Congress, the executive and judicial officers of a State, or the members of the legislature thereof, is denied to any of the male inhabitants of such State, being twenty-one years of age and citizens of the United States, or in any way abridged, except for participation in rebellion, or other crime, the basis of representation therein shall be reduced in the proportion which the number of such male citizens shall bear to the whole number of male citizens twenty-one years of age in such State.

Section 3.   No person shall be a Senator or Representative in Congress, or Elector of President and Vice-President, or hold any office, civil or military, under the United States, or under any State, who, having previously taken an oath, as a member of Congress, or as an officer of the United States, or as a member of any State legislature, or as an executive or judicial officer of any State, to support the Constitution of the United States, shall have engaged in insurrection or rebellion against the same, or given aid or comfort to the enemies thereof. Congress may, by a vote of two-thirds of each house, remove such disability.

Section 4.   The validity of the public debt of the United States, authorized by law, including debts incurred for payment of pensions and bounties for services in suppressing insurrection or rebellion, shall not be questioned. But neither the United States nor any State shall assume or pay any debt or obligation incurred in aid of insurrection or rebellion against the United States, or any claim for the loss of emancipation, of any slave; but all such debts, obligations, and claims shall be held illegal and void.

Section 5.   The Congress shall have the power to enforce, by appropriate legislation, the provisions of this article.

Article XV
[Adopted 1870]

Section 1.   The right of citizens of the United States to vote shall not be denied or abridged by the United States or by any State on account of race, color, or previous condition of servitude.

Section 2.   The Congress shall have power to enforce this article by appropriate legislation.

Article XVI
[Adopted 1913]

The Congress shall have power to lay and collect taxes on incomes, from whatever source derived, without apportionment among the several States, and without regard to any census or enumeration.

Article XVII
[Adopted 1913]

Section 1.   The Senate of the United States shall be composed of two Senators from each State, elected by the people thereof, for six years; and each Senator shall have one vote. The electors in each State shall have the qualifications requisite for electors of [voters for] the most numerous branch of the State legislatures.

Section 2.   When vacancies happen in the representation of any State in the Senate, the executive authority of such State shall issue writs of election to fill such vacancies: Provided, that the Legislature of any State may empower the executive thereof to make temporary appointments until the people fill the vacancies by election as the Legislature may direct.

Section 3.   This amendment shall not be so construed as to affect the election or term of any Senator chosen before it becomes valid as part of the Constitution.

Article XVIII
[Adopted 1919; Repealed 1933]

Section 1.   *After one year from the ratification of this article the manufacture, sale, or transportation of intoxicating liquors within, the importation thereof into, or the exportation thereof from the United States and all territory subject to the jurisdiction thereof, for beverage purposes, is hereby prohibited.*

Section 2.   *The Congress and the several States shall have concurrent power to enforce this article by appropriate legislation.*

Section 3.   *This article shall be inoperative unless it shall have been ratified as an amendment to the Constitution by the legislatures of the several States, as provided by the Constitution, within seven years from the date of the submission thereof to the States by the Congress.*

Article XIX
[Adopted 1920]

Section 1.   The right of citizens of the United States to vote shall not be denied or abridged by the United States or by any State on account of sex.

Section 2.   The Congress shall have the power to enforce this article by appropriate legislation.

Article XX
[Adopted 1933]

Section 1.   The terms of the President and Vice-President shall end at noon on the 20th day of January, and the terms of Senators and Representatives at noon on the 3d day of January, of the years in which such terms would have ended if this article had not been ratified; and the terms of their succesors shall then begin.

Section 2.   The Congress shall assemble at least once in every year, and such meeting shall begin at noon on the 3d day of January, unless they shall by law appoint a different day.

Section 3.   If, at the time fixed for the beginning of the term of the President, the President-elect shall have died, the Vice-President-elect shall become President. If a

President shall not have been chosen before the time fixed for the beginning of his term, or if the President-elect shall have failed to qualify, then the Vice-President-elect shall act as President until a President shall have qualified; and the Congress may by law provide for the case wherein neither a President-elect nor a Vice-President-elect shall have qualified, declaring who shall then act as President, or the manner in which one who is to act shall be selected, and such persons shall act accordingly until a President or Vice-President shall have qualified.

Section 4.   The Congress may by law provide for the case of the death of any of the persons from whom the House of Representatives may choose a President whenever the right of choice shall have devolved upon them, and for the case of the death of any persons from whom the Senate may choose a Vice-President whenever the right of choice shall have devolved upon them.

Section 5.   Sections 1 and 2 shall take effect on the 15th day of October following the ratification of this article.

Section 6.   This article shall be inoperative unless it shall have been ratified as an amendment to the Constitution by the Legislatures of three-fourths of the several States within seven years from the date of its submission.

Article XXI
[*Adopted 1933*]

Section 1.   The eighteenth article of amendment to the Constitution of the United States is hereby repealed.

Section 2.   The transportation or importation into any State, Territory, or Possession of the United States for delivery or use therein of intoxicating liquors, in violation of the laws thereof, is hereby prohibited.

Section 3.   This article shall be inoperative unless it shall have been ratified as an amendment to the Constitution by conventions in the several States, as provided in the Constitution, within seven years from the date of submission thereof to the States by the Congress.

Article XXII
[*Adopted 1951*]

Section 1.   No person shall be elected to the office of President more than twice, and no person who has held the office of President, or acted as President, for more than two years of a term to which some other person was elected President shall be elected to the office of President more than once. But this article shall not apply to any person holding the office of President when this article was proposed by the Congress, and shall not prevent any person who may be holding the office of President, or acting as President, during the term within which this article becomes operative from holding the office of President or acting as President during the remainder of such term.

Section 2. This article shall be inoperative unless it shall have been ratified as an amendment to the Constitution by the legislatures of three-fourths of the several States within seven years from the date of its submission to the States by the Congress.

Article XXIII
[Adopted 1961]

Section 1. The District constituting the seat of Government of the United States shall appoint in such manner as the Congress may direct:

A number of electors of President and Vice-President equal to the whole number of Senators and Representatives in Congress to which the District would be entitled if it were a State, but in no event more than the least populous State; they shall be in addition to those appointed by the States, but they shall be considered for the purposes of the election of President and Vice-President, to be electors appointed by a State; and they shall meet in the District and perform such duties as provided by the twelfth article of amendment.

Section 2. The Congress shall have the power to enforce this article by appropriate legislation.

Article XXIV
[Adopted 1964]

Section 1. The right of citizens of the United States to vote in any primary or other election for President or Vice-President, for electors for President or Vice-President, or for Senator or Representative in Congress, shall not be denied or abridged by the United States or any State by reason of failure to pay any poll tax or other tax.

Section 2. The Congress shall have the power to enforce this article by appropriate legislation.

Article XXV
[Adopted 1967]

Section 1. In case of the removal of the President from office or of his death or resignation, the Vice-President shall become President.

Section 2. Whenever there is a vacancy in the office of the Vice-President, the President shall nominate a Vice-President who shall take office upon confirmation by a majority vote of both Houses of Congress.

Section 3. Whenever the President transmits to the President pro tempore of the Senate and the Speaker of the House of Representatives his written declaration that he is unable to discharge the powers and duties of his office, and until he transmits to them a written declaration to the contrary, such powers and duties shall be discharged by the Vice-President as Acting President.

Section 4. Whenever the Vice-President and a majority of either the principal officers of the executive departments or of such other body as Congress may by law provide, transmit to the President pro tempore of the Senate and the Speaker of the House of Representatives their written declaration that the President is unable to discharge the powers and duties of his office, the Vice-President shall immediately assume the powers and duties of the office as Acting President.

Thereafter, when the President transmits to the President pro tempore of the Senate and the Speaker of the House of Representatives his written declaration that no inability exists, he shall resume the powers and duties of his office unless the Vice-President and a majority of either the principal officers of the executive department[s] or of such other body as Congress may by law provide, transmit within four days to the President pro tempore of the Senate and the Speaker of the House of Representatives their written declaration that the President is unable to discharge the powers and duties of his office. Thereupon Congress shall decide the issue, assembling within forty-eight hours for that purpose if not in session. If the Congress, within twenty-one days after receipt of the latter written declaration, or, if Congress is not in session, within twenty-one days after Congress is required to assemble, determines by two-thirds vote of both Houses that the President is unable to discharge the powers and duties of his office, the Vice-President shall continue to discharge the same as Acting President; otherwise, the President shall resume the powers and duties of his office.

Article XXVI
[Adopted 1971]

Section 1. The right of citizens of the United States, who are 18 years of age or older, to vote shall not be denied or abridged by the United States or by any State on account of age.

Section 2. The Congress shall have power to enforce this article by appropriate legislation.

Presidential Elections*

Election	Candidates	Parties	Popular Vote	Electoral Vote
1789	**George Washington**	No party designations		69
	John Adams			34
	Minor Candidates			35
1792	**George Washington**	No party designations		132
	John Adams			77
	George Clinton			50
	Minor Candidates			5
1796	**John Adams**	Federalist		71
	Thomas Jefferson	Democratic-Republican		68
	Thomas Pinckney	Federalist		59
	Aaron Burr	Democratic-Republican		30
	Minor Candidates			48
1800	**Thomas Jefferson**	Democratic-Republican		73
	Aaron Burr	Democratic-Republican		73
	John Adams	Federalist		65
	Charles C. Pinckney	Federalist		64
	John Jay	Federalist		1
1804	**Thomas Jefferson**	Democratic-Republican		162
	Charles C. Pinckney	Federalist		14
1808	**James Madison**	Democratic-Republican		122
	Charles C. Pinckney	Federalist		47
	George Clinton	Democratic-Republican		6
1812	**James Madison**	Democratic-Republican		128
	DeWitt Clinton	Federalist		89
1816	**James Monroe**	Democratic-Republican		183
	Rufus King	Federalist		34
1820	**James Monroe**	Democratic-Republican		231
	John Q. Adams	Independent Republican		1

---

*Candidates receiving less than 1% of the popular vote are omitted. Before the Twelfth Amendment (1804) the Electoral College voted for two presidential candidates, and the runner-up became vice-president. Basic figures are taken primarily from *Historical Statistics of the United States, 1789–1945* (1949), pp. 288–90; *Historical Statistics of the United States, Colonial Times to 1957* (1960), pp. 682–83; and *Statistical Abstract of the United States, 1969* (1969), pp. 355–57.

Election	Candidates	Parties	Popular Vote	Electoral Vote
1824	**John Q. Adams** (Min.)*	Democratic-Republican	108,740	84
	Andrew Jackson	Democratic-Republican	153,544	99
	William H. Crawford	Democratic-Republican	46,618	41
	Henry Clay	Democratic-Republican	47,136	37
1828	**Andrew Jackson**	Democratic	647,286	178
	John Q. Adams	National Republican	508,064	83
1832	**Andrew Jackson**	Democratic	687,502	219
	Henry Clay	National Republican	530,189	49
	William Wirt	Anti-Masonic	33,108	7
	John Floyd	National Republican		11
1836	**Martin Van Buren**	Democratic	762,678	170
	William H. Harrison	Whig		73
	Hugh L. White	Whig		26
	Daniel Webster	Whig	736,656	14
	W. P. Mangum	Whig		11
1840	**William H. Harrison**	Whig	1,275,016	234
	Martin Van Buren	Democratic	1,129,102	60
1844	**James K. Polk** (Min.)*	Democratic	1,337,243	170
	Henry Clay	Whig	1,299,062	105
	James G. Birney	Liberty	62,300	
1848	**Zachary Taylor** (Min.)*	Whig	1,360,099	163
	Lewis Cass	Democratic	1,220,544	127
	Martin Van Buren	Free Soil	291,263	
1852	**Franklin Pierce**	Democratic	1,601,274	254
	Winfield Scott	Whig	1,386,580	42
	John P. Hale	Free Soil	155,825	
1856	**James Buchanan** (Min.)*	Democratic	1,838,169	174
	John C. Frémont	Republican	1,341,264	114
	Millard Fillmore	American	874,534	8
1860	**Abraham Lincoln** (Min.)*	Republican	1,866,452	180
	Stephen A. Douglas	Democratic	1,375,157	12
	John C. Breckinridge	Democratic	847,953	72
	John Bell	Constitutional Union	590,631	39
1864	**Abraham Lincoln**	Union	2,213,665	212
	George B. McClellan	Democratic	1,802,237	21
1868	**Ulysses S. Grant**	Republican	3,012,833	214
	Horatio Seymour	Democratic	2,703,249	80
1872	**Ulysses S. Grant**	Republican	3,597,132	286
	Horace Greeley	Democratic and Liberal Republican	2,834,125	66

*"Min." indicates minority president—one receiving less than 50% of all popular votes.

Election	Candidates	Parties	Popular Vote	Electoral Vote
1876	**Rutherford B. Hayes** (Min.)*	Republican	4,036,298	185
	Samuel J. Tilden	Democratic	4,300,590	184
1880	**James A. Garfield** (Min.)*	Republican	4,454,416	214
	Winfield S. Hancock	Democratic	4,444,952	155
	James B. Weaver	Greenback-Labor	308,578	
1884	**Grover Cleveland** (Min.)*	Democratic	4,874,986	219
	James G. Blaine	Republican	4,851,981	182
	Benjamin F. Butler	Greenback-Labor	175,370	
	John P. St. John	Prohibition	150,369	
1888	**Benjamin Harrison** (Min.)*	Republican	5,439,853	233
	Grover Cleveland	Democratic	5,540,309	168
	Clinton B. Fisk	Prohibition	249,506	
	Anson J. Streeter	Union Labor	146,935	
1892	**Grover Cleveland** (Min.)*	Democratic	5,556,918	277
	Benjamin Harrison	Republican	5,176,108	145
	James B. Weaver	People's	1,041,028	22
	John Bidwell	Prohibition	264,133	
1896	**William McKinley**	Republican	7,104,779	271
	William J. Bryan	Democratic	6,502,925	176
1900	**William McKinley**	Republican	7,207,923	292
	William J. Bryan	Democratic; Populist	6,358,133	155
	John C. Woolley	Prohibition	208,914	
1904	**Theodore Roosevelt**	Republican	7,623,486	336
	Alton B. Parker	Democratic	5,077,911	140
	Eugene V. Debs	Socialist	402,283	
	Silas C. Swallow	Prohibition	258,536	
1908	**William H. Taft**	Republican	7,678,908	321
	William J. Bryan	Democratic	6,409,104	162
	Eugene V. Debs	Socialist	420,793	
	Eugene W. Chafin	Prohibition	253,840	
1912	**Woodrow Wilson** (Min.)*	Democratic	6,293,454	435
	Theodore Roosevelt	Progressive	4,119,538	88
	William H. Taft	Republican	3,484,980	8
	Eugene V. Debs	Socialist	900,672	
	Eugene W. Chafin	Prohibition	206,275	
1916	**Woodrow Wilson** (Min.)*	Democratic	9,129,606	277
	Charles E. Hughes	Republican	8,538,221	254
	A. L. Benson	Socialist	585,113	
	J. F. Hanly	Prohibition	220,506	
1920	**Warren G. Harding**	Republican	16,152,200	404
	James M. Cox	Democratic	9,147,353	127
	Eugene V. Debs	Socialist	919,799	
	P. P. Christensen	Farmer-Labor	265,411	

*"Min." indicates minority president—one receiving less than 50% of all popular votes.

Election	Candidates	Parties	Popular Vote	Electoral Vote
1924	**Calvin Coolidge**	Republican	15,725,016	382
	John W. Davis	Democratic	8,386,503	136
	Robert M. La Follette	Progressive	4,822,856	13
1928	**Herbert C. Hoover**	Republican	21,391,381	444
	Alfred E. Smith	Democratic	15,016,443	87
1932	**Franklin D. Roosevelt**	Democratic	22,821,857	472
	Herbert C. Hoover	Republican	15,761,841	59
	Norman Thomas	Socialist	881,951	
1936	**Franklin D. Roosevelt**	Democratic	27,751,597	523
	Alfred M. Landon	Republican	16,679,583	8
	William Lemke	Union, etc.	882,479	
1940	**Franklin D. Roosevelt**	Democratic	27,244,160	449
	Wendell L. Willkie	Republican	22,305,198	82
1944	**Franklin D. Roosevelt**	Democratic	25,602,504	432
	Thomas E. Dewey	Republican	22,006,285	99
1948	**Harry S Truman** (Min.)*	Democratic	24,105,812	303
	Thomas E. Dewey	Republican	21,970,065	189
	J. Strom Thurmond	States' Rights Democratic	1,169,063	39
	Henry A. Wallace	Progressive	1,157,172	
1952	**Dwight D. Eisenhower**	Republican	33,936,234	442
	Adlai E. Stevenson	Democratic	27,314,992	89
1956	**Dwight D. Eisenhower**	Republican	35,590,472	457
	Adlai E. Stevenson	Democratic	26,022,752	73
1960	**John F. Kennedy** (Min.)*	Democratic	34,226,731	303
	Richard M. Nixon	Republican	34,108,157	219
1964	**Lyndon B. Johnson**	Democratic	43,129,484	486
	Barry M. Goldwater	Republican	27,178,188	52
1968	**Richard M. Nixon** (Min.)*	Republican	31,785,480	301
	Hubert H. Humphrey, Jr.	Democratic	31,275,166	191
	George C. Wallace	American Independent	9,906,473	46
1972	**Richard M. Nixon**	Republican	45,767,218	520
	George S. McGovern	Democratic	28,357,668	17
1976	**Jimmy Carter**	Democratic	40,276,040	297
	Gerald R. Ford	Republican	38,532,630	241
1980	**Ronald W. Reagan**	Republican	43,899,248	489
	Jimmy Carter	Democratic	35,481,435	49
1984	**Ronald W. Reagan**	Republican	54,451,521	525
	Walter F. Mondale	Democratic	37,565,334	13
1988	**George H. W. Bush**	Republican	47,946,422	426
	Michael S. Dukakis	Democratic	41,016,429	112

*"Min." indicates minority president—one receiving less than 50% of all popular votes.

Presidents and Vice-Presidents

Term	President	Vice-President
1789–1793	George Washington	John Adams
1793–1797	George Washington	John Adams
1797–1801	John Adams	Thomas Jefferson
1801–1805	Thomas Jefferson	Aaron Burr
1805–1809	Thomas Jefferson	George Clinton
1809–1813	James Madison	George Clinton (d. 1812)
1813–1817	James Madison	Elbridge Gerry (d. 1814)
1817–1821	James Monroe	Daniel D. Tompkins
1821–1825	James Monroe	Daniel D. Tompkins
1825–1829	John Quincy Adams	John C. Calhoun
1829–1833	Andrew Jackson	John C. Calhoun (resigned 1832)
1833–1837	Andrew Jackson	Martin Van Buren
1837–1841	Martin Van Buren	Richard M. Johnson
1841–1845	William H. Harrison (d. 1841) John Tyler	John Tyler
1845–1849	James K. Polk	George M. Dallas
1849–1853	Zachary Taylor (d. 1850) Millard Fillmore	Millard Fillmore
1853–1857	Franklin Pierce	William R. D. King (d. 1853)
1857–1861	James Buchanan	John C. Breckinridge
1861–1865	Abraham Lincoln	Hannibal Hamlin
1865–1869	Abraham Lincoln (d. 1865) Andrew Johnson	Andrew Johnson
1869–1873	Ulysses S. Grant	Schuyler Colfax
1873–1877	Ulysses S. Grant	Henry Wilson (d. 1875)
1877–1881	Rutherford B. Hayes	William A. Wheeler
1881–1885	James A. Garfield (d. 1881) Chester A. Arthur	Chester A. Arthur
1885–1889	Grover Cleveland	Thomas A. Hendricks (d. 1885)
1889–1893	Benjamin Harrison	Levi P. Morton
1893–1897	Grover Cleveland	Adlai E. Stevenson
1897–1901	William McKinley	Garret A. Hobart (d. 1899)
1901–1905	William McKinley (d. 1901) Theodore Roosevelt	Theodore Roosevelt

Term	President	Vice-President
1905–1909	Theodore Roosevelt	Charles W. Fairbanks
1909–1913	William H. Taft	James S. Sherman (d. 1912)
1913–1917	Woodrow Wilson	Thomas R. Marshall
1917–1921	Woodrow Wilson	Thomas R. Marshall
1921–1925	Warren G. Harding (d. 1923) Calvin Coolidge	Calvin Coolidge
1925–1929	Calvin Coolidge	Charles G. Dawes
1929–1933	Herbert C. Hoover	Charles Curtis
1933–1937	Franklin D. Roosevelt	John N. Garner
1937–1941	Franklin D. Roosevelt	John N. Garner
1941–1945	Franklin D. Roosevelt	Henry A. Wallace
1945–1949	Franklin D. Roosevelt (d. 1945) Harry S Truman	Harry S Truman
1949–1953	Harry S Truman	Alben W. Barkley
1953–1957	Dwight D. Eisenhower	Richard M. Nixon
1957–1961	Dwight D. Eisenhower	Richard M. Nixon
1961–1965	John F. Kennedy (d. 1963) Lyndon B. Johnson	Lyndon B. Johnson
1965–1969	Lyndon B. Johnson	Hubert H. Humphrey, Jr.
1969–1974	Richard M. Nixon (resigned 1974)	Spiro T. Agnew (resigned 1973); Gerald R. Ford
1974–1977	Gerald R. Ford	Nelson A. Rockefeller
1977–1981	Jimmy Carter	Walter F. Mondale
1981–1985	Ronald W. Reagan	George H. W. Bush
1985–1989	Ronald W. Reagan	George H. W. Bush
1989–	George H. W. Bush	J. Danforth Quayle

Growth of U.S. Population and Area

Census	Population	Percent of Increase over Preceding Census	Land Area, Square Miles	Population per Square Mile
1790	3,929,214		867,980	4.5
1800	5,308,483	35.1	867,980	6.1
1810	7,239,881	36.4	1,685,865	4.3
1820	9,638,453	33.1	1,753,588	5.5
1830	12,866,020	33.5	1,753,588	7.3
1840	17,069,453	32.7	1,753,588	9.7
1850	23,191,876	35.9	2,944,337	7.9
1860	31,443,321	35.6	2,973,965	10.6
1870	39,818,449	26.6	2,973,965	13.4
1880	50,155,783	26.0	2,973,965	16.9
1890	62,947,714	25.5	2,973,965	21.2
1900	75,994,575	20.7	2,974,159	25.6
1910	91,972,266	21.0	2,973,890	30.9
1920	105,710,620	14.9	2,973,776	35.5
1930	122,775,046	16.1	2,977,128	41.2
1940	131,669,275	7.2	2,977,128	44.2
1950	150,697,361	14.5	2,974,726*	50.7
†1960	178,464,236	18.4	2,974,726	59.9
1970	204,765,770	14.7	2,974,726	68.8
1980	226,504,825	10.6	2,974,726	76.1
1990	249,632,692††	10.2	2,974,726	83.9

*As remeasured in 1940.

†Not including Alaska (pop. 226,167) and Hawaii (632,772).

††As released by U.S. Census Bureau, December 26, 1990. Critics of the census count have estimated that this figure may have undercounted the U.S. population by as much as 5 million persons.

· ILLUSTRATION CREDITS

The following abbreviations are used for some sources from which several illustrations were obtained:

AAS–American Antiquarian Society. DPH/SI–Division of Political History, Smithsonian Institution. LC–Library of Congress. MHS–Massachusetts Historical Society. NA–National Archives. NPG/SI–National Portrait Gallery, Smithsonian Institution. NW–North Wind Picture Archives. SI–Smithsonian Institution.

Part 1 p. 1, AAS.

Chapter 1 p. 6, Brown Brothers; p. 13, Nettie Lee Benson Collection, The General Libraries, University of Texas at Austin; p. 18, by kind permission of the Marquess of Tavistock and the Trustees of the Bedford Estate. Photo from the National Portrait Gallery, London; p. 20, National Portrait Gallery, London; p. 21, LC; p. 28, The Folger Shakespeare Library, Washington, D. C.

Chapter 2 p. 41, Richard Schlecht, National Geographic Society; p. 49, AAS; p. 52 (top), MHS; p. 52 (bottom), AAS; p. 55, Enoch Pratt Free Library; photograph from the Maryland Historical Society; p. 70, The Mansell Collection; p. 71, Historical Society of Pennsylvania.

Chapter 3 pp. 82, 83, The Folger Shakespeare Library, Washington, D. C.; p. 87, Harvard College Library; p. 94, Worcester Art Museum, Worcester, Mass.; p. 95, The Granger Collection, New York; p. 96, U.S. Department of the Interior, National Historic Site, Quincy, Mass.; p. 100, Courtesy, Virginia State Travel Service; p. 106, Arthur B. Mazmanian from his book *The Structure of Praise,* © The Beacon Press.

Chapter 4 p. 118, Rijksmuseum, Amsterdam; p. 123, The Charleston Library Society, Charleston, South Carolina; p. 127, The New York Historical Society, New York City; p. 131 (top), LC; p. 131 (bottom left), Virginia Historical Society; p. 131 (bottom right), The Metropolitan Museum of Art, Fletcher Fund, 1925, (25.108); p. 137, MHS; p. 144, LC.

Chapter 5 p. 151, LC; p. 155 (top), AAS; p. 155 (bottom), The Mabel Brady Garven Collection, Yale University Art Gallery; p. 156, Colonial Williamsburg Foundation; p. 164, The Saint Louis Art Museum, Museum Purchase; p. 170, Yale University Art Gallery, Bequest of Edward Phelps Edwards; p. 171, National Portrait Gallery, London; p. 181, Colonial Williamsburg Foundation.

Chapter 6 pp. 190, 195, LC; p. 198, AAS; p. 202, Philadelphia Museum of Art: Mr. and Mrs. Wharton Sinkler Collection; p. 203, Philadelphia Museum of Art: Gift of Mrs. John D. Rockefeller; p. 204, Houghton Library, Harvard University.

Part 2 p. 209, LC.

Chapter 7 p. 224, The Cleveland Museum of Art, gift of Mr. and Mrs. Lawrence S. Robbins; p. 226, LC; p. 228, MHS; p. 231 (top), LC; p. 231 (bottom), NW; p. 232, LC; p. 236, Deposited by the City of Boston. Courtesy, Museum of Fine Arts, Boston; p. 237, LC.

Chapter 8 p. 253, State Street Trust Company; p. 254, Division of Fine Arts, SI; p. 255, The National Gallery of Art, Washington, D. C.; p. 256, Copyright Yale University Art Gallery; p. 259, AAS; p. 263, The Brooklyn Museum, Dick S. Ramsey Fund; pp. 266, 269, LC.

Chapter 9 p. 275, LC; p. 276, The Houghton Library, Harvard University; pp. 287, 290, LC; p. 293, New York State Historical Association, Cooperstown, New York.

Chapter 10 p. 307, LC; p. 309, The Thomas Gilcrease Institute of American History and Art, Tulsa, Oklahoma; pp. 314, 317, 319, 329, LC; p. 331, NPG/SI.

Chapter 11 p. 336, LC; p. 338, I. N. Phelps Stokes Collection, Miriam & Ira D. Wallach Division of Art, Prints and Photographs, The New York Public Library, Astor, Lenox and Tilden Foundations; p. 347, Mrs. Walter Jennings and the Metropolitan Museum of Art; p. 348, Field Museum of Natural History, Chicago; p. 349, SI; p. 351, The Bettmann Archive; p. 357, LC; p. 366, Abby Rockefeller Collection of American Folk Art, Colonial Williamsburg Foundation.

Part 3 p. 373, LC.

Chapter 12 p. 381, LC; p. 385, Bureau of Public Roads, Department of Commerce; p. 388, LC; p. 391, LC; p. 393, Museum of American Textile History; p. 395, Collection of Business Americana, SI; p. 400, National Life Insurance Company, Montpelier, Vermont; p. 405, Woolaroc Museum, Bartlesville, Oklahoma.

Chapter 13 p. 420, LC; p. 426, Francis A. Countway Library of Medicine, Harvard University; pp. 428, 431, LC; p. 441, Division of Graphic Arts, SI; pp. 443, 445, LC; p. 447, National Museum of American Art, Washington, D. C./Art Resource, New York; p. 448, Munson-Williams-Proctor Institute, Museum of Art, Utica, New York; p. 449, NPG/SI.

Chapter 14 p. 455, United States National Museum, Washington, D. C.; pp. 458, 460, 462, 464, LC; p. 466, DPH/SI; p. 467, LC; p. 469, Division of Domestic Life, SI; p. 475, Harvard College Library; pp. 478, 482, LC.

Chapter 15 p. 492, LC; p. 495, NPG/SI; p. 498, LC; p. 499, NPG/SI, Gift of J. William Middendorf II; p. 502, NA; p. 507, Division of Cultural History, SI; p. 508, LC; p. 510, LC; p. 515, DPH/SI.

Chapter 16 pp. 529, 530, LC; p. 533, U.S. Signal Corps Photo, NA; p. 539, LC; p. 541 (top), Boston Public Library; p. 541 (bottom), AAS.

Chapter 17 p. 549, AAS; pp. 551, 554, LC; p. 558, The Metropolitan Museum of Art, Gift of I. N. Phelps Stokes, Edward S. Hawes, Alice Mary Hawes, Marion Augusta Hawes, 1937; p. 563, DPH/SI; p. 570, Print Collection, Miriam & Ira D. Wallach Division of Art, Prints and Photographs, The New York Public Library, Astor, Lenox and Tilden Foundations; p. 576, Illinois State Historical Society; p. 577, NPG/SI; p. 579, Kansas Historical Society, Topeka, Kansas; p. 581, LC.

Part 4 p. 587, LC.

Chapter 18 pp. 591, 593, 600 (right), LC; p. 600 (left), Eleanor S. Brockenbrough Library, The Museum of the Confederacy, Richmond, Virginia; p. 601, Chicago Historical Society; p. 610, LC; p. 617, NA.

Chapter 19 pp. 622, 637, 638, 640, LC; p. 650, Valentine Museum, Richmond, Virginia; pp. 651, 653, LC.

Chapter 20 pp. 663, 665, 666, 680, 682, 686, 687, LC; p. 690, R. B. Hayes Residential Center, Fremont, Ohio.

Chapter 21 pp. 697, 710, LC; p. 715 (top), DPH/SI; p. 715 (bottom), NW; p. 719, LC; p. 721, DPH/SI.

INDEX

Aberdeen, Lord, 531

Abolitionism, 412, 435–437, 443–444, 472–483. *See also* Antislavery

Abolitionists: and free blacks, 417, 439, 481–483; and women's movement, 442–445; critique of slavery, 465–468; southern, 470–471; values, 473–474, 476; propaganda barred from mails, 503, 509; Whigs and, 516; and Texas, 528, 530, 531; and crises of 1850s, 400–401, 555, 568; Douglas on, 565–566; John Brown and, 569, 578; Lincoln and, 574, 575, 576–577; during Civil War, 599, 636–637; Seward on, 608; and freedmen, 664

Acadians, 190

Act Concerning Religion (1649), 103

Act for Establishing Religious Freedom (1786), 104, 331, 354

Act of Settlement (1701), 138

Adams, Abigail, *293*

Adams, Charles Francis, 480, 607, 642

Adams, Henry, 707

Adams, John: on colonial experience, 3; on Revolution, 210, 249, 251, *256,* 277; on Boston Tea Party, 240; in imperial debate, 244; in Revolution, 249, 251, 256, 270, 277, 289, in Federalist period, 305, 308; as vice-president, 316; on public finance, 318–319; as president, 326, 327, 330, 332, 337, 350, 351; election of 1800, 330, 336; and Jefferson, 336; retirement, 341, 367; death, 486

Adams, John Quincy: and Jeffersonian Republicans, 341; as secretary of state, 342, 525, 527–528; on neutral rights, 362; election of 1824, 393–394, 518, 527; as president, 340, 486, 488–495, 496, 511–513; and antislavery, 479, 527–528, 544; on political parties, 486; as nationalist, 524; as Secretary of State, 525; as representative, 530

Adams, Samuel, 199, 235, *236,* 239, 249, 252, 276, 277, 303, 308

Adams-Onís Treaty. *See* Transcontinental Treaty

Adelantados, 12

Administrative systems: Spanish-American empire, 8–12; British Empire, 12, 113–114; Reconstruction period, 665–668. *See also* Bureaucracy; Government

Admiralty courts, 146, 251, 360, 368. *See also* Vice-admiralty courts

Adolescents. *See* Youth

Africa: in eighteenth-century wars, 188–190; slave trade from, 368, 436; demography, 379; and nineteenth-century humanitarianism, 435–437; and African-American culture, 467. *See also* Blacks; Slave trade; North Africa; West Africa

African-American culture, colonial period and nineteenth century, 83–84, 154, 463–468

African Americans. *See* Blacks; Slaves

Agassiz, Louis, 683

Age of Reason, 355

Agrarianism: republicanism and, 274, 275, 319, 324; and "safety-valve" theory, 399–401; Jacksonian and pre–Civil War periods, 567

Agriculture: colonial, 39–40, 56–57, 60, 67–68, 87–91, 121–124, 157–162, 165–166, 221; physiocrats on, 203; Revolutionary era, *275,* 286–288, 305; Indian, 347, 403; modernization, 380, 384–386; Jacksonian and pre–Civil War periods, 383–387; pre–Civil War southern, 454–455, 458, 500–501, 522; Civil War era, 604, 629; post-Civil War southern, 660, 670–673; breakup of plantation system, 671–673; tariff problem, Gilded Age, 701

Agriculture, Department of, creation, 630

Aix-la-Chappelle, Treaty of (1748), 187

Alabama: admission, 347, 489; Indians, 404, *407;* secession, 583, 585, *596,* 617; Reconstruction, 660, 661, *678,* 686–688, 691, 716, *717;* Gilded Age, 716; black voting rights, 720

Alabama, C.S.S., 628, 642, 698

Alamance, battle of the, 220, 245

Alamo, massacre at the, *529, 538*

Alaska, Russian occupation, 527, 533; purchase of, 699

Albany, N.Y., 60, 129, 136, 191, 299, 636

Albany Congress, 190, 249

Albany Evening Journal, 514

Albany Regency, 493, 496, 513–514

Albemarle, Duke of, 64

Albemarle, N.C., 65, 134

Albemarle Sound, 64

Alcohol: Indians and, 219; urban drunkenness, 398; abuse of, nineteenth century, 421, 435, *508. See also* Prohibition; Temperance

Alexander, General E. P., 660

Algonquians, 33

Alien and Sedition Acts (1798), 329–330, 332, 339

Allen, Ethan, 219, 355

Alliances: Franco-American (1778), 266, 271, 327, 359; Convention of 1800, 368

Ambergris, 27

Amendments to Articles of Confederation, 282, 303, 304, 306, 311

Amendments to Constitution: Bill of Rights, 315, 332; First, 358; Fifth, 573; Tenth, 315; Eleventh, 332; Twelfth, 337, 368; Thirteenth, 657, 658, 712, 718; Fourteenth, 656, 658, 675–678, 686, 712, 718; Fifteenth, 658, 712, 718; Seventeenth, 574; and Louisiana Purchase, 346; proposed by Hartford Convention, 368; and coming of Civil War, 555

America: Spanish conquest, 6–14; English colonization, 16–28, 33–75; seventeenth-century economy and society, 78–109, 119–132; consolidation of British Empire, 112–121, 186–199; and early modern European culture, 138–139, 199–206; eighteenth-century economy and society, 149–174; eighteenth-century politics, 174–181; American Revolution, 210–244, 248–270; U.S. expansion, 343–347, 365, 522–543. *See also* United States

American Anti-Slavery Society, 444, 476, 664

American Bible Society, 369, 437, 439

American Board of Commissioners for Foreign Missions, 369

American Board of Customs, 233, 244

American Civil War. *See* Civil War, American

American Colonization Society, 435, 473, 476

American Freedmen's Inquiry Commission, 664

American Indians. *See* Indians, American

American Missionary Association, 665

American Museum, 289

American party. *See* Know-Nothings

American Philosophical Society, 244

American Phrenological Journal, 426

American Red Cross, 711

American Review and Literary Journal, 332

American Revolution. *See* Revolution, American

American Society for the Promotion of Temperance, 435, 440

American Sunday School Union, 435, 439

American System, 493, 499, 511, 516

American system of manufacturing, 392

American Temperance Magazine, 442

American Tract Society, 369, 435, 440

Amherst, Lord Jeffrey, 191–192, 223

Anabaptists, 60

Anarchism, 427

Anderson, Joseph, 629

Anderson, Robert, 594–595

Andersonville (Ga.) prisoner-of-war camp, 659

Andover Theological Seminary, 437

Andrew, John A., 647

Andros, Edmund, 117–118, 137–138

Anglican church: origins, 44; in colonies, 99–103, 117, 168–169, 222, 224, *234, 239,* 244; contrast with Puritanism, 105–107; eighteenth-century Britain, 152, 175, 257; in Revolution, 354. *See also* Episcopalians

Anglicans: in colonies, 69, 99, *100,* 168; as loyalists, 286. *See also* Episcopalians

Anglo-Dutch War, 62–63

Anglo-French wars, 127–129, 186–193, *189,* 206–207, 217, 223, 227, 260, 264, 269–270, 325–327, 330, 332, 360–362, 365–367

Anglophobia, 436, 476, 487, 524, 527–528, 531, 543, 548, 552, 565, 583

Anglo-Spanish wars, 17–23, 63, 129, 186, 188, 206, 266, 269–271

Annapolis Convention, 305

Anne (queen of England), 146

Anthony, Susan B., 711

Anti-authoritarianism: colonial, 120–121, 152–153; of Locke, 203; Jacksonian and pre–Civil War periods, 424, 445

Anti-Catholicism: colonial and Revolutionary eras, 57–58, 136–137, 187, 227; nineteenth century, 413, 422, 440, 509, 547, 559–560, 563

Anti-Chinese movement, 682

Antietam, battle of, *614,* 616, 618, 622, 639

Antiexpansionism: post-Civil War, 656

Antifederalists, 311–313, 315, 322

Anti-Masonry, 438, 505, 509, 514, 516, 548

Antinomianism, 53

Antiquity, classical, 273, 274, 299, 315

Antiradicalism: Revolutionary era, 250–256, 299, 306–307; of Federalists, 320, 327–331

Anti-religious views, post-Revolutionary period, 334

Antislavery: of Quakers, 270; Revolutionary era, 294–295; Jacksonian period, 400, 415, 418, 429, 445, 468–483; riots, *478,* 491, 501, 504, 523–525; and expansion, 528–535, 537, 542, 543, 547, 549–552, 555–584; Lincoln and, 575, 580; European, and Civil War, 608, 641–642; and emancipation, 636–640. *See also* Abolitionism

Antwerp, as English wool market, 17, 29

Apaches, 406

Appalachian Mountains, 150, 215, 244, 282, 285, 295

Appleton, Nathan, 550

Appomattox Court House, Va., 651, 654, 660, 662, 663, 698

Apprentices: in Revolutionary society, 290; nineteenth century, 414, 426

Archduke Maximilian, 698

Architecture and architects: seventeenth century, *13, 100, 106;* eighteenth century, *106, 131, 144;* Jefferson and, 332

Argentina, Spanish conquest, 8, 29

Argyll, Duke of, 610

Aristocracy: in colonial society, 79, 91–92, 121–132; British, 157, 159, 160; in eighteenth-century political theory, 174; Enlightenment and, 205; proposed introduction in America, 234; republicanism and, 273, 274, 277, 289, 292; "natural," 277, 308, 313, 328; Tocqueville on, 373; absence of, in nineteenth-century U.S., 412, 445. *See also* Elites; Social class

Arizona: Spanish exploration, 8; Gadsden Purchase, 543

Arkansas: settlement, 348; slavery, 455, 490, 547, 549; pre–Civil War politics, 582; secession, 594, 596, 598, 617; in Civil War, 600; Reconstruction, 691, 678, 688, 716; Gilded Age, 716; black voting rights, 720

Armada, Spanish, 23

Armed forces, U.S.: under Constitution, 310; Federalist and Jeffersonian periods, 325, 339; War of 1812, 364–368. *See also specific branches*

Armies, Civil War, 599–604, *600, 601,* 620–621, blacks in, 636–637, 639–641. *See also* Army, Confederate; Army, U.S.

Army, British: in colonies, 114, 186–193, 219, 223, 233, 234, 236, 244; in Revolutionary War, 252, 253, 260–270, 286; War of 1812, 364–368

Army, Confederate: Indians in, 597; raising of, 600–601, 603; military operations, 610–617, *613, 614, 616,* 620, *623, 624–* 625, 647–652, *648, 649, 653,* 654, 679; desertions from, 643, condition of, 652, surrender, 660, 662–663

Army, Continental. *See* Continental army

Army, standing: fear of, Revolutionary era, 223, 240; Federalists and, 330; Jeffersonian Republicans and, 324, 339, 364; absence of, nineteenth-century U.S., 424

Army, U.S.: pre–Civil War Indian campaigns, 321–322, 348, 404, 405, 406, 407; Federalist and Jeffersonian periods, 330, 339, 346; War of 1812, 365, 369; Jacksonian period, 405; Mexican War, 535–541, *538;* "Mormon War," 433–434; Civil War, 592–594, 599–604, *600, 601,* 610–617, 620, 621–625, 639–640, 644–649; in Reconstruction, 677–679. *See also* Armed forces; Continental army

Arndt, Johann, 151

Arnold, Benedict, 254

Art, nineteenth century, 368, 446–449. *See also* Architecture and architects

Arthur, Chester A., 707

Articles of Confederation, 280–285, 298, 302–305, 337; amendments to, 282, 303, 304, 306, 311; text, Appendix

Artisans: immigrants to colonies, 79, 109, 195, 201; black, 84, 157; in colonial society, 93, 136, 162, 164, 221; in British political riots, 226; in Revolution, 232, 251, 254; in Revolutionary society, 288; Critical Period, 300, 306; and Jeffersonian Republicans, 324; religion, 421, 434; nineteenth-century immigrants, 381, 390, 391; in Jacksonian and pre–Civil War society, 399, 413, 414, *508,* 563; in Confederacy, 599. *See also* Labor; Working class

Ashley, James M., 679–680

Ashley Cooper, Sir Anthony (Earl of Shaftesbury), 64–65

Asia: in eighteenth-century colonial wars, 188, 191

Assemblies. *See* Legislatures

Assembly, freedom of, 315

Assumption Bill, 318, 332

Astor, John Jacob, 397, 422–423

Asylums, 435, 479, 512
Atchison, David R., 568
Atlanta, Ga., 649, 650, 654
Atlantic Ocean: sixteenth-century discoveries, 6, 16–23; early modern trade, 85–91, *163,* 165; nineteenth-century transportation, 388, 628
Auburn system, 437
Audiencias, 9
Austrian Empire: in eighteenth-century wars, 186, 188; nineteenth century, 560, 608
Aztecs, 6, 14

Babcock, Orville E., 706
Bacon, Nathaniel, 133–134
Bacon's Rebellion, 90, 132, 133–134, 145, 180
Badger, Joseph, *170*
Bagenal, Philip H., 382
Balance of payments, colonial, 194
Balboa, Vasco Nuñez de, 6, 7, 29
Baldwin, Theron, 419
Ballot, voting by, 251, 719–720
Baltimore, Md.: origins, 91, 166; and nineteenth-century railroads, 394, 396; slave trade, 475, Democratic convention (1860), 580, 585; in Civil War, 597; post-Civil War, 702; labor unions, 708
Baltimore and Ohio Railroad, 396
Bank charters: BUS, 340, 369; *McCulloch v. Maryland,* 352
Bank of North America, 303
Bank of the United States (BUS): First, 318, *319,* 320, 332, 339–340, 353, 365, 369; Second, 369, 504–506, 513, 518, 630
Bankruptcy: colonial, 130; in imperial crisis, 229; Federalist period, 345; Jacksonian period, 508, 519; post-Civil War South, 672
Banks and banking: colonial, 197–199; Revolutionary and Confederation periods, 246, 291, 303; in Hamiltonian program, 317, 318; Jeffersonian period, 340, 352–353; Panic of 1819, 369, 487; Jacksonian period, 429, 487, 493, 500, 504–507, 512, 518; pre–Civil War period, 533, 553, 555; Civil War era, 604–606, 630, 646; post-Civil War South, 672, 720
Bank War, 504–506, 511, 548
Baptism, 167
Baptists: in colonies, 66, 69, 222; Revolutionary period and early nineteenth century, 354–356; and slavery, 439

Barbados: colonization, 26; and Carolina, 64–66; and slavery, 83
Barbary pirates, 304, 339, 368
Barlow, Joel, 315
Barnburners, 550
Barrington, Lord, 237
Barrow, Bennet H., 461
Barton, Clara, 711
Bates, Edward, 645
Bayard family, 136
Beauregard, P. G. T., 540, 595, 689
Beecher, Catherine, 442
Beecher, Lyman, 413, 422, 434, 437, 438, 439, 442
Belcher, Andrew, 129, 132
Belgian immigrants, 381
Belknap, William W., 706
Bell, John, *582*
Bellows, Henry W., 378
Benevolent Empire, 435–442
Benjamin, Judah P., 603, 607, 642, 644, 645
Benton, Thomas Hart, 504, 533
Berkeley, Lord John, 64, 68
Berkeley, Sir William, 42, 125, 133–134, 143
Berlin Decree, 361
Bermuda, colonization of, 26, 27, 39
Bermuda Company, 27
Bernard, Francis, 235, 237
Bibb, Henry, 481
Bible: and American Indians, 140; colonial education and, 140; and Revolution, 255; propagation of, nineteenth century, 369, 415, 441; in abolitionist and feminist movements, 443–444; in proslavery arguments, 472; John Brown and, 578
Biddle, Nicholas, 506
Bigelow, Jacob, 425
Bill of Rights, American, enacted, 315, 332. *See also* Civil liberties; Civil rights
Bill of Rights, English. *See* English Bill of Rights
Bills of credit, 197, 288, 309
Bills of exchange, 86, 124
Bimetallism, 704
Birmingham, England, 241
Birney, James G., 480, 534
Birthrates: seventeenth century, 80–81; nineteenth century, 381–383
Bison, slaughter of, 386, 407
Black Belt, 468
Black code (colonial Carolina), 67
Black Codes (nineteenth century), 471, 674, 684
Black Kettle, Chief, 714
Black Reconstruction, 688

Blacks (African Americans): in Spanish-American empire, 15–16; population, colonial, 35, 83–84, 123–124, 149, 153–157; in southern colonies, 43, 67–68, 74, 83–84, 153–157; in northern colonies, 59, 67–68, 154; Revolutionary era, 294–295; economic condition of, pre–Civil War, 396, *460;* in pre–Civil War North, 416–417, 473; Mormons and, 429; and colonization, 435, 439, 473; free, 435, 439, 454, 468, 470, 473, 481–483, 490, 513, 523, 551–552, 570, 576, 636; population, nineteenth century, 455, 685; as abolitionists, 481–483; in pre–Civil War Far West, 551, 557; *Dred Scott* decision and, 572–573; during Civil War, 611, 635, 636–641, 646, 652, 659, 683–687; attitudes of, at end of Civil War, 661; freedmen, 465, 664–673; civil rights, Reconstruction period, 656, 658–659, 674–677; 683–687, 689, 716; in Union army, 661; and post-Civil War southern economy, 668–669; adjustment to freedom, 669–670; prejudice against, post-Civil War, 683–687; northern views toward, 683–684; state voting rights, post-Civil War, 683; suffrage amendment (1868), 683; population, post-Civil War, 685; in South Carolina legislature, 686; education, during Reconstruction, 687; in Southern governments, 688; discrimination against, post-Reconstruction South, 718–721. *See also* Race riots; Racism; Slavery
Black separatism: pre–Civil War, 482
Black suffrage, Reconstruction period, 683
Blaine, James G., 631
Bland, Giles, 133
Blast furnace, 196, 393
Blockade, of Confederacy, 605–609, 611, 627–629, 632, 634, 638, 642
Blodgett, Samuel, *319*
Bloody Lane, 616
Blount, William, 316
Board of Trade and Plantations, 113, 146
Boggs, L. W., 430
Bolivia: Spanish conquest, 8, 29
Bonaparte, Napoleon. *See* Napoleon I
Bonds, government: Revolutionary era, 288; and Hamiltonian program, 318, 323; Texan, 554; Civil War era, 605–606, 631–632; Reconstruction period, 664
Bonus Bill (1817), 369
Book of Mormon, 429
Boone, Daniel, 215

Booth, John Wilkes, 647, 659
Border Ruffians, 568, *569,* 597
Border states: and Crisis of 1850, 553; pre–Civil War politics, 562–566; at outbreak of Civil War, 593–594, 596–599; and emancipation, 639; in Civil War politics, 644–645
Boroughs, in colonial Virginia, 40, 42, 99–100
Boston, Mass.: foundation, 35, 49; and seventeenth-century trade, 86; and Andros's regime, 117, 146; eighteenth century, 132, 221; in Revolution, 235, 239, 252; post-Revolutionary, 287, and Embargo of 1807–09, 363; early nineteenth century, 379, 381, 398, 416–417; and industrialization, 392, 394; blacks in, pre–Civil War, 416; antislavery, 473, 475, 478; Civil War, 605; post-Civil War, 702
Boston Manufacturing Company, 390–391
Boston Massacre, 236, *237,* 245
Boston Tea Party, 240, 245
Bounties, Civil War, 635
Bourgeoisie. *See* Capitalism
Bouweries, 59
Bowdoin College, 417
Boycotts, Revolutionary era, 221, 230, 233, 235, 249. *See also* Embargos
Braddock, Edward, 189–190
Bradford, William, 45–47
Bragg, Braxton, 615, 623, 624, 626, 640, 654
Brandywine, battle of, *265,* 271
Bray, Thomas, 169
Brazil: Portuguese and, 10, 17; slavery, 455, 461, 463, 523; Confederate emigration to, 660
Breckinridge, John C., 580, 581, 582
Bridges, *287,* 291
Britain. *See* British Empire; England; Great Britain
Britain's Remembrancer, 205–206
British: as nineteenth-century immigrants, 380, 391, 513. *See also* English; Scotch
British and Foreign Bible Society, 436
British Empire: contrasts with Spanish-American empire, 5–6, 12–14; origins of, 16–27; early governance, 22–24; financing of early colonial ventures, 22–28; maps, *25, 63, 73, 128, 214;* establishment of North American colonies, 33–58, 62–75; consolidation, 112–121, 185–199; Anglo-American economic relations, 194–199, 220–223; imperial crisis, 193,

210, 223–244, 248–256, 311; Revolutionary War, 260–270; Madison on, 308
Brooklyn, urbanization of, 382
Brooks, Preston, *570*
Brown, Charles Brockden, 332
Brown, John (eighteenth-century writer), 206
Brown, John (abolitionist), 569, 578–580, *579, 584*
Brown, Joseph E., 634
Brown, Mather, 293
Brown, William Wells, 481
Brownson, Orestes A., 399, 676
Brown University (College of Rhode Island), 143, 172, 244
Bruce, Blanche K., 688
Bubble Act (1741), 198–199
Buchanan, James: and expansion, 540, 543; as president, 433, *551–557*, 567, 570, 571, 573, 583
"Bucktails," 492
Buell, Don Carlos, 613, 615, 623
Buffalo, N.Y., 388
Buffon, Count de, 202
Bull Run (Manassas), battle of: First, 612, *614,* 618; Second, *614,* 615, 618, 713
Bunker Hill, battle of, 253, *254,* 260, 270
Bureau of Refugees, Freedmen, and Abandoned Lands, 665
Bureaucracy: in Spanish-American empire, 8–12; absence of, in early British Empire, 113–114; Federalist and Jeffersonian periods, 339–340; industrial, nineteenth century, 396; educational, nineteenth century, 415; Jackson on, 497–498; during Civil War, 592; governmental, post–Civil War, 694; and women workers, Gilded Age, 711
Burgh, James, 205–206
Burgoyne, John, 253, 264, 265, 366
Burke, Edmund, 160, 225, 241
Burned-Over District, 429, 438
Burnside, Ambrose E., 622
Burr, Aaron, 336, 346–347, 368
Bushnell, Horace, 683
Business: Revolutionary and Confederation periods, 291; and law, nineteenth century, 353; agriculture as, 384–387; social effects of, nineteenth century, 421–424; and Emerson, 427; and political parties, Jacksonian period, 496, 509, 512, 513; and coming of Civil War, 555, 567; during Civil War, 630; small, post–Civil

War, 656. *See also* Capitalism; Commerce
Bute, Lord, 224, 225
Butler, Andrew, 570
Butler, Benjamin F., 621, 648
Byrd, Maria, *131*
Byrd, William II, 121, *131,* 139
Byrd family, 130, 132

Cabeza de Vaca, Álvar Nuñez, 7, 29
Cabinet, Confederate, 591–592, 644
Cabinet, U.S.: under Constitution, 310; Federalist period, 316, 323, 330; Jeffersonian period, 342; Jacksonian and pre–Civil War periods, 500; Civil War, 592, 609, 645; Reconstruction era, 681
Cabot, George, 326
Cabot, John and Sebastian, 16, 29
Cabot family, 286
Calhoun, John C.: as War Hawk, 364; presidential candidacy, 342, 493–494; as intellectual, 494; and Jackson, 496, *502;* and nullification, 501–502, 518; and Whigs, 512; as secretary of state, 532; and Crisis of 1850, 555
California: migration to, 406, 529; Mexico and, 528, 540; and U.S. commerce, pre–Civil War, 530; annexation, 535–536, 539, 540; admission, 548, 550–551; and slavery question, 551–557, 570; Gold Rush, *551,* 584; pre–Civil War politics, 563; and racism, Reconstruction period, 681–682
Calvert, Cecilius (Second Lord Baltimore), 54–56, *55,* 72, 75
Calvert, Charles, 55
Calvert, George (First Lord Baltimore), 54
Calvert, Leonard, 55, 57
Calvert family, 54–58, 103, 118, 136–137, 158
Calvinism: in colonial New England, 47–54; Horace Mann and, 415–416. *See also* Calvinists; Congregationists; Presbyterians; Puritanism
Calvinists: in New Netherland, 104–105; post-Revolutionary period, 355, 356, 357. *See also* Dutch Reformed Church; Puritans
Cambridge, Mass., 129
Camden, battle of, 267
Cameron, Simon, 602
Campbellites, 358
Camp meetings, 356
Canada: discovery and settlement, 16–17, 19, 24–26; French rule, 127–128; in

colonial wars, 127–129; 187–188, 190–192, 206, 212, 215; and Revolution, 254, 260, 264, *265,* 270; loyalist emigration to, 285; settlement of slaves in, 286; and U.S. Federalist period, 321; and U.S. expansion, 345; and U.S., period of War of 1812, *364, 365*–366, 369; Rush-Bagot convention, 369; nineteenth century, 381; immigrants, 456, flight of blacks to, pre–Civil War, 481, 532, 552; Webster-Ashburton Treaty, 531, 544; U.S. proposal to annex, 537, 699; Confederate emigration to, 660

Canals, 369, 374–375, 382, 387, 388, *389,* 394, 455, 458, 499, 506

Cane Ridge, Ky., 356, 368

Canning, George, 527

Cape Ann, 48, 49

Cape Breton Island, 187, *189,* 190, 206

Cape Cod, 45

Cape Fear, 65

Capital: and English colonization, 17–19, 24–29, 36–38, 39–40, 42

Capital, accumulation and investment of: colonial, 121–129, 159–162, 165, 195; Jacksonian and pre–Civil War periods, 374–376, 380, 384, 390–396, 423, 509, 512, 567

Capital, national: 323, 338, 366. *See also* Washington, D.C.

Capitalism: and early English colonization, 24–29; Puritan attitude toward, 85, 107–109; eighteenth-century attitude toward, 257; Revolutionary and Confederate periods, 287–288, 291; Jacksonian and pre–Civil War periods, 374–376, 380, 384, 390–396, 509, 512, 567; and slavery, 459, 472. *See also* Business, Capital; Joint-stock companies

Capital punishment. *See* Death penalty

Capitol building, 366

Caribbean region: Spanish exploration and conquest, 6–8, 29; English expansion, 17–19, 25–26, 186, 190, 192, 206; and colonial trade, 87–89, 221; U.S. and, nineteenth century, 346n, 523, 527, 535, 542–543, 583

Carlisle Commission, 265

Carnegie, Andrew, 630

Carolina: settlement, 61–66, *63,* 112; charter, 64–66, 118, 145; Indians, 65, 217; society and economy, 66–68; slavery, 67–68, 153–157; separation into North and South, 118; and colonial wars, 129; rebellions, 134–135, 145; popula-tion, 149–150, 215; religion, 169. *See also* North Carolina; South Carolina

"Carpetbaggers," 688

Carroll, John, 332

Carter, Landon, 160

Carter, Robert, 124

Carteret, Sir George, 68, 118, 158

Cartoons, political: presidential and con-gressional Reconstruction, 680

Cartwright, Peter, 420

Casa de Contratación (Board of Trade), 9, 29

Cass, Lewis, 540, 542

Castile, 9, 13

Catholicism. *See* Anti-Catholicism; Papacy; Roman Catholicism; Roman Catholic church

Catholics. *See* Roman Catholics

Caucus, congressional, 342

Cavalry, U.S., 407

Censorship, of abolitionist literature, 477–478, 503, 552

Centennial Exposition at Philadelphia of 1876, *697*

Central America: Spanish conquest, 6–8; filibustering, 346; U.S. and nineteenth century, 537, 543, 583; Isthmian canal, 543; Lincoln on colonization in, 639. *See also specific countries*

Central Pacific Railroad, 681

Champlain, Lake, 190, 215, 254, 264, 366

Chancellorsville, battle of, 622, *623,* 654

Chancery courts, 177

Channing, William Ellery, 412, 426

Chapman, Maria Weston, 443

Charity, public: eighteenth century, 163, 206; Revolutionary era, 215, 292–293; Civil War and Reconstruction, 665, 667

Charles I (king of England), 24, 48, 63, 74, 257, 274

Charles II (king of England), 63–64, 67, 71, 74, 112, 145, 158

Charles Stuart, "Bonnie Prince Charlie," 150, 224

Charles River, *287*

Charleston (Charles Town), S.C.: colonial, 66–67, 150; slave trade, 154–*155;* Revo-lutionary era, 232, 233, 267–268, 299; and railroads, 394; Denmark Vesey's plot, 461; and nullification crisis, 501–503; Democratic convention of 1860, 580, 585; in Civil War, 594, 595, 627, 628, 638, *663*

Charlestown, Mass., 35, 49, 253

Charter of Freedoms and Exemptions (New Netherland), 60

Charters: Virginia Company, 30, 36, 38, 42, 74; colonial Massachusetts, 46–47, 48, 49–50, 74, 117, 145, 146; colonial Rhode Island, 54, 75, 117, 145; colonial Maryland, 55, 75, 117, 145; Dutch West India Company, 58, 74; New Netherland, 60; Carolina, 64–66, 75, 117, 145; colonial Pennsylvania, 71–72, 75, 117, 145; colonial Connecticut, 107, 117, 145; colonial, James II's annulment of, 117, 145; in eighteenth century, 177, 189, 197; in Revolution, 271, 278, 283. *See also* Constitutions

Charters, bank: BUS, 340, 369; *McCulloch v. Maryland,* 352

Charters, corporate, Revolutionary and Confederation periods, 291, 300

Chase, Salmon P., 593, 631, 632, 645, 646, 647

Chase, Samuel, 350, 368

Chattanooga, Tenn., 623, 640, 654

Chattel slavery, 43, 459, 465. *See also* Blacks; Servitude; Slaves; Slavery

Cherokees, 217, *218,* 321, 403–405, *407,* 597

Cherokee War, 219

Chesapeake, U.S.S., 362, 368

Chesapeake Bay, 264, *268,* 269, 366. *See also* Chesapeake region

Chesapeake region: settlement, 36–43, 54–58; demography, 80–81, 83–84, 97, 343; slavery, 43, 83–84; colonial trade, 86, 88–89, *155,* 165, 167–168; economy, 42, 88–91, 125, 160, 165, 221; social tension, seventeenth century, 97–98; slavery, 154; religion and society, 168–169, 222; *See also* Maryland; Virginia

Cheyenne Indians, 714

Chicago, Ill., land speculation, 385; manufacturing, 390; railroads, 565; immigrant population of, 708

Chicago Tribune, 674

Chickamauga, battle of, 623, 654

Chickasaws, 217, *218,* 403, 404, *407,* 597

Chicopee, Mass., 391

Chief Black Kettle, 714

Child, Lydia Maria, 443

Child labor: nineteenth century, 391–392, 398, 414–415; of slaves, 463

Children: in colonial society, 81–82, 95–98, *96;* education, in colonial America, 140–145; under Halfway Covenant, 167; European notions about colonial American, 200; in Revolutionary society, 293–

294; in Jacksonian and pre–Civil War society, 379–380, 398, 413; slave, 463; black, post-Civil War South, 670; education of, Reconstruction period, 689. *See also* Child labor; Education; Youth

Chile, Spanish conquest, 8, *10, 11,* 29

China: U.S. trade with, 286, 533; Jefferson on, 360; and Chinese Exclusion Act, 682

Chinese and Chinese-Americans: and racism, Reconstruction period, 682; Gilded Age, 710

Chivington, John M., 714

Choate, Rufus, 486

Chocktaws, 217, *218,* 403, *407,* 597

Cholera epidemic (1848), 398

Christianity: and Spanish Empire, 13–14; and English expansion, 17; and slavery, 43, 418, 465–468, 479; and seventeenth-century society, 98–99; and Indians, 139, 143–144, 169; and rationalism, 355; in nineteenth-century U.S., 417, 420–422, 432. *See also* Religion; *specific denominations*

Church, established: in Great Britain, 43–44, 99, 101–102, 176, 257; in colonies, 99–109, 167–169, 222, 239; Revolution and early nineteenth century, 274, 318, 354–356, 417–418; effects of absence, 423. *See also* Anglican church

Church, the: Anglican-Puritan debate over, 105, 107–109; Enlightenment and, 202, 203. *See also* Clergy; Religion; *specific religions*

Church and state: in colonial New England, 50–51, 53, 54, 92, 103–104, 136–137; in seventeenth-century England, 69, 71; in seventeenth-century society, 98–99; in Chesapeake colonies, 100–103; First Great Awakening and, 169–173; in eighteenth-century Britain, 175; Revolutionary period and Second Great Awakening, 270–273; nineteenth century, 417, 436, 454; Mormons and, 433

Churches: and First Great Awakening, 169–173; in colonial society, 217, 222; post-Revolutionary society, 289–290; and nineteenth-century revivalism, 417–419, 421–423; splits in, nineteenth-century, 439–440; black, 461, 467–468, 471; and antislavery, 477, 479. *See also* Religion; *specific denominations*

Churchill, Sir Winston, 2

Church membership: in Puritanism, 50, 105–109; in colonial society, 122, 166–174; late eighteenth century, 354;

nineteenth century, 418, 421
Church of England. *See* Anglican church
Church of Jesus Christ of Latter-day Saints. *See* Mormonism
Cider tax, 223
Cincinnati, Ohio, 381, *461*
Cincinnati, Order of the, 289, 320, 331
Cincinnatus, 289, 315
Circuit courts, 350
Cities: colonial, c. 1700, 35; absence of, in early southern colonies, 91; eighteenth century, 162–166, *163;* Jacksonian and pre–Civil War periods, 380–382, 413, 414, 421–422, 486; post-Civil War southern, 660, 662, *663,* 669; rebuilding of, post-Civil War, 662; migration of blacks to, 670
Citizens, rights of: post-Civil War, 662
Citizenship: in colonies, 153; republicanism and, 274–275; and Alien and Sedition Acts, 330; and impressment, 361; of blacks, pre–Civil War, 482, 491, 572–574; issue of, 1850s, 559; post-Civil War, 656; Fourteenth Amendment and, 657, 658, 675, 686; of blacks, Reconstruction period, 658. *See also* Naturalization
Civil disobedience, pre–Civil War, 482
Civil liberties: colonial, 40, 72, 188; Revolutionary era, 240, 278–279; Bill of Rights, 315; and antislavery, 479–481, 503–504, 557, 572; during Civil War, 645; Reconstruction period, 658. *See also* Bill of Rights, American
Civil rights, of minorities: black, post-Civil War, 657, 658, 674, 675, 677, 683; of freedmen, 657; Reconstruction period, 658–659; 674–677; Chinese, 682; Civil Rights Act (1866), 675, 691; and Fourteenth Amendment, 676
Civil Rights Act (1866), 675, 691
Civil Service reform: as historical turning point, 656; and expansion of presidential powers, 657; and taxation, 659; views of Northerners toward South, 659; behavior of Union troops, 660; benefits of veterans, 662; service of blacks, 683; consequences of, 694; and nationalist sentiments, post-war, 695–697; Gilded Age, 706–708
Civil War, American, 286, 330; coming of, 547–584; course of, 588–618, 620–654; effects of, 658–661, 662–664, 688–689
Civil War, English. *See* English Civil War
Clarendon, Earl of, 64
Clarendon family, 119

Clark, George Rogers, 271, 316
Clark, William, *344, 345, 347,* 368
Class, social. *See* Social class
Classical learning, 139, 142–143
Clay, Henry: and War of 1812, 364; on social mobility, 397; and Missouri Compromise, 490–491; in Jacksonian-period politics, 493, 495, 499, 503–505, 511, 515, 516, 532; and Compromise of 1850, 553–554
Clayton-Bulwer Treaty (1850), 543
Cleburne, Patrick R., 640
Clemens, Samuel. *See* Twain, Mark
Clergy: in colonial New England, 50–54, *52,* 105–107, 168, 169–174; in southern colonies, 100–103, 168–169, 172; in New Netherland and colonial New York, 104–105, 169; and colonial colleges, 143–144, 172; Revolutionary era, 222, 230, 244, 354–356; and French Revolution, 325, 355; early nineteenth century, 418, 421, 422, 437, 562; black, nineteenth century, 467–468; and antislavery, 477–478; and southern education, 666
Clermont (steamship), 368, *388*
Cleveland, Ohio, immigrant population of, 708
Clinton, George, 325
Clinton, Sir Henry, 267, *268*
Cloth making, seventeenth century: Massachusetts, 85; England, 87. *See also* Cloth trade
Cloth trade: in sixteenth-century England, 17, 18, 29; colonial, 124; under Sugar Act, 230
Coal industry, 394, 396, 701, 703
Cobbaugh, Peter, 366
Cochin, Charles, 203
Coercive Acts (1774), 240, 245, 248, 249, 252, 270
Coffee trade, 229
Cohens v. *Virginia* (1821), 352
Coinage. *See* Currency
Coinage Act (1873), 703
Cold Harbor, battle of, 648, 654
Cole, Thomas, 446, *448*
Colfax, Schuyler, 706
Colleges: origins of, 143–145; late eighteenth century, 356; Jacksonian and pre–Civil War periods, 416–417, 419, 437; and antislavery, 477; landgrant, 630; Freedmen's Bureau and, 666. *See also* Education, higher; Universities
Colleton, Sir John, 64
Collinson, Peter, 202

Colonial wars, 127–129, 185, 186–193, 206–207, 212, 217, 219, 223

Colonies, British: foundation, 16–23, 33–58, 62–75; seventeenth-century society and economy, 78–109, 121–132; consolidation in British Empire, 112–120, 132–138, 185, 186–199; culture, 138–145, 199–206; eighteenth-century society and economy, 149–174, 212–223; eighteenth-century politics, 174–181; imperial crisis, 210–211, 223–244; struggle for independence, 248–256, 260–270

Colonies, Dutch, 58–62, 104–105

Colonies, Secretary of State for the, 235, 244

Colonies, Spanish: origins, 5–6, 8–14; independence movements, 11, 17, 523, 525

Colonization, North America, 5–29, 33–75

Colonization movement: and antislavery, 439; Lincoln and, 639

Colorado: Spanish exploration, 8; gold discovery, 714

Colton, Calvin, 510

Columbia, S.C., in Civil War, 651

Columbia University (King's College), 143

Columbus, Christopher, 6, 13, 29

Command of Army Act (1867), 691

Commerce: Spanish-American empire, 9; sixteenth-century England, 16–19, 29; seventeenth-century colonies, 39–40, 42, 58–59, 64–65, 84–91; and consolidation of British Empire, 114–116; as road to wealth, 121–125; and colonial wars, 127–129, 186; eighteenth-century colonies, 85–91, 162–166, *163,* 194, 220–222; and imperial crisis, 194, 230; Revolutionary era, 287; regulation of, under Constitution, 308–309; in Hamiltonian program, 318–319; U.S. and French Revolutionary wars, 325; and European wars, 360–363, *361;* and embargo of 1807, 362–363; with Indians, nineteenth century, 403; cotton trade, nineteenth century, 457–458, 507–508, 550; Jacksonian and pre–Civil War periods, 501, 547; Civil War era, 604, 608, 629, 631–634; in South, Reconstruction period, 660

Committees of Correspondence, 239, 245

Common law, English: in colonial Virginia, 40; in British Empire, 119, 133; and American law, 353

Common Sense, 259

Commonwealth (seventeenth-century England), 274

Commonwealth v. *Hunt* (1842), 399

Communal groups, nineteenth century, 445–446

Communications: colonial, 221; nineteenth century, 396, 438

Communitarianism, 445–446

Communities: seventeenth century, 33–36, 47–49, 81–82, 91–92, 96, 104, 108, 120, 121, 133; slave, 84, 154, 464–465; and colonial education, 141–145; eighteenth century, 163–164, 215–216; Revolutionary era, 248, 250, 275, 285, 289, 300; and Second Great Awakening, 355–356; Jacksonian and pre–Civil War periods, 375, 384, 416, 419, 421, 422, 434, 436, 466, 512; and modernization, 377, 384. *See also* Localism

Company of Cathay, 19

Competition, economic: in colonial society, 88, 89–90, 109, 132; in Revolutionary society, 289–290, 294; in Jacksonian and pre–Civil War society, 374–376, 397, 415, 422, 434. *See also* Capitalism; Instability, social; Laissez-faire policies

Compromise of 1850, 552–557, 547, *556,* 565, 584

Concepcion, Chile, 8

Concessions and Agreements (West Jersey), 68, 146

Concord, battle of. *See* Lexington and Concord, battle of

Concord, Mass.: foundation, 49; Revolution, 252, 260. *See also* Lexington and Concord, battle of

Confederate States of America: compared to North, 589–594, 598–599, 633, 652–654; establishment, 590, 591–592; and border states, 593–594, 596–599; conscription, 603, 634–635; finance, 604–606, 631–634; foreign relations, 606, 607–609, 642–643; military operations, 594–596, 610–617, *613, 614, 616,* 620, *623, 624*–625, 643–652, *648, 649, 653,* 654; economy, 629–634; emancipation question, 636–638, 640–641; politics, 643–644; defeat, *651*–654, *653;* postwar social and economic changes, 656; postwar treatment of leaders, 659–660, 663; postwar devastation, 662; postwar treatment of troops, 663; postwar rebuilding, 664; and national debt, 677

Confederation of New England Colonies (1643), 75

Congregationalism, 103; New England, 107–108; as post-Revolutionary official church, 354, 356, 417

Congregationalist Board of Commissioners for Foreign Missions, 402

Congregationalists: in colonial New Jersey, 69; and First Great Awakening, 166–168; and Second Great Awakening, 355, 356, 368; Indians and, 402; nineteenth century, 437, 439, 513. *See also* Puritans

Congress, Confederate, 592, 603, 626, 630, 634–635, 638, 641, 643–644, 645, 653

Congress, Continental. *See* Continental Congress

Congress, U.S.: Confederation period, 281–285, 288, 295, 302–304, 306, 307, 332, 331; under Constitution, 310–311; Federalist period, 305, 317, 319, 324, 327; Jeffersonian period, 340, 342, 347, 350, 352, 362, 363, 364, 369, 487; and Southern representation, post-Civil War, 657, 674; powers of, post-Civil War, 658; Reconstruction period, 658, 667, 675–679; establishment of administrative systems, post-Civil War, 665; 1865 session, 675; 1866 session, 677; second Reconstruction program, 677–679; policy toward president, during Reconstruction, 679–681; readmittance of Southern representatives, 688; special electoral commission, 1876, 717

Conkling, Roscoe, 707

Connecticut (colonial): origins, 50, 54, 75, 145; and New Netherland, 61; social control, 97; and Dominion of New England, 117; elite, 122; and colonial New York, 136; social and cultural change, 141; higher education, 145; religion, 168, 169, 170, 180; government, 177, 180; migration from, 215, 216

Connecticut (state): Revolution, 278, *283;* Critical Period, 305, 313; official church, 354, 356; and Embargo of 1807–09, 363; blacks' civil rights, after Civil War, 683

Connecticut Compromise, 310

Connecticut Moral Society, 369

Connecticut River, 86, 149, 169, 171, 206, 217

Conquistadores, 6–8, 23

Conscience Whigs, 550

Conscription, Civil War, 602–604, 629, 634–636, 643

Conservation, lack of concern for, nineteenth century, 384, 386, 672

Conservatism: of colonists, 2–3, 79, 84, 91–98, 107–109; critique of Enlightenment, 203; Revolutionary era, 210, 251,

256, 293; Critical and Federalist periods, 300, 311; of American reactions to French Revolution, 325, 354; Jacksonian and pre–Civil War periods, 415, 424, 512–513, of Jefferson Davis, 590; of Lincoln, 590; in Reconstruction period, 675

Considerations of the Propriety of Imposing Taxes, 242

Consignment system, 89–90, 161

Conspiracy laws, Gilded Age, 711

Constitution, British: eighteenth-century views of, 175–176, 180, 225, 257–258, 278. *See also* Political theory

Constitution, Confederate, 590, 603, 630, 641, 643

Constitution, U.S.: framing of, 298, 307–313; and slavery, 295, 310, 490, 501; Bill of Rights, 315; "strict" and "broad" constructions, 323, 346; and banking, 339–340; and commerce, 377; abolitionists and, 479, 480; and Republic of Texas constitution, 529; and coming of Civil War, 565–566, 573, 581; compared to Confederate Constitution, 589–590; and establishment of West Virginia, 598; post-Civil War amendments, 658; as limit to change during Reconstruction period and Gilded Age, 661–664; text, Appendix. *See also* Amendments to Constitution; Judicial review

Constitution, U.S.S., *366*

Constitutional amendments. *See* Amendments to Constitution

Constitutional Convention. *See* Philadelphia Convention

Constitutional conventions, state, 551, 571

Constitutionalism: post-Civil War, southern, 658; during Reconstruction period, 661–662; as limit to change, post-Civil War, 661–662; Gilded Age, 701; and voting rights, 720

Constitutionality: Virginia and Kentucky resolves, 330; of Louisiana Purchase, 346; of nullification, 501–502; of Bank Wars, 505; of Mexican War, 537; of *Dred Scott* decision, 573, 577; during Civil War, 634, 641; during Reconstruction period, 677–678. *See also* Judicial review

Constitutional Union party, *582, 592*

Constitutions, colonial: Carolina, 66; Pennsylvania, 72; Connecticut, 75; eighteenth century, 179. *See also* Charters

Constitutions, state: Revolutionary era, 277–280, 354; Critical Period, 301–302;

Jeffersonian period, 347; Jacksonian and pre–Civil War periods, 491, 551–552, 571, 575, 578, 584; post-Civil War northern, 683; post-Civil War southern, 678, 686–687, 691, 720
Construction, pre–Civil War, 380, 381
Continental army, 260, 262, 267, 270, 302–304, 306–307
Continental Association, 249, 270
Continental Congress: First, 249–250, 270; Second, 252–256, 260, 262, 270, 277–278
"Contrabands," *638*
Contracting, military: colonial wars, 127–129; Revolutionary War, 287–288; Civil War, 602, 604, 632
Convention, Annapolis. *See* Annapolis Convention
Convention, Constitutional. *See* Philadelphia Convention
Convention National Party, 498
Convention of 1800, 368
Convention of the Free People of Color, 481
Conway, Thomas, 266
Cooke, Jay, 631–632, 703, 709
Cooper, James Fenimore, 446, 448
Cooper, Peter, 710
Copley, John Singleton, 236
Copper trade, 115, 702
"Copperheads," 673
Corn. *See* Grain cultivation; Grain trade
Corn laws, 389
Cornbury, Lord, 119, 125
Cornwallis, Lord, *249,* 267, *268,* 269
Coronado, Francisco, 7, 29
Corporate charters. *See* Charters, corporate
Corporations: Revolutionary and Confederation periods, 291; early nineteenth century, 396, 512; Civil War, 604. *See also* Business; Capitalism; Monopoly
Corruption: colonial, 194, 213, 228; Britain, 257–258; Old World, 274, 277, 279; and Critical Period, 305; Jeffersonian Republican's view of, 320, 323–324, 328; Jackson's view of, 404; fear of, Jacksonian and pre–Civil War periods, 412, 413, 422–423, 474, 479, 487, 506; Reconstruction era and Gilded Age, 689, 705–706, 713
Corruption, political: Britain, 119–120, 178, 224, 225, 257, 486; colonial, 121, 125–126, 133–134, 178, 220; republican view of, 274, 277, 279; Hamiltonian program and, 320, 323–324; Jeffersonian

Republicans and, 328, 339; and Jackson's image, 496; Gilded Age, 705–706; Grant administration, 707
Cortés, Hernando, 6–8, 28
Cost of living. *See* Living standards
Cotton, John, 92
Cotton: and navigation acts, 115; and slavery, 379, 454–*459,* 462–463; cultivation, 386, 457, 522, 567; and Industrial Revolution, 379, 386, 390–392, 394; and Civil War, 608, *610,* 629, 631; post-Civil War South, 672
Cotton gin, 332, 454, *455,* 470
"Cotton Kingdom," 403, 454–459
Cotton mills, 332
Cotton trade, pre–Civil War, 457–459, 508, 550, 567; Civil War, 608, *610,* 629, 631
Cotton Whigs, 550
Council for New England, 46
Council of Fifty, 430, 431
Council of the Indies, 9–10, 29, 114
Councils, colonial, 40, 42, 50, 51, 57–58, 72, 117, 125, 130, 198, 234–235, 249
Country-Whig opposition, 257–258, 273, 278–279; tradition of, in Jeffersonian and Jacksonian periods, 323, 337, 493, 512
Court system: colonial, 49, 51, 103; British, in American colonies, 119; federal, creation of, 316, 350
Covenanted community, 46
Cowpens, battle of, 267, *268*
"Crackers," *469*
Craft, Ellen, 481
Crawford, William H., 342, 493
Credit, commercial: colonial, 86–88, 124–125, 160–161, 165, 221, 228–229; Revolutionary era, 286; Jeffersonian period, 345; Jacksonian and pre–Civil War periods, 386, 504, 552; post-Civil War South, 672–673
Credit, government, in Reconstruction period, 664
Credit, public: colonial, 197; Revolutionary era, 288; Critical Period, 303, 304; under Constitution, 309; Hamiltonian program and, 317–318; post-Civil War, 664, 703. *See also* Debt, government; Debt, national
Crédit Mobilier scandal (1872), 705
Creditors: colonial, 197–198; Revolutionary and Confederation periods, 300; and Gilded Age currency problems, 703–704
Creeks, 217, *218,* 321, 348, 369, 402, 403, *407,* 597

Creoles: in Spanish America, 15–16; defined, 200

Crime: punishment of, Revolutionary era, 292–293; nineteenth century, 398, 427, 435, 440; federal government and, nineteenth century, 662

"Crime of '73," and Gilded Age currency problems, 704

Critical Period, 298–307

Crittenden, John, 583

Crockett, David, 529

Cromwell, Oliver, 63, 138, 275

Crop-lien system, 672

Crown colonies: Virginia, 42, 74; New York, 116; New Hampshire, 116–117; Maryland, 236. *See also* Charters; Dominion of New England

Crystal Palace Exhibition, 392

Cuba: in eighteenth-century wars, 192; slavery, 531; U.S. and, nineteenth century, 523, 524, 527, 535–537, 542–543

Culpeper, John, 135

Culpeper's Rebellion, 132, 135–136, 145

Culture: African-American, 83–84, 153–157, 294–295, 463–468; colonial, 138–145, 165–166; American, and Enlightenment, 199–206; European, and late eighteenth-century America, 315–316; American, nineteenth century, 446–449, *447*

Currency: colonial, 197–199; and Stamp Act, 228; Revolutionary era, 281; Critical Period, 269, under Constitution, 310; in Hamiltonian program, 318–319; Jacksonian period, 487, 504; Civil War, 605–606, 632; Reconstruction period and Gilded Age, 702–705. *See also* Banks and banking

Currency Act (1751, 1764), 199, 229, 244

Curtis, Benjamin R., 573

Curtis, George William, 707

Customs duties: under navigation acts, 115; in imperial crisis, 228; and Constitution, 310; in Hamiltonian program, 318–319; Jacksonian and pre–Civil War periods, 554; Civil War, 605

Customs officials: colonial, 194; Revolutionary era, 228, 235, 238; in Federalist Treasury Department, 317. *See also* Officeholders

Cuzco, Peru, 7

Daily Intelligencer (Atlanta), 470

Dana, Richard Henry Jr., 675

Danish West Indies, Seward's proposal to purchase, 700

Dartmouth College: foundation, 143, 172; *Dartmouth College* cases, 291, 369; and blacks, 417

Darwin, Charles, 683

Daughters of Liberty, 235

Daval, P. S., *541*

Davies, Samuel, 172

Davis, Henry Winter, 647

Davis, Jefferson: in Mexican War, 540; on John Brown, 579; war aims, 589; as Confederate president, 589, 590, *591,* 606–607, 610, 617, 643–644, 647, 652, 653, 654; and Fort Sumter crisis, 595; and military operations, 643, 649; and emancipation question, 580, 641; Northern view of, 659; postwar fate, 659–660

Death penalty: Revolutionary era, 293; Garrisonians on, 479

DeBow's Review, 459

Debt: in colonial economy, 86–89, 164–165, 197–198, 221; in Critical Period, 300, 306; under Constitution, 309; in Federalist period, 326; in Jacksonian period, 506. *See also* Credit, commercial

Debt, government: colonial, 197–199; British, 223, Critical Period, 302–305; Republic of Texas, 554; Civil War, 631; of Confederacy, 676. *See also* Credit, public; Debt, national

Debt, national: in Hamiltonian program, 318, 340; Jeffersonian Republicans and, 326, 340; Reconstruction period, 677; Gilded Age, 704. *See also* Credit, public

Debt, state: post-Civil War, 658

Debts and debtors: of southern planters, Reconstruction period, 674–677; Gilded Age, 703–704

Decentralization. *See* Localism

Declaration of Independence: as end of Revolution, 211; adoption of, 252–256, 281; and nineteenth-century women's movement, 444; and antislavery, 476; in *Dred Scott* decision, 573; Lincoln on, 577; text, Appendix

Declaration of Sentiments, 336, 444

Declaration of the Causes and Necessities of Taking Up Arms, 252, 270

Declaratory Act (1766), 243, 244

Deference, social: colonial, 91–98; Revolutionary era, 289; Federalist period, 324; Jeffersonian period, 337–338; nineteenth-century Britain, 436. *See also* Elites

de Grasse, Admiral, 269
Deism, 355
DeLancey, Stephanus, 129
DeLancey family, 250
Delaney, Martin, 482
Delavan, Edward C., 437
Delaware (colonial), 72–73
Delaware (state): Revolution, 278; Critical Period, 301, 313; Jeffersonian period, 341; slavery, 469; pre–Civil war politics; 581, 594; Civil War, 594, *596, 597*
Delaware Indians, 217, *218*
Delaware River, 59, 68, 72, 263
De la Warr, Lord, 39
Demesne farms, 56
Demobilization, after Civil War, 662–663
Democracy: Puritan attitude toward, 92; town meeting as, 122; in colonial rebellions, 138; in eighteenth-century political theory, 174, 205–206; as American ideal, 211; Revolutionary era, 248–249; Critical Period, 298–302; Federalists and, 314; Jeffersonian Republicans and, 323, 335, 337, 348–349; views of, Jacksonian and pre–Civil War periods, 416, 417–418, 498, 509, 579; and nineteenth-century culture, 446, 448–449
Democratic party: origins and nature, 480–481, 486–487; Jacksonian period, 487, 496–511, 518; pre–Civil War period, 531, 534–535, 538, 542, 547, 549–550, 564, 571–572, 578, 580–581; Civil War, 645, 646, 654; post–Civil War, 664, 673, 689, 694, 701–702; Reconstruction period and Gilded Age, 664, 673–681, 688–689, 716, 717–718, 720; and tariffs, 702; and national debt policy, 704
Democratic-Republican party. *See* Republican party (Jeffersonian)
Demography: Spanish-American empire, 14–16; early modern England, 20, 22–24, 33, 79–83; early modern North America, 33–36, 78–84, 121–122, 149–153, 180–181, 213–217; nineteenth century, 377–380, 382–383, 455, *456–457,* 473
"Denization," 153
Denominationalism: seventeenth-century roots, 99–101; First Great Awakening and, 173–174; in Revolutionary period and Second Great Awakening, 356–359; Jacksonian and pre–Civil War periods, 417, 439

Dependency, social: colonial society, 92–93, 157–159, 162–166; Revolutionary era, 273–276, 288–290, 293–294; Jeffersonian Republicans' fear of, 323–325; of women, nineteenth century, 442; of slaves, 460–463; in pre–Civil War South, 470. *See also* Servitude
DePeyster, Johannes, *127*
Depressions: in colonial tobacco trade, 89–90, 167; late 1790s, 329; Panic of 1819, 369, 457; Jacksonian and pre–Civil War periods, 380, 440, 457, 557, 522, 524; Panic of 1837, 399, 422, 429, 457, 480, 507–508, 519, 524; Panic of 1857, 423, 522, 544; of 1873, 682, 709–711
Desegregation: pre–Civil War, 417; Reconstruction period, 677, 688–689
Deseret, State of, *432, 433*
Desertion, Civil War, 635, 643
de Soto, Hernando, 7, 29
Despotism. *See* Tyranny
Detroit, Mich.: War of 1812, 365, 369; immigrant population of, 708
Dickinson, John, 205, 235, 242, 244, 252
Dictatorship, of Cromwell, 275
Diderot, Denis, 202
Digger Indians, 406
Diplomacy, American: under Constitution, 305; Federalist period, 321–322; Jeffersonian period, 339, 345, 359–368; J. Q. Adams and, 495, 525–527; Jacksonian and pre–Civil War periods, 531–543; Civil War, 606–610, 641–643; post–Civil War, 697–700. *See also* Foreign relations
Disciples of Christ, 358
Discourse Concerning the Influence of America on the Mind, 411
Discrimination, racial: pre–Civil War, 416–417, 454, 470–472, 480–481; Reconstruction period, 659, 661, 684–687; "New South," 723. *See also* Blacks; Chinese and Chinese Americans; Racism
Disease: in colonial America, 14, 35, 37, 38, 45, 78, 81; and colonial slavery, 84, 154; in colonial wars, 187, 188; control of, in Revolutionary era, 293; yellow fever epidemic (1793), 332; during Industrial Revolution, 398; Civil War, 602
Disfranchisement: of ex-Confederates, 676; of blacks, 718–721. *See also* Suffrage, black
Disorder, social: colonial, 91–98, 107–109, 217, 236–237, 250–251; crisis of 1798–99, 327–330; Jacksonian and pre–Civil

War periods, 412, 421–422, 435–442, 475–476, 559–560, 568–569, 578–580; in pre–Civil War south, 461–462; Reconstruction period, 689–691; Gilded Age, 711. *See also* Instability, social; Mobs; Riots

Dissent, religious: in Massachusetts Bay Colony, 51, 53–54; in colonial Maryland, 103–104; eighteenth century, 168, 172–173, 175, 222; in nineteenth-century denominations, 358; Mormonism, 428–435. *See also* Persecution, religious; Toleration, religous

Dissent, social and political, Jacksonian and pre–Civil War period, 412, 428–435, 442–445, 472–483

District of Columbia: slavery, 480, 503, 516, 552, 554, 556–557; abolition of slavery, 639; segregation, 684. *See also* Capital, national; Washington, D.C.

Disunion: abolitionists and, 479, 482; Southern threats of, 488, 501–502, 553, 554, 580. *See also* Secession; Sectionalism

Divorce, in colonial society, 98

Dix, Dorothea, 711

Domesticity: Revolutionary era, 293–294; Jacksonian and pre–Civil War periods, 375, 524; Gilded Age, *666*

Dominican Republic, 698, 699

Dominion of New England, 116–118, 130, 132, 137, 145, 146

Doolittle, James R., 646

Dorchester, Mass., 253

Douglas, Stephen A., *577;* and expansion, 540, and Compromise of 1850, 555–556; and Kansas-Nebraska Act, 565–566, 568, 572, 573–574; and Lincoln, 585; presidential candidacy, 580; Johnson and, 677

Douglass, Frederick, 481, *482,* 636, 668

Douglass, William, 176

Downing, George, 138

Draft, military. *See* Conscription, Civil War

Drake, Sir Francis, 19, 22, 23, 29, 30

Drayton, William Henry, 251

Dred Scott decision, 572–575, 579, 584, 676

Due process of law, 676

Duke's Law (colonial New York), 145

Dulany, Daniel, 242, 250

Dunker Church, 616

Dunmore, Lord, 219

DuPont, Samuel F., 627

Durand, Asher B., 446

Dutch: religious tolerance of, 44; and New Netherland, 58–62; in British colonies, 68, 69, 136; and colonial trade, 86, 90

Dutch Guiana. *See* Surinam

Dutch Reformed church: in New Netherland and New York, 62, 104–105; in colonial New Jersey, 69, and education, 143; and First Great Awakening, 169–173

Dutch West India Company, 58–62, 74, 104

Dwight, Louis, 437

Dwight, Timothy, 294, 315

Early, Jubal A., 649, 660

East: Jacksonian and pre–Civil War periods, 387–388, 390–391; 394–398, 411–412

East Anglia (England), 23, 109

East Florida, 227, 270, 523, 524, 525. *See also* Florida

East India Company, 18, 239

Eastland Company, 18

Economy, American: colonial, 84–91, 121–125, 194–199, 220–223; Revolutionary and Confederation periods, 286–288; Jacksonian and pre–Civil War, 377–399, 389–390, 396–398; 401, 500, 507–508, 522; pre–Civil War South, 454–459; Civil War, 604–606, 629–634, 652; Reconstruction and Gilded Age, 656, 668–669; post-Civil War South, 663–664, 669–671

Economy, English, sixteenth century, 16–19, 23–27

Ecuador, Spanish conquest, 8, 29

Edict of Nantes, 150

Education: attitudes toward, colonial, 140–145; nineteenth century, 401, 413–417, 419, 424–425, 495; blacks and, nineteenth century, 416–417, 454, 459, 477, 687; during Reconstruction, 660, 665–666, 677–689

Education, adult: Jacksonian period, 425–427; Reconstruction, 665–666. *See also* Self-improvement

Education, higher: colonial, 101–102, 140–145; Revolutionary era, 292–294; post-Revolutionary, 292–293; Jacksonian and pre–Civil War periods, 417, 418, 437; women and, nineteenth century, 442; and antislavery, 477; land-grant colleges, 630; Freedmen's Bureau and, 665–666. *See also* Colleges; Universities; *specific institutions*

Education, primary and secondary: colonial Massachusetts, 75, 140–143; other colonies, 141; Revolutionary era, 291–293; Jacksonian and pre–Civil War periods, 413–414, 419; Reconstruction, 666–667

Education, public: absent in colonial America, 140; Revolutionary roots, 292; Jacksonian and pre–Civil War periods, 375, 413–414; religion and, 415; Gilded Age, 662; government controls, post-Civil War, 662; post-Civil War South, 687, 689; Gilded Age, 720

Edwards, Jonathan, 169–171, *170*

"Eight box" law, 719

El Dorado, 7

Elections: British, 176; colonial, 179; Critical Period, 300; as envisaged by framers of the Constitution, 310–313; Federalists and, 328–329; Mormons and, 429–431; nineteenth century, 488; Force Bill, 720

Elections, national: voting rights of Southern states, post-Civil War, 657; federal control of and Force Bill, 720. *See also* Elections, presidential

Elections, off-year: of 1810, 363; of 1854, 563, 585; of 1855, 568; of 1861 (Maryland), 597; of 1862, 645, 654; of 1863 (Confederate), 644; of 1865 (southern), 674; of 1866, 676–677, 691; of 1867 (southern), 686, 714; of 1874, 701; of 1878; 710

Elections, presidential: of 1796, 326, 332; of 1800, 330, 336–337, 350, 368; of 1804, 368, of 1808, 342; of 1812, 342, 369; of 1816, 342, 367, 369; of 1820, 341, 342, 368, 369, *488;* of 1824, 342, 487, *488,* 493–494, 518, 527; of 1828, 342, 487, *497–500, 487, 488, 498,* 518; of 1832, *488,* 505, 518; of 1836, *488,* 507, 518, 530; of 1840, 480, 482, *488,* 509, *515–517, 516,* 518, 581; of 1844, 430, 480, 482, *488,* 515, 518, 532–535, *533, 534;* of 1848, 480, 482, *488,* 509, 515, 539, 543, 550, 584; of 1852, *488,* 515, 561–562, 584; of 1856, *488,* 509, 543, 564, 567, 571, 584; of 1860, *581–584, 582,* 592; of 1864, 646–647, 653, 654; of 1868, 691, 704, 714, *715,* 722; of 1872, 700; of 1876, 716–718, *717,* 722; of 1880, 719

Electoral college: under Constitution, 310; election of 1800, 336; Twelfth Amendment, 336, 368; election of 1824, 494; election of 1876, 716–*717*

Elements of Technology, 425

Eliot, John, 139

Elites: Spanish-American, 14–15; colonial, 42, 56–58, 79, 88, 91–92, 94, 107, 120–132, 157–162, 179–181, 257–258; Revolution and, 285–286; threat to, in Critical Period, 300; and framing of Constitution, 307–308, 313; Federalists and, 324–325, 327–331, 340; Jeffersonian Republicans and, 336; and nineteenth-century religion, 357; Tocqueville on, 373–374, 397; Jacksonian and pre–Civil War periods, 398–399, 493–494; pre–Civil War southern, 470; Civil War era, 635; post-Civil War southern, 671–673. *See also* Aristocracy; Gentry; Social class

Elitism: of Federalists, 327–331; Jacksonian and pre–Civil War periods, 375, 424–426, 496, 505, 513–514

Elizabeth I (queen of England), 17–19, *18, 22,* 29, 44, 91

Elizabethan era (England): social and economic problems, 17–19; expansion, 17–28; social attitudes, 84, 91–92; educational attitudes, 140

Elmira (N.Y.) prisoner-of-war camp, 660

Emancipation: Revolutionary era, 286, 294–295; West Indies, 439, 501, 531, 542; pre–Civil War south, 470–471, 474, 481, 489, 490–491; Latin America, 524–525, 527, 528; Civil War, 636–641, 645, 656, 664, 669

Emancipation Bureau, 665

Emancipation Proclamation, 618, 639, 641, 645, 654, 657, 670

Embargo of 1807–09, 341, 362–363, 368

Emerson, Ralph Waldo, 427–*428, 588*

Emigration: loyalists, 285–286, 288; Confederates, 660

Emigrant Aid Society, 568, 569

Employers: colonial, 92–93, 163–164; Revolutionary and Confederation periods, 290; Jacksonian and pre–Civil War periods, 426; Civil War era, 633

Encomiendas, 12

Encyclopédie, 201, 202

Enforcement Acts (1870–1871), 714

England: origins of overseas expansion, 16–29; early modern society and economy, 17–19, 81–83, 89–90, 99–100, 107, 109, 196, 212, 213; religion, 17, 44, 47–48, 69, 99–100, 105, 107, 166, wars with Spain, 17, 20, 23; establishment of colonies, 33–58, 62–74; politics, 63–64, 133;

consolidation of British Empire, 112–121; education, 140–145; naturalization laws, 151–153; demography, nineteenth-century, 382. *See also* British Empire; Great Britain

English: and New Netherland, 58–59; in Nova Scotia, 129; view of Indians, 200; as immigrants, nineteenth century, 381

English Bill of Rights, 138

English Civil War, 63, 75; colonies and, 58, 103

Enlightenment: and America, 3–5, 199–206; and Revolution, 280, 292; and American religion, 358; legacy, nineteenth century, 424–427

Entail, 293

Entrepreneurs: colonial, 85, 88, 91, 124–125, 167–168; Revolutionary and Confederation period, 288, 291; Jeffersonian Republicans, 324; farmers as, 384–386; and industrialization, 390–396; Civil War, 630–631

"Enumerated" commodities, 115, 228

Enumerated powers, under Constitution, 309

Environment, lack of concern for, nineteenth century, 384–386, 672

Episcopalians, 358. *See also* Anglicans

Equality: as American ideal, 210–211; Revolutionary and Confederation period, 276, 277, 293–294; Hamilton's view of, 320; Jeffersonian Republicans and, 323–324; as Jackson's ideal, 374, 397, 486, 505; and proslavery arguments, 335; feminists and, 443–444; Lincoln as symbol of, 580. *See also* Feminism; Women's movement

Equality, racial: abolitionists and, 475–483; Lincoln on, 577; as Reconstruction period issue, 673–677, 683–687

Equal protection of the laws, 676, 687

Era of Good Feelings, 368, 486, 518

Ericsson, John, 628

Erie Canal, 382, 388, *384,* 396, 438

Essex decision, 360–361; 368

Established church. *See* Church, established

Estates, in early modern Britain, 159

Estimate of the Manners and Principles of the Times, 206

Ethics: and social control, nineteenth century, 375, 411–412, 415, 419–420, 424–425, 435–442, 445–446; and antislavery, 473–474. *See also* Moral Reform; Religion; Values

Europe: as model for American society, 91–109; and colonial trade, 86–91, 115, 194, 220–223; international relations, early modern, 127, 186–193; contrast with colonial society, 130; and colonial culture, 139–140, 199–204; and Revolutionary America, 280; and U.S., under Confederation, 304–305; and post-Revolutionary American culture, 315; and U.S., Federalist period, 321–322, 325–327, 330–331; and America, Jefferson on, 345, 346, 360, 362, 365; U.S. trade with, early nineteenth century, 359; and U.S., Jacksonian period, 374, 389, 396, 397, 402–403; immigration from, early nineteenth century, 380; and nineteenth-century American culture, 411, 446; cotton trade, 457–458; international relations, nineteenth century, 527; Monroe Doctrine and, 527–528, 535; and Civil War, 629, 641–643; relations with U.S., post-Civil War, 698–700

Evangelicalism: in First Great Awakening, 166–174; and Revolution and Second Great Awakening, 355, 356–359; Jacksonian and pre–Civil War periods, 417–424, 439–440, 467–468, 477, 483, 557

Evans, George Henry, 399

Executions, Sioux Indians (1862), 713

Executive power: fear of, Revolutionary and Confederation periods, 278–279; under Constitution, 308, 310; Federalist period, 320–321, 324; Jeffersonian period, 340–341, 346, 365; Jacksonian and pre–Civil War periods, 498–500; Civil War and Reconstruction, 679–681. *See also* Governors, colonial; Governors, state; Presidency

Expansion, in America: Spanish, 5–9, 29; Dutch, 58–62; English, 16–28, 33–58, 62–74; of colonial frontier, 90–91, 122, 149, 214–217, 219

Expansion and expansionism, U.S.: Federalist period, 321; Jefferson and, 343–349, 365–367, 522; War of 1812, 365; Jacksonian period, 375, 383, 423, 495, 498–499, 512, 529–531; pre–Civil War period, 454, 531–543, 547, 548, 564; post-Civil War period, 588. *See also* Frontier

Experiments and Observations on Electricity, 202

Exploration: European, in America, 5–9, 23, 29; Jeffersonian and Jacksonian periods, *344,* 345, 368, 386, 495, 535

Exports, American: colonial, 39, 46, 59, 67, 86, 88–91, 220–223; regulation under navigation acts, 115, 145; Revolutionary and Confederation periods, 286; Jeffersonian period, 360–363, *361,* Jacksonian and pre–Civil War periods, 377, 379, 389, 457–459, 500–501, 507, 531; Civil War era, 608–609, 629

Ex post facto laws, 309

Factionalism, political: colonial, 125, 127, 132–138, 176–179, 277; British, 224; Revolutionary era, 250; state, in Critical Period, 300–301; and origin of political parties, 327–331; in Jeffersonian Republican party, 341, 492–493, 495; Republican, during Civil War and Reconstruction period, 645–647, 654, 673–681. *See also* Parties, political

Factories: immigrant labor in, early nineteenth century, 380; Jacksonian and pre–Civil War periods, 391–392, 398–401, 512, 522; women in, 392; labor shortages, 19th century, 456; pre–Civil War south, 469; Civil War era, 604, 629–630, 635, 652; Gilded Age, 708–709. *See also* Child labor; Labor unions, Manufacturing; *specific industries*

"Factors," Scottish, 167, 222

Fairfax, Lord, 158

Fair Oaks (Seven Pines), battle of, 615

Faithful Narrative of the Surprising Work of God, 170

Fallen Timbers, battle of, 321, *322, 332*

Family: slave, colonial, 83–84, 153–157; colonial New England, 92–98; *95,* 140; white, and slavery, 153–154; 465; in Revolutionary society, 293; Jacksonian and pre–Civil War periods, 378, 379–380, 383, 384, 401, 415, 441; slave, nineteenth century, 463–465; Garrison on, 479; *Uncle Tom's Cabin* and, 557–558; freedmen and, 670. *See also* Children; Women

Famine: early Virginia, 40; potato famine, 380, 389; Civil War, 663, 666. *See also* "Starving times"

Faneuil family, 129

Farmers: as immigrants, 79, 109, 197; colonial, 165, 215, 220–221; in Revolution, 288; Republicanism and, 274, *275,* in Revolutionary society, *276,* 288; Critical Period, 300; Federalist period, 305, 306; Jeffersonian period, 345; and War

of 1812, 364; Jacksonian and pre–Civil War periods, 378, 383–388, 396, 454, 390, 394, 396, 399–400, 513; southern, nonslaveholding, 396, 456, 459, 462, 468, 500; Indians as, 403; Mormons and, 434; in Civil War, 629, 630, 634–635; post-Civil War, 656, 671–673; Gilded Age, 703. *See also* Agrarianism; Rural society

Farming: colonial, 122, 158, 197; Jacksonian and pre–Civil War periods, 384–386, 389–390, 419; Civil War era, 632; post-Civil War southern, 671–673. *See also* Agriculture; Farmers

Farragut, David G., 627, 652, 654

Far West: and slavery, 551. *See also* Northwest, Pacific; Oregon Country; *specific states*

Faulkner, William, 672

Federalism: origins of, 306–322, 325–331; and dissent, 329; end of, 336, 339–340, 367–368; and Embargo of 1807, 363

Federalist, The, 313, 320, 338, 352

Federalist period, 298–332

Federalists (quasi-party): Federalist period, 306–322, 325–331; election of 1800, 335–337, 339–340; Jeffersonian period, 341, 350, 355, 363, 367–368; 369; collapse of, 436, 486, 487, 496, 511

Feminism, nineteenth century, 438. *See also* Suffrage, Women's; Women; Women's movement

Ferdinand and Isabella (Spanish monarchs), 13

Fessenden, William Pitt, 632, 675, 681

Feudalism, 56

Filibuster (congressional), by J. Q. Adams, for antislavery, 530

Filibustering, Central American, 346

Fillmore, Millard, 509, 512, 556, 564

Finance. *See* Banks and banking; Capital, accumulation and investment; Currency; Credit, commercial; Credit, public; Debt, national; Fiscal policy; Investment; Monetary policy

Financial systems, reorganization, Reconstruction period, 687

Findley, William, 299

Finney, Charles Grandison, 421, 422–423, 438

"Fire-eaters," 502–503, 578, 579, 583, 592, 607

First Great Awakening. *See* Great Awakening, First

Fiscal policy: Hamiltonian, 316–319, 323–

325; Jeffersonian Republican, 323, 339; Jacksonian, 500, 504–507; Civil War, 604–606, 631–632

Fish, Hamilton, 699

Fisher, Samuel, 423

Fishing: sixteenth-century North American, 16; colonial, 46, *87,* 230, Newfoundland fisheries, 86–87, 269, New France, 127, 187; Rush-Bagot convention, 369

Fitzhugh, George, 472

"Five Civilized Nations," 597, 712

Fletcher, Benjamin, 125, 136, 169

Fletcher v. *Peck* (1810), 352, 369

Florida: discovery, 6, 29; and colonial wars, *128–129,* 186, 192, 212, 217; as Spanish possession, and U.S., 321, 346, 523; annexation, 369, 524, 525, 544; Indians, 403, 405, *407;* secession, 583, 589, 596, 617; in Civil War, 691; Reconstruction, *678,* 686, 688, 716; and Gilded Age, 716, 719, 720; and voting rights of blacks, 719, 720

Florida, C.S.S., 642

Flour milling, 136, 221, 394

Force Bill (1832), 503, 518–519

Force Bill (1889), 720

Foreign relations, U.S.: Revolutionary era, 254, 264–266, 269–270; under Confederation, 304–305; under Constitution, 309; Federalist period, 321, 325–326; Jeffersonian period, 341, 359–368, 523; J. Q. Adams and, 524, *526,* 530–531; Jacksonian period, 528–535; pre–Civil War period, 535–544; Civil War era, 606–609, 618, 641–643; post-Civil War, 697–700

Foreign trade. *See* Commerce; Exports; Free trade; Imports; Protectionism; Tariffs

Forrest, Nathan Bedford, 659, 690

Fort Dearborn, *364*

Fort Donelson, 613, 618

Fort Duquesne, *189,* 190, 191

Fort Fisher, 627

Fort Frontenac, *189,* 191

Fort Henry, 613, 618

Fort Herkimer, *189,* 191

Fort Monroe, 614, 621, 647, 659

Fort Necessity, 189

Fort Niagara, *189,* 191

Fort Orange, 59

Fort Pickens, 594, 595

Fort Pillow, 659

Fort Sumter, 594–595, 596, 599, 617

Fort Ticonderoga, *189,* 190, 191, 192, 254, 270

Fort Wagner, 640

Fort William Henry, *189,* 191

"Forty-Five," 226, 259

Forty-ninth parallel, *526,* 538, 544

Foster, John, 52, 132

Fourier, Charles, 445

Fowler, Orson and Lorenzo, 426

Fox Indians, 405, *407*

"Fractional currency," Gilded Age, 704

Frame of Government (colonial Pennsylvania), 72, 74

France: claim to North America, 29; and colonial trade, 86; and colonial wars, 127–129, 186–193, 207, 212, 217, 219, 244; and Revolution, 260, 266–267, 267–271, 280; and U.S., under Confederation, 305; French Revolution, and U.S., 325–327, 329–331, 355; and U.S., Napoleonic period, 345–346, 359–368, 523; and U.S., demography, nineteenth century, 382; Mormons and, 430; and Monroe Doctrine, 523, 527–528; and U.S., Jacksonian period, 536; Revolution of 1848, 560; and Civil War, 606–609, 643

Franchise, colonial, 51, *109,* 178–179. *See also* Suffrage; Town meeting; Voting

Franklin, Benjamin, *202, 203;* and American values, 3; early career, 74, 189, 199; and Enlightenment, 201–204; on British empire, 213, 222–223; as land speculator, 217; and Paxton Boys, 220; and Post Office, 221; and Revolution, 264, 266, 270

Franklin, battle of, 650

Fraternal organizations, Revolutionary era, 232

Freake, John and Elizabeth, *94*

Fredericksburg, battle of, 618, 622, *623,* 642, 645

Free blacks. *See* Blacks

Freedmen: Reconstruction, 657, 661, 664–668, 675–677. *See also* Blacks

Freedmen's Bureau, 664–669, *665, 666,* 670, 675, 686, 691

Freedmen's Bureau Act (1865), 665

Freedmen's Bureau bill, Johnson's veto of, 675

Freedmen's Union Industrial School, 666

Free enterprise. *See* Business; Capitalism; Competition, economic; Free-market economy; Laissez-faire policies

Freehold tenure: colonial, 157–158, 159,

162, 179; nineteenth century, 295. *See also* Landownership

Free-market economy: Jacksonian and pre–Civil War periods, 375, 377–379, 384–387, 404, 454, 548; and proslavery argument, 472. *See also* Capitalism

Freemasons. *See* Anti-Masonry

Freeport Doctrine, 578

Free-soil party, 480, 482, *549,* 550, 567, 584

Free trade: Enlightenment and, 359; Jacksonian and pre–Civil War periods, 500; Gilded Age, 701. *See also* Protectionism; Tariffs

Frémont, John C., 535–*536,* 540, 567, 597, 647

French: in New Amsterdam, 59; in British Colonies, 67, 69; as colonial enemy, 186–187, 188–193, 227; in British Canada, 227

French and Indian War (Seven Years' War, 1756–63), 188–193, *189,* 212, 217, 223, 244

French Revolution: and American Revolution, 3, 325; U.S. and, 325–327, 329–331, 355

French Revolutionary and Napoleonic wars (1792–1815), 327, 330, 345, 360, 363, 436

Frenchtown, battle of, *364,* 365

French West Indies, 194, 206, 230, 325, 360

Freylinghuysen, Theodore, 712

Friends, Society of. *See* Quakers

Fries, John, 330, 332

Frobisher, Martin, 19

Frontier: Spanish-American empire, 12; colonial, 133, 139, 150, 165, 172; and American education, 140–141; Revolutionary era, 215–220, *216,* 223, 227, 276, 283–285; Federalist period, 316, 317, 321; Jeffersonian period, 343–345, 346–347; religion, nineteenth century, 354–359, 417–424; and War of 1812, 364–365; and modernization, nineteenth century, 377, 384–386; as "safety valve," 399; in nineteenth-century literature, 448; Jackson and, 494. *See also* Expansion, U.S.; Northwest, Old; Southwest, Old; *specific regions*

Frost, Robert, 376

Fry, Joshua, 155

Fugitive Slave Law (1793), 480

Fugitive Slave Law (1850), 482, 555, 556, 572, 576

Fulton, Robert, 368, 388

Fundamental Constitutions of Carolina, 66, 145

Fundamentalism: nineteenth century, 356

Fundamental Orders (Connecticut), 75

Funding Bill, 318, 332

Fur trade: colonial, 46, 59, 67, 86, 219; and navigation acts, 115; in New France, 127; nineteenth century, 384

Gadsden, James, 543

Gadsden Purchase, 543

Gage, Thomas, 240, 252, 260

Gag rule, 479, 503–504, 552

Gall, Franz Joseph, 425

Gallatin, Albert, 339

Galloway, Joseph, 249, 270

Gardoqui, Diego de, 305

Garfield, James A., 706, 707, 718

Garment industry, 394, 604, 629, 709

Garnet, Henry, 481

Garrison, William Lloyd, 435, 443, 444, 445, 664

Gaspée, 239, 245

Gates, Horatio, 264, 267, *268*

Gayle, Sarah, 461

General Union for Promoting the Observance of the Christian Sabbath, 435

Genêt, Citizen, 325, 332

Gentry, American: Revolutionary era, 222, 231, 250, 254, 289; Federalist period, 298–299, 307–308, 323–324; Jeffersonian period, 335, 337–338, 341; Jacksonian period, 494. *See also* Elites; Planters

Gentry, English: 19, 24, 35–36, 48, 159, 223, 258

George, Henry, 709

George I (king of England), 146, 191, 224

George II (king of England), 206, 224

George III (king of England): *224,* imperial crisis, 223–226, 252, 254, 255, 270; insanity, 493

George IV (prince regent, king of England), 493

Georgia (colonial): slavery, 154; religion, 169; colonial wars, 186; founded, 206

Georgia (state): Revolution, 278, 280, 354; Critical period, 299, 301, 313; Jeffersonian period, 345; Indians, 348, 369, 403, 404, *407;* slavery, 455, 464, 475; Black Belt, 468, pre–Civil War politics, 562–564; secession, 583, 584, *596,* 617; in Civil War, 625, 634, 644, *649,* 650, 659; Reconstruction, 671–674, 678, 688, 716; post-Reconstruction period, 716, 719,

720; poll tax adopted, 719
Georgia Upcountry, 459
Germain, Lord George, 262
German Reformed church, 69
Germans and German Americans: in colonies, 69, *151*, 152–153
Germany: pietism in, 151, 166; immigration from, nineteenth century, 380, 381, 398; and nineteenth-century American culture, 427; revolutions of 1848, 560
Gettysburg, battle of, *623*, 626, 636, 640, 644, 654
Gettysburg Address, 652, 695
Ghent, Treaty of (1814), 366–367, 369, 511
Gibraltar, 270
Giddings, Joshua, 549
Gilbert, Sir Humphrey, 19–20, 22, 23, 30
Gilded Age: politics, 700–701; economic issues, 701; political corruption, 705–706; labor organization, 708–711
Gimbrede, Thomas, *495*
Ginger trade, 115
Glasgow, Scotland, 161–162
Glass, Carter, 720
Glorious Revolution, 118, 175; and colonial rebellions, 133, 135
Godkin, E. L., 707
Gold Rush, California, *536, 551*, 584, 714
Gold standard, 703
Gooch, William, 120
Gordon, John B., 718
Gordon, Thomas, 257
Gorgas, Josiah, 603, 653
Gorsuch, Edward, *557*
Government: powers of, post-Civil War, 658, 662, 665. *See also* Government, attitudes toward; Government, national; Government, role and expansion of
Government, attitudes toward: Enlightenment, 203; of Federalists, 314–322, 335, 337–342, 351–352; of Jeffersonian Republicans, 322, 325, 337–342, 350, 359–360
Government, local: reorganization, Reconstruction period, 687
Government, national: limits of power, during Reconstruction, 662–663
Government, role and expansion of: Spanish-American empire, 8–14; British Empire, 16–17, 19–23, 112–121, 210, 212, 223–244; seventeenth-century colonial, 40–43, 46–47, 51–52, 58–59, 64, 68, 125–127, 136–137; and religion, seventeenth century, 98–99; New France, 127; and colonial education, 140–145; eigh-

teenth-century British, 174–176; eighteenth-century colonial, 176–181; Revolutionary, 248–249, 275–276, 277–282; Critical Period, 300, 306; framing of Constitution, 307–313; Jacksonian period, 374–375; and western settlement, 387; during Civil War, 588, 589–590, 591–593, 630; Reconstruction period and Gilded Age, 656, 661–644, 667, 668, 669
Governors, colonial: 117–118, 132–133, 176–181, 193, 234, 248, 258; Virginia, 38–39, 219; Plymouth Plantation, 45–47; Massachusetts Bay, 50, 137, 187, 199, 239, 240, 243; Maryland, 55, 57–59, 136, 233; New Netherland, 61–62; Pennsylvania, 69–72; New Hampshire, 117; New York, 119, 136; Connecticut, 139
Governors, state: Revolutionary era, 278–279; Critical Period, 301–302, 307; Civil War, 597; Reconstruction period, 658, 688–689. *See also* Executive Power
Grace, in Puritan theology, 53, 105–109, 167
Grain cultivation: eighteenth century, 221; nineteenth century, 386, 387, 390, 455, 656
Grain trade: colonial, 220–221; and Whiskey Rebellion, 320
Grand Banks, 16
Grandfather clauses, 720
Grand Ohio Company, 227
Grant, Ulysses S.: in Mexican War, 540; in Civil War, *613, 616*, 618, 624–625, *648*-649, 651, 663, 667; and Johnson administration, 650, 652, 679; elections of 1868 and 1872, 700; currency policy, 704; as president, 714–715, 721–722
Granville, the Earl, 158
Great Awakening, First, 169–174, 206
Great Awakening, Second, 355–356
Great Britain: Quakers, 69, 202; eighteenth-century politics, 149, 165, 174–176, 185, 191–193, 205–206; eighteenth-century population, 149; naturalization laws, 151, 153; and eighteenth-century Ireland, 150, 259; eighteenth-century society and economy, 157, 159; Revolutionary era politics, 223–227, 229–232, 240–244; country-Whig opposition, 257–258; and U.S., post-Revolutionary period, 304, 314, 321, 322, 325–326; and U.S., Jeffersonian period, 339–340, 345–346, 522, 523; War of 1812, 364–367, 525; Irish famine, 380; Corn Laws, 389;

industrialization, 390, 454; emigration from, 399; U.S. trade with, early nineteenth-century, 394, 454–459, 507–508, 531; nineteenth-century social reform, 398–399, 411, 436, 477; and pre–Civil War U.S. reform movements, 421–422, 424–428, 435–437, 501; Mormons and, 429–434; U.S. Whigs and, 512–513; and Monroe Doctrine, 527–528; and U.S., Jacksonian and pre–Civil War periods, 528, 531–532, 542; and Civil War, 608–609, 642, 643; and U.S., post-Civil War, 698–700; Civil Service system, 706. *See also* Anglophobia; British Empire; England

Great Law (colonial Pennsylvania), 72
Great Migration, 26, 48–50, 75, 92, 109
Great Plains, 379
Great Railroad Strike (1877), 711
Great Revival, 418
Greece, ancient, 273, 275, 422, 472
Greek War for Independence, 528
Greeley, Horace, 399, 512, 515, 567, 700, 712
Green, Duff, 531–532
Greene, Nathanael, 267
Green Mountain Boys, 219
Greenough, Horatio, 446, *447*, 448
Greenville, Treaty of, 321, *322*, 332, 347
Greenwood, John, 164
Grenville, George, 225, 229, 230
Grimbede, Thomas, 495
Grimké, Angelina, 443
Grimké, Sarah, 443–444, 465–466
Griswold, Roger, *329*
Grundy, Felix, 364
Guadaloupe, 194. *See also* French West Indies
Guadalupe Hidalgo, Treaty of (1848), 540–541, 542, 544
Guatemala, Spanish conquest, 8, 29
Guilford Court House, battle of, 267, *268*, 271
Guinea Company, 18
Guiteau, Charles, 707
Gulf of Mexico, 316

Haiti: slave uprising, 316, 523, 661; and colonization, 482, 639; post-Civil War, 698. *See also* Santo Domingo
Hakluyt, Richard, 20, 22, 30
Hale, John R., 479
Halfway Covenant, 145, 167
Halleck, Henry Wagner, 613–614, 621–622, 624, 625

Hamilton, Alexander, *317;* in Critical Period, 303; and *The Federalist,* 313n, 331, 338, 352; in Washington administration, 314, 315, 323, 326, 330; financial program, 316–319, 339, 340, 365; political program, 320–322, 327, 330, 343, 355, 359–360, 365; and election of 1800, 336; killed by Burr, 336n, 368
Hampton, Wade, 660, 718
Hancock, John, 236, 244, 252
Handicapped persons, 435, 440, 664
Hanover, 191
Hanoverian dynasty (Great Britain), 146, 224
"Hard money." *See* Currency; Gold standard, Specie
Harper, Robert Goodloe, 341
Harper, William, 470
Harpers Ferry, W. Va., 578–579, 580
Harper's Weekly Magazine, 659, 705, 707
Harrington, James, 274
Harris, Isham, 596
Harrison, William Henry: 348, 365, 369, 402, 514
Hartford, Ct., 501
Hartford Convention, 367–368, 369
Hartford, Treaty of (1650), 61
Harvard, John, 143
Harvard University (Harvard College): foundation, 75, 143; in colonial culture, 144; and First Great Awakening, 172; blacks and, 417; nineteenth century, 437
Hasenclever iron works (New Jersey), 196
Hat Act (1732), 195
Haun's Mill, Mo., 430
Haverhill, Mass., 49, 221
Hawaii, 698
Hawkins, John, 19, 23
Hawthorne, Nathaniel, 394, 446, 449, 590
Hayes, John L., 702
Hayes, Rutherford B., 682, 701, 707, 716–718, 721, 722
Hayes-Tilden disputed election of 1876, 717
Headrights, 40, 57
Hegel, Georg Wilhelm Friedrich, 696
Hendrick, *190*
Henrico, Va., 39
Henry VII (king of England), 16
Henry VIII (king of England), 16–17, 25
Henry, Patrick, 222, *231,* 249, 308, 310
Higginson family, 286
"Higher law," 555
Highway networks, 456
Hill, Benjamin H., 590

Hillsborough, Lord, 235, 236, 238
H.L. Hunley (submarine), 627–628
Holland. *See* Netherlands
"Home rule" (post-Reconstruction South), 714–716
Homestead Act (1862), 580, 630, 632
Honduras, Spanish conquest, 8, 29
Hood, John B., 650
Hooker, Joseph, 622–623
Horseshoe Bend, battle of, 364, 369
Housatonic, U.S.S., 628
Household industry, 390. *See also* Family
House of Burgesses (colonial Virginia), 40, 42, 181, 222, 231
House of Commons, 174, 175–176, 194, 226, 237, 240, 242, 257
House of Lords, 174
House of Representatives (Massachusetts Bay Colony), 235, 243, 244
House of Representatives (U.S.): under Constitution, 310; Federalist period, 315, 323, 326; election of 1800, 336; Jeffersonian period, 350; Jacksonian and pre–Civil War periods, 489, 494, 530, 549; Reconstruction period, 674, 680, 689, 701; Gilded Age, 714, 717, 718, 720
Housing, urban, Jacksonian period, 397–398
Houston, Sam, 529, 540
Howard, Oliver O., 665, 666
Howe, Julia Ward, 695
Howe, Lord Richard, 262–263
Howe, Samuel Gridley, 440, 664
Howe, Timothy O., 684
Howe, William, 253, 260–264, 267
Huckleberry Finn, 413
Hudson Bay, 16, 19, 29, 128
Hudson River, 59, 60, 68, 86, 125, 126, 150, 159, 165, 265, 368, 382
Hudson River School, 446
Hudson's Bay Company, 533
Hughes, Bishop John, 415, 560
Huguenots, in colonial America, 67, 69, 150
Hull, William, 365
Humanitarianism: Enlightenment and Revolutionary, 199–206, 291–295; post-Revolutionary, 315; nineteenth century, 435–442; 472–483; Reconstruction period, 665–667
Humanitarian organizations, post-Civil War, 665–666
Hume, David, 312
"Hundreds," 40
Hunter, R. M. T., 607

Hunter, Robert, 120
Hurons, 217, 218
Hutchinson, Anne, 53, 54
Hutchinson, Thomas, 179, 232, 239, 243, 251, 198
Hutchinson family, 132

Ideology: Revolutionary, 210–211, 248–249; 354; Republican, 273–277; Federalist, 316–322; 335; Jeffersonian Republican, 323–325, 335, 337–349; Jacksonian and pre–Civil War, 374–375, 401, 423, 468; Free labor, 490, 548, 577, 582; Jacksonian Democratic, 496–497; proslavery, 468–470, 472, 501–503; Whig, 512–513. *See also* Democracy
Illinois: admission, 347; settlement, 401, Indians, 405, 407, culture, 19th century, 419; Mormons, 429–430; Jacksonian-period social reform, 437; antislavery, 478; pre–Civil War politics, 567, 574, 576–577
Illinois Central Railroad, 556, 574
Immigration and immigrants: to Spanish America, 14–15; from early modern England, 22; European, to colonies, 33, 35; to colonial Virginia, 36–40; Great Migration, 48–50; to colonial Maryland, 56–57; to New Netherlands, 59–60; to New France, 127; Revolutionary era, 288; Jacksonian and pre–Civil War period, 377, 380–381, 391–392, 396, 398, 413, 415, 422, 440, 456, 457, 496, 508, 513, 516, 522, 552, 553, 559–560, 561; Mormons and, 430; to Texas, 528; Civil War, 652; European and Chinese, Reconstruction period, 669, 710; Gilded Age and progressive era, 708
Impeachments: of Federalist judges, 350, 368; of Andrew Johnson, 679–681, 691
Imports: to colonies, 86, 220–221; regulation under Navigation Acts, 115; Revolutionary era, 220–221, 230, 235, 239–240, Confederation Period, 300, 306; in Hamiltonian program, 319, 326; Jeffersonian period, 361, 362–363; Jacksonian and pre–Civil War period, 377, 458, 500; Civil War, 611, 629, 632
Impressment, 326, 361, 362, 367
Impressment Act (Confederacy, 1863), 630
Incan empire, conquest of, 8
Indentured servants, 43, 57, 80, 92–93, 98, 123, 132, 153
Independence, American: origins of, 235,

238, 243–244; struggle for, 248–249, 252–270, 278–279; War of 1812 and, 363–365, 367; as secession from Britain, 583. *See also* Declaration of Indepenence
Independent Treasury Act (1840), 508, 519
Indian Appropriations Act (1851), 406
Indian Bureau, 713
Indian reservations, 219, 227, 406–407, 568
Indians, American (Native Americans): in Spanish America, 12–13; population, 14, 33–34; and Roanoke Colony, *21–22;* colonial Virginia, 36, 37, 40, 74, 133; New Netherland, 59, 60–62; Carolina, 67; and expansion of colonial frontier, 90, 133, 217–219, *218;* attempt to Christianize, 20, 139, 144; colonial wars, 187–188, *190;* English view of, 200; Enlightenment view of, 201; British officials and, 217, 219; Revolutionary War, 267; Jacksonian and pre–Civil War periods, 378, 401–*407, 405,* 379, 396, *556,* 557, 568, 570; Mormons and, 429; in nineteenth-century literature, 448; Garrison on, 478; during Civil War, 597; post-Civil War period, 656, 712–714
Indian Territory, 597
Indian tribes, 402–403, 406, 568, 597
Indian wars: colonial America, 40, 61–62, 121, 129, 219, 244; Federalist period, 321; Jeffersonian period, 348, 364; Jacksonian period, 405
Indigo, 67, 115, *123*
Industrial Revolution: British, 220, 388–391; U.S., 390–393; and slavery, 455
Industry: in Confederacy: 599, 603, 629; in North, Civil War era, 611, 627, 629, 652; tariff problem, Gilded Age, 701. *See also* Economy, American
Inequality, social: colonial, 91–98, 129–130, 132, 222; Republicanism and, 277, 289; pre–Civil War South, 461–462, 470, 505
Inflation, Revolutionary and Confederation periods, 288–302; Gilded Age, 703–704. *See also* Economy, American
Inflation Bill (1874), 703, 704
Ingersoll, Charles Jared, 411–412
Instability, social: seventeenth century, 91–98; 109, 132–138; and colonial education, 140–141; eighteenth century, 159, 173; Enlightenment and, 203; Critical Period, 298–299; and French Revolution, 325; crisis of 1798–1799, 327–331
Insurance, 165
Intellectuals: colonial, 138–139, 143–145,

204; Civil War generation, 683
Interest rates. *See* Credit, commercial
Internal Revenue Act (1862), 631
Internal Revenue Service, and political corruption, 706
International relations, nineteenth-century Europe, 698–700
International trade. *See* Commerce
Investment: English, in colonization, 16, 19, 20, 22, 24–27; Jacksonian and pre–Civil War periods, 387, 390, 499, 507; pre–Civil War South, 457, 459, 463, 477
Iowa: Indians, 406; Mormons, 431; politics, 551; blacks, 683; Reconstruction, 683
Ireland: and early modern English expansion, 24–26, *25,* 149–150; and British mercantilism, 115; demography, 213; struggle for liberty, eighteenth century, 224; potato famine, 380, 389
Irish and Irish Americans: as immigrants, 150, 380, 381, 401, 441, 456, 525
Iron industry, 40, 85, 196, 393–394, 596, 628, 701, 703
Iron trade, 124, 196, 228
Iroquois, 33, 402
Irving, Washington, 446
Isolationism: Washington and, 326; Jeffersonian period, 346, 359
Isthmus of Panama, exploration of, 6
Italy: early republics, 275; revolutions of 1848, 560
"Itinercy," 173

Jackson, Andrew: War of 1812, 363, 367, 369, 402; and Indians, 402, 406, 494, 496, 503; and Florida, 525; election of 1824, 494; election of 1828, 340, 342, 487, 497–500, *498;* as president, 496, 498–*499, 507,* 511, 517–518; and slavery, 477, 494, 503–504; and expansion, 496, 498, 529; as "monarch," *510,* 513, 548
Jackson, Thomas J. ("Stonewall"), 540, 603, 615, 622, 649
Jacksonian period: economy and society, 374–407; 411–428, 435–446, 454–483; politics, 496–518
Jacksonian revolution, 340, 496–500; 696
Jacobins, 646
Jamaica, 501
James I (king of England), 24, 30, 88, 257
James II (duke of York; king of England), 113, 116–118, 133
James River, 39, 40, 615, 648, 654
Jamestown, Va., 30, 36–39

Japan, Perry and, 547, 584
Jarratt, Devereux, 172
Jarvis, John Wesley, 255
Jay, John, 270, 305, 308, 313n, 321, 326, 341
Jay's Treaty (1795), 326, 327, 332, 361, 362
Jefferson, Peter, 155
Jefferson, Thomas, in imperial debate, 244; in Revolution, 211, 252, 255–256, 258, 268; political philosophy, 276, 277, 278, 293, 306, 308, 340; and religous toleration, 104, 354, 355; and slavery, 295; in Critical Period, 301, 302, 304, 305; on *The Federalist,* 313n; in Washington administration, 315; and origins of Republican party, 327, 330; as vice-president, 326; on French Revolution, 327; as president, 335, 336–337; 339, 340, 342, 343, 345–346, 347, 350, 352, 360, 362, 367, 368, 523; and Indians, 347, 403, 404; on war and peace, 362, 365, 368; as Anglophobe, 524; on Missouri crisis, 489; death, 486
Jeffersonianism: early nineteenth century, 335–342; 343, 359–368; and antislavery, 471; Republican party and, 567. *See also* Agrarianism
Jeffersonian Republicans. *See* Republican party (Jeffersonian)
Jeffersonian revolution, 335–342
Jenkins, Robert, 186
Jersey. *See* New Jersey (colonial)
Jesuits, 103
Jews: in colonies, 104, 153; in Revolution, 251; as immigrants, 381, 401
Jim Crow laws, 716–721
Johnson, Andrew: on religion, 418; nominated for vice-presidency, 647; as president, 654, 691; and Reconstruction, 657–658, 662, 667, 673–681; *680,* 684, 686, 691, 700; conflicts with Republican party, 676; impeachment, 679–681, 691; racism of, 684; on territorial expansion, 698
Johnson, Reverdy, 699
Johnston, Albert Sidney, 433
Johnston, Joseph E., 612, *613, 614,* 615, 649, 650, 651, 654, 625, 626, 640
Joint-stock companies: origins of, 17–19; financing English colonization, 26–28; and Plymouth Plantation, 45–46; suppressed, 198–199. *See also* Capitalism, Dutch West India Company; Massachusetts Bay Company; New England Company; Virginia Company

Jomini, Baron Henri, 611–617, 620–621, 622
Jones, J. B., 634
Journalism. *See* Press
Journeymen, 290
Juarez, Benito, 698
Judicial review: origins of, 350; Marshall and, *351*–353, 404. *See also* Constitutionality; Supreme Court
Judiciary, American: colonial, 132–133, 176–177, 353; Critical Period, 300–301; under Constitution, 310; federal, creation of, 316, 320; and crisis of 1798–99, 329–330; Jeffersonian period, 350–353; reorganization, Reconstruction period, 687. *See also* Court system; Supreme Court
Judiciary Act (1789), 316, 351, 352
Judiciary Act (1801), 350, 351, 368
Julian, George W., 684
Jurisprudence, history of, 656
Jury trial: absence in prerogative courts, 119, 177–178, 239, 240; Zenger trial, 206; absence of, under Fugitive Slave Law of 1850, 556–557

Kansas: Spanish exploration, 8; settlement, 400; slavery issue, in 1850s, 564–571, 572, 578, 584; admission, 571; in Civil War, 597–640; blacks, 683; Reconstruction, 683
Kansas-Nebraska Act (1854), 564, 565–*566,* 568, 574
Kant, Immanuel, 427
Kearney, Dennis, 681, *682*
Kearney, Stephen W., 540
Keayne, Robert, *52*
Kelley, Abby, 443
Kellogg, William, 583
Kendall, Amos, 504
Kenner, Duncan F., 643
Kentucky, settlement, 215, 289, 305; admission, 316, crisis of 1798–99, 330, 332; Second Great Awakening, 356, 368; religion, 356; and Jacksonian-period politics, 494; pre–Civil War politics, 582; in Civil War, 594, 597–598, 599, 612, *613,* 615, 618, 636, 645
Key, David M., 718
Kiefft, Willem, 61, 62
King, Rufus, 489, 491
King George's War (War of the Austrian Succession, 1740–48), 186–188, 206
King Philip's War (1675–76), 129
King's Mountain, battle of, 267

King William's War (War of the League of Augsburg, 1689–97), 127, 128; New York and, 135

Kinship: black, 154, 463–465, *464;* among colonial whites, 222

Kirby-Smith, Edmund, 615, *616,* 626, 651, 654

"Kitchen cabinet," 500, 504

Knights of the Golden Circle, 644

Knights of Labor, 709

Knowles, Charles, 188

Know-Nothings, 509, 549, 562–564, *563,* 580, 584

Knox, Henry, 320, 345

Knox, William, 243

Ku Klux Klan, 689–691, *690,* 714, *715–716*

Labor: in sixteenth-century England, 23–24; at Jamestown, 39–40; in seventeenth-century society, 56–57, 79–84, 92–93; availability of, in colonial society, 123; black, eighteenth century, 153–157; in eighteenth century, 162–163, 196; in Revolutionary society, 293–294; in Jacksonian and pre–Civil War society, 378, 390–394, *393,* 397, 398–401, 414, 421, 454; shortages, 456; slave, 463; free labor ideology, 490, 548, *549,* 582; during Civil War, 629, 633, 652; black, during Civil War, *637–638;* working conditions, post-Civil War, 656, 694; of freedmen, Reconstruction period, 666, 669–670; organization and conditions, Gilded Age, 708–711. *See also* Child labor; Labor unions; Slavery; Unemployment

Labor unions: Jacksonian and pre–Civil War periods, 399; late nineteenth century, 694; creation of, Gilded Age, 708–709. *See also* Working class; *specific unions*

Labrador, 16, 29

Lafayette, Marquis de, 269, 368

Laird shipyards (Liverpool, England), 628, 642

Laissez-faire policies: Jacksonian and pre–Civil War periods, 499, 509; Reconstruction period, 588, Gilded Age, 668–673. *See also* Capitalism; Free-market economy

Lake Champlain, 366–367

Lake Erie, battle of, *364,* 365, 369

Lamar, L. Q. C., 718

Land: availability of, in colonial society, 42, 50, 56–57, 60, 64–65, 72, 96, 132, 158–159; and churches, colonial Virginia, 99–100; and education, colonial New England, 141; and westward movement, Federalist and Jeffersonian periods, 345, 347; availability of, Jacksonian and pre–Civil War periods, 377, 384–385, 399–402, 455; freedmen and, 667, 670, *671,* 678. *See also* Landownership; Land speculation; "Safety-valve" theory

Land banks, 197–198

Land grant colleges, 630

Landlords: eighteenth century, 158–162; nineteenth-century British, 380; post-Civil War South, 669–673

Land Ordinance of 1785, *284, 285. See also* Northwest Ordinance

Landownership: Indian attitude toward, 33–34, 402–405; early seventeenth century, 42, 50, 55–58, 64, 92, 117; late seventeenth century and eighteenth centuries, 121–124, 158–162, 180–181; early modern Britain, 157, 159; republicanism and, 276; Jacksonian and pre–Civil War periods, 380, 387, 399–405; post-Civil War South, 670–672; Gilded Age, 709

Land policy, federal: Federalist and Jeffersonian periods, 345; Jacksonian and pre–Civil War periods, 377, 384, 386, 401–402; Homestead Act, 630; Gilded Age, 670. *See also* Land Ordinance of 1785; Northwest Ordinance

Land speculation: early colonial, 68; late seventeenth and eighteenth centuries, 21–24, 129–130, 139, 153, 158–159, 162, 181, 196; Revolutionary and Confederation periods, 215, 219, 282–285; Federalist and Jeffersonian periods, 345, 351; Jacksonian and pre–Civil War periods, 385, 386–387, 404, 568; post-Civil War, 667

Lane Theological Seminary, 477

Larkin, Thomas, 535, 539–540

Latin America: Spain's empire in, 5–6, 8–16; independence movement, 12, 523, 525; U.S. and, mid-nineteenth century, 527, 529. *See also* Central America; Monroe Doctrine; South America; Spanish-American empire; Western Hemisphere; *specific countries*

Laurens, Henry, 238

Law: colonial Virginia, 40; Carolina, 66; and social change, seventeenth century, 92–93, 98; English, and Dominion of New England, 117. *See also* Court system; Law, attitude toward; Judiciary; Vigilante groups

Law, attitude toward: colonial, 199; during Revolution, 230–231, 278–279; Critical Period, 300, 306; Jeffersonian period, 351–354; Jacksonian and pre–Civil War periods, 424, 479. *See also* Civil disobedience

Lawes Divine, Morall, and Martiall, 39, 40

Lawes and Libertyes, 51

Lawlessness. *See* Disorder

Lawrence, Abbott, 426, 550

Lawrence, Kansas, 568

League of Armed Neutrality, 266

Lecky, W. E. H., 150

Lecompton constitution, 571, 575, 577, 584

Lee, Arthur, 303

Lee, Richard Henry, 249, 277, 303, 308, 311

Lee, Robert E.: in Mexican War, 540; in Civil War, 603, *614,* 615–617, 618, 621, 622, 623, 626, 639, 641, 644, *648,* 649, *651,* 652, 660, 663

Legislatures: in Federalist political theory, 311–313; Jeffersonian period, 341–342

Legislatures, colonial, 40–43, 51, 57–58, 92–93, 133, 137–138, 141, 176–181, 197–199, 219–220, 229, 230–231, 233–234, 250–251, 257–258, 278–279

Legislatures, national: under Constitution, 308–311

Legislatures, state: Revolutionary and Confederate periods, 279–280, 291, 299–302, 306, 310, 342, 354, Federalist period, 299; Jeffersonian period, 347, and Marshall Court, 352; Jacksonian and pre–Civil War periods, 419, 475, 491, 493, 537, 553, 566, 577; Civil War, 596; Reconstruction period, 674; post-Reconstruction southern, 689; Gilded Age, 711

Leisler, Jacob, 135

Leisler's Rebellion, 132, 135–136

Leopard-Chesapeake Affair, 362, 368

Letcher, John, 596

Letters From a Farmer in Pennsylvania, 235, 242, 244

Levant Company, 18

Lewis, George Cornewall, 610

Lewis, Meriwether, *344*

Lewis and Clark expedition, *344,* 345, *347,* 368

Lexington, Mass., 252. *See also* Lexington and Concord, battle of

Lexington and Concord, battle of, 252, *253,* 260, *261,* 270

Liberalism: Enlightenment, 201–202, 359; Revolutionary era, 274–277, 291–295, 315, 359; in proslavery arguments, 472. *See also* Republicanism

Liberal Republican movement, during Grant administration, 700–701; and Civil Service reformers, Gilded Age, 707

Liberator, The, 475, 664

Liberia, 473

Liberty (ship), 236, 244

Liberty: seventeenth-century struggles for, 117–118, 132–133; in eighteenth-century America, 153, 205; Revolutionary era, 210, 226, 230, 240–244, 250–260; Critical Period, 274, 294–295; Federalist period, 306–307, 311–*314,* 327–331; Jeffersonian Republicans and, 326–327, 339, 343, 349; Jacksonian and pre–Civil War periods, 425, 481–482, 486; antislavery and, 477–481; Lincoln on, 576–577; South's view of, 583; Civil War, 634. *See also* Democracy; Equality

Liberty party, 480, 482, 534, 567

Library of Congress, 368

Lieber, Francis, 696

Life expectancy, seventeenth century, 81; nineteenth century, 398

Lima, Peru, 8

Lincoln, Abraham, *593;* character and beliefs, 538, 580; and Douglas, 574–578, 585; and slavery, 570, 574–578, 639; image of, 588; war aims, 589, 590, 620; election of 1860, *581*–584, 585; and border states, 596–599; and foreign relations, 606–607; and military operations, 614, 621–624; and emancipation, 618, 637, 639–640, 641, 646, 654; and Civil War politics and legislation, 630, 644–646, 652–653; and conscription, 635–636; and Gettysburg Address, 652, 695; Reconstruction plans, 657, 660; on union, 657, 660, 695; assassination, 647, 657, 659, 691; and Freedman's Bureau, 665

Lincoln, Benjamin, 267

Lincoln-Douglas debates, 574–578

Lindneux, Robert, 405

Literacy: colonial, 139, 142; nineteenth century, 413, 419, slave, 459; and post-Civil War southern blacks, *666,* 719

Literacy tests, blacks and, 720

Literature: colonial, 138, nineteenth century, 427, 448–449, 557, *558*

Livestock: colonial, 167; nineteenth century, 387, 390, 457

Living standards: colonial, 163–164, 221;

Revolutionary era, 288–289; Jacksonian and pre–Civil War periods, 378, 396, 398–401
Livingston, Robert (colonial New York oligarch), 125
Livingston, Robert R., 345
Livingston, William, 299
Livingston family 136, 250
Localism, post-Civil War, 656
Locke, John: and Fundamental Constitutions of Carolina, 65–66; as Enlightenment thinker, 203, 257; republicanism and, 292
Lodge, Henry Cabot, 511, 720
Log Cabin, The, 515
Lok, Michael, 19
London, England: economy and society, 23, *82–83,* 123, *163,* 164, 213, 381; and colonial economy, 222, 229; political riots, 225–226
Longfellow, Henry Wadsworth, 447
Long Island, 61, 136
Long Island, battle of, *261,* 263
Longstreet, James, 689
López, Narciso, 542
Lords of Trade, 113, 145
Loudoun, Lord, 190
Louis XIV (king of France), 114, 127
Louis XVI (king of France), 264, 332
Louisbourg, Nova Scotia, 187, *189,* 190, 206
Louisiana (French and Spanish), in colonial wars, *128,* 129, 192, 212; Spanish in, and U.S., 321, 345. *See also* Louisiana Purchase
Louisiana (state): admission, 347; slavery, 455, 461, 468, 549; sugar cultivation, 458; secession, 583, 589, *596,* 617; in Civil War, 600, 606, 627, 640; Reconstruction, 658, 672, *678,* 687–689; race riots, 677; post-Reconstruction and Gilded Age, 716, 718, 719; and black voting rights, 719, 720
Louisiana Purchase, *344,* 345–346, 368, 369, 565
Lovejoy, Elijah, 478
Lowell, Francis Cabot, 390–391
Lowell, James Russell, 447, 540
Lowell, Mass., 391
Lowell family, 286
Loyalists, 250–251, 257, 260–269, 285–286, 303
Lumber industry, 384, 394, 396, 458, 701–702
Lundy, Benjamin, 528–529
Luther, Martin, 44

Lutherans, 104, *151,* 168
Lyceums, 424–425
Lyon, Matthew, 328, *329*
Lyon, Nathaniel, 597

McClean, John, 573
McClellan, George B., 540, 612, *614–617,* 618, 621–622, 628, 639, 647, 654, 646–647, 654
McCormick, Cyrus Hall, 390, 629, 711
McCulloch, Hugh, 703, 704
McCulloch v. *Maryland,* 353–354, 369
Macdonough, Thomas, *364,* 369
McDowell, Irwin, 612
McGuffey readers, 416
Machiavelli, Niccolo, 274
Machines. *See* Mechanization
Machines, political, Jacksonian and pre-Civil War periods, 496, 498, 514, 517, 567
McKay, Gordon, 629
Macon, Nathaniel, 365, 489
Macon's Bill No. 2, 363, 368
Madison, James, 289, in Critical Period, 300, 303, 305; in Washington administration, 315, 320, 321; origin of Republican party, 319, 320, 322–323, 330; in Jefferson administration, 342, 351, 368; as president, 340, 342, 347, 363, 368, 525; and slavery, 295; on judicial review, 353; and religious liberty, 354; and Missouri Crisis, 489; and Monroe Doctrine, 527
Magruder, John B., 614
Mahan, Dennis Hart, 611
Maine (colonial): settlement, 36, 217; fur trade, 86; in colonial wars, 128–129
Maine (state): admission, *491,* 518; blacks, Reconstruction period, 683
Maine law, 442
Mallory, Stephen R., 627, 628
Mammonism, 422
Management: plantations, 159–162; railroads, 396
Manassas, battle of. *See* Bull Run, battle of
Manchester *Guardian,* 540
Manhates Indians, 59
Manhattan Island, 59–60, 75, 382
Manifest Destiny, 482, 537, 540, 698
Mann, Horace, 415–416, 426
Manorialism: seventeenth-century colonies, 56–58, 60; early modern Britain, 157, 159; in Southern self-image, 472. *See also* Landlords; Tenancy
Manufacturing: seventeenth-century colo-

nial, 40, 59, 85–86; eighteenth-century colonial, 195–196, 221, 239; Revolutionary era, 287, 291; Critical Period, 305; Hamiltonian's program and, 317, 319; and Embargo of 1807–09, 363; Jacksonian and pre–Civil War periods, 380, 390–394; slavery in, 458; Civil War era, 604, 611, 629–630, 632; Gilded Age, 702, 703. *See also* Factories; Industrialization; Labor; *specific industries*

Marbury v. *Madison*, 351–352, 368

Marine insurance, 165

Marion, Francis, 267

Markets and marketing: of agricultural produce, colonial, 88–91, 122, 167–168, 220–222; Revolutionary era, 286–287; Critical Period, 305; and War of 1812, 364; Jacksonian and pre–Civil War periods, 387, 390, 394, 422; pre–Civil War South, 457; Civil War era, 604, 629; post-Civil War, 656; Gilded Age, 703

Marlborough, Duke of, 119–120

"Maroons," 157

Marriage: seventeenth century, 81–82; Revolutionary era, 293; Jacksonian and pre–Civil War periods, 400; Mormons and, 430, 433, 434; in nineteenth-century women's movement, 442, 444; John Humphrey Noyes on, 445; of slaves, 459, 465; of freedmen, 670. *See also* Divorce; Domesticity; Family

Marshall, John, 350, *351–353*, 368, 404

Martial law, in post-Civil War southern states, 714

Martineau, Harriet, 385

Martin v. *Hunter's Lessee* (1816), 352

Martin's Hundred, *41*

Marx, Karl, 399

Mary I (queen of England), 17, 29

Mary II (queen of England). *See* William and Mary

Maryland (colonial): settlement, 54–58; religion, 54, 103, 169; and Pennsylvania, 73; population, 80; charter, 117, 118, 145; Protestant Association, 132, 136–137, 146; education, 142; eighteenth-century economy, 158, 159, 165–166, 196, 221; Pontiac's rebellion, 219; in imperial crisis, 250

Maryland (state): Revolution, 278, 282, 295, 354; Jeffersonian period, 341, 353; antislavery, 471; slavery, 482, 554; pre–Civil War politics, 582, in Civil War, *596–598, 614*, 616; *623, 645*

Mason-Dixon line, 73

Mason, Alice, *96*

Mason, George, 308

Masons. *See* Anti-Masonry

Massachusetts (colonial). *See* Massachusetts Bay Colony; Plymouth Plantation

Massachusetts (state): Revolution, 235, *252–253, 254* 270, 274, 277, 278, 282, *283,* 286, *287,* 291; Critical Period, 301, 302, 305, 306, 313, 331; Jeffersonian period, 341; Religion, 354, 356, 417, 421; urbanization and industrialization, 382, 390–391; labor unions, 399; education, 413, 415; blacks, 473, 481–482, 683; Jacksonian period politics, 511, 513; and Mexican War, 537; pre–Civil War politics, *549,* 550, 563; Reconstruction period, 677, 683

Massachusetts Anti-Slavery Society, 481

Massachusetts Bay Colony: and Plymouth Plantation, 45; establishment, 48; religion, 50–54, 107, 168, 169–170; seventeenth-century economy, 93; social control, 93–94; and Dominion of New England, 116–117, 132; and New Hampshire, 116; and colonial wars, 128–129, 132–133, 187; second charter, 144, 146; education, 145; eighteenth-century government, 177, 178; currency and banking problems, 197–198, 206; outflow of settlers, 215; eighteenth-century economy, 221; in imperial crisis, 252–253

Massachusetts Bay Company, 45, 75

Massachusetts General Colored Association, 473

Mather, Cotton, 142

Mather, Increase, *137*

Mather, Richard, *52*

Maximilian, Archduke, 642

Mayflower, 45

Mayflower Compact, 46

Mayhew, Jonathan, 185

May Resolves (1776), 277–278

Maysville Road Bill, 499, 518

Meade, George Gordon, 540, 623, 648

Mechanicsville, battle of, 615

Mechanization: in Industrial Revolution, 390–394, 456, 522

Melville, Herman, 449, 584

Memminger, Christopher G., 605, 606, 632

Memphis, Tenn., 613, 634, 677

Mercantilism: in Spanish-American empire, 9; in sixteenth-century England, 17; and consolidation of British Empire, 114–116, 212–213; in imperial crisis, 144, 227–229,

232–235; Enlightenment and, 203; and Revolution, 286

Merchants: Elizabethan English, and English expansion, 17–19, 24, 26–27; and settlement of Virginia, 36; and Great Migration, 48; in seventeenth-century Massachusetts, 86–88; Quaker, in colonial Pennsylvania, 72; and consolidation of British Empire, 112–113; in colonial society, 124, 130, 162–166, 221–222; in colonial wars, 127–129, 187, 193; in colonial New York, 136; and colonial currency problems, 196; in imperial crisis, 229–230, 235, 238; as loyalists, 286; and Revolution, 286; Critical Period, 300, 305; and rise of industrial capitalism, 390–394; and slavery, 475; post-Civil War southern, 672; Gilded Age, 703

Merrimack. See Virginia (ironclad)

Mestizos, in Spanish-America, 15–16

Methodism, First Great Awakening and, 166–172

Methodists: Revolutionary era, 222; and Second Great Awakening, 356; and slavery, 418, 439, 471; blacks as, 468

Mexican War: and Indians, 406; Mormons and, 431, 433; course of and outcome, 522, 536–542, *538, 539, 541,* 549, 574, 584

Mexico, Gulf of, 316, 388, *389,* 542, 552, 556

Mexico: Spanish conquests, 6, 29; and U.S., early nineteenth century, 346–347; independence, 523, 526–527; abolition of slavery, 523, 528, 544; Texas and, 528–530, 531, 535, 540–541, 544; Mormons and, 431; U.S. hopes to annex, 540–542; Franco-Spanish intervention; 607, 642; Confederates and, 626, 660; late nineteenth century, 698. *See also* Mexican War

Mexico City, Mexico, 540, *541,* 544

Michigan: Indians, 405; blacks, Reconstruction period, 683

Midway Islands, American occupation (1867), 699

Milan Decree, 362

Milbourne, Jacob, 135

Miliken's Bend, battle of, 640

Military Reconstruction Act (1867), 677–679, 686, 690, 691

Militia: colonial, 127–129, 186, 192, 220, 245; Revolutionary, 249, 252–*253,* 262, 263, 264, 285, 287, 303, 306; in Whiskey Rebellion, 321; War of 1812, 365

Millennialism: and Puritans, 53; in First Great Awakening, 170; in Second Great Awakening, 358–359, 445

Mills, and labor recuitment, 456

Milton, John, 274

Milwaukee, Wisconsin, 381, 708

Mind control, 425

Mingos, 217, *218*

Mining and miners: nineteenth-century U.S., 384, 386, 458, *551;* western interests, Gilded Age, 703

Ministry (Great Britain), 175, 212, 225, 229, 232–234, 239–240, 258–262, 265

Minnesota, Reconstruction period, 683

Minorca, 270

Minuit, Peter, 59, 61

Minutemen, 252

Miscegenation, obsession with, 465, 477, 548, 576, 646, 684

Missionary activities: Protestant, 402, 418–419, 424, 435–442, 477; Mormon, 430

Missions, Spanish, in Floridas, 129

Mississippi: admission, 347; Indians, 403–*407,* slavery, 461, 549; Black Belt, 468; secession, 583, *596,* 617; Reconstruction, 674, *678,* 687–689; Gilded Age, 716, 720

Mississippi River, 6, 192, 212, 215, 227, 270, 282, *283,* 295, 316, 321, 343, 345, 346, 347, 348, 383, 386, 388, 396, 490, 718

Missouri: settlement, 348; Indians, 406; Mormons, 429–430; and abolitionists, 478; slavery, 547, 572; pre–Civil War politics, 582, 594, 597; in Civil War, 597, 645; Reconstruction period, 683

Missouri Compromise, 369, 487, 488–491, 501, 518, 524, 549–552, 572, 573, 583

Missouri River, 396

Missouri Territory, 348

Mobile, Alabama, 627, 652, 654

Mobility, geographical: colonial, 80, 121, 149–150, 213–217, 227; Revolutionary era, 288–291; Federalist and Jeffersonian periods, 343, 345; Jacksonian and pre-Civil War periods, 374, 377–378, 382–383, 400–401; of slaves, 454–455, 470–471, of freedmen, 670. *See also* "Safety-valve" theory

Mobility, social: Spanish-American empire, 14–16; North American colonies, 88, 91–98, 121–127, 129–132; Revolutionary era, 287–288, 291; Federalist period, 299; Jacksonian and pre-Civil War periods, 398–401

Mobs: colonial, 163–164, 187; Britain, 225–226; Revolutionary, 229–230, 252–253, 236–237, 260; and American law, 253–254; Civil War, 597, 636; nineteenth-century urban, 430–431, 476–478, 682

Moby-Dick, 584

Modernization: Revolution and, 212–213; Jacksonian and pre–Civil War periods, 375–376, 411, 413, 422–423, 434

Mohawk Indians, *190*

Mohawk River, 150, 191, 215

Molasses, 115, 230

Molasses Act (1733), 194, 206, 229

Monarchy: Spanish, 8–14; British, and colonization, 16–23, 23–24; Puritan attitude toward, 92; in British Constitution and political theory, 133, 175, 196, 224, 255, 258, 274; imperial debate, 244; British, in Madison's political thought, 308; Antifederalists' fears of, 311; Federalists' use of monarchical forms, 320; as Jeffersonian Republican bugaboo, 327–331, 363, 367–368; as Jacksonian-era bugaboo, 496, 511, 548; and Monroe Doctrine, 528

Monetary policies, Gilded Age, 703

Money: shortage of, colonial society, 87, 197; and Revolutionary social relationships, 290; coinage of, under Constitution, 309; in Hamiltonian program, 318; and post-Civil War southern economy, 671. *See also* Currency; Paper money

"Money Power, The," 548

Monitor (ironclad), 618, 628

Monmouth, battle of, 271

Monongahela River, 189

Monopoly: in colonial New York, 136; republicanism and, 274, 291; Critical Period, 300; Jeffersonian Republicans' fear of, 324–325; Jacksonian attitudes toward, 504–505; post-Civil War, 656. *See also* Mercantilism

Monroe, James: as diplomat, 327, 362; as president, 340, 342, 367, 368, 486, 525; and Monroe Doctrine, 511–512; and presidency, 340–342; on Indians, 403, 404; as Revolutionary symbol, 486

Monroe Doctrine: formulation, 527–528, 544; Polk and, 544

Monroe-Pinkney Treaty (1806), 362, 368

Montcalm, Marquis de, 190, 192

Montesquieu, Baron de, 201

Montezuma, 6

Montgomery, Alabama, 589, 590, 598

Montgomery, Richard, 254, 270

Montreal, Canada, 192

Moore, Thomas, 339

Moral reform: Puritanism, 48–49, 92–98, 105, 107–109; Enlightenment, 199–203; Revolutionary era, 256–260; republicanism, 273–275, 291–295, 336–339, 356–359; Jacksonian and pre–Civil War periods, 374–376, 411–428, 435–449, 475–478. *See also* Prohibition

Morals. *See* Ethics; Moral reform; Sexual behavior

Morgan, Daniel, 267

Morgan, William, 514

Mormonism, 428–435, *432*, 436, 438, 439

Mormon War, 433

Morrill Act (1862), 630

Morrill Tariff (1861), 605

Morris, Gouverneur, 308

Morris, Robert, 303, 345

Morris, Thomas, 479

Morality: seventeenth-century colonies, 81; slave, eighteenth century, 154; Jacksonian and pre–Civil War periods, 379–380

Mott, Lucretia, 443, 444

Mount Vernon, Va., *160*

"Moving schools," 142

Mules (spinning machines), *391*

Mulford, Elisha, 696

Murfreesboro, battle of, *616*

Muscovy Company, 18–19

Napoleon I (Napoleon Bonaparte; emperor of the French), 330, 346, 360, 361–362, 363, 366, 369, 523, 525

Napoleon III (emperor of the French), 608, 642, 698

Napoleonic wars. *See* French Revolutionary and Napoleonic wars

Narragansett Bay, 54

Nashville, battle of, 640, 650

Nashville Convention, 553

Nast, Thomas, 705, 715

Nation, The, 695–707

Nation, The: The Foundations of Civil Order and Political Life In the United States, 696

National American Woman's Suffrage Association, 712

National Banking Act (1864), 630

National debt. *See* Debt, national

National Independent party, 710

Nationalism: economic, early nineteenth century, 342, 492–496; constitutional, early nineteenth century, 352–353; War of 1812 and, 367–368, 390–392; pre–Civil War, 524, 537, 559–560; Civil War and, 656; post-Civil War, 694–697

Nationalists, Critical Period, 302–313. *See also* Federalists; Nationalism

Nationalizing trends, Civil War, 656, 695–696; politics, Gilded Age, 696–701

National Labor Union, 708–709

National Reform Association, 399

National Republican party, 187, *488,* 496, 498, 505, 511. *See also* Republican party (Jeffersonian); Whig party

National Union Convention, 677

National Woman's Loyal League, 711

National Woman Suffrage Association, 712

National Women's Rights conventions, 444

Native Americans. *See* Indians, American

Nativism, nineteenth century, 421–422; 440, 509, 516, 559–560, 561–562, 564, 580, 584. *See also* Anti-Catholicism; Prejudice; Racism

Naturalization: in colonies, 151, 153; and Alien and Sedition Acts, 329; Jeffersonian period, 339; nineteenth-century immigrants, 516, 564; of Chinese, 682

Naturalization Law of 1740, 153

Natural resources: plunder of, nineteenth century, 386; of Confederacy, 599

Nauvoo, Ill., 430, 431

Navajo, 406

Naval Stores, 115

Navigation acts: Dutch and, 90; British, 115, 145; in imperial crisis, 193, 227–229. *See also* Mercantilism

Navy, British: and colonial administration, 114, in colonial wars, 188; in Revolutionary War, 239, 244, 252, 261, 269; in French Revolutionary and Napoleonic wars, 330, 360–362; in War of 1812, 365, 369

Navy, U.S.: Federalist and Jeffersonian periods, 339; War of 1812, 365, 369; Mexican War, 535, *538;* Civil War, 609, 611, 624, 627–629

Nayler, James, *70*

Nebraska: Mormon migration, 431; issue of, in 1850s, 565

"Necessary and proper" clause, 323, 352

Nelson, Horatio, 330

Netherlands: Pilgrims in, 44–45; as republic, 275, and U.S., under Confederation, 304. *See also* New Netherland

Neutrality, U.S., French Revolutionary wars, 325, 332; neutrality laws, 543

Neutral rights, in French Revolutionary and Napoleonic wars, 325, 361–362, 367

New Amsterdam, 59–60. *See also* New York City

Newburgh conspiracy, 303, 331

Newcastle, Duke of, 225

New England (colonial); earliest attempts at colonization, 19–23, Indian population c. 1600, 33; colonial settlement patterns, 43–54, 149, religion, 45–47, 50–55, 105, 107–109, 166–170; 215–217; demography, 81–83, 215–217; seventeenth-century economy, 85–88; and colonial wars, 122–123, 127–129, 186–193; education, 140–145; currency problems, 197–199. *See also specific colonies*

New England: Revolution, 252, 260–266, 270; Confederation period, 282, 292; loyalists, 286; Jeffersonian period, 341; and War of 1812, 364–367; industrialization, 390–392, 454; Jacksonian and pre–Civil War reform and dissent, 412, 415–420, 434–435, 436–437, 443, 475–478; literacy, 413; literature, 447–448; Jacksonian-period politics, 496–511; protectionism, 500–501; and Pacific trade, 529, 533; and Mexican War, 537

New England Company, 47–48

New England Emigrant Aid Company, 568

New England Freedmen's Aid Society, 665

New England Non-Resistance Society, 479

Newfoundland: discovery and colonization, 16, 24–26, 29; and colonial fisheries, 86; Great Britain secures title to, 129; in colonial wars, 187, fisheries, and Anglo-American relations, 269

New France, 127

New Hampshire (colonial): and New England Company, 47; social control, 97; origins, 117, 145; higher education, 145; settlement, 149, 217

New Hampshire (state): Revolution, 271, 278, Critical Period, 299, 301, 302; antislavery, 479; blacks, Reconstruction period, 683

New Harmony, Ind., 445

New Jersey (colonial): settlement, 68–69; religion, 68–69, 171; charter annulled, 117, 145; union of East and West Jersey, 118; higher education, 143–144; tenancy, 159; eighteenth-century economy, 166, 196

New Jersey (state): Revolution, 278, 286; Critical Period, 313; Sabbatarianism,

437–439; Jacksonian period politics, 496; pre–Civil War politics, 581, 582
New Jersey Plan, 308–309, 310–311
"New Light" party, 171
New Mexico: Spanish exploration, 8; Indians, 406; annexation, 536, 540; and Compromise of 1850, 552–559, *556,* 558, 565, 572
New Netherland, 58–59
New Orleans, La., 192; as Spanish possession, 321; Jefferson on, 345–346; early nineteenth century, *344, 523*; transportation, nineteenth century, 388, 457; wealth in, nineteenth century, 396–398; slave trade, 475; in Civil War, 600, 606, 627; race riot, 677; integration, Reconstruction period, 689
New Orleans, battle of, *364,* 366, 367, 369, 494
Newport, R.I.: foundation, 35; eighteenth century, 150, 217; in Revolution, 232; decline, 287
"New South," 720
New Spain, Viceroyalty of, 9–14, 29
Newspapers: Revolutionary era, 230, 235; Critical period, 299; Federalist period, 328–330, 350; Jacksonian and pre–Civil War periods, 401, 513, 537, 568, 572; abolitionist, 475; proslavery editorials, 552; during Civil War, 596, 612, 640, 644, 659; and exposure of corruption, 705
Newton, Sir Isaac, 355
New York (colonial): religion, 104, 169, 171; Duke of York and, 113; governors, 117–118, 125; political influence, 125, 127; and colonial wars, 129, 187, 189, 191; Leisler's Rebellion, 132, 135–136; education, 145; settlement patterns, 150, 215–217; tenancy, 159, 244, legislature, 179; Zenger trial, 206; Indians, 217–219; and Vermont, 219. *See also* New Netherland
New York (state): Revolution and Confederation period, 250, 271, 278, 286; Critical Period, 299, 301, 313; Jeffersonian period, 341; immigrants in, nineteenth century, 381; Erie Canal, 388, 389; Indians, 405; religion, 420–422, 434; Jacksonian-period politics, 492, 513; pre–Civil War politics, 534, 550, 567; in Civil War, 636; blacks, Reconstruction period, 683; political machine, Gilded Age, 707
New York Association for Improving the Condition of the Poor, 440

New York City: foundation, 35; seventeenth and early eighteenth centuries, 135–136; blacks in, colonial, 153–154; poor relief, colonial, 163–164; Revolution, 263, *265;* post-Revolutionary period, 271, 299, 304; population, early nineteenth century, 381, 382; Erie Canal and, 388, 396; railroads and, 396; economic inequalities, early ninteenth century, 398, 401, education, eighteenth and nineteenth centuries, 414, 416, 417, religion, nineteenth century, 420–422; social reform, early nineteenth century, 437, 438, 440; and cotton trade, 458; and antislavery, 476, 480; in Civil War, 636, 644; political scandals, Gilded Age, 705; immigrant population of, 708; unemployment, Gilded Age, 709. *See also* Manhattan Island; New Amsterdam
New York Public School Society, 414
New York State Anti-Slavery Society, 480
New York Sun, 705
New York Times, 669, 705
New York *Tribune,* 399, 567, 568, 573, 700, 712
New Zealand, Confederate emigration to, 660
Niagara region, and War of 1812, 365
Nicaragua, U.S. and, 543
Nicholson, Francis, 135
Nile, battle of the, 330
Nonconformists, British, 152, 168, 171, 175. *See also* Puritans; Separatists; *specific denominations*
Nonconformity. *See* Dissent, religious; Dissent, social and political
Nonimportation Act (1806), 362
Nonimportation agreements, 238
Nonintercourse Act (1809), 363, 368
Nonresistance, abolitionists and, 378–379. *See also* Civil disobedience; Pacifism
Nonslaveholding Southerners, 396, 457, 462–463; 468–469, 501
Norfolk, Va., 91, 221, 362, 628
Normal schools, 417
North, Lord, 225–226, 238–239, 252, 331
North (Civil War era), 375; religion, 423; and pre–Civil War South, 454, 482–483; ideals, 575, attitude toward South, 588; government, 591–593; and Fort Sumter crisis, 594–595; and border states, 596–599; army, 599–604; finance, 604–606; diplomacy, 606–611, 641–642; military and naval operations, 611–617, 620–629; emancipation issue, 636–640; politics,

644–647; view of defeated South, 659;
and post-Civil War southern economy,
672; racism, 681–684
North Africa, U.S. and, early nineteenth
century, 304
North America: early English exploration,
16, 19, 29; English colonization, 19–29,
33–58, 62–74; France and; 29, 127–129,
186–193, 212; Dutch colonization, 58–
62; and society, seventeenth century, 78–
109, 121–132; British empire and, 112–
121, 132–138, 185, 186–206, *214;* early
modern culture, 138–145, 199–206;
economy and society, eighteenth century,
149–181, 197–199, 212–223; American
Revolution, 210–211, 223–244, 272–295;
U.S. expansion in, 343–349, 522–544.
See also Canada; Mexico; United States
North Briton, 226, 259
North Carolina (colonial): Roanoke
Colony, 22-23, 29; detached from South
Carolina, 118, 206; population, 215;
backcountry disorder, 220, 245. *See also*
Carolina
North Carolina (state): Revolutionary and
Confederation periods, 267, 271, 278,
299, 313; Indians, 403, *407,* education,
417; pre–Civil War politics, 582; seces-
sion, 594, *596;* in Civil War, 627, 644,
649, 651; Reconstruction, *678,* 688; post-
Reconstruction period and Gilded Age,
716, 719, 720; and voting rights of
blacks, 719, 720
Northern colonies: Dominion of New
England, 117; colonial wars, 127–129;
slavery, 153–154
North Star, 381
Northup, Solomon, 481
Northwest, Old; British refusal to evacuate, 304; Federalist period, 321, 365;
Jeffersonian period, 348, 365; Indians,
402; religion and society, 419; self-
improvement movements, 424; and
expansion, 534, 551; and Crisis of 1850,
555; nativism, 564; in Civil War, 644
Northwest, Pacific: U.S. claims to, 526,
533–534, 544. *See also* Oregon Country;
specific states
Northwest Ordinance, 283–285, *284,* 295,
490
Notes on Virginia, 276, 301
Nova Scotia: discovery and colonization,
16, 19, 26, 29; in colonial wars, 127, 129,
187, *189;* immigration of New
Englanders, 215; enlargement, 227

Novus Ordo Seclorum, 424
Noyes, John Humphrey, 445–446
Nullification: and Embargo of 1807–09,
362–363; Jacksonian period, 501–503,
518, 583

Oberlin College, 417, 445, 477
Occultism, 425
Occupancy laws, 387
O'Connor, John, 635
Officeholders: and origins of the British
Empire, 119, in colonies, 119, 125;
Federalist and Jeffersonian periods, 320–
322, 339–340; Jacksonian and pre–Civil
War periods, 497; Civil War, 591–593,
601–602, 604–605; Reconstruction
period, 716–718. *See also* Bureaucracy;
Government; Patronage, political
Officers, military: Revolutionary War, 289,
303, 320; Burr conspiracy, 346–347; in
Reconstruction, 667, 688–689. *See also*
Army, British; Army, U.S.
Of Plymouth Plantation, 45–46
Ohio: Federalist period, 321, *322;* admission, 347; Second Great Awakening,
356; immigrants, nineteenth century,
381; canals, 388; religion, 421, 429;
antislavery, 475–480; politics, Jacksonian
and pre–Civil War periods, 514; in Civil
War, 599; blacks, 683; Reconstruction
period, 683
"Ohio Idea," and Gilded Age currency
problems, 704
Ohio River, 189, 191, 215, 227, *283,* 305,
388, 396, 490, 599
Oil industry. *See* Petroleum and petroleum
industry
Oklahoma: Spanish exploration, 8; Indian
removal to, 406, *407;* Missouri Compro-
mise and, 490. *See also* Indian Territory
Oligarchy: colonial, 57, 125, 133–136, 180;
eighteenth-century political theory, 174;
British, 174. *See also* Elites
Olive Branch Petition, 252, 254
Oliver, Andrew, 232
Omnibus Bill, 554, 556
On Civil Liberty and Self-Government, 696
Oneida, N.Y., 446
Onís, Luis de, 525
Opechancanough, 41
Order of the American Knights, 644
Order of the Cincinnati, 284
Order of the Heroes, 643
Order of the Star Spangled Banner, 562
Order of the White Camellia, 690

Order of United Americans, 561, 562
Ordinance of 1787, 285
Oregon: migration to, 406; racism, 551, 570; election of 1876, 716
Oregon Country: U.S. claims to, 527, 533–534, 535, *536;* annexation, 535–536, 538–540, 544
Oregon Trail, 534, *536, 544*
Origin of Species, 683
Oriskany, battle of, 264, *265*
Orkney, Earl of, 119–120
Osborn, Sir Danvers, 120
Ostend Manifesto, 543, 544
Otis, James, 242
Ottawa Indians, 219
Overseers, 460, 603, 635
Owen, Robert, 445
Oyster Point, 65–66

Pacific Ocean: discovery, 6, 29; Jefferson and expansion to, *344,* 345, 526; and U.S. commerce, 533–534; and Isthmian canal, 542; Missouri compromise line, extension to, 550, 553, 556, 583
Pacific Railroad Act (1862), 630
Pacifism: of Quakers, 69, 201, 220; of Enlightenment, 360; of Garrisonians, 478–479. *See also* Peace movement
Paine, Thomas, 254–*255,* 260, 263, 275, 355
Painting, 368. *See also* Art; *specific artists*
Palatinate, 151, *152*
Palmer, Elihu, 355
Palmerston, Lord, 609–610
Pamphlets: Revolutionary era, 230, 235, 241–242, 254; abolitionist, 473, 477–478
Panama, 8, 29
Panic of 1819, 369, 457, 487
Panic of 1837, 422, 429, 457–458, 480, 507–508
Panic of 1857, 423, 522, 544
Panic of 1873, 682, 709–711
Paoli, Pascal, 259
Papacy, 13–14, 415, 562
Paper money: colonial, 197–199, *198;* Revolutionary era, *198,* 253, 288; and Stamp Act, 229; Critical Period, 300; under Constitution, 310; in Hamiltonian program, 318; Jeffersonian period, 340; Jacksonian and pre–Civil War periods, 504–507; Civil War, 618, 632, 702–705; Gilded Age, 702–705
Parents: in colonial society, 94–98, 140, 167; in Jacksonian and pre–Civil War society, 413–415

Paris, Peace of (1763), 192, 212, 223, 244
Paris, Treaty of (1783), 270, 304, 331
Parker, Theodore, 548
Parliament (British): and English Civil War, 48, 63–64; and mercantilism, 115, 145, 194, 206; and Glorious Revolution, 118, 133; and Leisler's Rebellion, 135; and naturalization laws, 153; eighteenth century, 174–178, 279; and colonial wars, 186, 187, 191; and colonial currency problems, 199; and imperial crisis, 212, 225–231, 232–244; and Revolution, 257–258, 262; and West Indian slavery, 473, 501
Parochialism, post–Civil War, 656
Parochial schools, 415
Parson's Cause, 222, 244
"Particular plantation," *41*
Parties, political. *See* Political parties
Partisan loyalty, 510
Paterson, William, 309
Patriotism: Revolutionary era, 275; War of 1812, 364–368; Jacksonian and pre–Civil War periods, 417, 448, 486, *498,* 564; Civil War, 661. *See also* Nationalism
Patriots (Revolutionary era), 229–244, 262, 267, 285
Patronage, artistic, 448, 495
Patronage, political: British, 119–121, 165, 175–176, 212; colonial, 125, 133–138, 178–179; Hamiltonian program and, 316–322; Jeffersonian Republicans and, 324–325, 340; Jacksonian and pre–Civil War periods, 497, *498,* 510, 550, 553, 582; pre–Civil War South, 468–470; Civil War, 646, 647; Reconstruction period, 679, 718. *See also* Corruption, political
Patronage, social: colonial, 221–222, 252; British, 258; republican view of, 274–275, 278–279, 290. *See also* Dependency
Patroonships, 60
Paxton Boys, 220, 244
Peace movement, nineteenth century, 436, 478–479. *See also* Pacifism
Peale, Charles Wilson, 263
Peale, Rembrandt, 336
Pemberton, John C., *624, 625,* 626
Penal law: reform of, Revolutionary and Confederation periods, 293
Pendleton Act (1883), 707
Peninsula campaign, 614–615, 618
Penitentiaries, 293, 412, 440, 479, 512
Penn, William, 69–74, *71,* 151, 177, 201
Penn family, 118, 158

Pennsylvania (colony): foundation, 69–74, 145; religion, 69, 71, 168, 171; European immigrants, 72–73, 151; charter annulled, 117, 118, 145; higher education, 145; population, 150, 151, 216; eighteenth-century economy and society, 165, *221;* eighteenth-century politics, 177; and colonial wars, 187, 189–190, Enlightenment and, 201–204; backcountry disorder, 219–220
Pennsylvania (state): Revolution and Confederation periods, 274, 278, 280, *283,* 286, 293, 301; Federalist period, 308, 321; immigrants, nineteenth century, 381; canals, 388; education, nineteenth century, 417; Mormons and, 434; Jacksonian period politics, 494, 496, 513; pre–Civil War politics, 567; in Civil War, 622, 652; oil discovery in, 629; in Gilded Age, 702
Pennsylvania Academy of Fine Arts, 368
"Pennsylvania Dutch," 151
Pennsylvania Journal, 230
Peonage, 14
Pepperrell, Sir William, 187
Perfectionism, 438, 440, 445
Perry, Matthew, 547, 584
Perry, Oliver Hazard, *364,* 365, 369
Perryville, battle of, *616,* 623
Persecution, religous: of Separatists in England, 44–45; of Puritans in England, 48–50; of dissidents in New England, 51, 53–54; in New Netherland, 62; of Quakers in England, 68–69; of Huguenots in France, 150; of dissenters in Germany, 151; in nineteenth-century Europe, 381; of Mormons in U.S., 429–434
Personal liberty laws, 480, 552
Peru, Spanish conquest of, 8, *11,* 29
Peru, Viceroyalty of, 9, 14, 29
Petersburg, Va., *469, 648, 654*
Petition, freedom to, 315
Petroleum and petroleum industry, nineteenth century, 629, 632
Phelen, James, 635
Philadelphia, Pa.: foundation, 35, 72, 214; eighteenth century, 150, 165–166, 221; Revolutionary and post-Revolutionary periods, 233, 249, 251, 264, 267, 270, 294, 304; Federalist period, 304, 316, *319,* 338; culture in, early nineteenth century, 368; and nineteenth-century transportation, 388; economic inequalities in, nineteenth century, 397;

popular culture, nineteenth century, 421–422; social reform, nineteenth century, 414, 437; religion, nineteenth century, 421–423; in Civil War, 605, 633; Centennial Exposition of 1876, 697
Philadelphia Convention, 306–313, 488
Philadelphia Society of Friends, 665
Philadelphia Working Man's Party, 414
Philanthropy. *See* Charity, public; Humanitarianism; Settlement houses
Philip II (king of Spain), 17
Philips family, 136
Phillips, Wendell, 482
Philosophes, 201–204
Philosophical Letters, 201
Philosophy, Emerson and, 427–428
Phrenology, 425–427, *426*
Physiocrats, 203
Pickens, Francis, 595
Pickering, John, 350, 368
Pickering, Timothy, 341
Pierce, Franklin, 488, 542–543, 562, 565, 570
Pietism (eighteenth-century religious movement), *151,* 166
Pietism (political style), of Whigs, 515–516
Pike, Albert, 597
Pike, Zebulon, *344*
Pike's Peak trail, 714
Pilgrims: and "starving times," 27–29; character of, 43, 44, 47; in Netherlands, 44–45; Mayflower and Plymouth Plantation, 45–47
Pinckney, Charles, 489
Pinckney, Thomas, 321
Pinckney's Treaty (1795), 321, 332, *344*
"Pine tree shilling," 197
Pinkney, William, 362, 368
Piombo, Sebastiano del, 6
Pioneer Stage Line, 438
Pitt, William (Lord Chatham), 191–193, 223, 225
Pittsburgh, Pa.: and canals, 388
Pizarro, Francisco, 8, 29
Plains Indians, 406
Plains of Abraham, 192
Plan of Union, 368
Plan of Union (Galloway), 249, 270
Plantation Act. *See* Sugar Act
Plantations: seventeenth century, *41,* 42, 60, 67, 83, 88–91, 123–124; eighteenth century, 159–162, *160;* pre–Civil War, 460–468, 522; Civil War, 634–635; post-Civil War, 659, 661, 667, 669–673, 677; and breakup of plantation system, 671–673

Planter (steamship), 638

Planters: southern colonies, 42–43, 67, 90, 129, 137, 159–162, 222; West Indian, 67, 194; and Jeffersonian Republicans, 341; pre–Civil War; 454, 456, 468–470, 494, 501, 509, 513; Civil War, 604, 606; in Reconstruction, 688. *See also* Land-ownership

Plattsburgh, battle of, 369

Plow, steel, 390

Plymouth, Mass., 81

Plymouth Harbor, 45

Plymouth Plantation, 45–47

Pocahontas, 41

Poe, Edgar Allan, 448

Political machines, 707

Political parties: framers' attitude toward, 328; origins of, 316, 323–324, 326–331, 340–342, 368; in election of 1800, 334–337; Jeffersonian period, 340–341, 368; Jacksonian and pre–Civil War periods, 454, 487, 492–493, 496–500, 509–518, 532–533, 547–549, 562–563, 567, 580–581; Civil War, 653–654; Reconstruction period, 673–681. *See also specific parties*

Political reform: eighteenth-century Britain, 226, 257–258; Revolutionary era, 277–282; Jeffersonian period, 339–340

Political theory: eighteenth century, 174–176; Revolutionary era, 240–244, 257–258, 273–274, 275–280; and framing of Constitution, 307–313; of Calhoun, 501–503

Politics, American: seventeenth century, 42, 51, 57–58, 73–74, 119, 125, 132–138; eighteenth century, 174–181; Revolutionary era, 251, 277–285; Critical Period, 298, 313, 331–332; Federalist period, 314–316, 320–331, 332; Jeffersonian period, 335–354, 359–368, 527–534; Jacksonian period, 486–518, 528–537; pre–Civil War period, 479–483, 537–543, 546–584; Civil War, 589–599, 634–641, 643–647, 651–654; Reconstruction period, 657–658, 661–664, 673– 681, 688–689, 700–701, 705–708, 714, 716

Politics, British: seventeenth century, 47–48, 62–64, 69, 71, 112–113, 116–118, 257–258; eighteenth century, 149, 165, 174–175, 185, 191–194, 205–206, 223–241, 257–258. *See also* British Empire; England; Parliament

Polk, James K., *488,* 533, 540, 542, 549, 553

Poll taxes, 718–719

Polygamy, Mormon, 430, 433, 434

Ponce de Leon, Juan, 6, 29

Pontiac's Rebellion, 219, 227, 244

Pope, Alexander, 257

Pope, John, *614, 615*

Pope. *See* Papacy; Roman Catholic church

Popular sovereignty, 375, 403–404, 535, 550, 558–559, 565–566, 571–575, 580–581. *See also* Sovereignty

Population: Spanish-American empire, 14–16; and English expansion, 23–24; seventeenth century, 33, 62, 79–84, 121; colonial Virginia, 36, 38–43, 149; colonial Massachusetts, 46, 49; colonial Maryland, 56; New Netherland, 59; Carolina, 66–67; colonial New Jersey, 69; colonial Pennsylvania, 72–73, 150–151; and colonial church structures, 99–103; colonial South Carolina, 150; eighteenth century, 150–153, 157–158, 181; Revolutionary era, 211, 213–214, *218,* 280, 288–289; Federalist and Jeffersonian periods, *343, 347–348;* Jacksonian and pre–Civil War periods, 377, *378, 379–*380, 382–383, 396, 455, 470, 473; Civil War era, 598–599, 611, 652; black, nineteenth century, 685. *See also* Demography

Populism: Jacksonian origins, 505–506; post-Civil War, 720

Populist party, 720

Port Hudson, battle of, 640

Portugal: American empire, 8, *10,* 17; and British mercantilism, 115

Portuguese, 59

Post office: colonial, 221; nineteenth century, 339, 358, 437, 438, 582

Potato famine, 380, 389

Potomac River, 36, 55, 64, 323, 612, *614, 615,* 623

Pottawatomie massacre, 569, 584

Poverty: early modern England, 23–24, 109, 162–163; colonial, 132, 162; early modern Germany, 151; Revolutionary era, 215, 274, 292–293; Jacksonian and pre–Civil War urban, 397, 414, 440, *508,* post-Civil War South, 672–673, 719

"Powers," antirepublican: in Jacksonian and pre–Civil War politics, 509–511, 548, 583

Powhatan, 34–35, 41

Powhatan indians, 40–41

Predestination, 105

Preemption, 387

Prejudice: white, against Indians, 200, 401–407. *See also* Anti-Catholicism; Racism

Prerogative courts, 199, 177

Presbyterians: in Carolina, 66; in colonial New Jersey, 68–69; Scotch-Irish immigrants, 150, 152–153; and First Great Awakening, 168; Revolutionary era, 222, 354; post Revolutionary, 356; and Second Great Awakening, 355, 368; nineteenth century, 421–424, 439, 513

Presidency: under Constitution, 310; Federalist period, 315–316; two-term tradition, 326; Jeffersonian period, 329–331, 342, 367; Jacksonian and pre–Civil War periods, 496–498; expansion of powers, Civil War, 657. *See also specific presidents*

Press: Zenger trial, 206; eighteenth-century British, 226, 257; Revolutionary era, 231, 235, 239, 241; Critical Period, 299, 313, 332; Federalist period, 315, 328; reform, nineteenth century, 434; abolitionist, 473–482; political, Jacksonian and pre–Civil War periods, 515, 536, 537, 568, 573; Confederate, 588, 596, 640–641, 644; Northern, Civil War era, 612, 645, 659; Reconstruction period, 683–684

Price, Sterling, 597

Primogeniture, 23, 98, 293

Princeton, battle of, 263

Princeton University (College of New Jersey); foundation, 143, 172; Jonathan Edward's presidency of, 170; nineteenth century, 437

Principio iron works (Maryland), 196

Prison Discipline Society, 435

Prisoner-of-war camps, Civil War, 659, 660

Prison reform. *See* Penitentiaries

Privateers: French, 187; U.S., in French Revolutionary wars, 325; U.S., in War of 1812, 366; Confederate, 609, 642

"Private plantations," 28, 40

Privy Council, 19, 113, 145, 177, 193, 222

Prize Courts, 325, 360, 368

Proclamation of 1763, 227, 244

Productivity: Jacksonian and pre–Civil War periods, 378, 384, 390–396; of slaves, 459–460

Progress and Poverty, 709

Progressivism, Emerson as prophet of, 427

Prohibition, nineteenth century, 442, 562

Proletariat, 164–165, 401. *See also* Labor; Working class

Propaganda: Revolutionary era, 237, 254, 259–260, abolitionist, 479, 503; Jacksonian, Whig, 509–510, 513–516; free soil, *549;* Civil War, 631

Property, slaves as, 43, 459, 465, 549, 557–558, 572–573, 641; and suffrage, eighteenth-century, 179, 258, 274; and office holding, Jeffersonian period, 347; women and nineteenth century, 443–445; confiscation of post-Civil War, 660, 661, 667, 677, 668–669; blacks and, post-Civil War, 674, 683. *See also* Capitalism, Freehold tenure; Landownership

Proprietary colonies: Maryland, 55–56, 58, 75, 250; Carolina, 64–65, 75; New Jersey, 68, 75; Pennsylvania, 69–75; New York, 116, 145

Proprietors, colonial: Maryland, 55–56, 75, 136; Carolina, 64–65, 118; New Jersey, 68; Pennsylvania, 69–75; New York, 116–145; eighteenth century, 116, 158, 177

Prostitution, 413

Protectionism: Critical Period, 300; Jeffersonian period, 342, 368–369; and Industrial Revolution, 390; Jacksonian and pre–Civil War periods, 493, 496, 500, 503, 580, 584; Civil War era, 604, 629, 632; Gilded Age, 668, 700–702. *See also* Mercantilism

Protestant Association, 132, 136–137, 146

Protestant ethic. *See* Puritan ethic

Protestantism: and English expansion, 17; in colonial Maryland, 55–56, 103, 136–137; First Great Awakening and, 169–173; and Revolution, 354–356; in nineteenth-century American national consciousness, 415, 418, 423, 513, 516, 557, 562, 571; and pietistic politics, nineteenth century, 512–513. *See also* Denominationalism; Puritanism; Religion; *specific denominations*

Protestants: Scotch-Irish, immigration of, 150–152; German, persecution of, 152; American, anti-Catholicism of, 227; and French Revolution, 325, 354. *See also* Protestantism; *specific denominations*

Providence, R.I.: foundation, 54; and Embargo of 1807–09, 363

Providence Island Company, 27

Provincialism: of colonial America, 138–140; in early nineteenth-century culture, 445

Prude, Jonathan, 384

Prussia, 188, 191, 608

Public lands, U.S.: Federalist and Jeffersonian periods, 345; Jacksonian and pre–Civil War periods, 384, 386, 387, 401–402, 487, 507; Homestead Act, 630. *See also* Land policy, federal; Land Ordinance of 1785; Northwest Ordinance

Public relations: and Jacksonian and pre–Civil War reform, 439–440, 477

Public schools. *See* Education, public

Pulaski, Tenn., 690

Puritan ethic: seventeenth century, 109; nineteenth century, 434. *See also* Labor; Protestantism

Puritanism: origins and character, 23, 47–48, 105, 107–109; in eighteenth-century New England, 166–168. *See also* Calvinism; Protestantism

Puritans: and "starving times," 28; character, 43–44, 46, 48–49, 51, 53–54; Great Migration, 48–50; establish Massachusetts Bay Colony, 48; and religious dissent, 51, 53–54; social attitudes, 92–98, 105, 107–109; and Dominion of New England, 117, 137–138; and education, 140–143; as immigrants to colonies, 201; and British political culture, 257

Putney, Vermont, 446

"Putting out" system, 394

Quakers: colonial Rhode Island, 54; colonial New Jersey, 68; England, 69; colonial Pennsylvania, 69–74, 204, 220; eighteenth century, 153, 166, 168; Enlightenment view of, 201; and Revolution, 267; and antislavery, 270, 294, 443, 463, 529; and revivalism, 422–424; and freedmen, 665

Quantrill, William C., 537, 597

Quartering Act (1765), 233

Quasi-War (with France, 1798), 326–327, 330, 332

Quebec (province), 227, 254

Quebec, Canada, 187, 192, 207

Quebec, siege of, 254, *261,* 270

Quebec Act (1774), 227

Queen Anne's War (War of the Spanish Succession, 1702–1713), 127, 128, 132, 149, 186

Quitman, John A., 542–543

Quitrents, 117

Quorum of the Twelve Apostles, 431

Race riots: Civil War, 636; Reconstruction period, 677, 716; anti-Chinese, 682

Racially mixed populations: Spanish-American empire, 15; pre–Civil War South, 465, 470. *See also* Miscegenation, obsession with

Racism: colonial, 43, 67, 157; and slavery, Revolutionary era, 295; in Jacksonian and pre–Civil War society, 379, 406, 454, 473–475, 476–477, 480–481; as basis of pre–Civil War Southern unity, 470–471, 582–583, 669; in antislavery movement, 473–475; in North, during Civil War, 636, 639, 646–647; during Reconstruction, 677, 681–691, 718–721; and anti-Chinese movement, 682; and Southern "home rule," 714–716

Radicalism: of early Quakers, 69–70, 201; of Wilkes, 226; in Revolutionary era, 250–260; of republicanism, 273–277; and Constitution, 298, 308; of Jefferson, 335–342; of Mormons, 428–435, 478; of abolitionists, 473–483; of Lincoln, alleged by Douglas, 576, 577; of Radical Republicans, 645; in Reconstruction, 658–659, 676, 714. *See also* Anti-radicalism

Radical Reconstruction, 658

Radical Republicans, 646–647, 654, 668, 674–681, 714, 716

Radical Review, 709

Railroads: pre–Civil War, 387, 394–396, *395,* 398, 423, 456, 458, 522, 544, 547, 568, 574, 576; transcontinental, 406, 512, 565, 581, 718; in Civil War, 604, 611, 623, 630, 646, 649–650, 652, 662; post-Civil War, 656, 662, 664; 668, 712; Baltimore and Ohio strike, *710*

Raleigh, Sir Walter, *20, 21,* 23, 30

Randolph, Edmund, 308

Randolph, George Wythe, 603

Randolph, John, 350, 489

Rappites, 445

Rationalism: Enlightenment, 202, 203, 359; and post-Revolutionary religion, 355; in nineteenth-century religion, 437

Raymond, Daniel, 490

Reapers, mechanical, 390

Reason the Only Oracle of Man, 355

Rebellions: colonial, 57–58, 118, 132–138, 159; Confederation and Federalist periods, 306, 321, 330–331; "Mormon War," 433–434. *See also* Civil War, American; Revolution, American; Slave insurrections

Reconstruction, plans for, 646, 654

Reconstruction period, 417, 471, 656–691; and American revolution compared, 660, 661

"Redeemers," 716–721

Reform, political. *See* Political reform

Reform, social. *See* Social reform

Reformation, Protestant, 415

Reformed Calvinism, 62

Regulation, economic: Civil War, 631; Reconstruction period, 662–664, 668. *See also* Mercantilism; Protectionism

Regulators, 219, 220, 244

Religion: in Spanish-American empire, 13–14; and early English expansion, 17, 23; and first English colonies, 29; of blacks, 43, 154; of Pilgrims, 43–44, 47; seventeenth-century Puritanism, 47–48, 50–54, 92–98, 105, 107–109; seventeenth-century colonies, outside New England, 54–60, 62–68, 69–72; and colonial education, 140–145; First Great Awakening, 166, 169–174, Revolutionary era, 315; and French Revolution, 325, 355; "natural," 355; Second Great Awakening, 355–356; Jacksonian and pre–Civil War periods, 381, 418; in public education, 415; Mormonism, 428–435; and slavery, 368–381. *See also specific religions*

Remond, Charles Lenox, 481

Remond, Sarah Parker, 481

Rensselaerswyck Manor, 60, 125

Report on Public Credit, 317–319, 332

Representation: colonial, 50–51, 176–181, 220; British, 74–76, 258, "no taxation without representation," 235; virtual vs. actual, 241–242; Revolutionary era, 279–280, 311; in Critical Period, 298, 307; under Constitution, 310

Republicanism: Revolutionary era, 273–277, 285–291; Critical Period, 298–307, 311–313; during Washington administration, 314–316, 322–331, 354–355; and Jeffersonian revolution, 335–342, 354–355, 359–360, 362; and religion, 354–359; Era of Good Feelings, 486; Jacksonian and pre–Civil War periods, 412, 414, 567. *See also* Jeffersonianism; Republican party (Jeffersonian)

Republican party (Jeffersonian) (Democratic Republicans): Federalist period, 328, 330; Jeffersonian period, 340–342, 350, 359–356; Era of Good Feelings, 468; breakup of, 492–493, 511

Republican party (since 1854): origins, 399, 567, 573–578, 580–584; Civil War, 592–593, 639, 645–647; Reconstruction period and Gilded Age, 658, 661, 664, 658, 668, 673–681, 688–689, 694, 700–701, 714, 716–718, 720–721; and tariffs, 702

Republicans, Moderate, 676

Republicans, Radical, 646–647, 654, 668, 674–681, 714, 716

Reservations, Indian. *See* Indian reservations

Residences, 131. *See also* Housing, urban

Resolves of Suffolk County, 249

Resumption Act (1875), 704

Revelation, Book of, 695

Revels, Hiram R., 688

Revenue stamp, *228*

Revere, Paul, 236, *237,* 252

Revivalism: First Great Awakening, 166–174; Second Great Awakening, 355–356; Jacksonian and pre–Civil War periods, 412, 417–424, 474, 516

Revolution, American: character and significance, 2–3, 210–211; imperial crisis, 212–213, 233–240; Indians and, 220; imperial debate, 240–244; struggle for independence, 248–270; political changes, 273–285; social and economic consequences, 286–295; Critical Period, 298–307; completed in Jeffersonian revolution, 335; and religion, 354; tradition of, and abolitionists, 476; and Reconstruction period compared, 660, 661

Revolutionary War, 260–270; social and economic consequences, 286–290; and weakness of Congress, 302–303

Revolution of 1800. *See* Jeffersonian revolution

Revolutions of 1830, 381

Revolutions of 1848, 381, 607

Rhode Island (colonial): Roger Williams and, 54; and Dominion of New England, 117; higher education in, 145; religion in, 169; government of, 177; currency problems, 198, 199; in imperial crisis, 231, 239

Rhode Island (state): Revolution, 267, 271, 278, 282; Critical Period, 307, 312, 313; urbanization, 382; blacks, 683; Reconstruction period, 683

Rice cultivation: slavery and, 67, 123, 154; nineteenth century, 386, 458, 463

Rice trade, 115, 500

Richmond, Va.: origins, 39; becomes capital of Virginia, 299; architecture, 332; in Civil War, 599, 614, 615, 618, 629, 634, 641, *648, 649, 650,* 651, 663; blacks, during Reconstruction, *665, 666*

Rio Grande River, 536, 537, *538,* 539, 540, 544

Riots: New Jersey land riots, 159; urban, eighteenth century, 164, 188, 198; eighteenth-century Britain, 225; Revolutionary era, 232, 236–240; 1844 Philadelphia, 560; pre–Civil War period, 561; during Civil War, 636; Reconstruction period, 677, 716; anti-Chinese, 682. *See also* Disorder, social; Mobs; Race riots; Strikes

Ritual, religious, 105, 107

"River gods," 122

Roads: colonial, *216,* 221; Revolutionary and Confederation era, 287, 291; nineteenth century, 369, 375, 387, 456, 499, 506

Roanoke Colony, 22–23, *28*

Roberts, Jonathan, 489

Robinson, Harriet, 442

Rochambeau, Comte de, 269

Rochester, N.Y., 388, 421, 437–438

Rockefeller, John D., 630

Rockingham, Marquess of, 225

Rocky Mountains, 345, 433, 526, 533

Rolfe, John, 41

Roman Catholic church: and Spanish-American empire, 13–14; and Reformation, 105; first American bishop, 332

Roman Catholicism: colonial Maryland, 54–56, 103, 136; New Netherland, 59–60; as colonial enemy, 187, 227; Jacksonian and pre–Civil War periods, 415, 559, 560, 563

Roman Catholics: excluded from British naturalization, eighteenth century, 153; as immigrants, nineteenth century, 559

Rome, ancient, 273, 275, 280, 289, 315, 422, 472

Rosecrans, W. S., *616,* 623–624, 625

Ross, Chief John, 597

Rotten boroughs, 175, 178, 241

Rousseau, Jean-Jacques, 203

Royal Academy (London), 224

Royal African Company, 83

Royal colonies. *See* Crown colonies

Royal Society (London), 139

Ruins of Empire, 355

Rule of 1756, 325, 326, 360

Rum trade, *163,* 196, 230

Rural society: colonial, 42, 50, 56–57, 66–68, 83–84, 88–91, 157–158, 172, 217–218, 219–222; British, 157, 159; Revolutionary era, 276; Jacksonian and pre–Civil War periods, 382–390, 396–400, 403–404, 419–420, 498–499. *See also* Agrarianism; Farming

Rush, Benjamin, 276, 294

Rush-Bagot Convention (1818), 369

Russell, Lord John, 589, 607, 642

Russia: and eighteenth-century wars, 188; and Revolutionary War, 266; Mormons and, 430; and cotton trade, 458; and formulation of Monroe Doctrine, 527–528; and Civil War, 607, 609–610, 642; Alaskan purchase and, 699

Russian Revolution, and American Revolution, 3

Rutgers University (Queen's College), 143, 172

Sabbatarian movement, 358, 435, 437–439, 516

Sac Indians, 405, *407*

"Safety-valve" theory, 399–400

Sagadahoc, 36

Saint Aubin, Augustin, 203

St. Augustine, Fla., 63, 129, 186

St. Clair, Arthur, 321, *322,* 332

St. Lawrence River, 187, *188,* 192

St. Leger, Barry, 264

St. Louis, Mo.: early nineteenth century, 345; Lewis and Clark expedition, 345; Germans, 381; in Civil War, 597

St. Mary's, Md., settlement at, 56

Salem, Mass., 49, 146, 363

Salt Lake City, Utah, 431–433

Salt trade, 40, 115

Salvation: in Puritan theology, 79–80, 140; in First Great Awakening, 170–171; in Second Great Awakening, 356

Sandys, Sir Edwin, 40

Sandys, George, 138

San Francisco, Calif.: Jackson and, 529; in Mexican War, 535, 536, anti-Chinese agitation, *682*

San Ildefonso, Treaty of (1800), 345

Sanitation, public, 292

San Jacinto, battle of, 529, *530, 538*

Santa Anna, Antonio López de, *529*

Santa Fe Trail, 529, *530*

Santiago, Chile, 8

Santo Domingo: slave insurrection, 194, 295, 461, 523; Franco-Spanish intervention, 607. *See also* Dominican Republic; Haiti

Saratoga, battle of, 264–266, *265,* 271

Saugus, Mass., 85

Savage, Edward, *314*

Savannah, Ga., eighteenth century, 150;

Revolution, 251, 267, 268, 271, 299; in Civil War, 650
Say and Sele, Lord, 92
Saybrook Platform, 146, 168
"Scalawags," 688
Scandinavians and Scandinavian Americans, 380, 381, 434
Schurz, Carl, 607, 701
Schuyler brothers, 129
Schuyler family, 136
Science, in colonial America, 139; Franklin and, 202; Revolutionary era, 292; popularization, nineteenth century, 424–427; government and, nineteenth century, 495
Scotch: in colonies, 66, 68–69; and southern colonial economy, 161, 222. *See also* Scotch-Irish
Scotch-Irish, immigration to colonies, 150, 152–153, 244
Scotland: and British mercantilism, 115; demography, 213; and colonial economy, 220, 229. *See also* Scotch-Irish
Scott, Dred, 572
Scott, Sir Walter, 446
Scott, Winfield, 515, *538,* 539, 540, 544, 562
Sculpture, 446, *577*
Sea Islands, 468, 627, 640, 667
Secession: Hartford Convention, 367, 369; Southern justifications for, 468; and nullification, 502; and coming of Civil War, 555, 582–583, 585; Southern attitudes toward, 589; of Upper South, 593–594, *596*–599, 617; as dead issue, 657. *See also* Disunion; Sectionalism
Second Great Awakening. *See* Great Awakening, Second
Sectionalism: Critical Period, 304–305; Federalist period, 315, 323–324; Jeffersonian period, 342–343, 346–347, 349, 367; Jacksonian period, 487, 488–492, 501, 517; pre–Civil War, 472, 500–504, 522, 547–584; Civil War era, 588. *See also* Disunion; Secession
Seddon, James A., 603, 644
Sedition: Zenger trial, 206, "Wilkes and Liberty," 226; Revolutionary era, 252; crisis of 1798–99, 327–331, 339
Sedition Act (Federalist): *See* Alien and Sedition Acts
Segregation: in Jacksonian and pre–Civil War society, 416–417, 482; in Reconstruction period, 678, 684, 689. *See also* Jim Crow laws
Self-improvement movements: Jacksonian

and pre–Civil War periods, 411–412, 419, 424–428, 439–440, 574
Seminole Indians, 369, 403, 405, *407,* 525, 597
Semmes, Raphael, 628
Senate (U.S.): under Constitution, 310; Federalist period, 316, 325; Jeffersonian period, 350, 368; Jacksonian period, 489; pre–Civil War period, 542, 543, 555, 565, 569–570, 580; Reconstruction period and Gilded Age, 674, 680, 688, 717, 720
Senators, direct election of, 574–575
Seneca Falls Convention, 444
Senecas, 217, *218*
Separation of powers: Revolutionary era, 279; under Constitution, 308–310. *See also* Judicial review
Separatism, black. *See* Black separatism
Separatists, 44–45
Servants: in colonial families, 92–98; as immigrants to colonies, 201; in Revolutionary society, 276, 289; in nineteenth-century society, 378. *See also* Indentured servants
Servitude: in Spanish-American empire, 12, 13, 14; indentured servants, 42–43, 57, 67, 92–98; colonial and Revolutionary, 294; nineteenth century, 468
Seven Days (battle), 615
Seven Pines, battle of. *See* Fair Oaks, battle of
Seven Years' War. *See* French and Indian War
Seward, William H.: and Whig party, 514, 567; and Crisis of 1850, 555, 560; and slavery, 579; and Kansas-Nebraska Act, 565; presidential candidacy, 580; as secretary of state, during Civil War, 593, 606–607, 642, 645; Reconstruction, 673, 698, 699, 700
Sexism, 443–444. *See also* Women's movement; Suffrage, women's
Sex roles: colonial, 98; Revolutionary era, 293–294; nineteenth century, 442–445
Sexual behavior: and slavery, 157, 465–466; reform of, nineteenth century, 425, 446
Seymour, Horatio, 636, 704, 721
Shaftesbury, Earl of. *See* Ashley Cooper, Sir Anthony
Shakers, 445
Sharecropping, post-Civil War, 671–673
Sharpe, Horatio, 233
Shattucks, Jacob, *307*

Shawnee Indians, 217, *218,* 219, 348, 402, 514
Shays, Daniel, 306–307
Shays' Rebellion, 306, 331
Shenandoah Valley, in Civil War, 612, 649
Sheridan, Philip, 649
Sherman, John, 704, 718
Sherman, Roger, *256*
Sherman, William Tecumseh, 540, 624–625, 644, *649*–652, 653, 654, 661, 667
Shiloh, battle of, *613,* 614, 618
Shipbuilding, 40, 196
Shipping: under navigation acts, 115, 145; eighteenth century, 161, *163,* 165, 196; Revolutionary era, 254, 286, 287–288; Federalist period, 319, 325, 326; Jeffersonian period, 362; Jacksonian and pre–Civil War periods, 388, 530; Civil War, 627–629, 642
Shirley, William, 187, 190
Shoe industry, 221, 394, 629
Sidney, Algernon, 274
Silk, 40
Silliman, Benjamin, 426
Silver coinage, 703
Silver mining industry, 704
Simms, William Gilmore, 448
Sioux Indians, 713
Slater, Samuel, 332
Slave codes: colonial, 43, 67; pre–Civil War, 459, 558, 578, 580
Slave insurrections: colonial, 157; Santo Domingo, 295, 461, 523; pre–Civil War, 461–462, 471, 473, 491, 518, 548; abolitionists and, 481–482; Jamaica, 501; John Brown and, 578–580
Slavery, American: origins, 43, religion and, 43, 418; seventeenth century, 67, 83–84, 90, 121–124; eighteenth century, 154–157, *155,* 159, 195, 196; Revolutionary era, 282, 286, 294–295; Federalist period, 324; Jefferson and, 335; pre–Civil War, 378, 379; issue of, in northern states, 424, 472–483, 487, 488–491, 504; Mormons and, 429, 439; and the family, 463, 557, 558; Southern justifications of, 468–470, 471, 475–476, 491, 501, 522, 531–532; and pre–Civil War foreign policy, 523, 528, 531–532, 540–543; in Texas, 528–529, 531–534; and coming of Civil War, 548–558, 564–581, and *Dred Scott* decision, 572–575; Lincoln and, 574–578, 639; issue of, during Civil War, 588, 598–599, 608, 636–641; Confederate Constitution on, 589–590; emancipation, 636–641; end of, 567–568, 656, 657, 664, 668–669, 688, 714
Slavery, Cuban, 523, 542
Slavery, West Indian and Latin American, abolition of, 439, 525, 528, 542
Slaves: in Spanish-American empire, 13; colonial, 43, 67; geographical distribution of, eighteenth century, 149; and representation, under Constitution, 310; price of, pre–Civil War, 385, 457, 459; geographical distribution of, nineteenth century, 456; flight of, 465; community and family, 463–465; culture of, 466–468; Jamaican revolt, 501; suits for freedom, 572; in Civil War, 608, 621, 627, 636–641; quarters of, *671. See also* Slavery
"Slave Society," 468
Slave trade: African, seventeenth century, 83, 123; British and Spanish colonies, 129; eighteenth century, *155,* 186; abolition of, 295, 368, 437, 439, 473, 501, 523, 528, 531; to Brazil and Cuba, 455, 463; abolished in District of Columbia, 554, 556; attempt to reopen, 578, 579
Slidell, John, 536–537, 540, 544, 607–608
Sloughter, Henry, 135
Slums, nineteenth century, 397, 398
Smalls, Robert, 638
Smith, Adam, 196
Smith, Gerrit, 437
Smith, James McCune, 481
Smith, Captain John, 38, 40
Smith, Joseph Jr., 429–431
Smith, Sydney, 511
Smith, Sir Thomas, 24, 36, 40
Smith, William, 179
Smuggling: Colonial, 134; in Caribbean, 186; Revolutionary era, 194, 228, 235–236. *See also* Mercantilism
Social change: in early American history, 2–3; Pilgrims' attitude toward, 45–47; seventeenth-century attitude toward, 79, 91–98; and seventeenth-century religion, 98–109; emergence of colonial elites, 121–132; First Great Awakening and, 166–173; Revolutionary era, 210–211, 215–217, 219–220, 221–222, 274–277, 285–286, 286–295; eighteenth-century attitude toward, 257–258; Critical Period, 299; Jeffersonian Republicans and, 323–324; Federalists and, 335; and manipulative attitudes toward law, 353–354; as modernization, Jacksonian

period, 377–379, 396–401; in Jacksonian and pre–Civil War periods, 412–448, 512–513; post-Civil War, 659

Social class: in seventeenth-century colonies, 79, 88, 91–98, 107–109; beginnings of social stratification, 121–124, 129–132, 157–165; and First Great Awakening, 172; Revolutionary era, 254–256, 289–290; Jacksonian and pre–Civil War periods, 396–398, 422–424. *See also* Aristocracy; Elites; Working class

Social Darwinism, 683

Socialism, pre–Civil War, 445–456

Social reform: Enlightenment, 202, 203; Revolutionary era, 292–293; Jacksonian and pre–Civil War periods, 374–375, 411, 413–417, 427, 435–437, 439–446, 489, 512–516

Society for the Propagation of the Gospel in Foreign Parts (SPG), 101, 169

"Soft money." *See* Currency; Paper money

Soil, failure to conserve, nineteenth century, 386, 672

Sons of Liberty (American Revolution), 238, 250

Sons of Liberty (eighteenth-century Ireland), 259

South (U.S.): Revolution, 267–270, 282, 283, 286; anti-slavery, 295; Critical Period, 305, 306, Federalist period, 323; Jeffersonian period, 340, 346, 368; religion, nineteenth century, 351–358, 417–419, 435, 439; pre–Civil War economy and slavery, 375–376, 396, 454–472, 476, 532; Jacksonian period politics, 488–491, 496, 500–504, 509, 523, 531–532, 537, 542–543; education, pre–Civil War, 413–417; coming of Civil War, 547–559, 565–566, 571–573, 578–584; attitude toward North, 588; devastation caused by Civil War, 669; Reconstruction, 656–691; economic adjustments, 669–673; discrimination against blacks, 658, 714, 716, 718–721; per capita wealth (1880), 673; legislation regarding blacks (1865–1866), 674; ratification of constitution, 688; Reconstruction governments, 688–689; restoration of Home Rule, 714, 716

South America: Spanish conquest, 8–9; U.S. trade with, 286; demography, 379; independence movement, 524–527. *See also* Latin America; Spanish-American empire; Western Hemisphere

South Carolina (colonial): in early eighteenth century, 64–68, 123; detached from North Carolina, 118, 206; slavery, 123–124; black population, 149; in colonial wars, 186; Cherokee War, 219; Regulators, 219, 244; in imperial crisis, 232. *See also* Carolina

South Carolina (state): Revolution, 271, 278, *283*, 289, 354; Critical Period, 299, 301; slavery, 461, 468, 491; Jacksonian-period politics, 497, 500–504; secession, 582–583, 589, 596; in Civil War, 594, *596*, 627–628, 640, 645, *649*, 651, 654, 660, 667; Reconstruction, 667, 674, 677, *678*, 686–689, 714, 716, 718, 719, 720

South Carolina Exposition and Protest, 501–502, 518

Southeast (U.S.), Spanish exploration, 6, 29. *See also* South; *specific colonies, states*

Southern states. *See* South (U.S.)

Southwest (U.S.). Spanish exploration, 8, 29; Mexican War, *538*

Southwest, Old: Critical Period, 304; Federalist period, 321; and War of 1812, 365; Jacksonian and pre–Civil War periods, 384, 402–404

Sovereignty: in Glorious Revolution, 133; debate over, in imperial crisis, 242–244; Articles of Confederation, 281; and framing of Constitution, 311–312; American people as source of, 312, 353; Hamilton on, 352; and American law, 353–354; Mormons and, 434; state, pre–Civil War, 500–501, 547–548, 549–552, 572–573; state, in Confederacy, 589–590, 643–644; issue of, settled by Civil War, 657. *See also* Popular sovereignty

Spain: conquests in America, 5, 6–8; war with England, sixteenth century, 17–23, 24; and colonial economy, 86, 89, 197; and colonial wars, 186, 188, 192, 206; and Revolutionary War, 264; and U.S., Federalist and Jeffersonian periods, 304–305, 316, 321, 346, 369, 523, 525, 527; and U.S., mid-nineteenth century, 542–543, 607. *See also* Spanish-American empire

Spanish-American empire: origins, 6–12, *10, 11;* administration, 8–14; commerce, 9; political culture, 10–14; religion, 13–14; Indians, 9, 12, 14; independence movement, 12, 523, 525; racially mixed populations, 15–16; contrasts with British Empire, 12–14, 15, 16, 180

Spanish Armada, 23n

Spanish Main, 18–19, 186, 206

Specie: in colonial economy, 197; Critical Period, 303; in Hamiltonian program, 318; Jacksonian and pre–Civil War periods, 504, 507, 605–606
Specie circular, 507, 519
Specie payment, Gilded Age, 703
Speculation, land. *See* Land speculation
Speculators, post-Civil War, 700
Speech, freedom of, 315
Spinning, mechanized, *391*
Spiritualism, 425
Spoils system: Jacksonian and pre–Civil War, 497, 498, 510; Lincoln administration, 592; post-Civil War, 694, 706–708. *See also* Patronage, political
Spotswood, Alexander, 120, 121
Spotsylvania, battle of, 648, 654
Spurzheim, Johann Gaspar, 425–426
Squatters, 387, 404
Stamp Act, 229, 230–*232*, 233, 238, 240–241, 244
Stamp Act Congress, 231, 240, 242, 244
Stanton, Edwin M., 602, 622, 625, 580
Stanton, Elizabeth Cady, 444
Staple Act (1663), 115, 145
Stark, John, 264
"Starving times," 91; first English colonies, 27–29; at Jamestown, 38–39; at Plymouth, 45–46; in Carolina, 67
State, Department of, creation, 316
Staten Island, early settlement at, 61
States: and higher education, 143; Revolutionary and Confederation periods, 277–285, 288, 291, 299, 301–307; and framing of Constitution, 306, 308–310; and Bill of Rights, 315; Jeffersonian period, 352–353; Jacksonian and pre–Civil War periods, 379, 383, 404–406, 480; during Civil War, 604; and federal government, post-Civil War, 662–664; Reconstruction and, 675–676; and black suffrage, post-Civil War, 683, 718–721. *See also* Secession; *specific states*
States' rights: Jacksonian and pre–Civil War periods, 433, 491–493, 502–504, 511, 547, 548–550; in Confederacy, 589–590, 634–635, 643–644; issue of, during Reconstruction, 661–664
Status, social: colonial, 91–98, 121–132, 133–134, 157–166, 179–181; Revolutionary era, 288–290; Critical Period, 298–299, 307–308; and Jeffersonian revolution, 337–339; and Second Great Awakening, 355–359; Jacksonian and pre–Civil War periods, 374, 398–401,

411–412, 415–419, 421–424, 476, 495–496, 510, 513–514; pre–Civil War South, 468–470. *See also* Aristocracy; Elites; Gentry; Social class
Steamboats, 368, *388,* 394
Steam power, 394, 425, 430
Stephens, Alexander H., 550, 606, 636, 644, 659, 674, 684
Stephens, Uriah, 709
Stevens, Thaddeus, 646, 668, 674, 675, 681, 687
Stewart, Alvan, 480
Steward, Ira, 708
Stiles, Ezra, 217, 300
Stoddard, Solomon, 169
Stone, Lucy, 444, *445*
Stonites, 358
Story, Joseph, 426
Stowe, Harriet Beecher, 413, 442, 557, *558,* 584
Strategy and tactics: military, Revolutionary War, 260–269, *261, 265;* military, Civil War, 598–599, 610–617, 620–621, 624–625, 652–654; naval, Civil War, 627–629
Stratification, social. *See* Aristocracy; Elites; Social class; Status, social
Strikes: eighteenth century, 164; Revolutionary era, 290; Jacksonian and pre–Civil War periods, 399
Strong, George Templeton, 635
Stuart, Charles, 474
Stuart dynasty (England and Scotland), 63, 112–113, 150, 224. *See also specific monarchs*
Stuyvesant, Peter, 62, 104
Sudbury, Mass., 49
Suffolk County (Mass.) Resolves, 249
Suffrage: colonial, 178–179, 241–242; British, 240–241; Revolutionary era, 250, 280; Jeffersonian period, 347; Jacksonian and pre–Civil War periods, 454. *See also* Suffrage, black; Suffrage, women's; Town meeting
Suffrage, black: pre–Civil War, 480–481; post-Civil War, 675–677, 683, 684–688, 718–721; and fifthteenth amendment, 712
Suffrage, women's: Jacksonian and pre–Civil War periods, 444; post-Civil War, 711–712
Sugar Act (1765), 227–229, 230, 244
Sugar trade, 86, 115, 194, *195,* 206, 230
Sumner, Charles, 548; attacked in Senate, 569–*570;* and Lincoln, 637, 646; and Reconstruction, 646, 668, 675, 676, 677,

683, 696, 701; and women's suffrage, 712

Sumner, William Graham, 668

Sumptuary laws, 93

Sunday schools, 435, 436, 439

Supreme Court, U.S.: creation, 316; *Dartmouth College* case, 291; Marshall and, 350, *351*–353; and slavery, 480; and Bank War, 505; *Dred Scott* case, 572–574, 577; and citizenship, 676; and election of 1876, 717

Surinam, *164*

Surplus, federal, nineteenth century, 506

Swedes, 59, 72. *See also* Scandinavians and Scandinavian Americans

Swift, Jonathan, 257

Switzerland, 275

Sylvis, William H., 708, 709

Tallmadge, James Jr., 489

Taney, Robert B., 377

Tappan, Arthur, 437, 444, 477

Tappan, Lewis, 437, 438, 444

Tariff of Abominations, 496, 518

Tariffs: Critical Period, 300, 303; under Constitution, 309; Jeffersonian period, 342, 369; Jacksonian and pre–Civil War periods, 377, 391, 487, 493, 496, 500–501, 509, 518, 522, 553; Civil War, 605, 629, 632, 646; Gilded Age, 668, 689, 694, 700, 701–702. *See also* Customs duties; Protectionism

Tarleton, Banastre, 267, *268*

Taxation: and colonial churches, 100, 104, 168; Dominion of New England, 117; colonial Maryland, 136; and education, colonial New England, 141; Parliament and, 175, 229, 230, 238, 242, 252; and colonial currency problems, 197–199; colonial North Carolina, 220; Britain, 223; "internal" vs. "external," 232–235, 242–244; "no taxation without representation," 235; Revolutionary governments and, 281–282, 288; Critical Period, 300, 303; under Constitution, 281–282, 288; in Hamiltonian program, 320–322; Jeffersonian period, 339; *McCulloch* v. *Maryland* and, 352; and religion, Revolutionary era, 354; and War of 1812, 365; and nineteenth-century education, 414; and slavery, 501; Civil War, 605–606, 631; and cost of defeating Confederacy, 659

Taylor, Nathaniel William, 358

Taylor, Zachary, *488*, 509, 515, *538*–539, 542, 544, 547–556, 584

Tea Act (1773), 238, 239–240, 245

Teachers and teaching profession: colonial, 144, 294; Jacksonian and pre–Civil War periods, 413, 415–417, 419, 442; post-Civil War South, 665–667, *666*, 689

Technological change: early nineteenth century, 380, 390–396, 424–425, 477, 512, 574; and slavery, 454–455, 458–459

Tecumseh, *348, 365*, 515

Telegraph, 396, 423, 512

Temperance, nineteenth century: 440–442, *441*, 445, 474, 516, 574. *See also* Prohibition

Tenancy: in colonies, 57, 141, 157–159, 162, 181, 244; in Britain, 153, 157–158, 159, 162; in post–Civil War South, 671–673

Tennent, Gilbert, 171

Tennessee: settlement, 305; admission, 316; Indians, 348, 403, *407;* Second Great Awakening, 356; slavery, 469; Jackson's career in, 494; pre–Civil War politics, 582; secession, 594, *596,* 598, 617; in Civil War, *613,* 615, *616,* 623, 650, 659; Reconstruction period, 658, 677, *678, 685,* 716; post-Reconstruction period, 719–720

Tenure of Office Act (1867), 681, 691

Territories: slavery in, 375–376, 480, 489–490, 548, 551–559, *556,* 568–571, 572–573, 577–578, 579–580; Jacksonian and pre–Civil War periods, *383. See also* Northwest, Old; Northwest Ordinance; Southwest, Old

Terrorism, during Reconstruction, 689–691, 714–715

Texas: Indians, 406; Mormons, 430; slavery, 455, 468, 528–529, 531–532, 544, 547; Mexico and, 522, 526–527; independence, 528–535, 544; annexation, 523, 524, 528–531, 544, 547; Mexican War, 535–538, 540; secession, 583, 585, 589–590, *596,* 617; Reconstruction, 670, 678, 686, 687, 688, 716; post-Reconstruction, 720

Textile industry: early modern English, 17–18, 29; colonial, 85, 196, 221; in Industrial Revolution, 390–392, *391;* early nineteenth century, 455–459, 550; Civil War, 604, 629; European, and Civil War, 608

Thames, battle of the, *364, 365,* 369

Theyanoguin, *190*

Thomas, George H., *613,* 623, 625, 650

Thompson, Cephas, *351*

Thoreau, Henry David, *449*

Tilden, Samuel J., 709, 716, *717,* 722
Timber: trade, 39, 46, 114, 228; exploitation, 386
Tippecanoe, battle of, 348, 365, 369, *364*
Tithingmen, 98
Tobacco: in seventeenth-century Chesapeake region, 88–91, *155;* and colonial economy, 123, 161–162, 221–222; as medium of exchange, 101, 222; and navigation acts, 115; smuggling, 134; trade, Revolutionary era, 229, 286; cultivation and trade, nineteenth century, 386, 458, 463; Civil War, 629, 631; post-Civil War South, 672
Tocqueville, Alexis de, 374, 382–383, 386, 397, 517–518
Todd, John, 425
Toleration, religious: in seventeenth-century colonies, 55–56, 103–104; in eighteenth-century colonies, 168; of Quakers, 201; post-Revolutionary, 354–359; Mormons and, 434–435. *See also* Persecution, religious
Toombs, Robert, 553, 592, 594, 607
Tordesillas, Treaty of (1494), 17, 29
Tories (American). *See* Loyalists
Tories (British), 224, 257
Toronto, Canada, 365
Tory Legion, 267
Toussaint L'Ouverture, 461, 661
Town meeting, New England, 50–51, 117, 122, 232
Towns: colonial New England, 50, 122; absence of, in southern colonies, 91; and Dominion of New England, 117, in colonial society, 130, 150, 215; and New England education, 142–143; First Great Awakening and, 172; in Revolution, 255; religion in, post-Revolutionary, 354–355; Jacksonian and pre–Civil War period, 384. *See also* Cities; Communities; Urbanization; *specific cities, towns*
Townshend, Charles, 225, 233
Trade, foreign, 703. *See also* Commerce; Free trade; Tariffs; *specific commodities*
Trail of Tears, *405*
Transcendentalism, 427
Transcontinental railroad, 406
Transcontinental Treaty (Adams-Onís Treaty, 1819), 369, 523, 525–527, 544
Transportation: colonial, 196, *216,* 221; Revolutionary and post-Revolutionary periods, 287; Jacksonian and pre–Civil War periods, 382–385, 387–*389,* 394–396, *395,* 422, 446, 455, 487, 499, 565;

Civil War, 599, 604, 611, 630, 652. *See also* Canals; Roads; *specific means of transportation*
Treason: Patrick Henry accused of, 230; Burr tried for, 346, 368; Mormons accused of, 429–430, 435; Garrisonians and, 479; and nullification, 503; John Brown executed for, 578; Jefferson Davis indicted for, 659–660
Treasury, Department of the (Confederate), 592, 604–605, 631
Treasury, Department of the (U.S.): creation, 316, 322–323; Civil War, 604–605, 632; Gilded Age political corruption, 706
Treasury (Great Britain), 114, 115, 119, 233
Treaties, governing Indians, post-Civil War, 712. *See also specific treaties*
Tredegar Iron Works, 596, 629, 637
Trenchard, John, 257
Trenholm, George A., 632
Trent affair, 609–610, 618
Trenton, battle of, 261, 263, *265,* 271
"Triangular trade," 88
Trinity Church, 169
Trist, Nicholas, 540
Trollope, Frances, 524
Trumbull, John, *256, 269*
Trumbull, Lyman, 570
Tsar Alexander II, 699
Turkey, 528
Turner, Frederick Jackson, 399
Turner, Nat, 461, 471, 473
Twain, Mark, 413, 700
Two-party system: origins, 486–487, *488,* 501, 509–517; pre–Civil War breakdown, 547–548, 550, 564–567, 580–581; Civil War, 652–654. *See also* Political parties; *specific parties*
Two-Penny Acts, 222, 244
Two Years Before the Mast, 675
Tyler, John, 509, 515, 519, 531–535, 544
Tyranny: in eighteenth-century political theory, 174; view of, in Revolution, 222, 255, 259–260, 279, *334;* legislative, fear of, 299, 300, 306, 312–313; in Federalist-Antifederalist debate, 311–312; views of, in Jacksonian and pre–Civil War periods, 411–412, 414, 436, 443–446, 501, 502, 512, 537, 547–548, 555, 564

Ulster, Anglo-Scottish settlement of, 25–26, 150
Uncle Tom's Cabin, 557
Underground Railroad, 481–482

Underhill, John, 62
Unemployment: Jacksonian and pre–Civil
    War periods, 424, *506,* 564; late nine-
    teenth century, 682, 709
Union, question of: Jeffersonian period,
    348–349, 367; pre–Civil War, 375–376,
    479, 488–491, 502–503, 532, 537, 555,
    581–583; Lincoln and, 575, 576, 590,
    657; border states' attitude toward, 597–
    598; northern attitudes toward, 611,
    644–645; sentiment favoring, in Con-
    federacy, 643; Johnson on, 673–674
Union League, 661, 686
Union Industrial School, *666*
Union Pacific Railroad, 652, 705
Unions. *See* Labor unions; *specific unions*
Unitarians, 358, 513
United Kingdom. *See* Great Britain
United States: historical continuities, 2, 4–
    5; founding principles, 210–211; Revolu-
    tion, 248–270, 273–274, 279–281, 285–
    293; Constitution, 281–282, 298–307,
    331; Federalist and Jeffersonian periods,
    314–331; Jacksonian and pre–Civil War
    periods, 374–407, 411–448, 486–518;
    pre–Civil War slavery, 454–483; pre–
    Civil War expansion, 345–349, 522–543;
    coming of Civil War, 547–585; Civil
    War, 588–618, 620–654; Reconstruction,
    656–691. *See also* America; Colonies,
    British
United States v. *Peters,* 352
Universalists, 357
United States Review, 393
University of Pennsylvania (College of Phil-
    adelphia), 143
Unskilled labor, 397–401, 414, 422
Upshur, Abel P., 531, 532
Urbanization: absence of, in southern colo-
    nies, 91; early nineteenth century, 382–
    383, 384, 390, *397,* 522
Utah: Mormons, 431–433, 436; and Com-
    promise of 1850, 555–559, 565, 572
Utopianism: in Revolutionary ideology,
    273–274; Jacksonian period, 445
Utrecht, Treaty of (1713), 129

Valdivia, Pedro de, 9, 29
Valley Forge, Pa., 271
Values: colonial and Revolutionary, 2–5,
    79; Pilgrims, 46; Puritan, 84, 91–98,
    105–109, 140–143; Quaker, 69, 71; tradi-
    tional, in colonial America, 84, 91–93;
    cultural, in colonial America, 138–140;
    Enlightenment, 199–205; Revolutionary

era, 210–211, 256, 273–277, 288–290,
    293–295; Federalist, 315, 320, 324–325;
    Jeffersonian, 337–339, 349, 354–360;
    Jacksonian, 374–375, 397–399, 411–428,
    435–438, 454, 471–472, 498, 512–513,
    547–548, 575–580, 583; Mormon, 429–
    430, 434–435; abolitionist, 473–483
Van Buren, Martin: and origin of two-party
    system, 492–493, 496, 497; and Jackson
    administration, 500, 502; as president,
    488, 503, 507–508, 509, 530, 515, 517,
    544; and expansion, 530, 532; and Free
    Soil party, 550, 584
Van Cortlandt family, 136
Van Cortlandt Manor, 130
Vancouver Island, 538
van der Spriett, Jan, 137
Van Rensselaer, Kiliaen, 60–61
Vermont (colonial): settlement, 149, 159,
    217; and colonial wars, 187
Vermont (state): Revolution, 280; Critical
    Period, 300–301; admission, 316; migra-
    tion from, 401, 431; antislavery, 474;
    blacks, 683; Reconstruction period, 683
Vermont Council of Censors, 300
Verrazano, Giovanni da, 29
Vesey, Denmark, 461, 491, 518
Veterans: Revolutionary War, 289, 387;
    Civil War, 662; benefits of, post-Civil
    War, 662
Veto: Jackson, 499–500, 506, 518; Andrew
    Johnson, 675–679, 691
Vice-admiralty courts, 119, 177, 228, 233
Vicksburg campaign, 624–625, 626, 640,
    644, 654
Victoria (queen of England), 608
Vigilante groups: colonial and Revolution-
    ary, 219–220, 312; and American law,
    354; Reconstruction period, 690
Villiers, Elizabeth, 119
Vincent, Marvin R., 695
Violence. *See* Disorder; Mobs; Riots; Vig-
    ilante groups
Virginia (colonial): settlement, 36–43, 215;
    Indians, 38, 40, 219; governors, 40, 120,
    125, 219; as crown colony, 42, 116;
    economy and society, 42, 160–162, 221–
    222; slavery, 43, 83–84, 123; population,
    79–83, 149; religion, 99–103, 168, 172;
    culture and education, 142–143, 145;
    politics, 125, 180, 222, 244; Bacon's
    Rebellion, 132–134; colonial wars, 188;
    finance, 197; in imperial crisis, 231
Virginia (state): Revolution, 274, 277, 282–
    283, 286; Critical Period, 299; Federalist

period, 305, 306, 308, 330, 332; religious
liberty, 354; education, 417; slavery, 461,
469–473; in Missouri Crisis, 489; Jacksonian politics, 496; pre–Civil War, 563,
582, 595; secession, 593–594, *596,* 599,
617; in Civil War, *613–615, 614,* 621, *623,*
638, 640–643, 644, *648, 649;* Reconstruction, 658, 660, *678,* 688; black
voting rights, *687,* 720; post-Reconstruction, 714, 716, 720; Gilded Age, 716
Virginia (Merrimack, ironclad), 618, 628
Virginia and Kentucky resolutions, 330,
332
Virginia Company: economic ventures of,
28, 30, 36; chartered, 30, 36, 38, 41, 291;
and settlement of Virginia, 36–43;
failure of, 40–43, 116; and Pilgrims, 44;
and religion in Virginia, 99
Virginia Plan, 308, 309, 310
Virginia resolves, 230
Volney, Comte de, 355
Voltaire, 201, 203, 204
von Steuben, Baron, *269*
Vote and Proceedings (1772), 239
Voting: colonial, 178–179, 241–242; Britain, 240–241, 258; Revolutionary era,
250–251, 276, 279–280; Jeffersonian
period, 341; by blacks, pre–Civil War,
481; Jacksonian and pre–Civil War periods, 496, 534, 564, 580–581; election of
1864, 653–654; by blacks, post-Civil
War, 658–659, 670, 683, *687,* 691; by
former Confederates, 676, 684–687;
Fourteenth and Fifteenth amendments,
712; black disfranchisement, 718–721.
See also Elections; Suffrage; Town meeting

Wade, Benjamin F., 647, 684, 714, 715
Wade-Davis Bill, 647
Wages: seventeenth century, 93; eighteenth
century, 164; Revolutionary and Con-
federation periods, 288; Jacksonian and
pre–Civil War periods, 391–392, 397–
398, 416; women's, nineteenth century,
443, 633; of freedmen, 670
Walker, David, 473
Walker, Leroy P., 601, 603
Walker, William, 543
Walker Tariff (1846), 553, 584
Walpole, Sir Robert, 149, 165, 186, 224n,
257, 324
Waltham system, 391
War, attitudes toward: Indians, 34; Jeffer-
sonian Republicans, 364–365, 367; Gar-

risonians, 478–479. *See also* Pacifism;
Peace movement; *specific wars*
War, Department of (Confederate), 601,
603, 641
War, Department of (U.S.): Federalist and
Jeffersonian periods, 316, 339, 365; Civil
War, 601, 603, 664
War crimes, Civil War, 659
War Hawks, 364
Warner, Charles Dudley, 700
War of 1812, 314, 341, 359, *364–368,* 369
War Office (Great Britain), and colonial
administration, 114
War of Jenkins' Ear (1739–41), 186, 206
War of the Austrian Succession. *See* King
George's War
War of the League of Augsburg. *See* King
William's War
War of the Spanish Succession. *See* Queen
Anne's War
Warren, Peter, 187–188
Wars, French Revolutionary and
Napoleonic. *See* French Revolutionary
and Napoleonic wars
Washington, D.C.: Jeffersonian period,
338, 368, War of 1812, 366, 369; Civil
War, 597, 599, 649. *See also* Capital,
national
Washington, George: as land speculator,
227, 345; early career, 262; in Revolu-
tion, 253, 269, 270; French and Indian
War, 189, 190, 191; as Republican hero,
277, 315; and Order of the Cincinnati,
289; in Federalist period, 305, 313; and
Continental army, 260, 262–263, 264,
303, 306; as president, 315, 320, 321,
325, 332, 337; farewell address, 326,
332; in Crisis of 1798–99, 330; Greenough statue of, *447,* 448
Washington, Treaty of (1871), 699
Washingtonian societies, 441
Watie, Stand, 597
Watson, Tom, 720
Waud, A. W., *651*
Wayne, Anthony, 321, 332
Wealth, accumulation and distribution of:
in colonial society, 121–132; Revolution-
ary era, 287–290; Jacksonian and pre–
Civil War periods, 396–398, 422–424,
567; in pre–Civil War South, 457–459,
463, 469–470; during and after Civil
War, 632–634
Webster, Daniel, 500, 505, 511, 514, 531,
555, 558
Webster-Ashburton Treaty (1842), 531, 544

Weed, Thurlow, 513–515, 518
Weld, Theodore Dwight, 473, 477
Welfare and welfare agencies: nineteenth-century Britain, 398; nineteenth-century U.S., 381, 398. *See also* Charity, public
Welles, Gideon, 628, 673
Wells, David A., 701
West, Benjamin, *202, 224*
West: and national destiny, nineteenth century, 343–346, 348–349, 413, 547–548; settlement and economic development, Jacksonian and pre–Civil War periods, 374–375, 377–379, 380–387, 390–401, 522–523, 537; plundering of environment, 386; as "safety valve," 399; Indian removal to, 404–*407, 568;* religion, nineteenth century, 418–420, 423, 437, 476; and slavery, 455, 490, 555–556, 558; Clay and, 494, 511; Jackson and, 498–499; Calhoun and, 502. *See also* Frontier; *specific states*
West (Civil War theater), *613, 616, 624-625,* 626
West Africa, 154, 464, 473
West Coast. *See* Far West
West Country (England), 16, 19, 23, 24
Western Hemisphere, as U.S. sphere of influence: Hamilton on, 322; Jefferson on, *343,* 523–524; and formulation of Monroe Doctrine, 527–528
West Florida, 270, 369, 523
West Indies: Spanish exploration and conquest, 6; English raids, sixteenth century, 18–19; and Carolina, 64–68, 501; and seventeenth-century slavery, 83; in colonial trade, 194, 199, 221, 230; Britain and eighteenth century, 186; and Revolution, 267, 286; slave insurrections, 295, 461, 501; in French Revolutionary wars, 325; as "slave society," 468, 471, 473; slave emancipation, 455, 473, 501, 531, 542, 552
West Jersey. *See* New Jersey (colony)
Weston, Thomas, 45
"Westover," 130, *131–132*
West Point Military Academy, 611
West Virginia: slavery in, pre–Civil War, 469, 615; separation from Virginia and admission, 598
Wethersfield, Ct., 50
Whaling, 530
Wheat. *See* Grain cultivation; Grain trade
Whig party (U.S.): origins and nature, 257, 328, 487; and slavery, 471, 477, 479–480; Jacksonian-period politics, *488,*

503–504, 509–516; pre–Civil War politics, 531, 532–533, 537–538, 539, 547, 552–553; collapse of, 563–564, 567, 571, 581, 584
Whigs (British), 224, 232–233
Whiskey Rebellion, 321, 332
White, Hugh, 514
White, John, 22, 23
Whitefield, George, 170–*171,* 206
White House, 366
Whitman, Walt, 449, 593
Whitney, Eli, 332
Whittier, John Greenleaf, 430, 434, 447
Wilderness, battle of the, *648, 654*
Wiley, Calvin H., 660
Wilkes, Charles, 609
Wilkes, John, 226, 241, 259
Wilkinson, James, 346
William and Mary (king and queen of England), *118,* 119, 135
William and Mary, College of, 102, 143, *144,* 146
Williams, George, 712
Williams, Roger, 53–54, 138
Williamsburg, Va., 299
Wilmot, David, 549
Wilmot Proviso, 549–550, 584
Wilson, James, 308, 309, 310, 345
Wilson, Woodrow, 656
Windsor, Ct., 50
Wine trade, 40, 86, 229, 233
Winthrop, John, 48–*49,* 50
Winthrop, John Jr., 85, 139
Wirt, William, 505
Wirtz, Henry, 659
Wisconsin: Indians, 405, *407;* slavery issue, 572; in Civil War, 636; blacks, 683; Reconstruction period, 683
Wise, John, 117
Witchcraft hysteria, Salem, Mass., 146
Wolfe, James, 191–192
Wollaston, John, 171
Women: sent to Jamestown, 28, 38; in colonial society, 81, 95–96, 98; white, and slavery, 157, 465; European notions about American, 200; in Revolutionary society, 276, 293–294; in Jacksonian and pre–Civil War society, 374, 413, 416, 417, 442–443; and Industrial Revolution, 392, *393,* 398, 400; Indian, 402; slave, 465; in nineteenth-century literature, 448; and Civil War, 633; in Reconstruction, 666; working conditions, Gilded Age, 709; in late nineteenth century, 694, 711

Women's movement: nineteenth century, 437, 442–445, 481, 694, 711–712; Thirteenth Amendment, 712

Women workers, nineteenth century, 390–393, 416, 442

Woolen Act (1699), 146, 195

Wool industry: early modern England, 17, 29; nineteenth-century U.S., 390, 392, 500, 629; Gilded Age, 702. *See also* Cloth trade; Textile industry

Woolman, John, 463

Wool Manufacturers' Association, 702

Worcester v. *Georgia* (1832), 404

Working class: as immigrants to colonies, 20, 79–80; eighteenth-century urban, 162–165; Revolutionary era, 290; in Industrial Revolution, 390–394; attempts to organize, nineteenth century, 399; and education, nineteenth century, 413–417; and temperance, 440–442; racism among, nineteenth century, 473, 636; and politics, Jacksonian and pre–Civil War periods, 496, 513, 562–564; Civil War, 633, 636; Chinese immigrants, California, 681–682; Gilded Age, 708–711. *See also* Artisans; Labor; Labor unions; Women workers

Workingman's party, *682*

Working Men's party, 414

Wormley, James, 717–718

Wormley agreement, 717, 718

Wren, Christopher, 144

Writs of assistance, 228

Wyoming, Mormon migration, 431

Wythe, George, 302

XYZ Affair, 327, 330, 332

Yale University (Yale College), 217; foundation, 143; and First Great Awakening, 172

Yancey, William L., 591, 607

Yates, Abraham, 299

Yazoo land claims, 369

Yellow fever, 292, 332

York (Toronto), Canada, 365

York, Duke of, 72

Yorktown, battle of, *268,* 269, 271, 303

Young, Brigham, *431–433*

Youth: in seventeenth-century society, 81, 96; in Jacksonian and pre–Civil War society, 379–380, 414, 421, 426–427; in Civil War, 599–601. *See also* Child labor, Children; Family

Yucatán Peninsula, 542

Zenger, John Peter, 206

Zouaves, 600–601